Collins
LATIN
DICTIONARY
ESSENTIAL EDITION

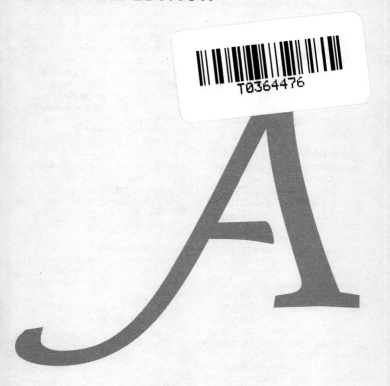

Published by Collins
An imprint of HarperCollins Publishers
Westerhill Road
Bishopbriggs
Glasgow G64 2QT

HarperCollins*Publishers*
Macken House, 39/40 Mayor Street
Upper Dublin 1, D01 C9W8, Ireland

First Edition 2020

10 9 8 7 6 5 4 3

© HarperCollins Publishers 2020

ISBN 978-0-00-837738-0

Collins® is a registered trademark of
HarperCollins Publishers Limited

collinsdictionary.com
collins.co.uk/dictionaries

Typeset by Davidson Publishing
Solutions, Glasgow

Printed and bound in the UK
using 100% renewable electricity
at CPI Group (UK) Ltd

A catalogue record for this book is
available from the British Library.

If you would like to comment on any
aspect of this book, please contact us
at the given address or online.
E-mail: dictionaries@harpercollins.co.uk
facebook.com/collinsdictionary
@collinsdict

Acknowledgements
We would like to thank those authors
and publishers who kindly gave
permission for copyright material to be
used in the Collins Corpus. We would
also like to thank Times Newspapers
Ltd for providing valuable data.

CONTENTS

Introduction	iv
Abbreviations	vi
Latin Alphabet	vii
Pronunciation	ix
LATIN–ENGLISH	1–236
Latin Grammar	1–18
Roman Culture	19–31
ENGLISH–LATIN	237–433

INTRODUCTION

Whether you are learning Latin for the first time or wish to "brush up" what you learned some time ago, this dictionary is designed to help you understand Latin and to express yourself in Latin, if you so wish.

HOW TO USE THE DICTIONARY
Entries are laid out as follows:

HEADWORD
This is shown in **bold type**. On the Latin-English side all long vowels are shown by placing a ‾ above them. Latin nouns show the genitive singular form in bold. Latin verbs show the first person singular of the present indicative as the headword, followed by the infinitive, and usually the first person singular of the perfect indicative and the past participle, all in bold type:

> **elegīa,-ae**
> **elementum, -ī**
> **ēmātūrēscō, -ēscere, -uī**

PART OF SPEECH
Next comes the part of speech (noun, verb, adjective etc), shown in *italics*. Part of speech abbreviations used in the dictionary are shown in the abbreviations list (p vi). Where a word has more than one part of speech, each new part of speech is preceded by a black triangle (▶). If a Latin headword is a preposition, the case taken by the preposition comes immediately after the part of speech, in *italics* and in brackets.

> **era, -ae** *f*
> **ticklish** *adj*
> **thunder** *n* tonitrus *m* ▶ *vi* tonare, intonare
> **ērgā** *prep* (*with acc*) towards; against

MEANINGS
Where a word or a part of speech has only one meaning, the translation comes immediately after the part of speech. However, many words have more than one meaning. Where the context is likely to show which translation is correct, variations in meaning are simply separated by a semicolon. But usually there will also be an "indicator" in *italics* and in brackets. Some meanings relate to specific subject areas, for example religion, politics, military matters etc – these indicators are in italic capitals.

ēnsiger, -ī *adj* with his sword
toy *n* crepundia *ntpl* ▶ *vi* ludere
toll collector *n* exactor *m*; portitor *m*
eō, īre, īvī *and* **iī, itum** *vi* to go; (*MIL*) to march; (*time*) to pass; (*event*) to proceed, turn out

TRANSLATIONS

Most words can be translated directly. On the English-Latin side, translations of nouns include the gender of the Latin noun in *italics*. However, sometimes a phrase is needed to show how a word is used, but in some cases a direct translation of a phrase would be meaningless – in these cases, an explanation in *italics* is given instead. In other cases, the user will need more information than simply the translation; in these cases, "indicators" are included in the translation(s), giving, for instance, the case required by a Latin verb or preposition or further details about a place or person.

> **thumb** *n* pollex *m*; **have under one's ~** in potestate sua habere
> **elephantomacha, -ae** *m fighter mounted on an elephant*
> **Erymanthus, Erymanthī** *m mountain range in Arcadia* (*where Hercules killed the boar*)
> **thwart** *vt* obstare (*dat*), officere (*dat*)

PRONUNCIATION

Since Latin pronunciation is regular and predictable provided you know the basic rules (see pp ix–x), the dictionary does not show phonetic transcriptions for each headword, but does show all long vowels.

OTHER INFORMATION

The dictionary also includes:
• a basic grammar section
• information about life in Roman times and key dates in Roman history

ABBREVIATIONS

abl	ablative	*m*	masculine
acc	accusative	*MATH*	mathematics
adj	adjective	*MED*	medicine
adv	adverb	*MIL*	military
AGR	agriculture	*n*	noun
ARCH	architecture	*NAUT*	nautical
art	article	*neg*	negative
ASTR	astronomy	*nom*	nominative
AUG	augury	*nt*	neuter
COMM	business	*num*	numeral
compar	comparative	*occ*	occasionally
conj	conjunction	*p*	participle
cpd	compound	*pass*	passive
dat	dative	*perf*	perfect
decl	declension	*pers*	person
defec	defective	*PHILOS*	philosophy
ECCL	ecclesiastical	*pl*	plural
esp	especially	*POL*	politics
excl	exclamatory	*ppa*	perfect participle active
f	feminine	*ppp*	perfect participle passive
fig	figurative	*prep*	preposition
fut	future	*pres*	present
gen	genitive	*pron*	pronoun
GEOG	geography	*prop*	properly
GRAM	grammar	*PROV*	proverb
imperf	imperfect	*rel*	relative
impers	impersonal	*RHET*	rhetoric
impv	imperative	*sg*	singular
indecl	indeclinable	*subj*	subjunctive
indic	indicative	*superl*	superlative
inf	informal	*THEAT*	theatre
infin	infinitive	*UNIV*	university
interj	interjection	*usu*	usually
interrog	interrogative	*vi*	intransitive verb
LIT	literature	*voc*	vocative
loc	locative	*vt*	transitive verb

LATIN ALPHABET

The Latin alphabet is the one which has been almost universally adopted by the modern languages of Europe and America. In the Classical period it had 23 letters, namely the English alphabet without letters **j**, **v** and **w**.

Letter v
The symbol **v** was the capital form of the letter **u**, but in a later age the small **v** came into use to represent the consonantal **u**, and as it is commonly so employed in modern editions of Latin authors, it has been retained as a distinct letter in this dictionary for convenience.

Letter j
The symbol **j** came to be used as the consonantal **i**, and is found in older editions of the Classics, but as it has been almost entirely discarded in modern texts, it is not used in this dictionary, and words found spelt with a **j** must therefore be looked up under **i**.

Letters w, y, z
The letter **w** may be seen in the Latinized forms of some modern names, e.g. **Westmonasterium**, Westminster. The letters **y** and **z** occur only in words of Greek origin.

ORTHOGRAPHY
Many Latin words which begin with a prefix can be spelled in two ways. The prefix can retain its original spelling, or it can be assimilated, changing a letter depending on the letter which follows it. Compare the following:

ad before **g**, **l**, **r** and **p**:

adpropinquare	appropinquare
adgredi	aggredi
adloquor	alloquor
adrogans	arrogans

ad is also often assimilated before **f** and **n**:

adfectus	affectus
adnexus	annexus

and **ad** is often shortened to **a** before **sc**:

adscendere	ascendere

in changes to **il** before **l**, to **im** before **m** or **p** and to **ir** before **r**.

con becomes **cor** when followed by another **r** and **col** when followed by **l**.

We have provided cross-references in the text to draw your attention to the alternative forms of words. Thus, although **arrogantia** does not appear in the Latin-English section, the cross-reference at **arr-** will point you to the entry for **adrogantia**, where the translation is given.

PRONUNCIATION

The ancient pronunciation of Latin has been established with a fair degree of certainty from the evidence of ancient authorities and inscriptions and inferences from the modern Romance languages. It is not possible, of course, to recapture the precise nuances of Classical Latin speech, but what follows is now generally accepted and generally understood as a reasonably accurate guide to the sounds of Latin as spoken by educated Romans during the two centuries from Cicero to Quintilian.

ACCENT

The Latin accent in the Classical period was a weak stress, perhaps with an element of pitch in it. It falls, as in English, on the second last syllable of the word if that syllable is long, and on the third last syllable if the second last is short. Disyllabic words take the accent on the first syllable, unless they have already lost a final syllable, e.g. **illīc(e)**.

Inflected words are commonly learned with the accent wrongly placed on the last syllable, for convenience in memorizing the inflexions. But it is advisable to get the accent as well as the ending right.

The correct accent of other words can easily be found by noting carefully the quantity of the second last syllable and then accenting the word as in English, according to the rule given above. Thus **fuērunt** is accented on the second last syllable because the **e** is long, whereas **fuerant** is accented on the third last, because the **e** is short.

VOWELS

Vowels are pure and should not be diphthongized as in certain sounds of Southern English. They may be long or short. Throughout this dictionary all vowels known or believed by the best authorities to be long are marked with a line above them; those unmarked are either known to be short or of uncertain quantity.

Short		*Long*	
agricola	rat	rāmus	rather
hedera	pen	avē	pay
itaque	kin	cīvis	keen
favor	rob	ampliō	robe
nebula	full	lūna	fool

y is a Greek sound and is pronounced (both short and long) as **u** in French ie **rue**.

DIPHTHONGS

aestas	try
audio	town
h**ei**	pa**yee**
m**eu**s	**ay-oo** *with the accent on first sound*
mo**e**cha	t**oy**
t**ui**tus	Lou**i**s

CONSONANTS

balneae	**b**a**b**y	
a**bs**temius	a**ps**e	
su**bt**ractus	a**pt**	
castra	**c**ar	
chorda	sepul**ch**re	
inter**d**o	**d**og	
cōn**f**lō	**f**ortune	
in**g**redior	**g**o	
habeō	**h**and	*(but faintly)*
iaceo	**y**es	*(consonantal i = j)*
Kalendae	oa**k**	
conge**l**ō	**l**et	
co**m**es	**m**an	*(final m was hardly sounded and may have simply nasalized the preceding vowel)*
pā**n**is	**n**o	
pa**ng**o	fi**ng**er	
stu**p**eō	a**p**t	
ra**ph**anus	**p**ill	
exse**qu**or	**qu**ite	
sup**r**emus	b**r**ae	*(Scottish)*
magnu**s**	**s**i**s**ter	*(never as in rose)*
lae**t**us	**st**op	
theātrum	**t**ake	
vapor *(and consonantal u)*	**w**in	
de**x**tra	si**x**	*(ks, not gs)*
zona	**z**ero	

Double consonants lengthen the sound of the consonant.

Latin – English

a

ā¹ *prep* (*with abl*) from; after, since; by, in respect of; **ab epistulīs**, **ā manū** secretary; **ab hāc parte** on this side; **ab integrō** afresh; **ā nōbīs** on our side; **ab integrō** afresh; **ā nōbīs** on our side; **ā tergō** in the rear; **cōpiōsus ā frūmentō** rich in corn; **usque ab** ever since

ā² *interj* ah!

ab *prep see* **ā¹**

abāctus *ppp of* **abigō**

abacus, -ī *m* tray; sideboard; gaming board; panel; counting table

abaliēnō, -āre, -āvī, -ātum *vt* to dispose of; to remove, estrange

Abantiadēs *m* Acrisius *or* Perseus

Abās, -antis *m* a king of Argos

abavus, -ī *m* great-great-grandfather

abbās, -ātis *m* abbot

abbātia *f* abbey

abbātissa *f* abbess

Abdēra, -ōrum *or* **-ae** *ntpl, fs* a town in Thrace

Abdērītānus *adj see* **Abdēra**

Abdērītēs *m* Democritus *or* Protagoras

abdicātiō, -ōnis *f* disowning, abdication

abdicō, -āre, -āvī, -ātum *vt* to disown; to resign; **sē abdicāre** abdicate

abdīcō, -īcere, -īxī, -ictum *vt* (AUG) to be unfavourable to

abditus *ppp of* **abdō**

abdō, -ere, -idī, -itum *vt* to hide; to remove

abdōmen, -inis *nt* paunch, belly; gluttony

abdūcō, -ūcere, -ūxī, -uctum *vt* to lead away, take away; to seduce

abductus *ppp of* **abdūcō**

abecedārium, -iī *nt* alphabet

abēgī *perf of* **abigō**

abeō, -īre, -iī, -itum *vi* to go away, depart; to pass away; to be changed; to retire (*from an office*)

abequitō, -āre, -āvī, -ātum *vi* to ride away

aberrātiō, -ōnis *f* relief (*from trouble*)

aberrō, -āre, -āvī, -ātum *vi* to stray; to deviate; to have respite

abfore *fut infin of* **absum**

abfuī *perf of* **absum**

abfutūrus *fut p of* **absum**

abhinc *adv* since, ago

abhorreō, -ēre, -uī *vi* to shrink from; to differ; to be inconsistent

abiciō, -icere, -iēcī, -iectum *vt* to throw away, throw down; to abandon, degrade

abiectus *ppp of* **abiciō ▸** *adj* despondent; contemptible

abiēgnus *adj* of fir

abiēns, -euntis *pres p of* **abeō**

abiēs, -etis *f* fir; ship

abigō, -igere, -ēgī, -āctum *vt* to drive away

abitus, -ūs *m* departure; exit

abiūdicō, -āre, -āvī, -ātum *vt* to take away (*by judicial award*)

abiūnctus *ppp of* **abiungō**

abiungō, -ungere, -ūnxī, -ūnctum *vt* to unyoke; to detach

abiūrō, -āre, -āvī, -ātum *vt* to deny on oath

ablātus *ppp of* **auferō**

ablēgātiō, -ōnis *f* sending away

ablēgō, -āre, -āvī, -ātum *vt* to send out of the way

abligurriō, -īre, -īvī, -ītum *vt* to spend extravagantly

ablocō, -āre, -āvī, -ātum *vt* to let (*a house*)

ablūdō, -dere, -sī, -sum *vi* to be unlike

abluō, -uere, -uī, -ūtum *vt* to wash clean; to remove

abnegō, -āre, -āvī, -ātum *vt* to refuse

abnepōs, -ōtis *m* great-great-grandson

abneptis *f* great-great-granddaughter

abnoctō, -āre *vi* to stay out all night

abnōrmis *adj* unorthodox

abnuō, -uere, -uī, -ūtum *vt* to refuse; to deny

aboleō, -ēre, -ēvī, -itum *vt* to abolish

abolēscō, -ēscere, -ēvī *vi* to vanish

abolitiō, -ōnis *f* cancelling

abolla, -ae *f* greatcoat

abōminātus *adj* accursed

abōminor, -ārī, -ātus *vt* to deprecate; to detest

Aborīginēs, -um *mpl* original inhabitants

aborior, -īrī, -tus *vi* to miscarry

abortiō, -ōnis *f* miscarriage

abortīvus *adj* born prematurely

abortus, -ūs *m* miscarriage

abrādō, -dere, -sī, -sum *vt* to scrape off, shave

abrāsus *ppp of* **abrādō**

abreptus *ppp of* **abripiō**

abripiō, -ipere, -ipuī, -eptum *vt* to drag away, carry off

abrogātiō, -ōnis *f* repeal

abrogō, -āre, -āvī, -ātum *vt* to annul

abrotonum, -ī *nt* southernwood

abrumpō, -umpere, -ūpī, -uptum *vt* to break off

abruptus *ppp of* **abrumpō ▸** *adj* steep; abrupt, disconnected

abs *etc see* **ā¹**

abscēdō, -ēdere, -essī, -essum *vi* to depart, withdraw; to cease

abscīdō, **-dere**, **-dī**, **-sum** vt to cut off

abscindō, **-ndere**, **-dī**, **-ssum** vt to tear off, cut off

abscissus ppp of **abscindō**

abscīsus ppp of **abscīdō** ▸ adj steep; abrupt

abscondō, **-ere**, **-ī** and **-idī**, **-itum** vt to conceal; to leave behind

absēns, **-entis** pres p of **absum** ▸ adj absent

absentia, **-ae** f absence

absiliō, **-īre**, **-iī** and **-uī** vi to spring away

absimilis adj unlike

absinthium, **-ī** and **-iī** nt wormwood

absis, **-īdis** f vault; (ECCL) chancel

absistō, **-istere**, **-titī** vi to come away; to desist

absolūtē adv fully, unrestrictedly

absolūtiō, **-ōnis** f acquittal; perfection

absolūtus ppp of **absolvō** ▸ adj complete; (RHET) unqualified

absolvō, **-vere**, **-vī**, **-ūtum** vt to release, set free; (LAW) to acquit; to bring to completion, finish off; to pay off, discharge

absonus adj unmusical; incongruous; ~ **ab** not in keeping with

absorbeō, **-bēre**, **-buī**, **-ptum** vt to swallow up; to monopolize

absp- etc see **asp-**

absque prep (with abl) without, but for

abstēmius adj temperate

abstergeō, **-gēre**, **-sī**, **-sum** vt to wipe away; (fig) to banish

absterreō, **-ēre**, **-uī**, **-itum** vt to scare away, deter

abstinēns, **-entis** adj continent

abstinenter adv with restraint

abstinentia, **-ae** f restraint, self-control; fasting

abstineō, **-inēre**, **-inuī**, **-entum** vt to withhold, keep off ▸ vi to abstain, refrain; **sē abstinēre** refrain

abstitī perf of **absistō**

abstō, **-āre** vi to stand aloof

abstractus ppp of **abstrahō**

abstrahō, **-here**, **-xī**, **-ctum** vt to drag away, remove; to divert

abstrūdō, **-dere**, **-sī**, **-sum** vt to conceal

abstrūsus ppp of **abstrūdō** ▸ adj deep, abstruse; reserved

abstulī perf of **auferō**

absum, **abesse**, **āfuī** vi to be away, absent, distant; to keep clear of; to be different; to be missing, fail to assist; **tantum abest ut** so far from; **haud multum āfuit quīn** I was (they were etc) within an ace of

absūmō, **-ere**, **-psī**, **-ptum** vt to consume; to ruin, kill; (time) to spend

absurdē adv out of tune; absurdly

absurdus adj unmusical; senseless, absurd

Absyrtus, **-ī** m brother of Medea

abundāns, **-antis** adj overflowing; abundant; rich; abounding in

abundanter adv copiously

abundantia, **-ae** f abundance, plenty; wealth

abundē adv abundantly, more than enough

abundō, **-āre**, **-āvī**, **-ātum** vi to overflow; to abound, be rich in

abūsiō, **-ōnis** f (RHET) catachresis

abusque prep (with abl) all the way from

abūtor, **-tī**, **-sus** vi (with abl) to use up; to misuse

Abydēnus adj see **Abȳdos**

Abȳdos, **Abȳdus**, **-ī** m a town on Dardanelles

ac etc see **atque**

Acadēmia, **-ae** f Plato's Academy at Athens; Plato's philosophy; Cicero's villa

Acadēmica ntpl book of Cicero on philosophy

Acadēmus, **-ī** m an Athenian hero

acalanthis, **-dis** f thistlefinch

acanthus, **-ī** m bear's-breech

Acarnānes, **-um** mpl the Acarnanians

Acarnānia, **-iae** f a district of N.W. Greece

Acarnānicus adj see **Acarnānia**

Acca Lārentia, **Accae Lārentiae** f Roman goddess

accēdō, **-ēdere**, **-essī**, **-essum** vi to come, go to, approach; to attack; to be added; to agree with; (duty) to take up; **ad rem pūblicam accēdere** to enter politics; **prope ~ ad** to resemble; **accēdit quod**, **hūc accēdit ut** moreover

accelerō, **-āre**, **-āvī**, **-ātum** vt, vi to hasten

accendō, **-endere**, **-endī**, **-ēnsum** vt to set on fire, light; to illuminate; (fig) to inflame, incite

accēnseō, **-ēre**, **-uī**, **-um** vt to assign

accēnsī mpl (MIL) supernumeraries

accēnsus¹ ppp of **accendō**, **accēnseō**

accēnsus², **-ī** m officer attending a magistrate

accentus, **-ūs** m accent

accēpī perf of **accipiō**

acceptiō, **-ōnis** f receiving

acceptum nt credit side (of ledger); **in ~ referre** place to one's credit

acceptus ppp of **accipiō** ▸ adj acceptable

accersō etc see **arcessō**

accessiō, **-ōnis** f coming, visiting; attack; increase, addition

accessus, **-ūs** m approach, visit; flood tide; admittance, entrance

Acciānus adj see **Accius**

accidō, **-ere**, **-ī** vi to fall (at, on); (senses) to strike; (usu misfortune) to befall, happen

accīdō, **-dere**, **-dī**, **-sum** vt to fell, cut into; to eat up, impair

accingō, **-gere**, **-xī**, **-ctum** vt to gird on, arm; (fig) to make ready

acciō, **-īre**, **-īvī**, **-ītum** vt to summon; to procure

accipiō, **-ipere**, **-ēpī**, **-eptum** vt to take, receive, accept; (guest) to treat; (information) to hear; to interpret, take as; to suffer; to approve

accipiter, **-ris** m hawk

accīsus ppp of **accīdō**

accītus¹ ppp of **acciō**

accītus², -ūs *m* summons

Accius, -ī *m* Roman tragic poet

acclāmātiō, -ōnis *f* shout (*of approval or disapproval*)

acclāmō, -āre, -āvī, -ātum *vi* to cry out against; to hail

acclārō, -āre, -āvī, -ātum *vt* to make known

acclīnātus *adj* sloping

acclīnis *adj* leaning against; inclined

acclīnō, -āre, -āvī, -ātum *vt* to lean against; **sē acclīnāre** incline towards

acclīvis *adj* uphill

acclīvitās, -ātis *f* gradient

accola, -ae *m* neighbour

accolō, -olere, -oluī, -ultum *vt* to live near

accommodātē *adv* suitably

accommodātiō, -ōnis *f* fitting together; compliance

accommodātus *adj* suited

accommodō, -āre, -āvī, -ātum *vt* to fit, put on; to adjust, adapt, bring to; to apply; **sē accommodāre** devote oneself

accommodus *adj* suitable

accrēdō, -ere, -idī, -itum *vi* to believe

accrēscō, -ēscere, -ēvī, -ētum *vi* to increase, be added

accrētiō, -ōnis *f* increasing

accubitiō, -ōnis *f* reclining (*at meals*)

accubō, -āre *vi* to lie near; to recline (*at meals*)

accumbō, -mbere, -buī, -bitum *vi* to recline at table; **in sinū accumbere** sit next to

accumulātē *adv* copiously

accumulō, -āre, -āvī, -ātum *vt* to pile up, amass; to load

accūrātē *adv* painstakingly

accūrātiō, -ōnis *f* exactness

accūrātus *adj* studied

accūrō, -āre, -āvī, -ātum *vt* to attend to

accurrō, -rrere, -currī *and* **-rrī, -rsum** *vi* to hurry to

accursus, -ūs *m* hurrying

accūsābilis *adj* reprehensible

accūsātiō, -ōnis *f* accusation

accūsātor, -ōris *m* accuser, prosecutor

accūsātōriē *adv* like an accuser

accūsātōrius *adj* of the accuser

accūsō, -āre, -āvī, -ātum *vt* to accuse, prosecute; to reproach; **ambitūs accūsāre** prosecute for bribery

acer, -is *nt* maple

ācer, -ris *adj* sharp; (*sensation*) keen, pungent; (*emotion*) violent; (*mind*) shrewd; (*conduct*) eager, brave; hasty, fierce; (*circumstances*) severe

acerbē *adv see* **acerbus**

acerbitās, -ātis *f* bitterness; (*fig*) harshness, severity; sorrow

acerbō, -āre, -āvī, -ātum *vt* to aggravate

acerbus *adj* bitter, sour; harsh; (*fig*) premature; (*person*) rough, morose, violent; (*things*) troublesome, sad

acernus *adj* of maple

acerra, -ae *f* incense box

acervātim *adv* in heaps

acervō, -āre, -āvī, -ātum *vt* to pile up

acervus, -ī *m* heap

acēscō, -ere, acuī *vt* to turn sour

Acestēs, -ae *m* a mythical Sicilian

acētum, -ī *nt* vinegar; (*fig*) wit

Achaemenēs, -is *m* first Persian king; type of Oriental wealth

Achaeus *adj* Greek

Achāia, -ae *f* a district in W. Greece; Greece; Roman province

Achāicus *adj see* **Achāia**

Achātēs, -ae *m* companion of Aeneas

Achelōius *adj see* **Achelōus**

Achelōus, -ī *m* river in N.W. Greece; river god

Acherōn, -ontis *m* river in Hades

Acherūsius *adj see* **Acherōn**

Achillēs, -is *m* Greek epic hero

Achillēus *adj see* **Achillēs**

Achīvus *adj* Greek

Acidālia, -ae *f* Venus

Acidālius *adj see* **Acidālia**

acidus *adj* sour, tart; (*fig*) disagreeable

aciēs, -ēī *f* sharp edge or point; (*eye*) sight, keen glance, pupil; (*mind*) power, apprehension; (*MIL*) line of troops, battle order, army, battle; (*fig*) debate; **prīma ~** van; **novissima ~** rearguard

acīnacēs, -is *m* scimitar

acinum, -ī *nt* berry, grape; fruit seed

acinus, -ī *m* berry, grape; fruit seed

acipēnser, -eris *m* sturgeon

acipēnsis, -is *m* sturgeon

aclys, -dis *f* javelin

aconītum, -ī *nt* monkshood; poison

acor, -ōris *m* sour taste

acquiēscō, -ēscere, -ēvī, -ētum *vi* to rest, die; to find pleasure (in); to acquiesce

acquīrō, -rere, -sīvī, -sītum *vt* to get in addition, acquire

Acragās, -antis *m see* **Agrigentum**

acrātophorum, -ī *nt* wine jar

acrēdula, -ae *f* a bird (*unidentified*)

ācriculus *adj* peevish

ācrimōnia, -ae *f* pungent taste; (*speech, action*) briskness, go

Acrisiōniadēs, -ae *m* Perseus

Acrisius, -ī *m* father of Danae

ācriter *adv see* **ācer**

ācroāma, -tis *nt* entertainment, entertainer

ācroāsis, -is *f* public lecture

Ācroceraunia, -ōrum *ntpl* a promontory in N.W. Greece

Ācrocorinthus, -ī *f* fortress of Corinth

acta, -ae *f* beach

ācta, -ōrum *ntpl* public records, proceedings; **~ diurna, ~ pūblica** daily gazette

Actaeus *adj* Athenian

āctiō, -ōnis *f* action, doing; official duties; negotiations; (*LAW*) action, suit, indictment, pleading, case, trial; (*RHET*) delivery; (*drama*) plot; **~ grātiārum** expression of thanks;

āctiōnem intendere, āctiōnem īnstituere bring an action

āctitō, -āre, -āvī, -ātum vt to plead, act often

Actium, -ī and **-iī** nt a town in N.W. Greece; *Augustus's great victory*

Actius, Actiacus adj see **Actium**

āctivus adj of action, practical

āctor, -ōris m driver, performer; (LAW) plaintiff, pleader; (COMM) agent; (RHET) orator; (drama) actor; **~ pūblicus** manager of public property; **~ summārum** cashier

āctuāria f pinnace

āctuāriolum, -ī nt small barge

āctuārius adj fast (ship)

āctuōsē adv actively

āctuōsus adj very active

āctus¹ ppp of **agō**

āctus², -ūs m moving, driving; right of way for cattle or vehicles; performance; (drama) playing a part, recital, act of a play

āctūtum adv immediately

acuī perf of **acēscō; acuō**

acula, -ae f small stream

aculeātus adj prickly; (words) stinging; quibbling

aculeus, -ī m sting, prickle, barb; (fig) sting

acūmen, -inis nt point, sting; (fig) shrewdness, ingenuity; trickery

acuō, -uere, -uī, -ūtum vt to sharpen; to exercise; (the mind) to stimulate; to rouse (to action)

acus, -ūs f needle, pin; **acū pingere** embroider; **rem acū tangere** hit the nail on the head

acūtē adv see **acūtus**

acūtulus adj rather subtle

acūtus adj sharp, pointed; (senses) keen; (sound) high-pitched; severe; intelligent

ad prep (with acc) to, towards, against; near, at; until; (num) about; with regard to, according to; for the purpose of, for; compared with; besides; **ad Castoris** to the temple of Castor; **ad dextram** on the right; **ad hōc** besides; **ad locum** on the spot; **ad manum** at hand; **ad rem** to the point; **ad summam** in short; **ad tempus** in time; **ad ūnum omnēs** all without exception; **ad urbem esse** wait outside the city gates; **ad verbum** literally; **nīl ad** nothing to do with; **usque ad** right up to

adāctiō, -ōnis f enforcing

adāctus¹ ppp of **adigō**

adāctus², -ūs m snapping (of teeth)

adaequē adv equally

adaequō, -āre, -āvī, -ātum vt to make equal, level; to equal, match ▶ vi to be equal

adamantēus, adamantinus adj see **adamās**

adamās, -antis m adamant, steel; diamond

adamō, -āre, -āvī, -ātum vt to fall in love with

adaperiō, -īre, -uī, -tum vt to throw open

adapertilis adj openable

adaquō, -āre, -āvī, -ātum vt (plants, animals) to water

adaquor vi to fetch water

adauctus, -ūs m growing

adaugeō, -gēre, -xī, -ctum vt to aggravate; (sacrifice) to consecrate

adaugēscō, -ere vi to grow bigger

adbibō, -ere, -ī vt to drink; (fig) to drink in

adbītō, -ere vi to come near

adc- etc see **acc-**

addecet, -ēre vt it becomes

addēnseō, -ēre vt to close (ranks)

addīcō, -īcere, -īxī, -ictum vi (AUG) to be favourable ▶ vt (LAW) to award; (auction) to knock down; (fig) to sacrifice, devote

addictiō, -ōnis f award (at law)

addictus ppp of **addīcō** ▶ m bondsman

addiscō, -scere, -dicī vt to learn more

additāmentum, -ī nt increase

additus ppp of **addō**

addō, -ere, -idī, -itum vt to add, put to, bring to; to impart; to increase; **addere gradum** quicken pace; **adde quod** besides

addoceō, -ēre, -uī, -tum vt to teach new

addubitō, -āre, -āvī, -ātum vi to be in doubt ▶ vt to question

addūcō, -ūcere, -ūxī, -uctum vt to take, bring to; to draw together, pull taut, wrinkle; (fig) to induce; (pass) to be led to believe

adductus ppp of **addūcō** ▶ adj contracted; (fig) severe

adedō, -edere, -ēdī, -ēsum vt to begin to eat; to eat up; to use up; to wear away

adēmī perf of **adimō**

ademptiō, -ōnis f taking away

ademptus ppp of **adimō**

adeō¹, -īre, -iī, -itum vt, vi to go to, approach; to address; to undertake, submit to, enter upon

adeō² adv so; (after pron) just; (after conj, adv, adj: for emphasis) indeed, very; (adding an explanation) for, in fact, thus; or rather; **~ nōn ... ut** so far from; **atque ~, sīve ~** or rather; **usque ~** so far, so long, so much

adeps, -ipis m/f fat; corpulence

adeptiō, -ōnis f attainment

adeptus ppa of **adipīscor**

adequitō, -āre, -āvī, -ātum vi to ride up (to)

adesdum come here!

adesse infin of **adsum**

adēsus ppp of **adedō**

adfābilis adj easy to talk to

adfābilitās, -ātis f courtesy

adfabrē adv ingeniously

adfatim adv to one's satisfaction, enough, ad nauseam

adfātur, -rī, -tus vt (defec) to speak to

adfātus¹ ppa of **adfātur**

adfātus², -ūs m speaking to

adfectātiō, -ōnis f aspiring; (RHET) affectation

adfectātus adj (RHET) studied

adfectiō, -ōnis f frame of mind, mood; disposition; goodwill; (ASTR) relative position

adfectō, -āre, -āvī, -ātum vt to aspire to, aim at; to try to win over; to make pretence of;

viam adfectāre ad try to get to

adfectus¹ ppp of **adficiō** ▸ adj affected with, experienced (abl); (person) disposed; (things) weakened; (explanation) well-advanced

adfectus², **-ūs** m disposition, mood; fondness; (pl) loved ones

adferō, **adferre**, **attulī**, **adlātum** and **allātum** vt to bring, carry to; to bring to bear, use against; to bring news; (explanation) to bring forward; (undertakings) to contribute (something useful)

adficiō, **-icere**, **-ēcī**, **-ectum** vt to affect; to endow, afflict with (abl); **exsiliō adficere** banish; **honōre adficere** honour (also used with other nouns to express the corresponding verbs)

adfictus ppp of **adfingō**

adfīgō, **-gere**, **-xī**, **-xum** vt to fasten, attach; to impress (on the mind)

adfingō, **-ngere**, **-nxī**, **-ctum** vt to make, form (as part of); invent

adfīnis, **-is** m/f neighbour; relation (by marriage) ▸ adj neighbouring; associated with (dat, gen)

adfīnitās, **-ātis** f relationship (by marriage)

adfirmātē adv with assurance

adfirmātiō, **-ōnis** f declaration

adfirmō, **-āre**, **-āvī**, **-ātum** vt to declare; to confirm

adfixus ppp of **adfīgō**

adflātus, **-ūs** m breath, exhalation; (fig) inspiration

adfleō, **-ēre** vi to weep (at)

adflīctātiō, **-ōnis** f suffering

adflīctō, **-āre**, **-āvī**, **-ātum** vt to harass, distress

adflīctor, **-ōris** m destroyer

adflīctus ppp of **adflīgō** ▸ adj distressed, ruined; dejected; depraved

adflīgō, **-īgere**, **-īxī**, **-īctum** vt to dash against, throw down; (fig) to impair, crush

adflō, **-āre**, **-āvī**, **-ātum** vt, vi to blow on, breathe upon

adfluēns, **-entis** adj rich (in)

adfluenter adv copiously

adfluentia, **-ae** f abundance

adfluō, **-ere**, **-xī**, **-xum** vi to flow; (fig) to flock in, abound in

adfore fut infin of **adsum**

adforem imperf subj of **adsum**

adfuī perf of **adsum**

adfulgeō, **-gēre**, **-sī** vi to shine on; to appear

adfundō, **-undere**, **-ūdī**, **-ūsum** vt to pour in; to rush (troops) to

adfūsus adj prostrate

adfutūrus fut p of **adsum**

adgemō, **-ere** vi to groan at

adglomerō, **-āre** vt to add on

adglūtinō, **-āre** vt to stick on

adgravēscō, **-ere** vi to become worse

adgravō, **-āre**, **-āvī**, **-ātum** vt to aggravate

adgredior, **-dī**, **-ssus** vt to approach, accost; to attack; (a task) to undertake, take up

adgregō, **-āre**, **-āvī**, **-ātum** vt to add, attach

adgressiō, **-ōnis** f introductory remarks

adgressus ppa of **adgredior**

adhaereō, **-rēre**, **-sī**, **-sum** vi to stick to; (fig) to cling to, keep close to

adhaerēscō, **-ere** vi to stick to or in; (speech) to falter

adhaesiō, **-ōnis** f clinging

adhaesus, **-ūs** m adhering

adhibeō, **-ēre**, **-uī**, **-itum** vt to bring, put, add; to summon, consult, treat; to use, apply (for some purpose)

adhinniō, **-īre**, **-īvī**, **-ītum** vi to neigh to; (fig) to go into raptures over

adhortātiō, **-ōnis** f exhortation

adhortātor, **-ōris** m encourager

adhortor, **-ārī**, **-ātus** vt to encourage, urge

adhūc adv so far; as yet, till now; still; ~ **nōn** not yet

adiaceō, **-ēre**, **-uī** vi to lie near, border on

adiciō, **-icere**, **-iēcī**, **-iectum** vt to throw to; to add; to turn towards (mind, eyes)

adiectiō, **-ōnis** f addition

adiectus¹ ppp of **adiciō**

adiectus², **-ūs** m bringing close

adigō, **-igere**, **-ēgī**, **-āctum** vt to drive (to); to compel; **iūs iūrandum adigere** put on oath; **in verba adigere** force to owe allegiance

adimō, **-imere**, **-ēmī**, **-emptum** vt to take away (from dat)

adipātum nt pastry

adipātus adj fatty; (fig) florid

adipīscor, **-ipīscī**, **-eptus** vt to overtake; to attain, acquire

aditus, **-ūs** m approach, access (to a person); entrance; (fig) avenue

adiūdicō, **-āre**, **-āvī**, **-ātum** vt to award (in arbitration); to ascribe

adiūmentum, **-ī** nt aid, means of support

adiūncta ntpl collateral circumstances

adiūnctiō, **-ōnis** f uniting; addition; (RHET) proviso; repetition

adiūnctus ppp of **adiungō** ▸ adj connected

adiungō, **-ungere**, **-ūnxī**, **-ūnctum** vt to yoke; to attach; (suspicion etc) to direct; (remark) to add

adiūrō, **-āre**, **-āvī**, **-ātum** vt, vi to swear, swear by

adiūtō, **-āre**, **-āvī**, **-ātum** vt to help

adiūtor, **-ōris** m helper; (MIL) adjutant; (POL) official; (THEAT) supporting cast

adiūtrīx, **-rīcis** f see **adiūtor**

adiūtus ppp of **adiuvō**

adiuvō, **-uvāre**, **-ūvī**, **-ūtum** vt to help; to encourage

adj- etc see **adi-**

adlābor, **-bī**, **-psus** vi to fall, move towards, come to

adlabōrō, **-āre**, **-āvī**, **-ātum** vi to work hard; to improve by taking trouble

adlacrimō, **-āre**, **-āvī**, **-ātum** vi to shed tears

adlāpsus¹ ppa of **adlābor**

adlāpsus², **-ūs** m stealthy approach

adlātrō, -āre, -āvī, -ātum vt to bark at; (fig) to revile

adlātus ppp of **adferō**

adlaudō, -āre, -āvī, -ātum vt to praise highly

adlectō, -āre, -āvī, -ātum vt to entice

adlectus ppp of **adliciō**

adlēctus ppp of **adlegō**

adlēgātī mpl deputies

adlēgātiō, -ōnis f mission

adlegō, -egere, -ēgī, -ēctum vt to elect

adlēgō, -āre, -āvī, -ātum vt to despatch, commission; to mention

adlevāmentum, -ī nt relief

adlevātiō, -ōnis f easing

adlevō, -āre, -āvī, -ātum vt to lift up; to comfort; to weaken

adliciō, -icere, -exī, -ectum vt to attract

adlīdō, -dere, -sī, -sum vt to dash (against); (fig) to hurt

adligō, -āre, -āvī, -ātum vt to tie up, bandage; (fig) to bind, lay under an obligation

adlinō, -inere, -ēvī, -itum vt to smear; (fig) to attach

adlīsus ppp of **adlīdō**

adlocūtiō, -ōnis f address, comforting words

adlocūtus ppa of **adloquor**

adloquium, -ī and -iī nt talk; encouragement

adloquor, -quī, -cūtus vt to speak to, address

adlūdiō, -āre, -āvī, -ātum vi to play (with)

adlūdō, -dere, -sī, -sum vi to joke, play

adluō, -ere, -ī vt to wash

adluviēs, -ēī f pool left by flood water

adluviō, -ōnis f alluvial land

admātūrō, -āre, -āvī, -ātum vt to hurry on

admētior, -tīrī, -nsus vt to measure out

adminiculor, -ārī, -ātus vt to prop

adminiculum, -ī nt (AGR) stake; (fig) support

administer, -rī m assistant

administrātiō, -ōnis f services; management

administrātor, -ōris m manager

administrō, -āre, -āvī, -ātum vt to manage, govern

admīrābilis adj wonderful, surprising

admīrābilitās, -ātis f wonderfulness

admīrābiliter adv admirably; paradoxically

admīrātiō, -ōnis f wonder, surprise, admiration

admīror, -ārī, -ātus vt to wonder at, admire; to be surprised at

admisceō, -scēre, -scuī, -xtum vt to mix in with, add to; (fig) to involve; **sē admīscēre** interfere

admissārius, -ī and -iī m stallion

admissum, -ī nt crime

admissus ppp of **admittō**

admittō, -ittere, -īsī, -issum vt to let in, admit; to set at a gallop; to allow; to commit (a crime); **equō admissō** charging

admixtiō, -ōnis f admixture

admixtus ppp of **admisceō**

admoderātē adv suitably

admoderor, -ārī, -ātus vt to restrain

admodum adv very, quite; fully; yes; (with neg) at all

admoneō, -ēre, -uī, -itum vt to remind, suggest, advise, warn

admonitiō, -ōnis f reminder, suggestion, admonition

admonitor, -ōris m admonisher (male)

admonitrīx, -rīcis f admonisher (female)

admonitū at the suggestion, instance

admordeō, -dēre, -sum vt to bite into; (fig) to cheat

admorsus ppp of **admordeō**

admōtiō, -ōnis f applying

admōtus ppp of **admoveō**

admoveō, -ovēre, -ōvī, -ōtum vt to move, bring up, apply; to lend (an ear), direct (the mind)

admurmurātiō, -ōnis f murmuring

admurmurō, -āre, -āvī, -ātum vi to murmur (of a crowd approving or disapproving)

admutilō, -āre, -āvī, -ātum vt to clip close; (fig) to cheat

adnectō, -ctere, -xuī, -xum vt to connect, tie

adnexus, -ūs m connection

adnīsus ppa of **adnītor**

adnītor, -tī, -sus and -xus vi to lean on; to exert oneself

adnīxus ppa of **adnītor**

adnō, -āre vt, vi to swim to

adnotō, -āre, -āvī, -ātum vt to comment on

adnumerō, -āre, -āvī, -ātum vt to pay out; to reckon along with

adnuō, -uere, -uī, -ūtum vi to nod; to assent, promise; to indicate

adoleō, -olēre, -oluī, -ultum vt to burn; to pile with gifts

adolēscen- etc see **adulēscen-**

adolēscō, -ēscere, -ēvī vi to grow up, increase; to burn

Adōnis, -is and -idis m a beautiful youth loved by Venus

adopertus adj covered

adoptātiō, -ōnis f adopting

adoptiō, -ōnis f adoption

adoptīvus adj by adoption

adoptō, -āre, -āvī, -ātum vt to choose; to adopt

ador, -ōris and -oris nt spelt

adōrea f glory

adōreus adj see **ador**

adorior, -īrī, -tus vt to accost; to attack; to set about

adōrnō, -āre, -āvī, -ātum vt to get ready

adōrō, -āre, -āvī, -ātum vt to entreat; to worship, revere

adortus ppa of **adorior**

adp- etc see **app-**

adrādō, -dere, -sī, -sum vt to shave close

Adrastus, -ī m a king of Argos

adrāsus ppp of **adrādō**

adrēctus ppp of **adrigō** ▸ adj steep

adrēpō, -ere, -sī, -tum vi to creep, steal into

adreptus *ppp of* **adripiō**

Adria *etc see* **Hadria** *etc*

adrīdeō, -dēre, -sī, -sum *vt, vi* to laugh, smile at; to please

adrigō, -igere, -ēxī, -ēctum *vt* to raise; (*fig*) to rouse

adripiō, -ipere, -ipuī, -eptum *vt* to seize; to appropriate; to take hold of; to learn quickly; (*LAW*) to arrest; to satirize

adrōdō, -dere, -sī, -sum *vt* to gnaw, nibble at

adrogāns, -antis *adj* arrogant, insolent

adroganter *adv see* **adrogāns**

adrogantia, -ae *f* arrogance, presumption, haughtiness

adrogātiō, -ōnis *f* adoption

adrogō, -āre, -āvī, -ātum *vt* to ask; to associate; to claim, assume; (*fig*) to award

adsc- *etc see* **asc-**

adsecla *etc see* **adsecula**

adsectātiō, -ōnis *f* attendance

adsectātor, -ōris *m* follower

adsector, -ārī, -ātus *vt* to attend on, follow (*esp a candidate*)

adsecula, -ae *m* follower (*derogatory*)

adsēdī *perf of* **adsīdeō; adsīdō**

adsēnsiō, -ōnis *f* assent, applause; (*PHILOS*) acceptance of the evidence of the senses

adsēnsor, -ōris *m* one in agreement

adsēnsus¹ *ppa of* **adsentiō**

adsēnsus², -ūs *m* assent, approval; echo; (*PHILOS*) acceptance of the evidence of the senses

adsentātiō, -ōnis *f* flattery

adsentātiuncula *f* trivial compliments

adsentātor, -ōris *m* flatterer (*male*)

adsentātōriē *adv* ingratiatingly

adsentātrīx, -rīcis *f* flatterer (*female*)

adsentiō, -entīre, -ēnsī, -ēnsum, adsentior, -entīrī, -ēnsus *vi* to agree, approve

adsentor, -ārī, -ātus *vi* to agree, flatter

adsequor, -quī, -cūtus *vt* to overtake; to attain; to grasp (*by understanding*)

adserō¹, -ere, -uī, -tum *vt* (*LAW*) to declare free (*usu with* **manū**), liberate (*a slave*), lay claim to, appropriate; **adsere in servitūtem** claim as a slave

adserō², -erere, -ēvī, -itum *vt* to plant near

adsertiō, -ōnis *f* declaration of status

adsertor, -ōris *m* champion

adserviō, -īre *vi* to assist

adservō, -āre, -āvī, -ātum *vt* to watch carefully; to keep, preserve

adsessiō, -ōnis *f* sitting beside

adsessor, -ōris *m* counsellor

adsessus, -ūs *m* sitting beside

adsevēranter *adv* emphatically

adsevērātiō, -ōnis *f* assertion; earnestness

adsevērō, -āre, -āvī, -ātum *vt* to do in earnest; to assert strongly

adsideō, -idēre, -ēdī, -essum *vi* to sit by; to attend, assist; to besiege; to resemble

adsīdō, -īdere, -ēdī *vi* to sit down

adsiduē *adv* continually

adsiduitās, -ātis *f* constant attendance; continuance, frequent recurrence

adsiduō *adv* continually

adsiduus¹ *adj* constantly in attendance, busy; continual, incessant

adsiduus², -ī *m* taxpayer

adsignātiō, -ōnis *f* allotment (*of land*)

adsignō, -āre, -āvī, -ātum *vt* to allot (*esp land*); assign; to impute, attribute; to consign

adsiliō, -ilīre, -iluī, -ultum *vi* to leap at *or* on to

adsimilis *adj* like

adsimiliter *adv* similarly

adsimulātus *adj* similar; counterfeit

adsimulō, -āre, -āvī, -ātum *vt, vi* to compare; to pretend, imitate

adsistō, -istere, -titī *vi* to stand (by); to defend

adsitus *ppp of* **adserō²**

adsoleō, -ēre *vi* to be usual

adsonō, -āre *vi* to respond

adsp- *etc see* **asp-**

adsternō, -ere *vt* to prostrate

adstipulātor, -ōris *m* supporter

adstipulor, -ārī, -ātus *vi* to agree with

adstitī *perf of* **adsistō; adstō**

adstō, -āre, -itī *vi* to stand near, stand up; to assist

adstrepō, -ere *vi* to roar

adstrictē *adv* concisely

adstrictus *ppp of* **adstringō ▶** *adj* tight, narrow; concise; stingy

adstringō, -ngere, -nxī, -ctum *vt* to draw close, tighten; to bind, oblige; to abridge

adstruō, -ere, -xī, -ctum *vt* to build on; to add

adstupeō, -ēre *vi* to be astonished

adsuēfaciō, -acere, -ēcī, -actum *vt* to accustom, train

adsuēscō, -scere, -vī, -tum *vi* to accustom, train

adsuētūdō, -inis *f* habit

adsuētus *ppp of* **adsuēscō ▶** *adj* customary

adsultō, -āre, -āvī, -ātum *vi* to jump; to attack

adsultus, -ūs *m* attack

adsum, -esse, -fuī *vi* to be present; to support, assist (*esp at law*); to come; to appear before (*a tribunal*); **animo adesse** pay attention; **iam aderō** I'll be back soon

adsūmō, -ere, -psī, -ptum *vt* to take for oneself, receive; to take also

adsūmptiō, -ōnis *f* taking up; (*LOGIC*) minor premise

adsūmptīvus *adj* (*LAW*) which takes its defence from extraneous circumstances

adsūmptum, -ī *nt* epithet

adsūmptus *ppp of* **adsūmō**

adsuō, -ere *vt* to sew on

adsurgō, -gere, -rēxī, -rēctum *vi* to rise, stand up; to swell, increase

adt- *etc see* **att-**
adulātiō, -ōnis *f (dogs)* fawning; servility
adulātor, -ōris *m* sycophant
adulātōrius *adj* flattering
adulēscēns, -entis *m/f* young man *or* woman (*usu from 15 to 30 years*)
adulēscentia, -ae *f* youth (*age 15 to 30*)
adulēscentula, -ae *f* girl
adulēscentulus, -ī *m* quite a young man
adulō, -āre, -āvī, -ātum, adulor, -ārī, -ātus *vt, vi* to fawn upon, flatter, kowtow
adulter, -ī *m*, **adultera, -ae** *f* adulterer, adulteress ▸ *adj* adulterous
adulterīnus *adj* forged
adulterium, -ī *and* **-iī** *nt* adultery
adulterō, -āre, -āvī, -ātum *vt, vi* to commit adultery; to falsify
adultus *ppp of* **adolēscō** ▸ *adj* adult, mature
adumbrātim *adv* in outline
adumbrātiō, -ōnis *f* sketch; semblance
adumbrātus *adj* false
adumbrō, -āre, -āvī, -ātum *vt* to sketch; to represent, copy
aduncitās, -ātis *f* curvature
aduncus *adj* hooked, curved
adurgeō, -ēre *vt* to pursue closely
adūrō, -rere, -ssī, -stum *vt* to burn; to freeze; (*fig*) to fire
adusque *prep* (*with acc*) right up to ▸ *adv* entirely
adūstus *ppp of* **adūrō** ▸ *adj* brown
advectīcius *adj* imported
advectō, -āre *vt* to carry frequently
advectus¹ *ppp of* **advehō**
advectus², -ūs *m* bringing
advehō, -here, -xī, -ctum *vt* to carry, convey; (*pass*) to ride
advēlō, -āre *vt* to crown
advena, -ae *m/f* stranger ▸ *adj* foreign
adveniō, -enīre, -ēnī, -entum *vi* to arrive, come
adventīcius *adj* foreign, extraneous; unearned
adventō, -āre, -āvī, -ātum *vi* to come nearer and nearer, advance rapidly
adventor, -ōris *m* visitor
adventus, -ūs *m* arrival, approach
adversāria *ntpl* daybook
adversārius, -ī *and* **-iī** *m* opponent ▸ *adj* opposing
adversātrīx, -īcis *f* antagonist
adversiō, -ōnis *f* turning (*the attention*)
adversor, -ārī, -ātus *vi* to oppose, resist
adversum, -ī *nt* opposite; misfortune ▸ *prep* (+ *acc*) towards, against ▸ *adv* to meet
adversus *ppp of* **advertō** ▸ *adj* opposite, in front; hostile; **adversō flūmine** upstream; **adversae rēs** misfortune ▸ *prep* (+ *acc*) towards, against ▸ *adv* to meet
advertō, -tere, -tī, -sum *vt* to turn, direct towards; to call attention; **animum advertere** notice, perceive; (*with* **ad**) to attend to; (*with* **in**) to punish

advesperāscit, -scere, -vit *vi* it is getting dark
advigilō, -āre *vi* to keep watch
advocātiō, -ōnis *f* legal assistance, counsel
advocātus, -ī *m* supporter in a lawsuit; advocate, counsel
advocō, -āre, -āvī, -ātum *vt* to summon; (*LAW*) to call in the assistance of
advolō, -āre, -āvī, -ātum *vi* to fly to, swoop down upon
advolvō, -vere, -vī, -ūtum *vt* to roll to; to prostrate
advor- *etc see* **adver-**
adytum, -ī *nt* sanctuary
Aeacidēs, -idae *m* Achilles; Pyrrhus
Aeacus, -ī *m* father of Peleus, and judge of the dead
Aeaea, -ae *f* Circe's island
Aeaeus *adj* of Circe
aedēs, -is *f* temple; (*pl*) house
aedicula, -ae *f* shrine; small house, room
aedificātiō, -ōnis *f* building
aedificātiuncula, -ae *f* little house
aedificātor, -ōris *m* builder
aedificium, -ī *and* **-iī** *nt* building
aedificō, -āre, -āvī, -ātum *vt* to build, construct
aedīlicius *adj* aedile's ▸ *m* ex-aedile
aedīlis, -is *m* aedile
aedīlitās, -ātis *f* aedileship
aedis, -is *see* **aedēs**
aeditumus, aedituus, -ī *m* temple-keeper
Aeduī, -ōrum *mpl* a tribe of central Gaul
Aeētēs, -ae *m* father of Medea
Aegaeus *adj* Aegean ▸ *nt* Aegean Sea
Aegātēs, -um *fpl* islands off Sicily
aeger, -rī *adj* ill, sick; sorrowful; weak
Aegīna, -ae *f* a Greek island
Aegīnēta, -ae *m* inhabitant of Aegīna
aegis, -dis *f* shield of Jupiter or Athena, aegis
Aegisthus, -ī *m* paramour of Clytemnestra
aegocerōs, -ōtis *m* Capricorn
aegrē *adv* painfully; with displeasure; with difficulty; hardly; **~ ferre** be annoyed
aegrēscō, -ere *vi* to become ill; to be aggravated
aegrimōnia, -ae *f* distress of mind
aegritūdō, -inis *f* sickness; sorrow
aegror, -ōris *m* illness
aegrōtātiō, -ōnis *f* illness, disease
aegrōtō, -āre, -āvī, -ātum *vi* to be ill
aegrōtus *adj* ill, sick
Aegyptius *adj see* **Aegyptus**
Aegyptus, -ī *f* Egypt ▸ *m* brother of Danaus
aelinos, -ī *m* dirge
Aemiliānus *adj esp* Scipio, destroyer of Carthage
Aemilius, -ī Roman family name; **Via Aemilia** road in N. Italy
aemulātiō, -ōnis *f* rivalry (*good or bad*); jealousy
aemulātor, -ōris *m* zealous imitator
aemulor, -ārī, -ātus *vt* to rival, copy; to be jealous

aemulus, -ī m rival ▸ adj rivalling; jealous
Aeneadēs, -ae m Trojan; Roman
Aenēās, -ae m Trojan leader and hero of Virgil's epic
Aenēis, -idis and **-idos** f Aeneid
Aenēius adj see **Aenēās**
aēneus adj of bronze
aenigma, -tis nt riddle, mystery
aēnum, -ī nt bronze vessel
aēnus adj of bronze
Aeolēs, -um mpl the Aeolians
Aeolia f Lipari Island
Aeolidēs m a descendant of Aeolus
Aeolis¹, -idis f Aeolia (N.W. of Asia Minor)
Aeolis², -idis f daughter of Aeolus
Aeolius adj see **Aeolus**
Aeolus, -ī m king of the winds
aequābilis adj equal; consistent, even; impartial
aequābilitās, -ātis f uniformity; impartiality
aequābiliter adv uniformly
aequaevus adj of the same age
aequālis adj equal, like; of the same age, contemporary; uniform
aequālitās, -ātis f evenness; (in politics, age) equality, similarity
aequāliter adv evenly
aequanimitās, -ātis f goodwill; calmness
aequātiō, -ōnis f equal distribution
aequē adv equally; (with 'ac', 'atque', 'et', 'quam') just as; justly
Aequī, -ōrum mpl a people of central Italy
Aequicus, Aequiculus adj see **Aequī**
Aequimaelium, -ī and **-iī** nt an open space in Rome
aequinoctiālis adj see **aequinoctium**
aequinoctium, -ī and **-iī** nt equinox
aequiperābilis adj comparable
aequiperō, -āre, -āvī, -ātum vt to compare; to equal
aequitās, -ātis f uniformity; fair dealing, equity; calmness of mind
aequō, -āre, -āvī, -ātum vt to make equal, level; to compare; to equal; **solō aequāre** raze to the ground
aequor, -is nt a level surface, sea
aequoreus adj of the sea
aequum, -ī nt plain; justice
aequus adj level, equal; favourable, friendly, fair, just; calm; **aequō animō** patiently; **aequō Marte** without deciding the issue; **aequum est** it is reasonable; **ex aequō** equally
āēr, āeris m air, weather; mist
aerāria f mine
aerārium nt treasury
aerārius adj of bronze; of money ▸ m a citizen of the lowest class at Rome; **tribūnī aerāriī** paymasters; a wealthy middle class at Rome
aerātus adj of bronze
aereus adj of copper or bronze
aerifer, -ī adj carrying cymbals
aeripēs, -edis adj bronze-footed

āērius adj of the air; lofty
aerūgō, -inis f rust; (fig) envy, avarice
aerumna, -ae f trouble, hardship
aerumnōsus adj wretched
aes, aeris nt copper, bronze; money; (pl) objects made of copper or bronze (esp statues, instruments, vessels; soldiers' pay); **aes aliēnum** debt; **aes circumforāneum** borrowed money; **aes grave** Roman coin, as
Aeschylus, -ī m Greek tragic poet
Aesculāpius, -ī m god of medicine
aesculētum, -ī nt oak forest
aesculeus adj see **aesculus**
aesculus, -ī f durmast oak
Aesōn, -onis m father of Jason
Aesonidēs, -ae m Jason
Aesōpius adj see **Aesōpus**
Aesōpus, -ī m Greek writer of fables
aestās, -ātis f summer
aestifer, -ī adj heat-bringing
aestimātiō, -ōnis f valuation, assessment; **lītis ~** assessment of damages
aestimātor, -ōris m valuer
aestimō, -āre, -āvī, -ātum vt to value, estimate the value of; **māgnī aestimāre** think highly of
aestīva, -ōrum ntpl summer camp, campaign
aestīvus adj summer
aestuārium, -ī and **-iī** nt tidal waters, estuary
aestuō, -āre, -āvī, -ātum vi to boil, burn; (movement) to heave, toss; (fig) to be excited; to waver
aestuōsus adj very hot; agitated
aestus, -ūs m heat; surge of the sea; tide; (fig) passion; hesitation
aetās, -ātis f age, life; time
aetātem adv for life
aetātula, -ae f tender age
aeternitās, -ātis f eternity
aeternō, -āre vt to immortalize
aeternus adj eternal, immortal; lasting; **in aeternum** for ever
aethēr, -eris m sky, heaven; air
aetherius adj ethereal, heavenly; of air
Aethiops, -is adj Ethiopian; (fig) stupid
aethra, -ae f sky
Aetna, -ae f Etna (in Sicily)
Aetnaeus, Aetnēnsis adj see **Aetna**
Aetōlia, -iae f a district of W. Greece
Aetōlus, Aetōlicus adj see **Aetōlia**
aevitās, -ātis old form of **aetās**
aevum, -ī nt age, lifetime; eternity; **in ~** for ever
Āfer, -rī adj African
āfore fut infin of **absum**
Āfrānius, -ī m Latin comic poet
Āfrica, -ae f Roman province (now Tunisia)
Āfricānae fpl panthers
Āfricānus adj name of two Scipios
Āfricus adj African ▸ m south-west (wind)
āfuī, āfutūrus perf, fut p of **absum**
Agamēmnōn, -onis m leader of Greeks against Troy

Agamēmnonius adj see **Agamēmnōn**
Aganippē, -ēs f a spring on Helicon
agāsō, -ōnis m ostler, footman
age, agedum come on!, well then
agellus, -ī m plot of land
Agēnōr, -oris m father of Europa
Agēnoreus adj see **Agēnōr**
Agēnoridēs, -ae m Cadmus; Perseus
agēns, -entis adj (RHET) effective
ager, -rī m land, field; countryside; territory
agg- etc see **adg-**
agger, -is m rampart; mound, embankment,
  any built-up mass
aggerō¹, -āre, -āvī, -ātum vt to pile up;
  to increase
aggerō², -rere, -ssī, -stum vt to carry, bring
aggestus, -ūs m accumulation
agilis adj mobile; nimble, busy
agilitās, -ātis f mobility
agitābilis adj light
agitātiō, -ōnis f movement, activity
agitātor, -ōris m driver, charioteer
agitō, -āre, -āvī, -ātum vt (animals) to
  drive; to move, chase, agitate; (fig) to excite
  (to action); to persecute, ridicule; to keep (a
  ceremony) ▸ vi to live; to deliberate
agmen, -inis nt forward movement,
  procession, train; army on the march;
  ~ **claudere** bring up the rear; **novissimum ~**
  rearguard; **prīmum ~** van
agna, -ae f ewe lamb; lamb (flesh)
agnāscor, -scī, -tus vi to be born after
agnātus, -ī m relation (by blood on father's side)
agnellus, -ī m little lamb
agnīnus adj of lamb
agnitiō, -ōnis f recognition, knowledge
agnitus ppp of **agnōscō**
agnōmen, -inis nt an extra surname (eg
  Africanus)
agnōscō, -ōscere, -ōvī, -itum vt to
  recognize; to acknowledge, allow; to
  understand
agnus, -ī m lamb
agō, agere, ēgī, āctum vt to drive, lead; to
  plunder; to push forward, put forth; (fig) to
  move, rouse, persecute; to do, act, perform;
  (time) to pass, spend; (undertakings) to manage,
  wage; (public speaking) to plead, discuss; to
  negotiate, transact; (THEAT) to play, act the part
  of; **agere cum populō** address the people; **age**
  come on!, well then; **age age** all right!; **āctum**
  est dē it is all up with; **aliud agere** not attend;
  animam agere expire; **annum quartum agere**
  be three years old; **causam agere** plead a cause;
  hōc age pay attention; **id agere ut** aim at; **lēge**
  agere go to law; **nīl agis** it's no use; **quid agis?**
  how are you?; **rēs agitur** interests are at stake;
  sē agere go, come
agrāriī mpl the land reform party
agrārius adj of public land; **lēx agrāria** land law
agrestis adj rustic; boorish, wild, barbarous
  ▸ m countryman

agricola, -ae m countryman, farmer
Agricola, -ae m a Roman governor of Britain; his
  biography by Tacitus
Agrigentīnus adj see **Agrigentum**
Agrigentum, -ī nt a town in Sicily
agripeta, -ae m landgrabber
Āgrippa, -ae m Roman surname (esp Augustus's
  minister)
Āgrippīna, -ae f mother of Nero; **Colōnia ~** or
  Āgrippīnēnsis Cologne
Agyīeus, -eī and **-eos** m Apollo
āh interj ah! (in sorrow or joy)
aha interj expressing reproof or laughter
ahēn- etc see **aēn-**
Āiāx, -ācis m Ajax (name of two Greek heroes at
  Troy)
āiō vt (defec) to say, speak; **ain tū?/ain vērō?**
  really?; **quid ais?** I say!
āla, -ae f wing; armpit; (MIL) wing of army
alabaster, -rī m perfume box
alacer, -ris adj brisk, cheerful
alacritās, -ātis f promptness, liveliness; joy,
  rapture
alapa, -ae f slap on the face; a slave's freedom
ālāriī mpl allied troops
ālārius adj (MIL) on the wing
ālātus adj winged
alauda, -ae f lark; name of a legion of Caesar's
alāzōn, -onis m braggart
Alba Longa, Albae Longae f a Latin town
  (precursor of Rome)
Albānus adj Alban; **Lacus ~, Mōns ~** lake and
  mountain near Alba Longa
albātus adj dressed in white
albeō, -ēre vi to be white; to dawn
albēscō, -ere vi to become white; to dawn
albicō, -āre vi to be white
albidus adj white
Albiōn, -ōnis f ancient name for Britain
albitūdō, -inis f whiteness
Albula, -ae f old name for the Tiber
albulus adj whitish
album, -ī nt white; records
Albunea, -ae f a spring at Tibur; a sulphur spring
  near Alban Lake
albus adj white, bright
Alcaeus, -ī m Greek lyric poet
alcēdō, -inis f kingfisher
alcēdōnia ntpl halcyon days
alcēs, -is f elk
Alcibiadēs, -is m brilliant Athenian politician
Alcīdēs, -ae m Hercules
Alcinous, -ī m king of Phaeacians in the Odyssey
ālea, -ae f gambling, dice; (fig) chance, hazard;
  iacta ~ est the die is cast; **in āleam dare** to risk
āleātor, -ōris m gambler
āleātōrius adj in gambling
ālec etc see **allēc**
āleō, -ōnis m gambler
āles, -itis adj winged; swift ▸ m/f bird; omen
alēscō, -ere vi to grow up
Alexander, -rī m a Greek name; Paris (prince of

Troy); Alexander (the Great) (*king of Macedon*)
Alexandrēa (*later* **-īa**), **-ēae** *f* Alexandria (*in Egypt*)
alga, -ae *f* seaweed
algeō, -gēre, -sī *vi* to feel cold; (*fig*) to be neglected
algēscō, -ere *vi* to catch cold
Algidus, -ī *m* mountain in Latium
algidus *adj* cold
algor, -ōris *m* cold
algū *abl sg m* with cold
aliā *adv* in another way
aliās *adv* at another time; at one time ... at another
alibī *adv* elsewhere; otherwise; in one place ... in another
alicubī *adv* somewhere
alicunde *adv* from somewhere
alid old form of **aliud**
aliēnātiō, -ōnis *f* transfer; estrangement
aliēnigena, -ae *m* foreigner
aliēnigenus *adj* foreign; heterogeneous
aliēnō, -āre, -āvī, -ātum *vt* to transfer (*property by sale*); to alienate, estrange; (*mind*) to derange
aliēnus *adj* of another, of others; alien, strange; (*with abl or ab*) unsuited to, different from; hostile ▶ *m* stranger
āliger, -ī *adj* winged
alimentārius *adj* about food
alimentum, -ī *nt* nourishment, food; obligation of children to parents; (*fig*) support
alimōnium, -ī *and* **-iī** *nt* nourishment
aliō *adv* in another direction, elsewhere; one way ... another way
aliōquī, aliōquīn *adv* otherwise, else; besides
aliōrsum *adv* in another direction; differently
ālipēs, -edis *adj* wing-footed; fleet
alīptēs, -ae *m* sports trainer
aliquā *adv* some way or other
aliquam *adv*: ~ **diū** for some time; ~ **multī** a considerable number
aliquandō *adv* sometime, ever; sometimes; once, for once; now at last
aliquantisper *adv* for a time
aliquantō *adv* (*with compar*) somewhat
aliquantulum *nt* a very little ▶ *adv* somewhat
aliquantulus *adj* quite small
aliquantum *adj* a good deal ▶ *adv* somewhat
aliquantus *adj* considerable
aliquātenus *adv* to some extent
aliquī, -quae, -quod *adj* some, any; some other
aliquid *adv* at all
aliquis, -quid *pron* somebody, something; someone or something important
aliquō *adv* to some place, somewhere else
aliquot *adj* (*indecl*) some
aliquotiēns *adv* several times
aliter *adv* otherwise, differently; in one way ... in another
alitus *ppp of* **alō**

ālium, -ī *and* **-iī** *nt* garlic
aliunde *adv* from somewhere else
alius, alia, aliud *adj* other, another; different; ~ ... ~ some ... others; ~ **ex aliō** one after the other; **in alia omnia īre** oppose a measure; **nihil aliud quam** only
all- *etc see* **adl-**
allēc, -is *nt* fish pickle
allex, -icis *m* big toe
Allia, -ae *f* tributary of the Tiber (*scene of a great Roman defeat*)
Alliēnsis *adj see* **Allia**
Allobrogēs, -um *mpl* a people of S.E. Gaul
Allobrogicus *adj see* **Allobrogēs**
almus *adj* nourishing; kindly
alnus, -ī *f* alder
alō, -ere, -uī, -tum *and* **-itum** *vt* to nourish, rear; to increase, promote
Alpēs, -ium *fpl* Alps
Alphēus, -ī *m* river of Olympia in S.W. Greece
Alpīnus *adj see* **Alpēs**
alsī *perf of* **algeō**
alsius, alsus *adj* cold
altāria, -ium *ntpl* altars, altar; altar top
altē *adv* on high, from above; deeply; from afar
alter, -īus *adj* the one, the other (*of two*); second, the next; fellow man; different; ~ **ego**, ~ **īdem** a second self; **alterum tantum** twice as much; **ūnus et** ~ one or two
altercātiō, -ōnis *f* dispute, debate
altercor, -ārī, -ātus *vi* to wrangle, dispute; to cross-examine
alternīs *adv* alternately
alternō, -āre, -āvī, -ātum *vt* to do by turns, alternate
alternus *adj* one after the other, alternate; elegiac (*verses*)
alteruter, -īusutrīus *adj* one or the other
altilis *adj* fat (*esp fowls*)
altisonus *adj* sounding on high
altitonāns, -antis *adj* thundering on high
altitūdō, -inis *f* height, depth; (*fig*) sublimity; (*mind*) secrecy
altivolāns, -antis *adj* soaring on high
altor, -ōris *m* foster father
altrīnsecus *adv* on the other side
altrīx, -īcis *f* nourisher, foster mother
altum, -ī *nt* heaven; sea (*usu out of sight of land*); **ex altō repetītus** far-fetched
altus *adj* high, deep; (*fig*) noble; profound
ālūcinor, -ārī, -ātus *vi* to talk wildly; (*mind*) to wander
aluī *perf of* **alō**
alumnus, -ī *m*, **alumna, -ae** *f* foster child; pupil
alūta, -ae *f* soft leather; shoe, purse, face patch
alveārium, -ī *and* **-iī** *nt* beehive
alveolus, -ī *m* basin
alveus, -eī *m* hollow; trough; (*ship*) hold; bath tub; riverbed
alvus, -ī *f* bowels; womb; stomach
amābilis *adj* lovely, lovable

amābilitās, -ātis f charm
amābiliter adv see amābilis
Amalthēa, -ae f nymph or she-goat; cornū
  Amalthēae horn of plenty
Amalthēum, -ī nt Atticus's library
āmandātiō f sending away
āmandō, -āre, -āvī, -ātum vt to send away
amāns, -antis adj fond ▸ m lover
amanter adv affectionately
āmanuēnsis, -is m secretary
amāracinum, -inī nt marjoram ointment
amāracum, -ī nt, amāracus, -ī m/f sweet
  marjoram
amārē adv see amārus
amāritiēs, -ēī f, amāritūdō, -inis f,
  amāror, -ōris m bitterness
amārus adj bitter; (fig) sad; ill-natured
amāsius, -ī and -iī m lover
Amathūs, -ūntis f town in Cyprus
Amathūsia f Venus
amātiō, -ōnis f lovemaking
amātor, -ōris m lover, paramour
amātorculus m poor lover
amātōriē adv amorously
amātōrius adj of love, erotic
amātrīx, -rīcis f mistress
Amāzōn, -onis f Amazon, warrior woman
Amāzonidēs fpl Amazons
Amāzonius adj see Amāzōn
ambāctus, -ī m vassal
ambāgēs, -is f windings; (speech)
  circumlocution, quibbling; enigma
ambedō, -edere, -ēdī, -ēsum vt to consume
ambēsus ppp of ambedō
ambigō, -ere vt, vi to wander about; to be in
  doubt; to argue; to wrangle
ambiguē adv doubtfully
ambiguitās, -ātis f ambiguity
ambiguus adj changeable, doubtful,
  unreliable; ambiguous
ambiō, -īre, -iī, -ītum vt to go round, encircle;
  (POL) to canvass for votes; (fig) to court (for a
  favour)
ambitiō, -ōnis f canvassing for votes; currying
  favour; ambition
ambitiōsē adv ostentatiously
ambitiōsus adj winding; ostentatious,
  ambitious
ambitus, -ūs m circuit, circumference;
  circumlocution; canvassing, bribery; lēx de
  ambitū a law against bribery
ambitus ppp of ambiō
ambō, ambae, ambō num both, two
Ambracia, -ae f district of N.W. Greece
Ambraciēnsis, Ambraciēnsus adj see
  Ambracia
ambrosia, -ae f food of the gods
ambrosius adj divine
ambūbāia, -ae f Syrian flute-girl
ambulācrum, -ī nt avenue
ambulātiō, -ōnis f walk, walking; walk (place)
ambulātiuncula f short walk

ambulō, -āre, -āvī, -ātum vi to walk, go;
  to travel
ambūrō, -rere, -ssī, -stum vt to burn up; to
  make frostbitten; (fig) to ruin
ambūstus ppp of ambūrō
amellus, -ī m Michaelmas daisy
āmēns, -entis adj mad, frantic; stupid
āmentia, -ae f madness; stupidity
āmentum, -ī nt strap (for throwing javelin)
ames, -itis m fowler's pole
amfr- etc see anfr-
amīca, -ae f friend; mistress
amiciō, -īre, -tus vt to clothe, cover
amīciter, -ē adv see amīcus
amīcitia, -ae f friendship; alliance
amictus¹ ppp of amiciō
amictus², -ūs m (manner of) dress; clothing
amiculum, -ī nt cloak
amīculus, -ī m dear friend
amīcus, -ī m friend ▸ adj friendly, fond
āmissiō, -ōnis f loss
āmissus ppp of āmittō
amita, -ae f aunt (on father's side)
āmittō, -ittere, -īsī, -issum vt to let go, lose
Ammōn, -is m Egyptian god identified with Jupiter
Ammōniacus adj see Ammōn
amnicola, -ae m/f something growing by a river
amniculus m brook
amnicus adj see amnis
amnis, -is m river
amō, -āre, -āvī, -ātum vt to love, like; (colloq)
  to be obliged to; ita mē dī ament bless my
  soul!; amābō please!
amoenitās, -ātis f delightfulness (esp of
  scenery)
amoenus adj delightful
āmōlior, -īrī, -ītus vt to remove
amōmum, -ī nt cardamom
amor, -ōris m love; (fig) strong desire; term of
  endearment; Cupid; (pl) love affairs
āmōtiō, -ōnis f removal
āmōtus ppp of āmoveō
āmoveō, -ovēre, -ōvī, -ōtum vt to remove;
  to banish
amphibolia, -ae f ambiguity
Amphīōn, -onis m musician and builder of Thebes
Amphīonius adj see Amphīōn
amphitheātrum, -ī nt amphitheatre
Amphitrītē, -ēs f sea goddess; the sea
Amphitryō, -ōnis m husband of Alcmena
Amphitryōniadēs m Hercules
amphora, -ae f a two-handled jar; liquid
  measure; (NAUT) measure of tonnage
Amphrȳsius adj of Apollo
Amphrȳsus, -ī m river in Thessaly
ample adv see amplus
amplector, -ctī, -xus vt to embrace, encircle;
  (mind) to grasp; (speech) to deal with; (fig) to
  cherish
amplexor, -ārī, -ātus vt to embrace, love
amplexus¹ ppa of amplector
amplexus², -ūs m embrace, encircling

amplificātiō, -ōnis f enlargement; (RHET) a passage elaborated for effect

amplificē adv splendidly

amplificō, -āre, -āvī, -ātum vt to increase, enlarge; (RHET) to enlarge upon

ampliō, -āre, -āvī, -ātum vt to enlarge; (LAW) to adjourn

ampliter adv see **amplūs**

amplitūdō, -inis f size; (fig) distinction; (RHET) fullness

amplius adv more (esp amount or number), further, longer; ~ ducentī more than 200; ~ nōn petere take no further legal action; ~ prōnūntiāre adjourn a case

amplūs adj large, spacious; great, abundant; powerful, splendid, eminent; (superl) distinguished

ampulla, -ae f a two-handled flask; (fig) high-flown language

ampullārius, -ārī m flask-maker

ampullor, -ārī vi to use high-flown language

amputātiō, -ōnis f pruning

amputatus adj (RHET) disconnected

amputō, -āre, -āvī, -ātum vt to cut off, prune; (fig) to lop off

Amūlius, -ī m king of Alba Longa, grand-uncle of Romulus

amurca, -ae f lees of olive oil

amussitātus adj nicely adjusted

Amӯclae, -ārum fpl town in S. Greece

Amӯclaeus adj see **Amӯclae**

amygdalum, -ī nt almond

amystis, -dis f emptying a cup at a draught

an conj or; perhaps; (with single question) surely not; **haud sciō an** I feel sure

Anacreōn, -ontis m Greek lyric poet

anadēma, -tis nt headband

anagnōstēs, -ae m reader

anapaestum, -ī nt poem in anapaests

anapaestus adj: ~ pēs anapaest

anas, -tis f duck

anaticula f duckling

anatīnus adj see **anas**

anatocismus, -ī m compound interest

Anaxagorās, -ae m early Greek philosopher

Anaximander, -rī m early Greek philosopher

anceps, -ipitis adj two-headed; double; wavering, doubtful; dangerous ▶ nt danger

Anchīsēs, -ae m father of Aeneas

Anchīsēus adj Aeneas

Anchīsiadēs m Aeneas

ancīle, -is nt oval shield (esp one said to have fallen from heaven in Numa's reign)

ancilla, -ae f servant

ancillāris adj of a young servant

ancillula f young servant

ancīsus adj cut round

ancora, -ae f anchor

ancorāle, -is nt cable

ancorārius adj see **ancora**

Ancus Marcius, Anci Marcii m 4th king of Rome

Ancӯra, -ae f Ankara (capital of Galatia)

andabata, -ae m blindfold gladiator

Andrius adj see **Andros**

androgynē, -ēs f hermaphrodite

androgynus, -ī m hermaphrodite

Andromachē, -ēs f wife of Hector

Andromeda, -ae f wife of Perseus; a constellation

Andronicus, -ī m Livius (earliest Latin poet)

Andros, Andrus, -ī f Aegean island

ānellus, -ī m little ring

anēthum, -ī nt fennel

ānfrāctus, -ūs m bend, orbit; roundabout way; (words) digression, prolixity

angelus, -ī m angel

angina, -ae f quinsy

angiportum, -ī nt alley

angiportus, -ūs m alley

angō, -ere vt to throttle; (fig) to distress, torment

angor, -ōris m suffocation; (fig) anguish

anguicomus adj with snakes for hair

anguiculus, -ī m small snake

anguifer, -ī adj snake-carrying

anguigena, -ae m one born of serpents; Theban

anguīlla, -ae f eel

anguimanus adj with a trunk

anguipēs, -edis adj serpent-footed

anguis, -is m/f snake, serpent; (constellation) Draco

Anguitenēns, -entis m Ophiuchus

angulātus adj angular

angulus, -ī m angle, corner; out-of-the-way place; **ad parēs angulōs** at right angles

angustē adv close, within narrow limits; concisely

angustiae, -ārum fpl defile, strait; (time) shortness; (means) want; (circumstances) difficulty; (mind) narrowness; (words) subtleties

angusticlāvius adj wearing a narrow purple stripe

angustō, -āre vt to make narrow

angustum, -ī nt narrowness; danger

angustus adj narrow, close; (time) short; (means) scanty; (mind) mean; (argument) subtle; (circumstances) difficult

anhēlitus, -ūs m panting; breath, exhalation

anhēlō, -āre, -āvī, -ātum vi to breathe hard, pant; to exhale

anhēlus adj panting

anicula, -ae f poor old woman

Aniēnsis, Aniēnus adj of the river Anio

Aniēnus m Anio

anīlis adj of an old woman

anīlitās, -tātis f old age

anīliter adv like an old woman

anima, -ae f wind, air; breath; life; soul, mind; ghost, spirit; **animam agere, animam efflāre** expire; **animam comprimere** hold one's breath

animadversiō, -ōnis f observation; censure, punishment

animadversor, -ōris m observer

animadvertō, -tere, -tī, -sum vt to pay attention to, notice; to realise; to censure, punish; **animadvertere in** punish

animal, -ālis nt animal; living creature

animālis adj of air; animate

animāns, -antis m/f/nt living creature; animal

animātiō, -ōnis f being

animātus adj disposed; in a certain frame of mind; courageous

animō, -āre, -āvī, -ātum vt to animate; to give a certain temperament to

animōsē adv boldly, eagerly

animōsus adj airy; lifelike; courageous, proud

animula, -ae f little soul

animulus, -ī m darling

animus, -ī m mind, soul; consciousness; reason, thought, opinion, imagination; heart, feelings, disposition; courage, spirit, pride, passion; will, purpose; term of endearment; **animī** in mind, in heart; **animī causā** for amusement; **animō fingere** imagine; **animō male est** I am fainting; **aequō animō esse** be patient, calm; **bonō animō esse** take courage; be well-disposed; **ex animō** sincerely; **ex animō effluere** be forgotten; **in animō habēre** purpose; **meō animō** in my opinion

Aniō, -ēnis m tributary of the Tiber

annālēs, -ium mpl annals, chronicle

annālis adj of a year; **lēx ~** law prescribing ages for public offices

Anna Perenna, Annae Perennae f Roman popular goddess

anne etc see **an**

anniculus adj a year old

anniversārius adj annual

annōn or not

annōna, -ae f year's produce; grain; price of corn; the market

annōsus adj aged

annōtinus adj last year's

annus, -ī m year; **~ māgnus** astronomical great year; **~ solidus** a full year

annuus adj a year's; annual

anquīrō, -rere, -sīvī, -sītum vt to search for; to make inquiries; (LAW) to institute an inquiry (dē) or prosecution (abl, gen)

ānsa, -ae f handle; (fig) opportunity

ānsātus adj with a handle; (comedy) with arms akimbo

ānser, -is m goose

ānserīnus adj see **ānser**

ante prep (with acc) before (in time, place, comparison) ▸ adv (place) in front; (time) before

anteā adv before, formerly

antecapiō, -apere, -ēpī, -eptum vt to take beforehand, anticipate

antecēdō, -ēdere, -essī, -essum vt to precede; to surpass

antecellō, -ere vi to excel, be superior

anteceptus ppp of **antecapiō**

antecessiō, -ōnis f preceding; antecedent cause

antecessor, -ōris m forerunner

antecursor, -ōris m forerunner, pioneer

anteeō, -īre, -iī vi to precede, surpass

anteferō, -ferre, -tulī, -lātum vt to carry before; to prefer; to anticipate

antefīxus adj attached (in front) ▸ ntpl ornaments on roofs of buildings

antegredior, -dī, -ssus vt to precede

antehabeō, -ēre vt to prefer

antehāc adv formerly, previously

antelātus ppp of **anteferō**

antelūcānus adj before dawn

antemerīdiānus adj before noon

antemittō, -ittere, -īsī, -issum vt to send on in front

antenna, -ae f yardarm

antepīlānī, -ōrum mpl (MIL) the front ranks

antepōnō, -ōnere, -osuī, -ositum vt to set before; to prefer

antequam conj before

Anterōs, -ōtis m avenger of slighted love

antēs, -ium mpl rows

antesignānus, -ī m (MIL) leader; (pl) defenders of the standards

antestō, antistō, -āre, -ētī vi to excel, distinguish oneself

antestor, -ārī, -ātus vi to call a witness

anteveniō, -enīre, -ēnī, -entum vt, vi to anticipate; to surpass

antevertō, -tere, -tī, -sum vt to precede; to anticipate; to prefer

anticipātiō, -ōnis f foreknowledge

anticipō, -āre, -āvī, -ātum vt to take before, anticipate

antīcus adj in front

Antigonē, -ēs f daughter of Oedipus

Antigonus, -ī m name of Macedonian kings

Antiochēnsis adj see **Antiochīa**

Antiochīa, -īae f Antioch (capital of Syria)

Antiochus, -ī m name of kings of Syria

antīquārius, -ī and **-iī** m antiquary

antīquē adv in the old style

antīquitās, -ātis f antiquity, the ancients; integrity

antīquitus adv long ago, from ancient times

antīquō, -āre, -āvī, -ātum vt to vote against (a bill)

antīquus adj ancient, former, old; good old-fashioned, honest, illustrious; **antīquior** more important; **antīquissimus** most important

antistēs, -itis m/f high priest, chief priestess; (fig) master (in any art)

Antisthenēs, -is and **-ae** m founder of Cynic philosophy

antistita, -ae f chief priestess

antistō etc see **antestō**

antitheton, -ī nt (RHET) antithesis

Antōnīnus, -ī m name of Roman emperors (esp Pius and Marcus Aurelius)

Antōnius, -ī m Roman name (esp the famous orator, and Mark Antony)

antrum, -ī nt cave, hollow

ānulārius, -i m ringmaker
ānulātus adj with rings on
ānulus, -ī m ring; equestrian rank
ānus, -ī m rectum; ring
anus, -ūs f old woman ▸ adj old
ānxiē adv see **ānxius**
ānxietās, -ātis f anxiety, trouble (of the mind)
ānxifer, -ī adj disquieting
ānxitūdō, -inis f anxiety
ānxius adj (mind) troubled; disquieting
Āones, -um adj Boeotian
Āonia f part of Boeotia
Āonius adj of Boeotia, of Helicon
Aornos, -ī m/f lake Avernus
apage interj away with!, go away!
apēliōtēs, -ae m east wind
Apellēs, -is m Greek painter
aper, -rī m boar
aperiō, -īre, -uī, -tum vt to uncover, disclose,
open; (country) to open up; (fig) to unfold,
explain, reveal
apertē adv clearly, openly
apertum, -ī nt open space; **in apertō esse** be
well known; be easy
apertus ppp of **aperiō** ▸ adj open, exposed;
clear, manifest; (person) frank
aperuī perf of **aperiō**
apex, -icis m summit; crown, priest's cap; (fig)
crown
aphractus, -ī f a long open boat
apiārius, -ī and -iī m beekeeper
Apīcius, -ī m Roman epicure
apicula, -ae f little bee
apis, -is f bee
apīscor, -īscī, -tus vt to catch, get, attain
apium, -ī and -iī nt celery
aplustre, -is nt decorated stern of a ship
apoclētī, -ōrum mpl committee of the Aetolian
League
apodytērium, -ī and -iī nt dressing room
Apollināris, -ineus adj: **lūdī Apollinārēs**
Roman games in July
Apollō, -inis m Greek god of music, archery,
prophecy, flocks and herds, and often identified with
the sun
apologus, -ī m narrative, fable
apophorēta, -ōrum ntpl presents for guests
to take home
apoproēgmena, -ōrum ntpl (PHILOS) what
is rejected
apostolicus adj see **apostolus**
apostolus, -ī m (ECCL) apostle
apothēca, -ae f storehouse, wine store
apparātē adv see **apparātus¹**
apparātiō, -ōnis f preparation
apparātus¹ adj ready, well-supplied,
sumptuous
apparātus², -ūs m preparation; equipment,
munitions; pomp, ostentation
appāreō, -ēre, -uī, -itum vi to come in sight,
appear; to be seen, show oneself; to wait upon
(an official); **appāret** it is obvious

appāritiō, -ōnis f service; domestic servants
appāritor, -ōris m attendant
apparō, -āre, -āvī, -ātum vt to prepare,
provide
appellātiō, -ōnis f accosting, appeal; title;
pronunciation
appellātor, -ōris m appellant
appellitātus adj usually called
appellō¹, -āre, -āvī, -ātum vt to speak to; to
appeal to; (for money) to dun; (LAW) to sue; to
call, name; to pronounce
appellō², -ellere, -ulī, -ulsum vt to drive,
bring (to); (NAUT) to bring to land
appendicula, -ae f small addition
appendix, -icis f supplement
appendō, -endere, -endī, -ensum vt to
weigh, pay
appetēns, -entis adj eager; greedy
appetenter adv see **appetēns**
appetentia, -ae f craving
appetītiō, -ōnis f grasping, craving
appetītus¹ ppp of **appetō**
appetītus², -ūs m craving; natural desire (as
opposed to reason)
appetō, -ere, -īvī, -ītum vt to grasp, try to get
at; to attack; to desire ▸ vi to approach
appingō, -ere vt to paint (in); (colloq) to write
more
Appius, -ī m Roman first name; **Via Appia** main
road from Rome to Capua and Brundisium
applaudō, -dere, -sī, -sum vt to strike, clap
▸ vi to applaud
applicātiō, -ōnis f applying (of the mind); **iūs**
applicātiōnis the right of a patron to inherit a
client's effects
applicātus, applicitus ppp of **applicō**
applicō, -āre, -āvī and -uī, -ātum and -itum
vt to attach, place close (to); (NAUT) to steer,
bring to land; **sē applicāre, animum applicāre**
devote self, attention (to)
applōrō, -āre vt to deplore
appōnō, -ōnere, -osuī, -ositum vt to put
(to, beside); (meal) to serve; to add, appoint;
to reckon
apporrēctus adj stretched nearby
apportō, -āre, -āvī, -ātum vt to bring, carry
(to)
apposcō, -ere vt to demand also
appositē adv suitably
appositus ppp of **appōnō** ▸ adj situated near;
(fig) bordering on; suitable
apposuī perf of **appōnō**
appōtus adj drunk
apprecor, -ārī, -ātus vt to pray to
apprehendō, -endere, -endī, -ēnsum vt
to take hold of; (MIL) to occupy; (argument) to
bring forward
apprīmē adv especially
apprimō, -imere, -essī, -essum vt to press
close
approbātiō, -ōnis f acquiescence; proof
approbātor, -ōris m approver

approbē adv very well

approbō, -āre, -āvī, -ātum vt to approve; to prove; to perform to someone's satisfaction

apprōmittō, -ere vt to promise also

approperō, -āre, -āvī, -ātum vt to hasten ▶ vi to hurry up

appropinquō, -āre, -āvī, -ātum vi to approach

appropinquātiō, -ōnis f approach

appugnō, -āre vt to attack

appulsus¹ ppp of **appellō²**

appulsus², -ūs m landing; approach

aprīcātiō, -ōnis f basking

aprīcor, -ārī vi to bask

aprīcus adj sunny; basking; **in aprīcum prōferre** bring to light

Aprīlis adj April, of April

aprūgnus adj of the wild boar

aps- etc see **abs-**

aptē adv closely; suitably, rightly

aptō, -āre, -āvī, -ātum vt to fit, put on; (fig) to adapt; to prepare, equip

aptus adj attached, joined together, fitted (with); suitable

apud prep (with acc) 1. (with persons) beside, by, with, at the house of, among, in the time of; (speaking) in the presence of, to; (judgment) in the opinion of; (influence) with; (faith) in; (authors) in 2. (with places) near, at, in; **est ~ mē** I have; **sum ~ mē** I am in my senses

Āpūlia, -iae f district of S.E. Italy

Āpūlus adj see **Āpūlia**

aput prep see **apud**

aqua, -ae f water; **~ mihī haeret** I am in a fix; **~ intercus** dropsy; **aquam adspergere** revive; **aquam praebēre** entertain; **aquam et terram petere** demand submission; **aquā et ignī interdīcere** outlaw

aquae fpl medicinal waters, spa

aquaeductus, -ūs m aqueduct; right of leading water

aquāliculus m belly

aquālis, -is m/f washbasin

aquārius adj of water ▶ m water carrier, water inspector; a constellation

aquāticus adj aquatic; humid

aquātilis adj aquatic

aquātiō, -ōnis f fetching water; watering place

aquātor, -ōris m water carrier

aquila, -ae f eagle; standard of a legion; (ARCH) gable; a constellation; **aquilae senectūs** a vigorous old age

Aquileia, -ae f town in N. Italy

Aquileiēnsis adj see **Aquileia**

aquilifer, -ī m chief standard-bearer

aquilīnus adj eagle's

aquilō, -ōnis m north wind; north

aquilōnius adj northerly

aquilus adj swarthy

Aquīnās, -ātis adj see **Aquīnum**

Aquīnum, -ī nt town in Latium

Aquītānia, -iae f district of S.W. Gaul

Aquītānus adj see **Aquītānia**

aquor, -ārī, -ātus vi to fetch water

aquōsus adj humid, rainy

aquula, -ae f little stream

āra, -ae f altar; (fig) refuge; a constellation; **ārae et focī** hearth and home

arabarchēs, -ae m customs officer (in Egypt)

Arabia, -iae f Arabia

Arabicē adv with all the perfumes of Arabia

Arabicus, Arabicius, Arabus adj see **Arabia**

Arachnē, -s f Lydian woman changed into a spider

arānea, -ae f spider; cobweb

arāneola f, **-olus** m small spider

arāneōsus adj full of spiders' webs

arāneum, -ī nt spider's web

arāneus, -ī m spider ▶ adj of spiders

Arar, -is m (river) Saône

Arātēus adj see **Arātus**

arātiō, -ōnis f ploughing, farming; arable land

arātiuncula f small plot

arātor, -ōris m ploughman, farmer; (pl) cultivators of public land

arātrum, -ī nt plough

Arātus, -ī m Greek astronomical poet

Araxēs, -is m river in Armenia

arbiter, -rī m witness; arbiter, judge, umpire; controller; **~ bibendī** president of a drinking party

arbitra, -ae f witness

arbitrāriō adv with some uncertainty

arbitrārius adj uncertain

arbitrātus, -ūs m decision; **meō arbitrātū** in my judgment

arbitrium, -ī and **-iī** nt decision (of an arbitrator), judgment; mastery, control

arbitror, -ārī, -ātus vt, vi to be a witness of; to testify; to think, suppose

arbor, arbōs, -oris f tree; ship, mast, oar; **~ īnfēlix** gallows

arboreus adj of trees, like a tree

arbustum, -ī nt plantation, orchard; (pl) trees

arbustus adj wooded

arbuteus adj of the strawberry tree

arbutum, -ī nt fruit of strawberry tree

arbutus, -ī f strawberry tree

arca, -ae f box; moneybox, purse; coffin; prison cell; **ex arcā absolvere** pay cash

Arcades, -um mpl Arcadians

Arcadia, -iae f district of E. Greece

Arcadicus, -ius adj see **Arcadia**

arcānō adv privately

arcānum, -ī nt secret, mystery

arcānus adj secret; able to keep secrets

arceō, -ēre, -uī, -tum vt to enclose; to keep off, prevent

arcessītū abl sg m at the summons

arcessītus ppp of **arcessō** ▶ adj far-fetched

arcessō, -ere, -īvī, -ītum vt to send for, fetch; (LAW) to summon, accuse; (fig) to derive

archetypus, -ī m original

Archilochus, -ī m Greek iambic and elegiac poet

archimagīrus, -ī *m* chief cook

Archimēdēs, -is *m* famous mathematician of Syracuse

archipīrāta, -ae *m* pirate chief

architectōn, -onis *m* master builder; master in cunning

architector, -ārī, -ātus *vt* to construct; (*fig*) to devise

architectūra, -ae *f* architecture

architectus, -ī *m* architect; (*fig*) author

archōn, -ontis *m* Athenian magistrate

Archytās, -ae *m* Pythagorean philosopher of Tarentum

arcitenēns, -entis *adj* holding a bow ▸ *m* Apollo

Arctophylax, -cis *m* (*constellation*) Boötes

arctos, -ī *f* Great Bear, Little Bear; north, north wind; night

Arctūrus, -ī *m* brightest star in Boötes

arctus *etc see* **artus¹** *etc*

arcuī *perf of* **arceō**

arcula, -ae *f* casket; (*RHET*) ornament

arcuō, -āre, -āvī, -ātum *vt* to curve

arcus, -ūs *m* bow; rainbow; arch, curve; (*MATH*) arc

ardea, -ae *f* heron

Ardea, -ae *f* town in Latium

ardeliō, -ōnis *m* busybody

ārdēns, -entis *adj* hot, glowing, fiery; (*fig*) eager, ardent

ārdenter *adv* passionately

ārdeō, -dēre, -sī, -sum *vi* to be on fire, burn, shine; (*fig*) to be fired, burn

ārdēscō, -ere *vi* to catch fire, gleam; (*fig*) to become inflamed, wax hotter

ārdor, -ōris *m* heat, brightness; (*fig*) ardour, passion

arduum, -ī *nt* steep slope; difficulty

arduus *adj* steep, high; difficult, troublesome

ārea, -ae *f* vacant site, open space, playground; threshing-floor; (*fig*) scope (*for effort*)

ārefaciō, -acere, -ēcī, -actum *vt* to dry

arēna *etc see* **harēna**

ārēns, -entis *adj* arid; thirsty

āreō, -ēre *vi* to be dry

āreola, -ae *f* small open space

Arēopagītēs *m* member of the court

Arēopagus, -ī *m* Mars' Hill in Athens; a criminal court

Arēs, -is *m* Greek god of war

ārēscō, -ere *vi* to dry, dry up

Arestoridēs, -ae *m* Argus

aretālogus, -ī *m* braggart

Arethūsa, -ae *f* spring near Syracuse

Arethūsis *adj* Syracusan

Argēī, -ōrum *mpl* sacred places in Rome; effigies thrown annually into the Tiber

argentāria, -ae *f* bank, banking; silver mine

argentārius *adj* of silver, of money ▸ *m* banker

argentātus *adj* silver-plated; backed with money

argenteus *adj* of silver, adorned with silver; silvery (*in colour*); of the silver age

argentum, -ī *nt* silver, silver plate; money

Argēus, Argīvus, Argolicus *adj* Argive; Greek

Argīlētānus *adj see* **Argīlētum**

Argīlētum, -ī *nt* part of Rome (*noted for bookshops*)

argilla, -ae *f* clay

Argō, -ūs *f* Jason's ship

Argolis, -olidis *f* district about Argos

Argonautae, -ārum *mpl* Argonauts

Argonauticus *adj see* **Argonautae**

Argos *nt*, **Argī, -ōrum** *mpl* town in S.E. Greece

Argōus *adj see* **Argō**

argūmentātiō, -ōnis *f* adducing proofs

argūmentor, -ārī, -ātus *vt*, *vi* to prove, adduce as proof; to conclude

argūmentum, -ī *nt* evidence, proof; (*LIT*) subject matter, theme, plot (*of a play*); (*art*) subject, motif

arguō, -uere, -uī, -ūtum *vt* to prove, make known; to accuse, blame, denounce

Argus, -ī *m* monster with many eyes

argūtē *adv* subtly

argūtiae, -ārum *fpl* nimbleness, liveliness; wit, subtlety, slyness

argūtor, -ārī, -ātus *vi* to chatter

argūtulus *adj* rather subtle

argūtus *adj* (*sight*) clear, distinct, graceful; (*sound*) clear, melodious, noisy; (*mind*) acute, witty, sly

argyraspis, -dis *adj* silver-shielded

Ariadna, -ae *f* daughter of Minos of Crete

Ariadnaeus *adj see* **Ariadna**

āridulus *adj* rather dry

āridum, -ī *nt* dry land

āridus *adj* dry, withered; meagre; (*style*) flat

ariēs, -etis *m* ram; 1st sign of Zodiac; battering ram; beam used as a breakwater

arietō, -āre *vt*, *vi* to butt, strike hard

Ariōn, -onis *m* early Greek poet and musician

Ariōnius *adj see* **Ariōn**

arista, -ae *f* ear of corn

Aristaeus, -ī *m* legendary founder of beekeeping

Aristarchus, -ī *m* Alexandrian scholar; a severe critic

Aristīdēs, -is *m* Athenian statesman noted for integrity

Aristippēus *adj see* **Aristippus**

Aristippus, -ī *m* Greek hedonist philosopher

aristolochia, -ae *f* birthwort

Aristophanēs, -is *m* Greek comic poet

Aristophanēus, Aristophanīus *adj see* **Aristophanēs**

Aristotelēs, -is *m* Aristotle (*founder of Peripatetic school of philosophy*)

Aristotelēus, Aristotelīus *adj see* **Aristotelēs**

arithmētica, -ōrum *ntpl* arithmetic

āritūdō, -inis *f* dryness

Ariūsius *adj* of Ariusia (*in Chios*)

arma, **-ōrum** ntpl armour, shield; arms, weapons (of close combat only); warfare, troops; (fig) defence, protection; implements, ship's gear

armāmenta, **-ōrum** ntpl implements, ship's gear

armāmentārium, **-ī** and **-iī** nt arsenal

armāriolum, **-ī** nt small chest

armārium, **-ī** and **-iī** nt chest, safe

armātū abl m armour; **gravī ~** with heavy-armed troops

armātūra, **-ae** f armour, equipment; **levis ~** light-armed troops

armātus adj armed

Armenia, **-ae** f Armenia

Armeniaca, **-acae** f apricot tree

Armeniacum, **-acī** nt apricot

Armenius adj see **Armenia**

armentālis adj of the herd

armentārius, **-ī** and **-iī** m cattle herd

armentum, **-ī** nt cattle (for ploughing), herd (cattle etc)

armifer, **-ī** adj armed

armiger, **-ī** m armour-bearer ▸ adj armed; productive of warriors

armilla, **-ae** f bracelet

armillātus adj wearing a bracelet

armipotēns, **-entis** adj strong in battle

armisonus adj resounding with arms

armō, **-āre**, **-āvī**, **-ātum** vt to arm, equip; to rouse to arms (against)

armus, **-ī** m shoulder (esp of animals)

Arniēnsis adj see **Arnus**

Arnus, **-ī** m (river) Arno

arō, **-āre**, **-āvī**, **-ātum** vt to plough, cultivate; to live by farming; (fig: sea, brow) to furrow

Arpīnās, **-ātis** adj see **Arpīnum**

Arpīnum, **-ī** nt town in Latium (birthplace of Cicero)

arquātus adj jaundiced

arr- etc see **adr-**

arrabō, **-ōnis** m earnest money

ars, **artis** f skill (in any craft); the art (of any profession); science, theory; handbook; work of art; moral quality, virtue; artifice, fraud

ārsī perf of **ārdeō**

ārsus ppp of **ārdeō**

artē adv closely, soundly, briefly

artēria¹, **-ae** f windpipe; artery

artēria², **-ōrum** ntpl trachea

arthrīticus adj gouty

articulō, **-āre**, **-āvī**, **-ātum** vt to articulate

articulōsus adj minutely subdivided

articulus, **-ī** m joint, knuckle; limb; (words) clause; (time) point, turning point; **in ipsō articulō temporis** in the nick of time

artifex, **-icis** m artist, craftsman, master; (fig) maker, author ▸ adj ingenious, artistic, artificial

artificiōsē adv skilfully

artificiōsus adj ingenious, artistic, artificial

artificium, **-ī** and **-iī** nt skill, workmanship; art, craft; theory, rule of an art; ingenuity, cunning

artō, **-āre** vt to compress, curtail

artolaganus, **-ī** m kind of cake

artopta, **-ae** m baker; baking tin

artus¹ adj close, narrow, tight; (sleep) deep; (fig) strict, straitened

artus², **-ūs** m joint; (pl) limbs, body; (fig) strength

ārula, **-ae** f small altar

arundō etc see **harundō** etc

arvīna, **-ae** f grease

arvum, **-ī** nt field; land, country, plain

arvus adj ploughed

arx, **arcis** f fortress, castle; height, summit; (fig) bulwark, stronghold; **arcem facere ē cloācā** make a mountain out of a molehill

ās, **assis** m (weight) pound; (coin) bronze unit, of low value; (inheritance) the whole (subdivided into 12 parts); **ad assem** to the last farthing; **hērēs ex asse** sole heir

Ascānius, **-ī** m son of Aeneas

ascendō, **-endere**, **-endī**, **-ēnsum** vt, vi to go up, climb, embark; (fig) to rise

ascēnsiō, **-ōnis** f ascent; (fig) sublimity

ascēnsus, **-ūs** m ascent, rising; way up

ascia, **-ae** f axe; mason's trowel

asciō, **-īre** vt to admit

ascīscō, **-īscere**, **-īvī**, **-ītum** vt to receive with approval; to admit (to some kind of association); to appropriate, adopt (esp customs); to arrogate to oneself

ascītus adj acquired, alien

Ascra, **-ae** f birthplace of Hesiod in Boeotia

Ascraeus adj of Ascra; of Hesiod; of Helicon

ascrībō, **-bere**, **-psī**, **-ptum** vt to add (in writing); to attribute, ascribe; to apply (an illustration); to enrol, include

ascrīptīcius adj enrolled

ascrīptiō, **-ōnis** f addition (in writing)

ascrīptīvus adj (MIL) supernumerary

ascrīptor, **-ōris** m supporter

ascrīptus ppp of **ascrībō**

asella, **-ae** f young ass

asellus, **-ī** m young ass

Āsia, **-ae** f Roman province; Asia Minor; Asia

asīlus, **-ī** m gad fly

asinus, **-ī** m ass; fool

Āsis, **-dis** f Asia

Āsius, **Āsiānus**, **Āsiāticus** adj see **Āsia**

Āsōpus, **-ī** m river in Boeotia

asōtus, **-ī** m libertine

asparagus, **-ī** m asparagus

aspargō etc see **aspergō¹**

aspectābilis adj visible

aspectō, **-āre** vt to look at, gaze at; to pay heed to; (places) to face

aspectus¹ ppp of **aspiciō**

aspectus², **-ūs** m look, sight, glance, sense of sight; aspect, appearance

aspellō, **-ere** vt to drive away

asper, **-ī** *adj* rough; (*taste*) bitter; (*sound*) harsh; (*weather*) severe; (*style*) rugged; (*person*) violent, exasperated, unkind, austere; (*animal*) savage; (*circumstances*) difficult

asperē *adv see* **asper**

aspergō¹, **-gere**, **-sī**, **-sum** *vt* to scatter, sprinkle; to bespatter, besprinkle; **aquam aspergere** revive

aspergō², **-inis** *f* sprinkling; spray

asperitās, **-ātis** *f* roughness, unevenness, harshness, severity; (*fig*) ruggedness, fierceness; trouble, difficulty

aspernātiō, **-ōnis** *f* disdain

aspernor, **-ārī**, **-ātus** *vt* to reject, disdain

asperō, **-āre**, **-āvī**, **-ātum** *vt* to roughen, sharpen; to exasperate

aspersiō, **-ōnis** *f* sprinkling

aspersus *ppp of* **aspergō¹**

aspiciō, **-icere**, **-exī**, **-ectum** *vt* to catch sight of, look at; (*places*) to face; (*fig*) to examine, consider

aspīrātiō, **-ōnis** *f* breathing (on); evaporation; pronouncing with an aspirate

aspīrō, **-āre**, **-āvī**, **-ātum** *vi* to breathe, blow; to favour; to aspire, attain (to) ▶ *vt* to blow, instil

aspis, **-dis** *f* asp

asportātiō, **-ōnis** *f* removal

asportō, **-āre** *vt* to carry off

aspreta, **-ōrum** *ntpl* rough country

ass- *etc see* **ads-**

Assaracus, **-ī** *m* Trojan ancestor of Aeneas

asser, **-is** *m* pole, stake

assula, **-ae** *f* splinter

assulātim *adv* in splinters

āssum, **-ī** *nt* roast; (*pl*) sweating-bath

āssus *adj* roasted

Assyria, **-ae** *f* country in W. Asia

Assyrius *adj* Assyrian; oriental

ast *conj* (*laws*) and then; (*vows*) then; (*strong contrast*) and yet

ast- *etc see* **adst-**

Astraea, **-ae** *f* goddess of Justice

Astraeus, **-ī** *m* father of winds; **Astraeī frātrēs** the winds

astrologia, **-ae** *f* astronomy

astrologus, **-ī** *m* astronomer; astrologer

astrum, **-ī** *nt* star, heavenly body, constellation; a great height; heaven, immortality, glory

astu *nt* (*indecl*) city (*esp Athens*)

astus, **-ūs** *m* cleverness, cunning

astūtē *adv* cleverly

astūtia, **-ae** *f* slyness, cunning

astūtus *adj* artful, sly

Astyanax, **-ctis** *m* son of Hector and Andromache

asȳlum, **-ī** *nt* sanctuary

asymbolus *adj* with no contribution

at *conj* (*adversative*) but, on the other hand; (*objecting*) but it may be said; (*limiting*) at least, but at least; (*continuing*) then, thereupon; (*transitional*) now; (*with passionate appeals*) but oh!, look now!; **at enim** yes, but; **at tamen** nevertheless

Atābulus, **-ī** *m* sirocco

atat *interj* (*expressing fright, pain, surprise*) oh!

atavus, **-ī** *m* great-great-great-grandfather; ancestor

Atella, **-ae** *f* Oscan town in Campania

Ātellānicus, **Atellānius** *adj see* **Atella**

Atellānus *adj*: **fābula Atellāna** kind of comic show popular in Rome

āter, **-rī** *adj* black, dark; gloomy, dismal; malicious; **diēs ātrī** unlucky days

Athamantēus *adj see* **Athamās**

Athamantiadēs *m* Palaemon

Athamantis *f* Helle

Athamās, **-antis** *m* king of Thessaly (*who went mad*)

Athēnae, **-ārum** *fpl* Athens

Athēnaeus, **Athēniēnsis** *adj see* **Athēnae**

atheos, **-ī** *m* atheist

athlēta, **-ae** *m* wrestler, athlete

athlēticē *adv* athletically

Athos (*dat* **-ō**, *acc* **-ō**, **-on**, **-ōnem**) *m* mount Athos (*in Macedonia*)

Atlantiadēs *m* Mercury

Atlanticus *adj*: **mare Atlanticum** Atlantic Ocean

Atlantis *f* lost Atlantic island; a Pleiad

Atlās, **-antis** *m* giant supporting the sky; Atlas mountains

atomus, **-ī** *m* atom

atque (*before consonants* **ac**) *conj* (*connecting words*) and, and in fact; (*connecting clauses*) and moreover, and then, and so, and yet; (*in comparison*) as, than, to, from; **~ adeō** and that too; or rather; **~ nōn** and not rather; **~ sī** as if; **alius ~** different from; **contrā ~** opposite to; **īdem ~** same as; **plūs ~** more than

atquī *conj* (*adversative*) and yet, nevertheless, yes but; (*confirming*) by all means; (*minor premise*) now; **~ sī** if now

ātrāmentum, **-ī** *nt* ink; blacking

ātrātus *adj* in mourning

Atreus, **-eī** *m* son of Pelops (*king of Argos*)

Atrīdēs *m* Agamemnon; Menelaus

ātriēnsis, **-is** *m* steward, major-domo

ātriolum, **-ī** *nt* anteroom

ātrium, **-ī** *and* **-iī** *nt* hall, open central room in Roman house; forecourt of a temple; hall (*in other buildings*)

atrōcitās, **-ātis** *f* hideousness; (*mind*) brutality; (*PHILOS*) severity

atrōciter *adv* savagely

Atropos, **-ī** *f* one of the Fates

atrōx, **-ōcis** *adj* hideous, dreadful; fierce, brutal, unyielding

attāctus¹ *ppp of* **attingō**

attāctus², **-ūs** *m* contact

attagēn, **-is** *m* heathcock

Attalica *ntpl* garments of woven gold

Attalicus *adj* of Attalus; of Pergamum; ornamented with gold cloth

Attalus, **-ī** *m* king of Pergamum (*who bequeathed his kingdom to Rome*)

attamen *conj* nevertheless

attat *see* **atat**

attegia, -ae *f* hut

attemperātē *adv* opportunely

attempto *etc see* **attentō**

attendō, -dere, -dī, -tum *vt* to direct (*the attention*); attend to, notice

attentē *adv* carefully

attentiō, -ōnis *f* attentiveness

attentō, -āre, -āvī, -ātum *vt* to test, try; (*loyalty*) to tamper with; to attack

attentus¹ *ppp of* **attendō** ▶ *adj* attentive, intent; businesslike, careful (*esp about money*)

attentus² *ppp of* **attineō**

attenuātē *adv* simply

attenuātus *adj* weak; (*style*) brief; refined; plain

attenuō, -āre, -āvī, -ātum *vt* to weaken, reduce; to diminish; to humble

atterō, -erere, -rīvī, -rītum *vt* to rub; to wear away; (*fig*) to impair, exhaust

attestor, -ārī, -ātus *vt* to confirm

attexō, -ere, -uī, -tum *vt* to weave on; (*fig*) to add on

Atthis, -dis *f* Attica

Attiānus *adj see* **Attius**

Attica, -ae *f* district of Greece about Athens

Atticē *adv* in the Athenian manner

Atticissō *vi* to speak in the Athenian manner

Atticus *adj* Attic, Athenian; (RHET) of a plain and direct style

attigī *perf of* **attingō**

attigō *see* **attingō**

attineō, -inēre, -inuī, -entum *vt* to hold fast, detain; to guard; to reach for ▶ *vi* to concern, pertain, be of importance, avail

attingō, -ingere, -igī, -āctum *vt* to touch; to strike, assault; to arrive at; to border on; to affect; to mention; to undertake; to concern, resemble

Attis, -dis *m* Phrygian priest of Cybele

Attius, -ī *m* Latin tragic poet

attollō, -ere *vt* to lift up, erect; (*fig*) to exalt, extol

attondeō, -ondēre, -ondī, -ōnsum *vt* to shear, prune, crop; (*fig*) to diminish; (*comedy*) to fleece

attonitus *adj* thunderstruck, terrified, astonished; inspired

attonō, -āre, -uī, -itum *vt* to stupefy

attōnsus *ppp of* **attondeō**

attorqueō, -ēre *vt* to hurl upwards

attractus *ppp of* **attrahō**

attrahō, -here, -xī, -ctum *vt* to drag by force, attract; (*fig*) to draw, incite

attrectō, -āre *vt* to touch, handle; to appropriate

attrepidō, -āre *vi* to hobble along

attribuō, -uere, -uī, -ūtum *vt* to assign, bestow; to add; to impute, attribute; to lay as a tax

attribūtiō, -ōnis *f* (*money*) assignment; (GRAM) predicate

attribūtum, -ī *nt* (GRAM) predicate

attribūtus *ppp of* **attribuō** ▶ *adj* subject

attrītus *ppp of* **atterō** ▶ *adj* worn; bruised; (*fig*) impudent

attulī *perf of* **adferō**

au *interj* (*expressing pain, surprise*) oh!

auceps, -upis *m* fowler; (*fig*) eavesdropper; a pedantic critic

auctārium, -ī *and* **-iī** *nt* extra

auctificus *adj* increasing

auctiō, -ōnis *f* increase; auction sale

auctiōnārius *adj* auction; **tabulae auctiōnāriae** catalogues

auctiōnor, -ārī, -ātus *vi* to hold an auction

auctitō, -āre *vt* to greatly increase

auctō, -āre *vt* to increase

auctor, -ōris *m/f* **1.** (*originator: of families*) progenitor; (: *of buildings*) founder; (: *of deeds*) doer **2.** (*composer: of writings*) author, historian; (: *of knowledge*) investigator, teacher; (: *of news*) informant **3.** (*instigator: of action*) adviser; (: *of measures*) promoter; (: *of laws*) proposer, supporter; ratifier **4.** (*person of influence: in public life*) leader; (: *of conduct*) model; (: *of guarantees*) witness, bail; (: *of property*) seller; (: *of women and minors*) guardian; (: *of others' welfare*) champion; **mē auctōre** at my suggestion

auctōrāmentum, -ī *nt* contract; wages

auctōrātus *adj* bound (*by a pledge*); hired out (*for wages*)

auctōritās, -ātis *f* **1.** source; lead, responsibility **2.** judgment; opinion; advice, support; bidding, guidance; (*of senate*) decree; (*of people*) will **3.** power; (*person*) influence, authority, prestige; (*things*) importance, worth; (*conduct*) example; (*knowledge*) warrant, document, authority; (*property*) right of possession

auctumn- *etc see* **autumn-**

auctus¹ *ppp of* **augeō** ▶ *adj* enlarged, great

auctus², -ūs *m* growth, increase

aucupium, -ī *and* **-iī** *nt* fowling; birds caught; (*fig*) hunting (*after*), quibbling

aucupō, -āre *vt* to watch for

aucupor, -ārī, -ātus *vi* to go fowling ▶ *vt* to chase; (*fig*) to try to catch

audācia, -ae *f* daring, courage; audacity, impudence; (*pl*) deeds of daring

audācter, audāciter *adv see* **audāx**

audāx, -ācis *adj* bold, daring; rash, audacious; proud

audēns, -entis *adj* bold, brave

audenter *adv see* **audēns**

audentia, -ae *f* boldness, courage

audeō, -dēre, -sus *vt, vi* to dare, venture; to be brave

audiēns, -entis *m* hearer ▶ *adj* obedient

audientia, -ae *f* hearing; **audientiam facere** gain a hearing

audiō, -īre, -īvī *and* **-iī, -ītum** *vt* to hear; to learn, be told; to be called; to listen, attend to, study under (*a teacher*); to examine (a case); to agree with; to obey, heed; **bene/male audīre** have a good/bad reputation

audītiō, -ōnis f listening; hearsay, news

audītor, -ōris m hearer; pupil

audītōrium, -ī and **-iī** nt lecture room, law court; audience

audītus, -ūs m (sense of) hearing; a hearing; rumour

auferō, auferre, abstulī, ablātum vt to take away, carry away; to mislead, lead into a digression; to take by force, steal; to win, obtain (as the result of effort); **aufer** away with!

Aufidus, -ō m river in Apulia

aufugiō, -ugere, -ūgī vi to run away ▸ vt to flee from

Augēās, -ae m king of Elis (whose stables Hercules cleaned)

augeō, -gēre, -xī, -ctum vt to increase; to enrich, bless (with); to praise, worship ▸ vi to increase

augēscō, -ere vi to begin to grow, increase

augmen, -inis nt growth

augur, -is m/f augur; prophet, interpreter

augurāle, -is nt part of camp where auspices were taken

augurālis adj augur's

augurātiō, -ōnis f soothsaying

augurātō adv after taking auspices

augurātus, -ūs m office of augur

augurium, -ī and **-iī** nt augury; an omen; prophecy, interpretation; presentiment

augurius adj of augurs

auguro, -āre vt, vi to take auguries; to consecrate by auguries; to forebode

auguror, -ārī, -ātus vt, vi to take auguries; to foretell by omens; to predict, conjecture

Augusta, -ae f title of the emperor's wife, mother, daughter or sister

Augustālis adj of Augustus; **lūdī Augustālēs** games in October; **praefectus ~** governor of Egypt; **sodālēs Augustālēs** priests of deified Augustus

augustē adv see **augustus**

Augustus, -ī m title given to C Octavius, first Roman emperor, and so to his successors ▸ adj imperial; (month) August, of August

augustus adj venerable, august, majestic

aula¹, -ae f courtyard (of a Greek house); hall (of a Roman house); palace, royal court; courtiers; royal power

aula² etc see **olla**

aulaeum, -ī nt embroidered hangings, canopy, covering; (THEAT) curtain

aulicī, -ōrum mpl courtiers

aulicus adj of the court

Aulis, -idis and **-is** f port in Boeotia from which the Greeks sailed for Troy

auloedus, -ī m singer accompanied by flute

aura, -ae f breath of air, breeze, wind; air, upper world; vapour, odour, sound, gleam; (fig) winds (of public favour), breeze (of prosperity), air (of freedom), daylight (of publicity)

aurāria, -ae f gold mine

aurārius adj of gold

aurātus adj gilt, ornamented with gold; gold

Aurēlius, -ī m Roman name; **lēx Aurēlia** law on the composition of juries; **via Aurēlia** main road running NW from Rome

aureolus adj gold; beautiful, splendid

aureus adj gold, golden; gilded; (fig) beautiful, splendid ▸ m gold coin

aurichalcum, -ī nt a precious metal

auricomus adj golden-leaved

auricula, -ae f the external ear; ear

aurifer, -ī adj gold-producing

aurifex, -icis m goldsmith

aurīga, -ae m charioteer, driver; groom; helmsman; a constellation

aurigena, -ae adj gold-begotten

auriger, -ī adj gilded

aurīgō, -āre vi to compete in the chariot race

auris, -is f ear; (RHET) judgment; (AGR) earthboard (of a plough); **ad aurem admonēre** whisper; **in utramvis aurem dormīre** sleep soundly

aurītulus, -ī m "Long-Ears"

aurītus adj long-eared; attentive

aurōra, -ae f dawn, morning; goddess of dawn; the East

aurum, -ī nt gold; gold plate, jewellery, bit, fleece etc; money; lustre; the Golden Age

auscultātiō, -ōnis f obedience

auscultātor, -ōris m listener

auscultō, -āre, -āvī, -ātum vt to listen to; to overhear ▸ vi (of servants) to wait at the door; to obey

ausim subj of **audeō**

Ausones, -um mpl indigenous people of central Italy

Ausonia f Italy

Ausonidae mpl Italians

Ausonius, -is adj Italian

auspex, -icis m augur, soothsayer; patron, commander; witness of a marriage contract

auspicātō adv after taking auspices; at a lucky moment

auspicātus adj consecrated; auspicious, lucky

auspicium, -ī and **-iī** nt augury, auspices; right of taking auspices; power, command; omen; **~ facere** give a sign

auspicō, -āre vi to take the auspices

auspicor, -ārī, -ātus vi to take the auspices; to make a beginning ▸ vt to begin, enter upon

auster, -rī m south wind; south

austērē adv see **austērus**

austēritās, -ātis f severity

austērus adj severe, serious; gloomy, irksome

austrālis adj southern

austrīnus adj from the south

ausum, -ī nt enterprise

ausus ppa of **audeō**

aut conj or; either … or; or else, or at least, or rather

autem conj (adversative) but, on the other hand; (in transitions, parentheses) moreover, now, and; (in dialogue) indeed

authepsa, -ae f stove

autographus adj written with his own hand

Autolycus, -ī m a robber

automaton, -ī nt automaton

automatus adj spontaneous

Automedōn, -ontis m a charioteer

autumnālis adj autumn, autumnal

autumnus, -ī m autumn ▸ adj autumnal

autumō, -āre vt to assert

auxī perf of **augeō**

auxilia, -iōrum ntpl auxiliary troops; military force

auxiliāris adj helping, auxiliary; of the auxiliaries ▸ mpl auxiliary troops

auxiliārius adj helping; auxiliary

auxiliātor, -ōris m helper

auxiliātus, -ūs m aid

auxilior, -ārī, -ātus vi to aid, support

auxilium, -ī and **-iī** nt help, assistance

avārē, avāriter adv see **avārus**

avāritia, -ae f greed, selfishness

avāritiēs, -ēī f avarice

avārus adj greedy, covetous; eager

avē, avēte, avētō impv hail!, farewell!

āvehō, -here, -xī, -ctum vt to carry away; (pass) to ride away

āvellō, -ellere, -ellī and **-ulsī (-olsī), -ulsum (-olsum)** vt to pull away, tear off; to take away (by force), remove

avēna, -ae f oats; (music) reed, shepherd's pipe

avēns, -entis adj eager

Aventīnum, -ī nt Aventine hill

Aventīnus, -ī m Aventine (hill) (in Rome) ▸ adj of Aventine

aveō, -ēre vt to desire, long for

Avernālis adj of lake Avernus

Avernus, -ī m lake near Cumae (said to be an entrance to the lower world); the lower world ▸ adj birdless; of Avernus; infernal

āverruncō, -āre vt to avert

āversābilis adj abominable

āversor¹, -ārī, -ātus vi to turn away ▸ vt to repulse, decline

āversor², -ōris m embezzler

āversum, -ī nt back

āversus ppp of **āvertō** ▸ adj in the rear, behind, backwards; hostile, averse

āvertō, -tere, -tī, -sum vt to turn aside, avert; to divert; to estrange; to embezzle ▸ vi to withdraw

avia¹, -ae f grandmother

avia², -ōrum ntpl wilderness

aviārium, -ī nt aviary, haunt of birds

aviārius adj of birds

avidē adv see **avidus**

aviditās, -ātis f eagerness, longing; avarice

avidus adj eager, covetous; avaricious, greedy; hungry; vast

avis, -is f bird; omen; ~ **alba** a rarity

avītus adj of a grandfather; ancestral

āvius adj out of the way, lonely, untrodden; wandering, astray

āvocāmentum, -ī nt relaxation

āvocātiō, -ōnis f diversion

āvocō, -āre vt to call off; to divert, distract; to amuse

āvolō, -āre vi to fly away, hurry away; to depart, vanish

āvolsus, avulsus ppp of **āvellō**

avunculus, -ī m uncle (on mother's side); ~ **māgnus** great-uncle

avus, -ī m grandfather; ancestor

Axenus, -ī m Black Sea

axicia, axitia, -ae f scissors

āxilla, -ae f armpit

axis, -is m axle, chariot; axis, pole, sky, clime; plank

azȳmus adj unleavened

babae *interj* (*expressing wonder or joy*) oho!
Babylōn, -ōnis *f* ancient city on the Euphrates
Babylōnia *f* the country under Babylon
Babylōnicus, Babylōniēnsis *adj see* **Babylōnia**
Babylōnius *adj* Babylonian; Chaldaean, versed in astrology
bāca, -ae *f* berry; olive; fruit; pearl
bācātus *adj* of pearls
bacca *etc see* **bāca**
baccar, -is *nt* cyclamen
Baccha, -ae *f* Bacchante
Bacchānal, -ālis *nt* place consecrated to Bacchus; (*pl*) festival of Bacchus
bacchātiō, -ōnis *f* revel
Bacchēus, Bacchīcus, Bacchius *adj see* **Bacchus**
Bacchiadae, -ārum *mpl* kings of Corinth (*founders of Syracuse*)
bacchor, -ārī, -ātus *vi* to celebrate the festival of Bacchus; to revel; rave; to rage
Bacchus, -ī *m* god of wine, vegetation, poetry, and religious ecstasy; vine, wine
bācifer *adj* olive-bearing
bacillum, -ī *nt* stick, lictor's staff
Bactra, -ōrum *ntpl* capital of Bactria in central Asia (*now Balkh*)
Bactriāna *f* Bactria
Bactriānus, Bactrius *adj* Bactrian
baculum, -ī *nt*, **baculus, -ī** *m* stick, staff
Baetica *f* Roman province (*now Andalusia*)
Baeticus *adj see* **Baetis**
Baetis, -is *m* river in Spain (*now Guadalquivir*)
Bagrada, -ae *m* river in Africa (*now Medjerda*)
Bāiae, -ārum *fpl* Roman spa on Bay of Naples
Bāiānus *adj see* **Bāiae**
bāiulō, -āre *vt* to carry (*something heavy*)
bāiulus, -ī *m* porter
bālaena, -ae *f* whale
balanus, -ī *f* balsam (*from an Arabian nut*); a shellfish
balatrō, -ōnis *m* jester
bālātus, -ūs *m* bleating
balbus *adj* stammering

balbūtiō, -īre *vt, vi* to stammer, speak indistinctly; (*fig*) to speak obscurely
Baleārēs, -ium *fpl* Balearic islands
Baleāris, Baleāricus *adj see* **Baleārēs**
balineum *etc see* **balneum** *etc*
ballista, -ae *f* (MIL) catapult for shooting stones and other missiles; (*fig*) weapon
ballistārium, -ī *and* **-iī** *nt* catapult
balneae, -ārum *fpl* bath, baths
balneāria, -ōrum *ntpl* bathroom
balneārius *adj* of the baths
balneātor, -ōris *m* bath superintendent
balneolum, -ī *nt* small bath
balneum, -ī *nt* bath
bālō, -āre *vi* to bleat
balsamum, -ī *nt* balsam, balsam tree
baltea, -ōrum *ntpl* belt (*esp swordbelt; woman's girdle; strapping*)
balteus, -ī *m* belt (*esp swordbelt; woman's girdle; strapping*)
Bandusia, -ae *f* spring near Horace's birthplace
baptisma, -tis *nt* baptism
baptizō, -āre *vt* (ECCL) to baptize
barathrum, -ī *nt* abyss; the lower world; (*fig*) a greedy person
barba, -ae *f* beard
barbarē *adv* in a foreign language (*to a Greek*), in Latin; in an uncivilized way; roughly, cruelly
barbaria, -ae, barbariēs (*acc* **-em**) *f* a foreign country (*outside Greece or Italy*); (*words*) barbarism; (*manners*) rudeness, stupidity
barbaricus *adj* foreign, outlandish (*to a Greek*), Italian
barbarus *adj* foreign, barbarous; (*to a Greek*) Italian; rude, uncivilized; savage, barbarous ▶ *m* foreigner, barbarian
barbātulus *adj* with a little beard
barbātus *adj* bearded, adult; ancient (*Romans*); of philosophers
barbiger, -ī *adj* bearded
barbitos (*acc* **-on**) *m* lyre, lute
barbula, -ae *f* little beard
Barcās, -ae *m* ancestor of Hannibal
Barcīnus *adj see* **Barcās**
bardus¹ *adj* dull, stupid
bardus², -ī *m* Gallic minstrel
bārō, -ōnis *m* dunce
barrus, -ī *m* elephant
bascauda, -ae *f* basket (*for the table*)
bāsiātiō, -ōnis *f* kiss
basilica, -ae *f* public building used as exchange and law court
basilicē *adv* royally, in magnificent style
basilicum, -ī *nt* regal robe
basilicus *adj* royal, magnificent ▶ *m* highest throw at dice
bāsiō, -āre *vt* to kiss
basis, -is *f* pedestal, base
bāsium, -ī *and* **-iī** *nt* kiss
Bassareus, -eī *m* Bacchus
Batāvī, -ōrum *mpl* people of Batavia (*now Holland*)

batillum, -ī nt firepan
Battiadēs, -ae m Callimachus
bātuō, -ere, -ī vt to beat
baubor, -ārī vi (of dogs) to howl
Baucis, -idis f wife of Philemon
beātē adv see **beātus**
beātitās, -ātis f happiness
beātitūdō, -inis f happiness
beātulus, -ī m the blessed man
beātus adj happy; prosperous, well-off; rich, abundant
Bēdriacēnsis adj see **Bēdriācum**
Bēdriācum, -ī nt village in N. Italy
Belgae, -ārum mpl people of N. Gaul (now Belgium)
Bēlides, -um fpl Danaids
Bēlidēs, -īdae m Danaus, Aegyptus, Lynceus
bellāria, -ōrum ntpl dessert, confectionery
bellātor, -ōris m warrior, fighter ▶ adj warlike
bellātōrius adj aggressive
bellātrīx, -īcis f warrioress ▶ adj warlike
bellē adv well, nicely; ~ **habēre** be well (in health)
Bellerophōn, -ontis m slayer of Chimaera, rider of Pegasus
Bellerophontēus adj see **Bellerophōn**
bellicōsus adj warlike
bellicus adj of war, military; **bellicum canere** give the signal for marching or attack
belliger, -ī adj martial
belligerō, -āre, -āvī, -ātum vi to wage war
bellipotēns, -entis adj strong in war
bellō, -āre, -āvī, -ātum vi to fight, wage war
Bellōna, -ae f goddess of war
bellor, -ārī vi to fight
bellulus adj pretty
bellum, -ī nt war, warfare; battle; ~ **gerere** wage war; **bellī** in war
bellus adj pretty, handsome; pleasant, nice
bēlua, -ae f beast, monster (esp large and fierce), any animal; (fig) brute; ~ **Gaetula** Indian elephant
bēluātus adj embroidered with animals
bēluōsus adj full of monsters
Bēlus, -ī m Baal; an oriental king
Bēnācus, -ī m lake in N. Italy (now Garda)
bene adv (compar **melius**, superl **optimē**) well; correctly; profitably; very ▶ interj bravo!, good!; ~ **dīcere** speak well; speak well of, praise; ~ **emere** buy cheap; ~ **est tibi** you are well off; ~ **facere** do well; do good to; ~ **facis** thank you; **rem ~ gerere** be successful; ~ **sē habēre** have a good time; ~ **habet** all is well, it's all right; ~ **merērī dē** do a service to; ~ **partum** honestly acquired; ~ **tē** your health!; ~ **vēndere** sell at a high price; ~ **vīvere** live a happy life
benedīcō, -īcere, -īxī, -ictum vt to speak well of, praise; (ECCL) to bless
benedictiō, -ōnis f (ECCL) blessing
beneficentia, -ae f kindness
beneficiāriī, -ōrum mpl privileged soldiers
beneficium, -ī and -iī nt benefit, favour; (POL, MIL) promotion; **beneficiō tuō** thanks to you

beneficus adj generous, obliging
Beneventānus adj see **Beneventum**
Beneventum, -ī nt town in S. Italy (now Benevento)
benevolē adv see **benevolus**
benevolēns, -entis adj kind-hearted
benevolentia, -ae f goodwill, friendliness
benevolus adj kindly, friendly; (of servants) devoted
benīgnē adv willingly, courteously; generously; (colloq) no thank you; ~ **facere** do a favour
benīgnitās, -ātis f kindness; liberality, bounty
benīgnus adj kind, friendly; favourable; liberal, lavish; fruitful, bounteous
beō, -āre, -āvī, -ātum vt to gladden, bless, enrich
Berecyntia f Cybele
Berecyntius adj of Berecyntus; of Cybele
Berecyntus, -ī m mountain in Phrygia sacred to Cybele
Berenīcē, -ēs f a queen of Egypt; **coma Berenīcēs** a constellation
bēryllus, -ī m beryl
bēs, bessis m two-thirds of the as; two-thirds
bēstia, -ae f beast; wild animal (for the arena)
bēstiārius adj of beasts ▶ m beast fighter (in the arena)
bēstiola, -ae f small animal
bēta¹, -ae f beet
bēta² nt indecl (Greek letter) beta
bibī perf of **bibō**
bibliopōla, -ae m bookseller
bibliothēca, -ae, bibliothēcē, -ēs f library
bibō, -ere, -ī vt to drink; to live on the banks of (a river); to drink in, absorb; (fig) to listen attentively, be imbued; **bibere aquas** be drowned; **Graecō mōre bibere** drink to someone's health
Bibulus, -ī m consul with Caesar in 59 BC
bibulus adj fond of drink, thirsty; (things) thirsty
biceps, -ipitis adj two-headed
biclīnium, -ī and -iī nt dining couch for two
bicolor, -ōris adj two-coloured
bicorniger, -ī adj two-horned
bicornis adj two-horned, two-pronged; (rivers) two-mouthed
bicorpor, -is adj two-bodied
bidēns, -entis adj with two teeth or prongs ▶ m hoe ▶ f sheep (or other sacrificial animal)
bidental, -ālis nt a place struck by lightning
biduum, -ī nt two days
biennium, -ī and -iī nt two years
bifāriam adv in two parts, twice
bifer, -ī adj flowering twice a year
bifidus adj split in two
biforis adj double-doored; double
bifōrmātus, bifōrmis adj with two forms
bifrōns, -ontis adj two-headed
bifurcus adj two-pronged, forked
bīgae, -ārum fpl chariot and pair
bīgātus adj stamped with a chariot and pair

biiugī, -ōrum mpl two horses yoked abreast; chariot with two horses

biiugis, biiugus adj yoked

bilībra, -ae f two pounds

bilībris adj holding two pounds

bilinguis adj double-tongued; bilingual; deceitful

bīlis, -is f bile, gall; (fig) anger, displeasure; ~ **ātra,** ~ **nigra** melancholy; madness

bilīx, -īcis adj double-stranded

bilūstris adj ten years

bimaris adj between two seas

bimarītus, -ī m bigamist

bimāter, -ris adj having two mothers

bimembris adj half man, half beast; (pl) Centaurs

bimēstris adj of two months, two months old

bīmulus, -ī adj only two years old

bīmus adj two years old, for two years

bīnī, bīnae, bīna num two each, two by two; a pair; (with pl nouns having a meaning different from sg) two

binoctium, -ī and **-iī** nt two nights

binōminis adj with two names

Biōn, -ōnis m satirical philosopher

Biōnēus adj satirical

bipalmis adj two spans long

bipartiō adv in two parts, in two directions

bipartītus adj divided in two

bipatēns, -entis adj double-opening

bipedālis adj two feet long, broad or thick

bipennifer, -ī adj wielding a battle-axe

bipennis adj two-edged ▶ f battle-axe

bipertītō etc see **bipartītō**

bipēs, -edis adj two-footed ▶ m biped

birēmis adj two-oared; with two banks of oars ▶ f two-oared skiff; galley with two banks of oars

bis adv twice, double; **bis ad eundem** make the same mistake twice; **bis diē, in diē** twice a day; **bis tantō, bis tantum** twice as much; **bis terque** frequently; **bis terve** seldom

bissextus, -ī m intercalary day after 24th Feb

Bistones, -um mpl people of Thrace

Bistonis f Thracian woman, Bacchante

Bistonius adj Thracian

bisulcilingua, -ae adj fork-tongued, deceitful

bisulcus adj cloven

Bīthȳnia, -iae f province of Asia Minor

Bīthȳnicus, Bīthȳnius adj see **Bīthȳnia**

bītō, -ere vi to go

bitūmen, -inis nt bitumen, a kind of pitch

bitūmineus adj see **bitūmen**

bivium nt two ways

bivius adj two-way

blaesus adj lisping, indistinct

blandē adv see **blandus**

blandidicus adj fair-spoken

blandiloquentia, -ae f attractive language

blandiloquus, blandiloquentulus adj fair-spoken

blandīmentum, -ī nt compliment, allurement

blandior, -īrī, -ītus vi to coax, caress; to flatter, pay compliments; (things) to please, entice

blanditia, -ae f caress, flattery; charm, allurement

blandītim adv caressingly

blandus adj smooth-tongued, flattering, fawning; charming, winsome

blaterō, -āre vi to babble

blatiō, -īre vt to babble

blatta, -ae f cockroach

blennus, -ī m idiot

bliteus adj silly

blitum, -ī nt kind of spinach

boārius adj of cattle; **forum boārium** cattle market in Rome

Bodotria, -ae f Firth of Forth

Boēotarchēs m chief magistrate of Boeotia

Boēotia, -iae f district of central Greece

Boēotius, Boēotus adj see **Boēotia**

boiae, -ārum fpl collar

Boiī, -ōrum mpl people of S.E. Gaul

Boiohaemī, -ōrum mpl Bohemians

bōlētus, -ī m mushroom

bolus, -ī m (dice) throw; (net) cast; (fig) haul, piece of good luck; titbit

bombus, -ī m booming, humming, buzzing

bombȳcinus adj of silk

bombȳx, -ȳcis m silkworm; silk

Bona Dea, Bonae Deae f goddess worshipped by women

bonitās, -ātis f goodness; honesty, integrity; kindness, affability

Bonōnia, -ae f town in N. Italy (now Bologna)

Bonōniēnsis adj see **Bonōnia**

bonum, -ī nt a moral good; advantage, blessing; (pl) property; **cuī bonō?** who was the gainer?

bonus adj (compar **melior,** superl **optimus**) good; kind; brave; loyal; beneficial; lucky ▶ mpl upper class party, conservatives; **bona aetās** prime of life; **bonō animō** of good cheer; well-disposed; **bonae artēs** integrity; culture, liberal education; **bona dicta** witticisms; **bona fidēs** good faith; **bonī mōrēs** morality; **bonī nummī** genuine money; **bona pars** large part; conservative party; **bonae rēs** comforts, luxuries; prosperity; morality; **bonā veniā** with kind permission; **bona verba** words of good omen; well-chosen diction; **bona vōx** loud voice

boō, -āre vi to cry aloud

Boōtēs, -ae nt constellation containing Arcturus

Boreās, -ae m north wind; north

Boreus adj see **Boreās**

Borysthenēs, -is m (river) Dnieper

Borysthenidae mpl dwellers near the Dnieper

Borysthenius adj see **Borysthenidae**

bōs, bovis m/f ox, cow; kind of turbot; **bōs Lūca** elephant; **bovī clitellās impōnere** put a round peg in a square hole

Bosporānus, **Bosporius** *adj see* **Bosporus**
Bosporus, **-ī** *m* strait from Black Sea to Sea of Marmora
Bosporus Cimmerius *m* strait from Sea of Azov to Black Sea
Boudicca, **-ae** *f* British queen (falsely called Boadicea)
bovārius *etc see* **boārius**
Bovillae, **-ārum** *fpl* ancient Latin town
Bovillānus *adj see* **Bovillae**
bovillus *adj* of oxen
brācae, **-ārum** *fpl* trousers
brācātus *adj* trousered; barbarian (*esp of tribes beyond the Alps*)
bracchiālis *adj* of the arm
bracchiolum, **-ī** *nt* dainty arm
bracchium, **-ī** *and* **-iī** *nt* arm, forearm; (*shellfish*) claw; (*tree*) branch; (*sea*) arm; (*NAUT*) yardarm; (*MIL*) outwork, mole; **levī bracchiō**, **mollī bracchiō** casually
bractea *etc see* **brattea**
brassica, **-ae** *f* cabbage
brattea, **-ae** *f* gold leaf
bratteola, **-ae** *f* very fine gold leaf
Brennus, **-ī** *m* Gallic chief who defeated the Romans
brevī *adv* shortly, soon; briefly, in a few words
brevia, **-ium** *ntpl* shoals
breviārium, **-ī** *and* **-iī** *nt* summary, statistical survey, official report
breviculus *adj* shortish
breviloquēns, **-entis** *adj* brief
brevis *adj* short, small, shallow; brief, short-lived; concise
brevitās, **-ātis** *f* shortness, smallness; brevity, conciseness
breviter *adv* concisely
Brigantēs, **-um** *mpl* British tribe in N. England
Briganticus *adj see* **Brigantēs**
Brīsēis, **-idos** *f* captive of Achilles
Britannia, **-iae** *f* Britain; the British Isles
Britannicus *m* son of emperor Claudius
Britannus, **Britannicus** *adj see* **Britannia**
Bromius, **-ī** *and* **-iī** *m* Bacchus
brūma, **-ae** *f* winter solstice, midwinter; winter
brūmālis *adj* of the winter solstice; wintry; **~ flexus** tropic of Capricorn
Brundisīnus *adj see* **Brundisium**
Brundisium, **-ī** *and* **-iī** *nt* port in S.E. Italy (now Brindisi)
Bruttiī, **-ōrum** *mpl* people of the toe of Italy
Bruttius *adj see* **Bruttiī**
Brūtus, **-ī** *m* liberator of Rome from kings; murderer of Caesar
brūtus *adj* heavy, unwieldy; stupid, irrational
bubīle, **-is** *nt* stall
būbo, **-ōnis** *m/f* owl
būbula, **-ae** *f* beef
bubulcitor, **-ārī** *vi* to drive oxen
bubulcus, **-ī** *m* ploughman
būbulus *adj* of cattle
būcaeda, **-ae** *m* flogged slave

bucca, **-ae** *f* cheek; mouth; ranter
buccō, **-ōnis** *m* babbler
buccula, **-ae** *f* visor
bucculentus *adj* fat-cheeked
būcerus *adj* horned
būcina, **-ae** *f* shepherd's horn; military trumpet; night watch
būcinātor, **-ōris** *m* trumpeter
būcolica, **-ōrum** *ntpl* pastoral poetry
būcula, **-ae** *f* young cow
būfō, **-ōnis** *m* toad
bulbus, **-ī** *m* bulb; onion
būlē, **-es** *f* Greek senate
būleuta *m* senator
būleutērium *nt* senate house
bulla, **-ae** *f* bubble; knob, stud; gold charm worn round the neck by children of noblemen
bullātus *adj* wearing the bulla; still a child
būmastus, **-ī** *f* kind of vine
būris, **-is** *m* plough-beam
Burrus *old form of* **Pyrrhus**
Busīris, **-idis** *m* Egyptian king killed by Hercules
bustirapus, **-ī** *m* graverobber
bustuārius *adj* at a funeral
bustum, **-ī** *nt* funeral place; tomb, grave
buxifer, **-ī** *adj* famed for its box trees
buxum, **-ī** *nt* boxwood; flute, top, comb, tablet
buxus, **-ī** *f* box tree; flute
Byzantium, **-ī** *and* **-iī** *nt* city on Bosporus (later Constantinople, now Istanbul)
Byzantius *adj see* **Byzantium**

C

caballīnus adj horse's

caballus, -ī m horse

cacātus adj impure

cachinnātiō, -ōnis f loud laughter

cachinnō¹, -āre vi to laugh, guffaw

cachinnō², -ōnis m scoffer

cachinnus, -ī m laugh, derisive laughter; (waves) splashing

cacō, -āre vi to evacuate the bowels

cacoēthes, -is nt (fig) itch

cacula, -ae m soldier's slave

cacūmen, -inis nt extremity, point, summit, treetop; (fig) height, limit

cacūminō, -āre vt to make pointed

Cācus, -ī m giant robber, son of Vulcan

cadāver, -is nt corpse, carcass

cadāverōsus adj ghastly

Cadmēa, -ēae f fortress of Thebes

Cadmēis, -ēidis f Agave; Ino; Semele

Cadmēus, Cadmēius adj of Cadmus; Theban

Cadmus, -ī m founder of Thebes

cadō, -ere, cecidī, cāsum vi to fall; to droop, die, be killed; (ASTR) to set; (dice) to be thrown; (events) to happen, turn out; (money) to be due; (strength, speech, courage) to diminish, cease, fail; (wind, rage) to subside; (words) to end; **cadere in** suit, agree with; come under; **cadere sub** be exposed to; **animīs cadere** be disheartened; **causā cadere** lose one's case

cādūceātor, -ōris m officer with flag of truce

cādūceus, -ī m herald's staff; Mercury's wand

cādūcifer, -ī adj with herald's staff

cādūcus adj falling, fallen; (fig) perishable, fleeting, vain; (LAW) without an heir ▶ nt property without an heir

Cadurcī, -ōrum mpl Gallic tribe

Cadurcum, -ī nt linen coverlet

cadus, -ī m jar, flask (esp for wine); urn

caecigenus adj born blind

Caeciliānus adj see Caecilius

Caecilius, -ī m Roman name (esp early Latin comic poet)

caecitās, -ātis f blindness

caecō, -āre, -āvī, -ātum vt to blind; to make obscure

Caecubum, -ī nt choice wine from the Ager Caecubus in S. Latium

caecus adj blind; invisible, secret; dark, obscure; (fig) aimless, unknown, uncertain; **appāret caecō** it's as clear as daylight; **domus caeca** a house with no windows; **caecā diē emere** buy on credit; **caecum corpus** the back

caedēs, -is f murder, massacre; gore; the slain

caedō, -ere, cecīdī, caesum vt to cut; to strike; to kill, cut to pieces; (animals) to sacrifice

caelāmen, -inis nt engraved work

caelātor, -ōris m engraver

caelātūra, -ae f engraving in bas-relief

caelebs, -ibis adj unmarried (bachelor or widower); (trees) with no vine trained on

caeles, -itis adj celestial ▶ mpl the gods

caelestis, -is adj of the sky, heavenly; divine; glorious ▶ mpl the gods ▶ ntpl the heavenly bodies

Caeliānus adj see Caelius

caelibātus, -ūs m celibacy

caelicola, -ae m god

caelifer, -ī adj supporting the sky

Caelius, -ī m Roman name; Roman hill

caelō, -āre, -āvī, -ātum vt to engrave (in relief on metals), carve (on wood); (fig) to compose

caelum¹, -ī nt engraver's chisel

caelum², -ī nt sky, heaven; air, climate, weather; (fig) height of success, glory; **~ ac terrās miscēre** create chaos; **ad ~ ferre** extol; **dē caelō dēlāpsus** a messiah; **dē caelō servāre** watch for omens; **dē caelō tangī** be struck by lightning; **digitō ~ attingere** be in the seventh heaven; **in caelumō esse** be overjoyed

caementum, -ī nt quarrystone, rubble

caenōsus adj muddy

caenum, -ī nt mud, filth

caepa, -ae f, **caepe, -is** nt onion

Caere (gen **-itis**, abl **-ēte**) nt indecl, f ancient Etruscan town

Caerēs, -itis and **-ētis** adj: **Caerite cērā dignī** like the disfranchised masses

caerimōnia, -ae f sanctity; veneration (for gods); religious usage, ritual

caeruleus, caerulus adj blue, dark blue, dark green, dusky ▶ ntpl the sea

Caesar, -is m Julius (great Roman soldier, statesman, author); Augustus; the emperor

Caesareus, Caesariānus, Caesarīnus adj see Caesar

caesariātus adj bushy-haired

caesariēs, -ēī f hair

caesīcius adj bluish

caesim adv with the edge of the sword; (RHET) in short clauses

caesius adj bluish grey, blue-eyed

caespes, -itis m sod, turf; mass of roots

caestus, -ūs m boxing glove

caesus ppp of **caedō**

caetra, -ae f targe

caetrātus adj armed with a targe

Caīcus, -ī m river in Asia Minor

Cāiēta, -ae, Cāiētē, -ēs f town in Latium

Cāius etc see **Gāius¹**

Calaber, -rī adj Calabrian

Calabria f S.E. peninsula of Italy

Calamis, -idis m Greek sculptor

calamister, -rī m, **calamisterum, -rī** nt curling iron; (RHET) flourish

calamistrātus adj curled; foppish

calamitās, -ātis f disaster; (MIL) defeat; (AGR) damage, failure

calamitōsē adv see **calamitōsus**

calamitōsus adj disastrous, ruinous; blighted, unfortunate

calamus, -ī m reed; stalk; pen, pipe, arrow, fishing rod

calathiscus, -ī m small basket

calathus, -ī m wicker basket; bowl, cup

calātor, -ōris m servant

calcāneum, -ī nt heel

calcar, -āris nt spur

calceāmentum, -ī nt shoe

calceātus ppp shod

calceolārius, -ī and -iī m shoemaker

calceolus, -ī m small shoe

calceus, -ī m shoe

Calchās, -antis m Greek prophet at Troy

calcitrō, -āre vi to kick; (fig) to resist

calcō, -āre, -āvī, -ātum vt to tread, trample on; (fig) to spurn

calculus, -ī m pebble, stone; draughtsman, counting stone, reckoning, voting stone; **calculum redūcere** take back a move; **calculōs subdūcere** compute; **ad calculōs vocāre** subject to a reckoning

caldārius adj with warm water

caldus etc see **calidus**

Calēdonia, -ae f the Scottish Highlands

Calēdonius adj see **Calēdonia**

calefaciō, calfaciō, -facere, -fēcī, -factum vt to warm, heat; (fig) to provoke, excite

calefactō, -āre vt to warm

Calendae see **Kalendae**

Calēnus adj of Cales ▸ nt wine of Cales

caleō, -ēre vi to be warm, be hot, glow; (mind) to be inflamed; (things) to be pursued with enthusiasm; to be fresh

Calēs, -ium fpl town in Campania

calēscō, -ere, -uī vi to get hot; (fig) to become inflamed

calidē adv promptly

calidus adj warm, hot; (fig) fiery, eager; hasty; prompt ▸ f warm water ▸ nt warm drink

caliendrum, -ī nt headdress of hair

caliga, -ae f soldier's boot

caligātus adj heavily shod

cālīginōsus adj misty, obscure

cālīgō¹, -inis f mist, fog; dimness, darkness; (mind) obtuseness; (circumstances) trouble

cālīgō², -āre vi to be misty, be dim; to cause dizziness

Caligula, -ae m emperor Gaius

calix, -cis m wine cup; cooking pot

calleō, -ēre vi to be thick-skinned; (fig) to be unfeeling; to be wise, be skilful ▸ vt to know, understand

callidē adv see **callidus**

calliditās, -ātis f skill; cunning

callidus adj skilful, clever; crafty

Callimachus, -ī m Greek poet of Alexandria

Calliopē, -ēs, Calliopēa, -ēae f Muse of epic poetry

callis, -is m footpath, mountain track; pass; hill pastures

Callistō, -ūs f daughter of Lycaon; (constellation) Great Bear

callōsus adj hard-skinned; solid

callum, -ī nt hard or thick skin; firm flesh; (fig) callousness

cālō, -ōnis m soldier's servant; drudge

calō, -āre, -āvī, -ātum vt to convoke

calor, -ōris m warmth, heat; (fig) passion, love

Calpē, -ēs f Rock of Gibraltar

Calpurniānus adj see **Calpurnius**

Calpurnius, -ī m Roman name

caltha, -ae f marigold

calthula, -ae f yellow dress

caluī perf of **calēscō**

calumnia, -ae f chicanery, sharp practice; subterfuge; misrepresentation; (LAW) dishonest accusation, blackmail; being convicted of malicious prosecution; **calumniam iūrāre** swear that an action is brought in good faith

calumniātor, -ōris m legal trickster, slanderer

calumnior, -ārī, -ātus vt to misrepresent, slander; (LAW) to bring an action in bad faith; **sē calumniārī** deprecate oneself

calva, -ae f bald head

calvitium, -ī and -iī nt baldness

calvor, -ārī vt to deceive

calvus adj bald

calx¹, -cis f heel; foot; **calce petere, calce ferīre** kick; **adversus stimulum calcēs** kicking against the pricks

calx², -cis f pebble; lime, chalk; finishing line, end; **ad carcerēs ā calce revocārī** have to begin all over again

Calydōn, -ōnis f town in Aetolia

Calydōnis adj Calydonian

Calydōnius f Deianira; **~ amnis** Achelous; **~ hērōs** Meleager; **Calydōnia rēgna** Daunia in S. Italy

Calypsō, -ūs (acc -ō) f nymph who detained Ulysses in Ogygia

camēlīnus adj camel's

camella, -ae f wine cup

camēlus, -ī m camel

Camēna, -ae f Muse; poetry

camera, -ae f arched roof

Camerīnum, -ī nt town in Umbria

Camers, -tis, -tīnus adj of Camerinum

Camillus, -ī m Roman hero (who saved Rome from the Gauls)

camīnus, -ī m furnace, fire; forge; **oleum addere camīnō** add fuel to the flames

cammarus, -ī m lobster

Campānia, -iae f district of W. Italy

Campānicus, Campānicius adj Campanian, Capuan

campē, -ēs f evasion

campester, -ris adj of the plain; of the Campus Martius ▶ nt loincloth ▶ ntpl level ground

campus, -ī m plain; sports field; any level surface; (fig) theatre, arena (of action, debate); **~ Martius** level ground by the Tiber (used for assemblies, sports, military drills)

Camulodūnum, -ī nt town of Trinobantes (now Colchester)

camur, -ī adj crooked

canālis, -is m pipe, conduit, canal

cancellī, -ōrum mpl grating, enclosure; barrier (in public places), bar of law court

cancer, -rī m crab; (constellation) Cancer; south, tropical heat; (MED) cancer

candefaciō, -ere vt to make dazzlingly white

candēla, -ae f taper, tallow candle; waxed cord; **candēlam appōnere valvīs** set the house on fire

candēlābrum, -ī nt candlestick, chandelier, lampstand

candēns, -entis adj dazzling white; white-hot

candeō, -ēre vi to shine, be white; to be white-hot

candēscō, -ere vi to become white; to grow white-hot

candidātōrius adj of a candidate

candidātus adj dressed in white ▶ m candidate for office

candidē adv in white; sincerely

candidulus adj pretty white

candidus adj white, bright; radiant, beautiful; clothed in white; (style) clear; (mind) candid, frank; (circumstances) happy; **candida sententia** acquittal

candor, -ōris m whiteness, brightness, beauty; (fig) brilliance, sincerity

cānēns, -entis adj white

cāneō, -ēre, -uī vi to be grey, be white

cānēscō, -ere vi to grow white; to grow old

canīcula, -ae f (dog) bitch; Dog Star, Sirius

canīnus adj dog's, canine; snarling, spiteful; **canīna littera** letter R

canis, -is m/f dog, bitch; (fig) shameless or angry person; hanger-on; (dice) lowest throw; (ASTR) Canis Major, Canis Minor; (myth) Cerberus

canistrum, -ī nt wicker basket

cānitiēs, -ēī f greyness; grey hair; old age

canna, -ae f reed; pipe; gondola

cannabis, -is f hemp

Cannae, -ārum fpl village in Apulia (scene of great Roman defeat by Hannibal)

Cannēnsis adj see **Cannae**

canō, canere, cecinī vt, vi to sing; to play; to sing about, recite, celebrate; to prophesy; (MIL) to sound; (birds) to sing, crow

canor, -ōris m song, tune, sound

canōrus adj musical, melodious; singsong ▶ nt melodiousness

Cantaber, -rī m Cantabrian

Cantabria, -riae f district of N Spain

Cantabricus adj see **Cantabria**

cantāmen, -inis nt charm

cantharis, -idis f beetle; Spanish fly

cantharus, -ī m tankard

canthērīnus adj of a horse

canthērius, -ī and **-iī** m gelding

canticum, -ī nt aria in Latin comedy; song

cantilēna, -ae f old song, gossip; **cantilēnam eandem canere** keep harping on the same theme

cantiō, -ōnis f song; charm

cantitō, -āre, -āvī, -atum vt to sing or play often

Cantium, -ī and **-iī** nt Kent

cantiunculae, -ārum fpl fascinating strains

cantō, -āre, -āvī, -ātum vt, vi to sing; to play; to sing about, recite, celebrate; to proclaim, harp on; to use magic spells; to sound; to drawl

cantor, -ōris m, **cantorīx, -rīcis** f singer, musician, poet; actor

cantus, -ūs m singing, playing, music; prophecy; magic spell

cānus adj white, grey, hoary; old ▶ mpl grey hairs

Canusīnus adj see **Canusium**

Canusium, -ī nt town in Apulia (famous for wool)

capācitās, -ātis f spaciousness

capāx, -ācis adj capable of holding, spacious, roomy; capable, able, fit

capēdō, -inis f sacrificial dish

capēduncula f small dish

capella, -ae f she-goat; (ASTR) bright star in Auriga

Capēna, -ae f old Etruscan town

Capēnās, Capēnus adj: **Porta Capēna** Roman gate leading to the Via Appia

caper, -rī m goat; odour of the armpits

caperrō, -āre vi to wrinkle

capessō, -ere, -īvī, -ītum vt to seize, take hold of, try to reach, make for; to take in hand, engage in; **rem pūblicam capessere** go in for politics

capillātus adj long-haired; ancient

capillus, -ī m hair (of head or beard), a hair

capiō, -ere, cēpī, captum vt to take, seize; to catch, capture; (MIL) to occupy, take prisoner; (NAUT) to make, reach (a goal); (fig) to captivate, charm, cheat; (pass) to be maimed, lose the use of; to choose; (appearance) to assume; (habit) to cultivate; (duty) to undertake; (ideas) to conceive, form; (feeling) to experience; (harm) to suffer; to receive, get, inherit; to contain, hold; (fig) to bear; (mind) to grasp; **cōnsilium capere** come to a decision; **impetum capere** gather momentum; **initium capere** start; **oculō capī** lose an eye; **mente captus** insane; **cupīdō eum cēpit** he felt a desire

capis, -dis f sacrificial bowl with one handle
capistrātus adj haltered
capistrum, -ī nt halter, muzzle
capital, -ālis nt capital crime
capitālis adj mortal, deadly, dangerous; (LAW) capital; important, excellent
capitō, -ōnis m bighead
Capitōlīnus adj of the Capitol; of Jupiter
Capitōlium, -ī nt Roman hill with temple of Jupiter
capitulātim adv summarily
capitulum, -ī nt small head; person, creature
Cappadocia, -ae f country of Asia Minor
capra, -ae f she-goat; odour of armpits; (ASTR) Capella
caprea, -ae f roe
Capreae, -ārum fpl island of Capri
capreolus, -ī m roebuck; (pl) crossbeams
Capricornus, -ī m (constellation) Capricorn (associated with midwinter)
caprifīcus, -ī f wild fig tree
caprigenus adj of goats
caprimulgus, -ī m goatherd, rustic
caprīnus adj of goats
capripēs, -edis adj goat-footed
capsa, -ae f box (esp for papyrus rolls)
capsō archaic fut of **capiō**
capsula, -ae f small box; **dē capsulā tōtus** out of a bandbox
Capta, -ae f Minerva
captātiō, -ōnis f catching at
captātor, -ōris m one who courts; legacy hunter
captiō, -ōnis f fraud; disadvantage; (argument) fallacy, sophism
captiōsē adv see **captiōsus**
captiōsus adj deceptive; dangerous; captious
captiuncula, -ae f quibble
captīvitās, -ātis f captivity; capture
captīvus adj captive, captured; of captives ▶ m/f prisoner of war
captō, -āre, -āvī, -ātum vt to try to catch, chase; to try to win, court, watch for; to deceive, trap
captus¹ ppp of **capiō** ▶ m prisoner
captus², -ūs m grasp, notion
Capua, -ae f chief town of Campania
capulāris adj due for a coffin
capulus, -ī m coffin; handle, hilt
caput, -itis nt head; top, extremity; (rivers) source; (more rarely) mouth; person, individual; life; civil rights; (person) chief, leader; (towns) capital; (money) principal; (writing) substance, chapter; principle, main point, the great thing; **~ cēnae** main dish; **capitis accūsāre** charge with a capital offence; **capitis damnāre** condemn to death; **capitis dēminūtiō** loss of political rights; **capitis poena** capital punishment; **capita cōnferre** confer in secret; **in capita** per head; **suprā ~ esse** be imminent
Cār, -is m Carian
carbaseus adj linen, canvas

carbasus, -ī f, **carbasa, -ōrum** ntpl Spanish flax, fine linen; garment, sail, curtain
carbō, -ōnis m charcoal, embers
carbōnārius, -ī and **-iī** m charcoal burner
carbunculus, -ī m small coal; precious stone
carcer, -is m prison; jailbird; barrier, starting place (for races); **ad carcerēs ā calce revocārī** have to begin all over again
carcerārius adj of a prison
carchēsium, -ī and **-iī** nt drinking cup; (NAUT) masthead
cardiacus, -ī m dyspeptic
cardō, -inis m hinge; (ASTR) pole, axis, cardinal point; (fig) juncture, critical moment
carduus, -ī m thistle
cārē adv see **cārus**
cārectum, -ī nt sedge
cāreō, -ēre, -uī vi (with abl) to be free from, not have, be without; to abstain from, be absent from; to want, miss
cārex, -icis f sedge
Cāria, -ae f district of S.W. Asia Minor
Cāricus adj Carian ▶ f dried fig
cariēs (acc **-em**, abl **-ē**) f dry rot
carīna, -ae f keel; ship
Carīnae, -ārum fpl district of Rome
carīnārius, -ī and **-iī** m dyer of yellow
cariōsus adj crumbling; (fig) withered
cāris, -idis f kind of crab
cāritās, -ātis f dearness, high price; esteem, affection
carmen, -inis nt song, tune; poem, poetry, verse; prophecy; (in law, religion) formula; moral text
Carmentālis adj see **Carmentis**
Carmentis, -is, Carmentia, -ae f prophetess, mother of Evander
carnārium, -ī and **-iī** nt fleshhook; larder
Carneadēs, -is m Greek philosopher (founder of the New Academy)
Carneadēus adj see **Carneadēs**
carnifex, -icis m executioner, hangman; scoundrel; murderer
carnificīna, -ae f execution; torture; **carnificīnam facere** be an executioner
carnificō, -āre vt to behead, mutilate
carnuf- etc see **carnif-**
cārō, -ere vt to card
carō, -nis f flesh
Carpathius adj see **Carpathus**
Carpathus, -ī f island between Crete and Rhodes
carpatina, -ae f leather shoe
carpentum, -ī nt two-wheeled coach
carpō, -ere, -sī, -tum vt to pick, pluck, gather; to tear off; to browse, graze on; (wool) to card; (fig) to enjoy, snatch; to carp at, slander; to weaken, wear down; to divide up; (journey) to go, travel
carptim adv in parts; at different points; at different times
carptor, -ōris m carver
carptus ppp of **carpō**

carrus, -ī m wagon

Carthāginiēnsis adj see **Carthāgō**

Carthāgō, -inis f Carthage (near Tunis); ~ **Nova** town in Spain (now Cartagena)

caruncula, -ae f piece of flesh

cārus adj dear, costly; dear, beloved

Carystēus adj see **Carystos**

Carystos, -ī f town in Euboea (famous for marble)

casa, -ae f cottage, hut

cascus adj old

cāseolus, -ī m small cheese

cāseus, -ī m cheese

casia, -ae f cinnamon; spurge laurel

Caspius adj Caspian

Cassandra, -ae f Trojan princess and prophetess, doomed never to be believed

cassēs, -ium mpl net, snare; spider's web

Cassiānus adj see **Cassius**

cassida, -ae f helmet

Cassiopēa, -ae, Cassiopē, -ēs f mother of Andromeda; a constellation

cassis, -idis f helmet

Cassius, -ī m Roman family name

cassō, -āre vi to shake

cassus adj empty; devoid of, without (abl); vain, useless; ~ **lūmine** dead; **in cassum** in vain

Castalia, -ae f spring on Parnassus, sacred to Apollo and the Muses

Castalides, -dum fpl Muses

Castalius, -is adj see **Castalia**

castanea, -ae f chestnut tree; chestnut

castē adv see **castus**

castellānus adj of a fortress ▸ mpl garrison

castellātim adv in different fortresses

castellum, -ī nt fortress, castle; (fig) defence, refuge

castēria, -ae f rowers' quarters

castīgābilis adj punishable

castīgātiō, -ōnis f correction, reproof

castīgātor, -ōris m reprover

castīgātus adj small, slender

castīgō, -āre, -āvī, -ātum vt to correct, punish; to reprove; to restrain

castimōnia, -ae f purity, morality; chastity, abstinence

castitās, -ātis f chastity

Castor, -oris m twin brother of Pollux (patron of sailors); star in Gemini

castor, -oris m beaver

castoreum, -ī nt odorous secretion of the beaver

castra, -ōrum ntpl camp; day's march; army life; (fig) party, sect; ~ **movēre** strike camp; ~ **mūnīre** construct a camp; ~ **pōnere** pitch camp; **bīna** ~ two camps

castrēnsis adj of the camp, military

castrō, -āre vt to castrate; (fig) to weaken

castrum, -ī nt fort

castus adj clean, pure, chaste, innocent; holy, pious

cāsū adv by chance

casula, -ae f little cottage

cāsus, -ūs m fall, downfall; event, chance, accident; misfortune, death; opportunity; (time) end; (GRAM) case

Catadūpa, -ōrum ntpl Nile cataract near Syene

catagraphus adj painted

Catamītus, -ī m Ganymede

cataphractēs, -ae m coat of mail

cataphractus adj wearing mail

cataplus, -ī m ship arriving

catapulta, -ae f (MIL) catapult; (fig) missile

catapultārius adj thrown by catapult

cataracta, -ae f waterfall; sluice; drawbridge

catasta, -ae f stage, scaffold

catē adv see **catus**

catēia, -ae f javelin

catella, -ae f small chain

catellus, -ī m puppy

catēna, -ae f chain; fetter; (fig) bond, restraint; series

catēnātus adj chained, fettered

caterva, -ae f crowd, band; flock; (MIL) troop, body; (THEAT) company

catervātim adv in companies

cathedra, -ae f armchair, sedan chair; teacher's chair

catholicus adj (ECCL) orthodox, universal

Catilīna, -ae m Catiline (conspirator suppressed by Cicero)

Catilīnārius adj see **Catilīna**

catīllō, -āre vt to lick a plate

catīllus, -ī m small dish

catīnus, -ī m dish, pot

Catō, -ōnis m famous censor and author, idealized as the pattern of an ancient Roman; famous Stoic and republican leader against Caesar

Catōniānus adj see **Catō**

Catōnīnī mpl Cato's supporters

catōnium, -ī and **-iī** nt the lower world

Catulliānus adj see **Catullus**

Catullus, -ī m Latin lyric poet

catulus, -ī m puppy; cub, young of other animals

catus adj clever, wise; sly, cunning

Caucasius adj see **Caucasus**

Caucasus, -ī m Caucasus (mountains)

cauda, -ae f tail; **caudam iactāre** fawn; **caudam trahere** be made a fool of

caudeus adj wooden

caudex, -icis m trunk; block of wood; book, ledger; (fig) blockhead

caudicālis adj of woodcutting

Caudīnus adj see **Caudium**

Caudium, -ī nt Samnite town

caulae, -ārum fpl opening; sheepfold

caulis, -is m stalk; cabbage

Cauneus adj Caunian

Caunus, -ī f town in Caria ▸ fpl dried figs

caupō, -ōnis m shopkeeper, innkeeper

caupōna, -ae f shop, inn

caupōnius adj see **caupō**

caupōnor, -ārī vt to trade in

caupōnula, -ae f tavern

Caurus, -ī m north-west wind

causa, **-ae** f cause, reason; purpose, sake; excuse, pretext; opportunity; connection, case, position; (*LAW*) case, suit; (*POL*) cause, party; (*RHET*) subject matter; **causam ōrāre** plead a case; **causam dēfendere** speak for the defence; **causam dīcere** defend oneself; **causā** for the sake of; **cum causā** with good reason; **quā dē causā** for this reason; **in causā esse** be responsible; **per causam** under the pretext

causārius adj (*MIL*) unfit for service

causia, **-ae** f Macedonian hat

causidicus, **-ī** m advocate

causificor, **-ārī** vi to make a pretext

causor, **-ārī**, **-ātus** vt, vi to pretend, make an excuse of

caussa etc see **causa**

causula, **-ae** f petty lawsuit; slight cause

cautē adv carefully, cautiously; with security

cautēla, **-ae** f caution

cautēs, **-is** f rock, crag

cautim adv warily

cautiō, **-ōnis** f caution, wariness; (*LAW*) security, bond, bail; **mihi ~ est** I must take care; **mea ~ est** I must see to it

cautor, **-ōris** m wary person; surety

cautus ppp of **caveō** ▸ adj wary, provident; safe, secure

cavaedium, **-ī** and **-iī** nt inner court (*of a house*)

cavea, **-ae** f cage, stall, coop, hive; (*THEAT*) auditorium; theatre; **prīma ~** upper class seats; **ultima ~** lower class seats

caveō, **-ēre**, **cāvī**, **cautum** vt to beware of, guard against ▸ vi (+ **ab** or **abl**) to be on one's guard against; (*with dat*) to look after; (*with nē*) to take care that ... not; (*with ut*) to take good care that; (*with dat* or *infin*) to take care not to, do not; (*LAW*) to stipulate, decree; (*COMM*) to get a guarantee, give a guarantee, stand security; **cavē** look out!

caverna, **-ae** f hollow, cave, vault; (*NAUT*) hold

cavilla, **-ae** f jeering

cavillātiō, **-ōnis** f jeering, banter; sophistry

cavillātor, **-ōris** m scoffer

cavillor, **-ārī**, **-ātus** vt to scoff at ▸ vi to jeer, scoff; to quibble

cavō, **-āre**, **-āvī**, **-ātum** vt to hollow, excavate

cavus adj hollow, concave, vaulted; (*river*) deep-channelled ▸ nt cavity, hole

Caystros, Caystrus, **-ī** m river in Lydia (*famous for swans*)

-ce demonstrative particle appended to pronouns and adverbs

Cēa, **-ae** f Aegean island (*birthplace of Simonides*)

cecidī perf of **cadō**

cecīdī perf of **caedō**

cecinī perf of **canō**

Cecropidēs, **-idae** m Theseus; Athenian

Cecropis, **-idis** f Aglauros; Procne; Philomela; Athenian, Attic

Cecropius adj Athenian ▸ f Athens

Cecrops, **-is** m ancient king of Athens

cedo (*pl* **cette**) impv give me, bring here; tell me; let me; look at!

cēdō, **-ere**, **cessī**, **cessum** vi to go, walk; to depart, withdraw, retreat; to pass away, die; (*events*) to turn out; to be changed (into); to accrue (to); to yield, be inferior (to) ▸ vt to give up, concede, allow; **cēdere bonīs**, **cēdere possessiōne** make over property (to); **cēdere forō** go bankrupt; **cēdere locō** leave one's post; **cēdere memoriā** be forgotten

cedrus, **-ī** f cedar, perfumed juniper; cedar oil

Celaenō, **-ūs** f a Harpy; a Pleiad

cēlāta ntpl secrets

celeber, **-ris** adj crowded, populous; honoured, famous; repeated

celebrātiō, **-ōnis** f throng; celebration

celebrātus adj full, much used; festive; famous

celebritās, **-ātis** f crowd; celebration; fame

celebrō, **-āre**, **-āvī**, **-ātum** vt to crowd, frequent; to repeat, practise; to celebrate, keep (*a festival*); to advertise, glorify

celer, **-is** adj quick, swift, fast; hasty

Celerēs, **-um** mpl royal bodyguard

celeripēs, **-edis** adj swift-footed

celeritās, **-ātis** f speed, quickness

celeriter adv see **celer**

celerō, **-āre** vt to quicken ▸ vi to make haste

cella, **-ae** f granary, stall, cell; garret, hut, small room; sanctuary (*of a temple*)

cellārius adj of the storeroom ▸ m steward

cellula, **-ae** f little room

cēlō, **-āre**, **-āvī**, **-ātum** vt to hide, conceal, keep secret; **id mē cēlat** he keeps me in the dark about it

celōx, **-ōcis** adj swift ▸ f fast ship, yacht

celsus adj high, lofty; (*fig*) great, eminent; haughty

Celtae, **-ārum** mpl Celts (*esp of central Gaul*) ▸ nt the Celtic nation

Celtibērī, **-ōrum** mpl people of central Spain

Celtibēria, **-iae** f Central Spain

Celtibēricus adj see **Celtibēria**

Celticus adj Celtic

cēna, **-ae** f dinner (*the principal Roman meal*); **inter cēnam** at table

cēnāculum, **-ī** nt dining-room; upper room, garret

cēnāticus adj of dinner

cēnātiō, **-ōnis** f dining-room

cēnātus ppa having dined, after dinner ▸ ppp spent in feasting

Cenchreae, **-ārum** fpl harbour of Corinth

cēnitō, **-āre** vi to be accustomed to dine

cēnō, **-āre**, **-āvī**, **-ātum** vi to dine ▸ vt to eat, dine on

cēnseō, **-ēre**, **-uī**, **-um** vt (*census*) to assess, rate, take a census, make a property return; (*fig*) to estimate, appreciate, celebrate; (*senate or other body*) to decree, resolve; (*member*) to express an opinion, move, vote; to advise; to judge, think, suppose, consider; **cēnsuī cēnsendō** for census purposes

cēnsiō, -ōnis f punishment; expression of opinion

cēnsor, -ōris m censor; (fig) severe judge, critic

cēnsōrius adj of the censors, to be dealt with by the censors; (fig) severe; **homō ~** an ex-censor

cēnsūra, -ae f censorship; criticism

cēnsus¹ ppp of **cēnseō; capite cēnsī** the poorest class of Roman citizens

cēnsus², -ūs m register of Roman citizens and their property, census; registered property; wealth; **cēnsum agere, cēnsum habēre** hold a census; **sine cēnsū** poor

centaurēum, -ī nt centaury

Centaurēus adj see **Centaurus**

Centaurus, -ī m Centaur, half man, half horse

centēnī, -um num a hundred each, a hundred

centēsimus adj hundredth ▸ f hundredth part; (interest) 1 per cent monthly (12 per cent per annum)

centiceps adj hundred-headed

centiēns, -ēs adv a hundred times

centimanus adj hundred-handed

centō, -ōnis m patchwork; **centōnēs sarcīre** tell tall stories

centum num a hundred

centumgeminus adj hundred-fold

centumplex adj hundred-fold

centumpondium, -ī and **-iī** nt a hundred pounds

centumvirālis adj of the centumviri

centumvirī, -ōrum mpl a bench of judges who heard special civil cases in Rome

centunculus, -ī m piece of patchwork, saddlecloth

centuria, -ae f (MIL) company; (POL) century (a division of the Roman people according to property)

centuriātim adv by companies, by centuries

centuriātus¹ adj divided by centuries; **comitia centuriāta** assembly which voted by centuries

centuriātus², -ūs m division into centuries; rank of centurion

centuriō¹, -āre, -āvī, -ātum vt (MIL) to assign to companies; (POL) to divide by centuries

centuriō², -ōnis m (MIL) captain, centurion

centussis, -is m a hundred asses

cēnula, -ae f little dinner

Cēōs (acc **-ō**) see **Cēa**

Cēphēis f Andromeda

Cēphēius adj of Cepheus

Cēpheus, -eī (acc **-ea**) m king of Ethiopia (father of Andromeda)

Cēphēus adj Ethiopian

Cēphīsis adj see **Cēphīsus**

Cēphīsius m Narcissus

Cēphīsus, -ī m river in central Greece

cēpī perf of **capiō**

cēra, -ae f wax; honey cells; writing tablet, notebook; seal; portrait of an ancestor; **prīma ~** first page

Ceramīcus, -ī m Athenian cemetery

cērārium, -ī and **-iī** nt seal-duty

cerastēs, -ae m a horned serpent

cerasus, -ī f cherry tree; cherry

cērātus adj waxed

Ceraunia, -ōrum nt, **Cerauniī** m mountains in Epirus

Cerbēreus adj see **Cerberus**

Cerberus, -ī m three-headed watchdog of Hades

cercopithēcus, -ī m monkey

cercūrus, -ī m Cyprian type of ship

cerdō, -ōnis m tradesman

Cereālia, -ium ntpl festival of Ceres

Cereālis adj of Ceres, of corn, of meal

cerebrōsus adj hot-headed

cerebrum, -ī nt brain; understanding; quick temper

Cerēs, -eris f goddess of agriculture; (fig) grain, bread

cēreus adj waxen; wax-coloured; (fig) supple, easily led ▸ m taper

cēriāria, -ae f taper maker

cērina, -ōrum ntpl wax-coloured clothes

cērintha, -ae f honeywort

cernō, -ere, -crēvī, crētum vt to see, discern; to understand, perceive; to decide, determine; (LAW) to decide to take up (an inheritance)

cernuus adj face downwards

cērōma, -atis nt wrestlers' ointment

cērōmaticus adj smeared with wax ointment

cerrītus adj crazy

certāmen, -inis nt contest, match; battle, combat; (fig) struggle, rivalry

certātim adv emulously

certātiō, -ōnis f contest; debate; rivalry

certē adv assuredly, of course; at least

certō¹ adv certainly, really

certō², -āre, -āvī, -ātum vi to contend, compete; (MIL) to fight it out; (LAW) to dispute; (with infin) to try hard

certus adj determined, fixed, definite; reliable, unerring; sure, certain; **mihi certum est** I have made up my mind; **certum scīre, prō certō habēre** know for certain, be sure; **certiōrem facere** inform

cērula, -ae f piece of wax; **~ miniāta** red pencil

cērussa, -ae f white lead

cērussātus adj painted with white lead

cerva, -ae f hind, deer

cervīcal, -ālis nt pillow

cervīcula, -ae f slender neck

cervīnus adj deer's

cervīx, -īcis f neck; **in cervīcibus esse** be a burden (to), threaten

cervus, -ī m stag, deer; (MIL) palisade

cessātiō, -ōnis f delaying; inactivity, idleness

cessātor, -ōris m idler

cessī perf of **cēdō**

cessiō, -ōnis f giving up

cessō, -āre, -āvī, -ātum vi to be remiss, stop; to loiter, delay; to be idle, rest, do nothing; (land) to lie fallow; to err

cestrosphendonē, -ēs f (MIL) engine for shooting stones

cestus, -ī m girdle (esp of Venus)
cētārium, -ī and **-iī** nt fishpond
cētārius, -ī and **-iī** m fishmonger
cētera adv in other respects
cēterī, -ōrum adj the rest, the others; (sg) the rest of
cēterōquī, cēterōquīn adv otherwise
cēterum adv for the rest, otherwise; but for all that; besides
Cethēgus, -ī m a conspirator with Catiline
cētr- etc see **caetr-**
cette etc see **cedo**
cētus, -ī m, **cētē** ntpl sea monster, whale
ceu adv just as, as if
Cēus adj see **Cēa**
Cēȳx, -ȳcis m husband of Alcyone, changed to a kingfisher
Chalcidēnsis, Chalcidiscus adj see **Chalcis**
Chalcis, -dis f chief town of Euboea
Chaldaeī, -aeōrum mpl Chaldeans; astrologers
Chaldāicus adj see **Chaldaeī**
chalybēius adj of steel
Chalybes, -um mpl a people of Pontus (famous as ironworkers)
chalybs, -is m steel
Chāones, -um mpl a people of Epirus
Chāonia, -iae f Epirus
Chāonius, -is adj see **Chāonia**
Chaos (abl **-ō**) nt empty space, the lower world, chaos
chara, -ae f an unidentified vegetable
charistia, -ōrum ntpl a Roman family festival
Charites, -um fpl the Graces
Charōn, -ontis m Charon (ferryman of Hades)
charta, -ae f sheet of papyrus, paper; writing
chartula, -ae f piece of paper
Charybdis, -is f monster personifying a whirlpool in the Straits of Messina; (fig) peril
Chattī, -ōrum mpl a people of central Germany
Chēlae, -ārum fpl (ASTR) the Claws (of Scorpio), Libra
chelydrus, -ī m watersnake
chelys (acc **-yn**) f tortoise; lyre
cheragra, -ae f gout in the hands
Cherronēsus, Chersonēsus, -ī f Gallipoli peninsula; Crimea
chīliarchus, -ī m officer in charge of 1000 men; chancellor of Persia
Chimaera, -ae f fire-breathing monster formed of lion, goat and serpent
Chimaeriferus adj birthplace of Chimaera
Chios, -ī f Aegean island (famous for wine)
chīrographum, -ī nt handwriting; document
Chīrōn, -ōnis m a learned Centaur (tutor of heroes)
chīronomos, -ī m/f, **chīronomōn, -untis** and **-ontis** m mime actor
chīrūrgia, -ae f surgery; (fig) violent measures
Chīus adj Chian ▶ nt Chian wine; Chian cloth
chlamydātus adj wearing a military cloak
chlamys, -dis f Greek military cloak

Choerilus, -ī m inferior Greek poet
chorāgium, -ī and **-iī** nt producing of a chorus
chorāgus, -ī m one who finances a chorus
choraulēs, -ae m flute-player (accompanying a chorus)
chorda, -ae f string (of an instrument); rope
chorēa, -ae f dance
chorēus, -ī m trochee
chorus, -ī m choral dance; chorus, choir of singers or dancers; band, troop
Christiānismus, -ī m Christianity
Christiānus adj Christian
Christus, -ī m Christ
Chrȳsēis, -ēidis f daughter of Chrȳsēs
Chrȳsēs, -ae m priest of Apollo in the Iliad
Chrȳsippēus adj see **Chrȳsippus**
Chrȳsippus, -ī m Stoic philosopher
chrȳsolithos, -ī m/f topaz
chrȳsos, -ī m gold
cibārius adj food (in cpds) ▶ ntpl rations
cibātus, -ūs m food
cibōrium, -ī and **-iī** nt kind of drinking cup
cibus, -ī m food, fodder, nourishment
cicāda, -ae f cicada, cricket
cicātrīcōsus adj scarred
cicātrīx, -īcis f scar; (plants) mark of an incision
ciccus, -ī m pomegranate pip
cicer, -is nt chickpea
Cicerō, -ōnis m great Roman orator and author
Cicerōniānus adj see **Cicerō**
cichorēum, -ī nt chicory
Cicōnes, -um mpl people of Thrace
cicōnia, -ae f stork
cicur, -is adj tame
cicūta, -ae f hemlock; pipe
cieō, ciēre, cīvī, citum vt to move, stir, rouse; to call, invoke; (fig) to give rise to, produce; **calcem ciēre** make a move (in chess)
Cilicia, -ae f country in S. Asia Minor (famous for piracy)
Ciliciēnsis, Ciliciēnsus adj see **Cilicia**
Cilix, -cis, Cilissa adj Cilician ▶ nt goats' hair garment
Cimbrī, -ōrum mpl people of N. Germany
Cimbricus adj see **Cimbrī**
cīmex, -icis m bug
Cimmeriī, -ōrum mpl people of the Crimea; mythical race in caves near Cumae
Cimmerius adj see **Cimmeriī**
cinaedus adj lewd
cinaedus, -ī m sodomite; lewd dancer
Cincinnātus, -ī m ancient Roman dictator
cincinnātus adj with curled hair
cincinnus, -ī m curled hair; (fig) rhetorical ornament
Cincius, -ī m Roman tribune; Roman historian
cincticulus, -ī m small girdle
cinctus¹ ppp of **cingō**
cinctus², -ūs m girding; ~ **Gabīnus** a ceremonial style of wearing the toga
cinctūtus adj girded
cinefactus adj reduced to ashes

cinerārius, -ī and **-iī** m hair curler

cingō, -gere, -xī, -ctum vt to surround, enclose; to gird, crown; (MIL) to besiege, fortify; to cover, escort; **ferrum cingor** I put on my sword

cingula, -ae f girth (of animals)

cingulum, -ī nt belt

cingulus, -ī m zone

ciniflō, -ōnis m hair curler

cinis, -eris m ashes; (fig) ruin

Cinna, -ae m colleague of Marius; poet friend of Catullus

cinnamōmum, cinnamum, -ī nt cinnamon

cinxī perf of **cingō**

Cīnyphius adj of the Cinyps (river of N. Africa); African

Cinyrās, -ae m father of Adonis

Cinyrēius adj see **Cinyrās**

cippus, -ī m tombstone; (pl) palisade

circā adv around, round about ▶ prep (with acc) (place) round, in the vicinity of, in; (time, number) about; with regard to

Circaeus adj see **Circē**

circamoerium, -ī and **-iī** nt space on both sides of a wall

Circē, -ēs and **-ae** f goddess with magic powers living in Aeaea

circēnsēs, -ium mpl the games

circēnsis adj of the Circus

circinō, -āre vt to circle through

circinus, -ī m pair of compasses

circiter adv (time, number) about ▶ prep (with acc) about, near

circueō, circumeō, -īre, -īvī and **-iī, -itum** vt, vi to go round, surround; (MIL) to encircle; to visit, go round canvassing; to deceive

circuitiō, -ōnis f (MIL) rounds; (speech) evasiveness

circuitus¹ ppp of **circueō**

circuitus², -ūs m revolution; way round, circuit; (RHET) period, periphrasis

circulātor, -ōris m pedlar

circulor, -ārī vi to collect in crowds

circulus, -ī m circle; orbit; ring; social group

circum adv round about ▶ prep (with acc) round, about; near; **~ īnsulās mittere** send to the islands round about

circumagō, -agere, -ēgī, -āctum vt to turn, move in a circle, wheel; (pass, time) to pass; (mind) to be swayed

circumarō, -āre vt to plough round

circumcaesūra, -ae f outline

circumcīdō, -dere, -dī, -sum vt to cut round, trim; to cut down, abridge

circumcircā adv all round

circumcīsus ppp of **circumcīdō** ▶ adj precipitous

circumclūdō, -dere, -sī, -sum vt to shut in, hem in

circumcolō, -ere vt to live round about

circumcursō, -āre vi to run about

circumdō, -are, -edī, -atum vt to put round; to surround, enclose

circumdūcō, -ūcere, -ūxī, -uctum vt to lead round, draw round; to cheat; (speech) to prolong, drawl

circumductus ppp of **circumdūcō**

circumeō etc see **circueō**

circumequitō, -āre vt to ride round

circumferō, -ferre, -tulī, -lātum vt to carry round, pass round; to spread, broadcast; to purify; (pass) to revolve

circumflectō, -ctere, -xī, -xum vt to wheel round

circumflō, -āre vt (fig) to buffet

circumfluō, -ere, -xī, -xum vt, vi to flow round; (fig) to overflow, abound

circumfluus adj flowing round; surrounded (by water)

circumforāneus adj itinerant; (money) borrowed

circumfundō, -undere, -ūdī, -ūsum vt to pour round, surround; (fig) to crowd round, overwhelm; (pass) to flow round

circumgemō, -ere vt to growl round

circumgestō, -āre vt to carry about

circumgredior, -dī, -ssus vt, vi to make an encircling move, surround

circumiaceō, -ēre vi to be adjacent

circumiciō, -icere, -iēcī, -iectum vt to throw round, put round; to surround

circumiecta ntpl neighbourhood

circumiectus¹ adj surrounding

circumiectus², -ūs m enclosure; embrace

circumit- etc see **circuit-**

circumitiō, -ōnis f see **circuitiō**

circumitus, -ūs m see **circuitus²**

circumlātus ppp of **circumferō**

circumligō, -āre, -āvī, -ātum vt to tie to, bind round

circumlinō, -ere, -tum vt to smear all over, bedaub

circumluō, -ere vt to wash

circumluviō, -ōnis f alluvial land

circummittō, -ittere, -īsī, -issum vt to send round

circummoeniō, circummūniō, -īre, -īvī, -ītum vt to fortify

circummūnītiō, -ōnis f investing

circumpadānus adj of the Po valley

circumpendeō, -ēre vi to hang round

circumplaudō, -ere vt to applaud on all sides

circumplector, -ctī, -xus vt to embrace, surround

circumplicō, -āre, -āvī, -ātum vt to wind round

circumpōnō, -pōnere, -posuī, -positum vt to put round

circumpōtātiō, -ōnis f passing drinks round

circumrētiō, -īre, -īvī, -ītum vt to ensnare

circumrōdō, -rodere, -rosī vt to nibble round about; (fig) to slander

circumsaepiō, -īre, -sī, -tum vt to fence round

circumscindō, -ere vt to strip

circumscrībō, -bere, -psī, -ptum vt to draw a line round; to mark the limits of; to restrict, circumscribe; to set aside; to defraud

circumscrīptē adv in periods

circumscrīptiō, -ōnis f circle, contour; fraud; (RHET) period

circumscrīptor, -ōris m defrauder

circumscrīptus ppp of **circumscrībō** ▶ adj restricted; (RHET) periodic

circumsecō, -āre vt to cut round

circumsedeō, -edēre, -ēdī, -essum vt to blockade, beset

circumsēpiō etc see **circumsaepiō**

circumsessiō, -ōnis f siege

circumsessus ppp of **circumsedeō**

circumsīdō, -ere vt to besiege

circumsiliō, -īre vi to hop about; (fig) to be rampant

circumsistō, -sistere, -stetī surround

circumsonō, -āre vi to resound on all sides ▶ vt to fill with sound

circumsonus adj noisy

circumspectātrīx, -īcis f spy

circumspectiō, -ōnis f caution

circumspectō, -āre vt, vi to look all round, search anxiously, be on the lookout

circumspectus[1] ppp of **circumspiciō** ▶ adj carefully considered, cautious

circumspectus[2] **, -ūs** m consideration; view

circumspiciō, -icere, -exī, -ectum vi to look all round; to be careful ▶ vt to survey; (fig) to consider, search for

circumstantēs, -antium mpl bystanders

circumstetī perf of **circumsistō; circumstō**

circumstō, -āre, -etī vt, vi to stand round; to besiege; (fig) to encompass

circumstrepō, -ere vt to make a clamour round

circumsurgēns, -entis pres p rising on all sides

circumtentus adj covered tightly

circumterō, -ere vt to crowd round

circumtextus adj embroidered round the edge

circumtonō, -āre, -uī vt to thunder about

circumvādō, -dere, -sī vt to assail on all sides

circumvagus adj encircling

circumvallō, -āre, -āvī, -ātum vt to blockade, beset

circumvectiō, -ōnis f carrying about; (sun) revolution

circumvector, -ārī vi to travel round, cruise round; (fig) describe

circumvehor, -hī, -ctus vt, vi to ride round, sail round; (fig) to describe

circumvēlō, -āre vt to envelop

circumveniō, -enīre, -ēnī, -entum vt to surround, beset; to oppress; to cheat

circumvertō, circumvortō, -ere vt to turn round

circumvestiō, -īre vt to envelop

circumvinciō, -īre vt to lash about

circumvīsō, -ere vt to look at all round

circumvolitō, -āre, -āvī, -ātum vt, vi to fly round; to hover around

circumvolō, -āre vt to fly round

circumvolvō, -vere vt to roll round

circus, -ī m circle; the Circus Maximus (famous Roman racecourse), a racecourse

Cirrha, -ae f town near Delphi (sacred to Apollo)

Cirrhaeus adj see **Cirrha**

cirrus, -ī m curl of hair; fringe

cis prep (with acc) on this side of; (time) within

Cisalpīnus adj on the Italian side of the Alps, Cisalpine

cisium, -ī and -iī nt two-wheeled carriage

Cissēis, -dis f Hecuba

cista, -ae f box, casket; ballot box

cistella, -ae f small box

cistellātrīx, -īcis f keeper of the moneybox

cistellula, -ae f little box

cisterna, -ae f reservoir

cistophorus, -ī m an Asiatic coin

cistula, -ae f little box

citātus adj quick, impetuous

citerior (superl **-imus**) adj on this side, nearer

Cithaerōn, -ōnis m mountain range between Attica and Boeotia

cithara, -ae f lyre, lute

citharista, -ae m, **citharistria, -ae** f lyre player

citharizō, -āre vi to play the lyre

citharoedus, -ī m a singer who accompanies himself on the lyre

citimus adj nearest

citō (compar **-ius**, superl **-issimē**) adv quickly, soon; **nōn** ~ not easily

citō, -āre, -āvī, -ātum vt to set in motion, rouse; to call (by name), appeal to, cite, mention

citrā adv on this side, this way, not so far ▶ prep (with acc) on this side of, short of; (time) before, since; apart from; ~ **quam** before

citreus adj of citrus wood

citrō adv hither, this way; **ultrō citrōque** to and fro

citrus, -ī f citrus tree; citron tree

citus ppp of **cieō** ▶ adj quick

cīvicus adj civic, civil; **corōna cīvica** civic crown (for saving a citizen's life in war)

cīvīlis adj of citizens, civil; political, civilian; courteous, democratic; **iūs cīvīle** civil rights; Civil Law; code of legal procedure

cīvīlitās, -ātis f politics; politeness

cīvīliter adv like citizens; courteously

cīvis, -is m/f citizen, fellow citizen

cīvitās, -ātis f citizenship; community, state; city; **cīvitāte dōnāre** naturalize

clādēs, -is f damage, disaster, ruin; defeat; (fig) scourge; **dare clādem** make havoc

clam adv secretly; unknown ▶ prep (with acc) unknown to; ~ **mē habēre** keep from me

clāmātor, -ōris m bawler

clāmitātiō, -ōnis f bawling

clāmitō, -āre, -āvī, -ātum vt, vi to bawl, screech, cry out

clāmō, -āre, -āvī, -ātum *vt, vi* to shout, cry out; to call upon, proclaim

clāmor, -ōris *m* shout, cry; acclamation

clāmōsus *adj* noisy

clanculum *adv* secretly ▶ *prep (with acc)* unknown to

clandestīnō *adv see* **clandestīnus**

clandestīnus *adj* secret

clangor, -ōris *m* clang, noise

clārē *adv* brightly, loudly, clearly, with distinction

clāreō, -ēre *vi* to be bright, be clear; to be evident; to be renowned

clārēscō, -ere, clāruī *vi* to brighten, sound clear; to become obvious; to become famous

clārigātiō, -ōnis *f* formal ultimatum to an enemy; fine for trespass

clārigō, -āre *vi* to deliver a formal ultimatum

clārisonus *adj* loud and clear

clāritās, -ātis *f* distinctness; (*RHET*) lucidity; celebrity

clāritūdō, -inis *f* brightness; (*fig*) distinction

Clarius *adj of* Claros ▶ *m* Apollo

clārō, -āre *vt* to illuminate; to explain; to make famous

Claros, -ī *f* town in Ionia (*famous for worship of Apollo*)

clārus *adj* (*sight*) bright; (*sound*) loud; (*mind*) clear; (*person*) distinguished; **~ intonāre** thunder from a clear sky; **vir clārissimus** *a courtesy title for eminent men*

classiārius *adj* naval ▶ *mpl* marines

classicula, -ae *f* flotilla

classicum, -ī *nt* battle-signal; trumpet

classicus *adj* of the first class; naval ▶ *mpl* marines

classis, -is *f* a political class; army; fleet

clāthrī, -ōrum *mpl* cage

clāthrātus *adj* barred

clāthrī, -ōrum *mpl see* **clāthrī**

claudeō, -ēre *vi* to limp; (*fig*) to be defective

claudicātiō, -ōnis *f* limping

claudicō, -āre *vi* to be lame; to waver, be defective

Claudius¹, -ī *m* patrician family name (*esp Appius Claudius Caecus, famous censor*); *Emperor Claudius*

Claudius², Claudiānus, Claudiālis *adj see* **Claudius¹**

claudō¹, -dere, -sī, -sum *vt* to shut, close; to cut off, block; to conclude; to imprison, confine, blockade; **agmen claudere** bring up the rear

claudō², -ere *etc see* **claudeō**

claudus *adj* lame; (*verse*) elegiac; (*fig*) wavering

clausī *perf of* **claudō¹**

claustra, -ōrum *ntpl* bar, bolt, lock; barrier, barricade, dam

clausula, -ae *f* conclusion; (*RHET*) ending of a period

clausum, -ī *nt* enclosure

clausus *ppp of* **claudō¹**

clāva, -ae *f* club, knotty branch; (*MIL*) foil

clāvārium, -ī *and* **-iī** *nt* money for buying shoe nails

clāvātor, -ōris *m* cudgel-bearer

clāvicula, -ae *f* vine tendril

clāviger, -ī *m* (*Hercules*) club bearer; (*Janus*) key-bearer

clāvis, -is *f* key

clāvus, -ī *m* nail; tiller, rudder; *purple stripe on the tunic* (*broad for senators, narrow for equites*); **clāvum annī movēre** reckon the beginning of the year

Cleanthēs, -is *m* Stoic philosopher

clēmēns, -entis *adj* mild, gentle, merciful; (*weather, water*) mild, calm

clēmenter *adv* gently, indulgently; gradually

clēmentia, -ae *f* mildness, forbearance, mercy

Cleopatra, -ae *f* queen of Egypt

clepō, -ere, -sī, -tum *vt* to steal

clepsydra, -ae *f* waterclock (*used for timing speakers*); **clepsydram dare** give leave to speak; **clepsydram petere** ask leave to speak

clepta, -ae *m* thief

cliēns, -entis *m* client, dependant; follower; vassal-state

clienta, -ae *f* client

clientēla, -ae *f* clientship, protection; clients

clientulus, -ī *m* insignificant client

clīnāmen, -inis *nt* swerve

clīnātus *adj* inclined

Cliō, -ūs *f* Muse of history

clipeātus *adj* armed with a shield

clipeus, -ī *m*, **clipeum, -ī** *nt* round bronze shield; disc; medallion on a metal base

clitellae, -ārum *fpl* packsaddle (*attribute of an ass*)

clitellārius *adj* carrying packsaddles

Clitumnus, -ī *m* river in Umbria

clīvōsus *adj* hilly

clīvus, -ī *m* slope, hill; **~ sacer** part of the Via Sacra

cloāca, -ae *f* sewer, drain

Cloācīna, -ae *f* Venus

Clōdius, -ī *m* Roman plebeian name (*esp the tribune, enemy of Cicero*)

Cloelia, -ae *f* Roman girl hostage (*who escaped by swimming the Tiber*)

Clōthō (*acc* **-ō**) *f* one of the Fates

clueō, -ēre, -eor, -ērī *vi* to be called, be famed

clūnis, -is *m/f* buttock

clūrīnus *adj* of apes

Clūsīnus *adj see* **Clūsium**

Clūsium, -ī *nt* old Etruscan town (*now Chiusi*)

Clūsius, -ī *m* Janus

Clytaemnēstra, -ae *f* wife of Agamemnon (*whom she murdered*)

Cnidius *adj see* **Cnidus**

Cnidus, -ī *f* town in Caria (*famous for worship of Venus*)

coacervātiō, -ōnis *f* accumulation

coacervō, -āre *vt* to heap, accumulate

coacēscō, -ēscere, -uī *vi* to become sour

coāctō, -āre *vt* to force

coāctor, -ōris *m* collector (*of money*);

coāctōrēs agminis *mpl* rearguard
coāctum, **-ī** *nt* thick coverlet
coāctus¹ *adj* forced
coāctus² *ppp of* **cōgō**
coāctus³, **-ūs** *m* compulsion
coaedificō, **-āre**, **-āvī**, **-ātum** *vt* to build on
coaequō, **-āre**, **-āvī**, **-ātum** *vt* to make equal, bring down to the same level
coagmentātiō, **-ōnis** *f* combination
coagmentō, **-āre**, **-āvī**, **-ātum** *vt* to glue, join together
coagmentum, **-ī** *nt* joining, joint
coāgulum, **-ī** *nt* rennet
coalēscō, **-ēscere**, **-uī**, **-itum** *vi* to grow together; (*fig*) to agree together; to flourish
coangustō, **-āre** *vt* to restrict
coarct- *etc see* **coart-**
coarguō, **-ere**, **-ī** *vt* to convict, prove conclusively
coartātiō, **-ōnis** *f* crowding together
coartō, **-āre**, **-āvī**, **-ātum** *vt* to compress, abridge
coccineus, coccinus *adj* scarlet
coccum, **-ī** *nt* scarlet
cochlea, coclea, **-ae** *f* snail
cocleāre, **-is** *nt* spoon
cocles, **-itis** *m* man blind in one eye; *surname of Horatius who defended the bridge*
coctilis *adj* baked; of bricks
coctus *ppp of* **coquō** ▸ *adj* (*fig*) well considered
cocus *etc see* **coquus**
Cōcȳtius *adj see* **Cōcȳtos**
Cōcȳtos, -us, **-ī** *m river in the lower world*
cōda *etc see* **cauda**
cōdex *etc see* **caudex**
cōdicillī, **-ōrum** *mpl* letter, note, petition; codicil
Codrus, **-ī** *m last king of Athens*
coēgī *perf of* **cōgō**
coel- *etc see* **cael-**
coemō, **-emere**, **-ēmī**, **-emptum** *vt* to buy up
coemptiō, **-ōnis** *f a form of Roman marriage; mock sale of an estate*
coemptiōnālis *adj* used in a mock sale; worthless
coen- *etc see* **caen-** *or* **cēn-**
coeō, **-īre**, **-īvī** *and* **-iī**, **-itum** *vi* to meet, assemble; to encounter; to combine, mate; (*wounds*) to close; to agree, conspire ▸ *vt*: **coīre societātem** make a compact
coepiō, **-ere**, **-ī**, **-tum** *vt, vi* begin (*esp in perf tenses*); **rēs agī coeptae sunt** things began to be done; **coepisse** to begin
coeptō, **-āre**, **-āvī**, **-ātum** *vt, vi* to begin, attempt
coeptum, **-ī** *nt* beginning, undertaking
coeptus¹ *ppp of* **coepiō**
coeptus², **-ūs** *m* beginning
coepulōnus, **-ī** *m* fellow-banqueter
coerātor *etc see* **cūrātor**
coerceō, **-ēre**, **-uī**, **-itum** *vt* to enclose; to confine, repress; (*fig*) to control, check, correct

coercitiō, **-ōnis** *f* coercion, punishment
coetus, coitus, **-ūs** *m* meeting, joining together; assembly, crowd
cōgitātē *adv* deliberately
cōgitātiō, **-ōnis** *f* thought, reflection; idea, plan; faculty of thought, imagination
cōgitātus *adj* deliberate ▸ *ntpl* ideas
cōgitō, **-āre**, **-āvī**, **-ātum** *vt, vi* to think, ponder, imagine; to feel disposed; to plan, intend
cognātiō, **-ōnis** *f* relationship (*by blood*); kin, family; (*fig*) affinity, resemblance
cognātus, **-ī** *m*, **cognāta**, **-ae** *f* relation ▸ *adj* related; (*fig*) connected, similar
cognitiō, **-ōnis** *f* acquiring of knowledge, knowledge; idea, notion; (*LAW*) judicial inquiry; (*comedy*) recognition
cognitor, **-ōris** *m* (*LAW*) attorney; witness of a person's identity; (*fig*) defender
cognitus¹ *adj* acknowledged
cognitus² *ppp of* **cognōscō**
cognōmen, **-inis** *nt* surname; name
cognōmentum, **-ī** *nt* surname, name
cognōminis *adj* with the same name
cognōminō, **-āre**, **-āvī**, **-ātum** *vt* to give a surname to; **verba cognōmināta** synonyms
cognōscō, **-ōscere**, **-ōvī**, **-itum** *vt* to get to know, learn, understand; to know, recognize, identify; (*LAW*) to investigate; (*MIL*) to reconnoitre
cōgō, **-ere**, **coēgī**, **coāctum** *vt* to collect, gather together; (*liquids*) to thicken, curdle; to contract, confine; to compel, force; to infer; **agmen cōgere** bring up the rear; **senātum cōgere** call a meeting of the senate
cohaerentia, **-ae** *f* coherence
cohaereō, **-rēre**, **-sī**, **-sum** *vi* to stick together, cohere; to cling to; (*fig*) to be consistent, harmonize; to agree, be consistent with
cohaerēscō, **-ere** *vi* to stick together
cohaesus *ppp of* **cohaereō**
cohērēs, **-ēdis** *m/f* co-heir
cohibeō, **-ēre**, **-uī**, **-itum** *vt* to hold together, encircle; to hinder, stop; (*fig*) to restrain, repress
cohonestō, **-āre** *vt* to do honour to
cohorrēscō, **-ēscere**, **-uī** *vi* to shudder all over
cohors, **-tis** *f* courtyard; (*MIL*) cohort (*about 600 men*); retinue (*esp of the praetor in a province*); (*fig*) company
cohortātiō, **-ōnis** *f* encouragement
cohorticula, **-ae** *f* small cohort
cohortor, **-ārī**, **-ātus** *vt* to encourage, urge
coitiō, **-ōnis** *f* encounter; conspiracy
coitus *etc see* **coetus**
colaphus, **-ī** *m* blow with the fist, box
Colchis¹, **-idis** *f Medea's country (at the E. end of the Black Sea)*
Colchis², Colchis, Colchicus *adj* Colchian
cōleus *etc see* **culleus**
cōlis *etc see* **caulis**
collābāscō, **-ere** *vi* to waver also

collabefactō, -āre vt to shake violently
collabefīō, -fierī, -factus vi to be destroyed
collābor, -bī, -psus vi to fall in ruin, collapse
collacerātus adj torn to pieces
collacrimātiō, -ōnis f weeping
collactea, -ae f foster-sister
collāpsus ppa of **collābor**
collāre, -is nt neckband
Collātia, -iae f ancient town near Rome
Collātīnus adj of Collatia ▶ m husband of Lucretia
collātiō, -ōnis f bringing together, combination; (money) contribution; (RHET) comparison; (PHILOS) analogy
collātor, -ōris m contributor
collātus ppp of **cōnferō**
collaudātiō, -ōnis f praise
collaudō, -āre, -āvī, -ātum vt to praise highly
collaxō, -āre vt to make porous
collēcta, -ae f money contribution
collēctīcius adj hastily gathered
collēctiō, -ōnis f gathering up; (RHET) recapitulation
collēctus¹ ppp of **colligō²**
collēctus², -ūs m accumulation
collēga, -ae m colleague; associate
collēgī perf of **colligō²**
collēgium, -ī and **-iī** nt association in office; college, guild (of magistrates, etc)
collībertus, -ī m fellow freedman
collibet, collubet, -uit and **-itum est** vi it pleases
collīdō, -dere, -sī, -sum vt to beat together, strike, bruise; (fig) to bring into conflict
colligātiō, -ōnis f connection
colligō¹, -āre, -āvī, -ātum vt to fasten, tie up; (fig) to combine; to restrain, check
colligō², -igere, -ēgī, -ēctum vt to gather, collect; to compress, draw together; to check; (fig) to acquire; to think about; to infer, conclude; **animum colligere, mentem colligere** recover, rally; **sē colligere** crouch; recover one's courage; **vāsa colligere** (MIL) pack up
Collīna Porta gate in N.E. of Rome
collīneō, -āre, vt, vi to aim straight
collinō, -inere, -ēvī, -itum vt to besmear; (fig) to deface
colliquefactus adj dissolved
collis, -is m hill, slope
collīsī perf of **collīdō**
collīsus ppp of **collīdō**
collitus ppp of **collinō**
collocātiō, -ōnis f arrangement; giving in marriage
collocō, -āre, -āvī, -ātum vt to place, station, arrange; to give in marriage; (money) to invest; (fig) to establish; to occupy, employ
collocuplētō, -āre, -āvī vt to enrich
collocūtiō, -ōnis f conversation
colloquium, -ī and **-iī** nt conversation, conference

colloquor, -quī, -cūtus vi to converse, hold a conference ▶ vt to talk to
collubet etc see **collibet**
collūceō, -ēre vi to shine brightly; (fig) to be resplendent
collūdō, -dere, -sī, -sum vi to play together or with; to practise collusion
collum, -ī nt neck; **~ torquēre, ~ obtorquēre, ~ obstringere** arrest
colluō, -uere, -uī, -ūtum vt to rinse, moisten
collus etc see **collum**
collūsiō, -ōnis f secret understanding
collūsor, -ōris m playmate, fellow gambler
collūstrō, -āre, -āvī, -ātum vt to light up; to survey
colluviō, -ōnis, colluviēs (acc **-em**, abl **-ē**) f sweepings, filth; (fig) dregs, rabble
collybus, -ī m money exchange, rate of exchange
collȳra, -ae f vermicelli
collȳricus adj see **collȳra**
collȳrium, -ī and **-iī** nt eye lotion
colō, -ere, -uī, cultum vt (AGR) to cultivate, work; (place) to live in; (human affairs) to cherish, protect, adorn; (qualities, pursuits) to cultivate, practise; (gods) to worship; (men) to honour, court; **vītam colere** live
colocāsia, -ae f, **colocāsia, -ōrum** ntpl Egyptian bean, caladium
colōna, -ae f country-woman
colōnia, -ae f settlement, colony; settlers
colōnicus adj colonial
colōnus, -ī m crofter, farmer; settler, colonist
color, colōs, -ōris m colour; complexion; beauty, lustre; (fig) outward show; (RHET) style, tone; colourful excuse; **colōrem mūtāre** blush, go pale; **homō nullīus colōris** an unknown person
colōrātus adj healthily tanned
colōrō, -āre, -āvī, -ātum vt to colour, tan; (fig) to give a colour to
colossus, -ī m gigantic statue (esp that of Apollo at Rhodes)
colostra, colustra, -ae f beestings
coluber, -rī m snake
colubra, -ae f snake
colubrifer, -ī adj snaky
colubrīnus adj wily
coluī perf of **colō**
cōlum, -ī nt strainer
columba, -ae f dove, pigeon
columbar, -āris nt kind of collar
columbārium, -ī and **-iī** nt dovecote
columbīnus adj pigeon's ▶ m little pigeon
columbus, -ī m dove, cock-pigeon
columella, -ae f small pillar
columen, -inis nt height, summit; pillar; (fig) chief; prop
columna, -ae f column, pillar; a pillory in the Forum Romanum; waterspout
columnārium, -ī and **-iī** nt pillar tax
columnārius, -ī m criminal

columnātus adj pillared
colurnus adj made of hazel
colus, -ī and **-ūs** m/f distaff
cōlȳphia, -ōrum ntpl food of athletes
coma, -ae f hair (of the head); foliage
comāns, -antis adj hairy, plumed; leafy
cōmarchus, -ī m burgomaster
comātus adj long-haired; leafy; **Gallia comāta** Transalpine Gaul
combibō¹, -ere, -ī vt to drink to the full, absorb
combibō², -ōnis m fellow-drinker
combūrō, -rere, -ssī, -stum vt to burn up; (fig) to ruin
combūstus ppp of **combūrō**
comedō, -esse, -ēdī, -ēsum and **-ēstum** vt to eat up, devour; (fig) to waste, squander; **sē comedesse** pine away
Cōmēnsis adj see **Cōmum**
comes, -itis m/f companion, partner; attendant, follower; one of a magistrate's or emperor's retinue; (medieval title) count
comēs, comēst pres of **comedō**
comēsus, comēsus ppp of **comedō**
comētēs, -ae m comet
cōmicē adv in the manner of comedy
cōmicus, -ī m comedy actor, comedy writer ▶ adj of comedy, comic
cōmis adj courteous, friendly
cōmissābundus adj carousing
cōmissātiō, -ōnis f Bacchanalian revel
cōmissātor, -ōris m reveller
cōmissor, -ārī, -ātus vi to carouse, make merry
cōmitās, -ātis f kindness, affability
comitātus, -ūs m escort, retinue; company
cōmiter adv see **cōmis**
comitia, -iōrum ntpl assembly for the election of magistrates and other business (esp the comitia centuriāta); elections
comitiālis adj of the elections; **~ morbus** epilepsy
comitiātus, -ūs m assembly at the elections
comitium, -ī and **-iī** nt place of assembly
comitō, -āre, -āvī, -ātum vt to accompany
comitor, -ārī, -ātus vt, vi to attend, follow
commaculō, -āre, -āvī, -ātum vt to stain, defile
commanipulāris, -is m soldier in the same company
commeātus, -ūs m passage; leave, furlough; convoy (of troops or goods); (MIL) lines of communication, provisions, supplies
commeditor, -ārī vt to practise
commeminī, -isse vt, vi to remember perfectly
commemorābilis adj memorable
commemorātiō, -ōnis f recollection, recounting
commemorō, -āre, -āvī, -ātum vt to recall, remind; to mention, relate
commendābilis adj praiseworthy

commendātīcius adj of recommendation or introduction
commendātiō, -ōnis f recommendation; worth, excellence
commendātor, -ōris m commender (male)
commendātrīx, -rīcis f commender (female)
commendātus adj approved, valued
commendō, -āre, -āvī, -ātum vt to entrust, commit, commend (to one's care or charge), recommend, set off to advantage
commēnsus ppa of **commētior**
commentāriolum, -ī nt short treatise
commentārius, -ī and **-iī** m, **commentārium, -ī** and **-iī** nt notebook; commentary, memoir; (LAW) brief
commentātiō, -ōnis f studying, meditation
commentīcius adj fictitious, imaginary; false
commentor¹, -ārī, -ātus vt, vi to study, think over, prepare carefully; to invent, compose, write
commentor², -ōris m inventor
commentum, -ī nt invention, fiction; contrivance
commentus ppa of **comminīscor** ▶ adj feigned, fictitious
commeō, -āre vi to pass to and fro; to go or come often
commercium, -ī and **-iī** nt trade, commerce; right to trade; dealings, communication
commercor, -ārī, -ātus vt to buy up
commereō, -ēre, -uī, -itum, commereor, -ērī, -itus vt to deserve; to be guilty of
commētior, -tīrī, -nsus vt to measure
commētō, -āre vi to go often
commictus ppp of **commingō**
commigrō, -āre, -āvī, -ātum vi to remove, migrate
commīlitium, -ī and **-iī** nt service together
commīlitō, -ōnis m fellow soldier
comminātiō, -ōnis f threat
commingō, -ingere, -īnxī, -īctum vt to pollute
comminīscor, -ī, commentus vt to devise, contrive
comminor, -ārī, -ātus vt to threaten
comminuō, -uere, -uī, -ūtum vt to break up, smash; to diminish; to impair
comminus adv hand to hand; near at hand
commīsceō, -scēre, -scuī, -xtum vt to mix together, join together
commiserātiō, -ōnis f (RHET) passage intended to arouse pity
commiserēscō, -ere vt to pity
commiseror, -ārī vt to bewail ▶ vi (RHET) to try to excite pity
commissiō, -ōnis f start (of a contest)
commissum, -ī nt enterprise; offence, crime; secret
commissūra, -ae f joint, connection
commissus ppp of **committō**
committō, -ittere, -īsī, -issum vt to join, connect, bring together; to begin, undertake; (battle) to join, engage in; (offence) to commit,

be guilty of; (*punishment*) to incur, forfeit; to entrust, trust; **sē urbī committere** venture into the city

commīxtus *ppp of* **commīsceō**

commodē *adv* properly, well; aptly, opportunely; pleasantly

commoditās, **-ātis** *f* convenience, ease, fitness; advantage; (*person*) kindliness; (*RHET*) apt expression

commodō, **-āre**, **-āvī**, **-ātum** *vt* to adjust, adapt; to give, lend, oblige with; (*with dat*) to oblige

commodulē, **-um** *adv* conveniently

commodum¹, **-ī** *nt* convenience; advantage, interest; pay, salary; loan; **commodō tuō** at your leisure; **commoda vītae** the good things of life

commodum² *adv* opportunely; just

commodus *adj* proper, fit, full; suitable, easy, opportune; (*person*) pleasant, obliging

commōlior, **-īrī** *vt* to set in motion

commonefaciō, **-facere**, **-fēcī**, **-factum** *vt* to remind, recall

commoneō, **-ēre**, **-uī**, **-itum** *vt* to remind, impress upon

commōnstrō, **-āre** *vt* to point out

commorātiō, **-ōnis** *f* delay, residence; (*RHET*) dwelling (*on a topic*)

commoror, **-ārī**, **-ātus** *vi* to sojourn, wait; (*RHET*) to dwell ▸ *vt* to detain

commōtiō, **-ōnis** *f* excitement

commōtiuncula *f* slight indisposition

commōtus *ppp of* **commoveō** ▸ *adj* excited, emotional

commoveō, **-ovēre**, **-ōvī**, **-ōtum** *vt* to set in motion, move, dislodge, agitate; (*mind*) to unsettle, shake, excite, move, affect; (*emotions*) to stir up, provoke

commūne, **-is** *nt* common property; state; **in ~** for a common end; equally; in general

commūnicātiō, **-ōnis** *f* imparting; (*RHET*) *making the audience appear to take part in the discussion*

commūnicō, **-āre**, **-āvī**, **-ātum** *vt* to share (*by giving or receiving*); to impart, communicate; **cōnsilia commūnicāre cum** make common cause with

commūniō¹, **-īre**, **-īvī** *and* **-iī**, **-ītum** *vt* to build (*a fortification*), fortify, strengthen

commūniō², **-ōnis** *f* sharing in common, communion

commūnis *adj* common, general, universal; (*person*) affable, democratic; **commūnia loca** public places; **commūnēs locī** general topics; **~ sēnsus** popular sentiment; **aliquid commūne habēre** have something in common

commūnitās, **-ātis** *f* fellowship; sense of fellowship; affability

commūniter *adv* in common, jointly

commūnītiō, **-ōnis** *f* preparing the way

commurmuror, **-ārī**, **-ātus** *vi* to mutter to oneself

commūtābilis *adj* changeable

commūtātiō, **-iōnis** *f* change

commūtātus, **-ūs** *m* change

commūtō, **-āre**, **-āvī**, **-ātum** *vt* to change, exchange, interchange

cōmō, **-ere**, **-psī**, **-ptum** *vt* to arrange, dress, adorn

cōmoedia, **-ae** *f* comedy

cōmoedicē *adv* as in comedy

cōmoedus, **-ī** *m* comic actor

cōmōsus *adj* shaggy

compāctiō, **-ōnis** *f* joining together

compāctus *ppp of* **compingō**

compāgēs, **-is**, **compāgō**, **-inis** *f* joint, structure, framework

compār, **-aris** *m/f* comrade, husband, wife ▸ *adj* equal

comparābilis *adj* comparable

comparātē *adv* by bringing in a comparison

comparātiō, **-ōnis** *f* comparison; (*ASTR*) relative positions; agreement; preparation, procuring

comparātīvus *adj* based on comparison

compāreō, **-ēre** *vi* to be visible; to be present, be realized

comparō, **-āre**, **-āvī**, **-ātum** *vt* to couple together, match; to compare; (*POL*) to agree (*about respective duties*); to prepare, provide; (*custom*) to establish; to procure, purchase, get

compāscō, **-ere** *vt* to put (cattle) to graze in common

compāscuus *adj* for common pasture

compecīscor, **-īscī**, **-tus** *vi* to come to an agreement

compectum, **-tī** *nt* agreement

compediō, **-īre**, **-ītum** *vt* to fetter

compēgī *perf of* **compingō**

compellātiō, **-ōnis** *f* reprimand

compellō¹, **-āre**, **-āvī**, **-ātum** *vt* to call, address; to reproach; (*LAW*) to arraign

compellō², **-ellere**, **-ulī**, **-ulsum** *vt* to drive, bring together, concentrate; to impel, compel

compendiārius *adj* short

compendium, **-ī** *and* **-iī** *nt* saving; abbreviating; short cut; **compendiī facere** save; abridge; **compendiī fierī** be brief

compēnsātiō, **-ōnis** *f* (*fig*) compromise

compēnsō, **-āre**, **-āvī**, **-ātum** *vt* to balance (against), make up for

compercō, **-cere**, **-sī** *vt*, *vi* to save; to refrain

comperendinātiō, **-iōnis** *f* adjournment for two days

comperendinātus, **-ūs** *m* adjournment for two days

comperendinō, **-āre** *vt* to adjourn for two days

comperiō, **-īre**, **-ī**, **-tum**, **comperior** *vt* to find out, learn; **compertus** detected; found guilty; **compertum habēre** know for certain

compēs, **-edis** *f* fetter, bond

compēscō, **-ere**, **-uī** *vt* to check, suppress

competītor, -ōris m, **competītrīx, -rīcis** f rival candidate

competō, -ere, -īvī and **-iī, -ītum** vi to coincide, agree; to be capable

compīlātiō, -ōnis f plundering; compilation

compīlō, -āre, -āvī, -ātum vt to pillage

compingō, -ingere, -ēgī, -āctum vt to put together, compose; to lock up, hide away

compitālia, -ium and **-iōrum** ntpl festival in honour of the Lares Compitales

compitālicius adj of the Compitalia

compitālis adj of crossroads

compitum, -ī nt crossroads

complaceō, -ēre, -uī and **-itus sum** vi to please (someone else) as well, please very much

complānō, -āre vt to level, raze to the ground

complector, -ctī, -xus vt to embrace, clasp; to enclose; (speech, writing) to deal with, comprise; (mind) to grasp, comprehend; to honour, be fond of

complēmentum, -ī nt complement

compleō, -ēre, -ēvī, -ētum vt to fill, fill up; (MIL) to man, make up the complement of; (time, promise, duty) to complete, fulfil, finish

complētus adj perfect

complexiō, -ōnis f combination; (RHET) period; (LOGIC) conclusion of an argument; dilemma

complexus, -ūs m embrace; (fig) affection, close combat; (speech) connection

complicō, -āre vt to fold up

complōrātiō, -iōnis f, **complōrātus, -ūs** m loud lamentation

complōrō, -āre, -āvī, -ātum vt to mourn for

complūrēs, -ium adj several, very many

complūriēns adv several times

complūsculī, -ōrum adj quite a few

compluvium, -ī and **-iī** nt roof opening in a Roman house

compōnō, -ōnere, -osuī, -ositum vt to put together, join; to compose, construct; to compare, contrast; to match, oppose; to put away, store up, stow; (dead) to lay out, inter; to allay, quieten, reconcile; to adjust, settle, arrange; to devise, prepare ▶ vi to make peace

comportō, -āre vt to collect, bring in

compos, -tis adj in control, in possession; sharing; **vōtī ~** having got one's wish

compositē adv properly, in a polished manner

compositiō, -ōnis f compounding, system; (words) arrangement; reconciliation; matching (of fighters)

compositor, -ōris m arranger

compositūra, -ae f connection

compositus ppp of **compōnō** ▶ adj orderly, regular; adapted, assumed, ready; calm, sedate; (words) compound; **compositō, ex compositō** as agreed

compōtātiō, -ōnis f drinking party

compotiō, -īre vt to put in possession (of)

compōtor, -ōris m, **compōtrīx, -rīcis** f fellow drinker

comprānsor, -ōris m fellow guest

comprecātiō, -ōnis f public supplication

comprecor, -ārī, -ātus vt, vi to pray to; to pray for

comprehendō, comprendō, -endere, -endī, -ēnsum vt to grasp, catch; to seize, arrest, catch in the act; (words) to comprise, recount; (thought) to grasp, comprehend; to hold in affection; **numerō comprehendere** count

comprehēnsibilis adj conceivable

comprehēnsiō, -ōnis f grasping, seizing; perception, idea; (RHET) period

comprehēnsus, comprēnsus ppp of **comprehendō**

comprendō etc see **comprehendō**

compressī perf of **comprimō**

compressiō, -ōnis f embrace; (RHET) compression

compressus[1] ppp of **comprimō**

compressus[2] **, -ūs** m compression, embrace

comprimō, -imere, -essī, -essum vt to squeeze, compress; to check, restrain; to suppress, withhold; **animam comprimere** hold one's breath; **compressīs manibus** with hands folded, idle

comprobātiō, -ōnis f approval

comprobātor, -ōris m supporter

comprobō, -āre, -āvī, -ātum vt to prove, make good; to approve

comprōmissum, -ī nt mutual agreement to abide by an arbitrator's decision

comprōmittō, -ittere, -īsī, -issum vt to undertake to abide by an arbitrator's decision

cōmpsī perf of **cōmō**

cōmptus[1] ppp of **cōmō** ▶ adj elegant

cōmptus[2] **, -ūs** m coiffure; union

compulī perf of **compellō**[2]

compulsus ppp of **compellō**[2]

compungō, -ungere, -ūnxī, -ūnctum vt to prick, sting, tattoo

computō, -āre, -āvī, -ātum vt to reckon, number

Cōmum, -ī nt (also **Novum Cōmum**) town in N. Italy (now Como)

cōnāmen, -inis nt effort; support

cōnāta, -ōrum ntpl undertaking, venture

cōnātus, -ūs m effort; endeavour; inclination, impulse

concaedēs, -ium fpl barricade of felled trees

concalefaciō, -facere, -fēcī, -factum vt to warm well

concaleō, -ēre vi to be hot

concalēscō, -ēscere, -uī vi to become hot, glow

concallēscō, -ēscere, -uī vi to become shrewd; to become unfeeling

concastīgō, -āre vt to punish severely

concavō, -āre vt to curve

concavus adj hollow; vaulted, bent

concēdō, -ēdere, -essī, -essum vi to withdraw, depart; to disappear, pass away,

pass; to yield, submit, give precedence, comply
▶ *vt* to give up, cede; to grant, allow; to pardon,
overlook

concelebrō, -āre, -āvī, -ātum *vt* to frequent,
fill, enliven; (*study*) to pursue eagerly; to
celebrate; to make known

concēnātiō, -ōnis *f* dining together

concentiō, -ōnis *f* chorus

concenturiō, -āre *vt* to marshal

concentus, -ūs *m* chorus, concert; (*fig*)
concord, harmony

conceptiō, -ōnis *f* conception; drawing up
legal formulae

conceptīvus *adj* (*holidays*) movable

conceptus¹ *ppp of* **concipiō**

conceptus², -ūs *m* conception

concerpō, -ere, -sī, -tum *vt* to tear up; (*fig*)
to abuse

concertātiō, -ōnis *f* controversy

concertātor, -ōris *m* rival

concertātōrius *adj* controversial

concertō, -āre, -āvī, -ātum *vi* to fight; to
dispute

concessiō, -ōnis *f* grant, permission; (*LAW*)
pleading guilty and asking indulgence

concessō, -āre *vi* to stop, loiter

concessus¹ *ppp of* **concēdō**

concessus², -ūs *m* permission

concha, -ae *f* mussel, oyster, murex; mussel
shell, oyster shell, pearl; purple dye; trumpet,
perfume dish

conchis, -is *f* kind of bean

conchīta, -ae *m* catcher of shellfish

conchȳliātus *adj* purple

conchȳlium, -ī *and* **-iī** *nt* shellfish, oyster,
murex; purple

concidō, -ere, -ī *vi* to fall, collapse; to subside,
fail, perish

concīdō, -dere, -dī, -sum *vt* to cut up, cut to
pieces, kill; (*fig*) to ruin, strike down; (*RHET*) to
dismember, enfeeble

**concieō, -iēre, -īvī, -itum, conciō, -īre,
-ītum** *vt* to rouse, assemble; to stir up, shake;
(*fig*) to rouse, provoke

conciliābulum, -ī *nt* place for public gatherings

conciliātiō, -ōnis *f* union; winning over
(*friends, hearers*); (*PHILOS*) inclination

conciliātor, -ōris *m* promoter

conciliātrīx, -īcis *m*, **conciliātrīcula, -ae** *f*
promoter, matchmaker

conciliātus¹, -ūs *m* combination

conciliātus² *adj* beloved; favourable

conciliō, -āre, -āvī, -ātum *vt* to unite; to win
over, reconcile; to procure, purchase, bring
about, promote

concilium, -ī *and* **-iī** *nt* gathering, meeting;
council; (*things*) union

concinnē *adv see* **concinnus**

concinnitās, -ātis, concinnitūdō, -ūdinis
f (*RHET*) rhythmical style

concinnō, -āre, -āvī, -ātum *vt* to arrange; to
bring about, produce; (*with adj*) to make

concinnus *adj* symmetrical, beautiful;
(*style*) polished, rhythmical; (*person*) elegant,
courteous; (*things*) suited, pleasing

concinō, -ere, -uī *vi* to sing, play, sound
together; (*fig*) to agree, harmonize ▶ *vt* to sing
about, celebrate, prophesy

concio- *etc see* **contio-**

conciō *etc see* **concieō**

concipiō, -ipere, -ēpī, -eptum *vt* to take to
oneself, absorb; (*women*) to conceive; (*senses*)
to perceive; (*mind*) to conceive, imagine,
understand; (*feelings, acts*) to harbour, foster,
commit; (*words*) to draw up, intimate formally

concīsiō, -ōnis *f* breaking up into short
clauses

concīsus *ppp of* **concīdō** ▶ *adj* broken up,
concise

concitātē *adv see* **concitātus**

concitātiō, -ōnis *f* acceleration; (*mind*)
excitement, passion; riot

concitātor, -ōris *m* agitator

concitātus *ppp of* **concitō** ▶ *adj* fast; excited

concitō, -āre, -āvī, -ātum *vt* to move rapidly,
bestir, hurl; to urge, rouse, impel; to stir up,
occasion

concitor, -ōris *m* instigator

concitus, concītus *ppp of* **concieō; conciō**

conclāmātiō, -ōnis *f* great shout

conclāmitō, -āre *vi* to keep on shouting

conclāmō, -āre, -āvī, -ātum *vt, vi* to
shout, cry out; to call to help; (*MIL*) to give the
signal; (*dead*) to call by name in mourning;
vāsa conclāmāre give the order to pack up;
conclāmātum est it's all over

conclāve, -is *nt* room

conclūdō, -dere, -sī, -sum *vt* to shut up,
enclose; to include, comprise; to end, conclude,
round off (*esp with a rhythmical cadence*); (*PHILOS*)
to infer, demonstrate

conclūsē *adv* with rhythmical cadences

conclūsiō, -ōnis *f* (*MIL*) blockade; end,
conclusion; (*RHET*) period, peroration; (*LOGIC*)
conclusion

conclūsiuncula, -ae *f* quibble

conclūsum, -ī *nt* logical conclusion

conclūsus *ppp of* **conclūdō**

concoctus *ppp of* **concoquō**

concolor, -ōris *adj* of the same colour

concomitātus *adj* escorted

concoquō, -quere, -xī, -ctum *vt* to boil
down; to digest; (*fig*) to put up with, stomach;
(*thought*) to consider well, concoct

concordia, -ae *f* friendship, concord, union;
goddess of Concord

concorditer *adv* amicably

concordō, -āre *vi* to agree, be in harmony

concors, -dis *adj* concordant, united,
harmonious

concrēbrēscō, -ēscere, -uī *vi* to gather
strength

concrēdō, -ere, -idī, -itum *vt* to entrust

concremō, -āre, -āvī, -ātum *vt* to burn

concrepō, -āre, -uī, -itum vi to rattle, creak, clash, snap (fingers) ▸ vt to beat

concrēscō, -scere, -vī, -tum vi to harden, curdle, congeal, clot; to grow, take shape

concrētiō, -ōnis f condensing; matter

concrētum, -ī nt solid matter, hard frost

concrētus ppp of **concrēscō** ▸ adj hard, thick, stiff, congealed; compounded

concrīminor, -ārī, -ātus vi to bring a complaint

concruciō, -āre vt to torture

concubīna, -ae f (female) concubine

concubīnātus, -ūs m concubinage

concubīnus, -ī m (male) concubine

concubitus, -ūs m reclining together (at table); sexual union

concubius adj: **concubiā nocte** during the first sleep ▸ nt the time of the first sleep

conculcō, -āre vt to trample under foot, treat with contempt

concumbō, -mbere, -buī, -bitum vi to lie together, lie with

concupīscō, -īscere, -īvī, -ītum vt to covet, long for, aspire to

concūrō, -āre vt to take care of

concurrō, -rere, -rī, -sum vi to flock together, rush in; (things) to clash, meet; (MIL) to join battle, charge; (events) to happen at the same time, concur

concursātiō, -ōnis f running together, rushing about; (MIL) skirmishing; (dreams) coherent design

concursātor, -ōris m skirmisher

concursiō, -ōnis f meeting, concourse; (RHET) repetition for emphasis

concursō, -āre vi to collide; to rush about, travel about; (MIL) to skirmish ▸ vt to visit, go from place to place

concursus, -ūs m concourse, gathering, collision; uproar; (fig) combination; (MIL) assault, charge

concussī perf of **concutiō**

concussus¹ ppp of **concutiō**

concussus², -ūs m shaking

concutiō, -tere, -ssī, -ssum vt to strike, shake, shatter; (weapons) to hurl; (power) to disturb, impair; (person) to agitate, alarm; (self) to search, examine; to rouse

condalium, -ī and -iī nt slave's ring

condecet, -ēre vt impers it becomes

condecorō, -āre vt to enhance

condemnātor, -ōris m accuser

condemnō, -āre, -āvī, -ātum vt to condemn, sentence; to urge the conviction of; to blame, censure; **ambitūs condemnāre** convict of bribery; **capitis condemnāre** condemn to death; **vōtī condemnātus** obliged to fulfil a vow

condēnsō, -āre, -eō, -ēre vt to compress, move close together

condēnsus adj very dense, close, thick

condiciō, -ōnis f arrangement, condition, terms; marriage contract, match; situation, position, circumstances; manner, mode; **eā condiciōne ut** on condition that; **sub condiciōne** conditionally; **hīs condiciōnibus** on these terms; **vītae ~** way of life

condīcō, -īcere, -īxī, -ictum vt, vi to talk over, agree upon, promise; **ad cēnam condīcere** have a dinner engagement

condidī perf of **condō**

condignē adv see **condignus**

condignus adj very worthy

condīmentum, -ī nt spice, seasoning

condiō, -īre, -īvī, -ītum vt to pickle, preserve, embalm; to season; (fig) to give zest to, temper

condiscipulus, -ī m school-fellow

condiscō, -scere, -dicī vt to learn thoroughly, learn by heart

conditiō etc see **condiciō**

condītiō, -ōnis f preserving, seasoning

conditor, -ōris m founder, author, composer

conditōrium, -ī and **-iī** nt coffin, urn, tomb

conditus ppp of **condō**

condītus¹ ppp of **condiō**

condītus² adj savoury; (fig) polished

condō, -ere, -idī, -itum vt **1.** (build, found: arts) to make, compose, write; (: institutions) to establish **2.** (put away for keeping, store up: fruit) to preserve; (: person) to imprison; (: dead) to bury; (: memory) to lay up; (: time) to pass, bring to a close **3.** (put out of sight, conceal: eyes) to close; (: sword) to sheathe, plunge; (: troops) to place in ambush

condocefaciō, -ere vt to train

condoceō, -ēre, -uī, -tum vt to train

condolēscō, -ēscere, -uī vi to begin to ache, feel very sore

condōnātiō, -ōnis f giving away

condōnō, -āre, -āvī, -ātum vt to give, present, deliver up; (debt) to remit; (offence) to pardon, let off

condormīscō, -īscere, -īvī vi to fall fast asleep

condūcibilis adj expedient

condūcō, -ūcere, -ūxī, -uctum vt to bring together, assemble, connect; to hire, rent, borrow; (public work) to undertake, get the contract for; (taxes) to farm ▸ vi to be of use, profit

conductī, -ōrum mpl hirelings, mercenaries

conductīcius adj hired

conductiō, -ōnis f hiring, farming

conductor, -ōris m hirer, tenant; contractor

conductum, -ī nt anything hired or rented

conductus ppp of **condūcō**

conduplicō, -āre vt to double

condūrō, -āre vt to make very hard

condus, -ī m steward

cōnectō, -ctere, -xuī, -xum vt to tie, fasten, link, join; (LOGIC) to state a conclusion

cōnexum, -ī nt logical inference

cōnexus¹ ppp of **cōnectō** ▸ adj connected; (time) following

cōnexus², -ūs m combination

cōnfābulor, -ārī, -ātus *vi* to talk (to), discuss
cōnfarreātiō, -ōnis *f* the most solemn of Roman marriage ceremonies
cōnfarreō, -āre, -ātum *vt* to marry by cōnfarreātiō
cōnfātālis *adj* bound by the same destiny
cōnfēcī *perf of* **cōnficiō**
cōnfectiō, -ōnis *f* making, completion; (*food*) chewing
cōnfector, -ōris *m* maker, finisher; destroyer
cōnfectus *ppp of* **cōnficiō**
cōnferciō, -cīre, -sī, -tum *vt* to stuff, cram, pack closely
cōnferō, -ferre, -tulī, -lātum *vt* to gather together, collect; to contribute; to confer, talk over; (*MIL*) to oppose, engage in battle; to compare; (*words*) to condense; to direct, transfer; to transform (into), turn (to); to devote, bestow; to ascribe, assign, impute; (*time*) to postpone; **capita cōnferre** put heads together, confer; **gradum cōnferre cum** walk beside; **sē cōnferre** go, turn (to); **sermōnēs cōnferre** converse; **signa cōnferre** join battle
cōnfertim *adv* in close order
cōnfertus *ppp of* **cōnferciō** ▶ *adj* crowded, full; (*MIL*) in close order
cōnfervēscō, -vēscere, -buī *vi* to boil up, grow hot
cōnfessiō, -ōnis *f* acknowledgement, confession
cōnfessus *ppa of* **cōnfiteor** ▶ *adj* acknowledged, certain; **in cōnfessō esse/in cōnfessum venīre** be generally admitted
cōnfestim *adv* immediately
cōnficiō, -icere, -ēcī, -ectum *vt* to make, effect, complete, accomplish; to get together, procure; to wear out, exhaust, consume, destroy; (*COMM*) to settle; (*space*) to travel; (*time*) to pass, complete; (*PHILOS*) to be an active cause; (*LOGIC*) to deduce; (*pass*) it follows
cōnfictiō, -ōnis *f* fabrication
cōnfictus *ppp of* **cōnfingō**
cōnfīdēns, -entis *pres p of* **cōnfīdō** ▶ *adj* self-confident, bold; presumptuous
cōnfīdenter *adv* fearlessly, insolently
cōnfīdentia, -ae *f* confidence, self-confidence; impudence
cōnfīdentiloquus *adj* outspoken
cōnfīdō, -dere, -sus sum *vi* to trust, rely, be sure; **sibi cōnfīdere** be confident
cōnfīgō, -gere, -xī, -xum *vt* to fasten together; to pierce, shoot; (*fig*) to paralyse
cōnfingō, -ingere, -inxī, -ictum *vt* to make, invent, pretend
cōnfīnis *adj* adjoining; (*fig*) akin
cōnfīnium, -ī *nt* common boundary; (*pl*) neighbours; (*fig*) close connection, borderland between
cōnfīō, -fierī *occ pass of* **cōnficiō**
cōnfirmātiō, -ōnis *f* establishing; (*person*) encouragement; (*fact*) verifying; (*RHET*) adducing of proofs
cōnfirmātor, -ōris *m* guarantor (*of money*)
cōnfirmātus *adj* resolute; proved, certain
cōnfirmō, -āre, -āvī, -ātum *vt* to strengthen, reinforce; (*decree*) to confirm, ratify; (*mind*) to encourage; (*fact*) to corroborate, prove, assert; **sē cōnfirmāre** recover; take courage
cōnfiscō, -āre *vt* to keep in a chest; to confiscate
cōnfisiō, -ōnis *f* assurance
cōnfisus *ppa of* **cōnfīdō**
cōnfiteor, -itērī, -essus *vt, vi* to confess, acknowledge; to reveal
cōnfixus *ppp of* **cōnfīgō**
cōnflagrō, -āre, -āvī, -ātum *vi* to burn, be ablaze
cōnflīctiō, -ōnis *f* conflict
cōnflīctō, -āre, -āvī, -ātum *vt* to strike down, contend (with); (*pass*) to fight, be harassed, be afflicted
cōnflīctus, -ūs *m* striking together
cōnflīgō, -gere, -xī, -ctum *vt* to dash together; (*fig*) to contrast ▶ *vi* to fight, come into conflict
cōnflō, -āre, -āvī, -ātum *vt* to ignite; (*passion*) to inflame; to melt down; (*fig*) to produce, procure, occasion
cōnfluēns, -entis, cōnfluēntēs, -entium *m* confluence of two rivers
cōnfluō, -ere, -xī *vi* to flow together; (*fig*) to flock together, pour in
cōnfodiō, -odere, -ōdī, -ossum *vt* to dig; to stab
cōnfore *fut infin of* **cōnsum**
cōnfōrmātiō, -ōnis *f* shape, form; (*words*) arrangement; (*voice*) expression; (*mind*) idea; (*RHET*) figure
cōnfōrmō, -āre, -āvī, -ātum *vt* to shape, fashion
cōnfossus *ppp of* **cōnfodiō** ▶ *adj* full of holes
cōnfrāctus *ppp of* **cōnfringō**
cōnfragōsus *adj* broken, rough; (*fig*) hard
cōnfrēgī *perf of* **cōnfringō**
cōnfremō, -ere, -uī *vi* to murmur aloud
cōnfricō, -āre *vt* to rub well
cōnfringō, -ingere, -ēgī, -āctum *vt* to break in pieces, wreck; (*fig*) to ruin
cōnfugiō, -ugere, -ūgī *vi* to flee for help (to), take refuge (with); (*fig*) to have recourse (to)
cōnfugium, -ī *and* **-iī** *nt* refuge
cōnfundō, -undere, -ūdī, -ūsum *vt* to mix, mingle, join; to mix up, confuse, throw into disorder; (*mind*) to perplex, bewilder; to diffuse, spread over
cōnfūsē *adv* confusedly
cōnfūsiō, -ōnis *f* combination; confusion, disorder; **ōris ~** going red in the face
cōnfūsus *ppp of* **cōnfundō** ▶ *adj* confused, disorderly, troubled
cōnfūtō, -āre, -āvī, -ātum *vt* to keep from boiling over; to repress; to silence, confute
congelō, -āre, -āvī, -ātum *vt* to freeze, harden ▶ *vi* to freeze over, grow numb

congeminō, -āre, -āvī, -ātum vt to double

congemō, -ere, -uī vi to groan, sigh ▸ vt to lament

conger, -rī m sea eel

congeriēs, -ēī f heap, mass, accumulation

congerō¹, -rere, -ssī, -stum vt to collect, accumulate, build; (missiles) to shower; (speech) to comprise; (fig) to heap (upon), ascribe

congerō², -ōnis m thief

congerrō, -ōnis m companion in revelry

congestīcius adj piled up

congestus¹ ppp of **congerō¹**

congestus², -ūs m accumulating; heap, mass

congiālis adj holding a congius

congiārium, -ī and -iī nt gift of food to the people, gratuity to the army

congius, -ī and -iī m Roman liquid measure (about 6 pints)

conglaciō, -āre vi to freeze up

conglīscō, -ere vi to blaze up

conglobātiō, -ōnis f mustering

conglobō, -āre, -āvī, -ātum vt to make round; to mass together

conglomerō, -āre vt to roll up

conglūtinātiō, -ōnis f gluing, cementing; (fig) combination

conglūtinō, -āre, -āvī, -ātum vt to glue, cement; (fig) to join, weld together; to contrive

congraecō, -āre vt to squander on luxury

congrātulor, -ārī, -ātus vt to congratulate

congredior, -dī, -ssus vt, vi to meet, accost; to contend, fight

congregābilis adj gregarious

congregātiō, -ōnis f union, society

congregō, -āre, -āvī, -ātum vt to collect, assemble, unite

congressiō, -ōnis f meeting, conference

congressus¹ ppa of **congredior**

congressus², -ūs m meeting, association, union; encounter, fight

congruēns, -entis adj suitable, consistent, proper; harmonious

congruenter adv in conformity

congruō, -ere, -ī vi to coincide; to correspond, suit; to agree, sympathize

congruus adj agreeable

coniciō, -icere, -iēcī, -iectum vt to throw together; to throw, hurl; to put, fling, drive, direct; to infer, conjecture; (AUG) to interpret; **sē conicere** rush, fly; devote oneself

coniectiō, -ōnis f throwing; conjecture, interpretation

coniectō, -āre vt to infer, conjecture, guess

coniector, -ōris m (male) interpreter, diviner

coniectrīx, -rīcis f (female) interpreter, diviner

coniectūra, -ae f inference, conjecture, guess; interpretation

coniectūrālis adj (RHET) involving a question of fact

coniectus¹ ppp of **coniciō**

coniectus², -ūs m heap, mass, concourse; throwing, throw, range; (eyes, mind) turning, directing

cōnifer, cōniger, -ī adj cone-bearing

cōnītor, -tī, -sus and -xus vi to lean on; to strive, struggle on; to labour

coniugālis adj of marriage, conjugal

coniugātiō, -ōnis f etymological relationship

coniugātor, -ōris m uniter

coniugiālis adj marriage- (in cpds)

coniugium, -ī and -iī nt union, marriage; husband, wife

coniugō, -āre vt to form (a friendship); **coniugāta verba** words related etymologically

coniūnctē adv jointly; on familiar terms; (LOGIC) hypothetically

coniūnctim adv together, jointly

coniūnctiō, -ōnis f union, connection, association; (minds) sympathy, affinity; (GRAM) conjunction

coniūnctum, -ī nt (RHET) connection; (PHILOS) inherent property (of a body)

coniūnctus ppp of **coniungō** ▸ adj near; connected, agreeing, conforming; related, friendly, intimate

coniungō, -ungere, -ūnxī, -ūnctum vt to yoke, join together, connect; (war) to join forces in; to unite in love, marriage, friendship; to continue without a break

coniūnx, -ugis m/f consort, wife, husband, bride

coniūrātī, -ōrum mpl conspirators

coniūrātiō, -ōnis f conspiracy, plot; alliance

coniūrātus adj (MIL) after taking the oath

coniūrō, -āre, -āvī, -ātum vi to take an oath; to conspire, plot

coniux etc see **coniūnx**

cōnīveō, -vēre, -vī and -xī vi to shut the eyes, blink; (fig) to be asleep; to connive at

conj- etc see **coni-**

conl- etc see **coll-**

conm- etc see **comm-**

conn- etc see **cōn-**

Conōn, -is m Athenian commander; Greek astronomer

cōnōpēum, cōnōpeum, -ēī nt mosquito net

cōnor, -ārī, -ātus vt to try, attempt, venture

conp- etc see **comp-**

conquassātiō, -ōnis f severe shaking

conquassō, -āre, -ātum vt to shake, upset, shatter

conqueror, -rī, -stus vt, vi to complain bitterly of, bewail

conquestiō, -ōnis f complaining; (RHET) appeal to pity

conquestus¹ ppa of **conqueror**

conquestus², -ūs m outcry

conquiēscō, -scere, -vī, -tum vi to rest, take a respite; (fig) to be at peace, find recreation; (things) to stop, be quiet

conquinīscō, -ere vi to cower, squat, stoop down

conquīrō, -rere, -sīvī, -sītum vt to search for, collect
conquīsītē adv carefully
conquīsītiō, -ōnis f search; (MIL) levy
conquīsītor, -ōris m recruiting officer; (theatre) claqueur
conquīsītus ppp of **conquīrō** ▸ adj select, costly
conr- etc see **corr-**
cōnsaepiō, -īre, -sī, -tum vt to enclose, fence round
cōnsaeptum, -tī nt enclosure
cōnsalūtātiō, -ōnis f mutual greeting
cōnsalūtō, -āre, -āvī, -ātum vt to greet, hail
cōnsānēscō, -ēscere, -uī vi to heal up
cōnsanguineus adj brother, sister, kindred ▸ mpl relations
cōnsanguinitās, -ātis f relationship
cōnscelerātus adj wicked
cōnscelerō, -āre, -āvī, -ātum vt to disgrace
cōnscendō, -endere, -endī, -ēnsum vt, vi to climb, mount, embark
cōnscēnsiō, -ōnis f embarkation
cōnscēnsus ppp of **cōnscendō**
cōnscientia, -ae f joint knowledge, being in the know; (sense of) consciousness; moral sense, conscience, guilty conscience
cōnscindō, -ndere, -dī, -ssum vt to tear to pieces; (fig) to abuse
cōnsciō, -īre vt to be conscious of guilt
cōnscīscō, -scere, -vī and -iī, -ītum vt to decide on publicly; to inflict on oneself; **mortem (sibi) cōnscīscere** commit suicide
cōnscīssus ppp of **cōnscindō**
cōnscītus ppp of **cōnscīscō**
cōnscius adj sharing knowledge, privy, in the know; aware, conscious (of); conscious of guilt ▸ m/f confederate, confidant
cōnscreor, -ārī vi to clear the throat
cōnscrībō, -bere, -psī, -ptum vt to enlist, enrol; to write, compose, draw up, prescribe
cōnscrīptiō, -ōnis f document, draft
cōnscrīptus ppp of **cōnscrībō**; **patrēs cōnscrīptī** patrician and elected plebeian members; senators
cōnsecō, -āre, -uī, -tum vt to cut up
cōnsecrātiō, -ōnis f consecration, deification
cōnsecrō, -āre, -āvī, -ātum vt to dedicate, consecrate, deify; (fig) to devote; to immortalise; **caput cōnsecrāre** doom to death
cōnsectārius adj logical, consequent ▸ ntpl inferences
cōnsectātiō, -ōnis f pursuit
cōnsectātrīx, -īcis f (fig) follower
cōnsectiō, -ōnis f cutting up
cōnsector, -ārī, -ātus vt to follow, go after, try to gain; to emulate, imitate; to pursue, chase
cōnsecūtiō, -ōnis f (PHILOS) consequences, effect; (RHET) sequence
cōnsēdī perf of **cōnsīdō**

cōnsenēscō, -ēscere, -uī vi to grow old, grow old together; (fig) to fade, pine, decay, become obsolete
cōnsēnsiō, -ōnis f agreement, accord; conspiracy, plot
cōnsēnsū adv unanimously
cōnsēnsus¹ ppp of **cōnsentiō**
cōnsēnsus², -ūs m agreement, concord; conspiracy; (PHILOS) common sensation; (fig) harmony
cōnsentāneus adj agreeing, in keeping with; **cōnsentāneum est** it is reasonable
cōnsentiō, -entīre, -ēnsī, -ēnsum vi to agree, determine together; to plot, conspire; (PHILOS) to have common sensations; (fig) to harmonize, suit, be consistent (with); **bellum cōnsentīre** vote for war
cōnsequēns, -entis pres p of **cōnsequor** ▸ adj coherent, reasonable; logical, consequent ▸ nt consequence
cōnsequor, -quī, -cūtus vt to follow, pursue; to overtake, reach; (time) to come after; (example) to follow, copy; (effect) to result, be the consequence of; (aim) to attain, get; (mind) to grasp, learn; (events) to happen to, come to; (standard) to equal, come up to; (speech) to do justice to
cōnserō¹, -erere, -ēvī, -itum vt to sow, plant; (ground) to sow with, plant with; (fig) to cover, fill
cōnserō², -ere, -uī, -tum vt to join, string together, twine; (MIL) to join battle; **manum/manūs ~** engage in close combat; **ex iūre manum ~** lay claim to (in an action for possession)
cōnsertē adv connectedly
cōnsertus ppp of **cōnserō²**
cōnserva, -ae f fellow slave
cōnservātiō, -ōnis f preserving
cōnservātor, -ōris m preserver
cōnservitium, -ī and -iī nt being fellow slaves
cōnservō, -āre, -āvī, -ātum vt to preserve, save, keep
cōnservus, -ī m fellow slave
cōnsessor, -ōris m companion at table, fellow spectator; (LAW) assessor
cōnsessus, -ūs m assembly; (LAW) court
cōnsēvī perf of **cōnserō¹**
cōnsīderātē adv cautiously, deliberately
cōnsīderātiō, -ōnis f contemplation
cōnsīderātus adj (person) circumspect; (things) well-considered
cōnsīderō, -āre, -āvī, -ātum vt to look at, inspect; to consider, contemplate
cōnsīdō, -īdere, -ēdī, -essum vi to sit down, take seats; (courts) to be in session; (MIL) to take up a position; (residence) to settle; (places) to subside, sink; (fig) to sink, settle down, subside
cōnsignō, -āre, -āvī, -ātum vt to seal, sign; to attest, vouch for; to record, register
cōnsilēscō, -ere vi to calm down
cōnsiliārius, -ī and -iī m adviser, counsellor; spokesman ▸ adj counselling

cōnsiliātor, -ōris m counsellor

cōnsilior, -ārī, -ātus vi to consult; (with dat) to advise

cōnsilium, -ī and **-iī** nt deliberation, consultation; deliberating body, council; decision, purpose; plan, measure, stratagem; advice, counsel; judgement, insight, wisdom; ~ **capere**, ~ **inīre** come to a decision, resolve; **cōnsilii esse** be an open question; **cōnsiliō** intentionally; **eō cōnsiliō ut** with the intention of; **prīvātō cōnsiliō** for one's own purposes

cōnsimilis adj just like

cōnsipiō, -ere vi to be in one's senses

cōnsistō, -istere, -titī vi to stand, rest, take up a position; to consist (of), depend (on); to exist, be; (fig) to stand firm, endure; (liquid) to solidify, freeze; to stop, pause, halt, come to rest; (fig) to come to a standstill, come to an end

cōnsitiō, -ōnis f sowing, planting

cōnsitor, -ōris m sower, planter

cōnsitus ppp of **cōnserō¹**

cōnsōbrīnus, -ī m, **cōnsōbrīna, -ae** f cousin

cōnsociātiō, -ōnis f society

cōnsociō, -āre, -āvī, -ātum vt to share, associate, unite

cōnsōlābilis adj consolable

cōnsōlātiō, -ōnis f comfort, encouragement, consolation

cōnsōlātor, -ōris m comforter

cōnsōlātōrius adj of consolation

cōnsōlor, -ārī, -ātus vt to console, comfort, reassure; (things) to relieve, mitigate

cōnsomniō, -āre vt to dream about

cōnsonō, -āre, -uī vi to resound; (fig) to accord

cōnsonus adj suitable; (fig) suitable

cōnsōpiō, -īre, -īvī, -ītum vt to put to sleep

cōnsors, -tis adj sharing in common; (things) shared in common ▸ m/f partner, colleague

cōnsortiō, -ōnis f partnership, fellowship

cōnsortium, -ī and **-iī** nt society, participation

cōnspectus¹ ppp of **cōnspiciō** ▸ adj visible; conspicuous

cōnspectus², -ūs m look, view, sight; appearing on the scene; (fig) mental picture, survey; **in cōnspectum venīre** come in sight, come near

cōnspergō, -gere, -sī, -sum vt to besprinkle; (fig) to spangle

cōnspiciendus adj noteworthy, distinguished

cōnspiciō, -icere, -exī, -ectum vt to observe, catch sight of; to look at (esp with admiration), contemplate; (pass) to attract attention, be conspicuous, be notorious; (mind) to see, perceive

cōnspicor, -ārī, -ātus vt to observe, see, catch sight of

cōnspicuus adj visible; conspicuous, distinguished

cōnspīrātiō, -ōnis f concord, unanimity; plotting, conspiracy

cōnspīrō, -āre, -āvī, -ātum vi to agree, unite; to plot, conspire; (music) to sound together

cōnspōnsor, -ōris m co-guarantor

cōnspuō, -ere vt to spit upon

cōnspurcō, -āre vt to pollute

cōnspūtō, -āre vt to spit upon (with contempt)

cōnstabiliō, -īre, -īvī, -itum vt to establish

cōnstāns, -antis pres p of **cōnstō** ▸ adj steady, stable, constant; consistent; faithful, steadfast

cōnstanter adv steadily, firmly, calmly; consistently

cōnstantia, -ae f steadiness, firmness; consistency, harmony; self- possession, constancy

cōnsternātiō, -ōnis f disorder, tumult; (horses) stampede; (mind) dismay, alarm

cōnsternō¹, -ernere, -rāvī, -rātum vt to spread, cover, thatch, pave; **cōnstrāta nāvis** decked ship

cōnsternō², -āre, -āvī, -ātum vt to startle, stampede; to alarm, throw into confusion

cōnstīpō, -āre vt to crowd together

cōnstitī perf of **cōnsistō**

cōnstituō, -uere, -uī, -ūtum vt to put, place, set down; (MIL) to station, post, halt; to establish, build, create; to settle, arrange, organize; to appoint, determine, fix; to resolve, decide; **bene cōnstitūtum corpus** a good constitution

cōnstitūtiō, -ōnis f state, condition; regulation, decree; definition, point at issue

cōnstitūtum, -ūtī nt agreement

cōnstō, -āre, -itī, -ātum vi to stand together; to agree, correspond, tally; to stand firm, remain constant; to exist, be; to consist (of), be composed (of); (facts) to be established, be well-known; (COMM) to cost; **sibi cōnstāre** be consistent; **inter omnēs cōnstat** it is common knowledge; **mihi cōnstat** I am determined; **ratiō cōnstat** the account is correct

cōnstrātum, -ī nt flooring, deck

cōnstrātus ppp of **cōnsternō¹**

cōnstringō, -ingere, -inxī, -ictum vt to tie up, bind, fetter; (fig) to restrain, restrict; (speech) to compress, condense

cōnstructiō, -ōnis f building up; (words) arrangement, sequence

cōnstruō, -ere, -xī, -ctum vt to heap up; to build, construct

cōnstuprātor, -ōris m debaucher

cōnstuprō, -āre vt to debauch, rape

cōnsuādeō, -ēre vi to advise strongly

Cōnsuālia, -ium ntpl festival of Consus

cōnsuāsor, -ōris m earnest adviser

cōnsūdō, -āre vi to sweat profusely

cōnsuēfaciō, -facere, -fēcī, -factum vt to accustom

cōnsuēscō, -scere, -vī, -tum vt to accustom, inure ▸ vi to get accustomed; to cohabit (with); (perf tenses) to be accustomed, be in the habit of

cōnsuētūdō, -inis f custom, habit; familiarity, social intercourse; love affair; (language) usage, idiom; **cōnsuētūdine/ex cōnsuētūdine** as usual; **epistulārum ~** correspondence

cōnsuētus ppp of **cōnsuēscō** ▸ adj customary, usual

cōnsuēvī perf of **cōnsuēscō**

cōnsul, -is m consul; **~ dēsignātus** consul elect; **~ ōrdinārius** regular consul; **~ suffectus** successor to a consul who has died during his term of office; **~ iterum/tertium** consul for the second/ third time; **cōnsulem creāre, cōnsulem dīcere, cōnsulem facere** elect to the consulship; **L. Domitiō App. Claudiō cōnsulibus** in the year 54 B.C.

cōnsulāris adj consular, consul's; of consular rank ▸ m ex-consul

cōnsulāriter adv in a manner worthy of a consul

cōnsulātus, -ūs m consulship; **cōnsulātum petere** stand for the consulship

cōnsulō, -ere, -uī, -tum vi to deliberate, take thought; (with dat) to look after, consult the interests of; (with dē or in) to take measures against, pass sentence on ▸ vt to consult, ask advice of; to consider; to advise (something); to decide; **bonī/optimī cōnsulere** take in good part, be satisfied with

cōnsultātiō, -ōnis f deliberation; inquiry; case

cōnsultē adv deliberately

cōnsultō[1] adv deliberately

cōnsultō[2]**, -āre, -āvī, -ātum** vt, vi to deliberate, reflect; to consult; (with dat) to consult the interests of

cōnsultor, -ōris m counsellor; **cōnsulter** client

cōnsultrīx, -īcis f protectress

cōnsultum, -ī nt decree (esp of the Senate); consultation; response (from an oracle)

cōnsultus ppp of **cōnsulō** ▸ adj considered; experienced, skilled ▸ m lawyer; **iūris ~** lawyer

cōnsuluī perf of **cōnsulō**

(cōnsum), -futūrum, -fore vi to be all right

cōnsummātus adj perfect

cōnsummō, -āre vt to sum up; to complete, perfect

cōnsūmō, -ere, -psī, -ptum vt to consume, use up, eat up; to waste, squander; to exhaust, destroy, kill; to spend, devote

cōnsūmptiō, -ōnis f wasting

cōnsūmptor, -ōris m destroyer

cōnsūmptus ppp of **cōnsūmō**

cōnsuō, -uere, -uī, -ūtum vt to sew up; (fig) to contrive

cōnsurgō, -gere, -rēxī, -rēctum vi to rise, stand up; to be roused (to); to spring up, start

cōnsurrēctiō, -ōnis f standing up

Cōnsus, -ī m ancient Roman god (connected with harvest)

cōnsusurrō, -āre vi to whisper together

cōnsūtus ppp of **cōnsuō**

contābefaciō, -ere vt to wear out

contābēscō, -ēscere, -uī vi to waste away

contābulātiō, -ōnis f flooring, storey

contābulō, -āre, -āvī, -ātum vt to board over, build in storeys

contāctus[1] ppp of **contingō**[1]

contāctus[2]**, -ūs** m touch, contact; contagion, infection

contāgēs, -is f contact, touch

contāgiō, -ōnis f, **contāgium, -ī** and **-iī** nt contact; contagion, infection; (fig) contamination, bad example

contāminātus adj impure, vicious

contāminō, -āre, -āvī, -ātum vt to defile; (fig) to mar, spoil

contechnor, -ārī, -ātus vi to think out plots

contegō, -egere, -ēxī, -ēctum vt to cover up, cover over; to protect; to hide

contemerō, -āre vt to defile

contemnō, -nere, -psī, -ptum vt to think light of, have no fear of, despise, defy; to disparage

contemplātiō, -ōnis f contemplation, surveying

contemplātor, -ōris m observer

contemplātus, -ūs m contemplation

contemplō, -āre, -āvī, -ātum, contemplor, -ārī, -ātus vt to look at, observe, contemplate

contempsī perf of **contemnō**

contemptim adv contemptuously, slightingly

contemptiō, -ōnis f disregard, scorn, despising

contemptor, -ōris m (male) despiser, defier

contemptrīx, -īcis f (female) despiser, defier

contemptus[1] ppp of **contemnō** ▸ adj contemptible

contemptus[2]**, -ūs** m despising, scorn; being slighted; **contemptuī esse** be despised

contendō, -dere, -dī, -tum vt to stretch, draw, tighten; (instrument) to tune; (effort) to strain, exert; (argument) to assert, maintain; (comparison) to compare, contrast; (course) to direct ▸ vi to exert oneself, strive; to hurry; journey, march; to contend, compete, fight; to entreat, solicit

contentē[1] adv (from **contendō**) earnestly, intensely

contentē[2] adv (from **contineō**) closely

contentiō, -ōnis f straining, effort; striving (after); struggle, competition, dispute; comparison, contrast, antithesis

contentus[1] ppp of **contendō** ▸ adj strained, tense; (fig) intent

contentus[2] ppp of **contineō** ▸ adj content, satisfied

conterminus adj bordering, neighbouring

conterō, -erere, -rīvī, -rītum vt to grind, crumble; to wear out, waste; (time) to spend, pass; (fig) to obliterate

conterreō, -ēre, -uī, -itum vt to terrify

contestātus adj proved

contestor, -ārī, -ātus vt to call to witness; **lītem ~** open a lawsuit by calling witnesses

contexō, -ere, -uī, -tum vt to weave, interweave; to devise, construct; (recital) to continue

contextē *adv* in a connected fashion

contextus¹ *adj* connected

contextus², -ūs *m* connection, coherence

conticēscō, conticīscō, -ēscere, -uī *vi* to become quiet, fall silent; (*fig*) to cease, abate

contigī *perf of* **contingō¹**

contignātiō, -ōnis *f* floor, storey

contignō, -āre *vt* to floor

contiguus *adj* adjoining, near; within reach

continēns, -entis *pres p of* **contineō** ▶ *adj* bordering, adjacent; (*time*) successive, continual, uninterrupted; (*person*) temperate, continent ▶ *nt* mainland, continent; essential point (*in an argument*)

continenter *adv* (*place*) in a row; (*time*) continuously; (*person*) temperately

continentia, -ae *f* moderation, self-control

contineō, -inēre, -inuī, -entum *vt* to hold, keep together; to confine, enclose; to contain, include, comprise; (*pass*) to consist of, rest on; to control, check, repress

contingō¹, -ingere, -igī, -āctum *vt* to touch, take hold of, partake of; to be near, border on; to reach, come to; to contaminate; (*mind*) to touch, affect, concern ▶ *vi* to happen, succeed

contingō², -ere *vt* to moisten, smear

continuātiō, -ōnis *f* unbroken succession, series; (*RHET*) period

continuī *perf of* **contineō**

continuō¹ *adv* immediately, without delay; (*argument*) necessarily

continuō², -āre, -āvī, -ātum *vt* to join together, make continuous; to continue without a break; **verba continuāre** form a sentence

continuus *adj* joined (to); continuous, successive, uninterrupted; **continuā nocte** the following night; **trīduum continuum** three days running

cōntiō, -ōnis *f* public meeting; speech, address; rostrum; **cōntiōnem habēre** hold a meeting; deliver an address; **prō cōntiōne** in public

cōntiōnābundus *adj* delivering a harangue, playing the demagogue

cōntiōnālis *adj* suitable for a public meeting, demagogic

cōntiōnārius *adj* fond of public meetings

cōntiōnātor, -ōris *m* demagogue

cōntiōnor, -ārī, -ātus *vi* to address a public meeting, harangue; to declare in public; to come to a meeting

cōntiuncula, -ae *f* short speech

contorqueō, -quēre, -sī, -tum *vt* to twist, turn; (*weapons*) to throw, brandish; (*words*) to deliver forcibly

contortē *adv* intricately

contortiō, -ōnis *f* intricacy

contortor, -ōris *m* perverter

contortulus *adj* somewhat complicated

contortuplicātus *adj* very complicated

contortus *ppp of* **contorqueō** ▶ *adj* vehement; intricate

contrā *adv* (*place*) opposite, face to face; (*speech*) in reply; (*action*) to fight, in opposition, against (*someone*); (*result, with* **esse**) adverse, unsuccessful; (*comparison*) the contrary, conversely, differently; (*argument*) on the contrary, on the other hand; **~ atque, ~ quam** contrary to what, otherwise than ▶ *prep* (*with acc*) facing, opposite to; against; contrary to, in violation of

contractiō, -ōnis *f* contracting; shortening; despondency

contractiuncula, -ae *f* slight despondency

contractus *ppp of* **contrahō** ▶ *adj* contracted, narrow; short; in seclusion

contrādīcō (*usu two words*), **-dīcere, -dīxī, -dictum** *vt*, *vi* to oppose, object; (*LAW*) to be counsel for the other side

contrādictiō, -ōnis *f* objection

contrahō, -here, -xī, -ctum *vt* to draw together, assemble; to bring about, achieve; (*COMM*) to contract, make a bargain; to shorten, narrow; to limit, depress; (*blame*) to incur; (*brow*) to wrinkle; (*sail*) to shorten; (*sky*) to overcast

contrāriē *adv* differently

contrārius *adj* opposite, from opposite; contrary; hostile, harmful ▶ *nt* opposite, reverse; **ex contrāriō** on the contrary

contrectābiliter *adv* so as to be felt

contrectātiō, -ōnis *f* touching

contrectō, -āre, -āvī, -ātum *vt* to touch, handle; (*fig*) to consider

contremīscō, -īscere, -uī *vi* to tremble all over; (*fig*) to waver ▶ *vt* to be afraid of

contremō, -ere *vi* to quake

contribuō, -uere, -uī, -ūtum *vt* to bring together, join, incorporate

contristō, -āre, -āvī, -ātum *vt* to sadden, darken, cloud

contrītus *ppp of* **conterō** ▶ *adj* trite, well-worn

contrōversia, -ae *f* dispute, argument, debate, controversy

contrōversiōsus *adj* much disputed

contrōversus *adj* disputed, questionable

contrucīdō, -āre, -āvī, -ātum *vt* to massacre

contrūdō, -dere, -sī, -sum *vt* to crowd together

contruncō, -āre *vt* to hack to pieces

contrūsus *ppp of* **contrūdō**

contubernālis, -is *m/f* tent companion; junior officer serving with a general; (*fig*) companion, mate

contubernium, -ī *and* **-iī** *nt* service in the same tent, mess; service as junior officer with a general; common tent, slaves' home

contueor, -ērī, -itus *vt* to look at, consider, observe

contuitus, -ūs *m* observing, view

contulī *perf of* **cōnferō**

contumācia, -ae *f* obstinacy, defiance

contumāciter *adv see* **contumāx**

contumāx, -ācis *adj* stubborn, insolent, pig-headed

contumēlia, -ae f (verbal) insult, libel, invective; (physical) assault, ill-treatment
contumēliōsē adv insolently
contumēliōsus adj insulting, outrageous
contumulō, -āre vt to bury
contundō, -undere, -udī, -ūsum vt to pound, beat, bruise; (fig) to suppress, destroy
contuor etc see **contueor**
conturbātiō, -ōnis f confusion, mental disorder
conturbātus adj distracted, diseased
conturbō, -āre, -āvī, -ātum vt to throw into confusion; (mind) to derange, disquiet; (money) to embarrass
contus, -ī m pole
contūsus ppp of **contundō**
contūtus see **contuitus**
cōnūbiālis adj conjugal
cōnūbium, -ī and **-iī** nt marriage; **iūs cōnūbī** right of intermarriage
cōnus, -ī m cone; (helmet) apex
convador, -ārī, -ātus vt (LAW) to bind over
convalēscō, -ēscere, -uī vi to recover, get better; (fig) to grow stronger, improve
convallis, -is f valley with hills on all sides
convāsō, -āre vt to pack up
convectō, -āre vt to bring home
convector, -ōris m fellow passenger
convehō, -here, -xī, -ctum vt to bring in, carry
convellō, -ellere, -ellī, -ulsum and **-olsum** vt to wrench, tear away; to break up; (fig) to destroy, overthrow; **signa convellere** decamp
convena, -ae adj meeting
convenae, -ārum mpl/fpl crowd of strangers, refugees
conveniēns, -entis pres p of **conveniō** ▸ adj harmonious, consistent; fit, appropriate
convenienter adv in conformity (with), consistently; aptly
convenientia, -ae f conformity, harmony
conveniō, -enīre, -ēnī, -entum vi to meet, assemble; (events) to combine, coincide; (person) to agree, harmonize; (things) to fit, suit; (impers) to be suitable, be proper ▸ vt to speak to, interview
conventīcium, -ī and **-iī** nt payment for attendance at assemblies
conventīcius adj visiting regularly
conventiculum, -ī nt gathering; meeting place
conventiō, -ōnis f agreement
conventum, -ī nt agreement
conventus¹ ppp of **conveniō**
conventus², -ūs m meeting; (LAW) local assizes; (COMM) corporation; agreement; **conventūs agere** hold the assizes
converrō, -rere, -rī, -sum vt to sweep up, brush together; (comedy) to give a good beating to
conversātiō, -ōnis f associating (with)

conversiō, -ōnis f revolution, cycle; change over; (RHET) well-rounded period; verbal repetition at end of clauses
conversō, -āre vt to turn round
conversus ppp **converrō**; **convertō**
convertō, -tere, -tī, -sum vt to turn round, turn back; (MIL) to wheel; to turn, direct; to change, transform; (writings) to translate ▸ vi to return, turn, change
convestiō, -īre, -īvī, -ītum vt to clothe, encompass
convexus adj vaulted, rounded; hollow; sloping ▸ nt vault, hollow
convīciātor, -ōris m slanderer
convīcior, -ārī, -ātus vt to revile
convīcium, -ī and **-iī** nt loud noise, outcry; invective, abuse; reproof, protest
convictiō, -ōnis f companionship
convictor, -ōris m familiar friend
convictus ppp of **convincō**
convictus, -ūs m community life, intercourse; entertainment
convincō, -incere, -īcī, -ictum vt to refute, convict, prove wrong; to prove, demonstrate
convīsō, -ere vt to search, examine; to pervade
convītium see **convīcium**
convīva, -ae m/f guest
convīvālis adj festive, convivial
convīvātor, -ōris m host
convīvium, -ī and **-iī** nt banquet, entertainment; guests
convīvor, -ārī, -ātus vi to feast together, carouse
convocātiō, -ōnis f assembling
convocō, -āre, -āvī, -ātum vt to call a meeting of, muster
convolnerō see **convulnerō**
convolō, -āre, -āvī, -ātum vi to flock together
convolsus see **convulsus**
convolvō, -vere, -vī, -ūtum vt to roll up, coil up; to intertwine
convomō, -ere vt to vomit over
convorrō see **converrō**
convortō see **convertō**
convulnerō, -āre vt to wound seriously
convulsus ppp of **convellō**
cooperiō, -īre, -uī, -tum vt to cover over, overwhelm
cooptātiō, -ōnis f electing, nominating (of new members)
cooptō, -āre, -āvī, -ātum vt to elect (as a colleague)
coorior, -īrī, -tus vi to rise, appear; to break out, begin
coortus, -ūs m originating
cōpa, -ae f barmaid
cophinus, -ī m basket
cōpia, -ae f abundance, plenty, number; resources, wealth, prosperity; (MIL, usu pl) troops, force; (words, thought) richness, fulness, store; (action) opportunity, facility, means,

access; **prō cōpiā** according to one's resources, as good as possible considering

cōpiolae, -ārum *fpl* small force

cōpiōsē *adv* abundantly, fully, at great length

cōpiōsus *adj* abounding, rich, plentiful; *(speech)* eloquent, fluent

cōpis *adj* rich

cōpula, -ae *f* rope, leash, grapnel; *(fig)* bond

cōpulātiō, -ōnis *f* coupling, union

cōpulātus *adj* connected, binding

cōpulō, -āre, -āvī, -ātum *vt* to couple, join; *(fig)* to unite, associate

coqua, -ae *f* cook

coquīnō, -āre *vi* to be a cook

coquīnus *adj* of cooking

coquō, -quere, -xī, -ctum *vt* to cook, boil, bake; to parch, burn; *(fruit)* to ripen; *(stomach)* to digest; *(thought)* to plan, concoct; *(care)* to disquiet, disturb

coquus, cocus, -ī *m* cook

cor, cordis *nt* heart; *(feeling)* heart, soul; *(thought)* mind, judgement; **cordī esse** please, be agreeable

cōram *adv* in one's presence; in person ▸ *prep (with abl)* in the presence of, before

corbis, -is *m/f* basket

corbīta, -ae *f* slow boat

corbula, -ae *f* little basket

corculum, -ī *nt* dear heart

Corcȳra, -ae *f* island off W. coast of Greece (now Corfu)

Corcȳraeus *adj see* **Corcȳra**

cordātē *adv see* **cordātus**

cordātus *adj* wise

cordolium, -ī and -iī *nt* sorrow

Corfiniēnsis *adj see* **Corfinium**

Corfinium, -ī *nt* town in central Italy

coriandrum, -ī *nt* coriander

Corinthiacus, Corinthiēnsis, Corinthius *adj*: **Corinthium aes** Corinthian brass *(an alloy of gold, silver and copper)*

Corinthus, -ī *f* Corinth

corium, -ī and -iī *nt*, **corius, -ī and -iī** *m* hide, skin; leather, strap

Cornēlia, -iae *f* mother of the Gracchi

Cornēliānus, Cornēlius *adj*: **lēgēs Cornēliae** Sulla's laws

Cornēlius, -ī *m* famous Roman family name *(esp Scipios, Gracchi, Sulla)*

corneolus *adj* horny

corneus¹ *adj* of horn

corneus² *adj* of the cornel tree, of cornel wood

cornicen, -cinis *m* horn-blower

cornīcula, -ae *f* little crow

corniculārius, -ī and -iī *m* adjutant

corniculum, -ī *nt* a horn-shaped decoration

corniger, -ī *adj* horned

cornipēs, -edis *adj* horn-footed

cornīx, -īcis *f* crow

cornū, -ūs, cornum, -ī *nt* horn; anything horn-shaped; *(army)* wing; *(bay)* arm; *(book)* roller-end; *(bow)* tip; *(helmet)* crest-socket; *(land)* tongue;

spit; *(lyre)* arm; *(moon)* horn; *(place)* side; *(river)* branch; *(yardarm)* point; anything made of horn: bow, funnel, lantern; *(music)* horn; *(oil)* cruet; anything like horn: beak, hoof, wart; *(fig)* strength, courage; **~ cōpiae** Amalthea's horn, symbol of plenty

cornum¹, -ī *nt* cornelian cherry

cornum² *see* **cornū**

cornus, -ī *f* cornelian cherry tree; javelin

corōlla, -ae *f* small garland

corōllārium, -ī and -iī *nt* garland for actors; present, gratuity

corōna, -ae *f* garland, crown; *(ASTR)* Corona Borealis; *(people)* gathering, bystanders; *(MIL)* cordon of besiegers or defenders; **sub corōnā vēndere, sub corōnā vēnīre** sell, be sold as slaves

Corōnaeus, Corōnēus, Corōnēnsis *adj see* **Corōnēa**

Corōnēa, -ēae *f* town in central Greece

corōnō, -āre, -āvī, -ātum *vt* to put a garland on, crown; to encircle

corporeus *adj* corporeal; of flesh

corpulentus *adj* corpulent

corpus, -oris *nt* body; substance, flesh; corpse; trunk, torso; person, individual; *(fig)* structure, corporation, body politic

corpusculum, -ī *nt* particle; term of endearment

corrādō, -dere, -sī, -sum *vt* to scrape together, procure

corrēctiō, -ōnis *f* amending, improving

corrēctor, -ōris *m* reformer, critic

corrēctus *ppp of* **corrigō**

corrēpō, -ere, -sī *vi* to creep, slink, cower

correptē *adv* briefly

correptus *ppp of* **corripiō**

corrīdeō, -ēre *vi* to laugh aloud

corrigia, -ae *f* shoelace

corrigō, -igere, -ēxī, -ēctum *vt* to make straight; to put right, improve, correct

corripiō, -ipere, -ipuī, -eptum *vt* to seize, carry off, get along quickly; *(speech)* to reprove, reproach, accuse; *(passion)* to seize upon, attack; *(time, words)* to cut short; **sē gradum corripere, sē viam corripere** hasten, rush

corrōborō, -āre, -āvī, -ātum *vt* to make strong, invigorate

corrōdō, -dere, -sī, -sum *vt* to nibble away

corrogō, -āre *vt* to gather by requesting

corrūgō, -āre *vt* to wrinkle

corrumpō, -umpere, -ūpī, -uptum *vt* to break up, ruin, waste; to mar, adulterate, falsify; *(person)* to corrupt, seduce, bribe

corruō, -ere, -ī *vi* to fall, collapse ▸ *vt* to overthrow, heap up

corruptē *adv* perversely; in a lax manner

corruptēla, -ae *f* corruption, bribery; seducer

corruptiō, -ōnis *f* bribing, seducing; corrupt state

corruptor, -ōris *m*, **corruptrīx, -rīcis** *f* corrupter, seducer

corruptus *ppp of* **corrumpō** ▸ *adj* spoiled, corrupt, bad

Corsus *adj* Corsican

cortex, -icis *m/f* bark, rind; cork

cortīna, -ae *f* kettle, cauldron; tripod of Apollo; (*fig*) vault, circle

corulus, -ī *f* hazel

Cōrus *see* **Caurus**

coruscō, -āre *vt* to butt; to shake, brandish ▸ *vi* to flutter, flash, quiver

coruscus *adj* tremulous, oscillating; shimmering, glittering

corvus, -ī *m* raven; (*MIL*) grapnel

Corybantēs, -ium *mpl priests of Cybele*

Corybantius *adj see* **Corybantēs**

cōrycus, -ī *m* punchball

corylētum, -ī *nt* hazel copse

corylus, -ī *f* hazel

corymbifer *m* Bacchus

corymbus, -ī *m* cluster (*esp of ivy berries*)

coryphaeus, -ī *m* leader

cōrytos, cōrytus, -ī *m* quiver

cōs, cōtis *f* hard rock, flint; grindstone

Cōs, Coī *f Aegean island (famous for wine and weaving)* ▸ *nt* Coan wine ▸ *ntpl* Coan clothes

cosmēta, -ae *m* master of the wardrobe

costa, -ae *f* rib; side, wall

costum, -ī *nt* an aromatic plant, perfume

cothurnātus *adj* buskined, tragic

cothurnus, -ī *m* buskin, hunting boot; tragedy, elevated style

cotīd- *see* **cottīd-**

cōtis *f see* **cōs**

cottabus, -ī *m game of throwing drops of wine*

cottana, -ōrum *ntpl Syrian figs*

cottīdiānō *adv* daily

cottīdiānus *adj* daily; everyday, ordinary

cottīdiē *adv* every day, daily

coturnīx, -īcis *f* quail

Cotyttia, -ōrum *ntpl festival of Thracian goddess Cotytto*

Cōus *adj* Coan

covinnārius, -ī *and* **-iī** *m* chariot fighter

covinnus, -ī *m* war chariot; coach

coxa, -ae, coxendīx, -īcis *f* hip

coxī *perf of* **coquō**

crābrō, -ōnis *m* hornet

crambē, -ēs *f* cabbage; ~ **repetīta** stale repetitions

Crantor, -oris *m Greek Academic philosopher*

crāpula, -ae *f* intoxication, hangover

crāpulārius *adj* for intoxication

crās *adv* tomorrow

crassē *adv* grossly, dimly

Crassiānus *adj see* **Crassus**

crassitūdō, -inis *f* thickness, density

crassus *adj* thick, gross, dense; (*fig*) dull, stupid

Crassus, -ī *m famous orator; wealthy politician, triumvir with Caesar and Pompey*

crāstinum, -ī *nt* the morrow

crāstinus *adj* of tomorrow; **diē crāstinī** tomorrow

crātēr, -is *m*, **crātēra, -ae** *f* bowl (*esp for mixing wine and water*); crater; *a constellation*

crātis, -is *f* wickerwork, hurdle; (*AGR*) harrow; (*MIL*) faggots for lining trenches; (*shield*) ribs; (*fig*) frame, joints

creātiō, -ōnis *f* election

creātor, -ōris *m*, **creātrīx, -rīcis** *f* creator, father, mother

creātus *m* (*with abl*) son of

crēber, -rī *adj* dense, thick, crowded; numerous, frequent; (*fig*) prolific, abundant

crēbrēscō, -ēscere, -uī *vi* to increase, become frequent

crēbritās, -ātis *f* frequency

crēbrō *adv* repeatedly

crēdibilis *adj* credible

crēdibiliter *adv see* **crēdibilis**

crēditor, -ōris *m* creditor

crēditum, -itī *nt* loan

crēdō, -ere, -idī, -itum *vt, vi* to entrust, lend; to trust, have confidence in; to believe; to think, suppose; **crēderēs** one would have thought

crēdulitās, -ātis *f* credulity

crēdulus *adj* credulous, trusting

cremō, -āre, -āvī, -ātum *vt* to burn, cremate

Cremōna, -ae *f town in N. Italy*

Cremōnēnsis *adj see* **Cremōna**

cremor, -ōris *m* juice, broth

creō, -āre, -āvī, -ātum *vt* to create, produce, beget; to elect (*to an office*); cause, occasion

creper, -ī *adj* dark; doubtful

crepida, -ae *f* sandal; **nē sūtor suprā crepidam** let the cobbler stick to his last

crepidātus *adj* wearing sandals

crepīdō, -inis *f* pedestal, base; bank, pier, dam

crepidula, -ae *f* small sandal

crepitāculum, -ī *nt* rattle

crepitō, -āre *vi* to rattle, chatter, rustle, creak

crepitus, -ūs *m* rattling, chattering, rustling, creaking

crepō, -āre, -uī, -itum *vi* to rattle, creak, snap (*fingers*) ▸ *vt* to make rattle, clap; to chatter about

crepundia, -ōrum *ntpl* rattle, babies' toys

crepusculum, -ī *nt* twilight, dusk; darkness

Crēs, -ētis *m* Cretan

crēscō, -scere, -vī, -tum *vi* to arise, appear, be born; to grow up, thrive, increase, multiply; to prosper, be promoted, rise in the world

Crēsius *adj* Cretan

Crēssa, -ae *f* Cretan

Crēta, -ae *f* Crete

crēta, -ae *f* chalk; good mark

Crētaeus, Crēticus, Crētis, -idis *adj see* **Crēta**

crētātus *adj* chalked; dressed in white

Crētē *see* **Crēta**

crēteus *adj* of chalk, of clay

crētiō, -ōnis *f* declaration of accepting an inheritance

crētōsus adj chalky, clayey

crētula, -ae f white clay for sealing

crētus ppp of **cernō** ▶ ppa of **crēscō** ▶ adj descended, born

Creūsa, -ae f wife of Jason; wife of Aeneas

crēvī perf of **cernō**; **crēscō**

crībrum, -ī nt sieve

crīmen, -inis nt accusation, charge, reproach; guilt, crime; cause of offence; **esse in crīmine** stand accused

crīminātiō, -ōnis f complaint, slander

crīminātor, -ōris m accuser

crīminō, -āre vt to accuse

crīminor, -ārī, -ātus dep to accuse, impeach; (things) to complain of, charge with

crīminōsē adv accusingly, slanderously

crīminōsus adj reproachful, slanderous

crīnālis adj for the hair, hair- (in cpds) ▶ nt hairpin

crīnis, -is m hair; (comet) tail

crīnītus adj long-haired; crested; **stēlla crīnīta** comet

crīspāns, -antis adj wrinkled

crīspō, -āre vt to curl, swing, wave

crīspus adj curled; curly-headed; wrinkled; tremulous

crista, -ae f cockscomb, crest; plume

cristātus adj crested, plumed

criticus, -ī m critic

croceus adj of saffron, yellow

crocinus adj yellow ▶ nt saffron oil

crōciō, -īre vi to croak

crocodīlus, -ī m crocodile

crocōtārius adj of saffron clothes

crocōtula, -ae f saffron dress

crocus, -ī m, **crocum, -ī** nt saffron; yellow

Croesus, -ī m king of Lydia (famed for wealth)

crotalistria, -ae f castanet dancer

crotalum, -ī nt rattle, castanet

cruciābilitās, -ātis f torment

cruciāmentum, -ī nt torture

cruciātus, -ūs m torture; instrument of torture; (fig) ruin, misfortune

cruciō, -āre, -āvī, -ātum vt to torture; to torment

crūdēlis adj hard-hearted, cruel

crūdēlitās, -ātis f cruelty, severity

crūdēliter adv see **crūdēlis**

crūdēscō, -ēscere, -uī vi to grow violent, grow worse

crūditās, -ātis f indigestion

crūdus adj bleeding; (food) raw, undigested; (person) dyspeptic; (leather) rawhide; (fruit) unripe; (age) immature, fresh; (voice) hoarse; (fig) unfeeling, cruel, merciless

cruentō, -āre vt to stain with blood, wound

cruentus adj bloody, gory; bloodthirsty, cruel; blood-red

crumēna, -ae f purse; money

crumilla, -ae f purse

cruor, -ōris m blood; bloodshed

cruppellāriī, -ōrum mpl mail-clad fighters

crūrifragius, -ī and -iī m one whose legs have been broken

crūs, -ūris nt leg, shin

crūsta, -ae f hard surface, crust; stucco, embossed or inlaid work

crūstulum, -ī nt small pastry

crūstum, -ī nt pastry

crux, -ucis f gallows, cross; (fig) torment; **abī in malam crucem** go and be hanged!

crypta, -ae f underground passage, grotto

cryptoporticus, -ūs f covered walk

crystallinus adj of crystal ▶ ntpl crystal vases

crystallum, -ī nt, **crystallus, -ī** m crystal

cubiculāris, cubiculārius adj of the bedroom ▶ m valet de chambre

cubiculum, -ī nt bedroom

cubīle, -is nt bed, couch; (animals) lair, nest; (fig) den

cubital, -ālis nt cushion

cubitālis adj a cubit long

cubitō, -āre vi to lie (in bed)

cubitum, -ī nt elbow; cubit

cubitus, -ūs m lying in bed

cubō, -āre, -uī, -itum vi to lie in bed; to recline at table; (places) to lie on a slope

cucullus, -ī m hood, cowl

cucūlus, -ī m cuckoo

cucumis, -eris m cucumber

cucurbita, -ae f gourd; cupping glass

cucurrī perf of **currō**

cūdō, -ere vt to beat, thresh; (metal) to forge; (money) to coin

cūiās, -tis pron of what country?, of what town?

cuicuimodī (gen of **quisquis** and **modus**) of whatever kind, whatever like

cūius pron (interrog) whose?; (rel) whose

culcita, -ae f mattress, pillow; eyepatch

cūleus see **culleus**

culex, -icis m/f gnat

culīna, -ae f kitchen; food

culleus, cūleus, -ī m leather bag for holding liquids; a fluid measure

culmen, -inis nt stalk; top, roof, summit; (fig) height, acme

culmus, -ī m stalk, straw

culpa, -ae f blame, fault; mischief; **in culpā sum, mea ~ est** I am at fault or to blame

culpātus adj blameworthy

culpitō, -āre vt to find fault with

culpō, -āre, -āvī, -ātum vt to blame, reproach

cultē adv in a refined manner

cultellus, -ī m small knife

culter, -rī m knife, razor

cultiō, -ōnis f cultivation

cultor, -ōris m cultivator, planter, farmer; inhabitant; supporter, upholder; worshipper

cultrīx, -īcis f inhabitant; (fig) nurse, fosterer

cultūra, -ae f cultivation, agriculture; (mind) care, culture; (person) courting

cultus¹ ppp of **colō** ▶ adj cultivated; (dress) well-dressed; (mind) polished, cultured ▶ ntpl cultivated land

cultus², **-ūs** *m* cultivation, care; (*mind*) training, culture; (*dress*) style, attire; (*way of life*) refinement, civilization; (*gods*) worship; (*men*) honouring

culullus, **-ī** *m* goblet

cūlus, **-ī** *m* buttocks

cum¹ *prep* (*with abl*) with; **cum decimō** tenfold; **cum eō quod**, **cum eō ut** with the proviso that; **cum prīmīs** especially; **cum māgnā calamitāte cīvitātis** to the great misfortune of the community; **cum perīculō suō** at one's own peril

cum² *conj* (*time*) when, whenever, while, as, after, since; (*cause*) since, as, seeing that; (*concession*) although; (*condition*) if; (*contrast*) while, whereas; **multī annī sunt cum in aere meō est** for many years now he has been in my debt; **aliquot sunt annī cum vōs dēlēgī** it is now some years since I chose you; **cum māximē** just when; just then, just now; **cum prīmum** as soon as; **cum ... tum** not only ... but also; both ... and

Cūmae, **-ārum** *fpl* town near Naples (*famous for its Sibyl*)

Cūmaeānum, **-ānī** *nt* Cicero's Cumaean residence

Cūmaeus, **-ānus** *adj see* **Cūmae**

cumba, **cymba**, **-ae** *f* boat, skiff

cumera, **-ae** *f* grain chest

cumīnum, **-ī** *nt* cumin

cumque, **quomque** *adv* -ever, -soever; at any time

cumulātē *adv* fully, abundantly

cumulātus *adj* increased; complete

cumulō, **-āre**, **-āvī**, **-ātum** *vt* to heap up; to amass, increase; to fill up, overload; (*fig*) to fill, overwhelm, crown, complete

cumulus, **-ī** *m* heap, mass; crowning addition, summit

cūnābula, **-ōrum** *ntpl* cradle

cūnae, **-ārum** *fpl* cradle

cunctābundus *adj* hesitant, dilatory

cunctāns, **-antis** *adj* dilatory, reluctant; sluggish, tough

cunctanter *adv* slowly

cunctātiō, **-ōnis** *f* delaying, hesitation

cunctātor, **-ōris** *m* loiterer; one given to cautious tactics (*esp Q Fabius Maximus*)

cunctor, **-ārī**, **-ātus** *vi* to linger, delay, hesitate; to move slowly

cūnctus *adj* the whole of; (*pl*) all together, all

cuneātim *adv* in the form of a wedge

cuneātus *adj* wedge-shaped

cuneus, **-ī** *m* wedge; (*MIL*) wedge-shaped formation of troops; (*theatre*) block of seats

cunīculus, **-ī** *m* rabbit; underground passage; (*MIL*) mine

cunque *see* **cumque**

cūpa, **-ae** *f* vat, tun

cupidē *adv* eagerly, passionately

Cupīdineus *adj see* **Cupīdō**

cupiditās, **-ātis** *f* desire, eagerness, enthusiasm; passion, lust; avarice, greed; ambition; partisanship

cupīdō, **-inis** *f* desire, eagerness; passion, lust; greed

Cupīdō, **-inis** *m* Cupid (*son of Venus*)

cupidus *adj* desirous, eager; fond, loving; passionate, lustful; greedy, ambitious; partial

cupiēns, **-entis** *pres p of* **cupiō** ▸ *adj* eager, desirous

cupienter *adv see* **cupiēns**

cupiō, **-ere**, **-īvī** *and* **-iī**, **-ītum** *vt* to wish, desire, long for; (*with dat*) to wish well

cupītor, **-ōris** *m* desirer

cupītus *ppp of* **cupiō**

cuppēdia¹, **-ae** *f* fondness for delicacies

cuppēdia², **-ōrum** *ntpl* delicacies

cuppēdinārius, **-ī** *m* confectioner

cuppēdō, **-inis** *f* longing, passion

cuppes, **-dis** *adj* fond of delicacies

cupressētum, **-ī** *nt* cypress grove

cupresseus *adj* of cypress wood

cupressifer, **-ī** *adj* cypress-bearing

cupressus, **-ī** *f* cypress

cūr *adv* why?; (*indirect*) why, the reason for

cūra, **-ae** *f* care, trouble, pains (bestowed); anxiety, concern, sorrow (felt); attention (to), charge (of), concern (for); (*MED*) treatment, cure; (*writing*) work; (*LAW*) trusteeship; (*poet*) love; (*person*) mistress, guardian; **~ est** I am anxious; **cūrae esse** be attended to, looked after

cūrābilis *adj* troublesome

cūralium, **-ī** *and* **-iī** *nt* red coral

cūrātē *adv* carefully

cūrātiō, **-ōnis** *f* charge, management; office; treatment, healing

cūrātor, **-ōris** *m* manager, overseer; (*LAW*) guardian

cūrātūra, **-ae** *f* dieting

cūrātus *adj* cared for; earnest, anxious

curculiō, **-ōnis** *m* weevil

curculiunculus, **-ī** *m* little weevil

Curēnsis *adj see* **Curēs**

Curēs, **-ium** *mpl* ancient Sabine town

Cūrētēs, **-um** *mpl* attendants of Jupiter in Crete

Cūrētis, **-idis** *adj* Cretan

cūria, **-ae** *f* earliest division of the Roman people; meeting-place of a curia; senate house; senate

cūriālis, **-is** *m* member of a curia

cūriātim *adv* by curiae

cūriātus *adj* of the curiae; **comitia cūriāta** earliest Roman assembly

cūriō¹, **-ōnis** *m* president of a curia; **~ māximus** head of all the curiae

cūriō², **-ōnis** *adj* emaciated

cūriōsē *adv* carefully; inquisitively

cūriōsitās, **-ātis** *f* curiosity

cūriōsus *adj* careful, thoughtful, painstaking; inquiring, inquisitive, officious; careworn

curis, **-ītis** *f* spear

cūrō, **-āre**, **-āvī**, **-ātum** *vt* to take care of, attend to; to bother about; (*with gerundive*) to

get something done; (*with infin*) to take the
trouble; (*with* ut) to see to it that; (*public life*)
to be in charge of, administer; (*MED*) to treat,
cure; (*money*) to pay, settle up; **aliud cūrā** never
mind; **corpus/cutem ~** take it easy; **prōdigia ~**
avert portents

curriculum, -ī *nt* running, race; course, lap;
(*fig*) career; **curriculō** at full speed

currō, -ere, cucurrī, cursum *vi* to run;
to hasten, fly ▶ *vt* to run through, traverse;
currentem incitāre spur a willing horse

currus, -ūs *m* car, chariot; triumph; team of
horses; ploughwheels

cursim *adv* quickly, at the double

cursitō, -āre *vi* to run about, fly hither and
thither

cursō, -āre *vi* to run about

cursor, -ōris *m* runner, racer; courier

cursūra, -ae *f* running

cursus, -ūs *m* running, speed; passage,
journey; course, direction; (*things*) movement,
flow; (*fig*) rapidity, flow, progress; **~ honōrum**
succession of magistracies; **~ rērum** course of
events; **cursum tenēre** keep on one's course;
cursū at a run; **māgnō cursū** at full speed

curtō, -āre *vt* to shorten

curtus *adj* short, broken off; incomplete

curūlis *adj* official, curule; **aedīlis ~** patrician
aedile; **sella ~** magistrates' chair; **equī ~** *horses
provided for the games by the state*

curvāmen, -inis *nt* bend

curvātūra, -ae *f* curve

curvō, -āre, -āvī, -ātum *vt* to curve, bend,
arch; (*fig*) to move

curvus *adj* bent, curved, crooked; (*person*) aged;
(*fig*) wrong

cuspis, -dis *f* point; spear, javelin, trident, sting

custōdēla, -ae *f* care, guard

custōdia, -ae *f* watch, guard, care; (*person*)
sentry, guard; (*place*) sentry's post, guardhouse;
custody, confinement, prison; **lībera ~**
confinement in one's own house

custōdiō, -īre, -īvī and **-iī, -ītum** *vt* to guard,
defend; to hold in custody, keep watch on; to
keep, preserve, observe

custōs, -ōdis *m/f* guard, bodyguard, protector,
protectress; jailer, warder; (*MIL*) sentry, spy;
container

cutīcula, -ae *f* skin

cutis, -is *f* skin; **cutem cūrāre** take it easy

cyathissō, -āre *vi* to serve wine

cyathus, -ī *m* wine ladle; (*measure*) one-twelfth
of a pint

cybaea, -ae *f* kind of merchant ship

Cybēbē, Cybelē, -ēs *f* Phrygian mother-goddess,
Magna Mater

Cybelēius *adj see* **Cybēbē**

Cyclades, -um *fpl group of Aegean islands*

cyclas, -adis *f* formal dress with a border

cyclicus *adj* of the traditional epic stories

Cyclōpius *adj see* **Cyclōps**

Cyclōps, -is *m* one-eyed giant (*esp Polyphemus*)

cycnēus *adj* of a swan, swan's

cycnus, -ī *m* swan

Cydōnius *adj* Cretan ▶ *ntpl* quinces

cygnus *see* **cycnus**

cylindrus, -ī *m* cylinder; roller

Cyllēnē, -ēs and **-ae** *f* mountain in Arcadia

Cyllēnēus, Cyllēnis, Cyllēnius *adj see*
Cyllēnē

Cyllēnius, -ī *m* Mercury

cymba *see* **cumba**

cymbalum, -ī *nt* cymbal

cymbium, -ī and **-iī** *nt* cup

Cynicē *adv* like the Cynics

Cynicus, -ī *m* a Cynic philosopher (*esp Diogenes*)
▶ *adj* Cynic

cynocephalus, -ī *m* dog-headed ape

Cynosūra, -ae *f* (constellation of) Ursa Minor

Cynosūris, -idis *adj see* **Cynosūra**

Cynthia, -iae *f* Diana

Cynthius, -ī *m* Apollo

Cynthus, -ī *m* hill in Delos (*birthplace of Apollo
and Diana*)

cyparissus, -ī *f* cypress

Cypris, -idis *f* Venus

Cyprius *adj* Cyprian; copper

Cyprus, -ī *f* (island of) Cyprus (*famed for its
copper and the worship of Venus*)

Cyrēnaeī, Cyrēnaicī *mpl followers of Aristippus*

Cyrēnaeus, Cyrēnaicus, Cyrēnēnsis *adj
see* **Cyrēnē**

Cyrēnē, -ēs *f,* **Cyrēnae, -ārum** *fpl town and
province of N. Africa*

Cyrnēus *adj* Corsican

Cȳrus, -ī *m* Persian king

Cytaeis, -idis *f* Medea

Cythēra, -ae *f* island S. of Greece (*famed for its
worship of Venus*)

**Cytherēa, -ēae, Cytherēia, -ēiae,
Cytherēis, -ēidis** *f* Venus

Cytherēus, Cythēriacus *adj* Cytherean; of
Venus

cytisus, -ī *m/f* cytisus (*a kind of clover*)

Cyzicēnus *adj see* **Cyzicum**

Cyzicum, -ī *nt,* **Cyzicus, -ī, Cyzicos, -ī** *f town
on Sea of Marmora*

d

Dācī, -ōrum mpl Dacians (a people on the lower Danube)

Dācia, -iae f the country of the Dacians (now Romania)

Dācicus, -icī m gold coin of Domitian's reign

dactylicus adj dactylic

dactylus, -ī m dactyl

Daedalēus adj see **Daedalus**

Daedalus, -ī m mythical Athenian craftsman and inventor

daedalus adj artistic, skilful in creating; skilfully made, variegated

Dalmatae, -ārum mpl Dalmatians (a people on the East coast of the Adriatic)

Dalmatia, -iae f Dalmatia

Dalmaticus adj see **Dalmatia**

dāma, -ae f deer; venison

Damascēnus adj see **Damascus**

Damascus, -ī f Damascus

damma f see **dāma**

damnātiō, -ōnis f condemnation

damnātōrius adj condemnatory

damnātus adj criminal; miserable

damnificus adj pernicious

damnō, -āre, -āvī, -ātum vt to condemn, sentence; to procure the conviction of; (heirs) to oblige; to censure; **capitis/capite damnāre** condemn to death; **māiestātis damnāre, dē māiestāte damnāre** condemn for treason; **vōtī damnāre** oblige to fulfil a vow

damnōsē adv ruinously

damnōsus adj harmful, ruinous; spendthrift; wronged

damnum, -ī nt loss, harm, damage; (LAW) fine, damages; ~ **facere** suffer loss

Danaē, -ēs f mother of Perseus

Danaēius adj see **Danaē**

Danaī, -ōrum and **-um** mpl the Greeks

Danaides, -idum fpl daughters of Danaus

Danaus¹, -ī m king of Argos and father of 50 daughters

Danaus² adj Greek

danista, -ae m moneylender

danisticus adj moneylending

danō see **dō**

Dānuvius, -ī m upper Danube

Daphnē, -ēs f nymph changed into a laurel tree

Daphnis, -idis (acc **-im** and **-in**) m mythical Sicilian shepherd

dapinō, -āre vt to serve (food)

daps, dapis f religious feast; meal, banquet

dapsilis adj sumptuous, abundant

Dardania, -iae f Troy

Dardanidēs, -idae m Trojan (esp Aeneas)

Dardanus¹, -ī m son of Jupiter and ancestor of Trojan kings

Dardanus², Dardanius, Dardanis, -idis adj Trojan

Darēus, -ī m Persian king

datārius adj to give away

datātim adv passing from one to the other

datiō, -ōnis f right to give away; (laws) making

datō, -āre vt to be in the habit of giving

dator, -ōris m giver; (sport) bowler

Daulias, -adis adj see **Daulis**

Daulis, -dis f town in central Greece (noted for the story of Procne and Philomela)

Daunias, -iadis f Apulia

Daunius adj Rutulian; Italian

Daunus, -ī m legendary king of Apulia (ancestor of Turnus)

dē prep (with abl) (movement) down from, from; (origin) from, of, out of; (time) immediately after, in; (thought, talk, action) about, concerning; (reason) for, because of; (imitation) after, in accordance with; **dē industriā** on purpose; **dē integrō** afresh; **dē nocte** during the night; **diem dē diē** from day to day

dea, -ae f goddess

dealbō, -āre vt to whitewash, plaster

deambulātiō, -ōnis f walk

deambulō, -āre, -āvī, -ātum vi to go for a walk

deamō, -āre, -āvī, -ātum vt to be in love with; to be much obliged to

dearmātus adj disarmed

deartuō, -āre, -āvī, -ātum vt to dismember, ruin

deasciō, -āre vt to smooth with an axe; (fig) to cheat

dēbacchor, -ārī, -ātus vi to rage furiously

dēbellātor, -ōris m conqueror

dēbellō, -āre, -āvī, -ātum vi to bring a war to an end ▶ vt to subdue; to fight out

dēbeō, -ēre, -uī, -itum vt to owe; (with infin) to be bound, ought, should, must; to have to thank for, be indebted for; (pass) to be destined

dēbilis adj frail, weak

dēbilitās, -ātis f weakness, infirmity

dēbilitātiō, -ōnis f weakening

dēbilitō, -āre, -āvī, -ātum vt to cripple, disable; (fig) to paralyse, unnerve

dēbitiō, -ōnis f owing

dēbitor, -ōris m debtor

dēbitum, -ī nt debt

dēblaterō, -āre vt to blab

dēcantō, **-āre**, **-āvī**, **-ātum** vt to keep on repeating ▶ vi to stop singing

dēcēdō, **-ēdere**, **-essī**, **-essum** vi to withdraw, depart; to retire from a province (after term of office); to abate, cease, die; (rights) to give up, forgo; (fig) to go wrong, swerve (from duty); **viā dēcēdere** get out of the way

decem num ten

December, **-ris** adj of December ▶ m December

decempeda, **-ae** f ten-foot rule

decempedātor, **-ōris** m surveyor

decemplex, **-icis** adj tenfold

decemprīmī, **-ōrum** mpl civic chiefs of Italian towns

decemscalmus adj ten-oared

decemvirālis adj of the decemviri

decemvirātus, **-ūs** m office of decemvir

decemvirī, **-ōrum** and **-um** mpl commission of ten men (for public or religious duties)

decennis adj ten years'

decēns, **-entis** adj seemly, proper; comely, handsome

decenter adv with propriety

decentia, **-ae** f comeliness

deceptus ppp of **dēcipiō**

dēcernō, **-ernere**, **-rēvī**, **-rētum** vt to decide, determine; to decree; to fight it out, decide the issue

dēcerpō, **-ere**, **-sī**, **-tum** vt to pluck off, gather; (fig) to derive, enjoy

dēcertātiō, **-ōnis** f deciding the issue

dēcertō, **-āre**, **-āvī**, **-ātum** vi to fight it out, decide the issue

dēcessiō, **-ōnis** f departure; retirement (from a province); deduction, disappearance

dēcessor, **-ōris** m retiring magistrate

dēcessus, **-ūs** m retirement (from a province); death; (tide) ebbing

decet, **-ēre**, **-uit** vt, vi it becomes, suits; it is right, proper

dēcidō, **-ere**, **-ī** vi to fall down, fall off; to die; (fig) to fail, come down

dēcīdō, **-dere**, **-dī**, **-sum** vt to cut off; to settle, put an end to

deciēns, **deciēs** adv ten times

decimus, **decumus** adj tenth; **cum decimō** tenfold; **decimum** for the tenth time

dēcipiō, **-ipere**, **-ēpī**, **-eptum** vt to ensnare; to deceive, beguile, disappoint

dēcīsiō, **-ōnis** f settlement

dēcīsus ppp of **dēcīdō**

Decius¹, **-ī** m Roman plebeian name (esp P Decius Mus, father and son, who devoted their lives in battle)

Decius², **Deciānus** adj see **Decius¹**

dēclāmātiō, **-ōnis** f loud talking; rhetorical exercise on a given theme

dēclāmātor, **-ōris** m apprentice in public speaking

dēclāmātōrius adj rhetorical

dēclāmitō, **-āre** vi to practise rhetoric; to bluster ▶ vt to practise pleading

dēclāmō, **-āre**, **-āvī**, **-ātum** vi to practise public speaking, declaim; to bluster

dēclārātiō, **-ōnis** f expression, making known

dēclārō, **-āre**, **-āvī**, **-ātum** vt to make known; to proclaim, announce, reveal, express, demonstrate

dēclīnātiō, **-ōnis** f swerving; avoidance; (RHET) digression; (GRAM) inflection

dēclīnō, **-āre**, **-āvī**, **-ātum** vt to turn aside, deflect; (eyes) to close; to evade, shun ▶ vi to turn aside, swerve; to digress

declive nt slope, decline

dēclīvis adj sloping, steep, downhill

dēclīvitās, **-ātis** f sloping ground

dēcocta, **-ae** f a cold drink

dēcoctor, **-ōris** m bankrupt

dēcoctus ppp of **dēcoquō** ▶ adj (style) ripe, elaborated

dēcolō, **-āre** vi to run out; (fig) to fail

dēcolor, **-ōris** adj discoloured, faded; **~ aetās** a degenerate age

dēcolōrātiō, **-ōnis** f discolouring

dēcolōrō, **-āre**, **-āvī**, **-ātum** vt to discolour, deface

dēcoquō, **-quere**, **-xī**, **-ctum** vt to boil down; to cook ▶ vi to go bankrupt

decor, **-ōris** m comeliness, ornament, beauty

decōrē adv becomingly, beautifully

decorō, **-āre**, **-āvī**, **-ātum** vt to adorn, embellish; (fig) to distinguish, honour

decōrum, **-ī** nt propriety

decōrus adj becoming, proper; beautiful, noble; adorned

dēcrepitus adj decrepit

dēcrēscō, **-scere**, **-vī**, **-tum** vi to decrease, wane, wear away; to disappear

dēcrētum, **-ī** nt decree, resolution; (PHILOS) doctrine

dēcrētus ppp of **dēcernō**

dēcrēvī perf **dēcernō**; **dēcrēscō**

decuma, **-ae** f tithe; provincial land tax; largesse

decumāna, **-ae** f wife of a tithe-collector

decumānus adj paying tithes; (MIL) of the 10th cohort or legion ▶ m collector of tithes; **decumānī decumānōrum** mpl men of the 10th legion; **porta decumāna** main gate of a Roman camp

decumātēs, **-ium** adj, pl subject to tithes

dēcumbō, **-mbere**, **-buī** vi to lie down; to recline at table; to fall (in fight)

decumus see **decimus**

decuria, **-ae** f group of ten; panel of judges; social club

decuriātiō, **-ōnis** f, **decuriātus**, **-ūs** m dividing into decuriae

decuriō¹, **-āre**, **-āvī**, **-ātum** vt to divide into decuriae or groups

decuriō², **-ōnis** m head of a decuria; (MIL) cavalry officer; senator of a provincial town or colony

dēcurrō, -rrere, -currī and **-rrī, -rsum** vt, vi to run down, hurry, flow, sail down; to traverse; (MIL) to parade, charge; (time) to pass through; (fig) to have recourse to

dēcursiō, -ōnis f military manoeuvre

dēcursus¹ ppp of **dēcurrō**

dēcursus², -ūs m descent, downrush; (MIL) manoeuvre, attack; (time) career

dēcurtātus adj mutilated

decus, -oris nt ornament, glory, beauty; honour, virtue; (pl) heroic deeds

dēcussō, -āre vt to divide crosswise

dēcutiō, -tere, -ssī, -ssum vt to strike down, shake off

dēdecet, -ēre, -uit vt it is unbecoming to, is a disgrace to

dēdecorō, -āre vt to disgrace

dēdecōrus adj dishonourable

dēdecus, -oris nt disgrace, shame; vice, crime

dedī perf of **dō**

dēdicātiō, -ōnis f consecration

dēdicō, -āre, -āvī, -ātum vt to consecrate, dedicate; to declare (property in a census return)

dēdidī perf of **dēdō**

dēdignor, -ārī, -ātus vt to scorn, reject

dēdiscō, -scere, -dicī vt to unlearn, forget

dēditīcius, -ī and **-iī** m one who has capitulated

dēditiō, -ōnis f surrender, capitulation

dēditus ppp of **dēdō** ▶ adj addicted, devoted; **dēditā operā** intentionally

dēdō, -ere, -idī, -itum vt to give up, yield, surrender; to devote

dēdoceō, -ēre vt to teach not to

dēdoleō, -ēre, -uī vi to cease grieving

dēdūcō, -ūcere, -ūxī, -uctum vt to bring down, lead away, deflect; (MIL) to lead, withdraw; (bride) to bring home; (colony) to settle; (hair) to comb out; (important person) to escort; (LAW) to evict, bring to trial; (money) to subtract; (sail) to unfurl; (ship) to launch; (thread) to spin out; (writing) to compose; (fig) to bring, reduce, divert, derive

dēductiō, -ōnis f leading off; settling a colony; reduction; eviction; inference

dēductor, -ōris m escort

dēductus ppp of **dēdūcō** ▶ adj finely spun

dēerrō, -āre, -āvī, -ātum vi to go astray

deesse infin of **dēsum**

dēfaecō, -āre, -āvī, -ātum vt to clean; (fig) to make clear, set at ease

dēfatīgātiō, -ōnis f tiring out; weariness

dēfatīgō, -āre, -āvī, -ātum vt to tire out, exhaust

dēfatīscor etc see **dēfetīscor**

dēfectiō, -ōnis f desertion; failure, faintness; (ASTR) eclipse

dēfector, -ōris m deserter, rebel

dēfectus¹ ppp of **dēficiō** ▶ adj weak, failing

dēfectus², -ūs m failure; eclipse

dēfendō, -dere, -dī, -sum vt to avert, repel; to defend, protect; (LAW) to speak in defence, urge, maintain; (THEAT) to play (a part); **crīmen dēfendere** answer an accusation

dēfēnsiō, -ōnis f defence, speech in defence

dēfēnsitō, -āre vt to defend often

dēfēnsō, -āre vt to defend

dēfēnsor, -ōris m averter; defender, protector, guard

dēferō, -ferre, -tulī, -lātum vt to bring down, bring, carry; to bear away; (power, honour) to offer, confer; (information) to report; (LAW) to inform against, indict; to recommend (for public services); **ad cōnsilium dēferre** take into consideration

dēfervēscō, -vēscere, -vī and **-buī** vi to cool down, calm down

dēfessus adj tired, exhausted

dēfetīgō etc see **dēfatīgō**

dēfetīscor, -tīscī, -ssus vi to grow weary

dēficiō, -icere, -ēcī, -ectum vt, vi to desert, forsake, fail; to be lacking, run short, cease; (ASTR) to be eclipsed; **animō dēficere** lose heart

dēfīgō, -gere, -xī, -xum vt to fix firmly; to drive in, thrust; (eyes, mind) to concentrate; (fig) to stupefy, astound; (magic) to bewitch

dēfingō, -ere vt to make, portray

dēfīniō, -īre, -īvī, -ītum vt to mark the limit of, limit; to define, prescribe; to restrict; to terminate

dēfīnītē adv precisely

dēfīnītiō, -ōnis f limiting, prescribing, definition

dēfīnītīvus adj explanatory

dēfīnītus adj precise

dēfīō, -ierī vi to fail

dēflagrātiō, -ōnis f conflagration

dēflagrō, -āre, -āvī, -ātum vi to be burned down, perish; to cool down, abate ▶ vt to burn down

dēflectō, -ctere, -xī, -xum vt to bend down, turn aside; (fig) to pervert ▶ vi to turn aside, deviate

dēfleō, -ēre, -ēvī, -ētum vt to lament bitterly, bewail ▶ vi to weep bitterly

dēflexus ppp of **dēflectō**

dēflōrēscō, -ēscere, -uī vi to shed blooms; (fig) to fade

dēfluō, -ere, -xī, -xum vi to flow down, float down; to fall, drop, droop; (fig) to come from, be derived; to flow past; (fig) to pass away, fail

dēfodiō, -ōdere, -ōdī, -ossum vt to dig, dig out; to bury; (fig) to hide away

dēfore fut infin of **dēsum**

dēfōrmis adj misshapen, disfigured, ugly; shapeless; (fig) disgraceful, disgusting

dēfōrmitās, -ātis f deformity, hideousness; baseness

dēfōrmō, -āre, -āvī, -ātum vt to form, sketch; to deform, disfigure; to describe; to mar, disgrace

dēfossus ppp of **dēfodiō**

dēfraudō, -āre vt to cheat, defraud; **genium dēfraudāre** deny oneself

dēfrēnātus adj unbridled

dēfricō, -āre, -uī, -ātum and **-tum** vt to rub down; (fig) to satirize

dēfringō, -ingere, -ēgī, -āctum vt to break off, break down

dēfrūdō etc see **dēfraudō**

dēfrutum, -ī nt new wine boiled down

dēfugiō, -ugere, -ūgī vt to run away from, shirk ▶ vi to flee

dēfuī perf of **dēsum**

dēfūnctus ppa of **dēfungor** ▶ adj discharged; dead

dēfundō, -undere, -ūdī, -ūsum vt to pour out

dēfungor, -ungī, -ūnctus vi (with abl) to discharge, have done with; to die

dēfutūrus fut p of **dēsum**

dēgener, -is adj degenerate, unworthy, base

dēgenerātum, -ātī nt degenerate character

dēgenerō, -āre, -āvī, -ātum vi to degenerate, deteriorate ▶ vt to disgrace

dēgerō, -ere vt to carry off

dēgō, -ere, -ī vt (time) to pass, spend; (war) to wage ▶ vi to live

dēgrandinat it is hailing heavily

dēgravō, -āre vt to weigh down, overpower

dēgredior, -dī, -ssus vi to march down, descend, dismount

dēgrunniō, -īre vi to grunt hard

dēgustō, -āre vt to taste, touch; (fig) to try, experience

dehinc adv from here; from now, henceforth; then, next

dehīscō, -ere vi to gape, yawn

dehonestāmentum, -ī nt disfigurement

dehonestō, -āre vt to disgrace

dehortor, -ārī, -ātus vt to dissuade, discourage

Dēianīra, -ae f wife of Hercules

dēiciō, -icere, -iēcī, -iectum vt to throw down, hurl, fell; to overthrow, kill; (eyes) to lower, avert; (LAW) to evict; (MIL) to dislodge; (ship) to drive off its course; (hopes, honours) to foil, disappoint

dēiectiō, -ōnis f eviction

dēiectus¹ ppp of **dēiciō** ▶ adj low-lying; disheartened

dēiectus², -ūs m felling; steep slope

dēierō, -āre, -āvī, -ātum vi to swear solemnly

dein etc see **deinde**

deinceps adv successively, in order

deinde, dein adv from there, next; then, thereafter; next in order

Dēiotarus, -ī m king of Galatia (defended by Cicero)

Dēiphobus, -ī m son of Priam (second husband of Helen)

dēiungō, -ere vt to sever

dēiuvō, -āre vt to fail to help

dej- etc see **dei-**

dēlābor, -bī, -psus vi to fall down, fly down, sink; (fig) to come down, fall into

dēlacerō, -āre vt to tear to pieces

dēlāmentor, -ārī vt to mourn bitterly for

dēlāpsus ppa of **dēlābor**

dēlassō, -āre vt to tire out

dēlātiō, -ōnis f accusing, informing

dēlātor, -ōris m informer, denouncer

dēlectābilis adj enjoyable

dēlectāmentum, -ī nt amusement

dēlectātiō, -ōnis f delight

dēlectō, -āre vt to charm, delight, amuse

dēlēctus¹ ppp of **dēligō**

dēlēctus², -ūs m choice; see also **dīlēctus²**

dēlēgātiō, -ōnis f assignment

dēlēgī perf of **dēligō**

dēlēgō, -āre, -āvī, -ātum vt to assign, transfer, make over; to ascribe

dēlēnificus adj charming

dēlēnimentum, -ī nt solace, allurement

dēlēniō, -īre, -īvī, -ītum vt to soothe, solace; to seduce, win over

dēlēnītor, -ōris m cajoler

dēleō, -ēre, -ēvī, -ētum vt to destroy, annihilate; to efface, blot out

Dēlia, -ae f Diana

Dēliacus adj of Delos

dēlīberābundus adj deliberating

dēlīberātiō, -ōnis f deliberating, consideration

dēlīberātīvus adj deliberative

dēlīberātor, -ōris m consulter

dēlīberātus adj determined

dēlīberō, -āre, -āvī, -ātum vt, vi to consider, deliberate, consult; to resolve, determine; **dēlīberārī potest** it is in doubt

dēlībō, -āre, -āvī, -ātum vt to taste, sip; to pick, gather; to detract from, mar

dēlībrō, -āre vt to strip the bark off

dēlibuō, -uere, -uī, -ūtum vt to smear, steep

dēlicātē adv luxuriously

dēlicātus adj delightful; tender, soft; voluptuous, spoiled, effeminate; fastidious

dēliciae, -ārum fpl delight, pleasure; whimsicalities, sport; (person) sweetheart, darling

dēliciolae, -ārum fpl darling

dēlicium, -ī and **-iī** nt favourite

dēlicō, -āre vt to explain

dēlictum, -ī nt offence, wrong

dēlicuus adj lacking

dēligō, -āre, -āvī, -ātum vt to tie up, make fast

dēligō, -igere, -ēgī, -ēctum vt to select, gather; to set aside

dēlingō, -ere vt to have a lick of

dēlīni- etc see **dēlēni-**

dēlinquō, -inquere, -īquī, -ictum vi to fail, offend, do wrong

dēliquēscō, -quēscere, -cuī vi to melt away; (fig) to pine away

dēliquiō, -ōnis f lack

dēlīrāmentum, -ī nt nonsense

dēlīrātiō, -ōnis f dotage

dēlīrō, -āre *vi* to be crazy, drivel
dēlīrus *adj* crazy
dēlitēscō, -ēscere, -uī *vi* to hide away, lurk; (*fig*) to skulk, take shelter under
dēlītigō, -āre *vi* to scold
Dēlius, -iacus *adj see* **Dēlos**
Delmatae *see* **Dalmatae**
Dēlos, -ī *f* sacred Aegean island (*birthplace of Apollo and Diana*)
Delphī, -ōrum *mpl* town in central Greece (*famous for its oracle of Apollo*); the Delphians
Delphicus *adj see* **Delphī**
delphīnus, -ī *m* dolphin
Deltōton, -ī *nt* (*constellation*) Triangulum
dēlubrum, -ī *nt* sanctuary, temple
dēluctō, -āre, dēluctor, -ārī *vi* to wrestle
dēlūdificō, -āre *vt* to make fun of
dēlūdō, -dere, -sī, -sum *vt* to dupe, delude
dēlumbis *adj* feeble
dēlumbō, -āre *vt* to enervate
dēmadēscō, -ēscere, -uī *vi* to be drenched
dēmandō, -āre *vt* to entrust, commit
dēmarchus, -ī *m* demarch (*chief of a village in Attica*)
dēmēns, -entis *adj* mad, foolish
dēmēnsum, -ī *nt* ration
dēmēnsus *ppa of* **dēmētior**
dēmenter *adv see* **dēmēns**
dēmentia, -ae *f* madness, folly
dēmentiō, -īre *vi* to rave
dēmereō, -ēre, -uī, -itum, dēmereor, -ērī *vt* to earn, deserve; to do a service to
dēmergō, -gere, -sī, -sum *vt* to submerge, plunge, sink; (*fig*) to overwhelm
dēmessus *ppp of* **dēmetō**
dēmētior, -tīrī, -nsus *vt* to measure out
dēmetō, -tere, -ssuī, -ssum *vt* to reap, harvest; to cut off
dēmigrātiō, -ōnis *f* emigration
dēmigrō, -āre *vi* to move, emigrate
dēminuō, -uere, -uī, -ūtum *vt* to make smaller, lessen, detract from; **capite dēminuere** deprive of citizenship
dēminūtiō, -ōnis *f* decrease, lessening; (*LAW*) right to transfer property; **capitis ~** loss of political rights
dēmīror, -ārī, -ātus *vt* to marvel at, wonder
dēmissē *adv* modestly, meanly
dēmissīcius *adj* flowing
dēmissiō, -ōnis *f* letting down; (*fig*) dejection
dēmissus *ppp of* **dēmittō** ▸ *adj* low-lying; drooping; humble, unassuming; dejected; (*origin*) descended
dēmītigō, -āre *vt* to make milder
dēmittō, -ittere, -īsī, -issum *vt* to let down, lower, sink; to send down, plunge; (*beard*) to grow; (*ship*) to bring to land; (*troops*) to move down; (*fig*) to cast down, dishearten, reduce, impress; **sē dēmittere** stoop; descend; be disheartened
dēmiūrgus, -ī *m* chief magistrate in a Greek state

dēmō, -ere, -psī, -ptum *vt* to take away, subtract
Dēmocriticus, Dēmocritius, Dēmocritēus *adj see* **Dēmocritus**
Dēmocritus, -ī *m* Greek philosopher (*author of the atomic theory*)
dēmōlior, -īrī *vt* to pull down, destroy
dēmōlītiō, -ōnis *f* pulling down
dēmōnstrātiō, -ōnis *f* pointing out, explanation
dēmōnstrātīvus *adj* (*RHET*) for display
dēmōnstrātor, -ōris *m* indicator
dēmōnstrō, -āre, -āvī, -ātum *vt* to point out; to explain, represent, prove
dēmorior, -ī, -tuus *vi* to die, pass away ▸ *vt* to be in love with
dēmoror, -ārī, -ātus *vi* to wait ▸ *vt* to detain, delay
dēmortuus *ppa of* **dēmorior**
Dēmosthenēs, -is *m* greatest Athenian orator
dēmoveō, -ovēre, -ōvī, -ōtum *vt* to remove, turn aside, dislodge
dēmpsī *perf of* **dēmō**
dēmptus *ppp of* **dēmō**
dēmūgītus *adj* filled with lowing
dēmulceō, -cēre, -sī *vt* to stroke
dēmum *adv* (*time*) at last, not till; (*emphasis*) just, precisely; **ibi ~** just there; **modo ~** only now; **nunc ~** now at last; **post ~** not till after; **tum ~** only then
dēmurmurō, -āre *vt* to mumble through
dēmūtātiō, -ōnis *f* change
dēmūtō, -āre *vt* to change, make worse ▸ *vi* to change one's mind
dēnārius, -ī and -iī *m* Roman silver coin
dēnārrō, -āre *vt* to relate fully
dēnāsō, -āre *vt* to take the nose off
dēnatō, -āre *vi* to swim down
dēnegō, -āre, -āvī, ātum *vt* to deny, refuse, reject ▸ *vi* to say no
dēnī, -ōrum *adj* ten each, in tens; ten; tenth
dēnicālis *adj* for purifying after a death
dēnique *adv* at last, finally; (*enumerating*) lastly, next; (*summing up*) in short, briefly; (*emphasis*) just, precisely
dēnōminō, -āre *vt* to designate
dēnōrmō, -āre *vt* to make irregular
dēnotō, -āre, -āvī, -ātum *vt* to point out, specify; to observe
dēns, dentis *m* tooth; ivory; prong, fluke
dēnsē *adv* repeatedly
dēnsō, -āre, -āvī, -ātum, dēnseō, -ēre *vt* to thicken; (*ranks*) to close
dēnsus *adj* thick, dense, close; frequent; (*style*) concise
dentālia, -ium *ntpl* ploughbeam
dentātus *adj* toothed; (*paper*) polished
dentiō, -īre *vi* to cut one's teeth; (*teeth*) to grow
dēnūbō, -bere, -psī, -ptum *vi* to marry, marry beneath one
dēnūdō, -āre, -āvī, -ātum *vt* to bare, strip; (*fig*) to disclose

dēnūntiātiō, -ōnis f intimation, warning
dēnūntiō, -āre, -āvī, -ātum vt to intimate, give notice of, declare; to threaten, warn; (LAW) to summon as witness
dēnuō adv afresh, again, once more
deonerō, -āre vt to unload
deorsum, deorsus adv downwards
deōsculor, -ārī vt to kiss warmly
dēpacīscor etc see **dēpecīscor**
dēpāctus adj driven in firmly
dēpāscō, -scere, -vī, -stum, dēpāscor, dēpāscī vt to feed on, eat up; (fig) to devour, destroy, prune away
dēpecīscor, -īscī, -tus vt to bargain for, agree about
dēpectō, -ctere, -xum vt to comb; (comedy) to flog
dēpectus ppa of **dēpecīscor**
dēpecūlātor, -ōris m embezzler
dēpecūlor, -ārī, -ātus vt to plunder
dēpellō, -ellere, -ulī, -ulsum vt to expel, remove, cast down; (MIL) to dislodge; (infants) to wean; (fig) to deter, avert
dēpendeō, -ēre vi to hang down, hang from; to depend on; to be derived
dēpendō, -endere, -endī, -ēnsum vt to weigh, pay up
dēperdō, -ere, -idī, -itum vt to lose completely, destroy, ruin
dēpereō, -īre, -iī vi to perish, be completely destroyed; to be undone ▶ vt to be hopelessly in love with
dēpexus ppp of **dēpectō**
dēpingō, -ingere, -inxī, -ictum vt to paint; (fig) to portray, describe
dēplangō, -gere, -xī vt to bewail frantically
dēplexus adj grasping
dēplōrābundus adj weeping bitterly
dēplōrō, -āre, -āvī, -ātum vi to weep bitterly ▶ vt to bewail bitterly, mourn; to despair of
dēpluit, -ere vi to rain down
dēpōnō, -ōnere, -osuī, -ositum vt to lay down; to set aside, put away, get rid of; to wager; to deposit, entrust, commit to the care of; (fig) to give up
dēpopulātiō, -ōnis f ravaging
dēpopulātor, -ōris m marauder
dēpopulor, -ārī, -ātus, dēpopulō, -āre vt to ravage, devastate; (fig) to waste, destroy
dēportō, -āre, -āvī, -ātum vt to carry down, carry off; to bring home (from a province); (LAW) to banish for life; (fig) to win
dēposcō, -scere, -poscī vt to demand, require, claim
dēpositum, -ī nt trust, deposit
dēpositus ppp of **dēpōnō** ▶ adj dying, dead, despaired of
dēprāvātē adv perversely
dēprāvātiō, -ōnis f distorting
dēprāvō, -āre, -āvī, -ātum vt to distort; (fig) to pervert, corrupt
dēprecābundus adj imploring

dēprecātiō, -ōnis f averting by prayer; imprecation, invocation; plea for indulgence
dēprecātor, -ōris m intercessor
dēprecor, -ārī, -ātus vt to avert (by prayer); deprecate, intercede for
dēprehendō, dēprendō, -endere, -endī, -ēnsum vt to catch, intercept; to overtake, surprise; to catch in the act, detect; (fig) to perceive, discover
dēprehēnsiō, -ōnis f detection
dēprehēnsus, dēprēnsus ppp of **dēprehendō**
dēpressī perf of **dēprimō**
dēpressus ppp of **dēprimō** ▶ adj low
dēprimō, -imere, -essī, -essum vt to press down, weigh down; to dig deep; (ship) to sink; (fig) to suppress, keep down
dēproelior, -ārī vi to fight it out
dēprōmō, -ere, psī, -ptum vt to fetch, bring out, produce
dēproperō, -āre vi to hurry up ▶ vt to hurry and make
depsō, -ere vt to knead
dēpudet, -ēre, -uit v impers not to be ashamed
dēpūgis adj thin-buttocked
dēpugnō, -āre, -āvī, -ātum vi to fight it out, fight hard
dēpulī perf of **dēpellō**
dēpulsiō, -ōnis f averting; defence
dēpulsō, -āre vt to push out of the way
dēpulsor, -ōris m repeller
dēpulsus ppp of **dēpellō**
dēpūrgō, -āre vt to clean
dēputō, -āre vt to prune; to consider, reckon
dēpȳgis etc see **dēpūgis**
dēque adv down
dērēctā, dērēctē, dērēctō adv straight
dērēctus ppp of **dērigō** ▶ adj straight, upright, at right angles; straightforward
dērelictiō, -ōnis f disregarding
dērelinquō, -inquere, -īquī, -ictum vt to abandon, forsake
dērepente adv suddenly
dērēpō, -ere vi to creep down
dēreptus ppp of **dēripiō**
dērīdeō, -dēre, -sī, -sum vt to laugh at, deride
dērīdiculum, -ī nt mockery, absurdity; object of derision
dērīdiculus adj laughable
dērigēscō, -ēscere, -uī vi to stiffen, curdle
dērigō, -igere, -ēxī, -ēctum vt to turn, aim, direct; (fig) to regulate
dēripiō, -ipere, -ipuī, -eptum vt to tear off, pull down
dērīsor, -ōris m scoffer
dērīsus¹ ppp of **dērīdeō**
dērīsus², -ūs m scorn, derision
dērīvātiō, -ōnis f diverting
dērīvō, -āre, -āvī, -ātum vt to lead off, draw off
dērogō, -āre vt (LAW) to propose to amend; (fig) to detract from

dērōsus adj gnawed away

dēruncinō, -āre vt to plane off; (comedy) to cheat

dēruō, -ere, -ī, -tum vt to demolish

dēruptus adj steep ▶ ntpl precipice

dēsaeviō, -īre vi to rage furiously; to cease raging

dēscendō, -endere, -endī, -ēnsum vi to come down, go down, descend, dismount; (MIL) to march down; (things) to fall, sink, penetrate; (fig) to stoop (to), lower oneself

dēscēnsiō, -ōnis f going down

dēscēnsus, -ūs m way down

dēscīscō, -īscere, -īvī and **-iī, -ītum** vi to desert, revolt; to deviate, part company

dēscrībō, -bere, -psī, -ptum vt to copy out; to draw, sketch; to describe; see also **dīscrībō**

dēscrīptiō, -ōnis f copy; drawing, diagram; description

dēscrīptus ppp of **dēscrībō**; see also **dīscrīptus**

dēsecō, -āre, -uī, -tum vt to cut off

dēserō, -ere, -uī, -tum vt to desert, abandon, forsake; (bail) to forfeit

dēsertor, -ōris m deserter

dēsertus ppp of **dēserō** ▶ adj desert, uninhabited ▶ ntpl deserts

dēserviō, -īre vi to be a slave (to), serve

dēses, -idis adj idle, inactive

dēsiccō, -āre vt to dry, drain

dēsideō, -idēre, -ēdī vi to sit idle

dēsīderābilis adj desirable

dēsīderātiō, -ōnis f missing

dēsīderium, -ī and **-iī** nt longing, sense of loss; want; petition; **mē ~ tenet urbis** I miss Rome

dēsīderō, -āre, -āvī, -ātum vt to feel the want of, miss; to long for, desire; (casualties) to lose

dēsidia, -ae f idleness, apathy

dēsidiōsē adv idly

dēsidiōsus adj lazy, idle; relaxing

dēsīdō, -īdere, -ēdī vi to sink, settle down; (fig) to deteriorate

dēsignātiō, -ōnis f specifying; election (of magistrates)

dēsignātor etc see **dissignātor**

dēsignātus adj elect

dēsignō, -āre, -āvī, -ātum vt to trace out; to indicate, define; (POL) to elect; (art) to depict

dēsiī perf of **dēsinō**

dēsiliō, -ilīre, -iluī, -ultum vi to jump down, alight

dēsinō, -nere, -ī vt to leave off, abandon ▶ vi to stop, desist; to end (in)

dēsipiēns, -ientis adj silly

dēsipientia, -ae f folly

dēsipiō, -ere vi to be stupid, play the fool

dēsistō, -istere, -titī, -titum vi to stop, leave off, desist

dēsitus ppp of **dēsinō**

dēsōlō, -āre, -āvī, -ātum vt to leave desolate, abandon

dēspectō, -āre vt to look down on, command a view of; to despise

dēspectus¹ ppp of **dēspiciō** ▶ adj contemptible

dēspectus², -ūs m view, prospect

dēspēranter adv despairingly

dēspērātiō, -ōnis f despair

dēspērātus adj despaired of, hopeless; desperate, reckless

dēspērō, -āre, -āvī, -ātum vt, vi to despair, give up hope of

dēspexī perf of **dēspiciō**

dēspicātiō, -ōnis f contempt

despicātus adj despised, contemptible

dēspicātus, -ūs m contempt

dēspicientia, -ae f contempt

dēspiciō, -icere, -exī, -ectum vt to look down on; to despise ▶ vi to look down

dēspoliātor, -ōris m robber

dēspoliō, -āre vt to rob, plunder

dēspondeō, -ondēre, -ondī and **-opondī, -ōnsum** vt to pledge, promise; to betroth; to devote; to give up, despair of; **animum dēspondēre** despair

dēspūmō, -āre vt to skim off

dēspuō, -ere vi to spit on the ground ▶ vt to reject

dēsquāmō, -āre vt to scale, peel

dēstillō, -āre vi to drop down ▶ vt to distil

dēstimulō, -āre vt to run through

dēstinātiō, -ōnis f resolution, appointment

dēstinātus adj fixed, decided

dēstinō, -āre, -āvī, -ātum vt to make fast; to appoint, determine, resolve; (archery) to aim at; (fig) to intend to buy ▶ nt ppp mark; intention; **dēstinātum est mihi** I have decided

dēstitī perf of **dēsistō**

dēstituō, -uere, -uī, -ūtum vt to set apart, place; to forsake, leave in the lurch

dēstitūtiō, -ōnis f defaulting

dēstitūtus ppp of **dēstituō**

dēstrictus ppp of **dēstringō** ▶ adj severe

dēstringō, -ingere, -inxī, -ictum vt (leaves) to strip; (body) to rub down; (sword) to draw; to graze, skim; (fig) to censure

dēstruō, -ere, -xī, -ctum vt to demolish; to destroy

dēsubitō adv all of a sudden

dēsūdāscō, -ere vi to sweat all over

dēsūdō, -āre vi to exert oneself

dēsuēfactus adj unaccustomed

dēsuētūdō, -inis f disuse

dēsuētus adj unaccustomed, unused

dēsultor, -ōris m circus rider; (fig) fickle lover

dēsultūra, -ae f jumping down

dēsum, deesse, -fuī vi to be missing, fail, fail in one's duty

dēsūmō, -ere, -psī, -ptum vt to select

dēsuper adv from above

dēsurgō, -ere vi to rise

dētegō, -egere, -ēxī, -ēctum vt to uncover, disclose; (fig) to reveal, detect

dētendō, -endere, -ēnsum vt (tent) to strike

dētentus *ppp of* **dētineō**

dētergō, -gere, -sī, -sum *vt* to wipe away, clear away; to clean; to break off

dēterior, -ōris *adj* lower; inferior, worse

dēterius *adv* worse

dēterminātiō, -ōnis *f* boundary, end

dēterminō, -āre, -āvī, -ātum *vt* to bound, limit; to settle

dēterō, -erere, -rīvī, -rītum *vt* to rub, wear away; (*style*) to polish; (*fig*) to weaken

dēterreō, -ēre, -uī, -itum *vt* to frighten away; to deter, discourage, prevent

dētersus *ppp of* **dētergō**

dētestābilis *adj* abominable

dētestātiō, -ōnis *f* execration, curse; averting

dētestor, -ārī, -ātus *vt* to invoke, invoke against; to curse, execrate; to avert, deprecate

dētexō, -ere, -uī, -tum *vt* to weave, finish weaving; (*comedy*) to steal; (*fig*) to describe

dētineō, -inēre, -inuī, -entum *vt* to hold back, detain; to keep occupied

dētondeō, -ondēre, -ondī, -ōnsum *vt* to shear off, strip

dētonō, -āre, -uī *vi* to cease thundering

dētorqueō, -quēre, -sī, -tum *vt* to turn aside, direct; to distort, misrepresent

dētractātiō, -ōnis *f* declining

dētractiō, -ōnis *f* removal, departure

dētractō *etc see* **dētrectō**

dētractus *ppp of* **dētrahō**

dētrahō, -here, -xī, -ctum *vt* to draw off, take away, pull down; to withdraw, force to leave; to detract, disparage

dētrectātor, -ōris *m* disparager

dētrectō, -āre, -āvī, -ātum *vt* to decline, shirk; to detract from, disparage

dētrīmentōsus *adj* harmful

dētrīmentum, -ī *nt* loss, harm; (*MIL*) defeat; **~ capere** suffer harm

dētrītus *ppp of* **dēterō**

dētrūdō, -dere, -sī, -sum *vt* to push down, thrust away; to dislodge, evict; to postpone; (*fig*) to force

dētruncō, -āre, -āvī, -ātum *vt* to cut off, behead, mutilate

dētrūsus *ppp of* **dētrūdō**

dēturbō, -āre, -āvī, -ātum *vt* to dash down, pull down; (*fig*) to cast down, deprive

Deucaliōn, -ōnis *m* son of Prometheus (survivor of the Flood)

Deucaliōnēus *adj see* **Deucaliōn**

deūnx, -cis *m* eleven twelfths

deūrō, -rere, -ssī, -stum *vt* to burn up; to frost

deus, -ī (*voc* **deus**, *pl* **dī, deos, deum, dis**) *m* god; **dī meliōra** Heaven forbid!; **dī tē ament** bless you!

deūstus *ppp of* **deūrō**

deūtor, -ī *vi* to maltreat

dēvastō, -āre *vt* to lay waste

dēvehō, -here, -xī, -ctum *vt* to carry down, convey; (*pass*) to ride down, sail down

dēvellō, -ellere, -ellī *and* **-olsī, -ulsum** *vt* to pluck, pull out

dēvēlō, -āre *vt* to unveil

dēveneror, -ārī *vt* to worship; to avert by prayers

dēveniō, -enīre, -ēnī, -entum *vi* to come, reach, fall into

dēverberō, -āre, -āvī, -ātum *vt* to thrash soundly

dēversor¹, -ārī *vi* to lodge, stay (*as guest*)

dēversor², -ōris *m* guest

dēversōriolum, -ī *nt* small lodging

dēversōrium, -ī *and* **-iī** *nt* inn, lodging

dēversōrius *adj* for lodging

dēverticulum, -ī *nt* by-road, by-pass; digression; lodging place; (*fig*) refuge

dēvertō, -tere, -tī, -sum *vi* to turn aside, put up; to have recourse to; to digress

dēvertor, -tī, -versus *vi see* **dēvertō**

dēvexus *adj* sloping, going down, steep

dēvinciō, -cīre, -xī, -ctum *vt* to tie up; (*fig*) to bind, lay under an obligation

dēvincō, -incere, -īcī, -ictum *vt* to defeat completely, win the day

dēvītātiō, -ōnis *f* avoiding

dēvītō, -āre *vt* to avoid

dēvius *adj* out of the way, devious; (*person*) solitary, wandering off the beaten track; (*fig*) inconstant

dēvocō, -āre, -āvī, -ātum *vt* to call down, fetch; to entice away

dēvolō, -āre *vi* to fly down

dēvolvō, -vere, -vī, -ūtum *vt* to roll down, fall; (*wool*) to spin off

dēvorō, -āre, -āvī, -ātum *vt* to swallow, gulp down; to engulf, devour; (*money*) to squander; (*tears*) to repress; (*trouble*) to endure patiently

dēvors-, dēvort- *see* **dēvers-, dēvert-**

dēvortia, -ōrum *ntpl* byways

dēvōtiō, -ōnis *f* devoting; (*magic*) spell

dēvōtō, -āre *vt* to bewitch

dēvōtus *ppp of* **dēvoveō** ▶ *adj* faithful; accursed

dēvoveō, -ovēre, -ōvī, -ōtum *vt* to devote, vow, dedicate; to give up; to curse; to bewitch

dēvulsus *ppp of* **dēvellō**

dextella, -ae *f* little right hand

dexter, -erī *and* **-rī** *adj* right, right-hand; handy, skilful; favourable

dexteritās, -ātis *f* adroitness

dextrā *prep* (*with acc*) on the right of

dextra *f* right hand, right-hand side; hand; pledge of friendship

dextrē (*compar* **-erius**) *adv* adroitly

dextrōrsum, dextrōrsus, dextrōvorsum *adv* to the right

dī *pl of* **deus**

diabathrārius, -ī *and* **-iī** *m* slipper maker

diabolus, -ī *m* devil

diāconus, -ī *m* (ECCL) deacon

diadēma, -tis *nt* royal headband, diadem

diaeta, -ae *f* diet; living room

dialectica, -ae, dialecticē, -ēs *f* dialectic, logic ▶ *ntpl* logical questions

dialecticē adv dialectically
dialecticus adj dialectical ▸ m logician
Diālis adj of Jupiter ▸ m high priest of Jupiter
dialogus, -ī m dialogue, conversation
Diāna, -ae f virgin goddess of hunting (also identified with the moon and Hecate, and patroness of childbirth)
Diānius adj of Diana ▸ nt sanctuary of Diana
diāria, -ōrum ntpl daily allowance of food or pay
dibaphus, -ī f Roman state robe
dica, -ae f lawsuit
dicācitās, -ātis f raillery, repartee
dicāculus adj pert
dicātiō, -ōnis f declaration of citizenship
dicāx, -ācis adj witty, smart
dichorēus, -ī m double trochee
diciō, -ōnis f power, sway, authority
dicis causā for the sake of appearance
dicō, -āre, -āvī, -ātum vt to dedicate, consecrate; to deify; to devote, give over
dīcō, -cere, -xī, dictum vt to say, tell; to mention, mean, call, name; to pronounce; (RHET) to speak, deliver; (LAW) to plead; (poetry) to describe, celebrate; (official) to appoint; (time, place) to settle, fix ▸ vi to speak (in public); **causam dīcere** plead; **iūs dīcere** deliver judgment; **sententiam dīcere** vote; **no** ~ **namely**; **dīxī** I have finished; **dictum factum** no sooner said than done
dicrotum, -ī nt bireme
Dictaeus adj Cretan
dictamnus, -ī f dittany (a kind of wild marjoram)
dictāta, -ōrum ntpl lessons, rules
dictātor, -ōris m dictator
dictātōrius adj dictator's
dictātūra, -ae f dictatorship
Dictē, -ēs f mountain in Crete (where Jupiter was brought up)
dictiō, -ōnis f speaking, declaring; style, expression, oratory; (oracle) response
dictitō, -āre vt to keep saying, assert; to plead often
dictō, -āre, -āvī, -ātum vt to say repeatedly; to dictate; to compose
dictum, -ī nt saying, word; proverb; bon mot, witticism; command
dictus ppp of **dīcō**
Dictynna, -ae f Britomartis; Diana
Dictynnaeus adj see **Dictynna**
didicī perf of **discō**
Dīdō, -ūs and **-ōnis** (acc **-ō**) f Queen of Carthage
dīdō, -ere, -idī, -itum vt to distribute, broadcast
dīdūcō, -ūcere, -ūxī, -uctum vt to separate, split, open up; (MIL) to disperse; (fig) to part, divide
diēcula, -ae f one little day
diērēctus adj crucified; **abī** ~ go and be hanged
diēs, -ēī m/f day; set day (usu fem); a day's journey; (fig) time; ~ **meus** my birthday; **diem dīcere** impeach; **diem obīre** die; **diem dē diē,**

diem ex diē from day to day; **in diem** to a later day; for today; **in diēs** daily
Diēspiter, -ris m Jupiter
diffāmō, -āre, -āvī, -ātum vt to divulge; to malign
differentia, -ae f difference, diversity; species
differitās, -ātis f difference
differō, -erre, distulī, dīlātum vt to disperse; to divulge, publish; (fig) to distract, disquiet; (time) to put off, delay ▸ vi to differ, be distinguished
differtus adj stuffed, crammed
difficilis adj difficult; (person) awkward, surly
difficiliter adv with difficulty
difficultās, -ātis f difficulty, distress, hardship; surliness
difficulter adv with difficulty
diffīdēns, -entis adj nervous
diffīdenter adv without confidence
diffīdentia, -ae f mistrust, diffidence
diffīdō, -dere, -sus vi to distrust, despair
diffindō, -ndere, -dī, -ssum vt to split, open up; (fig) to break off
diffingō, -ere vt to remake
diffissus ppp of **diffindō**
diffisus ppa of **diffīdō**
diffiteor, -ērī vt to disown
diffluēns, -entis adj (RHET) loose
diffluō, -ere vi to flow away; to melt away; (fig) to wallow
diffringō, -ere vt to shatter
diffugiō, -ugere, -ūgī vi to disperse, disappear
diffugium, -ī and **-iī** nt dispersion
diffunditō, -āre vt to pour out, waste
diffundō, -undere, -ūdī, -ūsum vt to pour off; to spread, diffuse; to cheer, gladden
diffūsē adv expansively
diffūsilis adj diffusive
diffūsus ppp of **diffundō** ▸ adj spreading; (writing) loose
Dīgentia, -ae f tributary of the Anio (near Horace's villa)
dīgerō, -rere, -ssī, -stum vt to divide, distribute; to arrange, set out; to interpret
dīgestiō, -ōnis f (RHET) enumeration
dīgestus ppp of **dīgerō**
digitulus, -ī m little finger
digitus, -ī m finger; toe; inch; (pl) skill in counting; **digitum porrigere, digitum prōferre** take the slightest trouble; **digitum trānsversum nōn discēdere** not swerve a finger's breadth; **attingere caelum digitō** reach the height of happiness; **licērī digitō** bid at an auction; **mōnstrārī digitō** be a celebrity; **extrēmī digitī, summī digitī** the fingertips; **concrepāre digitīs** snap the fingers
dīgladior, -ārī vi to fight fiercely
dignātiō, -ōnis f honour, dignity
dignē adv see **dignus**
dignitās, -ātis f worth, worthiness; dignity, rank, position; political office

dignō, -āre vt to think worthy

dignor, -ārī vt to think worthy; to deign

dīgnōscō, -ere, -ōvī vt to distinguish

dignus adj worth, worthy; (things) fitting, proper

dīgredior, -dī, -ssus vi to separate, part; to deviate, digress

dīgressiō, -ōnis f parting; deviation, digression

dīgressus¹ ppa of dīgredior

dīgressus², -ūs m parting

dīiūdicātiō, -ōnis f decision

dīiūdicō, -āre vt to decide; to discriminate

dīiun- etc see disiun-

dīlābor, -bī, -psus vi to dissolve, disintegrate; to flow away; (troops) to disperse; (fig) to decay, vanish

dīlacerō, -āre vt to tear to pieces

dīlāminō, -āre vt to split in two

dīlaniō, -āre, -āvī, -ātum vt to tear to shreds

dīlapidō, -āre vt to demolish

dīlāpsus ppa of dīlābor

dīlargior, -īrī vt to give away liberally

dīlātiō, -ōnis f putting off, adjournment

dīlātō, -āre, -āvī, -ātum vt to expand; (pronunciation) to broaden

dīlātor, -ōris m procrastinator

dīlātus ppp of differō

dīlaudō, -āre vt to praise extravagantly

dīlēctus¹ ppp of dīligō ▶ adj beloved

dīlēctus², -ūs m selection, picking; (MIL) levy; dīlēctum habēre hold a levy, recruit

dīlēxī perf of dīligō

dīligēns, -entis adj painstaking, conscientious, attentive (to); thrifty

dīligenter adv see dīligēns

dīligentia, -ae f carefulness, attentiveness; thrift

dīligō, -igere, -ēxī, -ēctum vt to prize especially, esteem, love

dīlōrīcō, -āre vt to tear open

dīlūceō, -ēre vi to be evident

dīlūcēscit, -ēscere, -xit vi to dawn, begin to grow light

dīlūcidē adv see dīlūcidus

dīlūcidus adj clear, distinct

dīlūculum, -ī nt dawn

dīlūdium, -ī and **-iī** nt interval

dīluō, -uere, -uī, -ūtum vt to wash away, dissolve, dilute; to explain; (fig) to weaken, do away with

dīluviēs, -iēī f, **dīluvium, -ī** and **-iī** nt flood, deluge

dīluviō, -āre vt to inundate

dīmānō, -āre vi to spread abroad

dīmēnsiō, -ōnis f measuring

dīmēnsus adj measured

dīmētior, -tīrī, -nsus vt to measure out

dīmētō, -āre, dīmētor, -ārī vt to mark out

dīmicātiō, -ōnis f fighting, struggle

dīmicō, -āre, -āvī, -ātum vi to fight, struggle, contend

dīmidiātus adj half, halved

dīmidius adj half ▶ nt half

dīmissiō, -ōnis f sending away; discharging

dīmissus ppp of dīmittō

dīmittō, -ittere, -īsī, -issum vt to send away, send round; to let go, lay down; (meeting) to dismiss; (MIL) to disband, detach; (fig) to abandon, forsake

dimminuō, -ere vt to dash to pieces

dīmoveō, -ovēre, -ōvī, -ōtum vt to part, separate; to entice away

Dindymēnē, -ēnēs f Cybele

Dindymus, -ī m mountain in Mysia (sacred to Cybele)

dīnōscō see dīgnōscō

dīnumerātiō, -ōnis f reckoning up

dīnumerō, -āre vt to count, reckon up; to pay out

diōbolāris adj costing two obols

dioecēsis, -is f district; (ECCL) diocese

dioecētēs, -ae m treasurer

Diogenēs, -is m famous Cynic philosopher; a Stoic philosopher

Diomēdēs, -is m Greek hero at the Trojan War

Diomēdēus adj see Diomēdēs

Diōnaeus adj see Diōnē

Diōnē, -ēs, Diōna, -ae f mother of Venus; Venus

Dīonȳsia, -iōrum ntpl Greek festival of Bacchus

Dionȳsius, -ī m tyrant of Syracuse

Dionȳsus, -ī m Bacchus

diōta, -ae f a two-handled wine jar

diplōma, -tis nt letter of recommendation

Dipylon, -ī nt Athenian gate

Dircaeus adj Boeotian

Dircē, -ēs f famous spring in Boeotia

dīrēctus ppp of dīrigō ▶ adj straight; straightforward, simple; see also dērēctus

dīrēmī perf of dirimō

diremptus¹ ppp of dirimō

diremptus², -ūs m separation

dīreptiō, -ōnis f plundering

dīreptor, -ōris m plunderer

dīreptus ppp of dīripiō

dīrēxī perf of dīrigō

dīribeō, -ēre vt to sort out (votes taken from ballot-boxes)

dīribitiō, -ōnis f sorting

dīribitor, -ōris m ballot-sorter

dīrigō, -igere, -ēxī, -ēctum vt to put in line, arrange; see also dērigō

dirimō, -imere, -ēmī, -emptum vt to part, divide; to interrupt, break off; to put an end to

dīripiō, -ipere, -ipuī, -eptum vt to tear in pieces; to plunder, ravage; to seize; (fig) to distract

dīritās, -ātis f mischief, cruelty

dīrumpō, disrumpō, -umpere, -ūpī, -uptum vt to burst, break in pieces; (fig) to break off; (pass) to burst (with passion)

dīruō, -ere, -ī, -tum vt to demolish; to scatter; aere dīrutus having one's pay stopped

dīruptus ppp of dīrumpō

dīrus adj ominous, fearful; (person) dread, terrible ▸ fpl bad luck; the Furies ▸ ntpl terrors
dīrutus ppp of **dīruō** ▸ adj bankrupt
Dīs, Dītis m Pluto
dīs, dītis adj rich
discēdō, -ēdere, -ēssī, -essum vi to go away, depart; to part, disperse; (MIL) to march away; (result of battle) to come off; (POL) to go over (to a different policy); to pass away, disappear; to leave out of consideration; **ab signīs discēdere** break the ranks; **victor discēdere** come off best
disceptātiō, -ōnis f discussion, debate
disceptātor, -ōris m, **disceptātrīx, -rīcis** f arbitrator
disceptō, -āre vt to debate, discuss; (LAW) to decide
discernō, -ernere, -rēvī, -rētum vt to divide, separate; to distinguish between
discerpō, -ere, -sī, -tum vt to tear apart, disperse; (fig) to revile
discessiō, -ōnis f separation, departure; (senate) division
discessus, -ūs m parting; departure; marching away
discidium, -ī and **-iī** nt disintegration; separation, divorce; discord
discīdō, -ere vt to cut in pieces
discinctus ppp of **discingō** ▸ adj ungirt; negligent; dissolute
discindō, -ndere, -dī, -ssum vt to tear up, cut open
discingō, -gere, -xī, -ctum vt to ungird
disciplīna, -ae f teaching, instruction; learning, science, school, system; training, discipline; habits
discipulus, -ī m, **discipula, -ae** f pupil, apprentice
discissus ppp of **discindō**
disclūdō, -dere, -sī, -sum vt to keep apart, separate out
discō, -ere, didicī vt to learn, be taught, be told
discolor, -ōris adj of a different colour; variegated; different
discondūcit it is not worthwhile
disconveniō, -īre vi to disagree, be inconsistent
discordābilis adj disagreeing
discordia, -ae f discord, disagreement
discordiōsus adj seditious
discordō, -āre vi to disagree, quarrel; to be unlike
discors, -dis adj discordant, at variance; inconsistent
discrepantia, -ae f disagreement
discrepātiō, -ōnis f dispute
discrepitō, -āre vi to be quite different
discrepō, -āre, -uī vi to be out of tune; to disagree, differ; to be disputed
discrētus ppp of **discernō**
dīscrībō, -bere, -psī, -ptum vt to distribute, apportion, classify

discrīmen, -inis nt interval, dividing line; distinction, difference; turning point, critical moment; crisis, danger
discrīminō, -āre vt to divide
dīscrīptē adv in good order
dīscrīptiō, -ōnis f apportioning, distributing
dīscrīptus ppp of **dīscrībō** ▸ adj secluded; well-arranged
discruciō, -āre vt to torture; (fig) to torment, trouble
discumbō, -mbere, -buī, -bitum vi to recline at table; to go to bed
discupiō, -ere vi to long
discurrō, -rrere, -currī and **-rrī, -rsum** vi to run about, run different ways
discursus, -ūs m running hither and thither
discus, -ī m quoit
discussus ppp of **discutiō**
discutiō, -tere, -ssī, -ssum vt to dash to pieces, smash; to scatter; to dispel
disertē, disertim adv distinctly; eloquently
disertus adj fluent, eloquent; explicit
disiciō, -icere, -iēcī, -iectum vt to scatter, cast asunder; to break up, destroy; (MIL) to rout
disiectō, -āre vt to toss about
disiectus¹ ppp of **disiciō**
disiectus², -ūs m scattering
disiūnctiō, -ōnis f separation, differing; (LOGIC) statement of alternatives; (RHET) a sequence of short co-ordinate clauses
disiūnctius adv rather in the manner of a dilemma
disiūnctus ppp of **disiungō** ▸ adj distinct, distant, removed; (speech) disjointed; (LOGIC) opposite
disiungō, -ungere, -ūnxī, -ūnctum vt to unyoke; to separate, remove
dispālēscō, -ere vi to be noised abroad
dispandō, -āndere, -andī, -ānsum and **-essum** vt to spread out
dispār, -aris adj unlike, unequal
disparilis adj dissimilar
disparō, -āre, -āvī, -ātum vt to segregate
dispart- etc see **dispert-**
dispectus ppp of **dispiciō**
dispellō, -ellere, -ulī, -ulsum vt to scatter, dispel
dispendium, -ī and **-iī** nt expense, loss
dispennō etc see **dispandō**
dispēnsātiō, -ōnis f management, stewardship
dispēnsātor, -ōris m steward, treasurer
dispēnsō, -āre, -āvī, -ātum vi to weigh out, pay out; to manage, distribute; (fig) to regulate
dispercutiō, -ere vt to dash out
disperdō, -ere, -idī, -itum vt to ruin, squander
dispereō, -īre, -iī vi to go to ruin, be undone
dispergō, -gere, -sī, -sum vt to disperse, spread over, space out
dispersē adv here and there
dispersus ppp of **dispergō**

dispertiō, -īre, -īvī, -ītum, dispertior, -īrī vt to apportion, distribute

dispertītiō, -ōnis f division

dispessus ppp of **dispandō**

dispiciō, -icere, -exī, -ectum vt to see clearly, see through; to distinguish, discern; (fig) to consider

displiceō, -ēre vi (with dat) to displease; **sibi displicēre** be in a bad humour

displōdō, -dere, -sī, -sum vt to burst with a crash

dispōnō, -ōnere, -osuī, -ositum vt to set out, arrange; (MIL) to station

dispositē adv methodically

dispositiō, -ōnis f arrangement

dispositūra, -ae f arrangement

dispositus¹ ppp of **dispōnō** ▸ adj orderly

dispositus², -ūs m arranging

dispudet, -ēre, -uit v impers to be very ashamed

dispulsus ppp of **dispellō**

disputātiō, -ōnis f argument

disputātor, -ōris m debater

disputō, -āre, -āvī, -ātum vt to calculate; to examine, discuss

disquīrō, -ere vt to investigate

disquīsītiō, -ōnis f inquiry

disrumpō etc see **dīrumpō**

dissaepiō, -īre, -sī, -tum vt to fence off, separate off

dissaeptum, -ī nt partition

dissāvior, -ārī vt to kiss passionately

dissēdī perf of **dissideō**

dissēminō, -āre vt to sow, broadcast

dissēnsiō, -ōnis f disagreement, conflict

dissēnsus, -ūs m dissension

dissentāneus adj contrary

dissentiō, -entīre, -ēnsī, -ēnsum vi to disagree, differ; to be unlike, be inconsistent

dissēp- etc see **dissaep-**

disserēnō, -āre vi to clear up

disserō¹, -erere, -ēvī, -itum vt to sow, plant at intervals

disserō², -ere, -uī, -tum vt to set out in order, arrange; to examine, discuss

disserpō, -ere vi to spread imperceptibly

dissertō, -āre vt to discuss, dispute

dissideō, -idēre, -ēdī, -essum vi to be distant; to disagree, quarrel; to differ, be unlike, be uneven

dissignātiō, -ōnis f arrangement

dissignātor, -ōris m master of ceremonies; undertaker

dissignō, -āre vt to arrange, regulate; see also **dēsignō**

dissiliō, -īre, -uī vi to fly apart, break up

dissimilis adj unlike, different

dissimiliter adv differently

dissimilitūdō, -inis f unlikeness

dissimulanter adv secretly

dissimulantia, -ae f dissembling

dissimulātiō, -ōnis f disguising, dissembling; Socratic irony

dissimulātor, -ōris m dissembler

dissimulō, -āre, -āvī, -ātum vt to dissemble, conceal, pretend that ... not, ignore

dissipābilis adj diffusible

dissipātiō, -ōnis f scattering, dispersing

dissipō, dissupō, -āre, -āvī, -ātum vt to scatter, disperse; to spread, broadcast; to squander, destroy; (MIL) to put to flight

dissitus ppp of **disserō¹**

dissociābilis adj disuniting; incompatible

dissociātiō, -ōnis f separation

dissociō, -āre, -āvī, -ātum vt to disunite, estrange

dissolūbilis adj dissoluble

dissolūtē adv loosely, negligently

dissolūtiō, -ōnis f breaking up, destruction; looseness; (LAW) refutation; (person) weakness

dissolūtum, -ī nt asyndeton

dissolūtus ppp of **dissolvō** ▸ adj loose; lax, careless; licentious

dissolvō, -vere, -vī, -ūtum vt to unloose, dissolve; to destroy, abolish; to refute; to pay up, discharge (debt); to free, release

dissonus adj discordant, jarring, disagreeing, different

dissors, -tis adj not shared

dissuādeō, -dēre, -sī, -sum vt to advise against, oppose

dissuāsiō, -ōnis f advising against

dissuāsor, -ōris m opposer

dissultō, -āre vi to fly asunder

dissuō, -ere vt to undo, open up

dissupō etc see **dissipō**

distaedet, -ēre v impers to weary, disgust

distantia, -ae f diversity

distendō, distenō, -dere, -dī, -tum vt to stretch out, swell

distentus ppp of **distendō** ▸ adj full ▸ ppp of **distineō** ▸ adj busy

disterminō, -āre vt to divide, limit

distichon, -ī nt couplet

distinctē adv distinctly, lucidly

distinctiō, -ōnis f differentiating, difference; (GRAM) punctuation; (RHET) distinction between words

distinctus¹ ppp of **distinguō** ▸ adj separate, distinct; ornamented, set off; lucid

distinctus², -ūs m difference

distineō, -inēre, -inuī, -entum vt to keep apart, divide; to distract; to detain, occupy; to prevent

distinguō, -guere, -xī, -ctum vt to divide, distinguish, discriminate; to punctuate; to adorn, set off

distō, -āre vi to be apart, be distant; to be different

distorqueō, -quēre, -sī, -tum vt to twist, distort

distortiō, -ōnis f contortion

distortus ppp of **distorqueō** ▸ adj deformed

distractiō, -ōnis f parting, variance

distractus ppp of **distrahō** ▸ adj separate

distrahō, -here, -xī, -ctum vt to tear apart, separate, estrange; to sell piecemeal, retail; (*mind*) to distract, perplex; **aciem distrahere** break up a formation; **contrōversiās distrahere** end a dispute; **vōcēs distrahere** leave a hiatus

distribuō, -uere, -uī, -ūtum vt to distribute, divide

distribūtē adv methodically

distribūtiō, -ōnis f distribution, division

districtus ppp of **distringō** ▶ adj busy, occupied; perplexed; severe

distringō, -ngere, -nxī, -ctum vt to draw apart; to engage, distract; (MIL) to create a diversion against

distruncō, -āre vt to cut in two

distulī perf of **differō**

disturbō, -āre, -āvī, -ātum vt to throw into confusion; to demolish; to frustrate, ruin

dītēscō, -ere vi to grow rich

dīthyrambicus adj dithyrambic

dīthyrambus, -ī m dithyramb

dītiae, -ārum fpl wealth

dītiō etc see **diciō**

dītō, -āre vt to enrich

diū (*compar* **diūtius**, *superl* **diūtissimē**) adv long, for a long time; long ago; by day

diurnum, -ī nt day-book; **ācta diurna** Roman daily gazette

diurnus adj daily, for a day; by day, day- (*in cpds*)

dīus adj divine, noble

diūtinē adv long

diūtinus adj long, lasting

diūtissimē, -ius etc see **diū**

diūturnitās, -ātis f long time, long duration

diūturnus adj long, lasting

dīva, -ae f goddess

dīvāricō, -āre vt to spread

dīvellō, -ellere, -ellī, -ulsum vt to tear apart, tear in pieces; (*fig*) to tear away, separate, estrange

dīvēndō, -ere, -itum vt to sell in lots

dīverberō, -āre vt to divide, cleave

dīverbium, -ī and **-iī** nt (*comedy*) passage in dialogue

dīversē adv in different directions, variously

dīversitās, -ātis f contradiction, disagreement, difference

dīversus, dīvorsus ppp of **dīvertō** ▶ adj in different directions, apart; different; remote; opposite, conflicting; hostile ▶ mpl individuals

dīvertō, -tere, -tī, -sum vi to turn away; differ

dīves, -itis adj rich

dīvexō, -āre vt to pillage

dīvidia, -ae f worry, concern

dīvidō, -idere, -īsī, -īsum vt to divide, break open; to distribute, apportion; to separate, keep apart; to distinguish; (*jewel*) to set off; **sententiam dīvidere** take the vote separately on the parts of a motion

dīviduus adj divisible; divided

dīvīnātiō, -ōnis f foreseeing the future, divination; (LAW) inquiry to select the most suitable prosecutor

dīvīnē adv by divine influence; prophetically; admirably

dīvīnitās, -ātis f divinity; divination; divine quality

dīvīnitus adv from heaven, by divine influence; excellently

dīvīnō, -āre, -āvī, -ātum vt to foresee, prophesy

dīvīnus adj divine, of the gods; prophetic; superhuman, excellent ▶ m soothsayer ▶ nt sacrifice; oath; **rēs dīvīna** religious service, sacrifice; **dīvīna hūmānaque** all things in heaven and earth; **dīvīnī crēdere** believe on oath

dīvīsī perf of **dīvidō**

dīvīsiō, -ōnis f division; distribution

dīvīsor, -ōris m distributor; bribery agent

dīvīsus¹ ppp of **dīvidō** ▶ adj separate

dīvīsus², -ūs m division

dīvitiae, -ārum fpl wealth; (*fig*) richness

dīvor- etc see **dīver-**

dīvortium, -ī and **-iī** nt separation; divorce (by consent), road fork, watershed

dīvulgātus adj widespread

dīvulgō, -āre, -āvī, -ātum vt to publish, make public

dīvulsus ppp of **dīvellō**

dīvum, -ī nt sky; **sub dīvō** in the open air

dīvus adj divine; deified ▶ m god

dīxī perf of **dīcō**

dō, dare, dedī, datum vt to give; to permit, grant; to put, bring, cause, make; to give up, devote; to tell; to impute; **fābulam dare** produce a play; **in fugam dare** put to flight; **litterās dare** post a letter; **manūs dare** surrender; **nōmen dare** enlist; **operam dare** take pains, do one's best; **poenās dare** pay the penalty; **vēla dare** set sail; **verba dare** cheat

doceō, -ēre, -uī, -tum vt to teach; to inform, tell; **fābulam docēre** produce a play

dochmius, -ī and **-iī** m dochmiac foot

docilis adj easily trained, docile

docilitās, -ātis f aptness for being taught

doctē adv skilfully, cleverly

doctor, -ōris m teacher, instructor

doctrīna, -ae f instruction, education, learning; science

doctus ppp of **doceō** ▶ adj learned, skilled; cunning, clever

documentum, -ī nt lesson, example, proof

Dōdōna, -ae f town in Epirus (famous for its oracle of Jupiter)

Dōdōnaeus, Dōdōnaeis, -idis adj see **Dōdōna**

dōdrāns, -antis m three-fourths

dogma, -tis nt philosophical doctrine

dolābra, -ae f pickaxe

dolēns, -entis pres p of **doleō** ▶ adj painful

dolenter adv sorrowfully

doleō, -ēre, -uī, -itum vt, vi to be in pain, be sore; to grieve, lament, be sorry (for); to pain; **cui dolet meminit** once bitten, twice shy

dōliāris adj tubby

dōliolum, -ī nt small cask

dōlium, -ī and -iī nt large wine jar

dolō¹, -āre, -āvī, -ātum vt to hew, shape with an axe

dolō², -ōnis m pike; sting; fore-topsail

Dolopes, -um mpl people of Thessaly

Dolopia, -iae f the country of the people of Thessaly

dolor, -ōris m pain, pang; sorrow, trouble; indignation, resentment; (RHET) pathos

dolōsē adv see **dolōsus**

dolōsus adj deceitful, crafty

dolus, -ī m deceit, guile, trick; ~ **malus** wilful fraud

domābilis adj tameable

domesticus adj domestic, household; personal, private; of one's own country, internal ▶ mpl members of a household; **bellum domesticum** civil war

domī adv at home

domicilium, -ī and -iī nt dwelling

domina, -ae f mistress, lady of the house; wife, mistress; (fig) lady

domināns, -antis pres p of **dominor** ▶ adj (words) literal ▶ m tyrant

dominātiō, -ōnis f mastery, tyranny

dominātor, -ōris m lord

dominātrīx, -rīcis f queen

dominātus, -ūs m mastery, sovereignty

dominicus adj (ECCL) the Lord's

dominium, -ī and -iī nt absolute ownership; feast

dominor, -ārī, -ātus vi to rule, be master; (fig) to lord it

dominus, -ī m master, lord; owner; host; despot; (ECCL) the Lord

Domitiānus adj, m Roman Emperor

Domitius, -ī m Roman plebeian name (esp with surname Ahenobarbus)

domitō, -āre vt to break in

domitor, -ōris m, **domitrīx, -rīcis** f tamer; conqueror

domitus¹ ppp of **domō**

domitus², -ūs m taming

domō, -āre, -uī, -itum vt to tame, break in; to conquer

domus, -ūs and -ī f house (esp in town); home, native place; family; (PHILOS) sect; **domī** at home; in peace; **domī habēre** have of one's own, have plenty of; **domum** home(wards); **domō** from home

dōnābilis adj deserving a present

dōnārium, -ī and -iī nt offering; altar, temple

dōnātiō, -ōnis f presenting

dōnātīvum, -ī nt largesse, gratuity

dōnec, dōnicum, dōnique conj until; while, as long as

dōnō, -āre, -āvī, -ātum vt to present, bestow; to remit, condone (for another's sake); (fig) to sacrifice

dōnum, -ī nt gift; offering

dorcas, -dis f gazelle

Dōrēs, -um mpl Dorians (mostly the Greeks of the Peloponnese)

Dōricus adj Dorian; Greek

Dōris, -dis f a sea nymph; the sea

dormiō, -īre, -īvī, -ītum vi to sleep, be asleep

dormītātor, -ōris m dreamer

dormītō, -āre vi to be drowsy, nod

dorsum, -ī nt back; mountain ridge

dōs, dōtis f dowry; (fig) gift, talent

Dossēnus, -ī m hunchback, clown

dōtālis adj dowry (in cpds), dotal

dōtātus adj richly endowed

dōtō, -āre vt to endow

drachma, drachuma, -ae f a Greek silver coin

dracō, -ōnis m serpent, dragon; (ASTR) Draco

dracōnigena, -ae adj sprung from dragon's teeth

drāpeta, -ae m runaway slave

Drepanum, -ī, Drepana, -ōrum nt town in W. Sicily

dromas, -dis m dromedary

dromos, -ī m racecourse (at Sparta)

Druidēs, -um, Druidae, -ārum mpl Druids

Drūsiānus adj see **Drūsus**

Drūsus, -ī m Roman surname (esp famous commander in Germany under Augustus)

Dryades, -um fpl wood nymphs, Dryads

Dryopes, -um mpl a people of Epirus

dubiē adv doubtfully

dubitābilis adj doubtful

dubitanter adv doubtingly, hesitatingly

dubitātiō, -ōnis f wavering, uncertainty, doubting; hesitancy, irresolution; (RHET) misgiving

dubitō, -āre, -āvī, -ātum vt, vi to waver, be in doubt, wonder, doubt; to hesitate, stop to think

dubium nt doubt

dubius adj wavering, uncertain; doubtful, indecisive; precarious; irresolute ▶ nt doubt; **in dubium vocāre** call in question; **in dubium venīre** be called in question; **sine dubiō, haud dubiē** undoubtedly

ducēnī, -ōrum adj 200 each

ducentēsima, -ae f one-half per cent

ducentī, -ōrum num two hundred

ducentiēs, -iēns adv 2 times

dūcō, -cere, -xī, ductum vt to lead, guide, bring, take; to draw, draw out; to reckon, consider; (MIL) to lead, march, command; (breath) to inhale; (ceremony) to conduct; (changed aspect) to take on, receive; (dance) to perform; (drink) to quaff; (metal) to shape, beat out; (mind) to attract, induce, deceive; (oars) to pull; (origin) to derive, trace; (time) to prolong, put off, pass; (udders) to milk; (wool) to spin; (a work) to construct, compose, make; (COMM) to

calculate; **īlia dūcere** become broken-winded;
in numerō hostium dūcere regard as an
enemy; **ōs dūcere** make faces; **parvī dūcere**
think little of; **ratiōnem dūcere** have regard for;
uxōrem dūcere marry
ductim adv in streams
ductitō, -āre vt to lead on, deceive; to marry
ductō, -āre vt to lead, draw; to take home;
to cheat
ductor, -ōris m leader, commander; guide,
pilot
ductus¹ ppp of **dūcō**
ductus², -ūs m drawing, drawing off; form;
command, generalship
dūdum adv a little while ago, just now; for long;
haud ~ not long ago; **iam ~ adsum** I have been
here a long time; **quam ~** how long
duellum etc see **bellum**
Duillius, -ī m consul who defeated the
Carthaginians at sea
duim pres subj of **dō**
dulce, dulciter adv see **dulcis**
dulcēdō, -inis f sweetness; pleasantness,
charm
dulcēscō, -ere vi to become sweet
dulciculus adj rather sweet
dulcifer, -ī adj sweet
dulcis adj sweet; pleasant, lovely; kind, dear
dulcitūdō, -inis f sweetness
dūlicē adv like a slave
Dūlichium, -ī nt island in the Ionian Sea near
Ithaca
Dūlichius adj of Dulichium; of Ulysses
dum conj while, as long as; provided that, if
only; until ▶ adv (enclitic) now, a moment; (with
neg) yet
dūmētum, -ī nt thicket, thornbushes
dummodo conj provided that
dūmōsus adj thorny
dumtaxat adv at least; only, merely
dūmus, -ī m thornbush
duo, duae, duo num two
duodeciēns, -ēs adv twelve times
duodecim num twelve
duodecimus adj twelfth
duodēnī, -ōrum adj twelve each, in dozens
duodēquadrāgēsimus adj thirty-eighth
duodēquadrāgintā num thirty-eight
duodēquīnquāgēsimus adj forty-eighth
duodētrīciēns adv twenty-eight times
duodētrīgintā num twenty-eight
duodēvīcēnī adj eighteen each
duodēvīgintī num eighteen
duoetvīcēsimānī, -ānōrum mpl soldiers of
the 22nd legion
duoetvīcēsimus adj twenty-second
duovirī, duumvirī, -ōrum mpl a board of
two men; colonial magistrates; **~ nāvālēs**
naval commissioners (for supply and repair);
~ sacrōrum keepers of the Sibylline Books
duplex, -icis adj double, twofold; both;
(person) false

duplicārius, -ī and **-iī** m soldier receiving
double pay
dupliciter adv doubly, on two accounts
duplicō, -āre, -āvī, -ātum vt to double,
increase; to bend
duplus adj double, twice as much ▶ nt double ▶ f
double the price
dupondius, -ī and **-iī** m coin worth two asses
dūrābilis adj lasting
dūrāmen, -inis nt hardness
dūrateus adj wooden
dūrē, dūriter adv stiffly; hardily; harshly,
roughly
dūrēscō, -ēscere, -uī vi to harden
dūritās, -ātis f harshness
dūritia, -ae, dūritiēs, -ēi f hardness;
hardiness; severity; want of feeling
dūrō, -āre, -āvī, -ātum vt to harden, stiffen;
to make hardy, inure; (mind) to dull ▶ vi to
harden; to be patient, endure; to hold out, last;
(mind) to be steeled
dūruī perf of **dūrēscō**
dūrus adj hard, harsh, rough; hardy, tough;
rude, uncultured; (character) severe, unfeeling,
impudent, miserly; (circumstances) hard, cruel
duumvirī etc see **duovirī**
dux, ducis m leader, guide; chief, head; (MIL)
commander, general
dūxī perf of **dūcō**
Dymantis, -antidis f Hecuba
Dymās, -antis m father of Hecuba
dynamis, -is f plenty
dynastēs, -ae m ruler, prince
Dyrrhachīnus adj see **Dyrrhachium**
Dyrrhachium, Dyrrachium, -ī nt Adriatic
port (now Durrës)

e

ē *prep see* **ex**
eā *adv* there, that way
ea *f, pron* she, it ▶ *adj see* **is**
eadem *f, pron see* **īdem**
eādem *adv* the same way; at the same time
eaīdem, eapse *f of* **ipse**
eapse *f of* **ipse**
eātenus *adv* so far
ebenus *etc see* **hebenus**
ēbibō, -ere, -ī *vt* to drink up, drain; to squander; to absorb
ēblandior, -īrī *vt* to coax out, obtain by flattery; **ēblandītus** obtained by flattery
Eborācum, -ī *nt* York
ēbrietās, ātis *f* drunkenness
ēbriolus *adj* tipsy
ēbriōsitās, -ātis *f* addiction to drink
ēbriōsus *adj* drunkard; (*berry*) juicy
ēbrius *adj* drunk; full; (*fig*) intoxicated
ēbulliō, -īre *vi* to bubble up ▶ *vt* to brag about
ebulus, -ī *m*, **ebulum, -ī** *nt* danewort, dwarf elder
ebur, -is *nt* ivory; ivory work
Eburācum, -ī *nt* York
eburātus *adj* inlaid with ivory
eburneolus *adj* of ivory
eburneus, eburnus *adj* of ivory; ivory-white
ēcastor *interj* by Castor!
ecce *adv* look!, here is!, there is!; lo and behold!; **ecca, eccam, eccillam, eccistam** here she is!; **eccum, eccillum** here he is!; **eccōs, eccās** here they are!
eccerē *interj* there now!
eccheuma, -tis *nt* pouring out
ecclēsia, -ae *f* a Greek assembly; (*ECCL*) congregation, church
eccum *etc see* **ecce**
ecdicus, -ī *m* civic lawyer
ecf- *see* **eff-**
echidna, -ae *f* viper; **~ Lernaea** hydra
echīnus, -ī *m* sea-urchin; hedgehog; a rinsing bowl
Echīōn, -onis *m* Theban hero
Echīonidēs *m* Pentheus

Echīonius *adj* Theban
Ēchō, -ūs *f* wood nymph; echo
ecloga, -ae *f* selection; eclogue
ecquandō *adv* ever
ecquī, -ae, -od *adj interrog* any
ecquid, ecquidī *adv* whether
ecquis, -id *pron interrog* anyone, anything
ecquō *adv* anywhere
eculeus, -ī *m* foal; rack
edācitās, -ātis *f* gluttony
edāx, -ācis *adj* gluttonous; (*fig*) devouring, carking
ēdentō, -āre *vt* to knock the teeth out of
ēdentulus *adj* toothless; old
edepol *interj* by Pollux, indeed
ēdī *perf of* **edō**
ēdīcō, -īcere, -īxī, -ictum *vt* to declare; to decree, publish by an edict
ēdictiō, -ōnis *f* decree
ēdictō, -āre *vt* to proclaim
ēdictum, -ī *nt* proclamation, edict (*esp a praetor's*)
ēdidī *perf of* **ēdō**
ēdiscō, -ere, ēdidicī *vt* to learn well, learn by heart
ēdisserō, -ere, -uī, -tum *vt* to explain in detail
ēdissertō, -āre *vt* to explain fully
ēditīcius *adj* chosen by the plaintiff
ēditiō, -ōnis *f* publishing, edition; statement; (*LAW*) designation of a suit
ēditus *ppp of* **ēdō** ▶ *adj* high; descended ▶ *nt* height; order
edō, edere *and* **ēsse, ēdī, ēsum** *vt* to eat; (*fig*) to devour
ēdō, -ere, -idī, -itum *vt* to put forth, discharge; to emit; to give birth to, produce; (*speech*) to declare, relate, utter; (*action*) to cause, perform; (*book*) to publish; (*POL*) to promulgate; **lūdōs ēdere** put on a show; **tribūs ēdere** nominate tribes of jurors
ēdoceō, -ere, -uī, -ctum *vt* to instruct clearly, teach thoroughly
ēdomō, -āre, -uī, -itum *vt* to conquer, overcome
Ēdōnus *adj* Thracian
ēdormiō, -īre *vi* to have a good sleep ▶ *vt* to sleep off
ēdormīscō, -ere *vt* to sleep off
ēducātiō, -ōnis *f* bringing up, rearing
ēducātor, -ōris *m* foster father, tutor
ēducātrīx, -īcis *f* nurse
ēducō, -āre, -āvī, -ātum *vt* to bring up, rear, train; to produce
ēdūcō, -ūcere, -ūxī, -uctum *vt* to draw out, bring away; to raise up, erect; (*LAW*) to summon; (*MIL*) to lead out, march out; (*ship*) to put to sea; (*young*) to hatch, rear, train
edūlis *adj* edible
ēdūrō, -āre *vi* to last out
ēdūrus *adj* very hard
effarciō *etc see* **efferciō**
effātus *ppa* (*occ pass*) *of* **effor** ▶ *adj* solemnly pronounced, declared ▶ *nt* axiom; (*pl*) predictions

effectiō, -ōnis f performing; efficient cause

effector, -ōris m, **effectrīx, -rīcis** f producer, author

effectus¹ ppp of **efficiō**

effectus², -ūs m completion, performance; effect

effēminātē adv see **effēminātus**

effēminātus adj effeminate

effēminō, -āre, -āvī, -ātum vt to make a woman of; to enervate

efferātus adj savage

efferciō, -cīre, -sī, -tum vt to cram full

efferitās, -ātis f wildness

efferō¹, -āre, -āvī, -ātum vt to make wild; (fig) to exasperate

efferō², ecferō, -re, extulī, ēlātum vt to bring out, carry out; to lift up, raise; (dead) to carry to the grave; (emotion) to transport; (honour) to exalt; (news) to spread abroad; (soil) to produce; (trouble) to endure to the end; **sē efferre** rise; be conceited

effertus ppp of **efferciō** ▶ adj full, bulging

efferus adj savage

effervēscō, -vēscere, -buī vi to boil over; (fig) to rage

effervō, -ere vi to boil up

effētus adj exhausted

efficācitās, -ātis f power

efficāciter adv effectually

efficāx, -ācis adj capable, effective

efficiēns, -entis pres p of **efficiō** ▶ adj effective, efficient

efficienter adv efficiently

efficientia, -ae f power, efficacy

efficiō, -icere, -ēcī, -ectum vt to make, accomplish; to cause, bring about; (numbers) to amount to; (soil) to yield; (theory) to make out, try to prove

effictus ppp of **effingō**

effigiēs, -ēī, effigia, -ae f likeness, copy; ghost; portrait, statue; (fig) image, ideal

effingō, -ngere, -nxī, -ctum vt to form, fashion; to portray, represent; to wipe clean; to fondle

efflāgitātiō, -ōnis f urgent demand

efflāgitātus, -ūs m urgent request

efflāgitō, -āre vt to demand urgently

efflīctim adv desperately

efflīctō, -āre vt to strike dead

efflīgō, -gere, -xī, -ctum vt to exterminate

efflō, -āre, -āvī, -ātum vt to breathe out, blow out ▶ vi to billow out; **animam efflāre** expire

efflōrēscō, -ēscere, -uī vi to blossom forth

effluō, -ere, -xī vi to run out, issue, emanate; (fig) to pass away, vanish; (rumour) to get known; **ex animō effluere** become forgotten

effluvium, -ī and **-iī** nt outlet

effodiō, -odere, -ōdī, -ossum vt to dig up; (eyes) to gouge out; (house) to ransack

effor, -ārī, -ātus vt to speak, utter; (AUG) to ordain; (LOGIC) to state a proposition

effossus ppp of **effodiō**

effrēnātē adv see **effrēnātus**

effrēnātiō, -ōnis f impetuousness

effrēnātus adj unbridled, violent, unruly

effrēnus adj unbridled

effringō, -ingere, -ēgī, -āctum vt to break open, smash

effugiō, -ugere, -ūgī vi to run away, escape ▶ vt to flee from, escape; to escape the notice of

effugium, -ī and **-iī** nt flight, escape; means of escape

effulgeō, -gēre, -sī vi to shine out, blaze

effultus adj supported

effundō, -undere, -ūdī, -ūsum vt to pour forth, pour out; (crops) to produce in abundance; (missiles) to shoot; (rider) to throw; (speech) to give vent to; (effort) to waste; (money) to squander; (reins) to let go; **sē effundere, sē effundī** rush out; indulge (in)

effūsē adv far and wide; lavishly, extravagantly

effūsiō, -ōnis f pouring out, rushing out; profusion, extravagance; exuberance

effūsus ppp of **effundō** ▶ adj vast, extensive; loose, straggling; lavish, extravagant

effūtiō, -īre vt to blab, chatter

ēgelidus adj mild, cool

egēns, -entis pres p of **egeō** ▶ adj needy

egēnus adj destitute

egeō, -ēre, -uī vi to be in want; (with abl or gen) to need, want

Ēgeria, -ae f nymph who taught Numa

ēgerō, -rere, -ssī, -stum vt to carry out; to discharge, emit

egestās, -ātis f want, poverty

ēgestus ppp of **ēgerō**

ēgī perf of **agō**

ego pron I; **egomet** I (emphatic)

ēgredior, -dī, -ssus vi to go out, come out; to go up, climb; (MIL) to march out; (NAUT) to disembark, put to sea; (speech) to digress ▶ vt to go beyond, quit; (fig) to overstep, surpass

ēgregiē adv uncommonly well, singularly

ēgregius adj outstanding, surpassing; distinguished, illustrious

ēgressus¹ ppa of **ēgredior**

ēgressus², -ūs m departure; way out; digression; (NAUT) landing; (river) mouth

eguī perf of **egeō**

ēgurgitō, -āre vt to lavish

ehem interj (expressing surprise) ha!, so!

ēheu interj (expressing pain) alas!

eho interj (expressing rebuke) look here!

ei interj (expressing alarm) oh!

eī dat of **is**

eia interj (expressing delight, playful remonstrance, encouragement) aha!, come now!, come on!

ēiaculor, -ārī vt to shoot out

ēiciō, -icere, -iēcī, -iectum vt to throw out, drive out, put out; (joint) to dislocate; (mind) to banish; (NAUT) to bring to land, run aground, wreck; (rider) to throw; (speech) to utter; (THEAT) to hiss off; **sē ēicere** rush out, break out

ēiectāmenta, -ōrum *ntpl* refuse

ēiectiō, -ōnis *f* banishment

ēiectō, -āre *vt* to throw up

ēiectus[1] *ppp of* **ēiciō ▸** *adj* shipwrecked

ēiectus[2], -ūs *m* emitting

ēierō, ēiūrō, -āre *vt* to abjure, reject on oath, forswear; (*office*) to resign; **bonam cōpiam ēierāre** declare oneself bankrupt

ēiulātiō, -ōnis *f*, **ēiulātus, -ūs** *m* wailing

ēiulō, -āre *vi* to wail, lament

ēius *pron* his, her, its; **ēiusmodī** such

ej- *etc see* **ei-**

ēlābor, -bī, -psus *vi* to glide away, slip off; to escape, get off; to pass away

ēlabōrātus *adj* studied

ēlabōrō, -āre, -āvī, -ātum *vi* to exert oneself, take great pains ▸ *vt* to work out, elaborate

ēlāmentābilis *adj* very mournful

ēlanguēscō, -ēscere, -ī *vi* to grow faint; to relax

ēlāpsus *ppa of* **ēlābor**

ēlātē *adv* proudly

ēlātiō, -ōnis *f* ecstasy, exaltation

ēlātrō, -āre *vt* to bark out

ēlātus *ppp of* **efferō[2] ▸** *adj* high; exalted

ēlavō, -avāre, -āvī, -autum *and* **-ōtum** *vt* to wash clean; (*comedy*) to rob

Ēlea, -ae *f* town in S. Italy (*birthplace of Parmenides*)

Ēleātēs, Ēleāticus *adj see* **Ēlea**

ēlecebra, -ae *f* snare

ēlēctē *adv* choicely

ēlēctilis *adj* choice

ēlēctiō, -ōnis *f* choice, option

ēlēctō, -āre *vt* to coax out

ēlēctō, -āre *vt* to select

Ēlectra, -ae *f a Pleiad* (*daughter of Atlas; sister of Orestes*)

ēlectrum, -ī *nt* amber; *an alloy of gold and silver*

ēlēctus[1] *ppp of* **ēligō ▸** *adj* select, choice

ēlēctus[2], -ūs *m* choice

ēlegāns, -antis *adj* tasteful, refined, elegant; fastidious; (*things*) fine, choice

ēleganter *adv* with good taste

ēlegantia, -ae *f* taste, finesse, elegance; fastidiousness

elegī, -ōrum *mpl* elegiac verses

ēlēgī *perf of* **ēligō**

elegīa, -ae *f* elegy

Eleleides, -eidum *fpl* Bacchantes

Eleleus, -eī *m* Bacchus

elementum, -ī *nt* element; (*pl*) first principles, rudiments; beginnings; letters (*of alphabet*)

elenchus, -ī *m* a pear-shaped pearl

elephantomacha, -ae *m fighter mounted on an elephant*

elephantus, -ī, elephās, -antis *m* elephant; ivory

Ēlēus, Ēlēius, Ēlēias *adj* Elean; Olympian

Eleusīn, -is *f* Eleusis (*Attic town famous for its mysteries of Demeter*)

Eleusīus *adj see* **Eleusīn**

eleutheria, -ae *f* liberty

ēlevō, -āre *vt* to lift, raise; to alleviate; to make light of, lessen, disparage

ēliciō, -ere, -uī, -itum *vt* to lure out, draw out; (*god*) to call down; (*spirit*) to conjure up; (*fig*) to elicit, draw

ēlīdō, -dere, -sī, -sum *vt* to dash out, squeeze out; to drive out; to crush, destroy

ēligō, -igere, -ēgī, -ēctum *vt* to pick, pluck out; to choose

ēlīminō, -āre *vt* to carry outside

ēlīmō, -āre *vt* to file; (*fig*) to perfect

ēlinguis *adj* speechless; not eloquent

ēlinguō, -āre *vt* to tear the tongue out of

Ēlis, -idis *f district and town in W. Peloponnese* (*famous for Olympia*)

Elissa, -ae *f* Dido

ēlīsus *ppp of* **ēlīdō**

ēlixus *adj* boiled

elleborōsus *adj* quite mad

elleborus, -ī *m*, **elleborum, -ī** *nt* hellebore

ellum, ellam there he/she is!

ēlocō, -āre *vt* to lease, farm out

ēlocūtiō, -ōnis *f* delivery, style

ēlocūtus *ppa of* **ēloquor**

ēlogium, -ī *and* **-iī** *nt* short saying; inscription; (*will*) clause

ēloquens, -entis *adj* eloquent

ēloquenter *adv see* **ēloquens**

ēloquentia, -ae *f* eloquence

ēloquium, -ī *and* **-iī** *nt* eloquence

ēloquor, -quī, -cūtus *vt, vi* to speak out, speak eloquently

ēlūceō, -cēre, -xī *vi* to shine out, glitter

ēluctor, -ārī, -ātus *vi* to struggle, force a way out ▸ *vt* to struggle out of, surmount

ēlūcubrō, -āre, ēlūcubror, -ārī, -ātus *vt* to compose by lamplight

ēlūdificor, -ārī, -ātus *vt* to cheat, play up

ēlūdō, -dere, -sī, -sum *vt* to parry, ward off, foil; to win off at play; to outplay, outmanoeuvre; to cheat, make fun of ▸ *vi* to finish one's sport

ēlūgeō, -gēre, -xī *vt* to mourn for

ēlumbis *adj* feeble

ēluō, -uere, -uī, -ūtum *vt* to wash clean; (*money*) to squander; (*fig*) to wash away, get rid of

ēlūsus *ppp of* **ēlūdō**

ēlūtus *ppp of* **ēluō ▸** *adj* insipid

ēluviēs (*acc* **-em**, *abl* **-ē**) *f* discharge; overflowing

ēluviō, -ōnis *f* deluge

Ēlysium, -ī *nt* Elysium

Ēlysius *adj* Elysian

em *interj* there you are!

ēmancipātiō, -ōnis *f giving a son his independence*; conveyance (*of property*)

ēmancipō, -āre *vt* to declare independent; to transfer, give up, sell

ēmānō, -āre, -āvī, -ātum *vi* to flow out; to spring (from); (*news*) to leak out, become known

Ēmathia, -ae f district of Macedonia; Macedonia, Thessaly

Ēmathidēs, -idum fpl Muses

Ēmathius adj Macedonian, Pharsalian

ēmātūrēscō, -ēscere, -uī vi to soften

emāx, -ācis adj fond of buying

emblēma, -tis nt inlaid work, mosaic

embolium, -ī and **-iī** nt interlude

ēmendābilis adj corrigible

ēmendātē adv see **ēmendātus**

ēmendātiō, -ōnis f correction

ēmendātor, -ōris m, **ēmendātrīx, -rīcis** f corrector

ēmendātus adj faultless

ēmendō, -āre, -āvī, -ātum vt to correct, improve

ēmēnsus ppa of **ēmētior** ▸ adj traversed

ēmentior, -īrī, -ītus vi to tell lies ▸ vt to pretend, fabricate; **ēmentītus** pretended

ēmercor, -ārī vt to purchase

ēmereō, -ēre, -uī, -itum, ēmereor, ēmerērī vt to earn fully, deserve; to lay under an obligation; to complete one's term of service

ēmergō, -gere, -sī, -sum vt to raise out; (fig) to extricate ▸ vi to rise, come up, emerge; (fig) to get clear, extricate oneself; (impers) it becomes evident

ēmeritus ppa of **ēmereor** ▸ adj superannuated, worn-out ▸ m veteran

ēmersus ppp of **ēmergō**

emetica, -ae f emetic

ēmētior, -tīrī, -nsus vt to measure out; to traverse, pass over; (time) to live through; (fig) to impart

ēmetō, -ere vt to harvest

ēmī perf of **emō**

ēmicō, -āre, -uī, -ātum vi to dart out, dash out, flash out; (fig) to shine

ēmigrō, -āre, -āvī, -ātum vi to remove, depart

ēminēns, -entis pres p of **ēmineō** ▸ adj high, projecting; (fig) distinguished, eminent

ēminentia, -ae f prominence; (painting) light

ēmineō, -ēre, -uī vi to stand out, project; to be prominent, be conspicuous, distinguish oneself

ēminor, -ārī vi to threaten

ēminus adv at or from a distance

ēmīror, -ārī vt to marvel at

ēmissārium, -ī and **-iī** nt outlet

ēmissārius, -ī and **-iī** m scout

ēmissīcius adj prying

ēmissiō, -ōnis f letting go, discharge

ēmissus¹ ppp of **ēmittō**

ēmissus², -ūs m emission

ēmittō, -ittere, -īsī, -issum vt to send out, let out; to let go, let slip; (missile) to discharge; (person) to release, free; (sound) to utter; (writing) to publish

emō, -ere, ēmī, emptum vt to buy, procure; to win over; **bene emere** buy cheap; **male emere** buy dear; **in diem emere** buy on credit

ēmoderor, -ārī vt to give expression to

ēmodulor, -ārī vt to sing through

ēmōlior, -īrī vt to accomplish

ēmolliō, -īre, -iī, -ītum vt to soften; to mollify; to enervate

ēmolumentum, -ī nt profit, advantage

ēmoneō, -ēre vt to strongly advise

ēmorior, -ī, -tuus vi to die; (fig) to pass away

ēmortuālis adj of death

ēmoveō, -ovēre, -ōvī, -ōtum vt to remove, drive away

Empedoclēs, -is m Sicilian philosopher

Empedoclēus adj see **Empedoclēs**

empīricus, -ī m empirical doctor

emporium, -ī and **-iī** nt market, market town

emptiō, -ōnis f buying; a purchase

emptitō, -āre vt to often buy

emptor, -ōris m purchaser

emptus ppp of **emō**

ēmulgeō, -ēre vt to drain

ēmunctus ppp of **ēmungō** ▸ adj discriminating

ēmungō, -gere, -xī, -ctum vt to blow the nose of; (comedy) to cheat

ēmūniō, -īre, -īvī, -ītum vt to strengthen, secure; to build up; to make roads through

ēn interj (drawing attention) look!, see!; (command) come now!

ēnārrābilis adj describable

ēnārrō, -āre, -āvī, -ātum vt to describe in detail

ēnāscor, -scī, -tus vi to sprout, grow

ēnatō, -āre vi to swim ashore; (fig) to escape

ēnātus ppa of **ēnāscor**

ēnāvigō, -āre vi to sail clear, clear ▸ vt to sail over

Enceladus, -ī m giant under Etna

endromis, -dis f sports wrap

Endymiōn, -ōnis m a beautiful youth loved by the Moon, and doomed to lasting sleep

ēnecō, -āre, -uī and **-āvī, -tum** and **-ātum** vt to kill; to wear out; to torment

ēnervātus adj limp

ēnervis adj enfeebled

ēnervō, -āre, -āvī, -ātum vt to weaken, unman

ēnicō etc see **ēnecō**

enim conj (affirming) yes, truly, in fact; (explaining) for, for instance, of course; **at ~** but it will be objected; **quid ~?** well?; **sed ~** but actually

enimvērō conj certainly, yes indeed

Enīpeus, -eī m river in Thessaly

ēnīsus ppa of **ēnītor**

ēniteō, -ēre, -uī vi to shine, brighten up; (fig) to be brilliant, distinguish oneself

ēnitēscō, -ēscere, -uī vi to shine, be brilliant

ēnītor, -tī, -sus and **-xus** vi to struggle up, climb; to strive, make a great effort ▸ vt to give birth to; to climb

ēnīxē adv earnestly

ēnīxus ppa of **ēnītor** ▸ adj strenuous

Enniānus adj see **Ennius**

Ennius, -ī m greatest of the early Latin poets

Ennosigaeus, -ī m Earthshaker, Neptune
ēnō, -āre, -āvī vi to swim out, swim ashore;
to fly away
ēnōdātē adv lucidly
ēnōdātiō, -ōnis f unravelling
ēnōdis adj free from knots; plain
ēnōdō, -āre, -āvī, -ātum vt to elucidate
ēnormis adj irregular; immense
ēnōtēscō, -ēscere, -uī vi to get known
ēnotō, -āre vt to make a note of
ēnsiculus, -ī m little sword
ēnsiger, -ī adj with his sword
ēnsis, -is m sword
enthymēma, -tis nt argument
ēnūbō, -bere, -psī vi to marry out of one's
station; to marry and go away
ēnucleātē adv plainly
ēnucleātus adj (style) straightforward; (votes)
honest
ēnucleō, -āre vt to elucidate
ēnumerātiō, -ōnis f enumeration; (RHET)
recapitulation
ēnumerō, -āre vt to count up; to pay out; to
relate
ēnūntiātiō, -ōnis f proposition
ēnūntiātum, -ī nt proposition
ēnūntiō, -āre vt to disclose, report; to express;
to pronounce
ēnūptiō, -ōnis f marrying out of one's station
ēnūtriō, -īre vt to feed, bring up
eō¹, īre, īvī and **iī, itum** vi to go; (MIL) to
march; (time) to pass; (event) to proceed, turn
out; **in alia omnia īre** vote against a bill; **in
sententiam īre** support a motion; **sīc eat** so
may he fare!; **ī** (mocking) go on!
eō² adv (place) thither, there; (purpose) with a
view to; (degree) so far, to such a pitch; (time) so
long; (cause) on that account, for the reason;
(with compar) the; **accēdit eō** besides; **rēs erat
eō locī** such was the state of affairs; **eō magis**
all the more
eōdem adv to the same place, purpose or
person; **~ locī** in the same place
Ēōs f dawn
Ēōus adj at dawn, eastern ▶ m morning star;
Oriental
Ēpamīnōndās, -ae m Theban general
ēpāstus adj eaten up
ephēbus, -ī m youth (18 to 20)
ephēmeris, -idis f diary
Ephesius adj see **Ephesus**
Ephesus, -ī f Ionian town in Asia Minor
ephippiātus adj riding a saddled horse
ephippium, -ī and **-iī** nt saddle
ephorus, -ī m a Spartan magistrate, ephor
Ephyra, -ae, Ephyrē, -ēs f Corinth
Ephyrēius adj see **Ephyra**
Epicharmus, -ī m Greek philosopher and comic
poet
epichysis, -is f kind of jug
epicōpus adj rowing
Epicūrēus adj Epicurean

Epicūrus, -ī m famous Greek philosopher
epicus adj epic
Epidaurius adj see **Epidaurus**
Epidaurus, -ī f town in E. Peloponnese
epidīcticus adj (RHET) for display
epigramma, -tis nt inscription; epigram
epilogus, -ī m peroration
epimēnia, -ōrum ntpl a month's rations
Epimēthis, -dis f Pyrrha (daughter of Epimetheus)
epirēdium, -ī and **-iī** nt trace
Ēpīrōtēs, -ōtae m native of Epirus
Ēpīrōticus, Ēpīrēnsis adj see **Ēpīrus**
Ēpīrus, Ēpīros, -ī f district of N.W. Greece
episcopus, -ī m bishop
epistolium, -ī and **-iī** nt short note
epistula, -ae f letter; **ab epistulīs** secretary
epitaphium, -ī and **-iī** nt funeral oration
epithēca, -ae f addition
epitoma, -ae, epitomē, -ēs f abridgement
epityrum, -ī nt olive salad
epops, -is m hoopoe
epos (pl **-ē**) nt epic
ēpōtō, -āre, -āvī, -um vt to drink up, drain; to
waste in drink; to absorb
epulae, -ārum fpl dishes; feast, banquet
epulāris adj at a banquet
epulō, -ōnis m guest at a feast; priest in charge
of religious banquets
epulor, -ārī, -ātus vi to be at a feast ▶ vt to
feast on
epulum, -ī nt banquet
equa, -ae f mare
eques, -itis m horseman, trooper; (pl) cavalry;
knight, member of the equestrian order
equester, -ris adj equestrian, cavalry- (in cpds)
equidem adv (affirming) indeed, of course, for
my part; (concessive) to be sure
equīnus adj horse's
equīria, -ōrum ntpl horseraces
equitātus, -ūs m cavalry
equitō, -āre vi to ride
equuleus etc see **eculeus**
equulus, -ī m colt
equus, -ī m horse; (ASTR) Pegasus; **~ bipēs**
seahorse; **equō merēre** serve in the cavalry;
equīs virīsque with might and main
era, -ae f mistress (of the house); (goddess) Lady
ērādīcō, -āre vt to root out, destroy
ērādō, -dere, -sī, -sum vt to erase, obliterate
Eratō f Muse of lyric poetry
Eratosthenēs, -is m famous Alexandrian
geographer
Erebēus adj see **Erebus**
Erebus, -ī m god of darkness; the lower world
Erechtheus, -eī m legendary king of Athens
Erechthēus adj see **Erechtheus**
Erechthīdae mpl Athenians
Erechthis, -idis f Orithyia; Procris
ērēctus ppp of **ērigō** ▶ adj upright, lofty; noble,
haughty; alert, tense; resolute
ērēpō, -ere, -sī vi to creep out, clamber up ▶ vt
to crawl over, climb

ēreptiō, -ōnis f seizure, robbery

ēreptor, -ōris m robber

ēreptus ppp of **ēripiō**

ergā prep (with acc) towards; against

ergastulum, -ī nt prison (esp for slaves); (pl) convicts

ergō adv therefore, consequently; (questions, commands) then, so; (resuming) well then; (with gen) for the sake of, because of

Erichthonius, -ī m a king of Troy; a king of Athens ▶ adj Trojan; Athenian

ēricius, -ī and **-iī** m hedgehog; (MIL) beam with iron spikes

Ēridanus, -ī m mythical name of river Po

erifuga, -ae m runaway slave

ērigō, -igere, -ēxī, -ēctum vt to make upright, raise up, erect; to excite; to encourage

Ērigonē, -ēs f (constellation) Virgo

Ērigonēius adj see **Ērigonē**

erīlis adj the master's, the mistress's

Erīnȳs, -yos f Fury; (fig) curse, frenzy

Eriphȳla, -ae f mother of Alcmaeon (who killed her)

ēripiō, -ipere, -ipuī, -eptum vt to tear away, pull away, take by force; to rob; to rescue; **sē ēripere** escape

ērogātiō, -ōnis f paying out

ērogitō, -āre vt to enquire

ērogō, -āre, -āvī, -ātum vt to pay out, expend; to bequeath

errābundus adj wandering

errāticus adj roving, shifting

errātiō, -ōnis f wandering, roving

errātum, -ī nt mistake, error

errātus, -ūs m wandering

errō¹, -āre, -āvī, -ātum vi to wander, stray, lose one's way; to waver; to make a mistake, err ▶ vt to traverse; **stēllae errantēs** planets

errō², -ōnis m vagabond

error, -ōris m wandering; meander, maze; uncertainty; error, mistake, delusion; deception

ērubēscō, -ēscere, -uī vi to blush; to feel ashamed ▶ vt to blush for, be ashamed of; to respect

ērūca, -ae f colewort

ēructō, -āre vt to belch, vomit; to talk drunkenly about; to throw up

ērudiō, -īre, -iī, -ītum vt to educate, instruct

ērudītē adv learnedly

ērudītiō, -ōnis f education, instruction; learning, knowledge

ērudītulus adj somewhat skilled

ērudītus ppp of **ērudiō** ▶ adj learned, educated, accomplished

ērumpō, -umpere, -ūpī, -uptum vt to break open; to make break out ▶ vi to burst out, break through; to end (in)

ēruō, -ere, -ī, -tum vt to uproot, tear out; to demolish, destroy; to elicit, draw out; to rescue

ēruptiō, -ōnis f eruption; (MIL) sally

ēruptus ppp of **ērumpō**

erus, -ī m master (of the house); owner

ērutus ppp of **ēruō**

ervum, -ī nt vetch

Erycīnus adj of Eryx; of Venus; Sicilian ▶ f Venus

Erymanthius, -is adj see **Erymanthus**

Erymanthus, Erymanthī m mountain range in Arcadia (where Hercules killed the boar)

Eryx, -cis m town and mountain in the extreme W. of Sicily

esca, -ae f food, titbits; bait

escārius adj of food; of bait ▶ ntpl dishes

ēscendō, -endere, -endī, -ēnsum vi to climb up, go up ▶ vt to mount

ēscēnsiō, -ōnis f raid (from the coast), disembarkation

esculentus adj edible, tasty

Esquiliae, -iārum fpl Esquiline hill (in Rome)

Esquilīnus adj Esquiline ▶ f Esquiline gate

essedārius, -ī and **-iī** m chariot fighter

essedum, -ī nt war chariot

essitō, -āre vt to usually eat

ēst pres of **edō**

ēstrīx, -īcis f glutton

ēsuriālis adj of hunger

ēsuriō, -īre, -ītum vi to be hungry ▶ vt to hunger for

ēsurītiō, -ōnis f hunger

ēsus ppp of **edō**

et conj and; (repeated) both ... and; (adding emphasis) in fact, yes; (comparing) as, than ▶ adv also, too; even

etenim conj (adding an explanation) and as a matter of fact, in fact

etēsiae, -ārum fpl Etesian winds

etēsius adj see **etēsiae**

ēthologus, -ī m mimic

etiam adv also, besides; (emphatic) even, actually; (affirming) yes, certainly; (indignant) really!; (time) still, as yet; again; ~ **atque** ~ again and again; ~ **cavēs** do be careful!; **nihil** ~ nothing at all

etiamdum adv still, as yet

etiamnum, etiamnunc adv still, till now, till then; besides

etiamsī conj even if, although

etiamtum, etiamtunc adv till then, still

Etrūria, -ae f district of Italy north of Rome

Etruscus adj Etruscan

etsī conj even if, though; and yet

etymologia, -ae f etymology

eu interj well done!, bravo!

Euan m Bacchus

Euander, Euanderus, -rī m Evander (ancient king on the site of Rome)

Euandrius adj see **Euander**

euax interj hurrah!

Euboea, -oeae f Greek island

Euboicus adj Euboean

euge, eugepae interj bravo!, cheers!

Euhan m Bacchus

euhāns, -antis adj shouting the Bacchic cry

Euhias f Bacchante

Euhius, -ī m Bacchus

euhoe interj ecstatic cry of Bacchic revellers

Euius, -i m Bacchus

Eumenides, -um fpl Furies

eunūchus, -ī m eunuch

Euphrātēs, -is m (river) Euphrates

Eupolis, -dis m Athenian comic poet

Eurīpidēs, -is m Athenian tragic poet

Eurīpidēus adj see **Eurīpidēs**

Eurīpus, -ī m strait between Euboea and mainland; a channel, conduit

Eurōpa, -ae, Eurōpē, -ēs f mythical princess of Tyre (who was carried by a bull to Crete); (continent of) Europe

Eurōpaeus adj see **Eurōpa**

Eurōtās, -ae m river of Sparta

Eurōus adj eastern

Eurus, -ī m east wind; south-east wind

Eurydicē, -ēs f wife of Orpheus

Eurystheus, -eī m king of Mycenae (who imposed the labours on Hercules)

euschēmē adv gracefully

Euterpē, -ēs f Muse of music

Euxīnus m the Black (Sea)

ēvādō, -dere, -sī, -sum vi to come out; to climb up; to escape; to turn out, result, come true ▸ vt to pass, mount; to escape from

ēvagor, -ārī, -ātus vi (MIL) to manoeuvre; (fig) to spread ▸ vt to stray beyond

ēvalēscō, -ēscere, -uī vi to grow, increase; to be able; to come into vogue

Ēvander etc see **Euander**

ēvānēscō, -ēscere, -uī vi to vanish, die away, lose effect

ēvangelium, -ī and **-iī** nt (ECCL) Gospel

ēvānidus adj vanishing

ēvāsī perf of **ēvādō**

ēvāstō, -āre vt to devastate

ēvehō, -here, -xī, -ctum vt to carry out; to raise up, exalt; to spread abroad; (pass) to ride, sail, move out

ēvellō, -ellere, -ellī, -ulsum vt to tear out, pull out; to eradicate

ēveniō, -enīre, -ēnī, -entum vi to come out; to turn out, result; to come to pass, happen, befall

ēventum, -ī nt result, issue; occurrence, event; fortune, experience

ēventus, -ūs m result, issue; success; fortune, fate

ēverberō, -āre vt to beat violently

ēverriculum, -ī nt dragnet

ēverrō, -rere, -rī, -sum vt to sweep out, clean out

ēversiō, -ōnis f overthrow, destruction

ēversor, -ōris m destroyer

ēversus ppp of **ēverrō; ēvertō**

ēvertō, -tere, -tī, -sum vt to turn out, eject; to turn up, overturn; to overthrow, ruin, destroy

ēvestīgātus adj tracked down

ēvictus ppp of **ēvincō**

ēvidens, -entis adj visible, plain, evident

ēvidenter adv see **ēvidens**

ēvidentia, -ae f distinctness

ēvigilō, -āre, -āvī, -ātum vi to be wide awake ▸ vt to compose carefully

ēvīlēscō, -ere vi to become worthless

ēvinciō, -cīre, -xī, -ctum vt to garland, crown

ēvincō, -incere, -īcī, -ictum vt to overcome, conquer; to prevail over; to prove

ēvirō, -āre vt to castrate

ēviscerō, -āre vt to disembowel, tear to pieces

ēvītābilis adj avoidable

ēvītō, -āre, -āvī, -ātum vt to avoid, clear

ēvocātī, -ōrum mpl veteran volunteers

ēvocātor, -ōris m enlister

ēvocō, -āre, -āvī, -ātum vt to call out, summon; to challenge; to call up; to call forth, evoke

ēvolō, -āre, -āvī, -ātum vi to fly out, fly away; to rush out; (fig) to rise, soar

ēvolūtiō, -ōnis f unrolling (a book)

ēvolvō, -vere, -vī, -ūtum vt to roll out, roll along; to unroll, unfold; (book) to open, read; (fig) to disclose, unravel, disentangle

ēvomō, -ere, -uī, -itum vt to vomit up, disgorge

ēvulgō, -āre, -āvī, -ātum vt to divulge, make public

ēvulsiō, -ōnis f pulling out

ēvulsus ppp of **ēvellō**

ex, ē prep (with abl) (place) out of, from, down from; (person) from; (time) after, immediately after, since; (change) from being; (source, material) of; (cause) by reason of, through; (conformity) in accordance with; **ex itinere** on the march; **ex parte** in part; **ex quō** since; **ex rē** for the good of; **ex ūsū** for the good of; **ē rē pūblicā** constitutionally; **ex sententiā** to one's liking; **aliud ex aliō** one thing after another; **ūnus ex** one of

exacerbō, -āre vt to exasperate

exāctiō, -ōnis f expulsion; supervision; tax; (debts) calling in

exāctor, -ōris m expeller; superintendent; tax collector

exāctus ppp of **exigō** ▸ adj precise, exact

exacuō, -uere, -uī, -ūtum vt to sharpen; (fig) to quicken, inflame

exadversum, exadversus adv, prep (with acc) right opposite

exaedificātiō, -ōnis f construction

exaedificō, -āre vt to build up; to finish the building of

exaequātiō, -ōnis f levelling

exaequō, -āre, -āvī, -ātum vt to level out; to compensate; to put on an equal footing; to equal

exaestuō, -āre vi to boil up

exaggerātiō, -ōnis f exaltation

exaggerō, -āre, -āvī, -ātum vt to pile up; (fig) to heighten, enhance

exagitātor, -ōris m critic

exagitō, -āre, -āvī, -ātum vt to disturb, harass; to scold, censure; to excite, incite

exagōga, -ae f export

exalbēscō, -ēscere, -uī vi to turn quite pale

exāmen, -inis nt swarm, crowd; tongue (of a balance); examining

examinō, -āre, -āvī, -ātum vt to weigh; to consider, test

examussim adv exactly, perfectly

exanclō, -āre vt to drain; to endure to the end

exanimālis adj dead; deadly

exanimātiō, -ōnis f panic

exanimis adj lifeless, breathless; terrified

exanimō, -āre, -āvī, -ātum vt to wind; to kill; to terrify, agitate; (pass) to be out of breath

exanimus see **exanimis**

exārdēscō, -dēscere, -sī, -sum vi to catch fire, blaze up; (fig) to be inflamed, break out

exārēscō, -ēscere, -uī vi to dry, dry up

exarmō, -āre vt to disarm

exarō, -āre, -āvī, -ātum vt to plough up; to cultivate, produce; (brow) to furrow; (writing) to pen

exārsī perf of **exārdēscō**

exasciātus adj hewn out

exasperō, -āre, -āvī, -ātum vt to roughen; (fig) to provoke

exauctōrō, -āre, -āvī, -ātum vt (MIL) to discharge, release; to cashier

exaudiō, -īre, -īvī, -ītum vt to hear clearly; to listen to; to obey

exaugeō, -ēre vt to increase

exaugurātiō, -ōnis f desecrating

exaugurō, -āre vt to desecrate

exauspicō, -āre vi to take an omen

exbibō etc see **ēbibō**

excaecō, -āre vt to blind; (river) to block up

excandēscentia, -ae f growing anger

excandēscō, -ēscere, -uī vi to burn, be inflamed

excantō, -āre vt to charm out, spirit away

excarnificō, -āre vt to tear to pieces

excavō, -āre vt to hollow out

excēdō, -ēdere, -essī, -essum vi to go out, go away; to die, disappear; to advance, proceed (to); to digress ▶ vt to leave; to overstep, exceed

excellēns, -entis pres p of **excellō** ▶ adj outstanding, excellent

excellenter adv see **excellēns**

excellentia, -ae f superiority, excellence

excellō, -ere vi to be eminent, excel

excelsē adv loftily

excelsitās, -ātis f loftiness

excelsum, -ī nt height

excelsus adj high, elevated; eminent, illustrious

exceptiō, -ōnis f exception, restriction; (LAW) objection

exceptō, -āre vt to catch, take out

exceptus ppp of **excipiō**

excernō, -ernere, -rēvī, -rētum vt to sift out, separate

excerpō, -ere, -sī, -tum vt to take out; to select, copy out extracts; to leave out, omit

excessus, -ūs m departure, death

excetra, -ae f snake

excidiō, -ōnis f destruction

excidium, -ī and -iī nt overthrow, destruction

excidō, -ere, -ī vi to fall out, fall; (speech) to slip out, escape; (memory) to get forgotten, escape; (person) to fail, lose; (things) to disappear, be lost

excīdō, -dere, -dī, -sum vt to cut off, hew out, fell; to raze; (fig) to banish

excieō vt see **exciō**

exciō, -īre, -īvī and -iī, -ītum and -ītum vt to call out, rouse, summon; to occasion, produce; to excite

excipiō, -ipere, -ēpī, -eptum vt to take out, remove; to exempt, make an exception of, mention specifically; to take up, catch, intercept, overhear; to receive, welcome, entertain; to come next to, follow after, succeed

excīsiō, -ōnis f destroying

excīsus ppp of **excīdō**

excitātus adj loud, strong

excitō, -āre, -āvī, -ātum vt to rouse, wake up, summon; to raise, build; to call on (to stand up); (fig) to encourage, revive, excite

excitus, excītus ppp of **exciō**

exclāmātiō, -ōnis f exclamation

exclāmō, -āre, -āvī, -ātum vi to cry out, shout ▶ vt to exclaim, call

exclūdō, -dere, -sī, -sum vt to shut out, exclude; to shut off, keep off; (egg) to hatch out; (eye) to knock out; (fig) to prevent, except

exclūsiō, -ōnis f shutting out

exclūsus ppp of **exclūdō**

excoctus ppp of **excoquō**

excōgitātiō, -ōnis f thinking out, devising

excōgitō, -āre, -āvī, -ātum vt to think out, contrive

excolō, -olere, -oluī, -ultum vt to work carefully; to perfect, refine

excoquō, -quere, -xī, -ctum vt to boil away; to remove with heat, make with heat; to dry up

excors, -dis adj senseless, stupid

excrēmentum, -ī nt excretion

excreō etc see **exscreō**

excrēscō, -scere, -vī, -tum vi to grow, rise up

excrētus ppp of **excernō**

excruciō, -āre, -āvī, -ātum vt to torture, torment

excubiae, -ārum fpl keeping guard, watch; sentry

excubitor, -ōris m sentry

excubō, -āre, -uī, -itum vi to sleep out of doors; to keep watch; (fig) to be on the alert

excūdō, -dere, -dī, -sum vt to strike out, hammer out; (egg) to hatch; (fig) to make, compose

exculcō, -āre vt to beat, tramp down

excultus ppp of **excolō**

excurrō, -rrere, -currī and -rī, -rsum vi to run out, hurry out; to make an excursion; (MIL) to make a sortie; (*place*) to extend, project; (*fig*) to expand

excursiō, -ōnis *f* raid, sortie; (*gesture*) stepping forward; (*fig*) outset

excursor, -ōris *m* scout

excursus, -ūs *m* excursion, raid, charge

excūsābilis *adj* excusable

excūsātē *adv* excusably

excūsātiō, -ōnis *f* excuse, plea

excūsō, -āre, -āvī, -ātum *vt* to excuse; to apologize for; to plead as an excuse

excussus *ppp of* **excutiō**

excūsus *ppp of* **excūdō**

excutiō, -tere, -ssī, -ssum *vt* to shake out, shake off; to knock out, drive out, cast off; (*fig*) to discard, banish; to examine, inspect

exdorsuō, -āre *vt* to fillet

exec- *etc see* **exsec-**

exedō, -esse, -ēdī, -ēsum *vt* to eat up; to wear away, destroy; (*feelings*) to prey on

exedra, -ae *f* hall, lecture room

exedrium, -ī *and* **-iī** *nt* sitting room

exēmī *perf of* **eximō**

exemplar, -āris *nt* copy; likeness; model, ideal

exemplārēs *mpl* copies

exemplum, -ī *nt* copy; example, sample, precedent, pattern; purport, nature; warning, object lesson; ~ **dare** set an example; **exemplī causā, exemplī grātiā** for instance

exemptus *ppp of* **eximō**

exenterō, -āre *vt* (*comedy*) to empty, clean out; to torture

exeō, -īre, -iī, -itum *vi* to go out, leave; to come out, issue; (*MIL*) to march out; (*time*) to expire; to spring up, rise ▶ *vt* to pass beyond; to avoid; **exīre ex potestāte** lose control

exeq- *etc see* **exseq-**

exerceō, -ēre, -uī, -itum *vt* to keep busy, supervise; (*ground*) to work, cultivate; (*MIL*) to drill, exercise; (*mind*) to engage, employ; (*occupation*) to practise, follow, carry on; (*trouble*) to worry, harass; **sē exercēre** practise, exercise

exercitātiō, -ōnis *f* practice, exercise, experience

exercitātus *adj* practised, trained, versed; troubled

exercitium, -ī *and* **-iī** *nt* exercising

exercitō, -āre *vt* to exercise

exercitor, -ōris *m* trainer

exercitus¹ *ppp of* **exerceō** ▶ *adj* disciplined; troubled; troublesome

exercitus², -ūs *m* army (*esp the infantry*); assembly; troop, flock; exercise

exerō *etc see* **exserō**

exēsor, -ōris *m* corroder

exēsus *ppp of* **exedō**

exhālātiō, -ōnis *f* vapour

exhālō, -āre *vt* to exhale, breathe out ▶ *vi* to steam; to expire

exhauriō, -rīre, -sī, -stum *vt* to drain off; to empty; to take away, remove; (*fig*) to exhaust, finish; (*trouble*) to undergo, endure to the end

exhērēdō, -āre *vt* to disinherit

exhērēs, -ēdis *adj* disinherited

exhibeō, -ere, -uī, -itum *vt* to hold out, produce (in public); to display, show; to cause, occasion

exhilarātus *adj* delighted

exhorrēscō, -ēscere, -uī *vi* to be terrified ▶ *vt* to be terrified at

exhortātiō, -ōnis *f* encouragement

exhortor, -ārī, -ātus *vt* to encourage

exigō, -igere, -ēgī, -āctum *vt* to drive out, thrust; (*payment*) to exact, enforce; to demand, claim; (*goods*) to dispose of; (*time*) to pass, complete; (*work*) to finish; (*news*) to ascertain; to test, examine, consider

exiguē *adv* briefly, slightly, hardly

exiguitās, -ātis *f* smallness, meagreness

exiguus *adj* small, short, meagre ▶ *nt* a little bit

exiliō *etc see* **exsiliō**

exīlis *adj* thin, small, meagre; poor; (*style*) flat, insipid

exīlitās, -ātis *f* thinness, meagreness

exīliter *adv* feebly

exilium *etc see* **exsilium**

exim *see* **exinde**

eximiē *adv* exceptionally

eximius *adj* exempt; select; distinguished, exceptional

eximō, -imere, -ēmī, -emptum *vt* to take out, remove; to release, free; to exempt; (*time*) to waste; (*fig*) to banish

exin *see* **exinde**

exināniō, -īre, -iī, -ītum *vt* to empty; to pillage

exinde *adv* (*place*) from there, next; (*time*) then, thereafter, next; (*measure*) accordingly

exīstimātiō, -ōnis *f* opinion, judgment; reputation, character; (*money*) credit

exīstimātor, -ōris *m* judge, critic

exīstimō, -āre, -āvī, -ātum *vt* to value, estimate, judge, think, consider

existō *etc see* **exsistō**

exīstumō *vt see* **exīstimō**

exitiābilis *adj* deadly, fatal

exitiālis *adj* deadly

exitiōsus *adj* pernicious, fatal

exitium, -ī *and* **-iī** *nt* destruction, ruin

exitus, -ūs *m* departure; way out, outlet; conclusion, end; death; outcome, result

exlēx, -ēgis *adj* above the law, lawless

exoculō, -āre *vt* to knock the eyes out of

exodium, -ī *and* **-iī** *nt* afterpiece

exolēscō, -scere, -vī, -tum *vi* to decay, become obsolete

exolētus *adj* full-grown

exonerō, -āre, -āvī, -ātum *vt* to unload, discharge; (*fig*) to relieve, exonerate

exoptātus *adj* welcome

exoptō, -āre, -āvī, -ātum *vt* to long for, desire

exōrābilis *adj* sympathetic

exōrātor, -ōris *m* successful pleader

exōrdior, -dīrī, -sus vt to lay the warp; to begin
exōrdium, -ī and **-iī** nt beginning; (RHET) introductory section
exorior, -īrī, -tus vi to spring up, come out, rise; to arise, appear, start
exōrnātiō, -ōnis f embellishment
exōrnātor, -ōris m embellisher
exōrnō, -āre, -āvī, -ātum vt to equip, fit out; to embellish, adorn
exōrō, -āre, -āvī, -ātum vt to prevail upon, persuade; to obtain, win by entreaty
exōrsus¹ ppa of **exōrdior** ▶ adj begun ▶ ntpl preamble
exōrsus², -ūs m beginning
exortus¹ ppa of **exorior**
exortus², -ūs m rising; east
exos, -ossis adj boneless
exōsculor, -ārī, -ātus vt to kiss fondly
exossō, -āre vt to bone
exōstra, -ae f stage mechanism; (fig) public
exōsus adj detesting
exōticus adj foreign
expallēscō, -ēscere, -uī vi to turn pale, be afraid
expalpō, -āre vt to coax out
expandō, -ere, -nsī, -nsum and **-ssum** vt to unfold
expatrō, -āre vt to squander
expavēscō, -ere, expāvī vi to be terrified ▶ vt to dread
expect- etc see **exspect-**
expediō, -īre, -īvī and **-iī, -ītum** vt to free, extricate, disentangle; to prepare, clear (for action); to put right, settle; to explain, relate; (impers) it is useful, expedient
expedītē adv readily, freely
expedītiō, -ōnis f (MIL) expedition, enterprise
expedītus ppp of **expediō** ▶ adj light-armed; ready, prompt; at hand ▶ m light-armed soldier; **in expedītō esse habēre** be, have in readiness
expellō, -ellere, -ulī, -ulsum vt to drive away, eject, expel; to remove, repudiate
expendō, -endere, -endī, -ēnsum vt to weigh out; to pay out; (penalty) to suffer; (mind) to ponder, consider, judge
expēnsum, -ī nt payment, expenditure
expergēfaciō, -facere, -fēcī, -factum vt to rouse, excite
expergīscor, -gīscī, -rēctus vi to wake up; to bestir oneself
expergō, -ere, -ī, -itum vt to awaken
experiēns, -entis pres p of **experior** ▶ adj enterprising
experientia, -ae f experiment; endeavour; experience, practice
experīmentum, -ī nt proof, test; experience
experior, -īrī, -tus vt to test, make trial of; to attempt, experience; (LAW) to go to law; (perf tenses) to know from experience
experrēctus ppa of **expergīscor**
expers, -tis adj having no part in, not sharing; free from, without

expertus ppa (occ pass) of **experior** ▶ adj proved, tried; experienced
expetessō, -ere vt to desire
expetō, -ere, -īvī and **-iī, -ītum** vt to aim at, tend towards; to desire, covet; to attack; to demand, require ▶ vi to befall, happen
expiātiō, -ōnis f atonement
expictus ppp of **expingō**
expīlātiō, -ōnis f pillaging
expīlātor, -ōris m plunderer
expīlō, -āre, -āvī, -ātum vt to rob, plunder
expingō, -ingere, -inxī, -ictum vt to portray
expiō, -āre, -āvī, -ātum vt to purify; to atone for, make amends for; to avert (evil)
expīrō etc see **exspīrō**
expiscor, -ārī, -ātus vt to try to find out, ferret out
explānātē adv see **explānātus**
explānātiō, -ōnis f explanation
explānātor, -ōris m interpreter
explānātus adj distinct
explānō, -āre, -āvī, -ātum vt to state clearly, explain; to pronounce clearly
explaudō etc see **explōdō**
explēmentum, -ī nt filling
expleō, -ēre, -ēvī, -ētum vt to fill up; to complete; (desire) to satisfy, appease; (duty) to perform, discharge; (loss) to make good; (time) to fulfil, complete
explētiō, -ōnis f satisfying
explētus ppp of **expleō** ▶ adj complete
explicātē adv plainly
explicātiō, -ōnis f uncoiling; expounding, analysing
explicātor, -ōris m, **explicātrīx, -rīcis** f expounder
explicātus¹ adj spread out; plain, clear
explicātus², -ūs m explanation
explicitus adj easy
explicō, -āre, -āvī and **-uī, -ātum** and **-itum** vt to unfold, undo, spread out; (book) to open; (MIL) to deploy, extend; (difficulty) to put in order, settle; (speech) to develop, explain; to set free
explōdō, -dere, -sī, -sum vt to hiss off, drive away; (fig) to reject
explōrātē adv with certainty
explōrātiō, -ōnis f spying
explōrātor, -ōris m spy, scout
explōrātus adj certain, sure
explōrō, -āre, -āvī, -ātum vt to investigate, reconnoitre; to ascertain; to put to the test
explōsī perf of **explōdō**
explōsiō, -ōnis f driving off (the stage)
explōsus ppp of **explōdō**
expoliō, -īre, -īvī, -ītum vt to smooth off, polish; (fig) to refine, embellish
expolītiō, -ōnis f smoothing off; polish, finish
expōnō, -ōnere, -osuī, -ositum vt to set out, put out; (child) to expose; (NAUT) to disembark; (money) to offer; (fig) to set forth, expose, display; (speech) to explain, expound

exporrigō, -igere, -ēxī, -ēctum vt to extend, smooth out

exportātiō, -ōnis f exporting

exportō, -āre, -āvī, -ātum vt to carry out, export

exposcō, -ere, expoposcī vt to implore, pray for; to demand

expositīcius adj foundling

expositiō, -ōnis f narration, explanation

expositus ppp of **expōnō** ▸ adj open, affable; vulgar

expostulātiō, -ōnis f complaint

expostulō, -āre, -āvī, -ātum vt to demand urgently; to complain of, expostulate

expōtus ppp of **ēpōtō**

expressus ppp of **exprimō** ▸ adj distinct, prominent

exprimō, -imere, -essī, -essum vt to squeeze out, force out; to press up; (fig) to extort, wrest; (art) to mould, model; (words) to imitate, portray, translate, pronounce

exprobrātiō, -ōnis f reproach

exprobrō, -āre, -āvī, -ātum vt to reproach, cast up

exprōmō, -ere, -psī, -ptum vt to bring out, fetch out; (acts) to exhibit, practise; (feelings) to give vent to; (speech) to disclose, state

expugnābilis adj capable of being taken by storm

expugnācior, -ōris adj more effective

expugnātiō, -ōnis f storming, assault

expugnātor, -ōris m stormer

expugnō, -āre, -āvī, -ātum vt to storm, reduce; to conquer; (fig) to overcome, extort

expulī perf of **expellō**

expulsiō, -ōnis f expulsion

expulsor, -ōris m expeller

expulsus ppp of **expellō**

expultrīx, -īcis f expeller

expungō, -ungere, -ūnxī, -ūnctum vt to prick out, cancel

expūrgātiō, -ōnis f excuse

expūrgō, -āre vt to purify; to justify

exputō, -āre vt to consider, comprehend

exquīrō, -rere, -sīvī, -sītum vt to search out, investigate; to inquire; to devise

exquīsītē adv with particular care

exquīsītus ppp of **exquīrō** ▸ adj well thought out, choice

exsaeviō, -īre vi to cease raging

exsanguis adj bloodless, pale; feeble

exsarciō, -cīre, -tum vt to repair

exsatiō, -āre vt to satiate, satisfy

exsaturābilis adj appeasable

exsaturō, -āre vt to satiate

exsce- etc see **esce-**

exscindō, -ndere, -dī, -ssum vt to extirpate

exscreō, -āre vt to cough up

exscrībō, -bere, -psī, -ptum vt to copy out; to note down

exsculpō, -ere, -sī, -tum vt to carve out; to erase; (fig) to extort

exsecō, -āre, -uī, -tum vt to cut out; to castrate

exsecrābilis adj cursing, deadly

exsecrātiō, -ōnis f curse; solemn oath

exsecrātus adj accursed

exsecror, -ārī, -ātus vt to curse; to take an oath

exsectiō, -ōnis f cutting out

exsecūtiō, -ōnis f management; discussion

exsecūtus ppa of **exsequor**

exsequiae, -ārum fpl funeral, funeral rites

exsequiālis adj funeral

exsequor, -quī, -cūtus vt to follow, pursue; to follow to the grave; (duty) to carry out, accomplish; (speech) to describe, relate; (suffering) to undergo; (wrong) to avenge, punish

exserciō vt see **exsarciō**

exserō, -ere, -uī, -tum vt to put out, stretch out; to reveal

exsertō, -āre vt to stretch out repeatedly

exsertus ppp of **exserō** ▸ adj protruding

exsībilō, -āre vt to hiss off

exsiccātus adj (style) uninteresting

exsiccō, -āre, -āvī, -ātum vt to dry up; to drain

exsicō etc see **exsecō**

exsignō, -āre vt to write down in detail

exsiliō, -īre, -uī, -sultum vi to jump up, spring out; to start

exsilium, -ī and -iī nt banishment, exile; retreat

exsistō, -istere, -titī, -titum vi to emerge, appear; to arise, spring (from); to be, exist

exsolvō, -vere, -vī, -ūtum vt to undo, loosen, open; to release, free; to get rid of, throw off; (debt, promise) to discharge, fulfil, pay up; (words) to explain

exsomnis adj sleepless, watchful

exsorbeō, -ēre, -uī vt to suck, drain; to devour, endure

exsors, -tis adj chosen, special; free from

exspargō etc see **exspergō**

exspatior, -ārī, -ātus vi to go off the course

exspectābilis adj to be expected

exspectātiō, -ōnis f waiting, expectation

exspectātus adj looked for, welcome

exspectō, -āre, -āvī, -ātum vt to wait for/till; to see; to expect; to hope for, dread; to require

exspergō, -gere, -sum vt to scatter; to diffuse

exspēs adj despairing

exspīrātiō, -ōnis f exhalation

exspīrō, -āre, -āvī, -ātum vt to breathe out, exhale; to emit ▸ vi to rush out; to expire, come to an end

exsplendēscō, -ere vi to shine

exspoliō, -āre vt to pillage

exspuō, -uere, -uī, -ūtum vt to spit out, eject; (fig) to banish

externō, -āre vt to terrify

exstillō, -āre vi to drip

exstimulātor, -ōris m instigator

exstimulō, -āre vt to goad on; to excite

exstinctiō, -ōnis f annihilation

exstinctor, -ōris m extinguisher; destroyer

exstinguō, -guere, -xī, -ctum vt to put out, extinguish; to kill, destroy, abolish

exstirpō, -āre vt to root out, eradicate

exstitī perf of **exsistō**

exstō, -āre vi to stand out, project; to be conspicuous, be visible; to be extant, exist, be

exstructiō, -ōnis f erection

exstruō, -ere, -xī, -ctum vt to heap up; to build up, construct

exsūdō, -āre vi to come out in sweat ▶ vt (fig) to toil through

exsūgō, -gere, -xī, -ctum vt to suck out

exsul, -is m/f exile

exsulō, -āre, -āvī, -ātum vi to be an exile

exsultātiō, -ōnis f great rejoicing

exsultim adv friskily

exsultō, -āre, -āvī, -ātum vi to jump up, prance; (fig) to exult, run riot, boast; (speech) to range at will

exsuperābilis adj superable

exsuperantia, -ae f superiority

exsuperō, -āre, -āvī, -ātum vi to mount up; to gain the upper hand, excel ▶ vt to go over; to surpass; to overpower

exsurdō, -āre vt to deafen; (fig) to dull

exsurgō, -gere, -rēxī, -rēctum vi to rise, stand up; to recover

exsuscitō, -āre vt to wake up; (fire) to fan; (mind) to excite

exta, -ōrum ntpl internal organs

extābēscō, -ēscere, -uī vi to waste away; to vanish

extāris adj sacrificial

extemplō adv immediately, on the spur of the moment; **quom ~** as soon as

extemporālis adj extempore

extempulō see **extemplō**

extendō, -dere, -dī, -tum and **extēnsum** vt to stretch out, spread, extend; to enlarge, increase; (time) to prolong; **sē extendere** exert oneself; **īre per extentum fūnem** walk the tightrope

extēnsus ppp of **extendō**

extentō, -āre vt to strain, exert

extentus ppp of **extendō** ▶ adj broad

extenuātiō, -ōnis f (RHET) diminution

extenuō, -āre, -āvī, -ātum vt to thin out, rarefy; to diminish, weaken

exter adj from outside; foreign

exterebrō, -āre vt to bore out; to extort

extergeō, -gēre, -sī, -sum vt to wipe off, clean; to plunder

exterior, -ōris adj outer, exterior

exterius adv on the outside

exterminō, -āre vt to drive out, banish; (fig) to put aside

externus adj outward, external; foreign, strange

exterō, -erere, -rīvī, -rītum vt to rub out, wear away

exterreō, -ēre, -uī, -itum vt to frighten

extersus ppp of **extergeō**

exterus see **exter**

extexō, -ere vt to unweave; (fig) to cheat

extimēscō, -ēscere, -uī vi to be very frightened ▶ vt to be very afraid of

extimus adj outermost, farthest

extin- etc see **exstin-**

extispex, -icis m diviner

extollō, -ere, -tulī vt to lift up, raise; (fig) to exalt, beautify; (time) to defer

extorqueō, -quēre, -sī, -tum vt to wrench out, wrest; to dislocate; (fig) to obtain by force, extort

extorris adj banished, in exile

extortor, -ōris m extorter

extortus ppp of **extorqueō**

extrā adv outside; **~ quam** except that, unless ▶ prep (with acc) outside, beyond; free from; except

extrahō, -here, -xī, -ctum vt to draw out, pull out; to extricate, rescue; to remove; (time) to prolong, waste

extrāneus, -ī m stranger ▶ adj external, foreign

extraōrdinārius adj special, unusual

extrārius adj external; unrelated ▶ m stranger

extrēmitās, -ātis f extremity, end

extrēmum¹, -ī nt end; **ad ~** at last

extrēmum² adv for the last time

extrēmus adj outermost, extreme; last; utmost, greatest, meanest

extrīcō, -āre, -āvī, -ātum vt to disentangle, extricate; to clear up

extrīnsecus adv from outside, from abroad; on the outside

extrītus ppp of **exterō**

extrūdō, -dere, -sī, -sum vt to drive out; to keep out; (sale) to push

extulī perf of **efferō²**

extumeō, -ēre vi to swell up

extundō, -undere, -udī, -ūsum vt to beat out, hammer out; (comedy) to extort; (fig) to form, compose

exturbō, -āre, -āvī, -ātum vt to drive out, throw out, knock out; (wife) to put away; (fig) to banish, disturb

exūberō, -āre vi to abound

exul etc see **exsul**

exulcerō, -āre, -āvī, -ātum vt to aggravate

exululō, -āre vi to howl wildly ▶ vt to invoke with cries

exūnctus ppp of **exungō**

exundō, -āre vi to overflow; to be washed up

exungō, -ere vt to anoint liberally

exuō, -uere, -uī, -ūtum vt to draw out, put off; to lay aside; to strip

exūrō, -rere, -ssī, -stum vt to burn up; to dry up; to burn out; (fig) to inflame

exūstiō, -ōnis f conflagration

exūtus ppp of **exuō**

exuviae, -ārum fpl clothing, arms; hide; spoils

f

faba, -ae f bean

fabālis adj bean- (in cpds)

fābella, -ae f short story, fable; play

faber, -rī m craftsman (in metal, stone, wood), tradesman, smith; (MIL) artisan; ~ **ferrārius** blacksmith; ~ **tignārius** carpenter ▸ adj skilful

Fabius¹, -ī m Roman family name (esp Q F Maximus Cunctator, dictator against Hannibal)

Fabius², Fabiānus adj see **Fabius¹**

fabrē adv skilfully

fabrēfaciō, -facere, -fēcī, -factum vt to make, build, forge

fabrica, -ae f art, trade; work of art; workshop; (comedy) trick

fabricātiō, -ōnis f structure

fabricātor, -ōris m artificer

Fabricius¹, -ī m Roman family name (esp C F Luscinus, incorruptible commander against Pyrrhus)

Fabricius², Fabriciānus adj see **Fabricius¹**

fabricō, -āre, fabricor, -ārī, -ātus vt to make, build, forge

fabrīlis adj artificer's ▸ ntpl tools

fābula, -ae f story; common talk; play, drama, fable; **fābulae** nonsense!; **lupus in fābulā** talk of the devil!

fābulor, -ārī, -ātus vi to talk, converse ▸ vt to say, invent

fābulōsus adj legendary

facessō, -ere, -īvī, -ītum vt to perform, carry out; to cause (trouble) ▸ vi to go away, retire

facētē adv humorously; brilliantly

facētiae, -ārum fpl wit, clever talk, humour

facētus adj witty, humorous; fine, genteel, elegant

faciēs, -ēī f form, shape; face, looks; appearance, aspect, character

facile adv easily; unquestionably; readily; pleasantly

facilis adj easy; well-suited; ready, quick; (person) good-natured, approachable; (fortune) prosperous

facilitās, -ātis f ease, readiness; (speech) fluency; (person) good nature, affability

facinorōsus adj criminal

facinus, -oris nt deed, action; crime

faciō, -ere, fēcī, factum (impv **fac**, pass **fīō**) vt to make, create, compose, cause; to do, perform; (profession) to practise; (property) to put under; (value) to regard, think of; (words) to represent, pretend, suppose ▸ vi to do, act; (religion) to offer (sacrifice); (with **ad** or **dat**) to be of use; **cōpiam facere** afford an opportunity; **damnum facere** suffer loss; **metum facere** excite fear; **proelium facere** join battle; **rem facere** make money; **verba facere** talk; **māgnī facere** think highly of; **quid tibi faciam?** how am I to answer you?; **quid tē faciam?** what am I to do with you?; **fac sciam** let me know; **fac potuisse** suppose one could have

factiō, -ōnis f making, doing; group, party, faction (esp in politics and chariot racing)

factiōsus adj factious, oligarchical

factitō, -āre, -āvī, -ātum vt to keep making or doing; to practise; to declare (to be)

factor, -ōris m (sport) batsman

factum, -ī nt deed, exploit

factus ppp of **faciō**

facula, -ae f little torch

facultās, -ātis f means, opportunity; ability; abundance, supply, resources

fācundē adv see **fācundus**

fācundia, -ae f eloquence

fācundus adj fluent, eloquent

faeceus adj impure

faecula, -ae f wine lees

faenebris adj of usury

faenerātiō, -ōnis f usury

faenerātō adv with interest

faenerātor, -ōris m moneylender

faenerō, -āre, faeneror, -ārī, -ātus vt to lend at interest; to ruin with usury; (fig) to trade in

faenīlia, -um ntpl hayloft

faenum, -ī nt hay; ~ **habet in cornū** he is dangerous

faenus, -oris nt interest; capital lent at interest; (fig) profit, advantage

faenusculum, -ī nt a little interest

Faesulae, -ārum fpl town in Etruria (now Fiesole)

Faesulānus adj see **Faesulae**

faex, faecis f sediment, lees; brine (of pickles); (fig) dregs

fāgineus, fāginus adj of beech

fāgus, -ī f beech

fala, -ae f siege tower (used in assaults); (Circus) pillar

falārica, -ae f a missile, firebrand

falcārius, -ī and -iī m sicklemaker

falcātus adj scythed; sickle-shaped

falcifer, -ī adj scythe-carrying

Falernus adj Falernian (of a district in N. Campania famous for its wine) ▸ nt Falernian wine

Faliscī, -ōrum mpl a people of S.E. Etruria (with chief town Falerii)

Faliscus adj see **Faliscī**

fallācia, -ae f trick, deception
fallāciter adv see **fallāx**
fallāx, -ācis adj deceitful, deceptive
fallō, -ere, fefellī, -sum vt to deceive, cheat, beguile; to disappoint, fail, betray; (promise) to break; to escape the notice of, be unknown to; (pass) to be mistaken; **mē fallit** I am mistaken; I do not know
falsē adv wrongly, by mistake; fraudulently
falsidicus adj lying
falsificus adj deceiving
falsiiūrius adj perjurious
falsiloquus adj lying
falsiparēns, -entis adj with a pretended father
falsō adv see **falsus**
falsus ppp of **fallō** ▶ adj false, mistaken; deceitful; forged, falsified; sham, fictitious ▶ nt falsehood, error
falx, falcis f sickle, scythe; pruning hook; (MIL) siege hook
fāma, -ae f talk, rumour, tradition; public opinion; reputation, fame; infamy
famēlicus adj hungry
famēs, -is f hunger; famine; (fig) greed; (RHET) poverty of expression
fāmigerātiō, -ōnis f rumour
fāmigerātor, -ōris m telltale
familia, -ae f domestics, slaves of a household; family property, estate; family, house; school, sect; **pater familiās** master of a household; **familiam dūcere** be head of a sect, company etc
familiāris adj domestic, household, family; intimate, friendly; (entrails) relating to the sacrificer ▶ m servant; friend
familiāritās, -ātis f intimacy, friendship
familiāriter adv on friendly terms
fāmōsus adj celebrated; infamous; slanderous
famula, -ae f maidservant, handmaid
famulāris adj of servants
famulātus, -ūs m slavery
famulor, -ārī vi to serve
famulus, -ī m servant, attendant ▶ adj serviceable
fānāticus adj inspired; frantic, frenzied
fandī gerund of **for**
fandum, -ī nt right
fānum, -ī nt sanctuary, temple
fār, farris nt spelt; corn; meal
farciō, -cīre, -sī, -tum vt to stuff, fill full
farīna, -ae f meal, flour
farrāgō, -inis f mash, hotch-potch; medley
farrātus adj of corn; filled with corn
farsī perf of **farciō**
fartem, -im f acc filling; mincemeat
fartor, -ōris m fattener, poulterer
fartus ppp of **farciō**
fās nt divine law; right; **fās est** it is lawful, possible
fascia, -ae f band, bandage; streak of cloud
fasciculus, -ī m bundle, packet
fascinō, -āre vt to bewitch (esp with the evil eye)

fascinum, -ī nt, **fascinus, -ī** m charm
fasciola, -ae f small bandage
fascis, -is m bundle, faggot; soldier's pack, burden; (pl) rods and axe (carried before the highest magistrates); high office (esp the consulship)
fassus ppa of **fateor**
fāstī, -ōrum mpl register of days for legal and public business; calendar; registers of magistrates and other public records
fastīdiō, -īre, -iī, -ītum vt to loathe, dislike, despise ▶ vi to feel squeamish, be disgusted; to be disdainful
fastīdiōsē adv squeamishly; disdainfully
fastīdiōsus adj squeamish, disgusted; fastidious, nice; disagreeable
fastīdium, -ī and -iī nt squeamishness, distaste; disgust, aversion; disdain, pride
fastīgātē adv in a sloping position
fastīgātus adj sloping up or down
fastīgium, -ī and -iī nt gable, pediment; slope; height, depth; top, summit; (fig) highest degree, acme, dignity; (speech) main headings
fāstus adj lawful for public business
fastus, -ūs m disdain, pride
Fāta ntpl the Fates
fātālis adj fateful, destined; fatal, deadly
fātāliter adv by fate
fateor, -tērī, -ssus vt to confess, acknowledge; to reveal, bear witness to
fāticanus, -inus adj prophetic
fātidicus adj prophetic ▶ m prophet
fātifer, -ī adj deadly
fatīgātiō, -ōnis f weariness
fatīgō, -āre, -āvī, -ātum vt to tire, exhaust; to worry, importune; to wear down, torment
fātiloqua, -ae f prophetess
fatīscō, -ere, fatīscor, -ī vi to crack, split; (fig) to become exhausted
fatuitās, -ātis f silliness
fātum, -ī nt divine word, oracle; fate, destiny; divine will; misfortune, doom, death; **fātō obīre** die a natural death
fātur, fātus 3rd pers and ppa of **for**
fatuus adj silly; unwieldy ▶ m fool
faucēs, -ium fpl throat; pass, narrow channel, chasm; (fig) jaws
Faunus, -ī m father of Latinus (god of forests and herdsmen, identified with Pan); (pl) woodland spirits, Fauns
faustē adv see **faustus**
faustitās, -ātis f good fortune, fertility
faustus adj auspicious, lucky
fautor, -ōris m supporter, patron
fautrīx, -īcis f protectress
favea, -ae f pet slave
faveō, -ēre, fāvī, fautum vi (with dat) to favour, befriend, support; **favēre linguīs** keep silence
favilla, -ae f embers, ashes; (fig) spark
favitor etc see **fautor**
Favōnius, -ī m west wind, zephyr

favor, **-ōris** m favour, support; applause
favōrābilis adj in favour; pleasing
favus, **-ī** m honeycomb
fax, **facis** f torch, wedding torch, funeral torch; marriage, death; (ASTR) meteor; (fig) flame, fire, instigator; guide; **facem praeferre** act as guide
faxim, **faxō** archaic subj and fut of **faciō**
febrīcula, **-ae** f slight fever
febris, **-is** f fever
Februārius, **-ī** m February ▶ adj of February
februum, **-ī** nt purification; **Februa** pl festival of purification in February
fēcī perf of **faciō**
fēcunditās, **-ātis** f fertility; (style) exuberance
fēcundō, **-āre** vt to fertilize
fēcundus adj fertile, fruitful; fertilizing; (fig) abundant, rich, prolific
fefellī perf of **fallō**
fel, **fellis** nt gall bladder, bile; poison; (fig) animosity
fēlēs, **-is** f cat
fēlīcitās, **-ātis** f happiness, good luck
fēlīciter adv abundantly; favourably; happily
fēlīx, **-īcis** adj fruitful; auspicious, favourable, fortunate, successful
fēmella, **-ae** f girl
fēmina, **-ae** f female, woman
fēmineus adj woman's, of women; unmanly
femur, **-oris** and **-inis** nt thigh
fēn- etc see **faen-**
fenestra, **-ae** f window; (fig) loophole
fera, **-ae** f wild beast
ferācius adv more fruitfully
Fērālis adj funereal; of the Feralia; deadly ▶ ntpl festival of the dead in February
ferāx, **-ācis** adj fruitful, productive
ferbuī perf of **ferveō**
ferculum, **-ī** nt litter, barrow; dish, course
ferē adv almost, nearly, about; quite, just; usually, generally, as a rule; (with neg) hardly; **nihil ~** hardly anything
ferentārius, **-ī** and **-iī** m a light-armed soldier
Feretrius, **-ī** m an epithet of Jupiter
feretrum, **-ī** nt bier
fēriae, **-ārum** fpl festival, holidays; (fig) peace, rest
fēriātus adj on holiday, idle
ferīnus adj of wild beasts ▶ f game
feriō, **-īre** vt to strike, hit; to kill, sacrifice; (comedy) to cheat; **foedus ferīre** conclude a treaty
feritās, **-ātis** f wildness, savagery
fermē see **ferē**
fermentum, **-ī** nt yeast; beer; (fig) passion, vexation
ferō, **ferre**, **tulī**, **lātum** vt to carry, bring, bear; to bring forth, produce; to move, stir, raise; to carry off, sweep away, plunder; (pass) to rush, hurry, fly, flow, drift; (road) to lead; (trouble) to endure, suffer, sustain; (feelings) to exhibit, show; (speech) to talk about, give out, celebrate;

(bookkeeping) to enter; (circumstances) to allow, require; **sē ferre** rush, move; profess to be, boast; **condiciōnem ferre**, **lēgem ferre** propose terms/a law; **iūdicem ferre** sue; **sententiam ferre**, **suffrāgium ferre** vote; **signa ferre** march; attack; **aegrē ferre**, **graviter ferre** be annoyed at; **laudibus ferre** extol; **in oculīs ferre** be very fond of; **prae sē ferre** show, declare; **fertur**, **ferunt** it is said, they say; **ut mea fert opīniō** in my opinion
ferōcia, **-ae** f courage; spirit; pride, presumption
ferōcitās, **-ātis** f high spirits, aggressiveness; presumption
ferōciter adv bravely; insolently
Fērōnia, **-ae** f old Italian goddess
ferōx, **-ōcis** adj warlike, spirited, daring; proud, insolent
ferrāmentum, **-ī** nt tool, implement
ferrārius adj of iron; **faber ~** blacksmith ▶ f iron-mine, iron-works
ferrātus adj ironclad, ironshod ▶ mpl men in armour
ferreus adj of iron, iron; (fig) hard, cruel; strong, unyielding
ferrūgineus adj rust-coloured, dark
ferrūgō, **-inis** f rust; dark colour; gloom
ferrum, **-ī** nt iron; sword; any iron implement; force of arms; **~ et ignis** devastation
fertilis adj fertile, productive; fertilizing
fertilitās, **-ātis** f fertility
ferula, **-ae** f fennel; staff, rod
ferus adj wild; uncivilized; cruel ▶ m beast
fervēfaciō, **-ere**, **-fēcī**, **-factum** vt to boil
fervēns, **-entis** pres p of **ferveō** ▶ adj hot; raging; (fig) impetuous, furious
ferventer adv hotly
ferveō, **-vēre**, **-buī** vi to boil, burn; (fig) to rage, bustle, be agitated
fervēscō, **-ere** vi to boil up, grow hot
fervidus adj hot, raging; (fig) fiery, violent
fervō, **-vere**, **-vī** vi see **ferveō**
fervor, **-ōris** m seething; heat; (fig) ardour, passion
Fescennīnus adj Fescennine (a kind of ribald song, perhaps from Fescennium in Etruria)
fessus adj tired, worn out
festīnanter adv hastily
festīnātiō, **-ōnis** f haste, hurry
festīnō, **-āre** vi to hurry, be quick ▶ vt to hasten, accelerate
festīnus adj hasty, quick
fēstīvē adv gaily; humorously
fēstīvitās, **-ātis** f gaiety, merriment; humour, fun
fēstīvus adj gay, jolly; delightful; (speech) humorous
festūca, **-ae** f rod (with which slaves were manumitted)
fēstus adj festal, on holiday ▶ nt holiday; feast
fētiālis, **-is** m priest who carried out the ritual in making war and peace

fētūra, -ae f breeding; brood
fētus¹ adj pregnant; newly delivered; (fig) productive, full of
fētus², -ūs m breeding, bearing, producing; brood, young; fruit, produce; (fig) production
fiber, -rī m beaver
fibra, -ae f fibre; section of lung or liver; entrails
fībula, -ae f clasp, brooch; clamp
fīcedula, -ae f fig pecker
fictē adv falsely
fictilis adj clay, earthen ▸ nt jar; clay figure
fictor, -ōris m sculptor; maker, inventor
fictrīx, -īcis f maker
fictūra, -ae f shaping, invention
fictus ppp of **fingō** ▸ adj false, fictitious ▸ nt falsehood
fīculnus adj of the fig tree
fīcus, -ī and **-ūs** f fig tree; fig
fīdēle adv faithfully, surely, firmly
fīdēlia, -ae f pot, pail; **dē eādem fīdēliā duōs parietēs dealbāre** kill two birds with one stone
fīdēlis adj faithful, loyal; trustworthy, sure
fīdēlitās, -ātis f faithfulness, loyalty
fīdēliter adv faithfully, surely, firmly
Fīdēnae, -ārum fpl ancient Latin town
Fīdēnās, -ātis adj see **Fīdēnae**
fīdens, -entis pres p of **fīdō** ▸ adj bold, resolute
fīdenter adv see **fīdens**
fīdentia, -ae f self-confidence
fīdēs¹, -ēī f trust, faith, belief; trustworthiness, honour, loyalty, truth; promise, assurance, word; guarantee, safe-conduct, protection; (COMM) credit; (LAW) good faith; **~ mala** dishonesty; **rēs fīdēsque** entire resources; **fidem facere** convince; **fidem servāre ergā** keep faith with; **dī vostram fidem** for Heaven's sake!; **ex fīdē bonā** in good faith
fīdēs², -is f (usu pl) stringed instrument, lyre, lute; (ASTR) Lyra
fīdī perf of **findō**
fīdicen, -inis m musician; lyric poet
fīdicina, -ae f music girl
fīdicula, -ae f small lute
Fīdius, -ī m an epithet of Jupiter
fīdō, -dere, -sus vi (with dat or abl) to trust, rely on
fīdūcia, -ae f confidence, assurance; self-confidence; (LAW) trust, security
fīdūciārius adj to be held in trust
fīdus adj trusty, reliable; sure, safe
fīgō, -gere, -xī, -xum vt to fix, fasten, attach; to drive in, pierce; (speech) to taunt
figulāris adj a potter's
figulus, -ī m potter; builder
figūra, -ae f shape, form; nature, kind; phantom; (RHET) figure of speech
figūrō, -āre vt to form, shape
fīlātim adv thread by thread
fīlia, -ae f daughter
fīlicātus adj with fern patterns
fīliola, -ae f little daughter
fīliolus, -ī m little son

fīlius, -ī and **-iī** m son; **terrae ~** a nobody
filix, -cis f fern
fīlum, -ī nt thread; band of wool, fillet; string, shred, wick; contour, shape; (speech) texture, quality
fimbriae, -ārum fpl fringe, end
fimus, -ī m dung; dirt
findō, -ndere, -dī, -ssum vt to split, divide; to burst
fingō, -ere, fīnxī, fictum vt to form, shape, make; to mould, model; to dress, arrange; to train; (mind, speech) to imagine, suppose, represent, sketch; to invent, fabricate; **vultum fingere** compose the features
fīniō, -īre, -īvī, -ītum vt to bound, limit; to restrain; to prescribe, define, determine; to end, finish, complete ▸ vi to finish, die
fīnis, -is m/f boundary, border; (pl) territory; bound, limit; end; death; highest point, summit; aim, purpose; **~ bonōrum** the chief good; **quem ad fīnem?** how long?; **fīne genūs** up to the knee
fīnītē adv within limits
fīnītimus adj neighbouring, adjoining; akin, like ▸ mpl neighbours
fīnītor, -ōris m surveyor
fīnītumus adj see **fīnitimus**
fīnītus ppp of **fīniō** ▸ adj (RHET) well-rounded
fīnxī perf of **fingō**
fīō, fierī, factus vi to become, arise; to be made, be done; to happen; **quī fit ut?** how is it that?; **ut fit** as usually happens; **quid mē fīet?** what will become of me?
firmāmen, -inis nt support
firmāmentum, -ī nt support, strengthening; (fig) mainstay
firmātor, -ōris m establisher
firmē adv powerfully, steadily
firmitās, -ātis f firmness, strength; steadfastness, stamina
firmiter adv see **firmē**
firmitūdō, -inis f strength, stability
firmō, -āre, -āvī, -ātum vt to strengthen, support, fortify; (mind) to encourage, steady; (fact) to confirm, prove, assert
firmus adj strong, stable, firm; (fig) powerful, constant, sure, true
fiscella, -ae f wicker basket
fiscina, -ae f wicker basket
fiscus, -ī m purse, moneybox; public exchequer; imperial treasury, the emperor's privy purse
fissilis adj easy to split
fissiō, -ōnis f dividing
fissum, -ī nt slit, fissure
fissus ppp of **findō**
fistūca, -ae f rammer
fistula, -ae f pipe, tube; panpipes; (MED) ulcer
fistulātor, -ōris m panpipe player
fīsus ppa of **fīdō**
fīxī perf of **fīgō**
fīxus ppp of **fīgō** ▸ adj fixed, fast, permanent
flābellifera, -ae f fanbearer

flābellum, -ī nt fan

flābilis adj airy

flābra, -ōrum ntpl blasts, gusts; wind

flacceō, -ēre vi to flag, lose heart

flaccēscō, -ere vi to flag, droop

flaccidus adj flabby, feeble

flaccus adj flap-eared

Flaccus, -ī m surname of Horace

flagellō, -āre vt to whip, lash

flagellum, -ī nt whip, lash; strap, thong; (vine) shoot; (polyp) arm; (feelings) sting

flāgitātiō, -ōnis f demand

flāgitātor, -ōris m demander, dun

flāgitiōsē adv infamously

flāgitiōsus adj disgraceful, profligate

flāgitium, -ī and **-iī** nt offence, disgrace, shame; scoundrel

flāgitō, -āre, -āvī, -ātum vt to demand, importune, dun; (LAW) to summon

flagrāns, -antis pres p of **flagrō** ▸ adj hot, blazing; brilliant; passionate

flagranter adv passionately

flagrantia, -ae f blazing; (fig) shame

flagrō, -āre vi to blaze, burn, be on fire; (feelings) to be excited, be inflamed; (ill-will) to be the victim of

flagrum, -ī nt whip, lash

flāmen¹, -inis m priest (of a particular deity)

flāmen², -inis nt blast, gale, wind

flāminica, -ae f wife of a priest

Flāminīnus, -ī m Roman surname (esp the conqueror of Philip V of Macedon)

flāminium, -ī and **-iī** nt priesthood

Flāminius¹, -ī m Roman family name (esp the consul defeated by Hannibal)

Flāminius², Flāminiānus adj: Via Flāminia road from Rome N.E. to Ariminum

flamma, -ae f flame, fire; torch, star; fiery colour; (fig) passion; danger, disaster

flammeolum, -ī nt bridal veil

flammēscō, -ere vi to become fiery

flammeus adj fiery, blazing; flame-coloured ▸ nt bridal veil

flammifer, -ī adj fiery

flammō, -āre, -āvī, -ātum vi to blaze ▸ vt to set on fire, burn; (fig) to inflame, incense

flammula, -ae f little flame

flātus, -ūs m blowing, breath; breeze; (fig) arrogance

flāvēns, -entis adj yellow, golden

flāvēscō, -ere vi to turn yellow

Flāviānus adj see **Flāvius**

Flāvius, -ī m Roman family name (esp the emperors Vespasian, Titus and Domitian)

flāvus adj yellow, golden

flēbilis adj lamentable; tearful, mournful

flēbiliter adv see **flēbilis**

flectō, -ctere, -xī, -xum vt to bend, turn; to turn aside, wheel; (promontory) to round; (mind) to direct, persuade, dissuade ▸ vi to turn, march

fleō, -ēre, -ēvī, -ētum vi to weep, cry ▸ vt to lament, mourn for

flētus, -ūs m weeping, tears

flexanimus adj moving

flexī perf of **flectō**

flexibilis adj pliant, flexible; fickle

flexilis adj pliant

flexiloquus adj ambiguous

flexiō, -ōnis f bending, winding; (voice) modulation

flexipēs, -edis adj twining

flexuōsus adj tortuous

flexūra, -ae f bending

flexus¹ ppp of **flectō** ▸ adj winding

flexus², -ūs m winding, bending; change

flīctus, -ūs m collision

flō, -āre, -āvī, -ātum vt, vi to blow; (money) to coin

floccus, -ī m bit of wool; triviality; **floccī nōn faciō** I don't care a straw for

Flōra, -ae f goddess of flowers

Flōrālis adj see **Flōra**

flōrēns, -entis pres p of **flōreō** ▸ adj in bloom; bright; prosperous, flourishing

flōreō, -ēre, -uī vi to blossom, flower; (age) to be in one's prime; (wine) to froth; (fig) to flourish, prosper; (places) to be gay with

flōrēscō, -ere vi to begin to flower; to grow prosperous

flōreus adj of flowers, flowery

flōridulus adj pretty little

flōridus adj of flowers, flowery; fresh, pretty; (style) florid, ornate

flōrifer, -ī adj flowery

flōrilegus adj flower-sipping

flōrus adj beautiful

flōs, -ōris m flower, blossom; (wine) bouquet; (age) prime, heyday; (youth) downy beard, youthful innocence; (fig) crown, glory; (speech) ornament

flōsculus, -ī m little flower; (fig) pride, ornament

flūctifragus adj surging

flūctuātiō, -ōnis f wavering

flūctuō, -āre vi to toss, wave; (fig) to rage, swell, waver

flūctuōsus adj stormy

flūctus, -ūs m wave; flowing, flood; (fig) disturbance; **flūctūs in simpulō** a storm in a teacup

fluēns, -entis pres p of **fluō** ▸ adj lax, loose, enervated; (speech) fluent

fluenta, -ōrum ntpl stream, flood

fluenter adv in a flowing manner

fluentisonus adj wave-echoing

fluidus adj flowing, fluid; lax, soft; relaxing

fluitō, -āre vi to flow, float about; to wave, flap, move unsteadily; (fig) to waver

flūmen, -inis nt stream, river; (fig) flood, flow, fluency; **adversō flūmine** upstream; **secundō flūmine** downstream

flūmineus adj river- (in cpds)

fluō, -ere, -xī, -xum vi to flow; to overflow, drip; (fig) to fall in, fall away, vanish; (speech) to run evenly; (*circumstances*) to proceed, tend

flūtō *etc see* **fluitō**

fluviālis *adj* river- (*in cpds*)

fluviātilis *adj* river- (*in cpds*)

flūvidus *etc see* **fluidus**

fluvius, -ī *and* **-iī** *m* river, stream

fluxī *perf of* **fluō**

fluxus *adj* flowing, loose, leaky; (*person*) lax, dissolute; (*thing*) frail, fleeting, unreliable

fōcāle, -is *nt* scarf

foculus, -ī *m* stove, fire

focus, -ī *m* hearth, fireplace; pyre, altar; (*fig*) home

fodicō, -āre *vt* to nudge, jog

fodiō, -ere, fōdī, fossum *vt* to dig; to prick, stab; (*fig*) to goad

foedē *adv see* **foedus¹**

foederātus *adj* confederated

foedifragus *adj* perfidious

foeditās, -ātis *f* foulness, hideousness

foedō, -āre, -āvī, -ātum *vt* to mar, disfigure; to disgrace, sully

foedus¹ *adj* foul, hideous, revolting; vile, disgraceful

foedus², -eris *nt* treaty, league; agreement, compact; law

foen- *etc see* **faen-**

foeteō, -ēre *vi* to stink

foetidus *etc see* **faetidus**

foetor, -ōris *m* stench

foetu- *etc see* **fētu-**

foliātum, -ī *nt* nard oil

folium, -ī *and* **-iī** *nt* leaf

folliculus, -ī *m* small bag; eggshell

follis, -is *m* bellows; punchball; purse

fōmentum, -ī *nt* poultice, bandage; (*fig*) alleviation

fōmes, -itis *m* tinder, kindling

fōns, fontis *m* spring, source; water; (*fig*) origin, fountainhead

fontānus *adj* spring- (*in cpds*)

fonticulus, -ī *m* little spring

for, fārī, fātus *vt, vi* to speak, utter

forābilis *adj* penetrable

forāmen, -inis *nt* hole, opening

forās *adv* out, outside

forceps, -ipis *m/f* tongs, forceps

forda, -ae *f* cow in calf

fore, forem *fut infin and imperf subj of* **sum**

forēnsis *adj* public, forensic; of the marketplace

foris, -is *f* (*usu pl*) door; (*fig*) opening, entrance

foris *adv* out of doors, outside, abroad; from outside, from abroad; ~ **cēnāre** dine out

fōrma, -ae *f* form, shape, appearance; mould, stamp, last; (*person*) beauty; (*fig*) idea, nature, kind

fōrmāmentum, -ī *nt* shape

fōrmātūra, -ae *f* shaping

Formiae, -ārum *fpl* town in S. Latium

Formiānus *adj* of Formiae ▸ *nt* villa at Formiae

formīca, -ae *f* ant

formīcinus *adj* crawling

formīdābilis *adj* terrifying

formīdō¹, -āre, -āvī, -ātum *vt, vi* to fear, be terrified

formīdō², -inis *f* terror, awe, horror; scarecrow

formīdolōsē *adv see* **formīdolōsus**

formīdolōsus *adj* fearful, terrifying; afraid

fōrmō, -āre, -āvī, -ātum *vt* to shape, fashion, form

fōrmōsitās, -ātis *f* beauty

fōrmōsus *adj* beautiful, handsome

fōrmula, -ae *f* rule, regulation; (*LAW*) procedure, formula; (*PHILOS*) principle

fornācula, -ae *f* small oven

fornāx, -ācis *f* furnace, oven, kiln

fornicātus *adj* arched

fornix, -icis *m* arch, vault; brothel

forō, -āre *vt* to pierce

Foroiūliēnsis *adj see* **Forum Iūli**

fors, fortis *f* chance, luck ▸ *adv* perchance; **forte** by chance, as it happened; perhaps; **nē forte** in case; **sī forte** if perhaps; in the hope that

forsan, forsit, forsitan *adv* perhaps

fortasse, -is *adv* perhaps, possibly; (*irony*) very likely

forticulus *adj* quite brave

fortis *adj* strong, sturdy; brave, manly, resolute

fortiter *adv* vigorously; bravely

fortitūdō, -inis *f* courage, resolution; strength

fortuītō *adv* by chance

fortuītus *adj* casual, accidental

fortūna, -ae *f* chance, luck, fortune; good luck, success; misfortune; circumstances, lot; (*pl*) possessions; **fortūnae fīlius** Fortune's favourite; **fortūnam habēre** be successful

fortūnātē *adv see* **fortūnātus**

fortūnātus *adj* happy, lucky; well off, rich, blessed

fortūnō, -āre *vt* to bless, prosper

forulī, -ōrum *mpl* bookcase

forum, -ī *nt* public place, market; market town; *Roman Forum between the Palatine and Capitol*; public affairs, law courts, business; ~ **boārium** cattle market; ~ **olitōrium** vegetable market; ~ **piscātōrium** fish market; ~ **agere** hold an assize; ~ **attingere** enter public life; **cēdere forō** go bankrupt; **utī forō** take advantage of a situation

Forum Iūli *colony in S. Gaul (now* Fréjus)

forus, -ī *m* gangway; block of seats; (*bees*) cell frame

fossa, -ae *f* ditch, trench

fossiō, -ōnis *f* digging

fossor, -ōris *m* digger

fossus *ppp of* **fodiō**

fōtus *ppp of* **foveō**

fovea, -ae *f* pit, pitfall

foveō, -ēre, fōvī, fōtum *vt* to warm, keep warm; (*MED*) to foment; to fondle, keep; (*fig*) to cherish, love, foster, pamper, encourage; **castra fovēre** remain in camp

frāctus *ppp of* **frangō** ▸ *adj* weak, faint

frāga, -ōrum *ntpl* strawberries

fragilis *adj* brittle, fragile; frail, fleeting

fragilitās, -ātis *f* frailness

fragmen, -inis *nt* (*usu pl*) fragment, ruin, wreck

fragmentum, -ī *nt* fragment, remnant

fragor, -ōris *m* crash, din; disintegration

fragōsus *adj* crashing, roaring, breakable; rough

frāgrāns, -antis *adj* fragrant

framea, -ae *f* German spear

frangō, -angere, -ēgī, -āctum *vt* to break, shatter, wreck; to crush, grind; (*fig*) to break down, weaken, humble; (*emotion*) to touch, move; **cervīcem frangere** strangle

frāter, -ris *m* brother; cousin; (*fig*) friend, ally

frāterculus, -ī *m* brother

frāternē *adv* like a brother

frāternitās, -ātis *f* brotherhood

frāternus *adj* brotherly, a brother's, fraternal

frātricīda, -ae *m* fratricide

fraudātiō, -ōnis *f* deceit, fraud

fraudātor, -ōris *m* swindler

fraudō, -āre, -āvī, -ātum *vt* to cheat, defraud; to steal, cancel

fraudulentus *adj* deceitful, fraudulent

fraus, -audis *f* deceit, fraud; delusion; error; offence, wrong; injury, damage; **lēgī fraudem facere** evade the law; **in fraudem incidere** be disappointed; **sine fraude** without harm

fraxineus, fraxinus *adj* of ash

fraxinus, -ī *f* ash tree; ashen spear

Fregellae, -ārum *fpl* town in S. Latium

Fregellānus *adj see* **Fregellae**

frēgī *perf of* **frangō**

fremebundus *adj* roaring

fremitus, -ūs *m* roaring, snorting, noise

fremō, -ere, -uī, -itum *vi* to roar, snort, grumble ▸ *vt* to shout for, complain

fremor, -ōris *m* murmuring

frendō, -ere *vi* to gnash the teeth

frēnō, -āre, -āvī, -ātum *vt* to bridle; (*fig*) to curb, restrain

frēnum, -ī *nt* (*pl* **-a, -ōrum** *nt*, **-ī, -ōrum** *m*) bridle, bit; (*fig*) curb, check; **frēnōs dare** give vent to; **~ mordēre** take the bit between one's teeth

frequēns, -entis *adj* crowded, numerous, populous; regular, repeated, frequent; **~ senatus** a crowded meeting of the senate

frequentātiō, -ōnis *f* accumulation

frequenter *adv* in large numbers; repeatedly, often

frequentia, -ae *f* full attendance, throng, crowd

frequentō, -āre, -āvī, -ātum *vt* to crowd, populate; to visit repeatedly, frequent; to repeat; (*festival*) to celebrate, keep

fretēnsis *adj* of the Straits of Messina

fretum, -ī *nt* strait; sea; (*fig*) violence; **~ Siciliēnse** Straits of Messina

fretus, -ūs *m* strait

frētus *adj* relying, confident

fricō, -āre, -uī, -tum *vt* to rub, rub down

frīctus *ppp of* **frīgō**

frīgefactō, -āre *vt* to cool

frīgeō, -ēre *vi* to be cold; (*fig*) to be lifeless, flag; to be coldly received, fall flat

frīgerāns *adj* cooling

frīgēscō, -ere, frixī *vi* to grow cold; to become inactive

frīgida, -ae *f* cold water

frīgidē *adv* feebly

frīgidulus *adj* rather cold, faint

frīgidus *adj* cold, cool; chilling; (*fig*) dull, torpid; (*words*) flat, uninteresting

frīgō, -gere, -xī, -ctum *vt* to roast, fry

frīgus, -oris *nt* cold; cold weather, winter; death; (*fig*) dullness, inactivity; coldness, indifference

friguttiō, -īre *vi* to stammer

friō, -āre *vt* to crumble

fritillus, -ī *m* dice box

frīvolus *adj* empty, paltry

frīxī *perf of* **frīgō**

frondātor, -ōris *m* vinedresser, pruner

frondeō, -ēre *vi* to be in leaf

frondēscō, -ere *vi* to become leafy, shoot

frondeus *adj* leafy

frondifer, -ī *adj* leafy

frondōsus *adj* leafy

frōns¹, -ondis *f* leaf, foliage; garland of leaves

frōns², -ontis *f* forehead, brow; front, facade; (*fig*) look, appearance, exterior; **frontem contrahere** frown; **ā fronte** in front; **in fronte** in breadth

frontālia, -um *ntpl* frontlet

frontō, -ōnis *m* a broad-browed man

frūctuārius *adj* productive; paid for out of produce

fructuōsus *adj* productive; profitable

frūctus¹ *ppa of* **fruor**

frūctus², -ūs *m* enjoyment; revenue, income; produce, fruit; (*fig*) consequence, reward; **frūctuī esse** be an asset (to); **frūctum percipere** reap the fruits (of)

frūgālis *adj* thrifty, worthy

frūgālitās, -ātis *f* thriftiness, restraint

frūgāliter *adv* temperately

frūgēs *etc see* **frūx**

frūgī *adj* (*indecl*) frugal, temperate, honest; useful

frūgifer, -ī *adj* fruitful, fertile

frūgiferēns, -entis *adj* fruitful

frūgilegus *adj* food-gathering

frūgiparus *adj* fruitful

frūmentārius *adj* of corn, corn- (*in cpds*) ▸ *m* corn dealer; **lēx frūmentāria** law about the distribution of corn; **rēs frūmentāria** commissariat

frūmentātiō, -ōnis *f* foraging

frūmentātor, -ōris *m* corn merchant, forager

frūmentor, -ārī, -ātus *vi* to go foraging

frūmentum, -ī *nt* corn, grain; (*pl*) crops

frūnīscor, -ī *vt* to enjoy

fruor, -uī, -ūctus vt, vi (usu with abl) to enjoy, enjoy the company of; (LAW) to have the use and enjoyment of

frūstillātim adv in little bits

frūstrā adv in vain, for nothing; groundlessly; in error; **~ esse** be deceived; **~ habēre** foil

frūstrāmen, -inis nt deception

frūstrātiō, -ōnis f deception, frustration

frūstrō, -āre, frūstror, -ārī, -ātus vt to deceive, trick

frūstulentus adj full of crumbs

frūstum, -ī nt bit, scrap

frutex, -icis m bush, shrub; (comedy) blockhead

fruticētum, -ī nt thicket

fruticor, -ārī vi to sprout

fruticōsus adj bushy

frūx, -ūgis f, **-ūgēs, -ūgum** pl fruits of the earth, produce; (fig) reward, success; virtue; **sē ad frūgem bonam recipere** reform

fuam old pres subj of **sum**

fūcātus adj counterfeit, artificial

fūcō, -āre, -āvī, -ātum vt to paint, dye (esp red)

fūcōsus adj spurious

fūcus¹, -ī m red dye, rouge; bee glue; (fig) deceit, pretence

fūcus², -ī m drone

fūdī perf of **fundō²**

fuga, -ae f flight, rout; banishment; speed, swift passing; refuge; (fig) avoidance, escape; **fugam facere, in fugam dare** put to flight

fugācius adv more timidly

fugāx, -ācis adj timorous, shy, fugitive; swift, transient; (with gen) avoiding

fūgī perf of **fugiō**

fugiēns, -entis pres p of **fugiō** ▸ adj fleeting, dying; averse (to)

fugiō, -ere, fūgī, -itum vi to flee, run away, escape; to go into exile; (fig) to vanish, pass swiftly ▸ vt to flee from, escape from; to shun, avoid; (fig) to escape, escape notice of; **fuge quaerere** do not ask; **mē fugit** I do not notice or know

fugitīvus, -ī m runaway slave, truant, deserter ▸ adj fugitive

fugitō, -āre vt to flee from, shun

fugō, -āre, -āvī, -ātum vt to put to flight; to banish; to rebuff

fulcīmen, -inis nt support

fulciō, -cīre, -sī, -tum vt to prop, support; to strengthen, secure; (fig) to sustain, bolster up

fulcrum, -ī nt bedpost; couch

fulgeō, -gēre, -sī vi to flash, lighten; to shine; (fig) to be illustrious

fulgidus adj flashing

fulgō etc see **fulgeō**

fulgor, -ōris m lightning; flash, brightness; (fig) splendour

fulgur, -is nt lightning; thunderbolt; splendour

fulgurālis adj of lightning (as an omen)

fulgurātor, -ōris m interpreter of lightning

fulgurītus adj struck by lightning

fulgurō, -āre vi to lighten

fulica, -ae f coot

fūlīgō, -inis f soot; black paint

fulix, -cis f see **fulica**

fullō, -ōnis m fuller

fullōnius adj fuller's

fulmen, -inis nt thunderbolt; (fig) disaster

fulmenta, -ae f heel (of a shoe)

fulmineus adj of lightning; (fig) deadly

fulminō, -āre vi to lighten; (fig) to threaten

fulsī perf of **fulciō; fulgeō**

fultūra, -ae f support

fultus ppp of **fulciō**

Fulvia, -iae f wife of M. Antony

Fulvius, -ī m Roman family name

fulvus adj yellow, tawny, dun

fūmeus adj smoking

fūmidus adj smoky, smoking

fūmifer, -ī adj smoking

fūmificō, -āre vi to burn incense

fūmificus adj steaming

fūmō, -āre vi to smoke, steam

fūmōsus adj smoky, smoked

fūmus, -ī m smoke, steam

fūnāle, -is nt cord; wax torch; chandelier

fūnambulus, -ī m tightrope walker

fūnctiō, -ōnis f performance

fūnctus ppa of **fungor**

fūnda, -ae f sling; dragnet

fundāmen, -inis nt foundation

fundāmentum, -ī nt foundation; **fundāmenta agere, fundāmenta iacere** lay the foundations

Fundānus adj see **Fundī**

fundātor, -ōris m founder

Fundī, -ōrum mpl coast town in Latium

funditō, -āre vt to sling

funditor, -ōris m slinger

funditus adv utterly, completely; at the bottom

fundō¹, -āre, -āvī, -ātum vt to found; to secure; (fig) to establish, make secure

fundō², -ere, fūdī, fūsum vt to pour, shed, spill; (metal) to cast; (solids) to hurl, scatter, shower; (MIL) to rout; (crops) to produce in abundance; (speech) to utter; (fig) to spread, extend

fundus, -ī m bottom; farm, estate; (LAW) authorizer

fūnebris adj funeral- (in cpds); murderous

fūnerātus adj killed

fūnereus adj funeral- (in cpds), fatal

fūnestō, -āre vt to pollute with murder, desecrate

fūnestus adj deadly, fatal; sorrowful, in mourning

fungīnus adj of a mushroom

fungor, -gi, fūnctus vt, vi (usu with abl) to perform, discharge, do; to be acted on

fungus, -ī m mushroom, fungus; (candle) clot on the wick

fūniculus, -ī m cord

fūnis, -is m rope, rigging; **fūnem dūcere** be the master

fūnus, -eris *nt* funeral; death; corpse; ruin, destruction

fūr, fūris *m* thief; slave

fūrācissimē *adv* most thievishly

fūrāx, -ācis *adj* thieving

furca, -ae *f* fork; fork-shaped pole; pillory

furcifer, -ī *m* gallows rogue

furcilla, -ae *f* little fork

furcillō, -āre *vt* to prop up

furcula, -ae *f* forked prop; **furculae Caudīnae** Pass of Caudium

furenter *adv* furiously

furfur, -is *m* bran; scurf

Furia, -ae *f* Fury, avenging spirit; madness, frenzy, rage

furiālis *adj* of the Furies; frantic, fearful; infuriating

furiāliter *adv* madly

furibundus *adj* mad, frenzied

furiō, -āre, -āvī, -ātum *vt* to madden

furiōsē *adv* in a frenzy

furiōsus *adj* mad, frantic

furnus, -ī *m* oven

furō, -ere *vi* to rave, rage, be mad, be crazy

furor, -ōris *m* madness, frenzy, passion

fūror, -ārī, -ātus *vt* to steal; to pillage; to impersonate

fūrtificus *adj* thievish

fūrtim *adv* by stealth, secretly

fūrtīvē *adv* secretly

fūrtīvus *adj* stolen; secret, furtive

fūrtō *adv* secretly

fūrtum, -ī *nt* theft, robbery; (*pl*) stolen goods; (*fig*) trick, intrigue

fūrunculus, -ī *m* pilferer

furvus *adj* black, dark

fuscina, -ae *f* trident

fuscō, -āre *vt* to blacken

fuscus *adj* dark, swarthy; (*voice*) husky, muffled

fūsē *adv* diffusely

fūsilis *adj* molten, softened

fūsiō, -ōnis *f* outpouring

fūstis, -is *m* stick, club, cudgel; (*MIL*) beating to death

fūstuārium, -ī and -iī *nt* beating to death

fūsus¹ *ppp of* **fundō²** ▶ *adj* broad, diffuse; copious

fūsus², -ī *m* spindle

futile *adv* in vain

futilis *adj* brittle; worthless

futilitās, -ātis *f* futility

futūrum, -ī *nt* future

futūrus *fut p of* **sum** ▶ *adj* future, coming

g

Gabiī, -iōrum *mpl* ancient town in Latium

Gabinius¹, -ī *m* Roman family name (*esp Aulus, tribune 67 B.C.*)

Gabinius², Gabiniānus *adj*: **lēx Gabinia** *law giving Pompey command against the pirates*

Gabīnus *adj see* **Gabiī**

Gādēs, -ium *fpl town in Spain (now Cadiz)*

Gāditānus *adj see* **Gādēs**

gaesum, -ī *nt* Gallic javelin

Gaetūlī, -ōrum *mpl African people N. of Sahara*

Gaetūlus, -icus *adj* Gaetulian; African

Gāius¹, -ī *m* Roman praenomen (*esp emperor Caligula*)

Gāius², Gāia *m/f* (*wedding ceremony*) bridegroom, bride

Galatae, -ārum *mpl* Galatians of Asia Minor

Galatia, -iae *f* Galatia

Galba, -ae *m* Roman surname (*esp emperor 68–9*)

galbaneus *adj* of galbanum (*a Syrian plant*)

galbinus *adj* greenish-yellow ▶ *ntpl* pale green clothes

galea, -ae *f* helmet

galeātus *adj* helmeted

galērītus *adj* rustic

galērum, -ī *nt*, **galērus, -ī** *m* leather hood, cap; wig

galla, -ae *f* oak apple

Gallī, -ōrum *mpl* Gauls (*people of what is now France and N. Italy*)

Gallia, -iae *f* Gaul

Gallicānus *adj* of Italian Gaul

Gallicus *adj* Gallic ▶ *f* a Gallic shoe

gallīna, -ae *f* hen; **gallīnae albae fīlius** fortune's favourite

gallīnāceus *adj* of poultry

gallīnārius, -ī and -iī *m* poultry farmer

Gallograecī, -ōrum *mpl* Galatians

Gallograecia, -iae *f* Galatia

Gallus, -ī *m* Gaul; Roman surname (*esp the lyric poet*); priest of Cybele

gallus, -ī *m* cock

ganēa, -ae *f* low eating house

ganeō, -ōnis *m* profligate

ganeum, -ī *nt* low eating house

Gangaridae, -ārum *mpl* a people on the Ganges
Gangēs, -is *m* (river) Ganges
Gangēticus *adj see* **Gangēs**
ganniō, -īre *vi* to yelp; (*fig*) to grumble
gannītus, -ūs *m* yelping
Ganymēdēs, -is *m* Ganymede (*cup bearer in Olympus*)
Garamantes, -um *mpl* N. African tribe
Garamantis, -idis *adj see* **Garamantes**
Gargānus, -ī *m* mountain in S. Italy
garriō, -īre *vi* to chatter
garrulitās, -ātis *f* chattering
garrulus *adj* talkative, babbling
garum, -ī *nt* fish sauce
Garumna, -ae *f* (river) Garonne
gaudeō, -ēre, gāvīsus *vt, vi* to rejoice, be pleased, delight (in); **in sē gaudēre, in sinū gaudēre** be secretly pleased
gaudium, -ī *and* **-iī** *nt* joy, delight, enjoyment
gaulus, -ī *m* bucket
gausape, -is *nt*, **gausapa, -ōrum** *pl* a woollen cloth, frieze
gāvīsus *ppa of* **gaudeō**
gāza, -ae *f* treasure, riches
gelidē *adv* feebly
gelidus *adj* cold, frosty; stiff, numb; chilling ▸ *f* cold water
gelō, -āre *vt* to freeze
Gelōnī, -ōrum *mpl* Scythian tribe (*in what is now Ukraine*)
gelū, -ūs *nt* frost, cold; chill
gemebundus *adj* groaning
gemellipara, -ae *f* mother of twins
gemellus *adj* twin, double; alike ▸ *m* twin
geminātiō, -ōnis *f* doubling
geminō, -āre, -āvī, -ātum *vt* to double, bring together; to repeat ▸ *vi* to be double
geminus, -ī *m* twin, double, both; similar ▸ *mpl* twins (*esp Castor and Pollux*)
gemitus, -ūs *m* groan, sigh, moaning sound
gemma, -ae *f* bud, precious stone, jewel; jewelled cup, signet
gemmātus *adj* bejewelled
gemmeus *adj* jewelled; sparkling
gemmifer, -ī *adj* gem-producing
gemmō, -āre *vi* to bud, sprout; to sparkle
gemō, -ere, -uī, -itum *vi* to sigh, groan, moan ▸ *vt* to bewail
Gemōniae, -ārum *fpl* steps in Rome on which bodies of criminals were thrown
genae, -ārum *fpl* cheeks; eyes, eye sockets
geneālogus, -ī *m* genealogist
gener, -ī *m* son-in-law
generālis *adj* of the species; universal
generāliter *adv* generally
generāscō, -ere *vi* to be produced
generātim *adv* by species, in classes; in general
generātor, -ōris *m* producer
generō, -āre, -āvī, -ātum *vt* to breed, procreate
generōsus *adj* high-born, noble; well-stocked; generous, chivalrous; (*things*) noble, honourable

genesis, -is *f* birth; horoscope
genethliacon, -ī *nt* birthday poem
genetīvus *adj* native, inborn
genetrīx, -īcis *f* mother
geniālis *adj* nuptial; joyful, genial
geniāliter *adv* merrily
geniculātus *adj* jointed
genista, -ae *f* broom
genitābilis *adj* productive
genitālis *adj* fruitful, generative; of birth
genitāliter *adv* fruitfully
genitor, -ōris *m* father, creator
genitus *ppp of* **gignō**
genius, -ī *and* **-iī** *m* guardian spirit; enjoyment, inclination; talent; **geniō indulgēre** enjoy oneself
gēns, gentis *f* clan, family, stock, race; tribe, people, nation; descendant; (*pl*) foreign peoples; **minimē gentium** by no means; **ubi gentium** where in the world
genticus *adj* national
gentīlicius *adj* family
gentīlis *adj* family, hereditary; national ▸ *m* kinsman
gentīlitās, -ātis *f* clan relationship
genū, -ūs *nt* knee
genuālia, -um *ntpl* garters
genuī *perf of* **gignō**
genuīnus¹ *adj* natural
genuīnus² *adj* of the cheek ▸ *mpl* back teeth
genus, -eris *nt* birth, descent, noble birth, descendant; race; kind, class, species, respect, way; (*LOGIC*) genus, general term; **id ~** of that kind; **in omnī genere** in all respects
geōgraphia, -ae *f* geography
geōmetrēs, -ae *m* geometer
geōmetria, -ae *f* geometry
geōmetricus *adj* geometrical ▸ *ntpl* geometry
germānē *adv* sincerely
Germānī, -ōrum *mpl* Germans
Germānia, -iae *f* Germany
Germānicus *adj, m* cognomen of Nero Claudius Drusus and his son
germānitās, -ātis *f* brotherhood, sisterhood; relation of sister colonies
germānus *adj* of the same parents, full (*brother/sister*); genuine, true ▸ *m* full brother ▸ *f* full sister
germen, -inis *nt* bud, shoot; embryo; (*fig*) germ
gerō¹, -rere, -ssī, -stum *vt* to carry, wear; to bring; (*plants*) to bear, produce; (*feelings*) to entertain, show; (*activity*) to conduct, manage, administer, wage; (*time*) spend; **mōrem gerere** comply, humour; **persōnam gerere** play a part; **sē gerere** behave; **sē medium gerere** be neutral; **prae sē gerere** exhibit; **rēs gestae** exploits
gerō², -ōnis *nt* carrier
gerrae, -ārum *fpl* trifles, nonsense
gerrō, -ōnis *m* idler
gerulus, -ī *m* carrier

Gēryōn, -onis m mythical three-bodied king killed by Hercules

gessī perf of **gerō¹**

gestāmen, -inis nt arms, ornaments; burden; litter, carriage

gestiō¹, -ōnis f performance

gestiō², -īre vi to jump for joy, be excited; to be very eager

gestitō, -āre vt to always wear or carry

gestō, -āre vt to carry about, usually wear; to fondle; to blab; (pass) to go for a ride, drive, sail

gestor, -ōris m telltale

gestus¹ ppp of **gerō¹**

gestus², -ūs m posture, gesture; gesticulation

Getae, -ārum mpl Thracian tribe on the lower Danube

Geticus adj Getan, Thracian

gibbus, -ī m hump

Gigantes, -um mpl Giants, sons of Earth

Gigantēus adj see **Gigantes**

gignō, -ere, genuī, genitum vt to beget, bear, produce; to cause

gilvus adj pale yellow, dun

gingīva, -ae f gum

glaber, -rī adj smooth, bald ▸ m favourite slave

glaciālis adj icy

glaciēs, -ēī f ice

glaciō, -āre vt to freeze

gladiātor, -ōris m gladiator; (pl) gladiatorial show

gladiātōrius adj of gladiators ▸ nt gladiators' pay

gladiātūra, -ae f gladiator's profession

gladius, -ī and **-iī** m sword; (fig) murder, death; **gladium stringere** draw the sword; **suō sibi gladiō iugulāre** beat at his own game

glaeba, -ae f sod, clod of earth; soil; lump

glaebula, -ae f small lump; small holding

glaesum etc see **glēsum**

glandifer, -ī adj acorn-bearing

glandium, -ī and **-iī** nt glandule (in meat)

glāns, -andis f acorn, nut; bullet

glārea, -ae f gravel

glāreōsus adj gravelly

glaucōma, -ae f cataract; **glaucōmam ob oculōs obicere** throw dust in the eyes of

glaucus adj bluish grey

glēba etc see **glaeba**

glēsum, -ī nt amber

glīs, -īris m dormouse

glīscō, -ere vi to grow, swell, blaze up

globōsus adj spherical

globus, -ī m ball, sphere; (MIL) troop; mass, crowd, cluster

glōmerāmen, -inis nt ball

glomerō, -āre, -āvī, -ātum vt to form into a ball, gather, accumulate

glomus, -eris nt ball of thread, clue

glōria, -ae f glory, fame; ambition, pride, boasting; (pl) glorious deeds

glōriātiō, -ōnis f boasting

glōriola, -ae f a little glory

glōrior, -ārī, -ātus vt, vi to boast, pride oneself

glōriōsē adv see **glōriōsus**

glōriōsus adj famous, glorious; boastful

glūten, -inis nt glue

glūtinātor, -ōris m bookbinder

gluttiō, -īre vt to gulp down

gnāruris, gnārus adj knowing, expert; known

gnātus see **nātus**

gnāvus see **nāvus**

Gnōsis, -idis f Ariadne

Gnōsius, Gnōsiacus, Gnōsias adj of Cnossos, Cretan ▸ f Ariadne

Gnōsus, -ī f Cnossos (ancient capital of Crete)

gōbiō, -ōnis, gōbius, -ī and **-iī** m gudgeon

Gorgiās, -ae m Sicilian sophist and teacher of rhetoric

Gorgō, -ōnis f mythical monster capable of turning men to stone, Medusa

Gorgoneus adj: **equus ~** Pegasus; **lacus ~** Hippocrene

Gortȳna, -ae f Cretan town

Gortȳnius, Gortȳniacus adj Gortynian, Cretan

gōrȳtos, -ī m quiver

grabātus, -ī m camp bed, low couch

Gracchānus adj see **Gracchus**

Gracchus, -ī m Roman surname (esp the famous tribunes Tiberius and Gaius)

gracilis adj slender, slight, meagre, poor; (style) plain

gracilitās, -ātis f slimness, leanness; (style) simplicity

grāculus, -ī m jackdaw

gradātim adv step by step, gradually

gradātiō, -ōnis f (RHET) climax

gradior, -adī, -essus vi to step, walk

Grādīvus, -ī m Mars

gradus, -ūs m step, pace; stage, step towards; firm stand, position, standing; (pl) stair, steps; (hair) braid; (MATH) degree, rank; **citātō gradū, plēnō gradū** at the double; **suspēnsō gradū** on tiptoe; **dē gradū deicī** be disconcerted

Graecē adv in Greek

Graecia, -iae f Greece; **Māgna ~** S. Italy

graecissō, -āre vi to ape the Greeks

graecor, -ārī vi to live like Greeks

Graeculus adj (contemptuous) Greek

Graecus adj Greek

Grāiugena, -ae m Greek

Grāius adj Greek

grallātor, -ōris m stiltwalker

grāmen, -inis nt grass; herb

grāmineus adj grassy; of cane

grammaticus adj literary, grammatical ▸ m teacher of literature and language ▸ f, ntpl grammar, literature, philology

grānāria, -ōrum ntpl granary

grandaevus adj aged, very old

grandēscō, -ere vi to grow

grandiculus adj quite big

grandifer, -ī adj productive

grandiloquus, -ī m grand speaker; boaster

grandinat, -āre vi it hails

grandis adj large, great, tall; old; strong; (style) grand, sublime; **~ nātū** old

granditās, -ātis f grandeur

grandō, -inis f hail

grānifer, -ī adj grain-carrying

grānum, -ī nt seed, grain

graphicē adv nicely

graphicus adj fine, masterly

graphium, -ī and **-iī** nt stilus, pen

grassātor, -ōris m vagabond; robber, footpad

grassor, -ārī, -ātus vi to walk about, prowl, loiter; (action) to proceed; (fig) to attack, rage against

grātē adv with pleasure; gratefully

grātēs fpl thanks

grātia, -ae f charm, grace; favour, influence, regard, friendship; kindness, service; gratitude, thanks; **grātiam facere** excuse; **grātiam referre** return a favour; **in grātiam redīre cum** be reconciled to; **grātiās agere** thank; **grātiās habēre** feel grateful; **grātiā** (with gen) for the sake of; **eā grātiā** on that account; **grātīs** for nothing

Grātiae, -ārum fpl the three Graces

grātificātiō, -ōnis f obligingness

grātificor, -ārī vi to do a favour, oblige ▸ vt to make a present of

grātiīs, grātīs adv for nothing

grātiōsus adj in favour, popular; obliging

grātor, -ārī, -ātus vi to rejoice, congratulate

grātuītō adv for nothing

grātuītus adj free, gratuitous

grātulābundus adj congratulating

grātulātiō, -ōnis f rejoicing; congratulation; public thanksgiving

grātulor, -ārī, -ātus vt, vi to congratulate; to give thanks

grātus adj pleasing, welcome, dear; grateful, thankful; (acts) deserving thanks; **grātum facere** do a favour

gravātē adv reluctantly, grudgingly

gravātim adv unwillingly

gravēdinōsus adj liable to colds

gravēdō, -inis f cold in the head

graveolēns, -entis adj strong-smelling

gravēscō, -ere vi to become heavy; to grow worse

graviditās, -ātis f pregnancy

gravidō, -āre vt to impregnate

gravidus adj pregnant; loaded, full

gravis adj heavy; loaded, pregnant; (smell) strong, offensive; (sound) deep, bass; (body) sick; (food) indigestible; (fig) oppressive, painful, severe; important, influential, dignified

gravitās, -ātis f weight, severity, sickness; importance, dignity, seriousness; **annōnae ~** high price of corn

graviter adv heavily; strongly, deeply; severely, seriously, violently; gravely, with dignity; **~ ferre** be vexed at

gravō, -āre vt to load, weigh down; to oppress, aggravate

gravor, -ārī vt, vi to feel annoyed, object to, disdain

gregālis adj of the herd, common ▸ m comrade

gregārius adj common; (MIL) private

gregātim adv in crowds

gremium, -ī nt bosom, lap

gressus¹ ppa of **gradior**

gressus², -ūs m step; course

grex, -egis m flock, herd; company, troop

grunniō, -īre vi to grunt

grunnītus, -ūs m grunting

grūs, -uis f crane

grȳps, -ȳpis m griffin

gubernāclum, gubernāculum, -ī nt rudder, tiller; helm, government

gubernātiō, -ōnis f steering, management

gubernātor, -ōris m steersman, pilot, governor

gubernātrīx, -īcis f directress

gubernō, -āre, -āvī, -ātum vt to steer, pilot; to manage, govern

gula, -ae f gullet, throat; gluttony, palate

gulōsus adj dainty

gurges, -itis m abyss, deep water, flood; (person) spendthrift

gurguliō, -ōnis f gullet, windpipe

gurgustium, -ī and **-iī** nt hovel, shack

gustātus, -ūs m sense of taste; flavour

gustō, -āre, -āvī, -ātum vt to taste; to have a snack; (fig) to enjoy, overhear; **prīmīs labrīs gustāre** have a superficial knowledge of

gustus, -ūs m tasting; preliminary dish

gutta, -ae f drop; spot, speck

guttātim adv drop by drop

guttur, -is nt throat, gluttony

gūttus, -ī m flask

Gyās, -ae m giant with a hundred arms

Gȳgaeus adj see **Gȳgēs**

Gȳgēs, -is and **-ae** m king of Lydia (famed for his magic ring)

gymnasiarchus, -ī m master of a gymnasium

gymnasium, -ī and **-iī** nt sports ground, school

gymnasticus adj gymnastic

gymnicus adj gymnastic

gynaecēum, -ēī, gynaecīum, -īī nt women's quarters

gypsātus adj coated with plaster

gypsum, -ī nt plaster of Paris; a plaster figure

gȳrus, -ī m circle, coil, ring; course

h

ha interj (expressing joy or laughter) hurrah!, ha ha!
habēna, -ae f strap; (pl) reins; (fig) control; **habēnās dare, habēnās immittere** allow to run freely
habeō, -ēre, -uī, -itum vt to have, hold; to keep, contain, possess; (fact) to know; (with infin) to be in a position to; (person) to treat, regard, consider; (action) to make, hold, carry out ▶ vi to have possessions; **ōrātiōnem habēre** make a speech; **in animō habēre** intend; **prō certō habēre** be sure; **sē habēre** find oneself, be; **sibi habēre, sēcum habēre** keep to oneself; (fight); **habet** a hit!; **bene habet** it is well; **sīc habet** so it is; **sīc habētō** be sure of this
habilis adj manageable, handy; suitable, nimble, expert
habilitās, -ātis f aptitude
habitābilis adj habitable
habitātiō, -ōnis f dwelling, house
habitātor, -ōris m tenant, inhabitant
habitō, -āre, -āvī, -ātum vt to inhabit ▶ vi to live, dwell; to reside, be always (in)
habitūdō, -inis f condition
habitus¹ ppp of **habeō** ▶ adj stout; in a humour
habitus², -ūs m condition, appearance; dress; character, quality; disposition, feeling
hāc adv this way
hāctenus adv thus far, so far; till now
Hadria, -ae f town in N. Italy; Adriatic Sea
Hadriānus, -ānī m (emperor) Hadrian
Hadriāticus, Hadriacus adj of (emperor) Hadrian
haedilia, -ae f little kid
haedinus adj kid's
haedulus, -ī m little kid
haedus, -ī m kid; (ASTR, usu pl) the Kids (a cluster in Auriga)
Haemonia, -ae f Thessaly
Haemonius adj Thessalian
Haemus, -ī m mountain range in Thrace
haereō, -rēre, -sī, -sum vi to cling, stick, be attached; (nearness) to stay close, hang on; (continuance) to linger, remain (at); (stoppage) to stick fast, come to a standstill, be at a loss

haerēscō, -ere vi to adhere
haeresis, -is f sect
haesī perf of **haereō**
haesitantia, -ae f stammering
haesitātiō, -ōnis f stammering; indecision
haesitō, -āre vi to get stuck; to stammer; to hesitate, be uncertain
hahae, hahahae see **ha**
haliaeetos, -ī m osprey
hālitus, -ūs m breath, vapour
hallex, -icis m big toe
hāllūcinor etc see **ālūcinor**
hālō, -āre vi to be fragrant ▶ vt to exhale
hālūcinor etc see **ālūcinor**
hama, -ae f water bucket
Hamādryas, -adis f wood nymph
hāmātilis adj with hooks
hāmātus adj hooked
Hamilcar, -is m father of Hannibal
hāmus, -ī m hook; talons
Hannibal, -is m famous Carthaginian general in 2nd Punic War
hara, -ae f sty, pen
harēna, -ae f sand; desert, seashore; arena (in the amphitheatre)
harēnōsus adj sandy
hariola, -ae f, **hariolus, -ī** m soothsayer
hariolor, -ārī vi to prophesy; to talk nonsense
harmonia, -ae f concord, melody; (fig) harmony
harpagō¹, -āre vt to steal
harpagō², -ōnis m grappling hook; (person) robber
harpē, -ēs f scimitar
Harpȳiae, -ārum fpl Harpies (mythical monsters, half woman, half bird)
harundifer, -ī adj reed-crowned
harundineus adj reedy
harundinōsus adj abounding in reeds
harundō, -inis f reed, cane; fishing rod; shaft, arrow; (fowling) limed twig; (music) pipe, flute; (toy) hobbyhorse; (weaving) comb; (writing) pen
haruspex, -icis m diviner (from entrails); prophet
haruspica, -ae f soothsayer
haruspicīnus adj of divination by entrails ▶ f art of such divination
haruspicium, -ī and **-iī** nt divination
Hasdrubal, -is m brother of Hannibal
hasta, -ae f spear, pike; sign of an auction sale; **sub hastā vēndere** put up for auction
hastātus adj armed with a spear ▶ mpl first line of Roman army in battle; **prīmus ~** 1st company of hastati
hastīle, -is nt shaft, spear, javelin; vine prop
hau, haud adv not, not at all
hauddum adv not yet
haudquāquam adv not at all, not by any means
hauriō, -rīre, -sī, -stum vt to draw, draw off, derive; to drain, empty, exhaust; to take in, drink, swallow, devour

haustus¹ *ppp of* **hauriō**

haustus², **-ūs** *m* drawing (*water*); drinking; drink, draught

haut *see* **hau**

hebdomas, **-dis** *f* week

Hēbē, **-ēs** *f* goddess of youth (*cup bearer to the gods*)

hebenus, **-ī** *f* ebony

hebeō, **-ēre** *vi* to be blunt, dull, sluggish

hebes, **-tis** *adj* blunt, dull, sluggish; obtuse, stupid

hebēscō, **-ere** *vi* to grow dim *or* dull

hebetō, **-āre** *vt* to blunt, dull, dim

Hebrus, **-ī** *m Thracian river (now* Maritza)

Hecatē, **-ēs** *f goddess of magic (and often identified with Diana)*

Hecatēius, **Hecatēis** *adj see* **Hecatē**

hecatombē, **-ēs** *f* hecatomb

Hector, **-is** *m son of Priam (chief warrior of the Trojans against the Greeks)*

Hectoreus *adj* of Hector; Trojan

Hecuba, **-ae**, **Hecubē**, **-ēs** *f wife of Priam*

hedera, **-ae** *f* ivy

hederiger, **-ī** *adj* wearing ivy

hederōsus *adj* covered with ivy

hēdychrum, **-ī** *nt* a cosmetic perfume

hei, **heia** *see* **eia**

Helena, **-ae**, **Helenē**, **-ēs** *f* Helen (*wife of Menelaus, abducted by Paris*)

Helenus, **-ī** *m son of Priam (with prophetic powers)*

Hēliades, **-um** *fpl* daughters of the Sun (*changed to poplars or alders, and their tears to amber*)

Helicē, **-ēs** *f* the Great Bear

Helicōn, **-ōnis** *m mountain in Greece sacred to Apollo and the Muses*

Helicōniades, **-um** *fpl* the Muses

Helicōnius *adj see* **Helicōn**

Hellas, **-dis** *f* Greece

Hellē, **-ēs** *f mythical Greek princess (carried by the golden-fleeced ram, and drowned in the Hellespont)*

Hellēspontius, **Hellēspontiacus** *adj see* **Hellēspontus**

Hellēspontus, **-ī** *m* Hellespont (*now* Dardanelles)

helluō, **-ōnis** *m* glutton

helluor, **-ārī** *vi* to be a glutton

helvella, **-ae** *f* a savoury herb

Helvētiī, **-ōrum** *mpl people of E. Gaul (now* Switzerland)

Helvētius, **Helvēticus** *adj see* **Helvētiī**

hem *interj (expressing surprise)* eh?, well well!

hēmerodromus, **-ī** *m* express courier

hēmicillus, **-ī** *m* mule

hēmicyclium, **-ī** *and* **-iī** *nt* semicircle with seats

hēmīna, **-ae** *f* half a pint

hendecasyllabī, **-ōrum** *mpl* hendecasyllabics, verses of eleven syllables per line

heptēris, **-is** *f* ship with seven banks of oars

hera *etc see* **era**

Hēra, **-ae** *f Greek goddess identified with Juno*

Hēraclītus, **-ī** *m early Greek philosopher*

Hēraea, **-aeōrum** *ntpl festival of Hera*

herba, **-ae** *f* blade, young plant; grass, herb, weed

herbēscō, **-ere** *vi* to grow into blades

herbeus *adj* grass-green

herbidus *adj* grassy

herbifer, **-ī** *adj* grassy

herbōsus *adj* grassy, made of turf; made of herbs

herbula, **-ae** *f* little herb

hercīscō, **-ere** *vt* to divide an inheritance

hercle *interj* by Hercules!

herctum, **-ī** *nt* inheritance

Hercule *interj* by Hercules!

Herculēs, **-is** *and* **-ī** *m mythical Greek hero, later deified*

Herculeus *adj*: **arbor ~** poplar; **urbs ~** Herculaneum

here *see* **herī**

hērēditārius *adj* inherited; about an inheritance

hērēditās, **-ātis** *f* inheritance; **~ sine sacrīs** a gift without awkward obligations

hērēdium, **-ī** *and* **-iī** *nt* inherited estate

hērēs, **-ēdis** *m/f* heir, heiress; (*fig*) master, successor

herī *adv* yesterday

herīlis *etc see* **erīlis**

Hermēs, **-ae** *m Greek god identified with Mercury;* Hermes pillar

Hernicī, **-ōrum** *mpl people of central Italy*

Hernicus *adj see* **Hernicī**

Hērodotus, **-ī** *m first Greek historian*

hērōicus *adj* heroic, epic

hērōīna, **-ae** *f* demigoddess

hērōis, **-dis** *f* demigoddess

hērōs, **-is** *m* demigod, hero

hērōus *adj* heroic, epic

herus *etc see* **erus**

Hēsiodēus, **-īus** *adj see* **Hēsiodus**

Hēsiodus, **-ī** *m* Hesiod (*Greek didactic poet*)

Hesperia, **-iae** *f* Italy; Spain

Hesperides, **-idum** *fpl keepers of a garden in the far West*

Hesperius, **-is** *adj* western

Hesperus, **-ī** *m* evening star

hesternus *adj* of yesterday

heu *interj (expressing dismay or pain)* oh!, alas!

heus *interj (calling attention)* ho!, hallo!

hexameter, **-rī** *m* hexameter verse

hexēris, **-is** *f* ship with six banks of oars

hiātus, **-ūs** *m* opening, abyss; open mouth, gaping; (*GRAM*) hiatus

Hibērēs, **-um** *mpl* Spaniards

Hibēria, **-iae** *f* Spain

hīberna, **-ōrum** *ntpl* winter quarters

hībernācula, **-ōrum** *ntpl* winter tents

Hibernia, **-ae** *f* Ireland

hībernō, **-āre** *vi* to winter, remain in winter quarters

hībernus *adj* winter, wintry
Hibērus¹, Hibēricus *adj* Spanish
Hibērus², -ī *m* (river) Ebro
hibīscum, -ī *nt* marsh mallow
hibrida, hybrida, -ae *m/f* (*dog*) mongrel
hīc¹, haec, hōc *pron, adj* this; he, she, it; my, the
  latter, the present; **hīc homō** I; **hōc magis** the
  more; **hōc est** that is
hīc² *adv* here; herein; (*time*) at this point
hīce, haece, hōce *emphatic forms of* **hīc¹,**
  haec, hōc
hīcine, haecine, hōcine *emphatic forms of*
  hīc¹, haec, hōc
hiemālis *adj* winter, stormy
hiemō, -āre *vi* to pass the winter; to be wintry,
  stormy
hiems (hiemps), -is *f* winter; stormy
  weather, cold
Hierōnymus, -ī *m* Jerome
Hierosolyma, -ōrum *ntpl* Jerusalem
Hierosolymārius *adj see* **Hierosolyma**
hietō, -āre *vi* to yawn
hilare *adv see* **hilaris**
hilaris *adj* cheerful, merry
hilaritās, -ātis *f* cheerfulness
hilaritūdō, -inis *f* merriment
hilarō, -āre *vt* to cheer, gladden
hilarulus *adj* a gay little thing
hilarus *etc see* **hilaris**
hīllae, -ārum *fpl* smoked sausage
Hīlōtae, -ārum *mpl* Helots (*of Sparta*)
hīlum, -ī *nt* something, a whit
hinc *adv* from here, hence; on this side; from this
  source, for this reason; (*time*) henceforth
hinniō, -īre *vi* to neigh
hinnītus, -ūs *m* neighing
hinnuleus, -ī *m* fawn
hiō, -āre *vi* to be open, gape, yawn; (*speech*) to
  be disconnected, leave a hiatus ▶ *vt* to sing
hippagōgī, -ōrum *fpl* cavalry transports
hippocentaurus, -ī *m* centaur
hippodromos, -ī *m* racecourse
Hippolytus, -ī *m* son of Theseus (*slandered by*
  stepmother Phaedra)
hippomanes, -is *nt* mare's fluid; membrane
  on foal's forehead
Hippōnactēus *adj* of Hipponax ▶ *m* iambic
  verse used by Hipponax
Hippōnax, -ctis *m* Greek satirist
hippotoxotae, -ārum *mpl* mounted
  archers
hīra, -ae *f* the empty gut
hircīnus *adj* of a goat
hircōsus *adj* goatish
hircus, -ī *m* he-goat; goatish smell
hirnea, -ae *f* jug
hirq- *etc see* **hirc-**
hirsūtus *adj* shaggy, bristly; uncouth
hirtus *adj* hairy, shaggy; rude
hirūdō, -inis *f* leech
hirundinīnus *adj* swallows'
hirundō, -inis *f* swallow

hīscō, -ere *vi* to gape; to open the mouth ▶ *vt*
  to utter
Hispānia, -iae *f* Spain
Hispāniēnsis, Hispānus *adj* Spanish
hispidus *adj* hairy, rough
Hister, -rī *m* lower Danube
historia, -ae *f* history, inquiry; story
historicus *adj* historical ▶ *m* historian
histricus *adj* of the stage
histriō, -ōnis *m* actor
histriōnālis *adj* of an actor
histriōnia, -ae *f* acting
hiulcē *adv* with hiatus
hiulcō, -āre *vt* to split open
hiulcus *adj* gaping, open; (*speech*) with hiatus
hodiē *adv* today; nowadays, now; up to the present
hodiernus *adj* today's
holitor, -ōris *m* market gardener
holitōrius *adj* for market gardeners
holus, -eris *nt* vegetables
holusculum, -ī *nt* small cabbage
Homēricus *adj see* **Homērus**
Homērus, -ī *m* Greek epic poet, Homer
homicīda, -ae *m* killer, murderer
homicīdium, -ī *and* **-iī** *nt* murder
homō, -inis *m/f* human being, man; (*pl*)
  people, the world; (*derogatory*) fellow, creature;
  inter hominēs esse be alive; see the world
homullus, -ī, homunciō, -ōnis,
  homunculus, -ī *m* little man, poor creature,
  mortal
honestās, -ātis *f* good character, honourable
  reputation; sense of honour, integrity; (*things*)
  beauty
honestē *adv* decently, virtuously
honestō, -āre *vt* to honour, dignify, embellish
honestus *adj* honoured, respectable;
  honourable, virtuous; (*appearance*) handsome
  ▶ *m* gentleman ▶ *nt* virtue, good; beauty
honor, -ōris *m* honour, esteem; public office,
  position, preferment; award, tribute, offering;
  ornament, beauty; **honōris causā** out of
  respect; **honōrem praefārī** apologize for a
  remark
honōrābilis *adj* as a mark of respect
honōrārius *adj* done out of respect, honorary
honōrātē *adv* honourably
honōrātus *adj* esteemed, distinguished; in
  high office; complimentary
honōrificē *adv* in complimentary terms
honōrificus *adj* complimentary
honōrō, -āre, -āvī, -ātum *vt* to do honour
  to, embellish
honōrus *adj* complimentary
honōs *etc see* **honor**
hōra, -ae *f* hour; time, season; (*pl*) clock; **in**
  hōrās hourly; **in hōram vīvere** live from hand
  to mouth
hōraeum, -ī *nt* pickle
Horātius¹, -ī *m* Roman family name (*esp the*
  defender of Rome against Porsenna); the lyric
  poet Horace

Horātius² *adj see* **Horātius¹**

hordeum, -ī *nt* barley

horia, -ae *f* fishing smack

hōrnō *adv* this year

hōrnōtinus *adj* this year's

hōrnus *adj* this year's

hōrologium, -ī *and* **-iī** *nt* clock

horrendus *adj* fearful, terrible; awesome

horrēns, -entis *pres p of* **horreō ▶** *adj* bristling, shaggy

horreō, -ēre, -uī *vi* to stand stiff, bristle; to shiver, shudder, tremble ▶ *vt* to dread; to be afraid, be amazed

horrēscō, -ere, horruī *vi* to stand on end, become rough; to begin to quake; to start, be terrified ▶ *vt* to dread

horreum, -ī *nt* barn, granary, store

horribilis *adj* terrifying; amazing

horridē *adv see* **horridus**

horridulus *adj* protruding a little; unkempt; (*fig*) uncouth

horridus *adj* bristling, shaggy, rough, rugged; shivering; (*manners*) rude, uncouth; frightening

horrifer, -ī *adj* chilling; terrifying

horrificē *adv* in awesome manner

horrificō, -āre *vt* to ruffle; to terrify

horrificus *adj* terrifying

horrisonus *adj* dread-sounding

horror, -ōris *m* bristling; shivering; ague; terror, fright, awe, a terror

hōrsum *adv* this way

hortāmen, -inis *nt* encouragement

hortāmentum, -ī *nt* encouragement

hortātiō, -ōnis *f* harangue, encouragement

hortātor, -ōris *m* encourager

hortātus, -ūs *m* encouragement

Hortēnsius, -ī *m* Roman family name (*esp an orator in Cicero's time*)

hortor, -ārī, -ātus *vt* to urge, encourage, exhort, harangue

hortulus, -ī *m* little garden

hortus, -ī *m* garden; (*pl*) park

hospes, -itis *m*, **hospita, -ae** *f* host, hostess; guest, friend; stranger, foreigner ▶ *adj* strange

hospitālis *adj* host's, guest's; hospitable

hospitālitās, -ātis *f* hospitality

hospitāliter *adv* hospitably

hospitium, -ī *and* **-iī** *nt* hospitality, friendship; lodging, inn

hostia, -ae *f* victim, sacrifice

hostiātus *adj* provided with victims

hosticus *adj* hostile; strange ▶ *nt* enemy territory

hostīlis *adj* of the enemy, hostile

hostīliter *adv* in hostile manner

hostīmentum, -ī *nt* recompense

hostiō, -īre *vt* to requite

hostis, -is *m/f* enemy

hūc *adv* hither, here; to this, to such a pitch; **hūc illūc** hither and thither

hui *interj* (*expressing surprise*) ho!, my word!

hūiusmodī such

hūmānē, hūmāniter *adv* humanly; gently, politely

hūmānitās, -ātis *f* human nature, mankind; humanity, kindness, courtesy; culture, refinement

hūmānitus *adv* in accordance with human nature; kindly

hūmānus *adj* human, humane, kind, courteous; cultured, refined, well-educated; **hūmānō māior** superhuman

humātiō, -ōnis *f* burying

hūme-, hūmi- *see* **ūme-, ūmi-**

humilis *adj* low, low-lying, shallow; (*condition*) lowly, humble, poor; (*language*) commonplace; (*mind*) mean, base

humilitās, -ātis *f* low position, smallness, shallowness; lowliness, insignificance; meanness, baseness

humiliter *adv* meanly, humbly

humō, -āre, -āvī, -ātum *vt* to bury

humus, -ī *f* earth, ground; land; **humī** on the ground

hyacinthinus *adj* of the hyacinthus

hyacinthus, -ī *m* iris, lily

Hyades, -um *fpl* Hyads (*a group of stars in Taurus*)

hyaena, -ae *f* hyena

hyalus, -ī *m* glass

Hybla, -ae *f* mountain in Sicily (*famous for bees*)

Hyblaeus *adj see* **Hybla**

hybrida *etc see* **hibrida**

Hydaspēs, -is *m* tributary of river Indus (*now Jhelum*)

Hȳdra, -ae *f* hydra (*a mythical dragon with seven heads*)

hydraulus, -ī *m* water organ

hydria, -ae *f* ewer

Hydrochous, -ī *m* Aquarius

hydrōpicus *adj* suffering from dropsy

hydrōps, -is *m* dropsy

hydrus, -ī *m* serpent

Hylās, -ae *m* a youth loved by Hercules

Hymēn, -enis, Hymenaeus, -ī *m* god of marriage; wedding song; wedding

Hymettius *adj see* **Hymettus**

Hymettus, -ī *m* mountain near Athens (*famous for honey and marble*)

Hypanis, -is *m* river of Sarmatia (*now Bug*)

Hyperboreī, -ōrum *mpl* fabulous people in the far North

Hyperboreus *adj see* **Hyperboreī**

Hyperiōn, -onis *m* father of the Sun; the Sun

hypodidascalus, -ī *m* assistant teacher

hypomnēma, -tis *nt* memorandum

Hyrcānī, -ōrum *mpl* people on the Caspian Sea

Hyrcānus *adj* Hyrcanian

Iacchus, -ī m Bacchus; wine

iaceō, -ēre, -uī vi to lie; to be ill, lie dead; (places) to be situated, be flat or low-lying, be in ruins; (dress) to hang loose; (fig) to be inactive, be downhearted; (things) to be dormant, neglected, despised

iaciō, -ere, iēcī, iactum vt to throw; to lay, build; (seed) to sow; (speech) to cast, let fall, mention

iactāns, -antis pres p of **iactō** ▶ adj boastful

iactanter adv ostentatiously

iactantia, -ae f boasting, ostentation

iactātiō, -ōnis f tossing, gesticulation; boasting, ostentation; **~ populāris** publicity

iactātus, -ūs m waving

iactitō vt to mention, bandy

iactō, -āre, -āvī, -ātum vt to throw, scatter; to shake, toss about; (mind) to disquiet; (ideas) to consider, discuss, mention; (speech) to boast of; **sē iactāre** waver, fluctuate; to behave ostentatiously, be officious

iactūra, -ae f throwing overboard; loss, sacrifice

iactus¹ ppp of **iaciō**

iactus², -ūs m throwing, throw; **intrā tēlī iactum** within spear's range

iacuī perf of **iaceō**

iaculābilis adj missile

iaculātor, -ōris m thrower, shooter; light-armed soldier

iaculātrīx, -īcis f huntress

iaculor, -ārī, -ātus vt to throw, hurl, shoot; to throw the javelin; to shoot at, hit; (fig) to aim at, attack

iaculum, -ī nt javelin; fishing net

iāien- etc see **iēn-**

iam adv (past) already, by then; (present) now, already; (future) directly, very soon; (emphasis) indeed, precisely; (inference) therefore, then surely; (transition) moreover, next; **iam dūdum** for a long time, long ago; immediately; **iam iam** right now, any moment now; **non iam** no longer; **iam ... iam** at one time ... at another; **iam nunc** just now; **iam prīdem** long ago, for

a long time; **iam tum** even at that time; **sī iam** supposing for the purpose of argument

iambēus adj iambic

iambus, -ī m iambic foot; iambic poetry

iānālis adj see **iānus**

iāniculum, -ī nt Roman hill across the Tiber

iānitor, -ōris m doorkeeper, porter

iānua, -ae f door; entrance; (fig) key

iānuārius adj of January ▶ m January

iānus, -ī m god of gateways and beginnings; archway, arcade

Iapetīonidēs, -ae m Atlas

Iapetus, -ī m a Titan (father of Atlas and Prometheus)

Iāpyx, -gis adj Iapygian; Apulian ▶ m west-north-west wind from Apulia

Iāsōn, -onis m Jason (leader of Argonauts, husband of Medea)

Iāsonius adj see **Iāsōn**

iaspis, -dis f jasper

Ībēr- etc see **Hibēr-**

ibi adv there; then; in this, at it

ibīdem adv in the same place; at that very moment

ibis, -is and **-idis** f ibis

Īcarium, -ī nt Icarian (Sea)

Īcarius adj see **Īcarus**

Īcarus, -ī m son of Daedalus (drowned in the Aegean)

īcō, -ere, -ī, ictum vt to strike; **foedus īcere** make a treaty

ictericus adj jaundiced

ictis, -dis f weasel

ictus¹ ppp of **īcō**

ictus², -ūs m stroke, blow; wound; (metre) beat

Īda, -ae, Īdē, -ēs f mountain in Crete; mountain near Troy

Īdaeus adj Cretan; Trojan

idcircō adv for that reason; for the purpose

īdem, eadem, idem pron the same; also, likewise

identidem adv repeatedly, again and again

ideō adv therefore, for this reason, that is why

idiōta, -ae m ignorant person, layman

īdōlon, -ī nt apparition

idōneē adv see **idōneus**

idōneus adj fit, proper, suitable, sufficient

Īdūs, -uum fpl Ides (the 15th March, May, July, October, the 13th of other months)

iēcī perf of **iaciō**

iecur, -oris and **-inoris** nt liver; (fig) passion

iecusculum, -ī nt small liver

iēiūniōsus adj hungry

iēiūnitās, -ātis f fasting; (fig) meagreness

iēiūnium, -ī and **-iī** nt fast; hunger; leanness

iēiūnus adj fasting, hungry; (things) barren, poor, meagre; (style) feeble

iēntāculum, -ī nt breakfast

igitur adv therefore, then, so

ignārus adj ignorant, unaware; unknown

ignāvē, ignāviter adv without energy

ignāvia, -ae f idleness, laziness; cowardice

ignāvus adj idle, lazy, listless; cowardly; relaxing

ignēscō, -ere vi to take fire, burn

igneus adj burning, fiery

igniculus, -ī m spark; (fig) fire, vehemence

ignifer, -ī adj fiery

ignigena, -ae m the fireborn (Bacchus)

ignipēs, -edis adj fiery-footed

ignipotēns, -entis adj fire-working (Vulcan)

ignis, -is m fire, a fire; firebrand, lightning; brightness, redness; (fig) passion, love

ignōbilis adj unknown, obscure; low-born

ignōbilitās, -ātis f obscurity; low birth

ignōminia, -ae f dishonour, disgrace

ignōminiōsus adj (person) degraded, disgraced; (things) shameful

ignōrābilis adj unknown

ignōrantia, -ae f ignorance

ignōrātiō, -ōnis f ignorance

ignōrō, -āre, -āvī, -ātum vt to not know, be unacquainted with; to disregard

ignōscō, -scere, -vī, -tum, vi to forgive, pardon

ignōtus adj unknown; low-born; ignorant

īlex, -icis f holm oak

Īlia, -ae f mother of Romulus and Remus

īlia, -um ntpl groin; entrails; ~ dūcere become broken-winded

Īliadēs, -adae m son of Ilia; Trojan

Īlias, -dis f the Iliad; a Trojan woman

īlicet adv it's all over, let us go; immediately

īlicō adv on the spot; instantly

īlignus adj of holm oak

Īlīthyia, -ae f Greek goddess of childbirth

Īlium, -ī nt, **Īlion, -ī** nt, **Īlios, -ī** f Troy

Īlius, Īliacus adj Trojan

illā adv that way

illābefactus adj unbroken

illābor, -bī, -psus vi to flow into, fall down

illabōrō, -āre vi to work (at)

illāc adv that way

illacessītus adj unprovoked

illacrimābilis adj unwept; inexorable

illacrimō, -āre, illacrimor, -ārī vi to weep over, lament; to weep

illaesus adj unhurt

illaetābilis adj cheerless

illāpsus ppa of **illābor**

illaqueō, -āre vt to ensnare

illātus ppp of **īnferō**

illaudātus adj wicked

ille, -a, -ud pron, adj that, that one; he, she, it; the famous; the former, the other; **ex illō** since then

illecebra, -ae f attraction, lure, bait, decoy bird

illecebrōsus adj seductive

illectus ppp of **illiciō**

illēctus adj unread

illepidē adv see **illepidus**

illepidus adj inelegant, churlish

illex, -icis m/f lure

illēx, -ēgis adj lawless

illexī perf of **illiciō**

illībātus adj unimpaired

illīberālis adj ungenerous, mean, disobliging

illīberālitās, -ātis f meanness

illīberāliter adv see **illīberālis**

illic, -aec, -ūc pron he, she, it; that

illīc adv there, yonder; in that matter

illiciō, -icere, -exī, -ectum vt to seduce, decoy, mislead

illicitātor, -ōris m sham bidder (at an auction)

illicitus adj unlawful

illīdō, -dere, -sī, -sum vt to strike, dash against

illigō, -āre, -āvī, -ātum vt to fasten on, attach; to connect; to impede, encumber, oblige

illim adv from there

illimis adj clear

illinc adv from there; on that side

illinō, -inere, -ēvī, -itum vt to smear over, cover, bedaub

illiquefactus adj melted

illīsī perf of **illīdō**

illisus ppp of **illīdō**

illitterātus adj uneducated, uncultured

illitus ppp of **illinō**

illō adv (to) there; to that end

illōtus adj dirty

illūc adv (to) there; to that; to him/her

illūceō, -ēre vi to blaze

illūcēscō, -cēscere, -xī vi to become light, dawn

illūdō, -dere, -sī, -sum, vi to play, amuse oneself; to abuse; to jeer at, ridicule

illūmināte adv luminously

illūminō, -āre, -āvī, -ātum vt to light up; to enlighten; to embellish

illūsiō, -ōnis f irony

illūstris adj bright, clear; distinct, manifest; distinguished, illustrious

illūstrō, -āre, -āvī, -ātum vt to illuminate; to make clear, explain; to make famous

illūsus ppp of **illūdō**

illuviēs, -ēī f dirt, filth; floods

Illyria, -ae f, **Illyricum, -cī** nt Illyria

Illyricus, Illyrius adj see **Illyria**

Illyriī, -ōrum mpl people E. of the Adriatic

Ilva, -ae f Italian island (now Elba)

imāginārius adj fancied

imāginātiō, -ōnis f fancy

imāginor, -ārī vt to picture to oneself

imāgō, -inis f likeness, picture, statue; portrait of ancestor; apparition, ghost; echo, mental picture, idea; (fig) semblance, mere shadow; (RHET) comparison

imbēcillē adv faintly

imbēcillitās, -ātis f weakness, helplessness

imbēcillus adj weak, frail; helpless

imbellis adj non-combatant; peaceful; cowardly

imber, -ris m rain, heavy shower; water; (fig) stream, shower

imberbis, **imberbus** *adj* beardless
imbibō, **-ere**, **-ī** *vt* (*mind*) to conceive; to resolve
imbrex, **-icis** *f* tile
imbricus *adj* rainy
imbrifer, **-ī** *adj* rainy
imbuō, **-uere**, **-uī**, **-ūtum** *vt* to wet, steep,
   dip; (*fig*) to taint, fill; to inspire, accustom, train;
   to begin, be the first to explore
imitābilis *adj* imitable
imitāmen, **-inis** *nt* imitation; likeness
imitāmenta, **-ōrum** *ntpl* pretence
imitātiō, **-ōnis** *f* imitation
imitātor, **-ōris** *m*, **imitātrīx**, **-rīcis** *f*
   imitator
imitātus *adj* copied
imitor, **-ārī**, **-ātus** *vt* to copy, portray; to
   imitate, act like
immadēscō, **-ēscere**, **-uī** *vi* to become wet
immāne *adv* savagely
immānis *adj* enormous, vast; monstrous,
   savage, frightful
immānitās, **-ātis** *f* vastness; savageness,
   barbarism
immānsuētus *adj* wild
immātūritās, **-ātis** *f* over-eagerness
immātūrus *adj* untimely
immedicābilis *adj* incurable
immemor, **-is** *adj* unmindful, forgetful,
   negligent
immemorābilis *adj* indescribable, not worth
   mentioning
immemorātus *adj* hitherto untold
immēnsitās, **-ātis** *f* immensity
immēnsum, **-ī** *nt* infinity, vast extent ▸ *adv*
   exceedingly
immēnsus *adj* immeasurable, vast, unending
immerēns, **-entis** *adj* undeserving
immergō, **-gere**, **-sī**, **-sum** *vt* to plunge,
   immerse
immeritō *adv* unjustly
immeritus *adj* undeserving, innocent;
   undeserved
immērsābilis *adj* never foundering
immersus *ppp of* **immergō**
immētātus *adj* unmeasured
immigrō, **-āre**, **-āvī**, **-ātum** *vi* to move (into)
immineō, **-ēre**, **-uī** *vi* to overhang, project;
   to be near, adjoin, impend; to threaten, be a
   menace to; to long for, grasp at
imminuō, **-uere**, **-uī**, **-ūtum** *vt* to lessen,
   shorten; to impair; to encroach on, ruin
imminūtiō, **-ōnis** *f* mutilation; (*RHET*)
   understatement
immisceō, **-scēre**, **-scuī**, **-xtum** *vt* to
   intermingle, blend; **sē immiscēre** join,
   meddle with
immiserābilis *adj* unpitied
immisericorditer *adv* unmercifully
immisericors, **-dis** *adj* pitiless
immissiō, **-ōnis** *f* letting grow
immissus *ppp of* **immittō**
immītis *adj* unripe; severe, inexorable

immittō, **-ittere**, **-īsī**, **-issum** *vt* to let in, put
   in; to graft on; to let go, let loose, let grow; to
   launch, throw; to incite, set on
immīxtus *ppp of* **immisceō**
immo *adv* (*correcting preceding words*) no, yes; on
   the contrary, or rather; ~ **sī** ah, if only
immōbilis *adj* motionless; immovable
immoderātē *adv* extravagantly
immoderātiō, **-ōnis** *f* excess
immoderātus *adj* limitless; excessive,
   unbridled
immodestē *adv* extravagantly
immodestia, **-ae** *f* licence
immodestus *adj* immoderate
immodicē *adv see* **immodicus**
immodicus *adj* excessive, extravagant, unruly
immodulātus *adj* unrhythmical
immolātiō, **-ōnis** *f* sacrifice
immolātor, **-ōris** *m* sacrificer
immōlītus *adj* erected
immolō, **-āre**, **-āvī**, **-ātum** *vt* to sacrifice;
   to slay
immorior, **-ī**, **-tuus** *vi* to die upon; to waste
   away
immorsus *adj* bitten; (*fig*) stimulated
immortālis *adj* immortal, everlasting
immortālitās, **-ātis** *f* immortality; lasting
   fame
immortāliter *adv* infinitely
immōtus *adj* motionless, unmoved,
   immovable
immūgiō, **-īre**, **-iī** *vi* to roar (in)
immulgeō, **-ēre** *vt* to milk
immundus *adj* unclean, dirty
immūniō, **-īre**, **-īvī** *vt* to strengthen
immūnis *adj* with no public obligations,
   untaxed, free from office; exempt, free (from)
immūnitās, **-ātis** *f* exemption, immunity,
   privilege
immūnītus *adj* undefended; (*roads*)
   unmetalled
immurmurō, **-āre** *vi* to murmur (at)
immūtābilis *adj* unalterable
immūtābilitās, **-ātis** *f* immutability
immūtātiō, **-ōnis** *f* exchange; (*RHET*)
   metonymy
immūtātus *adj* unchanged
immūtō, **-āre**, **-āvī**, **-ātum** *vt* to change;
   (*words*) to substitute by metonymy
impācātus *adj* aggressive
impāctus *ppp of* **impingō**
impār, **-aris** *adj* unequal, uneven, unlike; no
   match for, inferior; (*metre*) elegiac
imparātus *adj* unprepared, unprovided
impariter *adv* unequally
impāstus *adj* hungry
impatiēns, **-entis** *adj* unable to endure,
   impatient
impatienter *adv* intolerably
impatientia, **-ae** *f* want of endurance
impavidē *adv see* **impavidus**
impavidus *adj* fearless, undaunted

impedīmentum, -ī nt hindrance, obstacle; (pl) baggage, luggage, supply train

impediō, -īre, -īvī and **-iī, -ītum** vt to hinder, entangle; to encircle; (fig) to embarrass, obstruct, prevent

impedītiō, -ōnis f obstruction

impedītus adj (MIL) hampered with baggage, in difficulties; (place) difficult, impassable; (mind) busy, obsessed

impēgī perf of **impingō**

impellō, -ellere, -ulī, -ulsum vt to strike, drive; to set in motion, impel, shoot; to incite, urge on; (fig) to overthrow, ruin

impendeō, -ēre vi to overhang; to be imminent, threaten

impendiō adv very much

impendium, -ī and **-iī** nt expense, outlay; interest on a loan

impendō, -endere, -endī, -ēnsum vt to weigh out, pay out, spend; (fig) to devote

impenetrābilis adj impenetrable

impēnsa, -ae f expense, outlay

impēnsē adv very much; earnestly

impēnsus ppp of **impendō** ▸ adj (cost) high, dear; (fig) great, earnest

imperātor, -ōris m commander-in-chief, general; emperor; chief, master

imperātōrius adj of a general; imperial

imperātum, -ī nt order

imperceptus adj unknown

impercussus adj noiseless

imperditus adj not slain

imperfectus adj unfinished, imperfect

imperfossus adj not stabbed

imperiōsus adj powerful, imperial; tyrannical

imperītē adv awkwardly

imperītia, -ae f inexperience

imperitō, -āre vt, vi to rule, command

imperītus adj inexperienced, ignorant

imperium, -ī and **-iī** nt command, order; mastery, sovereignty, power; military command, supreme authority; empire; (pl) those in command, the authorities

impermissus adj unlawful

imperō, -āre, -āvī, -ātum vt, vi to order, command; to requisition, demand; to rule, govern, control; to be emperor

imperterritus adj undaunted

impertiō, -īre, -īvī and **-iī, -ītum** vt to share, communicate, impart

imperturbātus adj unruffled

impervius adj impassable

impetibilis adj intolerable

impetis (gen) (abl **-e**) m force; extent

impetrābilis adj attainable; successful

impetrātiō, -ōnis f favour

impetriō, -īre vt to succeed with the auspices

impetrō, -āre, -āvī, -ātum vt to achieve; to obtain, secure (a request)

impetus, -ūs m attack, onset; charge; rapid motion, rush; (mind) impulse, passion

impexus adj unkempt

impiē adv wickedly

impietās, -ātis f impiety, disloyalty, unfilial conduct

impiger, -rī adj active, energetic

impigrē adv see **impiger**

impigritās, -ātis f energy

impingō, -ingere, -ēgī, -āctum vt to dash, force against; to force upon; (fig) to bring against, drive

impiō, -āre vt to make sinful

impius adj (to gods) impious; (to parents) undutiful; (to country) disloyal; wicked, unscrupulous

implācābilis adj implacable

implācābiliter adv see **implācābilis**

implācātus adj unappeased

implacidus adj savage

impleō, -ēre, -ēvī, -ētum vt to fill; to satisfy; (time, number) to make up, complete; (duty) to discharge, fulfil

implexus adj entwined; involved

implicātiō, -ōnis f entanglement

implicātus adj complicated, confused

implicitē adv intricately

implicō, -āre, -āvī and **-uī, -ātum** and **-itum** vt to entwine, enfold, clasp; (fig) to entangle, involve; to connect closely, join

implōrātiō, -ōnis f beseeching

implōrō, -āre, -āvī, -ātum vt to invoke, entreat, appeal to

implūmis adj unfledged

impluō, -ere vi to rain upon

impluvium, -ī and **-iī** nt roof-opening of the Roman atrium; rain basin in the atrium

impolītē adv without ornament

impolītus adj unpolished, inelegant

impollūtus adj unstained

impōnō, -ōnere, -osuī, -ositum vt to put in, lay on, place; to embark; (fig) to impose, inflict, assign; to put in charge; (tax) to impose; (with dat) to impose upon, cheat

importō, -āre, -āvī, -ātum vt to bring in, import; (fig) to bring upon, introduce

importūnē adv see **importūnus**

importūnitās, -ātis f insolence, ill nature

importūnus adj unsuitable; troublesome; ill-natured, uncivil, bullying

importuōsus adj without a harbour

impos, -tis adj not master (of)

impositus, impostus ppp of **impōnō**

impotēns, -entis adj powerless, weak; with no control over; headstrong, violent

impotenter adv weakly; violently

impotentia, -ae f poverty; want of self-control, violence

impraesentiārum adv at present

imprānsus adj fasting, without breakfast

imprecor, -ārī vt to invoke

impressiō, -ōnis f (MIL) thrust, raid; (mind) impression; (speech) emphasis; (rhythm) beat

impressus ppp of **imprimō**

imprīmīs adv especially

imprimō, -imere, -essī, -essum vt to press upon, impress, imprint, stamp
improbātiō, -ōnis f blame
improbē adv badly, wrongly; persistently
improbitās, -ātis f badness, dishonesty
improbō, -āre, -āvī, -ātum vt to disapprove, condemn, reject
improbulus adj a little presumptuous
improbus adj bad, inferior (in quality); wicked, perverse, cruel; unruly, persistent, rebellious
imprōcērus adj undersized
imprōdictus adj not postponed
imprōmptus adj unready, slow
improperātus adj lingering
improsper, -ī adj unsuccessful
improsperē adv unfortunately
imprōvidē adv see **imprōvidus**
imprōvidus adj unforeseeing, thoughtless
imprōvīsus adj unexpected; **imprōvīsō, de imprōvīsō, ex imprōvīsō** unexpectedly
imprūdēns, -entis adj unforeseeing, not expecting; ignorant, unaware
imprūdenter adv thoughtlessly, unawares
imprūdentia, -ae f thoughtlessness; ignorance; aimlessness
impūbēs, -eris and **-is** adj youthful; chaste
impudens, -entis adj shameless, impudent
impudenter adv see **impudens**
impudentia, -ae f impudence
impudīcitia, -ae f lewdness
impudīcus adj shameless; immodest
impugnātiō, -ōnis f assault
impugnō, -āre, -āvī, -ātum vt to attack; (fig) to oppose, impugn
impulī perf of **impellō**
impulsiō, -ōnis f pressure; (mind) impulse
impulsor, -ōris m instigator
impulsus¹ ppp of **impellō**
impulsus², -ūs m push, pressure, impulse; (fig) instigation
impūne adv safely, with impunity
impūnitās, -ātis f impunity
impūnītē adv with impunity
impūnītus adj unpunished
impūrātus adj vile
impūrē adv see **impūrus**
impūritās, -ātis f uncleanness
impūrus adj unclean; infamous, vile
imputātus adj unpruned
imputō, -āre, -āvī, -ātum vt to put to one's account; to ascribe, credit, impute
īmulus adj little tip of
īmus adj lowest, deepest, bottom of; last
in prep (with abl) in, on, at; among; in the case of; (time) during; (with acc) into, on to, to, towards; against; (time) for, till; (purpose) for; **in armīs** under arms; **in equō** on horseback; **in eō esse ut** be in the position of; be on the point of; **in hōrās** hourly; **in modum** in the manner of; **in rem** of use; **in ūniversum** in general
inaccessus adj unapproachable
inacēscō, -ere vi to turn sour

Īnachidēs, -idae m Perseus; Epaphus
Īnachis, -idis f Io
Īnachius adj of Inachus, Argive, Greek
Īnachus, -ī m first king of Argos
inadsuētus adj unaccustomed
inadūstus adj unsinged
inaedificō, -āre, -āvī, -ātum vt to build on, erect; to wall up, block up
inaequābilis adj uneven
inaequālis adj uneven; unequal; capricious
inaequāliter adv see **inaequālis**
inaequātus adj unequal
inaequō, -āre vt to level up
inaestimābilis adj incalculable; invaluable; valueless
inaestuō, -āre vi to rage in
inamābilis adj hateful
inamārēscō, -ere vi to become bitter
inambitiōsus adj unambitious
inambulātiō, -ōnis f walking about
inambulō, -āre vi to walk up and down
inamoenus adj disagreeable
inanimus adj lifeless, inanimate
ināniō, -īre vt to make empty
inānis adj empty, void; poor, unsubstantial; useless, worthless, vain, idle ▶ nt (PHILOS) space; (fig) vanity
inānitās, -ātis f empty space; inanity
ināniter adv idly, vainly
inarātus adj fallow
inārdēscō, -dēscere, -sī vi to be kindled, flare up
inass- etc see **inads-**
inattenuātus adj undiminished
inaudāx, -ācis adj timorous
inaudiō, -īre vt to hear of, learn
inaudītus adj unheard of, unusual; without a hearing
inaugurātō adv after taking the auspices
inaugurō, -āre vi to take auspices ▶ vt to consecrate, inaugurate
inaurēs, -ium fpl earrings
inaurō, -āre, -āvī, -ātum vt to gild; (fig) to enrich
inauspicātō adv without taking the auspices
inauspicātus adj done without auspices
inausus adj unattempted
incaeduus adj uncut
incalēscō, -ēscere, -uī vi to grow hot; (fig) to warm, glow
incalfaciō, -ere vt to heat
incallidē adv unskilfully
incallidus adj stupid, simple
incandēscō, -ēscere, -uī vi to become hot; to turn white
incānēscō, -ēscere, -uī vi to grow grey
incantātus adj enchanted
incānus adj grey
incassum adv in vain
incastīgātus adj unrebuked
incautē adv negligently

incautus adj careless, heedless; unforeseen, unguarded

incēdō, -ēdere, -ēssī, -ēssum vi to walk, parade, march; (MIL) to advance; (feelings) to come upon

incelebrātus adj not made known

incēnātus adj supperless

incendiārius, -ī and **-iī** m incendiary

incendium, -ī and **-iī** nt fire, conflagration; heat; (fig) fire, vehemence, passion

incendō, -ere, -ī, incēnsum vt to set fire to, burn; to light, brighten; (fig) to inflame, rouse, incense

incēnsiō, -ōnis f burning

incēnsus¹ ppp of **incendō**

incēnsus² adj not registered

incēpī perf of **incipiō**

inceptiō, -ōnis f undertaking

inceptō, -āre vt to begin, attempt

inceptor, -ōris m originator

inceptum, -ī nt beginning, undertaking, attempt

inceptus ppp of **incipiō**

incērō, -āre vt to cover with wax

incertō adv not for certain

incertus adj uncertain, doubtful, unsteady ▶ nt uncertainty

incēssō, -ere, -īvī vt to attack; (fig) to assail

incēssus, -ūs m gait, pace, tramp; invasion; approach

incestē adv see **incestus¹**

incestō, -āre vt to pollute, dishonour

incestus¹ adj sinful; unchaste, incestuous ▶ nt incest

incestus², -ūs m incest

incho- etc see **incoh-**

incidō, -idere, -idī, -āsum vi to fall upon, fall into; to meet, fall in with, come across; to befall, occur, happen; **in mentem incidere** occur to one

incīdō, -dere, -dī, -sum vt to cut open; to cut up; to engrave, inscribe; to interrupt, cut short

incīle, -is nt ditch

incīlō, -āre vt to rebuke

incingō, -gere, -xī, -ctum vt to gird, wreathe; to surround

incinō, -ere vt to sing, play

incipiō, -ipere, -ēpī, -eptum vt, vi to begin

incipissō, -ere vt to begin

incīsē adv in short clauses

incīsim adv in short clauses

incīsiō, -ōnis f clause

incīsum, -ī nt clause

incīsus ppp of **incīdō**

incitāmentum, -ī nt incentive

incitātē adv impetuously

incitātiō, -ōnis f inciting; rapidity

incitātus ppp of **incitō** ▶ adj swift, rapid; **equō incitātō** at a gallop

incitō, -āre, -āvī, -ātum vt to urge on, rush; to rouse, encourage, excite; to inspire; to increase; **sē incitāre** rush; **currentem incitāre** spur a willing horse

incitus¹ adj swift

incitus² adj immovable; **ad incitās redigere, ad incita redigere** bring to a standstill

inclāmō, -āre vt, vi to call out, cry out to; to scold, abuse

inclārēscō, -ēscere, -uī vi to become famous

inclēmēns, -entis adj severe

inclēmenter adv harshly

inclēmentia, -ae f severity

inclīnātiō, -ōnis f leaning, slope; (fig) tendency, inclination, bias; (circumstances) change; (voice) modulation

inclīnātus adj inclined, prone; falling; (voice) deep

inclīnō, -āre, -āvī, -ātum vt to bend, turn; to turn back; (fig) to incline, direct, transfer; to change ▶ vi to bend, sink; (MIL) to give way; (fig) to change, deteriorate; to incline, tend, turn in favour

inclitus etc see **inclutus**

inclūdō, -dere, -sī, -sum vt to shut in, keep in, enclose; to obstruct, block; (fig) to include; (time) to close, end

inclūsiō, -ōnis f imprisonment

inclūsus ppp of **inclūdō**

inclutus adj famous, glorious

incoctus¹ ppp of **incoquō**

incoctus² adj uncooked, raw

incōgitābilis adj thoughtless

incōgitāns, -antis adj thoughtless

incōgitantia, -ae f thoughtlessness

incōgitō, -āre vt to contrive

incognitus adj unknown, unrecognized; (LAW) untried

incohātus adj unfinished

incohō, -āre, -āvī, -ātum vt to begin, start

incola, -ae m/f inhabitant, resident

incolō, -ere, -uī vt to live in, inhabit ▶ vi to live, reside

incolumis adj safe and sound, unharmed

incolumitās, -ātis f safety

incomitātus adj unaccompanied

incommendātus adj unprotected

incommodē adv inconveniently, unfortunately

incommoditās, -ātis f inconvenience, disadvantage

incommodō, -āre vi to be inconvenient, annoy

incommodum, -ī nt inconvenience, disadvantage, misfortune

incommodus adj inconvenient, troublesome

incommūtābilis adj unchangeable

incompertus adj unknown

incompositē adv see **incompositus**

incompositus adj in disorder, irregular

incōmptus adj undressed, inelegant

inconcēssus adj forbidden

inconciliō, -āre vt to win over (by guile); trick, inveigle, embarrass

inconcinnus adj inartistic, awkward

inconcussus adj unshaken, stable

inconditē adv confusedly

inconditus adj undisciplined, not organized; (language) artless

incōnsīderātē adv see **incōnsīderātus**

incōnsīderātus adj thoughtless, ill-advised

incōnsōlābilis adj incurable

incōnstāns, -antis adj fickle, inconsistent

incōnstanter adv inconsistently

incōnstantia, -ae f fickleness, inconsistency

incōnsultē adv indiscreetly

incōnsultū without consulting

incōnsultus adj indiscreet, ill-advised; unanswered; not consulted

incōnsūmptus adj unconsumed

incontāminātus adj untainted

incontentus adj untuned

incontinēns, -entis adj intemperate

incontinenter adv without self-control

incontinentia, -ae f lack of self-control

inconveniēns, -entis adj ill-matched

incoquō, -quere, -xī, -ctum vt to boil; to dye

incorrēctus adj unrevised

incorruptē adv justly

incorruptus adj unspoiled; uncorrupted, genuine

incrēbrēscō, increbēscō, -ēscere, -uī vi to increase, grow, spread

incrēdibilis adj incredible, extraordinary

incrēdibiliter adv see **incrēdibilis**

incrēdulus adj incredulous

incrēmentum, -ī nt growth, increase; addition; offspring

increpitō, -āre vt to rebuke; to challenge

increpō, -āre, -uī, -itum vi to make a noise, sound; (news) to be noised abroad ▶ vt to cause to make a noise; to exclaim against, rebuke

incrēscō, -scere, -vī vi to grow in, increase

incrētus adj sifted in

incruentātus adj unstained with blood

incruentus adj bloodless, without bloodshed

incrūstō, -āre vt to encrust

incubō, -āre, -uī, -itum vi to lie in or on; (fig) to brood over

incubuī perf of **incubō**; **incumbō**

inculcō, -āre, -āvī, -ātum vt to force in; to force upon, impress on

inculpātus adj blameless

incultē adv uncouthly

incultus¹ adj uncultivated; (fig) neglected, uneducated, rude

incultus², -ūs m neglect, squalor

incumbō, -mbere, -buī, -bitum vi to lean, recline on; to fall upon, throw oneself upon; to oppress, lie heavily upon; (fig) to devote attention to, take pains with; to incline

incūnābula, -ōrum ntpl swaddling clothes; (fig) cradle, infancy, birthplace, origin

incūrātus adj neglected

incūria, -ae f negligence

incūriōsē adv carelessly

incūriōsus adj careless, indifferent

incurrō, -rrere, -rrī and **-curri, -rsum** vi to run into, rush, attack; to invade; to meet with, get involved in; (events) to occur, coincide

incursiō, -ōnis f attack; invasion, raid; collision

incursō, -āre vt, vi to run into, assault; to frequently invade; (fig) to meet, strike

incursus, -ūs m assault, striking; (mind) impulse

incurvō, -āre vt to bend, crook

incurvus adj bent, crooked

incūs, -ūdis f anvil

incūsātiō, -ōnis f blaming

incūsō, -āre, -āvī, -ātum vt to find fault with, accuse

incussī perf of **incutiō**

incussus¹ ppp of **incutiō**

incussus², -ūs m shock

incustōdītus adj unguarded, unconcealed

incūsus adj forged

incutiō, -tere, -ssī, -ssum vt to strike, dash against; to throw; (fig) to strike into, inspire with

indāgātiō, -ōnis f search

indāgātor, -ōris m explorer

indāgātrīx, -rīcis f female explorer

indāgō¹, -āre vt to track down; (fig) to trace, investigate

indāgō², -inis f (hunt) drive, encirclement

indaudiō etc see **inaudiō**

inde adv from there, from that, from them; on that side; from then, ever since; after that, then

indēbitus adj not due

indēclīnātus adj constant

indecor, -is adj dishonourable, a disgrace

indecorē adv indecently

indecorō, -āre vt to disgrace

indecōrus adj unbecoming, unsightly

indēfēnsus adj undefended

indēfessus adj unwearied, tireless

indēflētus adj unwept

indēiectus adj undemolished

indēlēbilis adj imperishable

indēlībātus adj unimpaired

indemnātus adj unconvicted

indēplōrātus adj unlamented

indēprēnsus adj undetected

indeptus ppa of **indipīscor**

indēsertus adj unforsaken

indēstrictus adj unscathed

indētōnsus adj unshorn

indēvītātus adj unerring

index, -icis m forefinger; witness, informer; (book, art) title, inscription; (stone) touchstone; (fig) indication, pointer, sign

India, -iae f India

indicātiō, -ōnis f value

indīcente mē without my telling

indicium, -ī and **-iī** nt information, evidence; reward for information; indication, sign, proof; ~ profitērī, ~ offerre turn King's evidence; ~ postulāre, ~ dare ask, grant permission to give evidence

indicō, -āre, -āvī, -ātum vt to point out; to disclose, betray; to give information, give evidence; to put a price on

indīcō, -īcere, -īxī, -ictum vt to declare, proclaim, appoint

indictus¹ ppp of **indīcō**

indictus² adj not said, unsung; **causā indictā** without a hearing

Indicus adj see **India**

indidem adv from the same place or thing

indidī perf of **indō**

indifferēns, -entis adj neither good nor bad

indigena, -ae m native ▶ adj native

indigēns, -entis adj needy

indigentia, -ae f need; craving

indigeō, -ēre, -uī vi (with abl) to need, want, require; to crave

indiges, -etis m national deity

indīgestus adj confused

indignābundus adj enraged

indignāns, -antis adj indignant

indignātiō, -ōnis f indignation

indignē adv unworthily; indignantly

indignitās, -ātis f unworthiness, enormity; insulting treatment; indignation

indignor, -ārī, -ātus vt to be displeased with, be angry at

indignus adj unworthy, undeserving; shameful, severe; undeserved

indigus adj in want

indīligēns, -entis adj careless

indīligenter adv see **indīligēns**

indīligentia, -ae f carelessness

indipīscor, -ī, indeptus vt to obtain, get, reach

indīreptus adj unplundered

indiscrētus adj closely connected, indiscriminate, indistinguishable

indisertē adv without eloquence

indisertus adj not eloquent

indispositus adj disorderly

indissolūbilis adj imperishable

indistinctus adj confused, obscure

inditus ppp of **indō**

indīviduus adj indivisible; inseparable ▶ nt atom

indō, -ere, -idī, -itum vt to put in or on; to introduce; to impart, impose

indocilis adj difficult to teach, hard to learn; untaught

indoctē adv unskilfully

indoctus adj untrained, illiterate, ignorant

indolentia, -ae f freedom from pain

indolēs, -is f nature, character, talents

indolēscō, -ēscere, -uī vi to feel sorry

indomitus adj untamed, wild; ungovernable

indormiō, -īre vi to sleep on; to be careless

indōtātus adj with no dowry; unhonoured; (fig) unadorned

indubitō, -āre vi to begin to doubt

indubius adj undoubted

indūcō, -ūcere, -ūxī, -uctum vt to bring in, lead on; to introduce; to overlay, cover over; (fig) to move, persuade, seduce; (book-keeping) to enter; (dress) to put on; (public show) to exhibit; (writing) to erase; **animum indūcere, in animum indūcere** determine, imagine

inductiō, -ōnis f leading, bringing on; (mind) purpose, intention; (LOGIC) induction

inductus ppp of **indūcō**

indugredior etc see **ingredior**

induī perf of **induō**

indulgēns, -entis pres p of **indulgeō** ▶ adj indulgent, kind

indulgenter adv indulgently

indulgentia, -ae f indulgence, gentleness

indulgeō, -gēre, -sī vi (with dat) to be kind to, indulge, give way to; to indulge in ▶ vt to concede; **sibi indulgēre** take liberties

induō, -uere, -uī, -ūtum vt (dress) to put on; (fig) to assume, entangle

indup- etc see **imp-**

indūrēscō, -ēscere, -uī vi to harden

indūrō, -āre vt to harden

Indus¹, -ī m Indian; Ethiopian; mahout

Indus² adj see **India**

industria, -ae f diligence; **dē industriā, ex industriā** on purpose

industriē adv see **industrius**

industrius adj diligent, painstaking

indūtiae, -ārum fpl truce, armistice

indūtus¹ ppp of **induō**

indūtus², -ūs m wearing

induviae, -ārum fpl clothes

indūxī perf of **indūcō**

inēbriō, -āre vt to intoxicate; (fig) to saturate

inedia, -ae f starvation

inēditus adj unpublished

inēlegāns, -antis adj tasteless

inēleganter adv without taste

inēluctābilis adj inescapable

inēmorior, -ī vi to die in

inemptus adj unpurchased

inēnārrābilis adj indescribable

inēnōdābilis adj inexplicable

ineō, -īre, -īvī and -iī, -itum vi to go in, come in; to begin ▶ vt to enter; to begin, enter upon, form, undertake; **cōnsilium inīre** form a plan; **grātiam inīre** win favour; **numerum inīre** enumerate; **ratiōnem inīre** calculate, consider, contrive; **suffrāgium inīre** vote; **viam inīre** find out a way

ineptē adv see **ineptus**

ineptia, -ae f stupidity; (pl) nonsense

ineptiō, -īre vi to play the fool

ineptus adj unsuitable; silly, tactless, absurd

inermis, inermus adj unarmed, defenceless; harmless

inerrāns, -antis adj fixed

inerrō, -āre vi to wander about in

iners, -tis adj unskilful; inactive, indolent, timid; insipid

inertia, -ae f lack of skill; idleness, laziness

inērudītus *adj* uneducated

inescō, -āre *vt* to entice, deceive

inēvectus *adj* mounted

inēvītābilis *adj* inescapable

inexcītus *adj* peaceful

inexcūsābilis *adj* with no excuse

inexercitātus *adj* untrained

inexhaustus *adj* unexhausted

inexōrābilis *adj* inexorable; (*things*) severe

inexperrēctus *adj* unawakened

inexpertus *adj* inexperienced; untried

inexpiābilis *adj* inexpiable; implacable

inexplēbilis *adj* insatiable

inexplētus *adj* incessant

inexplicābilis *adj* inexplicable; impracticable, unending

inexplōrātō *adv* without making a reconnaissance

inexplōrātus *adj* unreconnoitred

inexpugnābilis *adj* impregnable, safe

inexspectātus *adj* unexpected

inexstinctus *adj* unextinguished; insatiable, imperishable

inexsuperābilis *adj* insurmountable

inextrīcābilis *adj* inextricable

īnfabrē *adv* unskilfully

īnfabricātus *adj* unfashioned

īnfacētus *adj* not witty, crude

īnfācundus *adj* ineloquent

īnfāmia, -ae *f* disgrace, scandal

īnfāmis *adj* infamous, disreputable

īnfāmō, -āre, -āvī, -ātum *vt* to disgrace, bring into disrepute

īnfandus *adj* unspeakable, atrocious

īnfāns, -antis *adj* mute, speechless; young, infant; tongue-tied; childish ▸ *m/f* infant, child

īnfantia, -ae *f* inability to speak; infancy; lack of eloquence

īnfatuō, -āre *vt* to make a fool of

īnfaustus *adj* unlucky

īnfector, -ōris *m* dyer

īnfectus¹ *ppp of* **īnficiō**

īnfectus² *adj* undone, unfinished; **rē īnfectā** without achieving one's purpose

īnfēcunditās, -ātis *f* infertility

īnfēcundus *adj* unfruitful

īnfēlīcitās, -ātis *f* misfortune

īnfēlīciter *adv see* **īnfēlīx**

īnfēlīcō, -āre *vt* to make unhappy

īnfēlīx, -īcis *adj* unfruitful; unhappy, unlucky

īnfēnsē *adv* aggressively

īnfēnsō, -āre *vt* to make dangerous, make hostile

īnfēnsus *adj* hostile, dangerous

īnferciō, -īre *vt* to cram in

īnferiae, -ārum *fpl* offerings to the dead

īnferior, -ōris *compar of* **īnferus**

īnferius *compar of* **īnfrā**

īnfernē *adv* below

īnfernus *adj* beneath; of the lower world, infernal ▸ *mpl* the shades ▸ *ntpl* the lower world

īnferō, -re, intulī, illātum *vt* to carry in, bring to, put on; to move forward; (*fig*) to introduce, cause; (*book-keeping*) to enter; (*LOGIC*) to infer; **bellum īnferre** make war (on); **pedem īnferre** advance; **sē īnferre** repair, rush, strut about; **signa īnferre** attack, charge

īnferus (*compar* **īnferior**, *superl* **īnfimus**) *adj* lower, below ▸ *mpl* the dead, the lower world ▸ *compar* lower; later; inferior ▸ *superl* lowest, bottom of; meanest, humblest

īnfervēscō, -vēscere, -buī *vi* to boil

īnfestē *adv* aggressively

īnfestō, -āre *vt* to attack

īnfestus *adj* unsafe; dangerous, aggressive

īnficet- *see* **īnfacēt-**

īnficiō, -icere, -ēcī, -ectum *vt* to dip, dye, discolour; to taint, infect; (*fig*) to instruct, corrupt, poison

īnfidēlis *adj* faithless

īnfidēlitās, -ātis *f* disloyalty

īnfidēliter *adv* treacherously

īnfidus *adj* unsafe, treacherous

īnfīgō, -gere, -xī, -xum *vt* to thrust, drive in; (*fig*) to impress, imprint

īnfimus *superl of* **īnferus**

īnfindō, -ere *vt* to cut into, plough

īnfīnitās, -ātis *f* boundless extent, infinity

īnfīnitē *adv* without end

īnfīnītiō, -ōnis *f* infinity

īnfīnītus *adj* boundless, endless, infinite; indefinite

īnfirmātiō, -ōnis *f* invalidating, refuting

īnfirmē *adv* feebly

īnfirmitās, -ātis *f* weakness; infirmity, sickness

īnfirmō, -āre *vt* to weaken; to invalidate, refute

īnfirmus *adj* weak, indisposed; weak-minded; (*things*) trivial

īnfit *vi* (*defec*) begins

īnfitiālis *adj* negative

īnfitiās eō deny

īnfitiātiō, -ōnis *f* denial

īnfitiātor, -ōris *m* denier (of a debt)

īnfitior, -ārī, -ātus *vt* to deny, repudiate

īnfīxus *ppp of* **īnfīgō**

īnflammātiō, -ōnis *f* (*fig*) exciting

īnflammō, -āre, -āvī, -ātum *vt* to set on fire, light; (*fig*) to inflame, rouse

īnflātē *adv* pompously

īnflātiō, -ōnis *f* flatulence

īnflātus, -ūs *m* blow; inspiration ▸ *adj* blown up, swollen; (*fig*) puffed up, conceited; (*style*) turgid

īnflectō, -ctere, -xī, -xum *vt* to bend, curve; to change; (*voice*) to modulate; (*fig*) to affect, move

īnflētus *adj* unwept

īnflexiō, -ōnis *f* bending

īnflexus *ppp of* **īnflectō**

īnflīgō, -gere, -xī, -ctum *vt* to dash against, strike; to inflict

īnflō, -āre, -āvī, -ātum vt to blow, inflate; (fig) to inspire, puff up

īnfluō, -ere, -xī, -xum vi to flow in; (fig) to stream, pour in

īnfodiō, -odere, -ōdī, -ossum vt to dig in, bury

īnfōrmātiō, -ōnis f sketch, idea

īnfōrmis adj shapeless; hideous

īnfōrmō, -āre, -āvī, -ātum vt to shape, fashion; to sketch; to educate

īnfortūnātus adj unfortunate

īnfortūnium, -ī and **-iī** nt misfortune

īnfossus ppp of **īnfodiō**

īnfrā (compar **īnferius**) adv underneath, below ▶ compar lower down ▶ prep (with acc) below, beneath, under; later than

īnfrāctiō, -ōnis f weakening

īnfrāctus ppp of **īnfringō**

īnfragilis adj strong

īnfremō, -ere, -uī vi to growl

īnfrēnātus¹ ppp of **īnfrēnō**

īnfrēnātus² adj without a bridle

īnfrendō, -ere vi to gnash

īnfrēnis, -us adj unbridled

īnfrēnō, -āre, -āvī, -ātum vt to put a bridle on, harness; (fig) to curb

īnfrequēns, -entis adj not crowded, infrequent; badly attended

īnfrequentia, -ae f small number; emptiness

īnfringō, -ingere, -ēgī, -āctum vt to break, bruise; (fig) to weaken, break down, exhaust

īnfrōns, -ondis adj leafless

īnfūcātus adj showy

īnfula, -ae f woollen band, fillet, badge of honour

īnfumus etc see **īnfimus**

īnfundō, -undere, -ūdī, -ūsum vt to pour in or on; to serve; (fig) to spread

īnfuscō, -āre vt to darken; to spoil, tarnish

īnfūsus ppp of **īnfundō**

ingeminō, -āre vt to redouble ▶ vi to be redoubled

ingemīscō, -īscere, -uī vi to groan, sigh ▶ vt to sigh over

ingemō, -ere, -uī vt, vi to sigh for, mourn

ingenerō, -āre, -āvī, -ātum vt to engender, produce, create

ingeniātus adj with a natural talent

ingeniōsē adv cleverly

ingeniōsus adj talented, clever; (things) naturally suited

ingenitus ppp of **ingignō** ▶ adj inborn, natural

ingenium, -ī and **-iī** nt nature; (disposition) bent, character; (intellect) ability, talent, genius; (person) genius

ingēns, -entis adj huge, mighty, great

ingenuē adv liberally, frankly

ingenuitās, -ātis f noble birth, noble character

ingenuus adj native, innate; free-born; noble, frank; delicate

ingerō, -rere, -ssī, -stum vt to carry in; to heap on; to throw, hurl; (fig) to press, obtrude

ingignō, -ignere, -enuī, -enitum vt to engender, implant

inglōrius adj inglorious

ingluviēs, -ēī f maw; gluttony

ingrātē adv unwillingly; ungratefully

ingrātiīs, ingrātīs adv against one's will

ingrātus adj disagreeable, unwelcome; ungrateful, thankless

ingravēscō, -ere vi to grow heavy, become worse, increase

ingravō, -āre vt to weigh heavily on; to aggravate

ingredior, -dī, -ssus vt, vi to go in, enter; to walk, march; to enter upon, engage in; to commence, begin to speak

ingressiō, -ōnis f entrance; beginning; pace

ingressus, -ūs m entrance; (MIL) inroad; beginning; walking, gait

ingruō, -ere, -ī vi to fall upon, assail

inguen, -inis nt groin

ingurgitō, -āre vt to pour in; **sē ingurgitāre** gorge oneself; (fig) to be absorbed in

ingustātus adj untasted

inhabilis adj unwieldy, awkward; unfit

inhabitābilis adj uninhabitable

inhabitō, -āre vt to inhabit

inhaereō, -rēre, -sī, -sum vi to stick in, cling to; to adhere, be closely connected with; to be always in

inhaerēscō, -ere vi to take hold, cling fast

inhālō, -āre vt to breathe on

inhibeō, -ēre, -uī, -itum vt to check, restrain, use, practise; **inhibēre rēmīs/nāvem** back water

inhibitiō, -ōnis f backing water

inhiō, -āre vi to gape ▶ vt to gape at, covet

inhonestē adv see **inhonestus**

inhonestō, -āre vt to dishonour

inhonestus adj dishonourable, inglorious; ugly

inhonōrātus adj unhonoured; unrewarded

inhonōrus adj unhonoured; ugly

inhorreō, -ēre, -uī vt to stand erect, bristle

inhorrēscō, -ēscere, -uī vi to bristle up; to shiver, shudder, tremble

inhospitālis adj inhospitable

inhospitālitās, -ātis f inhospitality

inhospitus adj inhospitable

inhūmānē adv savagely; uncivilly

inhūmānitās, -ātis f barbarity; discourtesy, churlishness, meanness

inhūmāniter adv = **inhūmānē**

inhūmānus adj savage, brutal; ill-bred, uncivil, uncultured

inhumātus adj unburied

inibi adv there, therein; about to happen

iniciō, -icere, -iēcī, -iectum vt to throw into, put on; (fig) to inspire, cause; (speech) to hint, mention; **manum īnicere** take possession

iniectus, -ūs m putting in, throwing over

inimīcē adv hostilely

inimīcitia, -ae f enmity

inimīcō, -āre vt to make enemies

inimīcus adj unfriendly, hostile; injurious ▶ m/f enemy; **inimīcissimus** greatest enemy
inīquē adv unequally, unjustly
inīquitās, -ātis f unevenness; difficulty; injustice, unfair demands
inīquus adj unequal, uneven; adverse, unfavourable, injurious; unfair, unjust; excessive; impatient, discontented ▶ m enemy
initiō, -āre vt to initiate
initium, -ī and **-iī** nt beginning; (pl) elements, first principles; holy rites, mysteries
initus¹ ppp of **ineō**
initus², -ūs m approach; beginning
iniūcundē adv see **iniūcundus**
iniūcunditās, -ātis f unpleasantness
iniūcundus adj unpleasant
iniungō, -ungere, -ūnxī, -ūnctum vt to join, attach; (fig) to impose, inflict
iniūrātus adj unsworn
iniūria, -ae f wrong, injury, injustice; insult, outrage; severity, revenge; unjust possession; **iniūriā** unjustly
iniūriōsē adv wrongfully
iniūriōsus adj unjust, wrongful; harmful
iniūrius adj wrong, unjust
iniūssū without orders (from)
iniūssus adj unbidden
iniūstē adv see **iniūstus**
iniūstitia, -ae f injustice, severity
iniūstus adj unjust, wrong; excessive, severe
inl- etc see **ill-**
inm- etc see **imm-**
innābilis adj that none may swim
innāscor, -scī, -tus vi to be born in, grow up in
innatō, -āre vt to swim in, float on; to swim, flow into
innātus ppa of **innāscor** ▶ adj innate, natural
innāvigābilis adj unnavigable
innectō, -ctere, -xuī, -xum vt to tie, fasten together, entwine; (fig) to connect; to contrive
innītor, -tī, -xus and **-sus** vi to rest, lean on; to depend
innō, -āre vi to swim in, float on, sail on
innocēns, -entis adj harmless, innocent; upright, unselfish
innocenter adv blamelessly
innocentia, -ae f innocence; integrity, unselfishness
innocuē adv innocently
innocuus adj harmless; innocent; unharmed
innōtēscō, -ēscere, -uī vi to become known
innovō, -āre vt to renew; **sē innovāre** return
innoxius adj harmless, safe; innocent; unharmed
innuba, -ae adj unmarried
innūbilus adj cloudless
innūbō, -bere, -psī vi to marry into
innumerābilis adj countless
innumerābilitās, -ātis f countless number
innumerābiliter adv innumerably
innumerālis adj numberless
innumerus adj countless

innuō, -ere, -ī vi to give a nod
innūpta, -ae adj unmarried
Īnō, -ūs f daughter of Cadmus
inoblītus adj unforgetful
inobrutus adj not overwhelmed
inobservābilis adj unnoticed
inobservātus adj unobserved
inoffēnsus adj without hindrance, uninterrupted
inofficiōsus adj irresponsible; disobliging
inolēns, -entis adj odourless
inolēscō, -scere, -vī vi to grow in
inōminātus adj inauspicious
inopia, -ae f want, scarcity, poverty, helplessness
inopīnāns, -antis adj unaware
inopīnātō adv unexpectedly
inopīnātus adj unexpected; off one's guard
inopīnus adj unexpected
inopiōsus adj in want
inops, -is adj destitute, poor, in need (of); helpless, weak; (speech) poor in ideas
inōrātus adj unpleaded
inōrdinātus adj disordered, irregular
inōrnātus adj unadorned, plain; uncelebrated
Īnōus adj see **Īnō**
inp- etc see **imp-**
inquam vt (defec) to say; (emphatic) I repeat, maintain
inquiēs, -ētis adj restless
inquiētō, -āre vt to unsettle, make difficult
inquiētus adj restless, unsettled
inquilīnus, -ī m inhabitant, tenant
inquinātē adv filthily
inquinātus adj filthy, impure
inquinō, -āre, -āvī, -ātum vt to defile, stain, contaminate
inquīrō, -rere, -sīvī, -sītum vt to search for, inquire into; (LAW) to collect evidence
inquīsītiō, -ōnis f searching, inquiry; (LAW) inquisition
inquīsītor, -ōris m searcher, spy; investigator
inquīsītus¹ ppp of **inquīrō**
inquīsītus² adj not investigated
inr- etc see **irr-**
īnsalūtātus adj ungreeted
īnsānābilis adj incurable
īnsānē adv madly
īnsānia, -ae f madness; folly, mania, poetic rapture
īnsāniō, -īre, -īvī, -ītum vi to be mad, rave; to rage; to be inspired
īnsānitās, -ātis f unhealthiness
īnsānum adv (slang) frightfully
īnsānus adj mad; frantic, furious; outrageous
īnsatiābilis adj insatiable; never cloying
īnsatiābiliter adv see **īnsatiābilis**
īnsatietās, -ātis f insatiateness
īnsaturābilis adj insatiable
īnsaturābiliter adv see **īnsaturābilis**
īnscendō, -endere, -endī, -ēnsum vt, vi to climb up, mount, embark

īnscēnsiō, -ōnis f going on board
īnscēnsus ppp of **īnscendō**
īnsciēns, -entis adj unaware; stupid
īnscienter adv ignorantly
īnscientia, -ae f ignorance, inexperience; neglect
īnscītē adv clumsily
īnscītia, -ae f ignorance, stupidity, inattention
īnscītus adj ignorant, stupid
īnscius adj unaware, ignorant
īnscrībō, -bere, -psī, -ptum vt to write on, inscribe; to ascribe, assign; (book) to entitle; (for sale) to advertise
īnscrīptiō, -ōnis f inscribing, title
īnscrīptus ppp of **īnscrībō**
īnsculpō, -ere, -sī, -tum vt to carve in, engrave on
īnsectātiō, -ōnis f hot pursuit; (words) abusing, persecution
īnsectātor, -ōris m persecutor
īnsector, -ārī, -ātus, īnsectō, -āre vt to pursue, attack, criticise
īnsectus adj notched
īnsēdābiliter adv incessantly
īnsēdī perf of **īnsīdō**
īnsenēscō, -ēscere, -uī vi to grow old in
īnsēnsilis adj imperceptible
īnsepultus adj unburied
īnsequēns, -entis pres p of **īnsequor** ▶ adj the following
īnsequor, -quī, -cūtus vt to follow, pursue hotly; to proceed; (time) to come after, come next; (fig) to attack, persecute
īnserō¹, -erere, -ēvī, -itum vt to graft; (fig) to implant
īnserō², -ere, -uī, -tum vt to let in, insert; to introduce, mingle, involve
īnsertō, -āre vt to put in
īnsertus ppp of **īnserō²**
īnserviō, -īre, -iī, -ītum vt, vi to be a slave (to); to be devoted, submissive (to)
īnsessus ppp of **īnsīdō**
īnsībilō, -āre vi to whistle in
īnsīdeō, -ēre vi to sit on or in; to remain fixed ▶ vt to hold, occupy
īnsidiae, -ārum fpl ambush; (fig) trap, trickery
īnsidiātor, -ōris nt soldier in ambush; (fig) waylayer, plotter
īnsidior, -ārī, -ātus vi to lie in ambush; (with dat) to lie in wait for, plot against
īnsidiōsē adv insidiously
īnsidiōsus adj artful, treacherous
īnsīdō, -īdere, -ēdī, -essum vi to settle on; (fig) to become fixed, rooted in ▶ vt to occupy
īnsigne, -is nt distinguishing mark, badge, decoration; (pl) insignia, honours; (speech) purple passages
īnsigniō, -īre vt to distinguish
īnsignis adj distinguished, conspicuous
īnsignītē adv remarkably
īnsilia, -um ntpl treadle (of a loom)
īnsiliō, -īre, -uī vi to jump into or onto

īnsimulātiō, -ōnis f accusation
īnsimulō, -āre, -āvī, -ātum vt to charge, accuse, allege (esp falsely)
īnsincērus adj adulterated
īnsinuātiō, -ōnis f ingratiating
īnsinuō, -āre, -āvī, -ātum vt to bring in, introduce stealthily ▶ vi to creep in, worm one's way in, penetrate; **sē īnsinuāre** ingratiate oneself; to make one's way into
īnsipiēns, -entis adj senseless, foolish
īnsipienter adv foolishly
īnsipientia, -ae f folly
īnsistō, -istere, -titī vi to stand on, step on; to stand firm, halt, pause; to tread on the heels, press on, pursue; to enter upon, apply oneself to, begin; to persist, continue
īnsitiō, -ōnis f grafting; grafting time
īnsitīvus adj grafted; (fig) spurious
īnsitor, -ōris m grafter
īnsitus ppp of **īnserō¹** ▶ adj innate; incorporated
īnsociābilis adj incompatible
īnsōlābiliter adv unconsolably
īnsolēns, -entis adj unusual, unaccustomed; excessive, extravagant, insolent
īnsolenter adv unusually; immoderately, insolently
īnsolentia, -ae f inexperience, novelty, strangeness; excess, insolence
īnsolēscō, -ere vi to become insolent, elated
īnsolidus adj soft
īnsolitus adj unaccustomed, unusual
īnsomnia, -ae f sleeplessness
īnsomnis adj sleepless
īnsomnium, -ī and **-iī** nt dream
īnsonō, -āre, -uī vi to resound, sound; to make a noise
īnsōns, -ontis adj innocent; harmless
īnsōpītus adj sleepless
īnspectō, -āre vt to look at
īnspectus ppp of **īnspiciō**
īnspērāns, -antis adj not expecting
īnspērātus adj unexpected; **īnspērātō, ex īnspērātō** unexpectedly
īnspergō, -gere, -sī, -sum vt to sprinkle on
īnspiciō, -icere, -exī, -ectum vt to look into; to examine, inspect; (MIL) to review; (mind) to consider, get to know
īnspīcō, -āre vt to sharpen
īnspīrō, -āre, -āvī, -ātum vt, vi to blow on, breathe into
īnspoliātus adj unpillaged
īnspūtō, -āre vt to spit on
īnstābilis adj unsteady, not firm; (fig) inconstant
īnstāns, -antis pres p of **īnstō** ▶ adj present; urgent; threatening
īnstanter adv vehemently
instantia, -ae f presence; vehemence
īnstar nt (indecl) likeness, appearance; as good as, worth
īnstaurātiō, -ōnis f renewal
īnstaurātīvus adj renewed

īnstaurō, -āre, -āvī, -ātum vt to renew, restore; to celebrate; to requite
īnsternō, -ernere, -rāvī, -rātum vt to spread over, cover
īnstīgātor, -ōris m instigator
īnstīgātrīx, -rīcis f female instigator
īnstīgō, -āre vt to goad, incite, instigate
īnstillō, -āre vt to drop on, instil
īnstimulātor, -ōris m instigator
īnstimulō, -āre vt to urge on
īnstinctor, -ōris m instigator
īnstinctus¹ adj incited, inspired
īnstinctus², -ūs m impulse, inspiration
īnstipulor, -ārī, -ātus vi to bargain for
īnstita, -ae f flounce (of a lady's tunic)
īnstitī perf of **īnstō**
īnstitiō, -ōnis f stopping
īnstitor, -ōris m pedlar
īnstituō, -uere, -uī, -ūtum vt to set, implant; to set up, establish, build, appoint; to marshal, arrange, organize; to teach, educate; to undertake, resolve on
īnstitūtiō, -ōnis f custom; arrangement; education; (pl) principles of education
īnstitūtum, -ī nt way of life, tradition, law; stipulation, agreement; purpose; (pl) principles
īnstō, -āre, -itī vi to stand on or in; to be close, be hard on the heels of, pursue; (events) to approach, impend; (fig) to press on, work hard at; (speech) to insist, urge
īnstrātus ppp of **īnsternō**
īnstrēnuus adj languid, slow
īnstrepō, -ere vi to creak
īnstructiō, -ōnis f building; setting out
īnstructius adv in better style
īnstructor, -ōris m preparer
īnstructus¹ ppp of **īnstruō** ▶ adj provided, equipped; prepared, versed
īnstructus², -ūs m equipment
īnstrūmentum, -ī nt tool, instrument; equipment, furniture, stock; (fig) means, provision; dress, embellishment
īnstruō, -ere, -xī, -ctum vt to erect, build up; (MIL) to marshal, array; to equip, provide, prepare; (fig) to teach, train
īnsuāsum, -ī nt a dark colour
īnsuāvis adj disagreeable
īnsūdō, -āre vi to perspire on
īnsuēfactus adj accustomed
īnsuēscō, -scere, -vī, -tum vt to train, accustom ▶ vi to become accustomed
īnsuētus¹ ppp of **īnsuēscō**
īnsuētus² adj unaccustomed, unused; unusual
īnsula, -ae f island; block (of houses)
īnsulānus, -ī m islander
īnsulsē adv see **īnsulsus**
īnsulsitās, -ātis f lack of taste, absurdity
īnsulsus adj tasteless, absurd, dull
īnsultō, -āre vt, vi to jump on, leap in; (fig) to exult, taunt, insult
īnsultūra, -ae f jumping on

īnsum, inesse, īnfuī vi to be in or on; to belong to
īnsūmō, -ere, -psī, -ptum vt to spend, devote
īnsuō, -uere, -uī, -ūtum vt to sew in, sew up in
īnsuper adv above, on top; besides, over and above ▶ prep (abl) besides
īnsuperābilis adj unconquerable, impassable
īnsurgō, -gere, -rēxī, -rēctum vi to stand up, rise to; to rise, grow, swell; to rise against
īnsusurrō, -āre vt, vi to whisper
īnsūtus ppp of **īnsuō**
intābēscō, -ēscere, -uī vi to melt away, waste away
intāctilis adj intangible
intāctus adj untouched, intact; untried; undefiled, chaste
intāminātus adj unsullied
intēctus¹ ppp of **integō**
intēctus² adj uncovered, unclad; frank
integellus adj fairly whole or pure
integer, -rī adj whole, complete, unimpaired, intact; sound, fresh, new; (mind) unbiased, free; (character) virtuous, pure, upright; (decision) undecided, open; **in integrum restituere** restore to a former state; **ab integrō, dē integrō, ex integrō** afresh; **integrum est mihi** I am at liberty (to)
integō, -egere, -ēxī, -ēctum vt to cover over; to protect
integrāscō, -ere vi to begin all over again
integrātiō, -ōnis f renewing
integrē adv entirely; honestly; correctly
integritās, -ātis f completeness, soundness; integrity, honesty; (language) correctness
integrō, -āre vt to renew, replenish, repair; (mind) to refresh
integumentum, -ī nt cover, covering, shelter
intellēctus¹ ppp of **intellegō**
intellēctus², -ūs m understanding; (word) meaning
intellegēns, -entis pres p of **intellegō** ▶ adj intelligent, a connoisseur
intellegenter adv intelligently
intellegentia, -ae f discernment, understanding; taste
intellegō, -egere, -ēxī, -ēctum vt to understand, perceive, realize; to be a connoisseur
intemerātus adj pure, undefiled
intemperāns, -antis adj immoderate, extravagant; incontinent
intemperanter adv extravagantly
intemperantia, -ae f excess, extravagance; arrogance
intemperātē adv dissolutely
intemperātus adj excessive
intemperiae, -ārum fpl inclemency; madness
intemperiēs, -ēī f inclemency, storm; (fig) fury
intempestīvē adv inopportunely
intempestīvus adj unseasonable, untimely
intempestus adj (night) the dead of; unhealthy

intemptātus *adj* untried

intendō, -dere, -dī, -tum *vt* to stretch out, strain, spread; (*weapon*) to aim; (*tent*) to pitch; (*attention, course*) to direct, turn; (*fact*) to increase, exaggerate; (*speech*) to maintain; (*trouble*) to threaten ▸ *vi* to make for, intend; **animō intendere** purpose; **sē intendere** exert oneself

intentē *adv* strictly

intentiō, -ōnis *f* straining, tension; (*mind*) exertion, attention; (*LAW*) accusation

intentō, -āre *vt* to stretch out, aim; (*fig*) to threaten with, attack

intentus¹ *ppp of* **intendō** ▸ *adj* taut; attentive, intent; strict; (*speech*) vigorous

intentus², -ūs *m* stretching out

intepeō, -ēre *vi* to be warm

intepēscō, -ēscere, -uī *vi* to be warmed

inter *prep* (*with acc*) between, among, during, in the course of; in spite of; **~ haec** meanwhile; **~ manūs** within reach; **~ nōs** confidentially; **~ sē** mutually, one another; **~ sīcāriōs** in the murder court; **~ viam** on the way

interāmenta, -ōrum *ntpl* ship's timbers

interaptus *adj* joined together

interārēscō, -ere *vi* to wither away

interbibō, -ere *vt* to drink up

interbītō, -ere *vi* to fall through

intercalāris *adj* intercalary

intercalārius *adj* intercalary

intercalō, -āre *vt* to intercalate

intercapēdō, -inis *f* interruption, respite

intercēdō, -ēdere, -essī, -essum *vi* to come between, intervene; to occur; to become surety; to interfere, obstruct; (*tribune*) to protest, veto

interceptiō, -ōnis *f* taking away

interceptor, -ōris *m* embezzler

interceptus *ppp of* **intercipiō**

intercessiō, -ōnis *f* (*LAW*) becoming surety; (*tribune*) veto

intercessor, -ōris *m* mediator, surety; interposer of the veto; obstructor

intercidō, -ere, -ī *vi* to fall short; to happen in the meantime; to get lost, become obsolete, be forgotten

intercīdō, -dere, -dī, -sum *vt* to cut through, sever

intercinō, -ere *vt* to sing between

intercipiō, -ipere, -ēpī, -eptum *vt* to intercept; to embezzle, steal; to cut off, obstruct

intercīsē *adv* piecemeal

intercīsus *ppp of* **intercīdō**

interclūdō, -dere, -sī, -sum *vt* to cut off, block, shut off, prevent; **animam interclūdere** suffocate

interclūsiō, -ōnis *f* stoppage

interclūsus *ppp of* **interclūdō**

intercolumnium, -ī *and* **-iī** *nt* space between two pillars

intercurrō, -ere *vi* to mingle with; to intercede; to hurry in the meantime

intercursō, -āre *vi* to crisscross; to attack between the lines

intercursus, -ūs *m* intervention

intercus, -tis *adj*: **aqua ~** dropsy

interdīcō, -īcere, -īxī, -ictum *vt, vi* to forbid, interdict; (*praetor*) to make a provisional order; **aquā et ignī interdīcere** banish

interdictiō, -ōnis *f* prohibiting, banishment

interdictum, -ī *nt* prohibition; provisional order (*by a praetor*)

interdiū *adv* by day

interdō, -are *vt* to make at intervals; to distribute; **nōn interdōuim** I wouldn't care

interductus, -ūs *m* punctuation

interdum *adv* now and then, occasionally

intereā *adv* meanwhile, in the meantime; nevertheless

interēmī *perf of* **interimō**

interemptus *ppp of* **interimō**

intereō, -īre, -iī, -itum *vi* to be lost, perish, die

interequitō, -āre *vt, vi* to ride between

interesse *infin of* **intersum**

interfātiō, -ōnis *f* interruption

interfātur, -ārī, -ātus *vi* to interrupt

interfectiō, -ōnis *f* killing

interfector, -ōris *m* murderer

interfectrīx, -rīcis *f* murderess

interfectus *ppp of* **interficiō**

interficiō, -icere, -ēcī, -ectum *vt* to kill, destroy

interfīō, -ierī *vi* to pass away

interfluō, -ere, -xī, -xum *vt, vi* to flow between

interfodiō, -ere *vt* to pierce

interfugiō, -ere *vi* to flee among

interfuī *perf of* **intersum**

interfulgeō, -ēre *vi* to shine amongst

interfūsus *ppp* lying between; marked here and there

interiaceō, -ēre *vi* to lie between

interibī *adv* in the meantime

intericiō, -icere, -iēcī, -iectum *vt* to put amongst *or* between, interpose, mingle; **annō interiectō** after a year

interiectus, -ūs *m* coming in between; interval

interiī *perf of* **intereō**

interim *adv* meanwhile, in the meantime; sometimes; all the same

interimō, -imere, -ēmī, -emptum *vt* to abolish, destroy, kill

interior, -ōris *adj* inner, interior; nearer, on the near side; secret, private; more intimate, more profound

interitiō, -ōnis *f* ruin

interitus, -ūs *m* destruction, ruin, death

interiūnctus *adj* joined together

interius *adv* inwardly; too short

interlābor, -ī *vi* to glide between

interlegō, -ere *vt* to pick here and there

interlinō, -inere, -ēvī, -itum *vt* to smear in parts; to erase here and there

interloquor, -quī, -cūtus vi to interrupt
interlūceō, -cēre, -xī vi to shine through, be clearly seen
interlūnia, -ōrum ntpl new moon
interluō, -ere vt to wash, flow between
intermēnstruus adj of the new moon ▶ nt new moon
interminātus¹ ppa (occ pass) of **interminor** ▶ adj forbidden
interminātus² adj endless
interminor, -ārī, -ātus vi to threaten; to forbid threateningly
intermisceō, -scēre, -scuī, -xtum vt to mix, intermingle
intermissiō, -ōnis f interruption
intermittō, -ittere, -īsī, -issum vt to break off; to interrupt; to omit, neglect; to allow to elapse ▶ vi to cease, pause
intermixtus ppp of **intermisceō**
intermorior, -ī, -tuus vi to die suddenly
intermortuus adj falling unconscious
intermundia, -ōrum ntpl space between worlds
intermūrālis adj between two walls
internātus adj growing among
internecīnus adj murderous, of extermination
intern@eciō, -ōnis f massacre, extermination
internecīus adj = **internecīnus**
internectō, -ere vt to enclasp
internōdia, -ōrum ntpl space between joints
internōscō, -scere, -vī, -tum vt to distinguish between
internūntia, -iae f messenger, mediator, go-between
internūntiō, -āre vi to exchange messages
internūntius, -ī and -iī m messenger, mediator, go-between
internus adj internal, civil ▶ ntpl domestic affairs
interō, -erere, -rīvī, -rītum vt to rub in; (fig) to concoct
interpellātiō, -ōnis f interruption
interpellātor, -ōris m interrupter
interpellō, -āre, -āvī, -ātum vt to interrupt; to disturb, obstruct
interpolis adj made up
interpolō, -āre vt to renovate, do up; (writing) to falsify
interpōnō, -ōnere, -osuī, -ositum vt to put between or amongst, insert; (time) to allow to elapse; (person) to introduce, admit; (pretext etc) to put forward, interpose; **fidem interpōnere** pledge one's word; **sē interpōnere** interfere, become involved
interpositiō, -ōnis f introduction
interpositus¹ ppp of **interpōnō**
interpositus², -ūs m obstruction
interpres, -tis m/f agent, negotiator; interpreter, explainer, translator
interpretātiō, -ōnis f interpretation, exposition, meaning
interpretātus adj translated

interpretor, -ārī, -ātus vt to interpret, explain, translate, understand
interprimō, -imere, -essī, -essum vt to squeeze
interpūnctiō, -ōnis f punctuation
interpūnctus adj well-divided ▶ ntpl punctuation
interquiēscō, -scere, -vī vi to rest awhile
interrēgnum, -ī nt regency, interregnum; interval between consuls
interrēx, -ēgis m regent; deputy consul
interritus adj undaunted, unafraid
interrogātiō, -ōnis f question; (LAW) cross-examination; (LOGIC) syllogism
interrogātiuncula, -ae f short argument
interrogō, -āre, -āvī, -ātum vt to ask, put a question; (LAW) to cross-examine, bring to trial
interrumpō, -umpere, -ūpī, -uptum vt to break up, sever; (fig) to break off, interrupt
interruptē adv interruptedly
intersaepiō, -īre, -sī, -tum vt to shut off, close
interscindō, -ndere, -dī, -ssum vt to cut off, break down
interserō¹, -erere, -ēvī, -itum vt to plant at intervals
interserō², -ere, -uī, -tum vt to interpose
intersitus ppp of **interserō¹**
interspīrātiō, -ōnis f pause for breath
interstinguō, -guere, -ctum vt to mark, spot; to extinguish
interstringō, -ere vt to strangle
intersum, -esse, -fuī vi to be between; to be amongst, be present at; (time) to elapse; **interest** there is a difference; it is of importance, it concerns, it matters; **meā interest** it is important for me
intertextus adj interwoven
intertrahō, -here, -xī vt to take away
intertrīmentum, -ī nt wastage; loss, damage
interturbātiō, -ōnis f confusion
intervallum, -ī nt space, distance, interval; (time) pause, interval, respite; difference
intervellō, -ere vt to pluck out; to tear apart
interveniō, -enīre, -ēnī, -entum vi to come on the scene, intervene; to interfere (with), interrupt; to happen, occur
interventor, -ōris m intruder
interventus, -ūs m appearance, intervention; occurrence
intervertō, -tere, -tī, -sum vt to embezzle; to rob, cheat
intervīsō, -ere, -ī, -um vt to have a look at, look and see; to visit occasionally
intervolitō, -āre vi to fly about, amongst
intervomō, -ere vt to throw up (amongst)
intervortō vt see **intervertō**
intestābilis adj infamous, wicked
intestātō adv without making a will
intestātus adj intestate; not convicted by witnesses
intestīnus adj internal ▶ nt, ntpl intestines, entrails

intexō, -ere, -uī, -tum vt to inweave, embroider, interlace

intibum, -ī nt endive

intimē adv most intimately, cordially

intimus adj innermost; deepest; secret; intimate ▸ m most intimate friend

intingō, intinguō, -gere, -xī, -ctum vt to dip in

intolerābilis adj unbearable; irresistible

intolerandus adj intolerable

intolerāns, -antis adj impatient; unbearable

intoleranter adv excessively

intolerantia, -ae f insolence

intonō, -āre, -uī, -ātum vi to thunder, thunder out

intōnsus adj unshorn, unshaven; long-haired, bearded; uncouth

intorqueō, -quēre, -sī, -tum vt to twist, wrap round; to hurl at

intortus ppp of **intorqueō** ▸ adj twisted, curled; confused

intrā adv inside, within; within ▸ prep (with acc) inside, within; (time) within, during; (amount) less than, within the limits of

intrābilis adj navigable

intractābilis adj formidable

intractātus adj not broken in; unattempted

intremīscō, -īscere, -uī vi to begin to shake

intremō, -ere vi to tremble

intrepidē adv see **intrepidus**

intrepidus adj calm, brave; undisturbed

intrīcō, -āre vt to entangle

intrīnsecus adv on the inside

intrītus adj not worn out

intrīvī perf of **interō**

intrō¹ adv inside, in

intrō², -āre, -āvī, -ātum vt, vi to go in, enter; to penetrate

intrōdūcō, -ūcere, -ūxī, -uctum vt to bring in, introduce, escort in; to institute

intrōductiō, -ōnis f bringing in

intrōeō, -īre, -iī, -itum vi to go into, enter

intrōferō, -ferre, -tulī, -lātum vt to carry inside

intrōgredior, -dī, -ssus vi to step inside

intrōitus, -ūs m entrance; beginning

intrōlātus ppp of **intrōferō**

intrōmittō, -ittere, -īsī, -issum vt to let in, admit

intrōrsum, intrōrsus adv inwards, inside

intrōrumpō, -ere vi to break into

intrōspectō, -āre vt to look in at

intrōspiciō, -icere, -exī, -ectum vt to look inside; to look at, examine

intubum etc see **intibum**

intueor, -ērī, -itus vt to look at, watch; to contemplate, consider; to admire

intumēscō, -ēscere, -uī vi to begin to swell, rise; to increase; to become angry

intumulātus adj unburied

intuor etc see **intueor**

inturbidus adj undisturbed; quiet

intus adv inside, within, in; from within

intūtus adj unsafe; unguarded

inula, -ae f elecampane

inultus adj unavenged; unpunished

inumbrō, -āre vt to shade; to cover

inundō, -āre, -āvī, -ātum vt, vi to overflow, flood

inunguō, -unguere, -ūnxī, -ūnctum vt to anoint

inurbānē adv see **inurbānus**

inurbānus adj rustic, unmannerly, unpolished

inurgeō, -ēre vi to push, butt

inūrō, -rere, -ssī, -stum vt to brand; (fig) to brand, inflict

inūsitātē adv strangely

inūsitātus adj unusual, extraordinary

inūstus ppp of **inūrō**

inūtilis adj useless; harmful

inūtilitās, -ātis f uselessness, harmfulness

inūtiliter adv unprofitably

invādō, -dere, -sī, -sum vt, vi to get in, make one's way in; to enter upon; to fall upon, attack, invade; to seize, take possession of

invalēscō, -ēscere, -uī vi to grow stronger

invalidus adj weak; inadequate

invāsī perf of **invādō**

invectiō, -ōnis f importing; invective

invectus ppp of **invehō**

invehō, -here, -xī, -ctum vt to carry in, bring in; **sē invehere** attack

invehor, -hī, -ctus vi to ride, drive, sail in or into, enter; to attack; to inveigh against

invēndibilis adj unsaleable

inveniō, -enīre, -ēnī, -entum vt to find, come upon; to find out, discover; to invent, contrive; to win, get

inventiō, -ōnis f invention; (RHET) compiling the subject-matter

inventor, -ōris m inventor, discoverer

inventrīx, -rīcis f inventor, discoverer

inventus ppp of **inveniō** ▸ nt invention, discovery

invenustus adj unattractive; unlucky in love

inverēcundus adj immodest, shameless

invergō, -ere vt to pour upon

inversiō, -ōnis f transposition; irony

inversus ppp of **invertō** ▸ adj upside down, inside out; perverted

invertō, -tere, -tī, -sum vt to turn over, invert; to change, pervert

invesperāscit, -ere vi it is dusk

investīgātiō, -ōnis f search

investīgātor, -ōris m investigator

investīgō, -āre, -āvī, -ātum vt to follow the trail of; (fig) to track down, find out

inveterāscō, -scere, -vī vi to grow old (in); to become established, fixed, inveterate; to grow obsolete

inveterātiō, -ōnis f chronic illness

inveterātus adj of long standing, inveterate

invexī perf of **invehō**

invicem adv in turns, alternately; mutually, each other

invictus adj unbeaten; unconquerable

invidentia, -ae f envy

invideō, -idēre, -īdī, -īsum vt, vi to cast an evil eye on; (with dat) to envy, grudge; to begrudge

invidia, -ae f envy, jealousy, ill-will; unpopularity

invidiōsē adv spitefully

invidiōsus adj envious, spiteful; enviable; invidious, hateful

invidus adj envious, jealous, hostile

invigilō, -āre vi to be awake over; to watch over, be intent on

inviolābilis adj invulnerable; inviolable

inviolātē adv inviolately

inviolātus adj unhurt; inviolable

invīsitātus adj unseen, unknown, strange

invīsō, -ere, -ī, -um vt to go and see, visit, have a look at; to inspect

invīsus¹ adj hateful, detested; hostile

invīsus² adj unseen

invītāmentum, -ī nt attraction, inducement

invītātiō, -ōnis f invitation; entertainment

invītātus, -ūs m invitation

invītē adv unwillingly

invītō, -āre, -āvī, -ātum vt to invite; to treat, entertain; to summon; to attract, induce

invītus adj against one's will, reluctant

invius adj trackless, impassable; inaccessible

invocātus¹ ppp of **invocō**

invocātus² adj unbidden, uninvited

invocō, -āre vt to call upon, invoke; to appeal to; to call

involātus, -ūs m flight

involitō, -āre vi to play upon

involō, -āre vi to fly at, pounce on, attack

involūcre, -is nt napkin

involūcrum, -ī nt covering, case

involūtus ppp of **involvō** ▸ adj complicated

involvō, -vere, -vī, -ūtum vt to roll on; to wrap up, envelop, entangle

involvolus, -ī m caterpillar

invulnerātus adj unwounded

iō interj (joy) hurrah!; (pain) oh!; (calling) ho there!

Iōannēs, -is m John

iocātiō, -ōnis f joke

iocor, -ārī, -ātus vt, vi to joke, jest

iocōsē adv jestingly

iocōsus adj humorous, playful

iocularis adj laughable, funny ▸ ntpl jokes

iocularius adj ludicrous

ioculātor, -ōris m jester

ioculor, -ārī vi to joke

ioculus, -ī m a bit of fun

iocus, -ī m, **ioca, -ōrum** ntpl joke, jest; **extrā iocum** joking apart; **per iocum** for fun

Iōnes, -um mpl Ionians

Iōnia, -iae f Ionia, coastal district of Asia Minor

Iōnium, -ī nt Ionian Sea (W. of Greece)

Iōnius, Iōnicus adj Ionian

iōta nt indecl Greek letter I

Iovis gen of **Iuppiter**

Iphianassa, -ae f Iphigenia

Iphigenīa, -ae f daughter of Agamemnon (who sacrificed her at Aulis to Diana)

ipse, -a, -um, -īus pron self, himself etc; in person, for one's own part, of one's own accord, by oneself; just, precisely, very; the master, the host

ipsissimus his very own self; **nunc ipsissimum** right now

īra, -ae f anger, rage; object of indignation

īrācundē adv angrily

īrācundia, -ae f irascibility, quick temper; rage, resentment

īrācundus adj irascible, choleric; resentful

īrāscor, -ī vi to be angry, get furious

īrātē adv see **īrātus**

īrātus adj angry, furious

īre infin of **eō¹**

Īris, -dis (acc **-m**) f messenger of the gods; the rainbow

īrōnīa, -ae f irony

irrāsus adj unshaven

irraucēscō, -cēscere, -sī vi to become hoarse

irredivīvus adj irreparable

irreligātus adj not tied

irreligiōsē adv see **irreligiōsus**

irreligiōsus adj impious

irremeābilis adj from which there is no returning

irreparābilis adj irretrievable

irrepertus adj undiscovered

irrēpō, -ere, -sī vi to steal into, insinuate oneself into

irreprehēnsus adj blameless

irrequiētus adj restless

irresectus adj unpared

irresolūtus adj not slackened

irrētiō, -īre, -iī, -ītum vt to ensnare, entangle

irretortus adj not turned back

irreverentia, -ae f disrespect

irrevocābilis adj irrevocable; implacable

irrevocātus adj without an encore

irrīdeō, -dēre, -sī, -sum vi to laugh, joke ▸ vt to laugh at, ridicule

irrīdiculē adv unwittily

irrīdiculum, -ī nt laughing stock

irrigātiō, -ōnis f irrigation

irrigō, -āre, -āvī, -ātum vt to water, irrigate; to inundate; (fig) to shed over, flood, refresh

irriguus adj well-watered, swampy; refreshing

irrīsiō, -ōnis f ridicule, mockery

irrīsor, -ōris m scoffer

irrīsus¹ ppp of **irrīdeō**

irrīsus², -ūs m derision

irrītābilis adj excitable

irrītāmen, -inis nt excitement, provocation

irrītātiō, -ōnis f incitement, irritation

irrītō, -āre, -āvī, -ātum vt to provoke, incite, enrage

irritus *adj* invalid, null and void; useless, vain, ineffective; (*person*) unsuccessful; **ad irritum cadere** come to nothing

irrogātiō, -ōnis *f* imposing

irrogō, -āre *vt* to propose (*a measure*) against; to impose

irrōrō, -āre *vt* to bedew

irrumpō, -umpere, -ūpī, -uptum *vt, vi* to rush in, break in; to intrude, invade

irruō, -ere, -ī *vi* to force a way in, rush in, attack; (*speech*) to make a blunder

irruptiō, -ōnis *f* invasion, raid

irruptus¹ *ppp of* **irrumpō**

irruptus² *adj* unbroken

is, ea, id *pron* he, she, it; this, that, the; such; **nōn is sum quī** I am not the man to; **id** (*with vi*) for this reason; **id quod** what; **ad id** hitherto; for the purpose; besides; **in eō est** it has come to this; one is on the point of; it depends on this

Ismara, -ōrum *ntpl*, **Ismarus, -ī** *m* Mt Ismarus (*in Thrace*)

Ismarius *adj* Thracian

Īsocratēs, -is *m* Athenian orator and teacher of rhetoric

istāc *adv* that way

iste, -a, -ud, -īus *pron* of yours; (*LAW*) your client, the plaintiff, the defendant; (*contemptuous*) the fellow; that, such

Isthmius *adj* Isthmian ▸ *ntpl* the Isthmian Games

Isthmus, Isthmos, -ī *m* Isthmus of Corinth

istic, -aec, -uc *and* **-oc** *pron* that of yours, that

istīc *adv* there; in this, on this occasion

istinc *adv* from there; of that

istīusmodī such, of that kind

istō, istōc *adv* to you, there, yonder

istōrsum *adv* in that direction

istūc *adv* (to) there, to that

ita *adv* thus, so; as follows; yes; accordingly; **itane** really?; **nōn ita** not so very; **ita ut** just as; **ita ... ut** so, to such an extent that; on condition that; only in so far as; **ita ... ut nōn** without; **ut ... ita** just as ... so; although ... nevertheless

Ītalī, -ōrum *mpl* Italians

Ītalia, -iae *f* Italy

Ītalicus, Ītalus *adj* Italian

itaque *conj* and so, therefore, accordingly

item *adv* likewise, also

iter, -ineris *nt* way, journey, march; a day's journey *or* march; route, road, passage; (*fig*) way, course; **~ mihi est** I have to go to; **~ dare** grant a right of way; **~ facere** to journey, march, travel; **ex itinere, in itinere** on the way, on the march; **māgnīs itineribus** by forced marches

iterātiō, -ōnis *f* repetition

iterō, -āre, -āvī, -ātum *vt* to repeat, renew; to plough again

iterum *adv* again, a second time; **~ atque ~** repeatedly

Ithaca, -ae, Ithacē, -ēs *f* island W. of Greece (*home of Ulysses*)

Ithacēnsis, Ithacus *adj* Ithacan

Ithacus, -ī *m* Ulysses

itidem *adv* in the same way, similarly

itiō, -ōnis *f* going

itō, -āre *vi* to go

itus, -ūs *m* going, movement, departure

iuba, -ae *f* mane; crest

Iuba, -ae *m* king of Numidia (*supporter of Pompey*)

iubar, -is *nt* brightness, light

iubātus *adj* crested

iubeō, -bēre, -ssī, -ssum *vt* to order, command, tell; (*greeting*) to bid; (*MED*) to prescribe; (*POL*) to decree, ratify, appoint

iūcundē *adv* agreeably

iūcunditās, -ātis *f* delight, enjoyment

iūcundus *adj* delightful, pleasing

Iūdaea, -ae *f* Judaea, Palestine

Iūdaeus¹, **-ī** *m* Jew

Iūdaeus², **Iūdaicus** *adj* Jewish

iūdex, -icis *m* judge; (*pl*) panel of jurors; (*fig*) critic

iūdicātiō, -ōnis *f* judicial inquiry; opinion

iūdicātum, -ī *nt* judgment, precedent

iūdicātus, -ūs *m* office of judge

iūdiciālis *adj* judicial, forensic

iūdiciārius *adj* judiciary

iūdicium, -ī *and* **-iī** *nt* trial; court of justice; sentence; judgment, opinion; discernment, taste, tact; **in ~ vocāre, iūdiciō arcessere** sue, summon

iūdicō, -āre, -āvī, -ātum *vt* to judge, examine, sentence, condemn; to form an opinion of, decide; to declare

iugālis *adj* yoked together; nuptial

iugātiō, -ōnis *f* training (*of a vine*)

iūgerum, -ī *nt* a land measure (*240 x 120 feet*)

iūgis *adj* perpetual, never-failing

iūglāns, -andis *f* walnut tree

iugō, -āre, -āvī, -ātum *vt* to couple, marry

iugōsus *adj* hilly

Iugulae, -ārum *fpl* Orion's Belt

iugulō, -āre, -āvī, -ātum *vt* to cut the throat of, kill, murder

iugulus, -ī *m*, **iugulum, -ī** *nt* throat

iugum, -ī *nt* (*animals*) yoke, collar; pair, team; (*MIL*) yoke of subjugation; (*mountain*) ridge, height, summit; (*ASTR*) Libra; (*loom*) crossbeam; (*ship*) thwart; (*fig*) yoke, bond

Iugurtha, -ae *m* king of Numidia (*rebel against Rome*)

Iugurthīnus *adj see* **Iugurtha**

Iūlēus *adj* of Iulus; of Caesar; of July

Iūlius¹, **-ī** *m* Roman family name (*esp Caesar*); (*month*) July

Iūlius², **Iūliānus** *adj see* **Iūlius**¹

Iūlus, -ī *m* son of Aeneas, Ascanius

iūmentum, -ī *nt* beast of burden, packhorse

iūnceus *adj* of rushes; slender

iūncōsus *adj* rushy

iūnctiō, -ōnis *f* union

iūnctūra, -ae *f* joint; combination; relationship

iūnctus *ppp of* **iungō** ▸ *adj* connected, attached

iuncus, -ī m rush

iungō, -gere, iūnxī, iūnctum vt to join together, unite; to yoke, harness; to mate; (river) to span, bridge; (fig) to bring together, connect, associate; (agreement) to make; (words) to compound

iūnior, -ōris adj younger

iūniperus, -ī f juniper

Iūnius¹, -ī m Roman family name; (month) June

Iūnius² adj of June

Iūnō, -ōnis f Roman goddess, wife of Jupiter, patroness of women and marriage

Iūnōnālis adj see **Iūnō**

Iūnōnicola, -ae m/f worshipper of Juno

Iūnōnigena, -ae m Vulcan

Iūnōnius adj = **Iūnōnālis**

Iuppiter, Iovis m Jupiter (king of the gods, god of sky and weather); ~ **Stygius** Pluto; **sub Iove** in the open air

iūrātor, -ōris m sworn judge

iūrecōnsultus etc see **iūriscōnsultus**

iūreiūrō, -āre vi to swear

iūreperītus etc see **iūrisperītus**

iūrgium, -ī and **-iī** nt quarrel, brawl

iūrgō, -āre vi to quarrel, squabble ▸ vt to scold

iūridiciālis adj of law, juridical

iūriscōnsultus, -ī m lawyer

iūrisdictiō, -ōnis f administration of justice; authority

iūrisperītus adj versed in the law

iūrō, -āre, -āvī, -ātum vi, vt to swear, take an oath; to conspire; **in nōmen ~** swear allegiance to; **in verba ~** take a prescribed form of oath; **iūrātus** having sworn, under oath

iūs¹, iūris nt broth, soup

iūs², iūris nt law, right, justice; law court; jurisdiction, authority; **iūs gentium** international law; **iūs pūblicum** constitutional law; **summum iūs** the strict letter of the law; **iūs dīcere** administer justice; **suī iūris** independent; **iūre** rightly, justly

iūsiūrandum, iūrisiūrandī nt oath

iussī perf of **iubeō**

iussū abl m by order

iussus ppp of **iubeō** ▸ nt order, command, prescription

iūstē adv duly, rightly

iūstificus adj just dealing

iūstitia, -ae f justice, uprightness, fairness

iūstitium, -ī and **-iī** nt cessation of legal business

iūstus adj just, fair; lawful, right; regular, proper ▸ nt right ▸ ntpl rights; formalities, obsequies

iūtus ppp of **iuvō**

iuvenālis adj youthful ▸ ntpl youthful games

Iuvenālis, -is m Juvenal (Roman satirist)

iuvenāliter adv vigorously, impetuously

iuvenca, -ae f heifer; girl

iuvencus, -ī m bullock; young man ▸ adj young

iuvenēscō, -ēscere, -uī vi to grow up; to grow young again

iuvenīlis adj youthful

iuvenīliter adv see **iuvenīlis**

iuvenis adj young ▸ m/f young man or woman (20-45 years), man, warrior

iuvenor, -ārī vi to behave indiscreetly

iuventa, -ae f youth

iuventās, -ātis f youth

iuventūs, -ūtis f youth, manhood; men, soldiers

iuvō, -āre, iūvī, iūtum vt to help, be of use to; to please, delight; **iuvat mē** I am glad

iuxtā adv near by, close; alike, just the same ▸ prep (with acc) close to, hard by; next to; very like, next door to; ~ **ac**, ~ **cum**, ~ **quam** just the same as

iuxtim adv near; equally

īvī perf of **eō¹**

Ixīōn, -onis m Lapith king (bound to a revolving wheel in Tartarus)

Ixīoneus adj see **Ixīōn**

Ixīonidae, -ārum mpl Centaurs

Ixīonidēs, -ae m Pirithous

j k

J- *see* **I**-

Kalendae, -ārum Kalends, first day
(*of each month*)
Karthāgō *see* **Carthāgō**

l

labāscō, -ere vi to totter, waver
lābēcula, -ae f aspersion
labefaciō, -facere, -fēcī, -factum (pass **-fīō**) vt to shake; (fig) to weaken, ruin
labefactō, -āre, -āvī, -ātum vt to shake; (fig) to weaken, destroy
labellum, -ī nt lip
lābellum, -ī nt small basin
Laberius, -ī m Roman family name (esp a writer of mimes)
lābēs¹, -is f sinking, fall; ruin, destruction
lābēs², -is f spot, blemish; disgrace, stigma; (person) blot
labia, -iae f lip
Labiēnus, -ī m Roman surname (esp Caesar's officer who went over to Pompey)
labiōsus adj large-lipped
labium, -ī and -iī nt lip
labō, -āre vi to totter, be unsteady, give way; to waver, hesitate, collapse
lābor, -bī, -psus vi to slide, glide; to sink, fall; to slip away, pass away; (fig) to fade, decline, perish; to be disappointed, make a mistake
labor, labōs, -ōris m effort, exertion, labour; work, task; hardship, suffering, distress; (ASTR) eclipse
labōrifer, -ī adj sore afflicted
labōriōsē adv laboriously, with difficulty
labōriōsus adj troublesome, difficult; industrious
labōrō, -āre, -āvī, -ātum vi to work, toil, take pains; to suffer, be troubled (with), be in distress; to be anxious, worried ▶ vt to work out, make, produce
labōs etc see **labor**
labrum, -ī nt lip; edge, rim; **prīmīs labrīs gustāre** acquire a smattering of
lābrum, -ī nt tub, vat; bath
lābrusca, -ae f wild vine
lābruscum, -ī nt wild grape
labyrinthēus adj labyrinthine
labyrinthus, -ī m labyrinth, maze (esp that of Cnossos in Crete)
lac, lactis nt milk

Lacaena, -ae f Spartan woman ▶ adj Spartan
Lacedaemōn, Lacedaemō, -onis (acc **-ona**) f Sparta
Lacedaemonius adj Spartan
lacer, -ī adj torn, mangled, lacerated; tearing
lacerātiō, -ōnis f tearing
lacerna, -ae f cloak (worn in cold weather)
lacernātus adj cloaked
lacerō, -āre, -āvī, -ātum vt to tear, lacerate, mangle; (ship) to wreck; (speech) to slander, abuse; (feeling) to torture, distress; (goods, time) to waste, destroy
lacerta, -ae f lizard; a sea fish
lacertōsus adj brawny
lacertus¹, -ī m upper arm, arm; (pl) brawn, muscle
lacertus², -ī m lizard; a sea fish
lacessō, -ere, -īvī and -iī, -ītum vt to strike, provoke, challenge; (fig) to incite, exasperate
Lachesis, -is f one of the Fates
lacinia, -ae f flap, corner (of dress)
Lacīnium, -ī nt promontory in S. Italy, with a temple of Juno
Lacīnius adj see **Lacīnium**
Lacō, Lacōn, -ōnis m Spartan; Spartan dog
Lacōnicus adj Spartan ▶ nt sweating bath
lacrima, -ae f tear; (plant) gumdrop
lacrimābilis adj mournful
lacrimābundus adj bursting into tears
lacrimō, -āre, -āvī, -ātum vt, vi to weep, weep for
lacrimōsus adj tearful; lamentable
lacrimula, -ae f tear, crocodile tear
lacrum- etc see **lacrim-**
lactāns, -antis adj giving milk; sucking
lactātiō, -ōnis f allurement
lactēns, -entis adj sucking; milky, juicy
lacteolus adj milk-white
lactēs, -ium fpl guts, small intestines
lactēscō, -ere vi to turn to milk
lacteus adj milky, milk-white
lactō, -āre vt to dupe, wheedle
lactūca, -ae f lettuce
lacūna, -ae f hole, pit; pool, pond; (fig) deficiency
lacūnar, -āris nt panelled ceiling
lacūnō, -āre vt to panel
lacūnōsus adj sunken
lacus, -ūs m vat, tank; lake; reservoir, cistern
laedō, -dere, -sī, -sum vt to hurt, strike, wound; (fig) to offend, annoy, break
Laelius, -ī m Roman family name (esp the friend of Scipio)
laena, -ae f a lined cloak
Lāērtēs, -ae m father of Ulysses
Lāērtiadēs m Ulysses
Lāērtius adj see **Lāērtēs**
laesī perf of **laedō**
laesiō, -ōnis f attack
Laestrygonēs, -um mpl fabulous cannibals of Campania, founders of Formiae
Laestrygonius adj see **Laestrygonēs**

laesus *ppp of* **laedō**
laetābilis *adj* joyful
laetē *adv* gladly
laetificō, -āre *vt* to gladden
laetificus *adj* glad, joyful
laetitia, -ae *f* joy, delight, exuberance
laetor, -ārī, -ātus *vi* to rejoice, be glad
laetus *adj* glad, cheerful; delighting (in); pleasing, welcome; (*growth*) fertile, rich; (*style*) exuberant
laevē *adv* awkwardly
laevus *adj* left; stupid; ill-omened, unfortunate; (*AUG*) lucky, favourable ▶ *f* left hand
laganum, -ī *nt* a kind of oilcake
lagēos, -ī *f* a Greek vine
lagoena, -ae *f* flagon
lagōis, -idis *f* a kind of grouse
lagōna, -ae *f* flagon
Lāiadēs, -ae *m* Oedipus
Lāius, -ī *m* father of Oedipus
lallō, -āre *vi* to sing a lullaby
lāma, -ae *f* bog
lamberō, -āre *vt* to tear to pieces
lambō, -ere, -ī *vt* to lick, touch; (*river*) to wash
lāmenta, -ōrum *ntpl* lamentation
lāmentābilis *adj* mournful, sorrowful
lāmentārius *adj* sorrowful
lāmentātiō, -ōnis *f* weeping, lamentation
lāmentor, -ārī, -ātus *vi* to weep, lament ▶ *vt* to weep for, bewail
lamia, -ae *f* witch
lāmina, lammina, lāmna, -ae *f* plate, leaf (of metal, wood); blade; coin
lampas, -dis *f* torch; brightness, day
Lamus, -ī *m* Laestrygonian king
lāna, -ae *f* wool
lānārius, -ī *and* **-iī** *m* wool-worker
lānātus *adj* woolly
lancea, -ae *f* spear, lance
lancinō, -āre *vt* to tear up; to squander
lāneus *adj* woollen
languefaciō, -ere *vt* to make weary
langueō, -ēre *vi* to be weary, be weak, droop; to be idle, dull
languēscō, -ēscere, -uī *vi* to grow faint, droop
languidē *adv see* **languidus**
languidulus *adj* languid
languidus *adj* faint, languid, sluggish; listless, feeble
languor, -ōris *m* faintness, fatigue, weakness; dullness, apathy
laniātus, -ūs *m* mangling; (*mind*) anguish
laniēna, -ae *f* butcher's shop
lānificium, -ī *and* **-iī** *nt* wool-working
lānificus *adj* wool-working
lāniger, -ī *adj* fleecy ▶ *m/f* ram, sheep
laniō, -āre, -āvī, -ātum *vt* to tear to pieces, mangle
lanista, -ae *m* trainer of gladiators, fencing master; (*fig*) agitator
lānitium, -ī *and* **-iī** *nt* woolgrowing

lanius, -ī *and* **-iī** *m* butcher
lanterna, -ae *f* lamp
lanternārius, -ī *and* **-iī** *m* guide
lānūgō, -inis *f* down, woolliness
Lānuvīnus *adj see* **Lānuvium**
Lānuvium, -ī *nt* Latin town on the Appian Way
lānx, lancis *f* dish, platter; (*balance*) scale
Lāomedōn, -ontis *m* king of Troy (father of Priam)
Lāomedontēus *adj*, **Lāomedontiadēs, -ae** *m* son of Lāomedōn; (*pl*) Trojans
Lāomedontius *adj* Trojan
lapathum, -ī *nt*, **lapathus, -ī** *f* sorrel
lapicīda, -ae *m* stonecutter
lapicīdīnae, -ārum *fpl* quarries
lapidārius *adj* stone- (in *cpds*)
lapidātiō, -ōnis *f* throwing of stones
lapidātor, -ōris *m* stone thrower
lapideus *adj* of stones, stone- (in *cpds*)
lapidō, -āre *vt* to stone ▶ *vi* to rain stones
lapidōsus *adj* stony; hard as stone
lapillus, -ī *m* stone, pebble; precious stone, mosaic piece
lapis, -dis *m* stone; milestone, boundary stone, tombstone; precious stone; marble; auctioneer's stand; (*abuse*) blockhead; **bis ad eundem lapidem (offendere)** make the same mistake twice; **Juppiter ~** the Jupiter stone
Lapithae, -ārum *and* **-um** *mpl* Lapiths, mythical people of Thessaly
Lapithaeus, -ēius *adj see* **Lapithae**
lappa, -ae *f* goosegrass
lāpsiō, -ōnis *f* tendency
lāpsō, -āre *vi* to slip, stumble
lāpsus¹ *ppa of* **lābor**
lāpsus², -ūs *m* fall, slide, course, flight; error, failure
laqueāria, -ium *ntpl* panelled ceiling
laqueātus *adj* panelled, with a panelled ceiling
laqueus, -ī *m* noose, snare, halter; (*fig*) trap
Lār, Laris *m* tutelary deity, household god; hearth, home
lārdum *etc see* **lāridum**
largē *adv* plentifully, generously, very much
largificus *adj* bountiful
largifluus *adj* copious
largiloquus *adj* talkative
largior, -īrī, -ītus *vt* to give freely, lavish; to bestow, confer ▶ *vi* to give largesse
largitās, -ātis *f* liberality, abundance
largiter *adv* = **largē**
largītiō, -ōnis *f* giving freely, distributing; bribery
largītor, -ōris *m* liberal giver, dispenser; spendthrift; briber
largus *adj* copious, ample; liberal, bountiful
lāridum, -ī *nt* bacon fat
Lārissa, Lārīsa, -ae *f* town in Thessaly
Lārissaeus, -ēnsis *adj see* **Lārissa**
Lārius, -ī *m* lake Como
larix, -cis *f* larch
larva, -ae *f* ghost; mask

larvātus adj bewitched
lasanum, -ī nt pot
lasārpīcifer, -ī adj producing asafoetida
lascīvia, -ae f playfulness; impudence, lewdness
lascīviō, -īre vi to frolic, frisk; to run wild, be irresponsible
lascīvus adj playful, frisky; impudent, lustful
laserpīcium, -ī and **-iī** nt silphium
lassitūdō, -inis f fatigue, heaviness
lassō, -āre vt to tire, fatigue
lassulus adj rather weary
lassus adj tired, exhausted
lātē adv widely, extensively; **longē lātēque** far and wide, everywhere
latebra, -ae f hiding place, retreat; (fig) loophole, pretext
latebricola, -ae adj low-living
latebrōsē adv in hiding
latebrōsus adj secret, full of coverts; porous
latēns, -entis pres p of **lateō** ▶ adj hidden, secret
latenter adv in secret
lateō, -ēre, -uī vi to lie hid, lurk, skulk; to be in safety, live a retired life; to be unknown, escape notice
later, -is m brick, tile; **laterem lavāre** waste one's time
laterāmen, -inis nt earthenware
laterculus, -ī m small brick, tile; kind of cake
latericius adj of bricks ▶ nt brickwork
lāterna etc see **lanterna**
latēscō, -ere vi to hide oneself
latex, -icis m water; any other liquid
Latiar, -iaris nt festival of Jupiter Latiaris
Latiaris adj Latin
latibulum, -ī nt hiding place, den, lair
lāticlāvius adj with a broad purple stripe ▶ m senator, patrician
lātifundium, -ī and **-iī** nt large estate
Latīnē adv in Latin, into Latin; **~ loquī** speak Latin, speak plainly, speak correctly; **~ reddere** translate into Latin
Latīnitās, -ātis f good Latin, Latinity; Latin rights
Latīnus adj Latin ▶ m legendary king of the Laurentians
lātiō, -ōnis f bringing; proposing
latitō, -āre vi to hide away, lurk, keep out of the way
lātitūdō, -inis f breadth, width; size; broad pronunciation
Latium, -ī nt district of Italy including Rome; Latin rights
Latius = Latiaris; Latīnus
Lātōis¹, -idis f Diana
Lātōis², -ius adj see **Lātōis¹**
lātom- etc see **lautum-**
Lātōna, -ae f mother of Apollo and Diana
Lātōnigenae, -ārum pl Apollo and Diana
Lātōnius adj, f Diana
lātor, -ōris m proposer

Lātōus adj of Latona ▶ m Apollo
lātrātor, -ōris m barker
lātrātus, -ūs m barking
lātrō, -āre vi to bark; to rant, roar ▶ vt to bark at; to clamour for
latrō, -ōnis m mercenary soldier; bandit, brigand; (chess) man
latrōcinium, -ī and **-iī** nt highway robbery, piracy
latrōcinor, -ārī, -ātus vi to serve as a mercenary; to be a brigand or pirate
latrunculus, -ī m brigand; (chess) man
lātumiae etc see **lautumiae**
lātus¹ ppp of **ferō**
lātus² adj broad, wide; extensive; (pronunciation) broad; (style) diffuse
latus, -eris nt side, flank; lungs; body; **~ dare** expose oneself; **~ tegere** walk beside; **lateris dolor** pleurisy; **ab latere** on the flank
latusculum, -ī nt little side
laudābilis adj praiseworthy
laudābiliter adv laudably
laudātiō, -ōnis f commendation, eulogy; panegyric, testimonial
laudātor, -ōris m, **laudātrīx, -rīcis** f praiser, eulogizer; speaker of a funeral oration
laudātus adj excellent
laudō, -āre, -āvī, -ātum vt to praise, commend, approve; to pronounce a funeral oration over; to quote, name
laurea, -ae f bay tree; crown of bay; triumph
laureātus adj crowned with bay; (despatches) victorious
Laurentēs, -um mpl Laurentians (people of ancient Latium)
Laurentius adj see **Laurentēs**
laureola, -ae f triumph
laureus adj of bay
lauricomus adj bay-covered
lauriger, -ī adj crowned with bay
laurus, -ī f bay tree; bay crown; victory, triumph
laus, laudis f praise, approval; glory, fame; praiseworthy act, merit, worth
lautē adv elegantly, splendidly; excellently
lautia, -ōrum ntpl State banquet
lautitia, -ae f luxury
lautumiae, -ārum fpl stone quarry; prison
lautus ppp of **lavō** ▶ adj neat, elegant, sumptuous; fine, grand, distinguished
lavābrum, -ī nt bath
lavātiō, -ōnis f washing, bath; bathing gear
Lāvīnium, -ī nt town of ancient Latium
Lāvīnius adj see **Lāvīnium**
lavō, -āre, lāvī, lautum, lavātum, lōtum vt to wash, bathe; to wet, soak, wash away
laxāmentum, -ī nt respite, relaxation
laxē adv loosely, freely
laxitās, -ātis f roominess
laxō, -āre, -āvī, -ātum vt to extend, open out; to undo; to slacken; (fig) to release, relieve; to relax, abate ▶ vi (price) to fall off
laxus adj wide, loose, roomy; (time) deferred; (fig) free, easy

lea, -ae f lioness

leaena, -ae f lioness

Leander, -rī m Hero's lover (who swam the Hellespont)

lebēs, -ētis m basin, pan, cauldron

lectīca, -ae f litter, sedan chair

lectīcārius, -ī and **-iī** m litter-bearer

lectīcula, -ae f small litter; bier

lēctiō, -ōnis f selecting; reading, calling the roll

lectisterniātor, -ōris m arranger of couches

lectisternium, -ī and **-iī** nt religious feast

lēctitō, -āre vt to read frequently

lēctiuncula, -ae f light reading

lēctor, -ōris m reader

lectulus, -ī m couch, bed

lectus, -ī m couch, bed; bier

lēctus ppp of **legō ▶** adj picked; choice, excellent

Lēda, -ae, Lēdē, -ēs f mother of Castor, Pollux, Helen and Clytemnestra

Lēdaeus adj see **Lēda**

lēgātiō, -ōnis f mission, embassy; members of a mission; (MIL) staff appointment, command of a legion; **lībera ~** free commission to visit provinces; **vōtīva ~** free commission for paying a vow in a province

lēgātor, -ōris m testator

lēgātum, -ī nt legacy, bequest

lēgātus, -ī m delegate, ambassador; deputy, lieutenant; commander (of a legion)

lēgifer, -ī adj law-giving

legiō, -ōnis f legion (up to 6000 men); (pl) troops, army

legiōnārius adj legionary

lēgirupa, -ae, lēgirupiō, -iōnis m lawbreaker

lēgitimē adv lawfully, properly

lēgitimus adj lawful, legal; right, proper

legiuncula, -ae f small legion

legō, -ere, lēgī, lēctum vt to gather, pick; to choose, select; (sail) to furl; (places) to traverse, pass, coast along; (view) to scan; (writing) to read, recite; **senātum legere** call the roll of the senate

lēgō, -āre, -āvī, -ātum vt to send, charge, commission; to appoint as deputy or lieutenant; (will) to leave, bequeath

lēgulēius, -ī and **-iī** m pettifogging lawyer

legūmen, -inis nt pulse, bean

lembus, -ī m pinnace, cutter

Lemnias f Lemnian woman

Lemnicola, -ae m Vulcan

lēmniscātus adj beribboned

lēmniscus, -ī m ribbon (hanging from a victor's crown)

Lēmnius adj see **Lēmnos**

Lēmnos, Lēmnus, -ī f Aegean island, abode of Vulcan

Lemurēs, -um mpl ghosts

lēna, -ae f procuress; seductress

Lēnaeus adj Bacchic ▶ m Bacchus

lēnīmen, -inis nt solace, comfort

lēnīmentum, -ī nt sop

lēniō, -īre, -īvī and **-iī, -ītum** vt to soften, soothe, heal, calm

lēnis adj soft, smooth, mild, gentle, calm

lēnitās, -ātis f softness, smoothness, mildness, tenderness

lēniter adv softly, gently; moderately, half-heartedly

lēnitūdō, -inis f smoothness, mildness

lēnō, -ōnis m pander, brothel keeper; go-between

lēnōcinium, -ī and **-iī** nt pandering; allurement; meretricious ornament

lēnōcinor, -ārī, -ātus vi to pay court to; to promote

lēnōnius adj pander's

lēns, lentis f lentil

lentē adv slowly; calmly, coolly

lentēscō, -ere vi to become sticky, soften; to relax

lentiscifer, -ī adj bearing mastic trees

lentiscus, -ī f mastic tree

lentitūdō, -inis f slowness, dullness, apathy

lentō, -āre vt to bend

lentulus adj rather slow

lentus adj sticky, sluggish; pliant; slow, lasting, lingering; (person) calm, at ease, indifferent

lēnunculus, -ī m skiff

leō, -ōnis m lion

Leōnidās, -ae m Spartan king who fell at Thermopylae

leōnīnus adj lion's

Leontīnī, -ōrum mpl town in Sicily

Leontīnus adj see **Leontīnī**

lepas, -dis f limpet

lepidē adv neatly, charmingly; (reply) very well, splendidly

lepidus adj pleasant, charming, neat, witty

lepōs, lepor, -ōris m pleasantness, charm; wit

lepus, -oris m hare

lepusculus, -ī m young hare

Lerna, -ae, Lernē, -ēs f marsh near Argos (where Hercules killed the Hydra)

Lernaeus adj Lernaean

Lesbias, -iadis f Lesbian woman

Lesbis, Lesbius, Lesbōus, Lesbiacus adj see **Lesbos**

Lesbos, Lesbus, -ī f Aegean island (home of Alcaeus and Sappho)

lētālis adj deadly

Lēthaeus adj of Lethe; infernal; soporific

lēthargicus, -ī m lethargic person

lēthargus, -ī m drowsiness

Lēthē, -ēs f river in the lower world, which caused forgetfulness

lētifer, -ī adj fatal

lētō, -āre vt to kill

lētum, -ī nt death; destruction

Leucadius adj see **Leucas**

Leucas, -dis, Leucadia, -diae f island off W. Greece

Leucothea, -ae, Leucotheē, -ēs f Ino (a sea goddess)

Leuctra, -ōrum *ntpl* battlefield in Boeotia
Leuctricus *adj see* **Leuctra**
levāmen, -inis *nt* alleviation, comfort
levāmentum, -ī *nt* mitigation, consolation
levātiō, -ōnis *f* relief; diminishing
lēvī *perf of* **linō**
leviculus *adj* rather vain
levidēnsis *adj* slight
levipēs, -edis *adj* light-footed
levis *adj* (*weight*) light; (*MIL*) light-armed; (*fig*) easy, gentle; (*importance*) slight, trivial; (*motion*) nimble, fleet; (*character*) fickle, unreliable
lēvis *adj* smooth; (*youth*) beardless, delicate
levisomnus *adj* light-sleeping
levitās, -ātis *f* lightness; nimbleness; fickleness, frivolity
lēvitās, -ātis *f* smoothness; fluency
leviter *adv* lightly; slightly; easily
levō, -āre *vt* to lighten, ease; (*fig*) to alleviate, lessen; to comfort, relieve; to impair; (*danger*) to avert; **sē levāre** rise
lēvō, -āre *vt* to smooth, polish
lēvor, -ōris *m* smoothness
lēx, lēgis *f* law, statute; bill; rule, principle; contract, condition; **lēgem ferre** propose a bill; **lēgem perferre** carry a motion; **lēge agere** proceed according to law; **sine lēge** out of control
lībāmen, -inis *nt* offering, libation
lībāmentum, -ī *nt* offering, libation
lībātiō, -ōnis *f* libation
lībella, -ae *f* small coin, as; level; **ad lībellam** exactly; **ex lībellā** sole heir
libellus, -ī *m* small book; notebook, diary, letter; notice, programme, handbill; petition, complaint; lampoon
libēns, -entis *adj* willing, glad
libenter *adv* willingly, with pleasure
liber, -rī *m* inner bark (*of a tree*); book; register
Līber, -ī *m* Italian god of fertility (*identified with Bacchus*)
līber, -ī *adj* free, open, unrestricted, undisturbed; (*with abl*) free from; (*speech*) frank; (*POL*) free, not slave, democratic
Lībera, -ae *f* Proserpine; Ariadne
Līberālia, -ālium *ntpl* festival of Liber in March
līberālis *adj* of freedom, of free citizens, gentlemanly, honourable; generous, liberal; handsome
līberālitās, -ātis *f* courtesy, kindness; generosity; bounty
līberāliter *adv* courteously, nobly; generously
līberātiō, -ōnis *f* delivery, freeing; (*LAW*) acquittal
līberātor, -ōris *m* liberator, deliverer
līberē *adv* freely, frankly, boldly
līberī, -ōrum *mpl* children
līberō, -āre, -āvī, -ātum *vt* to free, set free, release; to exempt; (*LAW*) to acquit; (*slave*) to give freedom to; **fidem līberāre** keep one's promise; **nōmina līberāre** cancel debts
līberta, -ae *f* freedwoman

lībertās, -ātis *f* freedom, liberty; status of a freeman; (*POL*) independence; freedom of speech, outspokenness
lībertīnus *adj* of a freedman, freed ▸ *m* freedman ▸ *f* freedwoman
lībertus, -ī *m* freedman
libet, lubet, -ēre, -uit *and* **-itum est** *vi* (*impers*) it pleases; **mihi ~** I like; **ut ~** as you please
lībīdinōsē *adv* wilfully
lībīdinōsus *adj* wilful, arbitrary, extravagant; sensual, lustful
lībīdō, lubīdō, -inis *f* desire, passion; wilfulness, caprice; lust
libita, -ōrum *ntpl* pleasure, fancy
Libitīna, -ae *f* goddess of burials
lībō, -āre, -āvī, -ātum *vt* to taste, sip, touch; to pour (*a libation*), offer; to extract, take out; to impair
lībra, -ae *f* pound; balance, pair of scales; **ad lībram** of equal size
lībrāmentum, -ī *nt* level surface, weight (*to give balance or movement*); (*water*) fall
lībrāria, -ae *f* head spinner
lībrāriolus, -ī *m* copyist
lībrārium, -ī *and* **-iī** *nt* bookcase
lībrārius *adj* of books ▸ *m* copyist
lībrātus *adj* level; powerful
lībrīlis *adj* weighing a pound
lībritor, -ōris *m* slinger
lībrō, -āre, -āvī, -ātum *vt* to poise, hold balanced; to swing, hurl
lībum, -ī *nt* cake
Liburna, -ae *f* a fast galley, frigate
Liburnī, -ōrum *mpl* people of Illyria
Liburnus *adj* Liburnian
Libya, -ae, Libyē, -ēs *f* Africa
Libycus *adj* African
Libyes, -um *mpl* Libyans, people in N. Africa
Libyssus, Libystinus, Libystis *adj* = **Libycus**
licēns, -entis *adj* free, bold, unrestricted
licenter *adv* freely, lawlessly
licentia, -ae *f* freedom, licence; lawlessness, licentiousness
liceō, -ēre, -uī *vi* to be for sale, value at
liceor, -ērī, -itus *vt, vi* to bid (*at an auction*), bid for
licet, -ēre, -uit *and* **-itum est** *vi* (*impers*) it is permitted, it is lawful; (*reply*) all right ▸ *conj* although; **mihi ~** I may
Licinius¹, -ī *m* Roman family name (*esp with surname Crassus*)
Licinius² *adj see* **Licinius¹**
licitātiō, -ōnis *f* bidding (*at a sale*)
licitor, -ārī *vi* to make a bid, bid
licitus *adj* lawful
līcium, -ī *and* **-iī** *nt* thread
lictor, -ōris *m* lictor (*an attendant with fasces preceding a magistrate*)
licuī *perf of* **liceō; liquēscō**
liēn, -ēnis *m* spleen
ligāmen, -inis *nt* band, bandage

ligāmentum, -ī nt bandage

Liger, -is m (river) Loire

lignārius, -ī and -iī m carpenter

lignātiō, -ōnis f fetching wood

lignātor, -ōris m woodcutter

ligneolus adj wooden

ligneus adj wooden

lignor, -ārī vi to fetch wood

lignum, -ī nt wood, firewood, timber; **in silvam ligna ferre** carry coals to Newcastle

ligō¹, -āre, -āvī, -ātum vt to tie up, bandage; (fig) to unite

ligō², -ōnis m mattock, hoe

ligula, -ae f shoestrap

Ligur, -ris m/f Ligurian

Liguria, -riae f district of N.W. Italy

ligūriō, ligurriō, -īre vt to lick; to eat daintily; (fig) to feast on, lust after

ligūrītiō, -ōnis f daintiness

Ligus, -ris m/f Ligurian

Ligusticus, -stīnus adj see **Ligus**

ligustrum, -ī nt privet

līlium, -ī and -iī nt lily; (MIL) spiked pit

līma, -ae f file; (fig) revision

līmātius adv more elegantly

līmātulus adj refined

līmāx, -ācis f slug, snail

limbus, -ī m fringe, hem

līmen, -inis nt threshold, lintel; doorway, entrance; house, home; (fig) beginning

līmes, -itis m path between fields, boundary; path, track, way; frontier; boundary line

līmō, -āre, -āvī, -ātum vt to file; (fig) to polish, refine; to file down, investigate carefully; to take away from

līmōsus adj muddy

limpidus adj clear, limpid

līmus¹ adj sidelong, askance

līmus², -ī m mud, slime, dirt

līmus³, -ī m ceremonial apron

līnea, -ae f line, string; plumbline; boundary; **ad līneam, rectā līneā** vertically; **extrēmā līneā amāre** love at a distance

līneāmentum, -ī nt line; feature; outline

līneus adj flaxen, linen

lingō, -ere vt to lick

lingua, -ae f tongue; speech, language; tongue of land; **~ Latīna** Latin

lingula, -ae f tongue of land

līniger, -ī adj linen-clad

linō, -ere, lēvī, litum vt to daub, smear; to overlay; (writing) to rub out; (fig) to befoul

linquō, -ere, līquī vt to leave, quit; to give up, let alone; (pass) to faint, swoon; **linquitur ut** it remains to

linteātus adj canvas

linteō, -ōnis m linen weaver

linter, -ris f boat; trough

linteum, -ī nt linen cloth, canvas; sail

linteus adj linen

lintriculus, -ī m small boat

līnum, -ī nt flax; linen; thread, line, rope; net

Lipara, -ae, Liparē, -ēs f island N. of Sicily (now Lipari)

Liparaeus, -ēnsis adj see **Lipara**

lippiō, -īre vi to have sore eyes

lippitūdō, -inis f inflammation of the eyes

lippus adj blear-eyed, with sore eyes; (fig) blind

liquefaciō, -facere, -fēcī, -factum (pass -fīō) vt to melt, dissolve; to decompose; (fig) to enervate

liquēns, -entis adj fluid, clear

liquēscō, -ere, licuī vi to melt; to clear; (fig) to grow soft, waste away

liquet, -ēre, licuit vi (impers) it is clear, it is evident; nōn ~ not proven

līquī perf of **linquō**

liquidō adv clearly

liquidus adj fluid, liquid, flowing; clear, transparent, pure; (mind) calm, serene ▶ nt liquid water

liquō, -āre vt to melt; to strain

liquor, -ōris m fluidity; liquid, the sea

liquor, -ī vi to flow; (fig) to waste away

Līris, -is m river between Latium and Campania

līs, lītis f quarrel, dispute; lawsuit; matter in dispute; **lītem aestimāre** assess damages

litātiō, -ōnis f favourable sacrifice

lītera etc see **littera**

lītigātor, -ōris m litigant

lītigiōsus adj quarrelsome, contentious; disputed

lītigium, -ī and -iī nt quarrel

lītigō, -āre vi to quarrel; to go to law

litō, -āre, -āvī, -ātum vi to offer an acceptable sacrifice, obtain favourable omens; (with dat) to propitiate ▶ vt to offer successfully

lītorālis adj of the shore

lītoreus adj of the shore

littera, -ae f letter (of the alphabet)

litterae, -ārum fpl writing; letter, dispatch; document, ordinance; literature; learning, scholarship; **litterās discere** learn to read and write; **homō trium litterārum** thief (from fur); **sine litterīs** uncultured

litterārius adj of reading and writing

litterātē adv in clear letters; literally

litterātor, -ōris m grammarian

litterātūra, -ae f writing, alphabet

litterātus adj with letters on it, branded; educated, learned

litterula, -ae f small letter; short note; (pl) studies

litūra, -ae f correction, erasure, blot

litus ppp of **linō**

lītus, -oris nt shore, beach, coast; bank; **~ arāre** labour in vain

lituus, -ī m augur's staff; trumpet; (fig) starter

līvēns, -entis pres p of **līveō** ▶ adj bluish, black and blue

līveō, -ēre vi to be black and blue; to envy

līvēscō, -ere vi to turn black and blue

Līviānus adj = **Līvius²**

līvidulus adj a little jealous

līvidus adj bluish, black and blue; envious, malicious

Līvius¹, -ī Roman family name (esp the first Latin poet); the famous historian, Livy

Līvius² adj see **Līvius¹**

līvor, -ōris m bluish colour; envy, malice

lixa, -ae m sutler, camp-follower

locātiō, -ōnis f leasing; lease, contract

locātōrius adj concerned with leases

locitō, -āre vt to let frequently

locō, -āre, -āvī, -ātum vt to place, put; to give in marriage; to let, lease, hire out; to contract for; (money) to invest

loculus, -ī m little place; (pl) satchel, purse

loculēs, -ētis adj rich, opulent; reliable, responsible

loculētō, -āre vt to enrich

locus, -ī (pl **-ī** m and **-a** nt) m place, site, locality, region; (MIL) post; (theatre) seat; (book) passage; (speech) topic, subject, argument; (fig) room, occasion; situation, state; rank, position; **locī** individual spots; **loca** regions, ground; **locī commūnēs** general arguments; **locō** (with gen) instead of; **in locō** opportunely; **eō locī** in the position; **intereā locī** meanwhile

lōcusta, -ae f locust

locūtiō, -ōnis f speech; pronunciation

locūtus ppa of **loquor**

lōdīx, -īcis f blanket

logica, -ōrum ntpl logic

logos, logus, -ī m word; idle talk; witticism

lōlīgō see **lollīgō**

lolium, -ī and **-iī** nt darnel

lollīgō, -inis f cuttlefish

lōmentum, -ī nt face cream

Londinium, -ī nt London

longaevus adj aged

longē adv far, far off; (time) long; (compar) by far, very much; **~ esse** be far away, of no avail; **~ latēque** everywhere

longinquitās, -ātis f length; distance; duration

longinquus adj distant, remote; foreign, strange; lasting, wearisome; (hope) long deferred

longitūdō, -inis f length; duration; **in longitūdinem** lengthwise

longiusculus adj rather long

longulē adv rather far

longulus adj rather long

longurius, -ī and **-iī** m long pole

longus adj long; vast; (time) long, protracted, tedious; (hope) far-reaching; **longa nāvis** warship; **longum est** it would be tedious; **nē longum faciam** to cut a long story short

loquācitās, -ātis f talkativeness

loquāciter adv see **loquāx**

loquāculus adj somewhat talkative

loquāx, -ācis adj talkative, chattering

loquella, -ae f language, words

loquor, -quī, cūtus vt, vi to speak, talk, say; to talk about, mention; (fig) to indicate; **rēs loquitur ipsa** the facts speak for themselves

lōrārius, -ī and **-iī** m flogger

lōrātus adj strapped

lōreus adj of leather strips

lōrīca, -ae f breastplate; parapet

lōrīcātus adj mailed

lōripēs, -edis adj bandylegged

lōrum, -ī nt strap; whip, lash; leather charm; (pl) reins

lōtos, lōtus, -ī f lotus

lōtus ppp of **lavō**

lubēns see **libēns**

lubentia, -ae f pleasure

lubet, lubīdō see **libet, libīdō**

lūbricō, -āre vt to make slippery

lūbricus adj slippery, slimy; gliding, fleeting; (fig) dangerous, hazardous

Lūca bōs f elephant

Lūcania, -iae f district of S. Italy

Lūcanica f kind of sausage

Lūcanus adj Lucanian ▸ m the epic poet Lucan

lūcar, -āris nt forest tax

lucellum, -ī nt small gain

lūceō, -cēre, -xī vi to shine, be light; (impers) to dawn, be daylight; (fig) to shine, be clear; **meridiē nōn lūcēre** (argue) that black is white

Lūcerēs, -um mpl a Roman patrician tribe

Lūceria, -iae f town in Apulia

Lūcerīnus adj see **Lūceria**

lucerna, -ae f lamp; (fig) midnight oil

lūcēscō, -ere vi to begin to shine, get light, dawn

lūcidē adv clearly

lūcidus adj bright, clear; (fig) lucid

lūcifer, -ī adj light-bringing ▸ m morning star, Venus; day

lūcifugus adj shunning the light

Lūcīlius, -ī m Roman family name (esp the first Latin satirist)

Lūcīna, -ae f goddess of childbirth

lūcīscō etc see **lūcēscō**

Lucmō, Lucumō, -ōnis m Etruscan prince or priest

Lucrētia, -iae f wife of Collatinus, ravished by Tarquin

Lucrētius, -ī m Roman family name (esp the philosophic poet)

lucrifuga, -ae m non-profiteer

Lucrīnēnsis adj see **Lucrīnus**

Lucrīnus, -ī m lake near Baiae (famous for oysters)

lucror, -ārī, -ātus vt to gain, win, acquire

lucrōsus adj profitable

lucrum, -ī nt profit, gain; greed; wealth; **lucrī facere** gain, get the credit of; **lucrō esse** be of advantage; **in lucrīs pōnere** count as gain

luctāmen, -inis nt struggle, exertion

luctātiō, -ōnis f wrestling; fight, contest

luctātor, -ōris m wrestler

lūctificus adj baleful

lūctisonus adj mournful

luctor, -ārī, -ātus vi to wrestle; to struggle, fight

lūctuōsus adj sorrowful, lamentable

lūctus, -ūs m mourning, lamentation; mourning (dress)

lūcubrātiō, -ōnis f work by lamplight, nocturnal study

lūcubrō, -āre, -āvī, -ātum vi to work by night ▶ vt to compose by night

lūculentē adv splendidly, right

lūculenter adv very well

lūculentus adj bright; (fig) brilliant, excellent, rich, fine

Lūcullus, -ī m Roman surname (esp the conqueror of Mithridates)

lūcus, -ī m grove; wood

lūdia, -ae f woman gladiator

lūdibrium, -ī and **-iī** nt mockery, derision; laughing stock; sport, play; **lūdibriō habēre** make fun of

lūdibundus adj playful; safely, easily

lūdicer, -rī adj playful; theatrical

lūdicrum, -ī nt public show, play; sport

lūdificātiō, -ōnis f ridicule; tricking

lūdificātor, -ōris m mocker

lūdificō, -āre, lūdificor, -ārī, -ātus vt to make a fool of, ridicule; to delude, thwart

lūdiō, -ōnis m actor

lūdius, -ī and **-iī** m actor; gladiator

lūdō, -dere, -sī, -sum vi to play; to sport, frolic; to dally, make love ▶ vt to play at; to amuse oneself with; to mimic, imitate; to ridicule, mock; to delude

lūdus, -ī m game, sport, play; (pl) public spectacle, games; school; (fig) child's play; fun, jest; (love) dalliance; **lūdum dare** humour; **lūdōs facere** put on a public show; make fun of

luella, -ae f atonement

luēs, -is f plague, pest; misfortune

Lugdūnēnsis adj see **Lugdūnum**

Lugdūnum, -ī nt town in S. Gaul (now Lyon)

lūgeō, -gēre, -xī, -ctum vt, vi to mourn; to be in mourning

lūgubris adj mourning; disastrous; (sound) plaintive ▶ ntpl mourning dress

lumbī, -ōrum mpl loins

lumbrīcus, -ī m worm

lūmen, -inis nt light; lamp, torch; day; eye; life; (fig) ornament, glory; clarity

lūmināre, -is nt window

lūminōsus adj brilliant

lūna, -ae f moon; month; crescent

lūnāris adj of the moon

lūnātus adj crescent-shaped

lūnō, -āre vt to bend into a crescent

luō, -ere, -ī vt to pay; to atone for; to avert by expiation

lupa, -ae f she-wolf; prostitute

lupānar, -āris nt brothel

lupātus adj toothed ▶ m, ntpl curb

Lupercal, -ālis nt a grotto sacred to Pan

Lupercālia, -ālium ntpl festival of Pan in February

Lupercus, -ī m Pan; priest of Pan

lupīnum, -ī nt lupin; sham money, counters

lupīnus¹ adj wolf's

lupīnus², -ī m lupin; sham money, counters

lupus, -ī m wolf; (fish) pike; toothed bit; grapnel; **~ in fābulā** talk of the devil

lūridus adj pale yellow, ghastly pallid

lūror, -ōris m yellowness

lūscinia, -ae f nightingale

luscitiōsus adj purblind

luscus adj one-eyed

lūsiō, -ōnis f play

Lūsītānia, -iae f part of W. Spain (including what is now Portugal)

Lūsītānus adj see **Lūsītānia**

lūsitō, -āre vi to play

lūsor, -ōris m player; humorous writer

lūstrālis adj lustral, propitiatory; quinquennial

lūstrātiō, -ōnis f purification; roving

lūstrō, -āre, -āvī, -ātum vt to purify; (motion) to go round, encircle, traverse; (MIL) to review; (eyes) to scan, survey; (mind) to consider; (light) to illuminate

lustror, -ārī vi to frequent brothels

lustrum, -ī nt den, lair; (pl) wild country; (fig) brothels; debauchery

lūstrum, -ī nt purificatory sacrifice; (time) five years

lūsus¹ ppp of **lūdō**

lūsus², -ūs m play, game, sport; dalliance

lūteolus adj yellow

Lutetia, -ae f town in N. Gaul (now Paris)

luteus adj of clay; muddy, dirty; (fig) vile

lūteus adj yellow, orange

lutitō, -āre vt to throw mud at

lutulentus adj muddy, filthy; (fig) foul

lutum, -ī nt mud, mire; clay

lūtum, -ī nt dyer's weed; yellow

lūx, lūcis f light; daylight; day; life; (fig) public view; glory, encouragement, enlightenment; **lūce** in the daytime; **prīmā lūce** at daybreak; **lūce carentēs** the dead

lūxī perf of **lūceō; lūgeō**

luxor, -ārī vi to live riotously

luxuria, -ae, luxuriēs, -ēī f frankness, profusion; extravagance, luxury

luxuriō, -āre, luxurior, -ārī vi to grow to excess, be luxuriant; (fig) to be exuberant, run riot

luxuriōsē adv voluptuously

luxuriōsus adj luxuriant; excessive; extravagant; voluptuous

luxus, -ūs m excess, debauchery, pomp

Lyaeus, -ī m Bacchus; wine

Lycaeus, -ī m mountain in Arcadia (sacred to Pan)

Lycāōn, -onis m father of Callisto, the Great Bear

Lycāonius adj see **Lycāōn**

Lycēum, Lycīum, -ī nt Aristotle's school at Athens

lychnūchus, -ī m lampstand

lychnus, -ī m lamp

Lycia, -ae f country in S.W. Asia Minor

Lycius adj Lycian

Lyctius *adj* Cretan
Lycurgus, -ī *m* Thracian king killed by Bacchus;
  Spartan lawgiver; Athenian orator
Lȳdia, -iae *f* country of Asia Minor
Lȳdius *adj* Lydian; Etruscan
Lȳdus, -ī *m* Lydian
lympha, -ae *f* water
lymphāticus *adj* crazy, frantic
lymphātus *adj* distracted
Lynceus, -eī *m* keen-sighted Argonaut
lynx, lyncis *m/f* lynx
lyra, -ae *f* lyre; lyric poetry
lyricus *adj* of the lyre, lyrical
Lysiās, -ae *m* Athenian orator

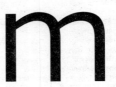

Macedō, -onis *m* Macedonian
Macedonia *f* Macedonia
Macedonicus, -onius *adj see* **Macedonia**
macellum, -ī *nt* market
maceō, -ēre *vi* to be lean
macer, -rī *adj* lean, meagre; poor
māceria, -ae *f* wall
mācerō, -āre *vt* to soften; (*body*) to enervate;
  (*mind*) to distress
macēscō, -ere *vi* to grow thin
machaera, -ae *f* sword
machaerophorus, -ī *m* soldier armed with
  a sword
Machāōn, -onis *m legendary Greek surgeon*
Machāonius *adj see* **Machāōn**
māchina, -ae *f* machine, engine; (*fig*) scheme,
  trick
māchināmentum, -ī *nt* engine
māchinātiō, -ōnis *f* mechanism, machine;
  (*fig*) contrivance
māchinātor, -ōris *m* engineer; (*fig*) contriver
māchinor, -ārī, -ātus *vt* to devise, contrive;
  (*fig*) to plot, scheme
maciēs, -ēī *f* leanness, meagreness; poorness
macilentus *adj* thin
macrēscō, -ere *vi* to grow thin
macritūdō, -inis *f* leanness
macrocollum, -ī *nt* large size of paper
mactābilis *adj* deadly
mactātus, -ūs *m* sacrifice
macte blessed; well done!
mactō¹, -āre, -āvī, -ātum *vt* to sacrifice; to
  punish, kill
mactō², -āre *vt* to glorify
macula, -ae *f* spot, stain; (*net*) mesh; (*fig*)
  blemish, fault
maculō, -āre, -āvī, -ātum *vt* to stain, defile
maculōsus *adj* dappled, mottled; stained,
  polluted
madefaciō, -facere, -fēcī, -factum
  (*pass* **-fīō**) *vt* to wet, soak
madeō, -ēre *vi* to be wet, be drenched;
  to be boiled soft; (*comedy*) to be drunk;
  (*fig*) to be steeped in

madēscō, -ere vi to get wet, become moist

madidus adj wet, soaked; sodden; drunk

madulsa, -ae m drunkard

Maeander, Maeandros, -rī m a winding river of Asia Minor; winding, wandering

Maecēnās, -ātis m friend of Augustus, patron of poets

maena, -ae f sprat

Maenala, -ōrum ntpl mountain range in Arcadia

Maenalis, -ius adj of Maenalus; Arcadian

Maenalus, Maenalos, -ī m Maenala

Maenas, -dis f Bacchante

Maeniānum nt balcony

Maenius, -ī m Roman family name; **Maenia columna** whipping post in the Forum

Maeonia, -ae f Lydia

Maeonidēs, -dae m Homer

Maeonius adj Lydian; Homeric; Etruscan

Maeōticus, Maeōtius adj Scythian, Maeotic

Maeōtis, -dis f Sea of Azov

maereō, -ēre vi to mourn, be sad

maeror, -ōris m mourning, sorrow, sadness

maestiter adv see maestus

maestitia, -ae f sadness, melancholy

maestus adj sad, sorrowful; gloomy; mourning

māgālia, -um ntpl huts

mage etc see magis

magicus adj magical

magis, mage adv more; **eō ~** the more, all the more

magister, -rī m master, chief, director; (school) teacher; (fig) instigator; **~ equitum** chief of cavalry, second in command (to a dictator); **~ mōrum** censor; **~ sacrōrum** chief priest

magisterium, -ī and **-iī** nt presidency, tutorship

magistra, -ae f mistress, instructress

magistrātus, -ūs m magistracy, office; magistrate, official

magnanimitās, -ātis f greatness

magnanimus adj great, brave

Magnēs, -ētis m Magnesian; magnet

Magnēsia f district of Thessaly

Magnēsius, Magnēssus, Magnētis adj see Magnēsia

magnidicus adj boastful

magnificē adv grandly; pompously

magnificentia, -ae f greatness, grandeur; pomposity

magnificō, -āre vt to esteem highly

magnificus (compar **-entior**, superl **-entissimus**) adj great, grand, splendid; pompous

magniloquentia, -ae f elevated language; pomposity

magniloquus adj boastful

magnitūdō, -inis f greatness, size, large amount; dignity

magnopere adv greatly, very much

magnus (compar **māior**, superl **māximus**) adj great, large, big, tall; (voice) loud; (age) advanced; (value) high, dear; (fig) grand, noble, important; **avunculus ~** great-uncle; **magna loquī** boast; **magnī aestimāre** think highly of; **magnī esse** be highly esteemed; **magnō stāre** cost dear; **magnō opere** very much

magus, -ī m wise man; magician ▶ adj magic

Māia, -ae f mother of Mercury

māiestās, -ātis f greatness, dignity, majesty; treason; **māiestātem laedere, māiestātem minuere** offend against the sovereignty of; **lēx māiestātis** law against treason

māior, -ōris compar of **magnus**; **~ nātū** older, elder; **in māius crēdere/ferre** exaggerate

māiōrēs, -ōrum mpl ancestors

Māius, -ī m May ▶ adj of May

māiusculus adj somewhat greater; a little older

māla, -ae f cheek, jaw

malacia, -ae f dead calm

malacus adj soft

male (compar **pēius**, superl **pessimē**) adv badly, wrongly, unfortunately; not; (with words having bad sense) very much; **~ est animō** I feel ill; **~ sānus** insane; **~ dīcere** abuse, curse; **~ facere** harm

maledicē adv abusively

maledictiō, -ōnis f abuse

maledictum, -ī nt curse

maledicus adj scurrilous

malefactum, -ī nt wrong

maleficē adv see maleficus

maleficium, -ī and **-iī** nt misdeed, wrong, mischief

maleficus adj wicked ▶ m criminal

malesuādus adj seductive

malevolēns, -entis adj spiteful

malevolentia, -ae f ill-will

malevolus adj ill-disposed, malicious

mālifer, -ī adj apple-growing

malignē adv spitefully; grudgingly

malignitās, -ātis f malice; stinginess

malignus adj unkind, ill-natured, spiteful; stingy; (soil) unfruitful; (fig) small, scanty

malitia, -ae f badness, malice; roguishness

malitiōsē adv see malitiōsus

malitiōsus adj wicked, crafty

maliv- etc see malev-

mālle infin of **mālō**

malleolus, -ī m hammer; (MIL) fire-brand

malleus, -ī m hammer, mallet, maul

mālō, -le, -uī vt to prefer; would rather

malobathrum, -ī nt an oriental perfume

māluī perf of **mālō**

malum, -ī nt evil, wrong, harm, misfortune; (interj) mischief

mālum, -ī nt apple, fruit

malus (compar **pēior**, superl **pessimus**) adj bad, evil, harmful; unlucky; ugly; **ī in malam rem** go to hell!

mālus[1], -ī f apple tree

mālus[2], -ī m mast, pole

malva, -ae f mallow

Māmers, -tis m Mars

Māmertīnī, -ōrum *mpl mercenary troops who occupied Messana*

mamma, -ae *f breast; teat*

mammilla, -ae *f breast*

mānābilis *adj penetrating*

manceps, -ipis *m purchaser; contractor*

mancipium, -ī *and* **-iī** *nt formal purchase; property; slave*

mancipō, -āre *vt to sell, deliver up*

mancup- *etc see* **mancip-**

mancus *adj crippled*

mandātum, -ī *nt commission, command; (LAW) contract*

mandātus, -ūs *m command*

mandō¹, -āre, -āvī, -ātum *vt to entrust, commit; to commission, command*

mandō², -ere, -ī, mānsum *vt to chew, eat, devour*

mandra, -ae *f drove of cattle*

mandūcus, -ī *m masked figure of a glutton*

māne *nt (indecl) morning* ▶ *adv in the morning, early*

maneō, -ēre, mānsī, mānsum *vi to remain; to stay, stop; to last, abide, continue* ▶ *vt to wait for, await;* **in condiciōne manēre** *abide by an agreement*

Mānēs, -ium *mpl ghosts, shades of the dead; the lower world; bodily remains*

mangō, -ōnis *m dealer*

manicae, -ārum *fpl sleeves, gloves; handcuffs*

manicātus *adj with long sleeves*

manicula, -ae *f little hand*

manifestō¹, -āre *vt to disclose*

manifestō² *adv clearly, evidently*

manifestus *adj clear, obvious; convicted, caught*

manipl- *etc see* **manipul-**

manipulāris *adj of a company* ▶ *m private (in the ranks); fellow soldier*

manipulātim *adv by companies*

manipulus, -ī *m bundle (esp of hay); (MIL) company*

Manlius¹, -ī *m Roman family name (esp the saviour of the Capitol from the Gauls); a severe disciplinarian*

Manlius², Manliānus *adj see* **Manlius¹**

mannus, -ī *m Gallic horse*

mānō, -āre, -āvī, -ātum *vi to flow, drip, stream; (fig) to spread, emanate*

mānsī *perf of* **maneō**

mānsiō, -ōnis *f remaining, stay*

mānsitō, -āre *vi to stay on*

mānsuēfaciō, -facere, -fēcī, -factum *(pass* **-fīō)** *vt to tame*

mānsuēscō, -scere, -vī, -tum *vt to tame* ▶ *vi to grow tame, grow mild*

mānsuētē *adv see* **mānsuētus**

mānsuētūdō, -inis *f tameness; gentleness*

mānsuētus *ppp of* **mānsuēscō** ▶ *adj tame; mild, gentle*

mānsus *ppp of* **mandō²; maneō**

mantēle, -is *nt napkin, towel*

mantēlum, -ī *nt cloak*

mantica, -ae *f knapsack*

manticinor, -ārī, -ātus *vi to be a prophet*

mantō, -āre *vi to remain, wait*

Mantua, -ae *f birthplace of Vergil in N. Italy*

manuālis *adj for the hand*

manubiae, -ārum *fpl money from sale of booty*

manūbrium, -ī *and* **-iī** *nt handle, haft*

manuleātus *adj with long sleeves*

manūmissiō, -ōnis *f emancipation (of a slave)*

manūmittō, -ittere, -īsī, -issum *vt to emancipate, make free*

manupretium, -ī *and* **-iī** *nt pay, wages, reward*

manus, -ūs *f hand; corps, band, company; (elephant) trunk; (art) touch; (work) handiwork, handwriting; (war) force, valour, hand to hand fighting; (fig) power;* **~ extrēma** *finishing touch;* **~ ferrea** *grappling iron;* **manum dare** *give up, yield;* **manū** *artificially;* **manū mittere** *emancipate;* **ad manum** *at hand;* **in manū** *obvious; subject;* **in manūs venīre** *come to hand;* **in manibus** *well known; at hand;* **in manibus habēre** *be engaged on; fondle;* **per manūs** *forcibly;* **per manūs trādere** *hand down*

mapālia, -um *ntpl huts*

mappa, -ae *f napkin, cloth*

Marathōn, -ōnis *f Attic village famous for Persian defeat*

Marathōnius *adj see* **Marathōn**

Marcellia, -iōrum *ntpl festival of the Marcelli*

Marcellus, -ī *m Roman surname (esp the captor of Syracuse)*

marceō, -ēre *vi to droop, be faint*

marcēscō, -ere *vi to waste away, grow feeble*

Marciānus *adj see* **Marcius¹**

marcidus *adj withered; enervated*

Marcius¹, -ī *m Roman family name (esp Ancus, fourth king)*

Marcius² *adj see* **Marcius¹**

mare, -is *nt sea;* **~ nostrum** *Mediterranean;* **~ inferum** *Tyrrhenian Sea;* **~ superum** *Adriatic*

Mareōticus *adj Mareotic; Egyptian*

margarīta, -ae *f pearl*

marginō, -āre *vt to put a border or kerb on*

margō, -inis *m/f edge, border, boundary;* **~ cēnae** *side dishes*

Mariānus *adj see* **Marius¹**

Marīca, -ae *f nymph of Minturnae*

marīnus *adj of the sea*

marītālis *adj marriage- (in cpds)*

maritimus *adj of the sea, maritime, coastal* ▶ *ntpl coastal area*

marītō, -āre *vt to marry*

marītus, -ī *m husband* ▶ *adj nuptial*

Marius¹, -ī *m Roman family name (esp the victor over Jugurtha and the Teutons)*

Marius² *adj see* **Marius¹**

marmor, -is *nt marble; statue, tablet; sea*

marmoreus *adj of marble; like marble*

Marō, -ōnis *m surname of Vergil*

marra, -ae f kind of hoe

Mars, Martis m god of war, father of Romulus and Remus; war, conflict; planet Mars; **aequō Marte** on equal terms; **suō Marte** by one's own exertions

Marsī, -ōrum mpl people of central Italy, famous as fighters

Marsicus, Marsus adj see **Marsī**

marsuppium, -ī and **-iī** nt purse

Mārtiālis adj of Mars

Mārticola, -ae m worshipper of Mars

Mārtigena, -ae m son of Mars

Mārtius adj of Mars; of March; warlike

mās, maris m male, man ▶ adj male; manly

māsculus adj male, masculine; manly

Masinissa, -ae m king of Numidia

massa, -ae f lump, mass

Massicum, -ī nt Massic wine

Massicus, -ī m mountain in Campania, famous for vines

Massilia, -ae f Greek colony in Gaul (now Marseille)

Massiliēnsis adj see **Massilia**

mastīgia, -ae nt scoundrel

mastrūca, -ae f sheepskin

mastrūcātus adj wearing sheepskin

matara, -ae, mataris, -is f Celtic javelin

matelliō, -ōnis m pot

māter, -ris f mother; **Magna ~** Cybele

mātercula, -ae f poor mother

māteria, -ae, māteriēs, -ēī f matter, substance; wood, timber; (fig) subject matter, theme; occasion, opportunity; (person) ability, character

māteriārius, -ī and **-iī** m timber merchant

māteriātus adj timbered

māteriēs etc see **māteria**

māterior, -ārī vi to fetch wood

māternus adj mother's

mātertera, -ae f aunt (maternal)

mathēmaticus, -ī m mathematician; astrologer

mātricīda, -ae m matricide

mātricīdium, -ī and **-iī** nt a mother's murder

mātrimōnium, -ī and **-iī** nt marriage

mātrimus adj whose mother is still alive

mātrōna, -ae f married woman, matron, lady

mātrōnālis adj a married woman's

matula, -ae f pot

mātūrē adv at the right time; early, promptly

mātūrēscō, -ēscere, -uī vi to ripen

mātūritās, -ātis f ripeness; (fig) maturity, perfection, height

mātūrō, -āre, -āvī, -ātum vt to bring to maturity; to hasten, be too hasty with ▶ vi to make haste

mātūrus adj ripe, mature; timely, seasonable; early

Mātūta, -ae f goddess of dawn

mātūtīnus adj morning, early

Mauritānia, -ae f Mauretania (now Morocco)

Maurus, -ī m Moor ▶ adj Moorish, African

Maurūsius adj see **Maurus**

Māvors, -tis m Mars

Māvortius adj see **Māvors**

maxilla, -ae f jaw

maximē adv most, very much, especially; precisely; just; certainly, yes; **cum ~** just as; **quam ~** as much as possible

maximitās, -ātis f great size

maximus superl of **magnus**

māxum- etc see **māxim-**

māzonomus, -ī m dish

meāpte my own

meātus, -ūs m movement, course

mēcastor interj by Castor!

mēcum with me

meddix tuticus m senior Oscan magistrate

Mēdēa, -ae f Colchian wife of Jason, expert in magic

Mēdēis adj magical

medentēs, -entum mpl doctors

medeor, -ērī vi (with dat) to heal, remedy

mediastīnus, -ī m drudge

mēdica, -ae f lucern (kind of clover)

medicābilis adj curable

medicāmen, -inis nt drug, medicine; cosmetic; (fig) remedy

medicāmentum, -ī nt drug, medicine; potion, poison; (fig) relief; embellishment

medicātus, -ūs m charm

medicīna, -ae f medicine; cure; (fig) remedy, relief

medicō, -āre, -āvī, -ātum vt to cure; to steep, dye

medicor, -ārī vt, vi to cure

medicus adj healing ▶ m doctor

medietās, -ātis f mean

medimnum, -ī nt, **medimnus, -ī** m bushel

mediocris adj middling, moderate, average

mediocritās, -ātis f mean, moderation; mediocrity

mediocriter adv moderately, not particularly; calmly

Mediolānēnsis adj see **Mediolānum**

Mediolānum, -ī nt town in N. Italy (now Milan)

meditāmentum, -ī nt preparation, drill

meditātiō, -ōnis f thinking about; preparation, practice

meditātus adj studied

mediterrāneus adj inland

meditor, -ārī, -ātus vt, vi to think over, contemplate, reflect; to practise, study

medius adj middle, the middle of; intermediate; intervening; middling, moderate; neutral ▶ nt middle; public ▶ m mediator; **medium complectī** clasp round the waist; **medium sē gerere** be neutral; **mediō** midway; **mediō temporis** meanwhile; **in medium** for the common good; **in medium prōferre** publish; **dē mediō tollere** do away with; **ē mediō abīre** die, disappear; **in mediō esse** be public; **in mediō positus** open to all; **in mediō relinquere** leave undecided

medius fidius interj by Heaven!

medix tuticus *see* **meddix tuticus**
medulla, -ae *f* marrow, pith
medullitus *adv* from the heart
medullula, -ae *f* marrow
Mēdus¹, -ī *m* Mede, Persian
Mēdus² *adj see* **Mēdus¹**
Medūsa, -ae *f* Gorgon, *whose look turned everything to stone*
Medūsaeus *adj:* ~ **equus** Pegasus
Megalēnsia, Megalēsia, -um *ntpl* festival of Cybele in April
Megara, -ae *f*, **Megara, -ōrum** *ntpl* town in Greece near the Isthmus
Megarēus, Megarīcus *adj* Megarean
megistānes, -um *mpl* grandees
mehercle, mehercule, mehercules *interj* by Hercules!
mēiō, -ere *vi* to make water
mel, mellis *nt* honey
melancholicus *adj* melancholy
melē *pl of* **melos**
Meleager, Meleagros, -rī *m* prince of Calydon
melicus *adj* musical; lyrical
melilōtos, -ī *f* kind of clover
melimēla, -ōrum *ntpl* honey apples
Mēlīnum, -ī *nt* Melian white
melior, -ōris *adj* better
melisphyllum, -ī *nt* balm
Melita, -ae *f* Malta
Melitēnsis *adj* Maltese
melius *nt of* **melior** ▸ *adv* better
meliusculē *adv* fairly well
meliusculus *adj* rather better
mellifer, -ī *adj* honey-making
mellītus *adj* honeyed; sweet
melos, -ī *nt* tune, song
Melpomenē, -ēs *f* Muse of tragedy
membrāna, -ae *f* skin, membrane, slough; parchment
membrānula, -ae *f* piece of parchment
membrātim *adv* limb by limb; piecemeal; in short sentences
membrum, -ī *nt* limb, member; part, division; clause
mēmet me *(emphatic)*
meminī, -isse *vi (with gen)* to remember, think of; to mention
Memnōn, -onis *m* Ethiopian king, killed at Troy
Memnonius *adj see* **Memnōn**
memor, -is *adj* mindful, remembering; in memory (of)
memorābilis *adj* memorable, remarkable
memorandus *adj* noteworthy
memorātus¹, -ūs *m* mention
memorātus² *adj* famed
memoria, -ae *f* memory, remembrance; time, lifetime; history; **haec ~** our day; **memoriae prōdere** hand down to posterity; **post hominum memoriam** since the beginning of history
memoriola, -ae *f* weak memory
memoriter *adv* from memory; accurately

memorō, -āre, -āvī, -ātum *vt* to mention, say, speak
Memphis, -is *and* **-idos** *f* town in middle Egypt
Memphītēs, Memphītis, Memphītīticus *adj* of Memphis; Egyptian
Menander, Menandros, -rī *m* Greek writer of comedy
Menandrēus *adj see* **Menander**
menda, -ae *f* fault
mendācium, -ī *and* **-iī** *nt* lie
mendāciunculum, -ī *nt* fib
mendāx, -ācis *adj* lying; deceptive, unreal ▸ *m* liar
mendīcitās, -ātis *f* beggary
mendīcō, -āre, mendīcor, -ārī *vi* to beg, go begging
mendīcus *adj* beggarly, poor ▸ *m* beggar
mendōsē *adv see* **mendōsus**
mendōsus *adj* faulty; wrong, mistaken
mendum, -ī *nt* fault, blunder
Menelāēus *adj see* **Menelāus**
Menelāus, -ī *m* brother of Agamemnon, husband of Helen
Menoetiadēs, -ae *m* Patroclus
mēns, mentis *f* mind, understanding; feelings, heart; idea, plan, purpose; courage; **venit in mentem** it occurs; **mente captus** insane; **eā mente ut** with the intention of
mēnsa, -ae *f* table; meal, course; counter, bank; **secunda ~** dessert
mēnsārius, -ī *and* **-iī** *m* banker
mēnsiō, -ōnis *f* (metre) quantity
mēnsis, -is *m* month
mēnsor, -ōris *m* measurer, surveyor
mēnstruālis *adj* for a month
mēnstruus *adj* monthly; for a month ▸ *nt* a month's provisions
mēnsula, -ae *f* little table
mēnsūra, -ae *f* measure, measurement; standard, standing; amount, size, capacity
mēnsus *ppa of* **mētior**
menta, -ae *f* mint
mentiēns, -ientis *m* fallacy
mentiō, -ōnis *f* mention, hint
mentior, -īrī, -ītus *vi* to lie, deceive ▸ *vt* to say falsely; to feign, imitate
mentītus *adj* lying, false
Mentor, -is *m* artist in metalwork; ornamental cup
Mentoreus *adj see* **Mentor**
mentum, -ī *nt* chin
meō, -āre *vi* to go, pass
mephītis, -is *f* noxious vapour, malaria
merācus *adj* pure
mercābilis *adj* buyable
mercātor, -ōris *m* merchant, dealer
mercātūra, -ae *f* commerce; purchase; goods
mercātus, -ūs *m* trade, traffic; market, fair
mercēdula, -ae *f* poor wages, small rent
mercēnārius *adj* hired, mercenary ▸ *m* servant
mercēs, -ēdis *f* pay, wages, fee; bribe; rent; (fig) reward, retribution, cost

mercimōnium, -ī *and* **-iī** *nt* wares, goods
mercor, -ārī, -ātus *vt* to trade in, purchase
Mercuriālis *adj see* **Mercurius**
Mercurius, -ī *m* messenger of the gods, god of trade, thieves, speech and the lyre; **stēlla Mercuriī** planet Mercury
merda, -ae *f* dung
merenda, -ae *f* lunch
mereō, -ēre, -uī, mereor, -ērī, -itus *vt, vi* to deserve; to earn, win, acquire; (MIL) to serve; **bene merēre dē** do a service to, serve well; **merēre equō** serve in the cavalry
meretrīcius *adj* a harlot's
meretrīcula, -ae *f* pretty harlot
meretrīx, -īcis *f* harlot
mergae, -ārum *fpl* pitchfork
merges, -itis *f* sheaf
mergō, -gere, -sī, -sum *vt* to dip, immerse, sink; (fig) to bury, plunge, drown
mergus, -ī *m* (bird) diver
merīdiānus *adj* midday; southerly
merīdiātiō, -ōnis *f* siesta
merīdiēs, -ēī *f* midday, noon; south
merīdiō, -āre *vi* to take a siesta
meritō¹, -āre *vt* to earn
meritō² *adv* deservedly
meritōrius *adj* money-earning ▸ *ntpl* lodgings
meritum, -ī *nt* service, kindness, merit; blame
meritus *ppp of* **mereō** ▸ *adj* deserved, just
merops, -is *f* bee-eater
mersī *perf of* **mergō**
mersō, -āre *vt* to immerse, plunge; to overwhelm
mersus *ppp of* **mergō**
merula, -ae *f* blackbird
merum, -ī *nt* neat wine
merus *adj* pure, undiluted; bare, mere
merx, mercis *f* goods, wares
Messalla, -ae *m* Roman surname (esp Messalla Corvīnus, Augustan orator, soldier and literary patron)
Messallīna, -īnae *f* wife of emperor Claudius; wife of Nero
Messāna, -ae *f* Sicilian town (now Messina)
messis, -is *f* harvest
messor, -ōris *m* reaper
messōrius *adj* a reaper's
messuī *perf of* **metō**
messus *ppp of* **metō**
mēta, -ae *f* pillar at each end of the Circus course; turning point, winning post; (fig) goal, end, limit
metallum, -ī *nt* mine, quarry; metal
mētātor, -ōris *m* surveyor
Metaurus, -ī *m* river in Umbria, famous for the defeat of Hasdrubal
Metellus, -ī *m* Roman surname (esp the commander against Jugurtha)
Mēthymna, -ae *f* town in Lesbos
Mēthymnaeus *adj see* **Mēthymna**
mētior, -tīrī, -nsus *vt* to measure, measure out; to traverse; (fig) to estimate, judge

metō, -tere, -ssuī, -ssum *vt* to reap, gather; to mow, cut down
mētor, -ārī, -ātus *vt* to measure off, lay out
metrēta, -ae *f* liquid measure (about 9 gallons)
metuculōsus *adj* frightful
metuō, -uere, -uī, -ūtum *vt* to fear, be apprehensive
metus, -ūs *m* fear, alarm, anxiety
meus *adj* my, mine
mī *dat of* **ego** ▸ *voc and mpl of* **meus**
mīca, -ae *f* crumb, grain
micō, -āre, -uī *vi* to quiver, flicker, beat, flash, sparkle
Midās, -ae *m* Phrygian king whose touch turned everything to gold
migrātiō, -ōnis *f* removal, change
migrō, -āre, -āvī, -ātum *vi* to remove, change, pass away ▸ *vt* to transport, transgress
mīles, -itis *m* soldier, infantryman; army, troops
Mīlēsius *adj see* **Mīlētus**
Mīlētus, -ī *f* town in Asia Minor
mīlia, -um *ntpl* thousands; **~ passuum** miles
mīliārium, milliārium, -ī *and* **-iī** *nt* milestone
mīlitāris *adj* military, a soldier's
mīlitāriter *adv* in a soldierly fashion
mīlitia, -ae *f* military service, war; the army; **mīlitiae** on service; **domī mīlitiaeque** at home and abroad
mīlitō, -āre *vi* to serve, be a soldier
milium, -ī *and* **-iī** *nt* millet
mīlle (pl **mīlia**) *num* a thousand; **~ passūs** a mile
mīllensimus, mīllēsimus *adj* thousandth
mīllia *etc see* **mīlia**
mīlliārium *etc see* **mīliārium**
mīlliēns, mīlliēs *adv* a thousand times
Milō, -ōnis *m* tribune who killed Clodius and was defended by Cicero
Milōniānus *adj see* **Milō**
Miltiadēs, -is *m* Athenian general, victor at Marathon
mīluīnus *adj* resembling a kite; rapacious
mīluus, mīlvus, -ī *m* kite; gurnard
mīma, -ae *f* actress
Mimallonis, -dis *f* Bacchante
mīmicē *adv see* **mīmicus**
mīmicus *adj* farcical
Mimnermus, -ī *m* Greek elegiac poet
mīmula, -ae *f* actress
mīmus, -ī *m* actor; mime, farce
mina, -ae *f* Greek silver coin
mināciter *adv see* **mināx**
minae, -ārum *fpl* threats; (wall) pinnacles
minanter *adv* threateningly
minātiō, -ōnis *f* threat
mināx, -ācis *adj* threatening; projecting
Minerva, -ae *f* goddess of wisdom and arts, esp weaving; (fig) talent, genius; working in wool; **sūs Minervam** "teach your grandmother!"
miniātulus *adj* painted red
miniātus *adj* red-leaded
minimē *adv* least, very little; (reply) no, not at all

minimus adj least, smallest, very small; youngest

miniō, -āre, -āvī, -ātum vt to colour red

minister, -rī m, **ministra, ministrae** f attendant, servant; helper, agent, tool

ministerium, -ī and **-iī** nt service, office, duty; retinue

ministrātor, -ōris m, **ministrātorrīx, ministrātorrīcis** f assistant, handmaid

ministrō, -āre vt to serve, supply; to manage

minitābundus adj threatening

minitor, -ārī, minitō, -āre vt, vi to threaten

minium, -ī and **-iī** nt vermilion, red lead

Mīnōis, -idis f Ariadne

Mīnōius, Mīnōus adj see **Mīnōs**

minor¹, -ārī, -ātus vt, vi to threaten; to project

minor², -ōris smaller, less, inferior; younger; (pl) descendants

Mīnōs, -is m king of Crete, judge in the lower world

Mīnōtaurus, -ī m monster of the Cretan labyrinth, half bull, half man

Minturnae, -ārum fpl town in S. Latium

Minturnēnsis adj see **Minturnae**

minum- etc see **minim-**

minuō, -uere, -uī, -ūtum vt to make smaller, lessen; to chop up; to reduce, weaken ▸ vi (tide) to ebb

minus nt = **minor²** ▸ adv less; not, not at all; **quō ~** (prevent) from

minusculus adj smallish

minūtal, -ālis nt mince

minūtātim adv bit by bit

minūtē adv in a petty manner

minūtus ppp of **minuō** ▸ adj small; paltry

mīrābilis adj wonderful, extraordinary

mīrābiliter adv see **mīrābilis**

mīrābundus adj astonished

mīrāculum, -ī nt marvel, wonder; amazement

mīrandus adj wonderful

mīrātiō, -ōnis f wonder

mīrātor, -ōris m admirer

mīrātrīx, -īcis adj admiring

mīrē adv see **mīrus**

mīrificē adv see **mīrificus**

mīrificus adj wonderful

mirmillō see **murmillō**

mīror, -ārī, -ātus vt to wonder at, be surprised at, admire ▸ vi to wonder, be surprised

mīrus adj wonderful, strange; **mīrum quam, mīrum quantum** extraordinarily

miscellānea, -ōrum ntpl (food) hotchpotch

misceō, -scēre, -scuī, -xtum vt to mix, mingle, blend; to join, combine; to confuse, embroil

misellus adj poor little

Mīsēnēnsis adj see **Mīsēnum**

Mīsēnum, -ī nt promontory and harbour near Naples

miser, -ī adj wretched, poor, pitiful, sorry

miserābilis adj pitiable, sad, plaintive

miserābiliter adv see **miserābilis**

miserandus adj deplorable

miserātiō, -ōnis f pity, compassion, pathos

miserē adv see **miser**

misereō, -ēre, -uī, misereor, -ērī, -itus vt, vi (with gen) to pity, sympathize with; **miseret mē** I pity, I am sorry

miserēscō, -ere vi to feel pity

miseria, -ae f misery, trouble, distress

misericordia, -ae f pity, sympathy, mercy

misericors, -dis adj sympathetic, merciful

miseriter adv sadly

miseror, -ārī, -ātus vt to deplore; to pity

mīsī perf of **mittō**

missa, -ae f (ECCL) mass

missilis adj missile

missiō, -ōnis f sending; release; (MIL) discharge; (gladiators) quarter; (events) end; **sine missiōne** to the death

missitō, -āre vt to send repeatedly

missus¹ ppp of **mittō**

missus², -ūs m sending; throwing; **~ sagittae** bowshot

mitella, -ae f turban

mītēscō, -ere vi to ripen; to grow mild

Mithridātēs, -is m king of Pontus, defeated by Pompey

Mithridātēus, Mithridāticus adj see **Mithridātēs**

mītigātiō, -ōnis f soothing

mītigō, -āre, -āvī, -ātum vt to ripen, soften; to calm, pacify

mītis adj ripe, mellow; soft, mild; gentle

mitra, -ae f turban

mittō, -ere, mīsī, missum vt to send, dispatch; to throw, hurl; to let go, dismiss; to emit, utter; (news) to send word; (gift) to bestow; (event) to end; (speech) to omit, stop; **sanguinem mittere** bleed; **ad cēnam mittere** invite to dinner; **missum facere** forgo

mītulus, -ī m mussel

mixtim adv promiscuously

mixtūra, -ae f mingling

Mnēmosynē, -ēs f mother of the Muses

mnēmosynon, -ī nt souvenir

mōbilis adj movable; nimble, fleet; excitable, fickle

mōbilitās, -ātis f agility, rapidity; fickleness

mōbiliter adv rapidly

mōbilitō, -āre vt to make rapid

moderābilis adj moderate

moderāmen, -inis nt control; government

moderanter adv with control

moderātē adv with restraint

moderātim adv gradually

moderātiō, -ōnis f control, government; moderation; rules

moderātor, -ōris m controller, governor

moderātrīx, -īcis f mistress, controller

moderātus adj restrained, orderly

moderor, -ārī, -ātus vt, vi (with dat) to restrain, check; (with acc) to manage, govern, guide

modestē adv with moderation; humbly

modestia, -ae f temperate behaviour, discipline; humility

modestus adj sober, restrained; well-behaved, disciplined; modest, unassuming

modiālis adj holding a peck

modicē adv moderately; slightly

modicus adj moderate; middling, small, mean

modificātus adj measured

modius, -ī and **-iī** m corn measure, peck

modo adv only; at all, in any way; (with imp) just; (time) just now, a moment ago, in a moment ▶ conj if only; non ~ not only; non ~ … sed not only … but also …; ~ nōn all but, almost; ~ … sometimes … sometimes; ~ … tum at first … then

modulātē adv melodiously

modulātor, -ōris m musician

modulātus, -is m played, measured

modulor, -ārī, -ātus vt to modulate, play, sing

modulus, -ī m measure

modus, -ī m measure; size; metre, music; way, method; limit, end; **ēius modī** such; **modō, in modum** like

moecha, -ae f adulteress

moechor, -ārī vi to commit adultery

moechus, -ī m adulterer

moenera etc see **mūnus**

moenia, -um ntpl defences, walls; town, stronghold

moeniō etc see **mūniō**

Moesī, -ōrum mpl people on lower Danube (now Bulgaria)

mola, -ae f millstone, mill; grains of spelt

molāris, -is m millstone; (tooth) molar

mōlēs, -is f mass, bulk, pile; dam, pier, massive structure; (fig) greatness, weight, effort, trouble

molestē adv see **molestus**

molestia, -ae f trouble, annoyance, worry; (style) affectation

molestus adj irksome, annoying; (style) laboured

mōlīmen, -inis nt exertion, labour; importance

mōlīmentum, -ī nt great effort

mōlior, -īrī, -ītus vt to labour at, work, build; to wield, move, heave; to undertake, devise, occasion ▶ vi to exert oneself, struggle

mōlītiō, -ōnis f laborious work

mōlītor, -ōris m builder

mollēscō, -ere vi to soften, become effeminate

molliculus adj tender

molliō, -īre, -īvī, -ītum vt to soften, make supple; to mitigate, make easier; to demoralize

mollis adj soft, supple; tender, gentle; (character) sensitive, weak, unmanly; (poetry) amatory; (opinion) changeable; (slope) easy

molliter adv softly, gently; calmly; voluptuously

mollitia, -ae, mollitiēs, -ēī f softness, suppleness; tenderness, weakness, effeminacy

mollitūdō, -inis f softness; susceptibility

molō, -ere vt to grind

Molossī, -ōrum mpl Molossians, people in Epirus

Molossicus, Molossus adj see **Molossī**

Molossis, -idis f country of the Molossians

Molossus, -ī m Molossian hound

mōly, -os nt a magic herb

mōmen, -inis nt movement, momentum

mōmentum, -ī nt movement; change; (time) short space, moment; (fig) cause, influence, importance; **nūllīus mōmentī** unimportant

momordī perf of **mordeō**

Mona, -ae f Isle of Man; Anglesey

monachus, -ī m monk

monēdula, -ae f jackdaw

moneō, -ēre, -uī, -itum vt to remind, advise, warn; to instruct, foretell

monēris, -is f galley with one bank of oars

monērula etc see **monēdula**

monēta, -ae f mint; money; stamp

monīle, -is nt necklace, collar

monim- etc see **monum-**

monitiō, -ōnis f admonishing

monitor, -ōris m admonisher; prompter; teacher

monitum, -ī nt warning; prophecy

monitus, -ūs m admonition; warning

monogrammus adj shadowy

monopodium, -ī and **-iī** nt table with one leg

mōns, montis m mountain

mōnstrātor, -ōris m shower, inventor

mōnstrātus adj distinguished

mōnstrō, -āre, -āvī, -ātum vt to point out, show; to inform, instruct; to appoint; to denounce

mōnstrum, -ī nt portent, marvel; monster

mōnstruōsus adj unnatural

montānus adj mountainous, mountain- (in cpds), highland

monticola, -ae m highlander

montivagus adj mountain-roving

montuōsus, montōsus adj mountainous

monumentum, -ī nt memorial, monument; record

Mopsopius adj Athenian

mora¹, -ae f delay, pause; hindrance; space of time, sojourn; **moram facere** put off

mora², -ae f division of the Spartan army

mōrālis adj moral

morātor, -ōris m delayer

mōrātus adj mannered, of a nature; (writing) in character

morbidus adj unwholesome

morbus, -ī m illness, disease; distress

mordāciter adv see **mordāx**

mordāx, -ācis adj biting, sharp, pungent; (fig) snarling, carking

mordeō, -dēre, momordī, -sum vt to bite; to bite into, grip; (cold) to nip; (words) to sting, hurt, mortify

mordicus adv with a bite; (fig) doggedly

mōres pl of **mōs**

morētum, -ī *nt* salad
moribundus *adj* dying, mortal; deadly
mōrigeror, -ārī, -ātus *vi* (*with dat*) to gratify, humour
mōrigerus *adj* obliging, obedient
morior, -ī, -tuus *vi* to die; to decay, fade
moritūrus *fut p of* **morior**
mōrologus *adj* foolish
moror, -ārī, -ātus *vi* to delay, stay, loiter ▶ *vt* to detain, retard; to entertain; (*with neg*) to heed, object; **nihil morārī** have no objection to; to not care for; to withdraw a charge against
mōrōsē *adv see* **mōrōsus**
mōrōsitās, -ātis *f* peevishness
mōrōsus *adj* peevish, difficult
Morpheus, -eos *m* god of dreams
mors, mortis *f* death; corpse; **mortem sibi cōnscīscere** commit suicide; **mortis poena** capital punishment
morsiuncula, -ae *f* little kiss
morsus¹ *ppp of* **mordeō** ▶ *ntpl* little bits
morsus², -ūs *m* bite; grip; (*fig*) sting, vexation
mortālis *adj* mortal; transient; man-made ▶ *m* human being
mortālitās, -ātis *f* mortality, death
mortārium, -ī *and* **-iī** *nt* mortar
mortifer, -ī *adj* fatal
mortuus *ppa of* **morior** ▶ *adj* dead ▶ *m* dead man
mōrum, -ī *nt* blackberry, mulberry
mōrus¹, -ī *f* black mulberry tree
mōrus² *adj* foolish ▶ *m* fool
mōs, mōris *m* nature, manner; humour, mood; custom, practice, law; (*pl*) behaviour, character, morals; **mōs māiōrum** national tradition; **mōrem gerere** oblige, humour; **mōre, in mōrem** like
Mosa, -ae *m* (river) Meuse
Mōsēs, -is *m* Moses
mōtiō, -ōnis *f* motion
mōtō, -āre *vt* to keep moving
mōtus¹ *ppp of* **moveō**
mōtus², -ūs *m* movement; dance, gesture; (*mind*) impulse, emotion; (POL) rising, rebellion; **terrae ~** earthquake
movēns, -entis *pres p of* **moveō** ▶ *adj* movable ▶ *ntpl* motives
moveō, -ēre, mōvī, mōtum *vt* to move, set in motion; to disturb; to change; to dislodge, expel; to occasion, begin; (*opinion*) to shake; (*mind*) to affect, influence, provoke ▶ *vi* to move; **castra movēre** strike camp; **sē movēre** budge; to dance
mox *adv* presently, soon, later on; next
Mō̆ysēs *see* **Mōsēs**
mūcidus *adj* snivelling; mouldy
Mūcius, -ī *m* Roman family name (*esp Scaevola, who burned his right hand before Porsena*)
mūcrō, -ōnis *m* point, edge; sword
mūcus, -ī *m* mucus
mūgilis, -is *m* mullet

muginor, -ārī *vi* to hesitate
mūgiō, -īre *vi* to bellow, groan
mūgītus, -ūs *m* lowing, roaring
mūla, -ae *f* she-mule
mulceō, -cēre, -sī, -sum *vt* to stroke, caress; to soothe, alleviate, delight
Mulciber, -is *and* **-ī** *m* Vulcan
mulcō, -āre, -āvī, -ātum *vt* to beat, ill-treat, damage
mulctra, -ae *f*, **mulctrārium, -ārī** *and* **-āriī**, **mulctrum, -ī** *nt* milkpail
mulgeō, -ēre, mulsī *vt* to milk
muliebris *adj* woman's, feminine; effeminate
muliebriter *adv* like a woman; effeminately
mulier, -is *f* woman; wife
mulierārius *adj* woman's
muliercula, -ae *f* girl
mulierōsitās, -ātis *f* fondness for women
mulierōsus *adj* fond of women
mūlīnus *adj* mulish
mūliō, -ōnis *m* mule driver
mūliōnius *adj* mule driver's
mullus, -ī *m* red mullet
mulsī *perf of* **mulceō; mulgeō**
mulsus¹ *ppp of* **mulceō**
mulsus² *adj* honeyed, sweet ▶ *nt* honey-wine, mead
multa, -ae *f* penalty, fine; loss
multangulus *adj* many-angled
multātīcius *adj* fine- (*in cpds*)
multātiō, -ōnis *f* fining
multēsimus *adj* very small
multicavus *adj* many-holed
multīcia, -ōrum *ntpl* transparent garments
multifāriam *adv* in many places
multifidus *adj* divided into many parts
multifōrmis *adj* of many forms
multiforus *adj* many-holed
multigeneris, multigenus *adj* of many kinds
multiiugis, multiiugus *adj* yoked together; complex
multiloquium, -ī *and* **-iī** *nt* talkativeness
multiloquus *adj* talkative
multimodīs *adv* variously
multiplex, -icis *adj* with many folds, tortuous; many-sided, manifold, various; (*comparison*) far greater; (*character*) fickle, sly
multiplicō, -āre, -āvī, -ātum *vt* to multiply, enlarge
multipotēns, -entis *adj* very powerful
multitūdō, -inis *f* great number, multitude, crowd
multivolus *adj* longing for much
multō¹ *adv* much, far, by far; (*time*) long
multō², -āre, -āvī, -ātum *vt* to punish, fine
multum *adv* much, very, frequently
multus (*compar* **plūs**, *superl* **plūrimus**) *adj* much, many; (*speech*) lengthy, tedious; (*time*) late; **multā nocte** late at night; **nē multa** to cut a long story short
mūlus, -ī *m* mule
Mulvius *adj* Mulvian (*a Tiber bridge above Rome*)

mundānus, -ī m world citizen

munditia, -ae, mundities, -ēī f cleanness; neatness, elegance

mundus¹ adj clean, neat, elegant; **in mundō esse** be in readiness

mundus², -ī m toilet gear; universe, world, heavens; mankind

mūnerigerulus, -ī m bringer of presents

mūnerō, -āre, mūneror, -ārī vt to present, reward

mūnia, -ōrum ntpl official duties

mūniceps, -ipis m/f citizen (of a municipium), fellow-citizen

mūnicipālis adj provincial

mūnicipium, -ī and **-iī** nt provincial town, burgh

mūnificē adv see **mūnificus**

mūnificentia, -ae f liberality

mūnificō, -āre vt to treat generously

mūnificus adj liberal

mūnīmen, -inis nt defence

mūnīmentum, -ī nt defencework, protection

mūniō, -īre, -iī, -ītum vt to fortify, secure, strengthen; (road) to build; (fig) to protect

mūnis adj ready to oblige

mūnītiō, -ōnis f building; fortification; (river) bridging

mūnītō, -āre vt (road) to open up

mūnītor, -ōris m sapper, builder

mūnus, -eris nt service, duty; gift; public show; entertainment; tax; (funeral) tribute; (book) work

mūnusculum, -ī nt small present

mūraena, -ae f a fish

mūrālis adj wall- (in cpds), mural, for fighting from or attacking walls

mūrex, -icis m purple-fish; purple dye, purple; jagged rock

muria, -ae f brine

murmillō, -ōnis m kind of gladiator

murmur, -is nt murmur, hum, rumbling, roaring

murmurillum, -ī nt low murmur

murmurō, -āre vi to murmur, rumble; to grumble

murra, -ae f myrrh

murreus adj perfumed; made of the stone called murra

murrina¹, -ae f myrrh wine

murrina², -ōrum ntpl murrine vases

murt- etc see **myrt-**

mūrus, -ī m wall; dam; defence

mūs, mūris m/f mouse, rat

Mūsa, -ae f goddess inspiring an art; poem; (pl) studies

mūsaeus adj poetic, musical

musca, -ae f fly

mūscipula, -ae f, **mūscipulum, -ī** nt mousetrap

mūscōsus adj mossy

mūsculus, -ī m mouse; muscle; (MIL) shed

mūscus, -ī m moss

mūsicē adv very pleasantly

mūsicus adj of music, of poetry ▶ m musician ▶ f music, culture ▶ ntpl music

mussitō, -āre vi to say nothing; to mutter ▶ vt to bear in silence

mussō, -āre vt, vi to say nothing, brood over; to mutter, murmur

mustāceum, -ī nt, **mustāceus, -ī** m wedding cake

mūstēla, -ae f weasel

mustum, -ī nt unfermented wine, must; vintage

mūtābilis adj changeable, fickle

mūtābilitās, -ātis f fickleness

mūtātiō, -ōnis f change, alteration; exchange

mutilō, -āre, -āvī, -ātum vt to cut off, maim; to diminish

mutilus adj maimed

Mutina, -ae f town in N. Italy (now Modena)

Mutinēnsis adj see **Mutina**

mūtiō etc see **muttiō**

mūtō, -āre, -āvī, -ātum vt to shift; to change, alter; to exchange, barter ▶ vi to change; **mūtāta verba** figurative language

muttiō, -īre vi to mutter, mumble

mūtuātiō, -ōnis f borrowing

mūtuē adv mutually, in turns

mūtuitō, -āre vt to try to borrow

mūtuō adv = **mūtuē**

mūtuor, -ārī, -ātus vt to borrow

mūtus adj dumb, mute; silent, still

mūtuum, -ī nt loan

mūtuus adj borrowed, lent; mutual, reciprocal; **mūtuum dare** lend; **mūtuum sūmere** borrow; **mūtuum facere** return like for like

Mycēnae, -ārum fpl Agamemnon's capital in S. Greece

Mycēnaeus, Mycēnēnsis adj see **Mycēnae**

Mycēnis, -idis f Mycenaean woman; Iphigenia

Mygdonius adj Phrygian

myoparō, -ōnis m pirate galley

myrīca, -ae f tamarisk

Myrmidones, -um mpl followers of Achilles

Myrōn, -ōnis m famous Greek sculptor

myropōla, -ae m perfumer

myropōlium, -ī and **-iī** nt perfumer's shop

myrothēcium, -ī and **-iī** nt perfume-box

myrrh- etc see **murr-**

myrtētum, -ī nt myrtle grove

myrteus adj myrtle- (in cpds)

Myrtōum mare sea N.W. of Crete

myrtum, -ī nt myrtle-berry

myrtus, -ī and **-ūs** f myrtle

Mȳsia, -iae f country of Asia Minor

Mȳsius, Mȳsus adj see **Mȳsia**

mysta, -ae m priest of mysteries

mystagōgus, -ī m initiator

mystērium, -ī and **-iī** nt secret religion, mystery; secret

mysticus adj mystic

Mytilēnae, -ārum fpl, **Mytilēnē, -es** f capital of Lesbos

Mytilēnaeus adj see **Mytilēnae**

Mytilēnēnsis adj see **Mytilēnae**

n

nablium, **-ī** *and* **-iī** *nt kind of harp*
nactus *ppa of* **nancīscor**
nae *etc see* **nē¹**
naenia *etc see* **nēnia**
Naeviānus *adj see* **Naevius**
Naevius, **-ī** *m early Latin poet*
naevus, **-ī** *m mole (on the body)*
Nāias, **-adis** *and* **Nāis**, **-dis** *f water nymph, Naiad*
Nāicus *adj see* **Nāias**
nam *conj (explaining)* for; *(illustrating)* for
example; *(transitional)* now; *(interrog)* but;
(enclitic) an emphatic particle
namque *conj* for, for indeed, for example
nancīscor, **-ī**, **nactus** *and* **nanctus** *vt to*
obtain, get; to come upon, find
nānus, **-ī** *m (with plants)* dwarf
Napaeae, **-ārum** *fpl* dell nymphs
nāpus, **-ī** *m* turnip
Narbō, **-ōnis** *m town in S. Gaul*
Narbōnēnsis *adj see* **Narbō**
narcissus, **-ī** *m* narcissus
nardus, **-ī** *f*, **nardum**, **-ī** *nt* nard, nard oil
nāris, **-is** *f* nostril; *(pl)* nose; *(fig)* sagacity, scorn
nārrābilis *adj* to be told
nārrātiō, **-ōnis** *f* narrative
nārrātor, **-ōris** *m* storyteller, historian
nārrātus, **-ūs** *m* narrative
nārrō, **-āre**, **-āvī**, **-ātum** *vt to* tell, relate, say;
male **nārrāre** bring bad news
narthēcium, **-ī** *and* **-iī** *nt* medicine chest
nāscor, **-scī**, **-tus** *vi to* be born; to originate,
grow, be produced
Nāsō, **-ōnis** *m surname of Ovid*
nassa, **-ae** *f wicker basket for catching fish; (fig)*
snare
nasturtium, **-ī** *and* **-iī** *nt* cress
nāsus, **-ī** *m* nose
nāsūtē *adv* sarcastically
nāsūtus *adj* big-nosed; satirical
nāta, **-ae** *f* daughter
nātālicius *adj of* one's birthday, natal ▶ *ntpl*
birthday party
nātālis *adj of* birth, natal ▶ *m* birthday ▶ *mpl*
birth, origin

natātiō, **-ōnis** *f* swimming
natātor, **-ōris** *m* swimmer
nātiō, **-ōnis** *f* tribe, race; breed, class
natis, **-is** *f (usu pl)* buttocks
nātīvus *adj* created; inborn, native, natural
natō, **-āre** *vi to* swim, float; to flow, overflow;
(eyes) to swim, fail; *(fig)* to waver
nātrīx, **-īcis** *f* watersnake
nātū *abl m* by birth, in age; **grandis ~**, **māgnō ~**
quite old; **māior ~** older; **māximus ~** oldest
nātūra, **-ae** *f* birth; nature, quality, character;
natural order of things; the physical world;
(physics) element; **rērum ~** Nature
nātūrālis *adj* by birth; by nature, natural
nātūrāliter *adv* by nature
nātus *ppa of* **nāscor** ▶ *m* son ▶ *adj* born, made
(for); old, of age; **prō rē nātā**, **ē rē nātā** under
the circumstances, as things are; **annōs**
vīgintī ~ 20 years old
nauarchus, **-ī** *m* captain
naucī: **nōn ~ esse**, **nōn ~ facere**, **nōn ~ habēre**
to be worthless, consider worthless
nauclēricus *adj* skipper's
nauclērus, **-ī** *m* skipper
naufragium, **-ī** *and* **-iī** *nt* shipwreck, wreck;
~ facere be shipwrecked
naufragus *adj* shipwrecked, wrecked; *(sea)*
dangerous to shipping ▶ *m* shipwrecked man;
(fig) ruined man
naulum, **-ī** *nt* fare
naumachia, **-ae** *f* mock sea fight
nausea, **-ae** *f* seasickness
nauseō, **-āre** *vi to* be sick; *(fig)* to disgust
nauseola, **-ae** *f* squeamishness
nauta, **nāvita**, **-ae** *m* sailor, mariner
nauticus *adj* nautical, sailors' ▶ *mpl* seamen
nāvālis *adj* naval, of ships ▶ *nt*, *ntpl* dockyard;
rigging
nāvicula, **-ae** *f* boat
nāviculāria, **-ae** *f* shipping business
nāviculārius, **-ī** *and* **-iī** *m* ship-owner
nāvifragus *adj* dangerous
nāvigābilis *adj* navigable
nāvigātiō, **-ōnis** *f* voyage
nāviger, **-ī** *adj* ship-carrying
nāvigium, **-ī** *and* **-iī** *nt* vessel, ship
nāvigō, **-āre**, **-āvī**, **-ātum** *vi to* sail, put to sea
▶ *vt to* sail across, navigate
nāvis, **-is** *f* ship; **~ longa** warship; **~ mercātōria**
merchantman; **~ onerāria** transport;
~ praetōria flagship; **nāvem dēdūcere** launch;
nāvem solvere set sail; **nāvem statuere** heave
to; **nāvem subdūcere** beach; **nāvibus atque**
quadrīgīs with might and main
nāvita *etc see* **nauta**
nāvitās, **-ātis** *f* energy
nāviter *adv* energetically; absolutely
nāvō, **-āre** *vt to* perform energetically; **operam**
nāvāre be energetic; to come to the assistance (of)
nāvus *adj* energetic
Naxos, **-ī** *f Aegean island (famous for wines and the*
story of Ariadne)

nē[1] *interj* truly, indeed

nē[2] *adv* not ▶ *conj* that not, lest; *(fear)* that; *(purpose)* so that ... not, to avoid, to prevent

-ne *enclitic* introducing a question

Neāpolis, -is *f* Naples

Neāpolītānus *adj see* **Neāpolis**

nebula, -ae *f* mist, vapour, cloud

nebulō, -ōnis *m* idler, good-for-nothing

nebulōsus *adj* misty, cloudy

nec *etc see* **neque**

necdum *adv* and not yet

necessāriē, necessāriō *adv* of necessity, unavoidably

necessārius *adj* necessary, inevitable; indispensable; *(kin)* related ▶ *m/f* relative ▶ *ntpl* necessities

necesse *adj (indecl)* necessary, inevitable; needful

necessitās, -ātis *f* necessity, compulsion; requirement, want; relationship, connection

necessitūdō, -inis *f* necessity, need, want; connection; friendship; *(pl)* relatives

necessum *etc see* **necesse**

necne *adv* or not

necnōn *adv* also, besides

necō, -āre, -āvī, -ātum *vt* to kill, murder

necopīnāns, -antis *adj* unaware

necopīnātō *adv see* **necopīnātus**

necopīnātus *adj* unexpected

necopīnus *adj* unexpected; unsuspecting

nectar, -is *nt* nectar *(the drink of the gods)*

nectareus *adj* of nectar

nectō, -ctere, -xī *and* **-xuī, -xum** *vt* to tie, fasten, connect; to weave; *(fig)* to bind, enslave *(esp for debt)*; to contrive, frame

nēcubi *conj* so that nowhere

nēcunde *conj* so that from nowhere

nēdum *adv* much less, much more

nefandus *adj* abominable, impious

nefāriē *adv see* **nefārius**

nefārius *adj* heinous, criminal

nefās *nt indecl* wickedness, sin, wrong ▶ *interj* horror!, shame!

nefāstus *adj* wicked; unlucky; *(days)* closed to public business

negātiō, -ōnis *f* denial

negitō, -āre *vt* to deny, refuse

neglēctiō, -ōnis *f* neglect

neglēctus[1] *ppp of* **neglegō**

neglēctus[2] **, -ūs** *m* neglecting

neglegēns, -entis *pres p of* **neglegō** ▶ *adj* careless, indifferent

neglegenter *adv* carelessly

neglegentia, -ae *f* carelessness, neglect, coldness

neglegō, -egere, -ēxī, -ēctum *vt* to neglect, not care for; to slight, disregard; to overlook

negō, -āre, -āvī, -ātum *vi* to say no; to say not, deny; to refuse, decline

negōtiālis *adj* business- *(in cpds)*

negōtiāns, -antis *m* businessman

negōtiātiō, -ōnis *f* banking business

negōtiātor, -ōris *m* businessman, banker

negōtiolum, -ī *nt* trivial matter

negōtior, -ārī, -ātus *vi* to do business, trade

negōtiōsus *adj* busy

negōtium, -ī *and* **-iī** *nt* business, work; trouble; matter, thing; **quid est negōtiī?** what is the matter?

Nēlēius *adj see* **Nēleus**[1]

Nēleus[1] **, -eī** *m* father of Nestor

Nēleus[2] *adj see* **Nēleus**[1]

Nemea[1] **, -ae** *f* town in S. Greece, where Hercules killed the lion

Nemea[2] **, -ōrum** *ntpl* Nemean Games

Nemeaeus *adj* Nemean

nēmō, -inis *m/f* no one, nobody ▶ *adj* no; **~ nōn** everybody; **nōn ~** many; **~ ūnus** not a soul

nemorālis *adj* sylvan

nemorēnsis *adj* of the grove

nemoricultrīx, -īcis *f* forest dweller

nemorivagus *adj* forest-roving

nemorōsus *adj* well-wooded; leafy

nempe *adv (confirming)* surely, of course, certainly; *(in questions)* do you mean?

nemus, -oris *nt* wood, grove

nēnia, -ae *f* dirge; incantation; song, nursery rhyme

neō, nēre, nēvī, nētum *vt* to spin; to weave

Neoptolemus, -ī *m* Pyrrhus *(son of Achilles)*

nepa, -ae *f* scorpion

nepōs, -ōtis *m* grandson; descendant; spendthrift

nepōtīnus, -ī *m* little grandson

neptis, -is *f* granddaughter

Neptūnius *adj*: **~ hērōs** Theseus

Neptūnus, -ī *m* Neptune *(god of the sea)*; sea

nēquam *adj (indecl)* worthless, bad

nēquāquam *adv* not at all, by no means

neque, nec *adv* not ▶ *conj* and not, but not; neither, nor; **~ ... et** not only not ... but also

nequeō, -īre, -īvī, -ītum *vi* to be unable, cannot

nēquior, nēquissimus *compar, superl of* **nēquam**

nēquīquam *adv* fruitlessly, for nothing; without good reason

nēquiter *adv* worthlessly, wrongly

nēquitia, -ae, nēquitiēs, -ēī *f* worthlessness, badness

Nērēis, -ēidis *f* Nereid, sea nymph

Nērēius *adj see* **Nērēis**

Nēreus, -eī *m* a sea god; the sea

Nēritius *adj* of Neritos; Ithacan

Nēritos, -ī *m* island near Ithaca

Nerō, -ōnis *m* Roman surname *(esp the emperor)*

Nerōniānus *adj see* **Nerō**

nervōsē *adv* vigorously

nervōsus *adj* sinewy, vigorous

nervulī, -ōrum *mpl* energy

nervus, -ī *m* sinew; string; fetter, prison; *(shield)* leather; *(pl)* strength, vigour, energy

nesciō, -īre, -īvī *and* **-iī, -ītum** *vt* to not know, be ignorant of; to be unable; **~ quis, ~ quid** somebody, something; **~ an** probably

nescius adj ignorant, unaware; unable; unknown

Nestor, -oris m Greek leader at Troy (famous for his great age and wisdom)

neu see **nēve**

neuter, -rī adj neither; neuter

neutiquam adv by no means, certainly not

neutrō adv neither way

nēve, neu conj and not; neither, nor

nēvī perf of **neō**

nex, necis f murder, death

nexilis adj tied together

nexum, -ī nt personal enslavement

nexus¹ ppp of **nectō**

nexus², -ūs m entwining, grip; (LAW) bond, obligation (esp enslavement for debt)

nī adv not ▶ conj if not, unless; that not; **quid nī?** why not?

nīcētērium, -ī and -iī nt prize

nictō, -āre vi to wink

nīdāmentum, -ī nt nest

nīdor, -ōris m steam, smell

nīdulus, -ī m little nest

nīdus, -ī m nest; (pl) nestlings; (fig) home

niger, -rī adj black, dark; dismal, ill-omened; (character) bad

nigrāns, -antis adj black, dusky

nigrēscō, -ere vi to blacken, grow dark

nigrō, -āre vi to be black

nigror, -ōris m blackness

nihil, nīl nt indecl nothing ▶ adv not; **~ ad nōs** it has nothing to do with us; **~ est** it's no use; **~ est quod** there is no reason why; **~ nisi** nothing but, only; **~ nōn** everything; **nōn ~** something

nihilum, -ī nt nothing; **nihilī esse** be worthless; **nihilō minus** none the less

nīl, nīlum see **nihil, nihilum**

Nīliacus adj of the Nile; Egyptian

Nīlus, -ī m Nile; conduit

nimbifer, -ī adj stormy

nimbōsus adj stormy

nimbus, -ī m cloud, rain, storm

nimiō adv much, far

nīmīrum adv certainly, of course

nimis adv too much, very much; **nōn ~** not very

nimium adv too, too much; very, very much

nimius adj too great, excessive; very great ▶ nt excess

ningit, ninguit, -ere vi it snows

ninguēs, -ium fpl snow

Nioba, -ae, Niobē, -ēs f daughter of Tantalus (changed to a weeping rock)

Niobēus adj see **Nioba**

Nīreus, -eī and -eos m handsomest of the Greeks at Troy

Nīsaeus, Nīsēius adj see **Nīsus**

Nīsēis, -edis f Scylla

nisi conj if not, unless; except, but

Nīsus, -ī m father of Scylla

nīsus¹ ppa of **nītor**

nīsus², -ūs m pressure, effort; striving, soaring

nītēdula, -ae f dormouse

nitēns, -entis pres p of **niteō** ▶ adj bright; brilliant, beautiful

niteō, -ēre vi to shine, gleam; to be sleek, be greasy; to thrive, look beautiful

nitēscō, -ere, nituī vi to brighten, shine, glow

nitidē adv magnificently

nitidiusculē adv rather more finely

nitidiusculus adj a little shinier

nitidus adj bright, shining; sleek; blooming; smart, spruce; (speech) refined

nitor, -ōris m brightness, sheen; sleekness, beauty; neatness, elegance

nītor, -tī, -sus and -xus vi to rest on, lean on; to press, stand firmly; to press forward, climb; to exert oneself, strive, labour; to depend on

nitrum, -ī nt soda

nivālis adj snowy

niveus adj of snow, snowy, snow-white

nivōsus adj snowy

nix, nivis f snow

nīxor, -ārī vi to rest on; to struggle

nīxus¹ ppp of **nītor**

nīxus², -ūs m pressure; labour

nō, nāre, nāvī vi to swim, float; to sail, fly

nōbilis adj known, noted, famous, notorious; noble, high-born; excellent

nōbilitās, -ātis f fame; noble birth; the nobility; excellence

nōbilitō, -āre, -āvī, -ātum vt to make famous or notorious

nocēns, -entis pres p of **noceō** ▶ adj harmful; criminal, guilty

noceō, -ēre, -uī, -itum vi (with dat) to harm, hurt

nocīvus adj injurious

noctifer, -ī m evening star

noctilūca, -ae f moon

noctivagus adj night-wandering

noctū adv by night

noctua, -ae f owl

noctuābundus adj travelling by night

nocturnus adj night- (in cpds), nocturnal

nōdō, -āre, -āvī, -ātum vt to knot, tie

nōdōsus adj knotty

nōdus, -ī m knot; knob; girdle; (fig) bond, difficulty

nōlō, -le, -uī vt, vi to not wish, be unwilling, refuse; **nōlī, nōlīte** do not

Nomas, -dis m/f nomad; Numidian

nōmen, -inis nt name; title; (COMM) demand, debt; (GRAM) noun; (fig) reputation, fame; account, pretext; **~ dare, ~ profitērī** enlist; **~ dēferre** accuse; **nōmina facere** enter the items of a debt

nōmenclātor, -ōris m slave who told his master the names of people

nōminātim adv by name, one by one

nōminātiō, -ōnis f nomination

nōminitō, -āre vt to usually name

nōminō, -āre, -āvī, -ātum vt to name, call; to mention; to make famous; to nominate; to accuse, denounce

nomisma, -tis nt coin

nōn adv not; no

Nōnae, -ārum fpl Nones (7th day of March, May, July, October, 5th of other months)

nōnāgēsimus adj ninetieth

nōnāgiēns, nōnāgiēs adv ninety times

nōnāgintā num ninety

nōnānus adj of the ninth legion

nōndum adv not yet

nōngentī, -ōrum num nine hundred

nonna, -ae f nun

nōnne adv do not?, is not? etc; (indirect) whether not

nōnnūllus adj some

nōnnunquam adv sometimes

nōnus adj ninth ▶ f ninth hour

nōnusdecimus adj nineteenth

Nōricum, -ī nt country between the Danube and the Alps

Nōricus adj see **Nōricum**

nōrma, -ae f rule

nōs pron we, us; I, me

nōscitō, -āre vt to know, recognize; to observe, examine

nōscō, -scere, -vī, -tum vt to get to know, learn; to examine; to recognize, allow; (perf) to know

nōsmet pron (emphatic) see **nōs**

noster, -rī adj our, ours; for us; my; (with names) my dear, good old ▶ m our friend ▶ mpl our side, our troops; **nostrī, nostrum** of us

nostrās, -ātis adj of our country, native

nota, -ae f mark, sign, note; (writing) note, letter; (pl) memoranda, shorthand, secret writing; (books) critical mark, punctuation; (wine, etc) brand, quality; (gesture) sign; (fig) sign, token; (censor's) black mark; (fig) stigma, disgrace

notābilis adj remarkable; notorious

notābiliter adv perceptibly

notārius, -ī and -iī m shorthand writer; secretary

notātiō, -ōnis f marking; choice; observation; (censor) stigmatizing; (words) etymology

nōtēscō, -ere, nōtuī vi to become known

nothus adj bastard; counterfeit

nōtiō, -ōnis f (LAW) cognisance, investigation; (PHILOS) idea

nōtitia, -ae, nōtitiēs, -ēī f fame; acquaintance; (PHILOS) idea, preconception

notō, -āre, -āvī, -ātum vt to mark, write; to denote; to observe; to brand, stigmatize

nōtuī perf of **nōtēscō**

Notus, Notos, -ī m south wind

nōtus ppp of **nōscō** ▶ adj known, familiar; notorious ▶ mpl acquaintances

novācula, -ae f razor

novālis, -is f, **novāle, -is** nt fallow land; field; crops

novātrīx, -īcis f renewer

novē adv unusually

novellus adj young, fresh, new

novem num nine

November, -ris adj of November ▶ m November

novendecim num nineteen

novendiālis adj nine days'; on the ninth day

novēnī, -ōrum adj in nines; nine

Novēnsilēs, -ium mpl new gods

noverca, -ae f stepmother

novercālis adj stepmother's

nōvī perf of **nōscō**

novīcius adj new

noviēns, noviēs adv nine times

novissimē adv lately; last of all

novissimus adj latest, last, rear

novitās, -ātis f newness, novelty; strangeness

novō, -āre, -āvī, -ātum vt to renew, refresh; to change; (words) to coin; **rēs novāre** effect a revolution

novus adj new, young, fresh, recent; strange, unusual; inexperienced; **~ homō** upstart, first of his family to hold curule office; **novae rēs** revolution; **novae tabulae** cancellation of debts; **quid novī** what news?

nox, noctis f night; darkness, obscurity; **nocte, noctū** by night; **dē nocte** during the night

noxa, -ae f hurt, harm; offence, guilt; punishment

noxia, -ae f harm, damage; guilt, fault

noxius adj harmful; guilty

nūbēcula, -ae f cloudy look

nūbēs, -is f cloud; (fig) gloom; veil

nūbifer, -ī adj cloud-capped; cloudy

nūbigena, -ae m cloudborn, Centaur

nūbilis adj marriageable

nūbilus adj cloudy; gloomy, sad ▶ ntpl clouds

nūbō, -bere, -psī, -ptum vi (women) to be married

nucleus, -ī m nut, kernel

nūdius day since, days ago; **~ tertius** the day before yesterday

nūdō, -āre, -āvī, -ātum vt to bare, strip, expose; (MIL) to leave exposed; to plunder; (fig) to disclose, betray

nūdus adj naked, bare; exposed, defenceless; wearing only a tunic; (fig) destitute, poor; mere; unembellished, undisguised; **vestīmenta dētrahere nūdō** draw blood from a stone

nūgae, -ārum fpl nonsense, trifles; (person) waster

nūgātor, -ōris m silly creature, liar

nūgātōrius adj futile

nūgāx, -ācis adj frivolous

nūgor, -ārī, -ātus vi to talk nonsense; to cheat

nūllus (gen **-īus**, dat **-ī**) adj no, none; not, not at all; non-existent, of no account ▶ m/f nobody

num interrog particle surely not?; (indirect) whether, if

Numa, -ae m second king of Rome

nūmen, -inis nt nod, will; divine will, power; divinity, god

numerābilis adj easy to count

numerātus adj in cash ▶ nt ready money

numerō¹, -āre, -āvī, -ātum vt to count, number; (money) to pay out; (fig) to reckon, consider as

numerō² adv just now, quickly, too soon

numerōsē adv rhythmically

numerōsus adj populous; rhythmical

numerus, -ī m number; many, numbers; (MIL) troop; (fig) a cipher; (pl) mathematics; rank, category, regard; rhythm, metre, verse; **in numerō esse, in numerō habērī** be reckoned as; **nūllō numerō** of no account

Numida adj see **Numidae**

Numidae, -ārum mpl Numidians (people of N. Africa)

Numidia, -iae f the country of the Numidians

Numidicus adj see **Numidia**

Numitor, -ōris m king of Alba (grandfather of Romulus)

nummārius adj money- (in cpds), financial; mercenary

nummātus adj moneyed

nummulī, -ōrum mpl some money, cash

nummus, -ī m coin, money, cash; (Roman coin) sestertius; (Greek coin) two-drachma piece

numnam, numne see **num**

numquam adv never; **~ nōn** always; **nōn ~** sometimes

numquid (question) do you? does he? etc; (indirect) whether

nunc adv now; at present, nowadays; but as it is; **~ ... ~** at one time ... at another

nuncupātiō, -ōnis f pronouncing

nuncupō, -āre, -āvī, -ātum vt to call, name; to pronounce formally

nūndinae, -ārum fpl market day; market; trade

nūndinātiō, -ōnis f trading

nūndinor, -ārī vi to trade, traffic; to flock together ▸ vt to buy

nūndinum, -ī nt market time; **trīnum ~** 17 days

nunq- etc see **numq-**

nūntiātiō, -ōnis f announcing

nūntiō, -āre, -āvī, -ātum vt to announce, report, tell

nūntius adj informative, speaking ▸ m messenger; message, news; injunction; notice of divorce ▸ nt message

nūper adv recently, lately

nūpsī perf of **nūbō**

nūpta, -ae f bride, wife

nūptiae, -ārum fpl wedding, marriage

nūptiālis adj wedding- (in cpds), nuptial

nurus, -ūs f daughter-in-law; young woman

nūsquam adv nowhere; in nothing, for nothing

nūtō, -āre vi to nod; to sway, totter, falter

nūtrīcius, -ī m tutor

nūtrīcō, -āre, nūtrīcor, -ārī vt to nourish, sustain

nūtrīcula, -ae f nurse

nūtrīmen, -inis nt nourishment

nūtrīmentum, -ī nt nourishment, support

nūtriō, -īre, -īvī, -ītum vt to suckle, nourish, rear, nurse

nūtrīx, -īcis f nurse, foster mother

nūtus, -ūs m nod; will, command; (physics) gravity

nux, nucis f nut; nut tree, almond tree

Nyctēis, -idis f Antiopa

nympha, -ae, nymphē, -ēs f bride; nymph; water

Nysa, -ae f birthplace of Bacchus

Nysaeus, Nysaēis, Nysaius adj see **Nysa**

O

ō *interj* (*expressing joy, surprise, pain, etc*) oh!; (*with voc*) O!

ob *prep* (*with acc*) in front of; for, on account of, for the sake of; **quam ob rem** accordingly

obaerātus *adj* in debt ▶ *m* debtor

obambulō, -āre *vi* to walk past, prowl about

obarmō, -āre *vt* to arm (*against*)

obarō, -āre *vt* to plough up

obc- *etc see* **occ-**

obdō, -ere, -idī, -itum *vt* to shut; to expose

obdormīscō, -īscere, -īvī *vi* to fall asleep ▶ *vt* to sleep off

obdūcō, -ūcere, -ūxī, -uctum *vt* to draw over, cover; to bring up; (*drink*) to swallow; (*time*) to pass

obductiō, -ōnis *f* veiling

obductō, -āre *vt* to bring as a rival

obductus *ppp of* **obdūcō**

obdūrēscō, -ēscere, -uī *vi* to harden; to become obdurate

obdūrō, -āre *vi* to persist, stand firm

obeō, -īre, -īvī *and* **-iī, -itum** *vi* to go to, meet; to die; (*ASTR*) to set ▶ *vt* to visit, travel over; to survey, go over; to envelop; (*duty*) to engage in, perform; (*time*) to meet; **diem obīre** die; (*LAW*) to appear on the appointed day

obequitō, -āre *vi* to ride up to

oberrō, -āre *vi* to ramble about; to make a mistake

obēsus *adj* fat, plump; coarse

ōbex, -icis *m/f* bolt, bar, barrier

obf- *etc see* **off-**

obg- *etc see* **ogg-**

obhaerēscō, -rēscere, -sī *vi* to stick fast

obiaceō, -ēre *vi* to lie over against

obiciō, -icere, -iēcī, -iectum *vt* to throw to, set before; (*defence*) to put up, throw against; (*fig*) to expose, give up; (*speech*) to taunt, reproach

obiectātiō, -ōnis *f* reproach

obiectō, -āre *vt* to throw against; to expose, sacrifice; to reproach; (*hint*) to let on

obiectus¹ *ppp of* **obiciō** ▶ *adj* opposite, in front of; exposed ▶ *ntpl* accusations

obiectus², -ūs *m* putting in the way, interposing

obīrātus *adj* angered

obiter *adv* on the way; incidentally

obitus¹ *ppp of* **obeō**

obitus², -ūs *m* death, ruin; (*ASTR*) setting; visit

obiūrgātiō, -ōnis *f* reprimand

obiūrgātor, -ōris *m* reprover

obiūrgātōrius *adj* reproachful

obiūrgitō, -āre *vt* to keep on reproaching

obiūrgō, -āre, -āvī, -ātum *vt* to scold, rebuke; to deter by reproof

oblanguēscō, -ēscere, -uī *vi* to become feeble

oblātrātrīx, -īcis *f* nagging woman

oblātus *ppp of* **offerō**

oblectāmentum, -ī *nt* amusement

oblectātiō, -ōnis *f* delight

oblectō, -āre, -āvī, -ātum *vt* to delight, amuse, entertain; to detain; (*time*) to spend pleasantly; **sē oblectāre** enjoy oneself

oblīdō, -dere, -sī, -sum *vt* to crush, strangle

obligātiō, -ōnis *f* pledge

obligō, -āre, -āvī, -ātum *vt* to tie up, bandage; to put under an obligation, embarrass; (*LAW*) to render liable, make guilty; to mortgage

oblīmō, -āre *vt* to cover with mud

oblinō, -inere, -ēvī, -itum *vt* to smear over; to defile; (*fig*) to overload

oblīquē *adv* sideways; indirectly

oblīquō, -āre *vt* to turn aside, veer

oblīquus *adj* slanting, downhill; from the side, sideways; (*look*) askance, envious; (*speech*) indirect

oblīsus *ppp of* **oblīdō**

oblītēscō, -ere *vi* to hide away

oblitterō, -āre, -āvī, -ātum *vt* to erase, cancel; (*fig*) to consign to oblivion

oblitus *ppp of* **oblinō**

oblītus *ppa of* **oblīvīscor**

oblīviō, -ōnis *f* oblivion, forgetfulness

oblīviōsus *adj* forgetful

oblīvīscor, -vīscī, -tus *vt*, *vi* to forget

oblīvium, -ī *and* **-iī** *nt* forgetfulness, oblivion

oblocūtor, -ōris *m* contradicter

oblongus *adj* oblong

obloquor, -quī, -cūtus *vi* to contradict, interrupt; to abuse; (*music*) to accompany

obluctor, -ārī *vi* to struggle against

obmōlior, -īrī *vt* to throw up (*as a defence*)

obmurmurō, -āre *vi* to roar in answer

obmūtēscō, -ēscere, -uī *vi* to become silent; to cease

obnātus *adj* growing on

obnītor, -tī, -xus *vi* to push against, struggle; to stand firm, resist

obnīxē *adv* resolutely

obnīxus *ppa of* **obnītor** ▶ *adj* steadfast

obnoxiē *adv* slavishly

obnoxiōsus *adj* submissive

obnoxius adj liable, addicted; culpable; submissive, slavish; under obligation, indebted; exposed (to danger)

obnūbō, -bere, -psī, -ptum vt to veil, cover

obnūntiātiō, -ōnis f announcement of an adverse omen

obnūntiō, -āre vt to announce an adverse omen

oboediēns, -entis pres p of **oboediō** ▶ adj obedient

oboedienter adv readily

oboedientia, -ae f obedience

oboediō, -īre vi to listen; to obey, be subject to

oboleō, -ēre, -uī vt to smell of

oborior, -īrī, -tus vi to arise, spring up

obp- etc see **opp-**

obrēpō, -ere, -sī, -tum vt, vi to creep up to, steal upon, surprise; to cheat

obrētiō, -īre vt to entangle

obrigēscō, -ēscere, -uī vi to stiffen

obrogō, -āre, -āvī, -ātum vt to invalidate (by making a new law)

obruō, -ere, -ī, -tum vt to cover over, bury, sink; to overwhelm, overpower ▶ vi to fall to ruin

obrussa, -ae f test, touchstone

obrutus ppp of **obruō**

obsaepiō, -īre, -sī, -tum vt to block, close

obsaturō, -āre vt to sate, glut

obscaen- etc see **obscen-**

obscēnē adv indecently

obscēnitās, -ātis f indecency

obscēnus adj filthy; indecent; ominous

obscūrātiō, -ōnis f darkening, disappearance

obscūrē adv secretly

obscūritās, -ātis f darkness; (fig) uncertainty; (rank) lowliness

obscūrō, -āre, -āvī, -ātum vt to darken; to conceal, suppress; (speech) to obscure; (pass) to become obsolete

obscūrus adj dark, shady, hidden; (fig) obscure, indistinct; unknown, ignoble; (character) reserved

obsecrātiō, -ōnis f entreaty; public prayer

obsecrō, -āre vt to implore, appeal to

obsecundō, -āre vi to comply with, back up

obsēdī perf of **obsideō**

obsēp- etc see **obsaep-**

obsequēns, -entis pres p of **obsequor** ▶ adj compliant; (gods) gracious

obsequenter adv compliantly

obsequentia, -ae f complaisance

obsequiōsus adj complaisant

obsequium, -ī and **-iī** nt compliance, indulgence; obedience, allegiance

obsequor, -quī, -cūtus vi to comply with, yield to, indulge

obserō¹, -āre vt to bar, close

obserō², -erere, -ēvī, -itum vt to sow, plant; to cover thickly

observāns, -antis pres p of **observō** ▶ adj attentive, respectful

observantia, -ae f respect

observātiō, -ōnis f watching; caution

observitō, -āre vt to observe carefully

observō, -āre, -āvī, -ātum vt to watch, watch for; to guard; (laws) to keep, comply with; (person) to pay respect to

obses, -idis m/f hostage; guarantee

obsessiō, -ōnis f blockade

obsessor, -ōris m frequenter; besieger

obsessus ppp of **obsideō**

obsideō, -idēre, -ēdī, -essum vt to sit at, frequent; (MIL) to blockade, besiege; to block, fill, take up; to guard, watch for ▶ vi to sit

obsidiō, -ōnis f siege, blockade; (fig) imminent danger

obsidium, -ī and **-iī** nt siege, blockade; hostageship

obsīdō, -ere vt to besiege, occupy

obsignātor, -ōris m sealer; witness

obsignō, -āre, -āvī, -ātum vt to seal up; to sign and seal; (fig) to stamp

obsistō, -istere, -titī, -titum vi to put oneself in the way, resist

obsitus ppp of **obserō²**

obsolefīō, -fierī vi to wear out, become degraded

obsolēscō, -scere, -vī, -tum vi to wear out, become out of date

obsolētius adv more shabbily

obsolētus ppa of **obsolēscō** ▶ adj worn out, shabby; obsolete; (fig) ordinary, mean

obsōnātor, -ōris m caterer

obsōnātus, -ūs m marketing

obsōnium, -ī and **-iī** nt food eaten with bread (usu fish)

obsonō, -āre vi to interrupt

obsōnō, -āre, obsōnor, -ārī vi to cater, buy provisions; to provide a meal

obsorbeō, -ēre vt to swallow, bolt

obstantia, -ium ntpl obstructions

obstetrīx, -īcis f midwife

obstinātē adv firmly, obstinately

obstinātiō, -ōnis f determination, stubbornness

obstinātus adj firm, resolute; stubborn

obstinō, -āre vi to be determined, persist

obstipēscō etc see **obstupēscō**

obstīpus adj bent, bowed, drawn back

obstitī perf of **obsistō**; **obstō**

obstō, -āre, -itī vi to stand in the way; to obstruct, prevent

obstrepō, -ere, -uī, -itum vi to make a noise; to shout against, cry down, molest ▶ vt to drown (in noise), fill with noise

obstrictus ppp of **obstringō**

obstringō, -ingere, -inxī, -ictum vt to bind up, tie round; (fig) to confine, hamper; to lay under an obligation

obstructiō, -ōnis f barrier

obstructus ppp of **obstruō**

obstrūdō, obtrūdō, -dere, -sī, -sum vt to force on to; to gulp down

obstruō, -ere, -xī, -ctum vt to build up against, block; to shut, hinder

obstupefaciō, -facere, -fēcī, -factum (pass **-fiō**) vt to astound, paralyse

obstupēscō, -ēscere, -uī vi to be astounded, paralysed

obstupidus adj stupefied

obsum, -esse, -fuī vi to be against, harm

obsuō, -uere, -uī, -ūtum vt to sew on, sew up

obsurdēscō, -ēscere, -uī vi to grow deaf; to turn a deaf ear

obsūtus ppp of **obsuō**

obtegō, -egere, -ēxī, -ēctum vt to cover over; to conceal

obtemperātiō, -ōnis f obedience

obtemperō, -āre, -āvī, -ātum vi (with dat) to comply with, obey

obtendō, -dere, -dī, -tum vt to spread over, stretch over against; to conceal; to make a pretext of

obtentus¹ ppp of **obtendō**; **obtineō**

obtentus², -ūs m screen; pretext

obterō, -erere, -rīvī, -rītum vt to trample on, crush; to disparage

obtestātiō, -ōnis f adjuring; supplication

obtestor, -ārī, -ātus vt to call to witness; to entreat

obtexō, -ere, -uī vt to overspread

obticeō, -ēre vi to be silent

obticēscō, -ēscere, -uī vi to be struck dumb

obtigī perf of **obtingō**

obtigō see **obtegō**

obtineō, -inēre, -inuī, -entum vt to hold, possess; to maintain; to gain, obtain ▶ vi to prevail, continue

obtingō, -ngere, -gī vi to fall to one's lot; to happen

obtorpēscō, -ēscere, -uī vi to become numb, lose feeling

obtorqueō, -quēre, -sī, -tum vt to twist about, wrench

obtrectātiō, -ōnis f disparagement

obtrectātor, -ōris m disparager

obtrectō, -āre vt, vi to detract, disparage

obtrītus ppp of **obterō**

obtrūdō etc see **obstrūdō**

obtruncō, -āre vt to cut down, slaughter

obtueor, -ērī, -or, -ī vt to gaze at, see clearly

obtulī perf of **offerō**

obtundō, -undere, -udī, -ūsum and **-ūnsum** vt to beat, thump; to blunt; (speech) to deafen, annoy

obturbō, -āre vt to throw into confusion; to bother, distract

obturgēscō, -ere vi to swell up

obtūrō, -āre vt to stop up, close

obtūsus, obtūnsus ppp of **obtundō** ▶ adj blunt; (fig) dulled, blurred, unfeeling

obtūtus, -ūs m gaze

obumbrō, -āre vt to shade, darken; (fig) to cloak, screen

obuncus adj hooked

obūstus adj burnt, hardened in fire

obvallātus adj fortified

obveniō, -enīre, -ēnī, -entum vi to come up; to fall to; to occur

obversor, -ārī vi to move about before; (visions) to hover

obversus ppp of **obvertō** ▶ adj turned towards ▶ mpl enemy

obvertō, -tere, -tī, -sum vt to direct towards, turn against

obviam adv to meet, against; **~ īre** to go to meet

obvius adj in the way, to meet; opposite, against; at hand, accessible; exposed

obvolvō, -vere, -vī, -ūtum vt to wrap up, muffle up; (fig) to cloak

occaecō, -āre, -āvī, -ātum vt to blind, obscure, conceal; to benumb

occallēscō, -ēscere, -uī vi to grow a thick skin; to become hardened

occanō, -ere vi to sound the attack

occāsiō, -ōnis f opportunity, convenient time; (MIL) surprise

occāsiuncula, -ae f opportunity

occāsus, -ūs m setting; west; downfall, ruin

occātiō, -ōnis f harrowing

occātor, -ōris m harrower

occēdō, -ere vi to go up to

occentō, -āre vt, vi to serenade; to sing a lampoon

occēpī perf of **occipiō**

occepsō archaic fut of **occipiō**

occeptō, -āre vt to begin

occidēns, -entis pres p of **occidō** ▶ m west

occīdiō, -ōnis f massacre; **occīdiōne occīdere** annihilate

occidō, -idere, -idī, -āsum vi to fall; to set; to die, perish, be ruined

occīdō, -dere, -dī, -sum vt to fell; to cut down, kill; to pester

occiduus adj setting; western; failing

occinō, -ere, -uī vi to sing inauspiciously

occipiō, -ipere, -ēpī, -eptum vt, vi to begin

occipitium, -ī and **-iī** nt back of the head

occīsiō, -ōnis f massacre

occīsor, -ōris m killer

occīsus ppp of **occīdō**

occlāmitō, -āre vi to bawl

occlūdō, -dere, -sī, -sum vt to shut up; to stop

occō, -āre vt to harrow

occubō, -āre vi to lie

occulcō, -āre vt to trample down

occulō, -ere, -uī, -tum vt to cover over, hide

occultātiō, -ōnis f concealment

occultātor, -ōris m hider

occultē adv secretly

occultō, -āre, -āvī, -ātum vt to conceal, secrete

occultus ppp of **occulō** ▶ adj hidden, secret; (person) reserved, secretive ▶ nt secret, hiding

occumbō, -mbere, -buī, -bitum vi to fall, die

occupātiō, -ōnis f taking possession; business; engagement

occupātus adj occupied, busy

occupō, -āre, -āvī, -ātum vt to take possession of, seize; to occupy, take up; to surprise, anticipate; (money) to lend, invest

occurrō, -rere, -rī, -sum vi to run up to, meet; to attack; to fall in with; to hurry to; (fig) to obviate, counteract; (words) to object; (thought) to occur, suggest itself

occursātiō, -ōnis f fussy welcome

occursō, -āre vi to run to meet, meet; to oppose; (thought) to occur

occursus, -ūs m meeting

Ōceanītis, -ītidis f daughter of Ocean

Ōceanus, -ī m Ocean, a stream encircling the earth; the Atlantic

ocellus, -ī m eye; darling, gem

ōcior, -ōris adj quicker, swifter

ōcius adv more quickly; sooner, rather; quickly

ocrea, -ae f greave

ocreātus adj greaved

Octāviānus adj of Octavius ▶ m Octavian (a surname of Augustus)

Octāvius, -ī m Roman family name (esp the emperor Augustus; his father)

octāvum adv for the eighth time

octāvus adj eighth ▶ f eighth hour

octāvusdecimus adj eighteenth

octiēns, octiēs adv eight times

octingentēsimus adj eight hundredth

octingentī, -ōrum num eight hundred

octipēs, -edis adj eight-footed

octō num eight

Octōber, -ris adj of October ▶ m October

octōgēnī, -ōrum adj eighty each

octōgēsimus adj eightieth

octōgiēns, octōgiēs adv eighty times

octōgintā num eighty

octōiugis adj eight together

octōnī, -ōrum adj eight at a time, eight each

octōphoros adj (litter) carried by eight bearers

octuplicātus adj multiplied by eight

octuplus adj eightfold

octussis, -is m eight asses

oculātus adj with eyes; visible; **oculātā diē vēndere** sell for cash

oculus, -ī m eye; sight; (plant) bud; (fig) darling, jewel; **oculōs adicere ad** glance at, covet; **ante oculōs pōnere** imagine; **ex oculīs** out of sight; **esse in oculīs** be in view; be a favourite

ōdī, -isse vt to hate, dislike

odiōsē adv see **odiōsus**

odiōsus adj odious, unpleasant

odium, -ī and -iī nt hatred, dislike, displeasure; insolence; **odiō esse** be hateful, be disliked

odor, odōs, -ōris m smell, perfume, stench; (fig) inkling, suggestion

odōrātiō, -ōnis f smelling

odōrātus¹ adj fragrant, perfumed

odōrātus², -ūs m sense of smell; smelling

odōrifer, -ī adj fragrant; perfume-producing

odōrō, -āre vt to perfume

odōror, -ārī, -ātus vt to smell, smell out; (fig) to search out; to aspire to; to get a smattering of

odōrus adj fragrant; keen-scented

odōs etc see **odor**

Odrysius adj Thracian

Odyssēa, -ae f Odyssey

Oeagrius adj Thracian

Oebalia, -iae f Tarentum

Oebalidēs, -idae m Castor, Pollux

Oebalis, -idis f Helen

Oebalius adj Spartan

Oebalus, -ī m king of Sparta

Oedipūs, -odis and **-ī** m king of Thebes; solver of riddles

oenophorum, -ī nt wine basket

Oenopia, -ae f Aegina

Oenotria, -ae f S.E. Italy

Oenotrius adj Italian

oestrus, -ī m gadfly; (fig) frenzy

Oeta, -ae, Oetē, -ēs f mountain range in Thessaly, associated with Hercules

Oetaeus adj see **Oeta**

ofella, -ae f morsel

offa, -ae f pellet, lump; swelling

offectus ppp of **officiō**

offendō, -endere, -endī, -ēnsum vt to hit; to hit on, come upon; to offend, blunder; to take offence; to fail, come to grief

offēnsa, -ae f displeasure, enmity; offence, injury

offēnsiō, -ōnis f stumbling; stumbling block; misfortune, indisposition; offence, displeasure

offēnsiuncula, -ae f slight displeasure; slight check

offēnsō, -āre vt, vi to dash against

offēnsus¹ ppp of **offendō** ▶ adj offensive; displeased ▶ nt offence

offēnsus², -ūs m shock; offence

offerō, -re, obtulī, oblātum vt to present, show; to bring forward, offer; to expose; to cause, inflict; **sē offerre** encounter

offerumenta, -ae f present

officīna, -ae f workshop, factory

officiō, -icere, -ēcī, -ectum vi to obstruct; to interfere with; to hurt, prejudice

officiōsē adv courteously

officiōsus adj obliging; dutiful

officium, -ī and -iī nt service, attention; ceremonial; duty, sense of duty; official duty, function

offīgō, -ere vt to fasten, drive in

offirmātus adj determined

offirmō, -āre vt, vi to persevere in

offlectō, -ere vt to turn about

offrēnātus adj checked

offūcia, -ae f (cosmetic) paint; (fig) trick

offulgeō, -gēre, -sī vi to shine on

offundō, -undere, -ūdī, -ūsum vt to pour out to; to pour over; to spread; to cover, fill

offūsus ppp of **offundō**

ogganniō, -īre vi to growl at

oggerō, -ere vt to bring, give

Ōgygius adj Theban

oh interj (expressing surprise, joy, grief) oh!

ohē interj (expressing surfeit) stop!, enough!

oi interj (expressing complaint, weeping) oh!, oh dear!

oiei interj (lamenting) oh dear!

Oīleus, -eī m father of the less famous Ajax

olea, -ae f olive; olive tree

oleāginus adj of the olive tree

oleārius adj oil- (in cpds) ▶ m oil seller

oleaster, -rī m wild olive

olēns, -entis pres p of **oleō** ▶ adj fragrant; stinking, musty

oleō, -ēre, -uī vt, vi to smell, smell of; (fig) to betray

oleum, -ī nt olive oil, oil; wrestling school; **~ et operam perdere** waste time and trouble

olfaciō, -facere, -fēcī, -factum vt to smell, scent

olfactō, -āre vt to smell at

olidus adj smelling, rank

ōlim adv once, once upon a time; at the time, at times; for a good while; one day (in the future)

olit- etc see **holit-**

olīva, -ae f olive, olive tree; olive branch, olive staff

olīvētum, -ī nt olive grove

olīvifer, -ī adj olive-bearing

olīvum, -ī nt oil; wrestling school; perfume

olla, -ae f pot, jar

olle, ollus see **ille**

olor, -ōris m swan

olōrīnus adj swan's

olus etc see **holus**

Olympia¹, -ae f site of the Greek games in Elis

Olympia², -ōrum ntpl Olympic Games

Olympiacus adj = **Olympicus**

Olympias, -adis f Olympiad, period of four years

Olympicus, Olympius adj Olympic

Olympionīcēs, -ae m Olympic winner

Olympus, -ī m mountain in N. Greece, abode of the gods; heaven

omāsum, -ī nt tripe; paunch

ōmen, -inis nt omen, sign; solemnity

ōmentum, -ī nt bowels

ōminor, -ārī, -ātus vt to forebode, prophesy

ōmissus ppp of **ōmittō** ▶ adj remiss

ōmittō, -ittere, -īsī, -issum vt to let go; to leave off, give up; to disregard, overlook; (speech) to pass over, omit

omnifer, -ī adj all-sustaining

omnigenus adj of all kinds

omnimodīs adv wholly

omnīnō adv entirely, altogether, at all; in general; (concession) to be sure, yes; (number) in all, just; **~ nōn** not at all

omniparēns, -entis adj mother of all

omnipotēns, -entis adj almighty

omnis adj all, every, any; every kind of; the whole of ▶ nt the universe ▶ mpl everybody ▶ ntpl everything

omnituēns, -entis adj all-seeing

omnivagus adj roving everywhere

omnivolus adj willing everything

onager, -rī m wild ass

onerārius adj (beast) of burden; (ship) transport

onerō, -āre, -āvī, -ātum vt to load, burden; (fig) to overload, oppress; to aggravate

onerōsus adj heavy, burdensome, irksome

onus, -eris nt load, burden, cargo; (fig) charge, difficulty

onustus adj loaded, burdened; (fig) filled

onyx, -chis m/f onyx; onyx box

opācitās, -ātis f shade

opācō, -āre vt to shade

opācus adj shady; dark

ope abl of **ops**

opella, -ae f light work, small service

opera, -ae f exertion, work; service; care, attention; leisure; time; (person) workman, hired rough; **operam dare** pay attention; do one's best; **operae pretium** worth while; **operā meā** thanks to me

operārius adj working ▶ m workman

operculum, -ī nt cover, lid

operīmentum, -ī nt covering

operiō, -īre, -uī, -tum vt to cover; to close; (fig) to overwhelm, conceal

operor, -ārī, -ātus vi to work, take pains, be occupied

operōsē adv painstakingly

operōsus adj active, industrious; laborious, elaborate

opertus ppp of **operiō** ▶ adj covered, hidden ▶ nt secret

opēs pl of **ops**

opicus adj barbarous, boorish

opifer, -ī adj helping

opifex, -icis m/f maker; craftsman, artisan

ōpiliō, -ōnis m shepherd

opīmitās, -ātis f abundance

opīmus adj rich, fruitful, fat; copious, sumptuous; (style) overloaded; **spolia opīma** spoils of an enemy commander killed by a Roman general

opīnābilis adj conjectural

opīnātiō, -ōnis f conjecture

opīnātor, -ōris m conjecturer

opīnātus, -ūs m supposition

opīniō, -ōnis f opinion, conjecture, belief; reputation, esteem; rumour; **contrā opīniōnem, praeter opīniōnem** contrary to expectation

opīniōsus adj dogmatic

opīnor, -ārī, -ātus vi to think, suppose, imagine ▶ adj imagined

opiparē adv see **opiparus**

opiparus adj rich, sumptuous

opitulor, -ārī, -ātus vi (with dat) to help

oportet, -ēre, -uit vi (impers) ought, should

oppēdō, -ere vi to insult

opperior, -īrī, -tus vt, vi to wait, wait for

oppetō, -ere, -īvī, -ītum vt to encounter; to die

oppidānus adj provincial ▶ mpl townsfolk

oppidō adv quite, completely, exactly

oppidulum, -ī nt small town

oppidum, -ī nt town

oppignerō, -āre vt to pledge

oppilō, -āre vt to stop up

oppleō, -ēre, -ēvī, -ētum vt to fill, choke up

oppōnō, -ōnere, -osuī, -ositum vt to put against, set before; to expose; to present; (*argument*) to adduce, reply, oppose; (*property*) to pledge, mortgage

opportūnē adv opportunely

opportūnitās, -ātis f suitableness, advantage; good opportunity

opportūnus adj suitable, opportune; useful; exposed

oppositiō, -ōnis f opposing

oppositus¹ ppp of **oppōnō** ▶ adj against, opposite

oppositus², -ūs m opposing

oppressiō, -ōnis f violence; seizure; overthrow

oppressus¹ ppp of **opprimō**

oppressus², -ūs m pressure

opprimō, -imere, -essī, -essum vt to press down, crush; to press together, close; to suppress, overwhelm, overthrow; to surprise, seize

opprobrium, -ī and **-iī** nt reproach, disgrace, scandal

opprobrō, -āre vt to taunt

oppsuī perf of **oppōnō**

oppugnātiō, -ōnis f attack, assault

oppugnātor, -ōris m assailant

oppugnō, -āre, -āvī, -ātum vt to attack, assault

Ops goddess of plenty

ops, opis f power, strength; help; (*pl*) resources, wealth

ops- etc see **obs-**

optābilis adj desirable

optātiō, -ōnis f wish

optātus adj longed for ▶ nt wish; **optātō** according to one's wish

optimās, -ātis adj aristocratic ▶ mpl the nobility

optimē adv best, very well; just in time

optimus adj best, very good; excellent; **optimō iūre** deservedly

optiō, -ōnis f choice ▶ m assistant

optīvus adj chosen

optō, -āre, -āvī, -ātum vt to choose; to wish for

optum- etc see **optim-**

opulēns, -entis adj rich

opulentē, -er adv sumptuously

opulentia, -ae f wealth; power

opulentō, -āre vt to enrich

opulentus adj rich, sumptuous, powerful

opus, -eris nt work, workmanship; (*art*) work, building, book; (*MIL*) siege work; (*colloq*) business; (*with* **esse**) need; **virō ~ est** a man is needed; **magnō opere** much, greatly

opusculum, -ī nt little work

ōra, -ae f edge, boundary; coast; country, region; (*NAUT*) hawser

ōrāculum, -ī nt oracle, prophecy

ōrātiō, -ōnis f speech, language; a speech, oration; eloquence; prose; emperor's message; **ōrātiōnem habēre** deliver a speech

ōrātiuncula, -ae f short speech

ōrātor, -ōris m speaker, spokesman, orator

ōrātōrius adj oratorical

ōrātrīx, -īcis f suppliant

ōrātus, -ūs m request

orbātor, -ōris m bereaver

orbiculātus adj round

orbis, -is m circle, ring, disc, orbit; world; (*movement*) cycle, rotation; (*style*) rounding off; **~ lacteus** Milky Way; **~ signifer** Zodiac; **~ fortūnae** wheel of Fortune; **~ terrārum** the earth, world; **in orbem cōnsistere** form a circle; **in orbem īre** go the rounds

orbita, -ae f rut, track, path

orbitās, -ātis f childlessness, orphanhood, widowhood

orbitōsus adj full of ruts

orbō, -āre, -āvī, -ātum vt to bereave, orphan, make childless

orbus adj bereaved, orphan, childless; destitute

orca, -ae f vat

orchas, -dis f kind of olive

orchēstra, -ae f senatorial seats (*in the theatre*)

Orcus, -ī m Pluto; the lower world; death

ōrdinārius adj regular

ōrdinātim adv in order, properly

ōrdinātiō, -ōnis f orderly arrangement

ōrdinātus adj appointed

ōrdinō, -āre, -āvī, -ātum vt to arrange, regulate, set in order

ōrdior, -dīrī, -sus vt, vi to begin, undertake

ōrdō, -inis m line, row, series; order, regularity, arrangement; (*MIL*) rank, line, company; (*pl*) captains; (*building*) course, layer; (*seats*) row; (*POL*) class, order, station; **ex ōrdine** in order, in one's turn; one after the other; **extrā ōrdinem** irregularly, unusually

Orēas, -dis f mountain nymph

Orestēs, -is and **-ae** m son of Agamemnon, whom he avenged by killing his mother

Orestēus adj see **Orestēs**

orexis, -is f appetite

organum, -ī nt instrument, organ

orgia, -ōrum ntpl Bacchic revels; orgies

orichalcum, -ī nt copper ore, brass

ōricilla, -ae f lobe

oriēns, -entis pres p of **orior** ▶ m morning; east

orīgō, -inis f beginning, source; ancestry, descent; founder

Ōrīōn, -onis and **-ōnis** m mythical hunter and constellation

orior, -īrī, -tus *vi* to rise; to spring, descend

oriundus *adj* descended, sprung

ōrnāmentum, -ī *nt* equipment, dress; ornament, decoration; distinction, pride of

ōrnātē *adv* elegantly

ōrnātus¹ *ppa of* **ōrnō** ▶ *adj* equipped, furnished; embellished, excellent

ōrnātus², -ūs *m* preparation; dress, equipment; embellishment

ōrnō, -āre, -āvī, -ātum *vt* to fit out, equip, dress, prepare; to adorn, embellish, honour

ornus, -ī *f* manna ash

ōrō, -āre, -āvī, -ātum *vt* to speak, plead; to beg, entreat; to pray

Orontēs, -is *and* **-ī** *m* river of Syria

Orontēus *adj* Syrian

Orpheus, -eī *and* **-eos** *(acc* **-ea)** *m* legendary Thracian singer, who went down to Hades for Eurydice

Orphēus, Orphēicus *adj see* **Orpheus**

ōrsus¹ *ppa of* **ōrdior** ▶ *ntpl* beginning; utterance

ōrsus², -ūs *m* beginning

ortus¹ *ppa of* **orior** ▶ *adj* born, descended

ortus², -ūs *m* rising; east; origin, source

Ortygia, -ae, Ortygiē, -ēs *f* Delos

Ortygius *adj see* **Ortygia**

oryx, -gis *m* gazelle

oryza, -ae *f* rice

os, ossis *nt* bone; *(fig)* very soul

ōs, ōris *nt* mouth; face; entrance, opening; effrontery; **ūnō ōre** unanimously; **in ōre esse** be talked about; **quō ōre redībō** how shall I have the face to go back?

oscen, -inis *m* bird of omen

ōscillum, -ī *nt* little mask

ōscitāns, -antis *pres p of* **ōscitō** ▶ *adj* listless, drowsy

ōscitanter *adv* half-heartedly

ōscitō, -āre, ōscitor, -ārī *vi* to yawn, be drowsy

ōsculātiō, -ōnis *f* kissing

ōsculor, -ārī, -ātus *vt* to kiss; to make a fuss of

ōsculum, -ī *nt* sweet mouth; kiss

Oscus *adj* Oscan

Osīris, -is *and* **-idis** *m* Egyptian god, husband of Isis

Ossa, -ae *f* mountain in Thessaly

osseus *adj* bony

ossifraga, -ae *f* osprey

ostendō, -dere, -dī, -tum *vt* to hold out, show, display; to expose; to disclose, reveal; *(speech)* to say, make known

ostentātiō, -ōnis *f* display; showing off, ostentation; pretence

ostentātor, -ōris *m* displayer, boaster

ostentō, -āre *vt* to hold out, proffer, exhibit; to show off, boast of; to make known, indicate

ostentum, -ī *nt* portent

ostentus¹ *ppp of* **ostendō**

ostentus², -ūs *m* display, appearance; proof

Ōstia, -ae *f*, **Ōstia, -ōrum** *ntpl* port at the Tiber mouth

ōstiārium, -ī *and* **-iī** *nt* door tax

ōstiātim *adv* from door to door

Ōstiēnsis *adj see* **Ōstia**

ōstium, -ī *and* **-iī** *nt* door; entrance, mouth

ostrea, -ae *f* oyster

ostreōsus *adj* rich in oysters

ostreum, -ī *nt* oyster

ostrifer, -ī *adj* oyster-producing

ostrīnus *adj* purple

ostrum, -ī *nt* purple; purple dress *or* coverings

ōsus, ōsūrus *ppa and fut p of* **ōdī**

Othō, -ōnis *m* author of a law giving theatre seats to Equites; Roman emperor after Galba

Othōniānus *adj see* **Othō**

ōtiolum, -ī *nt* bit of leisure

ōtior, -ārī *vi* to have a holiday, be idle

ōtiōsē *adv* leisurely; quietly; fearlessly

ōtiōsus *adj* at leisure, free; out of public affairs; neutral, indifferent; quiet, unexcited; *(things)* free, idle ▶ *m* private citizen, civilian

ōtium, -ī *and* **-iī** *nt* leisure, time (for), idleness, retirement; peace, quiet

ovātiō, -ōnis *f* minor triumph

ovīle, -is *nt* sheep fold, goat fold

ovillus *adj* of sheep

ovis, -is *f* sheep

ovō, -āre *vi* to rejoice; to celebrate a minor triumph

ōvum, -ī *nt* egg

p

pābulātiō, -ōnis f foraging
pābulātor, -ōris m forager
pābulor, -ārī vi to forage
pābulum, -ī nt food, fodder
pācālis adj of peace
pācātus adj peaceful, tranquil ▶ nt friendly country
Pachӯnum, -ī nt S.E. point of Sicily (now Cape Passaro)
pācifer, -ī adj peace-bringing
pācificātiō, -ōnis f peacemaking
pācificātor, -ōris m peacemaker
pācificātōrius adj peacemaking
pācificō, -āre vi to make a peace ▶ vt to appease
pācificus adj peacemaking
paciscor, -īscī, -tus vi to make a bargain, agree ▶ vt to stipulate for; to barter
pācō, -āre, -āvī, -ātum vt to pacify, subdue
pactiō, -ōnis f bargain, agreement, contract; collusion; (words) formula
Pactōlus, -ī m river of Lydia (famous for its gold)
pactor, -ōris m negotiator
pactum, -ī nt agreement, contract
pactus ppa of **paciscor** ▶ adj agreed, settled; betrothed
Pācuvius, -ī m Latin tragic poet
Padus, -ī m (river) Po
paeān, -ānis m healer, epithet of Apollo; hymn of praise, shout of joy; (metre) paeon
paedagōgus, -ī m slave who took children to school
paedor, -ōris m filth
paelex, -icis f mistress, concubine
paelicātus, -ūs m concubinage
Paelignī, -ōrum mpl people of central Italy
Paelignus adj see **Paelignī**
paene adv almost, nearly
paenīnsula, -ae f peninsula
paenitendus adj regrettable
paenitentia, -ae f repentance
paenitet, -ēre, -uit vt, vi (impers) to repent, regret, be sorry; to be dissatisfied; **an ~ is it not enough?**

paenula, -ae f travelling cloak
paenulātus adj wearing a cloak
paeōn, -ōnis m metrical foot of one long and three short syllables
paeōnius adj healing
Paestānus adj see **Paestum**
Paestum, -ī nt town in S. Italy
paetulus adj with a slight cast in the eye
paetus adj with a cast in the eye
pāgānus adj rural ▶ m villager, yokel
pāgātim adv in every village
pāgella, -ae f small page
pāgina, -ae f (book) page, leaf
pāginula, -ae f small page
pāgus, -ī m village, country district; canton
pāla, -ae f spade; (ring) bezel
palaestra, -ae f wrestling school, gymnasium; exercise, wrestling; (RHET) exercise, training
palaestricē adv in gymnastic fashion
palaestricus adj of the wrestling school
palaestrīta, -ae m head of a wrestling school
palam adv openly, publicly, well-known ▶ prep (with abl) in the presence of
Palātīnus adj Palatine; imperial
Palātium, -ī nt Palatine Hill (in Rome); palace
palātum, -ī nt palate; taste, judgment
palea, -ae f chaff
paleāria, -ium ntpl dewlap
Palēs, -is f goddess of shepherds
Palīlis adj of Pales ▶ ntpl festival of Pales
palimpsēstus, -ī m palimpsest
Palinūrus, -ī m pilot of Aeneas; promontory in S. Italy
paliūrus, -ī m Christ's thorn
palla, -ae f woman's robe; tragic costume
Palladium, -dī nt image of Pallas
Palladius adj of Pallas
Pallantēus adj see **Pallas**
Pallas, -dis and -dos f Athene, Minerva; oil; olive tree
Pallās, -antis m ancestor or son of Evander
pallēns, -entis pres p of **palleō** ▶ adj pale; greenish
palleō, -ēre, -uī vi to be pale or yellow; to fade; to be anxious
pallēscō, -escere, -uī vi to turn pale, turn yellow
palliātus adj wearing a Greek cloak
pallidulus adj palish
pallidus adj pale, pallid, greenish; in love
palliolum, -ī nt small cloak, cape, hood
pallium, -ī and -iī nt coverlet; Greek cloak
pallor, -ōris m paleness, fading; fear
palma, -ae f (hand) palm, hand; (oar) blade; (tree) palm, date; branch; (fig) prize, victory, glory
palmāris adj excellent
palmārius adj prizewinning
palmātus adj palm-embroidered
palmes, -itis m pruned shoot, branch
palmētum, -ī nt palm grove
palmifer, -ī adj palm-bearing

palmōsus adj palm-clad

palmula, -ae f oar blade

pālor, -ārī, -ātus vi to wander about, straggle

palpātiō, -ōnis f flatteries

palpātor, -ōris m flatterer

palpebra, -ae f eyelid

palpitō, -āre vi to throb, writhe

palpō, -āre, palpor, -ārī vt to stroke; to coax, flatter

palpus, -ī m coaxing

palūdāmentum, -ī nt military cloak

palūdātus adj in a general's cloak

palūdōsus adj marshy

palumbēs, -is m/f wood pigeon

pālus, -ī m stake, pale

palūs, -ūdis f marsh, pool, lake

palūster, -ris adj marshy

pampineus adj of vineshoots

pampinus, -ī m vineshoot

Pān, -ānos (acc **-āna**) m Greek god of shepherds, hills and woods, esp associated with Arcadia

panacēa, -ae f a herb supposed to cure all diseases

Panaetius, -ī m Stoic philosopher

Panchāeus, Panchāius adj see **Panchāia**

Panchāia, -iae f part of Arabia

panchrēstus adj good for everything

pancratium, -i and **-iī** nt all-in boxing and wrestling match

pandiculor, -āre vi to stretch oneself

Pandīōn, -onis m king of Athens, father of Procne and Philomela

Pandīonius adj see **Pandīōn**

pandō, -ere, -ī, pānsum and **passum** vt to spread out, stretch, extend; to open; (fig) to disclose, explain

pandus adj curved, bent

pangō, -ere, panxī and **pepigī, pāctum** vt to drive in, fasten; to make, compose; to agree, settle

pānicula, -ae f tuft

pānicum, -ī nt Italian millet

pānis, -is m bread, loaf

Pāniscus, -ī m little Pan

panniculus, -ī m rag

Pannonia, -ae f country on the middle Danube

Pannonius adj see **Pannonia**

pannōsus adj ragged

pannus, -ī m piece of cloth, rag, patch

Panormus, -ī f town in Sicily (now Palermo)

pānsa adj splayfoot

pānsus ppp of **pandō**

panthēra, -ae f panther

Panthoidēs, -ae m Euphorbus

Panthūs, -ī m priest of Apollo at Troy

panticēs, -um mpl bowels; sausages

panxī perf of **pangō**

papae interj (expressing wonder) ooh!

pāpas, -ae m tutor

papāver, -is nt poppy

papāvereus adj see **papāver**

Paphius adj see **Paphos**

Paphos, -ī f town in Cyprus, sacred to Venus

pāpiliō, -ōnis m butterfly

papilla, -ae f teat, nipple; breast

pappus, -ī m woolly seed

papula, -ae f pimple

papȳrifer, -ī adj papyrus-bearing

papȳrum, -ī nt papyrus; paper

papȳrus, -ī m/f papyrus; paper

pār, paris adj equal, like; a match for; proper, right ▸ m peer, partner, companion ▸ nt pair; **pār parī respondēre** return like for like; **parēs cum paribus facillimē congregantur** birds of a feather flock together; **lūdere pār impār** play at evens and odds

parābilis adj easy to get

parasīta, -ae f woman parasite

parasītaster, -rī m sorry parasite

parasīticus adj of a parasite

parasītus, -ī m parasite, sponger

parātē adv with preparation; carefully; promptly

parātiō, -ōnis f trying to get

paratragoedō, -āre vi to talk theatrically

parātus¹ ppp of **parō** ▸ adj ready; equipped; experienced

parātus², -ūs m preparation, equipment

Parca, -ae f Fate

parcē adv frugally; moderately

parcō, -cere, pepercī, -sum vt, vi (with dat) to spare, economize; to refrain from, forgo; (with infin) to forbear, stop

parcus adj sparing, thrifty; niggardly, scanty; chary

pardus, -ī m panther

pārēns, -entis pres p of **pāreō** ▸ adj obedient ▸ mpl subjects

parēns, -entis m/f parent, father, mother; ancestor; founder

parentālis adj parental ▸ ntpl festival in honour of dead ancestors and relatives

parentō, -āre vi to sacrifice in honour of dead parents or relatives; to avenge (with the death of another)

pāreō, -ēre, -uī, -itum vi to be visible, be evident; (with dat) to obey, submit to, comply with; **pāret** it is proved

pariēs, -etis m wall

parietinae, -ārum fpl ruins

Parīlia, -ium ntpl festival of Pales

parīlis adj equal

pariō, -ere, peperī, -tum vt to give birth to; to produce, create, cause; to procure

Paris, -idis m son of Priam, abductor of Helen

pariter adv equally, alike; at the same time, together

paritō, -āre vt to get ready

Parius adj see **Paros**

parma, -ae f shield, buckler

parmātus adj armed with a buckler

parmula, -ae f little shield

Parnāsis, -idis adj Parnassian

Parnāsius adj = **Parnāsis**

Parnāsus, -ī m Mount Parnassus in central Greece, sacred to the Muses

parō, -āre, -āvī, -ātum vt to prepare, get ready, provide; to intend, set about; to procure, get, buy; to arrange

parocha, -ae f provision of necessaries (to officials travelling)

parochus, -ī m purveyor; host

paropsis, -dis f dish

Paros, -ī f Aegean island (famous for white marble)

parra, -ae f owl

Parrhasis, -idis, Parrhasius adj Arcadian

parricīda, -ae m parricide, assassin; traitor

parricīdium, -ī and -iī nt parricide, murder; high treason

pars, -tis f part, share, fraction; party, side; direction; respect, degree; (with pl verb) some; (pl) stage part, role; duty, function; **māgna ~** the majority; **māgnam partem** largely; **in eam partem** in that direction, on that side, in that sense; **nullā parte** not at all; **omnī parte** entirely; **ex parte** partly; **ex alterā parte** on the other hand; **ex māgnā parte** to a large extent; **prō parte** to the best of one's ability; **partēs agere** play a part; **duae partēs** two-thirds; **trēs partēs** three-fourths; **multīs partibus** a great deal

parsimōnia, -ae f thrift, frugality

parthenicē, -ēs f a plant

Parthenopē, -ēs f old name of Naples

Parthenopēius adj see **Parthenopē**

Parthī, -ōrum mpl Parthians (Rome's great enemy in the East)

Parthicus, Parthus adj see **Parthī**

particeps, -ipis adj sharing, partaking ▶ m partner

participō, -āre vt to share, impart, inform

particula, -ae f particle

partim adv partly, in part; mostly; some ... others

partiō, -īre, -īvī, -ītum, partior, -īrī vt to share, distribute, divide

partītē adv methodically

partītiō, -ōnis f distribution, division

parturiō, -īre vi to be in labour; (fig) to be anxious ▶ vt to teem with, be ready to produce; (mind) to brood over

partus¹ ppp of **pariō** ▶ ntpl possessions

partus², -ūs m birth; young

parum adv too little, not enough; not very, scarcely

parumper adv for a little while

parvitās, -ātis f smallness

parvulus, parvolus adj very small, slight; quite young ▶ m child

parvus (compar **minor**, superl **minimus**) adj small, little, slight; (time) short; (age) young; **parvī esse** be of little value

Pascha, -ae f Easter

pāscō, -scere, -vī, -stum vt to feed, put to graze; to keep, foster; (fig) to feast, cherish ▶ vi to graze, browse

pāscuus adj for pasture ▶ nt pasture

Pāsiphaē, -ēs f wife of Minos (mother of the Minotaur)

passer, -is m sparrow; (fish) plaice; **~ marīnus** ostrich

passerculus, -ī m little sparrow

passim adv here and there, at random; indiscriminately

passum, -ī nt raisin wine

passus¹ ppp of **pandō** ▶ adj spread out, dishevelled; dried

passus² ppa of **patior**

passus³, -ūs m step, pace; footstep; **mille passūs** mile; **mīlia passuum** miles

pastillus, -ī m lozenge

pāstor, -ōris m shepherd

pāstōrālis adj shepherd's, pastoral

pāstōricius, pāstōrius adj shepherd's

pāstus¹ ppp of **pāscō**

pāstus², -ūs m pasture, food

Patara, -ae f town in Lycia (with oracle of Apollo)

Pataraeus, Patareus adj see **Patara**

Patavīnus adj see **Patavium**

Patavium, -ī nt birthplace of Livy (now Padua)

patefaciō, -facere, -fēcī, -factum (pass **-fīō**) vt to open, open up; to disclose

patefactiō, -ōnis f disclosing

patefīō etc see **patefaciō**

patella, -ae f small dish, plate

patēns, -entis pres p of **pateō** ▶ adj open, accessible, exposed; broad; evident

patenter adv clearly

pateō, -ēre, -uī vi to be open, accessible, exposed; to extend; to be evident, known

pater, -ris m father; (pl) forefathers; senators

patera, -ae f dish, saucer, bowl

paterfamiliās, patrisfamiliās m master of the house

paternus adj father's, paternal; native

patēscō, -ere vi to open out; to extend; to become evident

patibilis adj endurable; sensitive

patibulātus adj pilloried

patibulum, -ī nt fork-shaped yoke, pillory

patiēns, -entis pres p of **patior** ▶ adj able to endure; patient; unyielding

patienter adv patiently

patientia, -ae f endurance, stamina; forbearance; submissiveness

patina, -ae f dish, pan

patior, -tī, -ssus vt to suffer, experience; to submit to; to allow, put up with; **facile patī** be well pleased with; **aegrē patī** be displeased with

Patrae, -ārum fpl Greek seaport (now Patras)

patrātor, -ōris m doer

patrātus adj: **pater ~** officiating priest

Patrēnsis adj see **Patrae**

patria, -ae f native land, native town, home

patricius adj patrician ▶ m aristocrat

patrimōnium, -ī and -iī nt inheritance, patrimony

patrimus adj having a father living

patrissō, -āre vi to take after one's father
patrītus adj of one's father
patrius adj father's; hereditary, native
patrō, -āre, -āvī, -ātum vt to achieve, execute, complete
patrōcinium, -ī and **-iī** nt patronage, advocacy, defence
patrōcinor, -ārī vi (with dat) to defend, support
patrōna, -ae f patron goddess; protectress, safeguard
patrōnus, -ī m patron, protector; (LAW) advocate, counsel
patruēlis adj cousin's ▸ m cousin
patruus, -ī m (paternal) uncle ▸ adj uncle's
patulus adj open; spreading, broad
paucitās, -ātis f small number, scarcity
pauculus adj very few
paucus adj few, little ▸ mpl a few, the select few ▸ ntpl a few words
paulātim adv little by little, gradually
paulisper adv for a little while
Paullus, -ī m = **Paulus**
paulō adv a little, somewhat
paululus adj very little ▸ nt a little bit
paulum adv = **paulō**
paulus adj little
Paulus, -ī m a Roman surname (esp victor of Pydna)
pauper, -is adj poor; meagre ▸ mpl the poor
pauperculus adj poor
pauperiēs, -ēī f poverty
pauperō, -āre vt to impoverish; to rob
paupertās, -ātis f poverty, moderate means
pausa, -ae f stop, end
pauxillātim adv bit by bit
pauxillulus adj very little
pauxillus adj little
pavefactus adj frightened
paveō, -ēre, pāvī vi to be terrified, quake ▸ vt to dread, be scared of
pavēscō, -ere vt, vi to become alarmed (at)
pāvī perf of **pāscō**
pavidē adv in a panic
pavidus adj quaking, terrified
pavīmentātus adj paved
pavīmentum, -ī nt pavement, floor
paviō, -īre vt to strike
pavitō, -āre vi to be very frightened; to shiver
pāvō, -ōnis m peacock
pavor, -ōris m terror, panic
pāx, pācis f peace; (gods) grace; (mind) serenity ▸ interj enough!; **pāce tuā** by your leave
peccātum, -ī nt mistake, fault, sin
peccō, -āre, -āvī, -ātum vi to make a mistake, go wrong, offend
pecorōsus adj rich in cattle
pecten, -inis m comb; (fish) scallop; (loom) reed; (lyre) plectrum
pectō, -ctere, -xī, -xum vt to comb
pectus, -oris nt breast; heart, feeling; mind, thought
pecū nt flock of sheep; (pl) pastures

pecuārius adj of cattle ▸ m cattle breeder ▸ ntpl herds
pecūlātor, -ōris m embezzler
pecūlātus, -ūs m embezzlement
pecūliāris adj one's own; special
pecūliātus adj provided with money
pecūliōsus adj with private property
pecūlium, -ī and **-iī** nt small savings, private property
pecūnia, -ae f property; money
pecūniārius adj of money
pecūniōsus adj moneyed, well-off
pecus¹, -oris nt cattle, herd, flock; animal
pecus², -udis f sheep, head of cattle, beast
pedālis adj a foot long
pedārius adj (senator) without full rights
pedes, -itis m foot soldier, infantry ▸ adj on foot
pedester, -ris adj on foot, pedestrian; infantry-(in cpds); on land; (writing) in prose, prosaic
pedetemptim adv step by step, cautiously
pedica, -ae f fetter, snare
pedis, -is m louse
pedisequa, -ae f handmaid
pedisequus, -ī m attendant, lackey
peditātus, -ūs m infantry
pedum, -ī nt crook
Pēgaseus, Pēgasis, -idis adj Pegasean
Pēgasus, -ī m mythical winged horse (associated with the Muses)
pēgma, -tis nt bookcase; stage elevator
pēierō, -āre vi to perjure oneself
pēior, -ōris compar of **malus**
pēius adv worse
pelagius adj of the sea
pelagus, -ī (pl **-ē**) nt sea, open sea
pelamys, -dis f young tuna fish
Pelasgī, -ōrum mpl Greeks
Pelasgias, Pelasgis, Pelasgus adj Grecian
Pēleus, -eī and **-eos** (acc **-ea**) m king of Thessaly (father of Achilles)
Peliās, -ae m uncle of Jason
Pēlias, Pēliacus, Pēlius adj see **Pēlion**
Pēlīdēs, -īdae m Achilles; Neoptolemus
Pēlion, -ī nt mountain in Thessaly
Pella, -ae, Pellē, -ēs f town of Macedonia (birthplace of Alexander)
pellācia, -ae f attraction
Pellaeus adj of Pella; Alexandrian; Egyptian
pellāx, -ācis adj seductive
pellēctiō, -ōnis f reading through
pellectus ppp of **pelliciō**
pellegō etc see **perlegō**
pelliciō, -icere, -exī, -ectum vt to entice, inveigle
pellicula, -ae f skin, fleece
pelliō, -ōnis m furrier
pellis, -is f skin, hide; leather, felt; tent
pellītus adj wearing skins, with leather coats
pellō, -ere, pepulī, pulsum vt to push, knock, drive; to drive off, rout, expel; (lyre) to play; (mind) to touch, affect; (feeling) to banish
pellūc- etc see **perlūc-**

Pelopēis, Pelopēias, Pelopēius, Pelopēus
adj see **Pelops**
Pelopidae, -idārum mpl house of Pelops
Peloponnēsiacus, -ius adj see **Peloponnēsus**
Peloponnēsus, -ī f Peloponnese, S. Greece
Pelops, -is m son of Tantalus (grandfather of
Agamemnon)
pelōris, -idis f a large mussel
pelta, -ae f light shield
peltastae, -ārum mpl peltasts
peltātus adj armed with the pelta
Pēlūsiacus adj see **Pēlūsium**
Pēlūsium, -ī nt Egyptian town at the E. mouth
of the Nile
Pēlūsius adj see **Pēlūsium**
pelvis, -is f basin
penārius adj provision- (in cpds)
Penātēs, -ium mpl spirits of the larder,
household gods; home
penātiger, -ī adj carrying his home gods
pendeō, -ēre, pependī vi to hang; to
overhang, hover; to hang down, be flabby; (fig)
to depend; to gaze, listen attentively; (mind) to
be in suspense, be undecided
pendō, -ere, pependī, pēnsum vt to weigh;
to pay; (fig) to ponder, value ▸ vi to weigh
pendulus adj hanging; in doubt
Pēnēis adj see **Pēnēus**
Pēnelopē, -ēs, Pēnelopa, -ae f wife of Ulysses
(famed for her constancy)
Pēnelopēus adj see **Pēnelopē**
penes prep (with acc) in the power or possession
of; in the house of, with
penetrābilis adj penetrable; piercing
penetrālis adj penetrating; inner, inmost ▸ ntpl
inner room, interior, sanctuary; remote parts
penetrō, -āre, -āvī, -ātum vt, vi to put into,
penetrate, enter
Pēnēus, -ī m chief river of Thessaly
pēnicillus, -ī m painter's brush, pencil
pēniculus, -ī m brush; sponge
pēnis, -is m penis
penitē adj inwardly
penitus adv inside, deep within; deeply, from
the depths; utterly, thoroughly
penna, pinna, -ae f feather, wing; flight
pennātus adj winged
penniger, -ī adj feathered
pennipotēns, -entis adj winged
pennula, -ae f little wing
pēnsilis adj hanging, pendent
pēnsiō, -ōnis f payment, instalment
pēnsitō, -āre vt to pay; to consider
pēnsō, -āre, -āvī, -ātum vt to weight out; to
compensate, repay; to consider, judge
pēnsum, -ī nt spinner's work; task, duty;
weight, value; **pēnsī esse** be of importance;
pēnsī habēre care at all about
pēnsus ppp of **pendō**
pentēris, -is f quinquereme
Penteus, -eī and **-eos** m king of Thebes
(killed by Bacchantes)

pēnūria, -ae f want, need
penus, -ūs and **-ī** m/f, **penum, -ī** nt, **penus,
-oris** nt provisions, store of food
pependī perf of **pendeō**; **pendō**
pepercī perf of **parcō**
peperī perf of **pariō**
pepigī perf of **pangō**
peplum, -ī nt, **peplus, -ī** m state robe of
Athena
pepulī perf of **pellō**
per prep (with acc: space) through, all over;
(: time) throughout, during; (: means) by, by
means of; (: cause) by reason of, for the sake of;
per īram in anger; **per manūs** from hand to
hand; **per mē** as far as I am concerned; **per vim**
forcibly; **per ego tē deōs ōrō** in Heaven's name
I beg you
pēra, -ae f bag
perabsurdus adj very absurd
peraccommodātus adj very convenient
perācer, -ris adj very sharp
peracerbus adj very sour
peracēscō, -ēscere, -uī vi to get vexed
perāctiō, -ōnis f last act
perāctus ppp of **peragō**
peracūtē adv very acutely
peracūtus adj very sharp, very clear
peradulēscēns, -entis adj very young
peraequē adv quite equally, uniformly
peragitātus adj harried
peragō, -agere, -ēgī, -āctum vt to carry
through, complete; to pass through, pierce;
to disturb; (LAW) to prosecute to a conviction;
(words) to go over, describe
peragrātiō, -ōnis f travelling
peragrō, -āre, -āvī, -ātum vt to travel
through, traverse
peramāns, -antis adj very fond
peramānter adv devotedly
perambulō, -āre vt to walk through, traverse
peramoenus adj very pleasant
peramplus adj very large
perangustē adv see **perangustus**
perangustus adj very narrow
perantīquus adj very old
perappositus adj very suitable
perarduus adj very difficult
perargūtus adj very witty
perarō, -āre vt to furrow; to write (on wax)
perattentē adv see **perattentus**
perattentus adj very attentive
peraudiendus adj to be heard to the end
perbacchor, -ārī vt to carouse through
perbeātus adj very happy
perbellē adv very nicely
perbene adv very well
perbenevolus adj very friendly
perbenignē adv very kindly
perbibō, -ere, -ī vt to drink up, imbibe
perbītō, -ere vi to perish
perblandus adj very charming
perbonus adj very good

perbrevis adj very short
perbreviter adv very briefly
perca, -ae f perch
percalefactus adj quite hot
percalēscō, -ēscere, -uī vi to become quite hot
percallēscō, -ēscere, -uī vi to become quite hardened ▸ vt to become thoroughly versed in
percārus adj very dear
percautus adj very cautious
percelebrō, -āre vt to talk much of
perceler, -is adj very quick
perceleriter adv see **perceler**
percellō, -ellere, -ulī, -ulsum vt to knock down, upset; to strike; (fig) to ruin, overthrow; to discourage, unnerve
percēnseō, -ēre, -uī vt to count over; (place) to travel through; (fig) to review
perceptiō, -ōnis f harvesting; understanding, idea
perceptus ppp of **percipiō**
percieō, -iēre, -iō, -īre vt to rouse, excite
percipiō, -ipere, -ēpī, -eptum vt to take, get hold of; to gather in; (senses) to feel; (mind) to learn, grasp, understand
percitus ppp of **percieō** ▸ adj roused, excited; excitable
percoctus ppp of **percoquō**
percolō¹, -āre vt to filter through
percolō², -olere, -oluī, -ultum vt to embellish; to honour
percōmis adj very friendly
percommodē adv very conveniently
percommodus adj very suitable
percontātiō, -ōnis f asking questions
percontātor, -ōris m inquisitive person
percontor, -ārī, -ātus vt to question, inquire
percontumāx, -ācis adj very obstinate
percoquō, -quere, -xī, -ctum vt to cook thoroughly, heat, scorch, ripen
percrēbēscō, percrēbrēscō, -ēscere, -uī vi to be spread abroad
percrepō, -āre, -uī vi to resound
perculī perf of **percellō**
perculsus ppp of **percellō**
percultus ppp of **percolō²**
percunct- etc see **percont-**
percupidus adj very fond
percupiō, -ere vi to wish very much
percūriōsus adj very inquisitive
percūrō, -āre vt to heal completely
percurrō, -rrere, -currī and **-rrī, -rsum** vt to run through, hurry over; (fig) to run over, look over ▸ vi to run along; to pass
percursātiō, -ōnis f travelling through
percursiō, -ōnis f running over
percursō, -āre vi to rove about
percursus ppp of **percurrō**
percussiō, -ōnis f beating; (fingers) snapping; (music) time
percussor, -ōris m assassin
percussus¹ ppp of **percutiō**

percussus², -ūs m striking
percutiō, -tere, -ssī, -ssum vt to strike, beat; to strike through, kill; (feeling) to shock, impress, move; (colloq) to trick
perdēlīrus adj quite crazy
perdidī perf of **perdō**
perdifficilis adj very difficult
perdifficiliter adv with great difficulty
perdignus adj most worthy
perdīligēns, -entis adj very diligent
perdīligenter adv see **perdīligēns**
perdiscō, -scere, -dicī vt to learn by heart
perdisertē adv very eloquently
perditē adv desperately; recklessly
perditor, -ōris m destroyer
perditus ppp of **perdō** ▸ adj desperate, ruined; abandoned, profligate
perdiū adv for a very long time
perdiūturnus adj protracted
perdīves, -itis adj very rich
perdīx, -īcis m/f partridge
perdō, -ere, -idī, -itum vt to destroy, ruin; to squander, waste; to lose; **dī tē perduint** curse you!
perdoceō, -ēre, -uī, -tum vt to teach thoroughly
perdolēscō, -ēscere, -uī vi to take it to heart
perdomō, -āre, -uī, -itum vt to subjugate, tame completely
perdormīscō, -ere vi to sleep on
perdūcō, -ūcere, -ūxī, -uctum vt to bring, guide to; to induce, seduce; to spread over; to prolong, continue
perductō, -āre vt to guide
perductor, -ōris m guide; pander
perductus ppp of **perdūcō**
perduelliō, -ōnis f treason
perduellis, -is m enemy
perduim archaic subj of **perdō**
perdūrō, -āre vi to endure, hold out
peredō, -edere, -ēdī, -ēsum vt to consume, devour
peregrē adv away from home, abroad; from abroad
peregrīnābundus adj travelling
peregrīnātiō, -ōnis f living abroad, travel
peregrīnātor, -ōris m traveller
peregrīnitās, -ātis f foreign manners
peregrīnor, -ārī, -ātus vi to be abroad, travel; to be a stranger
peregrīnus adj foreign, strange ▸ m foreigner, alien
perēlegāns, -antis adj very polished
perēleganter adv in a very polished manner
perēloquēns, -entis adj very eloquent
perēmī perf of **perimō**
peremnia, -ium ntpl auspices taken on crossing a river
peremptus ppp of **perimō**
perendiē adv the day after tomorrow
perendinus adj (the day) after tomorrow
perennis adj perpetual, unfailing

perennitās, -ātis f continuance
perennō, -āre vi to last a long time
pereō, -īre, -iī, -itum vi to be lost, pass away, perish, die; (fig) to be wasted, be in love, be undone
perequitō, -āre vt, vi to ride up and down
pererrō, -āre, -āvī, -ātum vt to roam over, cover
perērudītus adj very learned
perēsus ppp of **peredō**
perexcelsus adj very high
perexiguē adv very meagrely
perexiguus adj very small, very short
perfacetē adv very wittily
perfacētus adj very witty
perfacilē adv very easily
perfacilis adj very easy; very courteous
perfamiliāris adj very intimate ▸ m very close friend
perfectē adv fully
perfectiō, -ōnis f completion, perfection
perfector, -ōris m perfecter
perfectus ppp of **perficiō** ▸ adj complete, perfect
perferō, -ferre, -tulī, -lātum vt to carry through, bring, convey; to bear, endure, put up with; (work) to finish, bring to completion; (LAW) to get passed; (message) to bring news
perficiō, -icere, -ēcī, -ectum vt to carry out, finish, complete; to perfect; to cause, make
perficus adj perfecting
perfidēlis adj very loyal
perfidia, -ae f treachery, dishonesty
perfidiōsē adv see **perfidiōsus**
perfidiōsus adj treacherous, dishonest
perfidus adj treacherous, faithless
perfigō, -gere, -xī, -xum vt to pierce
perflābilis adj that can be blown through
perflāgitiōsus adj very wicked
perflō, -āre vt to blow through, blow over
perfluctuō, -āre vt to flood through
perfluō, -ere, -xī vi to run out, leak
perfodiō, -odere, -ōdī, -ossum vt to dig through, excavate, pierce
perforō, -āre, -āvī, -ātum vt to bore through, pierce
perfortiter adv very bravely
perfossor, -ōris m: ~ parietum burglar
perfossus ppp of **perfodiō**
perfrāctus ppp of **perfringō**
perfrēgī perf of **perfringō**
perfremō, -ere vi to snort along
perfrequēns, -entis adj much frequented
perfricō, -āre, -uī, -tum and **-ātum** vt to rub all over; ōs perfricāre put on a bold face
perfrīgefaciō, -ere vt to make shudder
perfrīgēscō, -gēscere, -xī vi to catch a bad cold
perfrīgidus adj very cold
perfringō, -ingere, -ēgī, -āctum vt to break through, fracture, wreck; (fig) to violate; to affect powerfully

perfrīxī perf of **perfrīgēscō**
perfrūctus ppa of **perfruor**
perfruor, -uī, -ūctus vi (with abl) to enjoy to the full; to fulfil
perfuga, -ae m deserter
perfugiō, -ugere, -ūgī vi to flee for refuge, desert to
perfugium, -ī and **-iī** nt refuge, shelter
perfūnctiō, -ōnis f performing
perfūnctus ppa of **perfungor**
perfundō, -undere, -ūdī, -ūsum vt to pour over, drench, besprinkle; to dye; (fig) to flood, fill
perfungor, -gī, perfūnctus vi (with abl) to perform, discharge; to undergo
perfurō, -ere vi to rage furiously
perfūsus ppp of **perfundō**
Pergama, -ōrum ntpl Troy
Pergamēnus adj see **Pergama**
Pergameus adj Trojan
Pergamum, -ī nt town in Mysia (famous for its library)
pergaudeō, -ēre vi to be very glad
pergō, -gere, -rēxī, -rēctum vi to proceed, go on, continue ▸ vt to go on with, continue
pergraecor, -ārī vi to have a good time
pergrandis adj very large; very old
pergraphicus adj very artful
pergrātus adj very pleasant
pergravis adj very weighty
pergraviter adv very seriously
pergula, -ae f balcony; school; brothel
perhibeō, -ēre, -uī, -itum vt to assert, call, cite
perhīlum adv very little
perhonōrificē adv very respectfully
perhonōrificus adj very complimentary
perhorrēscō, -ēscere, -uī vi to shiver, tremble violently ▸ vt to have a horror of
perhorridus adj quite horrible
perhūmāniter adv see **perhūmānus**
perhūmānus adj very polite
Periclēs, -is and **-ī** m famous Athenian statesman and orator
perīclitātiō, -ōnis f experiment
perīclitor, -ārī, -ātus vt to test, try; to risk, endanger ▸ vi to attempt, venture; to run a risk, be in danger
perīculōsē adv see **perīculōsus**
perīculōsus adj dangerous, hazardous
perīculum, perīclum, -ī nt danger, risk; trial, attempt; (LAW) lawsuit, writ
peridōneus adj very suitable
periī perf of **pereō**
perillūstris adj very notable; highly honoured
perimbēcillus adj very weak
perimō, -imere, -ēmī, -emptum vt to destroy, prevent, kill
perincommodē adv see **perincommodus**
perincommodus adj very inconvenient
perinde adv just as, exactly as
perindulgēns, -entis adj very tender
perinfirmus adj very feeble

peringeniōsus *adj* very clever
periniquus *adj* very unfair; very discontented
perinsignis *adj* very conspicuous
perinvītus *adj* very unwilling
periodus, -ī *f* sentence, period
Peripatēticī, -ōrum *mpl* Peripatetics (followers of Aristotle)
peripetasmata, -um *ntpl* curtains
perīrātus *adj* very angry
periscelis, -dis *f* anklet
peristrōma, -atis *nt* coverlet
peristylum, -ī *nt* colonnade, peristyle
perītē *adv* expertly
perītia, -ae *f* practical knowledge, skill
perītus *adj* experienced, skilled, expert
periūcundē *adv see* **periūcundus**
periūcundus *adj* very enjoyable
periūrium, -ī *and* **-iī** *nt* perjury
periūrō *see* **pēierō**
periūrus *adj* perjured, lying
perlābor, -bī, -psus *vi* to glide along *or* through, move on
perlaetus *adj* very glad
perlāpsus *ppa of* **perlābor**
perlātē *adv* very extensively
perlateō, -ēre *vi* to lie quite hidden
perlātus *ppp of* **perferō**
perlegō, -egere, -ēgī, -ēctum *vt* to survey; to read through
perlevis *adj* very slight
perleviter *adv see* **perlevis**
perlibēns, -entis *adj* very willing
perlibenter *adv see* **perlibēns**
perlīberālis *adj* very genteel
perlīberāliter *adv* very liberally
perlibet, -ēre *vi (impers)* (I) should very much like
perliciō *etc see* **pelliciō**
perlītō, -āre, -āvī, -ātum *vi* to sacrifice with auspicious results
perlongē *adv* very far
perlongus *adj* very long, very tedious
perlub- *etc see* **perlib-**
perlūceō, -cēre, -xī *vi* to shine through, be transparent; *(fig)* to be quite intelligible
perlūcidulus *adj* transparent
perlūcidus *adj* transparent; very bright
perlūctuōsus *adj* very mournful
perluō, -ere *vt* to wash thoroughly; *(pass)* to bathe
perlūstrō, -āre *vt* to traverse; *(fig)* to survey
permāgnus *adj* very big, very great
permānanter *adv* by flowing through
permānāscō, -ere *vi* to penetrate
permaneō, -anēre, -ānsī, -ānsum *vi* to last, persist, endure to the end
permānō, -āre, -āvī, -ātum *vi* to flow *or* ooze through, penetrate
permānsiō, -ōnis *f* continuing, persisting
permarīnus *adj* of seafaring
permātūrēscō, -ēscere, -uī *vi* to ripen fully
permediocris *adj* very moderate

permēnsus *ppa of* **permētior**
permeō, -āre *vt, vi* to pass through, penetrate
permētior, -tīrī, -nsus *vt* to measure out; to traverse
permīrus *adj* very wonderful
permisceō, -scēre, -scuī, -xtum *vt* to mingle, intermingle; to throw into confusion
permissiō, -ōnis *f* unconditional surrender; permission
permissus¹ *ppp of* **permittō**
permissus², -ūs *m* leave, permission
permitiālis *adj* destructive
permitiēs, -ēī *f* ruin
permittō, -ittere, -īsī, -issum *vt* to let go, let pass; to hurl; to give up, entrust, concede; to allow, permit
permixtē *adv see* **permixtus**
permixtiō, -ōnis *f* mixture; disturbance
permixtus *ppp of* **permisceō** ▸ *adj* promiscuous, disordered
permodestus *adj* very moderate
permoleste *adv* with much annoyance
permolestus *adj* very troublesome
permōtiō, -ōnis *f* excitement; emotion
permōtus *ppp of* **permoveō**
permoveō, -ovēre, -ōvī, -ōtum *vt* to stir violently; *(fig)* to influence, induce; to excite, move deeply
permulceō, -cēre, -sī, -sum *vt* to stroke, caress; *(fig)* to charm, flatter; to soothe, appease
permulsus *ppp of* **permulceō**
permultus *adj* very much, very many
permūniō, -īre, -īvī, -ītum *vt* to finish fortifying; to fortify strongly
permūtātiō, -ōnis *f* change, exchange
permūtō, -āre, -āvī, -ātum *vt* to change completely; to exchange; *(money)* to remit by bill of exchange
perna, -ae *f* ham
pernecessārius *adj* very necessary; very closely related
pernecesse *adj* indispensable
pernegō, -āre *vi* to deny flatly
perniciābilis *adj* ruinous
perniciēs, -ēī *f* destruction, ruin, death
perniciōsē *adv see* **perniciōsus**
perniciōsus *adj* ruinous
pernīcitās, -ātis *f* agility, swiftness
pernīciter *adv* nimbly
pernimius *adj* much too much
pernīx, -īcis *adj* nimble, agile, swift
pernōbilis *adj* very famous
pernoctō, -āre *vi* to stay all night
pernōscō, -scere, -vī, -tum *vt* to examine thoroughly; to become fully acquainted with, know thoroughly
pernōtēscō, -ēscere, -uī *vi* to become generally known
pernōtus *ppp of* **pernōscō**
pernox, -octis *adj* all night long
pernumerō, -āre *vt* to count up

pĕrō, -ōnis m rawhide boot
perobscūrus adj very obscure
perodiōsus adj very troublesome
perofficiōsē adv very attentively
peroleō, -ēre vi to give off a strong smell
peropportūnē adv very opportunely
peropportūnus adj very timely
peroptātō adv very much to one's wish
peropus est it is most essential
perōrātiō, -ōnis f peroration
perōrnātus adj very ornate
perōrnō, -āre vt to give great distinction to
perōrō, -āre, -āvī, -ātum vt to plead at
  length; (speech) to bring to a close; to conclude
perōsus adj detesting
perpācō, -āre vt to quieten completely
perparcē adv very stingily
perparvulus adj very tiny
perparvus adj very small
perpāstus adj well fed
perpauculus adj very very few
perpaucus adj very little, very few
perpaulum, -ī nt a very little
perpauper, -is adj very poor
perpauxillum, -ī nt a very little
perpellō, -ellere, -ulī, -ulsum vt to urge,
  force, influence
perpendiculum, -ī nt plumbline; **ad ~**
  perpendicularly
perpendō, -endere, -endī, -ēnsum vt to
  weigh carefully, judge
perperam adv wrongly, falsely
perpes, -etis adj continuous
perpessiō, -ōnis f suffering, enduring
perpessus ppa of perpetior
perpetior, -tī, -ssus vt to endure patiently,
  allow
perpetrō, -āre, -āvī, -ātum vt to perform,
  carry out
perpetuitās, -ātis f continuity, uninterrupted
  duration
perpetuō¹ adv without interruption, forever,
  utterly
perpetuō², -āre vt to perpetuate, preserve
perpetuus adj continuous, entire; universal; **in
  perpetuum** forever
perplaceō, -ēre vi to please greatly
perplexē adv obscurely
perplexor, -ārī vi to cause confusion
perplexus adj confused, intricate, obscure
perplicātus adj interlaced
perpluō, -ere vi to let the rain through, leak
perpoliō, -īre, -īvī, -ītum vt to polish
  thoroughly
perpolītus adj finished, refined
perpopulor, -ārī, -ātus vt to ravage
  completely
perpōtātiō, -ōnis f drinking bout
perpōtō, -āre vi to drink continuously ▶ vt to
  drink off
perprimō, -ere vt to lie on
perpugnāx, -ācis adj very pugnacious

perpulcher, -rī adj very beautiful
perpulī perf of perpellō
perpūrgō, -āre, -āvī, -ātum vt to make quite
  clean; to explain
perpusillus adj very little
perquam adv very, extremely
perquīrō, -rere, -sīvī, -sītum vt to search for,
  inquire after; to examine carefully
perquīsītius adv more accurately
perrārō adv very seldom
perrārus adj very uncommon
perreconditus adj very abstruse
perrēpō, -ere vt to crawl over
perrēptō, -āre, -āvī, -ātum vt, vi to creep
  about or through
perrēxī perf of pergō
perrīdiculē adv see perrīdiculus
perrīdiculus adj very laughable
perrogātiō, -ōnis f passing (of a law)
perrogō, -āre vt to ask one after another
perrumpō, -umpere, -ūpī, -uptum vt, vi
  to break through, force a way through; (fig) to
  break down
perruptus ppp of perrumpō
Persae, -ārum mpl Persians
persaepe adv very often
persalsē adv see persalsus
persalsus adj very witty
persalūtātiō, -ōnis f greeting everyone in
  turn
persalūtō, -āre vt to greet in turn
persanctē adv most solemnly
persapiēns, -entis adj very wise
persapienter adv see persapiēns
perscienter adv very discreetly
perscindō, -ndere, -dī, -ssum vt to tear
  apart
perscītus adj very smart
perscrībō, -bere, -psī, -ptum vt to write
  in full; to describe, report; (record) to enter;
  (money) to make over in writing
perscrīptiō, -ōnis f entry; assignment
perscrīptor, -ōris m writer
perscrīptus ppp of perscrībō
perscrūtor, -ārī, -ātus vt to search, examine
  thoroughly
persecō, -āre, -uī, -tum vt to dissect; to do
  away with
persector, -ārī vt to investigate
persecūtiō, -ōnis f (LAW) prosecution
persecūtus ppa of persequor
persedeō, -edēre, -ēdī, -essum vi to remain
  sitting
persegnis adj very slow
Persēius adj see Perseus
persentiō, -entīre, -ēnsī vt to see clearly; to
  feel deeply
persentīscō, -ere vi to begin to see; to begin
  to feel
Persephonē, -ēs f Proserpine
persequor, -quī, -cūtus vt to follow all the
  way; to pursue, chase, hunt after; to overtake;

(*pattern*) to be a follower of, copy; (*enemy*) to proceed against, take revenge on; (*action*) to perform, carry out; (*words*) to write down, describe

Persēs¹, -ae m last king of Macedonia
Persēs², -ae m Persian
Perseus, -eī and **-eos** (acc **-ea**) m son of Danaë (killer of Medusa, rescuer of Andromeda)
Persēus adj see **Perseus**
persevērāns, -antis pres p of **persevērō** ▶ adj persistent
persevēranter adv see **persevērāns**
persevērantia, -ae f persistence
persevērō, -āre, -āvī, -ātum vi to persist ▶ vt to persist in
persevērus adj very strict
Persicum nt peach
Persicus adj Persian; of Perses
persīdō, -īdere, -ēdī, -essum vi to sink down into
persignō, -āre vt to record
persimilis adj very like
persimplex, -icis adj very simple
Persis, -idis f Persia
persistō, -istere, -titī vi to persist
persōlus adj one and only
persolūtus ppp of **persolvō**
persolvō, -vere, -vī, -ūtum vt to pay, pay up; to explain
persōna, -ae f mask; character, part; person, personality
persōnātus adj masked; in an assumed character
personō, -āre, -uī, -itum vi to resound, ring (with); to play ▶ vt to make resound; to cry aloud
perspectē adv intelligently
perspectō, -āre vt to have a look through
perspectus ppp of **perspiciō** ▶ adj well-known
perspeculor, -ārī vt to reconnoitre
perspergō, -gere, -sī, -sum vt to besprinkle
perspicāx, -ācis adj sharp, shrewd
perspicientia, -ae f full understanding
perspiciō, -icere, -exī, -ectum vt to see through; to examine, observe
perspicuē adv clearly
perspicuitās, -ātis f clarity
perspicuus adj transparent; clear, evident
persternō, -ernere, -rāvī, -rātum vt to pave all over
perstimulō, -āre vt to rouse violently
perstitī perf of **persistō; perstō**
perstō, -āre, -itī, -ātum vi to stand fast; to last; to continue, persist
perstrātus ppp of **persternō**
perstrepō, -ere vi to make a lot of noise
perstrictus ppp of **perstringō**
perstringō, -ingere, -inxī, -ictum vt to graze, touch lightly; (words) to touch on, belittle, censure; (senses) to dull, deaden
perstudiōsē adv very eagerly
perstudiōsus adj very fond

persuādeō, -dēre, -sī, -sum vi (with dat) to convince, persuade; **persuāsum habeō, mihi persuāsum est** I am convinced
persuāsiō, -ōnis f convincing
persuāsus, -ūs m persuasion
persubtīlis adj very fine
persultō, -āre vt, vi to prance about, frisk over
pertaedet, -dēre, -sum est vt (impers) to be weary of, be sick of
pertegō, -egere, -ēxī, -ēctum vt to cover over
pertemptō, -āre vt to test carefully; to consider well; to pervade, seize
pertendō, -ere, -ī vi to push on, persist ▶ vt to go on with
pertenuis adj very small, very slight
perterebrō, -āre vt to bore through
pertergeō, -gēre, -sī, -sum vt to wipe over; to touch lightly
perterrefaciō, -ere vt to scare thoroughly
perterreō, -ēre, -uī, -itum vt to frighten thoroughly
perterricrepus adj with a terrifying crash
perterritus adj terrified
pertexō, -ere, -uī, -tum vt to accomplish
pertica, -ae f pole, staff
pertimefactus adj very frightened
pertimēscō, -ēscere, -uī vt, vi to be very alarmed, be very afraid of
pertinācia, -ae f perseverance, stubbornness
pertināciter adv see **pertināx**
pertināx, -ācis adj very tenacious; unyielding, stubborn
pertineō, -ēre, -uī vi to extend, reach; to tend, lead to, concern; to apply, pertain, belong; **quod pertinet ad** as far as concerns
pertingō, -ere vi to extend
pertolerō, -āre vt to endure to the end
pertorqueō, -ēre vt to distort
pertractātē adv in a hackneyed fashion
pertractātiō, -ōnis f handling
pertractō, -āre vt to handle, feel all over; (fig) to treat, study
pertractus ppp of **pertrahō**
pertrahō, -here, -xī, -ctum vt to drag across, take forcibly; to entice
pertrect- etc see **pertract-**
pertristis adj very sad, very morose
pertulī perf of **perferō**
pertumultuōsē adv very excitedly
pertundō, -undere, -udī, -ūsum vt to perforate
perturbātē adv in confusion
perturbātiō, -ōnis f confusion, disturbance; emotion
perturbātrīx, -īcis f disturber
perturbātus ppp of **perturbō** ▶ adj troubled; alarmed
perturbō, -āre, -āvī, -ātum vt to throw into disorder, upset, alarm
perturpis adj scandalous
pertūsus ppp of **pertundō** ▶ adj in holes, leaky

perungō, -ungere, -ūnxī, -ūnctum vt to smear all over

perurbānus adj very refined; over-fine

perūrō, -rere, -ssī, -stum vt to burn up, scorch; to inflame, chafe; to freeze, nip

Perusia, -iae f Etruscan town (now Perugia)

Perusīnus adj see **Perusia**

perūstus ppp of **perūrō**

perūtilis adj very useful

pervādō, -dere, -sī, -sum vt, vi to pass through, spread through; to penetrate, reach

pervagātus adj widespread, well-known; general

pervagor, -ārī, -ātus vi to range, rove about; to extend, spread ▶ vt to pervade

pervagus adj roving

pervariē adv very diversely

pervāstō, -āre, -āvī, -ātum vt to devastate

pervāsus ppp of **pervādō**

pervectus ppp of **pervehō**

pervehō, -here, -xī, -ctum vt to carry, convey, bring through; (pass) to ride, drive, sail through; to attain

pervellō, -ere, -ī vt to pull, twitch, pinch; to stimulate; to disparage

perveniō, -enīre, -ēnī, -entum vi to come to, arrive, reach; to attain to

pervēnor, -ārī vi to chase through

perversē adv perversely

perversitās, -ātis f perverseness

perversus, pervorsus ppp of **pervertō** ▶ adj awry, squint; wrong, perverse

pervertō, -tere, -tī, -sum vt to overturn, upset; to overthrow, undo; (speech) to confute

pervesperī adv very late

pervestīgātiō, -ōnis f thorough search

pervestīgō, -āre, -āvī, -ātum vt to track down; to investigate

pervetus, -eris adj very old

pervetustus adj antiquated

pervicācia, -ae f obstinacy; firmness

pervicāciter adv see **pervicāx**

pervicāx, -ācis adj obstinate, wilful; dogged

pervictus ppp of **pervincō**

pervideō, -idēre, -īdī, -īsum vt to look over, survey; to consider; to discern

pervigeō, -ēre, -uī vi to continue to flourish

pervigil, -is adj awake, watchful

pervigilātiō, -ōnis f vigil

pervigilium, -ī and -iī nt vigil

pervigilō, -āre, -āvī, -ātum vt, vi to stay awake all night, keep vigil

pervīlis adj very cheap

pervincō, -incere, -īcī, -ictum vt, vi to conquer completely; to outdo, surpass; to prevail upon, effect; (argument) to carry a point, maintain, prove

pervius adj passable, accessible

pervīvō, -ere vi to survive

pervolgō etc see **pervulgō**

pervolitō, -āre vt, vi to fly about

pervolō¹, -āre, -āvī, -ātum vt, vi to fly through or over, fly to

pervolō², -elle, -oluī vi to wish very much

pervolūtō, -āre vt (books) to read through

pervolvō, -vere, -vī, -ūtum vt to tumble about; (book) to read through; (pass) to be very busy (with)

pervor- etc see **perver-**

pervulgātus adj very common

pervulgō, -āre, -āvī, -ātum vt to make public, impart; to haunt

pēs, pedis m foot; (length) foot; (verse) foot, metre; (sailrope) sheet; **pedem cōnferre** to close quarters; **pedem referre** go back; **ante pedēs** self-evident; **pedibus** on foot, by land; **pedibus īre in sententiam** take sides; **pedibus aequīs** (NAUT) with the wind right aft; **servus ā pedibus** footman

pessimē superl of **male**

pessimus superl of **malus**

pessulus, -ī m bolt

pessum adv to the ground, to the bottom; **~ dare** put an end to, ruin, destroy; **~ īre** sink, perish

pestifer, -ī adj pestilential; baleful, destructive

pestilēns, -entis adj unhealthy; destructive

pestilentia, -ae f plague, pest; unhealthiness

pestilitās, -ātis f plague

pestis, -is f plague, pest; ruin, destruction

petasātus adj wearing the petasus

petasunculus, -ī m small leg of pork

petasus, -ī m broadbrimmed hat

petessō, -ere vt to be eager for

petītiō, -ōnis f thrust, attack; request, application; (office) candidature, standing for; (LAW) civil suit, right of claim

petītor, -ōris m candidate; plaintiff

petīturiō, -īre vt to long to be a candidate

petītus¹ ppp of **petō**

petītus², -ūs m falling to

petō, -ere, -īvī and -iī, -ītum vt to aim at, attack; (place) to make for, go to; to seek, look for, demand, ask; to go and fetch; (LAW) to sue; (love) to court; (office) to stand for

petorritum, -ī nt carriage

petrō, -ōnis m yokel

Petrōnius, -ī m arbiter of fashion under Nero

petulāns, -antis adj pert, impudent, lascivious

petulanter adv see **petulāns**

petulantia, -ae f pertness, impudence

petulcus adj butting

pexus ppp of **pectō**

Phaeāces, -cum mpl fabulous islanders in the Odyssey

Phaeācius, Phaeācus, Phaeax adj Phaeacian

Phaedra, -ae f stepmother of Hippolytus

Phaedrus, -ī m pupil of Socrates; writer of Latin fables

Phaethōn, -ontis m son of the Sun (killed while driving his father's chariot)

Phaethonteus *adj see* **Phaethōn**
Phaethontiades, -um *fpl* sisters of Phaethon
phalangae, -ārum *fpl* wooden rollers
phalangītae, -ārum *mpl* soldiers of a phalanx
phalanx, -gis *f* phalanx; troops, battle order
Phalaris, -dis *m* tyrant of Agrigentum
phalerae, -ārum *fpl* medallions, badges;
(*horse*) trappings
phalerātus *adj* wearing medallions;
ornamented
Phalēreus, -icus *adj see* **Phalērum**
Phalērum, -ī *nt* harbour of Athens
pharetra, -ae *f* quiver
pharetrātus *adj* wearing a quiver
Pharius *adj see* **Pharus**
pharmaceutria, -ae *f* sorceress
pharmacopōla, -ae *m* quack doctor
Pharsālicus, -ius *adj see* **Pharsālus**
Pharsālus, Pharsālos, -ī *f* town in Thessaly
(*where Caesar defeated Pompey*)
Pharus, Pharos, -ī *f* island off Alexandria with a
famous lighthouse; lighthouse
phasēlus, -ī *m/f* French bean; (*boat*) pinnace
Phāsiacus *adj* Colchian
Phāsiāna, -āna *m/f* pheasant
Phāsis¹, -dis *and* **-dos** *m* river of Colchis
Phāsis² *adj see* **Phāsis¹**
phasma, -tis *nt* ghost
Pherae, -ārum *fpl* town in Thessaly (*home of
Admetus*)
Pheraeus *adj see* **Pherae**
phiala, -ae *f* saucer
Phīdiacus *adj see* **Phīdiās**
Phīdiās, -ae *m* famous Athenian sculptor
philēma, -tis *nt* kiss
Philippēus *adj see* **Philippus**
Philippī, -ōrum *mpl* town in Macedonia (*where
Brutus and Cassius were defeated*)
Philippicae *fpl* Cicero's speeches against Antony
Philippicus *adj see* **Philippus**
Philippus, -ī *m* king of Macedonia; gold coin
philitia, phīditia, -ōrum *ntpl* public meals
at Sparta
Philō, Philōn, -ōnis *m* Academic philosopher
(*teacher of Cicero*)
Philoctētēs, -ae *m* Greek archer who gave
Hercules poisoned arrows
philologia, -ae *f* study of literature
philologus *adj* scholarly, literary
Philomēla, -ae *f* sister of Procne; nightingale
philosophē *adv see* **philosophus**
philosophia, -ae *f* philosophy
philosophor, -ārī, -ātus *vi* to philosophize
philosophus, -ī *m* philosopher ▸ *adj*
philosophical
philtrum, -ī *nt* love potion
philyra, -ae *f* inner bark of the lime tree
phīmus, -ī *m* dice box
Phlegethōn, -ontis *m* a river of Hades
Phlegethontis *adj see* **Phlegethōn**
Phliāsius *adj see* **Phliūs**
Phliūs, -ūntis *f* town in Peloponnese

phōca, -ae *f* seal
Phōcaicus *adj see* **Phōcis**
Phōcēus *adj see* **Phōcis**
Phōcis, -idis *f* country of central Greece
Phōcius *adj see* **Phōcis**
Phoebas, -adis *f* prophetess
Phoebē, -ēs *f* Diana, the moon
Phoebēius, -ēus *adj see* **Phoebus**
Phoebigena, -ae *m* son of Phoebus, Aesculapius
Phoebus, -ī *m* Apollo; the sun
Phoenīcē, -cēs *f* Phoenicia
Phoenīces, -cum *mpl* Phoenicians
phoenīcopterus, -ī *m* flamingo
Phoenīssus *adj* Phoenician ▸ *f* Dido
phoenīx, -īcis *m* phoenix
Phoenīx, -īcis *m* friend of Achilles
Phorcis, -idos = **Phorcȳnis**
Phorcus, -ī *m* son of Neptune (*father of Medusa*)
Phorcȳnis, -ȳnidos *f* Medusa
Phraātēs, -ae *m* king of Parthia
phrenēsis, -is *f* delirium
phrenēticus *adj* mad, delirious
Phrixēus *adj see* **Phrixus**
Phrixus, -ī *m* Helle's brother (*who took the ram
with the golden fleece to Colchis*)
Phryges, -um *mpl* Phrygians; Trojans
Phrygia, -iae *f* Phrygia (*country of Asia Minor*);
Troy
Phrygius *adj* Phrygian, Trojan
Phthīa, -ae *f* home of Achilles in Thessaly
Phthīōta, -ōtēs, -ōtae *m* native of Phthia
phthisis *f* consumption
Phthīus *adj see* **Phthīa**
phy *interj* bah!
phylaca, -ae *f* prison
phylarchus, -ī *m* chieftain
physica, -ae, physicē, -ēs *f* physics
physicē *adv* scientifically
physicus *adj* of physics, natural ▸ *m* natural
philosopher ▸ *ntpl* physics
physiognōmōn, -onis *m* physiognomist
physiologia, -ae *f* natural philosophy, science
piābilis *adj* expiable
piāculāris *adj* atoning ▸ *ntpl* sin offerings
piāculum, -ī *nt* sin offering; victim; atonement;
punishment; sin, guilt
piāmen, -inis *nt* atonement
pīca, -ae *f* magpie
picāria, -ae *f* pitch hut
picea, -ae *f* pine
Picēns, -entis *adj* = **Picēnus**
Picēnum, -ēnī *nt* Picenum
Picēnus *adj* of Picenum in E. Italy
piceus *adj* pitch black; of pitch
pictor, -ōris *m* painter
pictūra, -ae *f* painting; picture
pictūrātus *adj* painted; embroidered
pictus *ppp of* **pingō** ▸ *adj* coloured, tattooed;
(*style*) ornate; (*fear*) unreal
pīcus, -ī *m* woodpecker
piē *adv* religiously, dutifully
Pīeris, -dis *f* Muse

Pīerius adj of the Muses, poetic
pietās, -ātis f sense of duty (to gods, family, country), piety, filial affection, love, patriotism
piger, -rī adj reluctant, slack, slow; numbing, dull
piget, -ēre, -uit vt (impers) to be annoyed, dislike; to regret, repent
pigmentārius, -ī and **-iī** m dealer in paints
pigmentum, -ī nt paint, cosmetic; (style) colouring
pignerātor, -ōris m mortgagee
pignerō, -āre vt to pawn, mortgage
pigneror, -ārī, -ātus vt to claim, accept
pignus, -oris and **-eris** nt pledge, pawn, security; wager, stake; (fig) assurance, token; (pl) children, dear ones
pigritia, -ae, pigritiēs, -ēī f sluggishness, indolence
pigrō, -āre, pigror, -ārī vi to be slow, be slack
pila, -ae f ball, ball game
pīla¹, -ae f mortar
pīla², -ae f pillar; pier
pīlānus, -ī m soldier of the third line
pīlātus adj armed with javelins
pīlentum, -ī nt carriage
pilleātus adj wearing the felt cap
pilleolus, -ī m skullcap
pilleum, -ī nt, **pilleus, -ī** m felt cap presented to freed slaves; (fig) liberty
pilōsus adj hairy
pīlum, -ī nt javelin
pilus, -ī m hair; a whit
pīlus, -ī m division of triarii; **prīmus ~** chief centurion
Pimplēa, -ae, Pimplēis, -idis f Muse
Pimplēus adj of the Muses
Pindaricus adj see **Pindarus**
Pindarus, -ī m Pindar (Greek lyric poet)
Pindus, -ī m mountain range in Thessaly
pīnētum, -ī nt pine wood
pīneus adj pine- (in cpds)
pingō, -ere, pinxī, pictum vt to paint, embroider; to colour; (fig) to embellish, decorate
pinguēscō, -ere vi to grow fat, become fertile
pinguis adj fat, rich, fertile; (mind) gross, dull; (ease) comfortable, calm; (weather) thick ▶ nt grease
pīnifer, -ī, pīniger, -ī adj pine-clad
pinna, -ae f feather; wing, arrow; battlement; (fish) fin
pinnātus adj feathered, winged
pinniger, -ī adj winged; finny
pinnipēs, -edis adj wing-footed
pinnirapus, -ī m plume-snatcher
pinnula, -ae f little wing
pīnotērēs, -ae m hermit crab
pīnsō, -ere vt to beat, pound
pīnus, -ūs and **-ī** f stone pine, Scots fir; ship, torch, wreath
pinxī perf of **pingō**
piō, -āre vt to propitiate, worship; to atone for, avert; to avenge

piper, -is nt pepper
pīpilō, -āre vi to chirp
Pīraea, -ōrum ntpl Piraeus (main port of Athens)
Pīraeeus, Pīraeus, -ī m main port of Athens
Pīraeus adj see **Pīraeeus**
pīrāta, -ae m pirate
pīrāticus adj pirate ▶ f piracy
Pīrēnē, -ēs f spring in Corinth
Pīrēnis, -idis adj see **Pīrēnē**
Pīrithous, -ī m king of the Lapiths
pirum, -ī nt pear
pirus, -ī f pear tree
Pīsa, -ae f Greek town near the Olympic Games site
Pīsae, -ārum fpl town in Etruria (now Pisa)
Pīsaeus adj see **Pīsae**
Pīsānus adj see **Pīsae**
piscārius adj fish- (in cpds), fishing- (in cpds)
piscātor, -ōris m fisherman
piscātōrius adj fishing- (in cpds)
piscātus, -ūs m fishing; fish; catch, haul
pisciculus, -ī m little fish
piscīna, -ae f fishpond; swimming pool
piscīnārius, -ī and **-iī** m person keen on fish ponds
piscis, -is m fish; (ASTR) Pisces
piscor, -ārī, -ātus vi to fish
piscōsus adj full of fish
pisculentus adj full of fish
Pīsistratidae, -idārum mpl sons of Pisistratus
Pīsistratus, -ī m tyrant of Athens
pistillum, -ī nt pestle
pistor, -ōris m miller; baker
pistrilla, -ae f little mortar
pīstrīnum, -ī nt mill, bakery; drudgery
pistris, -is, pistrīx, -īcis f sea monster, whale; swift ship
pithēcium, -ī and **-iī** nt little ape
pītuīta, -ae f phlegm; catarrh, cold in the head
pītuītōsus adj phlegmatic
pius adj dutiful, conscientious; godly, holy; filial, affectionate; patriotic; good, upright ▶ mpl the blessed dead
pix, picis f pitch
plācābilis adj easily appeased
plācābilitās, -ātis f readiness to condone
plācāmen, -inis, plācāmentum, -ī nt peace-offering
plācātē adv calmly
plācātiō, -ōnis f propitiating
plācātus ppp of **plācō** ▶ adj calm, quiet, reconciled
placenta, -ae f cake
Placentia, -iae f town in N. Italy (now Piacenza)
Placentīnus adj see **Placentia**
placeō, -ēre, -uī, -itum vi (with dat) to please, satisfy; **placet** it seems good, it is agreed, resolved; **mihi ~** I am pleased with myself
placidē adv peacefully, gently
placidus adj calm, quiet, gentle
placitum, -ī nt belief
placitus ppa of **placeō** ▶ adj pleasing; agreed on

plācō, -āre, -āvī, -ātum vt to calm, appease, reconcile

plaga¹, -ae f region, zone

plaga², -ae f hunting net, snare, trap

plāga, -ae f blow, stroke, wound

plagiārius, -ī and **-iī** m plunderer, kidnapper

plāgigerulus adj much flogged

plāgōsus adj fond of punishing

plagula, -ae f curtain

planctus, -ūs m beating the breast, lamentation

plānē adv plainly, clearly; completely, quite; certainly

plangō, -gere, -xī, -ctum vt, vi to beat noisily; to beat in grief; to lament loudly, bewail

plangor, -ōris m beating; loud lamentation

plānipēs, -edis m ballet dancer

plānitās, -ātis f perspicuity

plānitiēs, -ēī, plānitia, -ae f level ground, plain

planta, -ae f shoot, slip; sole, foot

plantāria, -ium ntpl slips, young trees

planus, -ī m impostor

plānus adj level, flat; plain, clear ▸ nt level ground; **dē plānō** easily

platalea, -ae f spoonbill

platea, -ae f street

Platō, -ōnis m Plato (founder of the Academic school of philosophy)

Platōnicus adj see **Platō**

plaudō, -dere, -sī, -sum vt to clap, beat, stamp ▸ vi to clap, applaud; to approve, be pleased with

plausibilis adj praiseworthy

plausor, -ōris m applauder

plaustrum, -ī nt wagon, cart; (ASTR) Great Bear; ~ **percellere** upset the applecart

plausus¹ ppp of **plaudō**

plausus², -ūs m flapping; clapping, applause

Plautīnus adj see **Plautus**

Plautus, -ī m early Latin comic poet

plēbēcula, -ae f rabble

plēbēius adj plebeian; common, low

plēbicola, -ae m friend of the people

plēbiscītum, -ī nt decree of the people

plēbs, plēbēs, -is f common people, plebeians; lower classes, masses

plēctō, -ere vt to punish

plēctrum, -ī nt plectrum; lyre, lyric poetry

Plēias, -dis f Pleiad; (pl) the Seven Sisters

plēnē adv fully, entirely

plēnus adj full, filled; (fig) sated; (age) mature; (amount) complete; (body) stout, plump; (female) pregnant; (matter) solid; (style) copious; (voice) loud; **ad plēnum** abundantly

plērumque adv generally, mostly

plērusque adj a large part, most; (pl) the majority, the most; very many

plexus adj plaited, interwoven

Plīas see **Plēias**

plicātrīx, -īcis f clothes folder

plicō, -āre, -āvī and **-uī, -ātum** and **-itum** vt to fold, coil

Plīnius, -ī m Roman family name (esp Pliny the Elder, who died in the eruption of Vesuvius; Pliny the Younger, writer of letters)

plōrātus, -ūs m wailing

plōrō, -āre, -āvī, -ātum vi to wail, lament ▸ vt to weep for, bewail

plōstellum, -ī nt cart

ploxenum, -ī nt cart box

pluit, -ere, -it vi (impers) it is raining

plūma, -ae f soft feather, down

plumbeus adj of lead; (fig) heavy, dull, worthless

plumbum, -ī nt lead; bullet, pipe, ruler; ~ **album** tin

plūmeus adj down, downy

plūmipēs, -edis adj feather-footed

plūmōsus adj feathered

plūrimus superl of **multus**

plūs, -ūris compar of **multus** ▸ adv more

plūsculus adj a little more

pluteus, -ī m shelter, penthouse; parapet; couch; bookcase

Plūtō, -ōnis m king of the lower world

Plūtōnius adj see **Plūtō**

pluvia, -ae f rain

pluviālis adj rainy

pluvius adj rainy, rain- (in cpds)

pōcillum, -ī nt small cup

pōculum, -ī nt cup; drink, potion

podagra, -ae f gout

podagrōsus adj gouty

podium, -ī and **-iī** nt balcony

poēma, -tis nt poem

poena, -ae f penalty, punishment; **poenas dare** to be punished

Poenī, -ōrum mpl Carthaginians

Poenus, Pūnicus adj Punic

poēsis, -is f poetry, poem

poēta, -ae m poet

poēticē adv poetically

poēticus adj poetic ▸ f poetry

poētria, -ae f poetess

pol interj by Pollux!, truly

polenta, -ae f pearl barley

poliō, -īre, -īvī, -ītum vt to polish; to improve, put in good order

polītē adv elegantly

polītia, -ae f Plato's Republic

politicus adj political

polītus adj polished, refined, cultured

pollen, -inis nt fine flour, meal

pollēns, -entis pres p of **polleō** ▸ adj powerful, strong

pollentia, -ae f power

polleō, -ēre vi to be strong, be powerful

pollex, -icis m thumb

polliceor, -ērī, -itus vt to promise, offer

pollicitātiō, -ōnis f promise

pollicitor, -ārī, -ātus vt to promise

pollicitum, -ī nt promise

Polliō, -ōnis m Roman surname (esp C. Asinius, soldier, statesman and literary patron under Augustus)

pollis, -inis m/f see **pollen**

pollūcibiliter adv sumptuously

pollūctus adj offered up ▶ nt offering

polluō, -uere, -uī, -ūtum vt to defile, pollute, dishonour

Pollūx, -ūcis m twin brother of Castor (famous as a boxer)

polus, -ī m pole, North pole; sky

Polyhymnia, -ae f a Muse

Polyphēmus, -ī m one-eyed Cyclops

pōlypus, -ī m polypus

pōmārium, -i and **-iī** nt orchard

pōmārius, -ī and **-iī** m fruiterer

pōmerīdiānus adj afternoon

pōmērium, -ī and **-iī** nt free space round the city boundary

pōmifer, -ī adj fruitful

pōmoerium see **pōmērium**

pōmōsus adj full of fruit

pompa, -ae f procession; retinue, train; ostentation

Pompeiānus adj see **Pompeiī**

Pompeiī, -ōrum mpl Campanian town buried by an eruption of Vesuvius

Pompeius¹, -ī m Roman family name (esp Pompey the Great)

Pompeius², -ānus adj see **Pompeius¹**

Pompilius¹, -ī m Numa (second king of Rome)

Pompilius² adj see **Pompilius¹**

Pomptīnus adj Pomptine (name of marshy district in S. Latium)

pōmum, -ī nt fruit; fruit tree

pōmus, -ī f fruit tree

ponderō, -āre vt to weigh; to consider, reflect on

ponderōsus adj heavy, weighty

pondō adv in weight; pounds

pondus, -eris nt weight; mass, burden; (fig) importance, authority; (character) firmness; (pl) balance

pōne adv behind

pōnō, -ere, posuī, positum vt to put, place, lay, set; to lay down, lay aside; (fig) to regard, reckon; (art) to make, build; (camp) to pitch; (corpse) to lay out, bury; (example) to take; (food) to serve; (hair) to arrange; (hope) to base, stake; (hypothesis) to suppose, assume; (institution) to lay down, ordain; (money) to invest; (sea) to calm; (theme) to propose; (time) to spend, devote; (tree) to plant; (wager) to put down ▶ vi (wind) to abate

pōns, pontis m bridge; drawbridge; (ship) gangway, deck

ponticulus, -ī m small bridge

Ponticus adj see **Pontus**

pontifex, -icis m high priest, pontiff

pontificālis adj pontifical

pontificātus, -ūs m high priesthood

pontificius adj pontiff's

pontō, -ōnis m ferryboat

Pontus, -ī m Black Sea; kingdom of Mithridates in Asia Minor

pontus, -ī m sea

popa, -ae m minor priest

popanum, -ī nt sacrificial cake

popellus, -ī m mob

popīna, -ae f eating house, restaurant

popīnō, -ōnis m glutton

popl- etc see **pūbl-**

poples, -itis m knee

poposcī perf of **poscō**

poppysma, -tis nt clicking of the tongue

populābilis adj destroyable

populābundus adj ravaging

populāris adj of, from, for the people; popular, democratic; native ▶ m fellow countryman ▶ mpl the people's party, the democrats

populāritās, -ātis f courting popular favour

populāriter adv vulgarly; democratically

populātiō, -ōnis f plundering; plunder

populātor, -ōris m ravager

pōpuleus adj poplar- (in cpds)

pōpulifer, -ī adj rich in poplars

populor, -ārī, -ātus, populō, -āre vt to ravage, plunder; to destroy, ruin

populus, -ī m people, nation; populace, the public; large crowds; district

pōpulus, -ī f poplar tree

porca, -ae f sow

porcella, -ae f, **porcellus, -ī** m little pig

porcīna, -ae f pork

porcīnārius, -ī and **-iī** m pork seller

Porcius¹, -ī m family name of Cato

Porcius² adj see **Porcius¹**

porculus, -ī m porker

porcus, -ī m pig, hog

porgō etc see **porrigō**

Porphyriōn, -ōnis m a Giant

porrēctiō, -ōnis f extending

porrēctus ppp of **porrigō** ▶ adj long, protracted; dead

porrēxī perf of **porrigō**

porriciō, -ere vt to make an offering of; **inter caesa et porrēcta** at the eleventh hour

porrigō, -igere, -ēxī, -ēctum vt to stretch, spread out, extend; to offer, hold out

porrigō, -inis f scurf, dandruff

porrō adv forward, a long way off; (time) in future, long ago; (sequence) next, moreover, in turn

porrum, -ī nt leek

Porsena, Porsenna, Porsinna, -ae f king of Clusium in Etruria

porta, -ae f gate; entrance, outlet

portātiō, -ōnis f carrying

portendō, -dere, -dī, -tum vt to denote, predict

portentificus adj marvellous

portentōsus adj unnatural

portentum, -ī nt omen, unnatural happening; monstrosity, monster; (story) marvel

porthmeus, -eī and **-eos** m ferryman

porticula, -ae f small gallery

porticus, -ūs m portico, colonnade; (MIL) gallery; (PHILOS) Stoicism

portiō, -ōnis f share, instalment; **prō portiōne** proportionally

portitor¹, -ōris m customs officer

portitor², -ōris m ferryman

portō, -āre, -āvī, -ātum vt to carry, convey, bring

portōrium, -ī and **-iī** nt customs duty, tax

portula, -ae f small gate

portuōsus adj well-off for harbours

portus, -ūs m harbour, port; (fig) safety, haven

pōsca, -ae f a vinegar drink

poscō, -ere, poposcī vt to ask, require, demand; to call on

Posidōnius, -ī m Stoic philosopher (teacher of Cicero)

positiō, -ōnis f position, climate

positor, -ōris m builder

positūra, -ae f position; formation

▶ **positus** ppp of **pōnō** ▶ adj situated

posse infin of **possum**

possēdī perf of **possideō; possīdō**

possessiō, -ōnis f seizing; occupation; possession, property

possessiuncula, -ae f small estate

possessor, -ōris m occupier, possessor

possessus ppp of **possideō; possīdō**

possideō, -idēre, -ēdī, -essum vt to hold, occupy; to have, possess

possīdō, -īdere, -ēdī, -essum vt to take possession of

possum, -sse, -tuī vi to be able, can; to have power, avail

post adv (place) behind; (time) after; (sequence) next ▶ prep (with acc) behind; after, since; **paulō ~** soon after; **~ urbem conditam** since the foundation of the city

posteā adv afterwards, thereafter; next, then; **~ quam** conj after

posterior, -ōris adj later, next; inferior, less important

posteritās, -ātis f posterity, the future

posterius adv later

posterus adj next, following ▶ mpl posterity

postferō, -re vt to put after, sacrifice

postgenitī, -ōrum mpl later generations

posthabeō, -ēre, -uī, -itum vt to put after, neglect

posthāc adv hereafter, in future

postibi adv then, after that

postīculum, -ī nt small back building

postīcus adj back- (in cpds), hind- (in cpds) ▶ nt back door

postideā adv after that

postillā adv afterwards

postis, -is m doorpost, door

postlīminium, -ī and **-iī** nt right of recovery

postmerīdiānus adj in the afternoon

postmodo, postmodum adv shortly, presently

postpōnō, -ōnere, -osuī, -ositum vt to put after, disregard

postputō, -āre vt to consider less important

postquam conj after, when

postrēmō adv finally

postrēmus adj last, rear; lowest, worst

postrīdiē adv next day, the day after

postscaenium, -ī and **-iī** nt behind the scenes

postscrībō, -ere vt to write after

postulātiō, -ōnis f demand, claim; complaint

postulātum, -ī nt demand, claim

postulātus, -ūs m claim

postulō, -āre, -āvī, -ātum vt to demand, claim; (LAW) to summon, prosecute; to apply for a writ (to prosecute)

postumus adj last, last-born

postus etc see **positus**

posuī perf of **pōnō**

pōtātiō, -ōnis f drinking

pōtātor, -ōris m toper

pote etc see **potis**

potēns, -entis adj able, capable; powerful, strong, potent; master of, ruling over; successful in carrying out

potentātus, -ūs m political power

potenter adv powerfully; competently

potentia, -ae f power, force, efficacy; tyranny

pōtērium, -ī and **-iī** nt goblet

potesse archaic infin of **possum**

potestās, -ātis f power, ability; control, sovereignty, authority; opportunity, permission; (person) magistrate; (things) property; **potestātem suī facere** allow access to oneself

potin can (you)?, is it possible?

potiō, -īre vt to put into the power of

pōtiō, -ōnis f drink, draught, philtre

potior¹, -īrī, -ītus vi (with gen and abl) to take possession of, get hold of, acquire; to be master of

potior², -ōris adj better, preferable

potis adj (indecl) able; possible

potissimum adv especially

potissimus adj chief, most important

pōtitō, -āre vt to drink much

potius adv rather, more

pōtō, -āre, -āvī, -ātum and **-um** vt to drink

pōtor, -ōris m drinker

pōtrīx, -īcis f woman tippler

potuī perf of **possum**

pōtulenta, -ōrum ntpl drinks

pōtus¹ ppp of **pōtō** ▶ adj drunk

pōtus², -ūs m drink

prae adv in front, before; in comparison ▶ prep (with abl) in front of; compared with; (cause) because of, for; **~ sē** openly; **~ sē ferre** display; **~ manū** to hand

praeacūtus adj pointed

praealtus adj very high, very deep

praebeō, -ēre, -uī, -itum vt to hold out, proffer; to give, supply; to show, represent; **sē praebēre** behave, prove

praebibō, -ere, -ī vt to toast

praebitor, -ōris m purveyor

praecalidus adj very hot

praecānus adj prematurely grey

praecautus ppp of **praecaveō**

praecaveō, -avēre, -āvī, -autum vt to guard against ▸ vi to beware, take precautions

praecēdō, -dere, -ssī, -ssum vt to go before; to surpass ▸ vi to lead the way; to excel

praecellō, -ere vi to excel, be distinguished ▸ vt to surpass

praecelsus adj very high

praecentiō, -ōnis f prelude

praecentō, -āre vi to sing an incantation for

praeceps, -ipitis adj head first, headlong; going down, precipitous; rapid, violent, hasty; inclined (to); dangerous ▸ nt edge of an abyss, precipice; danger ▸ adv headlong; into danger

praeceptiō, -ōnis f previous notion; precept

praeceptor, -ōris m teacher

praeceptrīx, -rīcis f teacher

praeceptum, -ī nt maxim, precept; order

praeceptus ppp of **praecipiō**

praecerpō, -ere, -sī, -tum vt to gather prematurely; to forestall

praecīdō, -dere, -dī, -sum vt to cut off, damage; (fig) to cut short, put an end to

praecinctus ppp of **praecingō**

praecingō, -ingere, -inxī, -inctum vt to gird in front; to surround

praecinō, -inere, -inuī, -entum vt to play before; to chant a spell ▸ vt to predict

praecipiō, -ipere, -ēpī, -ēptum vt to take beforehand, get in advance; to anticipate; to teach, admonish, order

praecipitanter adv at full speed

praecipitem acc of **praeceps**

praecipitō, -āre, -āvī, -ātum vt to throw down, throw away, hasten; (fig) to remove, carry away, ruin ▸ vi to rush headlong, fall; to be hasty

praecipuē adv especially, chiefly

praecipuus adj special; principal, outstanding

praecīsē adv briefly, absolutely

praecīsus ppp of **praecīdō** ▸ adj steep

praeclārē adv very clearly; excellently

praeclārus adj very bright; beautiful, splendid; distinguished, noble

praeclūdō, -dere, -sī, -sum vt to close, shut against; to close to, impede

praecō, -ōnis m crier, herald; auctioneer

praecōgitō, -āre vt to premeditate

praecognitus adj foreseen

praecolō, -olere, -oluī, -ultum vt to cultivate early

praecompositus adj studied

praecōnium, -ī and **-iī** nt office of a crier; advertisement; commendation

praecōnius adj of a public crier

praecōnsūmō, -ere, -ptum vt to use up beforehand

praecontrectō, -āre vt to consider beforehand

praecordia, -ōrum ntpl midriff; stomach; breast, heart; mind

praecorrumpō, -umpere, -ūpī, -uptum vt to bribe beforehand

praecox, -cis adj early, premature

praecultus ppp of **praecolō**

praecurrentia, -ium ntpl antecedents

praecurrō, -rrere, -currī and **-rrī, -rsum** vi to hurry on before, precede; to excel ▸ vt to anticipate; to surpass

praecursiō, -ōnis f previous occurrence; (RHET) preparation

praecursor, -ōris m advance guard; scout

praecutiō, -ere vt to brandish before

praeda, -ae f booty, plunder; (animal) prey; (fig) gain

praedābundus adj plundering

praedamnō, -āre vt to condemn beforehand

praedātiō, -ōnis f plundering

praedātor, -ōris m plunderer

praedātōrius adj marauding

praedēlassō, -āre vt to weaken beforehand

praedēstinō, -āre vt to predetermine

praediātor, -ōris m buyer of landed estates

praediātōrius adj relating to the sale of estates

praedicābilis adj laudatory

praedicātiō, -ōnis f proclamation; commendation

praedicātor, -ōris m eulogist

praedicō, -āre, -āvī, -ātum vt to proclaim, make public; to declare; to praise, boast

praedīcō, -īcere, -īxī, -ictum vt to mention beforehand, prearrange; to foretell; to warn, command

praedictiō, -ōnis f foretelling

praedictum, -ī nt prediction; command; prearrangement

praedictus ppp of **praedīcō**

praediolum, -ī nt small estate

praediscō, -ere vt to learn beforehand

praedispositus adj arranged beforehand

praeditus adj endowed, provided

praedium, -ī and **-iī** nt estate

praedīves, -itis adj very rich

praedō, -ōnis m robber, pirate

praedor, -ārī, -ātus vt, vi to plunder, rob; (fig) to profit

praedūcō, -ūcere, -ūxī, -uctum vt to draw in front

praedulcis adj very sweet

praedūrus adj very hard, very tough

praeēmineō, -ēre vt to surpass

praeeō, -īre, -īvī and **-iī, -itum** vi to lead the way, go first; (formula) to dictate, recite first ▸ vt to precede, outstrip

praeesse infin of **praesum**

praefātiō, -ōnis f formula; preface

praefātus ppa of **praefor**
praefectūra, -ae f superintendence; governorship; *Italian town governed by Roman edicts*, prefecture; district, province
praefectus ppp of **praeficiō ▶** m overseer, director, governor, commander; **~ classis** admiral; **~ legiōnis** colonel; **~ urbis** or **urbī** city prefect (*of Rome*)
praeferō, -ferre, -tulī, -lātum vt to carry in front, hold out; to prefer; to show, display; to anticipate; (*pass*) to hurry past, outflank
praeferōx, -ōcis adj very impetuous, very insolent
praefervidus adj very hot
praefestīnō, -āre vi to be too hasty; to hurry past
praefica, -ae f hired mourner
praeficiō, -icere, -ēcī, -ectum vt to put in charge, set up before; to tip, point; to transfix
praefīdēns, -entis adj over-confident
praefīgō, -gere, -xī, -xum vt to fasten in front, set up before; to tip, point; to transfix
praefīniō, -īre, -īvī and **-iī, -ītum** vt to determine, prescribe
praefiscinē, -ī adv without offence
praeflōrō, -āre vt to tarnish
praefluō, -ere vt, vi to flow past
praefocō, -āre vt to choke
praefodiō, -odere, -ōdī vt to dig in front of; to bury beforehand
praefor, -ārī, -ātus vt, vi to say in advance, preface; to pray beforehand; to predict
praefrāctē adv resolutely
praefrāctus ppp of **praefringō ▶** adj abrupt; stern
praefrīgidus adj very cold
praefringō, -ingere, -ēgī, -āctum vt to break off, shiver
praefuī perf of **praesum**
praefulciō, -cīre, -sī, -tum vt to prop up; to use as a prop
praefulgeō, -ulgēre, -ulsī vt to shine conspicuously; to outshine
praegelidus adj very cold
praegestiō, -īre vi to be very eager
praegnāns, -antis adj pregnant; full
praegracilis adj very slim
praegrandis adj very large, very great
praegravis adj very heavy; very wearisome
praegravō, -āre vt to weigh down; to eclipse
praegredior, -dī, -ssus vt, vi to go before; to go past; to surpass
praegressiō, -ōnis f precession, precedence
praegustātor, -ōris m taster
praegustō, -āre vt to taste beforehand
praehibeō, -ēre vt to offer, give
praeiaceō, -ēre vt to lie in front of
praeiūdicium, -ī and **-iī** nt precedent, example; prejudgment
praeiūdicō, -āre, -āvī, -ātum vt to prejudge, decide beforehand
praeiuvō, -āre vt to give previous assistance to

praelābor, -bī, -psus vt, vi to move past, move along
praelambō, -ere vt to lick first
praelātus ppp of **praeferō**
praelegō, -ere vt to coast along
praeligō, -āre vt to bind, tie up
praelongus adj very long, very tall
praeloquor, -quī, -cūtus vi to speak first
praelūceō, -cēre, -xī vi to light, shine; to outshine
praelūstris adj very magnificent
praemandāta ntpl warrant of arrest
praemandō, -āre, -āvī, -ātum vt to bespeak
praemātūrē adv too soon
praemātūrus adj too early, premature
praemedicātus adj protected by charms
praemeditātiō, -ōnis f thinking over the future
praemeditātus adj premeditated
praemeditor, -ārī, -ātus vt to think over, practise
praemetuenter adv anxiously
praemetuō, -ere vi to be anxious ▶ vt to fear the future
praemissus ppp of **praemittō**
praemittō, -ittere, -īsī, -issum vt to send in advance
praemium, -ī and **-iī** nt prize, reward
praemōlestia, -ae f apprehension
praemōlior, -īrī vt to prepare thoroughly
praemoneō, -ēre, -uī, -itum vt to forewarn, foreshadow
praemonitus, -ūs m premonition
praemōnstrātor, -ōris m guide
praemōnstrō, -āre vt to guide; to predict
praemordeō, -ēre vt to bite off; to pilfer
praemorior, -ī, -tuus vi to die too soon
praemūniō, -īre, -īvī, -ītum vt to fortify, strengthen, secure
praemūnītiō, -ōnis f (RHET) preparation
praenārrō, -āre vt to tell beforehand
praenatō, -āre vt to flow past
Praeneste, -is nt/f Latin town (now Palestrina)
Praenestīnus adj see **Praeneste**
praeniteō, -ēre, -uī vi to seem more attractive
praenōmen, -inis nt first name
praenōscō, -ere vt to foreknow
praenōtiō, -ōnis f preconceived idea
praenūbilus adj very gloomy
praenūntia, -iae f harbinger
praenūntiō, -āre vt to foretell
praenūntius, -ī and **-iī** m harbinger
praeoccupō, -āre, -āvī, -ātum vt to take first, anticipate
praeolit mihi I get a hint of
praeoptō, -āre, -āvī, -ātum vt to choose rather, prefer
praepandō, -ere vt to spread out; to expound
praeparātiō, -ōnis f preparation
praeparō, -āre, -āvī, -ātum vt to prepare, prepare for; **ex praeparātō** by arrangement

praepediō, -īre, -īvī, -ītum vt to shackle, tether; to hamper

praependeō, -ēre vi to hang down in front

praepes, -etis adj swift, winged; of good omen ▶ f bird

praepilātus adj tipped with a ball

praepinguis adj very rich

praepolleō, -ēre vi to be very powerful, be superior

praeponderō, -āre vt to outweigh

praepōnō, -ōnere, -osuī, -ositum vt to put first, place in front; to put in charge, appoint commander; to prefer

praeportō, -āre vt to carry before

praepositiō, -ōnis f preference; (GRAM) preposition

praepositus ppp of **praepōnō** ▶ m overseer, commander

praepossum, -sse, -tuī vi to gain the upper hand

praeposterē adv the wrong way round

praeposterus adj inverted, perverted; absurd

praepotēns, -entis adj very powerful

praeproperanter adv too hastily

praeproperē adv too hastily

praeproperus adj overhasty, rash

praepūtium, -ī and **-iī** nt foreskin

praequam adv compared with

praequestus adj complaining beforehand

praeradiō, -āre vt to outshine

praerapidus adj very swift

praereptus ppp of **praeripiō**

praerigēscō, -ēscere, -uī vi to become very stiff

praeripiō, -ipere, -ipuī, -eptum vt to take before, forestall; to carry off prematurely; to frustrate

praerōdō, -dere, -sum vt to bite the end of, nibble off

praerogātīva, -ae f tribe or century with the first vote, the first vote; previous election; omen, sure token

praerogātīvus adj voting first

praerōsus ppp of **praerōdō**

praerumpō, -umpere, -ūpī, -uptum vt to break off

praeruptus ppp of **praerumpō** ▶ adj steep, abrupt; headstrong

praes, -aedis m surety; property of a surety

praesaep- etc see **praesēp-**

praesāgiō, -īre vt to have a presentiment of, forebode

praesāgītiō, -ōnis f foreboding

praesāgium, -ī and **-iī** nt presentiment; prediction

praesāgus adj foreboding, prophetic

praesciō, -īre, -iī vt to know before

praescīscō, -ere vi to find out beforehand

praescius adj foreknowing

praescrībō, -bere, -psī, -ptum vt to write first; to direct, command; to dictate, describe; to put forward as a pretext

praescrīptiō, -ōnis f preface, heading; order, rule; pretext

praescrīptum, -ī nt order, rule

praescrīptus ppp of **praescrībō**

praesecō, -āre, -uī, -tum and **-ātum** vt to cut off, pare

praesēns, -entis adj present, in person; (things) immediate, ready, prompt; (mind) resolute; (gods) propitious ▶ ntpl present state of affairs; in ~ for the present; ~ in rē praesentī on the spot

praesēnsiō, -ōnis f foreboding; preconception

praesēnsus ppp of **praesentiō**

praesentārius adj instant, ready

praesentia, -ae f presence; effectiveness

praesentiō, -entīre, -ēnsī, -ēnsum vt to presage, have a foreboding of

praesēpe, -is nt, **praesēpēs, -is** f stable, fold, pen; hovel; hive

praesēpiō, -īre, -sī, -tum vt to barricade

praesēpis f = **praesēpe**

praesertim adv **especially**

praeserviō, -īre vi to serve as a slave

praeses, -idis m guardian, protector; chief, ruler

praesideō, -idēre, -ēdī vi to guard, defend; to preside over, direct

praesidiārius adj garrison-

praesidium, -ī and **-iī** nt defence, protection; support, assistance; guard, garrison, convoy; defended position, entrenchment

praesignificō, -āre vt to foreshadow

praesignis adj conspicuous

praesonō, -āre, -uī vi to sound before

praespargō, -ere vt to strew before

praestābilis adj outstanding; preferable

praestāns, -antis pres p of **praestō²** ▶ adj outstanding, pre-eminent

praestantia, -ae f pre-eminence

praestes, -itis adj presiding, guardian

praestīgiae, -ārum fpl illusion, sleight of hand

praestīgiātor, -ōris m, **praestīgiātrīx, -rīcis** f conjurer, cheat

praestinō, -āre vt to buy

praestitī perf of **praestō²**

praestituō, -uere, -uī, -ūtum vt to prearrange, prescribe

praestitus ppp of **praestō²**

praestō¹ adv at hand, ready

praestō², -āre, -itī, -itum and **-ātum** vi to be outstanding, be superior; (impers) it is better ▶ vt to excel; to be responsible for, answer for; (duty) to discharge, perform; (quality) to show, prove; (things) to give, offer, provide; sē **praestāre** behave, prove

praestōlor, -ārī, -ātus vt, vi to wait for, expect

praestrictus ppp of **praestringō**

praestringō, -ingere, -inxī, -ictum vt to squeeze; to blunt, dull; (eyes) to dazzle

praestruō, -ere, -xī, -ctum vt to block up; to build beforehand

praesul, -is m/f public dancer

praesultātor, -ōris m public dancer

praesultō, -āre vi to dance before

praesum, -esse, -fuī vi (with dat) to be at the head of, be in command of; to take the lead; to protect

praesūmō, -ere, -psī, -ptum vt to take first; to anticipate; to take for granted

praesūtus adj sewn over at the point

praetemptō, -āre vt to feel for, grope for; to test in advance

praetendō, -dere, -dī, -tum vt to hold out, put before, spread in front of; to give as an excuse, allege

praetentō etc see **praetemptō**

praetentus ppp of **praetendō** ▸ adj lying over against

praetepeō, -ēre, -uī vi to glow before

praeter adv beyond; excepting ▸ prep (with acc) past, along; except, besides; beyond, more than, in addition to, contrary to

praeteragō, -ere vt to drive past

praeterbītō, -ere vt, vi to pass by

praeterdūcō, -ere vt to lead past

praetereā adv besides; moreover; henceforth

praetereō, -īre, -īī, -itum vi to go past ▸ vt to pass, overtake; to escape, escape the notice of; to omit, leave out, forget, neglect; to reject, exclude; to transgress

praeterequitāns, -antis adj riding past

praeterfluō, -ere vt, vi to flow past

praetergredior, -dī, -ssus vt to pass, march past; to surpass

praeterhāc adv further, more

praeteritus ppp of **praetereō** ▸ adj past, gone by ▸ ntpl the past

praeterlābor, -bī, -psus vt to flow past, move past ▸ vi to slip away

praeterlātus adj driving, flying past

praetermeō, -āre vi to pass by

praetermissiō, -ōnis f omission, passing over

praetermittō, -ittere, -īsī, -issum vt to let pass; to omit, neglect; to make no mention of; to overlook

praeterquam adv except, besides

praetervectiō, -ōnis f passing by

praetervehor, -hī, -ctus vt, vi to ride past, sail past; to march past; to pass by, pass over

praetervolō, -āre vt, vi to fly past; to escape

praetexō, -ere, -uī, -tum vt to border, fringe; to adorn; to pretend, disguise

praetextātus adj wearing the toga praetexta, under age

praetextus¹ ppp of **praetexō** ▸ adj wearing the toga praetexta ▸ f toga with a purple border; Roman tragedy ▸ nt pretext

praetextus², -ūs m splendour; pretence

praetimeō, -ēre vi to be afraid in advance

praetinctus adj dipped beforehand

praetor, -ōris m chief magistrate, commander; praetor; propraetor, governor

praetōriānus adj of the emperor's bodyguard

praetōrium, -ī and **-iī** nt general's tent, camp headquarters; governor's residence; council of war; palace, grand building; emperor's bodyguard

praetōrius adj praetor's, praetorian; of a propraetor; of the emperor's bodyguard ▸ m ex-praetor; **praetōria cohors** bodyguard of general or emperor; **porta praetōria** camp gate facing the enemy

praetorqueō, -ēre vt to strangle first

praetrepidāns, -antis adj very impatient

praetruncō, -āre vt to cut off

praetulī perf of **praeferō**

praetūra, -ae f praetorship

praeumbrāns, -antis adj obscuring

praeūstus adj hardened at the point; frostbitten

praeut adv compared with

praevaleō, -ēre, -uī vi to be very powerful, have most influence, prevail

praevalidus adj very strong, very powerful; too strong

praevāricātiō, -ōnis f collusion

praevāricātor, -ōris m advocate guilty of collusion

praevāricor, -ārī, -ātus vi (with dat) to favour by collusion

praevehor, -hī, -ctus vi to ride, fly in front, flow past

praeveniō, -enīre, -ēnī, -entum vt, vi to come before; to anticipate, prevent

praeverrō, -ere vt to sweep before

praevertō, -ere, -ī, praevertor, -ī vt to put first, prefer; to turn to first, attend first to; to outstrip, to anticipate, frustrate, prepossess

praevideō, -idēre, -īdī, -īsum vt to foresee

praevitiō, -āre vt to taint beforehand

praevius adj leading the way

praevolō, -āre vi to fly in front

pragmaticus adj of affairs ▸ m legal expert

prandeō, -ēre, -ī vi to take lunch ▸ vt to eat

prandium, -ī and **-iī** nt lunch

prānsor, -ōris m guest at lunch

prānsus adj having lunched, fed

prasinus adj green

prātēnsis adj meadow (in cpds)

prātulum, -ī nt small meadow

prātum, -ī nt meadow; grass

prāvē adv wrongly, badly

prāvitās, -ātis f irregularity; perverseness, depravity

prāvus adj crooked, deformed; perverse, bad, wicked

Prāxitelēs, -is m famous Greek sculptor

Prāxitelius adj see **Prāxitelēs**

precāriō adv by request

precārius adj obtained by entreaty

precātiō, -ōnis f prayer

precātor, -ōris m intercessor

preces *pl see* **prex**

preciae, -ārum *fpl* kind of vine

precor, -ārī, -ātus *vt, vi* to pray, beg, entreat; to wish (well), curse

prehendō, -endere, -endī, -ēnsum *vt* to take hold of, catch; to seize, detain; to surprise; (*eye*) to take in; (*mind*) to grasp

prehēnsō *etc see* **prēnsō**

prehēnsus *ppp of* **prehendō**

prēlum, -ī *nt* wine press, oil press

premō, -mere, -ssī, -ssum *vt* to press, squeeze; to press together, compress; (*eyes*) to close; (*reins*) to tighten; (*trees*) to prune; to press upon, lie, sit, stand on, cover, conceal, surpass; to press hard on, follow closely; (*coast*) to hug; to press down, lower, burden; (*fig*) to overcome, rule; (*words*) to disparage; to press in, sink, stamp, plant; to press back, repress, check, stop

prendō *etc see* **prehendō**

prēnsātiō, -ōnis *f* canvassing

prēnsō, prehēnsō, -āre, -āvī, -ātum *vt* to clutch at, take hold of, buttonhole

prēnsus *ppp of* **prehendō**

presbyter, -ī *m* (ECCL) elder

pressē *adv* concisely, accurately, simply

pressī *perf of* **premō**

pressiō, -ōnis *f* fulcrum

pressō, -āre *vt* to press

pressus¹ *ppp of* **premō** ▶ *adj* (*style*) concise, compressed; (*pace*) slow; (*voice*) subdued

pressus², -ūs *m* pressure

prēster, -ēris *m* waterspout

pretiōsē *adv* expensively

pretiōsus *adj* valuable, expensive; extravagant

pretium, -ī *and* **-iī** *nt* price, value; worth; money, fee, reward; **māgnī pretiī, in pretiō** valuable; **operae ~** worth while

prex, -ecis *f* request, entreaty; prayer; good wish; curse

Priamēis, -ēidis *f* Cassandra

Priamēius *adj see* **Priamus**

Priamidēs, -idae *m* son of Priam

Priamus, -ī *m* king of Troy

Priāpus, -ī *m* god of fertility and of gardens

prīdem *adv* long ago, long

prīdiē *adv* the day before

prīmaevus *adj* youthful

prīmānī, -ōrum *mpl* soldiers of the 1st legion

prīmārius *adj* principal, first-rate

prīmigenus *adj* original

prīmipilāris, -is *m* chief centurion

prīmipilus, -ī *m* chief centurion

prīmitiae, -ārum *fpl* first fruits

prīmitus *adv* originally

prīmō *adv* at first; firstly

prīmōrdium, -ī *and* **-iī** *nt* beginning; **prīmōrdia rērum** atoms

prīmōris *adj* first, foremost, tip of; principal ▶ *mpl* nobles; (MIL) front line

prīmulum *adv* first

prīmulus *adj* very first

prīmum *adv* first, to begin with, in the first place; for the first time; **cum ~, ubi ~, ut ~** as soon as; **quam ~** as soon as possible; **~ dum** in the first place

prīmus *adj* first, foremost, tip of; earliest; principal, most eminent; **~ veniō** I am the first to come; **prima lux** dawn, daylight; **prīmō mēnse** at the beginning of the month; **prīmīs digitīs** with the fingertips; **prīmās agere** play the leading part; **prīmās dare** give first place to; **in prīmīs** in the front line; especially

prīnceps, -ipis *adj* first, in front, chief, most eminent ▶ *m* leader, chief; first citizen, emperor; (MIL) company, captain, captaincy ▶ *pl* (MIL) the second line

prīncipālis *adj* original; chief; the emperor's

prīncipātus, -ūs *m* first place; post of commander-in-chief; emperorship

prīncipiālis *adj* from the beginning

prīncipium, -ī *and* **-iī** *nt* beginning, origin; first to vote ▶ *pl* first principles; (MIL) front line; camp headquarters

prior, -ōris (*nt* **-us**) *adj* former, previous, first; better, preferable ▶ *mpl* forefathers

prīscē *adv* strictly

prīscus *adj* former, ancient, old-fashioned

prīstinus *adj* former, original; of yesterday

prius *adv* previously, before; in former times; **~ quam** before, sooner than

prīvātim *adv* individually, privately; at home

prīvātiō, -ōnis *f* removal

prīvātus *adj* individual, private; not in public office ▶ *m* private citizen

Prīvernās, -ātis *adj see* **Prīvernum**

Prīvernum, -ī *nt* old Latin town

prīvīgna, -ae *f* stepdaughter

prīvīgnus, -ī *m* stepson; (*pl*) stepchildren

prīvilēgium, -ī *and* **-iī** *nt* law in favour of or against an individual

prīvō, -āre, -āvī, -ātum *vt* to deprive, rob; to free

prīvus *adj* single, one each; own, private

prō¹ *adv* (with **ut** and **quam**) in proportion (as) ▶ *prep* (with *abl*) in front of, on the front of; for, on behalf of, instead of, in return for; as, as good as; according to, in proportion to, by virtue of; **prō eō ac** just as; **prō eō quod** just because; **prō eō quantum, prō eō ut** in proportion as

prō² *interj* (*expressing wonder or sorrow*) O!, alas!

proāgorus, -ī *m* chief magistrate (*in Sicilian towns*)

proavītus *adj* ancestral

proavus, -ī *m* great-grandfather, ancestor

probābilis *adj* laudable; credible, probable

probābilitās, -ātis *f* credibility

probābiliter *adv* credibly

probātiō, -ōnis *f* approval; testing

probātor, -ōris *m* approver

probātus *adj* tried, excellent; acceptable

probē *adv* well, properly; thoroughly, well done!

probitās, -ātis *f* goodness, honesty

probō, -āre, -āvī, -ātum vt to approve, approve of; to appraise; to recommend; to prove, show

probrōsus adj abusive; disgraceful

probrum, -ī nt abuse, reproach; disgrace; infamy, unchastity

probus adj good, excellent; honest, upright

procācitās, -ātis f impudence

procāciter adv insolently

procāx, -ācis adj bold, forward, insolent

prōcēdō, -ēdere, -essī, -essum vi to go forward, advance; to go out, come forth; (time) to go on, continue; (fig) to make progress, get on; (events) to turn out, succeed

procella, -ae f hurricane, storm; (MIL) charge

procellōsus adj stormy

procer, -is m chief, noble, prince

prōcēritās, -ātis f height; length

prōcērus adj tall; long

prōcessiō, -ōnis f advance

prōcessus, -ūs m advance, progress

prōcidō, -ere, -ī vi to fall forwards, fall down

prōcinctus, -ūs m readiness (for action)

prōclāmātor, -ōris m bawler

prōclāmō, -āre vi to cry out

prōclīnātus adj tottering

prōclīnō, -āre vt to bend

prōclīve adv downwards; easily

prōclīvis, prōclīvus adj downhill, steep; (mind) prone, willing; (act) easy; **in prōclīvī** easy

prōclīvitās, -ātis f descent; tendency

prōclīvus etc see **prōclīvis**

Procnē, -ēs f wife of Tereus (changed to a swallow); swallow

prōconsul, -is m proconsul, governor

prōconsulāris adj proconsular

prōconsulātus, -ūs m proconsulship

prōcrāstinātiō, -ōnis f procrastination

prōcrāstinō, -āre vt to put off from day to day

prōcreātiō, -ōnis f begetting

prōcreātor, -ōris m creator, parent

prōcreātrix, -īcis f mother

prōcreō, -āre vt to beget, produce

prōcrēscō, -ere vi to be produced, grow up

Procrūstēs, -ae m Attic highwayman (who tortured victims on a bed)

prōcubō, -āre vi to lie on the ground

prōcūdō, -dere, -dī, -sum vt to forge; to produce

procul adv at a distance, far, from afar

prōculcō, -āre vt to trample down

prōcumbō, -mbere, -buī, -bitum vi to fall forwards, bend over; to sink down, be broken down

prōcūrātiō, -ōnis f management; (religion) expiation

prōcūrātor, -ōris m administrator, financial agent; (province) governor

prōcūrātrix, -īcis f governess

prōcūrō, -āre, -āvī, -ātum vt to take care of, manage; to expiate ▸ vi to be a procurator

prōcurrō, -rrere, -currī and **-rrī, -rsum** vi to rush forward; to jut out

prōcursātiō, -ōnis f charge

prōcursātor, -ōris m skirmisher

prōcursō, -āre vi to make a sally

prōcursus, -ūs m charge

prōcurvus adj curving forwards

procus¹, -ī m nobleman

procus², -ī m wooer, suitor

Procyōn, -ōnis m Lesser Dog Star

prōdeambulō, -āre vi to go out for a walk

prōdeō, -īre, -iī, -itum vi to come out, come forward, appear; to go ahead, advance; to project

prōdesse infin of **prōsum**

prōdīcō, -īcere, -īxī, -ictum vt to appoint, adjourn

prōdictātor, -ōris m vice-dictator

prōdigē adv extravagantly

prōdigentia, -ae f profusion

prōdigiāliter adv unnaturally

prōdigiōsus adj unnatural, marvellous

prōdigium, -ī and **-iī** nt portent; unnatural deed; monster

prōdigō, -igere, -ēgī, -āctum vt to squander

prōdigus adj wasteful; lavish, generous

prōditiō, -ōnis f betrayal

prōditor, -ōris m traitor

prōditus ppp of **prōdō**

prōdō, -ere, -idī, -itum vt to bring forth, produce; to make known, publish; to betray, give up; (tradition) to hand down

prōdoceō, -ēre vt to preach

prodromus, -ī m forerunner

prōdūcō, -ūcere, -ūxī, -uctum vt to bring forward, bring out; to conduct; to drag in front; to draw out, extend; (acting) to perform; (child) to beget, bring up; (fact) to bring to light; (innovation) to introduce; (rank) to promote; (slave) to put up for sale; (time) to prolong, protract, put off; (tree) to cultivate; (vowel) to lengthen

prōductē adv long

prōductiō, -ōnis f lengthening

prōductō, -āre vt to spin out

prōductus ppp of **prōdūcō** ▸ adj lengthened, long

proēgmenon, -ī nt a preferred thing

proeliātor, -ōris m fighter

proelior, -ārī, -ātus vi to fight, join battle

proelium, -ī and **-iī** nt battle, conflict

profānō, -āre vt to desecrate

profānus adj unholy, common; impious; ill-omened

profātus ppa of **profor**

profectiō, -ōnis f departure; source

profectō adv really, certainly

profectus ppa of **proficīscor**

profectus¹ ppp of **prōficiō**

profectus², -ūs m growth, progress, profit

prōferō, -ferre, -tulī, -lātum vt to bring forward, forth or out; to extend, enlarge; (time) to prolong, defer; (*instance*) to mention, quote; (*knowledge*) to publish, reveal; **pedem prōferre** proceed; **signa prōferre** advance

professiō, -ōnis *f* declaration; public register; profession

professor, -ōris *m* teacher

professōrius *adj* authoritative

professus *ppa of* **profiteor**

profēstus *adj* not holiday, working

prōficiō, -icere, -ēcī, -ectum *vi* to make progress, profit; to be of use

prōficīscor, -icīscī, -ectus *vi* to set out, start; to originate, proceed

profiteor, -itērī, -essus *vt* to declare, profess; to make an official return of; to promise, volunteer

prōflīgātor, -ōris *m* spendthrift

prōflīgātus *adj* dissolute

prōflīgō, -āre, -āvī, -ātum *vt* to dash to the ground; to destroy, overthrow; to bring almost to an end; to degrade

prōflō, -āre *vt* to breathe out

prōfluēns, -entis *pres p of* **prōfluō** ▸ *adj* flowing; fluent ▸ *f* running water

prōfluenter *adv* easily

prōfluentia, -ae *f* fluency

prōfluō, -ere, -xī *vi* to flow on, flow out; (*fig*) to proceed

prōfluvium, -ī and -iī *nt* flowing

profor, -ārī, -ātus *vi* to speak, give utterance

profugiō, -ugere, -ūgī *vi* to flee, escape; to take refuge (with) ▸ *vt* to flee from

profugus *adj* fugitive; exiled; nomadic

prōfuī *perf of* **prōsum**

profundō, -undere, -ūdī, -ūsum *vt* to pour out, shed; to bring forth, produce; to prostrate; to squander; **sē profundere** burst forth, rush out

profundus *adj* deep, vast, high; infernal; (*fig*) profound, immoderate ▸ *nt* depths, abyss

profūsē *adv* in disorder, extravagantly

profūsus *ppp of* **profundō** ▸ *adj* lavish; excessive

prōgener, -ī *m* grandson-in-law

prōgenerō, -āre *vt* to beget

prōgeniēs, -ēī *f* descent; offspring, descendants

prōgenitor, -ōris *m* ancestor

prōgignō, -ignere, -enuī, -enitum *vt* to beget, produce

prōgnātus *adj* born, descended ▸ *m* son, descendant

Prognē *see* **Procnē**

prognōstica, -ōrum *ntpl* weather signs

prōgredior, -dī, -ssus *vi* to go forward, advance; to go out

prōgressiō, -ōnis *f* advancing, increase; (*RHET*) climax

prōgressus¹ *ppa of* **prōgredior**

prōgressus², -ūs *m* advance, progress; (*events*) march

prōh *interj see* **prō²**

prohibeō, -ēre, -uī, -itum *vt* to hinder, prevent; to keep away, protect; to forbid

prohibitiō, -ōnis *f* forbidding

prōiciō, -icere, -iēcī, -iectum *vt* to throw down, fling forwards; to banish; (*building*) to make project; (*fig*) to discard, renounce; to forsake; (*words*) to blurt out; (*time*) to defer; **sē prōicere** rush forward, run into danger; to fall prostrate

prōiectiō, -ōnis *f* forward stretch

prōiectus¹ *ppp of* **prōiciō** ▸ *adj* projecting, prominent; abject, useless; downcast; addicted (to)

prōiectus², -ūs *m* jutting out

proinde, proin *adv* consequently, therefore; just (as)

prōlābor, -bī, -psus *vi* to slide, move forward; to fall down; (*fig*) to go on, come to; to slip out; to fail, fall, sink into ruin

prōlāpsiō, -ōnis *f* falling

prōlāpsus *ppa of* **prōlābor**

prōlātiō, -ōnis *f* extension; postponement; adducing

prōlātō, -āre *vt* to extend; to postpone

prōlātus *ppp of* **prōferō**

prōlectō, -āre *vt* to entice

prōlēs, -is *f* offspring; child; descendants, race

prōlētārius, -ī and -iī *m* citizen of the lowest class

prōliciō, -cere, -xī *vt* to entice

prōlixē *adv* fully, copiously, willingly

prōlixus *adj* long, wide, spreading; (*person*) obliging; (*circumstances*) favourable

prōlogus, -ī *m* prologue

prōloquor, -quī, -cūtus *vt* to speak out

prōlubium, -ī and -iī *nt* inclination

prōlūdō, -dere, -sī, -sum *vi* to practise

prōluō, -uere, -uī, -ūtum *vt* to wash out, wash away

prōlūsiō, -ōnis *f* prelude

prōluviēs, -ēī *f* flood; excrement

prōmereō, -ēre, -uī, prōmereor, -ērī, -itus *vt* to deserve, earn

prōmeritum, -ī *nt* desert, merit, guilt

Prōmētheus, -eī and -eos *m* demigod who stole fire from the gods

Promēthēus *adj see* **Prōmētheus**

prōminēns, -entis *pres p of* **prōmineō** ▸ *adj* projecting ▸ *nt* headland, spur

prōmineō, -ēre, -uī *vi* to jut out, overhang; to extend

prōmiscam, prōmiscē, prōmiscuē *adv* indiscriminately

prōmiscuus, prōmiscus *adj* indiscriminate, in common; ordinary; open to all

prōmīsī *perf of* **prōmittō**

prōmissiō, -ōnis *f* promise

prōmissor, -ōris *m* promiser

prōmissum, -ī *nt* promise

prōmissus *ppp of* **prōmittō** ▸ *adj* long

prōmittō, -ittere, -īsī, -issum *vt* to let grow; to promise, give promise of

prōmō, -ere, -psī, -ptum *vt* to bring out, produce; to disclose

prōmontorium, -ī *and* **-iī** *nt* headland, promontory, ridge

prōmōtus *ppp of* **prōmoveō** ▶ *ntpl* preferable things

prōmoveō, -ovēre, -ōvī, -ōtum *vt* to move forward, advance; to enlarge; to postpone; to disclose

prōmpsī *perf of* **prōmō**

prōmptē *adv* readily; easily

prōmptō, -āre *vt* to distribute

prōmptū *abl m*: **in ~** at hand, in readiness; obvious, in evidence; easy

prōmptus *ppp of* **prōmō** ▶ *adj* at hand, ready; prompt, resolute; easy

prōmulgātiō, -ōnis *f* promulgating

prōmulgō, -āre, -āvī, -ātum *vt* to make public, publish

prōmulsis, -idis *f* hors d'oeuvre

prōmus, -ī *m* cellarer, butler

prōmūtuus *adj* as a loan in advance

prōnepōs, -ōtis *m* great-grandson

pronoea, -ae *f* providence

prōnōmen, -inis *nt* pronoun

prōnuba, -ae *f* matron attending a bride

prōnūntiātiō, -ōnis *f* declaration; (*RHET*) delivery; (*LOGIC*) proposition

prōnūntiātor, -ōris *m* narrator

prōnūntiātum, -ātī *nt* proposition

prōnūntiō, -āre, -āvī, -ātum *vt* to declare publicly, announce; to recite, deliver; to narrate; to nominate

prōnurus, -ūs *f* granddaughter-in-law

prōnus *adj* leaning forward; headlong, downwards; sloping, sinking; (*fig*) inclined, disposed, favourable; easy

prooemium, -ī *and* **-iī** *nt* prelude, preface

propāgātiō, -ōnis *f* propagating; extension

propāgātor, -ōris *m* enlarger

propāgō¹, -āre, -āvī, -ātum *vt* to propagate; to extend; to prolong

propāgō², -inis *f* (*plant*) layer, slip; (*men*) offspring, posterity

prōpalam *adv* openly, known

prōpatulum, -ī *nt* open space

prōpatulus *adj* open

prope *adv* (*compar* **propius**, *superl* **proximē**) near; nearly ▶ *prep* (*with acc*) near, not far from

propediem *adv* very soon

prōpellō, -ellere, -ulī, -ulsum *vt* to drive, push forward, impel; to drive away, keep off

propemodum, propemodo *adv* almost

prōpendeō, -endēre, -endī, -ēnsum *vi* to hang down; to preponderate; to be disposed (to)

propēnsē *adv* willingly

prōpēnsiō, -ōnis *f* inclination

prōpēnsus *adj* inclining; inclined, well-disposed; important

properanter *adv* hastily, quickly

properantia, -ae *f* haste

properātiō, -ōnis *f* haste

properātō *adv* quickly

properātus *adj* speedy

properē *adv* quickly

properipēs, -edis *adj* swiftfooted

properō, -āre, -āvī, -ātum *vt* to hasten, do with haste ▶ *vi* to make haste, hurry

Propertius, -ī *m* Latin elegiac poet

properus *adj* quick, hurrying

prōpexus *adj* combed forward

propīnō, -āre *vt* to drink as a toast; to pass on (*a cup*)

propinquitās, -ātis *f* nearness; relationship, friendship

propinquō, -āre *vi* to approach ▶ *vt* to hasten

propinquus *adj* near, neighbouring; related ▶ *m/f* relation ▶ *nt* neighbourhood

propior, -ōris *adj* nearer; more closely related, more like; (*time*) more recent

propitiō, -āre *vt* to appease

propitius *adj* favourable, gracious

propius *adv* nearer, more closely

prōpōla, -ae *f* retailer

prōpolluō, -ere *vt* to defile further

prōpōnō, -ōnere, -osuī, -ositum *vt* to set forth, display; to publish, declare; to propose, resolve; to imagine; to expose; (*LOGIC*) to state the first premise; **ante oculōs prōpōnere** picture to oneself

Propontiacus *adj see* **Propontis**

Propontis, -idis *and* **-idos** *f* Sea of Marmora

prōporrō *adv* furthermore; utterly

prōportiō, -ōnis *f* symmetry, analogy

prōpositiō, -ōnis *f* purpose; theme; (*LOGIC*) first premise

prōpositum, -ī *nt* plan, purpose; theme; (*LOGIC*) first premise

prōpositus *ppp of* **prōpōnō**

prōpraetor, -ōris *m* propraetor, governor; vice-praetor

propriē *adv* properly, strictly; particularly

proprietās, -ātis *f* peculiarity, property

proprītim *adv* properly

proprius *adj* one's own, peculiar; personal, characteristic; permanent; (*words*) literal, regular

propter *adv* near by ▶ *prep* (*with acc*) near, beside; on account of; by means of

proptereā *adv* therefore

prōpudium, -ī *and* **-iī** *nt* shameful act; villain

prōpugnāculum, -ī *nt* bulwark, tower; defence

prōpugnātiō, -ōnis *f* defence

prōpugnātor, -ōris *m* defender, champion

prōpugnō, -āre *vi* to make a sortie; to fight in defence

prōpulsātiō, -ōnis *f* repulse

prōpulsō, -āre, -āvī, -ātum *vt* to repel, avert

prōpulsus *ppp of* **prōpellō**

Propylaea, -ōrum *ntpl* gateway to the Acropolis of Athens

prō quaestōre m proquaestor

prōquam conj according as

prōra, -ae f prow, bows; ship

prōrēpō, -ere, -sī, -tum vi to crawl out

prōrēta, -ae m man at the prow

prōreus, -eī m man at the prow

prōripiō, -ipere, -ipuī, -eptum vt to drag out; to hurry away; **sē prōripere** rush out, run away

prōrogātiō, -ōnis f extension; deferring

prōrogō, -āre, -āvī, -ātum vt to extend, prolong, continue; to defer

prōrsum adv forwards; absolutely

prōrsus adv forwards; absolutely; in short

prōrumpō, -umpere, -ūpī, -uptum vt to fling out; (pass) to rush forth ▶ vi to break out, burst forth

prōruō, -ere, -ī, -tum vt to throw down, demolish ▶ vi to rush forth

prōruptus ppp of **prōrumpō**

prōsāpia, -ae f lineage

proscaenium, -ī and **-iī** nt stage

proscindō, -ndere, -dī, -ssum vt to plough up; (fig) to revile

prōscrībō, -bere, -psī, -ptum vt to publish in writing; to advertise; to confiscate; to proscribe, outlaw

prōscrīptiō, -ōnis f advertisement; proscription

prōscrīptūriō, -īre vi to want to have a proscription

prōscrīptus ppp of **prōscrībō** ▶ m outlaw

prōsecō, -āre, -uī, -tum vt to cut off (for sacrifice)

prōsēminō, -āre vt to scatter; to propagate

prōsentiō, -entīre, -ēnsī vt to see beforehand

prōsequor, -quī, -cūtus vt to attend, escort; to pursue, attack; to honour (with); (words) to proceed with, continue

Proserpina, -ae f Proserpine (daughter of Ceres and wife of Pluto)

proseucha, -ae f place of prayer

prōsiliō, -īre, -uī vi to jump up, spring forward; to burst out, spurt

prōsocer, -ī m wife's grandfather

prōspectō, -āre vt to look out at, view; to look forward to, await; (place) to look towards

prōspectus¹ ppp of **prōspiciō**

prōspectus², -ūs m sight, view, prospect; gaze

prōspeculor, -ārī vi to look out, reconnoitre. ▶ vt to watch for

prosper, prosperus adj favourable, successful

prosperē adv see **prosper**

prosperitās, -ātis f good fortune

prosperō, -āre vt to make successful, prosper

prosperus etc see **prosper**

prōspicientia, -ae f foresight

prōspiciō, -icere, -exī, -ectum vi to look out, watch; to see to, take precautions ▶ vt to descry, watch for; to foresee; to provide; (place) to command a view of

prōsternō, -ernere, -rāvī, -rātum vt to throw in front, prostrate; to overthrow, ruin; **sē prōsternere** fall prostrate; demean oneself

prōstibulum, -ī nt prostitute

prōstituō, -uere, -uī, -ūtum vt to put up for sale, prostitute

prōstō, -āre, -itī vi to project; to be on sale; to prostitute oneself

prōstrātus ppp of **prōsternō**

prōsubigō, -ere vt to dig up

prōsum, -desse, -fuī vi (with dat) to be useful to, benefit

Prōtagorās, -ae m Greek sophist (native of Abdera)

prōtēctus ppp of **prōtegō**

prōtegō, -egere, -ēxī, -ēctum vt to cover over, put a projecting roof on; (fig) to shield, protect

prōtēlō, -āre vt to drive off

prōtēlum, -ī nt team of oxen; (fig) succession

prōtendō, -dere, -dī, -tum vt to stretch out, extend

prōtentus ppp of **prōtendō**

prōterō, -erere, -rīvī, -rītum vt to trample down, crush; to overthrow

prōterreō, -ēre, -uī, -itum vt to scare away

protervē adv insolently; boldly

protervitās, -ātis f forwardness, insolence

protervus adj forward, insolent, violent

Prōtesilāeus adj see **Prōtesilāus**

Prōtesilāus, -ī m first Greek killed at Troy

Prōteus, -eī and **-eos** m sea god with power to assume many forms

prothȳmē adv gladly

prōtinam adv immediately

prōtinus adv forward, onward; continuously; right away, forthwith

prōtollō, -ere vt to stretch out; to put off

prōtractus ppp of **prōtrahō**

prōtrahō, -here, -xī, -ctum vt to draw on (to); to drag out; to bring to light, reveal

prōtrītus ppp of **prōterō**

prōtrūdō, -dere, -sī, -sum vt to thrust forward, push out; to postpone

prōtulī perf of **prōferō**

prōturbō, -āre, -āvī, -ātum vt to drive off; to overthrow

prout conj according as

prōvectus ppp of **prōvehō** ▶ adj advanced

prōvehō, -here, -xī, -ctum vt to carry along, transport; to promote, advance, bring to; (speech) to prolong; (pass) to drive, ride, sail on

prōveniō, -enīre, -ēnī, -entum vi to come out, appear; to arise, grow; to go on, prosper, succeed

prōventus, -ūs m increase; result, success

prōverbium, -ī and **-iī** nt saying, proverb

prōvidēns, -entis pres p of **prōvideō** ▶ adj prudent

prōvidenter adv with foresight

prōvidentia, -ae f foresight, forethought

prōvideō, -idēre, -īdī, -īsum vi to see ahead; to take care, make provision ▶ vt to foresee; to look after, provide for; to obviate

prōvidus adj foreseeing, cautious, prudent; provident

prōvincia, -ae f sphere of action, duty, province

prōvinciālis adj provincial ▶ mpl provincials

prōvīsiō, -ōnis f foresight; precaution

prōvīsō¹ adv with forethought

prōvīsō², -ere vi to go and see

prōvīsor, -ōris m foreseer; provider

prōvīsus¹ ppp of **prōvideō**

prōvīsus², -ūs m looking forward; foreseeing; providing, providence

prōvīvō, -vere, -xī vi to live on

prōvocātiō, -ōnis f challenge; appeal

prōvocātor, -ōris m kind of gladiator

prōvocō, -āre, -āvī, -ātum vt to challenge, call out; to provoke; to bring about ▶ vi to appeal

prōvolō, -āre vi to fly out, rush out

prōvolvō, -vere, -vī, -ūtum vt to roll forward, tumble over; (pass) to fall down, humble oneself, be ruined; **sē prōvolvere** wallow

prōvomō, -ere vt to belch forth

proximē adv next, nearest; (time) just before or after; (with acc) next to, very close to, very like

proximitās, -ātis f nearness; near relationship; similarity

proximus adj nearest, next; (time) previous, last, following, next; most akin, most like ▶ m next of kin ▶ nt next door

proxum- etc see **proxim-**

prūdēns, -entis adj foreseeing, aware; wise, prudent, circumspect; skilled, versed (in)

prūdenter adv prudently; skilfully

prūdentia, -ae f prudence, discretion; knowledge

pruīna, -ae f hoar frost

pruīnōsus adj frosty

prūna, -ae f live coal

prūnitius adj of plum tree wood

prūnum, -ī nt plum

prūnus, -ī f plum tree

prūriō, -īre vi to itch

prytanēum, -ī nt Greek town hall

prytanis, -is m Greek chief magistrate

psallō, -ere vi to play the lyre or lute

psaltērium, -ī and **-iī** nt kind of lute

psaltria, -ae f girl musician

psecas, -adis f slave who perfumed the ladies' hair

psēphisma, -tis nt decree of the people

Pseudocatō, -ōnis m sham Cato

pseudomenos, -ī m sophistical argument

pseudothyrum, -ī nt back door

psithius adj psithian (kind of Greek vine)

psittacus, -ī m parrot

psychomantēum, psychomantīum, -ī nt place of necromancy

-pte enclitic (to pronouns) self, own

ptisanārium, -ī and **-iī** nt gruel

Ptolemaeēus, Ptolemaeus adj see **Ptolemaeus**

Ptolemaeus, -ī m Ptolemy (name of Egyptian kings)

pūbēns, -entis adj full-grown; (plant) juicy

pūbertās, -ātis f manhood; signs of puberty

pūbēs¹, pūber, -eris adj grown up, adult; (plant) downy

pūbēs², -is f hair at age of puberty; groin; youth, men, people

pūbēscō, -ēscere, -uī vi to grow to manhood, become mature; to become clothed

pūblicānus adj of public revenue ▶ m tax farmer

pūblicātiō, -ōnis f confiscation

pūblicē adv by or for the State, at the public expense; all together

pūblicitus adv at the public expense; in public

pūblicō, -āre, -āvī, -ātum vt to confiscate; to make public

Pūblicola, -ae m P. Valerius (an early Roman consul)

pūblicum, -ī nt State revenue; State territory; public

pūblicus adj of the State, public, common ▶ m public official; **pūblica causa** criminal trial; **rēs pūblica** the State; **dē pūblicō** at the public expense; **in pūblicō** in public

Publius, -ī m Roman first name

pudendus adj shameful

pudēns, -entis adj bashful, modest

pudenter adv modestly

pudet, -ēre, -uit and **-itum est** vt impers to shame, be ashamed

pudibundus adj modest

pudīcē adv see **pudīcus**

pudīcitia, -ae f modesty, chastity

pudīcus adj modest, chaste

pudor, -ōris m shame, modesty, sense of honour; disgrace

puella, -ae f girl; sweetheart, young wife

puellāris adj girlish, youthful

puellula, -ae f little girl

puellus, -ī m little boy

puer, -ī m boy, child; son; slave

puerīlis adj boyish, child's; childish, trivial

puerīliter adv like a child; childishly

pueritia, -ae f childhood, youth

puerperium, -ī and **-iī** nt childbirth

puerperus adj to help childbirth ▶ f woman in labour

puertia etc see **pueritia**

puerulus, -ī m little boy, slave

pugil, -is m boxer

pugilātiō, -iōnis f, **pugilātus, -ūs** m boxing

pugillāris adj that can be held in the hand ▶ mpl, ntpl writing tablets

pugillātōrius adj: **follis ~** punchball

pugiō, -ōnis m dirk, dagger

pugiunculus, -ī m small dagger

pugna, -ae f fight, battle

pugnācitās, -ātis f fondness for a fight
pugnāciter adv aggressively
pugnāculum, -ī nt fortress
pugnātor, -ōris m fighter
pugnāx, -ācis adj fond of a fight, aggressive; obstinate
pugneus adj with the fist
pugnō, -āre, -āvī, -ātum vi to fight; to disagree; to struggle; **sēcum pugnāre** be inconsistent; **pugnātum est** the battle was fought
pugnus, -ī m fist
pulchellus adj pretty little
pulcher, -rī adj beautiful, handsome; fine, glorious
pulchrē adv excellently; well done!
pulchritūdō, -inis f beauty, excellence
pūlēium, pūlegium, -ī and **-iī** nt pennyroyal
pūlex, -icis m flea
pullārius, -ī and **-iī** m keeper of the sacred chickens
pullātus adj dressed in black
pullulō, -āre vi to sprout
pullus¹, -ī m young (of animals), chicken
pullus² adj dark-grey; mournful ▶ nt dark grey clothes
pulmentārium, -ārī and **-āriī, pulmentum, -ī** nt relish; food
pulmō, -ōnis m lung
pulmōneus adj of the lungs
pulpa, -ae f fleshy part
pulpāmentum, -ī nt titbits
pulpitum, -ī nt platform, stage
puls, pultis f porridge
pulsātiō, -ōnis f beating
pulsō, -āre, -āvī, -ātum vt to batter, knock, strike
pulsus¹ ppp of **pellō**
pulsus², -ūs m push, beat, blow; impulse
pultiphagus, -ī m porridge eater
pultō, -āre vt to beat, knock at
pulvereus adj of dust, dusty, fine as dust; raising dust
pulverulentus adj dusty; laborious
pulvillus, -ī m small cushion
pulvīnar, -āris nt sacred couch; seat of honour
pulvīnus, -ī m cushion, pillow
pulvis, -eris m dust, powder; arena; effort
pulvisculus, -ī m fine dust
pūmex, -icis m pumice stone; stone, rock
pūmiceus adj of soft stone
pūmicō, -āre vt to smooth with pumice stone
pūmiliō, -ōnis m/f person of small stature
pūnctim adv with the point
pūnctum, -ī nt point, dot; vote; (time) moment; (speech) short section
pūnctus ppp of **pungō**
pungō, -ere, pupugī, pūnctum vt to prick, sting, pierce; (fig) to vex
Pūnicānus adj in the Carthaginian style
Pūnicē adv in Punic
pūniceus adj reddish, purple

pūnicum, -ī nt pomegranate
Pūnicus adj Punic, Carthaginian; purple-red
pūniō, poeniō, -īre, pūnior, -īrī vt to punish; to avenge
pūnītor, -ōris m avenger
pūpa, -ae f doll
pūpilla, -ae f ward; (eye) pupil
pūpillāris adj of a ward, of an orphan
pūpillus, -ī m orphan, ward
puppis, -is f after part of a ship, stern; ship
pupugī perf of **pungō**
pūpula, -ae f (eye) pupil
pūpulus, -ī m little boy
pūrē adv cleanly, brightly; plainly, simply, purely, chastely
pūrgāmen, -inis nt sweepings, dirt; means of expiation
pūrgāmentum, -ī nt refuse, dirt
pūrgātiō, -ōnis f purging; justification
pūrgō, -āre, -āvī, -ātum vt to cleanse, purge, clear away; to exculpate, justify; to purify
pūriter adv cleanly, purely
purpura, -ae f purple-fish, purple; purple cloth; finery, royalty
purpurātus adj wearing purple ▶ m courtier
purpureus adj red, purple, black; wearing purple; bright, radiant
purpurissum, -ī nt kind of rouge
pūrus adj clear, unadulterated, free from obstruction or admixture; pure, clean; plain, unadorned; (moral) pure, chaste ▶ nt clear sky
pūs, pūris nt pus; (fig) malice
pusillus adj very little; petty, paltry
pūsiō, -ōnis m little boy
pūstula, -ae f pimple, blister
putāmen, -inis nt peeling, shell, husk
putātiō, -ōnis f pruning
putātor, -ōris m pruner
puteal, -ālis nt low wall round a well or sacred place
puteālis adj well- (in cpds)
pūteō, -ēre vi to stink
Puteolānus adj see **Puteolī**
Puteolī, -ōrum mpl town on the Campanian coast
puter, putris, -ris adj rotten, decaying; crumbling, flabby
putēscō, -ēscere, -uī vi to become rotten
puteus, -ī m well; pit
pūtidē adv see **pūtidus**
pūtidiusculus adj somewhat nauseating
pūtidus adj rotten, stinking; (speech) affected, nauseating
putō, -āre, -āvī, -ātum vt to think, suppose; to think over; to reckon, count; (money) to settle; (tree) to prune
pūtor, -ōris m stench
putrefaciō, -facere, -fēcī, -factum vt to make rotten; to make crumble
putrēscō, -ere vi to rot, moulder
putridus adj rotten, decayed; withered
putris etc see **puter**

putus¹ *adj* perfectly pure
putus², -ī *m* boy
pycta, pyctēs, -ae *m* boxer
Pydna, -ae *f* town in Macedonia
Pydnaeus *adj see* **Pydna**
pȳga, -ae *f* buttocks
Pygmaeus *adj* Pygmy
Pyladēs, -ae *and* **-is** *m* friend of Orestes
Pyladēus *adj see* **Pyladēs**
Pylae, -ārum *fpl* Thermopylae
Pylaicus *adj see* **Pylae**
Pylius *adj see* **Pylos**
Pylos, -ī *f* Pylus (*Peloponnesian town, home of Nestor*)
pyra, -ae *f* funeral pyre
Pȳramaeus *adj see* **Pȳramus**
pȳramis, -idis *f* pyramid
Pȳramus, -ī *m* lover of Thisbe
Pȳrēnē, -ēs *f* Pyrenees
pyrethrum, -ī *nt* Spanish camomile
Pyrgēnsis *adj see* **Pyrgī**
Pyrgī, -ōrum *mpl* ancient town in Etruria
pyrōpus, -ī *m* bronze
Pyrrha, -ae, Pyrrhē, -ēs *f* wife of Deucalion
Pyrrhaeus *adj see* **Pyrrha**
Pyrrhō, -ōnis *m* Greek philosopher (*founder of the Sceptics*)
Pyrrhōnēus *adj see* **Pyrrhō**
Pyrrhus, -ī *m* son of Achilles; king of Epirus, enemy of Rome
Pȳthagorās, -ae *m* Greek philosopher who founded a school in S. Italy
Pȳthagorēus, -icus *adj* Pythagorean
Pȳthius, Pȳthicus *adj* Pythian, Delphic ▶ *m* Apollo ▶ *f* priestess of Apollo ▶ *ntpl* Pythian Games
Pȳthō, -ūs *f* Delphi
Pȳthōn, -ōnis *m* serpent killed by Apollo
pȳtisma, -tis *nt* what is spat out
pȳtissō, -āre *vi* to spit out wine
pyxis, -dis *f* small box, toilet box

q

quā *adv* where, which way; whereby; as far as; partly ... partly
quācumque *adv* wherever; anyhow
quādam: ~ tenus *adv* only so far
quadra, -ae *f* square; morsel; table
quadrāgēnī, -ōrum *adj* forty each
quadrāgēsimus, -ī *and* **-iī** *adj* fortieth ▶ *f* 2.5 per cent tax
quadrāgiēns, quadrāgiēs *adv* forty times
quadrāgintā *num* forty
quadrāns, -antis *m* quarter; (*coin*) quarter as
quadrantārius *adj* of a quarter
quadrātum, -ī *nt* square; (ASTR) quadrature
quadrātus *ppp of* **quadrō** ▶ *adj* square; **quadrātō agmine** in battle order
quadriduum, -ī *nt* four days
quadriennium, -ī *and* **-iī** *nt* four years
quadrifāriam *adv* in four parts
quadrifidus *adj* split in four
quadrīga, -ae *f* team of four; chariot
quadrīgārius, -ī *and* **-iī** *m* chariot racer
quadrīgātus *adj* stamped with a chariot
quadrīgulae, -ārum *fpl* little four horse team
quadriiugī, -ōrum *mpl* team of four
quadriiugis, quadriiugus *adj* of a team of four
quadrilībris *adj* weighing four pounds
quadrīmulus *adj* four years old
quadrīmus *adj* four years old
quadringēnārius *adj* of four hundred each
quadringēnī, -ōrum *adj* four hundred each
quadringentēsimus *adj* four-hundredth
quadringentī, -ōrum *num* four hundred
quadringentiēns, quadringentiēs *adv* four hundred times
quadripertītus *adj* fourfold
quadrirēmis, -is *f* quadrireme
quadrivium, -ī *and* **-iī** *nt* crossroads
quadrō, -āre *vt* to make square; to complete ▶ *vi* to square, fit, agree
quadrum, -ī *nt* square
quadrupedāns, -antis *adj* galloping
quadrupēs, -edis *adj* four-footed, on all fours ▶ *m/f* quadruped
quadruplātor, -ōris *m* informer, twister

quadruplex, -icis adj four-fold

quadruplum, -ī nt four times as much

quaeritō, -āre vt to search diligently for; to earn (a living); to keep on asking

quaerō, -rere, -sīvī and **-siī, -sītum** vt to look for, search for; to seek, try to get; to acquire, earn; (plan) to think out, work out; (question) to ask, make inquiries; (LAW) to investigate; (with infin) to try, wish; **quid quaeris?** in short; **sī quaeris/quaerimus** to tell the truth

quaesītiō, -ōnis f inquisition

quaesītor, -ōris m investigator, judge

quaesītus ppp of **quaerō** ▸ adj special; far-fetched ▸ nt question ▸ ntpl gains

quaesīvī perf of **quaerō**

quaesō, -ere vt to ask, beg

quaesticulus, -ī m slight profit

quaestiō, -ōnis f seeking, questioning; investigation, research; criminal trial; court; **servum in quaestiōnem ferre** take a slave for questioning by torture; **quaestiōnēs perpetuae** standing courts

quaestiuncula, -ae f trifling question

quaestor, -ōris m quaestor, treasury official

quaestōrius adj of a quaestor ▸ m ex-quaestor ▸ nt quaestor's tent or residence

quaestuōsus adj lucrative, productive; money-making; wealthy

quaestūra, -ae f quaestorship; public money

quaestus, -ūs m profit, advantage; money-making, occupation; **quaestuī habēre** make money out of; **quaestum facere** make a living

quālibet adv anywhere; anyhow

quālis adj (interrog) what kind of?; (rel) such as, even as

quāliscumque adj of whatever kind; any, whatever

qualiscunque adj = **quāliscumque**

quālitās, -ātis f quality, nature

quāliter adv just as

quālubet adv anywhere; anyhow

quālus, -ī m wicker basket

quam adv (interrog, excl) how?, how much?; (comparison) as, than; (with superl) as ... possible; (emphatic) very; **dīmidium ~ quod** half of what; **quīntō diē ~** four days after

quamdiū adv how long?; as long as

quamlibet, quamlubet adv as much as you like, however

quamobrem adv (interrog) why?; (rel) why ▸ conj therefore

quamquam conj although; and yet

quamvīs adv however, ever so ▸ conj however much, although

quānam adv what way

quandō adv (interrog) when?; (rel) when; (with **sī, nē, num**) ever ▸ conj when; since

quandōcumque, quandocunque adv whenever, as often as; some day

quandōque adv whenever; some day ▸ conj seeing that

quandō quidem conj seeing that, since

quanquam etc see **quamquam**

quantillus adj how little, how much

quantopere adv how much; (after **tantopere**) as

quantulus adj how little, how small

quantuluscumque adj however small, however trifling

quantum adv how much; as much as; **quantumcumque** as much as ever; **quantumlibet** however much; **quantumvīs** as much as you like; although

quantus adj how great; so great as, such as; **quantī** how dear, how highly; **quantō** (with compar) how much; the; **in quantum** as far as

quantuscumque adj however great, whatever size

quantuslibet adj as great as you like

quantus quantus adj however great

quantusvīs adj however great

quāpropter adv why; and therefore

quāquā adv whatever way

quārē adv how, why; whereby; and therefore

quartadecumānī, -ōrum mpl men of the fourteenth legion

quartānus adj every four days ▸ f quartan fever ▸ mpl men of the fourth legion

quartārius, -ī and **-iī** m quarter pint

quartus adj fourth; **quartum/quartō** for the fourth time

quartusdecimus adj fourteenth

quasi adv as if; as it were; (numbers) about

quasillus, -ī m, **quasillum, -ī** nt wool basket

quassātiō, -ōnis f shaking

quassō, -āre, -āvī, -ātum vt to shake, toss; to shatter, damage

quassus ppp of **quatiō** ▸ adj broken

quatefaciō, -facere, -fēcī vt to shake, give a jolt to

quātenus adv (interrog) how far?; how long?; (rel) as far as; in so far as, since

quater adv four times; **~ deciēs** fourteen times

quaternī, -ōrum adj four each, in fours

quatiō, -tere, -ssī, -ssum vt to shake, disturb, brandish; to strike, shatter; (fig) to agitate, harass

quattuor num four

quattuordecim num fourteen

quattuorvirātus, -ūs m membership of quattuorviri

quattuorvirī, -ōrum mpl board of four officials

-que conj and; both ... and; (after neg) but

quemadmodum adv (interrog) how?; (rel) just as

queō, -īre, -īvī and **-iī, -itum** vi to be able, can

quercētum, -ī nt oak forest

querceus adj of oak

quercus, -ūs f oak; garland of oak leaves; acorn

querēla, querella, -ae f complaint; plaintive sound

queribundus adj complaining

querimōnia, -ae f complaint; elegy

queritor, -ārī vi to complain much

quernus adj oak- (in cpds)

queror, -rī, -stus vt, vi to complain, lament; (birds) to sing

querquetulānus adj of oakwoods

querulus adj complaining; plaintive, warbling

questus¹ ppa of **queror**

questus², -ūs m complaint, lament

quī¹, quae, quod pron (interrog) what?, which?; (rel) who, which, that; what; and this, he etc; (with **sī, nisi, nē, num**) any

quī² adv (interrog) how?; (rel) with which, whereby; (indef) somehow; (excl) indeed

quia conj because; **quianam** why?

quicquam nt see **quisquam**

quicque nt see **quisque**

quicquid nt see **quisquis**

quīcum with whom, with which

quīcumque, quīcunque pron whoever, whatever, all that; every possible

quid nt see **quis ▶** adv why?

quīdam, quaedam, quoddam pron a certain, a sort of, a ...

quiddam nt something

quidem adv (emphatic) in fact; (qualifying) at any rate; (conceding) it is true; (alluding) for instance; **nē ... ~** not even

quidlibet nt anything

quidnam nt see **quisnam**

quidnī adv why not?

quidpiam nt see **quispiam**

quidquam nt see **quisquam**

quidquid nt see **quisquis**

quiēs, -ētis f rest, peace, quiet; sleep, dream, death; neutrality; lair

quiēscō, -scere, -vī, -tum vi to rest, keep quiet; to be at peace, keep neutral; to sleep; (with acc and infin) to stand by and see; (with infin) to cease

quiētē adv peacefully, quietly

quiētus ppa of **quiēscō ▶** adj at rest; peaceful, neutral; calm, quiet, asleep

quīlibet, quaelibet, quodlibet pron any, anyone at all

quīn adv (interrog) why not?; (correcting) indeed, rather ▶ conj who not; but that, but, without; (preventing) from; (doubting) that

quīnam, quaenam, quodnam pron which?, what?

Quīnct- etc see **Quīnt-**

quīncūnx, -ūncis m five-twelfths; number five on a dice; **in quīncūncem dispositī** arranged in oblique lines

quīndeciēns, quīndeciēs adv fifteen times

quīndecim num fifteen; **~ prīmī** fifteen chief magistrates

quīndecimvirālis adj of the council of fifteen

quīndecimvirī, -ōrum mpl council of fifteen

quīngēnī, -ōrum adj five hundred each

quīngentēsimus adj five-hundredth

quīngentī, -ōrum num five hundred

quīngentiēns, quīngentiēs adv five hundred times

quīnī, -ōrum adj five each; five; **~ dēnī** fifteen each; **~ vīcēnī** twenty-five each

quīnquāgēnī, -ōrum adj fifty each

quīnquāgēsimus adj fiftieth ▶ f 2 per cent tax

quīnquāgintā num fifty

Quīnquātria, -iōrum and **-ium** ntpl festival of Minerva

Quīnquātrūs, -uum fpl festival of Minerva

quīnque num five

quīnquennālis adj quinquennial; lasting five years

quīnquennis adj five years old; quinquennial

quīnquennium, -ī and **-iī** nt five years

quīnquepartītus adj fivefold

quīnqueprīmī, -ōrum mpl five leading men

quīnquerēmis adj five-banked ▶ f quinquereme

quīnquevirātus, -ūs m membership of the board of five

quīnquevirī, -ōrum mpl board of five

quīnquiēns, quīnquiēs adv five times

quīnquiplicō, -āre vt to multiply by five

quīntadecimānī, -ōrum mpl men of the fifteenth legion

quīntānus adj of the fifth ▶ f street in a camp between the 5th and 6th maniples ▶ mpl men of the fifth legion

Quīntiliānus, -ī m Quintilian (famous teacher of rhetoric in Rome)

Quīntīlis adj of July

quīntum, quīntō adv for the fifth time

Quīntus, -ī m Roman first name

quīntus adj fifth

quīntusdecimus adj fifteenth

quippe adv (affirming) certainly, of course ▶ conj (explaining) for in fact, because, since; **~ quī** since I, he etc

quippiam etc see **quispiam**

quippinī adv certainly

Quirīnālis adj of Romulus; Quirinal (hill)

Quirīnus, -ī m Romulus ▶ adj of Romulus

Quirīs, -ītis m inhabitant of Cures; Roman citizen; citizen

quirītātiō, -ōnis f shriek

Quirītēs mpl inhabitants of Cures; Roman citizens

quirītō, -āre vi to cry out, wail

quis, quid pron who?, what?; (indef) anyone, anything

quīs poetic dat pl and abl pl of **quī¹**

quisnam, quaenam, quidnam pron who?, what?

quispiam, quaepiam, quodpiam and **quidpiam** pron some, someone, something

quisquam, quaequam, quicquam and **quidquam** pron any, anyone, anything; **nec ~** and no one

quisque, quaeque, quodque pron each, every, every one; **quidque, quicque** everything; **decimus ~** every tenth; **optimus ~** all the best; **prīmus ~** the first possible

quisquiliae, -ārum fpl refuse, rubbish

quisquis, quaequae, quodquod, quidquid and **quicquid** pron whoever, whatever, all

quīvīs, quaevīs, quodvīs, quidvīs pron any you please, anyone, anything

quīvīscumque, quaevīscumque, quodvīscumque pron any whatsoever

quō adv (interrog) where?; whither?; for what purpose?, what for?; (rel) where, to which (place), to whom; (with compar) the (more); (with sī) anywhere ▶ conj (with subj) in order that; **nōn quō** not that

quoad adv how far?; how long? ▶ conj as far as, as long as; until

quōcircā conj therefore

quōcumque adv whithersoever

quod conj as for, in that, that; because; why; **~ sī** but if

quōdam modo adv in a way

quoi old dat form of **quī** [1]

quoius old gen form of **quī** [1]

quōlibet adv anywhere, in any direction

quom etc conj see **cum** [2]

quōminus conj that not; (preventing) from

quōmodo adv (interrog) how?; (rel) just as; **quōmodocumque** howsoever; **quōmodonam** how?

quōnam adv where, where to?

quondam adv once, formerly; sometimes; (fut) one day

quōniam conj since, seeing that

quōpiam adv anywhere

quōquam adv anywhere

quoque adv also, too

quōquō adv to whatever place, wherever

quōquō modo adv howsoever

quōquō versus, quōquō versum adv in every direction

quōrsus, quōrsum adv where to?, in what direction?; what for?, to what end?

quot adj how many; as many as, every

quotannīs adv every year

quotcumque adj however many

quotēnī, -ōrum adj how many

quotīd- etc see **cottīd-**

quotiēns, quotiēs adv how often?; (rel) as often as

quotiēnscumque adv however often

quotquot adj however many

quotumus adj which number?, what date?

quotus adj what number, how many; **~ quisque** how few; **quota hōra** what time

quotuscumque adj whatever number, however big

quōusque adv how long, till when; how far

quōvīs adv anywhere

quum etc conj see **cum** [2]

rabidē adv furiously

rabidus adj raving, mad; impetuous

rabiēs (acc **-em**, abl **-ē**) f madness, rage, fury

rabiō, -ere vi to rave

rabiōsē adv wildly

rabiōsulus adj somewhat rabid

rabiōsus adj furious, mad

rabula, -ae m wrangling lawyer

racēmifer, -ī adj clustered

racēmus, -ī m stalk of a cluster; bunch of grapes; grape

radiātus adj radiant

rādīcitus adv by the roots; utterly

rādīcula, -ae f small root

radiō, -āre vt to irradiate ▶ vi to radiate, shine

radius, -ī and **-iī** m stick, rod; (light) beam, ray; (loom) shuttle; (MATH) rod for drawing figures, radius of a circle; (plant) long olive; (wheel) spoke

rādīx, -īcis f root; radish; (hill) foot; (fig) foundation, origin

rādō, -dere, -sī, -sum vt to scrape, shave, scratch; to erase; to touch in passing, graze, pass along

raeda, -ae f four-wheeled carriage

raedārius, -ī and **-iī** m driver

Raetī, -ōrum mpl Alpine people between Italy and Germany

Raetia, -iae f country of the Raetī

Raeticus, Raetius, Raetus adj see **Raetia**

rāmālia, -ium ntpl twigs, brushwood

rāmentum, -ī nt shavings, chips

rāmeus adj of branches

rāmex, -icis m rupture, blood vessels of the lungs

Ramnēnsēs, Ramnēs, -ium mpl one of the original Roman tribes; a century of equites

rāmōsus adj branching

rāmulus, -ī m twig, sprig

rāmus, -ī m branch, bough

rāna, -ae f frog; frogfish

rancēns, -entis adj putrid

rancidulus adj rancid

rancidus adj rank, rancid; disgusting

rānunculus, -ī m tadpole

rapācida, -ae m son of a thief
rapācitās, -ātis f greed
rapāx, -ācis adj greedy, grasping, ravenous
raphanus, -ī m radish
rapidē adv swiftly, hurriedly
rapiditās, -ātis f rapidity
rapidus adj tearing, devouring; swift, rapid; hasty, impetuous
rapīna, -ae f pillage, robbery; booty, prey
rapiō, -ere, -uī, -tum vt to tear, snatch, carry off; to seize, plunder; to hurry, seize quickly
raptim adv hastily, violently
raptiō, -ōnis f abduction
raptō, -āre, -āvī, -ātum vt to seize and carry off, drag away, move quickly; to plunder, lay waste; (passion) to agitate
raptor, -ōris m plunderer, robber, ravisher
raptus¹ ppp of **rapiō** ▶ nt plunder
raptus², -ūs m carrying off, abduction; plundering
rāpulum, -ī nt small turnip
rāpum, -ī nt turnip
rārēfaciō, -facere, -fēcī, -factum (pass **-fīō**) vt to rarefy
rārēscō, -ere vi to become rarefied, grow thin; to open out
rāritās, -ātis f porousness, open texture; thinness, fewness
rārō, rārē adv seldom
rārus adj porous, open in texture; thin, scanty; scattered, straggling, here and there; (MIL) in open order; few, infrequent; uncommon, rare
rāsī perf of **rādō**
rāsilis adj smooth, polished
rāstrum, -ī nt hoe, mattock
rāsus ppp of **rādō**
ratiō, -ōnis f 1. (reckoning of) account, calculation; list, register; affair, business 2. (relation) respect, consideration; procedure, method, system, way, kind 3. (reason) reasoning, thought; cause, motive; science, knowledge, philosophy; ~ atque ūsus theory and practice; ~ est it is reasonable; Stōicōrum ~ Stoicism; ratiōnem dūcere, ratiōnem inīre calculate; ratiōnem habēre take account of, have to do with, consider; ratiōnem reddere give an account of; cum ratiōne reasonably; meae ratiōnēs my interests; ā ratiōnibus accountant
ratiōcinātiō, -ōnis f reasoning; syllogism
ratiōcinātīvus adj syllogistic
ratiōcinātor, -ōris m accountant
ratiōcinor, -ārī, -ātus vt, vi to calculate; to consider; to argue, infer
ratiōnālis adj rational; syllogistic
ratis, -is f raft; boat
ratiuncula, -ae f small calculation; slight reason; petty syllogism
ratus ppa of **reor** ▶ adj fixed, settled, sure; valid; **prō ratā (parte)** proportionally; **ratum dūcere**, **ratum facere**, **ratum habēre** ratify
raucisonus adj hoarse

raucus adj hoarse; harsh, strident
raudus, -eris nt copper coin
raudusculum, -ī nt bit of money
Ravenna, -ae f port in N.E. Italy
Ravennās, -ātis adj see **Ravenna**
rāvis (acc **-im**) f hoarseness
rāvus adj grey, tawny
rea, -ae f defendant, culprit
reāpse adv in fact, actually
Reāte, -is nt ancient Sabine town
Reātīnus adj see **Reāte**
rebellātiō, -ōnis f revolt
rebellātrīx, -īcis adj rebellious
rebelliō, -ōnis f revolt
rebellis adj rebellious ▶ mpl rebels
rebellium, -ī and -iī nt revolt
rebellō, -āre vi to revolt
rebītō, -ere vi to return
reboō, -āre vi to re-echo ▶ vt to make resound
recalcitrō, -āre vi to kick back
recaleō, -ēre vi to be warm again
recalēscō, -ere vi to grow warm again
recalfaciō, -facere, -fēcī vt to warm again
recalvus adj bald in front
recandēscō, -ēscere, -uī vi to whiten (in response); to glow
recantō, -āre, -āvī, -ātum vt to recant; to charm away
reccidī perf of **recidō**
recēdō, -ēdere, -essī, -essum vi to move back, withdraw, depart; (place) to recede; (head) to be severed
recellō, -ere vi to spring back
recēns, -entis adj fresh, young, recent; (writer) modern; (with ab) immediately after ▶ adv newly, just
recēnseō, -ēre, -uī, -um vt to count; to review
recēnsiō, -ōnis f revision
recēnsus ppp of **recēnseō**
recēpī perf of **recipiō**
receptāculum, -ī nt receptacle, reservoir; refuge, shelter
receptō, -āre vt to take back; to admit, harbour; to tug hard at
receptor, -ōris m (male) receiver, shelterer
receptrīx, -īcis f (female) receiver, shelterer
receptum, -ī nt obligation
receptus¹ ppp of **recipiō**
receptus², -ūs m withdrawal; retreat; return; refuge; **receptuī canere** sound the retreat
recessī perf of **recēdō**
recessim adv backwards
recessus, -ūs m retreat, departure; recess, secluded spot; (tide) ebb
recidīvus adj resurrected; recurring
recidō, -idere, -cidī, -āsum vi to fall back; to recoil, relapse; (fig) to fall, descend
recīdō, -dere, -dī, -sum vt to cut back, cut off
recingō, -gere, -ctum vt to ungird, loose
recinō, -ere vt, vi to re-echo, repeat; to sound a warning

reciper- *etc see* **recuper-**
recipiō, -ipere, -ēpī, -eptum *vt* to take back, retake; to get back, regain, rescue; to accept, admit; (*MIL*) to occupy; (*duty*) to undertake; (*promise*) to pledge, guarantee; **sē recipere** withdraw, retreat; **nōmen recipere** receive notice of a prosecution
reciprocō, -āre *vt* to move to and fro; (*ship*) to bring round to another tack; (*proposition*) to reverse ▸ *vi* (*tide*) to rise and fall
reciprocus *adj* ebbing
recīsus *ppp of* **recīdō**
recitātiō, -ōnis *f* reading aloud, recital
recitātor, -ōris *m* reader, reciter
recitō, -āre, -āvī, -ātum *vt* to read out, recite
reclāmātiō, -ōnis *f* outcry (*of disapproval*)
reclāmitō, -āre *vi* to cry out against
reclāmō, -āre *vi* to cry out, protest; to reverberate
reclīnis *adj* leaning back
reclīnō, -āre, -āvī, -ātum *vt* to lean back
reclūdō, -dere, -sī, -sum *vt* to open up; to disclose
reclūsus *ppp of* **reclūdō**
recoctus *ppp of* **recoquō**
recōgitō, -āre *vi* to think over, reflect
recognitiō, -ōnis *f* review
recognōscō, -ōscere, -ōvī, -itum *vt* to recollect; to examine, review
recolligō, -igere, -ēgī, -ēctum *vt* to gather up; (*fig*) to recover, reconcile
recolō, -olere, -oluī, -ultum *vt* to recultivate; to resume; to reflect on, contemplate; to revisit
recomminīscor, -ī *vi* to recollect
recompositus *adj* rearranged
reconciliātiō, -ōnis *f* restoration, reconciliation
reconciliō, -āre, -āvī, -ātum *vt* to win back again, restore, reconcile
reconcinnō, -āre *vt* to repair
reconditus *ppp of* **recondō** ▸ *adj* hidden, secluded; abstruse, profound; (*disposition*) reserved
recondō, -ere, -idī, -itum *vt* to store away, stow; to hide away, bury
recōnflō, -āre *vt* to rekindle
recoquō, -quere, -xī, -ctum *vt* to cook again, boil again; to forge again, recast; (*fig*) to rejuvenate
recordātiō, -ōnis *f* recollection
recordor, -ārī, -ātus *vt, vi* to recall, remember; to ponder over
recreō, -āre, -āvī, -ātum *vt* to remake, reproduce; to revive, refresh
recrepō, -āre *vt, vi* to ring, re-echo
recrēscō, -scere *vi* to grow again
recrūdēscō, -ēscere, -uī *vi* (*wound*) to open again; (*war*) to break out again
rēctā *adv* straight forward, right on
rēctē *adv* straight; correctly, properly, well; quite; (*colloq*) good, all right, no thank you
rēctiō, -ōnis *f* government

rēctor, -ōris *m* guide, driver, helmsman; governor, master
rēctum, -ī *nt* right, virtue
rēctus *ppp of* **regō** ▸ *adj* straight; upright, steep; right, correct, proper; (*moral*) good, virtuous
recubō, -āre *vi* to lie, recline
recultus *ppp of* **recolō**
recumbō, -mbere, -buī *vi* to lie down, recline; to fall, sink down
recuperātiō, -ōnis *f* recovery
recuperātor, -ōris *m* recapturer; (*pl*) board of justices who tried civil cases requiring a quick decision, esp cases involving foreigners
recuperātōrius *adj* of the recuperatores
recuperō, -āre, -āvī, -ātum *vt* to get back, recover, recapture
recūrō, -āre *vt* to restore
recurrō, -ere, -ī *vi* to run back; to return, recur; to revert
recursō, -āre *vi* to keep coming back, keep recurring
recursus, -ūs *m* return, retreat
recurvō, -āre *vt* to bend back, curve
recurvus *adj* bent, curved
recūsātiō, -ōnis *f* refusal, declining; (*LAW*) objection, counterplea
recūsō, -āre, -āvī, -ātum *vt* to refuse, decline, be reluctant; (*LAW*) to object, plead in defence
recussus *adj* reverberating
redāctus *ppp of* **redigō**
redambulō, -āre *vi* to come back
redamō, -āre *vt* to love in return
redārdēscō, -ere *vi* to blaze up again
redarguō, -ere, -ī *vt* to refute, contradict
redauspicō, -āre *vi* to take auspices for going back
redditus *ppp of* **reddō**
reddō, -ere, -idī, -itum *vt* to give back, return, restore; to give in response, repay; to give up, deliver, pay; (*copy*) to represent, reproduce; (*speech*) to report, repeat, recite, reply; to translate; (*with adj*) to make; **iūdicium reddere** fix the date for a trial; **iūs reddere** administer justice
redēgī *perf of* **redigō**
redēmī *perf of* **redimō**
redemptiō, -ōnis *f* ransoming; bribing; (*revenue*) farming
redemptō, -āre *vt* to ransom
redemptor, -ōris *m* contractor
redemptūra, -ae *f* contracting
redemptus *ppp of* **redimō**
redeō, -īre, -iī, -itum *vi* to go back, come back, return; (*speech*) to revert; (*money*) to come in; (*circumstances*) to be reduced to, come to
redhālō, -āre *vt* to exhale
redhibeō, -ēre *vt* to take back
redigō, -igere, -ēgī, -āctum *vt* to drive back, bring back; (*money*) to collect, raise; (*to a condition*) to reduce, bring; (*number*) to reduce; **ad irritum redigere** make useless

rediī *perf of* **redeō**

redimīculum, **-ī** *nt* band

redimiō, **-īre**, **-iī**, **-ītum** *vt* to bind, crown, encircle

redimō, **-imere**, **-ēmī**, **-emptum** *vt* to buy back; to ransom, redeem; to release, rescue; (*good*) to procure; (*evil*) to avert; (*fault*) to make amends for; (*COMM*) to undertake by contract, hire

redintegrō, **-āre**, **-āvī**, **-ātum** *vt* to restore, renew, refresh

redipīscor, **-ī** *vt* to get back

reditiō, **-ōnis** *f* returning

reditus, **-ūs** *m* return, returning; (*money*) revenue

redivīvus *adj* renovated

redoleō, **-ēre**, **-uī** *vi* to give out a smell ▸ *vt* to smell of, smack of

redomitus *adj* broken in again

redōnō, **-āre** *vt* to restore; to give up

redūcō, **-ūcere**, **-ūxī**, **-uctum** *vt* to draw back; to lead back, bring back; to escort home; to marry again; (*troops*) to withdraw; (*fig*) to restore; (*to a condition*) to make into

reductiō, **-ōnis** *f* restoration

reductor, **-ōris** *m* man who brings back

reductus *ppp of* **redūcō** ▸ *adj* secluded, aloof

reduncus *adj* curved back

redundantia, **-ae** *f* extravagance

redundō, **-āre**, **-āvī**, **-ātum** *vi* to overflow; to abound, be in excess; (*fig*) to stream

reduvia, **-ae** *f* hangnail

redux, **-cis** *adj* (*gods*) who brings back; (*men*) brought back, returned

refectus *ppp of* **reficiō**

refellō, **-ere**, **-ī** *vt* to disprove, rebut

refierciō, **-cīre**, **-sī**, **-tum** *vt* to stuff, cram, choke full

referiō, **-īre** *vt* to hit back; to reflect

referō, **-ferre**, **-ttulī**, **-lātum** *vt* to bring back, carry back; to give back, pay back, repay; to repeat, renew; (*authority*) to refer to, trace back to; (*blame, credit*) to ascribe; (*likeness*) to reproduce, resemble; (*memory*) to recall; (*news*) to report, mention; (*opinion*) to reckon amongst; (*record*) to enter; (*senate*) to lay before, move; (*speech*) to reply, say in answer; **grātiam referre** be grateful, requite; **pedem referre**, **gradum referre** return; retreat; **ratiōnēs referre** present an account; **sē referre** return

rēfert, **-ferre**, **-tulit** *vi* (*impers*) it is of importance, it matters, it concerns; **meā ~** it matters to me

refertus *ppp of* **referciō** ▸ *adj* crammed, full

referveō, **-ēre** *vi* to boil over

refervēscō, **-ere** *vi* to bubble up

reficiō, **-icere**, **-ēcī**, **-ectum** *vt* to repair, restore; (*body, mind*) to refresh, revive; (*money*) to get back, get in return; (*POL*) to re-elect

refīgō, **-gere**, **-xī**, **-xum** *vt* to unfasten, take down; (*fig*) to annul

refingō, **-ere** *vt* to remake

refīxus *ppp of* **refīgō**

reflāgitō, **-āre** *vt* to demand back

reflātus, **-ūs** *m* contrary wind

reflectō, **-ctere**, **-xī**, **-xum** *vt* to bend back, turn back; (*fig*) to bring back ▸ *vi* to give way

reflexus *ppp of* **reflectō**

reflō, **-āre**, **-āvī**, **-ātum** *vi* to blow contrary ▸ *vt* to breathe out again

refluō, **-ere** *vi* to flow back, overflow

refluus *adj* ebbing

reformīdō, **-āre** *vt* to dread; to shun in fear

reformō, **-āre** *vt* to reshape

refōtus *ppp of* **refoveō**

refoveō, **-ovēre**, **-ōvī**, **-ōtum** *vt* to refresh, revive

refrāctāriolus *adj* rather stubborn

refrāctus *ppp of* **refringō**

refrāgor, **-ārī**, **-ātus** *vi* (*with dat*) to oppose, thwart

refrēgī *perf of* **refringō**

refrēnō, **-āre** *vt* to curb, restrain

refricō, **-āre**, **-uī**, **-ātum** *vt* to scratch open; to reopen, renew ▸ *vi* to break out again

refrīgerātiō, **-ōnis** *f* coolness

refrīgerō, **-āre**, **-āvī**, **-ātum** *vi* to cool, cool off; (*fig*) to flag

refrīgēscō, **-ēscere**, **-xī** *vi* to grow cold; (*fig*) to flag, grow stale

refringō, **-ingere**, **-ēgī**, **-āctum** *vt* to break open; to break off; (*fig*) to break, check

refrīxī *perf of* **refrīgēscō**

refugiō, **-ugere**, **-ūgī** *vi* to run back, flee, shrink ▸ *vt* to run away from, shun

refugium, **-ī** *and* **-iī** *nt* refuge

refugus *adj* fugitive, receding

refulgeō, **-gēre**, **-sī** *vi* to flash back, reflect light

refundō, **-undere**, **-ūdī**, **-ūsum** *vt* to pour back, pour out; (*pass*) to overflow

refūsus *ppp of* **refundō**

refūtātiō, **-ōnis** *f* refutation

refūtātus, **-ūs** *m* refutation

refūtō, **-āre**, **-āvī**, **-ātum** *vt* to check, repress; to refute, disprove

rēgālis *adj* king's, royal, regal

rēgāliter *adv* magnificently; tyrannically

regerō, **-rere**, **-ssī**, **-stum** *vt* to carry back, throw back

rēgia, **-ae** *f* palace; court; (*camp*) royal tent; (*town*) capital

rēgiē *adv* regally; imperiously

rēgificus *adj* magnificent

regignō, **-ere** *vt* to reproduce

Rēgillānus, **Rēgillēnsis** *adj see* **Rēgillus**

Rēgillus, **-ī** *m* Sabine town; *lake in Latium* (*scene of a Roman victory over the Latins*)

regimen, **-inis** *nt* guiding, steering; rudder; rule, command, government; ruler

rēgīna, **-ae** *f* queen, noblewoman

Rēgīnus *adj see* **Rēgium**

regiō, **-ōnis** *f* direction, line; boundary line; quarter, region; district, ward, territory; (*fig*) sphere, province; **ē regiōne** in a straight line; (with gen) exactly opposite

regiōnātim adv by districts

Rēgium, -ī and **-iī** nt town in extreme S. of Italy (now Reggio)

rēgius adj king's, kingly, royal; princely, magnificent

reglūtinō, -āre vt to unstick

rēgnātor, -ōris m ruler

rēgnātrīx, -īcis adj imperial

rēgnō, -āre, -āvī, -ātum vi to be king, rule, reign; to be supreme, lord it; (things) to prevail, predominate ▸ vt to rule over

rēgnum, -ī nt kingship, monarchy; sovereignty, supremacy; despotism; kingdom; domain

regō, -ere, rēxī, rēctum vt to keep straight, guide, steer; to manage, direct; to control, rule, govern; **regere fīnēs** (law) mark out the limits

regredior, -dī, -ssus vi to go back, come back, return; (MIL) to retire

regressus¹ ppa of **regredior**

regressus², -ūs m return; retreat

rēgula, -ae f rule, ruler; stick, board; (fig) rule, pattern, standard

rēgulus, -ī m petty king, chieftain; prince

Rēgulus, -ī m Roman consul taken prisoner by the Carthaginians

regustō, -āre vt to taste again

rēiciō, -icere, -iēcī, -iectum vt to throw back, throw over the shoulder, throw off; to drive back, repel; to cast off, reject; to reject with contempt, scorn; (jurymen) to challenge, refuse; (matter for discussion) to refer; (time) to postpone; **sē rēicere** fling oneself

rēiectāneus adj to be rejected

rēiectiō, -ōnis f rejection; (LAW) challenging

rēiectō, -āre vt to throw back

rēiectus ppp of **rēiciō**

relābor, -bī, -psus vi to glide back, sink back, fall back

relanguēscō, -ēscere, -ī vi to faint; to weaken

relātiō, -ōnis f (LAW) retorting; (pl) magistrate's report; (RHET) repetition

relātor, -ōris m proposer of a motion

relātus¹ ppp of **referō**

relātus², -ūs m official report; recital

relaxātiō, -ōnis f easing

relaxō, -āre, -āvī, -ātum vt to loosen, open out; (fig) to release, ease, relax, cheer

relēctus ppp of **relegō**

relēgātiō, -ōnis f banishment

relegō, -egere, -ēgī, -ēctum vt to gather up; (place) to traverse, sail over again; (speech) to go over again, reread

relēgō, -āre, -āvī, -ātum vt to send away, send out of the way; to banish; (fig) to reject; to refer, ascribe

relentēscō, -ere vi to slacken off

relēvī perf of **relinō**

relevō, -āre, -āvī, -ātum vt to lift up; to lighten; (fig) to relieve, ease, comfort

relictiō, -ōnis f abandoning

relictus ppp of **relinquō**

relicuus etc see **reliquus**

religātiō, -ōnis f tying up

rēligiō, -ōnis f religious scruple, reverence, awe; religion; superstition; scruples, conscientiousness; holiness, sanctity (in anything); object of veneration, sacred place; religious ceremony, observance

rēligiōsē adv devoutly; scrupulously, conscientiously

rēligiōsus adj devout, religious; superstitious; involving religious difficulty; scrupulous, conscientious; (objects) holy, sacred

religō, -āre, -āvī, -ātum vt to tie up, fasten behind; (ship) to make fast, moor; (fig) to bind

relinō, -inere, -ēvī vt to unseal

relinquō, -inquere, -īquī, -ictum vt to leave, leave behind; to bequeath; to abandon, forsake; (argument) to allow; (pass) to remain

rēliquiae, -ārum fpl leavings, remainder, relics

reliquus adj remaining, left; (time) subsequent, future; (debt) outstanding ▸ nt remainder, rest; arrears ▸ mpl the rest; **reliquum est** it remains, the next point is; **reliquī facere** leave behind, leave over, omit; **in reliquum** for the future

rell- etc see **rel-**

relūceō, -cēre, -xī vi to blaze

relūcēscō, -cēscere, -xī vi to become bright again

reluctor, -ārī, -ātus vi to struggle against, resist

remaneō, -anēre, -ānsī vi to remain behind; to remain, continue, endure

remānō, -āre vi to flow back

remānsiō, -ōnis f remaining behind

remedium, -ī and **-iī** nt cure, remedy, medicine

remēnsus ppa of **remētior**

remeō, -āre vi to come back, go back, return

remētior, -tīrī, -nsus vt to measure again; to go back over

rēmex, -igis m rower, oarsman

Rēmī, -ōrum mpl people of Gaul (in region of what is now Rheims)

rēmigātiō, -ōnis f rowing

rēmigium, -ī and **-iī** nt rowing; oars; oarsmen

rēmigō, -āre vi to row

remigrō, -āre vi to move back, return (home)

reminīscor, -ī vt, vi (usu gen) to remember, call to mind

remisceō, -scēre, -scuī, -xtum vt to mix up, mingle

remissē adv mildly, gently

remissiō, -ōnis f release; (tension) slackening, relaxing; (payment) remission; (mind) slackness, mildness, relaxation; (illness) abating

remissus ppp of **remittō** ▸ adj slack; negligent; mild, indulgent, cheerful

remittō, -ittere, -īsī, -issum vt to let go back, send back, release; to slacken, loosen, relax; to emit, produce; (mind) to relax, relieve; (notion) to discard, give up; (offence, penalty) to let off, remit; (*right*) to resign, sacrifice; (*sound*) to give back ▶ *vi* to abate

remixtus *ppp of* **remisceō**

remōlior, -īrī, -ītus *vt* to heave back

remōllēscō, -ere *vi* to become soft again, be softened

remōlliō, -īre *vt* to weaken

remora, -ae *f* hindrance

remorāmina, -um *ntpl* hindrances

remordeō, -dēre, -dī, -sum *vt* (*fig*) to worry, torment

remoror, -ārī, -ātus *vi* to linger, stay behind ▶ *vt* to hinder, delay, defer

remorsus *ppp of* **remordeō**

remōtē *adv* far

remōtiō, -ōnis *f* removing

remōtus *ppp of* **removeō** ▶ *adj* distant, remote; secluded; (*fig*) far removed, free from

removeō, -ovēre, -ōvī, -ōtum *vt* to move back, withdraw, set aside; to subtract

remūgiō, -īre *vi* to bellow in answer, re-echo

remulceō, -cēre, -sī *vt* to stroke; (*tail*) to droop

remulcum, -ī *nt* towrope

remūnerātiō, -ōnis *f* recompense, reward

remūneror, -ārī, -ātus *vt* to repay, reward

remurmurō, -āre *vi* to murmur in answer

Remus, -ī *m* brother of Romulus

rēmus, -ī *m* oar

renārrō, -āre *vt* to tell over again

renāscor, -scī, -tus *vi* to be born again; to grow, spring up again

renātus *ppa of* **renāscor**

renāvigō, -āre *vi* to sail back

reneō, -ēre *vt* to unspin, undo

rēnēs, -um *mpl* kidneys

renīdeō, -ēre *vi* to shine back, be bright; to be cheerful, smile, laugh

renīdēscō, -ere *vi* to reflect the gleam of

renītor, -ī *vi* to struggle, resist

renō, -āre *vi* to swim back

rēnō, -ōnis *m* fur

renōdō, -āre *vt* to tie back in a knot

renovāmen, -inis *nt* new condition

renovātiō, -ōnis *f* renewal; compound interest

renovō, -āre, -āvī, -ātum *vt* to renew, restore; to repair, revive, refresh; (*speech*) to repeat; **faenus renovāre** take compound interest

renumerō, -āre *vt* to pay back

renūntiātiō, -ōnis *f* report, announcement

renūntiō, -āre, -āvī, -ātum *vt* to report, bring back word; to announce, make an official statement; (*election*) to declare elected, return; (*duty*) to refuse, call off, renounce

renūntius, -ī *m* **and -iī** *m* reporter

renuō, -ere, -ī *vt, vi* to deny, decline, refuse

renūtō, -āre *vi* to refuse firmly

reor, rērī, ratus *vi* to think, suppose

repāgula, -ōrum *ntpl* (*door*) bolts, bars

repandus *adj* curving back, turned up

reparābilis *adj* retrievable

reparcō, -ere *vi* to be sparing with, refrain

reparō, -āre, -āvī, -ātum *vt* to retrieve, recover; to restore, repair; to purchase; (*mind, body*) to refresh; (*troops*) to recruit

repastinātiō, -ōnis *f* digging up again

repellō, -ellere, -pulī, -ulsum *vt* to push back, drive back, repulse; to remove, reject

rependō, -endere, -endī, -ēnsum *vt* to return by weight; to pay, repay; to requite, compensate

repēns, -entis *adj* sudden; new

repēnsus *ppp of* **rependō**

repentē *adv* suddenly

repentīnō *adv* suddenly

repentīnus *adj* sudden, hasty; upstart

repercō *etc see* **reparcō**

repercussus[1] *ppp of* **repercutiō**

repercussus[2], -ūs *m* reflection, echo

repercutiō, -tere, -ssī, -ssum *vt* to make rebound, reflect, echo

reperiō, -īre, repperī, -tum *vt* to find, find out; to get, procure; to discover, ascertain; to devise, invent

repertor, -ōris *m* discoverer, inventor, author

repertus *ppp of* **reperiō** ▶ *ntpl* discoveries

repetītiō, -ōnis *f* repetition; (*RHET*) anaphora

repetītor, -ōris *m* reclaimer

repetītus *ppp of* **repetō** ▶ *adj*: **altē/longē ~** far-fetched

repetō, -ere, -īvī and -iī, -ītum *vt* to go back to, revisit; to fetch back, take back; (*MIL*) to attack again; (*action, speech*) to resume, repeat; (*memory*) to recall, think over; (*origin*) to trace, derive; (*right*) to claim, demand back; **rēs repetere** demand satisfaction; reclaim one's property; **pecūniae repetundae** extortion

repetundae, -ārum *fpl* extortion (*by a provincial governor*)

repexus *adj* combed

repleō, -ēre, -ēvī, -ētum *vt* to fill up, refill; to replenish, make good, complete; to satiate, fill to overflowing

replētus *adj* full

replicātiō, -ōnis *f* rolling up

replicō, -āre *vt* to roll back, unroll, unfold

rēpō, -ere, -sī, -tum *vi* to creep, crawl

repōnō, -ōnere, -osuī, -ositum *vt* to put back, replace, restore; to bend back; to put (*in the proper place*); (*performance*) to repeat; (*something received*) to repay; (*store*) to lay up, put away; (*task*) to lay aside, put down; (*hope*) to place, rest; (*with* **prō**) substitute; **in numerō repōnere, in numerum repōnere** count, reckon among

reportō, -āre, -āvī, -ātum *vt* to bring back, carry back; (*prize*) to win, carry off; (*words*) to report

reposcō, -ere *vt* to demand back; to claim, require

repositus *ppp of* **repōnō** ▶ *adj* remote

repostor, -ōris *m* restorer

repostus *etc see* **repositus**
repōtia, -ōrum *ntpl* second drinking
repperī *perf of* **reperiō**
reppulī *perf of* **repellō**
repraesentātiō, -ōnis *f* vivid presentation; (COMM) cash payment
repraesentō, -āre, -āvī, -ātum *vt* to exhibit, reproduce; to do at once, hasten; (COMM) to pay cash
reprehendō, -endere, -endī, -ēnsum *vt* to hold back, catch, restrain; to hold fast, retain; to blame, rebuke, censure; to refute
reprehēnsiō, -ōnis *f* check; blame, reprimand, refutation
reprehēnsō, -āre *vt* to keep holding back
reprehēnsor, -ōris *m* censurer, critic, reviser
reprehēnsus *ppp of* **reprehendō**
reprendō *etc see* **reprehendō**
repressor, -ōris *m* restrainer
repressus *ppp of* **reprimō**
reprimō, -imere, -essī, -essum *vt* to keep back, force back; to check, restrain, suppress
reprōmissiō, -ōnis *f* counterpromise
reprōmittō, -ittere, -īsī, -issum *vt* to promise in return, engage oneself
rēptō, -āre *vi* to creep about, crawl along
repudiātiō, -ōnis *f* rejection
repudiō, -āre, -āvī, -ātum *vt* to reject, refuse, scorn; (wife) to divorce
repudium, -ī *and* **-iī** *nt* divorce; repudiation
repuerāscō, -ere *vi* to become a child again; to behave like a child
repugnanter *adv* reluctantly
repugnantia, -ium *ntpl* contradictions
repugnō, -āre, -āvī, -ātum *vi* to oppose, resist; to disagree, be inconsistent
repulsa, -ae *f* refusal, denial, repulse; (election) rebuff
repulsō, -āre *vi* to throb, reverberate
repulsus¹ *ppp of* **repellō**
repulsus², -ūs *m* (light) reflection; (sound) echoing
repungō, -ere *vt* to prod again
repūrgō, -āre, -āvī, -ātum *vt* to clear again, cleanse again; to purge away
reputātiō, -ōnis *f* pondering over
reputō, -āre, -āvī, -ātum *vt* to count back; to think over, consider
requiēs, -ētis *f* rest, relaxation, repose
requiēscō, -scere, -vī, -tum *vi* to rest, find rest; to cease ▶ *vt* to stay
requiētus *adj* rested, refreshed
requīritō, -āre *vt* to keep asking after
requīrō, -rere, -sīvī *and* **-siī, -sītum** *vt* to search for, look for; to ask, inquire after; (with ex or ab) to question; to need, want, call for; to miss, look in vain for
requīsītus *ppp of* **requīrō**
rēs, reī *f* thing, object; circumstance, case, matter, affair; business, transaction; fact, truth, reality; possessions, wealth, money; advantage, interest; (LAW) case; (MIL) campaign,

operations; (POL) politics, power, the State; (writing) subject matter, story, history; **rēs mihi est tēcum** I have to do with you; **rēs dīvīna** sacrifice; **rēs mīlitāris** war; **rēs pūblica** public affairs, politics, the State, republic; **rēs rūstica** agriculture; **rem facere** get rich; **rem gerere** wage war, fight; **ad rem** to the point, to the purpose; **in rem** usefully; **ob rem** to the purpose; **ob eam rem** therefore; **ī in malam rem** go to the devil!; **contrā rem pūblicam** unconstitutionally; **ē rē pūblicā** constitutionally; **rē vērā** in fact, actually; **eā rē** for that reason; **tuā rē, ex tuā rē** to your advantage; **ab rē** unhelpfully; **ē rē (nātā)** as things are; **prō rē** according to circumstances; **rēs adversae** failure, adversity; **rēs dubiae** danger; **rēs gestae** achievements, career; **rēs novae** revolution; **rēs prosperae, rēs secundae** success, prosperity; **rērum māximus** greatest in the world; **rērum scrīptor** historian
resacrō *etc see* **resecrō**
resaeviō, -īre *vi* to rage again
resalūtō, -āre *vt* to greet in return
resānēscō, -ēscere, -uī *vi* to heal up again
resarciō, -cīre, -tum *vt* to patch up, repair
rescindō, -ndere, -dī, -ssum *vt* to cut back, cut open, break down; to open up; (law, agreement) to repeal, annul
rescīscō, -īscere, -īvī *and* **-iī, -ītum** *vt* to find out, learn
rescissus *ppp of* **rescindō**
rescrībō, -bere, -psī, -ptum *vt* to write back, reply; to rewrite, revise; (emperors) to give a decision; (MIL) to transfer, re-enlist; (money) to place to one's credit, pay back
rescrīptus *ppp of* **rescrībō** ▶ *nt* imperial rescript
resecō, -āre, -uī, -tum *vt* to cut back, cut short; to curtail; **ad vīvum resecāre** cut to the quick
resecrō, -āre *vt* to pray again; to free from a curse
resectus *ppp of* **resecō**
resecūtus *ppa of* **resequor**
resēdī *perf of* **resideō; residō**
resēminō, -āre *vt* to reproduce
resequor, -quī, -cūtus *vt* to answer
reserō, -āre, -āvī, -ātum *vt* to unbar, unlock; to disclose
reservō, -āre, -āvī, -ātum *vt* to keep back, reserve; to preserve, save
reses, -idis *adj* remaining; inactive, idle; calm
resideō, -idēre, -ēdī *vi* to remain behind; to be idle, be listless; (fig) to remain, rest
residō, -īdere, -ēdī *vi* to sit down, sink down, settle; to subside; (fig) to abate, calm down
residuus *adj* remaining, left over; (money) outstanding
resignō, -āre *vt* to unseal, open; (fig) to reveal; (COMM) to cancel, pay back
resiliō, -īre, -uī *vi* to spring back; to recoil, rebound, shrink
resīmus *adj* turned up
rēsīna, -ae *f* resin

rēsinātus *adj* smeared with resin

resipiō, -ere *vt* to savour of, smack of

resipīscō, -īscere, -iī *and* **-uī** *vi* to come to one's senses

resistō, -istere, -titī *vi* to stand still, stop, halt; to resist, oppose; to rise again

resolūtus, -ūs *ppp of* **resolvō**

resolvō, -vere, -vī, -ūtum *vt* to unfasten, loosen, open, release; to melt, dissolve; to relax; (*debt*) to pay up; (*difficulty*) to banish, dispel; (*tax*) to abolish; (*words*) to explain

resonābilis *adj* answering

resonō, -āre *vi* to resound, re-echo ▶ *vt* to echo the sound of; to make resound

resonus *adj* echoing

resorbeō, -ēre *vt* to suck back, swallow again

respectō, -āre *vi* to look back; to gaze about, watch ▶ *vt* to look back at, look for; to have regard for

respectus¹ *ppp of* **respiciō**

respectus², -ūs *m* looking back; refuge; respect, regard

respergō, -gere, -sī, -sum *vt* to besprinkle, splash

respersiō, -ōnis *f* sprinkling

respersus *ppp of* **respergō**

respiciō, -icere, -exī, -ectum *vt* to look back at, see behind; (*help*) to look to; (*care*) to have regard for, consider, respect ▶ *vi* to look back, look

respīrāmen, -inis *nt* windpipe

respīrātiō, -ōnis *f* breathing; exhalation; taking breath, pause

respīrātus, -ūs *m* inhaling

respīrō, -āre, -āvī, -ātum *vt, vi* to breathe, blow back; to breathe again, revive; (*things*) to abate

resplendeō, -ēre *vi* to flash back, shine brightly

respondeō, -ondēre, -ondī, -ōnsum *vt* to answer, reply; (*lawyer, priest, oracle*) to advise, give a response; (*law court*) to appear; (*pledge*) to promise in return; (*things*) to correspond, agree, match; **pār parī respondēre** return like for like, give tit for tat

respōnsiō, -ōnis *f* answering; refutation

respōnsitō, -āre *vi* to give advice

respōnsō, -āre *vt, vi* to answer back; to defy

respōnsor, -ōris *m* answerer

respōnsum, -ī *nt* answer, reply; response, opinion, oracle

rēspūblica, reīpūblicae *f* public affairs, politics, the State, republic

respuō, -ere, -ī *vt* to spit out, eject; to reject, refuse

restagnō, -āre *vi* to overflow; to be flooded

restaurō, -āre *vt* to repair, rebuild

resticula, -ae *f* rope, cord

restinctiō, -ōnis *f* quenching

restinctus *ppp of* **restinguō**

restinguō, -guere, -xī, -ctum *vt* to extinguish, quench; (*fig*) to destroy

restiō, -ōnis *m* rope maker

restipulātiō, -ōnis *f* counterobligation

restipulor, -ārī *vt* to stipulate in return

restis, -is *f* rope

restitī *perf of* **resistō; restō**

restitō, -āre *vi* to stay behind, hesitate

restituō, -uere, -uī, -ūtum *vt* to replace, restore; to rebuild, renew; to give back, return; (*to a condition*) to reinstate; (*decision*) to quash, reverse; (*character*) to reform

restitūtiō, -ōnis *f* restoration; reinstating

restitūtor, -ōris *m* restorer

restitūtus *ppp of* **restituō**

restō, -āre, -itī *vi* to stand firm; to resist; to remain, be left; to be in store (for); **quod restat** for the future

restrictē *adv* sparingly; strictly

restrictus *ppp of* **restringō** ▶ *adj* tight, short; niggardly; severe

restringō, -ngere, -nxī, -ctum *vt* to draw back tightly, bind fast; (*teeth*) to bare; (*fig*) to check

resultō, -āre *vi* to rebound; to re-echo

resūmō, -ere, -psī, -ptum *vt* to take up again, get back, resume

resupīnō, -āre *vt* to turn back, throw on one's back

resupīnus *adj* lying back, face upwards

resurgō, -gere, -rēxī, -rēctum *vi* to rise again, revive

resuscitō, -āre *vt* to revive

retardātiō, -ōnis *f* hindering

retardō, -āre, -āvī, -ātum *vt* to retard, detain, check

rēte, -is *nt* net; (*fig*) snare

retēctus *ppp of* **retegō**

retegō, -egere, -ēxī, -ēctum *vt* to uncover, open; to reveal

retemptō, -āre *vt* to try again

retendō, -endere, -endī, -entum *and* **-ēnsum** *vt* to slacken, relax

retēnsus *ppp of* **retendō**

retentiō, -ōnis *f* holding back

retentō¹ *etc see* **retemptō**

retentō², -āre *vt* to keep back, hold fast

retentus *ppp of* **retendō; retineō**

retēxī *perf of* **retegō**

retexō, -ere, -uī, -tum *vt* to unravel; (*fig*) to break up, cancel; to renew

rētiārius, -ī *and* **-iī** *m* net-fighter

reticentia, -ae *f* saying nothing; pause

reticeō, -ēre, -uī *vi* to be silent, say nothing ▶ *vt* to keep secret

rēticulum, -ī *nt* small net, hairnet; network bag

retināculum, -ī *nt* tether, hawser

retinēns, -entis *pres p of* **retineō** ▶ *adj* tenacious, observant

retinentia, -ae *f* memory

retineō, -inēre, -inuī, -entum *vt* to hold back, detain, restrain; to keep, retain, preserve

retinniō, -īre *vi* to ring

retonō, **-āre** vi to thunder in answer

retorqueō, **-quēre**, **-sī**, **-tum** vt to turn back, twist

retorridus adj dried up, wizened

retortus ppp of **retorqueō**

retractātiō, **-ōnis** f hesitation

retractō, **-āre**, **-āvī**, **-ātum** vt to rehandle, take up again; to reconsider, revise; to withdraw ▶ vi to draw back, hesitate

retractus ppp of **retrahō** ▶ adj remote

retrahō, **-here**, **-xī**, **-ctum** vt to draw back, drag back; to withdraw, remove

retrectō etc see **retractō**

retribuō, **-uere**, **-uī**, **-ūtum** vt to restore, repay

retrō adv back, backwards, behind; (time) back, past

retrōrsum adv backwards, behind; in reverse order

retrūdō, **-dere**, **-sum** vt to push back; to withdraw

rettulī perf of **referō**

retundō, **-undere**, **-udī** and **-tudī**, **-ūsum** and **-ūnsum** vt to blunt; (fig) to check, weaken

retūnsus, **retūsus** ppp of **retundō** ▶ adj blunt, dull

reus, **-ī** m the accused, defendant; guarantor, debtor, one responsible; culprit, criminal; **vōtī ~** one who has had a prayer granted

revalēscō, **-ēscere**, **-uī** vi to recover

revehō, **-here**, **-xī**, **-ctum** vt to carry back, bring back; (pass) to ride, drive, sail back

revellō, **-ellere**, **-ellī**, **-ulsum (-olsum)** vt to pull out, tear off; to remove

revēlō, **-āre** vt to unveil, uncover

reveniō, **-enīre**, **-ēnī**, **-entum** vi to come back, return

rēvērā adv in fact, actually

reverendus adj venerable, awe-inspiring

reverēns, **-entis** pres p of **revereor** ▶ adj respectful, reverent

reverenter adv respectfully

reverentia, **-ae** f respect, reverence, awe

revereor, **-ērī**, **-itus** vt to stand in awe of; to respect, revere

reversiō, **revorsiō**, **-ōnis** f turning back; recurrence

reversus ppa of **revertor**

revertō, **-ere**, **-ī**, **revertor**, **-tī**, **-sus** vi to turn back, return; to revert

revexī perf of **revehō**

revictus ppp of **revincō**

revinciō, **-cīre**, **-xī**, **-ctum** vt to tie back, bind fast

revincō, **-incere**, **-īcī**, **-ictum** vt to conquer, repress; (words) to refute, convict

revinctus ppp of **revinciō**

revirēscō, **-ēscere**, **-uī** vi to grow green again; to be rejuvenated; to grow strong again, flourish again

revīsō, **-ere** vt, vi to come back to, revisit

revīvēscō, **-vīscō**, **-vīscere**, **-xī** vi to come to life again, revive

revocābilis adj revocable

revocāmen, **-inis** nt recall

revocātiō, **-ōnis** f recalling; (word) withdrawing

revocō, **-āre**, **-āvī**, **-ātum** vt to call back, recall; (action) to revoke; (former state) to recover, regain; (growth) to check; (guest) to invite in return; (judgment) to apply, refer; (LAW) to summon again; (performer) to encore; (troops) to withdraw

revolō, **-āre** vi to fly back

revolsus etc see **revulsus**

revolūbilis adj that may be rolled back

revolūtus ppp of **revolvō**

revolvō, **-vere**, **-vī**, **-ūtum** vt to roll back, unroll, unwind; (speech) to relate, repeat; (thought) to think over; (writing) to read over; (pass) to revolve, return, come round

revomō, **-ere**, **-uī** vt to disgorge

revor- etc see **rever-**

revulsus ppp of **revellō**

rēx, **rēgis** m king; tyrant, despot; leader; patron, rich man

rēxī perf of **regō**

Rhadamanthus, **-ī** m judge in the lower world

Rhaetī etc see **Raetī**

Rhamnūs, **-ūntis** f town in Attica (famous for its statue of Nemesis)

Rhamnūsis, **-ūsidis** f Nemesis

Rhamnūsius adj see **Rhamnūs**

rhapsōdia, **-ae** f a book of Homer

Rhea, **-ae** f Cybele

Rhea Silvia, **Rheae Silviae** f mother of Romulus and Remus

Rhēgium etc see **Rēgium**

Rhēnānus adj Rhenish

rhēnō etc see **rēnō**

Rhēnus, **-ī** m Rhine

Rhēsus, **-ī** m Thracian king (killed at Troy)

rhētor, **-oris** m teacher of rhetoric; orator

rhētorica, **-ae**, **rhētoricē**, **-ēs** f art of oratory, rhetoric

rhētoricē adv rhetorically, in an oratorical manner

rhētoricī, **-ōrum** mpl teachers of rhetoric

rhētoricus adj rhetorical, on rhetoric

rhīnocerōs, **-ōtis** m rhinoceros

rhō nt indecl (Greek letter) rho

Rhodanus, **-ī** m Rhone

Rhodius adj see **Rhodos**

Rhodopē, **-ēs** f mountain range in Thrace

Rhodopēius adj Thracian

Rhodos, **Rhodus**, **-ī** f (island) of Rhodes

Rhoetēum, **-ī** nt promontory on the Dardanelles (near Troy)

Rhoetēus adj Trojan

rhombus, **-ī** m magician's circle; (fish) turbot

rhomphaea, **-ae** f long barbarian javelin

rhythmicus, **-ī** m teacher of prose rhythm

rhythmos, **rhythmus**, **-ī** m rhythm, symmetry

rīca, -ae f sacrificial veil

rīcinium, -ī and **-iī** nt small cloak with hood

rictum, -ī nt, **rictus, -ūs** m open mouth, gaping jaws

rīdeō, -dēre, -sī, -sum vi to laugh, smile ▶ vt to laugh at, smile at; to ridicule

rīdibundus adj laughing

rīdiculāria, -ium ntpl jokes

rīdiculē adv jokingly; absurdly

rīdiculus adj amusing, funny; ridiculous, silly ▶ m jester ▶ nt joke

rigēns, -entis pres p of **rigeō** ▶ adj stiff, rigid, frozen

rigeō, -ēre vi to be stiff

rigēscō, -ēscere, -uī vi to stiffen, harden; to bristle

rigidē adv rigorously

rigidus adj stiff, rigid, hard; (fig) hardy, strict, inflexible

rigō, -āre vt to water, moisten, bedew; to convey (water)

rigor, -ōris m stiffness, hardness; numbness, cold; strictness, severity

riguī perf of **rigēscō**

riguus adj irrigating; watered

rīma, -ae f crack, chink

rīmor, -ārī, -ātus vt to tear open; to search for, probe, examine; to find out

rīmōsus adj cracked, leaky

ringor, -ī vi to snarl

rīpa, -ae f river bank; shore

Rīphaeī, -ōrum mpl mountain range in N. Scythia

Rīphaeus adj see **Rīphaeī**

rīpula, -ae f riverbank

riscus, -ī m trunk, chest

rīsī perf of **rīdeō**

rīsor, -ōris m scoffer

rīsus, -ūs m laughter, laugh; laughing stock

rīte adv with the proper formality or ritual; duly, properly, rightly; in the usual manner; fortunately

rītus, -ūs m ritual, ceremony; custom, usage; **rītū** after the manner of

rīvālis, -is m rival in love

rīvālitās, -ātis f rivalry in love

rīvulus, -ī m brook

rīvus, -ī m stream, brook; **ē rīvō flūmina magna facere** make a mountain of a molehill

rixa, -ae f quarrel, brawl, fight

rixor, -ārī, -ātus vi to quarrel, brawl, squabble

rōbīginōsus adj rusty

rōbīgō, -inis f rust; blight, mould, mildew

rōboreus adj of oak

rōborō, -āre vt to strengthen, invigorate

rōbur, -oris nt oak; hard wood; prison, dungeon (at Rome); (fig) strength, hardness, vigour; best part, élite, flower

rōbustus adj of oak; strong, hard, robust, mature

rōdō, -dere, -sī, -sum vt to gnaw; (rust) to corrode; (words) to slander

rogālis adj of a pyre

rogātiō, -ōnis f proposal, motion, bill; request; (RHET) question

rogātiuncula, -ae f unimportant bill; question

rogātor, -ōris m proposer; polling clerk

rogātus, -ūs m request

rogitō, -āre vt to ask for, inquire eagerly

rogō, -āre, -āvī, -ātum vt to ask, ask for; (bill) to propose, move; (candidate) to put up for election; **lēgem rogāre, populum rogāre** introduce a bill; **magistrātum populum rogāre** nominate for election to an office; **militēs sacrāmentō rogāre** administer the oath to the troops; **mālō emere quam rogāre** I'd rather buy it than borrow it

rogus, -ī m funeral pyre

Rōma, -ae f Rome

Rōmānus adj Roman

Rōmuleus, Rōmulus adj of Romulus; Roman

Rōmulidae, -idārum mpl the Romans

Rōmulus, -ī m founder and first king of Rome

rōrāriī, -ōrum mpl skirmishers

rōridus adj dewy

rōrifer, -ī adj dew-bringing

rōrō, -āre vi to distil dew; to drip, trickle ▶ vt to bedew, wet

rōs, rōris m dew; moisture, water; (plant) rosemary; **rōs marīnus** rosemary

rosa, -ae f rose; rose bush

rosāria, -ōrum ntpl rose garden

rōscidus adj dewy; wet

Roscius¹, -ī m: L. ~ **Othō** tribune in 67 BC, whose law reserved theatre seats for the equites; Q. ~ **Gallus** famous actor defended by Cicero; **Sex. ~** of Ameria, defended by Cicero

Roscius², -iānus adj see **Roscius¹**

rosētum, -ī nt rosebed

roseus adj rosy; of roses

rōsī perf of **rōdō**

rōstrātus adj beaked, curved; **columna rōstrāta** column commemorating a naval victory

rōstrum, -ī nt (bird) beak, bill; (animal) snout, muzzle; (ship) beak, end of prow; (pl) orators' platform in the Forum

rōsus ppp of **rōdō**

rota, -ae f wheel; potter's wheel, torture wheel; car, disc

rotō, -āre, -āvī, -ātum vt to turn, whirl, roll; (pass) to revolve

rotundē adv elegantly

rotundō, -āre vt to round off

rotundus adj round, circular, spherical; (style) well-turned, smooth

rubefaciō, -facere, -fēcī, -factum vt to redden

rubēns, -entis pres p of **rubeō** ▶ adj red; blushing

rubeō, -ēre vi to be red; to blush

ruber, -rī adj red; **mare rubrum** Red Sea; Persian Gulf; **ōceanus ~** Indian Ocean; **Saxa rubra** stone quarries between Rome and Veii

rubēscō, -ēscere, -uī *vi* to redden, blush
rubēta[1], -ae *f* toad
rubēta[2], -ōrum *ntpl* bramble bushes
rubeus *adj* of bramble
Rubicō, -ōnis *m* stream marking the frontier between Italy and Gaul
rubicundulus *adj* reddish
rubicundus *adj* red, ruddy
rūbīg- *etc see* **rōbīg-**
rubor, -ōris *m* redness; blush; bashfulness; shame
rubrīca, -ae *f* red earth, red ochre
rubuī *perf of* **rubēscō**
rubus, -ī *m* bramble bush; bramble, blackberry
ructō, -āre, ructor, -ārī *vi* to belch
ructus, -us *m* belching
rudēns, -entis *pres p of* **rudō** ▸ *m* rope; (*pl*) rigging
Rudiae, -iārum *fpl* town in E. Italy (*birthplace of Ennius*)
rudiārius, -ī *and* **-iī** *m* retired gladiator
rudīmentum, -ī *nt* first attempt, beginning
Rudīnus *adj see* **Rudiae**
rudis[1] *adj* unwrought, unworked, raw; coarse, rough, badly-made; (*age*) new, young; (*person*) uncultured, unskilled, clumsy; ignorant (of), inexperienced (in)
rudis[2], -is *f* stick, rod; foil (*for fighting practice*); (*fig*) discharge
rudō, -ere, -īvī, -ītum *vi* to roar, bellow, bray; to creak
rūdus[1], -eris *nt* rubble, rubbish; piece of copper
rūdus[2], -eris *nt* copper coin
Rūfulī, -ōrum *mpl* military tribunes (*chosen by the general*)
rūfulus *adj* red-headed
rūfus *adj* red, red-haired
rūga, -ae *f* wrinkle, crease
rūgō, -āre *vi* to become creased
rūgōsus *adj* wrinkled, shrivelled, corrugated
ruī *perf of* **ruō**
ruīna, -ae *f* fall, downfall; collapse, falling in; debris, ruins; destruction, disaster, ruin (*fig*)
ruīnōsus *adj* collapsing; ruined
rumex, -icis *f* sorrel
rūmificō, -āre *vt* to report
Rūmīna, -ae *f* goddess of nursing mothers; **fīcus Rūmīnālis** the fig tree of Romulus and Remus (*under which the she-wolf suckled them*)
rūminātiō, -ōnis *f* chewing the cud; (*fig*) ruminating
rūminō, -āre *vt, vi* to chew the cud
rūmor, -ōris *m* noise, cheering; rumour, hearsay; public opinion; reputation
rumpia *etc see* **rhomphaea**
rumpō, -ere, rūpī, ruptum *vt* to break, burst, tear; to break down, burst through; (*activity*) to interrupt; (*agreement*) to violate, annul; (*delay*) to put an end to; (*voice*) to give vent to; (*way*) to force through
rūmusculī, -ōrum *mpl* gossip
rūna, -ae *f* dart

runcō, -āre *vt* to weed
ruō, -ere, -ī, -tum *vi* to fall down, tumble; to rush, run, hurry; to come to ruin ▸ *vt* to dash down, hurl to the ground; to throw up, turn up
rūpēs, -is *f* rock, cliff
rūpī *perf of* **rumpō**
ruptor, -ōris *m* violator
ruptus *ppp of* **rumpō**
rūricola, -ae *adj* rural, country- (*in cpds*)
rūrigena, -ae *m* countryman
rūrsus, rūrsum, rūsum *adv* back, backwards; on the contrary, in return; again
rūs, rūris *nt* the country, countryside; estate, farm; **rūs** to the country; **rūrī** in the country; **rūre** from the country
ruscum, -ī *nt* butcher's-broom
russus *adj* red
rūsticānus *adj* country- (*in cpds*), rustic
rūsticātiō, -ōnis *f* country life
rūsticē *adv* in a countrified manner, awkwardly
rūsticitās, -ātis *f* country manners, rusticity
rūsticor, -ārī *vi* to live in the country
rūsticulus, -ī *m* yokel
rūsticus *adj* country- (*in cpds*), rural, rough, clownish ▸ *m* countryman
rūsum *see* **rūrsus**
rūta, -ae *f* (*herb*) rue; (*fig*) unpleasantness
ruta caesa *ntpl* minerals and timber on an estate
rutilō, -āre *vt* to colour red ▸ *vi* to glow red
rutilus *adj* red, auburn
rutrum, -ī *nt* spade, shovel, trowel
rūtula, -ae *f* little piece of rue
Rutulī, -ōrum *mpl* ancient Latin people
Rutulus *adj* Rutulian
Rutupiae, -iārum *fpl* seaport in Kent (*now Richborough*)
Rutupīnus *adj see* **Rutupiae**
rutus *ppp of* **ruō**

S

Saba, -ae f town in Arabia Felix

Sabaeus adj see Saba

Sabāzia, -iōrum ntpl festival of Bacchus

Sabāzius, -ī m Bacchus

sabbata, -ōrum ntpl Sabbath, Jewish holiday

Sabellus¹, -ī m Sabine, Samnite

Sabellus², -icus adj see Sabellus¹

Sabīnī, -ōrum mpl Sabines (a people of central
Italy)

Sabīnus adj Sabine ▶ f Sabine woman ▶ nt
Sabine estate; Sabine wine; herba Sabīna savin
(a kind of juniper)

Sabrīna, -ae f (river) Severn

saburra, -ae f sand, ballast

Sacae, -ārum mpl tribe of Scythians

saccipērium, -ī and -iī nt purse-pocket

saccō, -āre vt to strain, filter

sacculus, -ī m little bag, purse

saccus, -ī m bag, purse, wallet

sacellum, -ī nt chapel

sacer, -rī adj sacred, holy; devoted for sacrifice,
forfeited; accursed, criminal, infamous; Mōns ~
hill to which the Roman plebs seceded; Via sacra
street from the Forum to the Capitol

sacerdōs, -ōtis m/f priest, priestess

sacerdōtium, -ī and -iī nt priesthood

sacrāmentum, -ī nt deposit made by parties
to a lawsuit; civil lawsuit, dispute; (MIL) oath of
allegiance, engagement

sacrārium, -ī and -iī nt shrine, chapel

sacrātus adj holy, hallowed; sacrāta lēx a law
whose violation was punished by devotion to the
infernal gods

sacricola, -ae m/f sacrificing priest or priestess

sacrifer, -ī adj carrying holy things

sacrificālis adj sacrificial

sacrificātiō, -ōnis f sacrificing

sacrificium, -ī and -iī nt sacrifice

sacrificō, -āre vt, vi to sacrifice

sacrificulus, -ī m sacrificing priest; rēx ~ high
priest

sacrificus adj sacrificial

sacrilēgium, -ī and -iī nt sacrilege

sacrilegus adj sacrilegious; profane, wicked

▶ m temple-robber

sacrō, -āre, -āvī, -ātum vt to consecrate;
to doom, curse; to devote, dedicate; to make
inviolable; (poetry) to immortalize

sacrōsanctus adj inviolable, sacrosanct

sacruficō etc see sacrificō

sacrum, -rī nt holy thing, sacred vessel;
shrine; offering, victim; rite; (pl) sacrifice,
worship, religion; sacra facere sacrifice;
inter ~ saxumque with one's back to the wall;
hērēditās sine sacrīs a gift without any awkward
obligations

saeclum etc see saeculum

saeculāris adj centenary; (ECCL) secular, pagan

saeculum, -ī nt generation, lifetime, age; the
age, the times; century; in saecula (ECCL) for
ever

saepe adv often, frequently

saepe numerō adv very often

saepēs, -is f hedge, fence

saepīmentum, -ī nt enclosure

saepiō, -īre, -sī, -tum vt to hedge round, fence
in, enclose; (fig) to shelter, protect

saeptus ppp of saepiō ▶ nt fence, wall; stake,
pale; (sheep) fold; (Rome) voting area in the
Campus Martius

saeta, -ae f hair, bristle

saetiger, -ī adj bristly

saetōsus adj bristly, hairy

saevē, saeviter adv fiercely, cruelly

saevidicus adj furious

saeviō, -īre, -iī, -ītum vi to rage, rave

saevitia, -ae f rage; ferocity, cruelty

saevus adj raging, fierce; cruel, barbarous

sāga, -ae f fortune teller

sagācitās, -ātis f (dogs) keen scent; (mind)
shrewdness

sagāciter adv keenly; shrewdly

sagātus adj wearing a soldier's cloak

sagāx, -ācis adj (senses) keen, keen-scented;
(mind) quick, shrewd

sagīna, -ae f stuffing, fattening; food, rich
food; fatted animal

sagīnō, -āre vt to cram, fatten; to feed, feast

sāgiō, -īre vi to perceive keenly

sagitta, -ae f arrow

sagittārius, -ī and -iī m archer

sagittifer, -ī adj armed with arrows

sagmen, -inis nt tuft of sacred herbs (used as a
mark of inviolability)

sagulum, -ī nt short military cloak

sagum, -ī nt military cloak; woollen mantle

Saguntīnus adj see Saguntum

Saguntum, -ī nt, Saguntus, -ī, Saguntos,
-ī f town in E. Spain

sāgus adj prophetic

sāl, salis m salt; brine, sea; (fig) shrewdness,
wit, humour, witticism; good taste

salacō, -ōnis m swaggerer

Salamīnius adj see Salamīs

Salamīs, -inis f Greek island near Athens;
town in Cyprus

salapūtium, -ī *and* **-iī** *nt* manikin
salārius *adj* salt- (*in cpds*) ▸ *nt* allowance, salary
salāx, -ācis *adj* lustful, salacious
salebra, -ae *f* roughness, rut
Saliāris *adj* of the Salii; sumptuous
salictum, -ī *nt* willow plantation
salientēs, -ium *fpl* springs
salignus *adj* of willow
Saliī, -ōrum *mpl* priests of Mars
salillum, -ī *nt* little saltcellar
salīnae, -ārum *fpl* saltworks
salīnum, -ī *nt* saltcellar
saliō, -īre, -uī, -tum *vi* to leap, spring; to throb
saliunca, -ae *f* Celtic nard
salīva, -ae *f* saliva, spittle; taste
salix, -icis *f* willow
Sallustiānus *adj see* **Sallustius**
Sallustius, -ī *m* Sallust (*Roman historian*); *his wealthy grand-nephew*
Salmōneus, -eos *m* son of Aeolus (*punished in Tartarus for imitating lightning*)
Salmōnis, -idis *f* his daughter Tyro
salsāmentum, -ī *nt* brine, pickle; salted fish
salsē *adv* wittily
salsus *adj* salted; salt, briny; (*fig*) witty
saltātiō, -ōnis *f* dancing, dance
saltātor, -ōris *m* dancer
saltātōrius *adj* dancing- (*in cpds*)
saltātrīx, -īcis *f* dancer
saltātus, -ūs *m* dance
saltem *adv* at least, at all events; **nōn ~** not even
saltō, -āre *vt, vi* to dance
saltuōsus *adj* wooded
saltus¹, -ūs *m* leap, bound
saltus², -ūs *m* woodland pasture, glade; pass, ravine
salūber *adj see* **salūbris**
salūbris *adj* health-giving, wholesome; healthy, sound
salūbritās, -ātis *f* healthiness; health
salūbriter *adv* wholesomely; beneficially
saluī *perf of* **saliō**
salum, -ī *nt* sea, high sea
salūs, -ūtis *f* health; welfare, life; safety; greeting; **salūtem dīcere** greet; bid farewell
salūtāris *adj* wholesome, healthy; beneficial; **~ littera** letter A (*for* **absolvō** = *acquittal*)
salūtāriter *adv* beneficially
salūtātiō, -ōnis *f* greeting; formal morning visit, levee
salūtātor, -ōris *m* morning caller; male courtier
salūtātrīx, -rīcis *f* morning caller; female courtier
salūtifer, -ī *adj* health-giving
salūtigerulus *adj* carrying greetings
salūtō, -āre, -āvī, -ātum *vt* to greet, salute, wish well; to call on, pay respects to
salvē¹ *adv* well, in good health; all right
salvē² *impv of* **salveō**
salveō, -ēre *vi* to be well, be in good health;

salvē, salvētō, salvēte hail!, good day!, goodbye!; **salvēre iubeō** I bid good day
salvus, salvos *adj* safe, alive, intact, well; without violating; all right; **~ sīs** good day to you!; **salva rēs est** all is well; **salvā lēge** without breaking the law
Samaous *adj see* **Samē**
Samarobrīva, -ae *f* Belgian town (*now Amiens*)
sambūca, -ae *f* harp
sambūcistria, -ae *f* harpist
Samē, -ēs *f* old name of the Greek island Cephalonia
Samius *adj* Samian ▸ *ntpl* Samian pottery
Samnis, -ītis *adj* Samnite
Samnium, -ī *and* **-iī** *nt* district of central Italy
Samos, Samus, -ī *f* Aegean island off Asia Minor (*famous for its pottery and as the birthplace of Pythagoras*)
Samothrāces, -um *mpl* Samothracians
Samothrācia, -iae, Samothrāca, -ae *f* Samothrace (*island in the N. Aegean*)
Samothrācius *adj see* **Samothrācia**
sānābilis *adj* curable
sānātiō, -ōnis *f* healing
sanciō, -īre, -xī, -ctum *vt* to make sacred or inviolable; to ordain, ratify; to enact a punishment against
sanctimōnia, -ae *f* sanctity; chastity
sanctiō, -ōnis *f* decree, penalty for violating a law
sanctitās, -ātis *f* sacredness; integrity, chastity
sanctitūdō, -inis *f* sacredness
sanctō *adv* solemnly, religiously
sanctor, -ōris *m* enacter
sanctus *ppp of* **sanciō** ▸ *adj* sacred, inviolable; holy, venerable; pious, virtuous, chaste
sandaligerula, -ae *f* sandalbearer
sandalium, -ī *and* **-iī** *nt* sandal, slipper
sandapila, -ae *f* common bier
sandyx, -ycis *f* scarlet
sānē *adv* sensibly; (*intensive*) very, doubtless; (*ironical*) to be sure, of course; (*concessive*) of course, indeed; (*in answer*) certainly, surely; (*with impv*) then, if you please; **~ quam** very much; **haud ~** not so very, not quite
sanguen *etc see* **sanguis**
sanguināns, -antis *adj* bloodthirsty
sanguinārius *adj* bloodthirsty
sanguineus *adj* bloody, of blood; blood-red
sanguinolentus *adj* bloody; blood-red; sanguinary
sanguis, -inis *m* blood, bloodshed; descent, family; offspring; (*fig*) strength, life; **sanguinem dare** shed one's blood; **sanguinem mittere** let blood
saniēs (*acc* **-em**, *abl* **-ē**) *f* diseased blood, matter; venom
sānitās, -ātis *f* (*body*) health, sound condition; (*mind*) sound sense, sanity; (*style*) correctness, purity
sanna, -ae *f* grimace, mocking
sanniō, -ōnis *m* clown

sānō, -āre, -āvī, -ātum vt to cure, heal; (fig) to remedy, relieve

Sanquālis avis f osprey

sānus adj (body) sound, healthy; (mind) sane, sensible; (style) correct; **male ~** mad, inspired; **sānun es?** are you in your senses?

sanxī perf of **sanciō**

sapa, -ae f new wine

sapiēns, -entis pres p of **sapiō** ▸ adj wise, discreet ▸ m wise man, philosopher; man of taste

sapienter adv wisely, sensibly

sapientia, -ae f wisdom, discernment; philosophy; knowledge

sapiō, -ere, -īvī and **-uī** vi to have a flavour or taste; to have sense, be wise ▸ vt to taste of, smell of, smack of; to understand

sapor, -ōris m taste, flavour; (food) delicacy; (fig) taste, refinement

Sapphicus adj see **Sapphō**

Sapphō, -ūs f famous Greek lyric poetess, native of Lesbos

sarcina, -ae f bundle, burden; (MIL) pack

sarcinārius adj baggage- (in cpds)

sarcinātor, -ōris m patcher

sarcinula, -ae f little pack

sarciō, -cīre, -sī, -tum vt to patch, mend, repair

sarcophagus, -ī m sepulchre

sarculum, -ī nt light hoe

Sardēs, Sardis, -ium fpl Sardis (capital of Lydia)

Sardiānus adj see **Sardēs**

Sardinia, -iniae f (island of) Sardinia

sardonyx, -chis f sardonyx

Sardus, Sardōus, Sardiniēnsis adj see Sardinia

sariō, -īre, -īvī and **-uī** vt to hoe, weed

sarīsa, -ae f Macedonian lance

sarīsophorus, -ī m Macedonian lancer

Sarmatae, -ārum mpl Sarmatians (a people of S.E. Russia)

Sarmaticus, -is adj see **Sarmatae**

sarmentum, -ī nt twigs, brushwood

Sarpēdōn, -onis m king of Lycia

Sarra, -ae f Tyre

sarrācum, -ī nt cart

Sarrānus adj Tyrian

sarriō etc see **sariō**

sarsī perf of **sarciō**

sartāgō, -inis f frying pan

sartor, -ōris m hoer, weeder

sartus ppp of **sarciō**

sat etc see **satis**

satagō, -ere vi to have one's hands full, be in trouble; to bustle about, fuss

satelles, -itis m/f attendant, follower; assistant, accomplice

satiās, -ātis f sufficiency; satiety

satietās, -ātis f sufficiency; satiety

satin, satine see **satisne**

satiō¹, -āre, -āvī, -ātum vt to satisfy, appease; to fill, saturate; to glut, cloy, disgust

satiō², -ōnis f sowing, planting; (pl) fields

satis, sat adj enough, sufficient ▸ adv enough, sufficiently; tolerably, fairly, quite; **~ accipiō** take sufficient bail; **~ agō, ~ agitō** have one's hands full, be harassed; **~ dō** offer sufficient bail; **~ faciō** satisfy; give satisfaction, make amends; (creditor) pay

satisdatiō, -ōnis f giving security

satisdō see **satis**

satisfaciō see **satis**

satisfactiō, -ōnis f amends, apology

satisne adv quite, really

satius compar of **satis**; better, preferable

sator, -ōris m sower, planter; father; promoter

satrapēs, -is m satrap (Persian governor)

satur, -ī adj filled, sated; (fig) rich

satura, -ae f mixed dish; medley; (poem) satire; **per saturam** confusingly

saturēia, -ōrum ntpl (plant) savory

saturitās, -ātis f repletion; fulness, plenty

Saturnālia, -ium and **-iōrum** ntpl festival of Saturn in December

Saturnia, -iae f Juno

Saturnīnus, -ī m revolutionary tribune in 103 and 100 B.C.

Saturnius adj see **Saturnus**

Saturnus, -ī m Saturn (god of sowing, ruler of the Golden Age); (the planet) Saturn

saturō, -āre, -āvī, -ātum vt to fill, glut, satisfy; to disgust

satus¹ ppp of **serō¹** ▸ m son ▸ f daughter ▸ ntpl crops

satus², -ūs m sowing, planting; begetting

satyriscus, -ī m little satyr

satyrus, -ī m satyr

sauciātiō, -ōnis f wounding

sauciō, -āre vt to wound, hurt

saucius adj wounded, hurt; ill, stricken

Sauromatae etc see **Sarmatae**

sāviātiō, -ōnis f kissing

sāviolum, -ī nt sweet kiss

sāvior, -ārī vt to kiss

sāvium, -ī and **-iī** nt kiss

saxātilis adj rock- (in cpds)

saxētum, -ī nt rocky place

saxeus adj of rock, rocky

saxificus adj petrifying

saxōsus adj rocky, stony

saxulum, -ī nt small rock

saxum, -ī nt rock, boulder; the Tarpeian Rock

scaber, -rī adj rough, scurfy; mangy, itchy

scabiēs (acc **-em**, abl **-ē**) f roughness, scurf; mange, itch

scabillum, -ī nt stool; a castanet played with the foot

scabō, -ere, scābī vt to scratch

Scaea porta, Scaeae portae f the west gate of Troy

scaena, -ae f stage, stage setting; (fig) limelight, public life; outward appearance, pretext

scaenālis adj theatrical

scaenicus adj stage- (in cpds), theatrical ▶ m actor

Scaevola, -ae m early Roman who burned his hand off before Porsenna; famous jurist of Cicero's day

scaevus adj on the left; perverse ▶ f omen

scālae, -ārum fpl steps, ladder, stairs

scalmus, -ī m tholepin

scalpellum, -ī nt scalpel, lancet

scalpō, -ere, -sī, -tum vt to carve, engrave; to scratch

scalprum, -ī nt knife, penknife; chisel

scalpurriō, -īre vi to scratch

Scamander, -rī m river of Troy (also called Xanthus)

scammōnea, -ae f (plant) scammony

scamnum, -ī nt bench, stool; throne

scandō, -ere vt, vi to climb, mount

scapha, -ae f boat, skiff

scaphium, -ī and **-iī** nt a boat-shaped cup

scapulae, -ārum fpl shoulder blades; shoulders

scāpus, -ī m shaft; (loom) yarnbeam

scarus, -ī m (fish) scar

scatebra, -ae f gushing water

scateō, -ēre, scatō, -ere vi to bubble up, gush out; (fig) to abound, swarm

scatūrīginēs, -um fpl springs

scatūriō, -īre vi to gush out; (fig) to be full of

scaurus adj large-ankled

scelerātē adv wickedly

scelerātus adj desecrated; wicked, infamous, accursed; pernicious

scelerō, -āre vt to desecrate

scelerōsus adj vicious, accursed

scelestē adv wickedly

scelestus adj wicked, villainous, accursed; unlucky

scelus, -eris nt wickedness, crime, sin; (person) scoundrel; (event) calamity

scēn- etc see **scaen-**

scēptrifer, -ī adj sceptered

scēptrum, -ī nt staff, sceptre; kingship, power

scēptūchus, -ī m sceptre-bearer

scheda etc see **scida**

schēma, -ae f form, figure, style

Schoenēis, -ēidis f Atalanta

Schoenēius adj see **Schoenēis**

Schoeneus, -eī m father of Atalanta

schoenobatēs, -ae m rope dancer

schola, -ae f learned discussion, dissertation; school; sect, followers

scholasticus adj of a school ▶ m rhetorician

scida, -ae f sheet of paper

sciēns, -entis pres p of **scio** ▶ adj knowing, purposely; versed in, acquainted with

scienter adv expertly

scientia, -ae f knowledge, skill

scīlicet adv evidently, of course; (concessive) no doubt; (ironical) I suppose, of course

scilla etc see **squilla**

scindō, -ndere, -dī, -ssum vt to cut open, tear apart, split, break down; to divide, part

scintilla, -ae f spark

scintillō, -āre vi to sparkle

scintillula, -ae f little spark

sciō, -īre, -īvī, -ītum vt to know; to have skill in; (with infin) to know how to; **quod sciam** as far as I know; **scītō** you may be sure

Scīpiadēs, -ae m Scipio

scīpiō, -ōnis m staff

Scīpiō, -ōnis m famous Roman family name (esp Africanus, the conqueror of Hannibal, and Aemilianus, the destroyer of Carthage and patron of literature)

scirpeus adj rush (in cpds) ▶ f wickerwork frame

scirpiculus, -ī m rush basket

scirpus, -ī m bulrush

scīscitor, -ārī, -ātus, scīscitō, -āre vt to inquire; to question

scīscō, -scere, -vī, -tum vt to inquire, learn; (POL) to approve, decree, appoint

scissus ppp of **scindō** ▶ adj split; (voice) harsh

scītāmenta, -ōrum ntpl dainties

scītē adv cleverly, tastefully

scītor, -ārī, -ātus vt, vi to inquire; to consult

scītulus adj neat, smart

scītum, -ī nt decree, statute

scītus¹ ppp of **scio**; **scīscō** ▶ adj clever, shrewd, skilled; (words) sensible, witty; (appearance) fine, smart

scītus², -ūs m decree

sciūrus, -ī m squirrel

scīvī perf of **scio**; **scīscō**

scobis, -is f sawdust, filings

scomber, -rī m mackerel

scōpae, -ārum fpl broom

Scopās, -ae m famous Greek sculptor

scopulōsus adj rocky

scopulus, -ī m rock, crag, promontory; (fig) danger

scorpiō, -ōnis, scorpius, -ī, scorpios, -ī m scorpion; (MIL) a kind of catapult

scortātor, -ōris m fornicator

scorteus adj of leather

scortor, -ārī vi to associate with harlots

scortum, -ī nt harlot, prostitute

screātor, -ōris m one who clears his throat noisily

screātus, -ūs m clearing the throat

scrība, -ae m clerk, writer

scrībō, -bere, -psī, -ptum vt to write, draw; to write down, describe; (document) to draw up; (LAW) to designate; (MIL) to enlist

scrīnium, -ī and **-iī** nt book box, lettercase

scrīptiō, -ōnis f writing; composition; text

scrīptitō, -āre, -āvī, -ātum vt to write regularly, compose

scrīptor, -ōris m writer, author; secretary; rērum ~ historian

scrīptula, -ōrum ntpl lines of a squared board

scrīptum, -ī nt writing, book, work; (LAW) ordinance; **duōdecim scrīpta** Twelve Lines (a game played on a squared board)

scrīptūra, -ae f writing; composition; document; (POL) tax on public pastures; (will) provision

scrīptus¹ ppp of **scrībō**

scrīptus², -ūs m clerkship

scrīpulum, -ī nt small weight, scruple

scrobis, -is f ditch, trench; grave

scrōfa, -ae f breeding sow

scrōfipāscus, -ī m pig breeder

scrūpeus adj stony, rough

scrūpōsus adj rocky, jagged

scrūpulōsus adj stony, rough; (fig) precise

scrūpulum etc see **scrūpulum**

scrūpulus, -ī m small sharp stone; (fig) uneasiness, doubt, scruple

scrūpus, -ī m sharp stone; (fig) uneasiness

scrūta, -ōrum ntpl trash

scrūtor, -ārī, -ātus vt to search, probe into, examine; to find out

sculpō, -ere, -sī, -tum vt to carve, engrave

sculpōneae, -ārum fpl clogs

sculptilis adj carved

sculptor, -ōris m sculptor

sculptus ppp of **sculpō**

scurra, -ae m jester; dandy

scurrīlis adj jeering

scurrīlitās, -ātis f scurrility

scurror, -ārī vi to play the fool

scūtāle, -is nt sling strap

scūtātus adj carrying a shield

scutella, -ae f bowl

scutica, -ae f whip

scutra, -ae f flat dish

scutula¹, -ae f small dish

scutula² f wooden roller; secret letter

scutulāta, -ae f a checked garment

scūtulum, -ī nt small shield

scūtum, -ī nt shield

Scylla, -ae f dangerous rock or sea monster (in the Straits of Messina)

Scyllaeus adj see **Scylla**

scymnus, -ī m cub

scyphus, -ī m wine cup

Scyrius, -ias adj see **Scyros**

Scyros, Scyrus, -ī f Aegean island near Euboea

scytala see **scutula²**

Scytha, Scythēs, -ae m Scythian

Scythia, -iae f Scythia (country N.E. of the Black Sea)

Scythicus adj Scythian

Scythis, -idis f Scythian woman

sē pron himself, herself, itself, themselves; one another; **apud sē** at home; in his senses; **inter sē** mutually

sēbum, -ī nt tallow, suet, grease

sēcēdō, -ēdere, -essī, -essum vi to withdraw, retire; to revolt, secede

sēcernō, -ernere, -rēvī, -rētum vt to separate, set apart; to dissociate; to distinguish

sēcessiō, -ōnis f withdrawal; secession

sēcessus, -ūs m retirement, solitude; retreat, recess

sēclūdō, -dere, -sī, -sum vt to shut off, seclude; to separate, remove

sēclūsus ppp of **sēclūdō** ▸ adj remote

secō, -āre, -uī, -tum vt to cut; to injure; to divide; (MED) to operate on; (motion) to pass through; (dispute) to decide

sēcrētiō, -ōnis f separation

sēcrētō adv apart, in private, in secret

sēcrētum, -ī nt privacy, secrecy; retreat, remote place; secret, mystery

sēcrētus ppp of **sēcernō** ▸ adj separate; solitary, remote; secret, private

secta, -ae f path; method, way of life; (POL) party; (PHILOS) school

sectārius adj leading

sectātor, -ōris m follower, adherent

sectilis adj cut; for cutting

sectiō, -ōnis f auctioning of confiscated goods

sector¹, -ōris m cutter; buyer at a public sale

sector², -ārī, -ātus vt to follow regularly, attend; to chase, hunt

sectūra, -ae f digging

sectus ppp of **secō**

sēcubitus, -ūs m lying alone

sēcubō, -āre, -uī vi to sleep by oneself; to live alone

secuī perf of **secō**

sēcul- etc see **saecul-**

sēcum with himself etc

secundānī, -ōrum mpl men of the second legion

secundārius adj second-rate

secundō¹ adv secondly

secundō², -āre vt to favour, make prosper

secundum prep (place) behind, along; (time) after; (rank) next to; (agreement) according to, in favour of ▸ adv behind

secundus adj following, next, second; inferior; favourable, propitious, fortunate ▸ fpl (play) subsidiary part; (fig) second fiddle ▸ ntpl success, good fortune; **secundō flūmine** downstream; **rēs secundae** prosperity, success

sēcūricula, -ae f little axe

sēcūrifer, -ī adj armed with an axe

sēcūriger, -ī adj armed with an axe

sēcūris, -is f axe; (fig) death blow; (POL) authority, supreme power

sēcūritās, -ātis f freedom from anxiety, composure; negligence; safety, feeling of security

sēcūrus adj untroubled, unconcerned; carefree, cheerful; careless

secus¹ nt (indecl) sex

secus² adv otherwise, differently; badly; **nōn ~** even so

secūtor, -ōris m pursuer

sed conj but; but also, but in fact

sēdātē adv calmly

sēdātiō, -ōnis f calming

sēdātus ppp of **sēdō** ▸ adj calm, quiet, composed

sēdecim num sixteen

sēdēcula, -ae f low stool
sedentārius adj sitting
sedeō, -ēre, sēdī, sessum vi to sit; (army) to be encamped, blockade; (magistrates) to be in session; (clothes) to suit, fit; (places) to be low-lying; (heavy things) to settle, subside; (weapons) to stick fast; (inactivity) to be idle; (thought) to be firmly resolved
sēdēs, -is f seat, chair; abode, home; site, ground, foundation
sēdī perf of **sedeō**
sedīle, -is nt seat, chair
sēditiō, -ōnis f insurrection, mutiny
sēditiōsē adv seditiously
sēditiōsus adj mutinous, factious; quarrelsome; troubled
sēdō, -āre vt to calm, allay, lull
sēdūcō, -ūcere, -ūxī, -uctum vt to take away, withdraw; to divide
sēductiō, -ōnis f taking sides
sēductus ppp of **sēdūcō** ▶ adj remote
sēdulitās, -ātis f earnestness, assiduity; officiousness
sēdulō adv busily, diligently; purposely
sēdulus adj busy, diligent, assiduous; officious
seges, -itis f cornfield; crop
Segesta, -ae f town in N.W. Sicily
Segestānus adj see **Segesta**
segmentātus adj flounced
segmentum, -ī nt brocade
segne, segniter adv slowly, lazily
segnipēs, -edis adj slow of foot
segnis adj slow, sluggish, lazy
segnitia, -ae, segnitiēs (acc **-em**, abl **-ē**) f slowness, sluggishness, sloth
sēgregō, -āre, -āvī, -ātum vt to separate, put apart; to dissociate
sēiugātus adj separated
sēiugis, -is m chariot and six
sēiūnctim adv separately
sēiūnctiō, -ōnis f separation
sēiūnctus ppp of **sēiūngō**
sēiūngō, -gere, sēiūnxī, sēiūnctum vt to separate, part
sēlēctiō, -ōnis f choice
sēlēctus ppp of **sēligō**
Seleucus, -ī m king of Syria
sēlībra, -ae f half pound
sēligō, -igere, -ēgī, -ēctum vt to choose, select
sella, -ae f seat, chair, stool, sedan chair; **~ cūrūlis** chair of office for higher magistrates
sellisternia, -ōrum ntpl sacred banquets to goddesses
sellula, -ae f stool; sedan chair
sellulārius, -ī m mechanic
sēmanimus etc see **sēmianimis**
semel adv once; once for all; first; ever; **~ atque iterum** again and again; **~ aut iterum** once or twice
Semelē, -ēs f mother of Bacchus
Semelēius adj see **Semelē**

sēmen, -inis nt seed; (plant) seedling, slip; (men) race, child; (physics) particle; (fig) origin, instigator
sēmentifer, -ī adj fruitful
sēmentis, -is f sowing, planting; young corn
sēmentīvus adj of seed time
sēmermis etc see **sēmiermis**
sēmēstris adj half-yearly, for six months
sēmēsus adj half-eaten
sēmet pron self, selves
sēmiadapertus adj half-open
sēmianimis, -us adj half-dead
sēmiapertus adj half-open
sēmibōs, -ovis adj half-ox
sēmicaper, -rī adj half-goat
sēmicremātus, sēmicremus adj half-burned
sēmicubitālis adj half a cubit long
sēmideus adj half-divine ▶ m demigod
sēmidoctus adj half-taught
sēmiermis, -us adj half-armed
sēmiēsus adj half-eaten
sēmifactus adj half-finished
sēmifer, -ī adj half-beast; half-savage
sēmigermānus adj half-German
sēmigravis adj half-overcome
sēmigrō, -āre vi to go away
sēmihiāns adj half-opened
sēmihomō, -inis m half-man, half-human
sēmihōra, -ae f half an hour
sēmilacer, -ī adj half-mangled
sēmilautus adj half-washed
sēmilīber, -ī adj half-free
sēmilixa, -ae m not much better than a camp follower
sēmimarīnus adj half in the sea
sēmimās, -āris m hermaphrodite ▶ adj castrated
sēmimortuus adj half-dead
sēminārium, -ī and -iī nt nursery, seed plot
sēminātor, -ōris m originator
sēminecis adj half-dead
sēminium, -ī and -iī nt procreation; breed
sēminō, -āre vt to sow; to produce; to beget
sēminūdus adj half-naked; almost unarmed
sēmipāgānus adj half-rustic
sēmiplēnus adj half-full, half-manned
sēmiputātus adj half-pruned
Semīramis, -is and -idis f queen of Assyria
Semīramius adj see **Semīramis**
sēmirāsus adj half-shaven
sēmireductus adj half turned back
sēmirefectus adj half-repaired
sēmirutus adj half-demolished, half in ruins
sēmis, -issis m (coin) half an as; (interest) 1/2 per cent per month (i.e. 6 per cent per annum); (area) half an acre
sēmisepultus adj half-buried
sēmisomnus adj half-asleep
sēmisupīnus adj half lying back
sēmita, -ae f path, way
sēmitālis adj of byways

sēmitārius *adj* frequenting byways

sēmiūst- *etc see* **sēmūst-**

sēmivir, -ī *adj* half-man; emasculated; unmanly

sēmivīvus *adj* half-dead

sēmodius, -ī *and* **-iī** *m* half a peck

sēmōtus *ppp of* **sēmoveō** ▸ *adj* remote; distinct

sēmoveō, -ovēre, -ōvī, -ōtum *vt* to put aside, separate

semper *adv* always, ever, every time

sempiternus *adj* everlasting, lifelong

Semprōnius¹, -ī *m* Roman family name (esp the Gracchi)

Semprōnius², -iānus *adj see* **Semprōnius¹**

sēmūncia, -ae *f* half an ounce; a twenty-fourth

sēmūnciārius *adj* (interest) at the rate of one twenty-fourth

sēmustulātus *adj* half-burned

sēmūstus *adj* half-burned

sēnāculum, -ī *nt* open air meeting place (of the Senate)

sēnāriolus, -ī *m* little trimeter

sēnārius, -ī *and* **-iī** *m* (iambic) trimeter

senātor, -ōris *m* senator

senātōrius *adj* senatorial, in the Senate

senātus, -ūs *m* Senate; meeting of the Senate

senātūscōnsultum, -ī *nt* decree of the Senate

Seneca, -ae *m* Stoic philosopher, tutor of Nero

senecta, -ae *f* old age

senectus *adj* old, aged

senectūs, -ūtis *f* old age; old men

seneō, -ēre *vi* to be old

senēscō, -ēscere, -uī *vi* to grow old; (fig) to weaken, wane, pine away

senex, -is (*compar* **-ior**) *adj* old (over 45) ▸ *m/f* old man, old woman

sēnī, -ōrum *adj* six each, in sixes; six; **~ dēnī** sixteen each

senīlis *adj* of an old person, senile

sēniō, -ōnis *m* number six on a dice

senior *compar of* **senex**

senium, -ī *and* **-iī** *nt* weakness of age, decline; affliction; peevishness

Senonēs, -um *mpl* tribe of S. Gaul

sēnsī *perf of* **sentiō**

sēnsifer, -ī *adj* sensory

sēnsilis *adj* having sensation

sēnsim *adv* tentatively, gradually

sēnsus¹ *ppp of* **sentiō** ▸ *ntpl* thoughts

sēnsus², -ūs *m* (body) feeling, sensation, sense; (intellect) understanding, judgment, thought; (emotion) sentiment, attitude, frame of mind; (language) meaning, purport, sentence; **commūnis ~** universal human feelings, human sympathy, social instinct

sententia, -ae *f* opinion, judgment; purpose, will; (LAW) verdict, sentence; (POL) vote, decision; (language) meaning, sentence, maxim, epigram; **meā sententiā** in my opinion; **dē meā sententiā** in accordance with my wishes;

ex meā sententiā to my liking; **ex animī meī sententiā** to the best of my knowledge and belief; **in sententiam pedibus īre** support a motion

sententiola, -ae *f* phrase

sententiōsē *adv* pointedly

sententiōsus *adj* pithy

senticētum, -ī *nt* thornbrake

sentīna, -ae *f* bilge water; (fig) dregs, scum

sentiō, -īre, sēnsī, sēnsum *vt* (senses) to feel, see, perceive; (circumstances) to experience, undergo; (mind) to observe, understand; (opinion) to think, judge; (LAW) to vote, decide

sentis, -is *m* thorn, brier

sentīscō, -ere *vt* to begin to perceive

sentus *adj* thorny; untidy

senuī *perf of* **senēscō**

seorsum, seorsus *adv* apart, differently

sēparābilis *adj* separable

sēparātim *adv* apart, separately

sēparātiō, -ōnis *f* separation, severing

sēparātius *adv* less closely

sēparātus *adj* separate, different

sēparō, -āre, -āvī, -ātum *vt* to part, separate, divide; to distinguish

sepeliō, -elīre, -elīvī *and* **-eliī, -ultum** *vt* to bury; (fig) to overwhelm, overcome

sēpia, -ae *f* cuttlefish

Sēplasia, -ae *f* street in Capua where perfumes were sold

sēpōnō, -ōnere, -osuī, -ositum *vt* to put aside, pick out; to reserve; to banish; to appropriate; to separate

sēpositus *ppp of* **sēpōnō** ▸ *adj* remote; distinct, choice

sēpse *pron* oneself

septem *num* seven

September, -ris *m* September ▸ *adj* of September

septemdecim *etc see* **septendecim**

septemfluus *adj* with seven streams

septemgeminus *adj* sevenfold

septemplex, -icis *adj* sevenfold

septemtriō *etc see* **septentriō**

septemvirālis *adj* of the septemviri ▸ *mpl* the septemviri

septemvirātus, -ūs *m* office of septemvir

septemvirī, -ōrum *mpl* board of seven officials

septēnārius, -ī *and* **-iī** *m* verse of seven feet

septendecim *num* seventeen

septēnī, -ōrum *adj* seven each, in sevens

septentriō, -ōnis *m*, **septentriōnēs, -ōnum** *mpl* Great Bear, Little Bear; north; north wind

septentriōnālis *adj* northern ▸ *ntpl* northern regions

septiēns, septiēs *adv* seven times

septimānī, -ōrum *mpl* men of the seventh legion

septimum *adv* for the seventh time

septimus *adj* seventh; **~ decimus** seventeenth
septingentēsimus *adj* seven hundredth
septingentī, -ōrum *adj* seven hundred
septuāgēsimus *adj* seventieth
septuāgintā *adj* seventy
septuennis *adj* seven years old
septumus *adj* see **septimus**
septūnx, -ūncis *m* seven ounces, seven-twelfths
sepulcrālis *adj* funeral
sepulcrētum, -ī *nt* cemetery
sepulcrum, -ī *nt* grave, tomb
sepultūra, -ae *f* burial, funeral
sepultus *ppp of* **sepeliō**
Sequāna, -ae *f* (river) Seine
Sequānī, -ōrum *mpl* people of N. Gaul
sequāx, -ācis *adj* pursuing, following
sequēns, -entis *pres p of* **sequor** ▸ *adj* following, next
sequester, -rī *and* **-ris** *m* trustee; agent, mediator
sequestrum, -rī *nt* deposit
sēquius *compar of* **secus²**; otherwise; **nihilō ~** nonetheless
sequor, -quī, -cūtus *vt, vi* to follow; to accompany, go with; (*time*) to come after, come next, ensue; (*enemy*) to pursue; (*objective*) to make for, aim at; (*pulling*) to come away easily; (*share, gift*) to go to, come to; (*words*) to come naturally
sera, -ae *f* door bolt, bar
Serāpēum, -ēī *nt* temple of Serapis
Serāpis, -is *and* **-idis** *m* chief Egyptian god
serēnitās, -ātis *f* fair weather
serēnō, -āre *vt* to clear up, brighten up
serēnus *adj* fair, clear; (*wind*) fair-weather; (*fig*) cheerful, happy ▸ *nt* clear sky, fair weather
Sērēs, -um *mpl* Chinese
serēscō, -ere *vi* to dry off
sēria, -ae *f* tall jar
sērica, -ōrum *ntpl* silks
Sēricus *adj* Chinese; silk
seriēs (*acc* **-em**, *abl* **-ē**) *f* row, sequence, succession
sēriō *adv* in earnest, seriously
sēriola, -ae *f* small jar
Serīphius *adj see* **Serīphus**
Serīphus, Serīphos, -ī *f* Aegean island
sērius¹ *adj* earnest, serious
sērius² *compar of* **sērō**
sermō, -ōnis *m* conversation, talk; learned discussion, discourse; common talk, rumour; language, style; everyday language, prose; (*pl*) Satires (*of Horace*)
sermōcinor, -ārī *vi* to converse
sermunculus, -ī *m* gossip, rumour
serō¹, -ere, sēvī, -satum *vt* to sow, plant; (*fig*) to produce, sow the seeds of
serō², -ere, -tum *vt* to sew, join, wreathe; (*fig*) to compose, devise, engage in
sērō (*compar* **-ius**) *adv* late; too late

serpēns, -entis *m/f* snake, serpent; (*constellation*) Draco
serpentigena, -ae *m* offspring of a serpent
serpentipēs, -edis *adj* serpent-footed
serperastra, -ōrum *ntpl* splints
serpō, -ere, -sī, -tum *vi* to creep, crawl; (*fig*) to spread slowly
serpyllum, -ī *nt* wild thyme
serra, -ae *f* saw
serrācum *etc see* **sarrācum**
serrātus *adj* serrated, notched
serrula, -ae *f* small saw
Sertōriānus *adj see* **Sertōrius**
Sertōrius, -ī *m* commander under Marius, who held out against Sulla in Spain
sertus *ppp of* **serō²** ▸ *ntpl* garlands
serum, -ī *nt* whey, serum
sērum, -ī *nt* late hour
sērus *adj* late; too late; **sērā nocte** late at night
serva, -ae *f* maidservant, slave
servābilis *adj* that can be saved
servātor, -ōris *m* deliverer; watcher
servātrīx, -īcis *f* deliverer
servīlis *adj* of slaves, servile
servīliter *adv* slavishly
Servīlius¹, -ī *m* Roman family name of many consuls
Servīlius², -ānus *adj see* **Servīlius¹**
serviō, -īre, -īvī *and* **-iī, -ītum** *vi* to be a slave; (*with dat*) to serve, be of use to, be good for; (*property*) to be mortgaged
servitium, -ī *and* **-iī** *nt* slavery, servitude; slaves
servitūdō, -inis *f* slavery
servitūs, -ūtis *f* slavery, service; slaves; (*property*) liability
Servius, -ī *m* sixth king of Rome; famous jurist of Cicero's day
servō, -āre, -āvī, -ātum *vt* to save, rescue; to keep, preserve, retain; to store, reserve; to watch, observe, guard; (*place*) to remain in
servolus, -ī *m* young slave
servos, -ī *m see* **servus**
servula, -ae *f* servant girl
servulus, -ī *m* young slave
servus, -ī *m* slave, servant ▸ *adj* slavish, serving; (*property*) liable to a burden
sēsē *etc see* **sē**
seselis, -is *f* (*plant*) seseli
sesqui *adv* one and a half times
sesquialter, -ī *adj* one and a half
sesquimodius, -ī *and* **-iī** *m* a peck and a half
sesquioctāvus *adj* of nine to eight
sesquiopus, -eris *nt* a day and a half's work
sesquipedālis *adj* a foot and a half

sesquipēs, -edis m a foot and a half

sesquiplāga, -ae f a blow and a half

sesquiplex, -icis adj one and a half times

sesquitertius adj of four to three

sessilis adj for sitting on

sessiō, -ōnis f sitting; seat; session; loitering

sessitō, -āre, -āvī vi to sit regularly

sessiuncula, -ae f small meeting

sessor, -ōris m spectator; resident

sēstertium, -ī nt 1000 sesterces; **dēna sēstertia** 10,000 sesterces; **centēna mīlia ~** 100,000 sesterces; **deciēns ~** 1,000,000 sesterces

sēstertius, -ī and -iī m sesterce (a silver coin)

Sestius¹, -ī m tribune defended by Cicero

Sestius², -iānus adj of Sestius

Sestos, Sestus, -ī f town on Dardanelles (home of Hero)

Sestus adj see **Sestos**

sēt- etc see **saet-**

Sētia, -iae f town in S. Latium (famous for wine)

Sētiaīnus adj see **Sētia**

sētius compar of **secus²**

seu etc see **sīve**

sevērē adv sternly, severely

sevēritās, -ātis f strictness, austerity

sevērus adj strict, stern; severe, austere; grim, terrible

sēvī perf of **serō¹**

sēvocō, -āre vt to call aside; to withdraw, remove

sēvum etc see **sēbum**

sex num six

sexāgēnārius adj sixty years old

sexāgēnī, -ōrum adj sixty each

sexāgēsimus adj sixtieth

sexāgiēns, sexāgiēs adv sixty times

sexāgintā num sixty

sexangulus adj hexagonal

sexcēn- etc see **sescēn-**

sexcēnārius adj of six hundred

sexennis adj six years old, after six years

sexennium, -ī and -iī nt six years

sexiēns, sexiēs adv six times

sexprīmī, -ōrum mpl a provincial town council

sextadecimānī, -ōrum mpl men of the sixteenth legion

sextāns, -antis m a sixth; (coin, weight) a sixth of an as

sextārius, -ī and -iī m pint

Sextīlis, -is m August ▶ adj of August

sextula, -ae f a sixth of an ounce

sextum adv for the sixth time

sextus adj sixth; **~ decimus** sixteenth

sexus, -ūs m sex

sī conj if; if only; to see if; **sī forte** in the hope that; **sī iam** assuming for the moment; **sī minus** if not; **sī quandō** whenever; **sī quidem** if indeed; since; **sī quis** if anyone, whoever; **mīrum sī** surprising that; **quod sī** and if, but if

sībila, -ōrum ntpl whistle, hissing

sībilō, -āre vi to hiss, whistle ▶ vt to hiss at

sībilus¹, -ī m whistle, hissing

sībilus² adj hissing

Sibulla, Sibylla, -ae f prophetess, Sibyl

Sibyllīnus adj see **Sibulla**

sīc adv so, thus, this way, as follows; as one is, as things are; on this condition; yes

sīca, -ae f dagger

Sicānī, -ōrum mpl ancient people of Italy (later of Sicily)

Sicānia, -iae f Sicily

Sicānus, -ius adj Sicanian, Sicilian

sīcārius, -ī and -iī m assassin, murderer

siccē adv (speech) firmly

siccitās, -ātis f dryness, drought; (body) firmness; (style) dullness

siccō, -āre, -āvī, -ātum vt to dry; to drain, exhaust; (sore) to heal up

siccoculus adj dry-eyed

siccus adj dry; thirsty, sober; (body) firm, healthy; (argument) solid, sound; (style) flat, dull ▶ nt dry land

Sicilia, -ae f Sicily

sicilicula, -ae f little sickle

Siciliēnsis, Sicilis, -dis adj Sicilian

sīcine is this how?

sīcubi adv if anywhere, wheresoever

Siculus adj Sicilian

sīcunde adv if from anywhere

sīcut, sīcutī adv just as, as in fact; (comparison) like, as; (example) as for instance; (with subj) as if

Sicyōn, -ōnis f town in N. Peloponnese

Sicyōnius adj see **Sicyōn**

sīdereus adj starry; (fig) radiant

Sidicīnī, -ōrum mpl people of Campania

Sidicīnus adj see **Sidicīnī**

sīdō, -ere, -ī vi to sit down, settle; to sink, subside; to stick fast

Sīdōn, -ōnis f famous Phoenician town

Sīdōnis, -ōnidis adj Phoenician ▶ f Europa; Dido

Sīdōnius adj Sidonian, Phoenician

sīdus, -eris nt constellation; heavenly body, star; season, climate, weather; destiny; (pl) sky; (fig) fame, glory

siem archaic subj of **sum**

Sigambrī etc see **Sugambrī**

Sigēum, -ī nt promontory near Troy

Sīgēus, -ius adj Sigean

sigilla, -ōrum ntpl little figures; seal

sigillātus adj decorated with little figures

signātor, -ōris m witness (to a document)

signifer, -ī adj with constellations; **~ orbis** Zodiac ▶ m (MIL) standard-bearer

significanter adv pointedly, tellingly

significātiō, -ōnis f indication, signal, token; sign of approval; (RHET) emphasis; (word) meaning

significō, -āre, -āvī, -ātum vt to indicate, show; to betoken, portend; (word) to mean

signō, -āre, -āvī, -ātum vt to mark, stamp, print; (document) to seal; (money) to coin, mint; (fig) to impress, designate, note

signum, **-ī** *nt* mark, sign, token; (*MIL*) standard; signal, password; (*art*) design, statue; (*document*) seal; (*ASTR*) constellation; **signa cōnferre** join battle; **signa cōnstituere** halt; **signa convertere** wheel about; **signa ferre** move camp; attack; **signa inferre** attack; **signa prōferre** advance; **signa sequī** march in order; **ab signīs discēdere** leave the ranks; **sub signīs īre** march in order

Sīla, **-ae** *f forest in extreme S. Italy*

sīlānus, **-ī** *m* fountain, jet of water

silēns, **-entis** *pres p of* **sileō** ▶ *adj* still, silent ▶ *mpl* the dead

silentium, **-ī and -iī** *nt* stillness, silence; (*fig*) standstill, inaction

Sīlēnus, **-ī** *m old and drunken companion of Bacchus*

sileō, **-ēre**, **-uī** *vi* to be still, be silent; to cease ▶ *vt* to say nothing about

siler, **-is** *nt* willow

silēscō, **-ere** *vi* to calm down, fall silent

silex, **-icis** *m* flint, hard stone; rock

silicernium, **-ī and -iī** *nt* funeral feast

silīgō, **-inis** *f* winter wheat; fine flour

siliqua, **-ae** *f* pod, husk; (*pl*) pulse

sillybus, **-ī** *m* label bearing a book's title

Silurēs, **-um** *mpl British tribe in S. Wales*

silūrus, **-ī** *m* sheatfish

sīlus *adj* snub-nosed

silva, **-ae** *f* wood, forest; plantation, shrubbery; (*plant*) flowering stem; (*LIT*) material

Silvānus, **-ī** *m god of uncultivated land*

silvēscō, **-ere** *vi* to run to wood

silvestris *adj* wooded, forest- (in cpds), pastoral

silvicola, **-ae** *m/f* sylvan

silvicultrix, **-īcis** *adj* living in the woods

silvifragus *adj* tree-breaking

silvōsus *adj* woody

sīmia, **-ae** *f* ape

simile, **-is** *nt* comparison, parallel

similis *adj* like, similar; **~ atque** like what; **vērī ~** probable

similiter *adv* similarly

similitūdō, **-inis** *f* likeness, resemblance; imitation; analogy; monotony; (*RHET*) simile

sīmiolus, **-ī** *m* monkey

simītu *adv* at the same time, together

sīmius, **-ī and -iī** *m* ape

Simoīs, **-entis** *m river of Troy*

Simōnidēs, **-is** *m Greek lyric poet of Ceos (famous for dirges)*

Simōnidēus *adj see* **Simōnidēs**

simplex, **-icis** *adj* single, simple; natural, straightforward; (*character*) frank, sincere

simplicitās, **-ātis** *f* singleness; frankness; innocence

simpliciter *adv* simply, naturally; frankly

simplum, **-ī** *nt* simple sum

simpulum, **-ī** *nt* small ladle; **excitāre fluctūs in simpulō** raise a storm in a teacup

simpuvium, **-ī and -iī** *nt* libation bowl

simul *adv* at the same time, together, at once;

likewise, also; both … and; **~ ac**, **~ atque**, **~ ut** as soon as ▶ *conj* as soon as

simulācrum, **-ī** *nt* likeness, image, portrait, statue; phantom, ghost; (*writing*) symbol; (*fig*) semblance, shadow

simulāmen, **-inis** *nt* copy

simulāns, **-antis** *pres p of* **simulō** ▶ *adj* imitative

simulātē *adv* deceitfully

simulātiō, **-ōnis** *f* pretence, shamming, hypocrisy

simulātor, **-ōris** *m* imitator; pretender, hypocrite

simulatque *conj* as soon as

simulō, **-āre**, **-āvī**, **-ātum** *vt* to imitate, represent; to impersonate; to pretend, counterfeit

simultās, **-ātis** *f* feud, quarrel

sīmulus *adj* snub-nosed

sīmus *adj* snub-nosed

sīn *conj* but if; **sīn aliter**, **sīn minus** but if not

sināpi, **-is** *nt*, **sinapis**, **-is** *f* mustard

sincērē *adv* honestly

sincēritās, **-ātis** *f* integrity

sincērus *adj* clean, whole, genuine; (*fig*) pure, sound, honest

sincipitāmentum, **-ī** *nt* half a head

sinciput, **-itis** *nt* half a head; brain

sine *prep* (with abl) without, -less (in cpds)

singillātim *adv* singly, one by one

singulāris *adj* one at a time, single, sole; unique, extraordinary

singulāriter *adv* separately; extremely

singulārius *adj* single

singulī, **-ōrum** *adj* one each, single, one

singultim *adv* in sobs

singultō, **-āre** *vi* to sob, gasp, gurgle ▶ *vt* to gasp out

singultus, **-ūs** *m* sob, gasp, death rattle

singulus *etc see* **singulī**

sinister, **-rī** *adj* left; (*fig*) perverse, unfavourable; (*Roman auspices*) lucky; (*Greek auspices*) unlucky

sinistra, **-rae** *f* left hand, left-hand side

sinistrē *adv* badly

sinistrōrsus *adv* to the left

sinō, **-ere**, **sīvī**, **situm** *vt* to let, allow; to let be; **nē dī sīrint** God forbid!

Sinōpē, **-ēs** *f Greek colony on the Black Sea*

Sinōpēnsis, **-eus** *adj see* **Sinōpē**

Sinuessa, **-ae** *f town on the borders of Latium and Campania*

Sinuessānus *adj see* **Sinuessa**

sīnum *etc see* **sīnus**

sinuō, **-āre**, **-āvī**, **-ātum** *vt* to wind, curve

sinuōsus *adj* winding, curved

sinus, **-ūs** *m* curve, fold; (*fishing*) net; (*GEOG*) bay, gulf, valley; (*hair*) curl; (*ship*) sail; (*toga*) fold, pocket, purse; (*fig*) bosom; protection, love, heart, hiding place; **in sinū gaudēre** be secretly glad

sīnus, **-ī** *m* large cup

sīparium, -ī and **-iī** nt act curtain
sīphō, -ōnis m siphon; fire engine
sīquandō adv if ever
sīquī, sīquis pron if any, if anyone, whoever
sīquidem adv if in fact ▸ conj since
sirempse adj the same
Sīrēn, -ēnis f Siren
sīris, sīrit perf subj of **sinō**
Sīrius, -ī m Dog Star ▸ adj of Sirius
sirpe, -is nt silphium
sīrus, -ī m corn pit
sīs adv (for sī vīs) please
sistō, -ere, stitī, statum vt to place, set,
plant; (LAW) to produce in court; (monument) to
set up; (movement) to stop, arrest, check ▸ vi to
stand, rest; (LAW) to appear in court; (movement)
to stand still, stop, stand firm; **sē sistere**
appear, present oneself; **tūtum sistere** see
safe; **vadimōnium sistere** duly appear in court;
sistī nōn potest the situation is desperate
sistrum, -ī nt Egyptian rattle, cymbal
sisymbrium, -ī and **-iī** nt fragrant herb (perhaps
mint)
Sīsyphidēs, -idae m Ulysses
Sīsyphius adj see **Sīsyphus**
Sīsyphus, -ī m criminal condemned in Hades to roll
a rock repeatedly up a hill
sitella, -ae f lottery urn
Sīthonis, -idis adj Thracian
Sīthonius adj Thracian
siticulōsus adj thirsty, dry
sitiēns, -entis pres p of **sitiō** ▸ adj thirsty, dry;
parching; (fig) eager
sitienter adv eagerly
sitiō, -īre vi to be thirsty; to be parched ▸ vt to
thirst for, covet
sitis, -is f thirst; drought
sittybus etc see **sillybus**
situla, -ae f bucket
situs¹ ppp of **sinō** ▸ adj situated, lying; founded;
(fig) dependent
situs², -ūs m situation, site; structure; neglect,
squalor, mould; (mind) dullness
sīve conj or if, or; whether ... or
sīvī perf of **sinō**
smaragdus, -ī m/f emerald
smīlax, -acis f bindweed
Smintheus, -eī m Apollo
Smyrna, -ae f Ionian town in Asia Minor
Smyrnaeus adj see **Smyrna**
sobol- etc see **subol-**
sobriē adv temperately; sensibly
sobrīna, -ae f cousin (on the mother's side)
sobrīnus, -ī m cousin (on the mother's side)
sobrius adj sober; temperate, moderate; (mind)
sane, sensible
soccus, -ī m slipper (esp the sock worn by actors in
comedy); comedy
socer, -ī m father-in-law
sociābilis adj compatible
sociālis adj of allies, confederate; conjugal
sociāliter adv sociably

sociennus, -ī m friend
societās, -ātis f fellowship, association;
alliance
sociō, -āre, -āvī, -ātum vt to unite, associate,
share
sociofraudus, -ī m deceiver of friends
socius adj associated, allied ▸ m friend,
companion; partner, ally
sōcordia, -ae f indolence, apathy; folly
sōcordius adv more carelessly, lazily
sōcors, -dis adj lazy, apathetic; stupid
Sōcratēs, -is m famous Athenian philosopher
Sōcraticus adj of Socrates, Socratic ▸ mpl the
followers of Socrates
socrus, -ūs f mother-in-law
sodālicium, -ī and **-iī** nt fellowship; secret
society
sodālicius adj of fellowship
sodālis, -is m/f companion, friend; member of
a society, accomplice
sodālitās, -ātis f companionship, friendship;
society, club; secret society
sodālitius etc see **sodālicius**
sodēs adv please
sōl, sōlis m sun; sunlight, sun's heat; (poetry)
day; (myth) Sun god; **sōl oriēns, sōlis ortus**
east; **sōl occidēns, sōlis occāsus** west
sōlāciolum, -ī nt a grain of comfort
sōlācium, -ī and **-iī** nt comfort, consolation,
relief
sōlāmen, -inis nt solace, relief
sōlāris adj of the sun
sōlārium, -ī and **-iī** nt sundial; clock; balcony,
terrace
sōlātium etc see **sōlācium**
sōlātor, -ōris m consoler
soldūriī, -ōrum mpl retainers
soldus etc see **solidus**
solea, -ae f sandal, shoe; fetter; (fish) sole
soleārius, -ī and **-iī** m sandal maker
soleātus adj wearing sandals
soleō, -ēre, -itus vi to be accustomed, be in
the habit, usually do; **ut solēre** as usual
solidē adv for certain
soliditās, -ātis f solidity
solidō, -āre vt to make firm, strengthen
solidus adj solid, firm, dense; whole, complete;
(fig) sound, genuine, substantial ▸ nt solid
matter, firm ground
sōliferreum, -ī nt an all-iron javelin
sōlistimus adj (AUG) most favourable
sōlitārius adj solitary, lonely
sōlitūdō, -inis f solitariness, loneliness;
destitution; (place) desert
solitus ppa of **soleō** ▸ adj usual, customary
▸ nt custom; **plūs solitō** more than usual
solium, -ī and **-iī** nt seat, throne; tub; (fig) rule
sōlivagus adj going by oneself; single
sollemne, -is nt religious rite, festival; usage,
practice
sollemnis adj annual, regular; religious,
solemn; usual, ordinary

sollemniter adv solemnly

sollers, -tis adj skilled, clever, expert; ingenious

sollerter adv cleverly

sollertia, -ae f skill, ingenuity

sollicitātiō, -ōnis f inciting

sollicitō, -āre, -āvī, -ātum vt to stir up, disturb; to trouble, distress, molest; to rouse, urge, incite, tempt, tamper with

sollicitūdō, -inis f uneasiness, anxiety

sollicitus adj agitated, disturbed; (mind) troubled, worried, alarmed; (things) anxious, careful; (cause) disquieting

solliferreum etc see **sōliferreum**

sollistimus etc see **sōlistimus**

soloecismus, -ī m grammatical mistake

Solōn, -ōnis m famous Athenian lawgiver

sōlor, -ārī, -ātus vt to comfort, console; to relieve, ease

sōlstitiālis adj of the summer solstice; midsummer

sōlstitium, -ī and -iī nt summer solstice; midsummer, summer heat

solum, -ī nt ground, floor, bottom; soil, land, country; (foot) sole; (fig) basis; **solō aequāre** raze to the ground

sōlum adv only, merely

sōlus (gen -īus, dat -ī) see **vicis** ▸ adj only, alone; lonely, forsaken; (place) lonely, deserted

solūtē adv loosely, freely, carelessly, weakly, fluently

solūtiō, -ōnis f loosening; payment

solūtus ppp of **solvō** ▸ adj loose, free; (from distraction) at ease, at leisure, merry; (from obligation) exempt; (from restraint) free, independent, unprejudiced; (moral) lax, weak, insolent; (language) prose, unrhythmical; (speaker) fluent; **ōrātiō solūta, verba solūta** prose

solvō, -vere, -vī, -ūtum vt to loosen, undo; to free, release, acquit, exempt; to dissolve, break up, separate; to relax, slacken, weaken; to cancel, remove, destroy; to solve, explain; to pay, fulfil; (argument) to refute; (discipline) to undermine; (feelings) to get rid of; (hair) to let down; (letter) to open; (sail) to unfurl; (siege) to raise; (troops) to dismiss ▸ vi to set sail; to pay; **nāvem solvere** set sail; **poenās solvere** be punished; **praesēns solvere** pay cash; **rem solvere** pay; **sacrāmentō solvere** discharge; **solvendō esse** be solvent

Solyma, -ōrum ntpl Jerusalem

Solymus adj of the Jews

somniculōsē adv sleepily

somniculōsus adj sleepy

somnifer, -ī adj soporific; fatal

somniō, -āre vt to dream, dream about; to talk nonsense

somnium, -ī and -iī nt dream; nonsense, fancy

somnus, -ī m sleep; sloth

sonābilis adj noisy

sonipēs, -edis m steed

sonitus, -ūs m sound, noise

sonivius adj noisy

sonō, -āre, -uī, -itum vi to sound, make a noise ▸ vt to utter, speak, celebrate; to sound like

sonor, -ōris m sound, noise

sonōrus adj noisy, loud

sōns, sontis adj guilty

sonticus adj critical; important

sonus, -ī m sound, noise; (fig) tone

sophistēs, -ae m sophist

Sophoclēs, -is m famous Greek tragic poet

Sophoclēus adj of Sophocles, Sophoclean

sophus adj wise

sōpiō, -īre, -īvī, -ītum vt to put to sleep; (fig) to calm, lull

sopor, -ōris m sleep; apathy

sopōrifer, -ī adj soporific, drowsy

sopōrō, -āre vt to lull to sleep; to make soporific

sopōrus adj drowsy

Sōracte, -is nt mountain in S. Etruria

sorbeō, -ēre, -uī vt to suck, swallow; (fig) to endure

sorbillō, -āre vt to sip

sorbitiō, -ōnis f drink, broth

sorbum, -ī nt service berry

sorbus, -ī f service tree

sordeō, -ēre vi to be dirty, be sordid; to seem shabby; to be of no account

sordēs, -is f dirt, squalor, shabbiness; mourning; meanness; vulgarity; (people) rabble

sordēscō, -ere vi to become dirty

sordidātus adj shabbily dressed, in mourning

sordidē adv meanly, vulgarly

sordidulus adj soiled, shabby

sordidus adj dirty, squalid, shabby; in mourning; poor, mean; base, vile

sōrex, -icis m shrewmouse

sōricīnus adj of the shrewmouse

sōrītēs, -ae m chain syllogism

soror, -ōris f sister

sorōricīda, -ae m murderer of a sister

sorōrius adj of a sister

sors, sortis f lot; allotted duty; oracle, prophecy; fate, fortune; (money) capital, principal

sōrsum etc see **seorsum**

sortilegus adj prophetic ▸ m soothsayer

sortior, -īrī, -ītus vi to draw or cast lots ▸ vt to draw lots for, allot, obtain by lot; to distribute, share; to choose; to receive

sortītiō, -ōnis f drawing lots, choosing by lot

sortītus¹ ppa of **sortior** ▸ adj assigned, allotted; **sortītō** by lot

sortītus², -ūs m drawing lots

Sosius, -ī m Roman family name (esp two brothers Sosii, famous booksellers in Rome)

sōspes, -itis adj safe and sound, unhurt; favourable, lucky

sōspita, -ae f saviour

sōspitālis adj beneficial

sōspitō, -āre vt to preserve, prosper

sōtēr, -ēris *m* saviour

spādīx, -īcis *adj* chestnut-brown

spadō, -ōnis *m* eunuch

spargō, -gere, -sī, -sum *vt* to throw, scatter, sprinkle; to strew, spot, moisten; to disperse, spread abroad

sparsus *ppp of* **spargō ▸** *adj* freckled

Sparta, -ae, Spartē, -ēs *f* famous Greek city

Spartacus, -ī *m* gladiator who led a revolt against Rome

Spartānus, -icus *adj* Spartan

Spartiātēs, -iātae *m* Spartan

spartum, -ī *nt* Spanish broom

sparulus, -ī *m* bream

sparus, -ī *m* hunting spear

spatha, -ae *f* broadsword

spatior, -ārī, -ātus *vi* to walk; to spread

spatiōsē *adv* greatly; after a time

spatiōsus *adj* roomy, ample, large; (*time*) prolonged

spatium, -ī *and* **-iī** *nt* space, room, extent; (*between points*) distance; (*open space*) square, walk, promenade; (*race*) lap, track, course; (*time*) period, interval; (*opportunity*) time, leisure; (*metre*) quantity

speciēs, -ēī *f* seeing, sight; appearance, form, outline; (*thing seen*) sight; (*mind*) idea; (*in sleep*) vision, apparition; (*fair show*) beauty, splendour; (*false show*) pretence, pretext; (*classification*) species; **in speciem** for the sake of appearances; like; **per speciem** under the pretence; **sub speciē** under the cloak

specillum, -ī *nt* probe

specimen, -inis *nt* sign, evidence, proof; pattern, ideal

speciōsē *adv* handsomely

speciōsus *adj* showy, beautiful; specious, plausible

spectābilis *adj* visible; notable, remarkable

spectāclum, spectāculum, -ī *nt* sight, spectacle; public show, play; theatre, seats

spectāmen, -inis *nt* proof

spectātiō, -ōnis *f* looking; testing

spectātor, -ōris *m* onlooker, observer, spectator; critic

spectātrīx, -īcis *f* observer

spectātus *ppp of* **spectō ▸** *adj* tried, proved; worthy, excellent

spectiō, -ōnis *f* the right to take auspices

spectō, -āre, -āvī, -ātum *vt* to look at, observe, watch; (*place*) to face; (*aim*) to look to, bear in mind, contemplate, tend towards; (*judging*) to examine, test

spectrum, -ī *nt* spectre

specula, -ae *f* watchtower, lookout; height

spēcula, -ae *f* slight hope

speculābundus *adj* on the lookout

speculāris *adj* transparent ▸ *ntpl* window

speculātor, -ōris *m* explorer, investigator; (MIL) spy, scout

speculātōrius *adj* for spying, scouting ▸ *f* spy boat

speculātrīx, -īcis *f* watcher

speculor, -ārī, -ātus *vt* to spy out, watch for, observe

speculum, -ī *nt* mirror

specus, -ūs *m, nt* cave; hollow, chasm

spēlaeum, -ī *nt* cave, den

spēlunca, -ae *f* cave, den

spērābilis *adj* to be hoped for

spērāta, -ātae *f* bride

Sperchēis, -idis *adj see* **Sperchēus**

Sperchēus, Sperchēos, -ī *m* river in Thessaly

spernō, -ere, sprēvī, sprētum *vt* to remove, reject, scorn

spērō, -āre, -āvī, -ātum *vt* to hope, hope for, expect; to trust; to look forward to

spēs, speī *f* hope, expectation; **praeter spem** unexpectedly; **spē dēiectus** disappointed

Speusippus, -ī *m* successor of Plato in the Academy

sphaera, -ae *f* ball, globe, sphere

Sphinx, -ingis *f* fabulous monster near Thebes

spīca, -ae *f* (*grain*) ear; (*plant*) tuft; (ASTR) brightest star in Virgo

spīceus *adj* of ears of corn

spīculum, -ī *nt* point, sting; dart, arrow

spīna, -ae *f* thorn; prickle; fish bone; spine, back; (*pl*) difficulties, subtleties

spīnētum, -ī *nt* thorn hedge

spīneus *adj* of thorns

spīnifer, -ī *adj* prickly

spīnōsus *adj* thorny, prickly; (*style*) difficult

spintēr, -ēris *nt* elastic bracelet

spīnus, -ī *f* blackthorn, sloe

spīra, -ae *f* coil; twisted band

spīrābilis *adj* breathable, life-giving

spīrāculum, -ī *nt* vent

spīrāmentum, -ī *nt* vent, pore; breathing space

spīritus, -ūs *m* breath, breathing; breeze, air; inspiration; character, spirit, courage, arrogance

spīrō, -āre, -āvī, -ātum *vi* to breathe, blow; to be alive; to be inspired ▸ *vt* to emit, exhale; (*fig*) to breathe, express

spissātus *adj* condensed

spissē *adv* closely; slowly

spissēscō, -ere *vi* to thicken

spissus *adj* thick, compact, crowded; slow; (*fig*) difficult

splendeō, -ēre *vi* to be bright, shine; to be illustrious

splendēscō, -ere *vi* to become bright

splendidē *adv* brilliantly, magnificently, nobly

splendidus *adj* bright, brilliant, glittering; (*sound*) clear; (*dress, house*) magnificent; (*person*) illustrious; (*appearance*) showy

splendor, -ōris *m* brightness, lustre; magnificence; clearness; nobility

spoliātiō, -ōnis *f* plundering

spoliātor, -ōris *m* robber

spoliātrīx, -īcis *f* robber

spoliō, -āre, -āvī, -ātum *vt* to strip; to rob, plunder

spolium, **-ī** *and* **-iī** *nt* (*beast*) skin; (*enemy*) spoils, booty

sponda, **-ae** *f* bed frame; bed, couch

spondālium, **-ī** *and* **-iī** *nt* hymn accompanied *by the flute*

spondeō, **-ēre**, **spopondī**, **spōnsum** *vt* to promise, pledge, vow; (*LAW*) to go bail for; (*marriage*) to betroth

spondēus, **-ī** *m* spondee

spongia, **-ae** *f* sponge; coat of mail

spōnsa, **-ae** *f* fiancée, bride

spōnsālia, **-ium** *ntpl* engagement

spōnsiō, **-ōnis** *f* promise, guarantee; (*LAW*) agreement that the loser in a suit pays the winner *a sum*; bet

spōnsor, **-ōris** *m* guarantor, surety

spōnsus¹ *ppp of* **spondeō** ► *m* fiancé, bridegroom ► *nt* agreement, covenant

spōnsus², **-ūs** *m* contract, surety

sponte *f* (*abl*) voluntarily, of one's own accord; unaided, by oneself; spontaneously

spopondī *perf of* **spondeō**

sportella, **-ae** *f* fruit basket

sportula, **-ae** *f* small basket; gift to clients, dole

sprētiō, **-ōnis** *f* contempt

sprētor, **-ōris** *m* despiser

sprētus *ppp of* **spernō**

sprēvī *perf of* **spernō**

spūma, **-ae** *f* foam, froth

spūmēscō, **-ere** *vi* to become frothy

spūmeus *adj* foaming, frothy

spūmifer, **-ī** *adj* foaming

spūmiger, **-ī** *adj* foaming

spūmō, **-āre** *vi* to foam, froth

spūmōsus *adj* foaming

spuō, **-uere**, **-uī**, **-ūtum** *vi* to spit ► *vt* to spit out

spurcē *adv* obscenely

spurcidicus *adj* obscene

spurcificus *adj* obscene

spurcitia, **-ae**, **spurcitiēs**, **-ēī** *f* filth, smut

spurcō, **-āre** *vt* to befoul

spurcus *adj* filthy, nasty, foul

spūtātilicus *adj* despicable

spūtātor, **-ōris** *m* spitter

spūtō, **-āre** *vt* to spit out

spūtum, **-ī** *nt* spit, spittle

squāleō, **-ēre**, **-uī** *vi* to be rough, stiff, clotted; to be parched; to be neglected, squalid, filthy; to be in mourning

squālidē *adv* rudely

squālidus *adj* rough, scaly; neglected, squalid, filthy; (*speech*) unpolished

squālor, **-ōris** *m* roughness; filth, squalor

squāma, **-ae** *f* scale; scale armour

squāmeus *adj* scaly

squāmifer, **-ī** *adj* scaly

squāmiger, **-ī** *adj* scaly ► *mpl* fishes

squāmōsus *adj* scaly

squilla, **-ae** *f* prawn, shrimp

st *interj* sh!

stabilīmentum, **-ī** *nt* support

stabiliō, **-īre** *vt* to make stable; to establish

stabilis *adj* firm, steady; (*fig*) steadfast, unfailing

stabilitās, **-ātis** *f* firmness, steadiness, reliability

stabulō, **-āre** *vt* to house, stable ► *vi* to have a stall

stabulum, **-ī** *nt* stall, stable, steading; lodging, cottage; brothel

stacta, **-ae** *f* myrrh oil

stadium, **-ī** *and* **-iī** *nt* stade, furlong; racetrack

Stagīra, **-ōrum** *ntpl* town in Macedonia (*birthplace of Aristotle*)

Stagīrītēs, **-ītae** *m* Aristotle

stagnō, **-āre** *vi* to form pools; to be inundated ► *vt* to flood

stagnum, **-ī** *nt* standing water, pool, swamp; waters

stāmen, **-inis** *nt* warp; thread; (*instrument*) string; (*priest*) fillet

stāmineus *adj* full of threads

stata *adj*: **Stata māter** Vesta

statārius *adj* standing, stationary, steady; calm ► *f* refined comedy ► *mpl* actors in this comedy

statēra, **-ae** *f* scales

statim *adv* steadily; at once, immediately; ~ **ut** as soon as

statiō, **-ōnis** *f* standing still; station, post, residence; (*pl*) sentries; (*NAUT*) anchorage

Statius, **-ī** *m* Caecilius (*early writer of comedy*), Papinius (*epic and lyric poet of the Silver Age*)

statīvus *adj* stationary ► *ntpl* standing camp

Stator, **-ōris** *m* the Stayer (*epithet of Jupiter*)

stator, **-ōris** *m* attendant, orderly

statua, **-ae** *f* statue

statūmen, **-inis** *nt* (*ship*) rib

statuō, **-uere**, **-uī**, **-ūtum** *vt* to set up, place; to bring to a stop; to establish, constitute; to determine, appoint; to decide, settle; to decree, prescribe; (*with infin*) to resolve, propose; (*with acc and infin*) to judge, consider, conclude; (*army*) to draw up; (*monument*) to erect; (*price*) to fix; (*sentence*) to pass; (*tent*) to pitch; (*town*) to build; **condiciōnem statuere** dictate (to); **finem statuere** put an end (to); **iūs statuere** lay down a principle; **modum statuere** impose restrictions; **apud animum statuere** make up one's mind; **dē sē statuere** commit suicide; **gravius statuere in** deal severely with

statūra, **-ae** *f* height, stature

status¹ *ppp of* **sistō** ► *adj* appointed, due

status², **-ūs** *m* posture, attitude; position; (*social*) standing, status, circumstances; (*POL*) situation, state, form of government; (*nature*) condition; **reī pūblicae ~** the political situation; constitution; **dē statū movēre** dislodge

statūtus *ppp of* **statuō**

stega, **-ae** *f* deck

stēliō *see* **stēlliō**

stēlla, **-ae** *f* star; ~ **errāns** planet

stēllāns, -antis adj starry
stēllātus adj starred; set in the sky
stēllifer, -ī adj starry
stēlliger, -ī adj starry
stēlliō, -ōnis m newt
stemma, -tis nt pedigree
stercoreus adj filthy
stercorō, -āre vt to manure
stercus, -oris nt dung
sterilis adj barren, sterile; bare, empty; unprofitable, fruitless
sterilitās, -ātis f barrenness
sternāx, -ācis adj bucking
sternō, -ere, strāvī, strātum vt to spread, cover, strew; to smooth, level; to stretch out, extend; to throw to the ground, prostrate; to overthrow; (bed) to make; (horse) to saddle; (road) to pave
sternūmentum, -ī nt sneezing
sternuō, -ere, -ī vt, vi to sneeze
Steropē, -ēs f a Pleiad
sterquilīnium, -ī and -iī nt, **sterquilīnum, -ī** nt dung heap
stertō, -ere, -uī vi to snore
Stēsichorus, -ī m Greek lyric poet
stetī perf of **stō**
Sthenelēius, Sthenelēis, ēidis adj see **Sthenelus**
Sthenelus, -ī m father of Eurystheus; father of Cycnus
stigma, -tis nt brand
stigmatiās, -ae m branded slave
stilla, -ae f drop
stillicidium, -ī and -iī nt dripping water, rainfrom the eaves
stillō, -āre, -āvī, -ātum vi to drip, trickle ▸ vt to let fall in drops, distil
stilus, -ī m stake; pen; (fig) writing, composition, style; **stilum vertere** erase
stimulātiō, -ōnis f incentive
stimulātrīx, -īcis f provocative woman
stimuleus adj smarting
stimulō, -āre, -āvī, -ātum vt to goad; to trouble, torment; to rouse, spur on, excite
stimulus, -ī m goad; (MIL) stake; (pain) sting, pang; (incentive) spur, stimulus
stinguō, -ere vt to extinguish
stīpātiō, -ōnis f crowd, retinue
stīpātor, -ōris m attendant; (pl) retinue, bodyguard
stīpendiārius adj tributary, liable to a money tax; (MIL) receiving pay ▸ mpl tributary peoples
stīpendium, -ī and -iī nt tax, tribute; soldier's pay; military service, campaign; **~ merēre**, **~ merērī** serve; **~ ēmerērī** complete one's period of service
stīpes, -itis m log, trunk; tree; (insult) blockhead
stīpō, -āre, -āvī, -ātum vt to press, pack together; to cram, stuff full; to crowd round, accompany in a body
stips, stipis f donation, contribution

stipula, -ae f stalk, blade, stubble; reed
stipulātiō, -ōnis f promise, bargain
stipulātiuncula, -ae f slight stipulation
stipulātus adj promised
stipulor, -ārī vt, vi to demand a formal promise, bargain, stipulate
stīria, -ae f icicle
stirpēs etc see **stirps**
stirpitus adv thoroughly
stirps, -is f lower trunk and roots, stock; plant, shoot; family, lineage, progeny; origin; **ab stirpe** utterly
stīva, -ae f plough handle
stlattārius adj seaborne
stō, stāre, stetī, statum vi to stand; to remain in position, stand firm; to be conspicuous, (fig) to persist, continue; (battle) to go on; (hair) to stand on end; (NAUT) to ride at anchor; (play) to be successful; (price) to cost; (with **ab, cum, prō**) to be on the side of, support; (with **in**) to rest, depend on; (with **per**) to be the fault of; **stat sententia** one's mind is made up; **per Āfrānium stetit quōminus dīmicārētur** thanks to Afranius there was no battle
Stōicē adv like a Stoic
Stōicus adj Stoic ▸ m Stoic philosopher ▸ ntpl Stoicism
stola, -ae f long robe (esp worn by matrons)
stolidē adv stupidly
stolidus adj dull, stupid
stomachor, -ārī, -ātus vi to be vexed, be annoyed
stomachōsē adv see **stomachōsus**
stomachōsus adj angry, irritable
stomachus, -ī m gullet; stomach; taste, liking; dislike, irritation, chagrin
stōrea, storia, -ae f rush mat, rope mat
strāgēs, -is f heap, confused mass; havoc, massacre
strāgulus adj covering ▸ nt bedspread, rug
strāmen, -inis nt straw, litter
strāmentum, -ī nt straw, thatch; straw bed; covering, rug
strāmineus adj straw-thatched
strangulō, -āre, -āvī, -ātum vt to throttle, choke
strangūria, -ae f difficult discharge of urine
stratēgēma, -tis nt a piece of generalship, stratagem
stratēgus, -ī m commander, president
stratiōticus adj military
strātum, -ī nt coverlet, blanket; bed, couch; horsecloth, saddle; pavement
strātus ppp of **sternō** ▸ adj prostrate
strāvī perf of **sternō**
strēnuē adv energetically, quickly
strēnuitās, -ātis f energy, briskness
strēnuus adj brisk, energetic, busy; restless
strepitō, -āre vi to make a noise, rattle, rustle
strepitus, -ūs m din, clatter, crashing, rumbling; sound

strepō, -ere, -uī vi to make a noise, clang, roar, rumble, rustle etc ▸ vt to bawl out

striāta, -ae f scallop

strictim adv superficially, cursorily

strictūra, -ae f mass of metal

strictus ppp of **stringō** ▸ adj close, tight

strīdeō, -ēre, -ī, strīdō, -ere, -ī vi to creak, hiss, shriek, whistle

strīdor, -ōris m creaking, hissing, grating

strīdulus adj creaking, hissing, whistling

strigilis f scraper, strigil

strigō, -āre vi to stop, jib

strigōsus adj thin, scraggy; (style) insipid

stringō, -ngere, -nxī, -ctum vt to draw together, draw tight; to touch, graze; to cut off, prune, trim; (sword) to draw; (mind) to affect, pain

stringor, -ōris m twinge

strix, -igis f screech owl

stropha, -ae f trick

Strophades, -um fpl islands off S. Greece

strophiārius, -ī and **-iī** m maker of breastbands

strophium, -ī and **-iī** nt breastband; headband

structor, -ōris m mason, carpenter; (at table) server, carver

structūra, -ae f construction, structure; works

structus ppp of **struō**

struēs, -is f heap, pile

struix, -icis f heap, pile

strūma, -ae f tumour

strūmōsus adj scrofulous

struō, -ere, -xī, -ctum vt to pile up; to build, erect; to arrange in order; to make, prepare; to cause, contrive, plot

strūtheus adj sparrow- (in cpds)

strūthiocamēlus, -ī m ostrich

Strȳmōn, -onis m river between Macedonia and Thrace (now Struma)

Strȳmonius adj Strymonian, Thracian

studeō, -ēre, -uī vi (usu with dat) to be keen, be diligent, apply oneself to; to study; (person) to be a supporter of

studiōsē adv eagerly, diligently

studiōsus adj (usu with gen) keen on, fond of, partial to; studious ▸ m student

studium, -ī and **-iī** nt enthusiasm, application, inclination; fondness, affection; party spirit, partisanship; study, literary work

stultē adv foolishly

stultiloquentia, -ae f foolish talk

stultiloquium, -ī and **-iī** nt foolish talk

stultitia, -ae f folly, silliness

stultividus adj simple-sighted

stultus adj foolish, silly ▸ m fool

stupefaciō, -facere, -fēcī, -factum (pass **-fīō**) vt to stun, astound

stupeō, -ēre, -uī vi to be stunned, be astonished; to be brought to a standstill ▸ vt to marvel at

stupēscō, -ere vi to become amazed

stūpeus etc see **stuppeus**

stupiditās, -ātis f senselessness

stupidus adj senseless, astounded; dull, stupid

stupor, -ōris m numbness, bewilderment; dullness, stupidity

stuppa, -ae f tow

stuppeus adj of tow

stuprō, -āre, -āvī, -ātum vt to defile; to ravish

stuprum, -ī nt debauchery, unchastity

sturnus, -ī m starling

Stygius adj of the lower world, Stygian

stylus etc see **stilus**

Stymphalicus, Stymphalicius, Stymphalicis adj Stymphalian

Stymphalum, -ī nt, **Stymphalus, -ī** m district of Arcadia (famous for birds of prey killed by Hercules)

Styx, -ygis and **-ygos** f river of Hades

Styxius adj see **Styx**

suādēla, -ae f persuasion

suādeō, -dēre, -sī, -sum vi (with dat) to advise, urge, recommend

suāsiō, -ōnis f speaking in favour (of a proposal), persuasive type of oratory

suāsor, -ōris m adviser; advocate

suāsus¹ ppp of **suādeō**

suāsus², -ūs m advice

suāveolēns, -entis adj fragrant

suāviātiō etc see **sāviātiō**

suāvidicus adj charming

suāviloquēns, -entis adj charming

suāviloquentia, -ae f charm of speech

suāvior etc see **sāvior**

suāvis adj sweet, pleasant, delightful

suāvitās, -ātis f sweetness, pleasantness, charm

suāviter adv see **suāvis**

suāvium etc see **sāvium**

sub prep 1. (with abl: place) under, beneath; (: hills, walls) at the foot of, close to; (: time) during, at; (: order) next to; (: rule) under, in the reign of 2. (with acc: place) under, along under; (: hills, walls) up to, to; (: time) up to, just before, just after; **sub ictum venīre** come within range; **sub manum** to hand

subabsurdē adv see **subabsurdus**

subabsurdus adj somewhat absurd

subaccūsō, -āre vt to find some fault with

subāctiō, -ōnis f working (the soil)

subāctus ppp of **subigō**

subadroganter adv a little conceitedly

subagrestis adj rather boorish

subalāris adj carried under the arms

subamārus adj rather bitter

subaquilus adj brownish

subauscultō, -āre vt, vi to listen secretly, eavesdrop

subbasilicānus, -ī m lounger

subblandior, -īrī vi (with dat) to flirt with

subc- etc see **succ-**

subdidī perf of **subdō**

subdifficilis adj rather difficult
subdiffīdō, -ere vi to be a little doubtful
subditīcius adj sham
subditīvus adj sham
subditus ppp of **subdō** ▸ adj spurious
subdō, -ere, -idī, -itum vt to put under, plunge into; to subdue; to substitute, forge
subdoceō, -ēre vt to teach as an assistant
subdolē adv slily
subdolus adj sly, crafty, underhand
subdubitō, -āre vi to be a little undecided
subdūcō, -ūcere, -ūxī, -uctum vt to pull up, raise; to withdraw, remove; to take away secretly, steal; (account) to balance; (ship) to haul up, beach; **sē subdūcere** steal away, disappear
subductiō, -ōnis f (ship) hauling up; (thought) reckoning
subductus ppp of **subdūcō**
subedō, -ēsse, -ēdī vt to wear away underneath
subēgī perf of **subigō**
subeō, -īre, -iī, -itum vi to go under, go in; to come up to, climb, advance; to come immediately after; to come to the assistance; to come as a substitute, succeed; to come secretly, steal in; to come to mind, suggest itself ▸ vt to enter, plunge into; to climb; to approach, attack; to take the place of; to steal into; to submit to, undergo, suffer; (mind) to occur to
sūber, -is nt cork tree; cork
subesse infin of **subsum**
subf- etc see **suff-**
subg- etc see **sugg-**
subhorridus adj somewhat uncouth
subiaceō, -ēre, -uī vi to lie under, be close (to); to be connected (with)
subiciō, -icere, -iēcī, -iectum vt to put under, bring under; to bring up, throw up; to bring near; to submit, subject, expose; to subordinate, deal with under; to append, add on, answer; to adduce, suggest; to substitute; to forge; to suborn; **sē subicere** grow up
subiectē adv submissively
subiectiō, -ōnis f laying under; forging
subiectō, -āre vt to lay under, put to; to throw up
subiector, -ōris m forger
subiectus ppp of **subiciō** ▸ adj neighbouring, bordering; subject, exposed
subigitātiō, -ōnis f lewdness
subigitō, -āre vt to behave improperly to
subigō, -igere, -ēgī, -āctum vt to bring up to; to impel, compel; to subdue, conquer; (animal) to tame, break in; (blade) to sharpen; (boat) to row, propel; (cooking) to knead; (earth) to turn up, dig; (mind) to train
subiī perf of **subeō**
subimpudēns, -entis adj rather impertinent
subinānis adj rather empty
subinde adv immediately after; repeatedly

subīnsulsus adj rather insipid
subinvideō, -ēre vi to be a little envious of
subinvīsus adj somewhat odious
subinvītō, -āre vt to invite vaguely
subīrāscor, -scī, -tus vi to be rather angry
subīrātus adj rather angry
subitārius adj sudden, emergency (in cpds)
subitō adv suddenly
subitus ppp of **subeō** ▸ adj sudden, unexpected; (man) rash; (troops) hastily raised ▸ nt surprise, emergency
subiūnctus ppp of **subiungō**
subiungō, -ungere, -ūnxī, -ūnctum vt to harness; to add, affix; to subordinate, subdue
sublābor, -bī, -psus vi to sink down; to glide away
sublāpsus ppa of **sublābor**
sublātē adv loftily
sublātiō, -ōnis f elevation
sublātus ppp of **tollō** ▸ adj elated
sublectō, -āre vt to coax
sublēctus ppp of **sublegō**
sublegō, -egere, -ēgī, -ēctum vt to gather up; to substitute; (child) to kidnap; (talk) to overhear
sublestus adj slight
sublevātiō, -ōnis f alleviation
sublevō, -āre, -āvī, -ātum vt to lift up, hold up; to support, encourage; to lighten, alleviate
sublica, -ae f pile, palisade
sublicius adj on piles
sublīgāculum, -ī, sublīgar, -āris nt loincloth
sublīgō, -āre vt to fasten on
sublīmē adv aloft, in the air
sublīmis adj high, raised high, lifted up; (character) eminent, aspiring; (language) lofty, elevated
sublīmitās, -ātis f loftiness
sublīmus etc see **sublīmis**
sublingiō, -ōnis m scullion
sublinō, -inere, -ēvī, -itum vt: **ōs sublinere** to fool, bamboozle
sublitus ppp of **sublinō**
sublūceō, -ēre vi to glimmer
subl010uō, -ere vt (river) to flow past the foot of
sublūstris adj faintly luminous
sublūtus ppp of **subluō**
subm- etc see **summ-**
subnātus adj growing up underneath
subnectō, -ctere, -xuī, -xum vt to tie under, fasten to
subnegō, -āre vt to half refuse
subnexus ppp of **subnectō**
subniger, -rī adj darkish
subnīxus, subnīsus adj supported, resting (on); relying (on)
subnuba, -ae f rival
subnūbilus adj overcast
subō, -āre vi to be in heat
subobscēnus adj rather indecent
subobscūrus adj somewhat obscure

subodiōsus *adj* rather odious

suboffendō, -ere *vi* to give some offence

subolēs, -is *f* offspring, children

subolēscō, -ere *vi* to grow up

subolet, -ēre *vi* (*impers*) there is a faint scent; ~ **mihi** I detect, have an inkling

suborior, -īrī *vi* to rise up in succession

subōrnō, -āre, -āvī, -ātum *vt* to fit out, equip; to instigate secretly, suborn

subortus, -ūs *m* rising up repeatedly

subp- *etc see* **supp-**

subrancidus *adj* slightly tainted

subraucus *adj* rather hoarse

subrēctus *ppp of* **subrigō**

subrēmigō, -āre *vi* to paddle under (*water*)

subrēpō, -ere, -sī, -tum *vi* to creep along, steal up to

subreptus *ppp of* **subripiō**

subrīdeō, -dēre, -sī *vi* to smile

subrīdiculē *adv* rather funnily

subrigō, -igere, -ēxī, -ēctum *vt* to lift, raise

subringor, -ī *vi* to make a wry face, be rather vexed

subripiō, -ipere, -ipuī *and* **-upuī, -eptum** *vt* to take away secretly, steal

subrogō, -āre *vt* to propose as successor

subrōstrānī, -ōrum *mpl* idlers

subrubeō, -ēre *vi* to blush slightly

subrūfus *adj* ginger-haired

subruō, -ere, -ī, -tum *vt* to undermine, demolish

subrūsticus *adj* rather countrified

subrutus *ppp of* **subruō**

subscrībō, -bere, -psī, -ptum *vt* to write underneath; (*document*) to sign, subscribe; (*censor*) to set down; (*LAW*) to add to an indictment, prosecute; (*fig*) to record; (*with dat*) to assent to, approve

subscrīptiō, -ōnis *f* inscription underneath; signature; (*censor*) noting down; (*LAW*) subscription (*to an indictment*); register

subscrīptor, -ōris *m* subscriber (*to an indictment*)

subscrīptus *ppp of* **subscrībō**

subsecīvus *etc see* **subsicīvus**

subsecō, -āre, -uī, -ctum *vt* to cut off, clip

subsēdī *perf of* **subsīdō**

subsellium, -ī *and* **-iī** *nt* bench, seat; (*LAW*) the bench, the court

subsentiō, -entīre, -ēnsī *vt* to have an inkling of

subsequor, -quī, -cūtus *vt, vi* to follow closely; to support; to imitate

subserviō, -īre *vi* to be a slave; (*fig*) to comply (with)

subsicīvus *adj* left over; (*time*) spare; (*work*) overtime

subsidiārius *adj* in reserve ▶ *mpl* reserves

subsidium, -ī *and* **-iī** *nt* reserve ranks, reserve troops; relief, aid, assistance

subsīdō, -īdere, -ēdī, -essum *vi* to sit down, crouch, squat; to sink down, settle, subside; (*ambush*) to lie in wait; (*residence*) to stay, settle ▶ *vt* to lie in wait for

subsignānus *adj* special reserve (troops)

subsignō, -āre *vt* to register; to guarantee

subsiliō, -īre, -uī *vi* to leap up

subsistō, -istere, -titī *vi* to stand still, make a stand; to stop, halt; to remain, continue, hold out; (*with dat*) to resist ▶ *vt* to withstand

subsortior, -īrī, -ītus *vt* to choose as a substitute by lot

subsortītiō, -ōnis *f* choosing of substitutes by lot

substantia, -ae *f* means, wealth

substernō, -ernere, -rāvī, -rātum *vt* to scatter under, spread under; (*fig*) to put at one's service

substitī *perf of* **subsistō**

substituō, -uere, -uī, -ūtum *vt* to put next; to substitute; (*idea*) to present, imagine

substitūtus *ppp of* **substituō**

substō, -āre *vi* to hold out

substrātus *ppp of* **substernō**

substrictus *ppp of* **substringō** ▶ *adj* narrow, tight

substringō, -ngere, -nxī, -ctum *vt* to bind up; to draw close; to check

substructiō, -ōnis *f* foundation

substruō, -ere, -xī, -ctum *vt* to lay, pave

subsultō, -āre *vi* to jump up

subsum, -esse *vi* to be underneath; to be close to, be at hand; (*fig*) to underlie, be latent in

subsūtus *adj* fringed at the bottom

subtēmen, -inis *nt* woof; thread

subter *adv* below, underneath ▶ *prep* (*with acc and abl*) beneath; close up to

subterdūcō, -cere, -xī *vt* to withdraw secretly

subterfugiō, -ugere, -ūgī *vt* to escape from, evade

subterlābor, -ī *vt, vi* to flow past under; to slip away

subterrāneus *adj* underground

subtexō, -ere, -uī, -tum *vt* to weave in; to veil, obscure

subtīlis *adj* slender, fine; (*senses*) delicate, nice; (*judgment*) discriminating, precise; (*style*) plain, direct

subtīlitās, -ātis *f* fineness; (*judgment*) acuteness, exactness; (*style*) plainness, directness

subtīliter *adv* finely; accurately; simply

subtimeō, -ēre *vt* to be a little afraid of

subtractus *ppp of* **subtrahō**

subtrahō, -here, -xī, -ctum *vt* to draw away from underneath; to take away secretly; to withdraw, remove

subtristis *adj* rather sad

subturpiculus *adj* a little bit mean

subturpis *adj* rather mean

subtus *adv* below, underneath

subtūsus *adj* slightly bruised

subūcula, -ae *f* shirt, vest

sūbula, -ae *f* awl

subulcus, **-ī** m swineherd

Subūra, **-ae** f a disreputable quarter of Rome

Subūrānus adj see **Subūra**

suburbānitās, **-ātis** f nearness to Rome

suburbānus adj near Rome ▸ nt villa near Rome ▸ mpl inhabitants of the towns near Rome

suburbium, **-ī** and **-iī** nt suburb

suburgeō, **-ēre** vt to drive close (to)

subvectiō, **-ōnis** f transport

subvectō, **-āre** vt to carry up regularly

subvectus[1] ppp of **subvehō**

subvectus[2], **-ūs** m transport

subvehō, **-here**, **-xī**, **-ctum** vt to carry up, transport upstream

subveniō, **-enīre**, **-ēnī**, **-entum** vi (with dat) to come to the assistance of, relieve, reinforce

subventō, **-āre** vi (with dat) to come quickly to help

subvereor, **-ērī** vi to be a little afraid

subversor, **-ōris** m subverter

subversus ppp of **subvertō**

subvertō, **-tere**, **-tī**, **-sum** vt to turn upside down, upset; to overthrow, subvert

subvexī perf of **subvehō**

subvexus adj sloping upwards

subvolō, **-āre** vi to fly upwards

subvolvō, **-ere** vt to roll uphill

subvortō etc see **subvertō**

succavus adj hollow underneath

succēdō, **-ēdere**, **-essī**, **-essum** vt, vi (with dat) to go under, pass into, take on; (with dat, acc, **in**) to go up, climb; (with dat, acc, **ad**, **sub**) to march on, advance to; (with dat, **in**) to come to take the place of, relieve; (with dat, **in**, **ad**) to follow after, succeed, succeed to; (result) to turn out, be successful

succendō, **-endere**, **-endī**, **-ēnsum** vt to set fire to, kindle; (fig) to fire, inflame

succēnseō etc see **suscēnseō**

succēnsus ppp of **succendō**

succenturiātus adj in reserve

succenturiō, **-ōnis** m under-centurion

successī perf of **succēdō**

successiō, **-ōnis** f succession

successor, **-ōris** m successor

successus[1] ppp of **succēdō**

successus[2], **-ūs** m advance uphill; result, success

succīdia, **-ae** f leg or side of meat, flitch

succīdō, **-ere**, **-ī** vi to sink, give way

succīdō, **-dere**, **-dī**, **-sum** vt to cut off, mow down

succiduus adj sinking, failing

succinctus ppp of **succingō**

succingō, **-gere**, **-xī**, **-ctum** vt to gird up, tuck up; to equip, arm

succingulum, **-ī** nt girdle

succinō, **-ere** vi to chime in

succīsus ppp of **succīdō**

succlāmātiō, **-ōnis** f shouting, barracking

succlāmō, **-āre**, **-āvī**, **-ātum** vt to shout after, interrupt with shouting

succontumēliōsē adv somewhat insolently

succrēscō, **-ere** vi to grow up from or to

succrispus adj rather curly

succumbō, **-mbere**, **-buī**, **-bitum** vi to fall, sink under; to submit, surrender

succurrō, **-rere**, **-rī**, **-sum** vi to come quickly up; to run to the help of, succour; (idea) to occur

succus etc see **sūcus**

successus, **-ūs** m shaking

succustōs, **-ōdis** m assistant keeper

succutiō, **-tere**, **-ssī**, **-ssum** vt to toss up

sūcidus adj juicy, fresh, plump

sūcinum, **-ī** nt amber

sūctus ppp of **sūgō**

sucula[1], **-ae** f winch, windlass

sucula[2], **-ae** f piglet; (pl) the Hyads

sūcus, **-ī** m juice, sap; medicine, potion; taste, flavour; (fig) strength, vigour, life

sūdārium, **-ī** and **-iī** nt handkerchief

sūdātōrius adj for sweating ▸ nt sweating bath

sūdis, **-is** f stake, pile, pike, spike

sūdō, **-āre**, **-āvī**, **-ātum** vi to sweat, perspire; to be drenched with; to work hard ▸ vt to exude

sūdor, **-ōris** m sweat, perspiration; moisture; hard work, exertion

sūdus adj cloudless, clear ▸ nt fine weather

sueō, **-ēre** vi to be accustomed

suēscō, **-scere**, **-vī**, **-tum** vi to be accustomed ▸ vt to accustom

Suessa, **-ae** f town in Latium

Suessiōnēs, **-um** mpl people of Gaul (near what is now Soissons)

suētus ppp of **suēscō** ▸ adj accustomed; usual

Suēvī, **-ōrum** mpl people of N.E. Germany

sūfes, **-etis** m chief magistrate of Carthage

suffarcinātus adj stuffed full

suffectus ppp of **sufficiō** ▸ adj (consul) appointed to fill a vacancy during the regular term of office

sufferō, **-re** vt to support, undergo, endure

suffes etc see **sūfes**

sufficiō, **-icere**, **-ēcī**, **-ectum** vt to dye, tinge; to supply, provide; to appoint in place (of another), substitute ▸ vi to be adequate, suffice

suffīgō, **-gere**, **-xī**, **-xum** vt to fasten underneath, nail on

suffīmen, **-inis**, **suffīmentum**, **-ī** nt incense

suffiō, **-īre** vt to fumigate, perfume

suffīxus ppp of **suffīgō**

sufflāmen, **-inis** nt brake

sufflō, **-āre** vt to blow up; to puff up

suffocō, **-āre** vt to choke, stifle

suffodiō, **-odere**, **-ōdī**, **-ossum** vt to stab; to dig under, undermine

suffossus ppp of **suffodiō**

suffrāgātiō, **-ōnis** f voting for, support

suffrāgātor, **-ōris** m voter, supporter

suffrāgātōrius adj supporting a candidate

suffrāgium, **-ī** and **-iī** nt vote, ballot; right of suffrage; (fig) judgment, approval; ▸ ferre vote

suffrāgor, **-ārī**, **-ātus** vi to vote for; to support, favour

suffringō, **-ere** vt to break

suffugiō, -ugere, -ūgī *vi* to run for shelter ▶ *vt* to elude

suffugium, -ī *and* **-iī** *nt* shelter, refuge

suffulciō, -cīre, -sī, -tum *vt* to prop up, support

suffundō, -undere, -ūdī, -ūsum *vt* to pour in; to suffuse, fill; to tinge, colour; (*blush*) to overspread

suffūror, -ārī *vi* to filch

suffuscus *adj* darkish

suffūsus *ppp of* **suffundō**

Sugambrī, -ōrum *mpl* people of N.W. Germany

suggerō, -rere, -ssī, -stum *vt* to bring up to, supply; to add on, put next

suggestum, -ī *nt* platform

suggestus¹ *ppp of* **suggerō**

suggestus², -ūs *m* platform, stage

suggrandis *adj* rather large

suggredior, -dī, -ssus *vi* to come up close, approach ▶ *vt* to attack

sūgillātiō, -ōnis *f* affronting

sūgillātus *adj* bruised; insulted

sūgō, -gere, -xī, -ctum *vt* to suck

suī¹ *gen of* **sē**

suī² *perf of* **suō**

suillus *adj* of pigs

sulcō, -āre *vt* to furrow, plough

sulcus, -ī *m* furrow; trench; track

sulfur, -uris *n* sulphur

Sulla, -ae *m* famous Roman dictator

Sullānus *adj see* **Sulla**

sullāturiō, -īre *vi* to hanker after being a Sulla

Sulmō, -ōnis *m* town in E. Italy (*birthplace of Ovid*)

Sulmōnēnsis *adj see* **Sulmō**

sultis *adv* please

sum, esse, fuī *vi* to be, exist; **sum ab** belong to; **sum ad** be designed for; **sum ex** consist of; **est, sunt** there is, are; **est mihi** I have; **mihi tēcum nīl est** I have nothing to do with you; **est quod** something; there is a reason for; **est ubi** sometimes; **est ut** it is possible that; **est** (*with gen*) to belong to, be the duty of, be characteristic of; (*with infin*) it is possible, it is permissible; **sunt quī** some; **fuit Īlium** Troy is no more

sūmen, -inis *nt* udder, teat; sow

summa, -ae *f* main part, chief point, main issue; gist, summary; sum, amount, the whole; supreme power; ~ **rērum** the general interest, the whole responsibility; ~ **summārum** the universe; **ad summam** in short, in fact; in conclusion; **in summā** in all; after all

Summānus, -ī *m* god of nocturnal thunderbolts

summās, -ātis *adj* high-born, eminent

summātim *adv* cursorily, summarily

summātus, -ūs *m* sovereignty

summē *adv* in the highest degree, extremely

summergō, -gere, -sī, -sum *vt* to plunge under, sink

summersus *ppp of* **summergō**

sumministrō, -āre, -āvī, -ātum *vt* to provide, furnish

summissē *adv* softly; humbly, modestly

summissiō, -ōnis *f* flowering

summissus *ppp of* **summittō** ▶ *adj* low; (*voice*) low, calm; (*character*) mean, grovelling, submissive, humble

summittō, -ittere, -īsī, -issum *vt* (*growth*) to send up, raise, rear; to despatch, supply; to let down, lower, reduce, moderate; to supersede; to send secretly; **animum summittere** submit; **sē summittere** condescend

summolestē *adv* with some annoyance

summolestus *adj* a little annoying

summoneō, -ēre, -uī *vt* to drop a hint to

summōrōsus *adj* rather peevish

summōtor, -ōris *m* clearer

summōtus *ppp of* **summoveō**

summoveō, -ovēre, -ōvī, -ōtum *vt* to move away, drive off; to clear away (*to make room*), withdraw, remove, banish; (*fig*) to dispel

summum¹, -ī *nt* top, surface

summum² *adv* at the most

summus *adj* highest, the top of, the surface of; last, the end of; (*fig*) utmost, greatest, most important; (*person*) distinguished, excellent ▶ *m* head of the table

summūtō, -āre *vt* to substitute

sūmō, -ere, -psī, -ptum *vt* to take, take up; to assume, arrogate; (*action*) to undertake; (*argument*) to assume, take for granted; (*dress*) to put on; (*punishment*) to exact; (*for a purpose*) to use, spend

sūmptiō, -ōnis *f* assumption

sūmptuārius *adj* sumptuary

sūmptuōsē *adv see* **sūmptuōsus**

sūmptuōsus *adj* expensive, lavish, extravagant

sūmptus¹ *ppp of* **sūmō**

sūmptus², -ūs *m* expense, cost

Sūnium, -ī *and* **-iī** *nt* S.E. promontory of Attica

suō, suere, suī, sūtum *vt* to sew, stitch, join together

suōmet, suōpte *abl of* **suus**

suovetaurīlia, -ium *ntpl* sacrifice of a pig, sheep and bull

supellex, -ectilis *f* furniture, goods, outfit

super¹ *etc adj see* **superus**

super² *adv* above, on the top; besides, moreover; left, remaining ▶ *prep* (*with abl*) upon, above; concerning; besides; (*time*) at; (*with acc*) over, above, on; beyond; besides, over and above

superā *etc see* **suprā**

superābilis *adj* surmountable, conquerable

superaddō, -ere, -itum *vt* to add over and above

superāns, -antis *pres p of* **superō** ▶ *adj* predominant

superātor, -ōris *m* conqueror

superbē *adv* arrogantly, despotically

superbia, -ae *f* arrogance, insolence, tyranny; pride, lofty spirit

superbiloquentia, -ae *f* arrogant speech

superbiō, -īre vi to be arrogant, take a pride in; to be superb

superbus adj arrogant, insolent, overbearing; fastidious; superb, magnificent

supercilium, -ī and **-iī** nt eyebrow; (hill) brow, ridge; (fig) arrogance

superēmineō, -ēre vt to overtop

superesse infin of **supersum**

superficiēs, -ēī f surface; (LAW) a building (esp on another's land)

superfīō, -ieri vi to be left over

superfixus adj fixed on top

superfluō, -ere vi to overflow

superfuī perf of **supersum**

superfundō, -undere, -ūdī, -ūsum vt, vi to pour over, shower; (pass) to overflow, spread out

superfūsus ppp of **superfundō**

supergredior, -dī, -ssus vt to surpass

superiaciō, -iacere, -iēcī, -iectum and **-iactum** vt to throw over, overspread; to overtop; (fig) to exaggerate

superiectus ppp of **superiaciō**

superimmineō, -ēre vi to overhang

superimpendēns, -entis adj overhanging

superimpōnō, -ōnere, -osuī, -ositum vt to place on top

superimpositus ppp of **superimpōnō**

superincidēns, -entis adj falling from above

superincubāns, -antis adj lying upon

superincumbō, -ere vi to fling oneself down upon

superingerō, -ere vt to pour down

superiniciō, -icere, -iēcī, -iectum vt to throw upon, put on top

superiniectus ppp of **superiniciō**

superīnsternō, -ere vt to lay over

superior, -ōris adj higher, upper; (time, order) preceding, previous, former; (age) older; (battle) victorious, stronger; (quality) superior, greater

superlātiō, -ōnis f exaggeration

superlātus adj exaggerated

supernē adv at the top, from above

supernus adj upper; celestial

superō, -āre, -āvī, -ātum vi to rise above, overtop; to have the upper hand; to be in excess, be abundant; to be left over, survive ▶ vt to pass over, surmount, go beyond; to surpass, outdo; (MIL) to overcome, conquer; (NAUT) to sail past, double

superobruō, -ere vt to overwhelm

superpendēns, -entis adj overhanging

superpōnō, -ōnere, -osuī, -ositum vt to place upon; to put in charge of

superpositus ppp of **superpōnō**

superscandō, -ere vt to climb over

supersedeō, -edēre, -ēdī, -essum vi to forbear, desist from

superstes, -itis adj standing over; surviving

superstitiō, -ōnis f awful fear, superstition

superstitiōsē adv superstitiously; scrupulously

superstitiōsus adj superstitious; prophetic

superstō, -āre vt, vi to stand over, stand on

superstrātus adj spread over

superstruō, -ere, -xī, -ctum vt to build on top

supersum, -esse, -fuī vi to be left, remain; to survive; to be in abundance, be sufficient; to be in excess

supertegō, -ere vt to cover over

superurgēns, -entis adj pressing from above

superus (compar **-ior**, superl **suprēmus** and **summus**) adj upper, above ▶ mpl the gods above; the living ▶ ntpl the heavenly bodies; higher places; **mare superum** Adriatic Sea

supervacāneus adj extra, superfluous

supervacuus adj superfluous, pointless

supervādō, -ere vt to climb over, surmount

supervehor, -hī, -ctus vt to ride past, sail past

superveniō, -enīre, -ēnī, -entum vt to overtake, come on top of ▶ vi to come on the scene, arrive unexpectedly

superventus, -ūs m arrival

supervolitō, -āre vt to fly over

supervolō, -āre vt, vi to fly over

supīnō, -āre, -āvī, -ātum vt to upturn, lay on its back

supīnus adj lying back, face up; sloping, on a slope; backwards; (mind) indolent, careless

suppāctus ppp of **suppingō**

suppaenitet, -ēre vt impers to be a little sorry

suppalpor, -ārī vi to coax gently

suppār, -aris adj nearly equal

supparasītor, -ārī vi to flatter gently

supparus, -ī m, **supparum, -ī** nt woman's linen garment; topsail

suppeditātiō, -ōnis f abundance

suppeditō, -āre, -āvī, -ātum vi to be at hand, be in full supply, be sufficient; to be rich in ▶ vt to supply, furnish

suppēdō, -ere vi to break wind quietly

suppetiae, -ārum fpl assistance

suppetior, -ārī, -ātus vi to come to the assistance of

suppetō, -ere, -īvī and **-iī, -ītum** vi to be available, be in store; to be equal to, suffice for

suppīlō, -āre vt to steal

suppingō, -ingere, -āctum vt to fasten underneath

supplantō, -āre vt to trip up

supplēmentum, -ī nt full complement; reinforcements

suppleō, -ēre vt to fill up, make good, make up to the full complement

supplex, -icis adj suppliant, in entreaty

supplicātiō, -ōnis f day of prayer, public thanksgiving

suppliciter adv in supplication

supplicium, -ī and **-iī** nt prayer, entreaty; sacrifice; punishment, execution, suffering; **suppliciō afficere** execute

supplicō, -āre, -āvī, -ātum vi (with dat) to entreat, pray to, worship

supplōdō, -dere, -sī vt to stamp
supplōsiō, -ōnis f stamping
suppōnō, -ōnere, -osuī, -ositum vt to
put under, apply; to subject; to add on; to
substitute, falsify
supportō, -āre vt to bring up, transport
suppositīcius adj spurious
suppositiō, -ōnis f substitution
suppositus ppp of **suppōnō**
supposuī perf of **suppōnō**
suppressiō, -ōnis f embezzlement
suppressus ppp of **supprimō ▸** adj (voice) low
supprimō, -imere, -essī, -essum vt to sink;
to restrain, detain, put a stop to; to keep secret,
suppress
supprōmus, -ī m underbutler
suppudet, -ēre vt impers to be a little ashamed
suppūrō, -āre vi to fester
suppus adj head downwards
supputō, -āre vt to count up
suprā adv above, up on top; (time) earlier,
previously; (amount) more; **~ quam** beyond
what **▸** prep (with acc) over, above; beyond;
(time) before; (amount) more than, over
suprāscandō, -ere vt to surmount
suprēmum adv for the last time
suprēmus adj highest; last, latest; greatest,
supreme **▸** ntpl moment of death; funeral rites;
testament
sūra, -ae f calf (of the leg)
sūrculus, -ī m twig, shoot; graft, slip
surdaster, -rī adj rather deaf
surditās, -ātis f deafness
surdus adj deaf; silent
surēna, -ae m grand vizier (of the Parthians)
surgō, -ere, surrēxī, surrēctum vi to rise,
get up, stand up; to arise, spring up, grow
surpere etc = **subripere**
surr- etc see **subr-**
surrēxī perf of **surgō**
surruptīcius adj stolen
surrupuī perf of **subripiō**
sūrsum, sūrsus adv upwards, up, high up;
~ deōrsum up and down
sūs, suis m/f pig, boar, hog, sow
Sūsa, -ōrum ntpl ancient Persian capital
suscēnseō, -ēre, -uī vi to be angry,
be irritated
susceptiō, -ōnis f undertaking
susceptus ppp of **suscipiō**
suscipiō, -ipere, -ēpī, -eptum vt to take
up, undertake; to receive, catch; (child) to
acknowledge; to beget; to take under one's
protection
suscitō, -āre, -āvī, -ātum vt to lift, raise;
to stir, rouse, awaken; to encourage, excite
suspectō, -āre vt, vi to look up at, watch; **~**
to suspect, mistrust
suspectus¹ ppp of **suspiciō ▸** adj suspected,
suspicious
suspectus², -ūs m looking up; esteem
suspendium, -ī and -iī nt hanging

suspendō, -endere, -endī, -ēnsum vt to
hang, hang up; (death) to hang; (building) to
support; (mind) to keep in suspense; (movement)
to check, interrupt; (pass) to depend
suspēnsus ppp of **suspendō ▸** adj raised,
hanging, poised; with a light touch; (fig) in
suspense, uncertain, anxious; dependent;
suspēnsō gradū on tiptoe
suspicāx, -ācis adj suspicious
suspiciō, -icere, -exī, -ectum vt to look up
at, look up to; to admire, respect; to mistrust
suspīciō, -ōnis f mistrust, suspicion
suspīciōsē adv suspiciously
suspīciōsus adj suspicious
suspicor, -ārī, -ātus vt to suspect; to surmise,
suppose
suspīrātus, -ūs m sigh
suspīritus, -ūs m deep breath, difficult
breathing; sigh
suspīrium, -ī and -iī nt deep breath, sigh
suspīrō, -āre, -āvī, -ātum vi to sigh **▸** vt to
sigh for; to exclaim with a sigh
susque dēque adv up and down
sustentāculum, -ī nt prop
sustentātiō, -ōnis f forbearance
sustentō, -āre, -āvī, -ātum vt to hold up,
support; (fig) to uphold, uplift; (food, means)
to sustain, support; (enemy) to check, hold;
(trouble) to suffer; (event) to hold back, postpone
sustineō, -inēre, -inuī, -entum vt to hold
up, support; to check, control; (fig) to uphold,
maintain; (food, means) to sustain, support;
(trouble) to bear, suffer, withstand; (event) to
put off
sustollō, -ere vt to lift up, raise; to destroy
sustulī perf of **tollō**
susurrātor, -ōris m whisperer
susurrō, -āre vt, vi to murmur, buzz, whisper
susurrus¹, -ūs m murmuring, whispering
susurrus² adj whispering
sūtēla, -ae f trick
sūtilis adj sewn
sūtor, -ōris m shoemaker; **~ nē suprā
crepidam** let the cobbler stick to his last
sūtōrius adj shoemaker's; ex-cobbler
sūtrīnus adj shoemaker's
sūtūra, -ae f seam
sūtus ppp of **suō**
suus adj his, her, its, their; one's own, proper,
due, right **▸** mpl one's own troops, friends,
followers etc **▸** nt one's own property
Sybaris, -is f town in E. Italy (noted for its
debauchery)
Sybarīta, -ītae m Sybarite
Sychaeus, -ī m husband of Dido
sȳcophanta, -ae m slanderer, cheat,
sycophant
sȳcophantia, -ae f deceit
sȳcophantiōsē adv deceitfully
sȳcophantor, -ārī vi to cheat
Syēnē, -ēs f town in S. Egypt (now Aswan)
syllaba, -ae f syllable

syllabātim *adv* syllable by syllable

symbola, -ae *f* contribution

symbolus, -ī *m* token, symbol

symphōnia, -ae *f* concord, harmony

symphōniacus *adj* choir (*in cpds*)

Symplēgades, -um *fpl* clashing rocks in the Black Sea

synedrus, -ī *m* senator (*in Macedonia*)

Synephēbī, -ōrum *mpl* Youths Together (*comedy by Caecilius*)

syngrapha, -ae *f* promissory note

syngraphus, -ī *m* written contract; passport, pass

Synnada, -ōrum *ntpl* town in Phrygia (*famous for marble*)

Synnadēnsis *adj see* **Synnada**

synodūs, -ontis *m* bream

synthesis, -is *f* dinner service; suit of clothes; dressing gown

Syphāx, -ācis *m* king of Numidia

Syrācūsae, -ārum *fpl* Syracuse

Syrācūsānus, Syrācūsānius, Syrācosius *adj* Syracusan

Syria, -iae *f* country at the E. end of the Mediterranean

Syrius, Syriacus, Syriscus *adj* Syrian

syrma, -ae *f* robe with a train; (*fig*) tragedy

Syrtis, -is *f* Gulf of Sidra in N. Africa; sandbank

t

tabella, -ae *f* small board, sill; writing tablet, voting tablet, votive tablet; picture; (*pl*) writing, records, dispatches

tabellārius *adj* about voting ▸ *m* courier

tābeō, -ēre *vi* to waste away; to be wet

taberna, -ae *f* cottage; shop; inn; (*circus*) stalls

tabernāculum, -ī *nt* tent; ~ **capere** choose a site (*for auspices*)

tabernāriī, -ōrum *mpl* shopkeepers

tābēs, -is *f* wasting away, decaying, melting; putrefaction; plague, disease

tābēscō, -ēscere, -uī *vi* to waste away, melt, decay; (*fig*) to pine, languish

tābidulus *adj* consuming

tābidus *adj* melting, decaying; pining; corrupting, infectious

tābificus *adj* melting, wasting

tabula, -ae *f* board, plank; writing tablet; votive tablet; map; picture; auction; (*pl*) account books, records, lists, will; ~ **Sullae** Sulla's proscriptions; **XII tabulae** Twelve Tables of Roman laws; **tabulae novae** cancellation of debts

tabulārium, -ī *and* **-iī** *nt* archives

tabulātiō, -ōnis *f* flooring, storey

tabulātum, -ī *nt* flooring, storey; (*trees*) layer, row

tābum, -ī *nt* decaying matter; disease, plague

taceō, -ēre, -uī, -itum *vi* to be silent, say nothing; to be still, be hushed ▸ *vt* to say nothing about, not speak of

tacitē *adv* silently; secretly

taciturnitās, -ātis *f* silence, taciturnity

taciturnus *adj* silent, quiet

Tacitus, -ī *m* famous Roman historian

tacitus *ppp of* **taceō** ▸ *adj* silent, mute, quiet; secret, unmentioned; tacit, implied; **per tacitum** quietly

tāctilis *adj* tangible

tāctiō, -ōnis *f* touching; sense of touch

tāctus¹ *ppp of* **tangō**

tāctus², -ūs *m* touch, handling, sense of touch; influence

taeda, -ae *f* pitch pine, pinewood; torch; plank; (*fig*) wedding

taedet, -ēre, -uit and **-taesum est** vt (impers) to be weary (of), loathe

taedifer, -ī adj torch-bearing

taedium, -ī and **-iī** nt weariness, loathing

Taenaridēs, -idae m Spartan (esp Hyacinthus)

Taenarius, -is adj of Taenarus; Spartan

Taenarum, -ī nt, **Taenaron, -ī** nt, **Taenarus, -ī** m/f, **Taenaros, -ī** m/f town and promontory in S. Greece (now Matapan), lower world

taenia, -ae f hairband, ribbon

taesum est perf of **taedet**

taeter, -rī adj foul, hideous, repulsive

taetrē adv hideously

taetricus see **tetricus**

tagāx, -ācis adj light-fingered

Tagus, -ī m river of Lusitania (now Tagus)

tālāris adj reaching to the ankles ▸ ntpl winged sandals; a garment reaching to the ankles

tālārius adj of dice

Talāsius, -ī and **-iī** m god of weddings; wedding cry

tālea, -ae f rod, stake

talentum, -ī nt talent, a Greek weight about 25.4kg; a large sum of money (esp the Attic talent of 60 minae)

tāliō, -ōnis f retaliation in kind

tālis adj such; the following

talpa, -ae f mole

tālus, -ī m ankle; heel; (pl) knuckle bones, oblong dice

tam adv so, so much, so very

tamdiū adv so long, as long

tamen adv however, nevertheless, all the same

Tāmesis, -is, Tāmesa, -ae m Thames

tametsī conj although

tamquam adv as, just as, just like ▸ conj as if

Tanagra, -ae f town in Boeotia

Tanais, -is m river in Sarmatia (now Don)

Tanaquil, -ilis f wife of the elder Tarquin

tandem adv at last, at length, finally; (question) just

tangō, -ere, tetigī, tāctum vt to touch, handle; (food) to taste; (with force) to hit, strike; (with liquid) to sprinkle; (mind) to affect, move; (place) to reach; to border on; (task) to take in hand; (by trick) to take in, fool; (in words) to touch on, mention; **dē caelō tāctus** struck by lightning

tanquam see **tamquam**

Tantaleus adj see **Tantalus**

Tantalidēs, -idae m Pelops, Atreus, Thyestes or Agamemnon

Tantalis, -idis f Niobe or Hermione

Tantalus, -ī m father of Pelops (condemned to hunger and thirst in Tartarus, or to the threat of an overhanging rock)

tantillus adj so little, so small

tantisper adv so long, just for a moment

tantopere adv so much

tantulus adj so little, so small

tantum adv so much, so, as; only, merely; **~ modo** only; **~ nōn** all but, almost; **~ quod** only just

tantummodo adv only

tantundem adv just as much, just so much

tantus adj so great; so little ▸ nt so much; so little; **tantī esse** be worth so much, be so dear, be so important; **tantō** so much, so far; (with compar) so much the; **tantō opere** so much; **in tantum** to such an extent; **tria tanta** three times as much

tantusdem adj just so great

tapēta, -ae m, **tapētia, -ium** ntpl carpet, tapestry, hangings

Taprobanē, -ēs f Ceylon

tardē adv slowly, tardily

tardēscō, -ere vi to become slow, falter

tardipēs, -edis adj limping

tarditās, -ātis f slowness, tardiness; (mind) dullness

tardiusculus adj rather slow

tardō, -āre, -āvī, -ātum vt to retard, impede ▸ vi to delay, go slow

tardus adj slow, tardy, late; (mind) dull; (speech) deliberate

Tarentīnus adj Tarentine

Tarentum, -ī nt town in S. Italy (now Taranto)

tarmes, -itis m woodworm

Tarpēius adj Tarpeian; **mōns ~** the Tarpeian Rock on the Capitoline Hill from which criminals were thrown

tarpezīta, -ae m banker

Tarquiniēnsis adj of Tarquinii

Tarquiniī, -iōrum mpl ancient town in Etruria

Tarquinius¹ adj of Tarquin

Tarquinius², -ī m Tarquin (esp Priscus, the fifth king of Rome, and Superbus, the last king)

Tarracīna, -ae f, **Tarracīnae, -ārum** fpl town in Latium

Tarracō, -ōnis f town in Spain (now Tarragona)

Tarracōnēnsis adj see **Tarracō**

Tarsēnsis adj see **Tarsus**

Tarsus, -ī f capital of Cilicia

Tartareus adj infernal

Tartarus, -ī m, **Tartaros, -ī** m, **Tartara, -ōrum** ntpl Tartarus, the lower world (esp the part reserved for criminals)

tat interj hallo there!

Tatius¹, -ī m Sabine king (who ruled jointly with Romulus)

Tatius² adj see **Tatius¹**

Taum, -ī nt Firth of Tay

taureus adj bull's ▸ f whip of bull's hide

Taurī, -ōrum mpl Thracians of the Crimea

tauriformis adj bull-shaped

Taurīnī, -ōrum mpl people of N. Italy (near what is now Turin)

taurīnus adj bull's

Tauromenītānus adj see **Tauromenium**

Tauromenium, -ī and **-iī** nt town in E. Sicily

taurus, -ī m bull

Taurus, -ī m mountain range in S.E. Asia Minor

taxātiō, -ōnis f valuing

taxeus adj of yews

taxillus, -ī m small dice

taxō, -āre vt to value, estimate

taxus, -ī f yew

Tāygeta, -ōrum ntpl, **Tāygetus, -ī** m mountain range in S. Greece

Tāygetē, -ēs f a Pleiad

tē acc and abl of **tū**

-te suffix for **tū**

Teānēnsis adj see **Teānum**

Teānum, -ī nt town in Apulia; town in Campania

techina, -ae f trick

Tecmessa, -ae f wife of Ajax

tēctor, -ōris m plasterer

tēctōriolum, -ī nt a little plaster

tēctōrium, -ī and **-iī** nt plaster, stucco

tēctōrius adj of a plasterer

tēctum, -ī nt roof, ceiling, canopy; house, dwelling, shelter

tēctus ppp of **tegō** ▸ adj hidden; secret, reserved, close

tēcum with you

Tegea, -ae f town in Arcadia

Tegeaeus adj Arcadian ▸ m the god Pan ▸ f Atalanta

Tegeātae, -ātārum mpl Tegeans

teges, -etis f mat

tegillum, -ī nt hood, cowl

tegimen, -inis nt covering

tegimentum, -ī nt covering

tegimen- etc see **tegim-**

tegō, -ere, tēxī, tēctum vt to cover; to hide, conceal; to protect, defend; to bury; **latus tegere** walk by the side of

tēgula, -ae f tile; (pl) tiled roof

tegum- etc see **tegim-**

Tēius adj of Teos

tēla, -ae f web; warp; yarnbeam, loom; (fig) plan

Telamōn, -ōnis m father of Ajax

Tēlegonus, -ī m son of Ulysses and Circe

Tēlemachus, -ī m son of Ulysses and Penelope

Tēlephus, -ī m king of Mysia (wounded by Achilles' spear)

tellūs, -ūris f the earth; earth, ground; land, country

tēlum, -ī nt weapon, missile; javelin, sword; (fig) shaft, dart

temerārius adj accidental; rash, thoughtless

temerē adv by chance, at random; rashly, thoughtlessly; **nōn ~** not for nothing; not easily; hardly ever

temeritās, -ātis f chance, rashness, thoughtlessness

temerō, -āre, -āvī, -ātum vt to desecrate, disgrace

tēmētum, -ī nt wine, alcohol

temnō, -ere vt to slight, despise

tēmō, -ōnis m beam (of plough or carriage); (ASTR) the Plough

Tempē ntpl famous valley in Thessaly

temperāmentum, -ī nt moderation, compromise

temperāns, -antis pres p of **temperō** ▸ adj moderate, temperate

temperanter adv with moderation

temperantia, -ae f moderation, self-control

temperātē adv with moderation

temperātiō, -ōnis f proper mixture, composition, constitution; organizing power

temperātor, -ōris m organizer

temperātus ppp of **temperō** ▸ adj moderate, sober

temperī adv in time, at the right time

temperiēs, -ēī f due proportion; temperature, mildness

temperō, -āre, -āvī, -ātum vt to mix in due proportion, blend, temper; to regulate, moderate, tune; to govern, rule ▸ vi to be moderate, forbear, abstain; (with dat) to spare, be lenient to

tempestās, -ātis f time, season, period; weather; (fig) storm; (fig) storm, shower

tempestīvē adv at the right time, appropriately

tempestīvitās, -ātis f seasonableness

tempestīvus adj timely, seasonable, appropriate; ripe, mature; early

templum, -ī nt space marked off for taking auspices; open space, region, quarter; sanctuary; temple

temporārius adj for the time, temporary

temptābundus adj making repeated attempts

temptāmentum, -ī nt trial, attempt, proof

temptāmina, -um ntpl attempts, essays

temptātiō, -ōnis f trial, proof; attack

temptātor, -ōris m assailant

temptō, -āre, -āvī, -ātum vt to feel, test by touching; to make an attempt on, attack; to try, essay, attempt; to try to influence, tamper with, tempt, incite; **vēnās temptāre** feel the pulse

tempus, -oris nt time; right time, opportunity; danger, emergency, circumstance; (head) temple; (verse) unit of metre; (verb) tense; **tempore** at the right time, in time; **ad ~** at the right time; for the moment; **ante ~** too soon; **ex tempore** on the spur of the moment; to suit the circumstances; **in tempore** in time; **in ~** temporarily; **per ~** just in time; **prō tempore** to suit the occasion

tēmulentus adj intoxicated

tenācitās, -ātis f firm grip; stinginess

tenāciter adv tightly, firmly

tenāx, -ācis adj gripping, tenacious; sticky; (fig) firm, persistent; stubborn; stingy

tendicula, -ae f little snare

tendō, -ere, tetendī, tentum and **tēnsum** vt to stretch, spread; to strain; (arrow) to aim, shoot; (bow) to bend; (course) to direct; (lyre) to tune; (tent) to pitch; (time) to prolong; (trap) to lay ▸ vi to encamp; to go, proceed; to aim, tend; (with infin) to endeavour, exert oneself

tenebrae, -ārum *fpl* darkness, night;
unconsciousness, death, blindness; (*place*)
dungeon, haunt, the lower world; (*fig*)
ignorance, obscurity
tenebricōsus *adj* gloomy
tenebrōsus *adj* dark, gloomy
Tenedius *adj see* **Tenedos**
Tenedos, Tenedus, -ī *f Aegean island near Troy*
tenellulus *adj* dainty little
teneō, -ēre, -uī *vt* to hold, keep; to possess,
occupy, be master of; to attain, acquire;
(*argument*) to maintain, insist; (*category*) to
comprise; (*goal*) to make for; (*interest*) to
fascinate; (*LAW*) to bind, be binding on; (*mind*) to
grasp, understand, remember; (*movement*) to
hold back, restrain ▶ *vi* to hold on, last, persist;
(*rumour*) to prevail; **cursum tenēre** keep on
one's course; **sē tenēre** remain; to refrain
tener, -ī *adj* tender, delicate; young, weak;
effeminate; (*poet*) erotic
tenerāscō, -ere *vi* to grow weak
tenerē *adv* softly
teneritās, -ātis *f* weakness
tenor, -ōris *m* steady course; **ūnō tenōre**
without a break, uniformly
tēnsa, -ae *f* carriage bearing the images of the gods
in procession
tēnsus *ppp of* **tendō** ▶ *adj* strained
tentā- *etc see* **temptā-**
tentīgō, -inis *f* lust
tentō *etc see* **temptō**
tentōrium, -ī and -iī *nt* tent
tentus *ppp of* **tendō**
tenuiculus *adj* paltry
tenuis *adj* thin, fine; small, shallow; (*air*)
rarefied; (*water*) clear; (*condition*) poor, mean,
insignificant; (*style*) refined, direct, precise
tenuitās, -ātis *f* thinness, fineness; poverty,
insignificance; (*style*) precision
tenuiter *adv* thinly; poorly; with precision;
superficially
tenuō, -āre, -āvī, -ātum *vt* to make thin,
attenuate, rarefy; to lessen, reduce
tenus *prep* (*with gen or abl*) as far as, up to, down
to; **verbō ~** in name, nominally
Teos, -ī *f town on coast of Asia Minor* (*birthplace
of Anacreon*)
tepefaciō, -facere, -fēcī, -factum *vt* to
warm
tepeō, -ēre *vi* to be warm, be lukewarm; (*fig*)
to be in love
tepēscō, -ēscere, -uī *vi* to grow warm; to
become lukewarm, cool off
tepidus *adj* warm, lukewarm
tepor, -ōris *m* warmth; coolness
ter *adv* three times, thrice
terdeciēns, terdeciēs *adv* thirteen times
terebinthus, -ī *f* turpentine tree
terebra, -ae *f* gimlet
terebrō, -āre *vt* to bore
terēdō, -inis *f* grub
Terentia, -iae *f Cicero's wife*

Terentius¹, -ī *m Roman family name* (*esp the
comic poet Terence*)
Terentius², -iānus *adj see* **Terentius¹**
teres, -etis *adj* rounded (*esp cylindrical*),
smooth, shapely; (*fig*) polished, elegant
Tēreus, -eī and -eos *m king of Thrace* (*husband of
Procne, father of Itys*)
tergeminus *adj* threefold, triple
tergeō, -gēre, -sī, -sum *vt* to wipe off, scour,
clean; to rub up, burnish
tergīnum, -ī *nt* rawhide
tergiversātiō, -ōnis *f* refusal, subterfuge
tergiversor, -ārī, -ātus *vi* to hedge, boggle,
be evasive
tergō *etc see* **tergeō**
tergum, -ī *nt* back; rear; (*land*) ridge; (*water*)
surface; (*meat*) chine; (*skin*) hide, leather,
anything made of leather; **terga vertere** take to
flight; **ā tergō** behind, in the rear
tergus, -oris *see* **tergum**
termes, -itis *m* branch
Terminālia, -ium *ntpl Festival of the god of
Boundaries*
terminātiō, -ōnis *f* decision; (*words*) clausula
terminō, -āre, -āvī, -ātum *vt* to set bounds
to, limit; to define, determine; to end
terminus, -ī *m* boundary line, limit, bound; god
of boundaries
ternī, -ōrum *adj* three each; three
terō, -ere, -trīvī, trītum *vt* to rub, crush,
grind; to smooth, sharpen; to wear away, use
up; (*road*) to frequent; (*time*) to waste; (*word*) to
make commonplace
Terpsichorē, -ēs *f Muse of dancing*
terra, -ae *f* dry land, earth, ground, soil;
land, country; **orbis terrārum** the world; **ubi
terrārum** where in the world
terrēnus *adj* of earth; terrestrial, land- (*in cpds*)
▶ *nt* land
terreō, -ēre, -uī, -itum *vt* to frighten, terrify;
to scare away; to deter
terrestris *adj* earthly, on earth, land- (*in cpds*)
terribilis *adj* terrifying, dreadful
terricula, -ōrum *ntpl* scare, bogy
terrificō, -āre *vt* to terrify
terrificus *adj* alarming, formidable
terrigena, -ae *m* earth-born
terriloquus *adj* alarming
territō, -āre *vt* to frighten, intimidate
territōrium, -ī and -iī *nt* territory
territus *adj* terrified
terror, -ōris *m* fright, alarm, terror; a terror
tersī *perf of* **tergeō**
tersus *ppp of* **tergeō** ▶ *adj* clean; neat, terse
tertiadecimānī, -ōrum *mpl* men of the
thirteenth legion
tertiānus *adj* recurring every second day ▶ *f*
a fever ▶ *mpl* men of the third legion
tertiō *adv* for the third time; thirdly
tertium *adv* for the third time
tertius *adj* third; **~ decimus (decumus)**
thirteenth

terūncius, -ī *and* **-iī** *m* quarter-as; a fourth; (*fig*) farthing

tesqua, tesca, -ōrum *ntpl* waste ground, desert

tessella, -ae *f* cube of mosaic stone

tessera, -ae *f* cube, dice; (*MIL*) password; token (*for mutual recognition of friends*); ticket (*for doles*)

tesserārius, -ī *and* **-iī** *m* officer of the watch

testa, -ae *f* brick, tile; (*earthenware*) pot, jug, sherd; (*fish*) shell, shellfish

testāmentārius *adj* testamentary ▶ *m* forger of wills

testāmentum, -ī *nt* will, testament

testātiō, -ōnis *f* calling to witness

testātus *ppa of* **testor** ▶ *adj* public

testiculus, -ī *m* testicle

testificātiō, -ōnis *f* giving evidence, evidence

testificor, -ārī, -ātus *vt* to give evidence, vouch for; to make public, bring to light; to call to witness

testimōnium, -ī *and* **-iī** *nt* evidence, testimony; proof

testis¹, -is *m/f* witness; eyewitness

testis², -is *m* testicle

testor, -ārī, -ātus *vt* to give evidence, testify; to prove, vouch for; to call to witness, appeal to ▶ *vi* to make a will

testū (*abl* **-ū**) *nt* earthenware lid, pot

testūdineus *adj* of tortoiseshell, tortoise- (*in cpds*)

testūdō, -inis *f* tortoise; tortoiseshell; lyre, lute; (*MIL*) shelter for besiegers, covering of shields; (*building*) vault

testum, -ī *nt* earthenware lid, pot

tēte *emphatic acc of* **tū**

tetendī *perf of* **tendō**

tēter *etc see* **taeter**

Tēthys, -os *f* sea goddess; the sea

tetigī *perf of* **tangō**

tetrachmum, tetradrachmum, -ī *nt* four drachmas

tetraō, -ōnis *m* blackcock, grouse *or* capercaillie

tetrarchēs, -ae *m* tetrarch, ruler

tetrarchia, -ae *f* tetrarchy

tetricus *adj* gloomy, sour

tetulī *archaic perf of* **ferō**

Teucer, -rī *m* son of Telamon of Salamis; son-in-law of Dardanus

Teucrī, -rōrum *mpl* Trojans

Teucria, -riae *f* Troy

Teutonī, -ōrum, Teutones, -um *mpl* Teutons (*a German people*)

Teutonicus *adj* Teutonic, German

tēxī *perf of* **tegō**

texō, -ere, -uī, -tum *vt* to weave; to plait; to build, make; (*fig*) to compose, contrive

textilis *adj* woven ▶ *nt* fabric

textor, -ōris *m* weaver

textrīnum, -ī *nt* weaving; shipyard

textūra, -ae *f* web, fabric

textus¹ *ppp of* **texō** ▶ *nt* web, fabric

textus², -ūs *m* texture

texuī *perf of* **texō**

Thāis, -idis *f* an Athenian courtesan

thalamus, -ī *m* room, bedroom; marriage bed; marriage

thalassicus *adj* sea-green

thalassinus *adj* sea-green

Thalēs, -is *and* **-ētis** *m* early Greek philosopher (*one of the seven wise men*)

Thalia, -ae *f* Muse of comedy

thallus, -ī *m* green bough

Thamyrās, -ae *m* blinded Thracian poet

Thapsitānus *adj see* **Thapsus**

Thapsus, Thapsos, -ī *f* town in N. Africa (*scene of Caesar's victory*)

Thasius *adj see* **Thasus**

Thasus, Thasos, -ī *f* Greek island in N. Aegean

Thaumantias, -dis *f* Iris

theātrālis *adj* of the theatre, in the theatre

theātrum, -ī *nt* theatre; audience; (*fig*) theatre, stage

Thēbae, -ārum *fpl* Thebes (*capital of Boeotia*); town in Upper Egypt

Thēbais, -aidis *f* Theban woman; epic poem by Statius

Thēbānus *adj* Theban

thēca, -ae *f* case, envelope

Themis, -dis *f* goddess of justice

Themistoclēs, -ī *and* **-is** *m* famous Athenian statesman

Themistoclēus *adj see* **Themistoclēs**

thēnsaurārius *adj* of treasure

thēnsaurus *see* **thēsaurus**

theologus, -ī *m* theologian

Theophrastus, -ī *m* Greek philosopher (*successor to Aristotle*)

Theopompēus, -īnus *adj see* **Theopompus**

Theopompus, -ī *m* Greek historian

thermae, -ārum *fpl* warm baths

Thermōdōn, -ontis *m* river of Pontus (*where the Amazons lived*)

Thermōdontēus, -ontiacus *adj* Amazonian

thermopōlium *nt* restaurant serving warm drinks

thermopōtō, -āre *vt* to refresh with warm drinks

Thermopylae, -ārum *fpl* famous Greek pass defended by Leonidas

thēsaurus, -ī *m* treasure, store; storehouse, treasury

Thēseus, -eī *and* **-eos** *m* Greek hero (*king of Athens*)

Thēsēus, -ēius *adj* of Theseus, Athenian

Thēsīdēs, -īdae *m* Hippolytus; (*pl*) Athenians

Thespiae, -ārum *fpl* Boeotian town near Helicon

Thespiēnsis, Thespias, -adis *adj* Thespian

Thespis, -is *m* traditional founder of Greek tragedy

Thessalia, -iae *f* Thessaly (*district of N. Greece*)

Thessalicus, Thessalus, Thessalis, -idis *adj* Thessalian

Thetis, -idis *and* **-idos** *f* sea nymph (*mother of Achilles*); the sea

thiasus, -ī m Bacchic dance
Thoantēus adj see **Thoās**
Thoās, -antis m king of Crimea (killed by Orestes), king of Lemnos (father of Hypsipyle)
tholus, -ī m rotunda
thōrāx, -ācis m breastplate
Thrāca, -ae, Thrācē, -ēs, Thrācia, -iae f Thrace
Thrācius, Thrēicius adj Thracian
Thrasea, -ae m Stoic philosopher under Nero
Thrasymachus, -ī m Greek sophist
Thrāx, -ācis m Thracian; kind of gladiator
Thrēssa, -ae, Thrēissa, -ae f Thracian woman
Thrēx, -ēcis m kind of gladiator
Thūcydidēs, -is m famous Greek historian
Thūcydidius adj Thucydidean
Thūlē, -ēs f island in the extreme N. (perhaps Shetland)
thunnus see **thynnus**
thūr, -is nt = tūs
Thūriī, -iōrum mpl town in S. Italy
Thūrīnus adj see **Thūriī**
thūs see **tūs**
thȳa, thȳia, -ae f citrus tree
Thybris, -is and **-idis** m (river) Tiber
Thyestēs, -ae m brother of Atreus (whose son's flesh he served up to him to eat)
Thyestēus adj see **Thyestēs**
Thyestiadēs, -iadae m Aegisthus
Thyias, Thyas, -adis f Bacchante
Thȳlē see **Thūlē**
thymbra, -ae f savory
thymum, -ī nt garden thyme
Thȳnia, -iae f Bithynia
thynnus, -ī m tuna
Thȳnus, Thȳniacus, Thȳnias adj Bithynian
Thyōneus, -eī m Bacchus
thyrsus, -ī m Bacchic wand
tiāra, -ae f, **tiārās, -ae** m turban
Tiberiānus adj see **Tiberius**
Tiberīnus¹, Tiberīnis adj see **Tiberis**
Tiberīnus², -īnī m Tiber
Tiberis, Tibris, -is m (river) Tiber
Tiberius, -ī m Roman praenomen (esp the second emperor)
tibi dat of **tū**
tībia, -ae f shinbone; pipe, flute
tībīcen, -inis m flute player; pillar
tībīcina, -ae f flute player
tībīcinium, -ī and **-iī** nt flute playing
Tibullus, -ī m Latin elegiac poet
Tībur, -is nt town on the river Anio (now Tivoli)
Tīburs, -tis, Tīburtīnus, Tīburnus adj Tiburtine
Tīcīnus, -ī m tributary of the river Po
Tigellīnus, -ī m favourite of Nero
tigillum, -ī nt small log, small beam
tignārius adj working in wood; **faber ~** carpenter
tignum, -ī nt timber, trunk, log
Tigrānēs, -is m king of Armenia

tigris, -is and **-idis** f tiger
tīlia, -ae f lime tree
Tīmaeus, -ī m Sicilian historian; Pythagorean philosopher; a dialogue of Plato
timefactus adj frightened
timeō, -ēre, -uī vt, vi to fear, be afraid
timidē adv timidly
timiditās, -ātis f timidity, cowardice
timidus adj timid, cowardly
timor, -ōris m fear, alarm; a terror
tinctilis adj dipped in
tinctus ppp of **tingō**
tinea, -ae f moth, bookworm
tingō, -gere, -xī, -ctum vt to dip, soak; to dye, colour; (fig) to imbue
tinnīmentum, -ī nt ringing noise
tinniō, -īre vt, vi to ring, tinkle
tinnītus, -ūs m ringing, jingle
tinnulus adj ringing, jingling
tintinnābulum, -ī nt bell
tintinō, -āre vi to ring
tīnus, -ī m a shrub, laurustinus
tinxī perf of **tingō**
Tīphys, -os m helmsman of the Argo
tippula, -ae f water spider
Tīresiās, -ae m blind soothsayer of Thebes
Tīridātēs, -ae m king of Armenia
tīrō, -ōnis m recruit, beginner
Tīrō, -ōnis m Cicero's freedman secretary
tīrōcinium, -ī and **-iī** nt first campaign; recruits; (fig) first attempt, inexperience
Tīrōniānus adj see **Tīrō**
tīrunculus, -ī m young beginner
Tīryns, -this f ancient town in S.E. Greece (home of Hercules)
Tīrynthius adj of Tiryns, of Hercules ▶ m Hercules
tis archaic gen of **tū**
Tīsiphonē, -ēs f a Fury
Tīsiphonēus adj guilty
Tītān, -ānis, Tītānus, -ānī m Titan (an ancient race of gods); the sun
Tītānius, Tītāniacus, Tītānis adj see **Tītān**
Tīthōnius adj see **Tīthōnus**
Tīthōnus, -ī m consort of Aurora (granted immortality without youth)
tītillātiō, -ōnis f tickling
tītillō, -āre vt to tickle
titubanter adv falteringly
titubātiō, -ōnis f staggering
titubō, -āre vi to stagger, totter; to stammer; to waver, falter
titulus, -ī m inscription, label, notice; title of honour; fame; pretext
Tityos, -ī m giant punished in Tartarus
Tmōlus, -ī m mountain in Lydia
toculiō, -ōnis m usurer
tōfus, -ī m tufa
toga, -ae f toga (dress of the Roman citizen); (fig) peace; **~ candida** dress of election candidates; **~ picta** ceremonial dress of a victor in triumph; **~ praetexta** purple-edged toga of magistrates and children; **~ pūra, ~ virīlis** plain toga of manhood

togātus adj wearing the toga ▶ m Roman citizen; client ▶ f drama on a Roman theme

togula, -ae f small toga

tolerābilis adj bearable, tolerable; patient

tolerābiliter adv patiently

tolerāns, -antis pres p of tolerō ▶ adj patient

toleranter adv patiently

tolerantia, -ae f endurance

tolerātiō, -ōnis f enduring

tolerātus adj tolerable

tolerō, -āre, -āvī, -ātum vt to bear, endure; to support, sustain

tollēnō, -ōnis m crane, derrick, lift

tollō, -ere, sustulī, sublātum vt to lift, raise; to take away, remove; to do away with, abolish, destroy; (anchor) to weigh; (child) to acknowledge, bring up; (mind) to elevate, excite, cheer; (passenger) to take on board; **signa tollere** decamp

Tolōsa, -ae f Toulouse

Tolōsānus adj see **Tolōsa**

tolūtim adv at a trot

tomāculum, -ī nt sausage

tōmentum, -ī nt stuffing, padding

Tomis, -is f town on the Black Sea (to which Ovid was exiled)

Tomītānus adj see **Tomis**

Tonāns, -antis m Thunderer (epithet of Jupiter)

tondeō, -ēre, totondī, tōnsum vt to shear, clip, shave; to crop, reap, mow; to graze, browse on; (fig) to fleece, rob

tonitrālis adj thunderous

tonitrus, -ūs m, **tonitrua, -uōrum** ntpl thunder

tonō, -āre, -uī vi to thunder ▶ vt to thunder out

tōnsa, -ae f oar

tōnsillae, -ārum fpl tonsils

tōnsor, -ōris m barber

tōnsōrius adj for shaving

tōnstrīcula, -ae f barber girl

tōnstrīna, -ae f barber's shop

tōnstrīx, -īcis f woman barber

tōnsūra, -ae f shearing, clipping

tōnsus¹ ppp of **tondeō**

tōnsus², -ūs m coiffure

tōphus see **tōfus**

topiārius adj of ornamental gardening ▶ m topiarist ▶ f topiary

topicē, -ēs f the art of finding topics

toral, -ālis nt valance

torcular, -āris, torcularium, -ī nt press

toreuma, -tis nt embossed work, relief

tormentum, -ī nt windlass, torsion catapult, artillery; shot; rack, torture; (fig) torment, anguish

tormina, -um ntpl colic

torminōsus adj subject to colic

tornō, -āre, -āvī, -ātum vt to turn (in a lathe), round off

tornus, -ī m lathe

torōsus adj muscular

torpēdō, -inis f numbness, lethargy; (fish) electric ray

torpeō, -ēre vi to be stiff, be numb; to be stupefied

torpēscō, -ēscere, -uī vi to grow stiff, numb, listless

torpidus adj benumbed

torpor, -ōris m numbness, torpor, listlessness

torquātus adj wearing a neckchain

Torquātus, -ī m surname of Manlius

torqueō, -quēre, -sī, -tum vt to turn, twist, bend, wind; (missile) to whirl, hurl, brandish; (body) to rack, torture; (mind) to torment

torquēs, torquis, -is m/f neckchain, necklace, collar

torrēns, -entis pres p of torreō ▶ adj scorching, hot; rushing, rapid ▶ m torment

torreō, -ēre, -uī, tostum vt to parch, scorch, roast

torrēscō, -ere vi to become parched

torridus adj parched, dried up; frostbitten

torris, -is m brand, firebrand

torsī perf of **torqueō**

tortē adv awry

tortilis adj twisted, winding

tortor¹, -ārī vi to writhe

tortor², -ōris m torturer, executioner

tortuōsus adj winding; (fig) complicated

tortus¹ ppp of torqueō ▶ adj crooked; complicated

tortus², -ūs m twisting, writhing

torulus, -ī m tuft (of hair)

torus, -ī m knot, bulge; muscle, brawn; couch, bed; (earth) bank, mound; (language) ornament

torvitās, -ātis f wildness, grimness

torvus adj wild, grim, fierce

tostus ppp of **torreō**

tot adj (indecl) so many, as many

totidem adj (indecl) just as many, the same number of

totiēns, totiēs adv so often, as often

totondī perf of **tondeō**

tōtus (gen -īus, dat -ī) adj entire, the whole, all; entirely, completely taken up with; **ex tōtō** totally; **in tōtō** on the whole

toxicum, -ī nt poison

trabālis adj for beams; **clāvus ~** large nail

trabea, -ae f ceremonial robe

trabeātus adj wearing a ceremonial robe

trabs, -abis f beam, timber; tree; ship; roof

Trāchīn, -īnis f town in Thessaly (where Hercules cremated himself)

Trāchīnius adj see **Trāchīn**

tractābilis adj manageable, tractable

tractātiō, -ōnis f handling, treatment

tractātus, -ūs m handling

tractim adv slowly, little by little

tractō, -āre, -āvī, -ātum vt to maul; to handle, deal with, manage; (activity) to conduct, perform; (person) to treat; (subject) to discuss; consider

tractus¹ ppp of trahō ▶ adj fluent

tractus², **-ūs** m dragging, pulling, drawing; train, track; (*place*) extent, region, district; (*movement*) course; (*time*) lapse; (*word*) drawling

trādidī *perf of* **trādō**

trāditiō, **-ōnis** f surrender; handing down

trāditor, **-ōris** m traitor

trāditus *ppp of* **trādō**

trādō, **-ere**, **-idī**, **-itum** vt to hand over, deliver, surrender; to commit, entrust; to betray; to bequeath, hand down; (*narrative*) to relate, record; (*teaching*) to propound; **sē trādere** surrender, devote oneself

trādūcō, **trānsdūcō**, **-ūcere**, **-ūxī**, **-uctum** vt to bring across, lead over, transport across; to transfer; to parade, make an exhibition of (*in public*); (*time*) to pass, spend

trāductiō, **-ōnis** f transference; (*time*) passage; (*word*) metonymy

trāductor, **-ōris** m transferrer

trāductus *ppp of* **trādūcō**

trādux, **-ucis** m vine layer

tragicē *adv* dramatically

tragicocōmoedia, **-ae** f tragicomedy

tragicus *adj* of tragedy, tragic; in the tragic manner, lofty; terrible, tragic ▶ m writer of tragedy

tragoedia, **-ae** f tragedy; (*fig*) bombast

tragoedus, **-ī** m tragic actor

trāgula, **-ae** f kind of javelin

trahea, **-ae** f sledge

trahō, **-here**, **-xī**, **-ctum** vt to draw, drag, pull, take with one; to pull out, lengthen; to draw together, contract; to carry off, plunder; (*liquid*) to drink, draw; (*money*) to squander; (*wool*) to spin; (*fig*) to attract; (*appearance*) to take on; (*consequence*) to derive, get; (*praise, blame*) to ascribe, refer; (*thought*) to ponder; (*time*) to spin out

trāiciō, **-icere**, **-iēcī**, **-iectum** vt to throw across, shoot across; (*troops*) to get across, transport; (*with weapon*) to pierce, stab; (*river, etc*) to cross; (*fig*) to transfer ▶ vi to cross

trāiectiō, **-ōnis** f crossing, passage; (*fig*) transferring; (*RHET*) exaggeration; (*words*) transposition

trāiectus¹ *ppp of* **trāiciō**

trāiectus², **-ūs** m crossing, passage

trālāt- *etc see* **trānslāt-**

Trallēs, **-ium** fpl town in Lydia

Tralliānus *adj see* **Trallēs**

trālūceō *etc see* **trānslūceō**

trāma, **-ae** f woof, web

trāmes, **-itis** m footpath, path

trāmittō *etc see* **trānsmittō**

trānatō *etc see* **trānsnatō**

trānō, **-āre**, **-āvī**, **-ātum** vt, vi to swim across; (*air*) to fly through

tranquillē *adv* quietly

tranquillitās, **-ātis** f quietness, calm; (*fig*) peace, quiet

tranquillō, **-āre** vt to calm

tranquillus *adj* quiet, calm ▶ nt calm sea

trāns *prep* (*with acc*) across, over, beyond

trānsabeō, **-īre**, **-iī** vt to pierce

trānsāctor, **-ōris** m manager

trānsāctus *ppp of* **trānsigō**

trānsadigō, **-ere** vt to drive through, pierce

Trānsalpīnus *adj* Transalpine

trānscendō, **trānsscendō**, **-endere**, **-endī**, **-ēnsum** vt, vi to pass over, surmount; to overstep, surpass, transgress

trānscrībō, **trānsscrībō**, **-bere**, **-psī**, **-ptum** vt to copy out; (*fig*) to make over, transfer

trānscurrō, **-rere**, **-rī**, **-sum** vt, vi to run across, run past, traverse

trānscursus, **-ūs** m running through; (*speech*) cursory remark

trānsd- *etc see* **trād-**

trānsēgī *perf of* **trānsigō**

trānsenna, **-ae** f net, snare; trellis, latticework

trānseō, **-īre**, **-iī**, **-itum** vt, vi to pass over, cross over; to pass along or through; to pass by; to outstrip, surpass, overstep; (*change*) to turn into; (*speech*) to mention briefly, leave out, pass on; (*time*) to pass, pass away

trānsferō, **-ferre**, **-tulī**, **-lātum** vt to bring across, transport, transfer; (*change*) to transform; (*language*) to translate; (*RHET*) to use figuratively; (*time*) to postpone; (*writing*) to copy

trānsfīgō, **-gere**, **-xī**, **-xum** vt to pierce; to thrust through

trānsfīxus *ppp of* **trānsfīgō**

trānsfodiō, **-odere**, **-ōdī**, **-ossum** vt to run through, stab

trānsfōrmis *adj* changed in shape

trānsfōrmō, **-āre** vt to change in shape

trānsfossus *ppp of* **trānsfodiō**

trānsfuga, **-ae** m/f deserter

trānsfugiō, **-ugere**, **-ūgī** vi to desert, come over

trānsfugium, **-ī** and **-iī** nt desertion

trānsfundō, **-undere**, **-ūdī**, **-ūsum** vt to decant, transfuse

trānsfūsiō, **-ōnis** f transmigration

trānsfūsus *ppp of* **trānsfundō**

trānsgredior, **-dī**, **-ssus** vt, vi to step across, cross over, cross; to pass on; to exceed

trānsgressiō, **-ōnis** f passage; (*words*) transposition

trānsgressus¹ *ppa of* **trānsgredior**

trānsgressus², **-ūs** m crossing

trānsiciō *etc see* **trāiciō**

trānsigō, **-igere**, **-ēgī**, **-āctum** vt to carry through, complete, finish; (*difference*) to settle; (*time*) to pass, spend; (*with cum*) to put an end to; (*with weapon*) to stab

trānsiī *perf of* **trānseō**

trānsiliō, **trānssiliō**, **-īre**, **-uī** vi to jump across ▶ vt to leap over; (*fig*) to skip, disregard; to exceed

trānsitiō, **-ōnis** f passage; desertion; (*disease*) infection

trānsitō, -āre vi to pass through

trānsitus ppp of **trānseō**

trānsitus², -**ūs** m passing over, passage; desertion; passing by; transition

trānslātīcius, trālātīcius adj traditional, customary, common

trānslātiō, trālātiō, -ōnis f transporting, transferring; (language) metaphor

trānslātīvus adj transferable

trānslātor, -ōris m transferrer

trānslātus ppp of **trānsferō**

trānslegō, -ere vt to read through

trānslūceō, -ēre vi to be reflected; to shine through

trānsmarīnus adj overseas

trānsmeō, -āre vi to cross

trānsmigrō, -āre vi to emigrate

trānsmissiō, -ōnis f crossing

trānsmissus¹ ppp of **trānsmittō**

trānsmissus², -**ūs** m crossing

trānsmittō, -ittere, -īsī, -issum vt to send across, put across; to let pass through; to transfer, entrust, devote; to give up, pass over; (place) to cross over, go through, pass ▶ vi to cross

trānsmontānī adj beyond the mountains

trānsmoveō, -ovēre, -ōvī, -ōtum vt to move, transfer

trānsmūtō, -āre vt to shift

trānsnatō, trānatō, -āre vi to swim across ▶ vt to swim

trānsnō etc see **trānō**

Trānspadānus adj north of the Po

trānspectus, -ūs m view

trānspiciō, -ere vt to look through

trānspōnō, -ōnere, -osuī, -ositum vt to transfer

trānsportō, -āre vt to carry across, transport, remove

trānspositus ppp of **trānspōnō**

Trānsrhēnānus adj east of the Rhine

trānss- etc see **trāns-**

Trānstiberīnus adj across the Tiber

trānstineō, -ēre vi to get through

trānstrum, -ī nt thwart

trānstulī perf of **trānsferō**

trānsultō, -āre vi to jump across

trānsūtus adj pierced

trānsvectiō, -ōnis f crossing

trānsvectus ppp of **trānsvehō**

trānsvehō, -here, -xī, -ctum vt to carry across, transport

trānsvehor, -hī, -ctus vi to cross, pass over; (parade) to ride past; (time) to elapse

trānsverberō, -āre vt to pierce through, wound

trānsversus, trāversus adj lying across, crosswise, transverse; **digitum trānsversum** a finger's breadth; **dē trānsversō** unexpectedly; **ex trānsversō** sideways

trānsvolitō, -āre vt to fly through

trānsvolō, -āre vt, vi to fly across, fly through; to move rapidly across; to fly past, disregard

trānsvorsus etc see **trānsversus**

trapētus, -ī m olive mill, oil mill

trapezīta etc see **tarpezīta**

Trapezūs, -ūntis f Black Sea town (now Trabzon)

Trasumennus, Trasimēnus, -ī m lake in Etruria (where Hannibal defeated the Romans)

trāv- see **trānsv-**

trāvectiō etc see **trānsvectiō**

traxī perf of **trahō**

trecēnī, -ōrum adj three hundred each

trecentēsimus adj three-hundredth

trecentī, -ōrum num three hundred

trecentiēns, trecentiēs adv three hundred times

trechedīpna, -ōrum ntpl dinner shoes (of parasites)

tredecim num thirteen

tremebundus adj trembling

tremefaciō, -facere, -fēcī, -factum vt to shake

tremendus adj formidable, terrible

tremēscō, tremīscō, -ere vi to begin to shake ▶ vt to be afraid of

tremō, -ere, -uī vi to tremble, quake, quiver ▶ vt to tremble at, dread

tremor, -ōris m shaking, quiver, tremor; earthquake

tremulus adj trembling, shivering

trepidanter adv with agitation

trepidātiō, -ōnis f agitation, alarm, consternation

trepidē adv hastily, in confusion

trepidō, -āre, -āvī, -ātum vi to be agitated, bustle about, hurry; to be alarmed; to flicker, quiver ▶ vt to start at

trepidus adj restless, anxious, alarmed; alarming, perilous

trēs, trium num three

trēssis, -is m three asses

trēsvirī, triumvirōrum mpl three commissioners, triumvirs

Trēverī, -ōrum mpl people of E. Gaul (about what is now Trier)

Trēvericus adj see **Trēverī**

triangulum, -ī nt triangle

triangulus adj triangular

triāriī, -ōrum mpl the third line (in Roman battle order), the reserves

tribuārius adj of the tribes

tribūlis, -is m fellow tribesman

trībulum, -ī nt threshing sledge

tribulus, -ī m star thistle

tribūnal, -ālis nt platform; judgment seat; camp platform, cenotaph

tribūnātus, -ūs m tribuneship, rank of tribune

tribūnicius adj of a tribune ▶ m ex-tribune

tribūnus, -ī m tribune; ~ **plēbis** tribune of the people, a magistrate who defended the rights of the plebeians; ~ **mīlitum** or **mīlitāris** military tribune, an officer under the legatus; **tribūnī aerāriī** paymasters

tribuō, -uere, -uī, -ūtum vt to assign, allot; to give, bestow, pay; to concede, allow; to ascribe, attribute; (subject) to divide; (time) to devote

tribus, -ūs m tribe

tribūtārius adj: **tribūtāriae tabellae** letters of credit

tribūtim adv by tribes

tribūtiō, -ōnis f distribution

tribūtum, -ī nt contribution, tribute, tax

tribūtus¹ ppp of **tribuō**

tribūtus² adj arranged by tribes

trīcae, -ārum fpl nonsense; tricks, vexations

trīcēnī, -ōrum adj thirty each, in thirties

triceps, -ipitis adj three-headed

trīcēsimus adj thirtieth

trichila, -ae f arbour, summerhouse

trīciēns, trīciēs adv thirty times

trīclīnium, -ī and **-iī** nt dining couch; dining room

trīcō, -ōnis m mischief-maker

trīcor, -ārī vi to make mischief, play tricks

tricorpor, -is adj three-bodied

tricuspis, -idis adj three-pointed

trīdēns, -entis adj three-pronged ▶ m trident

tridentifer, -ī adj trident-wielding

tridentiger, -ī adj trident-wielding

trīduum, -ī nt three days

triennia, -ium ntpl a triennial festival

triennium, -ī and **-iī** nt three years

triēns, -entis m a third; (coin) a third of an as; (measure) a third of a pint

trientābulum, -ī nt land given by the State as a third of a debt

trientius adj sold for a third

triērarchus, -ī m captain of a trireme

triēris, -is f trireme

trietēricus adj triennial ▶ ntpl festival of Bacchus

trietēris, -idis f three years; a triennial festival

trifāriam adv in three parts, in three places

trifaux, -aucis adj three-throated

trifidus adj three-forked

trifōrmis adj triple

trifūr, -ūris m archthief

trifurcifer, -ī m hardened criminal

trigeminus adj threefold, triple ▶ mpl triplets

trīgintā num thirty

trigōn, -ōnis m a ball game

trilībris adj three-pound

trilinguis adj three-tongued

trilīx, -īcis adj three-ply, three-stranded

trīmēstris adj of three months

trimetrus, -ī m trimeter

trīmus adj three years old

Trīnacria, -iae f Sicily

Trīnacrius, Trīnacris, -idis adj Sicilian

trīnī, -ōrum adj three each, in threes; triple

Trinobantēs, -um mpl British tribe in East Anglia

trinōdis adj three-knotted

triōbolus, -ī m half-a-drachma

Triōnēs, -um mpl the Plough; the Little Bear

tripartītō adv in or into three parts

tripartītus, tripertītus adj divided into three parts

tripectorus adj three-bodied

tripedālis adj three-foot

tripert- etc see **tripart-**

tripēs, -edis adj three-legged

triplex, -icis adj triple, threefold ▶ nt three times as much ▶ mpl three-leaved writing tablet

triplus adj triple

Triptolemus, -ī m inventor of agriculture, judge in Hades

tripudiō, -āre vi to dance

tripudium, -ī and **-iī** nt ceremonial dance, dance; a favourable omen (when the sacred chickens ate greedily)

tripūs, -odis f tripod; the Delphic oracle

triquetrus adj triangular; Sicilian

trirēmis adj with three banks of oars ▶ f trireme

trīs etc see **trēs**

triscurria, -ōrum ntpl sheer fooling

trīstē adv sadly; severely

tristiculus adj rather sad

tristificus adj ominous

tristimōnia, -ae f sadness

tristis adj sad, glum, melancholy; gloomy, sombre, dismal; (taste) bitter; (smell) offensive; (temper) severe, sullen, ill-humoured

tristitia, -ae f sadness, sorrow, melancholy; moroseness, severity

tristitiēs, -ēī f sorrow

trisulcus adj three-forked

tritavus, -ī m great-great-great-grandfather

trītīceus adj of wheat, wheaten

trīticum, -ī nt wheat

Trītōn, -ōnis m sea god (son of Neptune); African lake (where Minerva was born)

Trītōnius, -ōniacus, -ōnis adj of Lake Triton, of Minerva ▶ f Minerva

trītūra, -ae f threshing

trītus¹ ppp of **terō** ▶ adj well-worn; (judgment) expert; (language) commonplace, trite

trītus², -ūs m rubbing, friction

triumphālis adj triumphal ▶ ntpl insignia of a triumph

triumphō, -āre, -āvī, -ātum vi to celebrate a triumph; to triumph, exult ▶ vt to triumph over, win by conquest

triumphus, -ī m triumphal procession, victory parade; triumph, victory

triumvir, -ī m commissioner, triumvir; mayor (of a provincial town)

triumvirālis adj triumviral

triumvirātus, -ūs m office of triumvir, triumvirate

triumvirī, -ōrum mpl three commissioners, triumvirs

trivenēfica, -ae f old witch

trīvī perf of **terō**

Trivia, -ae f Diana

triviālis adj common, popular

trivium, -ī and **-iī** nt crossroads; public street

trivius *adj* of the crossroads

Trōas, -adis *f the district of Troy*, Troad; Trojan woman ▶ *adj* Trojan

trochaeus, -ī *m* trochee; tribrach

trochlea, -ae *f* block and tackle

trochus, -ī *m* hoop

Trōglodytae, -ārum *mpl cave dwellers of Ethiopia*

Trōia, -ae *f* Troy

Trōilus, -ī *m son of Priam*

Trōiugena, -ae *m/f* Trojan; Roman

Trōius, Trōiānus, Trōicus *adj* Trojan

tropaeum, -ī *nt* victory memorial, trophy; victory; memorial, token

Trōs, -ōis *m king of Phrygia*; Trojan

trucīdātiō, -ōnis *f* butchery

trucīdō, -āre, -āvī, -ātum *vt* to slaughter, massacre

truculentē *adv see* **truculentus**

truculentia, -ae *f* ferocity, inclemency

truculentus *adj* ferocious, grim, wild

trudis, -is *f* pike

trūdō, -dere, -sī, -sum *vt* to push, thrust, drive; (*buds*) to put forth

trulla, -ae *f* ladle, scoop; washbasin

truncō, -āre, -āvī, -ātum *vt* to lop off, maim, mutilate

truncus, -ī *m* (*tree*) trunk, bole; (*human*) trunk, body; (*abuse*) blockhead ▶ *adj* maimed, broken, stripped (of); defective

trūsī *perf of* **trūdō**

trūsitō, -āre *vt* to keep pushing

trūsus *ppp of* **trūdō**

trutina, -ae *f* balance, scales

trux, -ucis *adj* savage, grim, wild

trygōnus, -ī *m* stingray

tū *pron* you, thou

tuātim *adv* in your usual fashion

tuba, -ae *f* trumpet, war trumpet

tuber, -is *f* kind of apple tree

tūber, -is *nt* swelling, lump; (*food*) truffle

tubicen, -inis *m* trumpeter

tubilūstria, -ōrum *ntpl* festival of trumpets

tuburcinor, -ārī *vi* to gobble up, guzzle

tubus, -ī *m* pipe

tuditō, -āre *vt* to strike repeatedly

tueor, -ērī, -itus *and* **-tūtus** *vt* to see, watch, look; to guard, protect, keep

tugurium, -ī *and* **-iī** *nt* hut, cottage

tuitiō, -ōnis *f* defence

tuitus *ppa of* **tueor**

tulī *perf of* **ferō**

Tulliānum, -ī *nt* State dungeon of Rome

Tulliānus *adj see* **Tullius**

Tulliola, -ae *f* little Tullia (*Cicero's daughter*)

Tullius, -ī *and* **-iī** *m* Roman family name (*esp the sixth king*), the orator Cicero

Tullus, -ī *m* third king of Rome

tum *adv* (*time*) then, at that time; (*sequence*) then, next ▶ *conj* moreover, besides; **tum ... tum** at one time ... at another; **tum ... cum** at the time when, whenever; **cum ... tum** not only ... but; **tum dēmum** only then; **tum ipsum** even then; **tum māximē** just then; **tum vērō** then more than ever

tumefaciō, -facere, -fēcī, -factum *vt* to make swell; (*fig*) to puff up

tumeō, -ēre *vi* to swell, be swollen; (*emotion*) to be excited; (*pride*) to be puffed up; (*language*) to be turgid

tumēscō, -ēscere, -uī *vi* to begin to swell, swell up

tumidus *adj* swollen, swelling; (*emotion*) excited, enraged; (*pride*) puffed up; (*language*) bombastic

tumor, -ōris *m* swelling, bulge; hillock; (*fig*) commotion, excitement

tumulō, -āre *vt* to bury

tumulōsus *adj* hilly

tumultuārius *adj* hasty; (*troops*) emergency

tumultuātiō, -ōnis *f* commotion

tumultuō, -āre, tumultuor, -ārī *vi* to make a commotion, be in an uproar

tumultuōsē *adv see* **tumultuōsus**

tumultuōsus *adj* uproarious, excited, turbulent

tumultus, -ūs *m* commotion, uproar, disturbance; (*MIL*) rising, revolt, civil war; (*weather*) storm; (*mind*) disorder

tumulus, -ī *m* mound, hill; burial mound, barrow

tunc *adv* (*time*) then, at that time; (*sequence*) then, next; **~ dēmum** only then; **~ quoque** then too; even so

tundō, -ere, tutudī, tūnsum *and* **tūsum** *vt* to beat, thump, hammer; (*grain*) to pound; (*speech*) to din, importune

Tūnēs, -ētis *m* Tunis

tunica, -ae *f* tunic; (*fig*) skin, husk

tunicātus *adj* wearing a tunic

tunicula, -ae *f* little tunic

tūnsus *ppp of* **tundō**

tuor *etc see* **tueor**

turba, -ae *f* disorder, riot, disturbance; brawl, quarrel; crowd, mob, troop, number

turbāmenta, -ōrum *ntpl* propaganda

turbātē *adv* in confusion

turbātiō, -ōnis *f* confusion

turbātor, -ōris *m* agitator

turbātus *ppp of* **turbō** ▶ *adj* troubled, disorderly

turbellae, -ārum *fpl* stir, row

turben *etc see* **turbō**[2]

turbidē *adv* in disorder

turbidus *adj* confused, wild, boisterous; (*water*) troubled, muddy; (*fig*) disorderly, troubled, alarmed, dangerous

turbineus *adj* conical

turbō[1]**, -āre, -āvī, -ātum** *vt* to disturb, throw into confusion; (*water*) to trouble, make muddy

turbō[2]**, -inis** *m* whirl, spiral, rotation; reel, whorl, spindle; (*toy*) top; (*wind*) tornado, whirlwind; (*fig*) storm

turbulentē, turbulenter *adv* wildly

turbulentus *adj* agitated, confused,
boisterous, stormy; troublemaking, seditious
turdus, -ī *m* thrush
tūreus *adj* of incense
turgeō, -gēre, -sī *vi* to swell, be swollen;
(*speech*) to be bombastic
turgēscō, -ere *vi* to swell up, begin to swell;
(*fig*) to become enraged
turgidulus *adj* poor swollen
turgidus *adj* swollen, distended; bombastic
tūribulum, -ī *nt* censer
tūricremus *adj* incense-burning
tūrifer, -ī *adj* incense-producing
tūrilegus *adj* incense-gathering
turma, -ae *f* troop, squadron (*of cavalry*); crowd
turmālis *adj* of a troop; equestrian
turmātim *adv* troop by troop
Turnus, -ī *m* Rutulian king (*chief opponent of
Aeneas*)
turpiculus *adj* ugly little; slightly indecent
turpificātus *adj* debased
turpilucricupidus *adj* fond of filthy lucre
turpis *adj* ugly, deformed, unsightly; base,
disgraceful ▸ *nt* disgrace
turpiter *adv* repulsively; shamefully
turpitūdō, -inis *f* deformity; disgrace, infamy
turpō, -āre *vt* to disfigure, soil
turriger, -ī *adj* turreted
turris, -is *f* tower, turret; siege tower; (*elephant*)
howdah; (*fig*) mansion
turrītus *adj* turreted; castellated; towering
tursī *perf of* **turgeō**
turtur, -is *m* turtledove
tūs, tūris *nt* incense, frankincense
Tusculānēnsis *adj* at Tusculum
Tusculānum, -ānī *nt* villa at Tusculum (*esp
Cicero's*)
Tusculānus *adj* Tusculan
Tusculum, -ī *nt* Latin town near Rome
tūsculum, -ī *nt* a little incense
Tusculus *adj* Tusculan
Tuscus *adj* Etruscan
tussiō, -īre *vi* to cough, have a cough
tussis, -is *f* cough
tūsus *ppp of* **tundō**
tūtāmen, -inis *nt* defence
tūtāmentum, -ī *nt* protection
tūte *emphatic form of* **tū**
tūtē *adv* safely, in safety
tūtēla, -ae *f* keeping, charge, protection;
(*of minors*) guardianship, wardship; (*person*)
watcher, guardian; ward, charge
tūtemet *emphatic form of* **tū**
tūtor¹, -ārī, -ātus, tūtō, -āre *vt* to watch,
guard, protect; to guard against
tūtor², -ōris *m* protector; (*LAW*) guardian
tutudī *perf of* **tundō**
tūtus *ppp of* **tueor** ▸ *adj* safe, secure; cautious
▸ *nt* safety
tuus *adj* your, yours, thy, thine; your own, your
proper; of you
Tȳdeus, -eī *and* **-eos** *m* father of Diomedes

Tȳdīdēs, -īdae *m* Diomedes
tympanotrība, -ae *m* timbrel player
tympanum, typanum, -ī *nt* drum, timbrel
(*esp of the priests of Cybele*); (*mechanism*) wheel
Tyndareus, -eī *m* king of Sparta (*husband of
Leda*)
Tyndaridae, -idārum *mpl* Castor and Pollux
Tyndaris, -idis *f* Helen; Clytemnestra
Typhōeus, -eos *m* giant under Etna
Typhōius, -is *adj see* **Typhōeus**
typus, -ī *m* figure
tyrannicē *adv see* **tyrannicus**
tyrannicīda, -ae *m* tyrannicide
tyrannicus *adj* tyrannical
tyrannis, -idis *f* despotism, tyranny
tyrannoctonus, -ī *m* tyrannicide
tyrannus, -ī *m* ruler, king; despot, tyrant
Tyrās, -ae *m* (river) Dniester
Tyrius *adj* Tyrian, Phoenician, Carthaginian;
purple
tȳrotarīchos, -ī *m* dish of salt fish and cheese
Tyrrhēnia, -iae *f* Etruria
Tyrrhēnus *adj* Etruscan, Tyrrhenian
Tyrtaeus, -ī *m* Spartan war poet
Tyrus, Tyros, -ī *f* Tyre (*famous Phoenician
seaport*)

ūber¹, -is *nt* breast, teat; (*fig*) richness

ūber², -is *adj* fertile, plentiful, rich (in); (*language*) full, copious

ūberius (*superl* **-rime**) *compar* more fully, more copiously

ūbertās, -ātis *f* richness, plenty, fertility

ūbertim *adv* copiously

ubī *adv* (*interrog*) where; (*rel*) where, in which, with whom; when

ubīcumque *adv* wherever; everywhere

Ubiī, -ōrum *mpl* German tribe on the lower Rhine

ubīnam *adv* where (in fact)?

ubīquāque *adv* everywhere

ubīque *adv* everywhere, anywhere

ubiubī *adv* wherever

ubīvīs *adv* anywhere

ūdus *adj* wet, damp

ulcerō, -āre *vt* to make sore, wound

ulcerōsus *adj* full of sores; wounded

ulcīscor, -ī, ultus *vt* to take vengeance on, punish; to take vengeance for, avenge

ulcus, -eris *nt* sore, ulcer; **~ tangere** touch on a delicate subject

ūlīgō, -inis *f* moisture, marshiness

Ulixēs, -is *m* Ulysses, Odysseus (*king of Ithaca, hero of Homer's Odyssey*)

ullus (*gen* **-īus**, *dat* **-ī**) *adj* any

ulmeus *adj* of elm

ulmus, -ī *f* elm; (*pl*) elm rods

ulna, -ae *f* elbow; arm; (*measure*) ell

ulterior, -ōris *compar* farther, beyond, more remote

ulterius *compar of* **ultrā**

ultimus *superl* farthest, most remote, the end of; (*time*) earliest, latest, last; (*degree*) extreme, greatest, lowest ▸ *ntpl* the end; **ultimum** for the last time; **ad ultimum** finally

ultiō, -ōnis *f* vengeance, revenge

ultor, -ōris *m* avenger, punisher

ultrā *adv* beyond, farther, besides ▸ *prep* (*with acc*) beyond, on the far side of; (*time*) past; (*degree*) over and above

ultrīx, -īcis *adj* avenging

ultrō *adv* on the other side, away; besides; of one's own accord, unasked, voluntarily

ultrō tribūta *ntpl* State expenditure for public works

ultus *ppa of* **ulcīscor**

ulula, -ae *f* screech owl

ululātus, -ūs *m* wailing, shrieking, yells, whoops

ululō, -āre, -āvī, -ātum *vi* to shriek, yell, howl ▸ *vt* to cry out to

ulva, -ae *f* sedge

umbella, -ae *f* parasol

Umber, -rī *adj* Umbrian ▸ *m* Umbrian dog

umbilīcus, -ī *m* navel; (*fig*) centre; (*book*) roller end; (*sea*) cockle *or* pebble

umbō, -ōnis *m* boss (*of a shield*); elbow

umbra, -ae *f* shadow, shade; (*dead*) ghost; (*diner*) uninvited guest; (*fish*) grayling; (*painting*) shade; (*place*) shelter, school, study; (*unreality*) semblance, mere shadow

umbrāculum, -ī *nt* arbour; school; parasol

umbrāticola, -ae *m* lounger

umbrāticus *adj* fond of idling; in retirement

umbrātilis *adj* in retirement, private, academic

Umbria, -riae *f* Umbria (*district of central Italy*)

umbrifer, -ī *adj* shady

umbrō, -āre *vt* to shade

umbrōsus *adj* shady

ūmectō, -āre *vt* to wet, water

ūmectus *adj* damp, wet

ūmeō, -ēre *vi* to be damp, be wet

umerus, -ī *m* upper arm, shoulder

ūmēscō, -ere *vi* to become damp, get wet

ūmidē *adv* with damp

ūmidulus *adj* dampish

ūmidus *adj* wet, damp, dank, moist

ūmor, -ōris *m* liquid, fluid, moisture

umquam, unquam *adv* ever, at any time

ūnā *adv* together

ūnanimāns, -antis *adj* in full agreement

ūnanimitās, -ātis *f* concord

ūnanimus *adj* of one accord, harmonious

ūncia, -ae *f* a twelfth; (*weight*) ounce; (*length*) inch

ūnciārius *adj* of a twelfth; (*interest*) 8 ⅓ per cent

ūnciātim *adv* little by little

uncīnātus *adj* barbed

ūnciola, -ae *f* a mere twelfth

ūnctiō, -ōnis *f* anointing

ūnctitō, -āre *vt* to anoint regularly

ūnctiusculus *adj* rather too unctuous

ūnctor, -ōris *m* anointer

ūnctūra, -ae *f* anointing (*of the dead*)

ūnctus *ppp of* **ungō** ▸ *adj* oiled; greasy, resinous; (*fig*) rich, sumptuous ▸ *nt* sumptuous dinner

uncus¹, -ī *m* hook, grappling-iron

uncus² *adj* hooked, crooked, barbed

unda, -ae *f* wave, water; (*fig*) stream, surge

unde *adv* from where, whence; from whom, from which; **~ petitur** the defendant; **~ unde** from wherever; somehow or other

ūndeciēns, ūndeciēs *adv* eleven times
ūndecim *num* eleven
ūndecimus *adj* eleventh
undecumque *adv* from wherever
ūndēnī, -ōrum *adj* eleven each, eleven
ūndēnōnāgintā *num* eighty-nine
ūndēoctōgintā *num* seventy-nine
ūndēquadrāgintā *num* thirty-nine
ūndēquīnquāgēsimus *adj* forty-ninth
ūndēquīnquāgintā *num* forty-nine
ūndēsexāgintā *num* fifty-nine
ūndētrīcēsimus *adj* twenty-ninth
ūndēvīcēsimānī, -ōrum *mpl* men of the
  nineteenth legion
ūndēvīcēsimus *adj* nineteenth
ūndēvīgintī *num* nineteen
undique *adv* from every side, on all sides,
  everywhere; completely
undisonus *adj* sea-roaring
undō, -āre *vi* to surge; (*fig*) to roll, undulate
undōsus *adj* billowy
ūnetvīcēsimānī, -ōrum *mpl* men of the
  twenty-first legion
ūnetvīcēsimus *adj* twenty-first
ungō, unguō, -gere, ūnxī, ūnctum *vt*
  to anoint, smear, grease
unguen, -inis *nt* fat, grease, ointment
unguentārius, -ī *and* **-iī** *m* perfumer
unguentātus *adj* perfumed
unguentum, -ī *nt* ointment, perfume
unguiculus, -ī *m* fingernail
unguis, -is *m* nail (*of finger or toe*); claw,
  talon, hoof; **ad unguem** with perfect finish;
  trānsversum unguem a hair's breadth;
  dē tenerō unguī from earliest childhood
ungula, -ae *f* hoof, talon, claw
unguō *etc see* **ungō**
ūnicē *adv* solely, extraordinarily
ūnicolor, -ōris *adj* all one colour
ūnicus *adj* one and only, sole; unparalleled,
  unique
ūnifōrmis *adj* simple
ūnigena, -ae *adj* only-begotten; of the same
  parentage
ūnimanus *adj* with only one hand
ūniō, -ōnis *m* a single large pearl
ūniter *adv* together in one
ūniversālis *adj* general
ūniversē *adv* in general
ūniversitās, -ātis *f* the whole; the universe
ūniversus *adj* all taken together, entire,
  general ▸ *mpl* the community as a whole ▸ *nt*
  the universe; **in ūniversum** in general
unquam *etc see* **umquam**
ūnus *num* one ▸ *adj* sole, single, only; one and
  the same; the outstanding one; an individual;
  ~ et alter one or two; **~ quisque** every single
  one; **nēmō ~** not a single one; **ad ūnum** to a
  man
ūnxī *perf of* **ungō**
ūpiliō, -ōnis *m* shepherd
upupa, -ae *f* hoopoe; crowbar

Ūrania, -ae, Ūraniē, -ēs *f* Muse of
  astronomy
urbānē *adv* politely; wittily, elegantly
urbānitās, -ātis *f* city life; refinement,
  politeness; wit
urbānus *adj* town (*in cpds*), city (*in cpds*);
  refined, polite; witty, humorous; impertinent
  ▸ *m* townsman
urbicapus, -ī *m* taker of cities
urbs, urbis *f* city; Rome
urceolus, -ī *m* jug
urceus, -ī *m* pitcher, ewer
ūrēdō, -inis *f* blight
urgeō, -gēre, -sī *vt, vi* to force on, push
  forward; to press hard on, pursue closely; to
  crowd, hem in; to burden, oppress; (*argument*)
  to press, urge; (*work, etc*) to urge on, ply hard,
  follow up
ūrīna, -ae *f* urine
ūrīnātor, -ōris *m* diver
urna, -ae *f* water jar, urn; voting urn, lottery
  urn, cinerary urn, money jar
urnula, -ae *f* small urn
ūrō, -ere, ūssi, ūstum *vt* to burn; to scorch,
  parch; (*cold*) to nip; (*MED*) to cauterize; (*rubbing*)
  to chafe, hurt; (*passion*) to fire, inflame;
  (*vexation*) to annoy, oppress
ursa, -ae *f* she-bear, bear; (*ASTR*) Great Bear,
  Lesser Bear
ursī *perf of* **urgeō**
ursīnus *adj* bear's
ursus, -ī *m* bear
urtīca, -ae *f* nettle
ūrus, -ī *m* wild ox
Usipetēs, -etum, Usipetiī, -iōrum *mpl*
  German tribe on the Rhine
ūsitātē *adv* in the usual manner
ūsitātus *adj* usual, familiar
uspiam *adv* anywhere, somewhere
usquam *adv* anywhere; in any way, at all
usque *adv* all the way (to, from), right on,
  right up to; (*time*) all the time, as long as,
  continuously; (*degree*) even, as much as;
  ~ quāque everywhere; every moment, on every
  occasion
ūssī *perf of* **ūrō**
ūstor, -ōris *m* cremator
ūstulō, -āre *vt* to burn
ūstus *ppp of* **ūrō**
ūsūcapiō[1], -apere, -ēpī, -aptum *vt*
  to acquire ownership of, take over
ūsūcapiō[2], -ōnis *f* ownership by use or
  possession
ūsūra, -ae *f* use, enjoyment; interest, usury
ūsūrārius *adj* for use and enjoyment; paying
  interest
ūsūrpātiō, -ōnis *f* making use (of)
ūsūrpō, -āre, -āvī, -ātum *vt* to make use of,
  employ, exercise; (*LAW*) to take possession of,
  enter upon; (*senses*) to perceive, make contact
  with; (*word*) to call by, speak of
ūsus[1] *ppa of* **ūtor**

ūsus², **-ūs** m use, enjoyment, practice; experience, skill; usage, custom; intercourse, familiarity; usefulness, benefit, advantage; need, necessity; ~ **est**, ~ **venit** there is need (of); **ūsuī esse**, **ex ūsū esse** be of use, be of service; **ūsū venīre** happen; ~ **et frūctus** use and enjoyment, usufruct

ut, **utī** adv how; (rel) as; (explaining) considering how, according as; (place) where; **ut in ōrātōre** for an orator ▶ conj 1. (with indic: manner) as; (: concessive) while, though; (: time) when, as soon as 2. (with subj: expressing the idea of a verb) that, to; (: purpose) so that, to; (: causal) seeing that; (: concessive) granted that, although; (: result) that, so that; (: fear) that not; **ut ... ita** while ... nevertheless; **ut nōn** without; **ut quī** seeing that I, he etc; **ut quisque māximē** the more

utcumque, **utcunque** adv however; whenever; one way or another

ūtēnsilis adj of use ▶ ntpl necessaries

uter (gen **-rīus**, dat **-rī**), **-ra**, **-rum** pron which (of two), the one that; one or the other

ūter, **-ris** m bag, skin, bottle

utercumque, **utracumque**, **utrumcumque** pron whichever (of two)

uterlibet, **utralibet**, **utrumlibet** pron whichever (of the two) you please, either one

uterque, **utraque**, **utrumque** pron each (of two), either, both

uterum, **-ī** nt, **uterus**, **-ī** m womb; child; belly

utervīs, **utravīs**, **utrumvīs** pron whichever (of two) you please; either

utī etc see **ut**

ūtī infin of **ūtor**

ūtibilis adj useful, serviceable

Utica, **-ae** f town near Carthage (where Cato committed suicide)

Uticēnsis adj see **Utica**

ūtilis adj useful, expedient, profitable; fit (for)

ūtilitās, **-ātis** f usefulness, expediency, advantage

ūtiliter adv usefully, advantageously

utinam adv I wish!, would that!, if only!

utique adv at least, by all means, especially

ūtor, **ūtī**, **ūsus** vi (with abl) to use, employ; to possess, enjoy; to practise, experience; (person) to be on intimate terms with, find; **ūtendum rogāre** borrow

utpote adv inasmuch as, as being

ūtrārius, **-ī** and **-iī** m watercarrier

ūtriculārius, **-ī** and **-iī** m bagpiper

utrimque, **utrinque** adv on both sides, on either side

utrō adv in which direction

utrobīque see **utrubīque**

utrōque adv in both directions, both ways

utrubī adv on which side

utrubīque adv on both sides, on either side

utrum adv whether

utut adv however

ūva, **-ae** f grape, bunch of grapes; vine; cluster

ūvēscō, **-ere** vi to become wet

ūvidulus adj moist

ūvidus adj wet, damp; drunken

uxor, **-ōris** f wife

uxorcula, **-ae** f little wife

uxōrius adj of a wife; fond of his wife

V

vacāns, -antis *pres p of* **vacō** ▸ *adj* unoccupied; *(woman)* single
vacātiō, -ōnis *f* freedom, exemption; exemption from military service; payment for exemption from service
vacca, -ae *f* cow
vaccīnium, -ī and -iī *nt* hyacinth
vaccula, -ae *f* heifer
vacēfiō, -ierī *vi* to become empty
vacillō, -āre *vi* to stagger, totter; to waver, be unreliable
vacīvē *adv* at leisure
vacīvitās, -ātis *f* want
vacīvus *adj* empty, free
vacō, -āre, -āvī, -ātum *vi* to be empty, vacant, unoccupied; to be free, aloof (from); to have time for, devote one's time to; **vacat** there is time
vacuātus *adj* empty
vacuēfaciō, -facere, -fēcī, -factum *vt* to empty, clear
vacuitās, -ātis *f* freedom, exemption; vacancy
vacuus *adj* empty, void, wanting; vacant; free (from); clear; disengaged, at leisure; *(value)* worthless; *(woman)* single ▸ *nt* void, space
vadimōnium, -ī and -iī *nt* bail, security; **~ sistere** appear in court; **~ dēserere** default
vādō, -ere *vi* to go, go on, make one's way
vador, -ārī, -ātus *vt* to bind over by bail
vadōsus *adj* shallow
vadum, -ī *nt* shoal, shallow, ford; water, sea; bottom
vae *interj* woe!, alas!
vafer, -rī *adj* crafty, subtle
vafrē *adv* artfully
vagē *adv* far afield
vāgīna, -ae *f* sheath, scabbard; *(grain)* husk
vāgiō, -īre *vi* to cry
vāgītus, -ūs *m* crying, bleating
vagor, -ārī, -ātus *vi* to wander, rove, go far afield; *(fig)* to spread
vāgor, -ōris *m* cry
vagus *adj* wandering, unsettled; *(fig)* fickle, wavering, vague

vah *interj (expressing surprise, joy, anger)* oh!, ah!
valdē *adv* greatly, intensely; very
valē, valēte *interj* goodbye, farewell
valēns, -entis *pres p of* **valeō** ▸ *adj* strong, powerful, vigorous; well, healthy
valenter *adv* strongly
valentulus *adj* strong
valeō, -ēre, -uī, -itum *vi* to be strong; to be able, have the power (to); to be well, fit, healthy; *(fig)* to be powerful, effective, valid; *(force)* to prevail; *(money)* to be worth; *(word)* to mean; **valēre apud** have influence over, carry weight with; **valēre iubeō** say goodbye to; **valē dīcō** say goodbye; **valeās** away with you!
valēscō, -ere *vi* to grow strong, thrive
valētūdinārium, -ī and -iī *nt* hospital
valētūdō, -inis *f* state of health, health; illness
valgus *adj* bow-legged
validē *adv* powerfully, very
validus *adj* strong, powerful, able; sound, healthy; effective
vallāris *adj (decoration)* for scaling a rampart
vallēs, vallis, -is *f* valley
vallō, -āre, -āvī, -ātum *vt* to palisade, entrench, fortify
vallum, -ī *nt* rampart, palisade, entrenchment
vallus, -ī *m* stake; palisade, rampart; *(comb)* tooth
valvae, -ārum *fpl* folding door
vānēscō, -ere *vi* to disappear, pass away
vānidicus, -ī *m* liar
vāniloquentia, -ae *f* idle talk
vāniloquus *adj* untruthful; boastful
vānitās, -ātis *f* emptiness; falsehood, worthlessness, fickleness; vanity
vānitūdō, -inis *f* falsehood
vannus, -ī *f* winnowing fan
vānus *adj* empty; idle, useless, groundless; false, untruthful, unreliable; conceited
vapidus *adj* spoilt, corrupt
vapor, -ōris *m* steam, vapour; heat
vapōrārium, -ī and -iī *nt* steam pipe
vapōrō, -āre *vt* to steam, fumigate, heat ▸ *vi* to burn
vappa, -ae *f* wine that has gone flat; *(person)* good-for-nothing
vāpulō, -āre *vi* to be flogged, beaten; to be defeated
variantia, -ae *f* diversity
variātiō, -ōnis *f* difference
vāricō, -āre *vi* to straddle
vāricōsus *adj* varicose
vāricus *adj* with feet wide apart
variē *adv* diversely, with varying success
varietās, -ātis *f* difference, diversity
variō, -āre, -āvī, -ātum *vt* to diversify, variegate; to make different, change, vary ▸ *vi* to change colour; to differ, vary
varius *adj* coloured, spotted, variegated; diverse, changeable, various; *(ability)* versatile; *(character)* fickle
Varius, -ī *m* epic poet *(friend of Vergil and Horace)*

varix, -icis f varicose vein

Varrō, -ōnis m consul defeated at Cannae; antiquarian writer of Cicero's day

Varrōniānus adj see **Varrō**

vārus adj knock-kneed; crooked; contrary

vas, vadis m surety, bail

vās, vāsis nt, **vāsa, -ōrum** ntpl vessel, dish; utensil, implement; (MIL) baggage

vāsārium, -ī and **-iī** nt furnishing allowance (of a governor)

vāsculārius, -ī and **-iī** m metalworker

vāsculum, -ī nt small dish

vastātiō, -ōnis f ravaging

vastātor, -ōris m ravager

vastē adv (size) enormously; (speech) coarsely

vastificus adj ravaging

vastitās, -ātis f desolation, desert; devastation, destruction

vastitiēs, -ēī f ruin

vastō, -āre, -āvī, -ātum vt to make desolate, denude; to lay waste, ravage

vastus adj empty, desolate, uncultivated; ravaged, devastated; (appearance) uncouth, rude; (size) enormous, vast

vāsum etc see **vās**

vātēs, -is m/f prophet, prophetess; poet, bard

Vāticānus adj Vatican (hill on right bank of Tiber)

vāticinātiō, -ōnis f prophesying, prediction

vāticinātor, -ōris m prophet

vāticinor, -ārī, -ātus vt, vi to prophesy; to celebrate in verse; to rave, rant

vāticinus adj prophetic

-ve conj or; either ... or

vēcordia, -ae f senselessness; insanity

vēcors, -dis adj senseless, foolish, mad

vectīgal, -ālis nt tax, honorarium (to a magistrate); income

vectiō, -ōnis f transport

vectis, -is m lever, crowbar; (door) bolt, bar

Vectis, -is f Isle of Wight

vectō, -āre vt to carry; (pass) to ride

vector, -ōris m carrier; passenger, rider

vectōrius adj transport (in cpds)

vectūra, -ae f transport; (payment) carriage, fare

vectus ppp of **vehō**

Vediovis, -is = **Vēiovis**

vegetus adj lively, sprightly

vēgrandis adj small

vehemēns, -entis adj impetuous, violent; powerful, strong

vehementer adv violently, eagerly; powerfully, very much

vehementia, -ae f vehemence

vehiculum, -ī nt carriage, cart; (sea) vessel

vehō, -here, -xī, -ctum vt to carry, convey; (pass) to ride, sail, drive

Vēiēns, -entis, Vēientānus, Vēius adj see **Vēiī**

Vēiī, -ōrum mpl ancient town in S. Etruria

Vēiovis, -is m ancient Roman god (anti-Jupiter)

vel conj or, or perhaps; or rather; or else; either ... or ▶ adv even, if you like; perhaps; for instance; **vel māximus** the very greatest

Vēlābrum, -ī nt low ground between Capitol and Palatine hills

vēlāmen, -inis nt covering, garment

vēlāmentum, -ī nt curtain; (pl) draped olive branches carried by suppliants

vēlārium, -ī and **-iī** nt awning

vēlātī, -ōrum mpl supernumerary troops

vēles, -itis m light-armed soldier, skirmisher

vēlifer, -ī adj carrying sail

vēlificātiō, -ōnis f sailing

vēlificō, -āre vi to sail ▶ vt to sail through

vēlificor, -ārī vi to sail; (with dat) to make an effort to obtain

Velīnus, -ī m a Sabine lake

vēlitāris adj of the light-armed troops

vēlitātiō, -ōnis f skirmishing

vēlitēs pl of **vēles**

vēlitor, -ārī vi to skirmish

vēlivolus adj sail-winged

velle infin of **volō²**

vellicō, -āre vt to pinch, pluck, twitch; (speech) to taunt, disparage

vellō, -ere, vellī and **vulsī, vulsum** vt to pluck, pull, pick; to pluck out, tear up

vellus, -eris nt fleece, pelt; wool; fleecy clouds

vēlō, -āre, -āvī, -ātum vt to cover up, clothe, veil; (fig) to conceal

vēlōcitās, -ātis f speed, rapidity

vēlōciter adv rapidly

vēlōx, -ōcis adj fast, quick, rapid

vēlum, -ī nt sail; curtain, awning; **rēmis vēlīsque** with might and main; **vēla dare** set sail

velut, velutī adv as, just as; for instance; just as if

vēmēns etc see **vehemēns**

vēna, -ae f vein, artery; vein of metal; water course; (fig) innermost nature of feelings, talent, strength; **vēnās temptāre** feel the pulse; **vēnās tenēre** have one's finger on the pulse (of)

vēnābulum, -ī nt hunting spear

Venāfrānus adj see **Venāfrum**

Venāfrum, -ī nt Samnite town famous for olive oil

vēnālicius adj for sale ▶ m slave dealer

vēnālis adj for sale; bribable ▶ m slave offered for sale

vēnāticus adj hunting- (in cpds)

vēnātiō, -ōnis f hunting; a hunt; public show of fighting wild beasts; game

vēnātor, -ōris m hunter

vēnātōrius adj hunter's

vēnātrix, -īcis f huntress

vēnātūra, -ae f hunting

vēnātus, -ūs m hunting

vēndibilis adj saleable; (fig) popular

vēnditātiō, -ōnis f showing off, advertising

vēnditātor, -ōris m braggart

vēnditiō, -ōnis f sale

vēnditō, -āre vt to try to sell; to praise up, advertise; **sē vēnditāre** ingratiate oneself (with)

vēnditor, -ōris m seller

vēndō (pass **vēneō**), **-ere, -idī, -itum** vt to sell; to betray; to praise up

venēficium, -ī and **-iī** nt poisoning; sorcery

venēficus adj poisonous; magic ▸ m sorcerer ▸ f sorceress

venēnātus adj poisonous; magic

venēnifer, -ī adj poisonous

venēnō, -āre vt to poison

venēnum, -ī nt drug, potion; dye; poison; magic charm; (fig) mischief; charm

vēneō, -īre, -iī, -itum vi to be sold

venerābilis adj honoured, venerable

venerābundus adj reverent

venerātiō, -ōnis f respect, reverence

venerātor, -ōris m reverencer

Venereus, Venerius adj of Venus ▸ m highest throw (at dice)

veneror, -ārī, -ātus vt to worship, revere, pray to; to honour, respect; to ask for, entreat

Venetia, -iae f district of the Veneti

Veneticus adj see **Venetia**

Venetus adj Venetian; (colour) blue

vēnī perf of **veniō**

venia, -ae f indulgence, favour, kindness; permission, leave; pardon, forgiveness; **bonā tuā veniā** by your leave; **bonā veniā audīre** give a fair hearing

vēniī perf of **vēneō**

veniō, -īre, vēnī, ventum vi to come; (fig) to fall into, incur, go as far as; **in amīcitiam venīre** make friends (with); **in spem venīre** entertain hopes

vēnor, -ārī, -ātus vt, vi to hunt, chase

venter, -ris m stomach, belly; womb, unborn child

ventilātor, -ōris m juggler

ventilō, -āre vt to fan, wave, agitate

ventiō, -ōnis f coming

ventitō, -āre vi to keep coming, come regularly

ventōsus adj windy; like the wind; fickle; conceited

ventriculus, -ī m belly; (heart) ventricle

ventriōsus adj pot-bellied

ventulus, -ī m breeze

ventus, -ī m wind

vēnūcula, -ae f kind of grape

vēnum, vēnō for sale

vēnumdō, vēnundō, -āre, -edī, -atum vt to sell, put up for sale

Venus, -eris f goddess of love; planet Venus; highest throw (at dice)

venus, -eris f charm, beauty; love, mating

Venusia, -iae f town in Apulia (birthplace of Horace)

Venusīnus adj see **Venusia**

venustās, -ātis f charm, beauty

venustē adv charmingly

venustulus adj charming little

venustus adj charming, attractive, beautiful

vēpallidus adj very pale

veprēcula, -ae f little brier bush

veprēs, -is m thornbush, bramblebush

vēr, vēris nt spring; **vēr sacrum** offerings of firstlings

vērātrum, -ī nt hellebore

vērāx, -ācis adj truthful

verbēna, -ae f vervain; (pl) sacred boughs carried by heralds or priests

verber, -is nt lash, scourge; (missile) strap; (pl) flogging, strokes

verberābilis adj deserving a flogging

verberātiō, -ōnis f punishment

verbereus adj deserving a flogging

verberō¹, -āre, -āvī, -ātum vt to flog, beat, lash

verberō², -ōnis m scoundrel

verbōsē adv verbosely

verbōsus adj wordy

verbum, -ī nt word; saying, expression; (GRAM) verb; (pl) language, talk; **~ ē verbō, ~ dē verbō, ~ prō verbō** literally; **ad ~** word for word; **verbī causa (grātiā)** for instance; **verbō** orally; briefly; **verba dare** cheat, fool; **verba facere** talk; **meīs verbīs** in my name

vērē adv really, truly, correctly

verēcundē adv see **verēcundus**

verēcundia, -ae f modesty, shyness; reverence, dread; shame

verēcundor, -ārī vi to be bashful, feel shy

verēcundus adj modest, shy, bashful

verendus adj venerable

vereor, -ērī, -itus vt, vi to fear, be afraid; to revere, respect

verētrum, -ī nt the private parts

Vergiliae, -ārum fpl the Pleiads

Vergilius, -ī m Vergil, Virgil (famous epic poet)

vergō, -ere vt to turn, incline ▸ vi to turn, incline, decline; (place) to face

vēridicus adj truthful

vērī similis adj probable

vērī similitūdō, -inis f probability

vēritās, -ātis f truth, truthfulness; reality, real life; (character) integrity; (language) etymology

veritus ppa of **vereor**

vermiculātus adj inlaid with wavy lines, mosaic

vermiculus, -ī m grub

vermina, -um ntpl stomach pains

vermis, -is m worm

verna, -ae f slave born in his master's home

vernāculus adj of home-born slaves; native

vernīlis adj slavish; (remark) smart

vernīliter adv slavishly

vernō, -āre vi to bloom, be spring-like; to be young

vernula, -ae f young home-born slave; native

vernus adj of spring

vērō adv in fact, assuredly; (confirming) certainly, yes; (climax) indeed; (adversative) but in fact; **minimē ~** certainly not

Vērōna, -ae *f* town in N. Italy (birthplace of Catullus)

Vērōnēnsis *adj see* **Vērōna**

verpus, -ī *m* circumcised man

Verrēs, -is *m* praetor prosecuted by Cicero

verrēs, -is *m* boar

verrīnus *adj* boar's, pork (*in cpds*)

Verrius, Verrīnus *adj see* **Verrēs**

verrō, -rere, -rī, -sum *vt* to sweep, scour; to sweep away, carry off

verrūca, -ae *f* wart; (*fig*) slight blemish

verrūcōsus *adj* warty

verruncō, -āre *vi* to turn out successfully

versābundus *adj* rotating

versātilis *adj* revolving; versatile

versicolor, -ōris *adj* of changing *or* various colours

versiculus, -ī *m* short line; (*pl*) unpretentious verses

versificātor, -ōris *m* versifier

versipellis *adj* of changed appearance; crafty ▶ *m* werewolf

versō, -āre, -āvī, -ātum *vt* to keep turning, wind, twist; (*fig*) to upset, disturb, ruin; (*mind*) to ponder, consider

versor, -ārī, -ātus *vi* to live, be, be situated; to be engaged (in), be busy (with)

versum *adv* turned, in the direction

versūra, -ae *f* borrowing to pay a debt; loan

versus¹ *ppp of* **vertō** ▶ *adv* turned, in the direction

versus², -ūs *m* line, row; verse; (*dance*) step

versūtē *adv* craftily

versūtiae, -ārum *fpl* tricks

versūtiloquus *adj* sly

versūtus *adj* clever; crafty, deceitful

vertex, -icis *m* whirlpool, eddy; whirlwind; crown of the head, head; top, summit; (*sky*) pole

verticōsus *adj* eddying, swirling

vertīgō, -inis *f* turning round; dizziness

vertō, -tere, -tī, -sum *vt* to turn; to turn over, invert; to turn round; to turn into, change, exchange; (*cause*) to ascribe, impute; (*language*) to translate; (*war*) to overthrow, destroy; (*pass*) to be (in), be engaged (in) ▶ *vi* to turn; to change; to turn out; **in fugam vertere** put to flight; **terga vertere** flee; **solum vertere** emigrate; **vitiō vertere** blame; **annō vertente** in the course of a year

Vertumnus, -ī *m* god of seasons

verū, -ūs *nt* spit; javelin

vērum¹ *adv* truly, yes; but actually; but, yet; ~ **tamen** nevertheless

vērum², -ī *nt* truth, reality; right; **vērī similis** probable

vērus *adj* true, real, actual; truthful; right, reasonable

verūtum, -ī *nt* javelin

verūtus *adj* armed with the javelin

vervēx, -ēcis *m* wether

vēsānia, -ae *f* madness

vēsāniēns, -entis *adj* raging

vēsānus *adj* mad, insane; furious, raging

vescor, -ī *vi* (*with abl*) to feed, eat; to enjoy

vescus *adj* little, feeble; corroding

vēsīca, -ae *f* bladder; purse; football

vēsīcula, -ae *f* small bladder, blister

vespa, -ae *f* wasp

Vespasiānus, -ī *m* Roman emperor

vesper, -is *and* **-ī** *m* evening; supper; evening star; west; **vespere, vesperī** in the evening

vespera, -ae *f* evening

vesperāscō, -ere *vi* to become evening, get late

vespertīliō, -ōnis *m* bat

vespertīnus *adj* evening (*in cpds*), in the evening; western

vesperūgō, -inis *f* evening star

Vesta, -ae *f* Roman goddess of the hearth

Vestālis *adj* Vestal ▶ *f* virgin priestess of Vesta

vester, -rī *adj* your, yours

vestibulum, -ī *nt* forecourt, entrance

vestīgium, -ī *and* **-iī** *nt* footstep, footprint, track; (*fig*) trace, sign, vestige; (*time*) moment, instant; **ē vestīgiō** instantly

vestīgō, -āre, -āvī, -ātum *vt* to track, trace, search for, discover

vestīmentum, -ī *nt* clothes

vestiō, -īre, -iī, -ītum *vt* to clothe, dress; to cover, adorn

vestipica, -ae *f* wardrobe woman

vestis, -is *f* clothes, dress; coverlet, tapestry, blanket; (*snake*) slough; **vestem mūtāre** change one's clothes; go into mourning

vestispica *etc see* **vestipica**

vestītus, -ūs *m* clothes, dress; covering; **mūtāre vestītum** go into mourning; **redīre ad suum vestītum** come out of mourning

Vesuvius, -ī *m* (the volcano) Vesuvius

veterānus *adj* veteran

veterāscō, -scere, -vī *vi* to grow old

veterātor, -ōris *m* expert, old hand; sly fox

veterātōriē *adv see* **veterātōrius**

veterātōrius *adj* crafty

veterīnus *adj* of burden ▶ *f and ntpl* beasts of burden

veternōsus *adj* lethargic, drowsy

veternus, -ī *m* lethargy, drowsiness

vetitus *ppp of* **vetō** ▶ *nt* prohibition

vetō, -āre, -uī, -itum *vt* to forbid, prohibit, oppose; (*tribune*) to protest

vetulus *adj* little old, poor old

vetus, -eris *adj* old, former ▶ *mpl* the ancients ▶ *fpl* the old shops (*in the Forum*) ▶ *ntpl* antiquity, tradition

vetustās, -ātis *f* age, long standing; antiquity; great age, future age

vetustus *adj* old, ancient; old-fashioned

vexāmen, -inis *nt* shaking

vexātiō, -ōnis *f* shaking; trouble, distress

vexātor, -ōris *m* troubler, opponent

vexī *perf of* **vehō**

vexillārius, -ī *and* **-iī** *m* standard-bearer, ensign; (*pl*) special reserve of veterans

vexillum, -ī nt standard, flag; company, troop; **~ prōpōnere** hoist the signal for battle

vexō, -āre, -āvī, -ātum vt to shake, toss, trouble, distress, injure, attack

via, -ae f road, street, way; journey, march; passage; (fig) way, method, fashion; the right way; **viā** properly; **inter viās** on the way

viālis adj of the highways

viārius adj for the upkeep of roads

viāticātus adj provided with travelling money

viāticus adj for a journey ▶ nt travelling allowance; (MIL) prizemoney, savings

viātor, -ōris m traveller; (LAW) summoner

vībix, -īcis f weal

vibrō, -āre, -āvī, -ātum vt to wave, shake, brandish, hurl, launch ▶ vi to shake, quiver, vibrate; to shimmer, sparkle

viburnum, -ī nt wayfaring-tree or guelder rose

vīcānus adj village (in cpds) ▶ mpl villagers

Vica Pota, Vicae Potae f goddess of victory

vicārius adj substituted ▶ m substitute, proxy; underslave

vīcātim adv from street to street; in villages

vice (with gen) on account of; like

vicem in turn; (with gen) instead of; on account of; like; **tuam ~** on your account

vīcēnārius adj of twenty

vīcēnī, -ōrum adj twenty each, in twenties

vicēs pl of **vicis**

vīcēsimānī, -ōrum mpl men of the twentieth legion

vīcēsimārius adj derived from the 5 per cent tax

vīcēsimus adj twentieth ▶ f a 5 per cent tax

vīcī perf of **vincō**

vicia, -ae f vetch

viciēns, vīciēs adv twenty times

vīcīnālis adj neighbouring

vīcīnia, -ae f neighbourhood, nearness

vīcīnitās, -ātis f neighbourhood, nearness

vīcīnus adj neighbouring, nearby; similar, kindred ▶ m/f neighbour ▶ nt neighbourhood

vicis gen (acc **-em**, abl **-e**) f interchange, alternation, succession; recompense, retaliation; fortune, changing conditions; duty, function, place; **in vicem** in turn, mutually

vicissim adv in turn, again

vicissitūdō, -inis f interchange, alternation

victima, -ae f victim, sacrifice

victimārius, -ī and -iī m assistant at sacrifices

victitō, -āre vi to live, subsist

victor, -ōris m conqueror, victor, winner ▶ adj victorious

victōria, -ae f victory

victōriātus, -ūs m silver coin stamped with Victory

Victōriola, -ae f little statue of Victory

victrīx, -īcis f conqueror ▶ adj victorious

victus ppp of **vincō**

victus, -ūs m sustenance, livelihood; way of life

vīculus, -ī m hamlet

vīcus, -ī m (city) quarter, street; (country) village, estate

vidēlicet adv clearly, evidently; (ironical) of course; (explaining) namely

videō, -ēre, vīdī, vīsum vt to see, look at; (mind) to observe, be aware, know; to consider, think over; to see to, look out for; to live to see; (pass) to seem, appear; to seem right, be thought proper; **mē vidē** rely on me; **vīderit** let him see to it; **mihi videor esse** I think I am; **sī (tibi) vidētur** if you like

viduāta adj widowed

viduitās, -ātis f bereavement, want; widowhood

vīdulus, -ī m trunk, box

viduō, -āre vt to bereave

viduus adj bereft, bereaved; unmarried; (with abl) without ▶ f widow; spinster

Vienna, -ae f town in Gaul on the Rhone (now Vienne)

viētus adj shrivelled

vigeō, -ēre, -uī vi to thrive, flourish

vigēscō, -ere vi to begin to flourish, become lively

vīgēsimus etc see **vīcēsimus**

vigil, -is adj awake, watching, alert ▶ m watchman, sentinel; (pl) the watch, police

vigilāns, -antis pres p of **vigilō** ▶ adj watchful

vigilanter adv vigilantly

vigilantia, -ae f wakefulness; vigilance

vigilāx, -ācis adj watchful

vigilia, -ae f lying awake, sleeplessness; keeping watch, guard; a watch; the watch, sentries; vigil; vigilance

vigilō, -āre, -āvī, -ātum vi to remain awake; to keep watch; to be vigilant ▶ vt to spend awake, make while awake at night

vīgintī num twenty

vīgintīvirātus, -ūs m membership of a board of twenty

vīgintīvirī, -ōrum mpl a board or commission of twenty men

vigor, -ōris m energy, vigour

vīlica, -ae f wife of a steward

vīlicō, -āre vi to be an overseer

vīlicus, -ī m overseer, manager of an estate, steward

vīlis adj cheap; worthless, poor, mean, common

vīlitās, -ātis f cheapness, low price; worthlessness

vīliter adv cheaply

vīlla, -ae f country house, villa

vīllic- etc see **vīlic-**

vīllōsus adj hairy, shaggy

vīllula, -ae f small villa

vīllum, -ī nt a drop of wine

villus, -ī m hair, fleece; (cloth) nap

vīmen, -inis nt osier; basket

vīmentum, -ī nt osier

Vīminālis adj Viminal (hill of Rome)

vīmineus adj of osiers, wicker

vīnāceus adj grape- (in cpds)

Vīnālia, -ium *ntpl* Wine festival

vīnārius *adj* of wine, wine (*in cpds*) ▸ *m* vintner ▸ *nt* wine flask

vincibilis *adj* easily won

vinciō, -cīre, -xī, -ctum *vt* to bind, fetter; to encircle; (*fig*) to confine, restrain, envelop, attach

vinclum *nt see* **vinculum**

vincō, -ere, vīcī, victum *vt* to conquer, defeat, subdue; to win, prevail, be successful; (*fig*) to surpass, excel; (*argument*) to convince, refute, prove conclusively; (*life*) to outlive

vinctus *ppp of* **vinciō**

vinculum, -ī *nt* bond, fetter, chain; (*pl*) prison

vīndēmia, -ae *f* vintage, grape harvest

vīndēmiātor, -ōris *m* vintager

vīndēmiola, -ae *f* small vintage

Vīndēmitor, -ōris *m* the Vintager (*a star in Virgo*)

vindex, -icis *m* champion, protector; liberator; avenger ▸ *adj* avenging

vindicātiō, -ōnis *f* punishment of offences

vindiciae, -ārum *fpl* legal claim; **vindiciās ab lībertāte in servitūtem dare** condemn a free person to slavery

vindicō, -āre, -āvī, -ātum *vt* to lay claim to; to claim, appropriate; to liberate, protect, champion; to avenge, punish; **in lībertātem vindicāre** emancipate

vindicta, -ae *f* rod used in manumitting a slave; defence, deliverance; revenge, punishment

vīnea, -ae *f* vineyard; vine; (*MIL*) penthouse (*for besiegers*)

vīnētum, -ī *nt* vineyard

vīnitor, -ōris *m* vine-dresser

vinnulus *adj* delightful

vīnolentia, -ae *f* wine drinking

vīnolentus *adj* drunk

vīnōsus *adj* fond of wine, drunken

vīnum, -ī *nt* wine

vinxī *perf of* **vinciō**

viola, -ae *f* violet; stock

violābilis *adj* vulnerable

violāceus *adj* violet

violārium, -ī *and* **-iī** *nt* violet bed

violārius, -ī *and* **-iī** *m* dyer of violet

violātiō, -ōnis *f* desecration

violātor, -ōris *m* violator, desecrater

violēns, -entis *adj* raging, vehement

violenter *adv* violently, furiously

violentia, -ae *f* violence, impetuosity

violentus *adj* violent, impetuous, boisterous

violō, -āre, -āvī, -ātum *vt* to do violence to, outrage, violate; (*agreement*) to break

vīpera, -ae *f* viper, adder, snake

vīpereus *adj* snake's, serpent's

vīperīnus *adj* snake's, serpent's

vir, virī *m* man; grown man; brave man, hero; husband; (*MIL*) footsoldier

virāgō, -inis *f* heroine, warrior maid

virecta, -ōrum *ntpl* grassy sward

vireō, -ēre, -uī *vi* to be green; (*fig*) to be fresh, flourish

vīrēs *pl of* **vīs¹**

virēscō, -ere *vi* to grow green

virga, -ae *f* twig; graft; rod, staff, walking stick, wand; (*colour*) stripe

virgātor, -ōris *m* flogger

virgātus *adj* made of osiers; striped

virgētum, -ī *nt* thicket of osiers

virgeus *adj* of brushwood

virgidēmia, -ae *f* crop of flogging

virginālis *adj* maidenly, of maids

virginārius *adj* of maids

virgineus *adj* maidenly, virgin, of virgins

virginitās, -ātis *f* maidenhood

virgō, -inis *f* maid, virgin; young woman, girl; (*constellation*) Virgo; *a Roman aqueduct*

virgula, -ae *f* wand

virgulta, -ōrum *ntpl* thicket, shrubbery; cuttings, slips

virguncula, -ae *f* little girl

viridāns, -antis *adj* green

viridārium, -ī *and* **-iī** *nt* plantation, garden

viridis *adj* green; fresh, young, youthful ▸ *ntpl* greenery

viriditās, -ātis *f* verdure, greenness; freshness

viridor, -ārī *vi* to become green

virīlis *adj* male, masculine; man's; adult; manly, brave, bold; ~ **pars** one's individual part *or* duty; **prō virīlī parte, prō virīlī portiōne** to the best of one's ability

virīlitās, -ātis *f* manhood

virīliter *adv* manfully

virītim *adv* individually, separately

vīrōsus *adj* slimy; rank

virtūs, -ūtis *f* manhood, full powers; strength, courage, ability, worth; (*MIL*) valour, prowess, heroism; (*moral*) virtue; (*things*) excellence, worth

vīrus, -ī *nt* slime; poison; offensive smell; salt taste

vīs¹ (*acc* **vim**, *abl* **vī**, *pl* **vīrēs**) *f* power, force, strength; violence, assault; quantity, amount; (*mind*) energy, vigour; (*word*) meaning, import; (*pl*) strength; (*MIL*) troops; **per vim** forcibly; **dē vī damnārī** be convicted of assault; **prō vīribus** with all one's might

vīs² *2nd pers of* **volō²**

viscātus *adj* limed

viscerātiō, -ōnis *f* public distribution of meat

viscō, -āre *vt* to make sticky

viscum, -ī *nt* mistletoe; bird lime

viscus, -eris (*pl* **-era, -erum**) *nt* internal organs; flesh; womb, child; (*fig*) heart, bowels

vīsendus *adj* worth seeing

vīsiō, -ōnis *f* apparition; idea

vīsitō, -āre *vt* to see often; to visit

vīsō, -ere, -ī, -um *vt* to look at, survey; to see to; to go and see, visit

Visurgis, -is *m* (river) Weser

vīsus¹ *ppp of* **videō** ▸ *nt* vision

vīsus², **-ūs** m sight, the faculty of seeing; a sight, vision

vīta, **-ae** f life, livelihood; way of life; career, biography

vītābilis adj undesirable

vītābundus adj avoiding, taking evasive action

vītālis adj of life, vital ▶ nt subsistence ▶ ntpl vitals

vītāliter adv with life

vītātiō, **-ōnis** f avoidance

Vitellius¹, **-ī** m Roman emperor in AD 69

Vitellius², **-iānus** adj see **Vitellius¹**

vitellus, **-ī** m little calf; (egg) yolk

vīteus adj of the vine

vīticula, **-ae** f little vine

vītigenus adj produced from the vine

vitilēna, **-ae** f procuress

vitiō, **-āre**, **-āvī**, **-ātum** vt to spoil, corrupt, violate; to falsify

vitiōsē adv badly, defectively

vitiōsitās, **-ātis** f vice

vitiōsus adj faulty, corrupt; wicked, depraved; ~ cōnsul a consul whose election had a religious flaw in it

vītis, **-is** f vine; vine branch, centurion's staff, centurionship

vītisator, **-ōris** m vine planter

vitium, **-ī** and **-iī** nt fault, flaw, defect; (moral) failing, offence, vice; (religion) flaw in the auspices

vītō, **-āre**, **-āvī**, **-ātum** vt to avoid, evade, shun

vītor, **-ōris** m basket maker, cooper

vitreus adj of glass; glassy ▶ ntpl glassware

vītricus, **-ī** m stepfather

vitrum, **-ī** nt glass; woad

vitta, **-ae** f headband, sacrificial fillet

vittātus adj wearing a fillet

vitula, **-ae** f (of cow) calf

vitulīnus adj of veal ▶ f veal

vītulor, **-ārī** vi to hold a celebration

vitulus, **-ī** m calf; foal; ~ marīnus seal

vituperābilis adj blameworthy

vituperātiō, **-ōnis** f blame, censure; scandalous conduct

vituperātor, **-ōris** m critic

vituperō, **-āre** vt to find fault with, disparage; (omen) to spoil

vīvārium, **-ī** and **-iī** nt fishpond, game preserve

vīvātus adj animated

vīvāx, **-ācis** adj long-lived; lasting; (sulphur) inflammable

vīvēscō, **-ere** vi to grow, become active

vīvidus adj full of life; (art) true to life, vivid; (mind) lively

vīvirādīx, **-īcis** f a rooted cutting, layer

vīvīscō etc see **vīvēscō**

vīvō, **-vere**, **-xī**, **-ctum** vi to live, be alive; to enjoy life; (fame) to last, be remembered; (with abl) to live on; **vīve** farewell!; **vīxērunt** they are dead

vīvus adj alive, living; (light) burning; (rock) natural; (water) running; **vīvō videntīque** before his very eyes; **mē vīvō** as long as I live, in my lifetime; **ad vīvum resecāre** cut to the quick; **dē vīvō dētrahere** take out of capital

vix adv with difficulty, hardly, scarcely

vixdum adv hardly, as yet

vīxī perf of **vīvō**

vocābulum, **-ī** nt name, designation; (GRAM) noun

vōcālis adj speaking, singing, tuneful ▶ f vowel

vocāmen, **-inis** nt name

vocātiō, **-ōnis** f invitation; (LAW) summons

vocātus, **-ūs** m summons, call

vōciferātiō, **-ōnis** f loud cry, outcry

vōciferor, **-ārī** vt to cry out loud, shout

vocitō, **-āre**, **-āvī**, **-ātum** vt to usually call; to shout

vocīvus etc see **vacīvus**

vocō, **-āre**, **-āvī**, **-ātum** vt to call, summon; to call, name; (gods) to call upon; (guest) to invite; (MIL) to challenge; (fig) to bring (into some condition or plight); **vocāre dē** name after; **in dubium vocāre** call in question; **in iūdicium vocāre** call to account

vōcula, **-ae** f weak voice; soft tone; gossip

volaema ntpl kind of large pear

Volaterrae, **-ārum** fpl old Etruscan town (now Volterra)

Volaterrānus adj see **Volaterrae**

volāticus adj winged; fleeting, inconstant

volātilis adj winged; swift; fleeting

volātus, **-ūs** m flight

Volcānius adj see **Volcānus**

Volcānus, **-ī** m Vulcan (god of fire), fire

volēns, **-entis** pres p of **volō³** ▶ adj willing, glad, favourable; **mihi volentī est** it is acceptable to me

volg- etc see **vulg-**

volitō, **-āre** vi to fly about, flutter; to hurry, move quickly; (fig) to hover, soar; to get excited

voln- etc see **vuln-**

volō¹, **-āre**, **-āvī**, **-ātum** vi to fly; to speed

volō², **velle**, **voluī** vt to wish, want; to be willing; to will, purpose, determine; (opinion) to hold, maintain; (word, action) to mean; ~ dīcere I mean; **bene velle** like; **male velle** dislike; **ōrātum tē** ~ I beg you; **paucīs tē** ~ a word with you!; **numquid vīs** (before leaving) is there anything else?; **quid sibi vult?** what does he mean?; what is he driving at?; **velim faciās** please do it; **vellem fēcissēs** I wish you had done it

volōnēs, **-um** mpl volunteers

volpēs etc see **vulpēs**

Volscī, **-ōrum** mpl people in S. Latium

Volscus adj Volscian

volsella, **-ae** f tweezers

volsus ppp of **vellō**

volt old 3rd pers sg of **volō²**

voltis old 2nd pers pl of **volō²**

Voltumna, **-ae** f patron goddess of Etruria

voltus *etc see* **vultus**

volūbilis *adj* spinning, revolving; (*fortune*) fickle; (*speech*) fluent

volubilitās, -ātis *f* whirling motion; roundness; fluency; inconstancy

volūbiliter *adv* fluently

volucer, -ris *adj* winged; flying, swift; fleeting

volucris, -is *f* bird; insect

volūmen, -inis *nt* roll, book; coil, eddy, fold

voluntārius *adj* voluntary ▸ *mpl* volunteers

voluntās, -ātis *f* will, wish, inclination; attitude, goodwill; last will, testament; **suā voluntāte** of one's own accord; **ad voluntātem** with the consent (of)

volup *adv* agreeably, to one's satisfaction

voluptābilis *adj* agreeable

voluptās, -ātis *f* pleasure, enjoyment; (*pl*) entertainments, sports

voluptuārius *adj* pleasureable, agreeable; voluptuous

volūtābrum, -ī *nt* wallowing place

volūtātiō, -ōnis *f* wallowing

volūtō, -āre *vt* to roll about, turn over; (*mind*) to occupy, engross; (*thought*) to ponder, think over; (*pass*) to wallow, flounder

volūtus *ppp of* **volvō**

volva, -ae *f* womb; (*dish*) sow's womb

volvō, -vere, -vī, -ūtum *vt* to roll, turn round; to roll along; (*air*) to breathe; (*book*) to open; (*circle*) to form; (*thought*) to ponder, reflect on; (*time*) to roll on; (*trouble*) to undergo; (*pass*) to roll, revolve ▸ *vi* to revolve, elapse

vōmer, -eris *m* ploughshare

vomica, -ae *f* sore, ulcer, abscess, boil

vōmis *etc see* **vōmer**

vomitiō, -ōnis *f* vomiting

vomitus, -ūs *m* vomiting, vomit

vomō, -ere, -uī, -itum *vt* to vomit, throw up; to emit, discharge

vorāgō, -inis *f* abyss, chasm, depth

vorāx, -ācis *adj* greedy, ravenous; consuming

vorō, -āre, -āvī, -ātum *vt* to swallow, devour; (*sea*) to swallow up; (*reading*) to devour

vors-, vort- *see* **vers-, vert-** *etc*

vōs *pron* you

Vosegus, -ī *m* Vosges (mountains)

voster *etc see* **vester**

vōtīvus *adj* votive, promised in a vow

votō *etc see* **vetō**

vōtum, -ī *nt* vow, prayer; votive offering; wish, longing; **vōtī damnārī** have one's prayer granted

vōtus *ppp of* **voveō**

voveō, -ēre, vōvī, vōtum *vt* to vow, promise solemnly; to dedicate; to wish

vōx, vōcis *f* voice; sound, cry, call; word, saying, expression; accent; **unā vōce** unanimously

Vulcānus *see* **Volcānus**

vulgāris *adj* common, general

vulgāriter *adv* in the common fashion

vulgātor, -ōris *m* betrayer

vulgātus *adj* common; generally known, notorious

vulgivagus *adj* roving; inconstant

vulgō¹ *adv* publicly, commonly, usually, everywhere

vulgō², -āre, -āvī, -ātum *vt* to make common, spread; to publish, divulge, broadcast; to prostitute; to level down

vulgus, -ī *nt* (*occ m*) the mass of the people, the public; crowd, herd; rabble, populace

vulnerātiō, -ōnis *f* wounding, injury

vulnerō, -āre, -āvī, -ātum *vt* to wound, hurt; to damage

vulnificus *adj* wounding, dangerous

vulnus, -eris *nt* wound, injury; (*things*) damage, hole; (*fig*) blow, misfortune, pain

vulpēcula, -ae *f* little fox

vulpēs, -is *f* fox; (*fig*) cunning

vulsī *perf of* **vellō**

vulsus *ppp of* **vellō**

vulticulus, -ī *m* a mere look (from)

vultum *etc see* **vultus**

vultuōsus *adj* affected

vultur, -is *m* vulture

vulturius, -ī *and* **-iī** *m* vulture, bird of prey; (*dice*) an unlucky throw

Vulturnus, -ī *m* river in Campania

vultus, -ūs *m* look, expression (*esp in the eyes*); face; (*things*) appearance

vulva *etc see* **volva**

X   Z

Xanthippē, -ēs *f wife of Socrates*
Xanthus, -ī *m river of Troy (identified with Scamander); river of Lycia*
xenium, -ī *and* **-iī** *nt present*
Xenocratēs, -is *m disciple of Plato*
Xenophanēs, -is *m early Greek philosopher*
Xenophōn, -ontis *m famous Greek historian*
Xenophontēus *adj see* **Xenophōn**
xērampelinae, -ārum *fpl dark-coloured clothes*
Xerxēs, -is *m Persian king defeated at Salamis*
xiphiās, -ae *m swordfish*
xystum, -ī *nt*, **xystus, -ī** *m open colonnade, walk, avenue*

Zacynthius *adj see* **Zacynthus**
Zacynthus, Zacynthos, -ī *f island off W. Greece (now Zante)*
Zama, -ae *f town in Numidia (where Scipio defeated Hannibal)*
Zamēnsis *adj see* **Zama**
zāmia, -ae *f harm*
Zanclaeus, Zanclēius *adj see* **Zanclē**
Zanclē, -ēs *f old name of Messana*
zēlotypus *adj jealous*
Zēnō, Zēnōn, -ōnis *m founder of Stoicism; a philosopher of Elea; an Epicurean teacher of Cicero*
Zephyrītis, -idis *f Arsinoe (queen of Egypt)*
Zephyrus, -ī *m west wind, zephyr; wind*
Zēthus, -ī *m brother of Amphion*
Zeuxis, -is *and* **-idis** *m famous Greek painter*
zmaragdus *etc see* **smaragdus**
Zmyrna *etc see* **Smyrna**
zōdiacus, -ī *m zodiac*
zōna, -ae *f belt, girdle; (GEOG) zone; (ASTR) Orion's Belt*
zōnārius *adj of belts;* **sector ~** *cutpurse* ▶ *m belt maker*
zōnula, -ae *f little belt*
zōthēca, -ae *f private room*
zōthēcula, -ae *f cubicle*

Latin Grammar

Declensions of nouns	2
Conjugations of verbs	6
Verbal nouns and adjectives	16
Irregular verbs	17

Declensions of nouns

1st Declension

	mainly f		*m*	
SINGULAR				
Nom.	terra	crambē	Aenēās	Anchīsēs
Voc.	terra	crambē	Aenēā	Anchīsā, -ē
Acc.	terram	crambēn	Aenēam, -ān	Anchīsam, -ēn
Gen.	terrae	crambes	Aenēae	Anchīsae
Dat.	terrae	crambae	Aenēae	Anchīsae
Abl.	terra	cramba	Aenēā	Anchīsā
PLURAL				
Nom.	terrae	crambae		
Voc.	terrae	crambae		
Acc.	terrās	crambās		
Gen.	terrārum	crambārum		
Dat.	terrīs	crambīs		
Abl.	terrīs	crambīs		

2nd Declension

	mainly m					*nt*
SINGULAR						
Nom.	modus	Lūcius	Dēlos (f)	puer	liber	dōnum
Voc.	mode	Lūcī	Dēle	puer	liber	dōnum
Acc.	modum	Lūcium	Dēlon	puerum	librum	dōnum
Gen.	modī	Lūcī	Dēlī	puerī	librī	dōnī
Dat.	modō	Lūciō	Dēlō	puerō	librō	dōnō
Abl.	modō	Lūciō	Dēlō	puerō	librō	dōnō
PLURAL						
Nom.	modī			puerī	librī	dōna
Voc.	modī			puerī	librī	dōna
Acc.	modōs			puerōs	librōs	dōna
Gen.	modōrum			puerōrum	librōrum	dōnōrum
Dat.	modīs			puerīs	librīs	dōnīs
Abl.	modīs			puerīs	librīs	dōnīs

2

3rd Declension

Group I: *Vowel stems, with gen pl in* **-ium**

	m and f		nt	
SINGULAR				
Nom.	clādēs	nāvis	rēte	animal
Voc.	clādēs	nāvis	rēte	animal
Acc.	clādem	nāvem, -im	rēte	animal
Gen.	clādis	nāvis	rētis	animālīs
Dat.	clādī	nāvī	rētī	animālī
Abl.	clāde	nāve, -ī	rētī	animālī
PLURAL				
Nom.	clādēs	nāvēs	rētia	animālia
Voc.	clādēs	nāvēs	rētia	animālia
Acc.	clādēs, -īs	nāvēs, -īs	rētia	animālia
Gen.	clādium	nāvium	rētium	animālium
Dat.	clādibus	nāvibus	rētibus	animālibus
Abl.	clādibus	nāvibus	rētibus	animālibus

Group II: *Consonant stems, some with gen pl in* **-ium**, *some in* **-um** *and some in either.*
Monosyllabic nouns ending in two consonants (e.g. **urbs** *below) regularly have* **-ium**.

	m and f				nt
SINGULAR					
Nom.	urbs	amāns	laus	aetās	os
Voc.	urbs	amāns	laus	aetās	os
Acc.	urbem	amantem	laudem	aetātem	os
Gen.	urbis	amantis	laudis	aetātis	ossis
Dat.	urbī	amantī	laudī	aetātī	ossī
Abl.	urbe	amante	laude	aetāte	osse
PLURAL					
Nom.	urbēs	amantēs	laudēs	aetātēs	ossa
Voc.	urbēs	amantēs	laudēs	aetātēs	ossa
Acc.	urbēs	amantēs	laudēs	aetātēs	ossa
Gen.	urbium	amantium, -um	laudum, -ium	aetātum, -ium	ossium
Dat.	urbibus	amantibus	laudibus	aetātibus	ossibus
Abl.	urbibus	amantibus	laudibus	aetātibus	ossibus

Group III: *Consonant stems, with gen pl in* **-um**

	m and f			nt	
SINGULAR					
Nom.	mōs	ratiō	pater	nōmen	opus
Voc.	mōs	ratiō	pater	nōmen	opus
Acc.	mōrem	ratiōnem	patrem	nōmen	opus
Gen.	mōris	ratiōnis	patris	nōminis	operis
Dat.	mōrī	ratiōnī	patrī	nōminī	operī
Abl.	mōre	ratiōne	patre	nōmine	opere
PLURAL					
Nom.	mōrēs	ratiōnēs	patrēs	nōmina	opera
Voc.	mōrēs	ratiōnēs	patrēs	nōmina	opera
Acc.	mōrēs	ratiōnēs	patrēs	nōmina	opera
Gen.	mōrum	ratiōnum	patrum	nōminum	operum
Dat.	mōribus	ratiōnibus	patribus	nōminibus	operibus
Abl.	mōribus	ratiōnibus	patribus	nōminibus	operibus

Group IV: *Greek nouns*

	m			f	nt
SINGULAR					
Nom.	āēr	hērōs	Periclēs	Naias	poēma
Voc.	āēr	hērōs	Periclē	Naias	poēma
Acc.	āera	hērōa	Periclem, Periclea	Naiada	poēma
Gen.	āeris	hērōis	Periclis, -i	Naiadis, -os	poēmatis
Dat.	āerī	hērōī	Periclī	Naiadī	poēmatī
Abl.	aere	hērōe	Pericle	Naiade	poēmate
PLURAL					
Nom.	āeres	hērōes		Naiades	poēmata
Voc.	āeres	hērōes		Naiades	poēmata
Acc.	āeras	hērōas		Naiadas	poēmata
Gen.	āerum	hērōum		Naiadum	poēmatōrum
Dat.	āeribus	hērōibus		Naiadibus	poēmatīs
Abl.	āeribus	hērōibus		Naiadibus	poēmatīs

	4th Declension		_5th Declension_	
	mainly m	_nt_	_mainly f_	
SINGULAR				
Nom.	portus	genū	diēs	rēs
Voc.	portus	genū	diēs	rēs
Acc.	portum	genū	diem	rem
Gen.	portūs	genūs	diēī	reī
Dat.	portuī	genū	diēī	reī
Abl.	portū	genū	diē	rē
PLURAL				
Nom.	portūs	genua	diēs	rēs
Voc.	portūs	genua	diēs	rēs
Acc.	portūs	genua	diēs	rēs
Gen.	portuum	genuum	diērum	rērum
Dat.	portibus, -ubus	genibus, -ubus	diēbus	rēbus
Abl.	portibus, -ubus	genibus, -ubus	diēbus	rēbus

Conjugations of verbs

ACTIVE
PRESENT TENSE

First	Second	Third	Fourth
parāre	habēre	sūmere	audīre
prepare	*have*	*take*	*hear*

Indicative				
SINGULAR				
1st pers	parō	habeō	sūmō	audiō
2nd pers	parās	habēs	sūmis	audīs
3rd pers	parat	habet	sūmit	audit
PLURAL				
1st pers	parāmus	habēmus	sūmimus	audīmus
2nd pers	parātis	habētis	sūmitis	audītis
3rd pers	parant	habent	sūmunt	audiunt

Subjunctive				
SINGULAR				
1st pers	parem	habeam	sūmam	audiam
2nd pers	parēs	habeās	sūmās	audiās
3rd pers	paret	habeat	sūmat	audiat
PLURAL				
1st pers	parēmus	habeāmus	sūmāmus	audiāmus
2nd pers	parētis	habeātis	sūmātis	audiātis
3rd pers	parent	habeant	sūmant	audiant

ACTIVE
IMPERFECT TENSE

Indicative				
SINGULAR				
1st pers	parābam	habēbam	sūmēbam	audiēbam
2nd pers	parābās	habēbās	sūmēbās	audiēbās
3rd pers	parābat	habēbat	sūmēbat	audiēbat
PLURAL				
1st pers	parābāmus	habēbāmus	sūmēbāmus	audiēbāmus
2nd pers	parābātis	habēbātis	sūmēbātis	audiēbātis
3rd pers	parābant	habēbant	sūmēbant	audiēbant

Subjunctive				
SINGULAR				
1st pers	parārem	habērem	sūmerem	audīrem
2nd pers	parārēs	habērēs	sūmerēs	audīrēs
3rd pers	parāret	habēret	sūmeret	audīret
PLURAL				
1st pers	parārēmus	habērēmus	sūmerēmus	audīrēmus
2nd pers	parārētis	habērētis	sūmerētis	audīrētis
3rd pers	parārent	habērent	sūmerent	audīrent

ACTIVE
FUTURE TENSE

Indicative				
SINGULAR				
1st pers	parābō	habēbō	sūmam	audiam
2nd pers	parābis	habēbis	sūmēs	audiēs
3rd pers	parābit	habēbit	sūmet	audiet
PLURAL				
1st pers	parābimus	habēbimus	sūmēmus	audiēmus
2nd pers	parābitis	habēbitis	sūmetis	audiētis
3rd pers	parābunt	habēbunt	sūment	audient

Subjunctive				
SINGULAR				
parātūrus, -a, -um		sim		essem
habitūrus, -a, -um		sīs	*or*	essēs
sūmptūrus, -a, -um		sit		esset
audītūrus, -a, -um				
PLURAL				
paratūrī, -ae, -a		sīmus		essēmus
habitūrī, -ae, -a		sītis	*or*	essētis
sūmptūrī, -ae, -a		sint		essent
audītūrī, -ae, -a				

ACTIVE
PERFECT TENSE

Indicative				
SINGULAR				
1st pers	parāvī	habuī	sūmpsī	audīvī
2nd pers	parāvistī	habuistī	sūmpsistī	audīvistī
3rd pers	parāvit	habuit	sūmpsit	audīvit
PLURAL				
1st pers	parāvimus	habuimus	sūmpsimus	audīvimus
2nd pers	parāvistis	habuistis	sūmpsistis	audīvistis
3rd pers	parāvērunt	habuērunt	sūmpsērunt	audīvērunt

Subjunctive				
SINGULAR				
1st pers	parāverim	habuerim	sūmpserim	audīverim
2nd pers	parāveris	habueris	sūmpseris	audīveris
3rd pers	parāverit	habuerit	sūmpserit	audīverit
PLURAL				
1st pers	parāverimus	habuerimus	sūmpserimus	audīverimus
2nd pers	parāveritis	habueritis	sūmpseritis	audīveritis
3rd pers	parāverint	habuerint	sūmpserint	audīverint

ACTIVE
PLUPERFECT TENSE

Indicative				
SINGULAR				
1st pers	parāveram	habueram	sūmpseram	audīveram
2nd pers	parāverās	habuerās	sūmpseras	audīveras
3rd pers	parāverat	habuerat	sūmpserat	audīverat
PLURAL				
1st pers	parāverāmus	habuerāmus	sūmpserāmus	audīveramus
2nd pers	parāverātis	habuerātis	sūmpserātis	audīverātis
3rd pers	parāverant	habuerant	sūmpserant	audīverant

Subjunctive				
SINGULAR				
1st pers	parāvissem	habuissem	sūmpsissem	audīvissem
2nd pers	parāvissēs	habuissēs	sūmpsissēs	audīvissēs
3rd pers	parāvisset	habuisset	sūmpsisset	audīvisset
PLURAL				
1st pers	parāvissēmus	habuissēmus	sūmpsissēmus	audīvissēmus
2nd pers	parāvissētis	habuissētis	sūmpsissētis	audīvissētis
3rd pers	parāvissent	habuissent	sūmpsissent	audīvissent

ACTIVE
FUTURE PERFECT TENSE

Indicative				
SINGULAR				
1st pers	parāverō	habuerō	sūmpserō	audīverō
2nd pers	parāveris	habueris	sūmpseris	audīveris
3rd pers	parāverit	habuerit	sūmpserit	audīverit
PLURAL				
1st pers	parāverimus	habuerimus	sūmpserimus	audīverimus
2nd pers	parāveritis	habueritis	sūmpseritis	audīveritis
3rd pers	parāverint	habuerint	sūmpserint	audīverint

ACTIVE
IMPERATIVE

Indicative				
SINGULAR	parā	habē	sūme	audī
PLURAL	parāte	habēte	sūmite	audīte

Future				
SINGULAR				
2nd pers	parātō	habētō	sūmitō	audītō
3rd pers	parātō	habētō	sūmitō	audītō
PLURAL				
2nd pers	parātōte	habētōte	sūmitōte	audītōte
3rd pers	parantō	habentō	sūmuntō	audiuntō

ACTIVE
INFINITIVE

Present			
parāre	habēre	sūmere	audīre
Perfect			
parāvisse	habuisse	sūmpsisse	audīvisse
Future			
parātūrus, -a, -um esse	habitūrus, -a, -um esse	sūmptūrus, -a, -um esse	audītūrus, -a, -um esse

PASSIVE
PRESENT TENSE

Indicative				
SINGULAR				
1st pers	paror	habeor	sūmor	audior
2nd pers	parāris	habēris	sūmeris	audīris
3rd pers	parātur	habētur	sūmitur	audītur
PLURAL				
1st pers	parāmur	habēmur	sūmimur	audīmur
2nd pers	parāminī	habēminī	sūmiminī	audīminī
3rd pers	parantur	habentur	sūmuntur	audiuntur

Subjunctive			
SINGULAR			
1st pers	parer	habear	sūmar	audiar
2nd pers	parēris	habeāris	sūmāris	audiāris
3rd pers	parētur	habeātur	sūmātur	audiātur
PLURAL			
1st pers	parēmur	habeāmur	sūmāmur	audiāmur
2nd pers	parēminī	habeāminī	sūmāminī	audiāminī
3rd pers	parentur	habeantur	sūmantur	audiantur

PASSIVE

IMPERFECT TENSE

Indicative			
SINGULAR			
1st pers	parābar	habēbar	sūmēbar	audiēbar
2nd pers	parābāris	habēbāris	sūmēbāris	audiēbāris
3rd pers	parābātur	habēbātur	sūmēbātur	audiēbātur
PLURAL			
1st pers	parābāmur	habēbāmur	sūmēbāmur	audiēbāmur
2nd pers	parābāmini	habēbāmini	sūmēbāminī	audiēbāminī
3rd pers	parābāntur	habēbantur	sūmēbantur	audiēbantur

Subjunctive			
SINGULAR			
1st pers	parārer	habērer	sūmerer	audīrer
2nd pers	parārēris	habērēris	sūmerēris	audīrēris
3rd pers	parārētur	habērētur	sūmerētur	audīrētur
PLURAL			
1st pers	parārēmur	habērēmur	sūmerēmur	audīrēmur
2nd pers	parārēminī	habērēminī	sūmerēminī	audīrēminī
3rd pers	parārentur	habērentur	sūmerentur	audīrentur

PASSIVE
FUTURE TENSE

Indicative				
SINGULAR				
1st pers	parābor	habēbor	sūmar	audiar
2nd pers	parāberis	habēberis	sūmēris	audiēris
3rd pers	parābitur	habēbitur	sūmētur	audiētur
PLURAL				
1st pers	parābimur	habēbimur	sūmēmur	audiēmur
2nd pers	parābiminī	habēbiminī	sūmēminī	audiēminī
3rd pers	parābuntur	habēbuntur	sūmentur	audientur

PASSIVE
PERFECT TENSE

Indicative			
SINGULAR		**PLURAL**	
parātus, -a, -um	sum/es/est	parātī, -ae, -a	sumus/estis/sunt
habitus, -a, -um	sum/es/est	habītī, -ae, -a	sumus/estis/sunt
sūmptus, -a, -um	sum/es/est	sūmptī, -ae, -a	sumus/estis/sunt
audītus, -a, -um	sum/es/est	audītī, -ae, -a	sumus/estis/sunt

Subjunctive			
SINGULAR		**PLURAL**	
parātus, -a, -um	sim/sīs/sit	parātī, -ae, -a	sīmus/sītis/sint
habitus, -a, -um	sim/sīs/sit	habītī, -ae, -a	sīmus/sītis/sint
sūmptus, -a, -um	sim/sīs/sit	sūmptī, -ae, -a	sīmus/sītis/sint
audītus, -a, -um	sim/sīs/sit	audītī, -ae, -a	sīmus/sītis/sint

PASSIVE
PLUPERFECT TENSE

Indicative			
SINGULAR		**PLURAL**	
parātus, -a, -um	eram/eras/erat	parātī, -ae, -a	eramus/eratis/erant
habitus, -a, -um	eram/eras/erat	habītī, -ae, -a	eramus/eratis/erant
sūmptus, -a, -um	eram/eras/erat	sūmptī, -ae, -a	eramus/eratis/erant
audītus, -a, -um	eram/eras/erat	audītī, -ae, -a	eramus/eratis/erant

Subjunctive			
SINGULAR		**PLURAL**	
parātus, -a, -um	essem/essēs/esset	parātī, -ae, -a	essēmus/essētis/essent
habitus, -a, -um	essem/essēs/esset	habītī, -ae, -a	essēmus/essētis/essent
sūmptus, -a, -um	essem/essēs/esset	sūmptī, -ae, -a	essēmus/essētis/essent
audītus, -a, -um	essem/essēs/esset	audītī, -ae, -a	essēmus/essētis/essent

PASSIVE
FUTURE PERFECT TENSE

Indicative			
SINGULAR		**PLURAL**	
parātus, -a, -um	erō/eris/erit	parātī, -ae, -a	erimus/eritis/erunt
habitus, -a, -um	erō/eris/erit	habītī, -ae, -a	erimus/eritis/erunt
sūmptus, -a, -um	erō/eris/erit	sūmptī, -ae, -a	erimus/eritis/erunt
audītus, -a, -um	erō/eris/erit	audītī, -ae, -a	erimus/eritis/erunt

PASSIVE
IMPERATIVE

Present				
SINGULAR	parāre	habēre	sūmere	audīre
PLURAL	parāminī	habēminī	sūmiminī	audīminī

Future				
SINGULAR				
2nd pers	parātor	habētor	sūmitor	audītor
3rd pers	parātor	habētor	sūmitor	audītor
PLURAL				
3rd pers	parantor	habentor	sūmuntor	audiuntor

PASSIVE
INFINITIVE

Present			
parārī	habērī	sūmī	audīrī
Perfect			
parātus, -a, -um esse	habitus, -a, -um esse	sūmptus, -a, -um esse	audītus, -a, -um esse
Future			
parātum īrī	habitum īrī	sūmptum īrī	audītum īrī

Note. *Some verbs of the 3rd conjugation have the present indicative ending in -io; e.g.* **capio**, *I capture.*

PRESENT TENSE			
INDICATIVE		**SUBJUNCTIVE**	
Active	**Passive**	**Active**	**Passive**
capio	capior	capiam	capiar
capis	caperis	capias	capiāris
capit	capitur	capiat	capiātur
capimus	capimur	capiāmus	capiāmur
capitis	capiminī	capiātis	capiāminī
capiunt	capiuntur	capiant	capiantur

IMPERFECT TENSE			
INDICATIVE		**SUBJUNCTIVE**	
Active	**Passive**	**Active**	**Passive**
capiēbam *etc.*	capiēbar *etc.*	caperem *etc.*	caperer *etc.*

FUTURE TENSE		INFINITIVE MOOD	
capiam	capiar	**Present Active**	capere
capiēs *etc.*	capiēris *etc.*	**Present Passive**	capī

PRESENT IMPERATIVE			
Active		**Passive**	
cape	capite	capere	capiminī

	PARTICIPLE	GERUND	GERUNDIVE
Present	capiēns	capiendum	capiendus, -a, -um

In all other tenses and moods **capere** *is similar to* **sumere**.

Verbal nouns and adjectives

Present Participle Active			
parāns	habēns	sūmēns	audiēns

Perfect Participle Passive			
parātus	habitus	sūmptus	audītus

Future Participle Active			
parātūrus	habitūrus	sūmptūrus	audītūrus

Gerund			
(acc, gen, dat and abl)			
parandum, -ī, -ō	habendum, -ī, -ō	sūmendum, -ī, -ō	audiendum, -ī, -ō

Gerundive			
parandus	habendus	sūmendus	audiendus

Supines				
1st	parātum	habitum	sūmptum	audītum
2nd	parātū	habitū	sūmptū	audītū

Irregular verbs

	esse	posse	velle	ire
	be	be able	wish	go

Present Indicative				
SINGULAR				
1st pers	sum	possum	volō	eō
2nd pers	es	potes	vīs	īs
3rd pers	est	potest	vult, volt	it
PLURAL				
1st pers	sumus	possumus	volumus	īmus
2nd pers	estis	potestis	vultis, voltis	ītis
3rd pers	sunt	possunt	volunt	eunt

Present Subjunctive				
SINGULAR				
1st pers	sim	possim	velim	eam
2nd pers	sīs	possīs	velīs	eās
3rd pers	sit	possit	velit	eat
PLURAL				
1st pers	sīmus	possīmus	velīmus	eāmus
2nd pers	sītis	possītis	velītis	eātis
3rd pers	sint	possint	velint	eant

Imperfect Indicative				
1st pers	eram	poteram	volēbam	ībam

Imperfect Subjunctive				
1st pers	essem	possem	vellem	īrem

Future Indicative				
1st pers	erō	poterō	volam	ībō

Future Subjunctive				
1st pers	futūrus, -a, -um sim *or* essem	—	—	itūrus, -a, -um sim *or* essem

Perfect Indicative			
1st pers	fuī	potuī	voluī	īvī, iī

Perfect Subjunctive			
1st pers	fuerim	potuerim	voluerim	īverim, ierim

Pluperfect Indicative			
1st pers	fueram	potueram	volueram	īveram, ieram

Pluperfect Subjunctive			
1st pers	fuissem	potuissem	voluissem	īvissem, iissem

Future Perfect Indicative			
1st pers	fuerō	potuerō	voluerō	īverō, ierō

Present Imperative			
SINGULAR	es	—	—	ī
PLURAL	este	—	—	īte

Future Imperative			
SINGULAR	estō	—	—	ītō
PLURAL	estōte	—	—	ītōte

Infinitives			
PRESENT	esse	posse	velle	īre
PERFECT	fuisse	potuisse	voluisse	īvisse, iisse
FUTURE	futūrus, -a, -um esse	—	—	itūrus, -a, -um esse

Participles			
PRESENT	—	—	—	iēns, euntis
FUTURE	futūrus	—	—	itūrus

Gerund and Supine			
GERUND	—	—	—	eundum
SUPINE	—	—	—	itum

Roman Culture

Key events in Roman History   20

Numbers   24

Dates   28

Measures   30

Money   31

Key events in Roman History

BCE

753	Foundation of Rome. Romulus became first king.
600–510	Rome ruled by Etruscan kings.
510	Expulsion of Tarquin and republic established.
507	Consecration of Temple of Jupiter on Capitol.
451	Code of Twelve Tables laid basis of Roman law.
390	Gauls sacked Rome.
367	Lex Liciniae Sextiae; plebeians allowed to be consul.
354	Treaty with Samnites.
343–341	First Samnite war; Romans occupied northern Campania.
340–338	Latin War; separate treaties made with Latins.
327–304	Second Samnite war; Rome increased influence in southern Italy.
321	Samnites defeated Romans at Caudine Forks; truce.
312	Appian Way, first Roman road, built.
298–290	Third Samnite war; Rome now all-powerful in southern Italy.
287	Hortensian Law; People's Assembly became a law-making body.
282–272	Wars with Tarentum and King Pyrrhus of Epirus.
270	Whole peninsula under Roman power.
264–241	First Punic war; Rome defended Greek cities in Sicily.
260	Fleet built; first naval victory at Mylae against Carthaginians.
241	Roman victory over Carthage secured Sicily, source of corn supply.
226	River Ebro treaty; Carthage should not cross into northern Spain.
218–201	Second Punic war against Hannibal.
216	Rome defeated at Battle of Cannae.
214–205	First Macedonian war with Philip V.
202	Scipio defeated Hannibal at Zama.
201	Peace concluded with Carthage; Rome now controlled the western Mediterranean.
200–196	Second Macedonian war; freedom of Greece proclaimed.
172–168	Third Macedonian war; Perseus crushed at Pydna.
148	Macedonia became a Roman province.

146	Carthage destroyed; Corinth destroyed.
133	Tiberius Gracchus became tribune; his assassination caused class conflict.
123–122	Gaius Gracchus carried out political/economic reforms.
121	Gaius was killed.
111–10	Marius and Sulla conducted war against Jugurtha of Numidia.
91–89	Social war between Rome and allies.
89–85	War with Mithridates VI of Pontus.
83–82	Civil war between Sulla and Marius; Sulla captured Rome.
81–79	Sulla, dictator, restored constitution, introduced reforms.
78	Death of Sulla.
77–72	Pompey fought Sertorius in Spain.
73–71	Spartacus's slave revolt.
70	Pompey and Crassus joint consuls; tribunes restored.
67	End of war against Mithridates; pirates controlled by Pompey.
63	Cicero suppressed Catiline's conspiracy.
60	First Triumvirate (Caesar, Pompey, Crassus) was formed.
58–51	Caesar conquered Gaul.
53	Battle of Carrhae; Rome defeated by Parthians; Crassus killed.
49	Caesar crossed Rubicon; civil war with Pompey began.
48	Pompey defeated by Caesar at Pharsalus; Caesar became dictator.
44	Caesar assassinated; Antony sought revenge against conspirators.
43	Second Triumvirate (Antony, Octavian, Lepidus).
42	Battle of Philippi; Triumvirate defeated Brutus and Cassius.
41–40	Antony and Octavian divided territory.
33–32	Rupture between Antony and Octavian.
31	Battle of Actium; Octavian defeated Antony and Cleopatra at sea.
27	Octavian returned powers to Senate; received name Augustus.
18	Julian laws promoted morality, condemned adultery, regulated divorce.
12	Augustus became Pontifex Maximus, head of state religion.
2	Augustus became 'pater patriae', father of his country; apex of his power.

CE

4	Tiberius adopted as Augustus's heir.
6	Annexation of Judaea.
9	Varus's three legions destroyed in Germany.
14	Death of Augustus.
14–37	Tiberius emperor; efficient administrator but unpopular.
14–16	Germanicus's successful campaign in Germany.
19	Germanicus died mysteriously; funeral at Antioch.
21–22	Sejanus organized Praetorian Guard.
26–31	Sejanus powerful in Rome; executed in 31.
37–41	Caligula emperor; cruel and tyrannical, was murdered by a tribune.
41–54	Claudius emperor; conquered Britain; showed political judgement.
57–68	Nero emperor; great fire (64); Christians persecuted.
68–69	Year of four emperors – Galba, Otho, Vitellius, Vespasian.
69–79	Vespasian began Flavian dynasty. Colosseum built.
70	Titus, Vespasian's son, captured Jerusalem, destroyed the Temple.
79–81	Titus emperor. Vesuvius erupted (79), Pompeii destroyed.
81–96	Domitian emperor. Border built in Germany; period ended in terror.
96–98	Nerva emperor after Domitian's assassination.
98–117	Trajan emperor – conqueror of Dacia and Parthian empire.
117–138	Hadrian, cultured traveller, soldier and administrator of empire.
122	Hadrian's Wall built between Solway and Tyne.
138–161	Antoninus Pius emperor; orderly, peaceful rule.
141–143	Antonine Wall built between Forth and Clyde.
161–180	Marcus Aurelius emperor; Commodus, his son, shared power (177–180).
162	War with Parthia.
175–180	War against Germans on the Danube.
180–192	Commodus emperor.
193–211	Septimius Severus became emperor after crisis; died in Britain. Authorized special benefits for army.
211–217	Deterioration under criminal rule of Caracalla.
212	All free men of the empire became citizens.

284–305	Diocletian and Maximian co-emperors, empire divided into 12 dioceses. Prices imposed throughout empire.
303	Christians persecuted by Diocletian.
312	Constantine's victory at Milvian Bridge gave him Rome.
313	Edict of Milan ended persecution of Christians.
324	Constantine became sole emperor.
325	Council of Nicaea made Christianity religion of the empire.
330	Constantine made Byzantium seat of government; renamed it Constantinople.
337	Constantine died a Christian, trying to reorganize the empire.
379–395	Emperor Theodosius kept empire formally intact.
410	Alaric and Goths captured and destroyed Rome.

Numbers

Cardinal

1	ūnus	I
2	duo	II
3	trēs	III
4	quattuor	IV
5	quīnque	V
6	sex	VI
7	septem	VII
8	octō	VIII
9	novem	IX
10	decem	X
11	undecim	XI
12	duodecim	XII
13	tredecim	XIII
14	quattuordecim	XIV
15	quīndecim	XV
16	sēdecim	XVI
17	septendecim	XVII
18	duodēvīgintī	XVIII
19	ūndēvīgintī	XIX
20	vīgintī	XX
21	vīgintī ūnus	XXI
28	duodētrīgintā	XXVIII
29	ūndētrīgintā	XXIX
30	trīgintā	XXX
40	quadrāgintā	XL
50	quīnquāgintā	L
60	sexāgintā	LX
70	septuāgintā	LXX
80	octōgintā	LXXX
90	nōnāgintā	XC
100	centum	C
101	centum et ūnus	CI
122	centum vīgintī duo	CXXII
200	ducentī	CC
300	trecentī	CCC
400	quadringentī	CCCC
500	quīngentī	D
600	sēscentī	DC
700	septingentī	DCC
800	octingentī	DCCC
900	nōngentī	DCCCC
1000	mīlle	M
1001	mīlle et ūnus	MI
1102	mīlle centum duo	MCII
3000	tria mīlia	MMM
5000	quīnque mīlia	IƆƆ
10,000	decem mīlia	CCIƆƆ
100,000	centum mīlia	CCCIƆƆƆ
1,000,000	deciēs centena mīlia	CCCCIƆƆƆƆ

Numbers cont.

	Ordinal	
1st	prīmus	I
2nd	secundus, alter	II
3rd	tertius	III
4th	quārtus	IV
5th	quīntus	V
6th	sextus	VI
7th	septimus	VII
8th	octāvus	VIII
9th	nōnus	IX
10th	decimus	X
11th	undecimus	XI
12th	duodecimus	XII
13th	tertius decimus	XIII
14th	quārtus decimus	XIV
15th	quīntus decimus	XV
16th	sextus decimus	XVI
17th	septimus decimus	XVII
18th	duodēvīcēsimus	XVIII
19th	ūndēvīcēsimus	XIX
20th	vīcēsimus	XX
21st	vīcēsimus prīmus	XXI
28th	duodētrīcēsimus	XXVIII
29th	ūndētrīcēsimus	XXIX
30th	trīcēsimus	XXX
40th	quadrāgēsimus	XL
50th	quīnquāgēsimus	L
60th	sexāgēsimus	LX
70th	septuāgēsimus	LXX
80th	octōgēsimus	LXXX
90th	nōnāgēsimus	XC
100th	centēsimus	C
101st	centēsimus prīmus	CI
122nd	centēsimus vīcēsimus alter	CXXII
200th	ducentēsimus	CC
300th	trecentēsimus	CCC
400th	quadringentēsimus	CCCC
500th	quīngentēsimus	D
600th	sēscentēsimus	DC
700th	septingentēsimus	DCC
800th	octingentēsimus	DCCC
900th	nōngentēsimus	DCCCC
1000th	mīllēsimus	M
1001st	mīllēsimus prīmus	MI
1102nd	mīllēsimus centēsimus alter	MCII
3000th	ter mīllēsimus	MMM
5000th	quīnquiēs mīllēsimus	IↃↃ
10,000th	deciēs mīllēsimus	CCIↃↃ
100,000th	centiēs mīllēsimus	CCCIↃↃↃ
1,000,000th	deciēs centiēs mīllēsimus	CCCCIↃↃↃↃ

Numbers cont.

Distributive

1	singulī	I
2	bīnī	II
3	ternī (trīnī)	III
4	quaternī	IV
5	quīnī	V
6	sēnī	VI
7	septēnī	VII
8	octōnī	VIII
9	novēnī	IX
10	dēnī	X
11	undēnī	XI
12	duodēnī	XII
13	ternī dēnī	XIII
14	quaternī dēnī	XIV
15	quīnī dēnī	XV
16	sēnī dēnī	XVI
17	septēni dēnī	XVII
18	duodēvīcēnī	XVIII
19	undēvīcēnī	XIX
20	vīcēnī	XX
21	vīcēnī singulī	XXI
28	duodētrīcēnī	XXVIII
29	ūndētrīcēnī	XXIX
30	trīcēnī	XXX
40	quadrāgēnī	XL
50	quīnquāgēnī	L
60	sexāgēnī	LX
70	septuāgēnī	LXX
80	octōgēnī	LXXX
90	nōnagēnī	XC
100	centēnī	C
101	centēnī singulī	CI
122	centēnī vīcēnī bīnī	CXXII
200	ducēnī	CC
300	trecēnī	CCC
400	quadringēnī	CCCC
500	quīngēnī	D
600	sexcēnī	DC
700	septingēnī	DCC
800	octingēnī	DCCC
900	nōngēnī	DCCCC
1000	singula mīlia	M
1001	singula mīlia singulī	MI
1102	singula mīlia centēnī bīnī	MCII
3000	trīna mīlia	MMM
5000	quīna mīlia	IↃↃ
10,000	dēna mīlia	CCIↃↃ
100,000	centēna mīlia	CCCIↃↃↃ
1,000,000	deciēs centēna mīlia	CCCCIↃↃↃↃ

26

Numbers cont.

	Adverb	
1st	semel	I
2nd	bis	II
3rd	ter	III
4th	quater	IV
5th	quīnquiēs	V
6th	sexiēs	VI
7th	septiēs	VII
8th	octiēs	VIII
9th	noviēs	IX
10th	deciēs	X
11th	undeciēs	XI
12th	duodeciēs	XII
13th	terdeciēs	XIII
14th	quattuordeciēs	XIV
15th	quīndeciēs	XV
16th	sēdeciēs	XVI
17th	septiēs deciēs	XVII
18th	duodēvīciēs	XVIII
19th	ūndēvīciēs	XIX
20th	vīciēs	XX
21st	semel et vīciēs	XXI
28th	duodētrīciēs	XXVIII
29th	ūndētrīciēs	XXIX
30th	trīciēs	XXX
40th	quadrāgiēs	XL
50th	quīnquāgiēs	L
60th	sexāgiēs	LX
70th	septuāgiēs	LXX
80th	octōgiēs	LXXX
90th	nōnāgiēs	XC
100th	centiēs	C
101st	semel et centiēs	CI
122nd	centiēs vīciēs bis	CXXII
200th	ducentiēs	CC
300th	trecentiēs	CCC
400th	quadringentiēs	CCCC
500th	quīngentiēs	D
600th	sexcentiēs	DC
700th	septingentiēs	DCC
800th	octingentiēs	DCCC
900th	nōngentiēs	DCCCC
1000th	mīlliēs	M
1001st	semel et mīlliēs	MI
1102nd	mīlliēs centiēs bis	MCII
3000th	ter mīlliēs	MMM
5000th	quīnquiēs mīlliēs	IƆƆ
10,000th	deciēs mīlliēs	CCIƆƆ
100,000th	centiēs mīlliēs	CCCIƆƆƆ
1,000,000th	mīlliēs mīlliēs	CCCCIƆƆƆƆ

Dates

Months

Iānuārius	January
Februārius	February
Martius	March
Āprīlis	April
Māius	May
Iūnius	June
Iulius (Quintīlis)	July
Augustus (Sextīlis)	August
September	September
Octōber	October
November	November
December	December

Three days of the month have special names:

Kalendae the 1st.

Nōnae the 5th of most months, but the 7th of March, May, July and October.

> "In March, July, October, May,
> The Nones are on the 7th day."

Idūs the 13th of most months, but the 15th of March, May, July and October.

If the date is one of these three days, it is expressed in the ablative, with the adjective of the month in agreement, *e.g.* 1st January, **Kalendīs Iānuāriīs**, usually abbreviated **Kal. Ian.**

The day immediately before any of these three is expressed by **prīdiē** with the accusative, *e.g.* 4th February, **prīdiē Nōnās Februāriās**, usually abbreviated **prid. Non. Feb.**

All other dates are expressed as so many days before the next named day, and in reckoning the interval both the date and the named day are counted, *e.g.* the 11th is the 5th day before the 15th.

The formula is all in the accusative, beginning with the words **ante diem**, *e.g.* 11th March, **ante diem quintum Idūs Martiās**, usually abbreviated **a.d. V Id. Mar.**

The selection of dates on the following page for April and May should be a sufficient guide to the dates of any month in the year.

April		May
Kal. Apr.	1	Kal. Mai.
a.d. IV Non. Apr.	2	a.d. VI Non. Mai.
a.d. III Non. Apr.	3	a.d. V Non. Mai.
prid. Non. Apr.	4	a.d. IV Non. Mai.
Non. Apr.	5	a.d. III Non. Mai.
a.d. VIII Id. Apr.	6	prid. Non. Mai.
a.d. VII Id. Apr.	7	Non. Mai.
a.d. VI Id. Apr .	8	a.d. VIII Id. Mai .
a.d. V Id. Apr.	9	a.d. VII Id. Mai.
a.d. IV Id. Apr.	10	a.d. VI Id. Mai.
a.d. III Id. Apr.	11	a.d. V Id. Mai.
prid. Id. Apr.	12	a.d. IV Id. Mai.
Id. Apr.	13	a.d. III Id. Mai.
a.d. XVIII Kal. Mai.	14	prid. Id. Mai.
a.d. XVII Kal. Mai.	15	Id. Mai.
a.d. XVI Kal. Mai.	16	a.d. XVII Kal. Iun.
a.d. XV Kal. Mai.	17	a.d. XVI Kal. Iun.
a.d. XII Kal. Mai.	20	a.d. XIII Kal. Iun.
a.d. VII Kal. Mai.	25	a.d. VIII Kal. Iun.
prid. Kal. Mai.	30	a.d. III Kal. Iun.
-	31	prid. Kal. Iun.

Years

A year is denoted either by giving the names of the consuls or by reckoning the number of years from the traditional date of the foundation of Rome, 753 BCE, to give the number *ab urbe condita* (abbreviated to a.u.c.). (To calculate the date a.u.c., a date BCE should be subtracted from 754, while a date CE should be added to 753.)

E.g. "In the year 218 BCE.," *either* P. Cornelio Scipione Ti. Sempronio Longo coss. *or* a. u. c. DXXXVI.

Measures

Length

12 ūnciae	=	1 pēs
5 pedēs	=	1 passus
125 passūs	=	1 stadium
8 stadia	=	mīlle passūs

The Roman mile was about 1.48km.

Area

100 pedēs quadrātī	=	1 scrīpulum
144 scrīpula	=	1 āctus quadrātus
2 āctūs quadrātī	=	1 iugerum
2 iugera	=	1 hērēdium
100 hērēdia	=	1 centuria

The **iugerum** was about 2529.28 square metres.

Capacity

4 cochleāria	=	1 cyathus
12 cyathī	=	1 sextārius
(*liquid*) 6 sextāriī	=	1 congius
8 congiī	=	1 amphora
20 amphorae	=	1 culleus
(*dry*) 8 sextārii	=	1 sēmodius
2 sēmodiī	=	1 modius

The **sextārius** was about half a litre, the **modius** about 9 litres.

Weight

4 scrīpula	=	1 sextula
6 sextulae	=	1 ūncia
12 ūnciae	=	1 lībra

The Roman lb. was about 326 g, and the **ūncia** was therefore about 27 g. The twelfths of the **lībra** have the following names, which are also used to denote fractions generally, *e.g.* **hērēs ex triente**, heir to a third of an estate.

1/12 ūncia	5/12 quīncūnx	3/4 dōdrāns
1/6 sextāns	1/2 sēmis	5/6 dextāns
1/4 quadrāns	7/12 septūnx	11/12 deūnx
1/3 triēns	2/3 bēs	

Money

Roman

$$2^{1}/_{2} \text{ assēs} = 1 \text{ sēstertius (or nummus)}$$
$$4 \text{ sēstertiī} = 1 \text{ dēnārius}$$
$$25 \text{ dēnāriī} = 1 \text{ aureus}$$

The sesterce is represented by a symbol for $2^{1}/_{2}$, properly **II S(ēmis)**, usually standardized in the form HS. The *ntpl* **sēstertia** with the distributive numeral denotes thousands of sesterces, and the numeral adverb with the *gen pl* **sēstertium** (understanding **centēna mīlia**) means hundred thousands, *e.g.*

$$10,000 \text{ sesterces} = \text{dēna sēstertia} = \text{HS X}$$
$$1,000,000 \text{ sesterces} = \text{deciēs sēstertium} = \text{HS IXI}$$

Greek

$$100 \text{ drachumae} = 1 \text{ mina}$$
$$60 \text{ minae} = 1 \text{ talentum}$$

English – Latin

a

a, an *art* not translated; *(a certain)* quīdam; **twice a day** bis in diē; **four acres a man** quaterna in singulōs iūgera

aback *adv*: **taken ~** dēprehēnsus

abaft *adv* in puppī ▶ *prep* post, pōne

abandon *vt* relinquere; *(wilfully)* dērelinquere, dēserere; *(to danger)* ōbicere; *(to pleasure)* dēdere; *(plan)* abicere; **~ hope** spem abicere

abandoned *adj* perditus

abase *vt* dēprimere; **~ oneself** sē prōsternere

abash *vt* perturbāre; rubōrem incutere *(dat)*

abate *vt* minuere, imminuere; *(a portion)* remittere ▶ *vi (fever)* dēcēdere; *(passion)* dēfervēscere; *(price)* laxāre; *(storm)* cadere

abatement *n* remissiō *f*, dēminūtiō *f*

abbess *n* abbātissa *f*

abbey *n* abbātia *f*

abbot *n* abbās *m*

abbreviate *vt* imminuere

abbreviation *n (writing)* nota *f*

abdicate *vt* sē abdicāre *(abl)*

abdication *n* abdicātiō *f*

abduct *vt* abripere

abduction *n* raptus *m*

aberration *n* error *m*

abet *vt* adiuvāre, adesse *(dat)*, favēre *(dat)*

abettor *n* adiūtor *m*, minister *m*, fautor *m*, socius *m*

abeyance *n*: **in ~** intermissus; **be in ~** iacēre

abhor *vt* ōdisse, invīsum habēre

abhorrence *n* odium *nt*

abhorrent *adj*: **~ to** aliēnus ab

abide *vi (dwell)* habitāre; *(tarry)* commorārī; *(last)* dūrāre; **~ by** *vt fus* stāre *(abl)*, perstāre in *(abl)*

abiding *adj* perpetuus, diūturnus

ability *n (to do)* facultās *f*, potestās *f*; *(physical)* vīrēs *fpl*; *(mental)* ingenium *nt*; **to the best of my ~** prō meā parte, prō virīlī parte

abject *adj* abiectus, contemptus; *(downcast)* dēmissus

abjectly *adv* humiliter, dēmissē

abjure *vt* ēiūrāre

ablative *n* ablātīvus *m*

ablaze *adj* flāgrāns, ardēns

able *adj* perītus, doctus; **be ~** posse, valēre

able-bodied *adj* rōbustus

ablution *n* lavātiō *f*

ably *adv* perītē, doctē

abnegation *n* abstinentia *f*

abnormal *adj* inūsitātus; *(excess)* immodicus

abnormally *adv* inūsitātē, praeter mōrem

aboard *adv* in nāvī; **go ~** nāvem cōnscendere; **put ~** impōnere

abode *n* domicilium *nt*, sēdēs *f*

abolish *vt* tollere, ē mediō tollere, abolēre; *(LAW)* abrogāre

abolition *n* dissolūtiō *f*; *(LAW)* abrogātiō *f*

abominable *adj* dētestābilis, nefārius

abominably *adv* nefāriē, foedē

abominate *vt* dētestārī

abomination *n* odium *nt*; *(thing)* nefas *nt*

aboriginal *adj* prīscus

aborigines *npl* aborīginēs *mpl*

abortion *n* abortus *m*

abortive *adj* abortīvus; *(fig)* inritus; **be ~** ad inritum redigī

abound *vi* abundāre, superesse; **~ in** abundāre *(abl)*, adfluere *(abl)*

abounding *adj* abundāns, adfluēns; cōpiōsus ab

about *adv (place)* usu expressed by compound verbs; *(number)* circiter, ferē, fermē ▶ *prep (place)* circā, circum *(acc)*; *(number)* circā, ad *(acc)*; *(time)* sub *(acc)*; *(concerning)* dē *(abl)*; **~ to die** moritūrus; **I am ~ to go** in eō est ut eam

above *adv* suprā; **from ~** dēsuper; **over and ~** īnsuper ▶ *prep* suprā *(acc)*; *(motion)* super *(acc)*; *(rest)* super *(abl)*; **be ~** *(conduct)* indignārī

abreast *adv (ships)* aequātīs prōrīs; **walk ~ of** latus tegere *(dat)*

abridge *vt* contrahere, compendī facere

abridgement *n* epitomē *f*

abroad *adv (out of doors)* forīs; **be ~** peregrīnārī; **from ~** peregrē

abrogate *vt* dissolvere; *(LAW)* abrogāre

abrupt *adj* subitus, repentīnus; *(speech)* concīsus

abscess *n* vomica *f*

abscond *vi* aufugere

absence *n* absentia *f*; **in my ~** mē absente; **leave of ~** commeātus *m*

absent *adj* absēns; **be ~** abesse; **~ oneself** *vi* deesse, nōn adesse

absent-minded *adj* immemor, parum attentus

absolute *adj* absolūtus, perfectus; *(not limited)* īnfīnītus; *(not relative)* simplex; **~ power** rēgnum *nt*, dominātus *m*; **~ ruler** rēx

absolutely *adv* absolūtē, omnīnō

absolution *n* venia *f*

absolve *vt* absolvere, exsolvere; *(from punishment)* condōnāre

absorb *vt* bibere, absorbēre; *(fig)* distringere; **I am absorbed in** tōtus sum in *(abl)*

absorbent *adj* bibulus

abstain vi abstinēre, sē abstinēre; (*from violence*) temperāre
abstemious adj sobrius
abstinence n abstinentia f, continentia f
abstinent adj abstinēns, sobrius
abstract adj mente perceptus, cōgitātiōne comprehēnsus ▶ n epitomē f ▶ vt abstrahere, dēmere
abstraction n (*idea*) nōtiō f; (*inattention*) animus parum attentus
abstruse adj reconditus, obscūrus, abstrūsus
absurd adj ineptus, absurdus
absurdity n ineptiae fpl, insulsitās f
absurdly adv ineptē, absurdē
abundance n cōpia f, abundantia f; **there is ~ of** abundē est (*gen*)
abundant adj cōpiōsus, abundāns, largus; **be ~** abundāre
abundantly adv abundē, abundanter, adfātim
abuse vt abūtī (*abl*); (*words*) maledīcere (*dat*) ▶ n probra ntpl, maledicta ntpl, convīcium nt, contumēlia f
abusive adj maledicus, contumēliōsus
abut vi adiacēre; **abutting on** cōnfīnis (*dat*), fīnitimus (*dat*)
abysmal adj profundus
abyss n profundum nt, vorāgō f; (*water*) gurges m; (*fig*) barathrum nt
academic adj scholasticus; (*style*) umbrātilis; (*sect*) Acadēmicus
academy n schola f; (*Plato's*) Acadēmīa f
accede vi adsentīrī; **~ to** accipere
accelerate vt, vi adcelerāre, festīnāre; (*process*) mātūrāre
accent n vōx f; (*intonation*) sonus m; (*mark*) apex m ▶ vt (*syllable*) acuere; (*word*) sonum admovēre (*dat*)
accentuate vt exprimere
accept vt accipere
acceptable adj acceptus, grātus, probābilis; **be ~** placēre
acceptation n significātiō f
access n aditus m; (*addition*) accessiō f; (*illness*) impetus m
accessary n socius m, particeps m
accessible adj (*person*) adfābilis, facilis; **be ~** (*place*) patēre; (*person*) facilem sē praebēre
accession n (*addition*) accessiō f; (*king's*) initium rēgnī
accident n cāsus m, calamitās f
accidental adj fortuītus
accidentally adv cāsū, fortuītō
acclaim vt adclāmāre
acclamation n clāmor m, studium nt
acclimatize vt aliēnō caelō adsuēfacere
accommodate vt accommodāre, aptāre; (*lodging*) hospitium parāre (*dat*); **~ oneself to** mōrigerārī (*dat*)
accommodating adj facilis
accommodation n hospitium nt
accompany vt comitārī; (*courtesy*) prōsequī; (*to Forum*) dēdūcere; (*music*) concinere (*dat*)

accomplice n socius m, particeps m, cōnscius m
accomplish vt efficere, perficere, patrāre
accomplished adj doctus, perītus
accomplishment n effectus m, perfectiō f, fīnis m; **accomplishments** pl artēs fpl
accord vi inter sē congruere, cōnsentīre ▶ vt dare, praebēre, praestāre ▶ n cōnsēnsus m, concordia f; (*music*) concentus m; **of one's own ~** suā sponte, ultrō; **with one ~** ūnā vōce
accordance n: **in ~ with** ex, ē (*abl*), secundum (*acc*)
according adv: **~ to** ex, ē (*abl*), secundum (*acc*); (*proportion*) prō (*abl*); **~ as** prōut
accordingly adv itaque, igitur, ergō
accost vt appellāre, adloquī, compellāre
account n ratiō f; (*story*) nārrātiō f, expositiō f; **on ~ of** ob (*acc*); propter (*acc*), causā (*gen*); **be of no ~** (*person*) nihilī aestimārī, nēquam esse; **on that ~** idcircō, ideō; **on your ~** tuā grātiā, tuō nōmine; **give an ~** ratiōnem reddere; **present an ~** ratiōnem referre; **take ~ of** ratiōnem habēre (*gen*); **put down to my ~** expēnsum ferre; **the accounts balance** ratiō cōnstat/convenit ▶ vi: **~ for** ratiōnēs reddere, adferre (*cūr*); **that accounts for it** haec causa est, (*proverb*) hinc illae lacrimae
accountable adj reus; **I am ~ for** mihi ratiō reddenda est (*gen*)
accountant n ā ratiōnibus, ratiōcinātor m
account book n tabulae fpl; cōdex acceptī et expēnsī
accoutred adj īnstructus, ōrnātus
accoutrements n ōrnāmenta ntpl, arma ntpl
accredited adj pūblicā auctōritāte missus
accretion n accessiō f
accrue vi (*addition*) cēdere; (*advantage*) redundāre
accumulate vt cumulāre, congerere, coacervāre ▶ vi crēscere, cumulārī
accumulation n cumulus m, acervus m
accuracy n cūra f; (*writing*) subtīlitās f
accurate adj (*work*) exāctus, subtīlis; (*worker*) dīligēns
accurately adv subtīliter, ad amussim, dīligenter
accursed adj sacer; (*fig*) exsecrātus, scelestus
accusation n (*act*) accūsātiō f; (*charge*) crīmen nt; (*unfair*) īnsimulātiō f; (*false*) calumnia f; **bring an ~ against** accūsāre; (*to a magistrate*) nōmen dēferre (*gen*)
accusative n (*case*) accūsātīvus m
accuse vt accūsāre, crīminārī, reum facere; (*falsely*) īnsimulāre; **the accused** reus; (*said by prosecutor*) iste
accuser n accūsātor m; (*civil suit*) petītor m; (*informer*) dēlātor m
accustom vt adsuēfacere; **~ oneself** adsuēscere, cōnsuēscere
accustomed adj adsuētus; **be ~** solēre; **become ~** adsuēscere, cōnsuēscere
ace n ūniō f; **I was within an ace of going** minimum āfuit quin īrem

acerbity n acerbitās f
ache n dolor m ▶ vi dolēre
achieve vt cōnficere, patrāre; (win) cōnsequī, adsequī
achievement n factum nt, rēs gesta
acid adj acidus
acknowledge vt (fact) agnōscere; (fault) fatērī, cōnfitērī; (child) tollere; (service) grātiās agere prō (abl); **I have to ~ your letter of 1st March** accēpī litterās tuās Kal. Mart. datās
acknowledgement n cōnfessiō f; grātia f
acme n fastīgium nt, flōs m
aconite n aconītum nt
acorn n glāns f
acoustics n rēs audītōria f
acquaint vt certiōrem facere, docēre; **~ oneself with** cognōscere; **acquainted with** gnārus (gen), perītus (gen)
acquaintance n (with fact) cognitiō f, scientia f; (with person) familiāritās f, ūsus m; (person) nōtus m, familiāris m
acquiesce vi (assent) adquiēscere; (submit) aequō animō patī
acquiescence n: **with your ~** tē nōn adversante, pāce tuā
acquire vt adquīrere, adipīscī, cōnsequī; nancīscī
acquirements n artēs fpl
acquisition n (act) comparātiō f, quaestus m; (thing) quaesītum nt
acquisitive adj quaestuōsus
acquit vt absolvere; **~ oneself** sē praestāre, officiō fungī
acquittal n absolūtiō f
acre n iūgerum nt
acrid adj asper, ācer
acrimonious adj acerbus, truculentus
acrimony n acerbitās f
acrobat n fūnambulus m
acropolis n arx f
across adv trānsversus ▶ prep trāns (acc)
act n factum nt, facinus nt; (play) āctus m; (POL) āctum nt, senātus cōnsultum nt, dēcrētum nt; **I was in the act of saying** in eō erat ut dīcerem; **caught in the act** dēprehēnsus ▶ vi facere, agere; (conduct) sē gerere; (stage) histriōnem esse, partēs agere; (pretence) simulāre ▶ vt: **act a part** partēs agere, persōnam sustinēre; **act the part of** agere; **act as** esse, munere fungī (gen); **act upon** (instructions) exsequī
action n (doing) āctiō f; (deed) factum nt, facinus nt; (legal) āctiō f, līs f; (MIL) proelium nt; (of play) āctiō f; (of speaker) gestus m; **bring an ~ against** lītem intendere, āctiōnem īnstituere (dat); **be in ~** agere, rem gerere; (MIL) pugnāre, in aciē dīmicāre; **man of ~** vir strēnuus
active adj impiger, strēnuus, sēdulus, nāvus
actively adv impigrē, strēnuē, nāviter
activity n (motion) mōtus m; (energy) industria f, sēdulitās f
actor n histriō m; (in comedy) cōmoedus m; (in tragedy) tragoedus m

actress n mīma f
actual adj vērus, ipse
actually adv rē vērā
actuate vt movēre, incitāre
acumen n acūmen nt, ingenī aciēs, argūtiae fpl
acute adj acūtus, ācer; (pain) ācer; (speech) argūtus, subtīlis
acutely adv acūtē, ācriter, argūtē
acuteness n (mind) acūmen nt, aciēs f, subtīlitās f
adage n prōverbium nt
adamant n adamās m ▶ adj obstinātus
adamantine adj adamantinus
adapt vt accommodāre
adaptable adj flexibilis, facile accommodandus
adaptation n accommodātiō f
add vt addere, adicere, adiungere; **be added** accēdere
adder n vīpera f
addicted adj dēditus
addition n adiūnctiō f, accessiō f; additāmentum nt, incrēmentum nt; **in ~** īnsuper, praetereā; **in ~ to** praeter (acc)
additional adj novus, adiūnctus
addled adj (egg) inritus; (brain) inānis
address vt compellāre, alloquī; (crowd) cōntiōnem habēre apud (acc); (letter) īnscrībere; **~ oneself** (to action) accingī ▶ n adloquium nt; (public) cōntiō f, ōrātiō f; (letter) īnscrīptiō f
adduce vt (argument) adferre; (witness) prōdūcere
adept adj perītus
adequate adj idōneus, dignus, pār; **be ~** sufficere
adequately adv satis, ut pār est
adhere vi haerēre, adhaerēre; **~ to** inhaerēre (dat), inhaerēscere in (abl); (agreement) manēre, stāre in (abl)
adherent n adsectātor m; (of party) fautor m; (of person) cliēns m
adhesive adj tenax
adieu interj valē, valēte; **bid ~ to** valēre iubēre
adjacent adj fīnitimus, vīcīnus; **be ~ to** adiacēre (dat)
adjoin vi adiacēre (dat)
adjoining adj fīnitimus, adiūnctus; proximus
adjourn vt (short time) differre; (longer time) prōferre; (case) ampliāre ▶ vi rem differre, prōferre
adjournment n dīlātiō f, prōlātiō f
adjudge vt addīcere, adiūdicāre
adjudicate vi dēcernere
adjudicator n arbiter m
adjunct n appendix f, accessiō f
adjure vt obtestārī, obsecrāre
adjust vt (adapt) accommodāre; (put in order) compōnere
adjutant n (MIL) optiō m; (civil) adiūtor m
administer vt administrāre, gerere; (justice) reddere; (oath to) iūreiūrandō adigere; (medicine) dare, adhibēre
administration n administrātiō f

administrator n administrātor m,
prōcūrātor m
admirable adj admīrābilis, ēgregius
admirably adv ēgregiē
admiral n praefectus classis; **admiral's ship**
nāvis praetōria
admiralty n praefectī classium
admiration n admīrātiō f, laus f
admire vt admīrārī; mīrārī
admirer n laudātor m; amātor m
admissible adj aequus
admission n (entrance) aditus m; (of guilt etc)
cōnfessiō f
admit vt (let in) admittere, recipere, accipere;
(to membership) adscīscere; (argument)
concēdere; (fault) fatērī; **~ of** patī, recipere
admittedly adv sānē
admonish vt admonēre, commonēre, hortārī
admonition n admonitiō f
ado n negōtium nt; **make much ado about
nothing** fluctūs in simpulō excitāre; **without
more ado** prōtinus, sine morā
adolescence n prīma adulēscentia f
adolescent adj adulēscēns ▶ n
adulēscentulus m
adopt vt (person) adoptāre; (custom) adscīscere;
~ a plan consilium capere
adoption n (person) adoptiō f; (custom)
adsūmptiō f; **by ~** adoptīvus
adoptive adj adoptīvus
adorable adj amābilis, venustus
adorably adv venustē
adoration n (of gods) cultus m; (of kings)
venerātiō f; (love) amor m
adore vt (worship) venerārī; (love) adamāre
adorn vt ōrnāre, exōrnāre, decorāre
adornment n ōrnāmentum nt, decus nt;
ōrnātus m
adrift adj fluctuāns; **be ~** fluctuāre
adroit adj sollers, callidus
adroitly adv callidē, scītē
adroitness n sollertia f, calliditās f
adulation n adūlātiō f, adsentātiō f
adulatory adj blandus
adult adj adultus
adulterate vt corrumpere, adulterāre
adulterer n adulter m
adulteress n adultera f
adulterous adj incestus
adultery n adulterium nt; **commit ~** adulterāre
adults npl pūberēs mpl
adumbrate vt adumbrāre
advance vt prōmovēre; (a cause) fovēre; (money)
crēdere; (opinion) dīcere; (to honours) prōvehere;
(time) mātūrāre ▶ vi prōcēdere, prōgredī,
adventāre; (MIL) signa prōferre, pedem īnferre;
(progress) prōficere; (walk) incēdere; **~ to the
attack** signa īnferre ▶ n prōgressus m,
prōcessus m; (attack) impetus m; (money)
mūtuae pecūniae; **in ~** mātūrius; **fix in ~**
praefinīre; **get in ~** praecipere
advanced adj prōvectus; **well ~** (task) adfectus

advancement n (POL) honōs m
advantage n (benefit) commodum nt, bonum
nt, ūsus m; (of place or time) opportūnitās f;
(profit) fructus m; (superiority) praestantia f; **it is
an ~ bono est; **be of ~ to** prōdesse (dat), ūsuī
esse (dat); **to your ~** in rem tuam; **it is to your ~**
tibi expedit, tuā interest; **take ~ of**
(circumstances) ūtī; (person) dēcipere, fallere;
have an ~ over praestāre (dat); **be seen to ~**
māximē placēre
advantageous adj ūtilis, opportūnus
advantageously adv ūtiliter, opportūnē
advent n adventus m
adventitious adj fortuītus
adventure n (exploit) facinus memorābile nt;
(hazard) perīculum nt
adventurer n vir audāx m; (social) parasītus m
adventurous adj audāx
adversary n adversārius m, hostis m
adverse adj adversus, contrārius, inimīcus
adversely adv contrāriē, inimīcē, male
adversity n rēs adversae fpl, calamitās f
advert vi: **~ to** attingere
advertise vt prōscrībere; vēnditāre
advertisement n prōscrīptiō f, libellus m
advice n cōnsilium nt; (POL) auctōritās f; (legal)
respōnsum nt; **ask ~ of** cōnsulere; **on the ~ of
Sulla** auctōre Sullā
advisable adj ūtilis, operae pretium
advise vt monēre, suādēre (dat), cēnsēre (dat);
~ against dissuādēre
advisedly adv cōnsultō
adviser n auctor m, suāsor m
advocacy n patrōcinium nt
advocate n patrōnus m, causidicus m;
(supporter) auctor m; **be an ~** causam dīcere ▶ vt
suādēre, cēnsēre
adze n ascia f
aedile n aedīlis m
aedile's adj aedīlicius
aedileship n aedīlitās f
aegis n aegis f; (fig) praesidium nt
Aeneid n Aenēis f
aerial adj āerius
aesthetic adj pulchritūdinis amāns,
artificiōsus
afar adv procul; **from ~** procul
affability n cōmitās f, facilitās f, bonitās f
affable adj cōmis, facilis, commodus
affably adv cōmiter
affair n negōtium nt, rēs f
affect vt afficere, movēre, commovēre;
(concern) attingere; (pretence) simulāre
affectation n simulātiō f; (RHET) adfectātiō f;
(in diction) īnsolentia f; quaesīta ntpl
affected adj (style) molestus, pūtidus
affectedly adv pūtidē
affecting adj miserābilis
affection n amor m, cāritās f, studium nt;
(family) pietās f
affectionate adj amāns, pius
affectionately adv amanter, piē

affiance vt spondēre
affidavit n testimōnium nt
affinity n affīnitās f, cognātiō f
affirm vt adfirmāre, adsevērāre
affirmation n adfirmātiō f
affirmative adj: **I reply in the ~** āiō
affix vt adfīgere, adiungere
afflict vt adflīctāre, angere, vexāre; afflīgere
affliction n miseria f, dolor m, rēs adversae fpl
affluence n cōpia f, opēs fpl
affluent adj dīves, opulentus, locuplēs
afford vt praebēre, dare; **I cannot ~** rēs mihi nōn
  suppetit ad
affray n rixa f, pugna f
affright vt terrēre ▶ n terror m, pavor m
affront vt offendere, contumēliam dīcere (dat)
  ▶ n iniūria f, contumēlia f
afield adv forīs; **far ~** peregrē
afloat adj natāns; **be ~** natāre
afoot adv pedibus; **be ~** gerī
aforesaid adj suprā dictus
afraid adj timidus; **be ~ of** timēre, metuere;
  verērī
afresh adv dēnuō, dē integrō
Africa n Africa f
aft adv in puppī, puppim versus
after adj posterior ▶ adv posthāc, posteā; **the
  day ~** postrīdiē ▶ conj postquam; **the day ~**
  postrīdiē quam ▶ prep post (acc); (in rank)
  secundum (acc); (in imitation) ad (acc), dē (abl);
  ~ all tamen, dēnique; **~ reading the book** librō
  lēctō; **one thing ~ another** aliud ex aliō;
  immediately ~ statim ab
aftermath n ēventus m
afternoon n: **in the ~** post merīdiem ▶ adj
  postmerīdiānus
afterthought n posterior cōgitātiō f
afterwards adv post, posteā, deinde
again adv rūrsus, iterum; **~ and ~** etiam atque
  etiam, identidem; **once ~** dēnuō; (new point in
  a speech) quid?
against prep contrā (acc), adversus (acc), in
  (acc); **~ the stream** adversō flūmine; **~ one's
  will** invītus
agape adj hiāns
age n (life) aetās f; (epoch) aetās f, saeculum nt;
  old age senectūs f; **he is of age** suī iūris est;
  he is eight years of age octō annōs nātus est,
  nōnum annum agit; **of the same age** aequālis
aged adj senex, aetāte prōvectus; (things)
  antīquus
agency n opera f; **through the ~ of** per (acc)
agent n āctor m, prōcūrātor m; (in crime)
  minister m
aggrandize vt augēre, amplificāre
aggrandizement n amplificātiō f
aggravate vt (wound) exulcerāre; (distress)
  augēre; **become aggravated** ingravēscere
aggravating adj molestus
aggregate n summa f
aggression n incursiō f, iniūria f
aggressive adj ferōx

aggressiveness n ferōcitās f
aggressor n oppugnātor m
aggrieved adj īrātus; **be ~** indignārī
aghast adj attonitus, stupefactus; **stand ~**
  obstupēscere
agile adj pernix, vēlōx
agility n pernīcitās f
agitate vt agitāre; (mind) commovēre,
  perturbāre
agitation n commōtiō f, perturbātiō f,
  trepidātiō f; (POL) tumultus m
agitator n turbātor m, concitātor m
aglow adj fervidus ▶ **be ~** fervēre
ago adv abhinc (acc); **three days ago** abhinc trēs
  diēs; **long ago** antīquitus, iamprīdem,
  iamdūdum; **a short time ago** dūdum
agog adj sollicitus, ērēctus
agonize vt cruciāre, torquēre
agonizing adj horribilis
agony n cruciātus m, dolor m
agrarian adj agrārius; **~ party** agrāriī mpl
agree vi (together) cōnsentīre, congruere; (with)
  adsentīrī (dat), sentīre cum; (bargain) pacīscī;
  (facts) cōnstāre, convenīre; (food) facilem esse
  ad concoquendum; **~ upon** cōnstituere,
  compōnere; **it is agreed** cōnstat (inter omnēs)
agreeable adj grātus, commodus, acceptus
agreeableness n dulcēdō f, iūcunditās f
agreeably adv iūcundē
agreement n (together) cōnsēnsus m,
  concordia f; (with) adsēnsus m; (pact) pactiō f,
  conventum nt, foedus nt; **according to ~**
  compāctō, ex compositō; **be in ~** cōnsentīre,
  congruere
agricultural adj rūsticus, agrestis
agriculture n rēs rūstica f, agrī cultūra f
aground adv: **be ~** sīdere; **run ~** in lītus ēicī,
  offendere
ague n horror m, febris f
ahead adv ante; **go ~** anteīre, praeīre; **go-ahead**
  adj impiger; **ships in line ~** agmen nāvium
aid vt adiuvāre, succurrere (dat), subvenīre (dat)
  ▶ n auxilium nt, subsidium nt
aide-de-camp n optiō m
ail vt dolēre ▶ vi aegrōtāre, labōrāre, languēre
ailing adj aeger, īnfirmus
ailment n morbus m, valētūdō f
aim vt intendere; **aim at** petere; (fig) adfectāre,
  spectāre, sequī; (with verb) id agere ut ▶ n fīnis
  m, prōpositum nt
aimless adj inānis, vānus
aimlessly adv sine ratiōne
aimlessness n vānitās f
air n āēr m; (breeze) aura f; (look) vultus m, speciēs
  f; (tune) modus m; **in the open air** sub dīvō; **airs**
  fastus m; **give oneself airs** sē iactāre
airily adv hilarē
airy adj (of air) āerius; (light) tenuis; (place)
  apertus; (manner) hilaris
aisle n āla f
ajar adj sēmiapertus
akin adj cōnsanguineus, cognātus

alacrity n alacritās f
alarm n terror m, formīdō f, trepidātiō f; (sound) clāmor m; **sound an ~** ad arma conclāmāre; **give the ~** increpāre; **be in a state of ~** trepidāre ▶ vt terrēre, perterrēre, perturbāre
alarming adj formīdolōsus
alas interj heu
albeit conj etsī, etiamsī
alcove n zōthēca f
alder n alnus f
alderman n decuriō m
ale n cervīsia f
alehouse n caupōna f, taberna f
alert adj prōmptus, alacer, vegetus
alertness n alacritās f
alien adj externus; **~ to** abhorrēns ab ▶ n peregrīnus m
alienate vt aliēnāre, abaliēnāre, āvertere, āvocāre
alienation n aliēnātiō f
alight adj: **be ~** ārdēre; **set ~** accendere ▶ vi (from horse) dēscendere, dēsilīre; (bird) īnsīdere
alike adj pār, similis ▶ adv aequē, pariter
alive adj vīvus; **be ~** vīvere
all adj omnis; (together) ūniversus, cūnctus; (whole) tōtus; **all but** paene; **all for** studiōsus (gen); **all in** cōnfectus; **all of** tōtus; **all over with** āctum dē (abl); **all the best men** optimus quisque; **all the more** eō plūs, tantō plūs; **at all** ullō modō, quid; **it is all up with** actum est de (abl); **not at all** haudquāquam ▶ n fortūnae fpl
allay vt sēdāre, mītigāre, lēnīre
allegation n adfirmātiō f; (charge) īnsimulātiō f
allege vt adfirmāre, praetendere; (in excuse) excūsāre
allegiance n fidēs f; **owe ~ to** in fidē esse (gen); **swear ~ to** in verba iūrāre (gen)
allegory n allēgoria f, immūtāta ōrātiō f
alleviate vt mītigāre, adlevāre, sublevāre
alleviation n levātiō f, levāmentum nt
alley n (garden) xystus m; (town) angiportus m
alliance n societās f, foedus nt
allied adj foederātus, socius; (friends) coniūnctus
alligator n crocodīlus m
allocate vt adsignāre, impertīre
allot vt adsignāre, distribuere; **be allotted** obtingere
allotment n (land) adsignātiō f
allow vt sinere, permittere (dat), concēdere (dat), patī; (admit) fatērī, concēdere; (approve) comprobāre; **it is allowed** licet (dat + infin); **~ for** vt ratiōnem habēre (gen)
allowance n venia f, indulgentia f; (pay) stīpendium nt; (food) cibāria ntpl; (for travel) viāticum nt; **make ~ for** indulgēre (dat), ignōscere (dat), excūsāre
alloy n admixtum nt
all right adj rēctē; **it is all right** bene est
allude vi: **~ to** dēsignāre, attingere, significāre
allure vt adlicere, pellicere
allurement n blanditia f, blandīmentum nt, illecebra f

alluring adj blandus
alluringly adv blandē
allusion n mentiō f, indicium nt
alluvial adj: **~ land** adluviō f
ally n socius m ▶ vt sociāre, coniungere
almanac n fāstī mpl
almighty adj omnipotēns
almond n (nut) amygdalum nt; (tree) amygdala f
almost adv paene, ferē, fermē, propemodum
alms n stipem (no nom) f
aloe n aloē f
aloft adj sublīmis ▶ adv sublīmē
alone adj sōlus, sōlitārius, ūnus ▶ adv sōlum
along prep secundum (acc), praeter (acc) ▶ adv porrō; **all ~** iamdūdum, ab initiō; **~ with** ūnā cum (abl)
alongside adv: **bring ~** adpellere; **come ~** ad crepīdinem accēdere
aloof adv procul; **stand ~** sē removēre ▶ adj sēmōtus
aloofness n sōlitūdō f, sēcessus m
aloud adv clārē, māgnā vōce
alphabet n elementa ntpl
Alps n Alpēs fpl
already adv iam
also adv etiam, et, quoque; īdem
altar n āra f
alter vt mūtāre, commūtāre; (order) invertere
alteration n mūtātiō f, commūtātiō f
altercation n altercātiō f, iūrgium nt
alternate adj alternus ▶ vt variāre
alternately adv invicem
alternation n vicem (no nom) f, vicissitūdō f
alternative adj alter, alius ▶ n optiō f
although conj quamquam (+ indic), etsī/ etiamsī (+ cond clause); quamvīs (subj)
altitude n altitūdō f
altogether adv omnīnō; (emphasis) plānē, prōrsus
altruism n beneficentia f
alum n alūmen nt
always adv semper
amalgamate vt miscēre, coniungere
amalgamation n coniūnctiō f, temperātiō f
amanuensis n librārius m
amass vt cumulāre, coacervāre
amateur n idiōta m
amatory adj amātōrius
amaze vt obstupefacere; attonāre; **be amazed** obstupēscere
amazement n stupor m; **in ~** attonitus, stupefactus
ambassador n lēgātus m
amber n sūcinum nt
ambidextrous adj utriūsque manūs compos
ambiguity n ambiguitās f; (RHET) amphibolia f
ambiguous adj ambiguus, anceps, dubius
ambiguously adv ambiguē
ambition n glōria f, laudis studium
ambitious adj glōriae cupidus, laudis avidus
amble vi ambulāre
ambrosia n ambrosia f

ambrosial adj ambrosius
ambuscade n īnsidiae fpl
ambush n īnsidiae fpl ▸ vt īnsidiārī (dat)
ameliorate vt corrigere, meliōrem reddere
amelioration n prōfectus m
amenable adj facilis, docilis
amend vt corrigere, ēmendāre
amendment n ēmendātiō f
amends n (apology) satisfactiō f; **make ~ for**
    expiāre; **make ~ to** satisfacere (dat)
amenity n (scenery) amoenitās f; (comfort)
    commodum nt
amethyst n amethystus f
amiability n benignitās f, suāvitās f
amiable adj benignus, suāvis
amiably adv benignē, suāviter
amicable adj amīcus, cōmis
amicably adv amīcē, cōmiter
amid, amidst prep inter (acc)
amiss adv perperam, secus, incommodē;
    take ~ aegrē ferre
amity n amīcitia f
ammunition n tēla ntpl
amnesty n venia f
among, amongst prep inter (acc), apud (acc)
amorous adj amātōrius, amāns
amorously adv cum amōre
amount vi: **~ to** efficere; (fig) esse ▸ n summa f
amours n amōrēs mpl
amphibious adj anceps
amphitheatre n amphitheātrum nt
ample adj amplus, satis
amplification n amplificātiō f
amplify vt amplificāre
amplitude n amplitūdō f, cōpia f
amputate vt secāre, amputāre
amuck adv: **run ~** bacchārī
amulet n amulētum nt
amuse vt dēlectāre, oblectāre
amusement n oblectāmentum nt, dēlectātiō f;
    for ~ animī causā
amusing adj rīdiculus, facētus
an indef art see **a**
anaemic adj exsanguis
analogous adj similis
analogy n prōportiō f, comparātiō f
analyse vt excutere, perscrūtārī
analysis n explicātiō f
anapaest n anapaestus m
anarchical adj sēditiōsus
anarchy n reī pūblicae perturbātiō, lēgēs nullae
    fpl, licentia f
anathema n exsecrātiō f; (object) pestis f
ancestor n proavus m; **ancestors** pl māiōrēs mpl
ancestral adj patrius
ancestry n genus nt, orīgō f
anchor n ancora f; **lie at ~** in ancorīs stāre;
    weigh ~ ancoram tollere ▸ vi ancoram iacere
anchorage n statiō f
ancient adj antīquus, prīscus, vetustus;
    ~ history, ~ world antīquitās f; **from/in ~ times**
    antīquitus; **the ancients** veterēs

and conj et, atque, ac, -que; **and ... not** nec,
    neque; **and so** itaque
anecdote n fābella f
anent prep dē (abl)
anew adv dēnuō, ab integrō
angel n angelus m
angelic adj angelicus; (fig) dīvīnus, eximius
anger n īra f ▸ vt inrītāre
angle n angulus m ▸ vi hāmō piscārī
angler n piscātor m
Anglesey n Mona f
angrily adv īrātē
angry adj īrātus; **be ~** īrāscī (dat)
anguish n cruciātus m, dolor m; (mind) angor m
angular adj angulātus
animal n animal nt; (domestic) pecus f; (wild) fera f
animate vt animāre
animated adj excitātus, vegetus
animation n ārdor m, alacritās f
animosity n invidia f, inimīcitia f
ankle n tālus m
annalist n annālium scrīptor
annals n annālēs mpl
annex vt addere
annexation n adiectiō f
annihilate vt dēlēre, exstinguere, perimere
annihilation n exstinctiō f, interneciō f
anniversary n diēs anniversārius; (public)
    sollemne nt
annotate vt adnotāre
annotation n adnotātiō f
announce vt nūntiāre; (officially) dēnūntiāre,
    prōnūntiāre; (election result) renūntiāre
announcement n (official) dēnūntiātiō f;
    (news) nūntius m
announcer n nūntius m
annoy vt inrītāre, vexāre; **be annoyed with**
    aegrē ferre
annoyance n molestia f, vexātiō f; (felt) dolor m
annoying adj molestus
annual adj annuus, anniversārius
annually adv quotannīs
annuity n annua ntpl
annul vt abrogāre, dissolvere, tollere
annulment n abrogātiō f
anoint vt ungere, illinere
anomalous adj novus
anomaly n novitās f
anon adv mox
anonymous adj incertī auctōris
anonymously adv sine nōmine
another adj alius; (second) alter; **of ~** aliēnus;
    one after ~ alius ex aliō; **one ~** inter sē, alius
    alium; **in ~ place** alibī; **to ~ place** aliō; **in ~ way**
    aliter; **at ~ time** aliās
answer vt respondēre (dat); (by letter) rescrībere
    (dat); (agree) respondēre, congruere; **~ a charge**
    crīmen dēfendere; **~ for** vt (surety) praestāre;
    (account) ratiōnem referre; (substitute) īnstar
    esse (gen) ▸ n respōnsum nt; (to a charge)
    dēfēnsiō f; **~ to the name of** vocārī; **give an ~**
    respondēre

answerable *adj* reus; **I am ~ for** ... ratiō mihī reddenda est ... *(gen)*

ant *n* formīca f

antagonism *n* simultās f, inimīcitia f

antagonist *n* adversārius m, hostis m

antarctic *adj* antarcticus

antecedent *adj* antecēdēns, prior

antediluvian *adj* prīscus, horridus, Deucaliōnēus

antelope *n* dorcas f

anterior *adj* prior

anteroom *n* vestibulum nt

anthology *n* excerpta ntpl; **make an ~** excerpere

anthropology *n* rēs hūmānae fpl

anticipate *vt (expect)* exspectāre; *(forestall)* antevenīre, occupāre; *(in thought)* animō praecipere

anticipation *n* exspectātiō f, spēs f; praesūmptiō f

antics *n* gestus m, ineptiae fpl

anticyclone *n* serēnitās f

antidote *n* remedium nt, medicāmen nt

antipathy *n* fastīdium nt, odium nt; *(things)* repugnantia f

antiphonal *adj* alternus

antiphony *n* alterna ntpl

antipodes *n* contrāria pars terrae

antiquarian *adj* historicus

antiquary *n* antīquārius m

antiquated *adj* prīscus, obsolētus

antique *adj* antīquus, prīscus

antiquity *n* antīquitās f, vetustās f, veterēs mpl

antithesis *n* contentiō f, contrārium nt

antlers *n* cornua ntpl

anvil *n* incūs f

anxiety *n* sollicitūdō f, metus m, cūra f; anxietās f

anxious *adj* sollicitus, anxius; avidus; cupidus

any *adj* ullus; *(interrog)* ecquī; *(after* sī, nisī, num, nē*)* quī; *(indef)* quīvīs, quīlibet; **hardly any** nullus ferē; **any further** longius; **any longer** *(of time)* diutius

anybody *pron* aliquis; *(indef)* quīvīs, quīlibet; *(after* sī, nisī, num, nē*)* quis; *(interrog)* ecquis, numquis; *(after neg)* quisquam; **hardly ~** nēmō ferē

anyhow *adv* ullō modō, quōquō modō

anyone *pron see* **anybody**

anything *pron* aliquid; quidvīs, quidlibet; *(interrog)* ecquid, numquid; *(after neg)* quicquam; *(after* sī, nisī, num, nē*)* quid; **hardly ~** nihil ferē

anywhere *adv* usquam, ubīvīs

apace *adv* citō, celeriter

apart *adv* seōrsum, sēparātim ▶ *adj* dīversus; **be six feet ~** sex pedēs distāre; **set ~** sēpōnere; **stand ~** distāre; **joking ~** remōtō iocō; **~ from** praeter *(acc)*

apartment *n* cubiculum nt, conclāve nt

apathetic *adj* lentus, languidus, ignāvus

apathy *n* lentitūdō f, languor m, ignāvia f

ape *n* sīmia f ▶ *vt* imitārī

aperture *n* hiātus m, forāmen nt, rīma f

apex *n* fastīgium nt

aphorism *n* sententia f

apiary *n* alveārium nt

apiece *adv* in singulōs; **two ~** bīnī

aplomb *n* cōnfīdentia f

apocryphal *adj* commentīcius

apologetic *adj* cōnfitēns, veniam petēns

apologize *vi* veniam petere, sē excūsāre

apology *n* excūsātiō f

apoplectic *adj* apoplēcticus

apoplexy *n* apoplēxis f

apostle *n* apostolus m

apothecary *n* medicāmentārius m

appal *vt* perterrēre, cōnsternere

appalling *adj* dīrus

apparatus *n* īnstrūmenta ntpl, ōrnāmenta ntpl

apparel *n* vestis f, vestīmenta ntpl

apparent *adj* manifestus, apertus, ēvidēns

apparently *adv* speciē, ut vidētur

apparition *n* vīsum nt, speciēs f

appeal *vi (to magistrate)* appellāre; *(to people)* prōvocāre ad; *(to gods)* invocāre, testārī; *(to senses)* placēre *(dat)* ▶ *n* appellātiō f, prōvocātiō f, testātiō f

appear *vi (in sight)* appārēre; *(in court)* sistī; *(in public)* prōdīre; *(at a place)* adesse, advenīre; *(seem)* vidērī

appearance *n (coming)* adventus m; *(look)* aspectus m, faciēs f; *(semblance)* speciēs f; *(thing)* vīsum nt; **for the sake of appearances** in speciem; *(formula)* dicis causā; **make one's ~** prōcēdere, prōdīre

appeasable *adj* plācābilis

appease *vt* plācāre, lēnīre, mītigāre, sēdāre

appeasement *n* plācātiō f; *(of enemy)* pācificātiō f

appellant *n* appellātor m

appellation *n* nōmen nt

append *vt* adiungere, subicere

appendage *n* appendix f, adiūnctum nt

appertain *vi* pertinēre

appetite *n* adpetītus m; *(for food)* famēs f

applaud *vt* plaudere; *(fig)* laudāre

applause *n* plausus m; *(fig)* adsēnsiō f, adprobātiō f

apple *n* pōmum nt; mālum nt; **~ tree** mālus f; **~ of my eye** ocellus meus; **upset the ~ cart** plaustrum percellere

appliance *n* māchina f, īnstrūmentum nt

applicable *adj* aptus, commodus; **be ~** pertinēre

applicant *n* petītor m

application *n (work)* industria f; *(mental)* intentiō f; *(asking)* petītiō f; *(MED)* fōmentum nt

apply *vt* adhibēre, admovēre; *(use)* ūtī *(abl)*; **~ oneself to** sē adplicāre, incumbere in *(acc)* ▶ *vi* pertinēre; *(to a person)* adīre *(acc)*; *(for office)* petere

appoint *vt (magistrate)* creāre, facere, cōnstituere; *(commander)* praeficere; *(guardian,* *heir)* īnstituere; *(time)* dīcere, statuere; *(for a purpose)* dēstināre; *(to office)* creāre

appointment *n* cōnstitūtum *nt; (duty)* mandātum *nt; (office)* magistrātus *m;* **have an ~ with** cōnstitūtum habēre cum; **keep an ~ ad** cōnstitūtum venīre

apportion *vt* dispertīre, dīvidere; *(land)* adsignāre

apposite *adj* aptus, appositus

appraisal *n* aestimātiō *f*

appraise *vt* aestimāre

appreciable *adj* haud exiguus

appreciate *vt* aestimāre

appreciation *n* aestimātiō *f*

apprehend *vt (person)* comprehendere; *(idea)* intellegere, mente comprehendere; *(fear)* metuere, timēre

apprehension *n* comprehēnsiō *f*; metus *m*, formīdō *f*

apprehensive *adj* anxius, sollicitus; **be ~ of** metuere

apprentice *n* discipulus *m*, tīrō *m*

apprenticeship *n* tīrōcinium *nt*

apprise *vt* docēre, certiōrem facere

approach *vt* appropinquāre ad *(acc)*, accēdere ad; *(person)* adīre ▸ *vi (time)* adpropinquāre; *(season)* appetere ▸ *n (act)* accessus *m*, aditus *m; (time)* adpropinquātiō *f; (way)* aditus *m;* **make approaches to** adīre ad, ambīre, petere

approachable *adj (place)* patēns; *(person)* facilis

approbation *n* adprobātiō *f*, adsēnsiō *f*

appropriate *adj* aptus, idōneus, proprius ▸ *vt* adscīscere, adsūmere

appropriately *adv* aptē, commodē

approval *n* adprobātiō *f*, adsēnsus *m*, favor *m*

approve *vi* ad probāre, comprobāre, adsentīrī *(dat); (LAW)* scīscere

approved *adj* probātus, spectātus

approximate *adj* propinquus ▸ *vi:* **~ to** accēdere ad

approximately *adv* prope, propemodum; *(number)* ad *(acc)*

appurtenances *n* īnstrūmenta *ntpl*, apparātus *m*

apricot *n* Armēniacum *nt;* **~ tree** *n* Armēniaca *f*

April *n* mēnsis Aprīlis *m;* **of ~** Aprīlis

apron *n* operīmentum *nt*

apropos of *prep* quod attinet ad

apse *n* apsis *f*

apt *adj* aptus, idōneus; *(pupil)* docilis, prōmptus; **apt to** prōnus, prōclīvis ad; **be apt to** solēre

aptitude *n* ingenium *f*, facultās *f*

aptly *adv* aptē

aquarium *n* piscīna *f*

aquatic *adj* aquātilis

aqueduct *n* aquae ductus *m*

aquiline *adj (nose)* aduncus

arable land *n* arvum *nt*

arbiter *n* arbiter *m*

arbitrarily *adv* ad libīdinem, licenter

arbitrary *adj* libīdinōsus *(act); (ruler)* superbus

arbitrate *vi* dīiūdicāre, disceptāre

arbitration *n* arbitrium *nt*, dīiūdicātiō *f*

arbitrator *n* arbiter *m*, disceptātor *m*

arbour *n* umbrāculum *nt*

arbutus *n* arbutus *f*

arc *n* arcus *m*

arcade *n* porticus *f*

arch *n* fornix *m*, arcus *m* ▸ *vt* arcuāre ▸ *adj* lascīvus, vafer

archaeologist *n* antīquitātis investīgātor *m*

archaeology *n* antīquitātis investīgātiō *f*

archaic *adj* prīscus

archaism *n* verbum obsolētum *nt*

archbishop *n* archiepiscopus *m*

arched *adj* fornicātus

archer *n* sagittārius *m*

archery *n* sagittāriōrum ars *f*

architect *n* architectus *m*

architecture *n* architectūra *f*

architrave *n* epistylium *nt*

archives *n* tabulae (pūblicae) *fpl*

arctic *adj* arcticus, septentriōnālis ▸ *n* septentriōnēs *mpl*

ardent *adj* ārdēns, fervidus, vehemēns

ardently *adv* ārdenter, ācriter, vehementer

ardour *n* ārdor *m*, fervor *m*

arduous *adj* difficilis, arduus

area *n* regiō *f*, *(MATH)* superficiēs *f*

arena *n* harēna *f*

argonaut *n* argonauta *m*

argosy *n* onerāria *f*

argue *vi (discuss)* disserere, disceptāre; *(dispute)* ambigere; disputāre; *(reason)* argūmentārī ▸ *vt (prove)* arguere

argument *n (discussion)* contrōversia *f*, disputātiō *f; (reason)* ratiō *f; (proof, theme)* argūmentum *nt*

argumentation *n* argūmentātiō *f*

argumentative *adj* lītigiōsus

aria *n* canticum *nt*

arid *adj* āridus, siccus

aright *adv* rectē, vērē

arise *vi* orīrī, coorīrī, exsistere; **~ from** nāscī ex, proficīscī ab

aristocracy *n* optimātēs *mpl*, nōbilēs *mpl; (govt)* optimātium dominātus *m*

aristocrat *n* optimās *m*

aristocratic *adj* patricius, generōsus

arithmetic *n* numerī *mpl*, arithmētica *ntpl*

ark *n* arca *f*

arm *n* bracchium *nt; (upper)* lacertus *m; (sea)* sinus *m; (weapon)* tēlum *nt* ▸ *vt* armāre ▸ *vi* arma capere

armament *n* bellī apparātus *m;* cōpiae *fpl*

armed *adj (men)* armātus; **light-armed troops** levis armātūra *f*, vēlitēs *mpl*

armistice *n* indutiae *fpl*

armlet *n* armilla *f*

armour *n* arma *ntpl; (kind of)* armātūra *f*

armourer *n* (armōrum) faber *m*

armoury *n* armāmentārium *nt*

armpit *n* āla *f*

arms *npl* (MIL) arma *ntpl*; **by force of ~** vī et
armīs; **under ~** in armīs
army *n* exercitus *m*; (*in battle*) aciēs *f*; (*on march*)
agmen *nt*
aroma *n* odor *m*
aromatic *adj* frāgrāns
around *adv* circum, circā ▶ *prep* circum (*acc*)
arouse *vt* suscitāre, ērigere, excitāre
arraign *vt* accūsāre
arrange *vt* (*in order*) compōnere, ōrdināre,
dīgerere, dispōnere; (*agree*) pacīscī; **~ a truce**
indūtiās compōnere
arrangement *n* ōrdō *m*, collocātiō *f*, dispositiō
f; pactum *nt*, cōnstitūtum *nt*
arrant *adj* summus
array *n* vestis *f*, habitus *m*; (MIL) aciēs *f* ▶ *vt*
vestīre, exōrnāre; (MIL) īnstruere
arrears *n* residuae pecūniae *fpl*, reliqua *ntpl*
arrest *vt* comprehendere, adripere; (*attention*)
in sē convertere; (*movement*) morārī, tardāre ▶ *n*
comprehēnsiō *f*
arrival *n* adventus *m*
arrive *vi* advenīre ('ad' + *acc*), pervenīre ('ad' + *acc*)
arrogance *n* superbia *f*, adrogantia *f*, fastus *m*
arrogant *adj* superbus, adrogāns
arrogantly *adv* superbē, adroganter
arrogate *vt* adrogāre
arrow *n* sagitta *f*
arsenal *n* armāmentārium *nt*
arson *n* incēnsiōnis crīmen *nt*
art *n* ars *f*, artificium *nt*; **fine arts** ingenuae
artēs
artery *n* artēria *f*
artful *adj* callidus, vafer, astūtus
artfully *adv* callidē, astūtē
artfulness *n* astūtia *f*, dolus *m*
artichoke *n* cinara *f*
article *n* rēs *f*, merx *f*; (*clause*) caput *nt*; (*term*)
condiciō *f*
articulate *adj* explānātus, distinctus ▶ *vt*
explānāre, exprimere
articulately *adv* explānātē, clārē
articulation *n* prōnūntiātiō *f*
artifice *n* ars *f*, artificium *nt*, dolus *m*
artificer *n* artifex *m*, opifex *m*, faber *m*
artificial *adj* (*work*) artificiōsus; (*appearance*)
fūcātus
artificially *adv* arte, manū
artillery *n* tormenta *ntpl*
artisan *n* faber *m*, opifex *m*
artist *n* artifex *m*; pictor *m*
artistic *adj* artificiōsus, ēlegāns
artistically *adv* artificiōsē, ēleganter
artless *adj* (*work*) inconditus; (*person*) simplex
artlessly *adv* incondītē; simpliciter, sine dolō
artlessness *n* simplicitās *f*
as *adv* (*before adj, adv*) tam; (*after* **aequus, īdem,
similis**) ac, atque; (*correlative*) quam, quālis,
quantus ▶ *conj* (*compar*) ut (+ *indic*), sīcut, velut,
quemadmodum; (*cause*) cum (+ *indic*), quōniam,
quippe quī; (*time*) dum, ut ▶ *rel pron* quī, quae,
quod (*subj*); **as being** utpote; **as follows** ita;

as for quod attinet ad; **as if** quasī, tamquam sī,
velut; (*while*) usu expressed by pres part; **as it were**
ut ita dīcam; **as yet** adhūc; **as soon as** simul
ac/atque (+ *perf indic*); **as ... as possible** quam
(+ *superl*) ▶ *n* (*coin*) as *m*
ascend *vt, vi* ascendere
ascendancy *n* praestantia *f*, auctōritās *f*
ascendant *adj* surgēns, potēns; **be in the ~**
praestāre
ascent *n* ascēnsus *m*; (*slope*) clīvus *m*
ascertain *vt* comperīre, cognōscere
ascetic *adj* nimis abstinēns, austērus
asceticism *n* dūritia *f*
ascribe *vt* adscrībere, attribuere, adsignāre
ash *n* (*tree*) fraxinus *f* ▶ *adj* fraxineus
ashamed *adj*: **I am ~** pudet mē; **~ of** pudet (+ *acc*
of person, + *gen* of thing)
ashen *adj* pallidus
ashes *n* cinis *m*
ashore *adv* (*motion*) in lītus; (*rest*) in lītore; **go ~**
ēgredī
Asia *n* Asia *f*
aside *adv* sēparātim, sē- (*in cpd*)
ask *vt* (*question*) rogāre, quaerere; (*request*)
petere, poscere; (*beg, entreat*) ōrāre; **ask for** *vt*
petere; rogāre; scīscitārī; percontārī
askance *adv* oblīquē; **look ~ at** līmīs oculīs
aspicere, invidēre (*dat*)
askew *adv* prāvē
aslant *adv* oblīquē
asleep *adj* sōpītus; **be ~** dormīre; **fall ~**
obdormīre, somnum inīre
asp *n* aspis *f*
asparagus *n* asparagus *m*
aspect *n* (*place*) aspectus *m*; (*person*) vultus *m*;
(*circumstances*) status *m*; **have a southern ~** ad
merīdiem spectāre; **there is another ~ to the
matter** aliter sē rēs habet
aspen *n* pōpulus *f*
asperity *n* acerbitās *f*
asperse *vt* maledīcere (*dat*), calumniārī
aspersion *n* calumnia *f*; **cast aspersions on**
calumniārī, īnfāmiā aspergere
asphalt *n* bitūmen *nt*
asphyxia *n* strangulātiō *f*
asphyxiate *vt* strangulāre
aspirant *n* petītor *m*
aspirate *n* (GRAM) aspīrātiō *f*
aspiration *n* spēs *f*; (POL) ambitiō *f*
aspire *vi*: **~ to** adfectāre, petere, spērāre,
contendere
ass *n* asinus *m*, asellus *m*; (*fig*) stultus
assail *vt* oppugnāre, adorīrī, aggredī
assailable *adj* expugnābilis
assailant *n* oppugnātor *m*
assassin *n* sīcārius *m*, percussor *m*
assassinate *vt* interficere, occīdere, iugulāre
assassination *n* caedēs *f*, parricīdium *nt*
assault *vt* oppugnāre, adorīrī, aggredī; (*speech*)
invehī in (*acc*) ▶ *n* impetus *m*, oppugnātiō *f*;
(*personal*) vīs *f*
assay *vt* (*metal*) spectāre; temptāre, cōnārī

assemble *vt* convocāre, congregāre, cōgere
▸ *vi* convenīre, congregārī

assembly *n* coetus *m*, conventus *m*; (*plebs*)
conciliam *nt*; (*Roman people*) comitia *ntpl*;
(*troops*) cōntiō *f*; (*things*) congeriēs *f*

assent *vi* adsentīrī, adnuere ▸ *n* adsēnsus *m*

assert *vt* adfirmāre, adsevērāre, dīcere

assertion *n* adfirmātiō *f*, adsevērātiō *f*, dictum
nt, sententia *f*

assess *vt* cēnsēre, aestimāre; **~ damages** lītem
aestimāre

assessment *n* cēnsus *m*, aestimātiō *f*

assessor *n* cēnsor *m*; (*assistant*) cōnsessor *m*

assets *npl* bona *ntpl*

assiduity *n* dīligentia *f*, sēdulitās *f*, industria *f*

assiduous *adj* dīligēns, sēdulus, industrius

assign *vt* tribuere, attribuere; (*land*) adsignāre;
(*in writing*) perscrībere; (*task*) dēlēgāre; (*reason*)
adferre

assignation *n* cōnstitūtum *nt*

assignment *n* adsignātiō *f*, perscrīptiō *f*; (*task*)
mūnus *nt*, pēnsum *nt*

assimilate *vt* aequāre; (*food*) concoquere;
(*knowledge*) concipere

assist *vt* adiuvāre, succurrere (*dat*), adesse (*dat*)

assistance *n* auxilium *nt*, opem (*no nom*) *f*;
come to the ~ of subvenīre (*dat*); **be of ~ to**
auxiliō esse (*dat*)

assistant *n* adiūtor *m*, minister *m*

assize *n* conventus *m*; **hold assizes** conventūs
agere

associate *vt* cōnsociāre, coniungere ▸ *vi* rem
inter sē cōnsociāre; **~ with** familiāriter ūtī (*abl*)
▸ *n* socius *m*, sodālis *m*

association *n* societās *f*; (*club*) sodālitās *f*

assort *vt* dīgerere, dispōnere ▸ *vi* congruere

assortment *n* (*of goods*) variae mercēs *fpl*

assuage *vt* lēnīre, mītigāre, sēdāre

assume *vt* (*for oneself*) adsūmere, adrogāre;
(*hypothesis*) pōnere; (*office*) inīre

assumption *n* (*hypothesis*) sūmptiō *f*,
positum *nt*

assurance *n* (*given*) fidēs *f*, pignus *nt*; (*felt*)
fīdūcia *f*; (*boldness*) cōnfidentia *f*

assure *vt* cōnfirmāre, prōmittere (*dat*)

assured *adj* (*person*) fīdēns; (*fact*) explōrātus,
certus

assuredly *adv* certō, certē, profectō, sānē

astern *adv* ā puppī; (*movement*) retrō; **~ of** post

asthma *n* anhēlitus *m*

astonish *vt* obstupefacere; attonāre

astonished *adj* attonitus, stupefactus; **be ~ at**
admīrārī

astonishing *adj* mīrificus, mīrus

astonishment *n* stupor *m*, admīrātiō *f*

astound *vt* obstupefacere

astray *adj* vagus; **go ~** errāre, aberrāre, deerrāre

astride *adj* vāricus

astrologer *n* Chaldaeus *m*, mathēmaticus *m*

astrology *n* Chaldaeōrum dīvīnātiō *f*

astronomer *n* astrologus *m*

astronomy *n* astrologia *f*

astute *adj* callidus, vafer

astuteness *n* callidītās *f*

asunder *adv* sēparātim, dis- (*in cpd*)

asylum *n* asȳlum *nt*

at *prep* in (*abl*), ad (*acc*); (*time*) *usu expressed by abl*;
(*towns, small islands*) *locative*; **at the house of**
apud (*acc*); **at all events** saltem; *see also* **dawn,
hand, house** *etc*

atheism *n* deōs esse negāre

atheist *n* atheos *m*; **be an ~** deōs esse negāre

Athenian *adj* Atheniensis

Athens *n* Athenae *fpl*; **at/from ~** Athenis; **to ~**
Athenas

athirst *adj* sitiens; (*fig*) avidus

athlete *n* athlēta *m*

athletic *adj* rōbustus, lacertōsus

athletics *n* athlētica *ntpl*

athwart *prep* trāns (*acc*)

atlas *n* orbis terrārum dēscrīptiō *f*

atmosphere *n* āēr *m*

atom *n* atomus *f*, corpus indīviduum *nt*

atone *vi*: **~ for** expiāre

atonement *n* expiātiō *f*, piāculum *nt*

atrocious *adj* immānis, nefārius, scelestus

atrociously *adv* nefāriē, scelestē

atrociousness *n* immānitās *f*

atrocity *n* nefas *nt*, scelus *nt*, flāgitium *nt*

atrophy *vi* marcēscere

attach *vt* adiungere, adfīgere, illigāre; (*word*)
subicere; **attached to** amāns (*gen*)

attachment *n* vinculum *nt*; amor *m*,
studium *nt*

attack *vt* oppugnāre, adorīrī, aggredī; impetum
facere in (*acc*); (*speech*) īnsequī, invehī in (*acc*);
(*disease*) ingruere in (*acc*) ▸ *n* impetus *m*,
oppugnātiō *f*, incursus *m*

attacker *n* oppugnātor *m*

attain *vt* adsequī, adipīscī, cōnsequī; **~ to**
pervenīre ad

attainable *adj* impetrābilis, in prōmptū

attainder *n*: **bill of ~** prīvilēgium *nt*

attainment *n* adeptiō *f*

attainments *npl* doctrīna *f*, ērudītiō *f*

attaint *vt* māiestātis condemnāre

attempt *vt* cōnārī, temptāre; (*with effort*) mōlīrī
▸ *n* cōnātus *m*, inceptum *nt*; (*risk*) perīculum *nt*;
first attempts rudīmenta *ntpl*

attend *vt* (*meeting*) adesse (*dat*), interesse (*dat*);
(*person*) prōsequī, comitārī; (*master*) appārēre
(*dat*); (*invalid*) cūrāre ▸ *vi* animum advertere,
animum attendere; **~ to** (*task*) adcūrāre; **~ upon**
prōsequī, adsectārī; **~ the lectures of** audīre;
not ~ aliud agere; **~ first to** praevertere (*dat*);
well attended frequēns; **thinly attended**
īnfrequēns

attendance *n* (*courtesy*) adsectātiō *f*; (*MED*)
cūrātiō *f*; (*service*) appāritiō *f*; **constant ~**
adsiduitās *f*; **full ~** frequentia *f*; **poor ~**
īnfrequentia *f*; **dance ~ on** haerēre (*dat*)

attendant *n* famulus *m*, minister *m*; (*on
candidate*) sectātor *m*; (*on nobleman*) adsectātor
m; (*on magistrate*) appāritor *m*

attention n animadversiō f, animī attentiō f;
(to work) cūra f; (respect) observantia f; **attract ~**
digitō mōnstrārī; **call ~ to** indicāre; **pay ~ to**
animadvertere, observāre; ratiōnem habēre
(gen); **attention!** hōc age!
attentive adj intentus; (to work) dīligēns
attentively adv intentē, dīligenter
attenuate vt attenuāre
attest vt cōnfirmāre, testārī
attestation n testificātiō f
attestor n testis m
attic n cēnāculum nt
attire vt vestīre ▶ n vestis f, habitus m
attitude n (body) gestus m, status m, habitus m;
(mind) ratiō f
attorney n āctor m; advocātus m
attract vt trahere, attrahere, adlicere
attraction n vīs attrahendī; illecebra f,
invītāmentum nt
attractive adj suāvis, venustus, lepidus
attractively adv suāviter, vēnustē, lepidē
attractiveness n venustās f, lepōs m
attribute vt tribuere, attribuere, adsignāre
▶ n proprium nt
attrition n attrītus m
attune vt modulārī
auburn adj flāvus
auction n auctiō f; (public) hasta f; **hold an ~**
auctiōnem facere; **sell by ~** sub hastā vēndere
auctioneer n praecō m
audacious adj audāx; protervus
audaciously adv audācter, protervē
audacity n audācia f, temeritās f
audible adj: **be ~** exaudīrī posse
audibly adv clārā vōce
audience n audītōrēs mpl; (interview) aditus m;
give an ~ to admittere
audit vt īnspicere ▶ n ratiōnum īnspectiō f
auditorium n cavea f
auditory adj audītōrius
auger n terebra f
augment vt augēre, adaugēre ▶ vi crēscere,
augērī
augmentation n incrēmentum nt
augur n augur m; **augur's staff** lituus m ▶ vi
augurārī; (fig) portendere
augural adj augurālis
augurship n augurātus m
augury n augurium nt, auspicium nt; ōmen nt;
take auguries augurārī; **after taking auguries**
augurātō
August n mēnsis Augustus, Sextīlis; **of ~** Sextīlis
august adj augustus
aunt n (paternal) amita f; (maternal) mātertera f
auspices n auspicium nt; **take ~** auspicārī;
after taking ~ auspicātō; **without taking ~**
inauspicātō
auspicious adj faustus, fēlīx
auspiciously adv fēlīciter, prosperē
austere adj austērus, sevērus, dūrus
austerely adv sevērē
austerity n sevēritās f, dūritia f

authentic adj vērus, certus
authenticate vt recognōscere
authenticity n auctōritās f, fidēs f
author n auctor m, inventor m; scrīptor m
authoress n auctor f
authoritative adj fīdus; imperiōsus
authority n auctōritās f, potestās f, iūs nt; (MIL)
imperium nt; (LIT) auctor m, scrīptor m;
enforce ~ iūs suum exsequī; **have great ~**
multum pollēre; **on Caesar's ~** auctōre Caesare;
an ~ on perītus (gen)
authorize vt potestātem facere (dat),
mandāre; (LAW) sancīre
autobiography n dē vītā suā scrīptus liber m
autocracy n imperium singulāre nt,
tyrannis f
autocrat n tyrannus m, dominus m
autocratic adj imperiōsus
autograph n manus f, chīrographum nt
automatic adj necessārius
automatically adv necessāriō
autonomous adj līber
autonomy n lībertās f
autumn n auctumnus m
autumnal adj auctumnālis
auxiliaries npl auxilia ntpl, auxiliāriī mpl
auxiliary adj auxiliāris ▶ n adiūtor m; **~ forces**
auxilia ntpl; novae copiae fpl
avail vi valēre ▶ vt prōdesse (dat); **~ oneself of**
ūtī (abl) ▶ n ūsus m; **of no ~** frustrā
available adj ad manum, in prōmptū
avalanche n montis ruīna f
avarice n avāritia f, cupīditās f
avaricious adj avārus, cupidus
avariciously adv avārē
avenge vt ulcīscī (abl), vindicāre
avenger n ultor m, vindex m
avenue n xystus m; (fig) aditus m, iānua f
aver vt adfirmāre, adsevērāre
average n medium nt; **on the ~** ferē
averse adj āversus (abl); **be ~ to** abhorrēre ab
aversion n odium nt, fastīdium nt
avert vt arcēre, dēpellere; (by prayer) dēprecārī
aviary n aviārium nt
avid adj avidus
avidity n aviditās f
avidly adv avidē
avoid vt vītāre, fugere, dēclīnāre; (battle)
dētrectāre
avoidance n fuga f, dēclīnātiō f
avow vt fatērī, cōnfitērī
avowal n cōnfessiō f
avowed adj apertus
avowedly adv apertē, palam
await vt exspectāre; (future) manēre
awake vt suscitāre, exsuscitāre ▶ vi expergīscī
▶ adj vigil
awaken vt exsuscitāre
award vt tribuere; (LAW) adiūdicāre ▶ n (decision)
arbitrium nt, iūdicium nt; (thing) praemium nt
aware adj gnārus; conscius (gen); **be ~** scīre;
become ~ of percipere

away *adv* ā-, ab- *(in cpd)*; **be ~** abesse ab *(abl)*;
  far ~ procul, longē; **make ~ with** dē mediō
  tollere
awe *n* formīdō *f*, reverentia *f*, rēligiō *f*; **stand in**
  awe of verērī; *(gods)* venerārī
awe-struck *adj* stupidus
awful *adj* terribilis, formīdolōsus, dīrus
awfully *adv* formīdolōsē
awhile *adv* aliquamdiū, aliquantisper,
  parumper
awkward *adj* incallidus, inconcinnus;
  (to handle) inhabilis; *(fig)* molestus
awkwardly *adv* incallidē, imperītē
awkwardness *n* imperītia *f*, īnscītia *f*
awl *n* sūbula *f*
awning *n* vēlum *nt*
awry *adj* prāvus, dissidēns
axe *n* secūris *f*
axiom *n* prōnūntiātum *nt*, sententia *f*
axiomatic *adj* ēvidēns, manifestus
axis *n* axis *m*
axle *n* axis *m*
aye *adv* semper; **for aye** in aeternum
azure *adj* caeruleus

b

baa *vi* bālāre ▸ *n* bālātus *m*
babble *vi* garrīre, blaterāre
babbler *n* garrulus *m*
babbling *adj* garrulus
babe *n* īnfāns *m/f*
babel *n* dissonae vōcēs *fpl*
baboon *n* sīmia *f*
baby *n* īnfāns *m/f*
Bacchanalian *adj* Bacchicus
Bacchante *n* Baccha *f*
bachelor *n* caelebs *m*; *(degree)* baccalaureus *m*
back *n* tergum *nt*; *(animal)* dorsum *nt*; *(head)*
  occipitium *nt*; **at one's ~** ā tergō; **behind one's ~**
  (fig) clam *(acc)*; **put one's ~ up** stomachum
  movēre *(dat)*; **turn one's ~ on** sē āvertere ab
  ▸ *adj* āversus, postīcus ▸ *adv* retrō, retrōrsum,
  re- *(in cpd)* ▸ *vt* obsecundāre *(dat)*, adesse *(dat)*;
  ~ water inhibēre rēmīs, inhibēre nāvem ▸ *vi*:
  ~ out of dētrectāre, dēfugere
backbite *vt* obtrectāre *(dat)*, maledīcere *(dat)*
backbone *n* spīna *f*
backdoor *n* postīcum *nt*
backer *n* fautor *m*
background *n* recessus *m*, umbra *f*
backing *n* fidēs *f*, favor *m*
backslide *vi* dēscīscere
backward *adj* āversus; *(slow)* tardus; *(late)*
  sērus
backwardness *n* tardītās *f*, pigritia *f*
backwards *adv* retrō, retrōrsum
bacon *n* lārdum *nt*
bad *adj* malus, prāvus, improbus, turpis; **go bad**
  corrumpī; **be bad for** obesse *(dat)*, nocēre *(dat)*
badge *n* īnsigne *nt*, īnfula *f*
badger *n* mēles *f* ▸ *vt* sollicitāre
badly *adv* male, prāvē, improbē, turpiter
badness *n* prāvitās *f*, nēquitia *f*, improbitās *f*
baffle *vt* ēlūdere, fallere, frustrārī
bag *n* saccus *m*, folliculus *m*; **handbag**
  mantica *f*
bagatelle *n* nūgae *fpl*, floccus *m*
baggage *n* impedīmenta *ntpl*, vāsa *ntpl*,
  sarcinae *fpl*; **~ train** impedīmenta *ntpl*;
  without ~ expedītus

bail n vadimōnium nt; (*person*) vas m;
  become ~ for spondēre prō (abl); **accept ~ for**
  vadārī; **keep one's ~** vadimōnium obīre ▸ vt
  spondēre prō (abl)
bailiff n (POL) apparitor m; (private) vīlicus m
bait n esca f, illecebra f ▸ vt lacessere
bake vt coquere, torrēre
bakehouse n pistrīna f
baker n pistor m
bakery n pistrīna f
balance n (scales) lībra f, trutina f; (equilibrium)
  lībrāmentum nt; (money) reliqua ntpl ▸ vt lībrāre;
  (fig) compēnsāre; **the account balances** ratiō
  cōnstat
balance sheet n ratiō acceptī et expēnsī
balcony n podium nt, Maeniānum nt
bald adj calvus; (style) āridus, iēiūnus
baldness n calvitium nt; (style) iēiūnitās f
bale n fascis m; **~ out** vt exhaurīre
baleful adj fūnestus, perniciōsus, tristis
balk n tignum nt ▸ vt frustrārī, dēcipere
ball n globus m; (play) pila f; (wool) glomus nt;
  (dance) saltātiō f
ballad n carmen nt
ballast n saburra f
ballet n saltātiō f
ballot n suffrāgium nt
ballot box urna f
balm n unguentum nt; (fig) sōlātium nt
balmy adj lēnis, suāvis
balsam n balsamum nt
balustrade n cancellī mpl
bamboozle vt cōnfundere
ban vt interdīcere (dat), vetāre ▸ n interdictum nt
banal adj trītus
banana n ariēna f; (tree) pāla f
band n vinculum nt, redimīculum nt; (head)
  īnfula f; (men) caterva f, manus f, grex f ▸ vi:
  ~ together cōnsociārī
bandage n fascia f, īnfula f ▸ vt obligāre,
  adligāre
bandbox n: **out of a ~** (fig) dē capsulā
bandeau n redimīculum nt
bandit n latrō m
bandy vt iactāre; **~ words** altercārī ▸ adj
  vārus
bane n venēnum nt, pestis f, perniciēs f
baneful adj perniciōsus, pestifer
bang n pulsāre ▸ n fragor m
bangle n armilla f
banish vt pellere, expellere, ēicere; (LAW) aquā
  et ignī interdīcere (dat); (temporarily) relēgāre;
  (feeling) abstergēre
banishment n (act) aquae et ignis interdictiō f;
  relēgātiō f; (state) exsilium nt, fuga f
bank n (earth) agger m; (river) rīpa f; (money)
  argentāria f
banker n argentārius m; (public) mēnsārius m
bankrupt adj: **be ~** solvendō nōn esse; **declare
  oneself ~** bonam cōpiam ēiūrāre; **go ~**
  dēcoquere ▸ n dēcoctor m
banner n vexillum nt

banquet n cēna f, epulae fpl; convīvium nt;
  (religious) daps f ▸ vi epulārī
banter n cavillātiō f ▸ vi cavillārī
baptism n baptisma nt
baptize vt baptizāre
bar n (door) sera f; (gate) claustrum nt; (metal)
  later m; (wood) asser m; (lever) vectis m; (obstacle)
  impedīmentum nt; (law-court) cancellī mpl;
  (barristers) advocātī mpl; (profession) forum nt; **of
  the bar** forēnsis; **practise at the bar** causās
  agere ▸ vt (door) obserāre; (way) obstāre (dat),
  interclūdere, prohibēre; (exception) excipere,
  exclūdere
barb n aculeus m, dēns m, hāmus m
barbarian n barbarus m ▸ adj barbarus
barbarism n barbaria f
barbarity n saevitia f, ferōcia f, immānitās f,
  inhūmānitās f
barbarous adj barbarus, saevus, immānis,
  inhūmānus
barbarously adv barbarē, inhūmānē
barbed adj hāmātus
barber n tōnsor m; **barber's shop** tōnstrīna f
bard n vātēs m/f; (Gallic) bardus m
bare adj nūdus; (mere) merus; **lay ~** nūdāre,
  aperīre, dētegere ▸ vt nūdāre
barefaced adj impudēns
barefoot adj nūdis pedibus
bare-headed adj capite apertō
barely adv vix
bargain n pactum nt, foedus nt; **make a ~**
  pacīscī; **make a bad ~** male emere; **into the ~**
  grātiīs ▸ vi pacīscī
barge n linter f
bark n cortex m; (dog) lātrātus m; (ship) nāvis f,
  ratis f ▸ vi lātrāre
barking n lātrātus m
barley n hordeum nt; **of ~** hordeāceus
barn n horreum nt
barrack vt obstrepere (dat)
barracks n castra ntpl
barrel n cūpa f; ligneum vās nt
barren adj sterilis
barrenness n sterilitās f
barricade n claustrum nt, mūnīmentum nt ▸ vt
  obsaepīre, obstruere; **~ off** intersaepīre
barrier n impedīmentum nt, claustra ntpl;
  (racecourse) carcer nt
barrister n advocātus m, patrōnus m,
  causidicus m
barrow n ferculum nt; (mound) tumulus m
barter vt mūtāre ▸ vi mercēs mūtāre ▸ n
  mūtātiō f, commercium nt
base adj turpis, vīlis; (birth) humilis, ignōbilis;
  (coin) adulterīnus ▸ n fundāmentum nt; (statue)
  basis f; (hill) rādīcēs fpl; (MIL) castra ntpl
baseless adj falsus, inānis
basely adv turpiter
basement n basis f; (storey) īmum tabulātum nt
baseness n turpitūdō f
bashful adj pudīcus, verēcundus
bashfully adv verēcundē

bashfulness n pudor m, verēcundia f
basic adj prīmus
basin n alveolus m, pelvis f; **washbasin** aquālis m
basis n fundāmentum nt
bask vi aprīcārī
basket n corbis f, fiscus m; (for bread) canistrum nt; (for wool) quasillum nt
basking n aprīcātiō f
bas-relief n toreuma nt
bass adj (voice) gravis
bastard adj nothus
bastion n prōpugnāculum nt
bat n vespertīliō m; (games) clāva f
batch n numerus m
Bath n Aquae Sulis fpl
bath n balneum nt; (utensil) lābrum nt, lavātiō f; Turkish ~ Lacōnicum nt; **cold** ~ frīgidārium nt; **hot** ~ calidārium nt; **~ superintendent** balneātor m ▸ vt lavāre
bathe vt lavāre ▸ vi lavārī, perluī
bathroom n balneāria ntpl
baths n (public baths) balneae fpl
batman n cālō m
baton n virga f, scīpiō m
battalion n cohors f
batter vt quassāre, pulsāre, verberāre
battering ram n ariēs m
battery n (assault) vīs f
battle n pugna f, proelium nt, certāmen nt; **a ~ was fought** pugnatum est; **pitched** ~ iūstum proelium nt; **line of** ~ aciēs f; **drawn** ~ anceps proelium ▸ vi pugnāre, contendere; **~ order** aciēs f
battle-axe n bipennis f
battlefield, battle-line n aciēs f
battlement n pinna f
bawl vt vōciferārī, clāmitāre
bay n (sea) sinus m; (tree) laurus f, laurea f; **of bay** laureus; **at bay** interclūsus ▸ adj (colour) spādīx ▸ vi (dog) lātrāre
be vi esse; (circumstances) versārī; (condition) sē habēre; **be at** adesse (dat); **be amongst** interesse (dat); **be in** inesse (dat); **consul-to-be** cōnsul dēsignātus; **how are you?** quid agis?; **so be it** estō; see also **absent, here** etc
beach n lītus nt, acta f ▸ vt (ship) subdūcere
beacon n ignis m
bead n pilula f
beadle n appāritor m
beak n rōstrum nt
beaked adj rōstrātus
beaker n cantharus m, scyphus m
beam n (wood) trabs f, tignum nt; (balance) iugum nt; (light) radius m; (ship) latus nt; **on the** ~ ā latere ▸ vi fulgēre; (person) adrīdēre
beaming adj hilaris
bean n faba f
bear n ursus m, ursa f; **Great Bear** septentriōnēs mpl, Arctos f; **Little Bear** septentriō minor m, Cynosūra f; **bear's** ursīnus ▸ vt (carry) ferre, portāre; (endure) ferre, tolerāre, patī; (produce)

ferre, fundere; (child) parere; **~ down upon** appropinquāre; **~ off** ferre; **~ out** vt arguere; **~ up** vi: **~ up under** obsistere (dat), sustinēre; **~ upon** innītī (dat); (refer) pertinēre ad; **~ with** vt indulgēre (dat); **~ oneself** sē gerere; **I cannot ~ to** addūcī nōn possum ut
bearable adj tolerābilis
beard n barba f ▸ vt ultrō lacessere
bearded adj barbātus
beardless adj imberbis
bearer n bāiulus m; (letter) tabellārius m; (litter) lectīcārius m; (news) nūntius m
bearing n (person) gestus m, vultus m; (direction) regiō f; **have no ~ on** nihil pertinēre ad; **I have lost my bearings** ubi sim nesciō
beast n bestia f; (large) bēlua f; (wild) fera f; (domestic) pecus f
beastliness n foedītās f, stuprum nt
beastly adj foedus
beast of burden n iūmentum nt
beat n ictus m; (heart) palpitātiō f; (music) percussiō f; (oars, pulse) pulsus m ▸ vt ferīre, percutere, pulsāre; (the body in grief) plangere; (punish) caedere; (whip) verberāre; (conquer) vincere, superāre ▸ vi palpitāre, micāre; **~ back** repellere; **~ in** perfringere; **~ out** excutere; (metal) extundere; **~ a retreat** receptuī canere; **~ about the bush** circuitiōne ūtī; **be beaten** vāpulāre; **dead** ~ cōnfectus
beating n verbera ntpl; (defeat) clādēs f; (time) percussiō f; **get a** ~ vāpulāre
beatitude n beātitūdō f, fēlīcitās f
beau n nitidus homō m; (lover) amāns m
beauteous adj pulcher, fōrmōsus
beautiful adj pulcher, fōrmōsus; (looks) decōrus; (scenery) amoenus
beautifully adv pulchrē
beautify vt exōrnāre, decorāre
beauty n fōrma f, pulchritūdō f, amoenitās f
beaver n castor m, fiber m; (helmet) buccula f
becalmed adj ventō dēstitūtus
because conj quod, quia, quōniam (+ indic), quippe quī; **~ of** propter (acc)
beck n nūtus m
beckon vt innuere, vocāre
become vi fierī; **what will ~ of me?** quid mē fīet? ▸ vt decēre, convenīre (acc)
becoming adj decēns, decōrus
becomingly adv decōrē, convenienter
bed n cubīle nt, lectus m, lectulus m; **go to bed** cubitum īre; **make a bed** lectum sternere; **be bedridden** lectō tenērī; **camp bed** grabātus m; **flowerbed** pulvīnus m; **marriage bed** lectus geniālis m; **riverbed** alveus m
bedaub vt illinere, oblinere
bedclothes n strāgula ntpl
bedding n strāgula ntpl
bedeck vt ōrnāre, exōrnāre
bedew vt inrōrāre
bedim vt obscūrāre
bedpost n fulcrum nt
bedraggled adj sordidus, madidus

bedroom n cubiculum nt
bedstead n sponda f
bee n apis f; **queen bee** rēx m
beech n fāgus f ▸ adj fāginus
beef n būbula f
beehive n alvus f
beekeeper n apiārius m
beer n cervīsia f, fermentum nt
beet n bēta f
beetle n (insect) scarabaeus m; (implement) fistūca f
beetling adj imminēns, mināx
befall vi, vt accidere, ēvenīre (dat); (good) contingere (dat)
befit vt decēre, convenīre in (acc)
before adv ante, anteā, antehāc ▸ prep ante (acc); (place) prō (abl); (presence) apud (acc), cōram (abl) ▸ conj antequam, priusquam
beforehand adv ante, anteā; prae (in cpd)
befoul vt inquināre, foedāre
befriend vt favēre (dat), adiuvāre; (in trouble) adesse (dat)
beg vt ōrāre, obsecrāre, precārī, poscere ab, petere ab; **beg for** petere ▸ vi mendīcāre
beget vt gignere, prōcreāre, generāre
begetter n generātor m, creātor m
beggar n mendīcus m
beggarly adj mendīcus, indigēns
beggary n mendīcitās f, indigentia f
begin vi, vt incipere, coepisse; (speech) exōrdīrī; (plan) īnstituere, incohāre; (time) inīre; **~ with** incipere ab
beginning n initium nt, prīncipium nt, exōrdium nt, inceptiō f; (learning) rudīmenta ntpl, elementa ntpl; (origin) orīgō f, fōns m; **at the ~ of spring** ineunte vēre
begone interj apage, tē āmovē
begotten adj genitus, nātus
begrudge vt invidēre (dat)
beguile vt dēcipere, fallere
behalf n: **on ~ of** prō (abl); **on my ~** meō nōmine
behave vi sē gerere, sē praebēre (with adj); **well behaved** bene mōrātus
behaviour n mōrēs mpl
behead vt dētruncāre, secūrī percutere
behest n iūssum nt
behind adv pōne, post, ā tergō ▸ prep post (acc), pōne (acc)
behindhand adv sērō; **be ~** parum prōficere
behold vt aspicere, cōnspicere, intuērī ▸ interj ecce, ēn
beholden adj obnoxius, obstrictus, obligātus
behoof n ūsus m
behove vt oportēre
being n (life) animātiō f; (nature) nātūra f; (person) homō m/f
bejewelled adj gemmeus, gemmātus
belabour vt verberāre, caedere
belated adj sērus
belch vi ructāre, ēructāre
beldam n anus f
beleaguer vt obsidēre, circumsedēre

belie vt abhorrēre ab, repugnāre
belief n fidēs f, opīniō f; (opinion) sententia f; **to the best of my ~** ex animī meī sententiā; **past ~** incrēdibilis
believe vt, vi (thing) crēdere; (person) crēdere (dat); (suppose) crēdere, putāre, arbitrārī, opīnārī; **~ in gods** deōs esse crēdere; **make ~** simulāre
believer n deōrum cultor m; Chrīstiānus m
belike adv fortasse
belittle vt obtrectāre
bell n tintinnābulum nt; (public) campāna f
belle n fōrmōsa f, pulchra f
belles-lettres n litterae fpl
bellicose adj ferōx
belligerent adj bellī particeps
bellow vi rūdere, mūgīre ▸ n mūgītus m
bellows n follis m
belly n abdōmen nt, venter m; (sail) sinus m ▸ vi tumēre
belong vi esse (gen), proprium esse (gen), inesse (dat); (concern) attinēre, pertinēre
belongings npl bona ntpl
beloved adj cārus, dīlectus, grātus
below adv īnfrā, subter ▸ adj īnferus ▸ prep īnfrā (acc), sub (abl, acc)
belt n zōna f; (sword) balteus m
bemoan vt dēplōrāre, lāmentārī
bemused adj stupefactus, stupidus
bench n subsellium nt; (rowing) trānstrum nt; (LAW) iūdicēs mpl; **seat on the ~** iūdicātus m
bend vt flectere, curvāre, inclīnāre; (bow) intendere; (course) tendere, flectere; (mind) intendere ▸ vi sē īnflectere; (person) sē dēmittere; **~ back** reflectere; **~ down** vi dēflectere; sē dēmittere ▸ n flexus m, ānfrāctus m
beneath adv subter ▸ prep sub (acc or abl)
benediction n bonae precēs fpl
benedictory adj faustus
benefaction n beneficium nt, dōnum nt
benefactor n patrōnus m; **be a ~** bene merērī (dē)
beneficence n beneficentia f, līberālitās f
beneficent adj beneficus
beneficial adj ūtilis, salūbris
benefit n beneficium nt; (derived) frūctus m; **have the ~ of** fruī (abl) ▸ vt prōdesse (dat), usuī esse (dat)
benevolence n benevolentia f, benignitās f
benevolent adj benevolus, benignus
benevolently adv benevolē, benignē
benighted adj nocte oppressus; (fig) ignārus, indoctus
benign adj benignus, cōmis
bent n (mind) inclīnātiō f, ingenium nt ▸ adj curvus, flexus; (mind) attentus; **be ~ on** studēre (dat)
benumb vt stupefacere
benumbed adj stupefactus, torpidus; **be ~** torpēre
bequeath vt lēgāre

bequest n lēgātum nt

bereave vt orbāre, prīvāre

bereavement n damnum nt

bereft adj orbus, orbātus, prīvātus

berry n bāca f

berth n statiō f; **give a wide ~ to** dēvītāre

beryl n bēryllus m

beseech vt implōrāre, ōrāre, obsecrāre

beset vt obsidēre, circumsedēre

beside prep ad (acc), apud (acc); (close) iuxtā (acc); **~ the point** nihil ad rem; **be ~ oneself** nōn esse apud sē

besides adv praetereā, accēdit quod; (in addition) īnsuper ▸ prep praeter (acc)

besiege vt obsidēre, circumsedēre

besieger n obsessor m

besmear vt illinere

besmirch vt maculāre

besom n scōpae fpl

besotted adj stupidus

bespatter vt aspergere

bespeak vt (order) imperāre; (denote) significāre

besprinkle vt aspergere

best adj optimus; **the ~ part** māior pars ▸ n flōs m, rōbur nt; **do one's ~** prō virīlī parte agere; **do one's ~ to** operam dare ut; **have the ~ of it** vincere; **make the ~ of** (a situation) aequō animō accipere; **to the ~ of one's ability** prō virīlī parte; **to the ~ of my knowledge** quod sciam ▸ adv optimē

bestial adj foedus

bestir vt movēre; **~ oneself** expergīscī

bestow vt dōnāre, tribuere, dare, cōnferre

bestride vt (horse) sedēre in (abl)

bet n pignus nt ▸ vt oppōnere ▸ vi pignore contendere

betake vt cōnferre, recipere; **~ oneself** sē cōnferre

bethink vt: **~ oneself** sē colligere; **~ oneself of** respicere

betide vi accidere, ēvenīre

betoken vt significāre; (foretell) portendere

betray vt prōdere, trādere; (feelings) arguere; **without betraying one's trust** salvā fidē

betrayal n prōditiō f

betrayer n prōditor m; (informer) index m

betroth vt spondēre, dēspondēre

betrothal n spōnsālia ntpl

better adj melior; **it is ~ to** praestat (infin); **get the ~ of** vincere, superāre; **I am ~** (in health) melius est mihī; **I had ~ go** praestat īre; **get ~** convalēscere; **think ~ of** sententiam mūtāre dē ▸ adv melius ▸ vt corrigere; **~ oneself** prōficere

betterment n prōfectus m

between prep inter (acc)

beverage n pōtiō f

bevy n manus f, grex f

bewail vt dēflēre, lāmentārī, dēplōrāre

beware vt cavēre

bewilder vt cōnfundere, perturbāre

bewildered adj attonitus

bewilderment n perturbātiō f, admīrātiō f

bewitch vt fascināre; (fig) dēlēnīre

beyond adv ultrā, suprā ▸ prep ultrā (acc), extrā (acc); (motion) trāns (acc); (amount) ultrā, suprā (acc); **go/pass ~** excēdere, ēgredī

bezel n pāla f

bias n inclīnātiō f; (party) favor m ▸ vt inclīnāre

biassed adj prōpēnsior

bibber n pōtor m, pōtātor m

Bible n litterae sacrae fpl

bibulous adj bibulus

bicephalous adj biceps

bicker vi altercārī, iūrgāre

bid vt iubēre; (guest) vocāre, invītāre ▸ vi (at auction) licērī; **bid for** licērī; **bid good day** salvēre iubēre; **he bids fair to make progress** spēs est eum prōfectūrum esse

biddable adj docilis

bidding n iussum nt; (auction) licitātiō f

bide vt manēre, opperīrī

biennial adj biennālis

bier n ferculum nt

bifurcate vi sē scindere

bifurcation n (road) trivium nt

big adj māgnus, grandis, amplus; (with child) gravida; **very big** permāgnus; **talk big** glōriārī

bight n sinus m

bigness n māgnitūdō f, amplitūdō f

bigot n nimis obstinātus fautor m

bigoted adj contumāx

bigotry n contumācia f, nimia obstinātiō f

bile n bīlis f, fel nt

bilge water n sentīna f

bilk vt fraudāre

bill n (bird) rōstrum nt; (implement) falx f; (LAW) rogātiō f, lēx f; (money) syngrapha f; (notice) libellus m, titulus m; **introduce a ~** populum rogāre, lēgem ferre; **carry a ~** lēgem perferre

billet n hospitium nt ▸ vt in hospitia dīvidere

billhook n falx f

billow n fluctus m

billowy adj undōsus

billy goat n caper m

bin n lacus m

bind vt adligāre, dēligāre, vincīre; (by oath) adigere; (by obligation) obligāre, obstringere; (wound) obligāre; **~ fast** dēvincīre; **~ together** conligāre; **~ over** vt vadārī

binding n compāgēs f ▸ adj (LAW) ratus; **it is ~ on** oportet

bindweed n convolvulus m

biographer n vītae nārrātor m

biography n vīta f

bipartite adj bipartītus

biped n bipēs m

birch n bētula f; (flogging) virgae ulmeae fpl

bird n avis f; **birds of a feather** parēs cum paribus facillimē congregantur; **kill two birds with one stone** ūnō saltū duōs aprōs capere, dē eādem fidēliā duōs parietēs dealbāre; **bird's-eye view of** dēspectus in (acc)

birdcatcher n auceps m

birdlime n viscum nt

birth n (act) partus m; (origin) genus nt; **low ~** ignōbilitās f; **high ~** nōbilitās f; **by ~** nātū, ortū
birthday n nātālis m
birthday party n nātālicia ntpl
birthplace n locus nātālis m; (fig) incūnābula ntpl
birthright n patrimōnium nt
bisect vt dīvidere
bishop n epīscopus m
bison n ūrus m
bit n pars f; (food) frustum nt; (broken off) fragmentum nt; (horse) frēnum nt; **bit by bit** minūtātim; **a bit** adv aliquantulum; **a bit sad** tristior
bitch n (dog) canis f
bite vt mordēre; (frost) ūrere ▶ n morsus m; **with a ~** mordicus
biting adj mordāx
bitter adj (taste) acerbus, amārus; (words) asper
bitterly adv acerbē, asperē
bittern n būtiō m, ardea f
bitterness n acerbitās f
bitumen n bitūmen nt
bivouac n excubiae fpl ▶ vi excubāre
bizarre adj īnsolēns
blab vt, vi garrīre, effūtīre
black adj (dull) āter; (glossy) niger; (dirt) sordidus; (eye) līvidus; (looks) trux; **~ and blue** līvidus ▶ n ātrum nt, nigrum nt; **dressed in ~** ātrātus; (in mourning) sordidātus
blackberry n mōrum nt
blackbird n merula f
blacken vt nigrāre, nigrum reddere; (character) īnfāmāre, obtrectāre (dat)
blackguard n scelestus, scelerātus m
blacking n ātrāmentum nt
blacklist n prōscrīptiō f
black magic n magicae artēs fpl
blackmail n minae fpl ▶ vt minīs cōgere
black mark n nota f
blacksmith n faber m
bladder n vēsīca f
blade n (grass) herba f; (oar) palma f; (sword) lāmina f
blame vt reprehendere, culpāre; **I am to ~** reus sum ▶ n reprehēnsiō f, culpa f
blameless adj innocēns
blamelessly adv innocenter
blamelessness n innocentia f, integritās f
blameworthy adj accūsābilis, nocēns
blanch vi exalbēscere, pallēscere
bland adj mītis, lēnis
blandishment n blanditiae fpl
blank adj vacuus, pūrus; (look) stolidus
blanket n lōdīx f; **wet ~** nimium sevērus
blare vi canere, strīdere ▶ n clangor m, strīdor m
blarney n lēnōcinium f
blaspheme vi maledīcere
blasphemous adj maledicus, impius
blasphemy n maledicta ntpl, impietās f
blast n flātus m, īnflātus m ▶ vt disicere, discutere; (crops) rōbīgine adficere

blatant adj raucus
blaze n flamma f, ignis m, fulgor m ▶ vi flāgrāre, ārdēre, fulgēre; **~ up** exārdēscere ▶ vt: **~ abroad** pervulgāre
blazon vt prōmulgāre
bleach vt candidum reddere
bleak adj dēsertus, tristis, inamoenus
bleary-eyed adj lippus
bleat vi bālāre ▶ n bālātus m
bleed vi sanguinem fundere ▶ vt sanguinem mittere (dat); **my heart bleeds** animus mihī dolet
bleeding adj crūdus, sanguineus ▶ n sanguinis missiō f
blemish n macula f, vitium nt ▶ vt maculāre, foedāre
blend vt miscēre, immiscēre, admiscēre ▶ n coniūnctiō f
bless vt beāre; laudāre; (ECCL) benedīcere; **~ with** augēre (abl); **~ my soul!** ita mē dī ament!
blessed adj beātus, fortūnātus; (emperors) dīvus
blessing n (thing) commodum nt, bonum nt; (ECCL) benedictiō f
blight n rōbīgō f, ūrēdō f ▶ vt rōbīgine adficere; (fig) nocēre (dat)
blind adj caecus; (in one eye) luscus; (fig) ignārus, stultus; (alley) nōn pervius; (forces) necessārius; **turn a ~ eye to** cōnīvēre in (abl) ▶ vt excaecāre, caecāre; (fig) occaecāre; (with light) praestringere
blindfold adj capite obvolūtō
blindly adv temerē
blindness n caecitās f; (fig) temeritās f, īnsipientia f
blink vi nictāre
bliss n fēlīcitās f, laetitia f
blissful adj fēlīx, beātus, laetus
blissfully adv fēlīciter, beātē
blister n pustula f
blithe adj hilaris, laetus
blithely adv hilare, laetē
blizzard n hiems f
bloated adj tumidus, turgidus
blob n gutta f, particula f
block n (wood) stīpes m, caudex m; (stone) massa f; (houses) īnsula f; **~ letter** quadrāta littera; **stumbling ~** offēnsiō f ▶ vt claudere, obstruere, interclūdere; **~ the way** obstāre
blockade n obsidiō f; **raise a ~** obsidiōnem solvere ▶ vt obsidēre, interclūdere
blockhead n caudex m, bārō m, truncus m
blockhouse n castellum nt
blond adj flāvus
blood n sanguis m; (shed) cruor m; (murder) caedēs f; (kin) genus nt; **let ~** sanguinem mittere; **staunch ~** sanguinem supprimere; **bad ~** simultās f; **in cold ~** cōnsultō; **own flesh and ~** cōnsanguineus
bloodless adj exsanguis; (victory) incruentus
bloodshed n caedēs f
bloodshot adj sanguineus
bloodstained adj cruentus

bloodsucker n hirūdō f
bloodthirsty adj sanguinārius
blood vessel n vēna f
bloody adj cruentus
bloom n flōs m; **in ~** flōrēns ▸ vi flōrēre, flōrēscere, vigēre
blooming adj flōrēns, flōridus
blossom n flōs m ▸ vi efflōrēscere, flōrēre
blot n macula f; (erasure) litūra f ▸ vt maculāre; **~ out** dēlēre, oblitterāre
blotch n macula f
blotched adj maculōsus
blow vt, vi (wind) flāre; (breath) adflāre, anhēlāre; (instrument) canere; (flower) efflōrēscere; (nose) ēmungere; **~ out** vi exstinguere; **~ over** vi (storm) cadere; (fig) abīre; **~ up** vt īnflāre; (destroy) discutere, disturbāre ▸ n ictus m; (on the cheek) alapa f; (fig) plāga f; (misfortune) calamitās f; **aim a ~ at** petere; **come to blows** ad manūs venīre
blowy adj ventōsus
bludgeon n fustis m
blue adj caeruleus; **black and ~** līvidus; **true ~** fīdissimus; **~ blood** nōbilitās f
bluff n rūpēs f, prōmontōrium nt ▸ adj inurbānus ▸ vt fallere, dēcipere, verba dare (dat), impōnere (dat)
blunder vi errāre, offendere ▸ n error m, errātum nt; (in writing) mendum nt
blunt adj hebes; (manners) horridus, rūsticus, inurbānus; **be ~** hebēre ▸ vt hebetāre, obtundere, retundere
bluntly adv līberius, plānē et apertē
blur n macula f ▸ vt obscūrāre
blurt vt: **~ out** ēmittere
blush vi rubēre, ērubēscere ▸ n rubor m
bluster vi dēclāmitāre, lātrāre
boa n boa f
Boadicea n Boudicca f
boar n verrēs m; (wild) aper m
board n tabula f; (table) mēnsa f; (food) vīctus m; (committee) concilium nt; (judicial) quaestiō f; (often men) decemvirī mpl; (gaming) abacus m, alveus m; **on ~** in nāvī; **go on ~** in nāvem cōnscendere; **go by the ~** intercidere, perīre; **above ~** sine fraude ▸ vt (building) contabulāre; (ship) cōnscendere; (person) vīctum praebēre (dat) ▸ vi: **~ with** dēvertere ad
boarder n hospes m
boast vi glōriārī, sē iactāre; **~ of** glōriārī dē (abl) ▸ n glōria f, glōriātiō f, iactātiō f
boastful adj glōriōsus
boastfully adv glōriōsē
boasting n glōriātiō f ▸ adj glōriōsus
boat n linter f, scapha f, cymba f; (ship) nāvis f; **be in the same ~** (fig) in eādem nāvī esse
boatman n nauta m
boatswain n hortātor m
bobbin n fūsus m
bode vt portendere, praesāgīre
bodiless adj sine corpore
bodily adj corporeus
bodkin n acus f

body n corpus nt; (dead) cadāver nt; (small) corpusculum nt; (person) homō m/f; (of people) globus m, numerus m; (of troops) manus f, caterva f; (of cavalry) turma f; (of officials) collēgium nt; (heavenly) astrum nt; **in a ~** ūniversī, frequentēs
bodyguard n custōs m, stīpātōrēs mpl; (emperor's) praetōriānī mpl
bog n palūs f
bogey n mōnstrum nt
boggle vi tergiversārī, haesitāre
boggy adj palūster
bogus adj falsus, fictus
Bohemian adj līberior, solūtior, libīdinōsus
boil vt coquere; (liquid) fervefacere; **~ down** dēcoquere ▸ vi fervēre, effervēscere; (sea) exaestuāre; (passion) exārdēscere, aestuāre; **~ over** effervēscere ▸ n (MED) fūrunculus m
boiler n cortīna f
boiling adj (hot) fervēns
boisterous adj (person) turbulentus, vehemēns; (sea) turbidus, agitātus; (weather) procellōsus, violentus
boisterously adv turbidē, turbulentē
boisterousness n tumultus m, violentia f
bold adj audāx, fortis, intrepidus; (impudent) impudēns, protervus; (language) līber; (headland) prōminēns; **make ~** audēre
boldly adv audācter, fortiter, intrepidē; impudenter
boldness n audācia f, cōnfīdentia f; impudentia f, petulantia f; (speech) lībertās f
bolster n pulvīnus m ▸ vt: **~ up** sustinēre, cōnfirmāre
bolt n (door) claustrum nt, pessulus m, sera f; (missile) tēlum nt, sagitta f; (lightning) fulmen nt; **make a ~ for it** sē prōripere, aufugere; **a ~ from the blue** rēs subita, rēs inopīnāta f ▸ vt (door) obserāre, obdere
bombard vt tormentīs verberāre; (fig) lacessere
bombast n ampullae fpl
bombastic adj tumidus, īnflātus; **be ~** ampullārī
bond n vinculum nt, catēna f, compes f; (of union) cōpula f, iugum nt, nōdus m; (document) syngrapha f; (agreement) foedus nt ▸ adj servus, addictus
bondage n servitūs f, famulātus m
bone n os nt; (fish) spīna f ▸ vt exossāre
boneless adj exos
bonfire n ignis festus m
bonhomie n festīvitās f
bon mot n dictum nt, sententia f
bonny adj pulcher, bellus
bony adj osseus
boo vt explōdere
book n liber m; (small) libellus m; (scroll) volūmen nt; (modern form) cōdex m; **books** (COMM) ratiōnēs fpl, tabulae fpl; **bring to ~** in iūdicium vocāre
bookbinder n glūtinātor m
bookcase n librārium nt, pēgma nt

bookish adj litterārum studiōsus
book-keeper n āctuārius m
bookseller n librārius m, bibliopōla m
bookshop n bibliothēca f, librāria taberna f
bookworm n tinea f
boom n (spar) longurius m; (harbour) ōbex m/f ▶ vi resonāre
boon n bonum nt, beneficium nt, dōnum nt ▶ adj festīvus; ~ **companion** sodālis m, compōtor m
boor n agrestis m, rūsticus m
boorish adj agrestis, rūsticus, inurbānus
boorishly adv rūsticē
boost vt efferre, margō f; (country) fīnis m
boot n calceus m; (MIL) caliga f; (rustic) pērō m; (tragic) cothurnus m ▶ vi prōdesse; **to** ~ īnsuper, praetereā
booted adj calceātus, caligātus
booth n taberna f
bootless adj inūtilis, vānus
bootlessly adv frustrā
booty n praeda f, spolia ntpl
border n ōra f, margō f; (country) fīnis m; (dress) limbus m ▶ vt praetexere, margināre; fīnīre ▶ vi: ~ **on** adiacēre (dat), imminēre (dat), attingere; (fig) fīnitimum esse (dat)
bordering adj fīnitimus
bore vt perforāre, perterebrāre; (person) obtundere, fatīgāre; ~ **out** exterebrāre ▶ n terebra f; (hole) forāmen nt; (person) homō importūnus m, ineptus m
boredom n lassitūdō f
borer n terebra f
born adj nātus m; **be** ~ nāscī
borough n mūnicipium nt
borrow vt mūtuārī
borrowed adj mūtuus; (fig) aliēnus
borrowing n mūtuātiō f; (to pay a debt) versūra f
bosky adj nemorōsus
bosom n sinus m; (fig) gremium nt; ~ **friend** familiāris m/f, sodālis m; **be a** ~ **friend of** ab latere esse (gen)
boss n bulla f; (shield) umbō m
botanist n herbārius m
botany n herbāria f
botch vt male sarcīre, male gerere
both pron ambō; uterque ▶ adv: ~ ... **and** et ... et, cum ... tum
bother n negōtium nt ▶ vt vexāre, molestus esse (dat) ▶ vi operam dare
bothersome adj molestus
bottle n lagoena f, amphora f ▶ vt (wine) diffundere
bottom n fundus m; (ground) solum nt; (ship) carīna f; **the** ~ **of** imus; **be at the** ~ **of** (cause) auctōrem esse; **go to the** ~ pessum īre, perīre; **send to the** ~ pessum dare; **from the** ~ funditus, ab īnfimō
bottomless adj profundus, fundō carēns
bottommost adj īnfimus
bough n rāmus m
boulder n saxum nt
boulevard n platea f

bounce vi salīre, resultāre
bound n fīnis m, modus m, terminus m; (leap) saltus m; **set bounds to** modum facere (dat) ▶ vt fīnīre, dēfīnīre, termināre ▶ vi salīre, saltāre ▶ adj adligātus, obligātus, obstrictus; **be** ~ **to** (duty) dēbēre; **it is** ~ **to happen** necesse est ēveniat; **be** ~ **for** tendere in (acc); **be stormbound** tempestāte tenērī
boundaries npl fīnēs mpl
boundary n fīnis m; (of fields) terminus m; (fortified) līmes m; ~ **stone** terminus m
boundless adj immēnsus, īnfīnītus
boundlessness n īnfīnitās f, immēnsum nt
bounteous adj see bountiful
bounteously adv largē, līberāliter, cōpiōsē
bountiful adj largus, līberālis, benignus
bounty n largitās f, līberālitās f; (store) cōpia f
bouquet n corollārium nt; (of wine) flōs m
bourn n fīnis m
bout n certāmen nt; (drinking) cōmissātiō f
bovine adj būbulus; (fig) stolidus
bow n arcus m; (ship) prōra f; (courtesy) salūtātiō f; **have two strings to one's bow** duplicī spē ūtī; **rainbow** arcus m ▶ vt flectere, inclīnāre ▶ vi caput dēmittere
bowels n alvus f; (fig) viscera ntpl
bower n umbrāculum nt, trichila f
bowl n (cooking) catīnus m; (drinking) calix m; (mixing wine) crātēra f; (ball) pila f ▶ vt volvere; ~ **over** prōruere
bow-legged adj valgus
bowler n (game) dator m
bowstring n nervus m
box n arca f, capsa f; (for clothes) cista f; (for medicine) pyxis f; (for perfume) alabaster m; (tree) buxus f; (wood) buxum nt; (blow on ears) alapa f ▶ vt inclūdere; **box the ears of** alapam dūcere (dat), colaphōs īnfringere (dat) ▶ vi (fight) pugnīs certāre
boxer n pugil m
boxing n pugilātiō f
boxing glove n caestus m
boy n puer m; **become a boy again** repuerāscere
boycott vt repudiāre
boyhood n pueritia f; **from** ~ ā puerō
boyish adj puerīlis
boyishly adv puerīliter
brace n (building) fībula f; (strap) fascia f; (pair) pār nt ▶ vt adligāre; (strengthen) firmāre
bracelet n armilla f
bracing adj (air) salūbris
bracken n filix f
bracket n uncus m
brackish adj amārus
bradawl n terebra f
brag vi glōriārī, sē iactāre
braggart n glōriōsus m
braid vt nectere
brain n cerebrum nt; ingenium nt
brainless adj sōcors, stultus
brainy adj ingeniōsus

brake n (wood) dūmētum nt; (on wheel) sufflāmen nt

bramble n rubus m

bran n furfur nt

branch n rāmus m; (kind) genus nt ▶ vi: ~ **out** rāmōs porrigere

branching adj rāmōsus

brand n (fire) torris m, fax f; (mark) nota f; (sword) ēnsis m; (variety) genus nt ▶ vt (mark) inūrere; (stigma) notāre; ~ **new** recēns

brandish vt vibrāre

brass n orichalcum nt

bravado n ferōcitās f; **out of** ~ per speciem ferōcitātis

brave adj fortis, ācer ▶ vt adīre, patī

bravely adv fortiter, ācriter

bravery n fortitūdō f, virtūs f

bravo interj bene, euge, macte

brawl n rixa f, iūrgium nt ▶ vi rixārī

brawn n lacertī mpl

brawny adj lacertōsus, rōbūstus

bray vi rūdere

brazen adj aēneus; (fig) impudēns

brazier n foculus m

breach n (in wall) ruīna f; (of friendship) dissēnsiō f ▶ vt perfringere; ~ **of trust** mala fidēs; **commit a** ~ **of promise** prōmissīs nōn stāre; ~ **of the peace** iūrgium nt, tumultus m

bread n pānis m

breadth n lātitūdō f; **in** ~ in lātitūdinem (acc)

break vt frangere, perfringere; ~ **down** vt īnfringere, dīruere; ~ **in** vt (animal) domāre; ~ **into pieces** dīrumpere; ~ **off** vt abrumpere, dēfringere; (action) dīrimere; ~ **open** effringere, solvere; ~ **through** vt interrumpere; ~ **up** vt dissolvere, interrumpere; ~ **one's word** fidem fallere, violāre; **without breaking the law** salvīs lēgibus ▶ vi rumpī, frangī; (day) illūcēscere; (strength) dēficere; ~ **off** vi dēsinere; ~ **into** intrāre; ~ **out** vi ērumpere; (sore) recrūdēscere; (trouble) exārdēscere; ~ **up** vi dīlābī, dissolvī; (meeting) dīmittī; ~ **through** vi inrumpere; ~ **with** dissidēre ab ▶ n intermissiō f, intervallum nt

breakable adj fragilis

breakage n frāctum nt

breakdown n (activity) mora f; (health) dēbilitās f

breaker n fluctus m

breakfast n iēntāculum nt, prandium nt ▶ vi ientāre, prandēre

breakwater n mōlēs f

bream n sparulus m

breast n pectus nt; (woman's) mamma f; **make a clean** ~ **of** cōnfitērī

breastplate n lōrīca f

breastwork n lōrīca f, pluteus m

breath n spīritus m, anima f; (bad) hālitus m; (quick) anhēlitus m; (of wind) aura f, adflātus m; **below one's** ~ mussitāns; **catch one's** ~ obstipēscere; **hold one's** ~ animam

comprimere, continēre; **take a** ~ spīritum dūcere; **take one's** ~ **away** exanimāre; **waste one's** ~ operam perdere; **out of** ~ exanimātus

breathable adj spīrābilis

breathe vt, vi spīrāre, respīrāre; (quickly) anhēlāre; ~ **again** respīrāre; ~ **in** vi spīritum dūcere; ~ **out** vt, vi exspīrāre, exhālāre; ~ **upon** īnspīrāre (dat), adflāre (dat); ~ **one's last** animam agere, efflāre

breathing n hālitus m, respīrātiō f

breathing space n respīrātiō f

breathless adj exanimātus

breeches n brācae fpl

breed n genus nt ▶ vt generāre, prōcreāre; (raise) ēducāre, alere; (fig) adferre, efficere; **well-bred** generōsus

breeder n (animal) mātrix f; (man) generātor m; (fig) nūtrix f

breeding n (act) fētūra f; (manners) mōrēs mpl; **good** ~ hūmānitās f

breeze n aura f, flātus m

breezy adj ventōsus; (manner) hilaris

brevity n brevitās f

brew vt coquere ▶ vi (fig) parārī, imminēre

bribe vt corrumpere ▶ vi largīrī ▶ n pecūnia f, mercēs f

briber n corruptor m, largītor m

bribery n ambitus m, largītiō f

brick n later m ▶ adj latericius

brickwork n latericium nt

bridal adj nūptiālis; (bed) geniālis ▶ n nūptiae fpl

bride n nūpta f

bridegroom n marītus m

bridge n pōns m ▶ vt pontem impōnere (dat)

bridle n frēnum nt ▶ vt frēnāre, īnfrēnāre

brief adj brevis; **to be** ~ nē longum sit, nē multa

briefly adv breviter, paucīs verbīs

briefness n brevitās f

brier n veprēs m, sentis m

brig n liburna f

brigade n legiō f; (cavalry) turma f

brigadier n lēgātus m

brigand n latrō m, praedō m

brigandage n latrōcinium nt

bright adj clārus, lūculentus; (sky) serēnus; (intellect) ingeniōsus; (manner) hilaris, laetus; **be** ~ lūcēre, splendēre

brighten vt illūstrāre; laetificāre ▶ vi lūcēscere; (person) hilarem fierī

brightly adv clārē

brightness n fulgor m, candor m; (sky) serēnitās f

brilliance n splendor m, fulgor m; (style) nitor m, lūmen nt, īnsignia ntpl

brilliant adj clārus, illūstris, splendidus; (fig) īnsignis, praeclārus, lūculentus

brilliantly adv splendidē, praeclārē, lūculentē

brim n lābrum nt, margō f; **fill to the** ~ explēre

brimstone n sulfur nt

brindled adj varius

brine n salsāmentum nt

bring vt ferre; (person) dūcere; (charge)

intendere; (*to a place*) adferre, addūcere, advehere, dēferre; (*to a destination*) perdūcere; (*to a worse state*) redigere; **~ about** vt efficere; **~ before** dēferre ad, referre ad; **~ back** vt (*thing*) referre; (*person*) redūcere; **~ down** vt dēdūcere, dēferre; **~ forth** (*from store*) dēprōmere; (*child*) parere; (*crops*) ferre, ēdere; **~ forward** vt (*for discussion*) iactāre, iacere; (*reason*) adferre; **~ home** (*bride*) dēdūcere; (*in triumph*) dēportāre; **~ home to** pervincere; **~ in** vt invehere, indūcere, intrōdūcere; (*import*) importāre; (*revenue*) reddere; **~ off** vt (*success*) reportāre; **~ on** īnferre, importāre; (*stage*) indūcere; **~ out** vt efferre; (*book*) ēdere; (*play*) dare; (*talent*) ēlicere; **~ over** perdūcere, trādūcere; **~ to bear** adferre; **~ to light** nūdāre, dētegere; **~ to pass** perficere, peragere; **~ to shore** ad litus appellere; **~ together** contrahere, cōgere; (*enemies*) conciliāre; **~ up** vt (*child*) ēducāre, tollere; (*troops*) admovēre; (*topic*) prōferre; **~ upon oneself** sibī cōnscīscere, sibī contrahere

brink n ōra f, margō f
briny adj salsus
brisk adj alacer, vegetus, ācer
briskly adv ācriter
briskness n alacritās f
bristle n sēta f ▸ vi horrēre, horrēscere
bristly adj horridus, hirsūtus
Britain n Britannia f
Britons n Britannī mpl
brittle adj fragilis
broach vt (*topic*) in medium prōferre
broad adj lātus; (*accent*) lātus; (*joke*) inurbānus; (*daylight*) multus
broadcast vt dissēmināre
broaden vt dīlātāre
broadly adv lātē
broadsword n gladius m
brocade n Attalica ntpl
brochure n libellus m
brogue n pērō m
broil n rixa f, iūrgium nt ▸ vt torrēre
broiling adj torridus
broken adj frāctus; (*fig*) cōnfectus; (*speech*) īnfrāctus
broken-hearted adj dolōre cōnfectus
broker n īnstitor m
bronze n aes nt ▸ adj aēneus, aerātus
brooch n fībula f
brood n fētus m; (*fig*) gēns f ▸ vi incubāre (*dat*); (*fig*) incubāre (*dat*), fovēre; **~ over** meditārī
brook n rīvus m ▸ vt ferre, patī
brooklet n rīvulus m
broom n (*plant*) genista f; (*brush*) scōpae fpl
broth n iūs nt
brother n frāter m; (*full*) germānus m
brotherhood n frāternitās f
brother-in-law n lēvir m, uxōris frāter m, sorōris marītus m
brotherly adj frāternus
brow n frōns f; (*eye*) supercilium nt; (*hill*) dorsum nt

browbeat vt obiūrgāre, exagitāre
brown adj fulvus, spādīx; (*skin*) adūstus
browse vi pāscī, dēpāscī
bruise vt atterere, frangere, contundere ▸ n vulnus nt
bruit vt pervulgāre
brunt n vīs f; **bear the ~ of** exhaurīre
brush n pēniculus m; (*artist's*) pēnicillus m; (*quarrel*) rixa f ▸ vt verrere, dētergēre; (*teeth*) dēfricāre; **~ aside** vt aspernārī, neglegere; **~ up** vt (*fig*) excolere
brushwood n virgulta ntpl; (*for cutting*) sarmenta ntpl
brusque adj parum cōmis
brutal adj atrōx, saevus, inhūmānus
brutality n atrōcitās f, saevitia f
brutally adv atrōciter, inhūmānē
brute n bēlua f, bestia f
brutish adj stolidus
bubble n bulla f ▸ vi bullāre; **~ over** effervēscere; **~ up** scatēre
buccaneer n praedō m, pīrāta m
buck n cervus m ▸ vi exsultāre
bucket n situla f, fidēlia f
buckle n fībula f ▸ vt fībulā nectere; **~ to** accingī
buckler n parma f
buckram n carbasus m
bucolic adj agrestis
bucolics n būcolica ntpl
bud n gemma f, flōsculus m ▸ vi gemmāre
budge vi movērī, cēdere
budget n pūblicae pecūniae ratiō f ▸ vi: **~ for** prōvidēre (*dat*)
buff adj lūteus
buffalo n ūrus m
buffet n (*blow*) alapa f; (*fig*) plāga f; (*sideboard*) abacus m ▸ vt iactāre, tundere
buffoon n scurra m, balatrō m
buffoonery n scurrilitās f
bug n cīmex m
bugbear n terricula ntpl, terror m
bugle n būcina f
bugler n būcinātor m
build vt aedificāre, struere; (*bridge*) facere; (*road*) mūnīre; **~ on** vt (*add*) adstruere; (*hopes*) pōnere; **~ on sand** in aquā fundāmenta pōnere; **~ up** vt exstruere; (*to block*) inaedificāre; (*knowledge*) īnstruere; **~ castles in the air** spem inānem pāscere ▸ n statūra f
builder n aedificātor m, structor m
building n (*act*) aedificātiō f; (*structure*) aedificium nt
bulb n bulbus m
bulge vi tumēre, tumēscere, prōminēre ▸ n tuberculum nt; (*of land*) locus prōminēns m
bulk n māgnitūdō f, amplitūdō f; (*mass*) mōlēs f; (*most*) plērīque, māior pars
bulky adj amplus, grandis
bull n taurus m; **bull's** taurīnus; **take the ~ by the horns** rem fortiter adgredī
bulldog n Molossus m
bullet n glāns f

bulletin n libellus m
bullion n aurum īnfectum nt, argentum īnfectum nt
bullock n iuvencus m
bully n obiūrgātor m, patruus m ▶ vt obiūrgāre, exagitāre
bulrush n scirpus m
bulwark n prōpugnāculum nt; (fig) arx f
bump n (swelling) tuber nt, tuberculum nt; (knock) ictus m
bumper n plēnum pōculum nt ▶ adj plēnus, māximus
bumpkin n rūsticus m
bumptious adj adrogāns
bunch n fasciculus m; (of berries) racēmus m
bundle n fascis m; (of hay) manipulus m ▶ vt obligāre
bung n obtūrāmentum nt ▶ vt obtūrāre
bungle vt male gerere
bunk n lectus m, lectulus m
buoy n cortex m ▶ vt sublevāre
buoyancy n levitās f
buoyant adj levis; (fig) hilaris
bur n lappa f
burden n onus nt; beast of ~ iūmentum nt ▶ vt onerāre; be a ~ oneri esse
burdensome adj gravis, molestus
bureau n scrīnium nt
burgeon vi gemmāre
burgess n mūniceps m
burgh n mūnicipium nt
burgher n mūniceps m
burglar n fūr m
burglary n fūrtum nt
burial n fūnes nt, humātiō f, sepultūra f
burin n caelum nt
burlesque n imitātiō f ▶ vt per iocum imitārī
burly adj crassus
burn vt incendere, ūrere; (to ashes) cremāre ▶ vi ārdēre, flāgrāre; ~ up ambūrere, combūrere, exūrere; be burned down dēflāgrāre; ~ out vi extinguī; ~ the midnight oil lūcubrāre ▶ n (MED) ambūstum nt
burning adj igneus
burnish vt polīre
burrow n cuniculus m ▶ vi dēfodere
burst vt rumpere, dīrumpere ▶ vi rumpī, dīrumpī; ~ in inrumpere; ~ into tears in lacrimās effundī; ~ open refringere; ~ out ērumpere, prōrumpere; ~ out laughing cachinnum tollere; ~ through perrumpere per (acc); ~ upon offerrī (dat), invādere ▶ n ēruptiō f; (noise) fragor m; ~ of applause clāmōrēs mpl; with a ~ of speed citātō gradū, citātō equō
bury vt sepelīre, humāre; (ceremony) efferre; (hiding) condere; (things) dēfodere; (fig) obruere; ~ the hatchet amīcitiam reconciliāre
bush n frutex m; dūmus m; beat about the ~ circuitiōne ūtī
bushel n medimnus m
bushy adj fruticōsus; (thick) dēnsus; (hair) hirsūtus

busily adv strēnuē, impigrē
business n negōtium nt; (occupation) ars f, quaestus m; (public life) forum nt; (matter) rēs f; it is your ~ tuum est; make it one's ~ to id agere ut; you have no ~ to nōn tē decet (infin); mind one's own ~ suum negōtium agere; ~ days diēs fāstī mpl
businessman negōtiātor m
buskin n cothurnus m
bust n imāgō f
bustle vi trepidāre, festīnāre; ~ about discurrere
busy adj negōtiōsus, occupātus; (active) operōsus, impiger, strēnuus; ~ in occupātus (abl); ~ on intentus (dat); keep ~ vt exercēre; ~ oneself with pertractāre, studēre (dat)
busybody n: be a ~ aliēnīs negōtīs sē immiscēre
but conj sed, at; (2nd place) autem, tamen ▶ adv modo ▶ prep praeter (acc); nothing but nihil nisī; but that, but what quīn; not but what nihilōminus
butcher n lanius m ▶ vt trucīdāre
butcher's shop n laniēna f
butchery n strāgēs f, occīdiō f
butler n prōmus m
butt n (cask) cadus m; (of ridicule) lūdibrium nt ▶ vi arietāre; ~ in interpellāre
butter n būtyrum nt
butterfly n pāpiliō m
buttock n clūnis m/f
button n bulla f
buttonhole vt (fig) dētinēre, prēnsāre
buttress n antērides fpl ▶ vt fulcīre
buxom adj nitidus
buy vt emere; buy provisions obsōnāre; buy back vt redimere; buy off vt redimere; buy up vt coemere
buyer n emptor m; (at auctions) manceps m
buzz n strīdor m, susurrus m ▶ vi strīdere, susurrāre
buzzard n būteō m
by prep (near) ad (acc), apud (acc); prope (acc); (along) secundum (acc); (past) praeter (acc); (agent) a, ab (abl); (instrument) abl; (time) ante (acc); (oath) per (acc) ▶ adv prope, iuxtā; by and by mox; be by adesse, adstāre; by force of arms vī et armīs; by land and sea terrā marique
bygone adj praeteritus
bystander n arbiter m ▶ pl circumstantēs mpl
byway n dēverticulum nt, trāmes m, sēmita f
byword n prōverbium nt

C

cabal n factiō f
cabbage n brassica f, caulis m
cabin n casa f; (ship) cubiculum nt
cabinet n armārium nt
cable n fūnis m; (anchor) ancorāle nt
cache n thēsaurus m
cachet n nota f
cackle vi strepere n, strepitus m, clangor m
cacophonous adj dissonus
cacophony n vōcēs dissonae fpl
cadaverous adj cadāverōsus
cadence n clausula numerōsa f, numerus m
cadet n (son) nātū minor; (MIL) contubernālis m
cage n cavea f ▶ vt inclūdere
caitiff n ignāvus m
cajole vt blandīrī, dēlēnīre
cake n placenta f
calamitous adj exitiōsus, calamitōsus
calamity n calamitās f, malum nt; (MIL) clādēs f
calculate vt ratiōnem dūcere, inīre
calculation n ratiō f
calculator n ratiōcinātor m
calendar n fāstī mpl
calends n Kalendae fpl
calf n (animal) vitulus m, vitula f; (leg) sūra f
calibre n (fig) ingenium nt, auctōritās f
call vt vocāre; (name) appellāre, nōmināre;
  (aloud) clāmāre; (to a place) advocāre,
  convocāre; **~ aside** sēvocāre; **~ down** (curse)
  dētestārī; **~ for** vt postulāre, requīrere; **~ forth**
  ēvocāre, excīre, ēlicere; **~ in** vt advocāre;
  ~ together convocāre; **~ on** vt (for help)
  implōrāre; (visit) salūtāre; **~ off** vt āvocāre,
  revocāre; **~ up** vt (dead)
  excitāre, ēlicere; (MIL) ēvocāre ▶ n vōx f, clāmor
  m; (summons) invītātiō f; (visit) salūtātiō f
caller n salūtātor m
calling n ars f, quaestus m
callous adj dūrus; **become ~** obdūrēscere
callow adj rudis
calm adj tranquillus, placidus; (mind) aequus
  ▶ vi: **~ down** (fig) dēfervēscere ▶ vt sēdāre,
  tranquillāre ▶ n tranquillitās f; **dead ~** (at sea)
  malacia f

calmly adv tranquillē, placidē; aequō animō
calumniate vt obtrectāre, crīminārī; (falsely)
  calumniārī
calumniator n obtrectātor m
calumny n opprobria ntpl, obtrectātiō f
calve vi parere
cambric n linteum nt
camel n camēlus m
camouflage n dissimulātiō f ▶ vt dissimulāre
camp n castra ntpl; **summer ~** aestīva ntpl;
  winter ~ hīberna ntpl; **in ~** sub pellibus; **pitch ~**
  castra pōnere; **strike ~** castra movēre ▶ adj
  castrēnsis ▶ vi tendere
campaign n stīpendium nt, bellum nt; (rapid)
  expedītiō f ▶ vi bellum gerere, stīpendium
  merēre
campaigner n mīles m; **old ~** veterānus m; (fig)
  veterātor m
campbed n grabātus m
camp followers n lixae mpl
can¹ n hirnea f
can² vi posse (infin); (know how) scīre
canaille n vulgus nt, plebs f
canal n fossa nāvigābilis f, eurīpus m
cancel vt indūcere, abrogāre
cancellation n (writing) litūra f; (LAW)
  abrogātiō f
cancer n cancer m; (fig) carcinōma nt, ulcus nt
cancerous adj (fig) ulcerōsus
candelabrum n candēlābrum nt
candid adj ingenuus, apertus, līber, simplex
candidate n petītor m; **be a ~ for** petere
candidature n petītiō f
candidly adv ingenuē
candle n candēla f
candlestick n candēlābrum nt
candour n ingenuitās f, simplicitās f, lībertās f
cane n (reed) harundō f; (for walking, punishing)
  virga f ▶ vt verberāre
canine adj canīnus
canister n capsula f
canker n (plants) rōbīgō f; (fig) aerūgō f,
  carcinōma nt ▶ vt corrumpere
Cannae n Cannae fpl
cannibal n anthrōpophagus m
cannon n tormentum nt
cannot nōn posse, nequīre; **I ~ help but ...**
  facere nōn possum quīn ... (subj), nōn possum
  nōn ... (infin)
canny adj prūdens, prōvidus, cautus,
  circumspectus
canoe n linter f
canon n nōrma f, rēgula f; (ECCL) canonicus m
canopy n aulaeum nt
cant n fūcus m, fūcāta verba ntpl ▶ vt
  oblīquāre
cantankerous adj importūnus
cantankerousness n importūnitās f
canter n lēnis cursus m ▶ vi lēniter currere
canticle n canticum nt
canto n carmen nt
canton n pāgus m

canvas n carbasus m, linteum nt ▸ adj
carbaseus; **under ~** sub pellibus
canvass vi ambīre ▸ vt prēnsāre, circumīre
canvassing n ambitus m, ambitiō f
cap n pilleus m; (priest's) galērus m, apex m
capability n facultās f, potestās f
capable adj capāx, doctus, perītus
capably adv bene, doctē
capacious adj capāx, amplus
capacity n capācitās f, amplitūdō f; (mind)
ingenium nt
caparison n ephippium nt
cape n (GEOG) prōmontōrium nt; (dress)
chlamys f
caper vi saltāre; (animal) lascīvīre ▸ n saltus m
capering n lascivia f
capital adj (chief) praecipuus, prīnceps;
(excellent) ēgregius; (LAW) capitālis; **convict of**
a ~ offence capitis damnāre ▸ n (town) caput nt;
(money) sors f; (class) negōtiātōrēs mpl;
make ~ out of ūtī (abl)
capitalist n faenerātor m
capital punishment n capitis supplicum nt
capitation tax n capitum exāctiō f
Capitol n Capitōlium nt
capitulate vi sē dēdere; **troops who have**
capitulated dēditīciī mpl
capitulation n dēditiō f
capon n capō m
caprice n libīdō f, incōnstantia f
capricious adj incōnstāns, levis
capriciously adv incōnstanter, leviter
capriciousness n incōnstantia f, libīdō f
capsize vt ēvertere ▸ vi ēvertī
captain n dux m, praefectus m, prīnceps m; (MIL)
centuriō m; (naval) nāvarchus m; (of merchant
ship) magister m ▸ vt praeesse (dat), dūcere
captaincy n centuriātus m
caption n caput nt
captious adj mōrōsus; (question) captiōsus
captiously adv mōrōsē
captiousness n mōrōsitās f
captivate vt capere, dēlēnīre, adlicere
captive n captīvus m
captivity n captīvitās f, vincula ntpl
captor n (by storm) expugnātor m; victor m
capture n (by storm) expugnātiō f ▸ vt capere
car n currus m
caravan n commeātus m
carbuncle n (MED) fūrunculus m; (stone)
acaustus m
carcass n cadāver nt
card n charta f; (ticket) tessera f; (wool) pecten nt
▸ vt pectere
cardamom n amōmum nt
cardinal adj praecipuus; **~ point** cardō m ▸ n
(ECCL) cardinālis
care n cūra f; (anxiety) sollicitūdō f; (attention)
dīligentia f; (charge) custōdia f; **take ~** cavēre;
take ~ of cūrāre ▸ vi cūrāre; **~ for** vt (look after)
cūrāre; (like) amāre; **I don't ~** nīl moror;
I couldn't ~ less about … floccī nōn faciō …,

pendō; **I don't ~ about** mittō, nihil moror; **for**
all I ~ per mē
career n curriculum nt; (POL) cursus honōrum;
(completed) rēs gestae fpl ▸ vi ruere, volāre
carefree adj sēcūrus
careful adj (cautious) cautus; (attentive) dīligēns,
attentus; (work) accūrātus
carefully adv cautē, dīligenter, attentē;
accūrātē
careless adj incautus, neglegēns
carelessly adv incautē, neglegenter
carelessness n incūria f, neglegentia f
caress vt fovēre, blandīrī ▸ n blandīmentum nt,
amplexus m
cargo n onus nt
caricature n (picture) gryllus m; (fig) imāgō
dētorta f ▸ vt dētorquēre
carmine n coccum nt ▸ adj coccineus
carnage n strāgēs f, caedēs f
carnal adj corporeus; (pleasure) libīdinōsus
carnival n fēriae fpl
carol n carmen nt ▸ vi cantāre
carouse vi perpōtāre, cōmissārī ▸ n cōmissātiō f
carp vi obtrectāre; **~ at** carpere, rōdere
carpenter n faber m, lignārius m
carpet n tapēte nt
carriage n (conveying) vectūra f; (vehicle)
vehiculum nt; (for journeys) raeda f, petorritum
nt; (for town) carpentum nt, pīlentum nt;
(deportment) gestus m, incessus m; **~ and pair**
bīgae fpl; **~ and four** quadrīgae fpl
carrier n vector m; (porter) bāiulus m; **letter ~**
tabellārius m
carrion n cadāver nt
carrot n carōta f
carry vt portāre, vehere, ferre, gerere; (LAW)
perferre; (by assault) expugnāre; **~ away** auferre,
āvehere; (by force) rapere; (with emotion) efferre;
~ all before one ēvincere; **~ along** (building)
dūcere; **~ back** reportāre; revehere, referre;
~ down dēportāre, dēvehere; **~ in** invehere,
intrōferre; **~ off** auferre, asportāre, āvehere; (by
force) abripere, ēripere; (prize) ferre, reportāre;
(success) bene gerere; **~ on** vt gerere; (profession)
exercēre; **~ out** vi efferre, ēgerere, ēvehere;
(task) exsequī; **~ out an undertaking** rem
suscipere; **~ over** trānsportāre, trānsferre;
~ the day vincere; **~ one's point** pervincere;
~ through perferre; **~ to** adferre, advehere; **~ up**
subvehere ▸ vi (sound) audīrī; **~ on** vi pergere;
(flirt) lascīvīre
cart n plaustrum nt; carrus nt; **put the ~ before**
the horse praeposterum dīcere ▸ vt plaustrō
vehere
Carthage n Carthāgō, Carthāginis f
Carthaginian adj Carthāginiēnsis; Pūnicus;
the Carthaginians Poenī mpl
carthorse n iūmentum nt
carve vt sculpere; (on surface) caelāre; (meat)
secāre; **~ out** exsculpere
carver n caelātor m
carving n caelātūra f

cascade n cataracta m
case n (*instance*) exemplum nt, rēs f; (*legal*) āctiō f, līs f, causa f; (*plight*) tempus nt; (GRAM) cāsus m; (*receptacle*) thēca f, involucrum nt; **in ~** sī; (*to prevent*) nē; **in any ~** utut est rēs; **in that ~** ergō; **such is the ~** sīc sē rēs habet; **civil ~** causa prīvāta; **criminal ~** causa pūblica; **win a ~** causam, lītem obtinēre; **lose a ~** causam, lītem āmittere
casement n fenestra f
cash n nummī mpl; (*ready*) numerātum nt, praesēns pecūnia f; **pay ~** ex arcā absolvere, repraesentāre
cash box n arca f
cashier n dispēnsātor m ▸ vt (MIL) exauctōrāre
cash payment n repraesentātiō f
cask n cūpa f
casket n arcula f, pyxis f
casque n galea f, cassis f
cast vt iacere; (*account*) inīre; (*eyes*) conicere; (*lots*) conicere; (*covering*) exuere; (*metal*) fundere; **~ ashore** ēicere; **~ away** prōicere; **~ down** dēicere; (*humble*) abicere; **~ in one's teeth** exprobrāre; **~ lots** sortīrī; **~ off** vi abicere, exuere; **~ out** dēicere, ēicere, pellere ▸ n iactus m; (*moulding*) typus m, fōrma f; **with a ~ in the eye** paetus
castanet n crotalum nt
castaway n ēiectus m
caste n ōrdō m
castigate vt animadvertere, castīgāre
castigation n animadversiō f, castīgātiō f
castle n arx f, castellum nt
castrate vt castrāre
casual adj fortuītus; (*person*) neglegēns
casually adv temerē
casualty n īnfortūnium nt ▸ pl: **casualties** occīsī mpl
casuist n sophistēs m
cat n fēlēs f
cataclysm n dīluvium nt, ruīna f
catalogue n index m
catapult n catapulta f, ballista f
cataract n cataracta f
catarrh n gravēdō f; **liable to ~** gravēdinōsus
catastrophe n calamitās f, ruīna f
catastrophic adj calamitōsus, exitiōsus
catch vt capere, dēprehendere, excipere; (*disease*) contrahere, nancīscī; (*fire*) concipere, comprehendere; (*meaning*) intellegere; **~ at** captāre; **~ out** vi dēprehendere; **~ up with** adsequī; **~ birds** aucupārī; **~ fish** piscārī ▸ n bolus m
categorical adj (*statement*) plānus
categorically adv sine exceptiōne
category n numerus m, genus nt
cater vi obsōnāre
cateran n praedātor m
caterer n obsōnātor m
caterpillar n ērūca f
caterwaul vi ululāre
catgut n chorda f

catharsis n pūrgātiō f
cathedral n aedēs f
catholic adj generālis
catkin n iūlus m
cattle n (*collectively*) pecus nt; (*singly*) pecus f; (*for plough*) armenta ntpl
cattle breeder n pecuārius m
cattle market n forum boārium nt
cattle thief n abāctor m
cauldron n cortīna f
cause n causa f; (*person*) auctor m; (LAW) causa f; (*party*) partēs fpl; **give ~ for** māteriam dare (*gen*); **make common ~ with** facere cum, stāre ab; **plead a ~** causam dīcere; **in the ~ of** prō (*abl*); **without ~** iniūriā ▸ vt efficere ut (*subj*), facere, facessere (*with 'ut'*), cūrāre (*with gerundive*); (*feelings*) movēre, inicere, ciēre
causeless adj vānus, sine causā
causeway n agger m
caustic adj (*fig*) mordāx
cauterize vt adūrere
caution n (*wariness*) cautiō f, prūdentia f; (*warning*) monitum nt ▸ vt monēre, admonēre
cautious adj cautus, prōvidus, prūdens
cautiously adv cautē, prūdenter
cavalcade n pompa f
cavalier n eques m ▸ adj adrogāns
cavalierly adv adroganter
cavalry n equitēs mpl, equitātus m ▸ adj equester; **troop of ~** turma f
cavalryman n eques m
cave n spēlunca f, caverna f; antrum nt; **~ in** vi concidere, conlābī
cavern n spēlunca f, caverna f
cavil vi cavillārī; **~ at** carpere, cavillārī ▸ n captiō f, cavillātiō f
cavity n caverna f, cavum nt
cavort vi saltāre
caw vi cornīcārī
cease vi dēsinere, dēsistere
ceaseless adj adsiduus, perpetuus
ceaselessly adv adsiduē, perpetuō
cedar n cedrus f ▸ adj cedrinus
cede vt cēdere, concēdere
ceiling n tēctum nt; (*panelled*) lacūnar nt, laqueārium nt
celebrate vt (*rite*) celebrāre, agitāre; (*in crowds*) frequentāre; (*person, theme*) laudāre, celebrāre, dīcere
celebrated adj praeclārus, illūstris, nōtus; **the ~** ille
celebration n celebrātiō f; (*rite*) sollemne nt
celebrity n celebritās f, fāma f; (*person*) vir illūstris
celerity n celeritās f, vēlōcitās f
celery n apium nt
celestial adj caelestis; dīvīnus
celibacy n caelibātus m
celibate n caelebs m
cell n cella f
cellar n cella f
cement n ferrūmen nt ▸ vt coagmentāre

cemetery n sepulchrētum nt
cenotaph n tumulus honōrārius, tumulus inānis m
censer n tūribulum nt, acerra f
censor n cēnsor m ▸ vt cēnsēre
censorious adj cēnsōrius, obtrectātor
censorship n cēnsūra f
censure n reprehēnsiō f, animadversiō f; (censor's) nota f ▸ vt reprehendere, animadvertere, increpāre; notāre
census n cēnsus m
cent n: **one per ~** centēsima f; **12 per ~ per annum** centēsima f (ie monthly)
centaur n centaurus m
centaury n (plant) centaurēum nt
centenarian n centum annōs nātus m, nāta f
centenary n centēsimus annus m
centesimal adj centēsimus
central adj medius
centralize vt in ūnum locum cōnferre; (power) ad ūnum dēferre
centre n centrum nt, media pars f; **the ~ of** medius
centuple adj centuplex
centurion n centuriō m
century n (MIL) centuria f; (time) saeculum nt
ceramic adj fictilis
cereal n frūmentum nt
ceremonial adj sollemnis ▸ n rītus m
ceremonious adj (rite) sollemnis; (person) officiōsus
ceremoniously adv sollemniter; officiōsē
ceremony n caerimōnia f, rītus m; (politeness) officium nt; (pomp) apparātus m; **master of ceremonies** dēsignātor m
cerise n coccum nt ▸ adj coccineus
certain adj (sure) certus; (future) explōrātus; **a ~** quīdam, quaedam, quoddam; **be ~ (know)** prō certō scīre/habēre
certainly adv certē, certō, sine dubiō; (yes) ita, māximē; (concessive) quidem
certainty n (thing) certum nt; (belief) fidēs f; **for a ~** prō certō, explōrātē; **regard as a ~** prō explōrātō habēre
certificate n testimōnium nt
certify vt (writing) recognōscere; (fact) adfirmāre, testificārī
cessation n fīnis m; (from labour) quiēs f; (temporary) intermissiō f; (of hostilities) indutiae fpl
chafe vt ūrere; (fig) inrītāre ▸ vi stomachārī
chaff n palea f ▸ vt lūdere
chaffinch n fringilla f
chagrin n dolor m, stomachus m ▸ vt stomachum facere (dat), sollicitāre
chain n catēna f; (for neck) torquis m; (sequence) seriēs f; **chains** pl vincula ntpl ▸ vt vincīre
chair n sella f; (of office) sella curūlis f; (sedan) sella gestātōria f, lectīca f; (teacher's) cathedra f
chairman n (at meeting) magister m; (of debate) disceptātor m
chalet n casa f

chalice n calix m
chalk n crēta f
chalky adj crētōsus
challenge n prōvocātiō f ▸ vt prōvocāre, lacessere; (statement) in dubium vocāre; (fig) invītāre, dēposcere
challenger n prōvocātor m
chamber n conclāve nt; (bed) cubiculum nt; (bridal) thalamus m; (parliament) cūria f
chamberlain n cubiculārius m
chambermaid n serva f, ancilla f
chameleon n chamaeleōn f
chamois n rūpicapra f
champ vt mandere
champion n prōpugnātor m, patrōnus m; (winner) victor m ▸ vt favēre (dat), adesse (dat)
chance n fors f, fortūna f, cāsus m; (opportunity) occāsiō f; potestās f, facultās f; (prospect) spēs f; **game of ~** ālea f; **by ~** cāsū, fortuītō; **have an eye to the main ~** forō ūtī; **on the ~ of** sī forte ▸ adj fortuītus ▸ vi accidere, ēvenīre; **it chanced that ... accidit ut ... (subj); ~ upon** incidere in, invenīre ▸ vt periclitārī
chancel n absis f
chancellor n cancellārius m
chancy adj dubius, perīculōsus
chandelier n candēlābrum nt
chandler n candēlārium propōla m
change n mūtātiō f, commūtātiō f, permūtātiō f; (POL) rēs novae fpl; (alternation) vicēs fpl, vicissitūdō f; (money) nummī minōrēs mpl ▸ vt mūtāre, commūtāre, permūtāre ▸ vi mūtārī; **~ hands** abaliēnārī; **~ places** ōrdinem permūtāre, inter sē loca permūtāre
changeable adj incōnstāns, mūtābilis
changeableness n incōnstantia f, mūtābilitās f
changeful adj varius
changeless adj cōnstāns, immūtābilis
changeling adj subditus m
channel n canālis m; (sea) fretum nt; (irrigation) rīvus m; (groove) sulcus m
chant vt cantāre, canere ▸ n cantus m
chaos n chaos nt; (fig) perturbātiō f
chaotic adj perturbātus
chap n rīma f; (man) homō m
chapel n sacellum nt, aedicula f
chaplain n diāconus m
chaplet n corōna f, sertum nt
chaps n (animal) mālae fpl
chapter n caput nt
char vt ambūrere
character n (inborn) indolēs f, ingenium nt, nātūra f; (moral) mōrēs mpl; (reputation) existimātiō f; (kind) genus nt; (mark) signum nt, littera f; (THEAT) persōna f, partēs fpl; **sustain a ~** persōnam gerere; **I know his ~** sciō quālis sit
characteristic adj proprius ▸ n proprium nt
characteristically adv suō mōre
characterize vt dēscrībere; proprium esse (gen)
charcoal n carbō m

charge n (LAW) accūsātiō f, crīmen nt; (MIL) impetus m, dēcursus m; (cost) impēnsa f; (task) mandātum nt, onus nt; (trust) cūra f, tūtēla f; **bring a ~ against** lītem intendere (dat); **entertain a ~ against** nōmen recipere (gen); **give in ~** in custōdiam trādere; **put in ~ of** praeficere (acc, dat); **be in ~ of** praeesse (dat) ▶ vt (LAW) accūsāre; (falsely) īnsimulāre; (MIL) incurrere in (acc), signa īnferre in (acc), impetum facere in (acc); (duty) mandāre; (cost) ferre, īnferre; (empty space) complēre; (trust) committere; (speech) hortārī; **~ to the account of** expēnsum ferre (dat)

chargeable adj obnoxius

charger n (dish) lānx f; (horse) equus m

charily adv cautē, parcē

chariot n currus m; (races) quadrīgae fpl; (war) essedum nt

charioteer n aurīga m; (war) essedārius m

charitable adj benevolus, benignus

charitably adv benevolē, benignē

charity n amor m, benignitās f; līberālitās f

charlatan n planus m

charm n (spell) carmen nt; (amulet) bulla f; (fig) blanditiae fpl, dulcēdō f, illecebra f; (beauty) venus f, lepōs m ▶ vt (magic) fascināre; (delight) dēlectāre, dēlēnīre

charming adj venustus, lepidus; (speech) blandus; (scenery) amoenus

charmingly adv venustē, blandē

chart n tabula f

charter n diplōma nt ▶ vt condūcere

chary adj (cautious) cautus; (sparing) parcus

chase vt fugāre; (hunt) vēnārī; (pursue) persequī, īnsequī; (engrave) caelāre; **~ away** pellere, abigere ▶ n vēnātus m, vēnātiō f; (pursuit) īnsectātiō f

chaser n (in metal) caelātor m

chasm n hiātus m

chaste adj castus, pudīcus; (style) pūrus

chasten vt castīgāre, corrigere

chastener n castīgātor m, corrēctor m

chastise vt castīgāre, animadvertere

chastisement n castīgātiō f, poena f

chastity n castitās f, pudīcitia f

chat vi colloquī, sermōcinārī ▶ n sermō m, colloquium nt

chatelaine n domina f

chattels n bona ntpl, rēs mancipī

chatter vi garrīre; (teeth) crepitāre ▶ n garrulitās f, loquācitās f

chatterbox n lingulāca m/f

chatterer n garrulus m, loquāx m

chattering adj garrulus, loquāx ▶ n garrulitās f, loquācitās f; (teeth) crepitus m

cheap adj vīlis; **hold ~** parvī aestimāre; **buy ~** bene emere

cheapen vt pretium minuere (gen)

cheaply adv vīliter, parvō pretiō

cheapness n vīlitās f

cheat vt dēcipere, fraudāre, dēfraudāre, frustrārī ▶ n fraudātor m

check vt cohibēre, coercēre; (movement) impedīre, inhibēre; (rebuke) reprehendere; (test) probāre ▶ n impedīmentum nt, mora f; (MIL) offēnsiō f; (rebuke) reprehēnsiō f; (test) probātiō f; (ticket) tessera f

checkmate n incitae calcēs fpl ▶ vt ad incitās redigere

cheek n gena f; (impudence) ōs nt; **cheeks** pl mālae fpl; **how have you the ~ to say?** quō ōre dīcis?

cheekbone n maxilla f

cheeky adj impudēns

cheep vi pīpilāre

cheer vt hilarāre, exhilarāre; hortārī; (in sorrow) cōnsōlārī ▶ vi clāmāre, adclāmāre; **~ up!** bonō animō es! ▶ n (shout) clāmor m, plausus m; (food) hospitium nt; (mind) animus m

cheerful adj alacer, hilaris, laetus

cheerfully adv hilare, laetē

cheerfulness n hilaritās f

cheerily adv hilare

cheerless adj tristis, maestus

cheerlessly adv triste

cheery adj hilaris

cheese n cāseus m

chef n coquus m

cheque n perscrīptiō f, syngrapha f

chequer vt variāre

chequered adj varius; (mosaic) tessellātus

cherish vt fovēre, colere

cherry n (fruit) cerasum nt; (tree) cerasus f

chess n latrunculī mpl

chessboard n abacus m

chest n (box) arca f, arcula f; (body) pectus nt; **~ of drawers** armārium nt

chestnut n castanea f ▶ adj (colour) spādīx

chevalier n eques m

chevaux-de-frise n ēricius m

chew vt mandere

chic adj expolītus, concinnus

chicanery n (LAW) calumnia f; (fig) dolus m

chick n pullus m

chicken n pullus m; **don't count your chickens before they're hatched** adhūc tua messis in herbā est

chicken-hearted adj timidus, ignāvus

chick-pea n cicer nt

chide vt reprehendere, increpāre, obiūrgāre

chief n prīnceps m, dux m ▶ adj praecipuus, prīmus; **~ point** caput nt

chief command n summa imperī

chiefly adv in prīmīs, praesertim, potissimum

chieftain n prīnceps m, rēgulus m

chilblain n pernīō m

child n īnfāns m/f; puer m, puerulus m, puella f; fīlius m, fīlia f; **child's play** lūdus m

childbed n puerperium nt

childbirth n partus m

childhood n pueritia f; **from ~** ā puerō

childish adj puerīlis

childishly adv puerīliter

childless adj orbus

childlessness n orbitās f
childlike adj puerīlis
children npl līberī mpl
chill n frīgus nt ▸ adj frīgidus ▸ vt refrīgerāre
chilly adj frīgidus, frīgidior
chime vi sonāre, canere; **~ in** interpellāre; (fig)
cōnsonāre ▸ n sonus m
chimera n chimaera f; (fig) somnium nt
chimerical adj commentīcius
chimney n camīnus m
chin n mentum nt
china n fictilia ntpl
chink n rīma f; (sound) tinnītus m ▸ vi crepāre,
tinnīre
chip n assula f, fragmentum nt ▸ vt dolāre
chirp vi pīpilāre
chirpy adj hilaris
chisel n scalprum nt, scalpellum nt ▸ vt sculpere
chit n (child) pūsiō m, puerulus m
chitchat n sermunculī mpl
chitterlings n hillae fpl
chivalrous adj generōsus
chivalry n virtūs f; (men) iuventūs f; (class)
equitēs mpl
chive n caepe nt
chock n cuneus m
chock-full adj refertus
choice n dēlēctus m, ēlēctiō f; (of alternatives)
optiō f ▸ adj lēctus, eximius, exquīsītus
choiceness n ēlegantia f, praestantia f
choir n chorus m
choke vt suffocāre; (emotion) reprimere;
(passage) obstruere
choler n bīlis f; (anger) īra f, stomachus m
choleric adj īrācundus
choose vt legere, ēligere, dēligere; (alternative)
optāre; (for office) dēsignāre; (with infin) velle,
mālle
chop vt concīdere; **~ off** praecīdere ▸ n (meat)
offa f
chopper n secūris f
choppy adj (sea) asper
choral adj symphōniacus
chord n (string) nervus m, chorda f
chortle vi cachinnāre
chorus n (singers) chorus m; (song) concentus m,
symphōnia f; **in ~** ūnā vōce
christen vt baptizāre
Christian adj Christiānus
Christianity n Christiānismus m
chronic adj inveterātus; **become ~**
inveterāscere
chronicle n annālēs mpl, ācta pūblica ntpl ▸ vt in
annālēs referre
chronicler n annālium scrīptor m
chronological adj: **in ~ order** servātō
temporum ōrdine; **make a ~ error** temporibus
errāre
chronology n temporum ratiō f, temporum
ōrdō m
chronometer n hōrologium nt
chubby adj pinguis

chuck vt conicere; **~ out** extrūdere
chuckle vi rīdēre ▸ n rīsus m
chum n sodālis m
church n ecclēsia f
churl n rūsticus m
churlish adj difficilis, importūnus; avārus
churlishly adv rūsticē, avārē
churlishness n mōrōsitās f, avāritia f
chute n (motion) lāpsus m; (place) dēclīve nt
cicada n cicāda f
cincture n cingulum nt
cinder n cinis m
cipher n numerus m, nihil nt; (code) notae fpl;
in ~ per notās
circle n orbis m, circulus m, gÿrus m; **form a ~**
in orbem cōnsistere ▸ vi sē circumagere,
circumīre
circlet n īnfula f
circuit n ambitus m, circuitus m; (assizes)
conventus m
circuitous adj longus; **a ~ route** circuitus m;
(speech) ambāgēs fpl
circular adj rotundus
circulate vt (news) pervulgāre ▸ vi circumagī;
(news) circumferrī, percrēbrēscere
circulation n ambitus m; **be in ~** in manibus
esse; **go out of ~** obsolēscere
circumcise vt circumcīdere
circumference n ambitus m
circumlocution n ambāgēs fpl, circuitiō f
circumnavigate vt circumvehī
circumscribe vt circumscrībere; (restrict)
coercēre, fīnīre
circumspect adj cautus, prūdēns
circumspection n cautiō f, prūdentia f,
circumspectiō f
circumspectly adv cautē, prūdenter
circumstance n rēs f; **circumstances** rērum
status m; (wealth) rēs f; **as circumstances arise**
ē rē nātā; **under the circumstances** cum haec
ita sint, essent; **under no circumstances**
nēquāquam
circumstantial adj adventīcius; (detailed)
accūrātus; **~ evidence** coniectūra f
circumstantially adv accūrātē, subtīliter
circumvallation n circummūnītiō f
circumvent vt circumvenīre, fallere
circus n circus m
cistern n lacus m, cisterna f
citadel n arx f
citation n (LAW) vocātiō f; (mention)
commemorātiō f
cite vt in iūs vocāre; (quote) commemorāre,
prōferre
citizen n cīvis m/f; (of provincial town) mūniceps
m; **fellow ~** cīvis m/f; **Roman citizens** Quirītēs
mpl ▸ adj cīvīlis, cīvicus
citizenship n cīvitās f; **deprived of ~** capite
dēminūtus; **loss of ~** capitis dēminūtiō f
citron n (fruit) citrum nt; (tree) citrus f
city n urbs f, oppidum nt
civic adj cīvīlis, cīvicus

civil adj (of citizens) cīvīlis; (war) cīvīlis, intestīnus, domesticus; (manners) urbānus, cōmis, officiōsus; (lawsuit) prīvātus

civilian n togātus m

civility n urbānitās f, cōmitās f; (act) officium nt

civilization n exculta hominum vīta f, cultus atque hūmānitās

civilize vt excolere, expolīre, ad hūmānum cultum dēdūcere

civil war n bellum cīvīle, bellum domesticum, bellum intestīnum

clad adj vestītus

claim vt (for oneself) adrogāre, adserere; (something due) poscere, postulāre, vindicāre; (at law) petere; (statement) adfirmāre ▶ n postulātiō f, postulātum nt; (at law) petītiō f, vindiciae fpl

claimant n petītor m

clam n chāma f

clamber vi scandere

clammy adj ūmidus, lentus

clamorous adj vōciferāns

clamour n strepitus m, clāmōrēs mpl ▶ vi: ~ against obstrepere (dat)

clamp n cōnfibula f

clan n gēns f

clandestine adj fūrtīvus

clandestinely adv clam, fūrtim

clang n clangor m, crepitus m ▶ vi increpāre

clangour n clangor m

clank n crepitus m ▶ vi crepitāre

clansman n gentīlis m

clap vi plaudere, applaudere; ~ eyes on cōnspicere; ~ in prison in vincula conicere ▶ n plausus m; (thunder) fragor m

clapper n plausor m

claptrap n iactātiō f

claque n plausōrēs mpl, operae fpl

clarify vt pūrgāre; (knowledge) illūstrāre ▶ vi liquēre

clarinet n tībia f

clarion n lituus m, cornū nt

clarity n perspicuitās f

clash n concursus m; (sound) strepitus m, crepitus m; (fig) discrepantia f ▶ vi concurrere; (sound) increpāre; (fig) discrepāre ▶ vt cōnflīgere

clasp n fībula f; (embrace) amplexus m ▶ vt implicāre; amplectī, complectī; ~ together interiungere

class n (POL) ōrdō m, classis f; (kind) genus nt; (school) classis f ▶ vt dēscrībere; ~ as in numerō (gen pl) referre, repōnere, habēre

classic n scrīptor classicus m

classical adj classicus; ~ literature litterae Graecae et Rōmānae

classics npl scrīptōrēs Graecī et Rōmānī

classify vt dēscrībere, in ōrdinem redigere

class-mate n condiscipulus m

clatter n crepitus m ▶ vi increpāre

clause n (GRAM) incīsum nt, membrum nt; (LAW) caput nt; (will) ēlogium nt; in short clauses incīsim

claw n unguis m, ungula f ▶ vt unguibus lacerāre

clay n argilla f; made of ~ fictilis

clayey adj argillāceus

claymore n gladius m

clean adj mundus; (fig) pūrus, castus; ~ slate novae tabulae fpl; make a ~ sweep of omnia tollere; show a ~ pair of heels sē in pedēs conicere; my hands are ~ innocēns sum ▶ adv prōrsus, tōtus ▶ vt pūrgāre

cleanliness n munditia f

cleanly adj mundus, nitidus ▶ adv mundē, pūrē

cleanse vt pūrgāre, abluere, dētergēre

clear adj clārus; (liquid) limpidus; (space) apertus, pūrus; (sound) clārus; (weather) serēnus; (fact) manifestus, perspicuus; (language) illūstris, dīlūcidus; (conscience) rēctus, innocēns; it is ~ liquet; ~ of līber (abl), expers (gen); be ~ about rēctē intellegere; keep ~ of ēvītāre; the coast is ~ arbitrī absunt ▶ vt (of obstacles) expedīre, pūrgāre; (of a charge) absolvere; (self) pūrgāre; (profit) lucrārī; ~ away āmovēre, tollere; ~ off vt (debt) solvere, exsolvere ▶ vi facessere; ~ out ēluere, dētergēre; ~ up vt (difficulty) illūstrāre, ēnōdāre, explicāre ▶ vi (weather) disserēnāscere

clearance n pūrgātiō f; (space) intervallum nt

clearing n (in forest) lūcus m

clearly adv clārē; manifestē, apertē, perspicuē; (with clause) vidēlicet

clearness n clāritās f; (weather) serēnitās f; (mind) acūmen nt; (style) perspicuitās f

clear-sighted adj sagāx, perspicāx

cleavage n discidium nt

cleave vt (cut) findere, discindere ▶ vi (cling): ~ to haerēre (dat), adhaerēre (dat)

cleaver n dolabra f

cleft n rīma f, hiātus m ▶ adj fissus, discissus

clemency n clēmentia f, indulgentia f; with ~ clēmenter

clement adj clēmēns, misericors

clench vt (nail) retundere; (hand) comprimere

clerk n scrība m; (of court) lēctor m

clever adj callidus, ingeniōsus, doctus, astūtus

cleverly adv doctē, callidē, ingeniōsē

cleverness n calliditās f, sollertia f

clew n glomus nt

cliché n verbum trītum nt

client n cliēns m/f; (lawyer's) cōnsultor m; body of clients clientēla f

clientele n clientēla f

cliff n rūpēs f, scopulus m

climate n caelum nt

climax n (RHET) gradātiō f; (fig) culmen nt

climb vt, vi scandere, ascendere; ~ down dēscendere ▶ n ascēnsus m

climber n scandēns m

clime n caelum nt, plāga f

clinch vt cōnfirmāre

cling vi adhaerēre; ~ together cohaerēre

clink vi tinnīre ▶ n tinnītus m

clip vt tondēre; praecīdere

clippers n forfex f

clique n factiō f
cloak n (rain) lacerna f; (travel) paenula f; (MIL) sagum nt; palūdāmentum nt; (Greek) pallium nt; (fig) involūcrum nt; (pretext) speciēs f ▸ vt tegere, dissimulāre
clock n hōrologium nt; (sun) sōlārium nt; (water) clepsydra f; **ten o'clock** quarta hōra
clockwise adv dextrōvorsum, dextrōrsum
clod n glaeba f
clog n (shoe) sculpōnea f; (fig) impedīmentum nt ▸ vt impedīre
cloister n porticus f
cloistered adj (fig) umbrātilis
close¹ adj (shut) clausus; (tight) artus; (narrow) angustus; (near) propinquus; (compact) refertus, dēnsus; (stingy) parcus; (secret) obscūrus; (weather) crassus; **~ together** dēnsus, refertus; **at ~ quarters** comminus; **be ~ at hand** īnstāre; **keep ~ to** adhaerēre; **~ to** prope (acc), iuxtā (acc) ▸ adv prope, iuxtā ▸ n angiportus m
close² vt claudere, operīre; (finish) perficere, fīnīre, conclūdere, termināre; (ranks) dēnsāre ▸ vi claudī; conclūdī, terminārī; (time) exīre; (wound) coīre; (speech) perōrāre; **~ with** (fight) manum cōnserere, signa cōnferre; (deal) pacīscī; (offer) accipere ▸ n fīnis m, terminus m; (action) exitus m; (sentence) conclūsiō f; **at the ~ of summer** aestāte exeunte
closely adv prope; (attending) attentē; (associating) coniūnctē; **follow ~** īnstāre (dat)
closeness n propinquitās f; (weather) gravitās f, crassitūdō f; (with money) parsimōnia f; (friends) coniūnctiō f; (manner) cautiō f
closet n cubiculum nt, cella f ▸ vt inclūdere
clot n (blood) concrētus sanguis m ▸ vi concrēscere
cloth n textile nt; (piece) pannus m; (linen) linteum nt; (covering) strāgulum nt
clothe vt vestīre
clothes n vestis f, vestītus m, vestīmenta ntpl
clothier n vestiārius m
clothing n vestis f, vestītus m, vestīmenta ntpl
clotted adj concrētus
cloud n nūbēs f; (storm) nimbus m; (dust) globus m; (disfavour) invidia f ▸ vt nūbibus obdūcere; (fig) obscūrāre
clouded adj obnūbilus
cloudiness n nūbilum nt
cloudless adj pūrus, serēnus
cloudy adj obnūbilus
clout n pannus m
cloven adj (hoof) bifidus
clover n trifolium nt
clown n (boor) rūsticus m; (comic) scurra m
clownish adj rūsticus, inurbānus
clownishness n rūsticitās f
cloy vt satiāre
cloying adj pūtidus
club n (stick) fustis m, clāva f; (society) sodālitās f; **~ together** vi in commūne cōnsulere, pecūniās cōnferre
club-footed adj scaurus

cluck vi singultīre ▸ n singultus m
clue n indicium nt, vestīgium nt
clump n massa f; (earth) glaeba f; (trees) arbustum nt; (willows) salictum nt
clumsily adv ineptē, inēleganter; inconditē, īnfabrē
clumsiness n īnscītia f
clumsy adj (person) inconcinnus, ineptus; (thing) inhabilis; (work) inconditus
cluster n cumulus m; (grapes) racēmus m; (people) corōna f ▸ vi congregārī
clutch vt prehendere, adripere; **~ at** captāre nt, comprehēnsiō f; **in one's clutches** ē manibus; **in one's clutches** in potestāte
clutter n turba f ▸ vt impedīre, obstruere
coach n currus m, raeda f, pīlentum nt; (trainer) magister m ▸ vt ēdocēre, praecipere (dat)
coachman n aurīga m, raedārius m
coagulate vt cōgere ▸ vi concrēscere
coagulation n concrētiō f
coal n carbō m; **carry coals to Newcastle** in silvam ligna ferre
coalesce vi coīre, coalēscere
coalition n coitiō f, cōnspīrātiō f
coarse adj (quality) crassus; (manners) rūsticus, inurbānus; (speech) īnfacētus
coarsely adv inurbānē, inēleganter
coarseness n crassitūdō f; rūsticitās f
coast n lītus nt, ōra maritima f ▸ vi: **~ along** legere, praetervehī
coastal adj lītorālis, maritimus
coastline n lītus nt
coat n pallium nt; (animals) pellis f ▸ vt indūcere, inlinere
coating n corium nt
coax vt blandīrī, dēlēnīre
coaxing adj blandus ▸ n blanditiae fpl
cob n (horse) mannus m; (swan) cygnus m
cobble n lapis m ▸ vt sarcīre
cobbler n sūtor m
cobweb n arāneum nt
cock n gallus m, gallus gallīnāceus m; (other birds) mās m; (tap) epitonium nt; (hay) acervus m
cockatrice n basiliscus m
cockchafer n scarabaeus m
cockcrow n gallī cantus m ▸ vt ērigere
cockerel n pullus m
cockroach n blatta f
cocksure adj cōnfīdēns
cod n callarias m
coddle vt indulgēre (dat), permulcēre
code n fōrmula f; (secret) notae fpl
codicil n cōdicillī mpl
codify vt in ōrdinem redigere
coequal adj aequālis
coerce vt cōgere
coercion n vīs f
coffer n arca f, cista f; (public) fiscus m
coffin n arca f
cog n dēns m
cogency n vīs f, pondus nt
cogent adj gravis, validus

cogitate *vi* cōgitāre, meditārī
cogitation *n* cōgitātiō f; meditātiō f
cognate *adj* cognātus
cognition *n* cognitiō f
cognizance *n* cognitiō f; **take ~ of** cognōscere
cognizant *adj* gnārus
cohabit *vi* cōnsuēscere
cohabitation *n* cōnsuētūdō f
coheir *n* cohērēs m/f
cohere *vi* cohaerēre; (*statement*) congruere
coherence *n* coniūnctiō f; (*fig*) convenientia f
coherent *adj* congruēns
cohesion *n* coagmentātiō f
cohesive *adj* tenāx
cohort *n* cohors f
coil *n* spīra f ▶ *vt* glomerāre
coin *n* nummus m ▶ *vt* cūdere; (*fig*) fingere
coinage *n* monēta f; (*fig*) fictum nt
coincide *vi* concurrere; (*opinion*) cōnsentīre
coincidence *n* concursus m; cōnsēnsus m;
  by a ~ cāsū
coincidental *adj* fortuītus
coiner *n* (*of money*) signātor m
col *n* iugum nt
colander *n* cōlum nt
cold *adj* frīgidus; (*icy*) gelidus; **very ~** perfrīgidus;
  be ~, feel ~ algēre, frīgēre; **get ~** algēscere,
  frīgēscere ▶ *n* frīgus nt; (*felt*) algor m; (*malady*)
  gravēdō f; **catch ~** algēscere, frīgus colligere;
  catch a ~ gravēdinem contrahere; **have a ~**
  gravēdine labōrāre
coldish *adj* frīgidulus, frīgidior
coldly *adv* (*manner*) sine studiō
coldness *n* frīgus nt, algor m
cold water *n* frīgida f
colic *n* tormina ntpl
collar *n* collāre nt
collarbone *n* iugulum nt
collate *vt* cōnferre, comparāre
collateral *adj* adiūnctus; (*evidence*)
  cōnsentāneus
collation *n* collātiō f; (*meal*) prandium nt,
  merenda f
colleague *n* collēga m
collect *vt* colligere, cōgere, congerere; (*persons*)
  congregāre, convocāre; (*taxes*) exigere;
  (*something due*) recipere; **~ oneself** animum
  colligere; **cool and collected** aequō animō
  ▶ *vi* convenīre, congregārī
collection *n* (*persons*) coetus m, conventus m;
  (*things*) congeriēs f; (*money*) exāctiō f
collective *adj* commūnis
collectively *adv* commūniter
collector *n* (*of taxes*) exāctor m
college *n* collēgium nt
collide *vi* concurrere, cōnflīctārī
collier *n* carbōnārius m
collision *n* concursus m
collocation *n* collocātiō f
collop *n* offa f
colloquial *adj* cottīdiānus
colloquy *n* sermō m, colloquium nt

collude *vi* praevāricārī
collusion *n* praevāricātiō f
collusive *adj* praevāricātor
colonel *n* lēgātus m
colonial *adj* colōnicus ▶ *n* colōnus m
colonist *n* colōnus m
colonization *n* dēductiō f
colonize *vt* colōniam dēdūcere, cōnstituere in
  (*acc*)
colonnade *n* porticus f
colony *n* colōnia f
colossal *adj* ingēns, vastus
colossus *n* colossus m
colour *n* color m; (*paint*) pigmentum nt;
  (*artificial*) fūcus m; (*complexion*) color m; (*pretext*)
  speciēs f; **take on a ~** colōrem dūcere;
  under ~ of per speciem (*gen*); **local ~** māteria dē
  regiōne sūmpta ▶ *vt* colōrāre; (*dye*) īnficere,
  fūcāre; (*fig*) praetendere (*dat*) ▶ *vi* rubēre,
  ērubēscere
colourable *adj* speciōsus
coloured *adj* (*naturally*) colōrātus; (*artificially*)
  fūcātus
colourful *adj* fūcōsus, varius
colouring *n* pigmentum nt; (*dye*) fūcus m
colourless *adj* perlūcidus; (*person*) pallidus; (*fig*)
  īnsulsus
colours *n* (MIL) signum nt, vexillum nt; (POL)
  partēs fpl; **sail under false ~** aliēnō nōmine ūtī;
  with flying ~ māximā cum glōriā
colour sergeant *n* signifer m
colt *n* equuleus m, equullus m
coltsfoot *n* farfarus m
column *n* columna f; (MIL) agmen nt
coma *n* sopor m
comb *n* pecten m; (*bird*) crista f; (*loom*) pecten m;
  (*honey*) favus m ▶ *vt* pectere
combat *n* pugna f, proelium nt, certāmen nt ▶ *vi*
  pugnāre, dīmicāre, certāre ▶ *vt* pugnāre cum
  (*abl*), obsistere (*dat*)
combatant *n* pugnātor m ▶ *adj* pugnāns;
  non-combatant imbellis
combative *adj* ferōx, pugnāx
combination *n* coniūnctiō f, cōnfūsiō f;
  (*persons*) cōnspīrātiō f; (*illegal*) coniūrātiō f
combine *vt* coniungere, iungere ▶ *vi* coīre,
  coniungī ▶ *n* societās f
combustible *adj* ignī obnoxius
combustion *n* dēflāgrātiō f, incendium nt
come *vi* venīre, advenīre; (*after a journey*)
  dēvenīre; (*interj*) age!; **how comes it that ...?**
  quī fit ut ...?; **~ across** *vi* invenīre, offendere;
  ~ after sequī, excipere, succēdere (*dat*); **~ again**
  revenīre, redīre; **~ away** *vi* abscēdere; (*when
  pulled*) sequī; **~ back** *vi* revenīre, redīre; regredī;
  ~ between intervenīre, intercēdere; **~ down** *vi*
  dēvenīre, dēscendere; (*from the past*) trādī,
  prōdī; **~ forward** *vi* prōcēdere, prōdīre; **~ from** *vi*
  (*origin*) dēfluere; **~ in** *vi* inīre, introīre; ingredī;
  (*revenue*) redīre; **~ near** accēdere ad (*acc*),
  appropinquāre (*dat*); **~ nearer and nearer**
  adventāre; **~ of** *vi* (*family*) ortum esse ab, ex

(abl); **~ off** vi ēvādere, discēdere; **~ on** vi
prōcēdere; (progress) prōficere; (interj) age,
agite; **~ on the scene** intervenīre, supervenīre,
adesse; **~ out** vi exīre, ēgredī; (hair, teeth) cadere;
(flower) flōrēscere; (book) ēdī; **~ over** vi trānsīre;
(feeling) subīre, occupāre; **~ to** vi advenīre ad, in
(acc); (person) adīre; (amount) efficere; **~ to the
help of** subvenīre (dat); succurrere (dat); **~ to
nought** ad nihilum recidere; **~ to pass** ēvenīre,
fierī; **~ together** convenīre, coīre; **~ up** vi subīre,
succēdere; (growth) prōvenīre; **~ upon** vt
invenīre; **he is coming to** animus eī redit
comedian n (actor) cōmoedus m; (writer)
cōmicus m
comedienne n mīma f
comedy n cōmoedia f
comeliness n decor m, decōrum nt
comely adj decōrus, pulcher
comestibles n vīctus m
comet n comētēs m
comfort vt sōlārī, cōnsōlārī, adlevāre ▶ n
sōlācium nt, cōnsōlātiō f
comfortable adj commodus; **make oneself ~**
corpus cūrāre
comfortably adv commodē
comforter n cōnsōlātor m
comfortless adj incommodus; **be ~** sōlātiō
carēre
comforts npl commoda ntpl
comic adj cōmicus; facētus ▶ n scurra m
comical adj facētus, rīdiculus
coming adj futūrus ▶ n adventus m
comity n cōmitās f
command vt iubēre (+ acc and infin), imperāre
(dat and ut + subj); dūcere; (feelings) regere;
(resources) fruī (abl); (view) prōspectāre ▶ n (MIL)
imperium nt; (sphere) prōvincia f; (order)
imperium nt, iussum nt, mandātum nt; **be
in ~ of** praeesse (dat); **put in ~ of** praeficere (dat);
~ of language fācundia f
commandant n praefectus m
commandeer vt pūblicāre
commander n dux m, praefectus m
commander in chief n imperātor m
commandment n mandātum nt
commemorate vt celebrāre, memoriae
trādere
commemoration n celebrātiō f
commence vt incipere, exōrdīrī, initium facere
(gen)
commencement n initium nt, exōrdium nt,
prīncipium nt
commend vt laudāre; (recommend)
commendāre; (entrust) mandāre; **~ oneself**
sē probāre
commendable adj laudābilis, probābilis
commendation n laus f, commendātiō f
commendatory adj commendātīcius
commensurable adj pār
commensurate adj congruēns, conveniēns
comment vi dīcere, scrībere; **~ on** interpretārī;
(with notes) adnotāre ▶ n dictum nt, sententia f

commentary n commentāriī mpl
commentator n interpres m
commerce n mercātūra f, commercium nt;
engage in ~ mercātūrās facere, negōtiārī
commercial dealings npl commercium nt
commercial traveller n īnstitor m
commination n minae fpl
comminatory adj mināx
commingle vt intermiscēre
commiserate vt miserērī (gen)
commiseration n misericordia f; (RHET)
commiserātiō f
commissariat n rēs frūmentāria f,
commeātus m; (staff) frūmentāriī mpl
commissary n lēgātus m; reī frūmentāriae
praefectus m
commission n (charge) mandātum nt; (persons)
triumvirī mpl, decemvirī mpl; (abroad) lēgātiō f;
get a ~ (MIL) tribūnum fierī; **standing ~** (LAW)
quaestiō perpetua f ▶ vt mandāre, adlēgāre
commissioner n lēgātus m; **three
commissioners** triumvirī mpl; **ten
commissioners** decemvirī mpl
commit vt (charge) committere, mandāre;
(crime) admittere; (to prison) conicere; (to an
undertaking) obligāre, obstringere; **~ to
memory** memoriae trādere; **~ to writing**
litterīs mandāre; **~ an error** errāre; **~ a theft**
fūrtum facere; see also **suicide**
commitment n mūnus nt, officium nt
committee n dēlēctī mpl
commodious adj capāx
commodity n merx f, rēs f
commodore n praefectus classis m
common adj (for all) commūnis; (ordinary)
vulgāris, cottīdiānus; (repeated) frequēns,
crēber; (inferior) nēquam ▶ n compāscuus ager m,
prātum nt; **~ man** homō plēbēius m; **~ soldier**
gregārius mīles m
commonalty n plēbs f
commoner n homō plēbēius m
common law n mōs māiōrum m
commonly adv ferē, vulgō
common people n plēbs f, vulgus nt
commonplace n trītum prōverbium nt; (RHET)
locus commūnis m ▶ adj vulgāris, trītus
commons npl plēbs f; (food) diāria ntpl
common sense n prūdentia f
commonwealth n cīvitās f, rēs pūblica f
commotion n perturbātiō f, tumultus m;
cause a ~ tumultuārī
communal adj commūnis
commune n pāgus m ▶ vi colloquī, sermōnēs
cōnferre
communicate vt commūnicāre; (information)
nūntiāre, patefacere ▶ vi: **~ with** commūnicāre
(dat), commercium habēre (gen), agere cum (abl)
communication n (dealings) commercium nt;
(information) litterae fpl, nūntius m; (passage)
commeātus m; **cut off the communications of**
interclūdere
communicative adj loquāx

communion n societās f
communiqué n litterae fpl, praedicātiō f
communism n bonōrum aequātiō f
community n cīvitās f, commūne nt; (participation) commūniō f
commutation n mūtātiō f
commute vt mūtāre, commūtāre
compact n foedus nt, conventum nt ▸ adj dēnsus ▸ vt dēnsāre
companion n socius m, comes m/f; (intimate) sodālis m; (at school) condiscipulus m; (in army) commīlitō m, contubernālis m
companionable adj facilis, commodus
companionship n sodālitās f, cōnsuētūdō f; (MIL) contubernium nt
company n societās f, cōnsuētūdō f; (gathering) coetus m, conventus m; (guests) cēnantēs mpl; (commercial) societās f; (magistrates) collēgium nt; (MIL) manipulus m; (THEAT) grex m, caterva f; **~ of ten** decuria f
comparable adj comparābilis, similis
comparative adj māgnus, sī cum aliīs cōnfertur
comparatively adv ut in tālī tempore, ut in eā regiōne, ut est captus hominum; **~ few** perpaucī, nullus ferē
compare vt comparāre, cōnferre; **compared with** ad (acc)
comparison n comparātiō f, collātiō f; (RHET) similitūdō f; **in ~ with** prō (abl)
compartment n cella f, pars f
compass n ambitus m, spatium nt, modus m; **pair of compasses** circinus m ▸ vt circumdare, cingere; (attain) cōnsequī
compassion n misericordia f
compassionate adj misericors, clēmēns
compassionately adv clēmenter
compatibility n convenientia f
compatible adj congruēns, conveniēns; **be ~** congruere
compatibly adv congruenter, convenienter
compatriot n cīvis m, populāris m
compeer n pār m; aequālis m
compel vt cōgere
compendious adj brevis
compendiously adv summātim
compendium n epitomē f
compensate vt compēnsāre, satisfacere (dat)
compensation n compēnsātiō f; pretium nt, poena f
compete vi certāre, contendere
competence n facultās f; (LAW) iūs nt; (money) quod sufficit
competent adj perītus, satis doctus, capāx; (witness) locuplēs; **it is ~** licet
competition n certāmen nt, contentiō f
competitor n competītor m, aemulus m
compilation n collectānea ntpl, liber m
compile vt compōnere
compiler n scrīptor m
complacency n amor suī m
complacent adj suī contentus

complain vi querī, conquerī; **~ of** (person) nōmen dēferre (gen)
complainant n accūsātor m, petītor m
complaint n questus m, querimōnia f; (LAW) crīmen nt; (MED) morbus m, valētūdō f
complaisance n cōmitās f, obsequium nt, indulgentia f
complaisant adj cōmis, officiōsus, facilis
complement n complēmentum nt; numerus suus m; **make up the ~** complēre
complete vt (amount, time) complēre, explēre; (work) cōnficere, perficere, absolvere, peragere ▸ adj perfectus, absolūtus, integer; (victory) iūstus; (amount) explētus
completely adv funditus, omnīnō, absolūtē, plānē; penitus
completeness n integritās f; (perfection) perfectiō f
completion n (process) absolūtiō f, cōnfectiō f; (end) finis m; **bring to ~** absolvere
complex adj implicātus, multiplex
complexion n color m
complexity n implicātiō f
compliance n accommodātiō f, obsequium nt, obtemperātiō f
compliant adj obsequēns, facilis
complicate vt implicāre, impedīre
complicated adj implicātus, involūtus, impedītus
complication n implicātiō f
complicity n cōnscientia f
compliment n blandīmentum nt, honōs m ▸ vt blandīrī, laudāre; **~ on** grātulārī (dat) dē (abl)
complimentary adj honōrificus, blandus
compliments npl (as greeting) salūs f
comply vi obsequī (dat), obtemperāre (dat); mōrem gerere (dat), mōrigerārī (dat)
component n elementum nt, pars f
comport vt gerere
compose vt (art) compōnere, condere, pangere; (whole) efficere, cōnflāre; (quarrel) compōnere, dīrimere; (disturbance) sēdāre; **be composed of** cōnsistere ex (abl), cōnstāre ex (abl)
composed adj tranquillus, placidus
composer n auctor m, scrīptor m
composite adj multiplex
composition n (process) compositiō f, scrīptūra f; (product) opus nt, poēma nt, carmen nt; (quality) structūra f
composure n sēcūritās f, aequus animus m; (face) tranquillitās f
compound vt miscēre; (words) duplicāre, iungere ▸ vi (agree) pacīscī ▸ adj compositus ▸ n (word) iūnctum verbum nt; (area) saeptum nt
compound interest n anatocismus m
comprehend vt intellegere, comprehendere; (include) continēre, complectī
comprehensible adj perspicuus
comprehension n intellegentia f, comprehēnsiō f
comprehensive adj capāx; **be ~** lātē patēre, multa complectī

compress vt comprimere, coartāre ▶ n fōmentum nt
compression n compressus m
comprise vt continēre, complectī, comprehendere
compromise n (by one side) accommodātiō f; (by both sides) comprōmissum nt ▶ vi comprōmittere ▶ vt implicāre, in suspiciōnem vocāre; **be compromised** in suspiciōnem venīre
comptroller n moderātor m
compulsion n necessitās f, vīs f; **under ~** coāctus
compulsory adj necesse, lēge imperātus; **use ~ measures** vim adhibēre
compunction n paenitentia f
computation n ratiō f
compute vt computāre, ratiōnem dūcere
comrade n socius m, contubernālis m
comradeship n contubernium nt
concatenation n seriēs f
concave adj concavus
conceal vt cēlāre, abdere, abscondere; (fact) dissimulāre
concealment n occultātiō f; (place) latebrae fpl; (of facts) dissimulātiō f; **in ~** abditus, occultus; **be in ~** latēre, latitāre; **go into ~** dēlitēscere
concede vt concēdere
conceit n (idea) nōtiō f; (wit) facētiae fpl; (pride) superbia f, adrogantia f, vānitās f
conceited adj glōriōsus, adrogāns
conceitedness n adrogantia f, vānitās f
conceive vt concipere, comprehendere, intellegere
concentrate vt (in one place) cōgere, congregāre; (attention) intendere, dēfīgere
concentrated adj dēnsus
concentration n animī intentiō f
concept n nōtiō f
conception n conceptus m; (mind) intellegentia f, īnfōrmātiō f; (idea) nōtiō f, cōgitātiō f, cōnsilium nt
concern vt (refer) attinēre ad (acc), interesse (gen); (worry) sollicitāre; **it concerns me** meā rēfert, meā interest; **as far as I am concerned** per mē ▶ n rēs f, negōtium nt; (importance) mōmentum nt; (worry) sollicitūdō f, cūra f; (regret) dolor m
concerned adj sollicitus, anxius; **be ~** dolēre; **be ~ about** molestē ferre
concerning prep dē (abl)
concernment n sollicitūdō f
concert n (music) concentus m; (agreement) cōnsēnsus m; **in ~** ex compositō, ūnō animō ▶ vt compōnere; (plan) inīre
concession n concessiō f; **by the ~ of** concessū (gen); **make a ~** concēdere, tribuere
conciliate vt conciliāre
conciliation n conciliātiō f
conciliator n arbiter m
conciliatory adj pācificus
concise adj brevis; (style) dēnsus

concisely adv breviter
conciseness n brevitās f
conclave n sēcrētus cōnsessus m
conclude vt (end) termināre, fīnīre, cōnficere; (settle) facere, compōnere, pangere; (infer) īnferre, colligere
conclusion n (end) fīnis m; (of action) exitus m; (of speech) perōrātiō f; (inference) coniectūra f; (decision) placitum nt, sententia f; **in ~** dēnique; **try conclusions with** contendere cum
conclusive adj certus, manifestus, gravis
conclusively adv sine dubiō
concoct vt coquere; (fig) cōnflāre
concoction n (fig) māchinātiō f
concomitant adj adiūnctus
concord n concordia f; (music) harmonia f
concordant adj concors
concordat n pactum nt, foedus nt
concourse n frequentia f, celebrātiō f; (moving) concursus m
concrete adj concrētus; **in the ~** rē
concretion n concrētiō f
concubine n concubīna f
concupiscence n libīdō f
concur vi (time) concurrere; (opinion) cōnsentīre, adsentīre
concurrence n (time) concursus m; (opinion) cōnsēnsus m
concurrent adj (time) aequālis; (opinion) cōnsentāneus; **be ~** concurrere, cōnsentīre
concurrently adv simul, ūnā
concussion n ictus m
condemn vt damnāre, condemnāre; (disapprove) improbāre; **~ to death** capitis damnāre; **~ for treason** dē māiestāte damnāre
condemnation n damnātiō f; condemnātiō f
condemnatory adj damnātōrius
condense vt dēnsāre; (words) premere
condescend vi dēscendere, sē submittere
condescending adj cōmis
condescension n cōmitās f
condiment n condīmentum nt
condition n (of body) habitus m; (external) status m, condiciō f, rēs f; (in society) locus m, fortūna f; (of agreement) condiciō f, lēx f; **conditions of sale** mancipī lēx f; **on ~ that** eā condiciōne ut (subj); **in ~** (animals) nitidus ▶ vt fōrmāre, regere
conditional adj: **the assistance is ~ on** eā condiciōne succurritur ut (subj)
conditionally adv sub condiciōne
conditioned adj (character) mōrātus
condole vi: **~ with** cōnsōlārī
condolence n cōnsōlātiō f
condonation n venia f
condone vt condōnāre, ignōscere (dat)
conduce vi condūcere (ad), prōficere (ad)
conducive adj ūtilis, accommodātus
conduct vt dūcere; (escort) dēdūcere; (to a place) addūcere, perdūcere; (business) gerere, administrāre; (self) gerere ▶ n mōrēs mpl; (past) vīta f, facta ntpl; (business) administrātiō f; **safe ~** praesidium nt

conductor n dux m, ductor m
conduit n canālis m, aquae ductus m
cone n cōnus m
coney n cunīculus m
confabulate vi colloquī
confection n cuppēdō f
confectioner n cuppēdinārius m
confectionery n dulcia ntpl
confederacy n foederātae cīvitātēs fpl, societās f
confederate adj foederātus ▶ n socius m
▶ vi coniūrāre, foedus facere
confederation n societās f
confer vt cōnferre, tribuere ▶ vi colloquī, sermōnem cōnferre; **~ about** agere dē (abl)
conference n colloquium nt, congressus m
conferment n dōnātiō f
confess vt fatērī, cōnfitērī
confessedly adv manifestō
confession n cōnfessiō f
confidant n cōnscius m
confide vi fīdere (dat), cōnfīdere (dat) ▶ vt crēdere, committere
confidence n fidēs f, fīdūcia f; **have ~ in** fīdere (dat), cōnfīdere (dat); **inspire ~ in** fidem facere (dat); **tell in ~** tūtīs auribus dēpōnere
confident adj fīdēns; **~ in** frētus (abl); **be ~ that** certō scīre, prō certō habēre
confidential adj arcānus, intimus
confidentially adv inter nōs
confidently adv fīdenter
confiding adj crēdulus
configuration n figūra f, fōrma f
confine vt (prison) inclūdere, in vincula conicere; (limit) termināre, circumscrībere; (restrain) coercēre, cohibēre; (to bed) dētinēre; **be confined** (women) parturīre
confinement n custōdia f, vincula ntpl, inclūsiō f; (women) puerperium nt
confines n fīnēs mpl
confirm vt (strength) corrōborāre, firmāre; (decision) sancīre, ratum facere; (fact) adfirmāre, comprobāre
confirmation n cōnfirmātiō f, adfirmātiō f
confirmed adj ratus
confiscate vt pūblicāre
confiscation n pūblicātiō f
conflagration n incendium nt, dēflāgrātiō f
conflict n (physical) concursus m; (hostile) certāmen nt, proelium nt; (verbal) contentiō f, contrōversia f; (contradiction) repugnantia f, discrepantia f ▶ vi inter sē repugnāre
conflicting adj contrārius
confluence n cōnfluēns m
confluent adj cōnfluēns
conform vt accommodāre ▶ vi sē cōnfōrmāre (ad), obsequī (dat), mōrem gerere (dat)
conformable adj accommodātus, conveniēns
conformably adv convenienter
conformation n structūra f, cōnfōrmātiō f
conformity n convenientia f, cōnsēnsus m

confound vt (mix) cōnfundere, permiscēre; (amaze) obstupefacere; (thwart) frustrārī; (suppress) opprimere, obruere; **~ you!** dī tē perduint
confounded adj miser, sacer, nefandus
confoundedly adv mīrum quantum nefāriē
confraternity n frāternitās f
confront vt sē oppōnere (dat), obviam īre (dat), sē cōram offerre
confuse vt permiscēre, perturbāre
confused adj perturbātus
confusedly adv perturbātē, prōmiscuē
confusion n perturbātiō f; (shame) rubor m
confutation n refūtātiō f
confute vt refūtāre, redarguere, convincere
congé n commeātus m
congeal vt congelāre, dūrāre ▶ vi concrēscere
congealed adj concrētus
congenial adj concors, congruēns, iūcundus
congeniality n concordia f, mōrum similitūdō f
congenital adj nātīvus
conger n conger m
congested adj refertus, dēnsus; (with people) frequentissimus
congestion n congeriēs f; frequentia f
conglomerate vt glomerāre
conglomeration n congeriēs f, cumulus m
congratulate vt grātulārī (dat)
congratulation n grātulātiō f
congratulatory adj grātulābundus
congregate vt congregāre, cōgere ▶ vi convenīre, congregārī
congregation n conventus m, coetus m
congress n conventus m, cōnsessus m, concilium nt; senātus m
congruence n convenientia f
congruent adj conveniēns, congruēns
congruently adv convenienter, congruenter
congruous adj see **congruent**
conical adj turbinātus
coniferous adj cōnifer
conjectural adj opīnābilis
conjecturally adv coniectūrā
conjecture n coniectūra f ▶ vt conicere, augurārī
conjoin vt coniungere
conjoint adj coniūnctus
conjointly adv coniūnctē, ūnā
conjugal adj coniugālis
conjugate vt dēclīnāre
conjugation n (GRAM) dēclīnātiō f
conjunct adj coniūnctus
conjunction n coniūnctiō f, concursus m
conjure vt (entreat) obtestārī, obsecrāre; (spirits) ēlicere, ciēre ▶ vi praestigiīs ūtī
conjurer n praestigiātor m
conjuring n praestigiae fpl
connate adj innātus, nātūrā īnsitus
connect vt iungere, coniungere, cōpulāre, connectere
connected adj coniūnctus; (unbroken) continēns; (by marriage) adfīnis; **be ~ with**

contingere; **be closely ~ with** inhaerēre (dat), cohaerēre cum (abl)

connectedly adv coniūnctē, continenter

connection n coniūnctiō f, contextus m, seriēs f; (kin) necessitūdō f; (by marriage) adfīnitās f; **~ between ... and ...** ratiō (gen) ... cum ... (abl); **I have no ~ with you** nīl mihī tēcum est

connivance n venia f, dissimulātiō f

connive vi connīvēre in (abl), dissimulāre

connoisseur n intellegēns m

connotation n vīs f, significātiō f

connote vt significāre

connubial adj coniugālis

conquer vt vincere, superāre

conquerable adj superābilis, expugnābilis

conqueror n victor m

conquest n victōria f; (town) expugnātiō f; (prize) praemium nt, praeda f; **the ~ of Greece** Graecia capta

conscience n cōnscientia f; **guilty ~** mala cōnscientia; **have a clear ~** nullīus culpae sibi cōnscium esse; **have no ~** nullam rēligiōnem habēre

conscientious adj probus, rēligiōsus

conscientiously adv bonā fidē, rēligiōsē

conscientiousness n fidēs f, rēligiō f

conscious adj sibī cōnscius; (aware) gnārus; (physically) mentis compos; **be ~** sentīre

consciously adv sciēns

consciousness n animus m; (of action) cōnscientia f; **he lost ~** animus eum relīquit

conscript n tīrō m ▶ vt cōnscrībere

conscription n dēlēctus m; (of wealth) pūblicātiō f

consecrate vt dēdicāre, cōnsecrāre; (self) dēvovēre

consecrated adj sacer

consecration n dēdicātiō f, cōnsecrātiō f; (self) dēvōtiō f

consecutive adj dēinceps, continuus

consecutively adv dēinceps, ōrdine

consensus n cōnsēnsus m

consent vi adsentīre (dat), adnuere (infin); (together) cōnsentīre ▶ n (one side) adsēnsus m; (all) cōnsēnsus m; **by common ~** omnium cōnsēnsū

consequence n ēventus m, exitus m; (LOGIC) conclūsiō f; (importance) mōmentum nt, auctōritās f; **it is of ~** interest; **what will be the ~ of?** quō ēvādet?

consequent adj cōnsequēns

consequential adj cōnsentāneus; (person) adrogāns

consequently adv itaque, igitur, proptereā

conservation n cōnservātiō f

conservative adj reī pūblicae cōnservandae studiōsus; (estimate) mediōcris; **~ party** optimātēs mpl

conservator n custōs m, cōnservātor m

conserve vt cōnservāre, servāre

consider vt cōnsīderāre, contemplārī; (reflect) sēcum volūtāre, meditārī, dēlīberāre, cōgitāre;

(deem) habēre, dūcere; (respect) respicere, observāre

considerable adj aliquantus, nōnnullus; (person) illūstris

considerably adv aliquantum; (with compar) aliquantō, multō

considerate adj hūmānus, benignus

considerately adv hūmānē, benignē

consideration n cōnsīderātiō f, contemplātiō f, dēlīberātiō f; (respect) respectus m, ratiō f; (importance) mōmentum nt; (reason) ratiō f; (pay) pretium nt; **for a ~** mercēde, datā mercēde; **in ~ of** propter (acc), prō (abl); **on no ~** nēquāquam; **with ~** cōnsultō; **without ~** temerē; **take into ~** ad cōnsilium dēferre; **show ~ for** respectum habēre (gen)

considered adj (reasons) exquīsītus

considering prep prō (abl), propter (acc) ▶ conj ut, quōniam

consign vt mandāre, committere

consist vi cōnstāre; **~ in** cōnstāre ex (abl), continērī (abl), positum esse in (abl); **~ with** congruere (dat), convenīre (dat)

consistence n firmitās f

consistency n cōnstantia f

consistent adj cōnstāns; (with) cōnsentāneus, congruens; (of movement) aequābilis; **be ~** cohaerēre

consistently adv constanter

consolable adj cōnsōlābilis

consolation n cōnsōlātiō f; (thing) sōlācium nt

consolatory adj cōnsōlātōrius

console vt cōnsōlārī

consoler n cōnsōlātor m

consolidate vt (liquid) cōgere; (strength) corrōborāre; (gains) obtinēre ▶ vi concrēscere

consolidation n concrētiō f; cōnfīrmātiō f

consonance n concentus m

consonant adj cōnsonus, haud absonus ▶ n cōnsōnāns f

consort n cōnsors m/f, socius m; (married) coniunx m/f ▶ vi: **~ with** familiāriter ūtī (abl), coniūnctissimē vīvere cum (abl)

conspectus n summārium nt

conspicuous adj ēminēns, īnsignis, manifestus; **be ~** ēminēre

conspicuously adv manifestō, palam, ante oculōs

conspiracy n coniūrātiō f

conspirator n coniūrātus m

conspire vi coniūrāre; (for good) cōnspīrāre

constable n lictor m

constancy n cōnstantia f, firmitās f; **with ~** cōnstanter

constant adj cōnstāns; (faithful) fīdus, fidēlis; (continuous) adsiduus

constantly adv adsiduē, saepe, crēbrō

constellation n sīdus nt

consternation n trepidātiō f, pavor m; **throw into ~** perterrēre, cōnsternere

constituency n suffrāgātōrēs mpl

constituent *adj*: ~ **part** elementum *nt* ▶ *n* (*voter*) suffrāgātor *m*

constitute *vt* creāre, cōnstituere; esse

constitution *n* nātūra *f*, status *m*; (*body*) habitus *m*; (*POL*) cīvitātis fōrma *f*, reī pūblicae status *m*, lēgēs *fpl*

constitutional *adj* lēgitimus, iūstus

constitutionally *adv* ē rē pūblicā

constrain *vt* cōgere

constraint *n* vīs *f*; **under ~** coāctus; **without ~** suā sponte

constrict *vt* comprimere, cōnstringere

constriction *n* contractiō *f*

construct *vt* aedificāre, exstruere

construction *n* aedificātiō *f*; (*method*) structūra *f*; (*meaning*) interpretātiō *f*; **put a wrong ~ on** in malam partem interpretārī

construe *vt* interpretārī

consul *n* cōnsul *m*; ~ **elect** cōnsul dēsignātus; **ex-consul** cōnsulāris *m*

consular *adj* cōnsulāris

consulship *n* cōnsulātus *m*; **stand for the ~** cōnsulātum petere; **hold the ~** cōnsulātum gerere; **in my ~** mē cōnsule

consult *vt* cōnsulere; ~ **the interests of** cōnsulere (*dat*) ▶ *vi* dēlīberāre, cōnsiliārī

consultation *n* (*asking*) cōnsultātiō *f*; (*discussion*) dēlīberātiō *f*

consume *vt* cōnsūmere, absūmere; (*food*) edere

consumer *n* cōnsūmptor *m*

consummate *adj* summus, perfectus ▶ *vt* perficere, absolvere

consummation *n* absolūtiō *f*; fīnis *m*, ēventus *m*

consumption *n* cōnsūmptiō *f*; (*disease*) tābēs *f*, phthisis *f*

consumptive *adj* pulmōnārius

contact *n* tāctus *m*, contāgiō *f*; **come in ~ with** contingere

contagion *n* contāgiō *f*

contagious *adj* tābificus; **be ~** contāgiīs vulgārī

contain *vt* capere, continēre; (*self*) cohibēre

container *n* vās *nt*

contaminate *vt* contāmināre, īnficere

contamination *n* contāgiō *f*, lābēs *f*

contemplate *vt* contemplārī, intuērī; (*action*) in animō habēre; (*prospect*) spectāre

contemplation *n* contemplātiō *f*; (*thought*) cōgitātiō *f*

contemplative *adj* cōgitāns, meditāns; **in a ~ mood** cōgitātiōnī dēditus

contemporaneous *adj* aequālis

contemporaneously *adv* simul

contemporary *adj* aequālis

contempt *n* contemptiō *f*; **be an object of ~** contemptuī esse; **treat with ~** contemptum habēre, conculcāre

contemptible *adj* contemnendus, abiectus, vīlis

contemptuous *adj* fastīdiōsus

contemptuously *adv* contemptim, fastīdiōsē

contend *vi* certāre, contendere; (*in battle*) dīmicāre, pugnāre; (*in words*) adfirmāre, adsevērāre

contending *adj* contrārius

content *adj* contentus ▶ *n* aequus animus *m* ▶ *vt* placēre (*dat*), satisfacere (*dat*); **be contented** satis habēre

contentedly *adv* aequō animō

contention *n* certāmen *nt*; contrōversia *f*; (*opinion*) sententia *f*

contentious *adj* pugnāx, lītigiōsus

contentiously *adv* pugnāciter

contentiousness *n* contrōversiae studium *nt*

contentment *n* aequus animus *m*

contents *n* quod inest, quae insunt; (*of speech*) argūmentum *nt*

conterminous *adj* adfīnis

contest *n* certāmen *nt*, contentiō *f* ▶ *vt* (*LAW*) lēge agere dē (*abl*); (*office*) petere; (*dispute*) repugnāre (*dat*), resistere (*dat*)

contestable *adj* contrōversus

contestant *n* petītor *m*, aemulus *m*

context *n* contextus *m*

contiguity *n* vīcīnia *f*, propinquitās *f*

contiguous *adj* vīcīnus, adiacēns; **be ~ to** adiacēre (*dat*), contingere

continence *n* continentia *f*, abstinentia *f*

continent *adj* continēns, abstinēns ▶ *n* continēns *f*

continently *adv* continenter, abstinenter

contingency *n* cāsus *m*, rēs *f*

contingent *adj* fortuītus ▶ *n* (*MIL*) numerus *m*

continual *adj* adsiduus, perpetuus

continually *adv* adsiduē, semper

continuance *n* perpetuitās *f*, adsiduitās *f*

continuation *n* continuātiō *f*; (*of a command*) prōrogātiō *f*; (*of a story*) reliqua pars *f*

continue *vt* continuāre; (*time*) prōdūcere; (*command*) prōrogāre ▶ *vi* (*action*) pergere; (*time*) manēre; (*endurance*) perstāre, dūrāre; ~ **to** *imperf indic*

continuity *n* continuātiō *f*; (*of speech*) perpetuitās *f*

continuous *adj* continuus, continēns, perpetuus

continuously *adv* perpetuō, continenter

contort *vt* contorquēre, dētorquēre

contortion *n* distortiō *f*

contour *n* fōrma *f*

contraband *adj* interdictus, vetitus

contract *n* pactum *nt*, mandātum *nt*, conventum *nt*; (*POL*) foedus *nt*; **trial for a breach of ~** mandātī iūdicium *nt* ▶ *vt* (*narrow*) contrahere, addūcere; (*short*) dēminuere; (*illness*) contrahere; (*agreement*) pacīscī; (*for work*) locāre; (*to do work*) condūcere ▶ *vi* pacīscī

contraction *n* contractiō *f*; (*word*) compendium *nt*

contractor *n* redemptor *m*, conductor *m*

contradict *vt* (*person*) contrādīcere (*dat*), refrāgārī (*dat*); (*statement*) īnfitiās īre (*dat*); (*self*) repugnāre (*dat*)

contradiction n repugnantia f, înfitiae fpl
contradictory adj repugnāns, contrārius;
be ~ inter sē repugnāre
contradistinction n oppositiō f
contraption n māchina f
contrariety n repugnantia f
contrariwise adv ē contrāriō
contrary adj contrārius, adversus; (person)
difficilis, mōrōsus; ~ **to** contrā (acc), praeter
(acc); ~ **to expectations** praeter opiniōnem
▶ n contrārium nt; **on the** ~ ē contrāriō, contrā;
(retort) immo
contrast n discrepantia f ▶ vt comparāre,
oppōnere ▶ vi discrepāre
contravene vt (LAW) violāre; (statement)
contrādīcere (dat)
contravention n violātiō f
contribute vt cōnferre, adferre, contribuere
▶ vi: ~ **towards** cōnferre ad (acc), adiuvāre; ~ **to**
the cost impēnsās cōnferre
contribution n conlātiō f; (money) stipem (no
nom) f
contributor n quī cōnfert
contributory adj adiūnctus
contrite adj paenitēns
contrition n paenitentia f
contrivance n māchinātiō f, excōgitātiō f;
(thing) māchina f; (idea) cōnsilium nt; (deceit)
dolus m
contrive vt māchinārī, excōgitāre, struere; (to
do) efficere ut
contriver n māchinātor m, artifex m, auctor m
control n (restraint) frēnum nt; (power)
moderātiō f, potestās f, imperium nt; **have** ~ **of**
praeesse (dat); **out of** ~ impotēns ▶ vt moderārī
(dat), imperāre (dat)
controller n moderātor m
controversial adj concertātōrius
controversy n contrōversia f, disceptātiō f
controvert vt redarguere, impugnāre, in
dubium vocāre
contumacious adj contumāx, pervicāx
contumaciously adv contumāciter,
pervicāciter
contumacy n contumācia f, pervicācia f
contusion n sūgillātiō f
conundrum n aenigma nt
convalesce vi convalēscere
convalescence n melior valētūdō f
convalescent adj convalēscēns
convene vt convocāre
convenience n opportūnitās f, commoditās f;
(thing) commodum nt; **at your** ~ commodō tuō
convenient adj idōneus, commodus,
opportūnus; **be** ~ convenīre; **very** ~
percommodus
conveniently adv opportūnē, commodē
convention n (meeting) conventus m;
(agreement) conventum nt; (custom) mōs m,
iūsta ntpl
conventional adj iūstus, solitus
conventionality n mōs m, cōnsuētūdō f

converge vi in medium vergere, in eundem
locum tendere
conversant adj perītus, doctus, exercitātus;
be ~ **with** versārī in (abl)
conversation n sermō m, colloquium nt
converse n sermō m, colloquium nt; (opposite)
contrārium nt ▶ vi colloquī, sermōnem cōnferre
▶ adj contrārius
conversely adv ē contrāriō, contrā
conversion n mūtātiō f; (moral) mōrum
ēmendātiō f
convert vt mūtāre, convertere; (to an opinion)
dēdūcere ▶ n discipulus m
convertible adj commūtābilis
convex adj convexus
convexity n convexum nt
convey vt vehere, portāre, convehere;
(property) abaliēnāre; (knowledge)
commūnicāre; (meaning) significāre; ~ **across**
trānsmittere, trādūcere, trānsvehere; ~ **away**
auferre, āvehere; ~ **down** dēvehere, dēportāre;
~ **into** importāre, invehere; ~ **to** advehere,
adferre; ~ **up** subvehere
conveyance n vehiculum nt; (property)
abaliēnātiō f
convict vt (prove guilty) convincere; (sentence)
damnāre ▶ n reus m
conviction n (LAW) damnātiō f; (argument)
persuāsiō f; (belief) fidēs f; **carry** ~ fidem facere;
have a ~ persuāsum habēre
convince vt persuādēre (dat); **I am firmly**
convinced mihi persuāsum habeō
convincing adj (argument) gravis; (evidence)
manifestus
convincingly adv manifestō
convivial adj convīvālis, festīvus
conviviality n festīvitās f
convocation n conventus m
convoke vt convocāre
convolution n spīra f
convoy n praesidium nt ▶ vt prōsequī
convulse vt agitāre; **be convulsed with**
laughter sē in cachinnōs effundere
convulsion n (MED) convulsiō f; (POL)
tumultus m
convulsive adj spasticus
coo vi gemere
cook vt coquere ▶ n coquus m
cookery n ars coquīnāria f
cool adj frīgidus; (conduct) impudens; (mind)
impavidus, lentus ▶ n frīgus nt ▶ vt refrīgerāre;
(passion) restinguere, sēdāre ▶ vi refrīgēscere,
refrīgerārī, dēfervēscere
coolly adv aequō animō; impudenter
coolness n frīgus nt; (mind) aequus animus m;
impudentia f
coop n hara f; (barrel) cūpa f ▶ vt inclūdere
co-operate vi operam cōnferre; ~ **with**
adiuvāre, socius esse (gen)
co-operation n cōnsociātiō f; auxilium nt,
opera f
co-operative adj (person) officiōsus

co-operator n socius m
co-opt vt cooptāre
coot n fulica f
copartner n socius m
copartnership n societās f
cope vi: ~ with contendere cum (abl); **able to ~ with** pār (dat); **unable to ~ with** impār (dat)
copier n librārius m
coping n fastīgium nt
copious adj cōpiōsus, largus, plēnus, abundāns
copiously adv cōpiōsē, abundanter
copiousness n cōpia f, ūbertās f
copper n aes nt ▶ adj aēneus
coppersmith n faber aerārius m
coppice, copse n dūmētum nt, virgultum nt
copy n exemplar nt ▶ vt imitārī; (writing) exscrībere, trānscrībere
copyist n librārius m
coracle n linter f
coral n cūrālium nt
cord n fūniculus m
cordage n fūnēs mpl
cordial adj cōmis, festīvus, amīcus; (greetings) multus
cordiality n cōmitās f, studium nt
cordially adv cōmiter, libenter, ex animō
cordon n corōna f
core n (fig) nucleus m
cork n sūber nt; (bark) cortex m
corn n frūmentum nt ▶ adj frūmentārius; (on the foot) clāvus m; **price of ~** annōna f
corndealer n frūmentārius m
cornel n (tree) cornus f
corner n angulus m
cornet n cornū nt
cornfield n seges f
cornice n corōna f
coronet n diadēma nt
corporal adj corporeus
corporal punishment n verbera ntpl
corporation n collēgium nt; (civic) magistrātūs mpl
corporeal adj corporeus
corps n manus f
corpse n cadāver nt
corpulence n obēsum corpus nt
corpulent adj obēsus, pinguis
corpuscle n corpusculum nt
corral n praesēpe nt
correct vt corrigere, ēmendāre; (person) castīgāre ▶ adj vērus; (language) integer; (style) ēmendātus
correction n ēmendātiō f; (moral) corrēctiō f; (punishment) castīgātiō f
correctly adv bene, vērē
correctness n (fact) vēritās f; (language) integritās f; (moral) probitās f
corrector n ēmendātor m, corrēctor m
correspond vi (agree) respondēre (dat), congruere (dat); (by letter) inter sē scrībere
correspondence n similitūdō f; epistulae fpl
correspondent n epistulārum scrīptor m

corresponding adj pār
correspondingly adv pariter
corridor n porticus f
corrigible adj ēmendābilis
corroborate vt cōnfīrmāre
corroboration n cōnfīrmātiō f
corrode vt ērōdere, edere
corrosive adj edāx
corrugate vt rūgāre
corrugated adj rūgōsus
corrupt vt corrumpere, dēprāvāre; (text) vitiāre ▶ adj corruptus, vitiātus; (person) prāvus, vēnālis; (text) vitiātus
corrupter n corruptor m
corruptible adj (matter) dissolūbilis; (person) vēnālis
corruption n (of matter) corruptiō f; (moral) corruptēla f, dēprāvātiō f; (bribery) ambitus m
corsair n pīrāta m
cortège n pompa f
coruscate vi fulgēre
coruscation n fulgor m
Corybant n Corybas m
Corybantic adj Corybantius
cosmetic n medicāmen nt
cosmic adj mundānus
cosmopolitan adj mundānus
cosmos n mundus m
cost vt emī, stāre (dat); **it ~ me dear** māgnō mihi stetit, male ēmī; **it ~ me a talent** talentō mihi stetit, talentō ēmī; **it ~ me my freedom** lībertātem perdidī ▶ n pretium nt, impēnsa f; **~ of living** annōna f; **to your ~** incommodō tuō, dētrīmentō tuō; **at the ~ of one's reputation** violātā fāmā, nōn salvā existimātiōne; **I sell at ~ price** quantī ēmī vēndō
costliness n sūmptus m; cāritās f
costly adj cārus; (furnishings) lautus, sūmptuōsus
costume n habitus m
cosy adj commodus
cot n lectulus m
cote n columbārium nt
cottage n casa f, tugurium nt
cottager n rūsticus m
cotton n (tree) gossympinus f; (cloth) xylinum nt
couch n lectus m ▶ vi recumbere ▶ vt (lance) intendere; (words) exprimere, reddere
cough n tussis f ▶ vi tussīre
council n concilium nt; (small) cōnsilium nt
councillor n (town) decuriō m
counsel n (debate) cōnsultātiō f; (advice) cōnsilium nt; (LAW) advocātus m, patrōnus m; **take ~** cōnsiliārī, dēlīberāre; **take ~ of** cōnsulere ▶ vt suādēre (dat), monēre
counsellor n cōnsiliārius m
count vt numerāre, computāre; **~ as** dūcere, habēre; **~ amongst** pōnere in (abl); **~ up** ēnumerāre; **~ upon** cōnfīdere (dat); **be counted among** in numerō esse (gen) ▶ vi aestimārī, habērī ▶ n ratiō f; (in indictment) caput nt; (title) comes m

countenance n faciēs f, vultus m, ōs nt; (fig) favor m; **put out of ~** conturbāre ▸ vt favēre (dat), indulgēre (dat)

counter n (for counting) calculus m; (for play) tessera f; (shop) mēnsa f ▸ adj contrārius ▸ adv contrā, obviam ▸ vt obsistere (dat), respondēre (dat)

counteract vt obsistere (dat), adversārī (dat); (malady) medērī (dat)

counterattack vt in vicem oppugnāre, adgredī

counterattraction n altera illecebra f

counterbalance vt compēnsāre, exaequāre

counterclockwise adv sinistrōrsus

counterfeit adj falsus, fūcātus, adsimulātus, fictus ▸ vt fingere, simulāre, imitārī

countermand vt renūntiāre

counterpane n lōdīx f, strāgulum nt

counterpart n pār m/f/nt

counterpoise n aequum pondus nt ▸ vt compēnsāre, exaequāre

countersign n (MIL) tessera f

counting table n abacus m

countless adj innumerābilis

countrified adj agrestis, rūsticus

country n (region) regiō f, terra f; (territory) fīnēs mpl; (native) patria f; (not town) rūs nt; (open) agrī mpl; **of our ~** nostrās; **live in the ~** rūsticārī; **living in the ~** rūsticātiō f

country house n vīlla f

countryman n agricola m; **fellow ~** populāris m, cīvis m

countryside n agrī mpl, rus nt

couple n pār nt; **a ~ of** duo ▸ vt cōpulāre, coniungere

couplet n distichon nt

courage n fortitūdō f, animus m; (MIL) virtūs f; **have the ~ to** audēre; **lose ~** animōs dēmittere; **take ~** bonō animō esse

courageous adj fortis, ācer; audāx

courageously adv fortiter, ācriter

courier n tabellārius m

course n (movement) cursus m; (route) iter nt; (sequence) seriēs f; (career) dēcursus f; (for races) stadium nt, circus m; (of dinner) ferculum nt; (of stones) ōrdō m; (of water) lāpsus m; **of ~** certē, sānē, scīlicet; **as a matter of ~** continuō; **in due ~** mox; **in the ~ of** inter (acc), in (abl); **keep on one's ~** cursum tenēre; **be driven off one's ~** dēicī; **second ~** secunda mēnsa

court n (space) ārea f; (of house) ātrium nt; (of king) aula f; (suite) cohors f, comitēs mpl; (LAW) iūdicium nt, iūdicēs mpl; **pay ~ to** ambīre, īnservīre (dat); **hold a ~** forum agere; **bring into ~** in iūs vocāre ▸ vt colere, ambīre; (danger) sē offerre (dat); (woman) petere

courteous adj cōmis, urbānus, hūmānus

courteously adv cōmiter, urbānē

courtesan n meretrīx f

courtesy n (quality) cōmitās f, hūmānitās f; (act) officium nt

courtier n aulicus m; **courtiers** pl aula f

courtly adj officiōsus

cousin n cōnsobrīnus m, cōnsobrīna f

cove n sinus m

covenant n foedus nt, pactum nt ▸ vi pacīscī

cover vt tegere, operīre; (hide) vēlāre; (march) claudere; **~ over** obdūcere; **~ up** vi obtegere ▸ n integumentum nt, operculum nt; (shelter) latebrae fpl, suffugium nt; (pretence) speciēs f; **under ~ of** sub (abl), sub speciē (gen); **take ~** dēlitēscere

covering n integumentum nt, involucrum nt, operculum nt; (of couch) strāgulum nt

coverlet n lōdīx f

covert adj occultus; (language) oblīquus ▸ n latebra f, perfugium nt; (thicket) dūmētum nt

covertly adv occultē, sēcrētō

covet vt concupīscere, expetere

covetous adj avidus, cupidus

covetously adv avidē, cupidē

covetousness n avidītās f, cupidītās f

covey n grex f

cow n vacca f ▸ vt terrēre

coward n ignāvus m

cowardice n ignāvia f

cowardly adj ignāvus

cower vi subsīdere

cowherd n bubulcus m

cowl n cucullus m

coxswain n rēctor m

coy adj pudens, verēcundus

coyly adv pudenter, modestē

coyness n pudor m, verēcundia f

cozen vt fallere, dēcipere

crab n cancer m

crabbed adj mōrōsus, difficilis

crack n (chink) rīma f; (sound) crepitus m ▸ vt findere, frangere; (whip) crepitāre (abl) ▸ vi (open) fatīscere; (sound) crepāre, crepitāre

crackle vi crepitāre

crackling n crepitus m

cradle n cūnae fpl; (fig) incūnābula ntpl

craft n ars f, (deceit) dolus m; (boat) nāvigium nt

craftily adv callidē, sollerter; dolōsē

craftsman n artifex m, faber m

craftsmanship n ars f, artificium nt

crafty adj callidus, sollers; dolōsus

crag n rūpēs f, scopulus m

cram vt farcīre, refercīre; (with food) sagīnāre

cramp n convulsiō f; (tool) cōnfibula f ▸ vt coercēre, coartāre

crane n (bird) grus f; (machine) māchina f, trochlea f

crank n uncus m; (person) ineptus m

crannied adj rīmōsus

cranny n rīma f

crash n (fall) ruīna f; (noise) fragor m ▸ vi ruere; strepere

crass adj crassus; **~ stupidity** mera stultitia

crate n crātēs fpl

crater n crātēr m

cravat n fōcāle nt

crave vt (desire) concupīscere, adpetere, exoptāre; (request) ōrāre, obsecrāre
craven adj ignāvus
craving n cupīdō f, dēsīderium nt, adpetītiō f
crawl vi (animal) serpere; (person) rēpere
crayfish n commarus m
craze n libīdō f ▶ vt mentem aliēnāre
craziness n dēmentia f
crazy adj dēmēns, fatuus
creak vi crepāre
creaking n crepitus m
cream n spūma lactis f; (fig) flōs m
crease n rūga f ▶ vt rūgāre
create vt creāre, facere, gignere
creation n (process) fabricātiō f; (result) opus nt; (human) hominēs mpl
creative adj (nature) creātrīx; (mind) inventor, inventrīx
creator n creātor m, auctor m, opifex m
creature n animal nt; (person) homō m/f
credence n fidēs f
credentials n litterae commendātīciae fpl; (fig) auctōritās f
credibility n fidēs f; (source) auctōritās f
credible adj crēdibilis; (witness) locuplēs
credit n (belief) fidēs f; (repute) existimātiō f; (character) auctōritās f, grātia f; (COMM) fidēs f; **be a ~ to** decus esse (gen); **it is to your ~** tibī laudī est; **give ~ for** laudem tribuere (gen); **have ~** fidē stāre ▶ vt crēdere (dat); (with money) acceptum referre (dat)
creditable adj honestus, laudābilis
creditably adv honestē, cum laude
creditor n crēditor m
credulity n crēdulitās f
credulous adj crēdulus
creed n dogma nt
creek n sinus m
creel n vīdulus m
creep vi (animal) serpere; (person) rēpere; (flesh) horrēre
cremate vt cremāre
crescent n lūna f
crescent-shaped adj lūnātus
cress n nasturtium nt
crest n crista f
crested adj cristātus
crestfallen adj dēmissus
crevasse n hiātus m
crevice n rīma f
crew n nautae mpl, rēmigēs mpl, grex f, turba f
crib n (cot) lectulus m; (manger) praesēpe nt
cricket n gryllus m
crier n praecō m
crime n scelus nt, facinus nt, flāgitium nt
criminal adj scelestus, facinorōsus, flāgitiōsus ▶ n reus m
criminality n scelus nt
criminally adv scelestē, flāgitiōsē
crimson n coccum nt ▶ adj coccineus
cringe vi adūlārī, adsentārī
crinkle n rūga f

cripple vt dēbilitāre, mūtilāre; (fig) frangere
crisis n discrīmen nt
crisp adj fragilis; (manner) alacer; (hair) crispus
crisscross adj in quīncūncem dispositus
criterion n index m, indicium nt; **take as a ~** referre ad (acc)
critic n iūdex m; (literary) criticus, grammaticus m; (adverse) castīgātor m
critical adj (mind) accūrātus, ēlegāns; (blame) cēnsōrius, sevērus; (danger) perīculōsus, dubius; **~ moment** discrīmen nt
critically adv accūrātē, ēleganter; sevērē; cum perīculō
criticism n iūdicium nt; (adverse) reprehēnsiō f
criticize vt iūdicāre; reprehendere, castīgāre
croak vi (raven) crōcīre; (frog) coaxāre
croaking n cantus m ▶ adj raucus
crock n olla f
crockery n fictilia ntpl
crocodile n crocodīlus m; **weep ~ tears** lacrimās cōnfingere
crocus n crocus m
croft n agellus m
crone n anus f
crony n sodālis m
crook n pedum nt ▶ vt incurvāre
crooked adj incurvus, aduncus; (deformed) prāvus; (winding) flexuōsus; (morally) perversus
crookedly adv perversē, prāvē
crookedness n prāvitās f
croon vt, vi cantāre
crop n (grain) segers f, messis f; (tree) fructus m; (bird) ingluviēs f ▶ vt (reap) metere; (graze) carpere, tondēre; **~ up** vi intervenīre
cross n (mark) decussis m; (torture) crux f ▶ adj trānsversus, oblīquus; (person) acerbus, īrātus ▶ vt trānsīre; (water) trāicere; (mountain) trānscendere; superāre; (enemy) obstāre (dat), frustrārī; **~ out** vt (writing) expungere ▶ vi trānsīre; **~ over** (on foot) trānsgredī; (by sea) trānsmittere
crossbar n iugum nt
crossbow n scorpiō m
cross-examination n interrogātiō f
cross-examine vt interrogāre, percontārī
cross-grained adj (fig) mōrōsus
crossing n trānsitus m; (on water) trāiectus m
cross purpose n: **be at cross purposes** dīversa spectāre
cross-question vt interrogāre
crossroads n quadrivium nt
crosswise adv ex trānsversō; **divide ~** decussāre
crotchety adj mōrōsus, difficilis
crouch vi subsīdere, sē submittere
crow n cornīx f; **as the ~ flies** rēctā regiōne ▶ vi cantāre; (fig) exsultāre, gestīre
crowbar n vectis m
crowd n turba f, concursus m, frequentia f; (small) grex m; multitūdō f; **in crowds** gregātim ▶ vi frequentāre, celebrāre ▶ vt (place) complēre; (person) stīpāre

crowded adj frequēns
crown n corōna f; (royal) diadēma nt; (of head) vertex m; (fig) apex m, flōs m; **the ~ of** summus ▶ vt corōnāre; (fig) cumulāre, fastīgium impōnere (dat)
crucial adj gravissimus, māximī mōmentī; **~ moment** discrīmen nt
crucifixion n crucis supplicium nt
crucify vt crucī suffīgere
crude adj crūdus; (style) dūrus, inconcinnus
crudely adv dūrē, asperē
crudity n asperitās f
cruel adj crūdēlis, saevus, atrōx
cruelly adv crūdēliter, atrōciter
cruelty n crūdēlitās f, saevitia f, atrōcitās f
cruise n nāvigātiō f ▶ vi nāvigāre
cruiser n speculātōria nāvis f
crumb n mīca f
crumble vi corruere, putrem fierī ▶ vt putrefacere, friāre
crumbling adj putris
crumple vt rūgāre
crunch vt dentibus frangere
crupper n postilēna f
crush vt frangere, contundere, obterere; (fig) adflīgere, opprimere, obruere ▶ n turba f, frequentia f
crust n crusta f; (bread) frustum nt
crusty adj (fig) stomachōsus
crutch n baculum nt
cry vt, vi clāmāre, clāmitāre; (weep) flēre; (infant) vāgīre; **cry down** dētrectāre; **cry out** exclāmāre, vōciferārī; **cry out against** adclāmāre, reclāmāre; **cry up** laudāre, vēnditāre ▶ n clāmor m, vōx f; (child's) vāgītus m; (of grief) plōrātus m
cryptic adj arcānus
crystal n crystallum nt ▶ adj crystallinus
cub n catulus m
cube n cubus m
cubit n cubitum nt
cuckoo n coccyx m
cucumber n cucumis m
cud n: **chew the cud** rūminārī
cudgel n fustis m ▶ vt verberāre
cue n signum nt, indicium nt
cuff n (blow) alapa f
cuirass n lōrīca f
culinary adj coquīnārius
cull vt legere, carpere, dēlibāre
culminate vi ad summum fastīgium venīre
culmination n fastīgium nt
culpability n culpa f, noxa f
culpable adj nocēns
culprit n reus m
cultivate vt (land) colere, subigere; (mind) excolere; (interest) fovēre, studēre (dat)
cultivation n cultus m, cultūra f
cultivator n cultor m, agricola m
cultural adj hūmānior
culture n hūmānitās f, bonae artēs fpl
cultured adj doctus, litterātus

culvert n cloāca f
cumber vt impedīre, obesse (dat); (load) onerāre
cumbersome adj molestus, gravis
cumulative adj alius ex aliō; **be ~** cumulārī
cuneiform adj cuneātus
cunning adj callidus, astūtus ▶ n ars f, astūtia f, calliditās f
cunningly adv callidē, astūtē
cup n pōculum nt; **drink the cup of** (fig) exanclāre, exhaurīre; **in one's cups** ēbrius, pōtus
cupboard n armārium nt
Cupid n Cupīdō m, Amor m
cupidity n avāritia f
cupola n tholus m
cupping glass n cucurbita f
cur n canis m
curable adj sānābilis
curative adj salūbris
curator n custōs m
curb vt frēnāre, īnfrēnāre; (fig) coercēre, cohibēre ▶ n frēnum nt
curdle vt cōgere ▶ vi concrēscere
curds n concrētum lac nt
cure vt sānāre, medērī (dat) ▶ n remedium nt; (process) sānātiō f
curio n dēliciae fpl
curiosity n studium nt; (thing) mīrāculum nt
curious adj (inquisitive) cūriōsus, cupidus; (artistic) ēlabōrātus; (strange) mīrus, novus
curiously adv cūriōsē; summā arte; mīrum in modum
curl n (natural) cirrus m; (artificial) cincinnus m ▶ vt (hair) crispāre ▶ vi (smoke) volvī
curling irons n calamistrī mpl
curly adj crispus
currency n (coin) monēta f; (use) ūsus m; **gain ~** (rumour) percrēbrēscere
current adj vulgāris, ūsitātus; (time) hīc ▶ n flūmen nt; **with the ~** secundō flūmine; **against the ~** adversō flūmine
currently adv vulgō
curriculum n īnstitūtiō f
curry vt (favour) aucupārī
curse n exsecrātiō f, maledictum nt; (formula) exsecrābile carmen nt; (fig) pestis f; **curses** interj malum! ▶ vt exsecrārī, maledīcere (dat)
cursed adj exsecrātus, sacer; scelestus
cursorily adv breviter, strictim
cursory adj brevis
curt adj brevis
curtail vt minuere, contrahere
curtailment n dēminūtiō f, contractiō f
curtain n aulaeum nt ▶ vt vēlāre
curule adj curūlis
curve n flexus m, arcus m ▶ vt flectere, incurvāre, arcuāre
cushion n pulvīnus m
custodian n custōs m
custody n custōdia f, tūtēla f; (prison) carcer m; **hold in ~** custōdīre
custom n mōs m, cōnsuētūdō f; (national) īnstitūtum nt; **customs** pl portōria ntpl

customarily adv plērumque, dē mōre, vulgō
customary adj solitus, ūsitātus; (rite)
sollemnis; **it is ~** mōs est
customer n emptor m
customs officer n portitor m
cut vt secāre, caedere, scindere; (corn) metere;
(branch) amputāre; (acquaintance) āversārī;
(hair) dētondēre; **cut away** abscindere,
resecāre; **cut down** rescindere, caedere,
succīdere; **cut into** incīdere; **cut off** vt
abscīdere, praecīdere; (exclude) exclūdere;
(intercept) interclūdere, intercipere; (head)
abscindere; **cut out** vt excīdere, exsecāre; (omit)
ōmittere; **cut out for** aptus ad, nātus ad (acc);
cut round circumcīdere; **cut short** praecīdere;
(speech) incīdere, interrumpere; **cut through**
intercīdere; **cut up** vt concīdere ▸ n vulnus nt
cutlass n gladius m
cutlery n cultrī mpl
cutter n sector m; (boat) lembus m
cutthroat n sīcārius m
cutting n (plant) propāgō f ▸ adj acūtus; (fig)
acerbus, mordāx
cuttlefish n sēpia f
cyclamen n baccar nt
cycle n orbis m
cyclone n turbō f
cylinder n cylindrus m
cymbal n cymbalum nt
cynic n (PHILOS) cynicus m
cynical adj mordāx, acerbus
cynically adv mordāciter, acerbē
cynicism n acerbitās f
cynosure n cynosūra f
cypress n cypressus f

d

dabble vi: **~ in** gustāre, leviter attingere
dactyl n dactylus m
dactylic adj dactylicus
dagger n sīca f, pugiō f
daily adj diūrnus, cottīdiānus ▸ adv cottīdiē,
in diēs
daintily adv molliter, concinnē; fastīdiōsē
daintiness n munditia f, concinnitās f;
(squeamish) fastīdium nt
dainty adj mundus, concinnus, mollis;
fastīdiōsus; **dainties** npl cuppēdia ntpl
dais n suggestus m
daisy n bellis f
dale n vallis f
dalliance n lascīvia f
dally vi lūdere; morārī
dam n mōlēs f, agger m; (animal) māter f ▸ vt
obstruere, exaggerāre
damage n damnum nt, dētrīmentum nt,
malum nt; (inflicted) iniūria f; (LAW) damnum nt;
assess damages lītem aestimāre ▸ vt laedere,
nocēre (dat); (by evidence) laedere; (reputation)
violāre
damageable adj fragilis
dame n mātrōna f, domina f
damn vt damnāre, exsecrārī
damnable adj dētestābilis, improbus
damnably adv improbē
damnation n malum nt
damp adj ūmidus ▸ n ūmor m ▸ vt madefacere;
(enthusiasm) restinguere, dēmittere
damsel n puella f, virgō f
damson n Damascēnum nt
dance vi saltāre ▸ n saltātiō f; (religious)
tripudium nt
dancer n saltātor m, saltātrīx f
dandruff n porrīgō f
dandy n dēlicātus m
danger n perīculum nt, discrīmen nt
dangerous adj perīculōsus, dubius; (in attack)
īnfestus
dangerously adv perīculōsē
dangle vt suspendere ▸ vi pendēre
dank adj ūmidus

dapper adj concinnus, nitidus
dapple vt variāre, distinguere
dappled adj maculōsus, distinctus
dare vt audēre; (challenge) prōvocāre; **I ~ say** haud sciō an
daring n audācia f ▸ adj audāx
daringly adv audācter
dark adj obscūrus, opācus; (colour) fuscus, āter; (fig) obscūrus; **it is getting ~** advesperāscit; **keep ~** silēre ▸ n tenebrae fpl; (mist) cālīgō f; **keep in the ~** cēlāre
darken vt obscūrāre, occaecāre
darkish adj subobscūrus
darkling adj obscūrus
darkness n tenebrae fpl; (mist) cālīgō f
darksome adj obscūrus
darling adj cārus, dīlēctus ▸ n dēliciae fpl, voluptās f
darn vt resarcīre
darnel n lolium nt
dart n tēlum nt; iaculum nt ▸ vi ēmicāre, sē conicere ▸ vt iaculārī, iacere
dash vt adflīgere; (hope) frangere; **~ against** illīdere, incutere; **~ down** dēturbāre; **~ out** ēlīdere; **~ to pieces** discutere; **~ to the ground** prōsternere ▸ vi currere, sē incitāre, ruere ▸ n impetus m; (quality) ferōcia f
dashing adj ferōx, animōsus
dastardly adj ignāvus
date n (fruit) palmula f; (time) tempus nt, diēs m; **out of ~** obsolētus; **become out of ~** exolēscere; **to ~** adhūc; **be up to ~** praesentī mōre ūtī ▸ vt (letter) diem adscrībere; (past event) repetere ▸ vi initium capere
dative n datīvus m
daub vt inlinere
daughter n fīlia f; (little) fīliola f
daughter-in-law n nurus f
daunt vt terrēre, perterrēre
dauntless adj impavidus, intrepidus
dauntlessly adv impavidē, intrepidē
dawdle vi cessāre, cunctārī
dawdler n cunctātor m
dawn n aurōra f, dīlūculum nt; (fig) orīgō f, prima lux f; **at ~** prīmā lūce. ▸ vi dīlūcēscere; **day dawns** diēs illūcēscit; **it dawns upon me** mente concipiō
day n diēs m/f; (period) aetās f; **day about** alternīs diēbus; **day by day** in diēs; cottīdiē; **by day** (adj) diūrnus; (adv) interdiū; **during the day** interdiū; **every day** cottīdiē; **from day to day** in diēs, diem dē diē; **late in the day** multō diē; **next day** postrīdiē; **one day/some day** ōlim; **the day after** (adv) postrīdiē; (conj) postrīdiē quam; **the day after tomorrow** perendiē; **the day before** (adv) prīdiē; (conj) prīdiē quam; **the day before yesterday** nūdius tertius; **the present day** haec aetās; **time of day** hōra; **twice a day** (in) diē; **days of old** praeteritum tempus; **days to come** posteritās; **better days** rēs prosperae; **evil days** rēs adversae; **three days** trīduum nt; **two days** bīduum nt; **win the day** vincere

daybook n adversāria ntpl
daybreak n aurōra f, prīma lūx f
daylight n diēs m; **become ~** illūcēscere
daystar n lūcifer m
daytime n diēs m; **in the ~** interdiū
daze vt obstupefacere ▸ n stupor m
dazzle vt praestringere
dazzling adj splendidus, nitēns
deacon n diāconus m
deaconess n diāconissa f
dead adj mortuus; (in battle) occīsus; (LIT) frīgidus; (place) iners, sōlitarius; (senses) hebes; **~ of night** nox intempesta f; **be ~ to** nōn sentīre; **in ~ earnest** sēriō ac vērō; **rise from the ~** revīvīscere ▸ adv prōrsus, omnīnō
dead beat adj cōnfectus
dead body n cadāver m
dead calm n malacia f
dead certainty n rēs certissima
deaden vt (senses) hebetāre, obtundere; (pain) restinguere
deadlock n incitae fpl; **reach a ~** ad incitās redigī
dead loss n mera iactūra
deadly adj fūnestus, exitiōsus, exitiābilis; (enmity) implācābilis; (pain) acerbissimus
dead weight n mōlēs f
deaf adj surdus; **become ~** obsurdēscere; **be ~ to** nōn audīre, obdūrēscere contrā
deafen vt (with noise) obtundere
deafness n surditās f
deal n (amount) cōpia f; **a good ~** aliquantum nt, bona pars f; (wood) abiēs f ▸ adj abiēgnus ▸ vt (blow) dare, īnflīgere; (share) dīvidere, partīrī ▸ vi agere, negōtiārī; **~ with** (person) agere cum (abl); (matter) tractāre
dealer n (wholesale) negōtiātor m, mercātor m; (retail) caupō m
dealings n commercium nt, negōtium nt, rēs f
dean n decānus m
dear adj (love) cārus, grātus; (cost) cārus, pretiōsus; **my ~ Quintus** mī Quīnte; (beginning of letter from Marcus) Marcus Quīntō salūtem; **~ me!** (sorrow) heil; (surprise) ehem!; **buy ~** male emere; **sell ~** bene vēndere
dearly adv (love) valdē, ārdenter; (value) magnī
dearness n cāritās f
dearth n inopia f, pēnūria f
death n mors f; (natural) obitus m; (violent) nex f, interitus m; **condemn to ~** capitis damnāre; **put to ~** interficere; **give the ~ blow to** interimere
deathbed n: **on one's ~** moriēns, moribundus
deathless adj immortālis
deathly adj pallidus
debar vt prohibēre, exclūdere
debase vt dēprāvāre, corrumpere; (coin) adulterāre; (self) prōsternere, dēmittere
debasement n dēdecus nt; (coin) adulterium nt
debatable adj ambiguus, dubius
debate vt disputāre, disceptāre ▸ n contrōversia f, disceptātiō f, altercātiō f
debater n disputātor m

debauch vt corrumpere, pellicere ▶ n cōmissātiō f
debauched adj perditus, prāvus
debauchee n cōmissātor m
debaucher n corruptor m
debauchery n luxuria f, stuprum nt
debilitate vt dēbilitāre
debility n īnfirmitās f
debit n expēnsum nt ▶ vt in expēnsum referre
debonair adj urbānus, cōmis
debouch vi exīre
debris n rūdus nt
debt n aes aliēnum nt; (booked) nōmen nt; (fig) dēbitum nt; **be in ~** in aere aliēnō esse; **pay off ~** aes aliēnum persolvere; **run up ~** aes aliēnum contrahere; **collect debts** nōmina exigere; **abolition of debts** novae tabulae fpl
debtor n dēbitor m
decade n decem annī mpl
decadence n occāsus m
decadent adj dēgener, dēterior
decamp vi (MIL) castra movēre; (fig) discēdere, aufugere
decant vt dēfundere, diffundere
decanter n lagoena f
decapitate vt dētruncāre
decay vi dīlābī, perīre, putrēscere; (fig) tābēscere, senēscere ▶ n ruīna f, lāpsus m; (fig) occāsus m, dēfectiō f
deceased adj mortuus
deceit n fraus f, fallācia f, dolus m
deceitful adj fallāx, fraudulentus, dolōsus
deceitfully adv fallāciter, dolōsē
deceive vt dēcipere, fallere, circumvenīre, fraudāre
deceiver n fraudātor m
December n mēnsis December m; **of ~** December
decemvir n decemvir m; **of the decemvirs** decemvirālis
decemvirate n decemvirātus m
decency n honestum nt, decōrum nt, pudor m
decent adj honestus, pudēns
decently adv honestē, pudenter
deception n fraus f, fallācia f
deceptive adj fallāx, fraudulentus
decide vt, vi (dispute) dīiūdicāre, dēcernere, dīrimere; **~ to do** statuere, cōnstituere (infin); **I have decided** mihī certum est; **~ the issue** dēcernere
decided adj certus, firmus
decidedly adv certē, plānē
deciduous adj cadūcus
decimate vt decimum quemque occīdere
decipher vt expedīre, ēnōdāre
decision n (of judge) iūdicium nt; (of council) dēcrētum nt; (of senate) auctōritās f; (of referee) arbitrium nt; (personal) sententia f; (quality) cōnstantia f
decisive adj certus, ~ **moment** discrīmen nt
decisively adv sine dubiō

deck vt ōrnāre, exōrnāre ▶ n (ship) pōns m; **with a ~** cōnstrātus
decked adj ōrnātus; (ship) cōnstrātus
declaim vt, vi dēclāmāre, prōnūntiāre
declamation n dēclāmātiō f
declamatory adj dēclāmātōrius
declaration n affirmātiō f, adsevērātiō f; (formal) professiō f; (of war) dēnūntiātiō f
declare vt affirmāre, adsevērāre; (secret) aperīre, expōnere; (proclamation) dēnūntiāre, ēdīcere; (property in census) dēdicāre; (war) indīcere
declension n dēclīnātiō f
declination n dēclīnātiō f
decline n (slope) dēclīve nt, dēiectus m; (of age) senium nt; (of power) dēfectiō f; (of nation) occāsus m ▶ vi inclīnāre, occidere; (fig) ruere, dēlābī, dēgenerāre ▶ vt dētrectāre, recūsāre; (GRAM) dēclīnāre
decode vt expedīre, ēnōdāre
decompose vt dissolvere ▶ vi putrēscere
decomposed adj putridus
decomposition n dissolūtiō f
decorate vt ōrnāre, decorāre
decoration n ōrnāmentum nt; (medal) īnsigne nt
decorous adj pudēns, modestus, decōrus
decorously adv pudenter, modestē
decorum n pudor m, honestum nt
decoy n illecebra f ▶ vt adlicere, inescāre
decrease n dēminūtiō f, dēcessiō f ▶ vt dēminuere, extenuāre ▶ vi dēcrēscere
decree n (of magistrate) dēcrētum nt, ēdictum nt; (of senate) cōnsultum nt, auctōritās f; (of people) scītum nt ▶ vt ēdīcere, dēcernere; (people) scīscere, iubēre; **the senate decrees** placet senātuī
decrepit adj īnfirmus, dēbilis, dēcrepitus
decrepitude n īnfirmitās f, dēbilitās f
decry vt obtrectāre, reprehendere
decurion n decuriō m
dedicate vt dēdicāre, cōnsecrāre; (life) dēvovēre
dedication n dēdicātiō f; dēvōtiō f
dedicatory adj commendātīcius
deduce vt colligere, conclūdere
deduct vt dēmere, dētrahere
deduction n (inference) conclūsiō f, cōnsequēns nt; (subtraction) dēductiō f, dēminūtiō f
deed n factum nt, facinus nt; gestum nt; (legal) tabulae fpl; **deeds** pl rēs gestae fpl
deem vt dūcere, cēnsēre, habēre
deep adj altus, profundus; (discussion) abstrūsus; (sleep) artus; (sound) gravis; (width) lātus; **three ~** (MIL) ternī in lātitūdinem ▶ n altum nt
deepen vt dēfodere, altiōrem reddere; (fig) augēre ▶ vi altiōrem fierī; (fig) crēscere
deepest adj īmus
deeply adv altē, graviter; (inside) penitus; **very ~** valdē, vehementer
deep-seated adj (fig) inveterātus

deer n cervus m, cerva f; (fallow) dāma f
deface vt dēfōrmāre, foedāre
defaced adj dēfōrmis
defacement n dēfōrmitās f
defalcation n pecūlātus m
defamation n calumnia f, opprobrium nt
defamatory adj contumēliōsus, probrōsus
defame vt īnfāmāre, obtrectāre, calumniārī
default vi dēesse; (money) nōn solvere ▶ n
  dēfectiō f, culpa f; **let judgment go by ~**
  vadimōnium dēserere, nōn respondēre
defaulter n reus m
defeat vt vincere, superāre; (completely)
  dēvincere; (plan) frustrārī, discere ▶ n clādēs f;
  (at election) repulsa f, offēnsiō f; (of plan)
  frustrātiō f
defeatism n patientia f
defeatist n imbellis m
defect n vitium nt
defection n dēfectiō f, sēditiō f
defective adj mancus, vitiōsus
defence n praesidium nt, tūtēla f; patrōcinium
  nt; (speech) dēfēnsiō f; **speak in ~** dēfendere
defenceless adj inermis, indēfēnsus; **leave ~**
  nūdāre
defences npl mūnīmenta ntpl, mūnītiōnēs fpl
defend vt dēfendere, tuērī, custōdīre
defendant n reus m
defender n dēfēnsor m, prōpugnātor m; (LAW)
  patrōnus m
defensible adj iūstus
defensive adj dēfēnsiōnis causā; **be on the ~**
  sē dēfendere
defensively adv dēfendendō
defer vt differre, prōlātāre ▶ vi mōrem gerere
  (dat); **I ~ to you in this** hōc tibī tribuō
deference n obsequium nt, observantia f;
  show ~ to observāre, īnservīre (dat)
deferential adj observāns, officiōsus
deferment n dīlātiō f, prōlātiō f
defiance n ferōcia f, minae fpl
defiant adj ferōx, mināx
defiantly adv ferōciter, mināciter
deficiency n vitium nt; (lack) pēnūria f, inopia f
deficient adj vitiōsus, inops; **be ~** dēesse,
  dēficere
deficit n lacūna f
defile n faucēs fpl, angustiae fpl ▶ vt inquināre,
  contāmināre
defilement n sordēs f, foeditās f
define vt (limits) fīnīre, dēfīnīre, termināre;
  (meaning) explicāre
definite adj certus, dēfīnītus
definitely adv dēfīnītē; prōrsus
definition n dēfīnītiō f, explicātiō f
definitive adj dēfīnītīvus
deflate vt laxāre
deflect vt dēdūcere, dēclīnāre ▶ vi dēflectere,
  dēgredī
deflection n dēclīnātiō f, flexus m
deform vt dēfōrmāre
deformed adj dēfōrmis, distortus

deformity n dēfōrmitās f, prāvitās f
defraud vt fraudāre, dēfraudāre
defrauder n fraudātor m
defray vt solvere, suppeditāre
deft adj habilis
deftly adv habiliter
defunct adj mortuus
defy vt contemnere, spernere, adversārī (dat);
  (challenge) prōvocāre, lacessere
degeneracy n dēprāvātiō f
degenerate adj dēgener ▶ vi dēgenerāre,
  dēscīscere
degradation n īnfāmia f, ignōminia f, nota f
degrade vt notāre, abicere; (from office) movēre
degrading adj turpis, indignus
degree n gradus m; (social) locus m; **in some ~**
  aliquā ex parte; **by degrees** gradātim, sēnsim
deification n apotheōsis f
deified adj (emperor) dīvus
deify vt cōnsecrāre, inter deōs referre
deign vi dignārī
deity n deus m
dejected adj adflīctus, dēmissus
dejectedly adv animō dēmissō
dejection n maestitia f
delay vt dēmorārī, dētinēre, retardāre ▶ vi
  cunctārī, cessāre ▶ n mora f, cunctātiō f
delayer n morātor m, cunctātor m
delectable adj iūcundus, amoenus
delegate vt lēgāre, mandāre, committere
  ▶ n lēgātus m
delegation n lēgātiō f, lēgātī mpl
delete vt dēlēre
deleterious adj perniciōsus, noxius
deletion n (writing) litūra f
deliberate vi dēlīberāre, cōnsulere ▶ adj (act)
  cōnsīderātus; (intention) certus; (manner)
  cōnsīderātus; (speech) lentus
deliberately adv dē industriā
deliberation n dēlīberātiō f
deliberative adj dēlīberātīvus
delicacy n (judgment) subtīlitās f, ēlegantia f;
  (manners) mollitia f, luxus m; (health) valētūdō f;
  (food) cuppēdia ntpl
delicate adj mollis; (health) īnfirmus; (shape)
  gracilis; (feelings) hūmānus
delicately adv molliter; hūmānē
delicious adj suāvis, lautus
delight n voluptās f, gaudium nt, dēlectātiō f
  ▶ vt dēlectāre, oblectāre, iuvāre ▶ vi gaudēre,
  dēlectārī
delightful adj iūcundus, dulcis, festīvus;
  (scenery) amoenus
delightfully adv iūcundē, suāviter
delimitation n dēfīnītiō f
delineate vt dēscrībere, dēpingere
delineation n dēscrīptiō f
delinquency n culpa f, dēlictum nt, noxa f
delinquent n nocēns m/f, reus m
delirious adj dēlīrus, āmēns, furiōsus; **be ~**
  furere, dēlīrāre
delirium n furor m, āmentia f

deliver vt (from) līberāre, exsolvere, ēripere; (blow) intendere; (message) referre; (speech) habēre; ~ **to** dēferre, trādere, dare; ~ **up** dēdere, trādere; **be delivered of** parere
deliverance n līberātiō f
deliverer n līberātor m
delivery n (of things due) trāditiō f; (of speech) āctiō f, prōnūntiātiō f; (of child) partus m
dell n convallis f
Delphi n Delphī mpl
delude vt dēcipere, frustrārī, dēlūdere
deluge n ēluviō f ▶ vt inundāre
delusion n error m, fraus f
delusive adj fallāx, inānis
delve vt fodere
demagogue n plēbicola m
demand vt poscere, postulāre, imperāre; (urgently) flāgitāre, poscere; (thing due) exigere; (answer) quaerere; ~ **back** repetere ▶ n postulātiō f, postulātum nt
demarcation n līmes m
demean vt (self) dēmittere
demeanour n gestus m, mōs m, habitus m
demented adj dēmēns, furiōsus
demerit n culpa f, vitium nt
demesne n fundus m
demigod n hērōs m
demise n obitus m ▶ vt lēgāre
democracy n cīvitās populāris f
democrat n homō populāris m/f
democratic adj populāris
demolish vt dēmōlīrī, dīruere, dēstruere; (argument) discutere
demolition n ruīna f, ēversiō f
demon n daemōn m
demonstrate vt (show) mōnstrāre, ostendere, indicāre; (prove) dēmōnstrāre
demonstration n exemplum nt; (proof) dēmōnstrātiō f
demonstrative adj (manner) vehemēns; (RHET) dēmōnstrātīvus
demoralization n corruptiō f, dēprāvātiō f
demoralize vt corrumpere, dēprāvāre, labefactāre
demote vt locō movēre
demur vi gravārī, recūsāre ▶ n mora f, dubitātiō f
demure adj modestus, verēcundus
demurely adv modestē, verēcundē
demureness n modestia f, verēcundia f, pudor m
demurrer n (LAW) exceptiō f
den n latibulum nt, latebra f; (of vice) lustrum nt
denarius n dēnārius m
denial n īnfitiātiō f, negātiō f
denigrate vt obtrectāre, calumniārī
denizen n incola m/f
denominate vt nōmināre, appellāre
denomination n nōmen nt; (religious) secta f
denote vt notāre, significāre
denouement n exitus m
denounce vt dēferre, incūsāre

denouncer n dēlātor m
dense adj dēnsus; (crowd) frequēns; (person) stolidus
density n crassitūdō f; (crowd) frequentia f
dent n nota f
dentate adj dentātus
denture n dentēs mpl
denudation n spoliātiō f
denude vt spoliāre, nūdāre
denunciation n (report) indicium nt, dēlātiō f; (threat) minae fpl
deny vt īnfitiārī, īnfitiās īre, negāre; (on oath) abiūrāre; ~ **oneself** genium dēfraudāre
depart vi discēdere (abl), abīre, exīre, ēgredī
department n (district) regiō f, pars f; (duty) prōvincia f, mūnus nt
departure n discessus m, abitus m, dīgressus m, exitus m; (change) mūtātiō f; (death) obitus m
depend vi pendēre; (be dependent) pendēre ex (abl), nītī (abl); (rely) fīdere, cōnfīdere; **depending on** frētus (abl)
dependable adj fīdus
dependant n cliēns m/f
dependence n clientēla f; (reliance) fīdūcia f
dependency n prōvincia f
dependent adj subiectus, obnoxius
depict vt dēscrībere, dēpingere; (to the life) expingere
deplete vt dēminuere
depletion n dēminūtiō f
deplorable adj turpis, nefandus, pessimus
deplorably adv turpiter, pessimē, miserē
deplore vt dēplōrāre, dēflēre, conquerī
deploy vt explicāre; instruere, dispōnere
depopulate vt vastāre, nūdāre
depopulation n vastātiō f, sōlitūdō f
deport vt (banish) dēportāre; (self) gerere
deportation n exsilium nt
deportment n gestus m, habitus m
depose vt dēmovēre, dēpellere; (evidence) testārī
deposit n fīdūcia f, dēpositum nt ▶ vt dēpōnere, mandāre
depositary n sequester m
deposition n (LAW) testimōnium nt, indicium nt
depository n apothēca f
depot n (for arms) armāmentārium nt; (for trade) emporium nt
deprave vt dēprāvāre, corrumpere
depraved adj prāvus
depravity n dēprāvātiō f, turpitūdō f
deprecate vt abōminārī, dēprecārī
deprecation n dēprecātiō f
depreciate vt obtrectāre, dētrectāre
depreciation n obtrectātiō f; (price) vīlitās f
depredation n praedātiō f, dīreptiō f
depress vt dēprimere; (mind) adflīgere, frangere; **be depressed** iacēre, animum dēspondēre
depressing adj maestus, tristis
depression n (place) cavum nt; (mind) tristitia f, sollicitūdō f

deprivation n prīvātiō f, spoliātiō f
deprive vt prīvāre, spoliāre
depth n altitūdō f; (place) profundum nt, gurges m
deputation n lēgātiō f, lēgātī mpl
depute vt lēgāre, mandāre
deputy n lēgātus m; (substitute) vicārius m
derange vt conturbāre
deranged adj īnsānus, mente captus
derangement n perturbātiō f; (mind) īnsānia f, dēmentia f
derelict adj dēsertus
dereliction n (of duty) neglegentia f
deride vt dērīdēre, inlūdere
derision n rīsus m, irrīsiō f
derisive adj mordāx
derivation n orīgō f
derive vt dūcere, trahere; (advantage) capere, parāre; (pleasure) dēcerpere, percipere; **be derived** dēfluere
derogate vi dērogāre, dētrahere; **~ from** imminuere, obtrectāre
derogation n imminūtiō f, obtrectātiō f
derogatory adj indignus; **~ remarks** obtrectātiō f
derrick n trochlea f
descant vt disserere ▶ n cantus m
descend vi dēscendere; (water) dēlābī; (from heaven) dēlābī; (by inheritance) pervenīre, prōdī; (morally) dēlābī, sē dēmittere; **be descended from** orīrī ex (abl)
descendant n prōgeniēs f; **descendants** pl minōrēs mpl, posterī mpl
descent n dēscēnsus m; (slope) clīvus m, dēiectus m; (birth) genus nt; (hostile) dēcursus m, incursiō f; **make a ~ upon** inrumpere in (acc), incursāre in (acc)
describe vt dēscrībere; (tell) nārrāre; (portray) dēpingere, exprimere
description n dēscrīptiō f; (tale) nārrātiō f; (kind) genus nt
descry vt cernere, cōnspicere, prōspectāre
desecrate vt prōfānāre, exaugurāre
desecration n exaugurātiō f, violātiō f
desert vt dēserere, dērelinquere, dēstituere ▶ vi dēscīscere, dēficere ▶ adj dēsertus, sōlitārius ▶ n (place) sōlitūdō f, loca dēserta ntpl; (merit) meritum nt
deserted adj dēsertus
deserter n dēsertor m; (MIL) trānsfuga m
desertion n dēfectiō f, trānsfugium nt
deserve vt merērī; dignus esse quī (subj); **~ well of** bene merērī dē (abl)
deserved adj meritus
deservedly adv meritō
deserving adj dignus
desiccate vt siccāre
design n (drawing) adumbrātiō f; (plan) cōnsilium nt, prōpositum nt; **by ~** cōnsultō ▶ vt adumbrāre, in animō habēre
designate vt dēsignāre, mōnstrāre; (as heir) scrībere; (as official) dēsignāre ▶ adj dēsignātus

designation n nōmen nt, titulus m
designedly adv dē industriā, cōnsultō
designer n auctor m, inventor m
designing adj vafer, dolōsus
desirable adj optābilis, expetendus, grātus
desire n cupiditās f; studium nt; (uncontrolled) libīdō f; (natural) appetītiō f ▶ vt cupere; (much) exoptāre, expetere; (command) iubēre
desirous adj cupidus, avidus, studiōsus
desist vi dēsistere
desk n scrīnium nt
desolate adj dēsertus, sōlitārius; (place) vastus ▶ vt vastāre
desolation n sōlitūdō f, vastitās f; (process) vastātiō f
despair vi dēspērāre dē (abl), animum dēspondēre ▶ n dēspērātiō f
despairingly adv dēspēranter
despatch see **dispatch**
desperado n homō dēspērātus m
desperate adj (hopeless) dēspērātus; (wicked) perditus; (dangerous) perīculōsus
desperately adv dēspēranter
desperation n dēspērātiō f
despicable adj dēspectus, abiectus, turpis
despicably adv turpiter
despise vt contemnere, dēspicere, spernere
despiser n contemptor m
despite n malevolentia f, odium nt
despoil vt spoliāre, nūdāre
despoiler n spoliātor m, praedātor m
despond vi animum dēspondēre, dēspērāre
despondency n dēspērātiō f
despondent adj abiectus, adflīctus, dēmissus; **be ~** animum dēspondēre
despondently adv animō dēmissō
despot n dominus m, rēx m
despotic adj imperiōsus, superbus
despotically adv superbē
despotism n dominātiō f, superbia f, rēgnum nt
dessert n secunda mēnsa f
destination n fīnis m
destine vt dēstināre, dēsignāre; **destined to be** futūrus
destiny n fātum nt; **of ~** fātālis
destitute adj inops, pauper, prīvātus; **~ of** expers (gen)
destitution n inopia f, egestās f
destroy vt dēlēre, ēvertere, dīrimere, perdere
destroyer n ēversor m
destructible adj fragilis
destruction n exitium nt, ēversiō f, excidium nt
destructive adj exitiābilis, perniciōsus
destructively adv perniciōsē
desuetude n dēsuētūdō f
desultorily adv carptim
desultory adj varius, incōnstāns
detach vt abiungere, sēiungere, āmovēre, sēparāre
detachment n (MIL) manus f, cohors f; (mind) integer animus m, līber animus m

detail n: in ~ singillātim ▸ vt exsequī; **details** pl singula ntpl
detain vt dēmorārī, dētinēre, distinēre, morārī
detect vt dēprehendere, patefacere
detection n dēprehēnsiō f
detective n inquīsītor m
detention n retentiō f; (prison) vincula ntpl
deter vt dēterrēre, absterrēre, impedīre
deteriorate vi dēgenerāre
deterioration n dēprāvātiō f, lāpsus m
determinate adj certus, fīnītus
determination n obstinātiō f, cōnstantia f; (intention) prōpositum nt, sententia f
determine vt (fix) fīnīre; (decide) statuere, cōnstituere
determined adj obstinātus; (thing) certus; **I am ~ to** mihī certum est (infin)
determinedly adv cōnstanter
deterrent n: **act as a ~ to** dēterrēre
detest vt ōdisse, dētestārī
detestable adj dētestābilis, odiōsus
detestation n odium nt, invidia f
dethrone vt rēgnō dēpellere
detour n circuitus m; **make a ~** iter flectere; (MIL) agmen circumdūcere
detract vi: ~ **from** dērogāre, dētrahere
detraction n obtrectātiō f
detractor n obtrectātor m, invidus m
detriment n damnum nt, dētrīmentum nt
detrimental adj damnōsus; **be ~ to** dētrīmentō esse (dat)
devastate vt vastāre, populārī
devastation n vastātiō f, populātiō f; (state) vastitās f
develop vt ēvolvere, explicāre; (person) ēducāre, alere ▸ vi crēscere; ~ **into** ēvādere in (acc)
development n explicātiō f; (of men) ēducātiō f; (of resources) cultus m; (of events) exitus m
deviate vi dēcēdere dē viā, aberrāre, dēclīnāre; (speech) dēgredī
deviation n dēclīnātiō f; (from truth) error m; (in speech) dīgressus m
device n (plan) cōnsilium nt; (machine) māchina f; (emblem) īnsigne nt
devil n diabolus m; **go to the ~** abī in malam crucem!; **talk of the ~** lupus in fābulā!
devilish adj scelestus, impius
devil-may-care adj praeceps, lascīvus
devilment n malitia f
devilry n magicae artēs fpl
devious adj dēvius, errābundus
devise vt excōgitāre, commentārī, fingere
devoid adj vacuus, expers; **be ~ of** carēre (abl)
devolve vi obtingere, obvenīre ▸ vt dēferre, committere
devote vt dēdicāre; (attention) dēdere, trādere; (life) dēvovēre
devoted adj dēditus, studiōsus; (victim) dēvōtus, sacer; **be ~ to** studēre (dat), incumbere (dat)
devotee n cultor m
devotion n amor m, studium nt; rēligiō f

devour vt dēvorāre, cōnsūmere; (fig) haurīre
devout adj pius, rēligiōsus
devoutly adv piē, rēligiōsē
dew n rōs m
dewy adj rōscidus
dexterity n ars f, sollertia f
dexterous adj sollers, habilis
dexterously adv sollerter, habiliter
diabolical adj scelestus, nefārius
diadem n diadēma nt
diagnose vt discernere, diiūdicāre
diagnosis n iūdicium nt
diagonal adj oblīquus
diagram n fōrma f
dial n sōlārium nt
dialect n dialectus f, sermō m
dialectic n ars disserendī f, dialēcticē f ▸ adj dialecticus
dialectician n dialecticus m
dialogue n dialogus m, colloquium nt
diameter n diametros f
diamond n adamās m
diaphanous adj perlūcidus
diaphragm n praecordia ntpl
diary n ephēmeris f
diatribe n convīcium nt
dice n tālus m, tessera f; **game of ~** ālea f
dictate vt dictāre ▸ n praeceptum nt; **dictates of nature** nātūrae iūdicia ntpl
dictation n dictāta ntpl; (fig) arbitrium nt
dictator n dictātor m; **dictator's** dictātōrius
dictatorial adj imperiōsus, superbus
dictatorship n dictātūra f
diction n (enunciation) ēlocūtiō f; (words) ōrātiō f
dictionary n verbōrum thēsaurus m
die n signum nt; **the die is cast** iacta ālea est ▸ vi morī, perīre, obīre; (in battle) cadere, occumbere; **die off** dēmorī; **die out** ēmorī; **be dying to** exoptāre
diet n (food) diaeta f; (meeting) conventus m
differ vi differre, discrepāre, dissentīre
difference n discrepantia f, dissimilitūdō f; (of opinion) dissēnsiō f; **there is a ~** interest
different adj dīversus, varius, dissimilis; ~ **from** alius ... ac; **in ~ directions** dīversī; **they say ~ things** alius aliud dīcit
differentiate vt discernere
differently adv dīversē, variē, alius aliter; ~ **from** aliter ... ac
difficult adj difficilis, arduus; **very ~** perdifficilis, perarduus
difficulty n difficultās f, labor m, negōtium nt; **with ~** difficulter, aegrē, vix; **be in ~** labōrāre
diffidence n diffīdentia f; (shyness) pudor m; **with ~** modestē
diffident adj diffīdēns; (shy) modestus, verēcundus
diffidently adv modestē
diffuse vt diffundere, dispergere; **be diffused** diffluere ▸ adj fūsus, diffūsus, cōpiōsus
diffusely adv diffūsē, cōpiōsē
diffuseness n cōpia f

dig vt fodere; dūcere; (*nudge*) fodicāre; **dig up** vt effodere, ēruere

digest vt coquere, concoquere ▶ n summārium nt

digestion n concoctiō f; **with a bad ~** crūdus

digger n fossor m

dignified adj gravis, augustus

dignify vt honōrāre, honestāre

dignity n gravitās f, māiestās f, amplitūdō f

digress vi dēvertere, dīgredī, dēclīnāre

digression n dēclīnātiō f, dīgressus m

dike n (*ditch*) fossa f; (*mound*) agger m

dilapidated adj ruīnōsus

dilapidation n ruīna f

dilate vt dīlātāre; (*speech*) plūra dīcere

dilatorily adv tardē, cunctanter

dilatoriness n mora f, cunctātiō f

dilatory adj tardus, lentus, segnis

dilemma n nōdus m, angustiae fpl; **be in a ~** haerēre; **be on the horns of a ~** auribus tenēre lupum

diligence n dīligentia f, industria f, cūra f

diligent adj dīligēns, industrius, sēdulus

diligently adv dīligenter, sēdulō

dill n anēthum nt

dilly-dally vi cessāre

dilute vt dīluere, temperāre

dim adj obscūrus; (*fig*) hebes ▶ vt obscūrāre; hebetāre

dimension n modus m; **dimensions** pl amplitūdō f, māgnitūdō f

diminish vt minuere, imminuere, extenuāre, īnfringere ▶ vi dēcrēscere

diminution n imminūtiō f, dēminūtiō f

diminutive adj parvulus, exiguus ▶ n (*word*) dēminūtum nt

diminutiveness n exiguitās f

dimly adv obscūrē

dimness n tenebrae fpl, cālīgō f

dimple n gelasīnus m

din n fragor m, strepitus m; **make a din** strepere ▶ vt obtundere

dine vi cēnāre

diner n convīva m

dinghy n scapha f

dingy adj sordidus; (*colour*) fuscus

dining room n cēnātiō f

dinner n cēna f

dinner party convīvium nt

dint n ictus m; **by ~ of** per (*acc*)

dip vt imbuere, mergere ▶ vi mergī; **dip into** (*study*) perstringere

diploma n diplōma nt

diplomacy n (*embassy*) lēgātiō f; (*tact*) iūdicium nt, sagācitās f

diplomat n lēgātus m

diplomatic adj sagāx, circumspectus

diptych n tabellae fpl

dire adj dīrus, horridus

direct vt regere, dīrigere; (*attention*) attendere, admovēre, advertere; (*course*) tendere; (*business*) administrāre, moderārī; (*letter*) īnscrībere; (*order*) imperāre (*dat*), iubēre; (*to a place*) viam mōnstrāre (*dat*); (*weapon*) intendere ▶ adj rēctus, dīrēctus; (*person*) simplex; (*language*) apertus ▶ adv rēctā

direction n (*of going*) cursus m, iter nt; (*of looking*) pars f, regiō f; (*control*) administrātiō f, regimen nt; (*order*) praeceptum nt, iussum nt; **in the ~ of Rome** Rōmam versus; **in all directions** passim, undique; **in both directions** utrōque

directly adv (*place*) prōtinus, continuō, statim; (*language*) apertē ▶ conj simulac

directness n (*fig*) simplicitās f

director n dux m, gubernātor m, moderātor m

dirge n nēnia f

dirk n pūgiō m

dirt n sordēs f; (*mud*) lūtum nt

dirty adj sordidus, foedus; (*speech*) inquinātus ▶ vt foedāre, inquināre

disability n vitium nt

disable vt dēbilitāre, imminuere

disabled adj mutilus, dēbilis

disabuse vt errōrem dēmere (*dat*)

disaccustom vt dēsuēfacere

disadvantage n incommodum nt, dētrīmentum nt; **it is a ~** dētrīmentō est

disadvantageous adj incommodus, inīquus

disadvantageously adv incommodē

disaffected adj aliēnātus, sēditiōsus

disaffection n aliēnātiō f, sēditiō f

disagree vi discrepāre, dissentīre, dissidēre

disagreeable adj molestus, incommodus, iniūcundus

disagreeably adv molestē, incommodē

disagreement n discordia f, dissēnsiō f, discrepantia f

disallow vt improbāre, abnuere, vetāre

disappear vi dēperīre, perīre, abīre, diffugere, ēvānēscere

disappearance n dēcessiō f, fuga f

disappoint vt dēcipere, spē dēicere, frustrārī; **be disappointed in a hope** ā spē dēcidere, dē spē dēicī

disappointment n frustrātiō f, malum nt

disapprobation n reprehēnsiō f, improbātiō f

disapproval n improbātiō f

disapprove vt, vi improbāre, reprehendere

disarm vt exarmāre, dearmāre; (*fig*) mītigāre

disarrange vt turbāre, cōnfundere

disarranged adj incompositus

disarrangement n turbātiō f

disarray n perturbātiō f ▶ vt perturbāre

disaster n calamitās f, cāsus m; (*MIL*) clādēs f

disastrous adj īnfēlīx, exitiōsus, calamitōsus

disavow vt diffitērī, īnfitiārī

disavowal n īnfitiātiō f

disband vt dīmittere

disbelief n diffīdentia f, suspiciō f

disbelieve vt diffīdere (*dat*)

disburden vt exonerāre

disburse vt ērogāre, expendere

disbursement n impēnsa f

disc n orbis m
discard vt mittere, pōnere, prōicere
discern vt cōnspicere, dīspicere, cernere; (fig) intellegere
discernment n iūdicium nt, intellegentia f, sagācitās f
discharge vt (load) exonerāre; (debt) exsolvere; (duty) fungī (abl), exsequī; (officer) exauctōrāre; (troops) missōs facere, dīmittere; (weapon) iacere, iaculārī; (prisoner) absolvere; (from body) ēdere, reddere ▶ vi (river) effundī, influere ▶ n (bodily) dēfluxiō f; (MIL) missiō f, dīmissiō f; (of a duty) perfūnctiō f
disciple n discipulus m
discipline n (MIL) modestia f; (punishment) castīgātiō f; (study) disciplīna f ▶ vt coercēre, castīgāre
disciplined adj modestus
disclaim vt renūntiāre, repudiāre, rēicere
disclaimer n repudiātiō f
disclose vt aperīre, patefacere, indicāre
disclosure n indicium nt
discoloration n dēcolōrātiō f
discolour vt dēcolōrāre
discoloured adj dēcolor
discomfit vt vincere, conturbāre, dēprehendere
discomfiture n clādēs f; (POL) repulsa f
discomfort n molestia f, incommodum nt
disconcert vt conturbāre, percellere
disconcerting adj molestus
disconnect vt abiungere, sēiungere
disconnected adj dissolūtus, abruptus
disconnectedly adv dissolūtē
disconsolate adj maestus, dēmissus
disconsolately adv animō dēmissō
discontent n offēnsiō f, fastīdium nt, taedium nt
discontented adj invidus, fastīdiōsus, parum contentus
discontentedly adv invītus, inīquō animō
discontinuance n intermissiō f
discontinue vt intermittere ▶ vi dēsistere, dēsinere
discord n discordia f; (music) dissonum nt
discordance n discrepantia f, dissēnsiō f
discordant adj discors, discrepāns; (music) dissonus, absonus
discount vt dētrahere; (fig) praetermittere ▶ n dēcessiō f; **be at a ~** iacēre
discountenance vt improbāre
discourage vt dēhortārī, dēterrēre; **be discouraged** animum dēmittere, animō dēficere
discouragement n animī abiectiō f; (cause) incommodum nt
discourse n sermō m; (lecture) ōrātiō f ▶ vi conloquī, disserere, disputāre
discourteous adj inurbānus, asper, inhūmānus
discourteously adv inhūmānē, rūsticē
discourtesy n inhūmānitās f, acerbitās f

discover vt (find) invenīre, reperīre; (detect) dēprehendere; (reveal) aperīre, patefacere; (learn) cognōscere
discoverer n inventor m
discovery n inventum nt
discredit vt notāre, fidem imminuere (gen) ▶ n invidia f, lābēs f; **be in ~** iacēre
discreditable adj inhonestus, turpis
discreditably adv inhonestē, turpiter
discreet adj prūdēns, sagāx, cautus
discreetly adv prūdenter, sagāciter, cautē
discrepancy n discrepantia f, dissēnsiō f
discretion n prūdentia f; (tact) iūdicium nt; (power) arbitrium nt, arbitrātus m; **at your ~** arbitrātū tuō; **surrender at ~** in dēditiōnem venīre, sine ullā pactiōne sē tradere; **years of ~** adulta aetās f
discretionary adj līber
discriminate vt, vi discernere, internōscere, distinguere
discriminating adj perspicāx, sagāx
discrimination n discrīmen nt, iūdicium nt
discursive adj vagus, loquāx; **be ~** excurrere
discuss vt agere, disputāre, disceptāre dē (abl); **~ terms of peace** dē pāce agere
discussion n disceptātiō f, disputātiō f
disdain vt contemnere, aspernārī, fastīdīre ▶ n contemptiō f, fastīdium nt
disdainful adj fastīdiōsus, superbus
disdainfully adv fastīdiōsē, superbē
disease n morbus m; pestilentia f
diseased adj aeger, aegrōtus
disembark vi ē nave ēgredī ▶ vt mīlitēs etc ē nāve expōnere
disembarkation n ēgressus m
disembodied adj sine corpore
disembowel vt exenterāre
disencumber vt exonerāre
disengage vt expedīre, līberāre; (mind) abstrahere, abdūcere
disengaged adj vacuus, ōtiōsus
disentangle vt expedīre, explicāre, exsolvere
disfavour n invidia f
disfigure vt dēfōrmāre, foedāre
disfigured adj dēfōrmis
disfigurement n dēfōrmātiō f
disfranchise vt cīvitātem adimere (dat)
disfranchised adj capite dēminūtus
disfranchisement n capitis dēminūtiō f
disgorge vt ēvomere
disgrace n dēdecus nt, ignōminia f, īnfāmia f ▶ vt dēdecorāre, dēdecorī esse (dat)
disgraceful adj ignōminiōsus, flāgitiōsus, turpis; **~ thing** flāgitium nt
disgracefully adv turpiter, flāgitiōsē
disgruntled adj mōrōsus, invidus
disguise n integumentum nt; (fig) speciēs f, simulātiō f; **in ~** mūtātā veste ▶ vt obtegere, involvere; (fact) dissimulāre; **~ oneself** vestem mūtāre
disgust vt displicēre (dat), fastīdium movēre (dat); **be disgusted** stomachārī; **I am disgusted**

mē taedet, mē piget ▶ n fastīdium nt,
taedium nt
disgusting adj taeter, foedus, dēfōrmis
disgustingly adv foedē
dish n lanx f; (course) ferculum nt
dishearten vt percellere; **be disheartened**
animō dēficere, animum dēmittere
dishevelled adj solūtus, passus
dishonest adj perfidus, inīquus, improbus
dishonestly adv improbē, dolō malō
dishonesty n mala fidēs f, perfidia f, fraus f
dishonour n dēdecus nt, ignōminia f, turpitūdō
f ▶ vt dēdecorāre
dishonourable adj ignōminiōsus, indecōrus,
turpis
dishonourably adv turpiter, inhonestē
disillusion vt errōrem adimere (dat)
disinclination n odium nt
disinclined adj invītus, āversus
disinfect vt pūrgāre
disingenuous adj dolōsus, fallāx
disingenuously adv dolōsē
disinherit vt abdicāre, exhērēdāre
disinherited adj exhērēs
disintegrate vt dissolvere ▶ vi dīlābī, dissolvī
disinter vt effodere, ēruere
disinterested adj grātuītus, favōris expers
disinterestedly adv sine favōre
disinterestedness n innocentia f, integritās f
disjoin vt sēiungere
disjointed adj parum cohaerēns
disk n orbis m
dislike n odium nt, offēnsiō f, invidia f ▶ vt
ōdisse; **I ~** mihī displicet, mē piget (gen)
dislocate vt extorquēre
dislocated adj luxus
dislodge vt dēmovēre, dēicere, dēpellere,
dētrūdere
disloyal adj īnfīdus, īnfīdēlis; (to gods, kin,
country) impius
disloyally adv īnfīdēliter
disloyalty n perfidia f, īnfīdēlitās f, impietās f
dismal adj fūnestus, maestus
dismally adv miserē
dismantle vt nūdāre; (building) dīruere
dismay n pavor m, formīdō f ▶ vt terrēre,
perturbāre
dismember vt discerpere
dismiss vt dīmittere; (troops) missōs facere;
(from service) exauctōrāre; (fear) mittere, pōnere
dismissal n missiō f, dīmissiō f
dismount vi dēgredī, (ex equō) dēscendere
disobedience n contumācia f
disobedient adj contumāx
disobediently adv contrā iussa
disobey vt nōn pārēre (dat), aspernārī
disoblige vt displicēre (dat), offendere
disobliging adj inofficiōsus, difficilis
disobligingly adv contrā officium
disorder n turba f, cōnfūsiō f; (MED) morbus m;
(POL) mōtus m, tumultus m ▶ vt turbāre,
miscēre, sollicitāre

disorderly adj immodestus, inōrdinātus,
incompositus; (POL) turbulentus, sēditiōsus; **in
a ~ manner** nullō ōrdine, temerē
disorganize vt dissolvere, perturbāre
disown vt (statement) īnfitiārī; (thing) abnuere,
repudiāre; (heir) abdicāre
disparage vt obtrectāre, dētrectāre
disparagement n obtrectātiō f, probrum nt
disparager n obtrectātor m, dētrectātor m
disparate adj dispār
disparity n discrepantia f, dissimilitūdō f
dispassionate adj studiī expers
dispassionately adv sine īrā et studiō
dispatch vt mittere, dīmittere; (finish)
absolvere, perficere; (kill) interficere ▶ n (letter)
litterae fpl; (speed) celeritās f
dispel vt dispellere, discutere
dispensation n (distribution) partītiō f;
(exemption) venia f; (of heaven) sors f; **by divine ~**
dīvīnitus
dispense vt dispertīrī, dīvidere ▶ vi: **~ with**
ōmittere, praetermittere, repudiāre
dispersal n dīmissiō f, diffugium nt
disperse vt dispergere, dissipāre, dīsicere ▶ vi
diffugere, dīlābī
dispirited adj dēmissō animō; **be ~** animō
dēficere, animum dēmittere
displace vt locō movēre
display n ostentātiō f, iactātiō f; **for ~** per
speciem ▶ vt exhibēre, ostendere, praestāre,
sē ferre
displease vt displicēre (dat), offendere; **be
displeased** aegrē ferre, stomachārī, indignārī
displeasing adj ingrātus, odiōsus
displeasure n invidia f, offēnsiō f, odium nt
disport vt: **~ oneself** lūdere
disposal n (sale) vēnditiō f; (power) arbitrium nt
dispose vt (troops) dispōnere; (mind) inclīnāre,
addūcere ▶ vi: **~ of** abaliēnāre, vēndere; (get rid)
tollere; (argument) refellere
disposed adj adfectus, inclīnātus, prōnus;
well ~ benevolus, bonō animō
disposition n animus m, adfectiō f, ingenium
nt, nātūra f; (of troops) dispositiō f
dispossess vt dētrūdere, spoliāre
disproportion n inconcinnitās f
disproportionate adj impār, inconcinnus
disproportionately adv inaequāliter
disprove vt refūtāre, redarguere, refellere
disputable adj dubius, ambiguus
disputation n disputātiō f
dispute n altercātiō f, contrōversia f; (violent)
iūrgium nt; **beyond ~** certissimus ▶ vi altercārī,
certāre, rixārī ▶ vt negāre, in dubium vocāre
disqualification n impedīmentum nt
disqualify vt impedīre
disquiet n sollicitūdō f ▶ vt sollicitāre
disquisition n disputātiō f
disregard n neglegentia f, contemptiō f ▶ vt
neglegere, contemnere, ōmittere
disrepair n vitium nt; **in ~** male sartus
disreputable adj inhonestus, īnfāmis

disrepute n înfâmia f

disrespect n neglegentia f, contumâcia f

disrespectful adj contumâx, însolêns

disrespectfully adv însolenter

disrobe vt nûdâre, vestem exuere (dat) ▶ vi vestem exuere

disrupt vt dîrumpere, dîvellere

disruption n discidium nt

dissatisfaction n molestia f, aegritûdô f, dolor m

dissatisfied adj parum contentus; **I am ~ with ...** mê taedet (gen) ...

dissect vt incîdere; (fig) investîgâre

dissemble vt, vi dissimulâre; mentîrî

dissembler n simulâtor m

disseminate vt dîvulgâre, dissêminâre

dissension n discordia f, dissênsiô f; (violent) iûrgium nt

dissent vi dissentîre, dissidêre ▶ n dissênsiô f

dissertation n disputâtiô f

disservice n iniûria f, incommodum nt

dissident adj discors

dissimilar adj dispâr, dissimilis

dissimilarity n discrepantia f, dissimilitûdô f

dissimulation n dissimulâtiô f

dissipate vt dissipâre, diffundere, disperdere

dissipated adj dissolûtus, lascîvus, luxuriôsus

dissipation n dissipâtiô f; (vice) luxuria f, licentia f

dissociate vt dissociâre, sêiungere

dissociation n sêparâtiô f, discidium nt

dissoluble adj dissolûbilis

dissolute adj dissolûtus, perditus, libîdinôsus

dissolutely adv libîdinôsê, luxuriôsê

dissoluteness n luxuria f

dissolution n dissolûtiô f, discidium nt

dissolve vt dissolvere; (ice) liquefacere; (meeting) dîmittere; (contract) dîrimere ▶ vi liquêscere; (fig) solvî

dissonance n dissonum nt

dissonant adj dissonus

dissuade vt dissuâdêre (dat), dêhortârî

dissuasion n dissuâsiô f

distaff n colus f

distance n intervallum nt, spatium nt; (long way) longinquitâs f; **at a ~** (far) longê; (within sight) procul; (fight) êminus; **at a ~ of ...** spatiô (gen) ...; **within striking ~** intrâ iactum têlî

distant adj longinquus; (measure) distâns; (person) parum familiâris; **be ~** abesse (abl)

distaste n fastîdium nt

distasteful adj molestus, iniûcundus

distemper n morbus m

distend vt distendere

distil vt, vi stillâre

distinct adj (different) dîversus; (separate) distinctus; (clear) clârus, argûtus; (marked) distinctus; (sure) certus; (well-drawn) expressus

distinction n discrîmen nt; (dissimilarity) discrepantia f; (public status) amplitûdô f; (honour) honôs m, decus nt; (mark) însigne nt; **there is a ~ interest; without ~** prômiscuê

distinctive adj proprius, însignîtus

distinctively adv propriê, însignîtê

distinctly adv clârê, distinctê, certê, expressê

distinguish vt distinguere, internôscere, dîiûdicâre, discernere; (honour) decorâre, ôrnâre; **~ oneself** êminêre

distinguished adj însignis, praeclârus, êgregius, amplissimus

distort vt dêtorquêre; (fig) dêprâvâre

distorted adj distortus

distortion n distortiô f; dêprâvâtiô f

distract vt distrahere, distinêre, âvocâre; (mind) aliênâre

distracted adj âmêns, însânus

distraction n (state) indîligentia f; (cause) invîtâmentum nt; (madness) furor m, dêmentia f; **to ~** efflîctim

distraught adj âmêns, dêmêns

distress n labor m, dolor m, aegrimônia f, aerumna f; **be in ~** labôrâre ▶ vt adflîgere, sollicitâre

distressed adj adflîctus, sollicitus; **be ~ at** rem etc aegrê ferre

distressing adj tristis, miser, acerbus

distribute vt distribuere, dîvidere, dispertîre

distribution n partîtiô f, distribûtiô f

district n regiô f, pars f

distrust n diffîdentia f ▶ vt diffîdere (dat), nôn crêdere (dat)

distrustful adj diffîdêns

distrustfully adv diffîdenter

disturb vt perturbâre, conturbâre; commovêre; (mind) sollicitâre

disturbance n turba f, perturbâtiô f; (POL) môtus m, tumultus m

disturber n turbâtor m

disunion n discordia f, discidium nt

disunite vt dissociâre, sêiungere

disuse n dêsuêtûdô f; **fall into ~** obsolêscere

disused adj dêsuêtus, obsolêtus

disyllabic adj disyllabus

ditch n fossa f, scrobis m

dithyrambic adj dithyrambicus

dittany n dictamnum nt

ditty n carmen nt, cantilêna f

diurnal adj diûrnus

divan n lectus m, lectulus m

dive vi dêmergî

diver n ûrînâtor m

diverge vi dêvertere, dîgredî; (road) sê scindere; (opinions) discrepâre

divergence n dîgressiô f; discrepantia f

divers adj complûrês

diverse adj varius, dîversus

diversify vt variâre

diversion n (of water) dêrîvâtiô f; (of thought) âvocâtiô f; (to amuse) oblectâmentum nt; **create a ~** (MIL) hostês dîstringere; **for a ~** animî causâ

diversity n varietâs f, discrepantia f

divert vt dêflectere, âvertere; (attention) âvocâre, abstrahere; (water) dêrîvâre; (to amuse) oblectâre, placêre (dat)

diverting adj iūcundus; (remark) facētus

divest vt exuere, nūdāre; ~ **oneself of** (fig) pōnere, mittere

divide vt dīvidere; (troops) dīdūcere; ~ **among** partīrī, distribuere; ~ **from** sēparāre ab, sēiungere ab; ~ **out** dispertīrī, dīvidere ▸ vi discēdere, sē scindere; (senate) in sententiam īre; **be divided** (opinions) discrepāre

divination n dīvīnātiō f; (from birds) augurium nt; (from entrails) haruspicium nt

divine adj dīvīnus ▸ vt dīvīnāre, augurārī, hariolārī; **by ~ intervention** dīvīnitus

divinely adv dīvīnē

diviner n dīvīnus m, augur m, haruspex m

divinity n (status) dīvīnitās f; (god) deus m, dea f

divisible adj dīviduus

division n (process) dīvīsiō f, partītiō f; (variance) discordia f, dissēnsiō f; (section) pars f; (grade) classis f; (of army) legiō f; (of time) discrīmen nt; (in senate) discessiō f

divorce n dīvortium nt, repudium nt ▸ vt (wife) nūntium mittere (dat); (things) dīvellere, sēparāre

divulge vt aperīre, patefacere, ēvulgāre, ēdere

dizziness n vertīgō f

dizzy adj vertīginōsus; (fig) attonitus

do vt facere, agere; (duty) fungī (abl); (wrong) admittere; **do away with** vt tollere; (kill) interimere; **do one's best to** id agere ut (subj); **do without** repudiāre; **do not ...** nōlī/nōlīte (infin); **how do you do?** quid agis?; **I have nothing to do with you** mihī tēcum nihil est commercī; **it has nothing to do with me** nihil est ad mē; **that will do** iam satis est; **be done** fierī; **have done with** dēfungī (abl)

docile adj docilis

docility n docilitās f

dock n (ships) nāvāle nt; (LAW) cancellī mpl ▸ vt praecīdere

dockyard n nāvālia ntpl

doctor n medicus m; (univ) doctor m ▸ vt cūrāre

doctrine n dogma nt, dēcrētum nt; (system) ratiō f

document n litterae fpl, tabula f

dodge vt dēclīnāre, ēvādere ▸ n dolus m

doe n cerva f

doer n āctor m, auctor m

doff vt exuere

dog n canis m/f; **dog star** Canīcula f; **dog's** canīnus ▸ vt īnsequī, īnstāre (dat)

dogged adj pertināx

doggedly adv pertināciter

dogma n dogma nt, praeceptum nt

dogmatic adj adrogāns

dogmatically adv adroganter

doing n factum nt

dole n sportula f ▸ vt: ~ **out** dispertīrī, dīvidere

doleful adj lūgubris, flēbilis, maestus

dolefully adv flēbiliter

dolefulness n maestitia f, miseria f

doll n pūpa f

dolorous adj lūgubris, maestus

dolour n maestitia f, dolor m

dolphin n delphīnus m

dolt n stīpes m, caudex m

domain n ager m; (king's) rēgnum nt

dome n tholus m, testūdō f

domestic adj domesticus, familiāris; (animal) mānsuētus ▸ n famulus m, servus m, famula f, ancilla f; **domestics** pl familia f

domesticate vt mānsuēfacere

domesticated adj mānsuētus

domesticity n larēs suī mpl

domicile n domicilium nt, domus f

dominant adj superior, praepotēns

dominate vt dominārī in (acc), imperāre (dat); (view) dēspectāre

domination n dominātiō f, dominātus m

domineer vi dominārī, rēgnāre

dominion n imperium nt, rēgnum nt

don vt induere ▸ n scholasticus m

donate vt dōnāre

donation n dōnum nt

donkey n asellus m

donor n dōnātor m

doom n fātum nt ▸ vt damnāre

door n (front) iānua f; (back) postīcum nt; (double) forēs fpl; **folding doors** valvae fpl; **out of doors** forīs; (to) forās; **next ~ to** iuxtā (acc)

doorkeeper n iānitor m

doorpost n postis m

doorway n ōstium nt

dormant adj sōpītus; **lie ~** iacēre

dormitory n cubiculum nt

dormouse n glīs m

dose n pōculum nt

dot n pūnctum nt

dotage n senium nt

dotard n senex dēlīrus m

dote vi dēsipere; ~ **upon** dēamāre

doting adj dēsipiēns, peramāns

dotingly adv perditē

double adj duplex; (amount) duplus; (meaning) ambiguus ▸ n duplum nt ▸ vt duplicāre; (promontory) superāre; (fold) complicāre ▸ vi duplicārī; (MIL) currere

double-dealer n fraudātor m

double-dealing adj fallāx, dolōsus ▸ n fraus f, dolus m

doublet n tunica f

doubly adv bis, dupliciter

doubt n dubium nt; (hesitancy) dubitātiō f; (distrust) suspīciō f; **give someone the benefit of the ~** innocentem habēre; **no ~** sānē; **I do not ~ that ...** nōn dubitō quīn ... (subj); **there is no ~ that ...** nōn dubium est quīn ... (subj) ▸ vt dubitāre; (distrust) diffīdere (dat), suspicārī

doubtful adj dubius, incertus; (result) anceps; (word) ambiguus

doubtfully adv dubiē; (hesitation) dubitanter

doubtless adv scīlicet, nīmīrum

doughty adj fortis, strēnuus

dove n columba f

dovecote n columbārium nt

dowdy adj inconcinnus
dower n dōs f ▸ vt dōtāre
dowerless adj indōtātus
down n plūmae fpl, lānūgō f; (thistle) pappus m
▸ adv deōrsum; **be ~** iacēre; **~ with!** perea(n)t;
up and ~ sūrsum deōrsum ▸ prep dē (abl); **~ from**
dē (abl)
downcast adj dēmissus, maestus
downfall n ruīna f; (fig) occāsus m
downhearted adj dēmissus, frāctus animī
downhill adj dēclīvis; (fig) prōclīvis ▸ adv in
praeceps
downpour n imber m
downright adj dīrectus; (intensive) merus
downstream adv secundō flūmine
downtrodden adj subiectus, oppressus
downward adj dēclīvis, prōclīvis
downwards adv deōrsum
downy adj plūmeus
dowry n dōs f
doyen n pater m
doze vi dormītāre
dozen n duodecim
drab adj sordidior
drachma n drachma f
draft n (writing) exemplum nt; (MIL) dīlēctus m;
(money) syngrapha f; (literary) silva f ▸ vt
scrībere; (MIL) mittere
drag vt trahere ▸ vi (time) trahī; **~ on** vi (war)
prōdūcere ▸ n harpagō m; (fig) impedīmentum nt
dragnet n ēverriculum nt
dragon n dracō m
dragoon n eques m
drain n cloāca f ▸ vt (water) dērīvāre; (land)
siccāre; (drink) exhaurīre; (resources) exhaurīre
drainage n dērīvātiō f
drake n anas m
drama n fābula f; **the ~** scaena f
dramatic adj scaenicus
dramatist n fābulārum scrīptor m
dramatize vt ad scaenam compōnere
drape vt vēlāre
drapery n vestīmenta ntpl
drastic adj vehemēns, efficāx
draught n (air) aura f; (drink) haustus m; (net)
bolus m
draughts n latrunculī mpl
draw vt dūcere, trahere; (bow) addūcere;
(inference) colligere; (picture) scrībere, pingere;
(sword) stringere, dēstringere; (tooth) eximere;
(water) haurīre; **~ aside** sēdūcere; **~ away**
āvocāre; **~ back** retrahere ▸ vi recēdere;
~ near adpropinquāre; **~ off** dētrahere; (water)
dērīvāre; **~ out** vt ēdūcere; (lengthen) prōdūcere;
~ over obdūcere; **~ taut** addūcere; **~ together**
contrahere; **~ up** vt (MIL) īnstruere; (document)
scrībere
drawback n scrūpulus m; **this was the only ~**
hōc ūnum dēfuit
drawing n dēscrīptiō f; (art) graphicē f
drawing room n sellāria f
drawings npl līneāmenta ntpl

drawl vi lentē dīcere
drawling adj lentus in dīcendō
dray n plaustrum nt
dread n formīdō f, pavor m, horror m ▸ adj dīrus
▸ vt expavēscere, extimēscere, formīdāre
dreadful adj terribilis, horribilis, formīdolōsus,
dīrus
dreadfully adv vehementer, atrōciter
dream n somnium nt ▸ vt, vi somniāre
dreamy adj somniculōsus
dreariness n (place) vastitās f; (mind) tristitia f
dreary adj (place) vastus; (person) tristis
dregs n faex f; (of oil) amurca f; **drain to the ~**
exhaurīre
drench vt perfundere
dress n vestis f, vestītus m, vestīmenta ntpl;
(style) habitus m ▸ vt vestīre; (wound) cūrāre;
(tree) amputāre ▸ vi induī; **~ up** vi vestum
induere
dressing n (MED) fōmentum nt
drift n (motion) mōtus m; (snow) agger m;
(language) vīs f; **I see the ~ of your speech** videō
quōrsum ōrātiō tua tendat ▸ vi fluitāre; (fig)
lābī, ferrī
drill n terebra f; (MIL) exercitātiō f ▸ vt (hole)
terebrāre; (MIL) exercēre; (pupil) īnstruere
drink vt, vi bibere, pōtāre; **~ a health** prōpīnāre,
Graecō mōre bibere; **~ deep of** exhaurīre; **~ in**
haurīre; **~ up** ēpōtāre ▸ n pōtiō f
drinkable adj pōtulentus
drinker n pōtor m
drinking bout n pōtātiō f
drip vi stillāre, dēstillāre
drive vt agere; (force) cōgere; **~ away** abigere;
(fig) pellere, prōpulsāre; **~ back** repellere;
~ home dēfīgere; **~ in/into** īnfigere in (acc);
(flock) cōgere in (acc); **~ off** dēpellere; **~ out**
exigere, expellere, exturbāre; **~ through**
trānsfīgere ▸ vi vehī; **~ away** āvehī; **~ back**
revehī; **~ in** invehī; **~ on** vt impellere; **~ round**
circumvehī; **~ past** praetervehī; **what are you
driving at?** quōrsum tua spectat ōrātiō? ▸ n
gestātiō f
drivel vi dēlīrāre
drivelling adj dēlīrus, ineptus ▸ n ineptiae fpl
driver n aurīga m; rēctor m
drizzle vi rōrāre
droll adj facētus, iocولāris
drollery n facētiae fpl
dromedary n dromas m
drone n (bee) fūcus m; (sound) bombus m ▸ vi
fremere
droop vi dēmittī; (flower) languēscere; (mind)
animum dēmittere
drooping adj languidus
drop n gutta f ▸ vi cadere; (liquid) stillāre ▸ vt
mittere; (anchor) iacere; (hint) ēmittere; (liquid)
īnstillāre; (work) dēsistere ab (abl) ▸ vi: **~ behind**
cessāre; **~ in** vīsere, supervenīre; **~ out**
excidere
dross n scōria f; (fig) faex f
drought n siccitās f

drouth n sitis f
drove n grex f
drover n bubulcus m
drown vt mergere, obruere; (noise) obscūrāre
▸ vi aquā perīre
drowse vi dormītāre
drowsily adv somniculōsē
drowsiness n sopor m
drowsy adj sēmisomnus, somniculōsus
drub vt pulsāre, verberāre
drudge n mediastīnus m ▸ vi labōrāre
drudgery n labor m
drug n medicāmentum nt ▸ vt medicāre
Druids n Druidae, Druidēs mpl
drum n tympanum nt; (container) urna f
drummer n tympanista m
drunk adj pōtus, ēbrius, tēmulentus
drunkard n ēbriōsus m
drunken adj ēbriōsus, tēmulentus
drunkenness n ēbrietās f
dry adj siccus, āridus; (thirst) sitiēns; (speech)
āridus, frīgidus; (joke) facētus; **be dry** ārēre
▸ vt siccāre ▸ vi ārēscere; **dry up** exārēscere
dryad n dryas f
dry rot n rōbīgō f
dual adj duplex
duality n duplex nātūra f
dubiety n dubium nt
dubious adj dubius, incertus; (meaning)
ambiguus
dubiously adv dubiē; ambiguē
duck n anas f ▸ vt dēmergere ▸ vi dēmergī, sē
dēmittere
duckling n anaticula f
duct n ductus m
dudgeon n dolor m, stomachus m
due adj dēbitus, meritus, iūstus; **be due** dēbērī;
it is due to me that ... not per mē stat
quōminus (subj); **be due to** orīrī ex, fierī (abl) ▸ n
iūs nt, dēbitum nt; (tax) vectīgal nt; (harbour)
portōrium nt; **give every man his due** suum
cuīque tribuere ▸ adv rēctā; **due to** ob (acc),
propter (acc)
duel n certāmen nt
dug n ūber nt
duke n dux m
dulcet adj dulcis
dull adj hebes; (weather) subnūbilus; (language)
frīgidus; (mind) tardus; **be ~** hebēre; **become ~**
hebēscere ▸ vt hebetāre, obtundere, retundere
dullard n stolidus m
dulness n (mind) tarditās f, stultitia f
duly adv rītē, ut pār est
dumb adj mūtus; **be struck ~** obmūtēscere
dun n flāgitātor m ▸ vt flāgitāre ▸ adj fuscus
dunce n bārō m
dune n tumulus m
dung n fimus m
dungeon n carcer m, rōbur nt
dupe vt dēlūdere, fallere ▸ n crēdulus m
duplicate n exemplar nt ▸ vt duplicāre
duplicity n fraus f, perfidia f

durability n firmitās f, firmitūdō f
durable adj firmus, perpetuus
durably adv firmē
duration n spatium nt; (long) diūturnitās f
duress n vīs f
during prep inter (acc), per (acc)
dusk n crepusculum nt, vesper m; **at ~** prīmā
nocte, prīmīs tenebrīs
dusky adj fuscus
dust n pulvis m; **throw ~ in the eyes of** tenebrās
offundere (dat) ▸ vt dētergēre
dusty adj pulverulentus
dutiful adj pius, officiōsus
dutifully adv piē, officiōsē
dutifulness n pietās f
duty n (moral) officium nt; (task) mūnus nt; (tax)
vectīgal nt; **be on ~** (MIL) statiōnem agere,
excubāre; **do one's ~** officiō fungī; **do ~ for**
(person) in locum sufficī (gen); (thing) adhibērī
prō (abl); **it is my ~** dēbeō, mē oportet, meum
est; **it is the ~ of a commander** ducis est; **sense
of ~** pietās f
duty call n salūtātiō f
duty-free adj immūnis
dwarf n (of plant) nānus m
dwell vi habitāre; **~ in** incolere; **~ upon** (theme)
commorārī in (abl)
dweller n incola m
dwelling n domus f, domicilium nt; (place)
sēdēs f
dwindle vi dēcrēscere, extenuārī
dye n fūcus m, color m ▸ vt īnficere, fūcāre
dyer n īnfector m
dying adj moribundus, moriēns
dynasty n domus (rēgia) f
dyspepsia n crūditās f

e

each adj, pron quisque; (of two) uterque; **~ other** inter sē; **one ~** singulī; **~ year** quotannīs

eager adj avidus, cupidus, alācer; **~ for** avidus (gen)

eagerly adv avidē, cupidē, ācriter

eagerness n cupīdō f, ārdor m, studium nt; alacritās f

eagle n aquila f

ear n auris f; (of corn) spīca f; **give ear** aurem praebēre, auscultāre; **go in at one ear and out at the other** surdīs auribus nārrārī; **prick up one's ears** aurēs ērigere; **with long ears** aurītus

earl n comes m

earlier adv ante; anteā

early adj (in season) mātūrus; (in day) mātūtīnus; (at beginning) prīmus; (in history) antīquus ▶ adv (in day) māne; (before time) mātūrē, temperī; **~ in life** ab ineunte aetāte

earn vt merērī, cōnsequī; **~ a living** vīctum quaerere, quaestum facere

earnest adj (serious) sērius; (eager) ācer, sēdulus ▶ n pignus nt; (money) arrabō m; **in ~** sēdulō, ēnīxē

earnestly adv sēriō, graviter, sēdulō

earnestness n gravitās f, studium nt

earnings n quaestus m

earring n elenchus m

earth n (planet) tellūs f; (inhabited) orbis terrārum m; (land) terra f; (soil) solum nt, humus f; (fox's) latibulum nt; **where on earth?** ubī gentium?; **of the ~** terrestris

earthen adj (ware) fictilis; (mound) terrēnus

earthenware n fictilia ntpl ▶ adj fictilis

earthly adj terrestris

earthquake n terrae mōtus m

earthwork n agger m

earthy adj terrēnus

ease n facilitās f; (leisure) ōtium nt; **at ~** ōtiōsus; (in mind) sēcūrus; **ill at ~** sollicitus ▶ vt laxāre, relevāre; (pain) mītigāre

easily adv facile; (gladly) libenter; (at leisure) ōtiōsē; **not ~** nōn temerē

easiness n facilitās f

east n Oriēns m, sōlis ortus m; **~ wind** eurus m

Easter n Pascha f

easterly, **eastern** adj orientālis

eastward adv ad orientem

easy adj facilis; (manner) adfābilis, facilis; (mind) sēcūrus; (speech) expedītus; (discipline) remissus; **~ circumstances** dīvitiae fpl, abundantia f

eat vt edere; cōnsūmere; vescī (abl); **eat away** rōdere; **eat up** exedere

eatable adj esculentus

eating n cibus m

eaves n suggrunda f

eavesdropper n sermōnis auceps m

ebb n dēcessus m, recessus m; **at ebbtide** minuente aestū; **be at a low ebb** (fig) iacēre ▶ vi recēdere

ebony n ebenus f

ebullient adj fervēns

ebullition n fervor m

eccentric adj īnsolēns

eccentricity n īnsolentia f

echo n imāgō f ▶ vt, vi resonāre

eclipse n dēfectus m, dēfectiō f ▶ vt obscūrāre; **be eclipsed** dēficere, labōrāre

eclogue n ecloga f

economic adj quaestuōsus, sine iactūrā

economical adj (person) frūgī, parcus

economically adv nūllā iactūrā factā

economics n reī familiāris dispēnsātiō f

economize vi parcere

economy n frūgālitās f

ecstasy n alacritās f, furor m

ecstatic adj gaudiō ēlātus

eddy n vertex m ▶ vi volūtārī

edge n ōra f, margō f; (of dish) labrum nt; (of blade) aciēs f; **take the ~ off** obtundere; **on ~** (fig) suspēnsō animō ▶ vt (garment) praetexere; (blade) acuere ▶ vi: **~ in** sē īnsinuāre

edging n limbus m

edible adj esculentus

edict n ēdictum nt, dēcrētum nt

edification n ērudītiō f

edifice n aedificium nt

edify vt ērudīre

edit vt recognōscere, recēnsēre

edition n ēditiō f

educate vt ērudīre, īnfōrmāre; **~ in** īnstituere ad (acc)

education n doctrīna f; (process) īnstitūtiō f

eel n anguilla f

eerie adj mōnstruōsus

efface vt dēlēre, tollere

effect n (result) ēventus m; (impression) vīs f, effectus m; (show) iactātiō f; **effects** pl bona ntpl; **for ~** iactātiōnis causā; **in ~** rē vērā; **to this ~** in hanc sententiam; **without ~** inritus ▶ vt efficere, facere, patrāre

effective adj valēns, validus; (RHET) gravis, ōrnātus

effectively adv validē, graviter, ōrnātē

effectiveness n vīs f

effectual adj efficāx, idōneus

effectually adv efficāciter
effectuate vt efficere, cōnsequī
effeminacy n mollitiēs f
effeminate adj mollis, effēminātus
effeminately adv molliter, effēminātē
effervesce vi effervēscere
effete adj effētus
efficacious adj efficāx
efficaciously adv efficāciter
efficacy n vīs f
efficiency n virtūs f, perītia f
efficient adj capāx, perītus; (LOGIC) efficiēns
efficiently adv perītē, bene
effigy n simulācrum nt, effigiēs f
effloresce vi flōrēscere
efflorescence n (fig) flōs m
effluvium n hālitus m
effort n opera f, cōnātus m; (of mind) intentiō f;
make an ~ ēnītī
effrontery n audācia f, impudentia f
effusive adj officiōsus
egg n ōvum nt; lay an egg ōvum parere ▸ vt
impellere, īnstīgāre
egoism n amor suī m
egoist n suī amāns m
egotism n iactātiō f
egotist n glōriōsus m
egregious adj singulāris
egress n exitus m
eight num octō; ~ each octōnī; ~ times octiēns
eighteen num duodēvīgintī
eighteenth adj duodēvīcēsimus
eighth adj octāvus
eight hundred num octingentī
eight hundredth adj octingentēsimus
eightieth adj octōgēsimus
eighty num octōgintā; ~ each octōgēnī; ~ times
octōgiēns
either pron alteruter, uterlibet, utervīs ▸ conj
aut, vel; ~ ... or aut ... aut, vel ... vel
ejaculation n clāmor m
eject vt ēicere, expellere
ejection n expulsiō f
eke vt: eke out parcendō prōdūcere
elaborate vt ēlabōrāre ▸ adj ēlabōrātus,
exquīsītus
elaborately adv summō labōre, exquīsītē
elan n ferōcia f
elapse vi abīre, intercēdere; allow to ~
intermittere; a year has elapsed since annus
est cum (+ indic)
elated adj ēlātus; be ~ efferrī
elation n laetitia f
elbow n cubitum nt
elder adj nātū māior, senior ▸ n (tree) sambūcus f
elderly adj aetāte prōvectus
elders npl patrēs mpl
eldest adj nātū māximus
elecampane n inula f
elect vt ēligere, dēligere; (magistrate) creāre;
(colleague) cooptāre ▸ adj dēsignātus;
(special) lēctus

election n (POL) comitia ntpl
electioneering n ambitiō f
elector n suffrāgātor m
elegance n ēlegantia f, lepōs m, munditia f,
concinnitās f
elegant adj ēlegāns, concinnus, nitidus
elegantly adv ēleganter, concinnē
elegiac adj: ~ verse elegī mpl, versūs alternī mpl
elegy n elegīa f
element n elementum nt; **elements** pl initia
ntpl, prīncipia ntpl; out of one's ~ peregrīnus
elementary adj prīmus
elephant n elephantus m, elephas m
elevate vt efferre, ērigere
elevated adj ēditus, altus
elevation n altitūdō f; (style) ēlātiō f
eleven num ūndecim; ~ each ūndēnī; ~ times
ūndeciēns
eleventh adj ūndecimus
elf n deus m
elicit vt ēlicere; (with effort) ēruere
elide vt ēlīdere
eligible adj idōneus, aptus
eliminate vt tollere, āmovēre
elite n flōs m, rōbur nt
elk n alcēs f
ell n ulna f
ellipse n (RHET) dētractiō f; (oval) ōvum nt
elm n ulmus f ▸ adj ulmeus
elocution n prōnūntiātiō f
elongate vt prōdūcere
elope vi aufugere
eloquence n ēloquentia f; (natural) fācundia f,
dīcendī vīs f
eloquent adj ēloquēns; (natural) fācundus;
(fluent) disertus
eloquently adv fācundē, disertē
else adv aliōquī, aliter ▸ adj alius; or ~ aliōquī;
who ~ quis alius
elsewhere adv alibī; ~ to aliō
elucidate vt ēnōdāre, illūstrāre
elucidation n ēnōdātiō f, explicātiō f
elude vt ēvītāre, frustrārī, fallere
elusive adj fallāx
emaciated adj macer
emaciation n maciēs f
emanate vi mānāre; (fig) ēmānāre, orīrī
emanation n exhālātiō f
emancipate vt ēmancipāre, manū mittere,
līberāre
emancipation n lībertās f
emasculate vt ēnervāre, dēlumbāre
embalm vt condīre
embankment n agger m, mōlēs f
embargo n interdictum nt
embark vi cōnscendere, nāvem cōnscendere;
~ upon (fig) ingredī ▸ vt impōnere
embarkation n cōnscēnsiō f
embarrass vt (by confusing) perturbāre; (by
obstructing) impedīre; (by revealing)
dēprehendere; be embarrassed haerēre
embarrassing adj incommodus, intempestīvus

embarrassment n (in speech) haesitātiō f; (in mind) sollicitūdō f; (in business) angustiae fpl, difficultās f; (cause) molestia f, impedīmentum nt
embassy n lēgātiō f
embedded adj dēfīxus
embellish vt adōrnāre, exōrnāre, decorāre
embellishment n decus nt, exōrnātiō f, ōrnāmentum nt
embers n cinis m, favilla f
embezzle vt pecūlārī, dēpecūlārī
embezzlement n pecūlātus m
embezzler n pecūlātor m
embitter vt exacerbāre
emblazon vt īnsignīre
emblem n īnsigne nt
embodiment n exemplar nt
embody vt repraesentāre; (MIL) cōnscrībere
embolden vt cōnfirmāre; ~ the hearts of animōs cōnfirmāre
emboss vt imprimere, caelāre
embrace vt amplectī, complectī; (items) continēre, comprehendere; (party) sequī; (opportunity) adripere ▶ n amplexus m, complexus m
embroider vt acū pingere
embroidery n vestis picta f
embroil vt miscēre, implicāre
emend vt ēmendāre, corrigere
emendation n ēmendātiō f, corrēctiō f
emerald n smaragdus m
emerge vi ēmergere, exsistere; ēgredī
emergency n tempus nt, discrīmen nt ▶ adj subitārius
emigrate vi migrāre, ēmigrāre
emigration n migrātiō f
eminence n (ground) tumulus m, locus ēditus m; (rank) praestantia f, amplitūdō f
eminent adj ēgregius, ēminēns, īnsignis, amplus
eminently adv ēgregiē, prae cēterīs, in prīmīs
emissary n lēgātus m
emit vt ēmittere
emolument n lucrum nt, ēmolumentum nt
emotion n animī mōtus m, commōtiō f, adfectus m
emotional adj (person) mōbilis; (speech) flexanimus
emperor n prīnceps m, imperātor m
emphasis n pondus nt; (words) impressiō f
emphasize vt exprimere
emphatic adj gravis
emphatically adv adsevēranter, vehementer
empire n imperium nt
employ vt ūtī (abl); (for purpose) adhibēre; (person) exercēre
employed adj occupātus
employees npl operae fpl
employer n redemptor m
employment n (act) ūsus m; (work) quaestus m
empower vt permittere (dat), potestātem facere (dat)

emptiness n inānitās f
empty adj inānis, vacuus; (fig) vānus, inritus ▶ vt exhaurīre, exinānīre ▶ vi (river) īnfluere
emulate vt aemulārī
emulation n aemulātiō f
emulous adj aemulus
emulously adv certātim
enable vt potestātem facere (dat); efficere ut (subj)
enact vt dēcernere, ēdīcere, scīscere; (part) agere
enactment n dēcrētum nt, lēx f
enamoured adj amāns; be ~ of dēamāre
encamp vi castra pōnere, tendere
encampment n castra ntpl
encase vt inclūdere
enchant vt fascināre; (fig) dēlectāre
enchantment n fascinātiō f; blandīmentum nt
enchantress n sāga f
encircle vt cingere, circumdare, amplectī
enclose vt inclūdere, saepīre
enclosure n saeptum nt, māceria f
encompass vt cingere, circumdare, amplectī
encounter vt obviam īre (dat), occurrere (dat); (in battle) concurrere cum (abl), congredī cum ▶ n occursus m, concursus m
encourage vt cōnfirmāre, (co)hortārī, sublevāre, favēre (dat)
encouragement n hortātiō f, favor m, auxilium nt
encroach vi invādere; ~ upon occupāre; (fig) imminuere
encrust vt incrustāre
encumber vt impedīre, onerāre
encumbrance n impedīmentum nt, onus nt
end n fīnis m; (aim) prōpositum nt; (of action) ēventus m, exitus m; (of speech) (time) exāctus; put an end to fīnem facere (dat), fīnem impōnere (dat); to the end that eō cōnsiliō ut (subj); to what end? quō?, quōrsum? ▶ vt fīnīre, cōnficere; (mutual dealings) dīrimere ▶ vi dēsinere; (event) ēvādere; (sentence) cadere; (speech) perōrāre; (time) exīre; end up as ēvādere; end with dēsinere in (acc)
endanger vt perīclitārī, in discrīmen addūcere
endear vt dēvincīre
endearing adj blandus
endearment n blanditiae fpl
endeavour vt cōnārī, ēnītī ▶ n cōnātus m
ending n fīnis m, exitus m
endive n intubum nt
endless adj īnfīnītus; (time) aeternus, perpetuus
endlessly adv sine fīne, īnfīnītē
endorse vt ratum facere
endow vt dōnāre, īnstruere
endowed adj praeditus (abl)
endowment n dōnum nt
endurance n patientia f

endure vi dūrāre, permanēre ▸ vt ferre, tolerāre, patī

enemy n (public) hostis m, hostēs mpl; (private) inimīcus m; **greatest ~** inimīcissimus m; **~ territory** hosticum nt

energetic adj impiger, nāvus, strēnuus; (style) nervōsus

energetically adv impigrē, nāviter, strēnuē

energy n impigritās f, vigor m, incitātiō f; (mind) contentiō f; (style) nervī mpl

enervate vt ēnervāre, ēmollīre

enervation n languor m

enfeeble vt īnfirmāre, dēbilitāre

enfold vt involvere, complectī

enforce vt (LAW) exsequī; (argument) cōnfirmāre

enfranchise vt cīvitāte dōnāre; (slave) manū mittere

engage vt (affection) dēvincīre; (attention) distinēre, occupāre; (enemy) manum cōnserere cum (abl); (hire) condūcere; (promise) spondēre, recipere; **~ the enemy** proelium cum hostibus committere; **be engaged in** versārī in (abl) ▸ vi: **~ in** ingredī, suscipere

engagement n (COMM) occupātiō f; (MIL) pugna f, certāmen nt; (agreement) spōnsiō f; **keep an ~** fidem praestāre; **break an ~** fidem fallere; **I have an ~ at your house** prōmīsī ad tē

engaging adj blandus

engender vt ingenerāre, ingignere

engine n māchina f

engineer n māchinātor m ▸ vt mōlīrī

engraft vt īnserere

engrave vt īnsculpere, incīdere, caelāre

engraver n sculptor m, caelātor m

engraving n sculptūra f, caelātūra f

engross vt dīstringere, occupāre; **engrossed in** tōtus in (abl)

engulf vt dēvorāre, obruere

enhance vt augēre, amplificāre, exaggerāre

enigma n aenigma nt, ambāgēs fpl

enigmatic adj ambiguus, obscūrus

enigmatically adv per ambāgēs, ambiguē

enjoin vt imperāre (dat), iniungere (dat)

enjoy vt fruī (abl); (advantage) ūtī (abl); (pleasure) percipere, dēcerpere; **~ oneself** dēlectārī, geniō indulgēre

enjoyable adj iūcundus

enjoyment n fructus m; dēlectātiō f, voluptās f

enlarge vt augēre, amplificāre, dīlātāre; (territory) prōpāgāre; **~ upon** amplificāre

enlargement n amplificātiō f, prōlātiō f

enlighten vt inlūstrāre; docēre, ērudīre

enlightenment n ērudītiō f, hūmānitās f

enlist vt scrībere, cōnscrībere; (sympathy) conciliāre ▸ vi nōmen dare

enliven vt excitāre

enmesh vt impedīre, implicāre

enmity n inimīcitia f, simultās f

ennoble vt honestāre, excolere

ennui n taedium nt

enormity n immānitās f; (deed) scelus nt, nefās nt

enormous adj immānis, ingēns

enormously adv immēnsum

enough adj satis (indecl, gen) ▸ adv satis; **more than ~** satis superque; **I have had ~ of …** mē taedet (gen) …

enquire vi quaerere, percontārī; **~ into** cognōscere, inquīrere in (acc)

enquiry n percontātiō f; (legal) quaestiō f

enrage vt inrītāre, incendere

enrapture vt dēlectāre

enrich vt dītāre, locuplētāre; **~ with** augēre (abl)

enrol vt adscrībere, cōnscrībere ▸ vi nōmen dare

enshrine vt dēdicāre; (fig) sacrāre

enshroud vt involvere

ensign n signum nt, īnsigne nt; (officer) signifer m

enslave vt in servitūtem redigere

enslavement n servitūs f

ensnare vt dēcipere, inlaqueāre, inrētīre

ensue vi īnsequī

ensure vt praestāre; **~ that** efficere ut (subj)

entail vt adferre

entangle vt impedīre, implicāre, inrētīre

entanglement n implicātiō f

enter vi inīre, ingredī, intrāre; (riding) invehī; **~ into** introīre in (acc); **~ upon** inīre, ingredī ▸ vt (place) intrāre; (account) ferre, indūcere; (mind) subīre

enterprise n inceptum nt; (character) prōmptus animus m

enterprising adj prōmptus, strēnuus

entertain vt (guest) invītāre, excipere; (state of mind) habēre, concipere; (to amuse) oblectāre

entertainer n acroāma nt

entertainment n hospitium nt; oblectāmentum nt; acroāma nt

enthral vt capere

enthusiasm n studium nt, fervor m; **~ for** studium nt (gen)

enthusiastic adj studiōsus, fervidus

enthusiastically adv summō studiō

entice vt inlicere, ēlicere, invītāre

enticement n illecebra f, lēnōcinium nt

entire adj integer, tōtus, ūniversus

entirely adv omnīnō, funditus, penitus

entitle vt (book) īnscrībere; **be entitled to** merērī, dignum esse quī (subj), iūs habēre (gen)

entity n rēs f

entomb vt humāre, sepelīre

entrails n intestīna ntpl, exta ntpl

entrance n aditus m, introitus m; (act) ingressiō f; (of house) vestibulum nt; (of harbour) ōstium nt ▸ vt fascināre, cōnsōpīre, capere

entreat vt implōrāre, obsecrāre; (successfully) exōrāre

entreaty n precēs fpl

entrenchment n mūnītiō f

entrust vt committere, crēdere, mandāre; (for keeping) dēpōnere

entry n introitus m, aditus m; **make an ~** (book) in tabulās referre

entwine vt implicāre, involvere

enumerate vt numerāre, dīnumerāre
enunciate vt ēdīcere; (word) exprimere
envelop vt implicāre, involvere
envelope n involucrum nt
enviable adj beātus
envious adj invidus, invidiōsus
enviously adv invidiōsē
environment n vīcīnia f; **our ~** ea in quibus versāmur
envoy n lēgātus m
envy n invidia f ▶ vt invidēre (dat)
enwrap vt involvere
ephemeral adj brevis
ephor n ephorus m
epic adj epicus ▶ n epos nt
epicure n dēlicātus m
epigram n sententia f; (poem) epigramma nt
epilepsy n morbus comitiālis m
epilogue n epilogus m
episode n ēventum nt
epistle n epistula f, litterae fpl
epitaph n epigramma nt, titulus m
epithet n adsūmptum nt
epitome n epitomē f
epoch n saeculum nt
equable adj aequālis; (temper) aequus
equal adj aequus, pār; **be ~ to** aequāre; (task) sufficere (dat) ▶ n pār m/f ▶ vt aequāre, adaequāre
equality n aequālitās f
equalize vt adaequāre, exaequāre
equally adv aequē, pariter
equanimity n aequus animus m
equate vt aequāre
equator n aequinoctiālis circulus m
equestrian adj equester
equidistant adj: **be ~** aequō spatiō abesse, idem distāre
equilibrium n lībrāmentum nt
equine adj equīnus
equinoctial adj aequinoctiālis
equinox n aequinoctium nt
equip vt armāre, īnstruere, ōrnāre
equipment n arma ntpl, īnstrūmenta ntpl, adparātus m
equipoise n lībrāmentum nt
equitable adj aequus, iūstus
equitably adv iūstē, aequē
equity n aequum nt, aequitās f
equivalent adj pār, īdem īnstar (gen)
equivocal adj anceps, ambiguus
equivocally adv ambiguē
equivocate vi tergiversārī
era n saeculum nt
eradicate vt ēvellere, exstirpāre
erase vt dēlēre, indūcere
erasure n litūra f
ere conj priusquam
erect vt ērigere; (building) exstruere; (statute) pōnere ▶ adj ērēctus
erection n (process) exstructiō f; (product) aedificium nt

erode vt rōdere
erotic adj amātōrius
err vi errāre, peccāre
errand n mandātum nt
errant adj vagus
erratic adj incōnstāns
erroneous adj falsus
erroneously adv falsō, perperam
error n error m; (moral) peccātum nt; (writing) mendum nt
erudite adj doctus
erudition n doctrīna f, ērudītiō f
erupt vi ērumpere
eruption n ēruptiō f
escapade n ausum nt
escape vi effugere, ēvādere ▶ vt fugere, ēvītāre; (memory) excidere ex (abl); **~ the notice of** fallere, praeterīre ▶ n effugium nt, fuga f; **way of ~** effugium nt
eschew vt vītāre
escort n praesidium nt; (private) dēductor m ▶ vt comitārī, prōsequī; (out of respect) dēdūcere
especial adj praecipuus
especially adv praecipuē, praesertim, māximē, in prīmīs
espionage n inquīsītiō f
espouse vt (wife) dūcere; (cause) fovēre
espy vt cōnspicere, cōnspicārī
essay n cōnātus m; (test) perīculum nt; (LIT) libellus m ▶ vt cōnārī, incipere
essence n vīs f, nātūra f
essential adj necesse, necessārius
essentially adv necessāriō
establish vt īnstituere, condere; (firmly) stabilīre
established adj firmus, certus; **be ~** cōnstāre; **become ~** (custom) inveterāscere
establishment n (act) cōnstitūtiō f; (domestic) familia f
estate n fundus m, rūs nt; (in money) rēs f; (rank) ōrdō m
esteem vt aestimāre, respicere ▶ n grātia f, opīniō f
estimable adj optimus
estimate vt aestimāre, ratiōnem inīre (gen) ▶ n aestimātiō f, iūdicium nt
estimation n opīniō f, sententia f
estrange vt aliēnāre, abaliēnāre
estrangement n aliēnātiō f, discidium nt
estuary n aestuārium nt
eternal adj aeternus, perennis
eternally adv semper, aeternum
eternity n aeternitās f
etesian winds n etēsiae fpl
ether n (sky) aethēr m
ethereal adj aetherius, caelestis
ethic, ethical adj mōrālis
ethics n mōrēs mpl, officia ntpl
Etruscan n Etruscus m ▶ adj Etruscus
etymology n verbōrum notātiō f
eulogist n laudātor m
eulogize vt laudāre, conlaudāre

eulogy n laudātiō f

eunuch n eunūchus m

euphony n sonus m

evacuate vt (place) exinānīre; (people) dēdūcere

evacuation n discessiō f

evade vt dēclīnāre, dēvītāre, ēlūdere

evaporate vt exhālāre ▶ vi exhālārī

evaporation n exhālātiō f

evasion n tergiversātiō f

evasive adj ambiguus

eve n vesper m; (before festival) pervigilium nt; **on the eve of** prīdiē (gen)

even adj aequus, aequālis; (number) pār ▶ adv et, etiam; (tentative) vel; **~ if** etsī, etiamsī; tametsī; **~ more** etiam magis; **so** nihilōminus; **~ yet** etiamnum; **not ~ ...** nē quidem ▶ vt aequāre

evening n vesper m ▶ adj vespertīnus; **~ is drawing on** invesperāscit; **in the ~** vesperī

evening star n Vesper m, Hesperus m

evenly adv aequāliter, aequābiliter

evenness n aequālitās f, aequābilitās f

event n ēventum nt; (outcome) ēventus m

eventide n vespertīnum tempus nt

eventuality n cāsus m

eventually adv mox, aliquandō, tandem

ever adv unquam; (after sī, nisī, num, nē) quandō; (always) semper; (after interrog) -nam, tandem; ever so nimium, nimium quantum; **best ~** omnium optimus; **for ~** in aeternum

everlasting adj aeternus, perpetuus, immortālis

evermore adv semper, in aeternum

every adj quisque, omnis; **~ four years** quintō quōque annō; **~ now and then** interdum; **in ~ direction** passim, undique; **~ other day** alternis diebus; **~ day** cottīdiē ▶ adj cottīdiānus

everybody pron quisque, omnēs mpl; **~ agrees** inter omnēs constat; **~ knows** nēmō est quīn sciat

everyday adj cottīdiānus

everyone pron see **everybody**

everything omnia ntpl; **your health is ~ to me** meā māximē interest tē valēre

everywhere adv ubīque, passim

evict vt dēicere, dētrūdere

eviction n dēiectiō f

evidence n testimōnium nt, indicium nt; (person) testis m/f; (proof) argūmentum nt; **on the ~ of** fidē (gen); **collect ~ against** inquīrere in (acc); **turn King's ~** indicium profitērī

evident adj manifestus, ēvidēns, clārus; **it is ~** appāret

evidently adv manifestō, clārē

evil adj malus, improbus, scelerātus

evildoer n scelerātus m, maleficus m

evil eye n fascinum nt, malum nt, improbitās f

evil-minded adj malevolus

evince vt praestāre

evoke vt ēvocāre, ēlicere

evolution n seriēs f, prōgressus m; (MIL) dēcursus m, dēcursiō f

evolve vt explicāre, ēvolvere ▶ vi crēscere

ewe n ovis f

ewer n hydria f

exacerbate vt exacerbāre, exasperāre

exact vt exigere ▶ adj accūrātus; (person) dīligēns; (number) exāctus

exaction n exāctiō f

exactly adv accūrātē; (reply) ita prōrsus; **~ as** perinde que

exactness n cūra f, dīligentia f

exaggerate vt augēre, in māius extollere

exalt vt efferre, extollere; laudāre

exaltation n ēlātiō f

examination n inquīsītiō f, scrūtātiō f; (of witness) interrogātiō f; (test) probātiō f

examine vt investīgāre, scrūtārī; īnspicere; (witness) interrogāre; (case) quaerere dē (abl); (candidate) probāre

examiner n scrūtātor m

example n exemplum nt, documentum nt; **for ~** exemplī grātiā; **make an ~ of** animadvertere in (acc); **I am an ~** exemplō sum

exasperate vt exacerbāre, inrītāre

exasperation n inrītātiō f

excavate vt fodere

excavation n fossiō f

excavator n fossor m

exceed vt excēdere, superāre

exceedingly adv nimis, valdē, nimium quantum

excel vt praestāre (dat), exsuperāre ▶ vi excellere

excellence n praestantia f, virtūs f

excellent adj ēgregius, praestāns, optimus

excellently adv ēgregiē, praeclārē

except vt excipere ▶ prep praeter (acc) ▶ adv nisī ▶ conj praeterquam, nisī quod

exception n exceptiō f; **make an ~ of** excipere; **take ~ to** gravārī quod; **with the ~ of** praeter (acc)

exceptional adj ēgregius, eximius

exceptionally adv ēgregiē, eximiē

excerpt vt excerpere ▶ n excerptum nt

excess n immoderātiō f, intemperantia f ▶ adj supervacāneus; **be in ~** superesse

excessive adj immoderātus, immodestus, nimius

excessively adv immodicē, nimis

exchange vt mūtāre, permūtāre ▶ n permūtātiō f; (of currencies) collybus m

exchequer n aerārium nt; (emperor's) fiscus m

excise n vectīgālia ntpl ▶ vt excīdere

excision n excīsiō f

excitable adj mōbilis

excite vt excitāre, concitāre; (to action) incitāre, incendere; (to hope) ērigere, exacuere; (emotion) movēre, commovēre

excitement n commōtiō f

exclaim vt exclāmāre; **~ against** adclāmāre (dat)

exclamation n clāmor m, exclāmātiō f

exclude vt exclūdere

exclusion n exclūsiō f

exclusive adj proprius

exclusively *adv* sōlum
excogitate *vt* excōgitāre
excrescence *n* tūber *nt*
excruciating *adj* acerbissimus
exculpate *vt* pūrgāre, absolvere
excursion *n* iter *nt*; (*MIL*) excursiō *f*
excuse *n* excūsātiō *f*; (*false*) speciēs *f* ▶ *vt* excūsāre, ignōscere (*dat*); (*something due*) remittere; **plead in ~** excūsāre; **put forward as an ~** praetendere
execrable *adj* dētestābilis, sacer, nefārius
execrate *vt* dētestārī, exsecrārī
execration *n* dētestātiō *f*, exsecrātiō *f*
execute *vt* efficere, patrāre, exsequī; suppliciō afficere; (*behead*) secūrī percutere
execution *n* effectus *m*; (*penalty*) supplicium *nt*, mors *f*
executioner *n* carnifex *m*
exemplar *n* exemplum *nt*
exempt *adj* immūnis, līber ▶ *vt* līberāre
exemption *n* (*from tax*) immūnitās *f*; (*from service*) vacātiō *f*
exercise *n* exercitātiō *f*, ūsus *m*; (*school*) dictāta *ntpl* ▶ *vt* exercēre, ūtī (*abl*); (*mind*) acuere
exert *vt* extendere, intendere, ūtī (*abl*); **~ oneself** mōlīrī, ēnītī, sē intendere
exertion *n* mōlīmentum *nt*; (*mind*) intentiō *f*
exhalation *n* exhālātiō *f*, vapor *m*
exhale *vt* exhālāre, exspīrāre
exhaust *vt* exhaurīre; (*tire*) dēfatīgāre, cōnficere
exhaustion *n* dēfatīgātiō *f*
exhaustive *adj* plēnus
exhibit *vt* exhibēre, ostendere, expōnere; (*on stage*) ēdere
exhibition *n* expositiō *f*, ostentātiō *f*
exhilarate *vt* exhilarāre
exhort *vt* hortārī, cohortārī
exhortation *n* hortātiō *f*, hortāmen *nt*
exhume *vt* ēruere
exigency *n* necessitās *f*
exile *n* exsilium *nt*, fuga *f*; (*temporary*) relēgātiō *f*; (*person*) exsul *m*; **live in ~** exsulāre ▶ *vt* in exsilium pellere, dēportāre; (*temporarily*) relēgāre
exist *vi* esse
existence *n* vīta *f*
exit *n* exitus *m*, ēgressus *m*
exodus *n* discessus *m*
exonerate *vt* absolvere
exorbitant *adj* nimius, immoderātus
exotic *adj* peregrīnus
expand *vt* extendere, dīlātāre
expanse *n* spatium *nt*, lātitūdō *f*
expatiate *vi*: **~ upon** amplificāre
expatriate *vt* extermināre ▶ *n* extorris *m*
expect *vt* exspectāre, spērāre
expectancy, expectation *n* spēs *f*, exspectātiō *f*; opīniō *f*
expediency *n* ūtile *nt*, ūtilitās *f*
expedient *adj* ūtilis, commodus; **it is ~** expedit ▶ *n* modus *m*, ratiō *f*

expediently *adv* commodē
expedite *vt* mātūrāre
expedition *n* (*MIL*) expedītiō *f*
expeditious *adj* prōmptus, celer
expeditiously *adv* celeriter
expel *vt* pellere, expellere, ēicere
expend *vt* impendere, expendere
expenditure *n* impēnsae *fpl*, sūmptus *m*
expense *n* impēnsae *fpl*, impendia *ntpl*; **at my ~** meō sūmptū; **at the public ~** dē pūblicō
expensive *adj* cārus, pretiōsus; (*furnishings*) lautus
expensively *adv* sūmptuōsē, māgnō pretiō
experience *n* ūsus *m*, experientia *f* ▶ *vt* experīrī, patī
experienced *adj* perītus, expertus (*gen*)
experiment *n* experīmentum *nt* ▶ *vi*: **~ with** experīrī
expert *adj* perītus, sciēns
expertly *adv* perītē, scienter
expertness *n* perītia *f*
expiate *vt* expiāre, luere
expiation *n* (*act*) expiātiō *f*; (*penalty*) piāculum *nt*
expiatory *adj* piāculāris
expiration *n* (*breath*) exspīrātiō *f*; (*time*) exitus *m*
expire *vi* exspīrāre; (*die*) animam agere, animam efflāre; (*time*) exīre
expiry *n* exitus *m*, fīnis *m*
explain *vt* explicāre, expōnere, explānāre, interpretārī; (*lucidly*) ēnōdāre; (*in detail*) ēdisserere
explanation *n* explicātiō *f*, ēnōdātiō *f*, interpretātiō *f*
explicit *adj* expressus, apertus
explicitly *adv* apertē
explode *vt* discutere ▶ *vi* dīrumpī
exploit *n* factum *nt*, ausum *nt*; **exploits** *pl* rēs gestae *fpl* ▶ *vt* ūtī (*abl*), fruī (*abl*)
explore *vt, vi* explōrāre, scrūtārī
explorer *n* explōrātor *m*
explosion *n* fragor *m*
exponent *n* interpres *m*, auctor *m*
export *vt* exportāre ▶ *n* exportātiō *f*
exportation *n* exportātiō *f*
expose *vt* dētegere, dēnūdāre, patefacere; (*child*) expōnere; (*to danger*) obicere; (*MIL*) nūdāre; (*for sale*) prōpōnere; **~ oneself** sē obicere
exposed *adj* apertus, obnoxius
exposition *n* explicātiō *f*, interpretātiō *f*
expostulate *vi* expostulāre, conquerī
expostulation *n* expostulātiō *f*
exposure *n* (*of child*) expositiō *f*; (*of guilt*) dēprehēnsiō *f*; (*to hardship*) patientia *f*
expound *vt* expōnere, interpretārī
expounder *n* interpres *m*
express *vt* (*in words*) exprimere, dēclārāre, ēloquī; (*in art*) effingere ▶ *adj* expressus; (*speed*) celerrimus
expression *n* significātiō *f*; (*word*) vōx *f*, verbum *nt*; (*face*) vultus *m*

expressive *adj* significāns; **~ of** index (*gen*);
be very **~** māximam vim habēre
expressively *adv* significanter
expressiveness *n* vīs *f*
expressly *adv* plānē
expulsion *n* expulsiō *f*, ēiectiō *f*
expurgate *vt* pūrgāre
exquisite *adj* ēlegāns, exquīsītus, eximius;
(*judgment*) subtīlis
exquisitely *adv* ēleganter, exquīsītē
ex-service *adj* ēmeritus
extant *adj* superstes; **be ~** exstāre
extempore *adv* ex tempore, subitō ▸ *adj*
extemporālis
extemporize *vi* subita dīcere
extend *vt* extendere, dīlātāre; (*hand*) porrigere;
(*line*) dūcere; (*office*) prōrogāre; (*territory*)
propāgāre ▸ *vi* patēre, porrigī; **~ into** incurrere
in (*acc*)
extension *n* prōductiō *f*, prōlātiō *f*; (*of office*)
prōrogātiō *f*; (*of territory*) propāgātiō *f*; (*extra*)
incrēmentum *nt*
extensive *adj* effūsus, amplus, lātus
extensively *adv* lātē
extent *n* spatium *nt*, amplitūdō *f*; **to a large ~**
māgnā ex parte; **to some ~** aliquā ex parte;
to this ~ hāctenus; **to such an ~** adeō
extenuate *vt* levāre, mītigāre
exterior *adj* externus, exterior ▸ *n* speciēs *f*
exterminate *vt* occīdiōne occīdere, interimere
extermination *n* occīdiō *f*, interneciō *f*
external *adj* externus
externally *adv* extrīnsecus
extinct *adj* mortuus; (*custom*) obsolētus
extinction *n* exstinctiō *f*, interitus *m*
extinguish *vt* exstinguere, restinguere
extinguisher *n* exstinctor *m*
extirpate *vt* exstirpāre, excīdere
extol *vt* laudāre, laudibus efferre
extort *vt* extorquēre, exprimere
extortion *n* (*offence*) rēs repetundae *fpl*
extortionate *adj* inīquus, rapāx
extra *adv* īnsuper, praetereā ▸ *adj* additus
extract *vt* excerpere, extrahere ▸ *n*: **make
extracts** excerpere
extraction *n* ēvulsiō *f*; (*descent*) genus *nt*
extraneous *adj* adventīcius, aliēnus
extraordinarily *adv* mīrificē, eximiē
extraordinary *adj* extraōrdinārius; (*strange*)
mīrus, novus; (*outstanding*) eximius, īnsignis
extravagance *n* intemperantia *f*; (*language*)
immoderātiō *f*, luxuria *f*; (*spending*) sūmptus *m*
extravagant *adj* immoderātus, immodestus;
(*spending*) sūmptuōsus, prōdigus
extreme *adj* extrēmus, ultimus
extremely *adv* valdē, vehementer
extremity *n* extrēmum *nt*, fīnis *m*; (*distress*)
angustiae *fpl*; **the ~ of** extrēmus
extricate *vt* expedīre, absolvere; **~ oneself**
ēmergere
exuberance *n* ūbertās *f*, luxuria *f*
exuberant *adj* ūber, laetus, luxuriōsus

exuberantly *adv* ūbertim
exude *vt* exsūdāre ▸ *vi* mānāre
exult *vi* exsultārī, laetārī, gestīre
exultant *adj* laetus
exultantly *adv* laetē
exultation *n* laetitia *f*
eye *n* oculus *m*; (*needle*) forāmen *nt*; **cast eyes on**
oculōs conicere in (*acc*); **have an eye to**
spectāre; **in your eyes** iūdice tē; **keep one's
eyes on** oculōs dēfigere in (*abl*); **lose an eye**
alterō oculō capī; **see eye to eye** cōnsentīre;
set eyes on cōnspicere; **shut one's eyes to**
cōnīvēre in (*abl*); **take one's eyes off** oculōs
dēicere ab (*abl*); **up to the eyes in** tōtus in (*abl*);
with a cast in the eye paetus; **with sore eyes**
lippus; **sore eyes** lippitūdō *f*; **with one's own
eyes** cōram; **with one's eyes open** sciēns ▸ *vt*
intuērī, aspicere
eyeball *n* pūpula *f*
eyebrow *n* supercilium *nt*
eyelash *n* palpebrae pilus *m*
eyelid *n* palpebra *f*
eyeshot *n* oculōrum coniectus *m*
eyesight *n* aciēs *f*, oculī *mpl*
eyesore *n* turpe *nt*; **it is an ~ to me** oculī meī
dolent
eye tooth *n* dēns canīnus *m*
eyewash *n* sycophantia *f*
eyewitness *n* arbiter *m*; **be an ~ of**
interesse (*dat*)

f

fable n fābula f, apologus m
fabled adj fābulōsus
fabric n (built) structūra f; (woven) textile nt
fabricate vt fabricārī, (fig) comminīscī, fingere
fabricated adj commentīcius
fabrication n (process) fabricātiō f; (thing) commentum nt
fabricator n auctor m
fabulous adj commentīcius, fictus
fabulously adv incrēdibiliter
facade n frōns f
face n faciēs, ōs nt; (aspect) aspectus m; (impudence) ōs nt; **~ to ~** cōram; **how shall I have the ~ to go back?** quō ōre redībō?; **on the ~ of it** ad speciem, prīmō aspectū; **put a bold ~ on** fortem sē praebēre; **save ~** factum pūrgāre; **set one's ~ against** adversārī (dat) ▶ vt spectāre ad (acc); (danger) obviam īre (dat), sē oppōnere (dat) ▶ vi (place) spectāre, vergere; **~ about** (MIL) signa convertere
facetious adj facētus, salsus
facetiously adv facētē, salsē
facetiousness n facētiae fpl, salēs mpl
facile adj facilis
facilitate vt expedīre
facilities npl opportūnitās f
facility n facilitās f
facing adj adversus ▶ prep exadversus (acc)
facsimile n exemplār nt
fact n rēs f, vērum nt; **as a matter of ~** enimvērō; **the ~ that** quod; **in ~** rē vērā ▶ conj etenim; (climax) dēnique
faction n factiō f
factious adj factiōsus, sēditiōsus
factiously adv sēditiōsē
factor n prōcūrātor m
factory n officīna f
faculty n facultās f, vīs f
fad n libīdō f
fade vi dēflōrēscere, marcēscere
faded adj marcidus
faggot n (twigs) sarmentum nt
fail vi dēficere, dēesse; (fig) cadere, dēcidere; (in business) forō cēdere; **~ to** nōn posse; **~ to come**

nōn venīre ▶ vt dēficere, dēstituere
failing n culpa f, vitium nt
failure n (of supply) dēfectiō f; (in action) offēnsiō f; (at election) repulsa f
fain adv libenter
faint adj (body) languidus, dēfessus; (impression) hebes, levis; (courage) timidus; (colour) pallidus; **be ~** languēre; hebēre ▶ vi intermorī, animō linquī; **I feel ~** animō male est
faint-hearted adj animo dēmissus; timidus
faintly adv languidē; leviter
faintness n dēfectiō f, languor m; levitās f
fair adj (appearance) pulcher, fōrmōsus; (hair) flāvus; (skin) candidus; (weather) serēnus; (wind) secundus; (copy) pūrus; (dealings) aequus; (speech) speciōsus, blandus; (ability) mediocris; (reputation) bonus ▶ n nūndinae fpl; **~ and square** sine fūcō ac fallāciīs
fairly adv iūre, iūstē; mediocriter
fairness n aequitās f
fair play n aequum et bonum nt
fairy n nympha f
faith n fidēs f; **in good ~** bonā fidē
faithful adj fidēlis, fīdus
faithfully adv fidēliter
faithfulness n fidēlitās f
faithless adj īnfidēlis, īnfīdus, perfidus
faithlessly adv īnfidēliter
faithlessness n īnfidēlitās f
fake vt simulāre
falchion n falx f
falcon n falcō m
fall vi cadere; (gently) lābī; (morally) prōlābī; (dead) concidere, occidere; (fortress) expugnārī, capī; **~ at** accidere; **~ away** dēficere, dēscīscere; **~ back** recidere; (MIL) pedem referre; **~ between** intercidere; **~ behind** cessāre; **~ by the way** intercidere; **~ down** dēcidere, dēlābī; (building) ruere, corruere; **~ due** cadere; **~ flat** sē prōsternere; (speech) frīgēre; **~ forward** prōlābī; **~ foul of** incurrere in (acc); **~ headlong** sē praecipitāre; **~ in, ~ into** incidere; **~ in with** occurrere (dat); **~ off** dēcidere; (fig) dēscīscere; **~ on** incumbere in (acc), incidere in (acc); **~ out** excidere; (event) ēvenīre; (hair) dēfluere; **~ short of** deesse ab; **~ to** (by lot) obtingere, obvenīre (dat); **~ to the ground** (case) iacēre; **~ upon** invādere, ingruere in (acc); (someone's neck) in collum invādere ▶ n cāsus m; (building) ruīna f; (moral) lāpsus m; (season) autumnus m; **the ~ of Capua** Capua capta
fallacious adj captiōsus, fallāx
fallaciously adv fallāciter
fallacy n captiō f
fallible adj: **be ~** errāre solēre
fallow adj (land) novālis ▶ n novāle nt; **lie ~** cessāre
false adj falsus, fictus
falsehood n falsum nt, mendācium nt; **tell a ~** mentīrī
falsely adv falsō
falsify vt vitiāre, interlinere

falter vi (speech) haesitāre; (gait) titubāre

faltering adj (speech) īnfrāctus; (gait) titubāns ▸ n haesitātiō f

fame n fāma f, glōria f, nōmen nt

famed adj illūstris, praeclārus

familiar adj (friend) intimus; (fact) nōtus; (manner) cōmis; ~ **spirit** genius m; **be ~ with** nōvisse; **be on ~ terms with** familiāriter ūtī (abl)

familiarity n ūsus m, cōnsuētūdō f

familiarize vt adsuēfacere

familiarly adv familiāriter

family n domus f, gēns f ▸ adj domesticus, familiāris; ~ **property** rēs familiāris f

famine n famēs f

famished adj famēlicus

famous adj illūstris, praeclārus, nōbilis; **make ~** nōbilitāre; **the ~** ille

fan n flābellum nt; (winnowing) vannus f ▸ vt ventilāre; **fan the flames of** (fig) īnflammāre

fanatic n (religious) fānāticus m

fanciful adj (person) incōnstāns; (idea) commentīcius

fancy n (faculty) mēns f; (idea) opīniātiō f; (caprice) libīdō f; **take a ~ to** amāre incipere; ~ **oneself** se amāre ▸ vt animō fingere, imāginārī, sibi prōpōnere; ~ **you thinking …!** tē crēdere …! ▸ adj dēlicātus

fancy-free adj sēcūrus, vacuus

fang n dēns m

fantastic adj commentīcius, mōnstruōsus

fantasy n imāginātiō f; (contemptuous) somnium nt

far adj longinquus ▸ adv longē, procul; (with compar) multō; **be far from** longē abesse ab; **be not far from doing** haud multum abest quīn (subj); **by far** longē; **how far?** quātenus?, quoūsque?; **so far** hāctenus, eātenus; (limited) quādam tenus; **thus far** hāctenus; **far and wide** lātē; **far be it from me to say** equidem dīcere nōlim; **far from thinking …** I adeō nōn crēdō … ut; **as far as** prep tenus (abl) ▸ adv ūsque ▸ conj quātenus; (know) quod

farce n mīmus m

farcical adj rīdiculus

fare vi sē habēre, agere ▸ n vectūra f; (boat) naulum nt; (food) cibus m

farewell interj valē, valēte; **say ~ to** valēre iubēre

far-fetched adj quaesītus, arcessītus, altē repetītus

farm n fundus m, praedium nt ▸ vt (soil) colere; (taxes) redimere; ~ **out** locāre

farmer n agricola m; (of taxes) pūblicānus m

farming n agrīcultūra f

farrow vt parere ▸ n fētus m

far-sighted adj prōvidus, prūdēns

farther adv longius, ultrā ▸ adj ulterior

farthest adj ultimus, extrēmus ▸ adv longissimē

fasces n fascēs mpl

fascinate vt dēlēnīre, capere

fascination n dulcēdō f, dēlēnīmenta ntpl, lēnōcinia ntpl

fashion n mōs m, ūsus m; (manner) modus m, ratiō f; (shape) fōrma f ▸ vt fingere, fōrmāre; **after the ~ of** rītū (gen); **come into ~** in mōrem venīre; **go out of ~** obsolēscere

fashionable adj ēlegāns; **it is ~** mōris est

fashionably adv ēleganter

fast adj (firm) firmus; (quick) celer; **make ~** dēligāre ▸ adv firmē; celeriter; **be ~ asleep** artē dormīre ▸ vi iēiūnus esse, cibō abstinēre ▸ n iēiūnium nt

fasten vt fīgere, ligāre; ~ **down** dēfīgere; ~ **on** inligāre; ~ **to** adligāre; ~ **together** conligāre, cōnfīgere

fastening n iūnctūra f

fastidious adj dēlicātus, ēlegāns

fastidiously adv fastīdiōsē

fastidiousness n fastīdium nt

fasting n iēiūnium nt, inedia f ▸ adj iēiūnus

fastness n arx f, castellum nt

fat adj pinguis, opīmus, obēsus; **grow fat** pinguēscere ▸ n adeps m/f

fatal adj (deadly) fūnestus, exitiābilis; (fated) fātālis

fatality n fātum nt, cāsus m

fatally adv: **be ~ wounded** vulnere perīre

fate n fātum nt, fortūna f, sors f

fated adj fātālis

fateful adj fātālis; fūnestus

Fates npl (goddesses) Parcae fpl

father n pater m; (fig) auctor m ▸ vt gignere; ~ **upon** addīcere, tribuere

father-in-law n socer m

fatherland n patria f

fatherless adj orbus

fatherly adj paternus

fathom n sex pedēs mpl ▸ vt (fig) exputāre

fathomless adj profundus

fatigue n fatīgātiō f, dēfatīgātiō f ▸ vt fatīgāre, dēfatīgāre

fatness n pinguitūdō f

fatten vt sagīnāre

fatty adj pinguis

fatuity n īnsulsitās f, ineptiae fpl

fatuous adj fatuus, īnsulsus, ineptus

fault n culpa f, vitium nt; (written) mendum nt; **count as a ~** vitiō vertere; **find ~ with** incūsāre; **it is not your ~ that …** nōn per tē stat quōminus (subj)

faultily adv vitiōsē, mendōsē

faultiness n vitium nt

faultless adj ēmendātus, integer

faultlessly adv ēmendātē

faulty adj vitiōsus, mendōsus

faun n faunus m

fauna n animālia ntpl

favour n grātia f, favor m; (done) beneficium nt; **win ~ with** grātiam inīre apud; **by your ~** bonā veniā tuā ▸ vt favēre (dat), indulgēre (dat)

favourable adj faustus, prosperus, secundus

favourably adv faustē, fēlīciter, benignē

favourite adj dīlectus, grātissimus ▸ n dēliciae fpl

favouritism n indulgentia f, studium nt
fawn n hinnuleus m ▶ adj (colour) gilvus ▶ vi:
~ **upon** adūlārī
fawning adj blandus ▶ n adūlātiō f
fear n timor m, metus m, formīdō f ▶ vt timēre,
metuere, formīdāre, verērī; **fearing that** veritus
ne (+ imperf subj)
fearful adj timidus; horrendus, terribilis,
formīdolōsus
fearfully adv timidē; formīdolōsē
fearless adj impavidus, intrepidus
fearlessly adv impavidē, intrepidē
fearlessness n fīdentia f, audācia f
fearsome adj formīdolōsus
feasible adj: **it is ~** fierī potest
feast n epulae fpl; (private) convīvium nt; (public)
epulum nt; (religious) daps f; (festival) festus diēs
m ▶ vi epulārī, convīvārī; (fig) pāscī ▶ vt: ~ **one's
eyes on** oculōs pāscere (abl)
feat n factum nt, facinus nt
feather n penna f; (downy) plūma f; **birds of
a ~ flock together** parēs cum paribus facillimē
congregantur
feathered adj pennātus
feathery adj plūmeus
feature n līneāmentum nt; (fig) proprium nt
February n mēnsis Februārius m; **of ~**
Februārius
federal adj sociālis, foederātus
federate vi societātem facere
federated adj foederātus
federation n societās f, foederātae cīvitātēs fpl
fee n honōs m, mercēs f
feeble adj imbēcillus, īnfirmus, dēbilis
feebleness n imbēcillitās f, īnfirmitās f
feebly adv īnfirmē
feed vt alere, pāscere ▶ vi pāscī; ~ **on** vescī (abl)
▶ n pābulum nt
feel vt sentīre; (with hand) tractāre, tangere;
(emotion) capere, afficī (abl); (opinion) cēnsēre,
sentīre; ~ **one's way** pedetemptim prōgredī ▶ vi
sentīre; **I ~ glad** gaudeō; ~ **sure** prō certō habēre
feeling n sēnsus m, tāctus m; (mind) animus m,
adfectus m; (pity) misericordia f; **good ~**
voluntās f; **bad ~** invidia f
feign vt simulāre, fingere
feignedly adv simulātē, fictē
feint n simulātiō f
felicitate vt grātulārī (dat)
felicitation n grātulātiō f
felicitous adj fēlīx, aptus
felicity n fēlīcitās f
feline adj fēlīnus
fell vt (tree) succīdere; (enemy) sternere, caedere
▶ adj dīrus, crūdēlis, atrōx ▶ n mōns m; (skin) pellis f
fellow n socius m, aequālis m; (contemptuous)
homō m
fellow citizen n cīvis m/f
fellow countryman n cīvis m/f, populāris m/f
fellow feeling n misericordia f
fellowship n societās f, sodālitās f
fellow slave n cōnservus m

fellow soldier n commīlitō m
fellow student n condiscipulus m
felon n nocēns m
felonious adj scelestus, scelerātus
felony n scelus nt, noxa f
felt n coāctum nt
female adj muliebris ▶ n fēmina f
feminine adj muliebris
fen n palūs f
fence n saepēs f; **sit on the ~** quiēscere, medium
sē gerere ▶ vt saepīre; ~ **off** intersaepīre ▶ vi
bātuere, rudibus lūdere
fencing n rudium lūdus m; ~ **master** lānista m
fend vt arcēre ▶ vi prōvidēre
fennel n ferula f
fenny adj palūster
ferment n fermentum nt; (fig) aestus m ▶ vt
fermentāre; (fig) excitāre, accendere ▶ vi fervēre
fermentation n fervor m
fern n filix f
ferocious adj ferōx, saevus, truculentus
ferociously adv truculentē
ferocity n ferōcitās f, saevitia f
ferret n viverra m ▶ vt: ~ **out** rīmārī, ēruere
ferry n trāiectus m; (boat) cymba f, pontō m ▶ vt
trānsvehere
ferryman n portitor m
fertile adj fertilis, fēcundus
fertility n fertilitās f, fēcunditās f
fertilize vt fēcundāre, laetificāre
fervent adj fervidus, ārdēns
fervently adv ārdenter
fervid adj fervidus
fervour n ārdor m, fervor m
festal adj festus
fester vi exulcerārī
festival n diēs festus m, sollemne nt
festive adj (time) festus; (person) festīvus
festivity n hilaritās f; (event) sollemne nt
festoon n sertum nt ▶ vt corōnāre
fetch vt arcessere, addūcere; (price) vēnīre (gen);
~ **out** dēprōmere; ~ **water** aquārī
fetching adj lepidus, blandus
fetid adj foetidus, pūtidus
fetter n compēs f, vinculum nt ▶ vt compedēs
inicere (dat), vincīre; (fig) impedīre
fettle n habitus m, animus m
feud n simultās f, inimīcitia f
fever n febris f
feverish adj febrīculōsus; (fig) sollicitus
few adj paucī; **very few** perpaucī; **how few?**
quotus quisque?
fewness n paucitās f
fiancé n spōnsus m
fiasco n calamitās f; **be a ~** frīgēre
fiat n ēdictum nt
fibre n fibra f
fickle adj incōnstāns, levis, mōbilis
fickleness n incōnstantia f, levitās f, mōbilitās f
fiction n fābula f, commentum nt
fictitious adj fictus, falsus, commentīcius;
(character) persōnātus

fictitiously adv fictē
fidelity n fidēlitās f, fidēs f
fidget vi sollicitārī
field n ager m; (ploughed) arvum nt; (of grain)
seges f; (MIL) campus m, aciēs f; (scope) campus
m, locus m; **in the ~** (MIL) mīlitiae; **hold the ~**
vincere, praevalēre; **~ of vision** cōnspectus m
fiend n diabolus m
fiendish adj nefārius, improbus
fierce adj saevus, ācer, atrōx; (look) torvus
fiercely adv ācriter, atrōciter, saevē
fierceness n saevitia f, atrōcitās f
fieriness n ārdor m, fervor m
fiery adj igneus, flammeus; (fig) ārdēns, fervidus
fife n tībia f
fifteen num quīndecim; **~ each** quīndēnī;
~ times quīndeciēns
fifteenth adj quīntus decimus
fifth adj quīntus ▶ n quīnta pars f
fiftieth adj quīnquāgēsimus
fifty num quīnquāgintā
fig n fīcus f; (tree) fīcus f; **of fig** fīculnus; **not care
a fig for** floccī nōn facere
fight n pugna f, proelium nt ▶ vi pugnāre,
dīmicāre; **~ it out** dēcernere, dēcertāre; **~ to the
end** dēpugnāre ▶ vt (battle) committere; (enemy)
pugnāre cum (abl)
fighter n pugnātor m
fighting n dīmicātiō f
figment n commentum nt
figurative adj trānslātus; **in ~ language**
trānslātīs per similitūdinem verbīs; **use
figuratively** trānsferre
figure n figūra f, fōrma f; (in art) signum nt; (of
speech) figūra f, trānslātiō f; (pl, on pottery) sigilla
ntpl ▶ vt figūrāre, fōrmāre; (art) fingere,
effingere; **~ to oneself** sibi prōpōnere
figured adj sigillātus
figurehead n (of ship) īnsigne nt
filament n fibra f
filch vt fūrārī, surripere
file n (tool) līma f; (line) ōrdō m, agmen nt; (of
papers) fasciculus m; **files** pl tabulae fpl; **in
single ~** simplicī ōrdine; **the rank and ~** gregāriī
mīlitēs ▶ vt līmāre
filial adj pius
filigree n diatrēta ntpl
fill vt implēre, explēre, complēre; (office) fungī
(abl); **~ up** supplēre
fillet n īnfula f, vitta f ▶ vt (fish) exossāre
fillip n stimulus m
filly n equula f
film n membrāna f
filter n cōlum nt ▶ vt dēliquāre ▶ vi percōlārī
filth n sordēs f, caenum nt
filthily adv foedē, inquinātē
filthiness n foedītās f, impūritās f
filthy adj foedus, impūrus; (speech) inquinātus
fin n pinna f
final adj ultimus, postrēmus, extrēmus
finally adv dēnique, tandem, postrēmō
finance n rēs nummāria f; (state) vectīgālia ntpl

financial adj aerārius
financier n faenerātor m
finch n fringilla f
find vt invenīre, reperīre; (supplies) parāre;
(verdict) iūdicāre; (pleasure) capere; **~ fault with**
incūsāre; **~ guilty** damnāre; **~ out** comperīre,
cognōscere
finder n inventor m
finding n iūdicium nt, sententia f
fine n (LAW) multa f, damnum nt; **in ~** dēnique
▶ vt multāre ▶ adj (thin) tenuis, subtīlis; (refined)
ēlegāns, mundus, decōrus; (beautiful) pulcher,
venustus; (showy) speciōsus; (of weather)
serēnus
finely adv pulchrē, ēleganter, subtīliter
fineness n tenuitās f; ēlegantia f; pulchritūdō f;
speciēs f; serēnitās f
finery n ōrnātus m, munditiae fpl
finesse n astūtia f, ars f, argūtiae fpl
finger n digitus m; **a finger's breadth**
trānsversus digitus; **not lift a ~** (in effort) nē
manum quidem vertere ▶ vt pertractāre
fingertips npl extrēmī digitī
finish n fīnis m; (art) perfectiō f ▶ vt fīnīre,
perficere; cōnficere; (with art) perficere, expolīre
▶ vi dēsinere; **~ off** trānsigere, peragere,
absolvere
finishing post n mēta f
finishing touch n manus extrēma f
finite adj circumscrīptus
fir n abiēs f; **of fir** abiēgnus
fire n ignis m; (conflagration) incendium nt; (in
hearth) focus m; (fig) ārdor m, calor m, impetus
m; **be on ~** ārdēre, flagrāre; **catch ~** flammam
concipere, ignem comprehendere; **set on ~**
accendere, incendere ▶ vt incendere; (fig)
īnflammāre; (missile) iaculārī
firebrand n fax f
fire brigade n vigilēs mpl
fireplace n focus m
fireside n focus m
firewood n lignum nt
firm n societās f ▶ adj firmus, stabilis; (mind)
cōnstāns; **stand ~** perstāre
firmament n caelum nt
firmly adv firmē, cōnstanter
firmness n firmitās f, firmitūdō f; cōnstantia f
first adj prīmus, prīnceps; (of two) prior ▶ adv
prīmum; **at ~** prīmō, prīncipiō; **at ~ hand** ipse,
ab ipsō; **come in ~** vincere; **give ~ aid to** ad
tempus medērī (dat); **I was the ~ to see** prīmus
vīdī
first-class adj classicus
first fruits npl prīmitiae fpl
firstly adv prīmum
first-rate adj eximius, lūculentus
firth n aestuārium nt, fretum nt
fiscal adj vectīgālis, aerārius
fish n piscis m ▶ vi piscārī; (fig) expiscārī
fisher, fisherman n piscātor m
fishing n piscātus m ▶ adj piscātōrius
fishing-rod n harundō f

fish market n forum piscārium nt
fishmonger n piscārius m
fish pond n piscīna f
fissile adj fissilis
fissure n rīma f
fist n pugnus m
fit n (MED) convulsiō f; (of anger, illness) impetus m; **by fits and starts** temerē, carptim ▶ vt aptāre, accommodāre; (dress) sedēre (dat); **fit out** armāre, īnstruere ▶ adj aptus, idōneus, dignus; **I see fit to** mihi vidētur; **fit for** aptus ad (acc)
fitful adj dubius, incōnstāns
fitfully adv incōnstanter
fitly adv dignē, aptē
fitness n convenientia f
fitting n adparātus m, īnstrūmentum nt ▶ adj idōneus, dignus; **it is ~** convenit, decet
fittingly adv dignē, convenienter
five num quīnque; **~ each** quīnī; **~ times** quīnquiēns; **~ years** quīnquennium nt, lūstrum nt; **~ sixths** quīnque partēs
five hundred num quīngentī; **five hundred each** quīngēnī; **five hundred times** quīngentiēns
five hundredth adj quīngentēsimus
fix vt fīgere; (time) dīcere, cōnstituere; (decision) statuere ▶ n angustiae fpl; **put in a fix** dēprehendere
fixed adj fīxus; (attention) intentus; (decision) certus; (star) inerrāns; **be firmly ~ in** īnsidēre (dat)
fixedly adv intentē
fixity n stabilitās f; (of purpose) cōnstantia f
fixtures npl adfīxa ntpl
flabbergast vt obstupefacere
flabbiness n mollitia f
flabby adj flaccidus, mollis
flag n vexillum nt; **~ officer** praefectus classis m ▶ vi flaccēre, flaccēscere, languēscere
flagellate vt verberāre
flagon n lagoena f
flagrant adj manifestus; flāgitiōsus
flagrantly adv flāgitiōsē
flagship n nāvis imperātōria f
flail n fūstis m
flair n iūdicium nt
flake n squāma f; **flakes** pl (snow) nix f
flame n flamma f ▶ vi flagrāre, exārdēscere
flaming adj flammeus
flamingo n phoenīcopterus m
flank n latus nt; cornū nt; **on the ~** ā latere, ad latus ▶ vt latus tegere (gen)
flap n flābellum nt; (dress) lacinia f ▶ vt plaudere (abl)
flare n flamma f, fulgor m ▶ vi exārdēscere, flagrāre
flash n fulgor m; (lightning) fulgur nt; (time) mōmentum nt ▶ vi fulgēre; (motion) micāre
flashy adj speciōsus
flask n ampulla f

flat adj plānus; (ground) aequus; (on back) supīnus; (on face) prōnus; (music) gravis; (style) āridus, frīgidus; **fall ~** (fig) frīgēre ▶ n (land) plānitiēs f; (sea) vadum nt; (house) tabulātum nt
flatly adv prōrsus
flatness n plānitiēs f
flatten vt aequāre, complānāre
flatter vt adūlārī (dat), adsentārī (dat), blandīrī (dat)
flatterer n adsentātor m
flattering adj blandus
flatteringly adv blandē
flattery n adūlātiō f, adsentātiō f, blanditiae fpl
flatulence n īnflātiō f
flatulent adj īnflātus
flaunt vt iactāre ▶ vi iactāre, glōriārī
flaunting n iactātiō f ▶ adj glōriōsus
flauntingly adv glōriōsē
flautist n tībīcen m
flavour n gustātus m, sapor m ▶ vt imbuere, condīre
flavouring n condītiō f
flavourless adj īnsulsus
flaw n vitium nt
flawless adj ēmendātus
flax n līnum nt
flaxen adj flāvus
flay vt dēglūbere
flea n pūlex m
fleck n macula f ▶ vt variāre
fledged adj pennātus
flee vi fugere, effugere; (for refuge) cōnfugere
fleece n vellus nt ▶ vt tondēre; (fig) spoliāre
fleecy adj lāneus
fleet n classis f ▶ adj vēlōx, celer
fleeting adj fugāx
fleetness n vēlōcitās f, celeritās f
flesh n cārō f; (fig) corpus nt; **in the ~** vīvus; **one's own ~ and blood** cōnsanguineus; **put on ~** pinguēscere
fleshiness n corpus nt
fleshliness n libīdō f
fleshly adj libīdinōsus
fleshy adj pinguis
flexibility n lentitia f
flexible adj flexibilis, lentus
flicker vi coruscāre
flickering adj tremulus
flight n (flying) volātus m; (fleeing) fuga f; (steps) scāla f; **put to ~** fugāre, in fugam conicere; **take to ~** sē in fugam dare, terga vertere
flightiness n mōbilitās f
flighty adj mōbilis, incōnstāns
flimsy adj tenuis, pertenuis
flinch vi recēdere
fling vt iacere, conicere; (missile) intorquēre; **~ away** abicere, prōicere; **~ open** patefacere; **~ in someone's teeth** obicere (dat); **~ to the ground** prōsternere ▶ vi sē incitāre ▶ n iactus m
flint n silex m
flinty adj siliceus
flippancy n lascīvia f

flippant adj lascīvus, protervus
flippantly adv petulanter
flirt vi lūdere, lascīvīre ▸ n lascīvus m, lascīva f
flit vi volitāre
flitch n succīdia f
float vi innāre, fluitāre; (in air) volitāre; ~ **down**
  dēfluere
flock n grex m; (wool) floccus m ▸ vi concurrere,
  congregārī, cōnfluere; ~ **in** adfluere
flog vt verberāre, virgīs caedere
flogging n verbera ntpl
flood n (deluge) ēluviō f; (river) torrēns m; (tide)
  accessus m; (fig) flūmen nt ▸ vt inundāre
floodgate n cataracta f
floor n solum nt; (paved) pavīmentum nt; (storey)
  tabulātum nt; (threshing) ārea f ▸ vt contabulāre;
  be floored (in argument) iacēre
flora n herbae fpl
floral adj flōreus
florid adj flōridus
flotilla n classicula f
flounce vi sē concitāre ▸ n īnstita f
flounder vi volutāre; (in speech) haesitāre
flour n farīna f
flourish vi flōrēre, vigēre ▸ vt vibrāre, iactāre
  ▸ n (RHET) calamistrī mpl; (music) clangor m
flout vt aspernārī, inlūdere (dat)
flow vi fluere, mānāre; (tide) accēdere; ~ **back**
  recēdere; ~ **between** interfluere; ~ **down**
  dēfluere; ~ **into** īnfluere in (acc); ~ **out** prōfluere,
  ēmānāre; ~ **past** praeterfluere; ~ **through**
  permānāre; ~ **together** cōnfluere; ~ **towards**
  adfluere ▸ n flūmen nt, cursus m; (tide) accessus
  m; (words) flūmen nt
flower n flōs m, flōsculus m ▸ vi flōrēre,
  flōrēscere
floweret n flōsculus m
flowery adj flōridus
flowing adj prōfluēns; ~ **with** abundāns (abl)
flowingly adv prōfluenter
flown adj īnflātus
fluctuate vi aestuāre, fluctuāre
fluctuating adj incōnstāns, incertus
fluctuation n aestus m, dubitātiō f
fluency n fācundia f, verbōrum cōpia f
fluent adj disertus, prōfluēns
fluently adv disertē, prōfluenter
fluid adj liquidus ▸ n liquor m
fluidity n liquor m
fluke n (anchor) dēns m; (luck) fortuītum nt
flurry n trepidātiō f ▸ vt sollicitāre, turbāre
flush n rubor m; **in the first ~ of victory** victōriā
  ēlātus ▸ vi ērubēscere ▸ adj (full) abundāns;
  (level) aequus
fluster n trepidātiō f ▸ vt turbāre, sollicitāre
flute n tībia f; **play the ~** tībiā canere
fluted adj striātus
flutter n tremor m; (fig) trepidātiō f ▸ vi
  (heart) palpitāre; (mind) trepidāre; (bird)
  volitāre
fluvial adj fluviātilis
flux n fluxus m; **be in a state of ~** fluere

fly n musca f ▸ vi volāre; (flee) fugere; **fly apart**
  dissilīre; **fly at** involāre in (acc); **fly away**
  āvolāre; **fly from** fugere; **fly in the face of**
  obviam īre (dat); **fly out** ēvolāre; **fly to** advolāre
  ad (acc); **fly up** ēvolāre, subvolāre; **let fly at**
  immittere in (acc)
flying adj volucer, volātilis; (time) fugāx
foal n equuleus m, equulus m ▸ vt parere
foam n spūma f ▸ vi spūmāre; (with rage) saevīre
foaming adj spūmeus
focus vt (mind) intendere
fodder n pābulum nt
foe n hostis m; (private) inimīcus m
fog n cālīgō f, nebula f
foggy adj cālīginōsus, nebulōsus
foible n vitium nt
foil n (metal) lāmina f; (sword) rudis f ▸ vt ēlūdere,
  ad inritum redigere
foist vt inculcāre, interpōnere
fold n sinus m; (sheep) ovīle nt ▸ vt plicāre,
  complicāre; (hands) comprimere; (sheep)
  inclūdere; ~ **back** replicāre; ~ **over** plicāre;
  ~ **together** complicāre; ~ **up in** involvere in (abl)
folding doors npl valvae fpl
foliage n frondēs fpl
folk n hominēs mpl ▸ adj patrius
follow vt sequī; (calling) facere; (candidate)
  adsectārī; (enemy) īnsequī; (example) imitārī;
  (instructions) pārēre (dat); (predecessor)
  succēdere (dat); (road) pergere; (speaker)
  intellegere; ~ **closely** īnsequī; ~ **hard on the**
  heels of īnsequī, īnstāre (dat), īnstāre (dat);
  ~ **out** exsequī; ~ **to the grave** exsequī; ~ **up**
  subsequī, īnsistere (dat) ▸ vi (time) īnsequī;
  (inference) sequī; **as follows** ita, in hunc modum
follower n comes m; (of candidate) adsectātor
  m; (of model) imitātor m; (of teacher) audītor m
following adj tālis; īnsequēns, proximus,
  posterus; **on the ~ day** postrīdiē, postero diē,
  proximo diē ▸ n adsectātōrēs mpl
folly n stultitia f, dēmentia f, īnsipientia f
foment vt fovēre; (fig) augēre
fond adj amāns, studiōsus; ineptus; **be ~ of**
  amāre
fondle vt fovēre, mulcēre
fondly adv amanter; inepte
food n cibus m; (fig) pābulum nt
fool n stultus m, ineptus m; (jester) scurra m;
  make a ~ of ludibriō habēre; ~ **play the ~** dēsipere
  ▸ vt dēcipere, lūdere; ~ **away** disperdere ▸ vi
  dēsipere
foolery n ineptiae fpl, nūgae fpl
foolhardy adj temerārius
foolish adj stultus, ineptus, īnsipiēns
foolishly adv stultē, inepte
foolishness n stultitia f, īnsipientia f
foot n pēs m; (MIL) peditātus m; **a ~ long** pedālis;
  on ~ pedes; **set ~ on** īnsistere (dat); **set on ~**
  īnstituere; **the ~ of** īmus ▸ vt (bill) solvere
football n follis m
footing n locus m, status m; **keep one's ~**
  īnsistere; **on an equal ~** ex aequō

footman n pedisequus m
footpad n grassātor m
footpath n sēmita f, trāmes m
footprint n vestīgium nt
foot soldier n pedes m
footstep n vestīgium nt; **follow in the footsteps of** vestīgiīs ingredī (gen)
foppish adj dēlicātus
for prep (advantage) dat; (duration) acc; (after noun) gen; (price) abl; (behalf) prō (abl); (cause) propter (acc), causā (gen); (after neg) prae (abl); (feelings) erga (acc); (lieu) prō (abl); (purpose) ad, in (acc); (time fixed) in (acc) ▶ conj namque; nam (1st word), enim (2nd word); (with pron) quippe quī; **for a long time** diū; **for some time** aliquamdiū
forage n pābulum nt ▶ vi pābulārī, frūmentārī
forager n pābulātor m, frūmentātor m
foraging n pābulātiō f, frūmentātiō f
forasmuch as conj quōniam
foray n incursiō f
forbear vi parcere (dat), supersedēre (infin)
forbearance n venia f, indulgentia f
forbears n māiōrēs mpl
forbid vt vetāre (+ acc and infin), interdīcere (dat and 'quominus' and subj); **Heaven ~!**, dī meliōra!
forbidding adj tristis
force n vīs f; (band of men) manus m; **by ~ of arms** vī et armīs ▶ vt cōgere, impellere; (way) rumpere, mōlīrī; (growth) festīnāre; **~ an engagement** hostēs proeliārī cōgere; **~ down** dētrūdere; **~ out** extrūdere, expellere, exturbāre; **~ upon** inculcāre; **~ a way in** intrōrumpere, inrumpere
forced adj (march) māgnus; (style) quaesītus; **~ march** māgnum iter
forceful adj validus
forceps n forceps m/f
forces npl (MIL) cōpiae fpl
forcible adj validus; (fig) gravis
forcibly adv vī, violenter; (fig) graviter
ford n vadum nt ▶ vt vadō trānsīre
fore adj prior; **to the ~** praestō ▶ adv: **~ and aft** in longitūdinem
forearm n bracchium nt ▶ vt: **be forearmed** praecavēre
forebode vt ōminārī, portendere; praesentīre
foreboding n praesēnsiō f; ōmen nt
forecast n praedictiō f ▶ vt praedīcere, prōvidēre
forecourt n vestibulum nt
forefathers n māiōrēs mpl
forefinger n index m
foreground n ēminentia ntpl
forehead n frōns f
foreign adj peregrīnus, externus; (goods) adventīcius; **~ to** aliēnus ab; **~ ways** peregrīnitās f
foreigner n peregrīnus m, advena m
foreknow vt praenōscere
foreknowledge n prōvidentia f
foreland n prōmontōrium nt

foremost adj prīmus, prīnceps
forenoon n antemerīdiānum tempus nt
forensic adj forēnsis
forerunner n praenūntius m
foresee vt praevidēre
foreshadow vt praemonēre
foresight n prōvidentia f
forest n silva f
forestall vt occupāre, antevenīre
forester n silvicola m
foretaste vt praegustāre
foretell vt praedīcere, vāticinārī
forethought n prōvidentia f
forewarn vt praemonēre
foreword n praefātiō f
forfeit n multa f, damnum nt ▶ vt āmittere, perdere, multārī (abl); (bail) dēserere
forfeiture n damnum nt
forgather vi congregārī, convenīre
forge n fornāx f ▶ vt fabricārī, excūdere; (document) subicere; (will) suppōnere; (signature) imitārī; (money) adulterīnōs nummōs percutere
forged adj falsus, adulterīnus, commentīcius
forger n (of will) subiector m
forgery n falsum nt, commentum nt
forget vt oblīvīscī (gen); (thing learnt) dēdiscere; **be forgotten** memoriā cadere, ex animō effluere
forgetful adj immemor; (by habit) oblīviōsus
forgetfulness n oblīviō f
forgive vt ignōscere (dat), veniam dare (dat)
forgiveness n venia f
forgo vt dīmittere, renūntiāre; (rights) dēcēdere dē iūre
fork n furca f; (small) furcula f; (road) trivium nt
forlorn adj inops, dēstitūtus, exspēs
form n fōrma f, figūra f; (of procedure) fōrmula f; (condition) vigor m; (etiquette) mōs m; (seat) scamnum nt; (school) schola f; (hare's) latibulum nt ▶ vt fōrmāre, fingere, efficere; (MIL) īnstruere; (plan) inīre, capere
formal adj iūstus; (rite) sollemnis
formality n iūsta ntpl, rītus m; **as a ~** dicis causā; **with due ~** rītē
formally adv rītē
formation n fōrma f, figūra f; (process) cōnfōrmātiō f; **in ~** (MIL) īnstructus
former adj prior, prīstinus, vetus; **the ~** ille
formerly adv anteā, ōlim, quondam
formidable adj formīdolōsus
formidably adv formīdolōsē
formula n fōrmula f; (dictated) praefātiō f
formulate vt compōnere
forsake vt dērelinquere, dēstituere, dēserere
forswear vt pēierāre, abiūrāre
fort n castellum nt
forth adv forās; (time) posthāc
forthwith adv extemplō, statim, prōtinus
fortieth adj quadrāgēsimus
fortification n (process) mūnītiō f; (place) mūnīmentum nt, arx f

fortify vt mūnīre, ēmūnīre, commūnīre; (fig) cōnfirmāre

fortitude n fortitūdō f

fortnight n quīndecim diēs mpl

fortnightly adv quīntō decimō quōque diē

fortress n arx f, castellum nt

fortuitous adj fortuītus

fortuitously adv fortuītō, cāsū

fortunate adj fēlīx, fortūnātus

fortunately adv fēlīciter, bene

fortune n fortūna f, fors f; (wealth) rēs f, dīvitiae fpl; **good ~** fēlīcitās f, secundae rēs fpl; **bad ~** adversae rēs fpl; **make one's ~** rem facere, rem quaerere; **tell fortunes** hariolārī

fortune-hunter n captātor m

fortune-teller n hariolus m, sāga f

forty num quadrāgintā; **~ each** quadrāgēnī; **~ times** quadrāgiēns

forum n forum nt

forward adj (person) protervus, audāx; (fruit) praecox ▶ adv porrō, ante; **bring ~** prōferre; **come ~** prōdīre ▶ vt (letter) perferre; (cause) adiuvāre, favēre (dat)

forwardness n audācia f, alacritās f

forwards adv porrō, prōrsus; **backwards and ~** rursum prōrsum, hūc illūc

fosse n fossa f

foster vt alere, nūtrīre; (fig) fovēre

foster child n alumnus m, alumna f

foster father n altor m, ēducātor m

foster mother n altrīx f, nūtrīx f

foul adj foedus; (speech) inquinātus; **fall ~ of** inruere in (acc)

foully adv foedē, inquinātē

foul-mouthed adj maledicus

foulness n foed1itās f

found vt condere, fundāre, īnstituere; (metal) fundere

foundation n fundāmenta ntpl

founder n fundātor m, conditor m ▶ vi submergī, naufragium facere

foundling n expositīcius m, expositīcia f

fount n fōns m

fountain n fōns m

fountainhead n fōns m, orīgō f

four num quattuor (indecl); **~ each** quaternī; **~ times** quater; **~ days** quadriduum nt; **~ years** quadriennium nt

fourfold adj quadruplex ▶ adv quadrifāriam

four hundred num quadringentī; **four hundred each** quadringēnī; **four hundred times** quadringentiēns

four hundredth adj quadringentēsimus

fourteen num quattuordecim; **~ each** quaternī dēnī; **~ times** quater deciēns

fourteenth adj quartus decimus

fourth adj quartus ▶ n quadrāns m; **three fourths** dōdrāns m, trēs partēs fpl

fowl n avis f; gallīna f

fowler n auceps m

fox n vulpēs f; **fox's** vulpīnus

foxy adj astūtus, vafer

fracas n rīxa f

fraction n pars f

fractious adj difficilis

fracture n frāctum os nt ▶ vt frangere

fragile adj fragilis

fragility n fragilitās f

fragment n fragmentum nt

fragrance n odor m

fragrant adj suāvis

fragrantly adv suāviter

frail adj fragilis, īnfirmus, dēbilis

frailty n dēbilitās f; (moral) error m

frame vt fabricārī, fingere, effingere; (document) compōnere ▶ n fōrma f; (of mind) adfectiō f, habitus m; **in a ~ of mind** animātus

framer n fabricātor m, opifex m; (of law) lātor m

framework n compāgēs f

franchise n suffrāgium nt, cīvitās f

frank adj ingenuus, apertus; (speech) līber

frankincense n tūs nt

frankly adv ingenuē, apertē; līberē

frankness n ingenuitās f; (speech) lībertās f

frantic adj furēns, furiōsus, dēlīrus

frantically adv furenter

fraternal adj frāternus

fraternally adv frāternē

fraternity n frāternitās f; (society) sodālitās f; (guild) collēgium nt

fraternize vi amīcitiam iungere

fratricide n frātricīda m; (act) frātris parricīdium nt

fraud n fraus f, dolus m, falsum nt; (criminal) dolus malus m

fraudulence n fraus f

fraudulent adj fraudulentus, dolōsus

fraudulently adv dolōsē, dolō malō

fraught adj plēnus

fray n pugna f, rīxa f ▶ vt terere

freak n mōnstrum nt; (caprice) libīdō f

freckle n lentīgō f

freckly adj lentīginōsus

free adj līber; (disengaged) vacuus; (generous) līberālis; (from cost) grātuītus; (from duty) immūnis; (from encumbrance) expedītus; **be ~ from** vacāre (abl); **I am still ~ to** integrum est mihī (infin); **set ~** absolvere, līberāre; (slave) manū mittere ▶ adv grātīs, grātuītō ▶ vt līberāre, expedīre, exsolvere

freebooter n praedō m

freeborn adj ingenuus

freedman n lībertus m

freedom n lībertās f; (from duty) immūnitās f

freehold n praedium līberum nt ▶ adj immūnis

freely adv līberē; (lavishly) cōpiōsē, largē; (frankly) apertē; (voluntarily) ultrō, suā sponte

freeman n cīvis m

free will n voluntās f; **of one's own free will** suā sponte

freeze vt gelāre, glaciāre ▶ vi concrēscere

freezing adj gelidus; **it is ~** gelat

freight n vectūra f; (cargo) onus nt ▶ vt onerāre

freighter n nāvis onerāria f

frenzied adj furēns, furiōsus, fānāticus

frenzy n furor m, īnsania f

frequency n adsiduitās f

frequent adj frequēns, crēber ▶ vt frequentāre, commeāre in (acc)

frequently adv saepe, saepenumerō, frequenter

fresh adj (new) recēns, novus; (vigorous) integer; (water) dulcis; (wind) ācer

freshen vt renovāre ▶ vi (wind) incrēbrēscere

freshly adv recenter

freshman n tīrō m

freshness n novitās f, viriditās f

fret vi maerēre, angī ▶ vt sollicitāre

fretful adj mōrōsus, querulus

fretfulness n mōrōsitās f

fretted adj laqueātus

friable adj puter

friction n trītus m

friend n amīcus m, familiāris m/f, hospes m, sodālis m; **make friends with** sē cōnferre ad amīcitiam (gen)

friendless adj sine amīcīs

friendliness n cōmitās f, officium nt

friendly adj cōmis, facilis, benīgnus; **on ~ terms** familiāriter

friendship n amīcitia f, familiāritās f

frigate n liburna f

fright n horror m, pavor m, terror m; **take ~** extimēscere, expavēscere

frighten vt terrēre, exterrēre, perterrēre; **~ away** absterrēre; **~ off** dēterrēre; **~ the life out of** exanimāre

frightful adj horribilis, immānis; (look) taeter

frightfully adv foedē

frigid adj frīgidus

frigidity n frīgus nt

frill n fimbriae fpl; (RHET) calamistrī mpl

fringe n fimbriae fpl

frisk vi lascīvīre, exsultāre

frisky adj lascīvus

fritter vt: **~ away** dissipāre; (time) extrahere

frivolity n levitās f

frivolous adj levis, inānis

frivolously adv ināniter

fro adv: **to and fro** hūc illūc

frock n stola f

frog n rāna f

frolic n lūdus m ▶ vi lūdere, lascīvīre

frolicsome adj lascīvus, hilaris

from prep ab (abl), ā before consonants; (out) ē, ex (abl); (cause) propter (acc); (prevention) quōminus, quīn; **~ all directions** undique

front n frōns f; **in ~** ā fronte, adversus; **in ~ of** prō (abl)

frontier n līmes m, cōnfīnia ntpl; **frontiers** fīnēs mpl

front line n prīma aciēs

frost n gelū nt

frostbitten adj: **be ~** vī frīgoris ambūrī

frosty adj gelidus, glaciālis

froth n spūma f ▶ vi spūmās agere

frothy adj spūmeus

froward adj contumāx

frown n frontis contractiō f ▶ vi frontem contrahere

frozen adj glaciālis

fructify vt fēcundāre

frugal adj parcus, frūgī

frugality n frūgālitās f, parsimōnia f

frugally adv parcē, frūgāliter

fruit n frūctus m; (tree) māla ntpl; (berry) bāca f; (fig) frūctus m; **fruits** pl (of earth) frūgēs fpl

fruiterer n pōmārius m

fruitful adj fēcundus, frūctuōsus

fruitfully adv ferāciter

fruitfulness n fēcunditās f, ūbertās f

fruition n frūctus m

fruitless adj inūtilis, vānus

fruitlessly adv nēquīquam, frustrā

fruit tree n pōmum nt

frustrate vt frustrārī, ad inritum redigere

frustration n frustrātiō f

fry vt frīgere

frying pan n sartāgō f; **out of the frying pan into the fire** incidit in Scyllam quī vult vītāre Charybdim

fuel n fōmes m

fugitive adj fugitīvus ▶ n fugitīvus m, trānsfuga m; (from abroad) extorris m

fulfil vt (duty) explēre, implēre; (promise) praestāre; (order) exsequī, perficere

fulfilment n absolūtiō f

full adj plēnus (abl), refertus, explētus; (entire) integer; (amount) solidus; (brother) germānus; (measure) iūstus; (meeting) frequēns; (style) cōpiōsus; **at ~ length** porrēctus; **at ~ speed** citātō gradū, citātō equō

fuller n fullō m

full-grown adj adultus

full moon n lūna plēna

fullness n (style) cōpia f; (time) mātūritās f

fully adv plēnē, penitus, funditus

fulminate vi intonāre

fulsome adj fastīdiōsus, pūtidus

fumble vi haesitāre

fume n fūmus m, hālitus m ▶ vi stomachārī

fumigate vt suffīre

fun n iocus m, lūdus m; **for fun** animī causā; **make fun of** inlūdere, dēlūdere, lūdibriō habēre

function n officium nt, mūnus nt

fund n cōpia f

fundamental adj prīmus ▶ n prīncipium nt, elementum nt

funds npl sors f, pecūniae fpl

funeral n fūnus nt, exsequiae fpl ▶ adj fūnebris

funeral pile n rogus m

funeral pyre n rogus m

funeral rites npl exsequiae fpl, īnferiae fpl

funereal adj fūnebria, lūgubris

funnel n īnfundibulum nt

funny adj ioculāris, rīdiculus

fur n pellis m

furbelow n īnstita f

furbish vt expolīre; **~ up** interpolāre
Furies npl Furiae fpl
furious adj saevus, vehemēns, perīrātus
furiously adv furenter, saevē, vehementer
furl vt (sail) legere
furlong n stadium nt
furlough n commeātus m
furnace n fornāx f
furnish vt praebēre, suppeditāre; (equip) īnstruere, ōrnāre
furniture n supellex f
furrow n sulcus m ▸ vt sulcāre
furry adj villōsus
further adj ulterior ▸ adv ultrā, porrō; amplius ▸ vt adiuvāre, cōnsulere (dat)
furtherance n prōgressus m; (means) īnstrūmentum nt
furthermore adv praetereā, porrō
furthest adj ultimus ▸ adv longissimē
furtive adj fūrtīvus, clandestīnus
furtively adv clam, fūrtim
fury n furor m, saevitia f; īra f
fuse vt fundere; (together) coniungere
fusion n coniūnctiō f
fuss n importūnitās f, querimōnia f ▸ vi conquerī, sollicitārī
fussy adj importūnus, incommodus
fusty adj mūcidus
futile adj inānis, inūtilis, futilis
futility n vānitās f, futilitās f
future adj futūrus, posterus ▸ n posterum nt, reliquum nt; **in ~** posthāc; **for the ~** in posterum
futurity n posterum tempus nt, posteritās f

g

gabble vi garrīre
gable n fastīgium nt
gadfly n tabānus m
gag vt ōs praeligāre (dat), ōs obvolvere (dat)
gage n pignus nt
gaiety n laetitia f, hilaritās f, festīvitās f
gaily adv hilare, festīve
gain n lucrum nt, quaestus m ▸ vt comparāre; adipīscī; (profit) lucrārī; (thing) parāre, cōnsequī, capere; (case) vincere; (place) pervenīre ad; (possession of) potīrī (gen); (victory) reportāre; **~ over** conciliāre; **~ ground** incrēbrēscere; **~ possession of** potior (abl); **~ the upper hand** rem obtinēre
gainful adj quaestuōsus
gainsay vt contrādīcere (dat)
gait n incessus m, ingressiō f
gaiters n ocreae fpl
gala n diēs festus m
galaxy n circulus lacteus m
gale n ventus m
gall n fel nt, bīlis m ▸ vt ūrere
gallant adj fortis, audāx; (courteous) officiōsus
gallantly adv fortiter; officiōsē
gallantry n virtūs f; urbānitās f
gall bladder n fel nt
gallery n porticus f
galley n nāvis āctuāria f; (cook's) culīna f
galling adj amārus, mordāx
gallon n congius m
gallop n cursus m; **at the ~** citātō equō, admissō equō ▸ vi admissō equō currere
gallows n īnfēlīx arbor m, furca f
gallows bird n furcifer m
galore adv adfatim
gamble n ālea f ▸ vi āleā lūdere
gambler n āleātor m
gambling n ālea f
gambol n lūsus m ▸ vi lūdere, lascīvīre, exsultāre
game n lūdus m; (with dice) ālea f; (hunt) praeda f; **play the ~** rēctē facere; **public games** lūdī mpl; **Olympic games** Olympia ntpl; **the game's up** āctum est ▸ adj animōsus
gamester n āleātor m

gammon n perna f
gander n ānser m
gang n grex m, caterva f
gangster n grassātor m
gangway n forus m
gaol n carcer m
gaoler n custōs m
gap n hiātus m, lacūna f
gape vi hiāre, inhiāre; (opening) dēhiscere
garb n habitus m, amictus m ▶ vt amicīre
garbage n quisquiliae fpl
garden n hortus m; (public) hortī mpl
gardener n hortulānus m; (ornamental)
    topiārius m
gardening n hortī cultūra f; (ornamental)
    topiāria f
gargle vi gargarissāre
garish adj speciōsus, fūcātus
garland n sertum nt, corōna f ▶ vt corōnāre
garlic n ālium nt
garment n vestis f, vestīmentum nt
garnish vt ōrnāre, decorāre
garret n cēnāculum nt
garrison n praesidium nt, dēfēnsōrēs mpl ▶ vt
    praesidiō mūnīre, praesidium collocāre in (abl)
garrotte vt laqueō gulam frangere (dat)
garrulity n garrulitās f
garrulous adj garrulus, loquāx
gas n vapor m
gash n vulnus nt ▶ vt caedere, lacerāre
gasp n anhēlitus m, singultus m ▶ vi anhēlāre
gastronomy n gula f
gate n porta f
gather vt colligere, cōgere; (fruit) legere;
    (inference) colligere, conicere ▶ vi congregārī
gathering n conventus m, coetus m
gauche adj inconcinnus, illepidus
gaudily adv splendidē, speciōsē
gaudy adj speciōsus, fūcātus, lautus
gauge n modulus m ▶ vt mētīrī
Gaul n Gallia f; (person) Gallus m
gaunt adj macer
gauntlet n manica f
gauze n Coa ntpl
gay adj hilaris, festīvus, laetus
gaze vi intuērī; ~ at intuērī, adspectāre,
    contemplārī
gazelle n oryx m
gazette n ācta diūrna ntpl, ācta pūblica ntpl
gear n īnstrūmenta ntpl; (ship's) armāmenta ntpl
gelding n cantērius m
gelid adj gelidus
gem n gemma f
gender n genus nt
genealogical adj dē stirpe
genealogical table n stemma nt
genealogist n geneālogus m
genealogy n geneālogia f
general adj generālis, ūniversus; (usual)
    vulgāris, commūnis; **in ~** omnīnō ▶ n dux m,
    imperātor m; **general's tent** praetōrium nt
generalissimo n imperātor m

generality n vulgus nt, plērīque mpl
generalize vi ūniversē loquī
generally adv ferē, plērumque; (discuss) īnfīnītē
generalship n ductus m
generate vt gignere, generāre
generation n aetās f, saeculum nt
generic adj generālis
generically adv genere
generosity n līberālitās f, largitās f
generous adj līberālis, largus, benīgnus
generously adv līberāliter, largē, benīgnē
genesis n orīgō f, prīncipium nt
genial adj cōmis, hilaris
geniality n cōmitās f, hilaritās f
genially adv cōmiter, hilare
genitive n genitīvus m
genius n (deity) genius m; (talent) ingenium nt,
    indolēs f; **of ~** ingeniōsus
genre n genus nt
genteel adj urbānus, polītus
gentility n urbānitās f, ēlegantia f
gentle adj (birth) ingenuus; (manner) hūmānus,
    indulgēns, mītis; (slope) lēnis, mollis; (thing)
    placidus, lēnis
gentleman n vir m, ingenuus m, vir honestus m
gentlemanly adj ingenuus, līberālis, honestus
gentleness n hūmānitās f, indulgentia f,
    lēnitās f
gentlewoman n ingenua f, mulier honesta f
gently adv lēniter, molliter, placidē
gentry n ingenuī mpl, optimātēs mpl; (contempt)
    hominēs mpl
genuine adj vērus, germānus, sincērus
genuinely adv germānē, sincērē
genuineness n fidēs f
geographical adj geōgraphicus; ~ **position**
    situs m
geography n geōgraphia f
geometrical adj geōmetricus
geometry n geōmetria f
Georgics n Geōrgica ntpl
germ n germen nt, sēmen nt
germane adj adfīnis
germinate vi gemmāre
gesticulate vi sē iactāre, gestū ūtī
gesticulation n gestus m
gesture n gestus m, mōtus m
get vt adipīscī, nancīscī, parāre; (malady)
    contrahere; (request) impetrāre; (return) capere;
    (reward) ferre; **get something done** cūrāre (with
    gerundive); **get somebody to do** persuādēre
    (dat), addūcere; **get by heart** ēdiscere; **get in**
    repōnere; **get the better of** superāre; **go and
    get** arcessere ▶ vi fierī; **get about** (rumour)
    palam fierī, percrēbrēscere; **get away** effugere;
    get at (intent) spectāre; **get behind** cessāre;
    get off absolvī; **get on** prōficere; **get out**
    effugere, ēvādere; **get out of hand** lascīvīre;
    get out of the way dē viā dēcēdere; **get ready**
    parāre; **get rid of** abicere, tollere; **get to**
    pervenīre ad; **get to know** cognōscere; **get
    together** congregārī; **get up** exsurgere

get-up n ōrnātus m
ghastliness n pallor m
ghastly adj pallidus; (sight) taeter
ghost n larva f, īdōlon nt; **ghosts** pl mānēs mpl; **give up the ~** animam agere, efflāre
giant n Gigas m
gibberish n barbaricus sermō m
gibbet n furca f
gibe vi inrīdēre
giddiness n vertīgō f
giddy adj vertīginōsus; (fig) levis
gift n dōnum nt; (small) mūnusculum nt; **gifts** pl (mind) ingenium nt
gifted adj ingeniōsus
gig n cisium nt
gigantic adj ingēns, immānis
gild vt inaurāre
gill n (measure) quartārius m; (fish) branchia f
gilt adj aurātus
gimlet n terebra f
gin n pedica f, laqueus m
ginger n zingiberī nt
gingerly adv pedetemptim
giraffe n camēlopardālis f
gird vt circumdāre; **~ on** accingere; **~ oneself** cingī; **~ up** succingere
girder n tignum nt
girdle n cingulus m ▶ vt cingere
girl n puella f, virgō f
girlhood n aetās puellāris f
girlish adj puellāris
girth n ambitus m, amplitūdō f
gist n firmāmentum nt
give vt dare, dōnāre, tribuere; (thing due) reddere; **~ away** largīrī; (bride) in matrimōnium collocāre; (secret) prōdere; **~ back** reddere, restituere; **~ birth (to)** pārere; **~ in** (name) profiterī; **~ off** ēmittere; **~ out** (orders) ēdere; (sound) ēmittere; **~ thanks** gratias agere; **~ up** dēdere, trādere; (hope) dēspērāre; (rights) dēcēdere dē, renūntiāre; **~ way** cēdere; (MIL) inclīnāre ▶ vi labāre; **~ in** sē victum fatērī; (MIL) manūs dare; **~ out** (fail) dēficere; (pretend) ferre; **~ up** dēsistere; **~ way** cēdere
giver n dator m
glacial adj glaciālis
glad adj laetus, alacer, hilaris; **be ~** gaudēre
gladden vt exhilarāre, oblectāre
glade n saltus m
gladiator n gladiātor m
gladiatorial adj gladiātōrius; **present a ~ show** gladiātōrēs dare
gladly adv laetē, libenter
gladness n laetitia f, alacritās f, gaudium nt
glamorous adj venustus
glamour n venustās f
glance n aspectus m ▶ vi oculōs conicere; **~ at** aspicere; (fig) attingere, perstringere; **~ off** stringere
glare n fulgor m ▶ vi fulgēre; **~ at** torvīs oculīs intuērī
glaring adj (look) torvus; (fault) manifestus;

be ~ ante pedēs positum esse
glass n vitrum nt; (mirror) speculum nt
glassy adj vitreus
glaze vt vitrō obdūcere
gleam n fulgor m, lūx f ▶ vi fulgēre, lūcēre
gleaming adj splendidus, nitidus
glean vi spīcās legere
gleaning n spīcilegium nt
glebe n fundus m
glee n hilaritās f, gaudium nt
gleeful adj hilaris, festīvus, laetus
gleefully adv hilare, laetē
glen n vallis f
glib adj prōfluēns, fācundus
glibly adv prōfluenter
glide n lāpsus m ▶ vi lābī; **~ away** ēlābī
glimmer vi sublūcēre ▶ n: **a ~ of hope** spēcula f
glimpse n aspectus m ▶ vt cōnspicārī
glint vi renīdēre
glisten vi fulgēre, nitēre
glitter vi micāre
gloaming n crepusculum nt
gloat vi: **~ over** inhiāre, animō haurīre, oculōs pāscere (abl)
globe n globus m, sphaera f; (inhabited) orbis terrārum m
globular adj globōsus
globule n globulus m, pilula f
gloom n tenebrae fpl; tristitia f
gloomy adj tenebricōsus; tristis, dēmissus
glorify vt illūstrāre, extollere, laudāre
glorious adj illūstris, praeclārus, splendidus
gloriously adv praeclārē, splendidē
glory n laus f, glōria f, decus nt ▶ vi glōriārī, sē iactāre
gloss n nitor m ▶ vt: **~ over** (fig) dissimulāre
glossy adj nitidus
glove n manica f
glow n (light) lūmen nt; (heat) ārdor m; (passion) calor m ▶ vi lūcēre, ārdēre, calēre, candēre
glowing adj candēns, ārdēns, calidus
glue n glūten nt ▶ vt glūtināre
glum adj tristis, maestus
glut vt explēre, saturāre ▶ n satietās f, abundantia f
glutton n gāneō m, helluō m
gluttonous adj edāx, vorāx, avidus
gluttony n gula f, edācitās f
gnarled adj nōdōsus
gnash vt, vi frendere; **~ one's teeth** dentibus frendere
gnat n culex m
gnaw vt rōdere; **~ away** ērōdere
gnawing adj mordāx
go vi īre, vādere; (depart) abīre, discēdere; (event) ēvādere; (mechanism) movērī; **go about** incipere, adgredī; **go after** īnsequī; **go away** abīre, discēdere; **go back** redīre, regredī; **go before** anteīre, praeīre; **go by** praeterīre; (rule) sequī, ūtī (abl); **go down** dēscendere; (storm) cadere; (star) occidere; **go for** petere; **go forward** prōgredī; **go in** intrāre, ingredī;

go in for (*profession*) facere, exercēre; **go off** abīre; **go on** pergere; (*event*) agī; **go out** exīre, ēgredī; (*fire*) extinguī; **go over** trānsīre; (*to enemy*) dēscīscere; (*preparation*) meditārī; (*reading*) legere; (*work done*) retractāre; **go round** circumīre, ambīre; **go through** percurrere; penetrāre; (*suffer*) perferre; **go to** adīre, petere; **go up** ascendere; **go to the help of** subvenīre (*dat*); **go to meet** obviam īre; **go with** comitārī; **go without** carēre (*abl*), sē abstinēre (*abl*) ▸ n vīs f, ācrimōnia f

goad n stimulus m ▸ vt irrītāre; pungere; (*fig*) stimulāre

go-ahead adj impiger

goal n fīnis m, mēta f

goat n caper m, capra f

gobble vt dēvorāre

go-between n internūntius m, internūntia f; (*bribery*) sequester m

goblet n pōculum nt, scyphus m

god n deus m

goddess n dea f

godhead n dīvīnitās f, nūmen nt

godless adj impius

godlike adj dīvīnus

godliness n pietās f, religiō f

godly adj pius

godsend n quasi caelō dēmissus

going n itiō f; (*way*) iter nt; (*departure*) profectiō f, discessus m

goitre n strūma nt

gold n aurum nt ▸ adj aureus

golden adj aureus; (*hair*) flāvus

gold leaf n bractea f

goldmine n aurāria f

goldsmith n aurārius m, aurifex m

good adj bonus, probus; (*fit*) idōneus, aptus; (*considerable*) magnus; ~ **day!** salvē, salvētē! ~ **looks** fōrma f, pulchritūdō f; ~ **nature** facilitās f, cōmitās f ▸ n bonum nt, commodum nt; **do ~ to** prōdesse (*dat*); **make ~** supplēre, praestāre; **seem ~** vidērī ▸ interj bene

goodbye interj valē, valēte; **say ~ to** valēre iubēre

good-for-nothing adj nēquam

good-humoured adj cōmis

good-looking adj pulcher

goodly adj pulcher; (*size*) amplus

good nature n facilitās f, cōmitās f

good-natured adj facilis, benīgnus, benevolus

goodness n bonitās f; (*character*) virtūs f, probitās f, pietās f

goods npl bona ntpl, rēs f, (*for sale*) merx f

good-tempered adj mītis, lēnis

goodwill n benevolentia f, favor m, grātia f

goose n ānser m/f

goose flesh n horror m

gore n cruor m ▸ vt cornibus cōnfodere

gorge n faucēs fpl, gula f; (GEOG) angustiae fpl ▸ vt: ~ **oneself** sē ingurgitāre

gorgeous adj lautus, splendidus

gorgeously adv lautē, splendidē

gorgeousness n lautitia f

gormandize vi helluārī

gory adj cruentus

gospel n ēvangelium nt

gossip n (*talk*) sermunculus m, rūmusculus m, fāma f; (*person*) lingulāca f ▸ vi garrīre

gouge vt ēruere

gourd n cucurbita f

gourmand n helluō m, gāneō m

gout n podagra f, articulāris morbus m

gouty adj arthrīticus

govern vt (*subjects*) regere; (*state*) administrāre, gubernāre; (*emotion*) moderārī (*dat*), cohibēre

governess n ēducātrīx f

government n gubernātiō f, administrātiō f; (*men*) magistrātūs mpl

governor n gubernātor m, moderātor m; (*province*) prōcōnsul m, prōcūrātor m

gown n (*men*) toga f; (*women*) stola f

grab vt adripere, corripere

grace n grātia f, lepōs m, decor m; (*favour*) grātia f, venia f; (*of gods*) pāx f; **be in the good graces of** in grātiā esse apud (*acc*); **with a bad ~** invītus ▸ vt decorāre, ōrnāre

graceful adj decōrus, venustus, lepidus

gracefully adv venustē, lepidē

graceless adj illepidus, impudēns

gracious adj benīgnus, prōpitius, misericors

graciously adv benīgnē, līberāliter

graciousness n benīgnitās f, līberālitās f

gradation n gradus m

grade n gradus m

gradient n clīvus m

gradual adj lēnis

gradually adv gradātim, sēnsim, paulātim

graft n surculus m; (POL) ambitus m ▸ vt īnserere

grafting n īnsitiō f

grain n frūmentum nt; (*seed*) grānum nt; **against the ~** invītā Minervā

grammar n grammatica f

grammarian n grammaticus m

granary n horreum nt

grand adj (*person*) amplus, illūstris, ēgregius; (*way of life*) lautus, māgnificus; (*language*) grandis, sublīmis

granddaughter n neptis f; **great ~** prōneptis f

grandeur n māiestās f, māgnificentia f; (*style*) granditās f

grandfather n avus m; **great ~** proavus m; **great-great-grandfather** abavus m; **of a ~** avītus

grandiloquence n māgniloquentia f

grandiloquent adj grandiloquus, tumidus

grandiose adj māgnificus

grandmother n avia f; **great ~** proavia f

grandson n nepōs m; **great ~** prōnepōs m

grant vt dare, concēdere, tribuere; (*admit*) fatērī ▸ n concessiō f

grape n ūva f

graphic adj expressus; **give a ~ account of** ante oculōs pōnere, oculīs subicere

grapnel n manus ferrea f, harpagō f

grapple vi luctārī
grappling iron n manus ferrea f
grasp vt prēnsāre, comprehendere; (with mind) complectī, adsequī, percipere, intellegere; **~ at** captāre, adpetere ▸ n manus f, comprehēnsiō f; (mind) captus m
grasping adj avārus, rapāx
grass n herba f
grasshopper n gryllus m
grassy adj herbōsus; herbidus
grate n focus m ▸ vt atterere; **~ upon** offendere
grateful adj grātus; **feel ~** grātiam habēre
gratefully adv grātē
gratification n voluptās f
gratify vt mōrem gerere (dat), mōrigerārī (dat), grātificārī (dat)
gratifying adj iūcundus
gratis adv grātuītō, grātīs
gratitude n grātia f; **show ~** grātiam referre
gratuitous adj grātuītus
gratuitously adv grātuītō
gratuity n stips f; (MIL) dōnātīvum nt
grave n sepulchrum nt ▸ adj gravis, austērus ▸ vt scalpere
gravel n glārea f
gravely adv graviter, sevērē
gravitate vi vergere
gravity n (person) sevēritās f, tristitia f; (circumstances) gravitās f, mōmentum nt; (physics) nūtus m; **by force of ~** nūtū suō
gray adj rāvus; (hair) cānus
graze vi pāscī ▸ vt (cattle) pāscere; (by touch) stringere
grazing n pāstus m
grease n arvīna f ▸ vt ungere
greasy adj pinguis, ūnctus
great adj māgnus, grandis, ingēns, amplus; (fame) īnsignis, praeclārus; **as ~ as ...** tantus ... quantus; **~ deal** plūrimum; **~ many** plūrimī; **how ~** quantus; **very ~** permāgnus
greatcoat n lacerna f
greatest adj māximus
greatly adv multum, māgnopere
greave n ocrea f
greed n avāritia f
greedily adv avārē, cupidē
greedy adj avārus, cupidus; avidus
Greek adj Graecus
green adj viridis; (unripe) crūdus; **be ~** virēre
greenness n viriditās f
greens n olus nt
greet vt salūtāre
greeting n salūs f, salūtātiō f
grey adj rāvus; (hair) cānus
greyhound n vertagus m
grief n dolor m, maeror m, lūctus m; **come to ~** perīre
grievance n querimōnia f; iniūria f
grieve vi dolēre, maerēre, lūgēre
grievous adj tristis, lūctuōsus; molestus, gravis, acerbus
grievously adv graviter, valdē

grim adj trux, truculentus; atrōx
grimace n ōris dēprāvātiō f; **make a ~** ōs dūcere
grime n sordēs f, lutum nt
grimy adj sordidus, lutulentus
grin n rīsus m ▸ vi adrīdēre
grind vt contundere; (corn) molere; (blade) acuere; **~ down** (fig) opprimere
grindstone n cōs f
grip vt comprehendere, arripere ▸ n comprehēnsiō f; **come to grips with** in complexum venīre (gen)
gripe n tormina ntpl
grisly adj horridus, dīrus
grist n (fig) ēmolumentum nt
grit n harēna f
groan n gemitus m ▸ vi gemere, ingemere
groin n inguen nt
groom n agāsō m
groove n canālis m, stria f
grope vi praetentāre
gross adj crassus, pinguis; (morally) turpis, foedus
grossly adv foedē, turpiter; (very) valdē
grossness n crassitūdō f; turpitūdō f
grotto n spēlunca f, antrum nt
ground n (bottom) solum nt; (earth) terra f, humus f; (cause) ratiō f, causa f; (sediment) faex f; **on the ~** humī; **on the grounds that** quod (subj); **to the ~** humum; **gain ~** prōficere; (rumour) incrēbrēscere; **lose ~** cēdere; (MIL) inclīnāre ▸ vt īnstituere ▸ vi (ship) sīdere
grounding n īnstitūtiō f
groundless adj vānus, inānis
groundlessly adv frustrā, temerē
grounds n faex f; (property) praedium nt; (reason) causa f; **I have good ~ for doing** nōn sine causā faciō, iūstīs dē causīs faciō
groundwork n fundāmentum nt
group n globus m, circulus m ▸ vt dispōnere
grouse n (bird) tetraō m; (complaint) querēla f ▸ vi querī
grove n nemus nt, lūcus m
grovel vi serpere, sē prōsternere, sē advolvere
grovelling adj humilis, abiectus
grow vi crēscere, glīscere; (spread) percrēbrēscere; (become) fierī; **~ old** (con) senēscere; **~ up** adolēscere, pūbēscere; **let ~** (hair) prōmittere ▸ vt (crops) colere; (beard) dēmittere
growl n fremitus m ▸ vi fremere
grown-up adj adultus, grandis
growth n incrēmentum nt, auctus m
grub n vermiculus m
grudge n invidia f ▸ vt invidēre (dat); (thing) gravārī
grudgingly adv invītus, gravātē
gruesome adj taeter
gruff adj acerbus, asper
grumble vi querī, mussāre ▸ n querēla f
grumpy adj mōrōsus, querulus
grunt n grunnītus m ▸ vi grunnīre
guarantee n (money) spōnsiō f; (promise) fidēs f; (person) praes m ▸ vt spondēre, praestāre

guarantor n spōnsor m

guard n custōdia f, praesidium nt; (person) custōs m; **on ~** in statiōne; **be on one's ~** cavēre; **keep ~** statiōnem agere; **off one's ~** imprūdēns, inopīnāns; **be taken off one's ~** dē gradū dēicī ▸ vt custōdīre, dēfendere; (keep) cōnservāre; **~ against** cavēre

guarded adj cautus

guardedly adv cautē

guardhouse n custōdia f

guardian n custōs m; (of minors) tūtor m

guardianship n custōdia f, tūtēla f

guardian spirit n genius m

gudgeon n gōbius m

guerdon n praemium nt, mercēs f

guess n coniectūra f ▸ vt dīvīnāre, conicere

guest n hospes m, hospita f; (at dinner) convīva m; **uninvited ~** umbra f; **guest's** hospitālis

guffaw n cachinnus m ▸ vi cachinnāre

guidance n moderātiō f; **under the ~ of God** dūcente deō

guide n dux m, ductor m; (in policy) auctor m ▸ vt dūcere; (steer) regere; (control) moderārī

guild n collēgium nt

guile n dolus m, fraus f

guileful adj dolōsus, fraudulentus

guilefully adv dolōsē

guileless adj simplex, innocēns

guilelessly adv sine fraude

guilt n culpa f, scelus nt

guiltless adj innocēns, īnsōns

guiltlessly adv integrē

guilty adj nocēns, sōns; **find ~** damnāre

guise n speciēs f

guitar n fidēs fpl; **play the ~** fidibus canere

gulf n sinus m; (chasm) hiātus m

gull n mergus m ▸ vt dēcipere

gullet n gula f, guttur nt

gullible adj crēdulus

gulp vt dēvorāre, haurīre

gum n gummī nt; (mouth) gingīva f

gumption n prūdentia f

gurgle vi singultāre

gush vi sē prōfundere, ēmicāre ▸ n scatūrīginēs fpl

gust n flāmen nt, impetus m

gusto n studium nt

gusty adj ventōsus

gut n intestīnum nt ▸ vt exenterāre; (fig) extergēre

gutter n canālis m

guzzle vi sē ingurgitāre

gymnasium n gymnasium nt, palaestra f; **head of a ~** gymnasiarchus m

gymnastic adj gymnicus; **gymnastics** pl palaestra f

gyrate vi volvī

h

habit n mōs m, cōnsuētūdō f; (dress) habitus m, vestītus m; **be in the ~ of** solēre

habitable adj habitābilis

habitation n domus f, domicilium nt; (place) sēdēs f

habitual adj ūsitātus

habitually adv ex mōre, persaepe

habituate vt adsuēfacere, īnsuēscere

hack vt caedere, concīdere ▸ n (horse) caballus m

hackneyed adj trītus

Hades n īnferī mpl

haft n manubrium nt

hag n anus f

haggard adj ferus

haggle vi altercārī

hail n grandō f ▸ vi: **it hails** grandinat ▸ vt salūtāre, adclāmāre ▸ interj avē, avēte; salvē, salvēte; **I ~ from Rome** Rōma mihi patria est

hair n capillus m; crīnis m; (single) pīlus m; (animals) sēta f, villus nt; **deviate a hair's breadth from** trānsversum digitum discēdere ab; **split hairs** cavillārī

hairdresser n tōnsor m

hairless adj (head) calvus; (body) glaber

hairpin n crīnāle nt

hairsplitting adj captiōsus ▸ n cavillātiō f

hairy adj pilōsus

halberd n bipennis f

halcyon n alcēdō f; **~ days** alcēdōnia ntpl

hale adj validus, rōbustus ▸ vt trahere, rapere

half n dīmidium nt, dīmidia pars f ▸ adj dīmidius, dīmidiātus; **~ as much again** sesquī; **well begun is ~ done** dīmidium factī quī coepit habet

half-asleep adj sēmisomnus

half-baked adj (fig) rudis

half-dead adj sēmianimis, sēmivīvus

half-full adj sēmiplēnus

half-hearted adj incūriōsus, sōcors

half-heartedly adv sine studiō

half-hour n sēmihōra f

half-moon n lūna dīmidiāta f

half-open adj sēmiapertus

half pound n sēlībra f

half-way adj medius; **~ up the hill** in mediō colle

half-yearly adj sēmestris

hall n ātrium nt; (public) exedra f

hallo interj heus

hallow vt sacrāre

hallucination n error m, somnium nt

halo n corōna f

halt vi īnsistere, cōnsistere ▶ vt sistere ▶ n: **come to a ~** cōnsistere, agmen cōnstituere ▶ adj claudus

halter n capistrum nt; (fig) laqueus m

halve vt bipartīre

ham n perna f

hamlet n vīcus m

hammer n malleus m ▶ vt tundere; **~ out** excūdere

hamper n corbis f ▶ vt impedīre; (with debt) obstringere

hamstring vt poplitem succīdere (dat)

hand n manus f; **left ~** laeva f, sinistra f; **right ~** dextra f; **an old ~** veterātor m; **at ~** praestō, ad manum; **be at ~** adesse; **at first ~** ipse; **at second ~** ab aliō; **on the one ~ ... on the other** et ... et, quidem ... at; **near at ~** in expedītō, inibī; **the matter in ~** quod nunc īnstat, quae in manibus sunt; **get out of ~** lascīvīre; **have a ~ in** interesse (dat); **lay hands on** manum adferre, inicere (dat); **live from ~ to mouth** ad hōram vīvere; **pass from ~ to ~** per manūs trādere; **take in ~** suscipere; **hands** pl (workmen) operae fpl ▶ vt trādere, porrigere; **~ down** trādere, prōdere; **~ over** dēferre, reddere

handbill n libellus m

handbook n ars f

handcuffs n manicae fpl

handful n manipulus m

handicap n impedīmentum nt

handicraft n artificium nt, ars operōsa f

handily adv habiliter

handiness n habilitās f; commoditās f

handiwork n opus nt, manus f

handkerchief n sūdārium nt

handle n (cup) ānsa f; (knife) manubrium nt; (fig) ānsa f, occāsiō f ▶ vt tractāre

handling n tractātiō f

handmaid n famula f

handsome adj fōrmōsus, pulcher; (gift) līberālis

handsomely adv pulchrē; līberāliter

handsomeness n pulchritūdō f, fōrma f

hand-to-hand adv: **fight ~** manum cōnserere, comminus pugnāre

handwriting n manus f

handy adj (to use) habilis; (near) praestō

hang vt suspendere; (head) dēmittere; (wall) vestīre ▶ vi pendēre; **~ back** gravārī, dubitāre; **~ down** dēpendēre; **~ on to** haerēre (dat); **~ over** imminēre (dat), impendēre (dat); **go and be hanged** abī in malam crucem!

hanger-on n cliēns m/f, assecla m/f

hanging n (death) suspendium nt; **hangings** pl aulaea ntpl ▶ adj pendulus

hangman n carnifex m

hanker vi: **~ after** appetere, exoptāre

hap n fors f

haphazard adj fortuītus

hapless adj miser, īnfēlīx

haply adv fortasse

happen vi accidere, ēvenīre, contingere; (become) fierī; **as usually happens** ut fit; **~ upon** incidere in (acc); **it happens that** accidit ut (subj)

happily adv fēlīciter, beātē, bene

happiness n fēlīcitās f

happy adj fēlīx, beātus; laetus; (in some respect) fortūnātus

harangue n cōntiō f ▶ vt cōntiōnārī apud (acc), hortārī

harass vt vexāre, lacessere, exagitāre, sollicitāre

harassing adj molestus

harbinger n praenūntius m

harbour n portus m ▶ vt recipere

harbour dues npl portōria ntpl

hard adj dūrus; (circumstances) asper, inīquus; (task) difficilis, arduus; **~ of hearing** surdaster; **grow ~** dūrēscere ▶ adv sēdulō, valdē; **~ by** prope, iuxtā; **I am ~ put to it to do** aegerrimē faciō

hard cash n praesēns pecūnia f

harden vt dūrāre ▶ vi dūrēscere; (fig) obdūrēscere; **become hardened** obdūrēscere

hard-fought adj atrōx

hard-hearted adj crūdēlis, dūrus, inhūmānus

hardihood n audācia f

hardily adv sevērē

hardiness n rōbur nt; dūritia f

hardly adv vix, aegrē; (severely) dūriter, acerbē; **~ any** nūllus ferē

hardness n dūritia f; (fig) asperitās f, inīquitās f; (difficulty) difficultās f; **~ of hearing** surditās f

hard-pressed adj: **be ~** labōrāre

hardship n labor m, malum nt, iniūria f

hard-working adj industrius, nāvus, sēdulus

hardy adj dūrus, rōbustus, sevērus

hare n lepus m

hark interj auscultā, auscultāte ▶ vi: **~ back to** repetere

harm n iniūria f, damnum nt, malum nt, dētrīmentum nt; **come to ~** dētrīmentum capere, accipere ▶ vt laedere, nocēre (dat)

harmful adj damnōsus, noxius

harmfully adv male

harmless adj innocēns

harmlessly adv innocenter; (escape) salvus, incolumis, inviolātus

harmonious adj cōnsonus, canōrus; (fig) concors; (things) congruēns

harmoniously adv modulātē; concorditer; convenienter

harmonize vi concinere, cōnsentīre, congruere

harmony n concentus m; (fig) concordia f, cōnsēnsus m

harness n arma ntpl ▶ vt înfrēnāre, iungere
harp n fidēs fpl; **play the ~** fidibus canere ▶ vi:
~ **on** (fig) cantāre, dictitāre; **be always harping
on the same thing** cantilēnam eandem canere
harpist n fidicen m, fidicina f
harpoon n iaculum nt
harpy n Harpyia f
harrow n rāstrum nt ▶ vt occāre
harrower n occātor m
harrowing adj horrendus
harry vt vexāre, dīripere
harsh adj dūrus, acerbus, asper; (person)
inclēmēns, sevērus
harshly adv acerbē, asperē; sevērē
harshness n acerbitās f, asperitās f; crūdēlitās f
hart n cervus m
harvest n messis f ▶ vt metere, dēmetere
harvester n messor m
hash n farrāgō f ▶ vt comminuere
haste n festīnātiō f, properātiō f; **in ~**
festīnanter; **in hot ~** incitātus; **make ~** festīnāre
hasten vt mātūrāre, adcelerāre ▶ vi festīnāre,
properāre, mātūrāre
hastily adv properē, raptim; temerē,
incōnsultē; īrācundē
hastiness n temeritās f; (temper) īrācundia f
hasty adj properus, celer; (action) incōnsultus,
temerārius; (temper) īrācundus, ācer; **over ~**
praeproperus
hat n petasus m
hatch vt exclūdere, parere
hatchet n dolābra f
hate n odium nt, invidia f ▶ vt ōdisse
hated adj: **to be ~** (by somebody) odiō esse (dat)
hateful adj odiōsus, invīsus
hatefully adv odiōsē
hatred n odium nt
haughtily adv adroganter, superbē, insolenter
haughtiness n fastus m, adrogantia f, superbia f
haughty adj adrogāns, superbus, īnsolēns
haul vt trahere ▶ n bolus m
haulage n vectūra f
haulm n culmus m
haunch n femur nt
haunt vt frequentāre ▶ n locus m; (animals)
lustrum nt
have vt habēre, tenēre; (get done) cūrāre (with
gerundive); **I ~ a house** est mihī domus; **I ~ to go**
mihī abeundum est; **~ it out with** rem
dēcernere cum; **~ on** gerere, gestāre, indui;
I had better go melius est īre, praestat īre;
I had rather mālim, māllem
haven n portus m; (fig) perfugium nt
havoc n exitium nt, vastātiō f, ruīna f
hawk n accipiter m ▶ vt (wares) circumferre
hawker n īnstitor m
hay n faenum nt; **make hay while the sun
shines** forō ūtī
hazard n perīculum nt, discrīmen nt, ālea f ▶ vt
perīclitārī, in āleam dare
hazardous adj perīculōsus
haze n nebula f

hazel n corylus f
hazy adj nebulōsus; (fig) incertus
he pron hic, ille, is
head n caput nt; (person) dux m, prīnceps m;
(composition) caput nt; (mind) animus m,
ingenium nt; **~ over heels** cernuus; **off one's ~**
dēmēns; **be at the ~ of** dūcere, praeesse (dat);
come to a ~ caput facere; (fig) in discrīmen
addūcī; **give someone his ~** indulgēre (dat),
habēnās immittere (dat); **keep one's ~** praesentī
animō ūtī; **lose one's ~** suī compotem nōn esse;
shake one's ~ abnuere ▶ vt dūcere, praeesse
(dat); **~ off** intercipere ▶ vi (in a direction) tendere
headache n capitis dolor m
headfirst adj praeceps
heading n caput nt
headland n prōmontōrium nt
headlong adj praeceps ▶ adv in praeceps;
rush ~ sē praecipitāre
headquarters n (MIL) praetōrium nt
headship n prīncipātus m
headsman n carnifex m
headstrong adj impotēns, pervicāx
headway n prōfectus m
heady adj incōnsultus; (wine) vehemēns
heal vt sānāre, medērī (dat) ▶ vi sānēscere;
~ over obdūcī
healer n medicus m
healing adj salūbris
health n valētūdō f, salūs f; **state of ~** valētūdō
f; **ill ~** valētūdō f; **be in good ~** valēre; **drink
the ~ of** propīnāre (dat)
healthful adj salūbris
healthiness n sānitās f
healthy adj sānus, integer; (conditions) salūber
heap n acervus m, cumulus m; **in heaps**
acervātim ▶ vt acervāre; **~ together** congerere;
~ up adcumulāre, coacervāre, congerere
hear vt audīre; (case) cognōscere; **~ clearly**
exaudīre; **~ in secret** inaudīre
hearer n audītor m
hearing n (sense) audītus m; (act) audītiō f; (of
case) cognitiō f; **get a ~** sibī audientiam facere;
hard of ~ surdaster; **without a ~** indictā causā
hearken vi auscultāre
hearsay n fāma f, rūmor m
heart n cor nt; (emotion) animus m, pectus nt;
(courage) animus m; (interior) viscera ntpl; **by ~**
memoriā, memoriter; **learn by ~** ēdiscere;
the ~ of the matter rēs ipsa; **lose ~** animum
dēspondēre; **take to ~** graviter ferre
heartache n dolor m, angor m
heartbroken adj animī frāctus, aeger; **be ~**
animō labōrāre
heartburning n invidia f
heartfelt adj sincērus
hearth n focus m; **~ and home** ārae et focī
heartily adv vehementer, valdē
heartiness n studium nt, vigor m
heartless adj dūrus, inhūmānus, crūdēlis
heartlessly adv inhūmānē
heartlessness n inhūmānitās f, crūdēlitās f

hearty *adj* studiōsus, vehemēns; (*health*) rōbustus; (*feeling*) sincērus

heat *n* ārdor *m*, calor *m*; (*emotion*) ārdor *m*, aestus *m*; (*race*) missus *m* ▶ *vt* calefacere, fervefacere; (*fig*) accendere; **become heated** incalēscere

heatedly *adv* ferventer, ārdenter

heath *n* inculta loca *ntpl*

heathcock *n* attagēn *m*

heathen *n* pāgānus *m*

heather *n* erīcē *f*

heave *vt* tollere; (*missile*) conicere; (*sigh*) dūcere ▶ *vi* tumēre, fluctuāre

heaven *n* caelum *nt*, dī *mpl*; **~ forbid!** dī meliōra; **from ~** dīvīnitus; **in heaven's name** prō deum fidem!; **be in seventh ~** digitō caelum attingere

heavenly *adj* caelestis, dīvīnus

heavily *adv* graviter

heaviness *n* gravitās *f*, pondus *nt*; (*of spirit*) maestitia *f*

heavy *adj* gravis; (*air*) crassus; (*spirit*) maestus; (*shower*) māgnus, dēnsus

heckle *vt* interpellāre

heckler *n* interpellātor *m*

hectic *adj* violēns, ācer, fervidus

hector *vt* obstrepere (*dat*)

hedge *n* saepēs *f* ▶ *vt* saepīre; **~ off** intersaepīre ▶ *vi* tergiversārī

hedgehog *n* echīnus *m*, ēricius *m*

heed *vt* cūrāre, respicere ▶ *n* cūra *f*, opera *f*; **pay ~** animum attendere; **take ~** cavēre

heedful *adj* attentus, cautus, dīligēns

heedfully *adv* attentē, cautē

heedfulness *n* cūra *f*, dīligentia *f*

heedless *adj* incautus, immemor, neglegēns

heedlessly *adv* incautē, neglegenter, temerē

heedlessness *n* neglegentia *f*

heel *n* calx *f*; **take to one's heels** sē in pedēs conicere ▶ *vi* sē inclīnāre

hegemony *n* prīncipātus *m*

heifer *n* būcula *f*

height *n* altitūdō *f*; (*person*) prōcēritās *f*; (*hill*) collis *m*, iugum *nt*; (*fig*) fastīgium *nt*; **the ~ of** summus

heighten *vt* augēre, exaggerāre

heinous *adj* atrōx, nefārius

heinously *adv* atrōciter, nefāriē

heinousness *n* atrōcitās *f*

heir *n* hērēs *m*; **sole ~** hērēs ex asse

heiress *n* hērēs *f*

heirship *n* hērēditās *f*

hell *n* Tartarus *m*, īnfernī *mpl*

hellish *adj* īnfernus, scelestus

helm *n* gubernāculum *nt*, clāvus *m*

helmet *n* galea *f*

helmsman *n* gubernātor *m*

helots *n* Hīlōtae *mpl*

help *n* auxilium *nt*, subsidium *nt*; **I am a ~** auxiliō sum ▶ *vt* iuvāre (*acc*), auxiliārī, subvenīre (*dat*), succurrere (*dat*) ▶ *vi* prōdesse; **I cannot ~** facere nōn possum quīn (*subj*); **it can't be helped** fierī nōn potest aliter; **so ~ me God** ita mē dī ament

helper *n* adiūtor *m*, adiūtrix *f*

helpful *adj* ūtilis; **be ~ to** auxiliō esse (*dat*)

helpless *adj* inops

helplessness *n* inopia *f*

hem *n* ōra *f*, limbus *m* ▶ *vt*: **hem in** interclūdere, circumsedēre

hemlock *n* cicūta *f*

hemp *n* cannabis *f*

hen *n* gallīna *f*

hence *adv* hinc; (*consequence*) igitur, ideō

henceforth, henceforward *adv* dehinc, posthāc, ex hōc tempore

her *adj* suus, ēius

herald *n* praecō *m*; (*POL*) fētiālis *m* ▶ *vt* praenūntiāre

herb *n* herba *f*, olus *nt*

herbage *n* herbae *fpl*

herd *n* pecus *nt*; grex *f*, armentum *nt* ▶ *vi* congregārī

herdsman *n* pāstor *m*

here *adv* hīc; **be ~** adesse; **~ and there** passim; **~ ... there** alibī ... alibī; **from ~** hinc; **~ is ...** ecce (*acc*) ...

hereabouts *adv* hīc ferē

hereafter *adv* posthāc, posteā

hereat *adv* hīc

hereby *adv* ex hōc, hinc

hereditary *adj* hērēditārius, patrius

heredity *n* genus *nt*

herein *adv* hīc

hereinafter *adv* īnfrā

hereof *adv* ēius reī

hereupon *adv* hīc, quō factō

herewith *adv* cum hōc, ūnā

heritable *adj* hērēditārius

heritage *n* hērēditās *f*

hermaphrodite *n* androgynus *m*

hermit *n* homō sōlitārius *m*

hero *n* vir fortissimus *m*; (*demigod*) hērōs *m*

heroic *adj* fortissimus, māgnanimus; (*epic*) hērōicus; (*verse*) hērōus

heroically *adv* fortissimē, audācissimē

heroism *n* virtūs *f*, fortitūdō *f*

heron *n* ardea *f*

hers *pron* suus, ēius

herself *pron* ipsa *f*; (*reflexive*) sē

hesitancy *n* dubitātiō *f*

hesitant *adj* incertus, dubius

hesitate *vi* dubitāre, haesitāre

hesitating *adj* dubius

hesitatingly *adv* cunctanter

hesitation *n* dubitātiō *f*; **with ~** dubitanter

heterogeneous *adj* dīversus, aliēnigenus

hew *vt* dolāre, caedere; **hew down** excīdere, interscindere

hexameter *n* hexameter *m*

heyday *n* flōs *m*

hiatus *n* hiātus *m*

hiccup *n* singultus *m* ▶ *vi* singultīre

hide *vt* cēlāre, abdere, abscondere, occultāre; **~ away** abstrūdere; **~ from** cēlāre (*acc*) ▶ *vi* sē abdere, latēre; **~ away** dēlitēscere ▶ *n* pellis *f*, corium *nt*

hideous *adj* foedus, dēfōrmis, turpis
hideously *adv* foedē
hideousness *n* foeditās *f*, dēfōrmitās *f*
hiding *n* (*place*) latebra *f*
hierarchy *n* ōrdinēs *mpl*
high *adj* altus, excelsus; (*ground*) ēditus; (*pitch*) acūtus; (*rank*) amplus; (*price*) cārus; (*tide*) māximus; (*wind*) māgnus; **~ living** luxuria *f*; **~ treason** māiestās *f*; **~ and mighty** superbus; **on ~** sublīmis ▶ *adv* altē
highborn *adj* nōbilis, generōsus
high-class *adj* (*goods*) lautus
high-flown *adj* īnflātus, tumidus
high-handed *adj* superbus, īnsolēns
high-handedly *adv* superbē, licenter
high-handedness *n* licentia *f*, superbia *f*
highland *adj* montānus
highlander *n* montānus *m*
highlands *npl* montāna *ntpl*
highly *adv* (*value*) māgnī; (*intensity*) valdē
highly-strung *adj* trepidus
high-minded *adj* generōsus
high-spirited *adj* ferōx, animōsus
highway *n* via *f*
highwayman *n* grassātor *m*, latrō *m*
hilarious *adj* festīvus, hilaris
hilariously *adv* festīvē, hilare
hilarity *n* festīvitās *f*, hilaritās *f*
hill *n* collis *m*, mōns *m*; (*slope*) clīvus *m*
hillock *n* tumulus *m*
hilly *adj* montuōsus, clīvōsus
hilt *n* manubrium *nt*, capulus *m*
himself *pron* ipse; (*reflexive*) sē
hind *n* cerva *f*
hinder *vt* impedīre, obstāre (*dat*), morārī
hindmost *adj* postrēmus; (*in column*) novissimus
hindrance *n* impedīmentum *nt*, mora *f*
hinge *n* cardō *f*
hint *n* indicium *nt*, suspiciō *f*; **throw out a ~** inicere ▶ *vt* subicere, significāre
hip *n* coxendīx *f*
hippodrome *n* spatium *nt*
hire *vt* condūcere; **~ out** locāre ▶ *n* conductiō *f*, locātiō *f*; (*wages*) mercēs *f*
hired *adj* mercennārius, conductus
hireling *n* mercennārius *m*
hirsute *adj* hirsūtus
his *adj* suus, ēius
hiss *vi* sībilāre ▶ *vt*: **~ off stage** explōdere, exsībilāre ▶ *n* sībilus *m*
historian *n* historicus *m*, rērum scrīptor *m*
historical *adj* historicus
history *n* historia *f*; **the ~ of Rome** rēs Rōmānae *fpl*; **since the beginning of ~** post hominum memoriam; **ancient ~** antīquitās *f*
histrionic *adj* scaenicus
hit *n* ictus *m*, plāga *f*; **a hit!** (*in duel*) habet! ▶ *vt* ferīre, icere, percutere; **hit against** offendere; **hit upon** invenīre
hitch *n* mora *f* ▶ *vt* implicāre; **~ up** succingere
hither *adv* hūc; **~ and thither** hūc illūc ▶ *adj* citerior

hitherto *adv* adhūc, hāctenus, hūcusque
hive *n* alveārium *nt*
hoar *adj* cānus ▶ *n* pruīna *f*
hoard *n* thēsaurus *m*, acervus *m* ▶ *vt* condere, recondere
hoarfrost *n* pruīna *f*
hoarse *adj* raucus, fuscus
hoarsely *adv* raucā vōce
hoary *adj* cānus
hoax *n* fraus *f*, fallācia *f*, lūdus *m* ▶ *vt* dēcipere, fallere
hobble *vi* claudicāre
hobby *n* studium *nt*
hob-nob *vi* familiāriter ūtī (*abl*)
hocus-pocus *n* trīcae *fpl*
hoe *n* sarculum *nt* ▶ *vt* sarrīre
hog *n* sūs *m*, porcus *m*; **hog's** porcīnus
hogshead *n* dōlium *nt*
hoist *vt* tollere; (*sail*) vēla dare
hold *n* (*grasp*) comprehēnsiō *f*; (*power*) potestās *f*; (*ship*) alveus *m*; **gain a ~ over** obstringere, sibi dēvincīre; **get ~ of** potīrī (*abl*); **keep ~ of** retinēre; **lose ~ of** ōmittere; **take ~ of** prehendere, comprehendere ▶ *vt* tenēre, habēre; (*possession*) obtinēre, possidēre; (*office*) gerere, fungī (*abl*); (*capacity*) capere; (*meeting*) habēre; **~ a meeting** concilium habēre; **~ one's own with** parem esse (*dat*); **~ over** differre, prōlātāre; **~ water** (*fig*) stāre ▶ *vi* manēre, dūrāre; (*opinion*) dūcere, existimāre, affirmāre; **~ back** *vt* retinēre, inhibēre ▶ *vi* gravārī, dubitāre; **~ cheap** parvī facere; **~ fast** *vt* retinēre, amplectī ▶ *vi* haerēre; **~ good** valēre; **~ out** *vt* porrigere, extendere; (*hope*) ostendere ▶ *vi* dūrāre, perstāre; **~ together** cohaerēre; **~ up** tollere; (*falling*) sustinēre; (*movement*) obstāre (*dat*), morārī; **~ with** adsentīre (*dat*)
holdfast *n* fībula *f*
holding *n* (*land*) agellus *m*
hole *n* forāmen *nt*, cavum *nt*; **make a ~ in** pertundere, perforāre
holiday *n* ōtium *nt*; festus diēs *m*; **on ~** fēriātus; **holidays** *pl* fēriae *fpl*
holily *adv* sanctē
holiness *n* sanctitās *f*
hollow *adj* cavus, concavus; (*fig*) inānis, vānus ▶ *n* cavum *nt*, caverna *f* ▶ *vt* excavāre
hollowness *n* (*fig*) vānitās *f*
holly *n* aquifolium *nt*
holy *adj* sanctus
homage *n* observantia *f*, venerātiō *f*; **pay ~ to** venerārī, colere
home *n* domus *f*; (*town, country*) patria *f*; **at ~** domī; **from ~** domō ▶ *adj* domesticus ▶ *adv* domum
homeless *adj* profugus
homely *adj* simplex, rūsticus; (*speech*) plēbēius
homestead *n* fundus *m*
homewards *adv* domum
homicide *n* (*act*) homicīdium *nt*, caedēs *f*; (*person*) homicīda *m*
homily *n* sermō *m*

homogeneous adj aequābilis
homologous adj cōnsimilis
hone n cōs f ▸ vt acuere
honest adj probus, frūgī, integer
honestly adv probē, integrē
honesty n probitās f, fidēs f
honey n mel nt
honeycomb n favus m
honeyed adj mellītus, mulsus
honorarium n stips f
honorary adj honōrārius
honour n honōs m; (repute) honestās f;
existimātiō f; (chastity) pudor m; (trust) fidēs f;
(rank) dignitās f; (award) decus nt, īnsigne nt;
(respect) observantia f ▸ vt honōrāre, decorāre;
(respect) observāre, colere; **do ~ to** honestāre
honourable adj honestus, probus; (rank)
illūstris, praeclārus
honourably adv honestē
hood n cucullus m
hoodwink vt verba dare (dat)
hoof n ungula f
hook n uncus m, hāmus m ▸ vt hāmō capere
hooked adj aduncus, hāmātus
hoop n circulus m; (toy) trochus m
hoot vi obstrepere; **~ off** (stage) explōdere
hop n saltus m; **catch on the hop** in ipsō articulō
opprimere ▸ vi salīre
hope n spēs f; **in the ~ that** sī forte; **give up ~**
spem dēpōnere, dēspērāre; **past ~** dēspērātus;
entertain hopes spem habēre ▸ vt spērāre
hopeful adj bonae speī; **be ~** aliquam spem
habēre
hopefully adv nōn sine spē
hopeless adj dēspērātus
hopelessly adv dēspēranter
hopelessness n dēspērātiō f
horde n multitūdō f
horizon n fīniēns m
horizontal adj aequus, lībrātus
horizontally adv ad lībram
horn n cornū nt; (shepherd's) būcina f
horned adj corniger
hornet n crabrō m; **stir up a hornet's nest**
crabrōnēs inrītāre
horny adj corneus
horoscope n sīdus nātālicium nt
horrible adj horrendus, horribilis, dīrus, foedus
horribly adv foedē
horrid adj horribilis
horrify vt terrēre, perterrēre
horror n horror m, terror m; odium nt
horse n equus m; (cavalry) equitēs mpl; **flog a
dead ~** asellum currere docēre; **spur a willing ~**
currentem incitāre; **horse's** equīnus
horseback n: **ride on ~** in equō vehī; **fight on ~**
ex equō pugnāre
horseman n eques m
horseradish n armoracia f
horse soldier n eques m
horticulture n hortōrum cultus m
hospitable adj hospitālis

hospitably adv hospitāliter
hospital n valētūdinārium nt
hospitality n hospitālitās f, hospitium nt
host n hospes m; (inn) caupō m; (number)
multitūdō f; (MIL) exercitus m
hostage n obses m/f
hostelry n taberna f, dēversōrium nt
hostile adj hostīlis, īnfēnsus, inimīcus; īnfestus;
in a ~ manner īnfensē, hostīliter, inimīcē
hostility n inimīcitia f; **hostilities** pl bellum nt
hot adj calidus, fervidus, aestuōsus; (boiling)
fervēns; (fig) ārdēns; **be hot** calēre, fervēre,
ārdēre; **get hot** calēscere
hotch-potch n farrāgō f
hotel n dēversōrium nt
hot-headed adj ārdēns, temerārius, praeceps
hotly adv ārdenter, ācriter
hot-tempered adj īrācundus
hot water n calida f
hound n canis m ▸ vt īnstāre (dat)
hour n hōra f
hourly adv in hōrās
house n domus f, aedēs fpl; (country) vīlla f;
(family) domus f, gēns f; **at the ~ of** apud (acc);
full ~ frequēns senātus, frequēns theātrum ▸ vt
hospitiō accipere, recipere; (things) condere
household n familia f, domus f ▸ adj familiāris,
domesticus
householder n paterfamiliās m, dominus m
housekeeping n reī familiāris cūra f
housemaid n ancilla f
housetop n fastīgium nt
housewife n māterfamiliās f, domina f
housing n hospitium nt; (horse) ōrnāmenta ntpl
hovel n gurgustium nt
hover vi pendēre; (fig) impendēre
how adv (interrog) quemadmodum; quōmodō,
quō pactō; (excl) quam; **how great/big/large**
quantus; **how long** (time) quamdiū; **how many**
quot; **how much** quantum; **how often**
quotiēns
howbeit adv tamen
however adv tamen; autem, nihilōminus;
utcumque, quōquō modō; **~ much** quamvīs,
quantumvīs; **~ great** quantuscumque
howl n ululātus m ▸ vi ululāre; (wind) fremere
howsoever adv utcumque
hub n axis m
hubbub n tumultus m
huckster n īnstitor m, propōla m
huddle n turba f ▸ vi congregārī
hue n color m; **hue and cry** clāmor m
huff n offēnsiō f ▸ vt offendere
hug n complexus m ▸ vt complectī
huge adj ingēns, immānis, immēnsus, vastus
hugely adv vehementer
hugeness n immānitās f
hulk n alveus m
hull n alveus m
hum n murmur nt, fremitus m ▸ vi murmurāre,
fremere
human adj hūmānus

human being n homō m/f
humane adj hūmānus, misericors
humanely adv hūmānē, hūmāniter
humanism n litterae fpl
humanist n homō litterātus m
humanity n hūmānitās f; misericordia f
humanize vt excolere
humanly adv hūmānitus
human nature n hūmānitās f
humble adj humilis, modestus ▸ vt dēprimere; (oneself) summittere
humbleness n humilitās f
humbly adv summissē, modestē
humbug n trīcae fpl
humdrum adj vulgāris; (style) pedester
humid adj ūmidus, madidus; **be ~** madēre
humidity n ūmor m
humiliate vt dēprimere, dēdecorāre
humiliation n dēdecus nt
humility n modestia f, animus summissus m
humorist n homō facētus m
humorous adj facētus, ioculāris, rīdiculus
humorously adv facētē
humour n facētiae fpl; (disposition) ingenium nt; (mood) libīdō f; **be in a bad ~** sibī displicēre ▸ vt indulgēre (dat), mōrem gerere (dat), mōrigerārī (dat)
hump n gibbus m
hunchback n gibber m
hundred num centum; **~ each** centēnī; **~ times** centiēns
hundredth adj centēsimus
hundredweight n centumpondium nt
hunger n famēs f ▸ vi ēsurīre
hungrily adv avidē
hungry adj ēsuriēns, iēiūnus, avidus; **be ~** ēsurīre
hunt n vēnātiō f, vēnātus m ▸ vt vēnārī, indāgāre, exagitāre
hunter n vēnātor m
hunting n vēnātiō f; (fig) aucupium nt
hunting spear n vēnābulum nt
huntress n vēnātrix f
huntsman n vēnātor m
hurdle n crātēs f; (obstacle) obex m/f
hurl vt conicere, ingerere, iaculārī, iācere
hurly-burly n turba f, tumultus m
hurrah interj euax, iō
hurricane n procella f
hurried adj praeproperus, praeceps, trepidus
hurriedly adv properātō, cursim, festīnanter
hurry vt adcelerāre, mātūrāre ▸ vi festīnāre, properāre; **~ along** vt rapere; **~ away** vi discēdere, properāre; **~ about** vi discurrere; **~ on** vt mātūrāre; **~ up** vi properāre ▸ n festīnātiō f; **in a ~** festīnanter, raptim
hurt n iniūria f, damnum nt; vulnus nt ▸ vt laedere, nocēre (dat); **it hurts** dolet
hurtful adj nocēns, damnōsus
hurtfully adv nocenter, damnōsē
hurtle vi volāre; sē praecipitāre
husband n vir m, marītus m ▸ vt parcere (dat)

husbandry n agrī cultūra f; (economy) parsimōnia f
hush n silentium nt ▸ vt silentium facere (dat), lēnīre ▸ vi tacēre, silēre; **~ up** comprimere, cēlāre ▸ interj st!
hushed adj tacitus
husk n folliculus m, siliqua f ▸ vt dēglūbāre
husky adj fuscus, raucus
hustle vt trūdere, īnstāre (dat)
hut n casa f, tugurium nt
hutch n cavea f
hyacinth n hyacinthus m
hybrid n hibrida m/f
hydra n hydra f
hyena n hyaena f
hygiene n salūbritās f
hygienic adj salūbris
hymeneal adj nūptiālis
hymn n carmen nt ▸ vt canere
hyperbole n superlātiō f
hypercritical adj quasi Aristarchus
hypocaust n hypocaustum nt
hypocrisy n simulātiō f, dissimulātiō f
hypocrite n simulātor m, dissimulātor m
hypocritical adj simulātus, fictus
hypothesis n positum nt, sūmptiō f, coniectūra f
hypothetical adj sūmptus

I *pron* ego

iambic *adj* iambēus

iambus *n* iambus *m*

ice *n* glaciēs *f*

icicle *n* stīria *f*

icon *n* simulacrum *nt*

icy *adj* glaciālis, gelidus

idea *n* nōtiō *f*, nōtitia *f*, imāgō *f*; (*Platonic*) fōrma *f*; (*expressed*) sententia *f*; **conceive the ~ of** īnfōrmāre

ideal *adj* animō comprehēnsus; (*perfect*) perfectus, optimus ▸ *n* specimen *nt*, speciēs *f*, exemplar *nt*

identical *adj* īdem, cōnsimilis

identify *vt* agnōscere

identity *n*: **establish the ~ of** cognōscere quis sit

Ides *n* Īdūs *fpl*

idiocy *n* animī imbēcillitās *f*

idiom *n* proprium *nt*, sermō *m*

idiomatic *adj* proprius

idiomatically *adv* sermōne suō, sermōne propriō

idiosyncrasy *n* proprium *nt*, libīdō *f*

idiot *n* excors *m*

idiotic *adj* fatuus, stultus

idiotically *adv* stultē, ineptē

idle *adj* ignāvus, dēses, iners; (*unoccupied*) ōtiōsus, vacuus; (*useless*) inānis, vānus; **be ~** cessāre, dēsidēre; **lie ~** (*money*) iacēre ▸ *vi* cessāre

idleness *n* ignāvia *f*, dēsidia *f*, inertia *f*; ōtium *nt*

idler *n* cessātor *m*

idly *adv* ignāvē; ōtiōsē; frustrā, nēquīquam

idol *n* simulacrum *nt*; (*person*) dēliciae *fpl*

idolater *n* falsōrum deōrum cultor *m*

idolatry *n* falsōrum deōrum cultus *m*

idolize *vt* venerārī

idyll *n* carmen Theocritēum *nt*

if *conj* sī; (*interrog*) num, utrum; **if anyone** sī quis; **if ever** sī quandō; **if not** nisī; **if only** dum, dummodo; **if ... or** sīve ... sīve; **as if** quasi, velut; **but if** sīn, quodsī; **even if** etiamsī

igneous *adj* igneus

ignite *vt* accendere, incendere ▸ *vi* ignem concipere

ignoble *adj* (*birth*) ignōbilis; (*repute*) illīberālis, turpis

ignominious *adj* ignōminiōsus, īnfāmis, turpis

ignominiously *adv* turpiter

ignominy *n* ignōminia *f*, īnfāmia *f*, dēdecus *nt*

ignoramus *n* idiōta *m*, indoctus *m*

ignorance *n* īnscītia *f*, ignōrātiō *f*

ignorant *adj* ignārus, indoctus; (*of something*) īnscītus, rudis; (*unaware*) īnscius; **be ~ of** nescīre, ignōrāre

ignorantly *adv* īnscienter, īnscītē, indoctē

ignore *vt* praetermittere

ilex *n* īlex *f*

Iliad *n* Īlias *f*

ill *adj* aeger, aegrōtus, invalidus; (*evil*) malus; **be ill** aegrōtāre; **fall ill** in morbum incidere; **ill at ease** sollicitus ▸ *adv* male, improbē ▸ *n* malum *nt*, incommodum *nt*, aerumna *f*, damnum *nt*

ill-advised *adj* incōnsultus

ill-bred *adj* agrestis, inurbānus

ill-disposed *adj* malevolus, invidus

illegal *adj* illicitus, vetitus

illegally *adv* contrā lēgēs

ill-fated *adj* īnfēlīx

ill-favoured *adj* turpis

ill-gotten *adj* male partus

ill-health *n* valētūdō *f*

illicit *adj* vetitus

illimitable *adj* īnfīnītus

illiteracy *n* litterārum īnscītia *f*

illiterate *adj* illitterātus, inērudītus

ill-natured *adj* malevolus, malignus

illness *n* morbus *m*, valētūdō *f*

illogical *adj* absurdus

ill-omened *adj* dīrus, īnfaustus

ill-starred *adj* īnfēlīx

ill-tempered *adj* īrācundus, amārus, stomachōsus

ill-timed *adj* immātūrus, intempestīvus

ill-treat *vt* malefacere (*dat*)

illuminate *vt* illūmināre, illūstrāre

illumination *n* lūmina *ntpl*

illusion *n* error *m*, somnium *nt*

illusive, illusory *adj* fallāx

illustrate *vt* illūstrāre; (*with instances*) exemplō cōnfīrmāre

illustration *n* exemplum *nt*

illustrious *adj* illūstris, īnsignis, praeclārus

illustriously *adv* praeclārē

ill will *n* invidia *f*

image *n* imāgō *f*, effigiēs *f*; (*idol*) simulacrum *nt*; (*verbal*) figūra *f*, similitūdō *f*

imagery *n* figūrae *fpl*

imaginary *adj* commentīcius, fictus

imagination *n* cōgitātiō *f*, opīniō *f*

imaginative *adj* ingeniōsus

imagine *vt* animō fingere, animum indūcere, ante oculōs pōnere; (*think*) opīnārī, arbitrārī

imbecile *adj* animō imbēcillus, fatuus, mente captus

imbecility n animī imbēcillitās f
imbibe vt adbibere; (fig) imbuī (abl)
imbrue vt īnficere
imbue vt imbuere, īnficere, tingere
imitable adj imitābilis
imitate vt imitārī
imitation n imitātiō f; (copy) imāgō f
imitator n imitātor m, imitātrix f, aemulātor m
immaculate adj integer, ēmendātus
immaculately adv integrē, sine vitiō
immaterial adj indifferēns
immature adj immātūrus
immeasurable adj immēnsus, īnfīnītus
immediate adj īnstāns, praesēns; (neighbour) proximus
immediately adv statim, extemplō, cōnfestim
immemorial adj antīquissimus; **from time ~** post hominum memoriam
immense adj immēnsus, immānis, ingēns, vastus
immensely adv vehementer
immensity n immēnsum nt, māgnitūdō f
immerse vt immergere, mergere
immigrant n advena m
immigrate vi migrāre
imminent adj īnstāns, praesēns; **be ~** imminēre, impendēre
immobile adj fīxus, immōbilis
immoderate adj immoderātus, immodestus
immoderately adv immoderātē, immodestē
immodest adj impudīcus, inverēcundus
immolate vt immolāre
immoral adj prāvus, corruptus, turpis
immorality n corruptī mōrēs mpl, turpitūdō f
immorally adv prāvē, turpiter
immortal adj immortālis, aeternus
immortality n immortālitās f
immortalize vt in astra tollere
immortally adv aeternum
immovable adj fīxus, immōbilis
immune adj immūnis, vacuus
immunity n immūnitās f, vacātiō f
immure vt inclūdere
immutability n immūtābilitās f
immutable adj immūtābilis
imp n puer improbus m
impact n ictus m, incussus m
impair vt imminuere, corrumpere
impale vt induere, īnfīgere
impalpable adj tenuissimus
impart vt impertīre, commūnicāre; (courage) addere
impartial adj aequus, medius
impartiality n aequābilitās f
impartially adv sine favōre
impassable adj invius; (mountains) inexsuperābilis; (fig) inexplicābilis
impasse n mora f, incitae fpl
impassioned adj violēns, fervidus
impassive adj rigidus, sēnsū carēns
impatience n aviditās f; (of anything) impatientia f

impatient adj trepidus, avidus; impatiēns
impatiently adv aegrē
impeach vt diem dīcere (dat), accūsāre
impeachment n accūsātiō f, crīmen nt
impeccable adj ēmendātus
impecunious adj pauper
impede vt impedīre, obstāre (dat)
impediment n impedīmentum nt
impel vt impellere, incitāre
impend vi impendēre, imminēre, īnstāre
impenetrable adj impenetrābilis; (country) invius, impervius
impenitent adj: **I am ~** nīl mē paenitet
imperative adj necessārius
imperceptible adj tenuissimus, obscurus
imperceptibly adv sēnsim
imperfect adj imperfectus, vitiōsus
imperfection n vitium nt
imperfectly adv vitiōsē
imperial adj imperātōrius, rēgius
imperil vt in discrīmen addūcere, labefactāre
imperious adj imperiōsus, superbus
imperiously adv superbē
imperishable adj immortālis, aeternus
impersonate vt partēs agere (gen)
impertinence n importūnitās f, protervitās f
impertinent adj importūnus, protervus, ineptus
impertinently adv importūnē, ineptē, protervē
imperturbable adj immōtus, gravis
impervious adj impervius, impenetrābilis
impetuosity n ārdor m, violentia f, vīs f
impetuous adj violēns, fervidus, effrēnātus
impetuously adv effrēnātē
impetus n impetus m
impiety n impietās f
impinge vi incidere
impious adj impius, profānus; **it is ~** nefas est
impiously adv impiē
impish adj improbus
implacable adj implācābilis, inexōrābilis, dūrus
implacably adv dūrē
implant vt īnserere, ingignere
implement n īnstrūmentum nt ▸ vt implēre, exsequī
implicate vt implicāre, impedīre
implication n indicium nt
implicit adj tacitus; absolūtus
implicitly adv absconditē; (trust) omnīnō, summā fidē
implore vt implōrāre, obsecrāre
imply vt significāre, continēre; **be implied** inesse
impolite adj inurbānus, illepidus
impolitely adv inurbānē
impolitic adj incōnsultus, imprūdēns
imponderable adj levissimus
import vt importāre, invehere; (mean) velle ▸ n significātiō f
importance n gravitās f, mōmentum nt; (rank)

dignitās f, amplitūdō f, auctōritās f; **it is of great ~ to me** meā māgnī rēfert

important adj gravis, magnī mōmentī; **it is ~ interest** (gen), rēfert; **more ~, most ~** antīquior, antīquissimus

importation n invectiō f

imports npl importātīcia ntpl

importunate adj molestus

importune vt flāgitāre, īnstāre (dat)

impose vt impōnere; (by order) indīcere, iniungere; **~ upon** illūdere, fraudāre, abūtī (abl)

imposing adj māgnificus, lautus

imposition n fraus f; (tax) tribūtum nt

impossible adj: **it is ~** fierī nōn potest

impost n tribūtum nt, vectīgal nt

impostor n planus m, fraudātor m

imposture n fraus f, fallācia f

impotence n īnfirmitās f

impotent adj īnfirmus, dēbilis; (with rage) impotēns

impotently adv frustrā; (rage) impotenter

impound vt inclūdere; (confiscate) pūblicāre

impoverish vt in inopiam redigere

impracticable adj: **be ~** fierī nōn posse

imprecate vt exsecrārī

imprecation n exsecrātiō f

impregnable adj inexpugnābilis

impregnate vt imbuere, īnficere

impress vt imprimere; (on mind) īnfīgere; (person) permovēre; (MIL) invītum scrībere

impression n (copy) exemplar nt; (mark) signum nt; (feeling) impulsiō f; (belief) opīniō f; **make an ~ of** exprimere; **make an ~ on** commovēre; **have the ~** opīnārī

impressionable adj crēdulus

impressive adj gravis

impressively adv graviter

impressiveness n gravitās f

imprint n impressiō f, signum nt ▶ vt imprimere; (on mind) īnfīgere, inūrere

imprison vt inclūdere, in vincula conicere

imprisonment n custōdia f, vincula ntpl

improbable adj incrēdibilis, haud vērīsimilis

impromptu adv ex tempore

improper adj indecōrus, ineptus

improperly adv prāvē, perperam

impropriety n culpa f, offēnsa f

improve ▶ vt ēmendāre, corrigere; (mind) excolere ▶ vi prōficere, meliōrem fierī

improvement n ēmendātiō f, prōfectus m

improvident adj imprōvidus; (with money) prōdigus

improvidently adv imprōvidē; prōdigē

improvise vt ex tempore compōnere, excōgitāre

imprudence n imprūdentia f

imprudent adj imprūdēns

imprudently adv imprūdenter

impudence n impudentia f, audācia f

impudent adj impudēns, audāx

impudently adv impudenter, protervē

impugn vt impugnāre, in dubium vocāre

impulse n impetus m, impulsus m

impulsive adj praeceps, violentus

impulsively adv impetū quōdam animī

impulsiveness n impetus m, violentia f

impunity n impūnitās f; **with ~** impūne

impure adj impūrus, incestus, inquinātus

impurely adv impūrē, inceste, inquinātē

impurity n impūritās f, sordēs fpl

imputation n crīmen nt

impute vt attribuere, adsignāre; **~ as a fault** vitiō vertere

in prep in (abl); (with motion) in (acc); (authors) apud (acc); (time) abl; **in my youth** adulēscēns; **in that** quod ▶ adv (rest) intrā; (motion) intrō

inaccessible adj inaccessus

inaccuracy n neglegentia f, incūria f; (error) mendum nt

inaccurate adj parum dīligēns, neglegēns

inaccurately adv neglegenter

inaction n inertia f

inactive adj iners, quiētus; **be ~** cessāre

inactivity n inertia f, ōtium nt

inadequate adj impār, parum idōneus

inadequately adv parum

inadvertency n imprūdentia f

inadvertent adj imprūdēns

inadvertently adv imprūdenter

inane adj inānis, vānus; ineptus, stultus

inanely adv ineptē

inanimate adj inanimus

inanity n ineptiae fpl, stultitia f

inapplicable adj: **be ~** nōn valēre

inappropriate adj aliēnus, parum aptus

inarticulate adj īnfāns

inartistic adj sine arte, dūrus, inēlegāns

inasmuch as conj quōniam, cum (subj)

inattention n incūria f, neglegentia f

inattentive adj neglegēns

inattentively adv neglegenter

inaudible adj: **be ~** audīrī nōn posse

inaugurate vt inaugurāre, cōnsecrāre

inauguration n cōnsecrātiō f

inauspicious adj īnfaustus, īnfēlīx

inauspiciously adv malīs ōminibus

inborn adj innātus

incalculable adj inaestimābilis

incantation n carmen nt

incapable adj inhabilis, indocilis; **be ~** nōn posse

incapacitate vt dēbilitāre

incapacity n inertia f, īnscītia f

incarcerate vt inclūdere, in vincula conicere

incarnate adj hūmānā speciē indūtus

incautious adj incautus, temerārius

incautiously adv incautē

incendiary adj incendiārius

incense n tūs nt ▶ vt inrītāre, stomachum movēre (dat); **be incensed** stomachārī

incentive n incitāmentum nt, stimulus m

inception n initium nt, exōrdium nt

incessant adj adsiduus

incessantly adv assiduē
incest n incestus m
inch n digitus m, ūncia f
incident n ēventum nt, cāsus m, rēs f
incidental adj fortuītus
incidentally adv cāsū
incipient adj prīmus
incisive adj ācer
incite vt īnstīgāre, impellere, hortārī, incitāre
incitement n invītāmentum nt, stimulus m
inciter n īnstimulātor m
incivility n importūnitās f, inhūmānitās f
inclemency n (weather) intemperiēs f
inclement adj asper, tristis
inclination n inclīnātiō f, animus m, libīdō f;
(slope) clīvus m
incline vt inclīnāre; (person) indūcere ▸ vi
inclīnāre, incumbere; ~ **towards** sē adclīnāre
▸ n adclīvitās f, clīvus m
inclined adj inclīnātus, prōpēnsus; **I am ~ to**
think haud sciō an
include vt inclūdere, continēre, complectī
incognito adv clam
incoherent adj interruptus; **be ~ nōn**
cohaerēre
income n frūctus m, mercēs f
incommensurate adj dispār
incommode vt molestiam adferre (dat)
incomparable adj singulāris, eximius
incompatibility n discrepantia f, repugnantia f
incompatible adj īnsociābilis, repugnāns;
be ~ with dissidēre ab, repugnāre (dat)
incompetence n inertia f, īnscītia f
incompetent adj iners, īnscītus
incomplete adj imperfectus
incomprehensible adj incrēdibilis
inconceivable adj incrēdibilis
inconclusive adj inānis
incongruous adj absonus, aliēnus
inconsiderable adj exiguus
inconsiderate adj imprōvidus, incōnsultus
inconsistency n discrepantia f, incōnstantia f
inconsistent adj; **be ~ discrepāre;**
be ~ with abhorrēre ab, repugnāre (dat)
inconsistently adv incōnstanter
inconsolable adj nōn cōnsōlābilis
inconspicuous adj obscūrus; **be ~ latēre**
inconstancy n incōnstantia f, levitās f
inconstant adj incōnstāns, levis, mōbilis
inconstantly adv incōnstanter
incontestable adj certus
incontinence n incontinentia f
incontinent adj intemperāns
inconvenience n incommodum nt ▸ vt
incommodāre
inconvenient adj incommodus
inconveniently adv incommodē
incorporate vt īnserere, adiungere
incorrect adj falsus; **be ~ nōn cōnstāre**
incorrectly adv falsō, perperam
incorrigible adj improbus, perditus
incorruptibility n integritās f

incorruptible adj incorruptus
increase n incrēmentum nt, additāmentum nt,
auctus m ▸ vt augēre, amplificāre ▸ vi crēscere,
incrēscere
increasingly adv magis magisque
incredible adj incrēdibilis
incredibly adv incrēdibiliter
incredulous adj incrēdulus
increment n incrēmentum nt
incriminate vt crīminārī
inculcate vt inculcāre, īnfīgere
incumbent adj: **it is ~ on** oportet
incur vt subīre; (guilt) admittere
incurable adj īnsānābilis
incursion n incursiō f
indebted adj obnoxius; **be ~ dēbēre**
indecency n obscēnitās f
indecent adj obscēnus, impudīcus
indecently adv obscēnē
indecision n dubitātiō f
indecisive adj anceps, dubius; **the battle is ~**
ancipitī Marte pugnātur
indecisively adv incertō ēventū
indecorous adj indecōrus
indeed adv profectō, sānē; (concessive) quidem;
(interrog) itane vērō?; (reply) certē, vērō; (with
pron) dēmum; (with adj, adv, conj) adeō
indefatigable adj impiger
indefensible adj: **be ~ dēfendī nōn posse;**
(belief) tenērī nōn posse; (offence) excūsārī nōn
posse
indefinite adj incertus, ambiguus, īnfīnītus
indefinitely adv ambiguē; (time) in incertum
indelicate adj pūtidus, indecōrus
independence n lībertās f
independent adj līber, suī iūris
indescribable adj inēnārrābilis
indestructible adj perennis
indeterminate adj incertus
index n index m
indicate vt indicāre, significāre
indication n indicium nt, signum nt
indict vt diem dīcere (dat), accūsāre, nōmen
dēferre (gen)
indictment n accūsātiō f
indifference n neglegentia f, languor m
indifferent adj (manner) neglegēns, frīgidus,
sēcūrus; (quality) mediocris
indifferently adv neglegenter; mediocriter;
(without distinction) prōmiscuē, sine discrīmine
indigence n indigentia f, egestās f
indigenous adj indigena
indigent adj indigēns, egēnus
indigestible adj crūdus
indigestion n crūditās f
indignant adj indignābundus, īrātus; **be ~**
indignārī
indignantly adv īrātē
indignation n indignātiō f, dolor m
indignity n contumēlia f, indignitās f
indigo n Indicum nt
indirect adj oblīquus

indirectly adv oblīquē, per ambāgēs
indirectness n ambāgēs fpl
indiscipline n lascīvia f, licentia f
indiscreet adj incōnsultus, imprūdēns
indiscreetly adv incōnsultē, imprūdenter
indiscretion n imprūdentia f; (act) culpa f
indiscriminate adj prōmiscuus
indiscriminately adv prōmiscuē, sine
discrīmine
indispensable adj necesse, necessārius
indisposed adj īnfirmus, aegrōtus; (will)
āversus, aliēnātus; **be ~** aegrōtāre; abhorrēre,
aliēnārī
indisposition n īnfirmitās f, valētūdō f
indisputable adj certus, manifestus
indisputably adv certē, sine dubiō
indissoluble adj indissolūbilis
indistinct adj obscūrus, obtūsus; (speaker)
balbus
indistinctly adv obscūrē; **pronounce ~**
opprimere; **speak ~** balbūtīre
individual adj proprius ▶ n homō m/f, prīvātus
m; **individuals** pl singulī mpl
individuality n proprium nt
individually adv singulātim, prīvātim
indivisible adj indīviduus
indolence n dēsidia f, ignāvia f, inertia f
indolent adj dēses, ignāvus, iners
indolently adv ignāvē
indomitable adj indomitus
indoor adj umbrātilis
indoors adv intus; (motion) intrā
indubitable adj certus
indubitably adv sine dubiō
induce vt indūcere, addūcere, persuādēre (dat)
inducement n illecebra f, praemium nt
induction n (LOGIC) inductiō f
indulge vt indulgēre (dat)
indulgence n indulgentia f, venia f; (favour)
grātia f
indulgent adj indulgēns, lēnis
indulgently adv indulgenter
industrious adj industrius, impiger, dīligēns
industriously adv industriē
industry n industria f, dīligentia f, labor m
inebriated adj ēbrius
inebriation n ēbrietās f
ineffable adj eximius
ineffective adj inūtilis, invalidus
ineffectively adv ināniter
ineffectual adj inritus
inefficient adj īnscītus, parum strēnuus
inelegant adj inēlegāns, inconcinnus
inelegantly adv inēleganter
inept adj ineptus
ineptly adv ineptē
inequality n dissimilitūdō f, inīquitās f
inert adj iners, sōcors, immōbilis
inertia n inertia f
inertly adv tardē, lentē
inestimable adj inaestimābilis
inevitable adj necessārius

inevitably adv necessāriō
inexact adj parum subtīlis
inexhaustible adj perennis
inexorable adj inexōrābilis
inexpediency n inūtilitās f, incommodum nt
inexpedient adj inūtilis; **it is ~** nōn expedit
inexpensive adj vīlis
inexperience n imperītia f, īnscītia f
inexperienced adj imperītus, rudis, īnscītus
inexpert adj imperītus
inexpiable adj inexpiābilis
inexplicable adj inexplicābilis, inēnōdābilis
inexpressible adj inēnārrābilis
inextricable adj inexplicābilis
infallible adj certus, errōris expers
infamous adj īnfāmis, flāgitiōsus
infamously adv flāgitiōsē
infamy n īnfāmia f, flāgitium nt, dēdecus nt
infancy n īnfantia f; (fig) incūnābula ntpl
infant n īnfāns m/f
infantile adj puerīlis
infantry n peditēs mpl, peditātus m
infantryman n pedes m
infatuate vt īnfatuāre
infatuated adj dēmēns
infatuation n dēmentia f
infect vt īnficere
infection n contāgiō f
infer vt īnferre, colligere
inference n conclūsiō f
inferior adj (position) īnferior; (quality) dēterior
infernal adj īnfernus
infest vt frequentāre
infidel adj impius
infidelity n perfidia f, īnfidēlitās f
infiltrate vi sē īnsinuāre
infinite adj īnfīnītus, immēnsus
infinitely adv longē, immēnsum
infinitesimal adj minimus
infinity n īnfīnitās f
infirm adj īnfirmus, invalidus
infirmary n valētūdinārium nt
infirmity n morbus m
inflame vt accendere, incendere, īnflammāre;
be inflamed exārdēscere
inflammation n (MED) īnflātiō f
inflate vt īnflāre
inflated adj (fig) īnflātus, tumidus
inflexible adj rigidus
inflexion n (GRAM) flexūra f; (voice) flexiō f
inflict vt īnflīgere, incutere; (burden) impōnere;
(penalty) sūmere; **be inflicted with** labōrāre ex
infliction n poena f; malum nt
influence n (physical) impulsiō f, mōmentum
nt; (moral) auctōritās f; (partial) grātia f; **have ~**
valēre; **have great ~ with** plūrimum posse
apud; **under the ~ of** īnstinctus (abl) ▶ vt
impellere, movēre, addūcere
influential adj gravis, potēns; grātiōsus
influenza n gravēdō f
inform vt docēre, certiōrem facere; **~ against**
nōmen dēferre (gen)

informant n index m, auctor m
information n indicium nt, nūntius m
informer n index m, dēlātor m; **turn ~** indicium profitērī
infrequent adj rārus
infrequently adv rārō
infringe vt violāre, imminuere
infringement n violātiō f
infuriate vt efferāre
infuriated adj furibundus
infuse vt īnfundere; (fig) inicere
ingenious adj ingeniōsus, callidus; (thing) artificiōsus
ingeniously adv callidē, summā arte
ingenuity n ars f, artificium nt, acūmen nt
ingenuous adj ingenuus, simplex
ingenuously adv ingenuē, simpliciter
ingenuousness n ingenuitās f
ingle n focus m
inglorious adj inglōrius, ignōbilis, inhonestus
ingloriously adv sine glōriā, inhonestē
ingot n later m
ingrained adj īnsitus
ingratiate vt: **~ oneself with** grātiam inīre ab, sē īnsinuāre in familiāritātem (gen); **~ oneself into** sē īnsinuāre in (acc)
ingratitude n ingrātus animus m
ingredient n pars f
inhabit vt incolere, habitāre in (abl)
inhabitable adj habitābilis
inhabitant n incola m/f
inhale vt haurīre
inharmonious adj dissonus
inherent adj īnsitus; **be ~ in** inhaerēre (dat), inesse (dat)
inherently adv nātūrā
inherit vt excipere
inheritance n hērēditās f, patrimōnium nt; **divide an ~** herctum ciēre; **come into an ~** hērēditātem adīre
inheritor n hērēs m/f
inhibit vt prohibēre, inhibēre
inhospitable adj inhospitālis
inhuman adj inhūmānus, immānis, crūdēlis
inhumanity n inhūmānitās f, crūdēlitās f
inhumanly adv inhūmānē, crūdēliter
inimical adj inimīcus
inimitable adj singulāris, eximius
iniquitous adj inīquus, improbus, nefārius
iniquity n scelus nt, flāgitium nt
initial adj prīmus
initiate vt initiāre; (with knowledge) imbuere
initiative n initium nt; **take the ~** initium capere, facere; occupāre (inf)
inject vt inicere
injudicious adj incōnsultus, imprūdēns
injunction n iussum nt, praeceptum nt
injure vt laedere, nocēre (dat)
injurious adj damnōsus, nocēns
injury n iniūria f, damnum nt; (bodily) vulnus nt
injustice n iniūria f, inīquitās f
ink n ātrāmentum nt

inkling n audītiō f, suspiciō f
inland adj mediterrāneus; **further ~** interior
inlay vt īnserere
inlet n sinus m, aestuārium nt
inly adv penitus
inmate n inquilīnus m
inmost adj intimus
inn n dēversōrium nt; caupōna f, taberna f
innate adj innātus, īnsitus
inner adj interior
innermost adj intimus
innkeeper n caupō m
innocence n innocentia f
innocent adj innocēns, īnsōns; (character) integer, castus
innocently adv innocenter, integrē, castē
innocuous adj innoxius
innovate vt novāre
innovation n novum nt, nova rēs f
innovator n novārum rērum auctor m
innuendo n verbum inversum nt
innumerable adj innumerābilis
inoffensive adj innocēns
inoffensively adv innocenter
inopportune adj intempestīvus
inopportunely adv intempestīvē
inordinate adj immodicus, immoderātus
inordinately adv immoderātē
inquest n quaestiō f; **hold an ~ on** quaerere dē
inquire vi exquīrere, rogāre; **~ into** inquīrere in (acc), investigāre
inquiry n quaestiō f, investīgātiō f; (asking) interrogātiō f; **make ~** exquīrere; **make inquiries about** inquīrere in (acc); **hold an ~ on** quaerere dē, quaestiōnem īnstituere dē
inquisition n inquīsītiō f
inquisitive adj cūriōsus
inquisitiveness n cūriōsitās f
inquisitor n inquīsītor m
inroad n incursiō f, impressiō f; **make an ~** incursāre
insane adj īnsānus, mente captus; **be ~** īnsānīre
insanity n īnsānia f, dēmentia f
insatiable adj īnsatiābilis, inexplēbilis, īnsaturābilis
insatiably adv īnsaturābiliter
inscribe vt īnscrībere
inscription n epigramma nt; (written) īnscrīptiō f
inscrutable adj obscūrus
insect n bestiola f
insecure adj īnstabilis, intūtus
insecurity n perīcula ntpl
insensate adj ineptus, stultus
insensible adj torpidus; (fig) dūrus
insensitive adj dūrus
inseparable adj coniūnctus; **be the ~ companion of** ab latere esse (gen)
inseparably adv coniūnctē
insert vt īnserere, immittere, interpōnere
insertion n interpositiō f
inshore adv prope lītus

inside adv intus; (motion) intrō ▶ adj interior ▶ n pars f interior ▶ prep intrā (acc); **get right ~** sē īnsinuāre in (acc); **turn ~ out** excutere; **on the ~** interior

insidious adj īnsidiōsus, subdolus

insidiously adv īnsidiōsē

insight n intellegentia f, cognitiō f

insignia n īnsignia ntpl

insignificance n levitās f

insignificant adj levis, exiguus, nullīus mōmentī; (position) humilis

insincere adj simulātus, fūcōsus

insincerely adv simulātē

insincerity n simulātiō f, fraus f

insinuate vt īnsinuāre; (hint) significāre ▶ vi sē īnsinuāre

insinuating adj blandus

insinuation n ambigua verba ntpl

insipid adj īnsulsus, frīgidus

insipidity n īnsulsitās f

insist vi īnstāre; **~ on** postulāre

insistence n pertinācia f

insistent adj pertināx

insolence n īnsolentia f, contumācia f, superbia f

insolent adj īnsolēns, contumāx, superbus

insolently adv īnsolenter

insoluble adj inexplicābilis

insolvency n reī familiāris naufragium nt

insolvent adj: **be ~** solvendō nōn esse

inspect vt īnspicere; (MIL) recēnsēre

inspection n cognitiō f; (MIL) recēnsiō f

inspector n cūrātor m

inspiration n adflātus m, īnstinctus m

inspire vt īnstinguere, incendere

instability n mōbilitās f

install vt inaugurāre

instalment n pēnsiō f

instance n exemplum nt; **for ~** exemplī causā, grātiā; **at the ~** admonitū; **at my ~** mē auctōre ▶ vt memorāre

instant adj īnstāns, praesēns ▶ n temporis pūnctum nt, mōmentum nt

instantaneous adj praesēns

instantaneously adv continuō, īlicō

instantly adv īlicō, extemplō

instead of prep prō (abl), locō (gen); (with verb) nōn ... sed

instigate vt īnstīgāre, impellere

instigation n impulsus m, stimulus m; auctōritās f; **at my ~** mē auctōre

instigator n īnstimulātor m, auctor m

instil vt imbuere, adspīrāre, inicere

instinct n nātūra f, ingenium nt, sēnsus m

instinctive adj nātūrālis

instinctively adv nātūrā, ingeniō suō

institute vt īnstituere, inaugurāre

institution n īnstitūtum nt; societās f

instruct vt docēre, īnstituere, īnstruere; ērudīre; (order) praecipere (dat)

instruction n doctrīna f, disciplīna f; praeceptum nt; **give instructions** dēnūntiāre, praecipere

instructor n doctor m, praeceptor m

instructress n magistra f

instrument n īnstrūmentum nt; (music) fidēs fpl; (legal) tabulae fpl

instrumental adj ūtilis

instrumentalist n fidicen m, fidicina f

instrumentality n opera f

insubordinate adj turbulentus, sēditiōsus

insubordination n intemperantia f, licentia f

insufferable adj intolerandus, intolerābilis

insufficiency n inopia f

insufficient adj minor; **be ~** nōn sufficere

insufficiently adv parum

insulate vt sēgregāre

insult n iniūria f, contumēlia f, probrum nt ▶ vt maledīcere (dat), contumēliam impōnere (dat)

insulting adj contumēliōsus

insultingly adv contumēliōsē

insuperable adj inexsuperābilis

insupportable adj intolerandus, intolerābilis

insurance n cautiō f

insure vi cavēre

insurgent n rebellis m

insurmountable adj inexsuperābilis

insurrection n mōtus m, sēditiō f

intact adj integer, intāctus, incolumis

integrity n integritās f, innocentia f, fidēs f

intellect n ingenium nt, mēns f, animus m

intellectual adj ingeniōsus

intelligence n intellegentia f, acūmen nt; (MIL) nūntius m

intelligent adj ingeniōsus, sapiēns, argūtus

intelligently adv ingeniōsē, sapienter, satis acūtē

intelligible adj perspicuus, apertus

intemperance n intemperantia f, licentia f

intemperate adj intemperāns, intemperātus

intemperately adv intemperanter

intend vt (with infin) in animō habēre, velle; (with object) dēstināre

intense adj ācer, nimius

intensely adv valdē, nimium

intensify vt augēre, amplificāre; **be intensified** ingravēscere

intensity n vīs f

intensive adj ācer, multus, adsiduus

intensively adv summō studiō

intent adj ērēctus, intentus; **be ~ on** animum intendere in (acc) ▶ n cōnsilium nt; **with ~** cōnsultō

intention n cōnsilium nt, prōpositum nt; **it is my ~** mihi in animō est; **with the ~ of** eā mente, eō cōnsiliō ut (subj)

intentionally adv cōnsultō, dē industriā

inter vt humāre

intercalary adj intercalāris

intercalate vt intercalāre

intercede vi intercēdere, dēprecārī

intercept vt excipere, intercipere; (cut off) interclūdere

intercession n dēprecātiō f; (tribune's) intercessiō f

intercessor n dēprecātor m
interchange vt permūtāre ▶ n permūtātiō f, vicissitūdō f
intercourse n commercium nt, ūsus m, cōnsuētūdō f
interdict n interdictum nt ▶ vt interdīcere (dat), vetāre
interest n (advantage) commodum nt; (study) studium nt; (money) faenus nt, ūsūra f; compound ~ anatocismus m; rate of ~ faenus nt; ~ at 12 per cent (per annum) centēsimae fpl; it is of ~ interest; it is in my interests meā interest; consult the interests of cōnsulere (dat); take an ~ in animum intendere (dat) ▶ vt dēlectāre, capere; (audience) tenēre; ~ oneself in studēre (dat)
interested adj attentus, (for gain) ambitiōsus
interesting adj iūcundus, novus
interfere vi intervenīre; (with) sē interpōnere (dat); sē admiscēre ad; (hinder) officere (dat)
interference n interventus m, intercessiō f
interim n: in the ~ interim, intereā
interior adj interior ▶ n pars interior f; (country) interiōra ntpl
interject vt exclāmāre
interjection n interiectiō f
interlace vt intexere
interlard vt variāre
interlock vt implicāre
interloper n interpellātor m
interlude n embolium nt
intermarriage n cōnūbium nt
intermediary adj medius ▶ n internūntius m
intermediate adj medius
interment n humātiō f
interminable adj sempiternus, longus
intermingle vt sē immiscēre ▶ vi sē immiscēre
intermission n intercapēdō f, intermissiō f
intermittent adj interruptus
intermittently adv interdum
intern vt inclūdere
internal adj internus; (POL) domesticus
internally adv intus, domī
international adj: ~ law iūs gentium
internecine adj internecīvus
interplay n vicēs fpl
interpolate vt interpolāre
interpose vt interpōnere ▶ vi intercēdere
interposition n intercessiō f
interpret vt interpretārī
interpretation n interpretātiō f
interpreter n interpres m/f
interrogate vt interrogāre, percontārī
interrogation n interrogātiō f, percontātiō f
interrupt vt (action) intercipere; (speaker) interpellāre; (talk) dirimere; (continuity) intermittere
interrupter n interpellātor m
interruption n interpellātiō f; intermissiō f
intersect vt dīvidere, secāre
intersperse vt distinguere
interstice n rīma f

intertwine vt intexere, implicāre
interval n intervallum nt, spatium nt; after an ~ spatiō interpositō; after an ~ of a year annō interiectō; at intervals interdum; at frequent intervals identidem; leave an ~ intermittere
intervene vt intercēdere, intervenīre
intervention n intercessiō f, interventus m; by the ~ of intercursū (gen)
interview n colloquium nt, aditus m ▶ vt convenīre
interweave vt implicāre, intexere
intestate adj intestātus ▶ adv intestātō
intestine adj intestīnus; (POL) domesticus ▶ npl intestīna ntpl; (victim's) exta ntpl
intimacy n familiāritās f
intimate adj familiāris; be an ~ friend of ab latere esse (gen); a very ~ friend perfamiliāris m/f ▶ vt dēnūntiāre
intimately adv familiāriter
intimation n dēnūntiātiō f; (hint) indicium nt
intimidate vt minārī (dat), terrōrem inicere (dat)
intimidation n metus m, minae fpl
into prep in (acc), intrā (acc)
intolerable adj intolerandus, intolerābilis
intolerably adv intoleranter
intolerance n impatientia f
intolerant adj impatiēns, intolerāns
intonation n sonus m, flexiō f
intone vt cantāre
intoxicate vt ēbrium reddere
intoxicated adj ēbrius
intoxication n ēbrietās f
intractable adj indocilis, difficilis
intransigent adj obstinātus
intrepid adj intrepidus, impavidus
intrepidity n audācia f, fortitūdō f
intricacy n implicātiō f
intricate adj implicātus, involūtus
intricately adv implicitē
intrigue n factiō f, artēs fpl, fallācia f ▶ vi māchinārī, fallāciīs ūtī
intriguing adj factiōsus; blandus
intrinsic adj vērus, innātus
intrinsically adv per sē
introduce vt indūcere, īnferre, importāre; (acquaintance) commendāre; (custom) īnstituere
introduction n exōrdium nt, prooemium nt; (of person) commendātiō f; letter of ~ litterae commendātīciae fpl
intrude vi sē interpōnere, intervenīre
intruder n interpellātor m, advena m; (fig) aliēnus m
intrusion n interpellātiō f
intuition n sēnsus m, cognitiō f
inundate vt inundāre
inundation n ēluviō f
inure vt dūrāre, adsuēfacere
invade vt invādere
invalid adj aeger, dēbilis; (null) inritus
invalidate vt īnfirmāre

invaluable adj inaestimābilis
invariable adj cōnstāns, immūtābilis
invariably adv semper
invasion n incursiō f
invective n convīcium nt
inveigh vi: ~ **against** invehī in (acc), īnsectārī
inveigle vt illicere, pellicere
invent vt fingere, comminīscī, invenīre
invention n inventum nt; (faculty) inventiō f
inventor n inventor m, auctor m
inverse adj inversus
inversely adv inversō ōrdine
invert vt invertere
invest vt (in office) inaugurāre; (MIL) obsidēre, circumsedēre; (money) locāre
investigate vt investīgāre, indāgāre; (case) cognōscere
investigation n investīgātiō f, indāgātiō f; (case) cognitiō f
investment n (MIL) obsessiō f; (money) locāta pecūnia f
inveterate adj inveterātus, vetus; **become ~** inveterāscere
invidious adj invidiōsus
invidiously adv invidiōsē
invigorate vt recreāre, reficere
invincible adj invictus
inviolable adj inviolātus; (person) sacrōsanctus
inviolably adv inviolātē
inviolate adj integer
invisible adj caecus; **be ~** vidērī nōn posse
invitation n invītātiō f; **at the ~ of** invītātū (gen)
invite vt invītāre, vocāre
inviting adj suāvis, blandus
invitingly adv blandē, suāviter
invocation n testātiō f
invoke vt invocāre, testārī
involuntarily adv īnscienter, invītus
involuntary adj coāctus
involve vt implicāre, involvere; **be involved in** inligārī (abl)
invulnerable adj inviolābilis; **be ~** vulnerārī nōn posse
inward adj interior
inwardly adv intus
inwards adv intrōrsus
inweave vt intexere
inwrought adj intextus
irascibility n īrācundia f
irascible adj īrācundus
irate adj īrātus
ire n īra f
iris n hyacinthus m
irk vt incommodāre; **I am irked** mē piget
irksome adj molestus
irksomeness n molestia f
iron n ferrum nt; **of ~** ferreus ▶ adj ferreus
ironical adj inversus
ironically adv inversīs verbīs
iron mine n ferrāria f
ironmonger n negōtiātor ferrārius m

ironmongery n ferrāmenta ntpl
iron ore n ferrum īnfectum nt
iron-tipped adj ferrātus
irony n illūsiō f, verbōrum inversiō f, dissimulātiō f
irradiate vt illūstrāre
irrational adj absurdus, ratiōnis expers; (animal) brūtus
irrationally adv absurdē, sine ratiōne
irreconcilable adj repugnāns, īnsociābilis
irrefutable adj certus, invictus
irregular adj incompositus; (ground) inaequālis; (meeting) extraōrdinārius; (troops) tumultuāriu**s**
irregularity n inaequālitās f; (conduct) prāvitās f, licentia f; (election) vitium nt
irregularly adv nullō ōrdine; (elected) vitiō
irrelevant adj aliēnus
irreligion n impietās f
irreligious adj impius
irremediable adj īnsānābilis
irreparable adj inrevocābilis
irreproachable adj integer, innocēns
irresistible adj invictus
irresolute adj dubius, anceps
irresolutely adv dubitanter
irresolution n dubitātiō f
irresponsibility n licentia f
irresponsible adj lascīvus, levis
irretrievable adj inrevocābilis
irreverence n impietās f
irreverent adj impius
irreverently adv impiē
irrevocable adj inrevocābilis
irrigate vt inrigāre
irrigation n inrigātiō f
irritability n īrācundia f
irritable adj īrācundus
irritate vt inrītāre, stomachum movēre (dat)
irritation n īrācundia f, stomachus m
island n īnsula f
islander n īnsulānus m
isle n īnsula f
isolate vt sēgregāre, sēparāre
isolation n sōlitūdō f
issue n (result) ēventus m, exitus m; (children) prōlēs f; (question) rēs f; (book) ēditiō f; **decide the ~** dēcernere, dēcertāre; **the point at ~** quā dē rē agitur ▶ vt distribuere; (book) ēdere; (announcement) prōmulgāre; (coin) ērogāre ▶ vi ēgredī, ēmānāre; (result) ēvādere, ēvenīre
isthmus n isthmus m
it pron hōc, id
itch n (disease) scabiēs f; (fig) cacoēthes nt ▶ vi prūrīre
item n nōmen nt, rēs f
iterate vt iterāre
itinerant adj vāgus, circumforāneus
itinerary n iter nt
its adj suus, ēius
itself pron ipse, ipsa, ipsum
ivory n ebur nt ▶ adj eburneus
ivy n hedera f

jabber vi blaterāre
jackdaw n grāculus m
jaded adj dēfessus, fatīgātus
jagged adj serrātus
jail n carcer m
jailer n custōs m, carcerārius m
jam vt comprimere; (way) obstruere
jamb n postis m
jangle vi crepitāre; rixārī
janitor n iānitor m
January n mēnsis Iānuārius m; **of ~** Iānuārius
jar n urna f; (for wine) amphora f; (for water) hydria f; (sound) offēnsa f; (quarrel) rixa f ▸ vi offendere
jasper n iaspis f
jaundice n morbus arquātus
jaundiced adj ictericus
jaunt n: **take a ~** excurrere
jauntily adv hilare, festīvē
jauntiness n hilaritās f
jaunty adj hilaris, festīvus
javelin n iaculum nt, pīlum nt; **throw the ~** iaculārī
jaw n māla f; **jaws** pl faucēs fpl
jay n grāculus m
jealous adj invidus; **be ~ of** invidēre (dat)
jealousy n invidia f
jeer n irrīsiō f ▸ vi irrīdēre; **~ at** illūdere
jejune adj iēiūnus, exīlis
jeopardize vt in perīculum addūcere
jeopardy n perīculum nt
jerk n subitus mōtus m
jest n iocus m
jester n scurra m
jet n (mineral) gagātēs m; (of water) saltus m ▸ vi salīre
jetsam n ēiectāmenta ntpl
jettison vt ēicere
jetty n mōlēs f
Jew n Iūdaeus m
jewel n gemma f
Jewish adj Iūdaicus
jig n tripudium nt
jilt vt repudiāre

jingle n nēnia f ▸ vi crepitāre, tinnīre
job n opus nt
jocose adj see **jocular**
jocular adj facētus, ioculāris
jocularity n facētiae fpl
jocularly adv facētē, per iocum
jocund adj hilaris, festīvus
jog vt fodicāre; (fig) stimulāre ▸ vi ambulāre
join vt iungere, coniungere, cōpulāre ▸ vi coniungī, sē coniungere; **~ in** interesse (dat), sē immiscēre (dat); **~ battle with** proelium committere (abl)
joiner n faber m
joint adj commūnis ▸ n commissūra f; (of body) articulus m, nōdus m; **by ~** articulātim
jointed adj geniculātus
joint-heir n cohērēs m/f
jointly adv ūnā, coniūnctē
joist n tignum nt
joke n iocus m ▸ vi iocārī, lūdere
joking n iocus m; **~ apart** remōtō iocō
jokingly adv per iocum
jollity n hilaritās f, festīvitās f
jolly adj hilaris, festīvus
jolt vt iactāre
jolting n iactātiō f
jostle vt agitāre, offendere
jot n minimum nt; **not a jot** nihil; **not care a jot** nōn floccī facere
journal n ācta diūrna ntpl
journey n iter nt
journeyman n opifex m
Jove n Iuppiter m
jovial adj hilaris
joviality n hilaritās f
jovially adv hilare
jowl n māla f; **cheek by ~** iuxtā
joy n gaudium nt, laetitia f, alacritās f
joyful adj laetus, hilaris
joyfully adv laetē, hilare
joyfulness n gaudium nt, laetitia f
joyless adj tristis, maestus
joyous adj see **joyful**
joyously adv see **joyfully**
jubilant adj laetus, gaudiō exsultāns
judge n iūdex m, arbiter m ▸ vt iūdicāre; (think) exīstimāre, cēnsēre; **~ between** dīiūdicāre
judgeship n iūdicātus m
judgment n iūdicium nt, arbitrium nt; (opinion) sententia f; (punishment) poena f; (wisdom) iūdicium nt; **in my ~** meō animō, meō arbitrātū; **pass ~ on** statuere dē; **sit in ~** iūdicium exercēre
judgment seat n tribūnal nt
judicature n iūrisdictiō f; (men) iūdicēs mpl
judicial adj iūdiciālis; (LAW) iūdiciārius
judiciary n iūdicēs mpl
judicious adj prūdēns, cōnsīderātus
judiciously adv prūdenter
jug n hydria f, urceus m
juggler n praestīgiātor m
juggling n praestīgiae fpl
juice n liquor m, sūcus m

juicy adj sūcī plēnus
July n mēnsis Quīnctīlis, Iūlius m; **of ~** Quīnctīlis, Iūlius
jumble n congeriēs f ▸ vt cōnfundere
jump n saltus m ▸ vi salīre; **~ across** transilīre; **~ at** (opportunity) captāre, adripere, amplectī; **~ down** dēsilīre; **~ on to** īnsilīre in (acc)
junction n coniūnctiō f
juncture n tempus nt
June n mēnsis Iūnius; **of ~** Iūnius
junior adj iūnior, nātū minor
juniper n iūniperus f
Juno n Iūnō, Iūnōnis f
Jupiter n Iuppiter, Iovis m
juridical adj iūdiciārius
jurisconsult n iūriscōnsultus m
jurisdiction n iūrisdictiō f, diciō f; **exercise ~** iūs dīcere
jurisprudence n iūrisprūdentia f
jurist n iūriscōnsultus m
juror n iūdex m
jury n iūdicēs mpl
just adj iūstus, aequus ▸ adv (exactly) prōrsus; (only) modo; (time) commodum, modo; (with adv) dēmum, dēnique; (with pron) adeō dēmum, ipse; **~ as** (comparison) aequē ac, perinde ac, quemadmodum; sīcut; **~ before** (time) cum māximē, sub (acc); **~ now** modo, nunc; **~ so** ita prōrsus, sānē; **only ~** vix
justice n iūstitia f, aequitās f, iūs nt; (person) praetor m; **administer ~** iūs reddere
justiciary n praetor m
justifiable adj iūstus
justifiably adv iūre
justification n pūrgātiō f, excūsātiō f
justify vt excūsāre, pūrgāre
justly adv iūstē, aequē; iūre, meritō
jut vi prōminēre, excurrere
jutting adj prōiectus
juvenile adj iuvenīlis, puerīlis

k

keel n carīna f
keen adj ācer; (mind) acūtus, argūtus; (sense) sagāx; (pain) acerbus; **I am ~ on** studeō
keenly adv ācriter, sagāciter, acūtē, acerbē
keenness n (scent) sagācitās f; (sight) aciēs f; (pain) acerbitās f; (eagerness) studium nt, ārdor m
keep vt servāre, tenēre, habēre; (celebrate) agere, celebrāre; (guard) custōdīre; (obey) observāre; (preserve) cōnservāre; (rear) alere, pāscere; (store) condere; **~ apart** distinēre; **~ away** arcēre; **~ back** dētinēre, reservāre; **~ down** comprimere; (exuberance) dēpāscere; **~ in** cohibēre, claudere; **~ in with** grātiam sequī (gen); **~ off** arcēre, dēfendere; **~ one's word** fidem praestāre; **~ one's hands off** manūs abstinēre; **~ house** domī sē retinēre; **~ secret** cēlāre; **~ together** continēre; **~ up** sustinēre, cōnservāre; **~ up with** subsequī; **~ waiting** dēmorārī ▸ vi dūrāre, manēre ▸ n arx f
keeper n custōs m
keeping n custōdia f; **in ~ with** prō (abl); **be in ~ with** convenīre (dat)
keg n cadus m
ken n cōnspectus m
kennel n stabulum nt
kerb n crepīdō f
kernel n grānum nt, nucleus m
kettle n lebēs f
key n clāvis f; (fig) claustra ntpl, iānua f; **key position** cardō m
kick vi calcitrāre ▸ vt calce ferīre
kid n haedus m
kidnap vt surripere
kidnapper n plagiārius m
kidney n rēn m
kidney bean n phasēlus m
kid's adj haedīnus
kill vt interficere, interimere; (in battle) occīdere; (murder) necāre, iugulāre; (time) perdere
killer n interfector m
kiln n fornāx f
kin n cognātī mpl, propinquī mpl; **next of kin** proximī mpl

kind *adj* bonus, benīgnus, benevolus, cōmis
▶ *n* genus *nt*; **of such a ~** tālis; **what ~ of** quālis
kindle *vt* incendere, succendere, īnflammāre
kindliness *n* cōmitās *f*, hūmānitās *f*
kindling *n* (*fuel*) fōmes *m*
kindly *adv* benīgnē
kindness *n* benīgnitās *f*, benevolentia *f*; (*act*) beneficium *nt*, officium *nt*, grātia *f*
kindred *n* necessitūdō *f*, cognātiō *f*; propinquī *mpl*, cognātī *mpl* ▶ *adj* cognātus, adfīnis
king *n* rēx *m*
kingdom *n* rēgnum *nt*
kingfisher *n* alcēdō *f*
kingly *adj* rēgius, rēgālis
kingship *n* rēgnum *nt*
kink *n* vitium *nt*
kinsfolk *n* cognātī *mpl*, necessāriī *mpl*
kinsman *n* cognātus *m*, propinquus *m*, necessārius *m*
kinswoman *n* cognāta *f*, propinqua *f*, necessāria *f*
kismet *n* fātum *nt*
kiss *n* ōsculum *nt* ▶ *vt* ōsculārī
kit *n* (MIL) sarcina *f*
kitchen *n* culīna *f*
kitchen garden *n* hortus *m*
kite *n* mīluus *m*
kite's *adj* mīluīnus
knack *n* calliditās *f*, artificium *nt*; **have the ~ of** callēre
knapsack *n* sarcina *f*
knave *n* veterātor *m*
knavish *adj* improbus
knavishly *adv* improbē
knead *vt* dēpsere, subigere
knee *n* genū *nt*
kneel *vi* genibus nītī
knife *n* culter *m*; (*surgeon's*) scalprum *nt*
knight *n* eques *m* ▶ *vt* in ōrdinem equestrem recipere
knighthood *n* ōrdō equester *m*
knightly *adj* equester
knit *vt* texere; (*brow*) contrahere
knob *n* bulla *f*
knock *vt* ferīre, percutere; **~ at** pulsāre; **~ against** offendere; **~ down** dēicere, adflīgere; (*at auction*) addīcere; **~ off** dēcutere; (*work*) dēsistere ab; **~ out** ēlīdere, excutere; (*unconscious*) exanimāre; (*fig*) dēvincere; **~ up** suscitāre ▶ *n* pulsus *m*, ictus *m*
knock-kneed *adj* vārus
knoll *n* tumulus *m*
knot *n* nōdus *m* ▶ *vt* nectere
knotty *adj* nōdōsus; **~ point** nōdus *m*
know *vt* scīre; (*person*) nōvisse; **~ all about** explōrātum habēre; **~ again** agnōscere; **~ how to** scīre; **not ~** ignōrāre, nescīre; **let me ~** fac sciam, fac mē certiōrem; **get to ~** cognōscere ▶ *n*: **in the ~** cōnscius
knowing *adj* prūdēns, callidus
knowingly *adv* cōnsultō, sciēns

knowledge *n* scientia *f*, doctrīna *f*; (*practical*) experientia *f*; (*of something*) cognitiō *f*
knowledgeable *adj* gnārus, doctus
known *adj* nōtus; **make ~** dēclārāre
knuckle *n* articulus *m*
knuckle bone *n* tālus *m*
kowtow *vi* adulārī
kudos *n* glōria *f*, laus *f*

l

label n titulus m ▶ vt titulō īnscrībere
laboratory n officīna f
laborious adj labōriōsus, operōsus
laboriously adv operōsē
laboriousness n labor m
labour n labor m, opera f; (work done) opus nt; (work allotted) pēnsum nt; (workmen) operae fpl; **be in ~** parturīre ▶ vi labōrāre, ēnītī; **~ at** ēlabōrāre; **~ under a delusion** errōre fallī
laboured adj adfectātus
labourer n operārius m; **labourers** pl operae fpl
labyrinth n labyrinthus m
lace n texta rēticulāta ntpl; (shoe) ligula f ▶ vt nectere
lacerate vt lacerāre
laceration n lacerātiō f
lack n inopia f, dēfectiō f ▶ vt egēre (abl), carēre (abl)
lackey n pedisequus m
laconic adj brevis
laconically adv ūnō verbō, paucīs verbīs
lacuna n lacūna f
lad n puer m
ladder n scāla f
lade vt onerāre
laden adj onustus, onerātus
lading n onus nt
ladle n trulla f
lady n domina f, mātrōna f, mulier f
ladylike adj līberālis, honestus
lag vi cessāre
lagoon n stagnum nt
lair n latibulum nt
lake n lacus m
lamb n agnus m; (flesh) agnīna f; **ewe ~** agna f
lame adj claudus; (argument) inānis; **be ~** claudicāre
lameness n claudicātiō f
lament n lāmentātiō f, lāmentum nt ▶ vt lūgēre, lāmentārī; (regret) dēplōrāre
lamentable adj lāmentābilis, miserābilis
lamentably adv miserābiliter
lamentation n lāmentātiō f
lamp n lucerna f, lychnus m

lampoon n satura f ▶ vt carmine dēstringere
lance n hasta f, lancea f
lancer n hastātus m
lancet n scalpellum nt
land n terra f; (country) terra f, regiō f; (territory) fīnēs mpl; (native) patria f; (property) praedium nt, ager m; (soil) solum nt ▶ vt expōnere ▶ vi ē nāve ēgredī ▶ adj terrēnus, terrestris
landfall n adpulsus m
landing place n ēgressus m
landlady n caupōna f
landlord n dominus m; (inn) caupō m
landmark n lapis m; **be a ~** ēminēre
landscape n agrōrum prōspectus m
landslide n terrae lābēs f, lāpsus m
landwards adv terram versus
lane n (country) sēmita f; (town) angiportus m
language n lingua f; (style) ōrātiō f, sermō m; (diction) verba ntpl; **bad ~** maledicta ntpl
languid adj languidus, remissus
languidly adv languidē
languish vi languēre, languēscere; (with disease) tābēscere
languor n languor m
lank, lanky adj exīlis, gracilis
lantern n lanterna f, lucerna f
lap n gremium nt, sinus m ▶ vt lambere; (cover) involvere
lapse n (time) lāpsus m; (mistake) errātum nt; **after the ~ of a year** interiectō annō ▶ vi lābī; (agreement) inritum fierī; (property) revertī
larceny n fūrtum nt
larch n larix f ▶ adj larignus
lard n adeps m/f
larder n cella pēnāria f
large adj māgnus, grandis, amplus; **at ~** solūtus; **very ~** permāgnus; **as ~ as ...** tantus ... quantus
largely adv plērumque
largesse n largītiō f; (MIL) dōnātīvum nt; (civil) congiārium nt; **give ~** largīrī
lark n alauda f
lascivious adj libīdinōsus
lasciviously adv libīdinōsē
lasciviousness n libīdō f
lash n flagellum nt, lōrum nt; (eye) cilium nt ▶ vt verberāre; (tie) adligāre; (with words) castīgāre
lashing n verbera ntpl
lass n puella f
lassitude n languor m
last adj ultimus, postrēmus, suprēmus; (in line) novissimus; (preceding) proximus; **at ~** tandem, dēmum, dēnique; **for the ~ time** postrēmum ▶ n fōrma f; **let the cobbler stick to his ~** nē sūtor suprā crepidam ▶ vi dūrāre, permanēre
lasting adj diūtinus, diūturnus
lastly adv postrēmō, dēnique
latch n pessulus m
latchet n corrigia f
late adj sērus; (date) recēns; (dead) dēmortuus; (emperor) dīvus; **~ at night** multā nocte; **till ~ in the day** ad multum diem ▶ adv sērō; **too ~** sērō; **too ~ to** sērius quam quī (subj); **of ~** nūper

lately adv nūper
latent adj occultus, latitāns
later adj posterior ▶ adv posteā, posthāc, mox
latest adj novissimus
lath n tigillum nt
lathe n tornus m
lather n spūma f
Latin adj Latīnus; **speak ~** Latīnē loquī;
  understand ~ Latīnē scīre; **translate into ~**
  Latīnē reddere; **in ~** Latīnē
Latinity n Latīnitās f
latitude n (GEOG) caelum nt; (scope) lībertās f,
  licentia f
latter adj posterior; **the ~** hīc
latterly adv nūper
lattice n trānsenna f
laud n laus f ▶ vt laudāre
laudable adj laudābilis, laude dignus
laudatory adj honōrificus
laugh n rīsus m; (loud) cachinnus m ▶ vi rīdēre,
  cachinnāre; **~ at** (joke) rīdēre; (person) dērīdēre;
  ~ up one's sleeve in sinū gaudēre
laughable adj rīdiculus
laughing stock n lūdibrium nt
laughter n rīsus m
launch vt (missile) contorquēre; (ship) dēdūcere;
  ~ an attack impetum dare ▶ vi: **~ out into**
  ingredī in (acc) ▶ n celōx f, lembus m
laureate adj laureātus
laurel n laurus m ▶ adj laureus
lave vt lavāre
lavish adj prōdigus, largus ▶ vt largīrī,
  profundere
lavishly adv prōdigē, effūsē
lavishness n largitās f
law n lēx f; (system) iūs nt; (divine) fās nt; **civil law**
  iūs cīvīle; **constitutional law** iūs pūblicum;
  international law iūs gentium; **go to law** lēge
  agere, lītigāre; **break the law** lēgēs violāre;
  pass a law (magistrate) lēgem perferre; (people)
  lēgem iubēre
law-abiding adj bene mōrātus
law court n iūdicium nt; (building) basilica f
lawful adj lēgitimus; (morally) fās
lawfully adv lēgitimē, lēge
lawgiver n lēgum scrīptor m
lawless adj exlēx
lawlessly adv licenter
lawlessness n licentia f
lawn n prātulum nt
law-suit n līs f, āctiō f
lawyer n iūriscōnsultus m, causidicus m
lax adj dissolūtus, remissus
laxity n dissolūtiō f
lay adj (ECCL) lāicus ▶ vt pōnere, locāre; (ambush)
  collocāre, tendere; (disorder) sēdāre; (egg)
  parere; (foundation) iacere; (hands) inicere; (plan)
  capere, inīre; (trap) tendere; (wager) facere; **lay
  aside** pōnere; (in store) repōnere; **lay by**
  repōnere; **lay down** dēpōnere; (rule) statuere;
  lay hold of prehendere, adripere; **lay in**
  condere; **lay a motion before** referre ad; **lay on**

impōnere; **lay open** patefacere; (to attack)
  nūdāre; **lay out** (money) impendere, ērogāre;
  (camp) mētārī; **lay siege to** obsidēre; **lay to
  heart** in pectus dēmittere; **lay up** recondere;
  lay upon iniungere, impōnere; **lay violent
  hands on** vim adferre, adhibēre (dat); **whatever
  they could lay hands on** quod cuïque in
  manum vēnisset; **lay waste** vastāre ▶ n carmen
  nt, melos nt
layer n corium nt; (stones) ōrdō m; (plant) propāgō f
layout n dēsignātiō f
laze vi ōtiārī
lazily adv ignāvē, ōtiōsē
laziness n ignāvia f, dēsidia f, pigritia f
lazy adj ignāvus, dēsidiōsus, piger
lea n prātum nt
lead[1] vt dūcere; (life) agere; (wall) perdūcere;
  (water) dērīvāre; **~ across** trādūcere; **~ around**
  circumdūcere; **~ astray** in errōrem indūcere;
  ~ away abdūcere; **~ back** redūcere; **~ down**
  dēdūcere; **~ in** intrōdūcere; **~ on** addūcere;
  ~ out ēdūcere; **~ over** trādūcere; **~ the way**
  dūcere, praeīre; **~ up to** tendere ad, spectāre ad;
  the road leads … via fert …
lead[2] n plumbum nt ▶ adj plumbeus
leaden adj (colour) līvidus
leader n dux m, ductor m
leadership n ductus m
leading adj prīmus, prīnceps, praecipuus
leaf n folium nt, frōns f; (paper) scheda f; **put
  forth leaves** frondēscere
leaflet n libellus m
leafy adj frondōsus
league n foedus nt, societās f; (distance) tria
  mīlia passuum ▶ vi coniūrāre, foedus facere
leagued adj foederātus
leak n rīma f ▶ vi mānāre, rīmās agere
leaky adj rīmōsus
lean adj macer, exīlis, gracilis ▶ vi nītī; **~ back**
  sē reclīnāre; **~ on** innītī in (abl), incumbere (dat);
  ~ over inclīnāre
leaning n prōpēnsiō f ▶ adj inclīnātus
leanness n gracilitās f, maciēs f
leap n saltus m ▶ vi salīre; (for joy) exsultāre;
  ~ down dēsilīre; **~ on to** īnsilīre in (acc)
leap year n annus bissextilis m
learn vt discere; (news) accipere, audīre; (by
  heart) ēdiscere; (discover) cognōscere
learned adj doctus, ērudītus, litterātus
learnedly adv doctē
learner n tīrō m, discipulus m
learning n doctrīna f, ērudītiō f, litterae fpl
lease n (taken) conductiō f; (given) locātiō f ▶ vt
  condūcere; locāre
leash n cōpula f
least adj minimus ▶ adv minimē; **at ~** saltem;
  to say the ~ ut levissimē dīcam; **not in the ~**
  haudquāquam
leather n corium nt, alūta f
leathery adj lentus
leave n (of absence) commeātus m; (permission)
  potestās f, venia f; **ask ~** veniam petere; **give ~**

potestātem facere; **obtain ~** impetrāre; **by your ~** pace tuā, bonā tuā veniā ▶ *vt* relinquere, dēserere; (*legacy*) lēgāre; **~ alone** nōn tangere, manum abstinēre ab; **~ behind** relinquere; **~ in the lurch** dēstituere, dērelinquere; **~ off** dēsinere, dēsistere ab; (*temporarily*) intermittere; (*garment*) pōnere; **~ out** praetermittere, ōmittere ▶ *vi* discēdere ab (*abl*), abīre

leaven *n* fermentum *nt*

leavings *n* rēliquiae *fpl*

lecherous *adj* salāx

lecture *n* acroāsis *f*, audītiō *f* ▶ *vi* docēre, scholam habēre

lecturer *n* doctor *m*

lecture room *n* audītōrium *nt*

ledge *n* līmen *nt*

ledger *n* cōdex acceptī et expēnsī

lee *n* pars ā ventō tūta

leech *n* hirūdō *f*

leek *n* porrum *nt*

leer *vi* līmīs oculīs intuērī

lees *n* faex *f*; (*of oil*) amurca *f*

left *adj* sinister, laevus ▶ *n* sinistra *f*, laeva *f*; **on the ~** ā laevā, ad laevam, ā sinistrā

leg *n* crūs *nt*; (*of table*) pēs *m*

legacy *n* lēgātum *nt*; **~ hunter** captātor *m*

legal *adj* lēgitimus

legalize *vt* sancīre

legally *adv* secundum lēgēs, lēge

legate *n* lēgātus *m*

legation *n* lēgātiō *f*

legend *n* fābula *f*; (*inscription*) titulus *m*

legendary *adj* fābulōsus

legerdemain *n* praestīgiae *fpl*

legging *n* ocrea *f*

legible *adj* clārus

legion *n* legiō *f*; **men of the 10th ~** decumānī *mpl*

legionary *n* legiōnārius *m*

legislate *vi* lēgēs scrībere, lēgēs facere

legislation *n* lēgēs *fpl*, lēgēs scrībendae

legislator *n* lēgum scrīptor *m*

legitimate *adj* lēgitimus

legitimately *adv* lēgitimē

leisure *n* ōtium *nt*; **at ~** ōtiōsus, vacuus; **have ~ for** vacāre (*dat*)

leisured *adj* ōtiōsus

leisurely *adj* lentus

lend *vt* commodāre, mūtuum dare; (*at interest*) faenerārī; (*ear*) aurēs praebēre, admovēre; **~ a ready ear** aurēs patefacere; **~ assistance** opem ferre

length *n* longitūdō *f*; (*time*) diūturnitās *f*; **at ~** tandem, dēmum, dēnique; (*speech*) cōpiōsē

lengthen *vt* extendere; (*time*) prōtrahere; (*sound*) prōdūcere

lengthwise *adv* in longitūdinem

lengthy *adj* longus, prōlixus

leniency *n* clēmentia *f*

lenient *adj* clēmēns, mītis

leniently *adv* clēmenter

lentil *n* lēns *f*

leonine *adj* leōnīnus

leopard *n* pardus *m*

less *adj* minor ▶ *adv* minus; **~ than** (*num*) intrā (*acc*); **much ~, still ~** nēdum

lessee *n* conductor *m*

lessen *vt* minuere, imminuere, dēminuere ▶ *vi* dēcrēscere

lesson *n* documentum *nt*; **be a ~ to** documentō esse (*dat*); **lessons** *pl* dictāta *ntpl*; **give lessons** scholās habēre; **give lessons in** docēre

lessor *n* locātor *m*

lest *conj* nē (*subj*)

let *vt* (*allow*) sinere; (*lease*) locāre; (*imper*) fac; **let alone** ōmittere; (*mention*) nē dīcam; **let blood** sanguinem mittere; **let down** dēmittere; **let fall** ā manibus mittere; (*word*) ēmittere; **let fly** ēmittere; **let go** mittere, āmittere; (*ship*) solvere; **let in** admittere; **let loose** solvere; **let off** absolvere, ignōscere (*dat*); **let oneself go** geniō indulgēre; **let out** ēmittere; **let slip** āmittere, ōmittere

lethal *adj* mortifer

lethargic *adj* veternōsus

lethargy *n* veternus *m*

letter *n* epistula *f*, litterae *fpl*; (*of alphabet*) littera *f*; **the ~ of the law** scrīptum *nt*; **to the ~** ad praescrīptum; **by ~** per litterās; **letters** (*learning*) litterae *fpl*; **man of letters** scrīptor *m*

lettered *adj* litterātus

lettuce *n* lactūca *f*

levee *n* salūtātiō *f*

level *adj* aequus, plānus ▶ *n* plānitiēs *f*; (*instrument*) lībra *f*; **do one's ~ best** prō virīlī parte agere; **put on a ~ with** exaequāre cum ▶ *vt* aequāre, adaequāre, inaequāre; (*to the ground*) solō aequāre, sternere; (*weapon*) intendere

level-headed *adj* prūdēns

levelled *adj* (*weapon*) īnfestus

lever *n* vectis *m*

levity *n* levitās *f*; (*fun*) iocī *mpl*, facētiae *fpl*

levy *vt* (*troops*) scrībere; (*tax*) exigere ▶ *n* dīlectus *m*

lewd *adj* impudīcus

lewdness *n* impudīcitia *f*

liable *adj* obnoxius; **render ~** obligāre

liaison *n* cōnsuētūdō *f*

liar *n* mendāx *m*

libel *n* probrum *nt*, calumnia *f* ▶ *vt* calumniārī

libellous *adj* probrōsus, fāmōsus

liberal *adj* līberālis; (*in giving*) largus, benīgnus; **~ education** bonae artēs *fpl*

liberality *n* līberālitās *f*, largitās *f*

liberally *adv* līberāliter, largē, benīgnē

liberate *vt* līberāre; (*slave*) manū mittere

liberation *n* līberātiō *f*

liberator *n* līberātor *m*

libertine *n* libīdinōsus *m*

liberty *n* lībertās *f*; (*excess*) licentia *f*; **I am at ~ to** mihī licet (*infin*); **I am still at ~ to** integrum est mihī (*infin*); **take a ~ with** licentius ūtī (*abl*), familiārius sē gerere in (*acc*)

libidinous adj libīdinōsus
librarian n librārius m
library n bibliothēca f
licence n (permission) potestās f; (excess) licentia f
license vt potestātem dare (dat)
licentious adj dissolūtus
licentiousness n libīdō f, licentia f
lick vt lambere; mulcēre
lictor n lictor m
lid n operculum nt
lie n mendācium nt; **give the lie to** redarguere; **tell a lie** mentīrī ▶ vi mentīrī; **lie down** iacēre; (place) situm esse; (consist) continērī; **as far as in me lies** quantum in mē est; **lie at anchor** stāre; **lie between** interiacēre; **lie down** cubāre, discumbere; **lie heavy on** premere; **lie hid** latēre; **lie in wait** īnsidiārī; **lie low** dissimulāre; **lie on** incumbere (dat); **lie open** patēre; hiāre
lien n nexus m
lieu n: **in ~ of** locō (gen)
lieutenant n decuriō m; lēgātus m
life n vīta f; (in danger) salūs f, caput nt; (biography) vīta f; (breath) anima f; (RHET) sanguis m; (time) aetās f; **come to ~ again** revīvīscere; **draw to the ~** exprimere; **for ~** aetātem; **matter of ~ and death** capitāle nt; **prime of ~** flōs aetātis; **way of ~** mōrēs mpl
lifeblood n sanguis m
life-giving adj almus, vītālis
lifeguard n custōs m; (emperor's) praetōriānus m
lifeless adj exanimis; (style) exsanguis
lifelike adj expressus
lifelong adj perpetuus
lifetime n aetās f
lift vt tollere, sublevāre; **~ up** efferre, attollere
light n lūx f, lūmen nt; (painting) lūmen nt; **bring to ~** in lūcem prōferre; **see in a favourable ~** in meliōrem partem interpretārī; **throw ~ on** lūmen adhibēre (dat) ▶ vt accendere, incendere; (illuminate) illūstrāre, illūmināre; **be lit up** collūcēre ▶ vi: **~ upon** invenīre, offendere ▶ adj illūstris; (movement) agilis; (weight) levis; **grow ~** illūcēscere, dīlūcēscere; **make ~ of** parvī pendere
light-armed adj expedītus
lighten vi fulgurāre ▶ vt levāre
lighter n linter f
light-fingered adj tagāx
light-footed adj celer, pernīx
light-headed adj levis, volāticus
light-hearted adj hilaris, laetus
lightly adv leviter; pernīciter
lightness n levitās f
lightning n fulgur nt; (striking) fulmen nt; **be hit by ~** dē caelō percutī; **of ~** fulgurālis
like adj similis, pār; **~ this** ad hunc modum ▶ adv similiter, sīcut, rītū (gen) ▶ vt amāre; **I ~** mihī placet, mē iuvat; **I ~ to** libet (infin); **I don't ~** nīl moror, mihī displicet; **look ~** similem esse, referre

likelihood n vērī similitūdō f
likely adj vērī similis ▶ adv sānē
liken vt comparāre, aequiperāre
likeness n imāgō f, īnstar nt, similitūdō f
likewise adv item; (also) etiam
liking n libīdō f, grātia f; **to one's ~** ex sententiā
lily n līlium nt
limb n membrum nt, artus m
lime n calx f; (tree) tilia f
limelight n celebritās f; **enjoy the ~** mōnstrārī digitō
limestone n calx f
limit n fīnis m, terminus m, modus m; **mark the limits of** dētermināre ▶ vt fīnīre, dēfīnīre, termināre; (restrict) circumscrībere
limitation n modus m
limp adj mollis, flaccidus ▶ vi claudicāre
limpid adj limpidus
linden n tilia f
line n līnea f; (battle) aciēs f; (limit) modus m; (outline) līneāmentum nt; (writing) versus m; **in a straight ~** ē regiōne; **~ of march** agmen nt; **read between the lines** dissimulātā dispicere; **ship of the ~** nāvis longa; **write a ~** pauca scrībere ▶ vt (street) saepīre
lineage n genus nt, stirps f
lineal adj (descent) līneus
lineaments n līneāmenta ntpl, ōris ductūs mpl
linen n linteum nt ▶ adj linteus
liner n nāvis f
linger vi cunctārī, cessāre, dēmorārī
lingering adj tardus ▶ n cunctātiō f
linguist n: **be a ~** complūrēs linguās callēre
link n ānulus m; (fig) nexus m, vinculum nt ▶ vt coniungere
lintel n līmen superum nt
lion n leō m; **lion's** leōnīnus; **lion's share** māior pars
lioness n leaena f
lip n lābrum nt; **be on everyone's lips** in ōre omnium hominum esse, per omnium ōra ferrī
lip service n: **pay lip service to** verbō tenus obsequī (dat)
liquefy vt liquefacere
liquid adj liquidus ▶ n liquor m
liquidate vt persolvere
liquor n liquor m; vīnum nt
lisp vi balbutīre
lisping adj blaesus
lissom adj agilis
list n index m, tabula f; (ship) inclīnātiō f ▶ vt scrībere ▶ vi (lean) sē inclīnāre; (listen) auscultāre; (wish) cupere
listen vi auscultāre; **~ to** auscultāre, audīre
listener n audītor m, auscultātor m
listless adj languidus
listlessness n languor m
literally adv ad verbum
literary adj (man) litterātus; **~ pursuits** litterae fpl, studia ntpl
literature n litterae fpl
lithe adj mollis, agilis

litigant n lītigātor m
litigate vi lītigāre
litigation n līs f
litigious adj lītigiōsus
litter n (carriage) lectīca f; (brood) fētus m; (straw) strāmentum nt; (mess) strāgēs f ▶ vt sternere; (young) parere
little adj parvus, exiguus; (time) brevis; **very ~** perexiguus, minimus; **~ boy** puerulus m ▶ n paulum nt, aliquantulum nt; **for a ~** paulisper, parumper; **~ or nothing** vix quicquam ▶ adv paulum, nōnnihil; (with compar) paulō; **by ~** paulātim, sēnsim, gradātim; **think ~ of** parvī aestimāre; **too ~** parum (gen)
littleness n exiguitās f
littoral n lītus nt
live vi vīvere, vītam agere; (dwell) habitāre; **~ down** (reproach) ēluere; **~ on** (food) vescī (abl) ▶ adj vīvus
livelihood n vīctus m
liveliness n alacritās f, hilaritās f
livelong adj tōtus
lively adj alacer, hilaris
liven vt exhilarāre
liver n iecur nt
livery n vestis famulāris f
livid adj līvidus; **be ~** līvēre
living adj vīvus ▶ n vīctus m; (earning) quaestus m
lizard n lacerta f
lo interj ecce
load n onus nt ▶ vt onerāre
loaf n pānis m ▶ vi grassārī
loafer n grassātor m
loam n lutum nt
loan n mūtuum nt, mūtua pecūnia f
loathe vt fastīdīre, ōdisse
loathing n fastīdium nt
loathsome adj odiōsus, taeter
lobby n vestibulum nt
lobe n fibra f
lobster n astacus m
local adj indigena, locī
locality n locus m
locate vt reperīre; **be located** situm esse
location n situs m
loch n lacus m
lock n (door) sera f; (hair) coma f ▶ vt obserāre
locomotion n mōtus m
locust n locusta f
lodge n casa f ▶ vi dēversārī ▶ vt īnfīgere; (complaint) dēferre
lodger n inquilīnus m
lodging n hospitium nt, dēversōrium nt
loft n cēnāculum nt
loftiness n altitūdō f, sublīmitās f
lofty adj excelsus, sublīmis
log n stīpes m; (fuel) lignum nt
loggerhead n: **be at loggerheads** rixārī
logic n dialecticē f
logical adj dialecticus, ratiōne frētus
logically adv ex ratiōne

logician n dialecticus m
loin n lumbus m
loiter vi grassārī, cessāre
loiterer n grassātor m, cessātor m
loll vi recumbere
lone adj sōlus, sōlitārius
loneliness n sōlitūdō f
lonely, lonesome adj sōlitārius
long adj longus; (hair) prōmissus; (syllable) prōductus; (time) longus, diūturnus; **in the ~ run** aliquandō; **for a ~ time** diū; **to make a ~ story short** nē longum sit, nē longum faciam ▶ adv diū; **~ ago** iamprīdem, iamdūdum; **as ~ as** (conj) dum; **before ~** mox; **for ~** diū; **how ~** quamdiū, quōusque; **I have ~ been wishing** iam prīdem cupiō; **not ~ after** haud multō post; **any longer** (time) diūtius; (distance) longius; **no longer** nōn iam ▶ vi: **~ for** dēsīderāre, exoptāre, expetere; **~ to** gestīre
longevity n vīvācitās f
longing n dēsīderium nt, cupīdō f ▶ adj avidus
longingly adv avidē
longitudinally adv in longitūdinem
long-lived adj vīvāx
long-suffering adj patiēns
long-winded adj verbōsus, longus
longwise adv in longitūdinem
look n aspectus m; (expression) vultus m ▶ vi aspicere; (seem) vidērī, speciem praebēre; **~ about** circumspicere; **~ after** prōvidēre (dat), cūrāre; **~ at** spectāre ad (acc), aspicere, intuērī; (with mind) contemplārī; **~ back** respicere; **~ down on** dēspectāre; (fig) dēspicere; **~ for** quaerere, petere; **~ forward to** exspectāre; **~ here** heus tu, ehodum; **~ into** īnspicere, intrōspicere; **~ out** prōspicere; (beware) cavēre; **~ round** circumspicere; **~ through** perspicere; **~ to** ratiōnem habēre (gen); (leader) spem pōnere in (abl); **~ towards** spectāre ad; **~ up** suspicere; **~ up to** suspicere; **~ upon** habēre
looker-on n arbiter m
lookout n (place) specula f; (man) vigil m, excubiae fpl
looks npl speciēs f; **good ~** fōrma f, pulchritūdō f
loom n tēla f ▶ vi in cōnspectum sē dare
loop n orbis m, sinus m
loophole n fenestra f
loose adj laxus, solūtus, remissus; (morally) dissolūtus; **let ~ on** immittere in (acc) ▶ vt (undo) solvere; (slacken) laxāre
loosely adv solūtē, remissē
loosen vt (re)solvere; (structure) labefacere
looseness n dissolūtiō f, dissolūtī mōrēs mpl
loot n praeda f, rapīna f
lop vt amputāre
lopsided adj inaequālis
loquacious adj loquāx
loquacity n loquācitās f
lord n dominus m ▶ vi: **~ it** dominārī
lordliness n superbia f
lordly adj superbus; (rank) nōbilis
lordship n dominātiō f, imperium nt

lore n litterae fpl, doctrīna f
lose vt āmittere, perdere; ~ **an eye** alterō oculō capī; ~ **heart** animum dēspondēre; ~ **one's way** deerrāre ▸ vi (in contest) vincī
loss n damnum nt, dētrīmentum nt; **be at a** ~ haerēre, haesitāre; **suffer** ~ damnum accipere, facere; **losses** (in battle) caesī mpl
lost adj āmissus, absēns; **be** ~ perīre, interīre; **give up for** ~ dēplōrāre
lot n sors f; **be assigned by lot** sorte obvenīre; **draw a lot** sortem dūcere; **draw lots for** sortīrī; **a lot of** multus, plūrimus
loth adj invītus
lottery n sortēs fpl; (fig) ālea f
lotus n lōtos f
loud adj clārus, māgnus
loudly adv māgnā vōce
loudness n māgna vōx f
lounge vi ōtiārī
louse n pedis m/f
lout n agrestis m
lovable adj amābilis
love n amor m; **be hopelessly in** ~ dēperīre; **fall in** ~ **with** adamāre ▸ vt amāre, dīligere; **I** ~ **to** mē iuvat (infin)
love affair n amor m
loveless adj amōre carēns
loveliness n grātia f, venustās f
lovely adj pulcher, amābilis, venustus
love poem n carmen amātōrium nt
lover n amāns m, amātor m
lovesick adj amōre aeger
loving adj amāns
lovingly adv amanter
low adj humilis; (birth) ignōbilis; (price) vīlis; (sound) gravis; (spirits) dēmissus; (voice) dēmissus; **at low water** aestūs dēcessū; **be low** iacēre; **lay low** interficere ▸ vi mūgīre
lower adj īnferior; **the** ~ **world** īnferī mpl; **of the** ~ **world** īnfernus ▸ adv īnferius ▸ vt dēmittere, dēprimere ▸ vi (cloud) obscūrārī, minārī
lowering adj mināx
lowest adj īnfimus, īmus
lowing n mūgītus m
lowland adj campestris
lowlands n campī mpl
lowliness n humilitās f
lowly adj humilis, obscūrus
low-lying adj dēmissus; **be** ~ sedēre
lowness n humilitās f; (spirit) tristitia f
loyal adj fidēlis, fīdus; (citizen) bonus
loyally adv fidēliter
loyalty n fidēs f, fidēlitās f
lubricate vt ungere
lucid adj clārus, perspicuus
lucidity n perspicuitās f
lucidly adv clārē, perspicuē
luck n fortūna f, fors f; **good** ~ fēlicitās f; **bad** ~ īnfortūnium nt
luckily adv fēlīciter, faustē, prosperē
luckless adj īnfēlīx

lucky adj fēlīx, fortūnātus; (omen) faustus
lucrative adj quaestuōsus
lucre n lucrum nt, quaestus m
lucubration n lūcubrātiō f
ludicrous adj rīdiculus
ludicrously adv rīdiculē
lug vt trahere
luggage n impedīmenta ntpl, sarcina f
lugubrious adj lūgubris, maestus
lukewarm adj tepidus; (fig) segnis, neglegēns; **be** ~ tepēre
lukewarmly adv segniter, neglegenter
lukewarmness n tepor m; (fig) neglegentia f, incūria f
lull vt sōpīre; (storm) sēdāre ▸ n intermissiō f
lumber n scrūta ntpl
luminary n lūmen nt, astrum nt
luminous adj lūcidus, illūstris
lump n massa f; (on body) tuber nt
lumpish adj hebes, crassus, stolidus
lunacy n īnsānia f
lunar adj lūnāris
lunatic n īnsānus m
lunch n prandium nt ▸ vi prandēre
lung n pulmō m; (pl, RHET) latera ntpl
lunge n ictus m ▸ vi prōsilīre
lurch n: **leave in the** ~ dērelinquere, dēstituere ▸ vi titubāre
lure n esca f ▸ vt allicere, illicere, ēlicere
lurid adj lūridus
lurk vi latēre, latitāre, dēlitēscere
luscious adj praedulcis
lush adj luxuriōsus
lust n libīdō f ▸ vi libīdine flagrāre, concupīscere
lustful adj libīdinōsus
lustily adv validē, strēnuē
lustiness n vigor m, nervī mpl
lustration n lūstrum nt
lustre n fulgor m, splendor m
lustrous adj illūstris
lusty adj validus, lacertōsus
lute n cithara f, fidēs fpl
lute player n citharista m, citharistria f, fidicen m, fidicina f
luxuriance n luxuria f
luxuriant adj luxuriōsus
luxuriate vi luxuriārī
luxuries npl lautitiae fpl
luxurious adj luxuriōsus, sūmptuōsus, lautus
luxuriously adv sūmptuōsē, lautē
luxury n luxuria f, luxus m
lynx n lynx m/f; **lynx-eyed** lyncēus
lyre n lyra f, fidēs fpl; **play the** ~ fidibus canere
lyric adj lyricus ▸ n carmen nt
lyrist n fidicen m, fidicina f

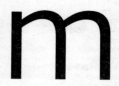

mace n scīpiō m
machination n dolus m
machine n māchina f
mackerel n scomber m
mad adj īnsānus, furiōsus, vēcors, dēmēns; **be mad** īnsānīre, furere
madam n domina f
madden vt furiāre, mentem aliēnāre (dat)
madly adv īnsānē, furiōsē, dēmenter
madness n īnsānia f, furor m, dēmentia f; (animals) rabiēs f
maelstrom n vertex m
magazine n horreum nt, apothēca f
maggot n vermiculus m
magic adj magicus ▶ n magicae artēs fpl
magician n magus m, veneficus m
magistracy n magistrātus m
magistrate n magistrātus m
magnanimity n māgnanimitās f, līberalitās f
magnanimous adj generōsus, līberālis, māgnanimus
magnet n magnēs m
magnificence n māgnificentia f, adparātus m
magnificent adj māgnificus, amplus, splendidus
magnificently adv māgnificē, amplē, splendidē
magnify vt amplificāre, exaggerāre
magnitude n māgnitūdō f
magpie n pīca f
maid n virgō f; (servant) ancilla f
maiden n virgō f
maidenhood n virginitās f
maidenly adj virginālis
mail n (armour) lōrīca f; (letters) epistulae fpl
maim vt mutilāre
maimed adj mancus
main adj prīnceps, prīmus; ~ **point** caput nt ▶ n (sea) altum nt, pelagus nt; **with might and** ~ manibus pedibusque, omnibus nervīs
mainland n continēns f
mainly adv praecipuē, plērumque
maintain vt (keep) tenēre, servāre; (keep up) sustinēre; (keep alive) alere, sustentāre; (argue) adfirmāre, dēfendere

maintenance n (food) alimentum nt
majestic adj augustus, māgnificus
majestically adv augustē
majesty n māiestās f
major adj māior
majority n māior pars f, plērīque; **have attained one's** ~ suī iūris esse
make vt facere, fingere; (appointment) creāre; (bed) sternere; (cope) superāre; (compulsion) cōgere; (consequence) efficere; (craft) fabricārī; (harbour) capere; (living) quaerere; (sum) efficere; (with adj) reddere; (with verb) cōgere; ~ **away with** tollere, interimere; ~ **good** supplēre, resarcīre; ~ **light of** parvī facere; ~ **one's way** iter facere; ~ **much of** māgnī aestimāre, multum tribuere (dat); ~ **for** petere; ~ **out** arguere; ~ **over** dēlēgāre, trānsferre; ~ **ready** parāre; ~ **a speech** ōrātiōnem habēre; ~ **a truce** indutiās compōnere; ~ **war on** bellum īnferre; ~ **up** (loss) supplēre; (total) efficere; (story) fingere; **be made** fierī
make-believe n simulātiō f
maker n fabricātor m, auctor m
make-up n medicāmina ntpl
maladministration n (charge) repetundae fpl
malady n morbus m
malcontent adj novārum rērum cupidus
male adj mās, māsculus
malefactor n nocēns m, reus m
malevolence n malevolentia f
malevolent adj malevolus, malignus
malevolently adv malignē
malformation n dēprāvātiō f
malice n invidia f, malevolentia f; **bear** ~ **towards** invidēre (dat)
malicious adj invidiōsus, malevolus, malignus
maliciously adv malignē
malign adj malignus, invidiōsus ▶ vt obtrectāre
malignant adj malevolus
maligner n obtrectātor m
malignity n malevolentia f
malleable adj ductilis
mallet n malleus m
mallow n malva f
malpractices npl dēlicta ntpl
maltreat vt laedere, vexāre
malversation n pecūlātus m
man n (human being) homō m/f; (male) vir m; (MIL) mīles m; (chess) latrunculus m; **to a man** omnēs ad ūnum; **man who** is quī; **old man** senex m; **young man** adulēscēns m; **man of war** nāvis longa f ▶ vt (ship) complēre; (walls) praesidiō firmāre
manacle n manicae fpl ▶ vt manicās inicere (dat)
manage vt efficere, gerere, gubernāre, administrāre; (horse) moderārī; (with verb) posse
manageable adj tractābilis, habilis
management n administrātiō f, cūra f; (finance) dispēnsātiō f
manager n administrātor m, moderātor m; dispēnsātor m

mandate n mandātum nt
mane n iuba f
manful adj virīlis, fortis
manfully adv virīliter, fortiter
manger n praesēpe nt
mangle vt dīlaniāre, lacerāre
mangy adj scaber
manhood n pūbertās f, toga virīlis f
mania n īnsānia f
maniac n furiōsus m
manifest adj manifestus, apertus, clārus ▶ vt
dēclārāre, aperīre
manifestation n speciēs f
manifestly adv manifestō, apertē
manifesto n ēdictum nt
manifold adj multiplex, varius
manikin n homunciō m, homunculus m
manipulate vt tractāre
manipulation n tractātiō f
mankind n hominēs mpl, genus hūmānum nt
manliness n virtūs f
manly adj fortis, virīlis
manner n modus m, ratiō f; (custom) mōs m,
ūsus m; **manners** pl mōrēs mpl; **after the ~ of**
rītū, mōre (gen); **good manners** hūmānitās f,
modestia f
mannered adj mōrātus
mannerism n mōs m
mannerly adj bene mōrātus, urbānus
manoeuvre n (MIL) dēcursus m, dēcursiō f; (fig)
dolus m ▶ vi dēcurrere; (fig) māchinārī
manor n praedium nt
mansion n domus f
manslaughter n homicīdium nt
mantle n pallium nt; (women's) palla f
manual adj: **~ labour** opera f ▶ n libellus m, ars f
manufacture n fabrica f ▶ vt fabricārī
manumission n manūmissiō f
manumit vt manū mittere, ēmancipāre
manure n fimus m, stercus m ▶ vt stercorāre
manuscript n liber m, cōdex m
many adj multī; **as ~ as** tot ... quot; **how many?**
quot?; **so ~** tot; **in ~ places** multifāriam; **a**
good ~ complūrēs; **too ~** nimis multī; **the ~**
vulgus nt; **very ~** permultī, plūrimī
map n tabula f ▶ vt: **map out** dēscrībere,
dēsignāre
maple n acer nt ▶ adj acernus
mar vt corrumpere, dēfōrmāre
marauder n praedātor m, dēpopulātor m
marble n marmor nt ▶ adj marmoreus
March n mēnsis Martius m; **of** ~ Martius
march n iter nt; **line of** ~ agmen nt; **by forced**
marches māgnīs itineribus; **on the** ~ ex itinere,
in itinere; **quick** ~ plēnō gradū; **a regular day's** ~
iter iūstum m ▶ vi contendere, iter facere,
incēdere, īre; **~ out** exīre; **~ on** signa prōferre,
prōgredī ▶ vt dūcere; **~ out** ēdūcere; **~ in**
intrōdūcere
mare n equa f
margin n margō f; (fig) discrīmen nt
marigold n caltha f

marine adj marīnus ▶ n mīles classicus m
mariner n nauta m
marital adj marītus
maritime adj maritimus
marjoram n amāracus m
mark n nota f; (of distinction) scopos m; (trace) vestīgium nt; (target)
scopos m; (trace) vestīgium nt; **beside the** ~ nihil
ad rem; **it is the** ~ **of a wise man to** sapientis est
(infin); **be wide of the** ~ errāre ▶ vt notāre,
dēsignāre; (observe) animadvertere, animum
attendere; ~ **out** (site) mētārī, dēsignāre; (for
purpose) dēnotāre
marked adj īnsignis, manifestus
markedly adv manifestō
marker n index m
market n macellum nt; ~ **day** nūndinae fpl;
~ **town** emporium nt; **cattle** ~ forum boārium
nt; **fish** ~ forum piscārium nt
marketable adj vēndibilis
marketplace n forum nt
market prices npl annōna f
market town n emporium nt
marking n macula f
maroon vt dērelinquere
marriage n mātrimōnium nt, coniugium nt;
(ceremony) nūptiae fpl; **give in** ~ collocāre; ~ **bed**
lectus geniālis m
marriageable adj nūbilis
marrow n medulla f
marry vt (a wife) dūcere, in mātrimōnium
dūcere; (a husband) nūbere (dat)
marsh n palūs f
marshal n imperātor m ▶ vt īnstruere
marshy adj palūster
mart n forum nt
marten n mēlēs f
martial adj bellicōsus, ferōx
martyr n dēvōtus m; (ECCL) martyr m/f
marvel n mīrāculum nt, portentum nt ▶ vi
mīrārī; ~ **at** admīrārī
marvellous adj mīrus, mīrificus, mīrābilis
marvellously adv mīrē, mīrum quantum
masculine adj mās, virīlis
mash n farrāgō f ▶ vt commiscēre, contundere
mask n persōna f ▶ vt persōnam induere (dat);
(fig) dissimulāre
mason n structor m
masonry n lapidēs mpl, caementum nt
masquerade n simulātiō f ▶ vi vestem mūtāre;
~ **as** speciem sibi induere (gen), persōnam ferre
(gen)
mass n mōlēs f; (of small things) congeriēs f; (of
people) multitūdō f; (ECCL) missa f; **the masses**
vulgus nt, plēbs f ▶ vt congerere, coacervāre
massacre n strāgēs f, caedēs f, interneciō f ▶ vt
trucīdāre
massive adj ingēns, solidus
massiveness n mōlēs f, soliditās f
mast n mālus m
master n dominus m; (school) magister m;
be ~ of dominārī in (abl); (skill) perītum esse
(gen); **become ~ of** potīrī (abl); **be one's own** ~

suī iūris esse; **not ~ of** impotēns (gen); **a past ~** veterātor m ▶ vt dēvincere; (skill) ēdiscere; (passion) continēre
masterful adj imperiōsus
masterly adj doctus, perītus
masterpiece n praeclārum opus nt
mastery n dominātiō f, imperium nt, arbitrium nt
masticate vt mandere
mastiff n Molossus m
mat n storea f
match n (person) pār m/f; (marriage) nūptiae fpl; (contest) certāmen nt; **a ~ for** pār (dat); **no ~ for** impār (dat) ▶ vt exaequāre, adaequāre ▶ vi congruere
matchless adj singulāris, ūnicus
mate n socius m; (married) coniunx m/f ▶ vi coniungī
material adj corporeus; (significant) haud levis ▶ n māteriēs f; (literary) silva f
materialize vi ēvenīre
materially adv māgnopere
maternal adj māternus
mathematical adj mathēmaticus
mathematician n mathēmaticus m, geōmetrēs m
mathematics n ars mathēmatica f, numerī mpl
matin adj mātūtīnus
matricide n (act) mātrīcīdium nt; (person) mātrīcīda m
matrimony n mātrimōnium nt
matrix n fōrma f
matron n mātrōna f
matter n māteria f, corpus nt; (affair) rēs f; (MED) pūs nt; **what is the ~ with you?** quid tibī est? ▶ vi: **it matters** interest, rēfert
matting n storea f
mattock n dolābra f
mattress n culcita f
mature adj mātūrus; (age) adultus ▶ vi mātūrēscere
maturity n mātūritās f; (age) adulta aetās f
maul n fistūca f ▶ vt contundere, dīlaniāre
maw n luluviēs f
mawkish adj pūtidus
mawkishly adv pūtidē
maxim n dictum nt, praeceptum nt, sententia f
maximum adj quam māximus, quam plūrimus
May n mēnsis Māius m; **of May** Māius
may vi posse; **I may** licet mihī
mayor n praefectus m
maze n labyrinthus m
mead n (drink) mulsum nt; (land) prātum nt
meagre adj exīlis, iēiūnus
meagrely adv exīliter, iēiūnē
meagreness n exīlitās f
meal n (flour) farīna f; (repast) cibus m
mealy-mouthed adj blandiloquus
mean adj humilis, abiectus; (birth) ignōbilis; (average) medius, mediocris ▶ n modus m, mediocritās f ▶ vt dīcere, significāre; (word) valēre; (intent) velle, in animō habēre

meander vi sinuōsō cursū fluere
meaning n significātiō f, vīs f, sententia f; **what is the ~ of?** quid sibī vult?, quōrsum spectat?
meanly adv abiectē, humiliter
meanness n humilitās f; (conduct) illīberālitās f, avāritia f
means n īnstrūmentum nt; (of doing) facultās f; (wealth) opēs fpl; **by ~ of** per (acc); **by all** māximē; **by no ~** nūllō modō, haudquāquam; **of small ~** pauper
meantime, meanwhile adv intereā, interim
measles n boa f
measure n modus m, mēnsūra f; (rhythm) numerī mpl; (plan) cōnsilium nt; (LAW) rogātiō f, lēx f; **beyond ~** nimium; **in some ~** aliquā ex parte; **take measures** cōnsulere; **take the ~ of** quālis sit cognōscere; **without ~** immoderātē ▶ vt mētīrī; **~ out** dīmētīrī; (land) mētārī
measured adj moderātus
measureless adj īnfīnītus, immēnsus
measurement n mēnsūra f
meat n carō f
mechanic n opifex m, faber m
mechanical adj mēchanicus
mechanical device māchinātiō f
mechanics n māchinālis scientia f
mechanism n māchinātiō f
medal n īnsigne nt
meddle vi sē interpōnere
meddlesome adj cūriōsus
Medes n Mēdī mpl
mediate vi intercēdere; **~ between** compōnere, conciliāre
mediator n intercessor m, dēprecātor m
medical adj medicus
medicate vt medicāre
medicinal adj medicus, salūbris
medicine n (art) medicīna f; (drug) medicāmentum nt
medicine chest n narthēcium nt
mediocre adj mediocris
mediocrity n mediocritās f
meditate vi meditārī, cōgitāre, sēcum volūtāre
meditation n cōgitātiō f, meditātiō f
medium n internūntius m; (means) modus m ▶ adj mediocris
medley n farrāgō f
meek adj mītis, placidus
meekly adv summissō animō
meet adj idōneus, aptus ▶ n conventus m ▶ vi convenīre ▶ vt obviam īre (dat), occurrere (dat); (fig) obīre; **~ with** invenīre, excipere
meeting n cōnsilium nt, conventus m
melancholic adj melancholicus
melancholy n ātra bīlis f; tristitia f, maestitia f ▶ adj tristis, maestus
mêlée n turba f, concursus m
mellow adj mītis; (wine) lēnis; **become ~** mītēscere; **make ~** mītigāre
mellowness n mātūritās f
melodious adj canōrus, numerōsus
melodiously adv numerōsē

melody n melos nt, modī mpl
melt vt liquefacere, dissolvere; (fig) movēre ▸ vi liquēscere, dissolvī; (fig) commovērī; **~ away** dēliquēscere
member n membrum nt; (person) socius m
membrane n membrāna f
memento n monumentum nt
memoir n commentārius m
memorable adj memorābilis, commemorābilis
memorandum n hypomnēma nt
memorial n monumentum nt
memorize vt ēdiscere
memory n memoria f; **from ~** memoriter
menace n minae fpl ▸ vt minārī, minitārī; (things) imminēre (dat)
menacing adj mināx
menacingly adv mināciter
menage n familia f
mend vt sarcīre, reficere ▸ vi meliōrem fierī; (health) convalēscere
mendacious adj mendāx
mendacity n mendācium nt
mendicant n mendīcus m
mendicity n mendīcitās f
menial adj servīlis, famulāris ▸ n servus m, famulus m
menstrual adj mēnstruus
mensuration n mētiendī ratiō f
mental adj cōgitātiōnis, mentis
mentality n animī adfectus m, mēns f
mentally adv cōgitātiōne, mente
mention n mentiō f ▸ vt memorāre, mentiōnem facere (gen); (casually) inicere; (briefly) attingere; **omit to ~** praetermittere
mentor n auctor m, praeceptor m
mercantile adj mercātōrius
mercenary adj mercennārius, vēnālis ▸ n mercennārius mīles m
merchandise n mercēs fpl
merchant n mercātor m
merchantman n nāvis onerāria f
merchant ship n nāvis onerāria f
merciful adj misericors, clēmens
mercifully adv clēmenter
merciless adj immisericors, inclēmens, inhūmānus
mercilessly adv inhūmānē
mercurial adj hilaris
mercy n misericordia f, clēmentia f, venia f; **at the ~ of** obnoxius (dat), in manū (gen)
mere n lacus m ▸ adj merus, ipse
merely adv sōlum, tantum, dumtaxat
meretricious adj meretricius; **~ attractions** lēnōcinia ntpl
merge vt cōnfundere ▸ vi cōnfundī
meridian n merīdiēs m ▸ adj merīdiānus
merit n meritum nt, virtūs f ▸ vt merērī
meritorious adj laudābilis
meritoriously adv optimē
mermaid n nympha f
merrily adv hilare, festīvē
merriment n hilaritās f, festīvitās f

merry adj hilaris, festīvus; **make ~** lūdere
merrymaking n lūdus m, festīvitās f
mesh n macula f
mess n (dirt) sordēs f, squālor m; (trouble) turba f; (food) cibus m; (MIL) contubernālēs mpl
message n nūntius m
messenger n nūntius m
messmate n contubernālis m
metal n metallum nt ▸ adj ferreus, aereus
metamorphose vt mūtāre, trānsfōrmāre
metamorphosis n mūtātiō f
metaphor n trānslātiō f
metaphorical adj trānslātus
metaphorically adv per trānslātiōnem
metaphysics n dialectica ntpl
mete vt mētīrī
meteor n fax caelestis f
meteorology n prognōstica ntpl
methinks vi: **~ I am** mihī videor esse
method n ratiō f, modus m
methodical adj dispositus; (person) dīligēns
methodically adv dispositē
meticulous adj accūrātus
meticulously adv accūrātē
meticulousness n cūra f
metonymy n immūtātiō f
metre n numerī mpl, modī mpl
metropolis n urbs f
mettle n ferōcitās f, virtūs f
mettlesome adj ferōx, animōsus
mew n (bird) larus m; **mews** pl stabula ntpl ▸ vi vāgīre
miasma n hālitus m
mid adj medius ▸ prep inter (acc)
midday n merīdiēs m ▸ adj merīdiānus
middle adj medius ▸ n medium nt; **in the ~** medius, in mediō; **~ of** medius
middling adj mediocris
midge n culex m
midget n (offensive) pūmiliō m/f
midland adj mediterrāneus
midnight n media nox f
midriff n praecordia ntpl
midst n medium nt; **in the ~** medius; **in the ~ of** inter (acc); **through the ~ of** per medium
midsummer n sōlstitium nt ▸ adj sōlstitiālis
midway adv medius
midwife n obstetrix f
midwinter n brūma f ▸ adj brūmālis
mien n aspectus m, vultus m
might n vīs f, potentia f; **with ~ and main** omnibus nervīs, manibus pedibusque
mightily adv valdē, magnopere
mighty adj ingēns, validus
migrate vi abīre, migrāre
migration n peregrīnātiō f
migratory adj advena
mild adj mītis, lēnis, clēmēns
mildew n rōbīgō f
mildly adv lēniter, clēmenter
mildness n clēmentia f, mānsuētūdō f; (weather) caelī indulgentia f

mile n mīlle passūs mpl; **miles** pl mīlia passuum

milestone n lapis m, mīliārium nt

militant adj ferōx

military adj mīlitāris ▶ n mīlitēs mpl

military service n mīlitia f

militate vi: **~ against** repugnāre (dat), facere contrā (acc)

militia n mīlitēs mpl

milk n lac nt ▶ vt mulgēre

milk pail n mulctra f

milky adj lacteus

mill n pistrīnum nt

milled adj (coin) serrātus

millennium n mīlle annī mpl

miller n pistor m

millet n mīlium nt

million num deciēs centēna mīlia ntpl

millionaire n rēx m

millstone n mola f, molāris m

mime n mīmus m

mimic n imitātor m, imitātrīx f ▶ vt imitārī

mimicry n imitātiō f

minatory adj mināx

mince vt concīdere; **not ~ words** plānē apertēque dīcere ▶ n minūtal nt

mind n mēns f, animus m, ingenium nt; (opinion) sententia f; (memory) memoria f; **be in one's right ~** mentis suae esse; **be of the same ~** eadem sentīre; **be out of one's ~** īnsānīre; **bear in ~** meminisse (gen), memorem esse (gen); **call to ~** memoriā repetere, recordārī; **have a ~ to** libet; **have in ~** in animō habēre; **put one's ~ to** animum applicāre (acc); **make up one's ~** animum indūcere, animō obstināre, statuere; **put in ~ of** admonēre (gen); **speak one's ~** sententiam suam aperīre; **to one's ~** ex sententiā ▶ vt cūrāre, attendere; **~ one's own business** suum negōtium agere ▶ vi gravārī; **I don't ~** nīl moror; **never ~** mitte

minded adj animātus

mindful adj memor

mine n metallum nt; (MIL) cuniculus m; (fig) thēsaurus m ▶ vi fodere; (MIL) cuniculum agere ▶ pron meus

miner n fossor m

mineral n metallum nt

mingle vt miscēre, commiscēre ▶ vi sē immiscēre

miniature n minima pictūra f

minimize vt dētrectāre

minimum n minimum nt ▶ adj quam minimus

minion n cliēns m/f, dēlicātus m

minister n administer m ▶ vi ministrāre, servīre

ministry n mūnus nt, officium nt

minor adj minor ▶ n pupillus m, pupilla f

minority n minor pars f; **in one's ~** nōndum suī iūris

Minotaur n Mīnōtaurus m

minstrel n fidicen m

minstrelsy n cantus m

mint n (plant) menta f; (money) Monēta f ▶ vt cūdere

minute[1] n temporis mōmentum nt

minute[2] adj minūtus, exiguus, subtīlis

minutely adv subtīliter

minuteness n exiguitās f, subtīlitas f

minutiae n singula ntpl

minx n lascīva f

miracle n mīrāculum nt, mōnstrum nt

miraculous adj mīrus, mīrābilis

miraculously adv dīvīnitus

mirage n falsa speciēs f

mire n lutum nt

mirror n speculum nt ▶ vt reddere

mirth n hilaritās f, laetitia f

mirthful adj hilaris, laetus

mirthfully adv hilare, laetē

miry adj lutulentus

misadventure n īnfortūnium nt, cāsus m

misapply vt abūtī (abl); (words) invertere

misapprehend vt male intellegere

misapprehension n error m

misappropriate vt intervertere

misbegotten adj nothus

misbehave vi male sē gerere

miscalculate vi errāre, fallī

miscalculation n error m

miscall vt maledīcere (dat)

miscarriage n abortus m; (fig) error m

miscarry vi aborīrī; (fig) cadere, inritum esse

miscellaneous adj prōmiscuus, varius

miscellany n farrāgō f

mischance n īnfortūnium nt

mischief n malum nt, facinus nt, maleficīum nt; (children) lascīvia f

mischievous adj improbus, maleficus; lascīvus

misconceive vt male intellegere

misconception n error m

misconduct n dēlictum nt, culpa f

misconstruction n prāva interpretātiō f

misconstrue vt male interpretārī

miscreant n scelerātus m

misdeed n maleficium nt, dēlictum nt

misdemeanour n peccātum nt, culpa f

miser n avārus m

miserable adj miser, īnfēlīx; **make oneself ~** sē cruciāre

miserably adv miserē

miserliness n avāritia f

miserly adj avārus

misery n miseria f, aerumna f

misfortune n malum nt, īnfortūnium nt, incommodum nt, rēs adversae fpl

misgiving n suspiciō f, cūra f; **have misgivings** parum cōnfīdere

misgovern vt male regere

misgovernment n prāva administrātiō f

misguide vt fallere, dēcipere

misguided adj dēmēns

mishap n īnfortūnium nt

misinform vt falsa docēre

misinterpret vt male interpretārī

misinterpretation n prāva interpretātiō f

misjudge vt male iūdicāre

mislay vt āmittere
mislead vt dēcipere, indūcere, auferre
mismanage vt male gerere
misnomer n falsum nōmen nt
misogyny n mulierum odium nt
misplace vt in aliēnō locō collocāre
misplaced adj (fig) vānus
misprint n mendum nt
mispronounce vt prāvē appellāre
misquote vt perperam prōferre
misrepresent vt dētorquēre, invertere; (person) calumniārī
misrepresentation n calumnia f
misrule n prāva administrātiō f
miss vt (aim) aberrāre (abl); (loss) requīrere, dēsīderāre; (notice) praetermittere ▶ n error m; (girl) virgō f
misshapen adj distortus, dēfōrmis
missile n tēlum nt
missing adj absēns; **be ~** dēesse, dēsīderārī
mission n lēgātiō f
missive n litterae fpl
misspend vt perdere, dissipāre
misstatement n falsum nt, mendācium nt
mist n nebula f, cālīgō f
mistake n error m; (writing) mendum nt; **full of mistakes** mendōsus ▶ vt: **~ for** habēre prō (abl); **be mistaken** errāre, fallī
mistletoe n viscum nt
mistranslate vt prāvē reddere
mistress n domina f; (school) magistra f; (lover) amīca f
mistrust n diffīdentia f, suspiciō f ▶ vt diffīdere (dat)
mistrustful adj diffīdēns
mistrustfully adv diffīdenter
misty adj nebulōsus
misunderstand vt male intellegere ▶ vi errāre
misunderstanding n error m; (quarrel) discidium nt
misuse n malus ūsus m ▶ vt abūtī (abl)
mite n parvulus m; (insect) vermiculus m
mitigate vt mītigāre, lēnīre
mitigation n mītigātiō f
mix vt miscēre; **mix in** admiscēre; **mix together** commiscēre; **get mixed up with** admiscērī cum, sē interpōnere (dat)
mixed adj prōmiscuus
mixture n (act) temperātiō f; (state) dīversitās f
mnemonic n artificium memoriae nt
moan n gemitus m ▶ vi gemere
moat n fossa f
mob n vulgus nt, turba f ▶ vt circumfundī in (acc)
mobile adj mōbilis, agilis
mobility n mōbilitās f, agilitās f
mobilize vt (MIL) ēvocāre
mock vt irrīdēre, lūdibriō habēre, lūdificārī; (ape) imitārī; **~ at** inlūdere ▶ n lūdibrium nt ▶ adj simulātus, fictus
mocker n dērīsor m
mockery n lūdibrium nt, irrīsus m
mode n modus m, ratiō f

model n exemplar nt, exemplum nt ▶ vt fingere
modeller n fictor m
moderate adj (size) modicus; (conduct) moderātus ▶ vt temperāre; (emotion) temperāre (dat) ▶ vi mītigārī
moderately adv modicē, moderātē, mediocriter
moderation n moderātiō f, modus m; (mean) mediocritās f
moderator n praefectus m
modern adj recēns
modernity n haec aetās f
modest adj pudīcus, verēcundus
modestly adv verēcundē, pudenter
modesty n pudor m, verēcundia f
modicum n paullulum nt, aliquantulum nt
modification n mūtātiō f
modify vt immūtāre; (LAW) derogāre aliquid dē
modulate vt (voice) īnflectere
modulation n flexiō f, inclīnātiō f
moiety n dīmidia pars f
moist adj ūmidus
moisten vt ūmectāre, rigāre
moisture n ūmor m
molar n genuīnus m
mole n (animal) talpa f; (on skin) naevus m; (pier) mōlēs f
molecule n corpusculum nt
molehill n: **make a mountain out of a ~** ē rīvō flūmina māgna facere, arcem facere ē cloācā
molest vt sollicitāre, vexāre
molestation n vexātiō f
mollify vt mollīre, lēnīre
molten adj liquefactus
moment n temporis mōmentum nt, temporis pūnctum nt; **for a ~** parumper; **in a ~** iam; **without a moment's delay** nūllā interpositā morā; **be of great ~** māgnō mōmentō esse; **it is of ~ interest**
momentary adj brevis
momentous adj gravis, māgnī mōmentī
momentum n impetus m
monarch n rēx m, tyrannus m
monarchical adj rēgius
monarchy n rēgnum nt
monastery n monastērium nt
monetary adj pecūniārius
money n pecūnia f; (cash) nummī mpl; **for ~** mercēde; **ready ~** nummī, praesēns pecūnia; **make ~** rem facere, quaestum facere
moneybag n fiscus m
moneyed adj nummātus, pecūniōsus
moneylender n faenerātor m
moneymaking n quaestus m
mongoose n ichneumōn m
mongrel n (dog) hibrida m
monitor n admonitor m
monk n monachus m
monkey n sīmia f
monograph n libellus m
monologue n ōrātiō f
monopolize vt absorbēre, sibī vindicāre

monopoly n arbitrium nt
monosyllabic adj monosyllabus
monosyllable n monosyllabum nt
monotonous adj aequābilis
monotony n taedium nt
monster n mōnstrum nt, portentum nt, bēlua f
monstrosity n mōnstrum nt
monstrous adj immānis, mōnstruōsus;
 improbus
month n mēnsis m
monthly adj mēnstruus
monument n monumentum nt
monumental adj ingēns
mood n affectiō f, adfectus m, animus m; (GRAM)
 modus m; **I am in the ~ for** libet (infin)
moody adj mōrōsus, tristis
moon n lūna f; **new ~** interlūnium nt
moonlight n: **by ~** ad lūnam
moonshine n somnia ntpl
moonstruck adj lūnāticus
moor vt religāre ▶ n tesqua ntpl
moorings n ancorae fpl
moot n conventus m; **it is a ~ point** discrepat
 ▶ vt iactāre
mop n pēniculus m ▶ vt dētergēre
mope vi maerēre
moral adj honestus, probus; (opposed to physical)
 animī; (PHILOS) mōrālis ▶ n documentum nt
morale n animus m; **~ is low** iacet animus
morality n bonī mōrēs mpl, virtūs f
moralize vi dē officiīs disserere
morally adv honestē
morals npl mōrēs mpl
morass n palūs f
moratorium n mora f
morbid adj aeger
mordant adj mordāx
more adj plūs, plūris (in sg + gen, in pl + adj) ▶ adv
 plūs, magis, amplius; (extra) ultrā; **~ than**
 amplius quam; **~ than three feet** amplius trēs
 pedēs; **~ and ~** magis magisque; **never ~** immo;
 ~ or less ferē; **no ~** (time) nōn diūtius, nunquam
 posteā
moreover adv tamen, autem, praetereā
moribund adj moribundus
morning n māne nt; **early in the ~** bene māne;
 this ~ hodiē māne; **good ~** salvē ▶ adj mātūtīnus
morning call n salūtātiō f
morning watch n (NAUT) tertia vigilia f
moron n (offensive) sōcors m
morose adj acerbus, tristis
moroseness n acerbitās f, tristitia f
morrow n posterus diēs m; **on the ~** posterō
 diē, postrīdiē
morsel n offa f
mortal adj mortālis, hūmānus; (wound)
 mortifer ▶ n mortālis m/f, homō m/f; **poor ~**
 homunculus m
mortality n mortālitās f; (death) mors f;
 the ~ was high plūrimī periērunt
mortally adv: **be ~ wounded** mortiferum
 vulnus accipere

mortar n mortārium nt
mortgage n pignus nt, fīdūcia f ▶ vt obligāre
mortification n dolor m, angor m
mortified adj: **be ~** aegrē ferre
mortify vt mordēre, vexāre; (lust) coercēre ▶ vi
 putrēscere
mortise vt immittere
mosaic n emblēma nt, lapillī mpl ▶ adj
 tessellātus
mosquito n culex m
mosquito net n cōnōpēum nt
moss n muscus m
mossy adj muscōsus
most adj plūrimus, plērusque; **for the ~ part**
 māximam partem ▶ adv māximē, plūrimum
mostly adv plērumque, ferē
mote n corpusculum nt
moth n tinea f
mother n māter f; **of a ~** māternus
mother-in-law n socrus f
motherless adj mātre orbus
motherly adj māternus
mother tongue n patrius sermō m
mother wit n Minerva f
motif n argūmentum nt
motion n mōtus m; (for law) rogātiō f; (in debate)
 sententia f; **propose a ~** ferre; **set in ~** movēre
 ▶ vt innuere
motionless adj immōbilis
motive n causa f, ratiō f; **I know your ~ in
 asking** sciō cūr rogēs
motley adj versicolor, varius
mottled adj maculōsus
motto n sententia f
mould n fōrma f; (soil) humus f; (fungus) mūcor
 m ▶ vt fingere, fōrmāre
moulder vi putrēscere ▶ n fictor m
mouldering adj puter
mouldiness n situs m
mouldy adj mūcidus
moult vi pennas exuere
mound n agger m, tumulus m
mount n mōns m; (horse) equus m ▶ vt scandere,
 cōnscendere, ascendere ▶ vi ascendere; **~ up**
 ēscendere
mountain n mōns m
mountaineer n montānus m
mountainous adj montuōsus
mourn vi maerēre, lūgēre ▶ vt dēflēre, lūgēre
mourner n plōrātor m; (hired) praefica f
mournful adj (cause) lūctuōsus, acerbus;
 (sound) lūgubris, maestus
mournfully adv maestē
mourning n maeror nt, lūctus m; (dress) sordēs
 fpl; **in ~** fūnestus; **be in ~** lūgēre; **put on ~**
 vestem mūtāre, sordēs suscipere; **wearing ~**
 ātrātus
mouse n mūs m
mousetrap n mūscipulum nt
mouth n ōs nt; (river) ōstium nt
mouthful n bucca f
mouthpiece n interpres m

movable adj mōbilis; **movables** npl rēs fpl, supellex f

move vt movēre; (emotion) commovēre; ~ **backwards and forwards** reciprocāre; ~ **out of the way** dēmovēre; ~ **up** admovēre ▶ vi movērī; (residence) dēmigrāre; (proposal) ferre, cēnsēre; ~ **into** immigrāre in (acc); ~ **on** prōgredī

movement n mōtus m; (process) cursus m; (society) societās f

mover n auctor m

moving adj flēbilis, flexanimus

mow vt secāre, dēmetere

mower n faenisex m

much adj multus ▶ adv multum; (with compar) multō; **as ~ as** tantum quantum; **so ~** tantum; (with verbs) adeo; ~ **less** nēdum; **too ~** nimis ▶ n multum nt

muck n stercus nt

mud n lutum nt

muddle n turba f ▶ vt turbāre

muffle vt involvere; ~ **up** obvolvere

muffled adj surdus

mug n pōculum nt

mulberry n mōrum nt; (tree) mōrus f

mule n mūlus m

muleteer n mūliō m

mulish adj obstinātus

mullet n mullus m

multifarious adj multiplex, varius

multiform adj multifōrmis

multiply vt multiplicāre ▶ vi crēscere

multitude n multitūdō f

multitudinous adj crēberrimus

mumble vt (words) opprimere ▶ vi murmurāre

munch vt mandūcāre

mundane adj terrestris

municipal adj mūnicipālis

municipality n mūnicipium nt

munificence n largitās f

munificent adj largus, mūnificus

munificently adv mūnificē

munitions n bellī adparātus m

mural adj mūrālis

murder n parricīdium nt, caedēs f; **charge with ~** inter sīcāriōs accūsāre; **trial for ~** quaestiō inter sīcāriōs ▶ vt interficere, iūgulāre, necāre

murderer n sīcārius m, homicīda m, parricīda m, percussor m

murderess n interfectrīx f

murderous adj cruentus

murky adj tenebrōsus

murmur n murmur nt; (angry) fremitus m ▶ vi murmurāre; fremere

murmuring n admurmurātiō f

muscle n torus m

muscular adj lacertōsus

muse vi meditārī ▶ n Mūsa f

mushroom n fungus m, bōlētus m

music n (art) mūsica f; (sound) cantus m, modī mpl

musical adj (person) mūsicus; (sound) canōrus

musician n mūsicus m; (strings) fidicen m; (wind) tībīcen m

muslin n sindōn f

must n (wine) mustum nt ▶ vi dēbēre; **I ~ go** mē oportet īre, mihī eundum est

mustard n sināpi nt

muster vt convocāre, cōgere; (review) recēnsēre ▶ vi convenīre, coīre ▶ n conventus m; (review) recēnsiō f

muster roll n album nt

mustiness n situs m

musty adj mūcidus

mutability n incōnstantia f

mutable adj incōnstāns, mūtābilis

mute adj mūtus

mutilate vt mūtilāre, truncāre

mutilated adj mūtilus, truncus

mutilation n lacerātiō f

mutineer n sēditiōsus m

mutinous adj sēditiōsus

mutiny n sēditiō f ▶ vi sēditiōnem facere

mutter vi mussitāre

mutton n carō ovilla f

mutual adj mūtuus

mutually adv mūtuō, inter sē

muzzle n ōs nt, rōstrum nt; (guard) fiscella f ▶ vt fiscellā capistrāre

my adj meus

myriad n decem mīlia; (any large number) sēscentī

myrmidon n satelles m

myrrh n murra f

myrtle n myrtus f ▶ adj myrteus

myrtle grove n myrtētum nt

myself pron ipse, egomet; (reflexive) mē

mysterious adj arcānus, occultus

mysteriously adv occultē

mystery n arcānum nt; (rites) mystēria ntpl; (fig) latebra f

mystic adj mysticus

mystical adj mysticus

mystification n fraus f, ambāgēs fpl

mystify vt fraudāre, cōnfundere

myth n fābula f

mythical adj fābulōsus

mythology n fābulae fpl

nabob n rēx m
nadir n fundus m
nag n caballus m ▶ vt obiūrgītāre
naiad n nāias f
nail n clāvus m; (finger) unguis m; **hit the ~ on the head** rem acū tangere ▶ vt clāvīs adfīgere
naive adj simplex
naively adv simpliciter
naiveté n simplicitās f
naked adj nūdus
nakedly adv apertē
name n nōmen nt; (repute) existimātiō f; (term) vocābulum nt; **by ~** nōmine; **have a bad ~** male audīre; **have a good ~** bene audīre; **in the ~ of** verbīs (gen); (oath) per ▶ vt appellāre, vocāre, nōmināre; (appoint) dīcere
nameless adj nōminis expers, sine nōmine
namely adv nempe, dīcō
namesake n gentīlis m/f
nanny goat n capra f
nap n brevis somnus m; (cloth) villus nt
napkin n linteum nt
narcissus n narcissus m
narcotic adj somnifer
nard n nardus f
narrate vt nārrāre, ēnārrāre
narration n nārrātiō f
narrative n fābula f
narrator n nārrātor m
narrow adj angustus ▶ vt coartāre ▶ vi coartārī
narrowly adv aegrē, vix
narrowness n angustiae fpl
narrows n angustiae fpl
nasal adj nārium
nascent adj nāscēns
nastily adv foedē
nastiness n foeditās f
nasty adj foedus, taeter, impūrus
natal adj nātālis
nation n populus m; (foreign) gēns f
national adj pūblicus, cīvīlis; (affairs) domesticus
nationality n cīvitās f

native adj indigena; (speech) patrius ▶ n incola m, indigena m/f
native land n patria f
nativity n ortus m
natural adj nātūrālis; (innate) nātīvus, genuīnus, īnsitus
naturalization n cīvitās f
naturalize vt cīvitāte dōnāre
naturalized adj (person) cīvitāte dōnātus; (thing) īnsitus
naturally adv nātūrāliter, secundum nātūram; (of course) scīlicet, certē
nature n nātūra f; rērum nātūra f; (character) indolēs f, ingenium nt; (species) genus nt; **course of ~** nātūra f; **I know the ~ of** sciō quālis sit
naught n nihil nt; **set at ~** parvī facere
naughty adj improbus
nausea n nausea f; (fig) fastīdium nt
nauseate vt fastīdium movēre (dat); **be nauseated with** fastīdīre
nauseous adj taeter
nautical adj nauticus, maritimus
naval adj nāvālis
navel n umbilīcus m
navigable adj nāvigābilis
navigate vt, vi nāvigāre
navigation n rēs nautica f; (sailing) nāvigātiō f
navigator n nauta m, gubernātor m
navy n classis f, cōpiae nāvālēs fpl
nay adv nōn; **nay more** immo
near adv prope ▶ adj propinquus ▶ prep prope (acc), ad (acc); **lie ~** adiacēre (dat) ▶ vt adpropinquāre (dat)
nearby adj iuxtā
nearer adj propior
nearest adj proximus
nearly adv paene, prope, fermē
neat adj nitidus, mundus, concinnus; (wine) pūrus
neatly adv mundē, concinnē
neatness n munditia f
nebulous adj nebulōsus; (fig) incertus
necessaries n rēs ad vīvendum necessāriae fpl
necessarily adv necessāriō, necesse
necessary adj necessārius, necesse; **it is ~** oportet (+ acc and infin or gerundive of vt)
necessitate vt cōgere (infin), efficere ut (subj)
necessitous adj egēnus, pauper
necessity n necessitās f; (thing) rēs necessāria f; (want) paupertās f, egestās f
neck n collum nt
neckcloth n fōcāle nt
necklace n monīle nt, torquis m
nectar n nectar nt
need n (necessity) necessitās f; (want) egestās f, inopia f, indigentia f; **there is ~ of** opus est (abl); **there is no ~ to** nihil est quod, cūr (subj) ▶ vt egēre (abl), carēre, indigēre (abl); **I ~** opus est mihī (abl)
needful adj necessārius
needle n acus f
needless adj vānus, inūtilis

needlessly adv frustrā, sine causā
needs adv necesse ▸ npl necessitātēs fpl
needy adj egēns, inops, pauper
nefarious adj nefārius, scelestus
negation n negātiō f, īnfītiātiō f
negative adj negāns ▸ n negātiō f; **answer in the ~** negāre ▸ vt vetāre, contrādīcere (dat)
neglect n neglegentia f, incūria f; (of duty) dērelictiō f ▸ vt neglegere, ōmittere
neglectful adj neglegēns, immemor
negligence n neglegentia f, incūria f
negligent adj neglegēns, indīligēns
negligently adv neglegenter, indīligenter
negligible adj levissimus, minimī mōmentī
negotiate vi agere dē ▸ vt (deal) peragere; (difficulty) superāre
negotiation n āctiō f, pactum nt
negotiator n lēgātus m, conciliātor m
negro n (offensive) Aethiops m
neigh vi hinnīre
neighbour n vīcīnus m, fīnitimus m
neighbourhood n vīcīnia f, vīcīnitās f
neighbouring adj vīcīnus, fīnitimus, propinquus
neighbourly adj hūmānus, amīcus
neighing n hinnītus m
neither adv neque, nec; nēve, neu ▸ pron neuter ▸ adj neuter, neutra, neutrum (like alter); **neither... nor** nec/neque ... nec/neque
neophyte n tīrō m
nephew n frātris fīlius m, sorōris fīlius m
Nereid n Nērēis f
nerve n nervus m; (fig) audācia f; **nerves** pl pavor m, trepidātiō f; **have the ~ to** audēre ▸ vt cōnfirmāre
nervous adj diffīdēns, sollicitus, trepidus
nervously adv trepidē
nervousness n sollicitūdō f, diffīdentia f
nest n nīdus m ▸ vi nīdificāre
nestle vi recubāre
nestling n pullus m
net n rēte nt ▸ vt inrētīre
nether adj īnferior
nethermost adj īnfimus, īmus
netting n rēticulum nt
nettle n urtīca f ▸ vt inrītāre, ūrere
neuter adj neuter
neutral adj medius; **be ~** neutrī partī sē adiungere, medium sē gerere
neutralize vt compēnsāre
never adv nunquam
nevertheless adv nihilōminus, at tamen
new adj novus, integer, recēns
newcomer n advena m/f
newfangled adj novus, inaudītus
newly adv nūper, modo
newness n novitās f
news n nūntius m; **what news?** quid novī?; **~ was brought that** nūntiātum est (+ acc and infin)
newspaper n ācta diūrna/pūblica ntpl
newt n lacerta f

next adj proximus; (time) īnsequēns ▸ adv deīnde, deīnceps; **~ day** postrīdiē; **~ to** iuxtā; **come ~ to** excipere
nibble vi rōdere
nice adj bellus, dulcis; (exact) accūrātus; (particular) fastīdiōsus
nicely adv bellē, probē
nicety n subtīlitās f
niche n aedicula f
nick n: **in the ~ of time** in ipsō articulō temporis
nickname n cognōmen nt
niece n frātris fīlia f, sorōris fīlia f
niggardliness n illīberālitās f, avāritia f
niggardly adj illīberālis, parcus, avārus
nigh adv prope
night n nox f; **by ~** noctū; **all ~** pernox; **spend the ~** pernoctāre; **be awake all ~** pervigilāre ▸ adj nocturnus
night bird n noctua f
nightfall n prīmae tenebrae fpl; **at ~** sub noctem
nightingale n luscinia f
nightly adj nocturnus ▸ adv noctū
nightmare n incubus m
night work n lūcubrātiō f
nimble adj agilis, pernīx
nimbleness n agilitās f, pernīcitās f; (mind) argūtiae fpl
nimbly adv pernīciter
nine num novem; **~ each** novēnī; **~ times** noviēns; **~ days'** novendiālis
nine hundred num nōngentī
nine hundredth adj nōngentēsimus
nineteen num ūndēvīgintī; **~ each** ūndēvīcēnī; **~ times** deciēns et noviēns
nineteenth adj ūndēvīcēsimus
ninetieth adj nōnāgēsimus
ninety num nōnāgintā; **~ each** nōnāgēnī; **~ times** nōnāgiēns
ninth adj nōnus
nip vt vellicāre; (frost) ūrere
nippers n forceps m
nipple n papilla f
no adv nōn; (correcting) immo; **say no** negāre ▸ adj nūllus
nobility n nōbilitās f; (persons) optimātēs mpl, nōbilēs mpl
noble adj nōbilis; (birth) generōsus; (appearance) decōrus
nobleman n prīnceps m, optimās m
nobly adv nōbiliter, praeclārē
nobody n nēmō m
nocturnal adj nocturnus
nod n nūtus m ▸ vi nūtāre; (sign) adnuere; (sleep) dormītāre
noddle n caput nt
node n nōdus m
noise n strepitus m, sonitus m; (loud) fragor m; **make a ~** increpāre, strepere ▸ vt: **~ abroad** ēvulgāre; **be noised abroad** percrēbrēscere
noiseless adj tacitus
noiselessly adv tacitē

noisily *adv* cum strepitū
noisome *adj* taeter, gravis
noisy *adj* clāmōsus
nomadic *adj* vagus
nomenclature *n* vocābula *ntpl*
nominally *adv* nōmine, verbō
nominate *vt* nōmināre, dīcere; (*in writing*) scrībere
nomination *n* nōminātiō *f*
nominative *adj* nōminātīvus
nominee *n* nōminātus *m*
nonappearance *n* absentia *f*
nonce *n*: for the ~ semel
nonchalance *n* aequus animus *m*
nonchalantly *adv* aequō animō
noncombatant *adj* imbellis
noncommittal *adj* circumspectus
nondescript *adj* īnsolitus
none *adj* nullus ▶ *pron* nēmō *m*
nonentity *n* nihil *nt*, nullus *m*
nones *n* Nōnae *fpl*
nonexistent *adj* quī nōn est
nonplus *vt* ad incitās redigere
nonresistance *n* patientia *f*
nonsense *n* nūgae *fpl*, ineptiae *fpl*
nonsensical *adj* ineptus, absurdus
nook *n* angulus *m*
noon *n* merīdiēs *m* ▶ *adj* merīdiānus
no one *pron* nēmō *m*
noose *n* laqueus *m*
nor *adv* neque, nec; nēve, neu
norm *n* nōrma *f*
normal *adj* solitus
normally *adv* plērumque
north *n* septentriōnēs *mpl* ▶ *adj* septentriōnālis
northeast *adv* inter septentriōnēs et orientem
northerly *adj* septentriōnālis
northern *adj* septentriōnālis
North Pole *n* arctos *f*
northwards *adv* ad septentriōnēs versus
northwest *adv* inter septentriōnēs et occidentem ▶ *adj*: ~ wind Cōrus *m*
north wind *n* aquilō *m*
nose *n* nāsus *m*, nārēs *fpl*; **blow the ~** ēmungere; **lead by the ~** labiīs ductāre ▶ *vi* scrūtārī
nostril *n* nāris *f*
not *adv* nōn, haud; **not at all** haudquāquam; **not as if** nōn quod, nōn quō; **not but what** nōn quīn; **not even** nē ... quidem; **not so very** nōn ita; **not that** nōn quō; **and not** neque; **does not, did not** (*interrog*) nonne; **if ... not** nisi; **that not** (*purpose*) nē; (*fear*) nē nōn; **not long after** haud multō post; **not only ... but also** nōn modo/solum ... sed etiam; **not yet** nōndum
notability *n* vir praeclārus *m*
notable *adj* īnsignis, īnsignītus, memorābilis
notably *adv* īnsignītē
notary *n* scrība *m*
notation *n* notae *fpl*
notch *n* incīsūra *f* ▶ *vt* incīdere
note *n* (*mark*) nota *f*; (*comment*) adnotātiō *f*; (*letter*) litterulae *fpl*; (*sound*) vōx *f*; **make a ~ of** in commentāriōs referre ▶ *vt* notāre; (*observe*) animadvertere
notebook *n* pugillārēs *mpl*
noted *adj* īnsignis, praeclārus, nōtus
noteworthy *adj* memorābilis
nothing *n* nihil, nīl *nt*; **~ but** merus, nīl nisi; **come to ~** in irritum cadere; **for ~** frustrā; (*gift*) grātīs, grātuītō; **good for ~** nēquam; **think ~ of** nihilī facere
notice *n* (*official*) prōscrīptiō *f*; (*private*) libellus *m*; **attract ~** cōnspicī; **escape ~** latēre; **escape the ~ of** fallere; **give ~ of** dēnūntiāre; **take ~ of** animadvertere ▶ *vt* animadvertere, cōnspicere
noticeable *adj* cōnspicuus, īnsignis
noticeably *adv* īnsignītē
notification *n* dēnūntiātiō *f*
notify *vt* (*event*) dēnūntiāre, indicāre; (*person*) renūntiāre (*dat*), certiōrem facere
notion *n* nōtiō *f*, īnfōrmātiō *f*; suspiciō *f*
notoriety *n* īnfāmia *f*
notorious *adj* fāmōsus, īnfāmis; (*thing*) manifestus
notoriously *adv* manifestō
notwithstanding *adv* nihilōminus, tamen ▶ *prep*: ~ **the danger** in tantō discrīmine
nought *n* nihil, nīl *nt*
noun *n* nōmen *nt*
nourish *vt* alere, nūtrīre
nourisher *n* altor *m*, altrīx *f*
nourishment *n* cibus *m*, alimenta *ntpl*
novel *adj* novus, inaudītus ▶ *n* fābella *f*
novelty *n* rēs nova *f*; novitās *f*, īnsolentia *f*
November *n* mēnsis November *m*; **of ~** November
novice *n* tīrō *m*
now *adv* nunc; (*past*) iam; **now and then** interdum; **just now** nunc; (*lately*) dūdum, modo; **now ... now** modo ... modo ▶ *conj* at, autem
nowadays *adv* nunc, hodiē
nowhere *adv* nusquam
nowise *adv* nullō modō, haudquāquam
noxious *adj* nocēns, noxius
nuance *n* color *m*
nucleus *n* sēmen *nt*
nude *adj* nūdus
nudge *vt* fodicāre
nudity *n* nūdātum corpus *nt*
nugget *n* massa *f*
nuisance *n* malum *nt*, incommodum *nt*
null *adj* inritus
nullify *vt* inritum facere; (*LAW*) abrogāre
numb *adj* torpēns, torpidus; **be ~** torpēre; **become ~** torpēscere
number *n* numerus *m*; **a ~ of** complūrēs, aliquot; **a great ~** multitūdō *f*, frequentia *f*; **a small ~** īnfrequentia *f*; **in large numbers** frequentēs ▶ *vt* numerāre, ēnumerāre
numberless *adj* innumerābilis
numbness *n* torpor *m*
numerous *adj* frequēns, crēber, plūrimī
nun *n* monacha *f*

nuptial *adj* nūptiālis
nuptials *n* nūptiae *fpl*
nurse *n* nūtrix *f* ▶ *vt* (*child*) nūtrīre; (*sick*) cūrāre; (*fig*) fovēre
nursery *n* (*children*) cubiculum *nt*; (*plants*) sēminārium *nt*
nursling *n* alumnus *m*, alumna *f*
nurture *n* ēducātiō *f*
nut *n* nux *f*
nutrition *n* alimenta *ntpl*
nutritious *adj* salūbris
nutshell *n* putāmen *nt*
nut tree *n* nux *f*
nymph *n* nympha *f*

O *interj* ō!
oaf *n* agrestis *m*
oak *n* quercus *f*; (*evergreen*) īlex *f*; (*timber*) rōbur *nt* ▶ *adj* quernus, īlignus, rōboreus; **oak forest** quercētum *nt*
oakum *n* stuppa *f*
oar *n* rēmus *m*
oarsman *n* rēmex *m*
oaten *adj* avēnāceus
oath *n* iūsiūrandum *nt*; (*MIL*) sacrāmentum *nt*; (*imprecation*) exsecrātiō *f*; **false ~** periūrium *nt*; **take an ~** iūrāre; **take an ~ of allegiance to** in verba iūrāre (*gen*)
oats *n* avēna *f*
obduracy *n* obstinātus animus *m*
obdurate *adj* obstinātus, pervicāx
obdurately *adv* obstinātē
obedience *n* oboedientia *f*, obsequium *nt*
obedient *adj* oboediēns, obsequēns; **be ~ to** pārēre (*dat*), obtemperāre (*dat*), obsequī (*dat*)
obediently *adv* oboedienter
obeisance *n* obsequium *nt*; **make ~ to** adōrāre
obelisk *n* obeliscus *m*
obese *adj* obēsus, pinguis
obesity *n* obēsitās *f*, pinguitūdō *f*
obey *vt* pārēre (*dat*), obtemperāre (*dat*), oboedīre (*dat*); **~ orders** dictō pārēre
obituary *n* mortēs *fpl*
object *n* rēs *f*; (*aim*) fīnis *m*, prōpositum *nt*; **be an ~ of hate** odiō esse; **with what ~** quō cōnsiliō ▶ *vi* recūsāre, gravārī; **but, it is objected** at enim; **~ to** improbāre
objection *n* recūsātiō *f*, mora *f*; **I have no ~** nīl moror
objectionable *adj* invīsus, iniūcundus
objective *adj* externus ▶ *n* prōpositum *nt*, fīnis *m*
objurgate *vt* obiūrgāre, culpāre
oblation *n* dōnum *nt*
obligation *n* (*legal*) dēbitum *nt*; (*moral*) officium *nt*; **lay under an ~** obligāre, obstringere
obligatory *adj* dēbitus, necessārius
oblige *vt* (*force*) cōgere; (*contract*) obligāre, obstringere; (*compliance*) mōrem gerere (*dat*),

mōrigerārī (dat); (person) amāre, grātiam habēre (dat); **I am obliged to** (action) dēbeō (infin)
obliging adj cōmis, officiōsus
obligingly adv cōmiter, officiōsē
oblique adj oblīquus
obliquely adv oblīquē
obliquity n (moral) prāvitās f
obliterate vt dēlēre, oblitterāre
obliteration n litūra f
oblivion n oblīviō f
oblivious adj oblīviōsus, immemor
oblong adj oblongus
obloquy n vītuperātiō f, opprobrium nt
obnoxious adj invīsus
obscene adj obscaenus, impūrus
obscenity n obscaenitās f, impūritās f
obscure adj obscūrus, caecus ▸ vt obscūrāre, officere (dat)
obscurely adv obscūrē; (speech) per ambāgēs
obscurity n obscūritās f; (speech) ambāgēs fpl
obsequies n exsequiae fpl
obsequious adj officiōsus, ambitiōsus
obsequiously adv officiōsē
obsequiousness n adsentātiō f
observance n observantia f; (rite) rītus m
observant adj attentus, dīligēns
observation n observātiō f, animadversiō f; (remark) dictum nt
observe vt animadvertere, contemplārī; (see) cernere, cōnspicere; (remark) dīcere; (adhere to) cōnservāre, observāre
observer n spectātor m, contemplātor m
obsess vt occupāre; **I am obsessed by** tōtus sum in (abl)
obsession n studium nt
obsolescent adj: **be ~** obsolēscere
obsolete adj obsolētus; **become ~** exolēscere
obstacle n impedīmentum nt, mora f
obstinacy n pertinācia f, obstinātus animus m
obstinate adj pertināx, obstinātus
obstinately adv obstinātō animō
obstreperous adj clāmōsus, ferus
obstruct vt impedīre, obstruere, obstāre (dat); (POL) intercēdere (dat); (fig) officere (dat)
obstruction n impedīmentum nt; (POL) intercessiō f
obstructionist n intercessor m
obtain vt adipīscī, nancīscī, cōnsequī; comparāre; (by request) impetrāre ▸ vi tenēre, obtinēre
obtrude vi sē inculcāre ▸ vt ingerere
obtrusive adj importūnus, molestus
obtuse adj hebes, stolidus
obtusely adv stolidē
obtuseness n stupor m
obverse adj obversus
obviate vt tollere, praevertere
obvious adj ēvidēns, manifestus, apertus; **it is ~** appāret
obviously adv ēvidenter, apertē, manifestō
occasion n occāsiō f, locus m; (reason) causa f ▸ vt movēre, facessere, auctōrem esse (gen)

occasional adj fortuïtus
occasionally adv interdum, nōnnunquam
occidental adj occidentālis
occult adj arcānus
occupancy n possessiō f
occupant n habitātor m, possessor m
occupation n quaestus m, occupātiō f
occupier n possessor m
occupy vt possidēre; (MIL) occupāre; (space) complēre; (attention) distinēre, occupāre
occur vi ēvenīre, accidere; (to mind) occurrere, in mentem venīre
occurrence n ēventum nt; rēs f
ocean n mare nt, ōceanus m
October n mēnsis October m; **of ~** October
ocular adj oculōrum; **give ~ proof of** ante oculōs pōnere, videntī dēmōnstrāre
odd adj (number) impār; (moment) subsecīvus; (appearance) novus, īnsolitus
oddity n novitās f; (person) homō rīdiculus m
oddly adv mīrum in modum
odds n praestantia f; **be at ~ with** dissidēre cum; **the ~ are against us** imparēs sumus; **the ~ are in our favour** superiōrēs sumus
ode n carmen nt
odious adj invīsus, odiōsus
odium n invidia f
odorous adj odōrātus
odour n odor m
of prep gen; (origin) ex, dē; (cause) abl; **all of us** nōs omnēs; **the city of Rome** urbs Rōma
off adv procul; (prefix) ab-; **off and on** interdum; **off with you** aufer tē; **come off** ēvādere; **well off** beātus; **well off for** abundāns (abl)
offal n quisquiliae fpl
offence n offēnsiō f; (legal) dēlictum nt; **commit an ~** dēlinquere
offend vt laedere, offendere; **be offended** aegrē ferre ▸ vi dēlinquere; **~ against** peccāre in (acc), violāre
offender n reus m
offensive adj odiōsus; (smell) gravis; (language) contumēliōsus; **take the ~** bellum īnferre
offensively adv odiōsē; graviter
offer vt offerre, dare, praebēre; (hand) porrigere; (violence) adferre; (honour) dēferre; (with verb) profitērī, pollicērī; **~ for sale** venditāre ▸ n condiciō f
offering n dōnum nt; (to the dead) īnferiae fpl
off-hand adj neglegēns, incūriōsus
office n (POL) magistrātus m, mūnus nt, honōs m; (kindness) officium nt; (place) mēnsa f
officer n praefectus m; lēgātus m
official adj pūblicus ▸ n adiūtor m, minister m
officially adv pūblicē
officiate vi operārī, officiō fungī
officious adj molestus
officiously adv molestē
officiousness n occursātiō f
offing n: **in the ~** procul
offset vt compēnsāre
offspring n prōgeniēs f, līberī mpl; (animal) fētus m

often *adv* saepe, saepenumerō; **as ~ as** quotiēns; totiēs … quotiēs; **how often?** quotiēns?; **so ~** totiēs; **very ~** persaepe

ogle *vi*: **~ at** līmīs oculīs intuērī

ogre *n* mōnstrum *nt*

oh *interj* (joy, surprise) ōh!; (sorrow) prō!

oil *n* oleum *nt* ▶ *vt* ungere

oily *adj* oleōsus

ointment *n* unguentum *nt*

old *adj* (person) senex; (thing) vetus; (ancient) antīquus, prīscus; **old age** senectūs *f*; **be ten years old** decem annōs habēre; **ten years old** decem annōs nātus; **two years old** bīmus; **good old** antīquus; **good old days** antīquitās *f*; **grow old** senēscere; **of old** quondam

olden *adj* prīscus, prīstinus

older *adj* nātū māior, senior

oldest *adj* nātū māximus

old-fashioned *adj* antīquus, obsolētus

old man *n* senex *m*

oldness *n* vetustās *f*

old woman *n* anus *f*

oligarchy *n* paucōrum dominātiō *f*, optimātium factiō *f*

olive *n* olea *f*; **~ orchard** olīvētum *nt*

Olympiad *n* Olympias *f*

Olympic *adj* Olympicus; **win an ~ victory** Olympia vincere

Olympic Games *npl* Olympia *ntpl*

omen *n* ōmen *nt*, auspicium *nt*; **announce a bad ~** obnūntiāre; **obtain favourable omens** litāre

ominous *adj* īnfaustus, mināx

omission *n* praetermissiō *f*, neglegentia *f*

omit *vt* ōmittere, praetermittere

omnipotence *n* īnfīnīta potestās *f*

omnipotent *adj* omnipotēns

on *prep* (place) in (abl), in- (prefix); (time) abl; (coast of) ad (acc); (subject) dē (abl); (side) ab (abl) ▶ *adv* porrō, usque; **and so on** ac deinceps; **on hearing the news** nūntiō acceptō; **on equal terms** (in battle) aequō Marte; **on the following day** posterō/proximō diē, postrīdiē; **on this side of** citrā (acc)

once *adv* semel; (past) ōlim, quondam; **at ~** extemplō, statim; (together) simul; **for ~** aliquandō; **~ and for all** semel; **~ more** dēnuō, iterum; **~ upon a time** ōlim, quondam

one *num* ūnus ▶ *pron* quīdam; (of two) alter, altera, alterum; **one and the same** ūnus; **one another** inter sē, alius alium; **one or the other** alteruter; **one day** ōlim; **one each** singulī; **one would have thought** crēderēs; **be one of** in numerō esse (gen); **be at one** idem sentīre; **it is all one** nihil interest; **the one** alter, hic; **this is the one** hōc illud est

one-eyed *adj* luscus

oneness *n* ūnitās *f*

onerous *adj* gravis

oneself *pron* ipse; (reflexive) sē

one-sided *adj* inaequālis, inīquus

onion *n* caepe *nt*

onlooker *n* spectātor *m*

only *adj* ūnus, sōlus; (son) ūnicus ▶ *adv* sōlum, tantum, modo; (with clause) nōn nisi, nīl nisi, nihil aliud quam; (time) dēmum; **if ~** sī modo; (wish) utinam

onrush *n* incursus *m*

onset *n* impetus *m*

onslaught *n* incursus *m*; **make an ~ on** (words) invehī in (acc)

onto *prep* in (acc)

onus *n* officium *nt*

onward, onwards *adv* porrō

onyx *n* onyx *m*

ooze *vi* mānāre, stillāre

opaque *adj* haud perlūcidus

open *adj* apertus; (wide) patēns, hiāns; (ground) pūrus, apertus; (question) integer; **lie ~** patēre; **stand ~** hiāre; **throw ~** adaperīre, patefacere; **it is ~ to me to** mihī integrum est (infin); **while the question is still ~** rē integrā ▶ *vt* aperīre, patefacere; (book) ēvolvere; (letter) resolvere; (speech) exōrdīrī; (with ceremony) inaugurāre; (will) resignāre ▶ *vi* aperīrī, hīscere; (sore) recrūdēscere; **~ out** extendere, pandere; **~ up** (country) aperīre

open air *n*: **in the open air** sub dīvō

open-handed *adj* largus, mūnificus

open-handedness *n* largitās *f*

open-hearted *adj* ingenuus

opening *n* forāmen *nt*, hiātus *m*; (ceremony) cōnsecrātiō *f*; (opportunity) occāsiō *f*, ānsa *f* ▶ *adj* prīmus

openly *adv* palam, apertē

open-mouthed *adj*: **stand ~ at** inhiāre

operate *vi* rem gerere ▶ *vt* movēre

operation *n* opus *nt*, āctiō *f*; (MED) sectiō *f*

operative *adj* efficāx

ophthalmia *n* lippitūdō *f*

opiate *adj* somnifer

opine *vi* opīnārī, existimāre

opinion *n* sententia *f*; (of person) existimātiō *f*; **public ~** fāma *f*; **in my ~** meō iūdiciō, meō animō

opponent *n* adversārius *m*, hostis *m*

opportune *adj* opportūnus, tempestīvus

opportunely *adv* opportūnē

opportunity *n* occāsiō *f*; (to act) facultās *f*, potestās *f*

oppose *vt* (barrier) obicere; (contrast) oppōnere ▶ *vi* adversārī (dat), resistere (dat), obstāre (dat); **be opposed to** adversārī (dat); (opinion) dīversum esse ab

opposite *adj* (facing) adversus; (contrary) contrārius, dīversus ▶ *prep* contrā (acc), adversus (acc); **directly ~** ē regiōne (gen) ▶ *adv* ex adversō

opposition *n* repugnantia *f*; (party) factiō adversa *f*

oppress *vt* opprimere, adflīgere; (burden) premere, onerāre

oppression *n* iniūria *f*, servitūs *f*

oppressive *adj* gravis, inīquus; **become more ~** ingravēscere

oppressor n tyrannus m
opprobrious adj turpis
opprobriously adv turpiter
opprobrium n dēdecus nt, ignōminia f
optical adj oculōrum
optical illusion n oculōrum lūdibrium nt
optimism n spēs f
option n optiō f, arbitrium nt; **I have no ~** nōn est arbitriī meī
optional adj: **it is ~ for you** optiō tua est
opulence n opēs fpl, cōpia f
opulent adj dīves, cōpiōsus
or conj aut, vel, -ve; (after 'utrum') an; **or else** aliōquīn; **or not** (direct) annōn; (indirect) necne
oracle n ōrāculum nt
oracular adj fātidicus; (fig) obscūrus
oral adj: **give an ~ message** vōce nūntiāre
orally adv vōce, verbīs
oration n ōrātiō f
orator n ōrātor m
oratorical adj ōrātōrius
oratory n ēloquentia f, rhētoricē f; (for prayer) sacellum nt; **of ~** dīcendī, ōrātōrius
orb n orbis m
orbit n orbis m, ambitus m
orchard n pōmārium nt
ordain vt ēdīcere, sancīre
ordeal n labor m
order n (arrangement) ōrdō m; (class) ōrdō m; (battle) aciēs f; (command) iussum nt, imperium nt; (money) perscrīptiō f; **in ~** dispositus; (succession) deinceps; **in ~ that/to** ut (subj); **in ~ that not** nē (subj); **put in ~** dispōnere, ōrdināre; **by ~ of** iussū (gen); **out of ~** incompositus; **without orders from** iniussū (gen) ▶ vt (arrange) dispōnere, ōrdināre; (command) iubēre (+ acc and infin), imperāre (dat and 'ut' + subj or 'nē' + subj)
orderly adj ōrdinātus; (conduct) modestus ▶ n accēnsus m
ordinance n ēdictum nt, īnstitūtum nt
ordinarily adv plērumque, ferē
ordinary adj ūsitātus, solitus, cottīdiānus
ordnance n tormenta ntpl
ordure n stercus m
ore n aes nt; **iron ore** ferrum īnfectum nt
Oread n (myth) Oreas f
organ n (bodily) membrum nt; (musical) organum nt, hydraulus m
organic adj nātūrālis
organically adv nātūrā
organization n ōrdinātiō f, structūra f
organize vt ōrdināre, īnstituere, adparāre
orgies n orgia ntpl
orgy n cōmissātiō f
orient n oriēns m
oriental adj Asiāticus
orifice n ōstium nt
origin n orīgō f, prīncipium nt; (source) fōns m; (birth) genus nt
original adj prīmus, prīstinus; (LIT) proprius ▶ n exemplar nt

originally adv prīncipiō, antīquitus
originate vt īnstituere, auctōrem esse (gen) ▶ vi exorīrī; **~ in** innāscī in (abl), initium dūcere ab
originator n auctor m
orisons n precēs fpl
ornament n ōrnāmentum nt; (fig) decus nt ▶ vt ōrnāre, decorāre
ornamental adj decōrus; **be ~** decorī esse
ornamentally adv ōrnātē
ornate adj ōrnātus
ornately adv ōrnātē
orphan n orbus m, orba f
orphaned adj orbātus
orthodox adj antīquus
orthography n orthographia f
oscillate vi reciprocāre
osculate vt ōsculārī
osier n vīmen nt ▶ adj vīmineus
osprey n haliaeetos m
ostensible adj speciōsus
ostensibly adv per speciem
ostentation n iactātiō f, ostentātiō f
ostentatious adj glōriōsus, ambitiōsus
ostentatiously adv glōriōsē
ostler n agāsō m
ostrich n strūthiocamēlus m
other adj alius; (of two) alter; **one or the ~** alteruter; **every ~ year** tertiō quōque annō; **on the ~ side of** ultrā (acc); **of others** aliēnus
otherwise adv aliter; (if not) aliōquī
otter n lutra f
ought vi dēbēre (+ infin or gerundive of vt); **I ~** mē oportet; **I ~ to have said** dēbuī dīcere
ounce n ūncia f; **two ounces** sextāns m; **three ounces** quadrāns m; **four ounces** triēns m; **five ounces** quīncūnx m; **six ounces** sēmis m; **seven ounces** septūnx m; **eight ounces** bēs m; **nine ounces** dōdrāns m; **ten ounces** dextāns m; **eleven ounces** deūnx m
our adj noster
ourselves pron ipsī; (reflexive) nōs
oust vt extrūdere, ēicere
out adv (rest) forīs; (motion) forās; **out of** dē, ē/ex (abl); (cause) propter (acc); (beyond) extrā, ultrā (acc); **be out** (book) in manibus esse; (calculation) errāre; (fire) exstinctum esse; (secret) palam esse
outbreak n initium nt, ēruptiō f
outburst n ēruptiō f
outcast n profugus m
outcome n ēventus m, exitus m
outcry n clāmor m, adclāmātiō f; **raise an ~ against** obstrepere (dat)
outdistance vt praevertere
outdo vt superāre
outdoor adj sub dīvō
outer adj exterior
outermost adj extrēmus
outfit n īnstrūmenta ntpl; vestīmenta ntpl
outflank vt circumīre
outgrow vt excēdere ex
outing n excursiō f
outlandish adj barbarus

outlaw n prōscrīptus m ▶ vt prōscrībere, aquā et ignī interdīcere (dat)
outlawry n aquae et ignis interdictiō f
outlay n impēnsa f, sūmptus m
outlet n ēmissārium nt, exitus m
outline n ductus m, adumbrātiō f ▶ vt adumbrāre
outlive vt superesse (dat)
outlook n prōspectus m
outlying adj longinquus, exterior
outnumber vt numerō superiōrēs esse, multitūdine superāre
out-of-doors adv forīs
outpost n statiō f
outpouring n effūsiō f
output n frūctus m
outrage n flāgitium nt, iniūria f ▶ vt laedere, violāre
outrageous adj flāgitiōsus, indignus
outrageously adv flāgitiōsē
outrider n praecursor m
outright adv penitus, prōrsus; semel
outrun vt praevertere
outset n initium nt
outshine vt praelūcēre (dat)
outside adj externus ▶ adv extrā, forīs; (motion to) forās; ~ in inversus; from ~ extrīnsecus ▶ n exterior pars f; (show) speciēs f; at the ~ summum, ad summum; on the ~ extrīnsecus ▶ prep extrā (acc)
outsider n aliēnus m; (POL) novus homō m
outskirts n suburbānus ager m; on the ~ suburbānus
outspoken adj līber
outspokenness n lībertās f
outspread adj patulus
outstanding adj ēgregius, īnsignis, singulāris; (debt) residuus
outstep vt excēdere
outstretched adj passus, porrēctus, extentus
outstrip vt praevertere
outvote vt suffrāgiīs superāre
outward adj externus; ~ form speciēs f ▶ adv domō, forās
outweigh vt praeponderāre
outwit vt dēcipere, circumvenīre
outwork n prōpugnāculum nt, bracchium nt
outworn adj exolētus
oval adj ōvātus ▶ n ōvum nt
ovation n (triumph) ovātiō f; receive an ~ cum laudibus excipī
oven n furnus m, fornāx f
over prep (above) super (abl), suprā (acc); (across) super (acc); (extent) per (acc); (time) inter (acc); ~ and above super (acc), praeter (acc); all ~ per; ~ against adversus (acc) ▶ adv suprā; (excess) nimis; (done) cōnfectus; ~ again dēnuō; ~ and above īnsuper; ~ and ~ identidem; be left ~ superesse, restāre; it is all ~ with āctum est dē
overall adj tōtus ▶ adv ubīque, passim
overawe vt formīdinem inicere (dat)
overbalance vi titubāre

overbearing adj superbus
overboard adv ē nāvī, in mare; throw ~ excutere, iactāre
overbold adj importūnus
overburden vt praegravāre
overcast adj nūbilus
overcoat n paenula f, lacerna f
overcome vt superāre, vincere
overconfidence n cōnfidentia f
overconfident adj cōnfidēns
overdo vt modum excēdere in (abl)
overdone adj (style) pūtidus
overdraw vt (style) exaggerāre
overdue adj (money) residuus
overestimate vt māiōris aestimāre
overflow n ēluviō f ▶ vi abundāre, redundāre ▶ vt inundāre
overgrown adj obsitus; be ~ luxuriāre
overhang vt, vi impendēre, imminēre (dat)
overhaul vt reficere
overhead adv īnsuper
overhear vt excipere, auscultāre
overjoyed adj nimiō gaudiō ēlātus
overladen adj praegravātus
overland adv terrā
overlap vt implicāre
overlay vt indūcere
overload vt (fig) obruere
overlook vt (place) dēspectāre, imminēre (dat); (knowledge) ignōrāre; (notice) neglegere, praetermittere; (fault) ignōscere (dat)
overlord n dominus m
overmaster vt dēvincere
overmuch adv nimis, plūs aequō
overnight adj nocturnus ▶ adv noctū
overpower vt superāre, domāre, obruere, opprimere
overpraise vt in māius extollere
overrate vt māiōris aestimāre
overreach vt circumvenīre
overriding adj praecipuus
overrule vt rescindere
overrun vt pervagārī; (fig) obsidēre
oversea adj trānsmarīnus
oversee vt praeesse (dat)
overseer n cūrātor m, custōs m
overset vt ēvertere
overshadow vt officere (dat)
overshoot vt excēdere
oversight n neglegentia f
overspread vt offendere (dat), obdūcere
overstep vt excēdere
overt adj apertus
overtake vt cōnsequī; (surprise) opprimere, dēprehendere
overtax vt (fig) abūtī (abl)
overthrow vt ēvertere; (destroy) prōflīgāre, dēbellāre ▶ n ēversiō f, ruīna f
overtly adv palam
overtop vt superāre
overture n exōrdium nt; make overtures to temptāre, agere cum, lēgātōs mittere ad

overturn vt ēvertere
overweening adj superbus, adrogāns, īnsolēns
overwhelm vt obruere, dēmergere, opprimere
overwhelming adj īnsignis, vehementissimus
overwhelmingly adv mīrum quantum
overwork vi plūs aequō labōrāre ▶ vt cōnficere ▶ n immodicus labor m
overwrought adj (emotion) ēlātus; (style) ēlabōrātus
owe vt dēbēre
owing adj: **be ~** dēbērī; **~ to** (person) per; (cause) ob/propter (acc)
owl n būbō m; ulula f
own adj proprius; **my own** meus; **have of one's own** domī habēre; **hold one's own** parem esse ▶ vt possidēre, habēre; (admit) fatērī, cōnfitērī
owner n dominus m, possessor m
ownership n possessiō f, mancipium nt
ox n bōs m
ox herd n bubulcus m
oyster n ostrea f

pace n passus m; (speed) gradus m; **keep ~** gradum cōnferre ▶ vi incēdere; **~ up and down** spatiārī, inambulāre
pacific adj pācificus; (quiet) placidus
pacification n pācificātiō f
pacifist n imbellis m
pacify vt (anger) plācāre; (rising) sēdāre
pack n (MIL) sarcina f; (animals) grex m; (people) turba f ▶ vt (kit) colligere; (crowd) stīpāre; **~ together** coartāre; **~ up** colligere, compōnere ▶ vi vāsa colligere; **send packing** missum facere ▶ adj (animal) clītellārius
package n fasciculus m, sarcina f
packet n fasciculus m; (ship) nāvis āctuāria f
packhorse n iūmentum nt
packsaddle n clītellae fpl
pact n foedus nt, pactum nt
pad n pulvillus m
padding n tōmentum nt
paddle n rēmus m ▶ vi rēmigāre
paddock n saeptum nt
paean n paeān m
pagan adj pāgānus
page n (book) pāgina f; (boy) puer m
pageant n pompa f, spectāculum nt
pageantry n adparātus m
pail n situla f
pain n dolor m; **be in ~** dolēre ▶ vt dolōre adficere
painful adj acerbus; (work) labōriōsus
painfully adv acerbē, labōriōsē
painless adj dolōris expers
painlessly adv sine dolōre
painlessness n indolentia f
pains npl opera f; **take ~** operam dare; **take ~ with** (art) ēlabōrāre
painstaking adj dīligēns, operōsus
painstakingly adv dīligenter, summā cūrā
paint n pigmentum nt; (cosmetic) fūcus m ▶ vt pingere; (red) fūcāre; (in words) dēpingere; (portrait) dēpingere
paintbrush n pēnicillus m
painter n pictor m
painting n pictūra f

pair n pār nt ▶ vt coniungere, compōnere
palace n rēgia f
palatable adj suāvis, iūcundus
palate n palātum nt
palatial adj rēgius
palaver n colloquium nt, sermunculī mpl
pale n pālus m, vallus m; **beyond the ~**
  extrāneus ▶ adj pallidus; **look ~** pallēre; **grow ~**
  pallēscere; **~ brown** subfuscus; **~ green**
  subviridis ▶ vi pallēscere
paleness n pallor m
palimpsest n palimpsēstus m
paling n saepēs f
palisade n (MIL) vallum nt
palish adj pallidulus
pall n (funeral) pallium nt ▶ vi taedēre
pallet n grabātus m
palliasse n strāmentum nt
palliate vt extenuāre, excūsāre
palliation n excūsātiō f
palliative n lēnīmentum nt
pallid adj pallidus
pallor n pallor m
palm n (hand) palma f; (tree) palma f ▶ vt: **~ off**
  impōnere
palmy adj flōrēns
palpable adj tractābilis; (fig) manifestus
palpably adv manifestō, propalam
palpitate vi palpitāre, micāre
palpitation n palpitātiō f
palsied adj membrīs captus
palsy n paralysis f
paltry adj vīlis, frīvolus
pamper vt indulgēre (dat)
pampered adj dēlicātus
pamphlet n libellus m
pan n patina f, patella f; (frying) sartāgō f;
  (of balance) lanx f
pancake n laganum nt
pander n lēnō m ▶ vi: **~ to** lēnōcinārī (dat)
panegyric n laudātiō f
panegyrist n laudātor m
panel n (wall) abacus m; (ceiling) lacūnar nt;
  (judges) decuria f
panelled adj laqueātus
pang n dolor m
panic n pavor m ▶ vi trepidāre
panic-stricken adj pavidus
panniers n clītellae fpl
panoply n arma ntpl
panorama n prōspectus m
panpipe n fistula f
pant vi anhēlāre
panther n panthēra f
panting n anhēlitus m
pantomime n mīmus m
pantry n cella penāria f
pap n mamma f
paper n charta f
papyrus n papyrus f
par n: **on a par with** pār (dat)
parable n parabolē f

parade n pompa f; (show) adparātus m ▶ vt
  trādūcere, iactāre ▶ vi pompam dūcere,
  incēdere
paradox n verba sēcum repugnantia;
  paradoxes pl paradoxa ntpl
paragon n exemplar nt, specimen nt
paragraph n caput nt
parallel adj parallēlus; (fig) cōnsimilis
paralyse vt dēbilitāre; (with fear) percellere;
  be paralysed torpēre
paralysis n dēbilitās f; (fig) torpēdō f
paramount adj prīnceps, summus
paramour n adulter m
parapet n lōrīca f
paraphernalia n adparātus m
paraphrase vt vertere
parasite n parasītus m
parasol n umbella f
parboiled adj subcrūdus
parcel n fasciculus m ▶ vt: **~ out** distribuere,
  dispertīre
parch vt torrēre
parched adj torridus, āridus; **be ~** ārēre
parchment n membrāna f
pardon n venia f ▶ vt ignōscere (dat); (offence)
  condōnāre
pardonable adj ignōscendus
pare vt dēglūbere; (nails) resecāre
parent n parēns m/f, genitor m, genetrīx f
parentage n stirps f, genus nt
parental adj patrius
parenthesis n interclūsiō f
parings n praesegmina ntpl
parish n (ECCL) paroecia f
parity n aequālitās f
park n hortī mpl
parlance n sermō m
parley n colloquium nt ▶ vi colloquī, agere
parliament n senātus m; **house of ~** cūria f
parliamentary adj senātōrius
parlour n exedrium nt
parlous adj difficilis, perīculōsus
parochial adj mūnicipālis
parody n carmen ioculāre nt ▶ vt calumniārī
parole n fidēs f
paronomasia n agnōminātiō f
paroxysm n accessus m
parricide n (doer) parricīda m; (deed) parricīdium
  nt
parrot n psittacus m
parry vt ēlūdere, prōpulsāre
parsimonious adj parcus
parsimoniously adv parcē
parsimony n parsimōnia f, frūgālitās f
part n pars f; (play) partēs fpl, persōna f; (duty)
  officium nt; **parts** loca ntpl; (ability) ingenium
  nt; **for my ~** equidem; **for the most ~** māximam
  partem; **on the ~ of** ab; **act the ~ of** persōnam
  sustinēre, partēs agere; **have no ~ in** expers
  esse (gen); **in ~** partim; **it is the ~ of a wise man**
  sapientis est; **play one's ~** officiō satisfacere;
  take ~ in interesse (dat), particeps esse (gen);

take in good ~ in bonam partem accipere; **take someone's ~** adesse alicuī, dēfendere aliquem; **from all parts** undique; **in foreign parts** peregrē; **in two parts** bifāriam; (MIL) bipartītō; **in three parts** trifāriam; (MIL) tripartītō; **of parts** ingeniōsus ▶ vt dīvidere, sēparāre, dirimere; **~ company** dīversōs discēdere ▶ vi dīgredī, discēdere; (things) dissilīre; **~ with** renūntiāre

partake vi interesse, particeps esse; **~ of** gustāre

partial adj (biased) inīquus, studiōsus; (incomplete) mancus; **be ~ to** favēre (dat), studēre (dat); **win a ~ victory** aliquā ex parte vincere

partiality n favor m, studium nt

partially adv partim, aliquā ex parte

participant n particeps m/f

participate vi interesse, particeps esse

participation n societās f

particle n particula f

parti-coloured adj versicolor, varius

particular adj (own) proprius; (special) praecipuus; (exact) dīligēns, accūrātus; (fastidious) fastīdiōsus; **a ~ person** quīdam ▶ n rēs f; **with full particulars** subtīliter; **give all the particulars** omnia exsequī; **in ~** praesertim

particularity n subtīlitās f

particularize vt singula exsequī

particularly adv praecipuē, praesertim, in prīmīs, māximē

parting n dīgressus m, discessus m ▶ adj ultimus

partisan n fautor m, studiōsus m

partisanship n studium nt

partition n (act) partītiō f; (wall) pariēs m; (compartment) loculāmentum nt ▶ vt dīvidere

partly adv partim, ex parte

partner n socius m; (in office) collēga m

partnership n societās f; **form a ~** societātem inīre

partridge n perdīx m/f

parturition n partus m

party n (POL) factiō f, partēs fpl; (entertainment) convīvium nt; (MIL) manus f; (individual) homō m/f; (associate) socius m, cōnscius m

party spirit n studium nt

parvenu n novus homō m

pass n (hill) saltus m; (narrow) angustiae fpl, faucēs fpl; (crisis) discrīmen nt; (document) diplōma nt; (fighting) petītiō f; **things have come to such a ~** in eum locum ventum est, adeō rēs rediit ▶ vi īre, praeterīre, trānsīre; (time) trānsīre; (property) pervenīre; **~ away** abīre; (die) morī, perīre; (fig) dēfluere; **~ by** praeterīre; **~ for** habērī prō (abl); **~ off** abīre; **~ on** pergere; **~ over** trānsīre; **come to ~** fierī, ēvenīre; **let ~** intermittere, praetermittere ▶ vt praeterīre; (riding) praetervehī; (by hand) trādere; (LAW) iubēre; (limit) excēdere; (sentence) interpōnere, dīcere; (test) satisfacere (dat); (time) dēgere, agere; **~ accounts** ratiōnēs ratās habēre; **~ the day** diem cōnsūmere; **~ a law** lēgem ferre; **~ a**

decree dēcernere; **~ off** ferre; **~ over** praeterīre, mittere; (fault) ignōscere (dat); **~ round** trādere; **~ through** trānsīre

passable adj (place) pervius; (standard) mediocris

passably adv mediocriter

passage n iter nt, cursus m; (land) trānsitus m; (sea) trānsmissiō f; (book) locus m; **of ~** (bird) advena

passenger n vector m

passer-by n praeteriēns m

passing n obitus m ▶ adj admodum

passion n animī mōtus m, permōtiō f, ārdor m; (anger) īra f; (lust) libīdō f

passionate adj ārdēns, impotēns, ācer; īrācundus

passionately adv vehementer, ārdenter; īrācundē; **be ~ in love** amōre ārdēre

passive adj iners

passiveness n inertia f, patientia f

passport n diplōma nt

password n tessera f

past adj praeteritus; (recent) proximus ▶ n praeterita ntpl ▶ prep praeter (acc); (beyond) ultrā (acc)

paste n glūten nt ▶ vt glūtināre

pastime n lūdus m, oblectāmentum nt

pastoral adj pastōrālis; (poem) būcolicus

pastry n crustum nt

pasture n pāstus m, pāscuum nt ▶ vt pāscere

pat vt dēmulcēre ▶ adj opportūnus

patch n pannus m ▶ vt resarcīre

patchwork n centō m

pate n caput nt

patent adj apertus, manifestus ▶ n prīvilēgium nt

patently adv manifestō

paternal adj paternus

path n sēmita f, trāmes m

pathetic adj miserābilis

pathetically adv miserābiliter

pathfinder n explorātor m

pathless adj āvius

pathos n misericordia f; (RHET) dolor m

pathway n sēmita f

patience n patientia f

patient adj patiēns ▶ n aeger m

patiently adv patienter, aequō animō

patois n sermō m

patrician adj patricius ▶ n patricius m

patrimony n patrimōnium nt

patriot n amāns patriae m

patriotic adj pius, amāns patriae

patriotically adv prō patriā

patriotism n amor patriae m

patrol n excubiae fpl ▶ vi circumīre

patron n patrōnus m, fautor m

patronage n patrōcinium nt

patroness n patrōna f, fautrīx f

patronize vt favēre (dat), fovēre

patronymic n nōmen nt

patter vi crepitāre ▶ n crepitus m

pattern n exemplar nt, exemplum nt, nōrma f; (*ideal*) specimen nt; (*design*) figūra f
paucity n paucitās f
paunch n abdōmen nt, venter m
pauper n pauper m
pause n mora f, intervallum nt ▶ vi īnsistere, intermittere
pave vt sternere; **~ the way** (*fig*) viam mūnīre
pavement n pavīmentum nt
pavilion n tentōrium nt
paw n pēs m ▶ vt pede pulsāre
pawn n (*chess*) latrunculus m; (*COMM*) pignus nt, fiдūcia f ▶ vt oppignerāre
pawnbroker n pignerātor m
pay n mercēs f; (*MIL*) stīpendium nt; (*workman*) manupretium nt ▶ vt solvere, pendere; (*debt*) exsolvere; (*in full*) persolvere; (*honour*) persolvere; (*MIL*) stīpendium numerāre (*dat*); (*penalty*) dare, luere; **pay down** numerāre; **pay for** condūcere; **pay off** dissolvere, exsolvere; **pay out** expendere; (*publicly*) ērogāre; **pay up** dēpendere; **pay a compliment to** laudāre; **pay respects to** salūtāre ▶ vi respondēre; **it pays** expedit
payable adj solvendus
paymaster n (*MIL*) tribūnus aerārius m
payment n solūtiō f; (*money*) pēnsiō f
pea n pīsum nt; **like as two peas** tam similis quam lac lactī est
peace n pāx f; **~ and quiet** ōtium nt; **breach of the ~** vīs f; **establish ~** pācem conciliāre; **hold one's ~** reticēre; **sue for ~** pācem petere
peaceable adj imbellis, placidus
peaceably adv placidē
peaceful adj tranquillus, placidus, pācātus
peacefully adv tranquillē
peacemaker n pācificus m
peace-offering n piāculum nt
peach n Persicum nt
peacock n pāvō m
peak n apex m, vertex m
peal n (*bell*) sonitus m; (*thunder*) fragor m ▶ vi sonāre
pear n pirum nt; (*tree*) pirus f
pearl n margarīta f
pearly adj gemmeus; (*colour*) candidus
peasant n agricola m, colōnus m
peasantry n agricolae mpl
pebble n calculus m
pebbly adj lapidōsus
peccadillo n culpa f
peck n (*measure*) modius m ▶ vt vellicāre
peculate vi pecūlārī
peculation n pecūlātus m
peculiar adj (*to one*) proprius; (*strange*) singulāris
peculiarity n proprietās f, nota f
peculiarly adv praecipuē, praesertim
pecuniary adj pecūniārius
pedagogue n magister m
pedant n scholasticus m
pedantic adj nimis dīligens

pedantically adv dīligentius
pedantry n nimia dīligentia f
peddle vt circumferre
pedestal n basis f
pedestrian adj pedester ▶ n pedes m
pedigree n stirps f, stemma nt ▶ adj generōsus
pediment n fastīgium nt
pedlar n īnstitor m, circumforāneus m
peel n cortex m ▶ vt glūbere
peep vi dīspicere ▶ n aspectus m; **at ~ of day** prīmā lūce
peer vi: **~ at** intuērī ▶ n pār m; (*rank*) patricius m
peerless adj ūnicus, ēgregius
peevish adj stomachōsus, mōrōsus
peevishly adv stomachōsē, mōrōsē
peevishness n stomachus m, mōrōsitās f
peg n clāvus m; **put a round peg in a square hole** bovī clītellās impōnere ▶ vt clāvīs dēfīgere
pelf n lucrum nt
pellet n globulus m
pell-mell adv prōmiscuē, turbātē
pellucid adj perlūcidus
pelt n pellis f ▶ vt petere ▶ vi violenter cadere
pen n calamus m, stilus m; (*cattle*) saeptum nt ▶ vt scrībere
penal adj poenālis
penalize vt poenā adficere, multāre
penalty n poena f, damnum nt; (*fine*) multa f; **pay the ~** poenās dare
penance n supplicium nt
pencil n graphis f
pending adj sub iūdice ▶ prep inter (*acc*)
penetrable adj pervius
penetrate vt penetrāre
penetrating adj ācer, acūtus; (*mind*) perspicāx
penetration n (*mind*) acūmen nt
peninsula n paenīnsula f
penitence n paenitentia f
penitent adj: **I am ~** mē paenitet
penknife n scalpellum nt
penmanship n scrīptiō f, manus f
pennant n vexillum nt
penny n dēnārius m
pension n annua ntpl
pensioner n ēmeritus m
pensive adj attentus
pensiveness n cōgitātiō f
pent adj inclūsus
penthouse n (*MIL*) vīnea f
penurious adj parcus, avārus, tenāx
penuriousness n parsimōnia f, tenācitās f
penury n egestās f, inopia f
people n hominēs mpl; (*nation*) populus m, gēns f; **common ~** plēbs f ▶ vt frequentāre
peopled adj frequēns
pepper n piper nt
peradventure adv fortasse
perambulate vi spatiārī, inambulāre
perceive vt sentīre, percipere, intellegere
perceptible adj: **be ~** sentīrī posse, audīrī posse
perception n sēnsus m
perch n (*bird's*) pertica f; (*fish*) perca f ▶ vi īnsidēre

perchance adv fortasse, forsitan (subj)
percolate vi permānāre
percussion n ictus m
perdition n exitium nt
peregrinate vi peregrīnārī
peregrination n peregrīnātiō f
peremptorily adv praecīsē, prō imperiō
peremptory adj imperiōsus
perennial adj perennis
perfect adj perfectus, absolūtus; (entire)
integer; (faultless) ēmendātus ▶ vt perficere,
absolvere
perfection n perfectiō f, absolūtiō f
perfectly adv perfectē, ē, ēmendātē; (quite)
plānē
perfidious adj perfidus, perfidiōsus
perfidiously adv perfidiōsē
perfidy n perfidia f
perforate vt perforāre, terebrāre
perforation n forāmen nt
perforce adv per vim, necessāriō
perform vt perficere, peragere; (duty) exsequī,
fungī (abl); (play) agere
performance n (process) exsecūtiō f, fūnctiō f;
(deed) factum nt; (stage) fābula f
performer n āctor m; (music) tībīcen m, fidicen
m; (stage) histriō m
perfume n odor m, unguentum nt ▶ vt odōrāre
perfumer n unguentārius m
perfumery n unguenta ntpl
perfunctorily adv neglegenter
perfunctory adj neglegēns
perhaps adv fortasse, forsitan (subj), nesciō an
(subj); (tentative) vel; (interrog) an
peril n perīculum m, discrīmen nt
perilous adj perīculōsus
perilously adv perīculōsē
perimeter n ambitus m
period n tempus nt, spatium nt; (history) aetās f;
(end) terminus m; (sentence) complexiō f,
ambitus m
periodic adj (style) circumscrīptus
periodical adj status
periodically adv certīs temporibus, identidem
peripatetic adj vagus; (sect) peripatēticus
periphery n ambitus m
periphrasis n circuitus m
perish vi perīre, interīre
perishable adj cadūcus, fragilis, mortālis
peristyle n peristȳlium nt
perjure vi: ~ oneself pēierāre
perjured adj periūrus
perjurer n periūrus m
perjury n periūrium nt; **commit ~** pēierāre
permanence n cōnstantia f, stabilitās f
permanent adj stabilis, diūturnus, perpetuus
permanently adv perpetuō
permeable adj penetrābilis
permeate vt penetrāre ▶ vi permānāre
permissible adj licitus, concessus; **it is ~** licet
permission n potestās f; **ask ~** veniam petere;
give ~ veniam dare, potestātem facere; **by ~ of**

permissū (gen); **with your kind ~** bonā tuā
veniā; **without your ~** tē invītō
permit vt sinere, permittere (dat); **I am
permitted** licet mihī
pernicious adj perniciōsus, exitiōsus
perorate vi perōrāre
peroration n perōrātiō f, epilogus m
perpendicular adj dīrēctus.
perpendicularly adv ad perpendiculum, ad
līneam
perpetrate vt facere, admittere
perpetual adj perpetuus, perennis,
sempiternus
perpetually adv perpetuō
perpetuate vt continuāre, perpetuāre
perpetuity n perpetuitās f
perplex vt sollicitāre, cōnfundere
perplexing adj ambiguus, perplexus
perplexity n haesitātiō f
perquisite n pecūlium nt
persecute vt īnsectārī, exagitāre; persequī
persecution n īnsectātiō f
persecutor n īnsectātor m
perseverance n persevērantia f, cōnstantia f
persevere vi persevērāre, perstāre; **~ in** tenēre
Persian n Persa m
persist vt īnstāre, perstāre, persevērāre
persistence, persistency n pertinācia f,
persevērantia f
persistent adj pertināx
persistently adv pertināciter, persevēranter
person n homō m/f; (counted) caput nt;
(character) persōna f; (body) corpus nt; **in ~** ipse
praesēns
personage n vir m
personal adj prīvātus, suus
personality n nātūra f; (person) vir ēgregius m
personally adv ipse, cōram
personal property n pecūlium nt
personate vt persōnam gerere (gen)
personification n prosōpopoeia f
personify vt hūmānam nātūram tribuere (dat)
personnel n membra ntpl, sociī mpl
perspective n scaenographia f
perspicacious adj perspicāx, acūtus
perspicacity n perspicācitās f, acūmen nt
perspicuity n perspicuitās f
perspicuous adj perspicuus
perspiration n sūdor m
perspire vi sūdāre
persuade vt persuādēre (dat); (by entreaty)
exōrāre
persuasion n persuāsiō f
persuasive adj blandus
persuasively adv blandē
pert adj procāx, protervus
pertain vi pertinēre, attinēre
pertinacious adj pertināx
pertinaciously adv pertināciter
pertinacity n pertinācia f
pertinent adj appositus; **be ~** ad rem pertinēre
pertinently adv appositē

pertly adv procāciter, protervē
perturb vt perturbāre
perturbation n animī perturbātiō f, trepidātiō f
peruke n capillāmentum nt
perusal n perlēctiō f
peruse vt perlegere; (book) ēvolvere
pervade vt permānāre per, complēre; (emotion) perfundere
pervasive adj crēber
perverse adj perversus, prāvus
perversely adv perversē
perversion n dēprāvātiō f
perversity n perversitās f
pervert vt dēprāvāre; (words) dētorquēre; (person) corrumpere
perverter n corruptor m
pessimism n dēspērātiō f
pest n pestis f
pester vt sollicitāre
pestilence n pestilentia f, pestis f
pestilential adj pestilēns, nocēns
pestle n pistillum nt
pet n dēliciae fpl ▶ vt in dēliciīs habēre, dēlēnīre
petard n: be hoist with his own ~ suō sibī gladiō iugulārī
petition n precēs fpl; (POL) libellus m ▶ vt ōrāre
petrify vt (fig) dēfīgere; be petrified stupēre, obstupēscere
pettifogger n lēgulēius m
pettiness n levitās f
pettish adj stomachōsus
petty adj levis, minūtus
petulance n protervitās f
petulant adj protervus, petulāns
petulantly adv petulanter
pew n subsellium nt
phalanx n phalanx f
phantasy n commentīcia ntpl
phantom n simulacrum nt, īdōlon nt
phases npl vicēs fpl
pheasant n phāsiānus m
phenomenal adj eximius, singulāris
phenomenon n rēs f, novum nt, spectāculum nt
philander vi lascīvīre
philanthropic adj hūmānus, beneficus
philanthropically adv hūmānē
philanthropy n hūmānitās f, beneficia ntpl
Philippic n Philippica f
philologist n grammaticus m
philology n grammatica ntpl
philosopher n philosophus m, sapiēns m
philosophical adj philosophus; (temperament) aequābilis
philosophize vi philosophārī
philosophy n philosophia f, sapientia f
philtre n philtrum nt
phlegm n pituīta f; (temper) lentitūdō f
phlegmatic adj lentus
phoenix n phoenīx m
phrase n locūtiō f, (GRAM) incīsum nt

phraseology n verba ntpl, ōrātiō f
physic n medicāmentum nt; **physics** pl physica ntpl
physical adj physicus; (of body) corporis
physician n medicus m
physicist n physicus m
physique n corpus nt, vīrēs fpl
piazza n forum nt
pick n (tool) dolabra f; (best part) lēctī mpl, flōs m ▶ vt (choose) legere, dēligere; (pluck) carpere; ~ out ēligere, excerpere; ~ up colligere
pickaxe n dolabra f
picked adj ēlēctus, dēlēctus
picket n (MIL) statiō f
pickle n muria f ▶ vt condīre
picture n pictūra f, tabula f ▶ vt dēpingere; (to oneself) ante oculōs pōnere
picturesque adj (scenery) amoenus
pie n crustum nt
piebald adj bicolor, varius
piece n pars f; (broken off) fragmentum nt; (food) frustum nt; (coin) nummus m; (play) fābula f; **break in pieces** comminuere; **fall to pieces** dīlābī; **take to pieces** dissolvere; **tear in pieces** dīlaniāre
piecemeal adv membrātim, minūtātim
pied adj maculōsus
pier n mōlēs f
pierce vt perfodere, trānsfīgere; (bore) perforāre; (fig) pungere
piercing adj acūtus
piety n pietās f, religiō f
pig n porcus m, sūs m/f; **buy a pig in a poke** spem pretiō emere; **pig's** suillus
pigeon n columba f; **wood ~** palumbēs f
pig-headed adj pervicāx
pigment n pigmentum nt
pigsty n hara f
pike n dolō m, hasta f
pikeman n hastātus m
pile n acervus, cumulus m; (funeral) rogus m; (building) mōlēs f; (post) sublica f ▶ vt cumulāre, congerere; ~ up exstruere, adcumulāre, coacervāre
pile-driver n fistūca f
pilfer vt fūrārī, surripere
pilferer n fūr m, fūrunculus m
pilgrim n peregrīnātor m
pilgrimage n peregrīnātiō f
pill n pilula f
pillage n rapīna f, dēpopulātiō f, expīlātiō f ▶ vt dīripere, dēpopulārī, expīlāre
pillager n expīlātor m, praedātor m
pillar n columen nt, columna f
pillory n furca f
pillow n pulvīnus nt, culcita f
pilot n gubernātor m, ductor m ▶ vt regere, gubernāre
pimp n lēnō m
pimple n pustula f
pin n acus f ▶ vt adfīgere
pincers n forceps m/f

pinch vt pervellere, vellicāre; (shoe) ūrere; (for room) coartāre
pine n pīnus f ▸ vi tābēscere; **~ away** intābēscere; **~ for** dēsīderāre
pinion n penna f
pink adj rubicundus
pinnace n lembus m
pinnacle n fastīgium nt
pint n sextārius m
pioneer n antecursor m
pious adj pius, religiōsus
piously adv piē, religiōsē
pip n grānum nt
pipe n (music) fistula f, tībia f; (water) canālis m ▸ vi fistulā canere
piper n tībīcen m
pipkin n olla f
piquancy n sāl m, vīs f
piquant adj salsus, argūtus
pique n offēnsiō f, dolor m ▸ vt offendere
piracy n latrōcinium nt
pirate n pīrāta m, praedō m
piratical adj pīrāticus
piscatorial adj piscātōrius
piston n embolus m
pit n fovea f, fossa f; (THEAT) cavea f
pitch n pix f; (sound) sonus m ▸ vt (camp) pōnere; (tent) tendere; (missile) conicere
pitch-black adj piceus
pitched battle n proelium iustum nt
pitcher n hydria f
pitchfork n furca f
pitch pine n picea f
piteous adj miserābilis, flēbilis
piteously adv miserābiliter
pitfall n fovea f
pith n medulla f
pithy adj (style) dēnsus; **~ saying** sententia f
pitiable adj miserandus
pitiful adj miser, miserābilis; misericors
pitifully adv miserē, miserābiliter
pitiless adj immisericors, immītis
pitilessly adv crūdēliter
pittance n (food) dēmēnsum nt; (money) stips f
pity n misericordia f; **take ~ on** miserērī (+acc of person, gen of things); **it is a ~ that** male accidit quod ▸ vt miserērī (gen); **I ~** mē miseret (gen)
pivot n cardō m
placability n plācābilitās f
placable adj plācābilis
placard n libellus m
placate vt plācāre
place n locus m; **in another ~** alibī; **in the first ~** prīmum; **in ~ of** locō (gen), prō (abl); **to this ~** hūc; **out of ~** intempestīvus; **give ~ to** cēdere (dat); **take ~** fierī, accidere; **take the ~ of** in locum (gen) succēdere ▸ vt pōnere, locāre, collocāre; **~ beside** adpōnere; **~ over** (in charge) praepōnere; **~ round** circumdare; **~ upon** impōnere
placid adj placidus, tranquillus, quiētus
placidity n tranquillitās f, sedātus animus m

placidly adv placidē, quiētē
plagiarism n fūrtum nt
plagiarize vt fūrārī
plague n pestilentia f, pestis f
plain adj (lucid) clārus, perspicuus; (unadorned) subtīlis, simplex; (frank) sincērus; (ugly) invenustus ▸ n campus m, plānitiēs f; **of the ~** campester
plainly adv perspicuē; simpliciter, sincērē
plainness n perspicuitās f; simplicitās f
plaint n querella f
plaintiff n petītor m
plaintive adj flēbilis, queribundus
plaintively adv flēbiliter
plait vt implicāre, nectere
plan n cōnsilium nt; (of a work) fōrma f, dēsignātiō f; (of living) ratiō f; (intent) prōpositum nt; (drawing) dēscrīptiō f ▸ vt (a work) dēsignāre, dēscrībere; (intent) cōgitāre, meditārī; cōnsilium capere or inīre; (with verb) in animō habēre (infin)
plane n (surface) plānitiēs f; (tree) platanus f; (tool) runcīna f ▸ adj aequus, plānus ▸ vt runcīnāre
planet n stēlla errāns f
plank n tabula f
plant n herba f, planta f ▸ vt (tree) serere; (field) cōnserere; (colony) dēdūcere; (feet) pōnere; **~ firmly** īnfīgere
plantation n arbustum nt
planter n sator m, colōnus m
plaque n tabula f
plaster n albārium nt, tectōrium nt; (MED) emplastrum nt; **~ of Paris** gypsum nt ▸ vt dealbāre
plasterer n albārius m
plastic adj ductilis, fūsilis
plate n (dish) catillus m; (silver) argentum nt; (layer) lāmina f ▸ vt indūcere
platform n suggestus m; rōstrum nt, tribūnal nt
platitude n trīta sententia f
platter n patella f, lanx f
plaudit n plausus m
plausibility n vērīsimilitūdō f
plausible adj speciōsus, vērī similis
play n lūdus m; (THEAT) fābula f; (voice) inclīnātiō f; (scope) campus m; (hands) gestus m; **~ on words** agnōminātiō f; **fair ~** aequum et bonum ▸ vi lūdere; (fountain) scatēre ▸ vt (music) canere; (instrument) canere (abl); (game) lūdere (abl); (part) agere; **~ the part of** agere; **~ a trick on** lūdificārī, impōnere (dat)
playbill n ēdictum nt
player n lūsor m; (at dice) āleātor m; (on flute) tībīcen m; (on lyre) fidicen m; (on stage) histriō m
playful adj lascīvus; (words) facētus
playfully adv per lūdum, per iocum
playfulness n lascīvia f; facētiae fpl
playground n ārea f
playmate n collūsor m
playwright n fābulārum scrīptor m
plea n causa f; (in defence) dēfēnsiō f, excūsātiō f

plead vi causam agere, causam ōrāre, causam dīcere; (in excuse) dēprecārī, excūsāre; ~ with obsecrāre

pleader n āctor m, causidicus m

pleasant adj iūcundus, dulcis, grātus; (place) amoenus

pleasantly adv iūcundē, suāviter

pleasantry n facētiae fpl, iocus m

please vt placēre (dat), dēlectāre; try to ~ īnservīre (dat); just as you ~ quod commodum est; if you ~ sīs; pleased with contentus (abl); be pleased with oneself sibī placēre ▸ adv amābō

pleasing adj grātus, iūcundus, amoenus; be ~ to cordī esse (dat)

pleasurable adj iūcundus

pleasure n voluptās f; (decision) arbitrium nt; it is my ~ libet; derive ~ voluptātem capere ▸ vt grātificārī (dat)

pleasure grounds n hortī mpl

pleasure-loving adj dēlicātus

plebeian adj plēbēius ▸ n: the plebeians plēbs f

plebiscite n suffrāgium nt

plectrum n plēctrum nt

pledge n pignus nt ▸ vt obligāre; ~ oneself prōmittere, spondēre; ~ one's word fidem obligāre, fidem interpōnere

Pleiads n Plēiadēs fpl

plenary adj īnfīnītus

plenipotentiary n lēgātus m

plenitude n cōpia f, mātūritās f

plentiful adj cōpiōsus, largus

plentifully adv cōpiōsē, largē

plenty n cōpia f, abundantia f; (enough) satis

pleonasm n redundantia f

pleurisy n lateris dolor m

pliable adj flexibilis, mollis, lentus

pliant adj flexibilis, mollis, lentus

pliers n forceps m/f

plight n habitus m, discrīmen nt ▸ vt spondēre

plod vi labōrāre, operam īnsūmere

plot n coniūrātiō f, īnsidiae fpl; (land) agellus m; (play) argūmentum nt ▸ vi coniūrāre, mōlīrī

plotter n coniūrātus m

plough n arātrum nt ▸ vt arāre; (sea) sulcāre; ~ up exarāre

ploughing n arātiō f

ploughman n arātor m

ploughshare n vōmer m

pluck n fortitūdō f ▸ vt carpere, legere; ~ out ēvellere; ~ up courage animum recipere, animō adesse

plucky adj fortis

plug n obtūrāmentum nt ▸ vt obtūrāre

plum n prūnum nt; (tree) prūnus f

plumage n plūmae fpl

plumb n perpendiculum nt ▸ adj dīrēctus ▸ adv ad perpendiculum ▸ vt (building) ad perpendiculum exigere; (depth) scrūtārī

plumber n artifex plumbārius m

plumb line n līnea f, perpendiculum nt

plume n crista f ▸ vt: ~ oneself on iactāre, prae sē ferre

plummet n perpendiculum nt

plump adj pinguis

plumpness n nitor m

plunder n (act) rapīna f; (booty) praeda f ▸ vi praedārī ▸ vt dīripere, expīlāre

plunderer n praedātor m, spoliātor m

plundering n rapīna f ▸ adj praedābundus

plunge vt mergere, dēmergere; (weapon) dēmittere ▸ vi mergī, sē dēmergere

plural adj plūrālis

plurality n multitūdō f, plūrēs pl

ply vt exercēre

poach vt surripere

pocket n sinus m

pocket money n pecūlium nt

pod n siliqua f

poem n poēma nt, carmen nt

poesy n poēsis f

poet n poēta m

poetess n poētria f

poetic adj poēticus

poetical adj = poetic

poetically adv poēticē

poetry n (art) poētica f; (poems) poēmata ntpl, carmina ntpl

poignancy n acerbitās f

poignant adj acerbus, acūtus

poignantly adv acerbē, acūtē

point n (dot) pūnctum nt; (place) locus m; (item) caput nt; (sharp end) aciēs f; (of sword) mucrō m; (of epigram) acūleī mpl; ~ of honour officium nt; beside the ~ ab rē; to the ~ ad rem; from this ~ hinc; to that ~ eō; up to this ~ hāctenus, adhūc; without ~ īnsulsus; in ~ of fact nempe; make a ~ of doing cōnsultō facere; on the ~ of death moritūrus; on the ~ of happening inibī; I was on the ~ of saying in eō erat ut dīcerem; matters have reached such a ~ eō rēs recidit; come to the ~ ad rem redīre; the ~ at issue is illud quaeritur; the main ~ cardō m, caput nt; turning ~ articulus temporis m ▸ vt acuere, exacuere; (aim) intendere; (punctuate) distinguere; ~ out indicāre, dēmōnstrāre; ostendere

point-blank adj simplex ▸ adv praecīsē

pointed adj acūtus; (criticism) acūleātus; (wit) salsus

pointedly adv apertē, dīlūcidē

pointer n index m

pointless adj īnsulsus, frīgidus

pointlessly adv īnsulsē

point of view n iūdicium nt, sententia f

poise n lībrāmen nt; (fig) urbānitās f ▸ vt lībrāre

poison n venēnum nt ▸ vt venēnō necāre; (fig) īnficere

poisoned adj venēnātus

poisoner n venēficus m

poisoning n venēficium nt

poisonous adj noxius

poke vt trūdere, fodicāre

polar *adj* septentriōnālis
pole *n* asser *m*, contus *m*; (ASTR) polus *m*
poleaxe *n* bipennis *f*
polemic *n* contrōversia *f*
police *n* lictōrēs *mpl*; (*night*) vigilēs *mpl*
policy *n* ratiō *f*, cōnsilium *nt*; **honesty is the best** = ea māximē condūcunt quae sunt rēctissima
polish *n* (*appearance*) nitor *m*; (*character*) urbānitās *f*; (LIT) līma *f* ▶ *vt* polīre; (*fig*) expolīre
polished *adj* polītus, mundus; (*person*) excultus, urbānus; (*style*) līmātus
polite *adj* urbānus, hūmānus, cōmis
politely *adv* urbānē, cōmiter
politeness *n* urbānitās *f*, hūmānitās *f*, cōmitās *f*
politic *adj* prūdēns, circumspectus
political *adj* cīvīlis, pūblicus; ~ **life** rēs pūblica *f*
politician *n* magistrātus *m*
politics *n* rēs pūblica *f*; **take up** ~ ad rem pūblicam accēdere
polity *n* reī pūblicae fōrma *f*
poll *n* caput *nt*; (*voting*) comitia *ntpl* ▶ *vi* suffrāgia inīre
poll tax *n* tribūtum *nt* in singula capita impositum
pollute *vt* inquināre, contāmināre
pollution *n* corruptēla *f*
poltroon *n* ignāvus *m*
pomegranate *n* mālum Pūnicum *nt*
pomp *n* adparātus *m*
pomposity *n* māgnificentia *f*, glōria *f*
pompous *adj* māgnificus, glōriōsus
pompously *adv* māgnificē, glōriōsē
pompousness *n* māgnificentia *f*
pond *n* stagnum *nt*, lacūna *f*
ponder *vi* sēcum reputāre ▶ *vt* animō volūtāre, in mente agitāre
ponderous *adj* gravis, ponderōsus
ponderously *adv* graviter
poniard *n* pugiō *m*
pontiff *n* pontifex *m*
pontifical *adj* pontificālis, pontificius
pontoon *n* pontō *m*
pony *n* mannus *m*
pooh-pooh *vt* dērīdēre
pool *n* lacūna *f*, stagnum *nt* ▶ *vt* cōnferre
poop *n* puppis *f*
poor *adj* pauper, inops; (*meagre*) exīlis; (*inferior*) improbus; (*pitiable*) miser; ~ **little** misellus
poorly *adj* aeger, aegrōtus ▶ *adv* parum, tenuiter
pop *n* crepitus *m* ▶ *vi* ēmicāre
pope *n* pāpa *m*
poplar *n* pōpulus *f*
poppy *n* papāver *nt*
populace *n* vulgus *nt*, plēbs *f*
popular *adj* grātus, grātiōsus; (*party*) populāris
popularity *n* populī favor *m*, studium *nt*
popularly *adv* vulgō
populate *vt* frequentāre
population *n* populus *m*, cīvēs *mpl*

populous *adj* frequēns
porcelain *n* fictilia *ntpl*
porch *n* vestibulum *nt*
porcupine *n* hystrīx *f*
pore *n* forāmen *nt* ▶ *vi*: ~ **over** scrūtārī, incumbere in (*acc*)
pork *n* porcīna *f*
porous *adj* rārus
porridge *n* puls *f*
port *n* portus *m* ▶ *adj* (*side*) laevus, sinister
portage *n* vectūra *f*
portal *n* porta *f*
portcullis *n* cataracta *f*
portend *vt* portendere
portent *n* mōnstrum *nt*, portentum *nt*
portentous *adj* mōnstruōsus
porter *n* iānitor *m*; (*carrier*) bāiulus *m*
portico *n* porticus *f*
portion *n* pars *f*; (*marriage*) dōs *f*; (*lot*) sors *f*
portliness *n* amplitūdō *f*
portly *adj* amplus, opīmus
portrait *n* imāgō *f*, effigiēs *f*
portray *vt* dēpingere, exprimere, effingere
pose *n* status *m*, habitus *m* ▶ *vt* pōnere ▶ *vi* habitum sūmere
poser *n* nōdus *m*
posit *vt* pōnere
position *n* (GEOG) situs *m*; (*body*) status *m*, gestus *m*; (*rank*) dignitās *f*; (*office*) honōs *m*; (MIL) locus *m*; **be in a** ~ **to** habēre (*infin*); **take up a** ~ (MIL) locum capere
positive *adj* certus; **be** ~ **about** adfirmāre
positively *adv* certō, adfirmātē, rē vērā
posse *n* manus *f*
possess *vt* possidēre, habēre; (*take*) occupāre, potīrī (*abl*)
possession *n* possessiō *f*; **possessions** *pl* bona *ntpl*, fortūnae *fpl*; **take** ~ **of** potīrī (*abl*), occupāre, manum inicere (*dat*); (*inheritance*) obīre; (*emotion*) invādere, incēdere (*dat*); **gain** ~ **of** potior (*abl*)
possessor *n* possessor *m*, dominus *m*
possibility *n* facultās *f*; **there is a** ~ fierī potest
possible *adj*: **it is** ~ fierī potest; **as big as** ~ quam māximus
possibly *adv* fortasse
post *n* pālus *m*; (MIL) statiō *f*; (*office*) mūnus *nt*; (*courier*) tabellārius *m*; **leave one's** ~ locō cēdere, signa relinquere ▶ *vt* (*troops*) locāre, collocāre; (*at intervals*) dispōnere; (*letter*) dare, tabellāriō dare; (*entry*) in cōdicem referre; **be posted** (MIL) in statiōne esse
postage *n* vectūra *f*
poster *n* libellus *m*
posterior *adj* posterior
posterity *n* posterī *mpl*; (*time*) posteritās *f*
postern *n* postīcum *nt*
posthaste *adv* summā celeritāte
posthumous *adj* postumus
posthumously *adv* (*born*) patre mortuō; (*published*) auctōre mortuō
postpone *vt* differre, prōferre

postponement n dīlātiō f
postscript n: add a ~ adscrībere, subicere
postulate vt sūmere ▶ n sūmptiō f
posture n gestus m, status m
pot n olla f, matella f
pot-bellied adj ventriōsus
potency n vīs f
potent adj efficāx, valēns
potentate n dynastēs m, tyrannus m
potential adj futūrus
potentiality n facultās f
potentially adv ut fierī posse vidētur; ~ **an
  emperor** capāx imperiī
potently adv efficienter
potion n pōtiō f
pot-pourri n farrāgō f
potsherd n testa f
pottage n iūs nt
potter n figulus m; **potter's** figulāris
pottery n fictilia ntpl
pouch n pēra f, sacculus m
poultice n fōmentum nt, emplastrum nt
poultry n gallīnae fpl
pounce vi involāre, īnsilīre
pound n lībra f; **five pounds** (weight) **of gold**
  aurī quīnque pondo ▶ vt conterere; pulsāre
pour vt fundere; ~ **forth** effundere; ~ **in**
  īnfundere; ~ **on** superfundere; ~ **out** effundere
  ▶ vi fundī, fluere; ~ **down** ruere, sē praecipitāre
pouring adj (rain) effūsus
poverty n paupertās f, egestās f, inopia f; (style)
  iēiūnitās f
powder n pulvis m
powdery adj pulvereus
power n potestās f; (strength) vīrēs fpl; (excessive)
  potentia f; (supreme) imperium nt; (divine)
  nūmen nt; (legal) auctōritās f; (of father) manus f;
  as far as is in my ~ quantum in mē est; **have
  great ~** multum valēre, posse; **have ~ of
  attorney** capiōnem esse; **it is still in my ~ to**
  integrum est mihī (infin)
powerful adj validus, potēns
powerfully adv valdē
powerless adj impotēns, imbēcillus; **be ~** nihil
  valēre
powerlessness n imbēcillitas f
practicable adj in apertō; **be ~** fierī posse
practical adj (person) habilis
practical joke n lūdus m
practical knowledge n ūsus m
practically adv ferē, paene
practice n ūsus m, exercitātiō f; (RHET)
  meditātiō f; (habit) cōnsuētūdō f, mōs m;
  corrupt practices malae artēs
practise vt (occupation) exercēre, facere;
  (custom) factitāre; (RHET) meditārī ▶ vi (MED)
  medicīnam exercēre; (LAW) causās agere
practised adj exercitātus, perītus
practitioner n (MED) medicus m
praetor n praetor nt; **praetor's** praetōrius
praetorian adj praetōrius
praetorian guards npl praetōriānī mpl

praetorship n praetūra f
praise n laus f ▶ vt laudāre
praiser n laudātor m
praiseworthy adj laudābilis, laude dignus
prance vi exsultāre
prank n lūdus m
prate vi garrīre
prating adj garrulus
pray vi deōs precārī, deōs venerārī ▶ vt precārī,
  ōrāre; ~ **for** petere, precārī; ~ **to** adōrāre
prayer, prayers n precēs fpl
prayerful adj supplex
preach vt, vi docēre, praedicāre
preacher n ōrātor m
preamble n exōrdium nt
prearranged adj cōnstitūtus
precarious adj dubius, perīculōsus
precariousness n discrīmen nt
precaution n cautiō f, prōvidentia f; **take
  precautions** cavēre, praecavēre
precede vt praeīre (dat), anteīre (dat),
  antecēdere
precedence n prīmārius locus m; **give ~ to**
  cēdere (dat); **take ~** (thing) antīquius esse;
  (person) prīmās agere
precedent n exemplum nt; (LAW) praeiūdicium
  nt; **breach of ~** īnsolentia f; **in defiance of ~**
  īnsolenter
preceding adj prior, superior
precept n praeceptum nt
preceptor n doctor m, magister m
precinct n terminus m, templum nt
precious adj cārus; pretiōsus; (style) pūtidus
precious stone n gemma f
precipice n locus praeceps m, rūpēs f
precipitancy n festīnātiō f
precipitate vt praecipitāre ▶ adj praeceps;
  praeproperus
precipitation n festīnātiō f
precipitous adj dēruptus, praeceps,
  praeruptus
precise adj certus, subtīlis; (person) accūrātus
precisely adv dēmum
precision n cūra f
preclude vt exclūdere, prohibēre
precocious adj praecox
precocity n festīnāta mātūritās f
preconceive vt praecipere; **preconceived idea**
  praeiūdicāta opīniō f
preconception n praeceptiō f
preconcerted adj ex compositō factus
precursor n antenūntius m
predatory adj praedātōrius
predecessor n dēcessor m; **my ~** cuī succēdō
predestination n fātum nt, necessitās f
predestine vt dēvovēre
predetermine vt praefīnīre
predicament n angustiae fpl, discrīmen nt
predicate n attribūtum nt
predict vt praedīcere, augurārī
prediction n praedictiō f
predilection ▶ n amor m, studium nt

predispose vt inclīnāre, praeparāre
predisposition n inclīnātiō f
predominance n potentia f, praestantia f
predominant adj praepotēns, praecipuus
predominantly adv plērumque
predominate vi pollēre, dominārī
pre-eminence n praestantia f
pre-eminent adj ēgregius, praecipuus, excellēns
pre-eminently adv ēgregiē, praecipuē, excellenter
preface n prooemium nt, praefātiō f ▸ vi praefārī
prefect n praefectus m
prefecture n praefectūra f
prefer vt (charge) dēferre; (to office) anteferre; (choice) antepōnere (acc and dat), posthabēre (dat and acc); (with verb) mālle
preferable adj potior
preferably adv potius
preference n favor m; **give ~ to** antepōnere, praeoptāre; **in ~ to** potius quam
preferment n honōs m, dignitās f
prefix vt praetendere ▸ n praepositiō f
pregnancy n graviditās f
pregnant adj gravida
prejudge vt praeiūdicāre
prejudice n praeiūdicāta opīniō f; (harmful) invidia f, incommodum nt; **without ~** cum bonā veniā ▸ vt obesse (dat); **be prejudiced against** invidēre (dat), male opīnārī dē (abl)
prejudicial adj damnōsus; **be ~ to** obesse (dat), nocēre (dat), officere (dat), dētrīmentō esse (dat)
preliminaries npl praecurrentia ntpl
preliminary adj prīmus ▸ n prōlūsiō f
prelude n prooemium nt
premature adj immātūrus; (birth) abortīvus
prematurely adv ante tempus
premeditate vt praecōgitāre, praemeditārī
premeditated adj praemeditātus
premier adj prīnceps, praecipuus
premise n (major) prōpositiō f; (minor) adsūmptiō f; **premises** pl aedēs fpl, domus f
premium n praemium nt; **be at a ~** male emī
premonition n monitus m
preoccupation n sollicitūdō f
preoccupied adj sollicitus, districtus
preordain vt praefinīre
preparation n (process) adparātiō f, comparātiō f; (product) adparātus m; (of speech) meditātiō f; **make preparations for** īnstruere, exōrnāre, comparāre
prepare vt parāre, adparāre, comparāre; (speech) meditārī; (with verb) parāre; **prepared for** parātus ad (acc)
preponderance n praestantia f
preponderate vi praepollēre, vincere
preposition n praepositiō f
prepossess vt commendāre (dat and acc), praeoccupāre
prepossessing adj suāvis, iūcundus
prepossession n favor m

preposterous adj absurdus
prerogative n iūs nt
presage n ōmen nt ▸ vt ōminārī, portendere
prescience n prōvidentia f
prescient adj prōvidus
prescribe vt imperāre; (MED) praescrībere; (limit) fīnīre
prescription n (MED) compositiō f; (right) ūsus m
presence n praesentia f; (appearance) aspectus m; **~ of mind** praesēns animus m; **in the ~ of** cōram (abl); apud (abl); **in my ~** mē praesente
present adj praesēns, īnstāns; **be ~** adesse; **be ~ at** interesse (dat) ▸ n praesēns tempus nt; (gift) dōnum nt; **at ~** in praesentī, nunc; **for the ~** in praesēns ▸ vt dōnāre, offerre; (on stage) indūcere; (in court) sistere; **~ itself** occurrere
presentable adj spectābilis
presentation n dōnātiō f
presentiment n augurium nt
presently adv mox
preservation n cōnservātiō f
preserve vt cōnservāre, tuērī; (food) condīre
preside vi praesidēre (dat)
presidency n praefectūra f
president n praefectus m
press n prēlum nt ▸ vt premere; (crowd) stīpāre; (urge) īnstāre (dat); **~ for** flāgitāre; **~ hard** (pursuit) īnsequī, īnstāre (dat), īnsistere (dat); **~ out** exprimere; **~ together** comprimere
pressing adj īnstāns, gravis
pressure n pressiō f, nīsus m
prestige n auctōritās f, opīniō f
presumably adv sānē
presume vt sūmere, conicere ▸ vi audēre, cōnfīdere; **I ~** opīnor, crēdō
presuming adj adrogāns
presumption n coniectūra f; (arrogance) adrogantia f, licentia f
presumptuous adj adrogāns, audāx
presumptuously adv adroganter, audacter
presuppose vt praesūmere
pretence n simulātiō f, speciēs f; **under ~ of** per speciem (gen); **under false pretences** dolō malō
pretend vt simulāre, fingere; **~ that ... not** dissimulāre
pretender n captātor m
pretension n postulātum nt; **make pretensions to** adfectāre, sibī adrogāre
pretentious adj adrogāns, glōriōsus
pretext n speciēs f; **under ~ of** per speciem (gen); **on the ~ that** quod (subj)
prettily adv pulchrē, bellē
prettiness n pulchritūdō f, lepōs m
pretty adj formōsus, pulcher, bellus ▸ adv admodum, satis
prevail vi vincere; (custom) tenēre, obtinēre; **~ upon** persuādēre (dat); (by entreaty) exōrāre
prevailing adj vulgātus
prevalent adj vulgātus; **be ~** obtinēre; **become ~** incrēbrēscere
prevaricate vi tergiversārī

prevarication n tergiversātiō f
prevaricator n veterātor m
prevent vt impedīre (+ quōminus/quīn +subj),
  prohibēre (+ acc and infin)
prevention n impedītiō f
previous adj prior, superior
previously adv anteā, antehāc
prevision n prōvidentia f
prey n praeda f ▶ vi: ~ **upon** īnsectārī; (fig)
  vexāre, carpere
price n pretium nt; (of corn) annōna f; **at a high** ~
  māgnī; **at a low** ~ parvī ▶ vt pretium cōnstituere
  (gen)
priceless adj inaestimābilis
prick vt pungere; (goad) stimulāre; ~ **up the ears**
  aurēs adrigere
prickle n aculeus m
prickly adj aculeātus, horridus
pride n superbia f, fastus m; (boasting) glōria f;
  (object) decus nt; (best part) flōs m ▶ vt: ~ **oneself
  on** iactāre, prae sē ferre
priest n sacerdōs m; (especial) flāmen m; **high** ~
  pontifex m, antistēs m
priestess n sacerdōs f; **high** ~ antistita f
priesthood n sacerdōtium nt, flāminium nt
prig n homō fastīdiōsus m
priggish adj fastīdiōsus
prim adj modestior
primarily adv prīncipiō, praecipuē
primary adj prīmus, praecipuus
prime adj prīmus, ēgregius; ~ **mover** auctor m
  ▶ n flōs m; **in one's** ~ flōrēns ▶ vt īnstruere,
  ērudīre
primeval adj prīscus
primitive adj prīstinus, incultus
primordial adj prīscus
prince n rēgulus m; rēgis fīlius m; prīnceps m
princely adj rēgālis
princess n rēgis fīlia f
principal adj praecipuus, prīnceps, māximus
  ▶ n (person) prīnceps m/f; (money) sors f
principally adv in prīmīs, māximē, māximam
  partem
principle n prīncipium nt; (rule) fōrmula f, ratiō
  f; (character) fidēs f; **principles** pl īnstitūta ntpl,
  disciplīna f; **first principles** elementa ntpl,
  initia ntpl
print n nota f, signum nt; (foot) vestīgium nt
  ▶ vt imprimere
prior adj prior, potior
priority n: **give** ~ **to** praevertere (dat)
prise vt sublevāre; ~ **open** vectī refringere
prison n carcer m, vincula ntpl; **put in** ~ in
  vincula conicere
prisoner n reus m; (for debt) nexus m; (of war)
  captīvus m; ~ **at the bar** reus m, rea f; **take** ~
  capere
pristine adj prīscus, prīstinus, vetus
privacy n sēcrētum nt
private adj (individual) prīvātus; (home)
  domesticus; (secluded) sēcrētus ▶ n (MIL)
  gregārius mīles m

privately adv clam, sēcrētō
private property n res familiāris f
privation n inopia f, egestās f
privet n ligustrum nt
privilege n iūs nt, immūnitās f
privileged adj immūnis
privy adj sēcrētus; ~ **to** cōnscius (gen)
prize n praemium nt; (captured) praeda f;
  ~ **money** manubiae fpl ▶ vt māgnī aestimāre
pro-Athenian adj rērum Athēniēnsium
  studiōsus
probability n vērī similitūdō f
probable adj vērī similis; **more** ~ vērō propior
probably adv fortasse
probation n probātiō f
probationer n tīrō m
probe vt īnspicere, scrūtārī
probity n honestās f, integritās f
problem n quaestiō f; **the** ~ **is** illud quaeritur
problematical adj dubius, anceps
procedure n ratiō f, modus m; (LAW) fōrmula f
proceed vi pergere, prōcēdere, prōgredī;
  (narrative) īnsequī; ~ **against** persequī, lītem
  intendere (dat); ~ **from** orīrī, proficīscī ex
proceedings npl ācta ntpl
proceeds n fructus m, reditus m
process n ratiō f; (LAW) āctiō f; **in the** ~ **of time**
  post aliquod tempus
procession n pompa f; (fig) agmen nt
proclaim vt ēdīcere, prōnūntiāre, praedicāre,
  dēclārāre; ~ **war against** bellum indīcere (dat)
proclamation n ēdictum nt
proclivity n prōpēnsiō f
proconsul n prōcōnsul m
proconsular adj prōcōnsulāris
proconsulship n prōcōnsulātus m
procrastinate vt differre, prōferre ▶ vi cunctārī
procrastination n prōcrāstinātiō f, mora f
procreate vt generāre, prōcreāre
procreation n prōcreātiō f
procreator n generātor m
procumbent adj prōnus
procurator n prōcūrātor m
procure vt parāre, adipīscī, adquīrere; (by
  request) impetrāre
procurer n lēnō m
prod vt stimulāre
prodigal adj prōdigus ▶ n nepōs m
prodigality n effūsiō f
prodigally adv effūsē
prodigious adj ingēns, immānis
prodigy n prōdigium nt, portentum nt; (fig)
  mīrāculum nt
produce vt ēdere; (young) parere; (crops) ferre;
  (play) dare, docēre; (line) prōdūcere; (in court)
  sistere; (into view) prōferre; (from store) prōmere,
  dēprōmere ▶ n fructus m; (of earth) frūgēs fpl; (in
  money) reditus m
product n opus nt; ~ **of** fructus (gen)
production n opus nt
productive adj fēcundus, ferāx, fructuōsus
productivity n fēcunditās f, ūbertās f

profanation n violātiō f
profane adj profānus, impius ▶ vt violāre, polluere
profanely adv impiē
profanity n impietās f
profess vt profitērī, prae sē ferre; ~ **to be** profitērī sē
profession n professiō f; (occupation) ars f, haeresis f
professor n doctor m
proffer vt offerre, pollicērī
proficiency n prōgressus m, perītia f; **attain ~** prōficere
proficient adj perītus
profile n ōris līneāmenta ntpl; (portrait) oblīqua imāgō f
profit n lucrum nt, ēmolumentum nt, fructus m; **make a ~ out of** quaestuī habēre ▶ vt prōdesse (dat) ▶ vi: ~ **by** fruī (abl), ūtī (abl); (opportunity) arripere
profitable adj fructuōsus, ūtilis
profitably adv ūtiliter
profligacy n flāgitium nt, perditī mōrēs mpl
profligate adj perditus, dissolūtus ▶ n nepōs m
profound adj altus; (discussion) abstrūsus
profoundly adv penitus
profundity n altitūdō f
profuse adj prōdigus, effūsus
profusely adv effūsē
profusion n abundantia f, adfluentia f; **in ~** abundē
progenitor n auctor m
progeny n prōgeniēs f, prōlēs f
prognostic n signum nt
prognosticate vt ōminārī, augurārī, praedīcere
prognostication n ōmen nt, praedictiō f
programme n libellus m
progress n prōgressus m; **make ~** prōficere ▶ vi prōgredī
progression n prōgressus m
progressively adv gradātim
prohibit vt vetāre, interdīcere (dat)
prohibition n interdictum nt
project n prōpositum nt ▶ vi ēminēre, exstāre; (land) excurrere ▶ vt prōicere
projectile n tēlum nt
projecting adj ēminēns
projection n ēminentia f
proletarian adj plēbēius
proletariat n plēbs f
prolific adj fēcundus
prolix adj verbōsus, longus
prolixity n redundantia f
prologue n prologus m
prolong vt dūcere, prōdūcere; (office) prōrogāre
prolongation n (time) propāgātiō f; (office) prōrogātiō f
promenade n ambulātiō f ▶ vi inambulāre, spatiārī
prominence n ēminentia f
prominent adj ēminēns, īnsignis; **be ~** ēminēre

promiscuous adj prōmiscuus
promiscuously adv prōmiscuē
promise n prōmissum nt; **break a ~** fidem fallere; **keep a ~** fidem praestāre; **make a ~** fidem dare; **a youth of great ~** summae speī adulēscēns ▶ vt prōmittere, pollicērī; (in marriage) dēspondēre; ~ **in return** reprōmittere ▶ vi: ~ **well** bonam spem ostendere
promising adj bonae speī
promissory note n syngrapha f
promontory n prōmunturium nt
promote vt favēre (dat); (growth) alere; (in rank) prōdūcere
promoter n auctor m, fautor m
promotion n dignitās f
prompt adj alacer, prōmptus ▶ vt incitāre, commovēre; (speaker) subicere
prompter n monitor m
promptitude n alacritās f, celeritās f
promptly adv extemplō, citō
promulgate vt prōmulgāre, palam facere
promulgation n prōmulgātiō f
prone adj prōnus; (mind) inclīnātus
prong n dēns m
pronounce vt ēloquī, appellāre; (oath) interpōnere; (sentence) dīcere, prōnūntiāre
pronounced adj manifestus, īnsignis
pronouncement n ōrātiō f, adfirmātiō f
pronunciation n appellātiō f
proof n documentum nt, argūmentum nt; (test) probātiō f ▶ adj immōtus, impenetrābilis
prop n adminiculum nt, firmāmentum nt ▶ vt fulcīre
propaganda n documenta ntpl
propagate vt propāgāre
propagation n propāgātiō f
propel vt incitāre, prōpellere
propensity n inclīnātiō f
proper adj idōneus, decēns, decōrus; rēctus; **it is ~** decet
properly adv decōrē; rēctē
property n rēs f, rēs mancipī, bona ntpl; (estate) praedium nt; (attribute) proprium nt; (slave's) pecūlium nt
prophecy n vāticinium nt, praedictiō f
prophesy vt vāticinārī, praedīcere
prophet n vātēs m, fātidicus m
prophetess n vātēs f
prophetic adj dīvīnus, fātidicus
prophetically adv dīvīnitus
propinquity n (place) vīcīnitās f; (kin) propinquitās f
propitiate vt plācāre
propitiation n plācātiō f, litātiō f
propitious adj fēlīx, faustus; (god) praesēns
proportion n mēnsūra f; **in ~** prō portiōne, prō ratā parte; **in ~ to** prō (abl)
proportionately adv prō portiōne, prō ratā parte
proposal n condiciō f
propose vt prōpōnere; (motion) ferre, rogāre; (penalty) inrogāre; (candidate) rogāre magistrātum

proposer n auctor m, lātor m
proposition n (offer) condiciō f; (plan) cōnsilium nt, prōpositum nt; (LOGIC) prōnūntiātum nt
propound vt expōnere, in medium prōferre
propraetor n prōpraetor m
proprietor n dominus m
propriety n decōrum nt; (conduct) modestia f; **with ~** decenter
propulsion n impulsus m
prorogation n prōrogātiō f
prorogue vt prōrogāre
prosaic adj pedester
proscribe vt prōscrībere
proscription n prōscrīptiō f
prose n ōrātiō f, ōrātiō solūta f
prosecute vt (task) exsequī, gerere; (at law) accūsāre, lītem intendere (dat)
prosecution n exsecūtiō f; (at law) accūsātiō f; (party) accūsātor m
prosecutor n accūsātor m
prosody n numerī mpl
prospect n prōspectus m; (fig) spēs f ▶ vi explōrāre
prospective adj futūrus, spērātus
prosper vi flōrēre, bonā fortūnā ūtī ▶ vt fortūnāre
prosperity n fortūna f, rēs secundae fpl, fēlīcitās f
prosperous adj fēlīx, fortūnātus, secundus
prosperously adv prosperē
prostrate adj prōstrātus, adflīctus; **lie ~** iacēre ▶ vt prōsternere, dēicere; **~ oneself** prōcumbere, sē prōicere
prostration n frāctus animus m
prosy adj longus
protagonist n prīmārum partium āctor m
protect vt tuērī, dēfendere, custōdīre, prōtegere
protection n tūtēla f, praesidium nt; (LAW) patrōcinium nt; (POL) fidēs f; **put oneself under the ~ of** in fidem venīre (gen); **take under one's ~** in fidem recipere
protector n patrōnus m, dēfēnsor m, custōs m
protectress n patrōna f
protégé n cliēns m
protest n obtestātiō f; (POL) intercessiō f ▶ vi obtestārī, reclāmāre; (POL) intercēdere
protestation n adsevērātiō f
prototype n archetypum nt
protract vt dūcere, prōdūcere
protrude vi prōminēre
protruding adj exsertus
protuberance n ēminentia f, tūber nt
protuberant adj ēminēns, turgidus
proud adj superbus, adrogāns, īnsolēns; **be ~** superbīre; **be ~ of** iactāre
proudly adv superbē
prove vt dēmōnstrāre, arguere, probāre; (test) experīrī ▶ vi (person) se praebēre; (event) ēvādere; **~ oneself** sē praebēre, sē praestāre; **not proven** nōn liquet

proved adj expertus
provenance n orīgō f
provender n pābulum nt
proverb n prōverbium nt
proverbial adj trītus; **become ~** in prōverbium venīre
provide vt parāre, praebēre; **~ for** prōvidēre (dat); **the law provides** lēx iubet; **~ against** praecavēre
provided that conj dum, dummodo (subj)
providence n prōvidentia f; Deus m
provident adj prōvidus, cautus
providential adj dīvīnus; secundus
providentially adv dīvīnitus
providently adv cautē
providing conj dum, dummodo
province n prōvincia f
provincial adj prōvinciālis; (contemptuous) oppidānus, mūnicipālis
provision n parātus m; **make ~ for** prōvidēre (dat); **make ~** cavēre
provisionally adv ad tempus
provisions n cibus m, commeātus m, rēs frūmentāria f
proviso n condiciō f; **with this ~** hāc lēge
provocation n inrītāmentum nt, offēnsiō f
provocative adj (language) molestus, invidiōsus
provoke vt inrītāre, lacessere; (to action) excitāre
provoking adj odiōsus, molestus
provost n praefectus m
prow n prōra f
prowess n virtūs f
prowl vi grassārī, vagārī
proximate adj proximus
proximity n propinquitās f, vīcīnia f
proxy n vicārius m
prude n fastīdiōsa f
prudence n prūdentia f
prudent adj prūdēns, cautus, sagāx
prudently adv prūdenter, cautē
prudery n fastīdiōsa quaedam pudīcitia f
prudish adj fastīdiōsus
prune vt amputāre
pruner n putātor m
pruning hook n falx f
pry vi inquīrere; **pry into** scrūtārī
pseudonym n falsum nōmen nt
psychology n animī ratiō f
Ptolemy n Ptolemaeus m
puberty n pūbertās f
public adj pūblicus; (speech) forēnsis; **~ life** rēs pūblica f, forum nt; **in ~** forīs; **appear in ~** in medium prōdīre; **make ~** in mediō pōnere, forās perferre; **make a ~ case of** in medium vocāre; **act for the ~ good** in medium cōnsulere; **be a ~ figure** in lūce versārī, digitō mōnstrārī ▶ n vulgus nt, hominēs mpl
publican n (taxes) pūblicānus m; (inn) caupō m
publication n ēditiō f, prōmulgātiō f; (book) liber m

publicity n lūx f, celebritās f
publicly adv palam; (by the state) pūblicē
public opinion n fāma f
publish vt vulgāre, dīvulgāre; (book) ēdere
pucker vt corrūgāre
puerile adj puerīlis
puerility n ineptiae fpl
puff n aura f ▶ vt īnflāre ▶ vi anhēlāre
puffed up adj īnflātus, tumidus
pugilism n pugilātus m
pugilist n pugil m
pugnacious adj pugnāx
pugnacity n ferōcitās f
puissance n potentia f, vīrēs fpl
puissant adj potēns
pull n tractus m; (of gravity) contentiō f ▶ vt
trahere, tractāre; ~ **apart** distrahere; ~ **at**
vellicāre; ~ **away** āvellere; ~ **back** retrahere;
~ **down** dēripere, dētrahere; (building) dēmōlīrī;
~ **off** āvellere; ~ **out** ēvellere, extrahere;
~ **through** vi pervincere; (illness) convalēscere;
~ **up** (plant) ēruere; (movement) coercēre; ~ **to**
pieces dīlaniāre
pullet n pullus gallīnāceus m
pulley n trochlea f
pulmonary adj pulmōneus
pulp n carō f
pulpit n suggestus m
pulsate vi palpitāre, micāre
pulse n (plant) legūmen nt; (of blood) vēnae fpl;
feel the ~ vēnās temptāre
pulverize vt contundere
pumice stone n pūmex m
pummel vt verberāre
pump n antlia f ▶ vt haurīre; ~ **out** exhaurīre
pumpkin n cucurbita f
pun n agnōminātiō f
punch n ictus m ▶ vt pertundere, percutere
punctilious adj religiōsus
punctiliousness n religiō f
punctual adj accūrātus, dīligēns
punctuality n dīligentia f
punctually adv ad hōram, ad tempus
punctuate vt distinguere
punctuation n interpūnctiō f
puncture n pūnctiō f ▶ vt pungere
pundit n scholasticus m
pungency n ācrimōnia f; (in debate)
aculeī mpl
pungent adj ācer, mordāx
punish vt pūnīre, animadvertere in (acc);
poenam sūmere dē (abl); **be punished** poenās
dare
punishable adj poenā dignus
punisher n vindex m, ultor m
punishment n poena f, supplicium nt; (censors')
animadversiō f; **capital ~** capitis supplicium nt;
corporal ~ verbera ntpl; **inflict ~ on** poenā
adficere, poenam capere dē (abl), supplicium
sūmere dē (abl); **submit to ~** poenam subīre;
undergo ~ poenās dare, pendere, solvere
punitive adj ulcīscendī causā

punt n pontō m
puny adj pusillus
pup n catulus m ▶ vi parere
pupil n discipulus m, discipula f; (eye) aciēs f,
pūpula f
pupillage n tūtēla f
puppet n pūpa f
puppy n catulus m
purblind adj luscus
purchase n emptiō f; (formal) mancipium nt ▶ vt
emere
purchaser n emptor m; (at auction) manceps m
pure adj pūrus, integer; (morally) castus; (mere)
merus
purely adv pūrē, integrē; (solely) sōlum, nīl nisi;
(quite) omnīnō, plānē
purgation n pūrgātiō f
purge vt pūrgāre, expūrgāre
purification n lūstrātiō f, pūrgātiō f
purify vt pūrgāre, expūrgāre
purist n fastīdiōsus m
purity n integritās f, castitās f
purloin vt surripere, fūrārī
purple n purpura f ▶ adj purpureus
purport n sententia f; (of words) vīs f; **what is**
the ~ of? quō spectat?, quid vult? ▶ vt velle
spectāre ad
purpose n prōpositum nt, cōnsilium nt, mēns f;
for that ~ eō; **for the ~ of** ad (acc), ut (subj), eā
mente ut, eō cōnsiliō ut (subj); **on ~** cōnsultō, dē
industriā; **to the ~** ad rem; **to what purpose?**
quō?, quōrsum?; **to no ~** frustrā, nēquīquam;
without achieving one's ~ rē īnfectā ▶ vt in
animō habēre, velle
purposeful adj intentus
purposeless adj inānis
purposely adv cōnsultō, dē industriā
purr n murmur nt ▶ vi murmurāre
purse n marsupium nt, crumēna f; **privy ~** fiscus
m ▶ vt adstringere
pursuance n exsecūtiō f; **in ~ of** secundum
(acc)
pursue vt īnsequī, īnsectārī, persequī; (closely)
īnstāre (dat), īnsistere (dat); (aim) petere;
(course) īnsistere
pursuer n īnsequēns m; (LAW) accūsātor m
pursuit n īnsectātiō f; (hunt) vēnātiō f;
(ambition) studium nt
purvey vt parāre; (food) obsōnāre
purveyance n prōcūrātiō f
purveyor n obsōnātor m
purview n prōvincia f
pus n pūs nt
push n pulsus m, impetus m ▶ vt impellere,
trūdere, urgēre; ~ **back** repellere; ~ **down**
dēprimere, dētrūdere; ~ **forward** prōpellere; ~ **in** intrūdere; ~ **on**
incitāre; ~ **through** perrumpere
pushing adj cōnfīdēns
pusillanimity n ignāvia f, timor m
pusillanimous adj ignāvus, timidus
pustule n pustula f

put *vt* (*in a state*) dare; (*in a position*) pōnere; (*in words*) reddere; (*argument*) pōnere; (*spur*) subdere; (*to some use*) adhibēre; **put an end to** fīnem facere (*dat*); **put a question to** interrogāre; **put against** adpōnere; **put among** intericere; **put aside** sēpōnere; **put away** pōnere, dēmovēre; (*store*) repōnere; **put back** repōnere; repellere; **put beside** adpōnere; **put between** interpōnere; **put by** condere; **put down** dēpōnere; (*revolt*) opprimere; **put forth** extendere; (*growth*) mittere; **put forward** ostentāre; (*plea*) adferre; **put in** immittere, īnserere; (*ship*) adpellere; **put off** differre; **put on** impōnere; (*clothes*) induere; (*play*) dare; **put out** ēicere; (*eye*) effodere; (*fire*) exstinguere; (*money*) pōnere; (*tongue*) exserere; **put out of the way** dēmovēre; **put out to sea** in altum ēvehi, solvere; **put over** superimpōnere; **put to** adpōnere; (*flight*) dare in (*acc*), fugāre, prōflīgāre; in fugam conicere; (*sea*) solvere; **put together** cōnferre; **put up** (*for sale*) prōpōnere; (*lodge*) dēvertere, dēversārī apud; **put up with** ferre, patī; **put upon** impōnere

putrefaction *n* pūtor *m*
putrefy *vi* putrēscere
putrid *adj* putridus
puzzle *n* nōdus *m* ▶ *vt* impedīre, sollicitāre; **be puzzled** haerēre
puzzling *adj* ambiguus, perplexus
pygmy *n* pygmaeus *m*
pyramid *n* pŷramis *f*
pyramidal *adj* pŷramidātus
pyre *n* rogus *m*
Pyrenees *npl* Pyrenaeī (montēs) *mpl*
python *n* pŷthōn *m*

q

quack *n* (*doctor*) circulātor *m* ▶ *vi* tetrinnīre
quadrangle *n* ārea *f*
quadruped *n* quadrupēs *m/f*
quadruple *adj* quadruplex
quaestor *n* quaestor *m*; **quaestor's** quaestōrius
quaestorship *n* quaestūra *f*
quaff *vt* ēpōtāre, haurīre
quagmire *n* palūs *f*
quail *n* (*bird*) coturnīx *f* ▶ *vi* pāvēscere, trepidāre
quaint *adj* novus, īnsolitus
quaintness *n* īnsolentia *f*
quake *vi* horrēre, horrēscere ▶ *n* (*earth*) mōtus *m*
quaking *n* horror *m*, tremor *m* ▶ *adj* tremulus
qualification *n* condiciō *f*; (*limitation*) exceptiō *f*
qualified *adj* (*for*) aptus, idōneus, dignus; (*in*) perītus, doctus
qualify *vi* prōficere ▶ *vt* temperāre, mītigāre
qualities *npl* ingenium *nt*
quality *n* nātūra *f*, vīs *f*; indolēs *f*; (*rank*) locus *m*, genus *nt*; **I know the ~ of** sciō quālis sit
qualm *n* religiō *f*, scrūpulus *m*
quandary *n* angustiae *fpl*; **be in a ~** haerēre
quantity *n* cōpia *f*, numerus *m*; (*metre*) vōcum mēnsiō *f*; **a large ~** multum *nt*, plūrimum *nt*; **a small ~** aliquantulum *nt*
quarrel *n* dissēnsiō *f*, contrōversia *f*; (*violent*) rixa *f*, iūrgium *nt* ▶ *vi* rixārī, altercārī
quarrelsome *adj* pugnāx, lītigiōsus
quarry *n* lapicīdinae *fpl*, metallum *nt*; (*prey*) praeda *f* ▶ *vt* excīdere
quart *n* duō sextāriī *mpl*
quartan *n* (*fever*) quartāna *f*
quarter *n* quarta pars *f*, quadrāns *m*; (*sector*) regiō *f*; (*direction*) pars *f*, regiō *f*; (*respite*) missiō *f*; **quarters** castra *ntpl*; (*billet*) hospitium *nt*; **come to close quarters** manum cōnserere; (*armies*) signa cōnferre; **winter quarters** hīberna *ntpl* ▶ *vt* quadrifidam dīvidere; (*troops*) in hospitia dīvidere
quarterdeck *n* puppis *f*
quarterly *adj* trimestris ▶ *adv* quartō quōque mēnse

quartermaster n (navy) gubernātor m; (army) castrōrum praefectus m
quarterstaff n rudis f
quash vt comprimere; (decision) rescindere
quatrain n tetrastichon nt
quaver n tremor m ▶ vi tremere
quavering adj tremebundus
quay n crepīdō f
queasy adj fastīdiōsus
queen n rēgīna f; (bee) rēx m
queer adj insolēns, rīdiculus
quell vt opprimere, domāre, dēbellāre
quench vt exstinguere, restinguere; (thirst) sēdāre, explēre
querulous adj querulus, queribundus
query n interrogātiō f ▶ vt in dubium vocāre ▶ vi rogāre
quest n investīgātiō f; **go in ~ of** investīgāre, anquīrere
question n interrogātiō f; (at issue) quaestiō f, rēs f; (in doubt) dubium nt; **ask a ~** rogāre, quaerere, scīscitārī, percontārī; **call in ~** in dubium vocāre, addubitāre; **out of the ~** indignus; **be out of the ~** improbārī, fierī nōn posse; **there is no ~ that** illud quaeritur; **there is no ~ that** nōn dubium est quīn (subj); **without ~** sine dubiō ▶ vt interrogāre; (closely) percontārī; (doubt) in dubium vocāre ▶ vi dubitāre
questionable adj incertus, dubius
questioner n percontātor m
questioning n interrogātiō f
queue n agmen nt
quibble n captiō f ▶ vi cavillārī
quibbler n cavillātor m
quibbling adj captiōsus
quick adj (speed) celer, vēlōx, citus; (to act) alacer, impiger; (to perceive) sagāx; (with hands) facilis; (living) vīvus; **be ~** properāre, festīnāre; **cut to the ~** ad vīvum resecāre; (fig) mordēre
quicken vt adcelerāre; (with life) animāre
quickening adj vītālis
quickly adv celeriter, citō; (haste) properē; (mind) acūtē; **as ~ as possible** quam celerrimē
quickness n celeritās f, vēlōcitās f; (to act) alacritās f; (to perceive) sagācitās f, sollertia f
quicksand n syrtis f
quick-tempered adj īrācundus
quick-witted adj acūtus, sagāx, perspicāx
quiescence n inertia f, ōtium nt
quiescent adj iners, ōtiōsus
quiet adj tranquillus, quiētus, placidus; (silent) tacitus; **be ~** quiēscere; silēre ▶ n quiēs f, tranquillitās f; silentium nt; (peace) pāx f ▶ vt pācāre, compōnere
quietly adv tranquillē, quiētē; tacitē, per silentium; aequō animō
quietness n tranquillitās f; silentium nt
quill n penna f
quince n cydōnium nt
quinquennial adj quinquennālis
quinquereme n quinquerēmis f
quintessence n flōs m, vīs f

quip n sāl m, facētiae fpl
quirk n captiuncula f; **quirks** pl trīcae fpl
quit vt relinquere ▶ adj līber, solūtus
quite adv admodum, plānē, prōrsus; **not ~** minus, parum; (time) nōndum
quits n parēs mpl
quiver n pharetra f ▶ vi tremere, contremere
quivering adj tremebundus, tremulus
quoit n discus m
quota n pars f, rata pars f
quotation n (act) commemorātiō f; (passage) locus m
quote vt prōferre, commemorāre
quoth vt inquit

r

rabbit n cunīculus m
rabble n turba f; (class) vulgus nt, plēbēcula f
rabid adj rabidus
rabidly adv rabidē
race n (descent) genus nt, stirps f; (people) gēns f, nōmen nt; (contest) certāmen nt; (fig) cursus m, curriculum nt; (water) flūmen nt; **run a ~** cursū certāre; **run the ~** (fig) spatium dēcurrere ▶ vi certāre, contendere
racecourse n (foot) stadium nt; (horse) spatium nt
racer n cursor m
racial adj gentīlis
rack n (torture) tormentum nt; (shelf) pluteus m; **be on the ~** (fig) cruciārī ▶ vt torquēre, cruciāre; **~ off** (wine) diffundere
racket n (noise) strepitus m
racy adj (style) salsus
radiance n splendor m, fulgor m
radiant adj splendidus, nitidus
radiantly adv splendidē
radiate vi fulgēre; (direction) dīversōs tendere ▶ vt ēmittere
radical adj insitus, innātus; (thorough) tōtus ▶ n novārum rērum cupidus m
radically adv omnīnō, penitus, funditus
radish n rādix f
radius n radius m
raffish adj dissolūtus
raffle n ālea f ▶ vt āleā vēndere
raft n ratis f
rafter n trabs f, tignum nt
rag n pannus m
rage n īra f, furor m; **be all the ~** in ōre omnium esse; **spend one's ~** exsaevīre ▶ vi furere, saevīre; (furiously) dēbacchārī
ragged adj pannōsus
raid n excursiō f, incursiō f, impressiō f; **make a ~** excurrere ▶ vt incursiōnem facere in (acc)
rail n longurius m ▶ vt saepīre ▶ vi: **~ at** maledīcere (dat), convīcia facere (dat)
railing n saepēs f, cancellī mpl
raillery n cavillātiō f
raiment n vestis f

rain n pluvia f, imber m ▶ vi pluere; **it is raining** pluit
rainbow n arcus m
rainstorm n imber m
rainy adj pluvius
raise vt tollere, ēlevāre; (army) cōgere, cōnscrībere; (children) ēducāre; (cry) tollere; (from dead) excitāre; (laugh) movēre; (money) cōnflāre; (price) augēre; (siege) exsolvere; (structure) exstruere; (to higher rank) ēvehere; **~ up** ērigere, sublevāre
raisin n astaphis f
rajah n dynastēs m
rake n rastrum nt; (person) nepōs m ▶ vt rādere; **~ in** conrādere; **~ up** (fig) ēruere
rakish adj dissolūtus
rally n conventus m ▶ vt (troops) in ōrdinem revocāre; (with words) hortārī; (banter) cavillārī ▶ vi sē colligere
ram n ariēs m; (battering) ariēs m ▶ vt: **ram down** fistūcāre; **ram home** (fact) inculcāre
ramble n errātiō f ▶ vi vagārī, errāre
rambling adj vagus; (plant) errāticus; (speech) fluēns
ramification n rāmus m
rammer n fistūca f
rampage vi saevīre
rampant adj ferōx
rampart n agger m, vallum nt
ranch n lātifundium nt
rancid adj pūtidus
rancour n odium nt, acerbitās f, invidia f
random adj fortuītus; **at ~** temerē
range n ōrdō m, seriēs f; (mountain) iugum nt; (of weapon) iactus m; **within ~** intrā tēlī iactum; **come within ~** sub ictum venīre ▶ vt ōrdināre ▶ vi ēvagārī, pervagārī; (in speech) excurrere
rank n (line) ōrdō m; (class) ōrdō m; (position) locus m, dignitās f; **~ and file** gregāriī mīlitēs mpl; **keep the ranks** ōrdinēs observāre; **the ranks** (MIL) aciēs, aciēī f; **leave the ranks** ōrdine ēgredī, ab signīs discēdere; **reduce to the ranks** in ōrdinem redigere ▶ adj luxuriōsus; (smell) gravis, foetidus ▶ vt numerāre ▶ vi in numerō habērī
rankle vi exulcerāre
rankness n luxuriēs f
ransack vt dīripere, spoliāre
ransom n redemptiō f, pretium nt ▶ vt redimere
rant vi latrāre
ranter n rabula m, latrātor m
rap n ictus m ▶ vt ferīre
rapacious adj rapāx, avidus
rapaciously adv avidē
rapacity n rapācitās f, aviditās f
rape n raptus m
rapid adj rapidus, vēlōx, citus, incitātus
rapidity n celeritās f, vēlōcitās f, incitātiō f
rapidly adv rapidē, vēlōciter, citō
rapine n rapīna f
rapt adj intentus
rapture n laetitia f, alacritās f

rare adj rārus; (occurrence) īnfrequēns; (quality) singulāris
rarefy vt extenuāre
rarely adv rārō
rarity n rāritās f; (thing) rēs īnsolita f
rascal n furcifer m, scelestus m
rascally adj improbus
rash adj temerārius, audāx, incōnsultus; praeceps
rashly adv temerē, incōnsultē
rashness n temeritās f, audācia f
rat n mūs m/f
rate n (cost) pretium nt; (standard) nōrma f; (tax) vectīgal nt; (speed) celeritās f; **at any ~** (concessive) utique, saltem; (adversative) quamquam, tamen ▶ vt (value) aestimāre; (scold) increpāre, obiūrgāre
rather adv potius, satius; (somewhat) aliquantum; (with compar) aliquantō; (with verbs) mālō; (correcting) immo; **~ sad** tristior; **I would ~** mālō; **I ~ think** haud sciō an; **~ than** magis quam, potius quam
ratification n (formal) sanctiō f
ratify vt ratum facere, sancīre; (LAW) iubēre
rating n taxātiō f, aestimātiō f; (navy) nauta m; (scolding) obiūrgātiō f
ratiocinate vi ratiōcinārī
ratiocination n ratiōcinātiō f
ration n dēmēnsum nt
rational adj animō praeditus; **be ~** sapere
rationality n ratiō f
rationally adv ratiōne
rations npl cibāria ntpl, diāria ntpl
rattle n crepitus m; (toy) crotalum nt ▶ vi crepitāre, increpāre
raucous adj raucus
ravage vt dēpopulārī, vastāre, dīripere
rave vi furere, īnsānīre; (fig) bacchārī, saevīre
raven n cornīx f
ravenous adj rapāx, vorāx
ravenously adv avidē
ravine n faucēs fpl, hiātus m
raving adj furiōsus, īnsānus ▶ n furor m
ravish vt rapere; (joy) efferre
raw adj crūdus; (person) rudis, agrestis
ray n radius m; **the first ray of hope appeared** prīma spēs adfulsit
raze vt excīdere, solō aequāre
razor n novācula f
reach n (space) spatium nt; (mind) captus m; (weapon) ictus m; **out of ~** of extrā (acc); **within ~** ad manum ▶ vt advenīre ad (acc); (space) pertinēre ad; (journey) pervenīre ad
react vi adficī; **~ to** ferre
reaction n: **what was his ~ to?** quō animō tulit?
read vt legere; (a book) ēvolvere; (aloud) recitāre; **~ over** perlegere
reader n lēctor m
readily adv facile, libenter, ultrō
readiness n facilitās f; **in ~** ad manum, in prōmptū, in expedītō
reading n lēctiō f

readjust vt dēnuō accommodāre
ready adj parātus, prōmptus; (manner) facilis; (money) praesēns; **get ~, make ~** parāre, expedīre, adōrnāre
reaffirm vt iterum adfirmāre
real adj vērus, germānus
real estate n fundus m, solum nt
realism n vēritās f
realistic adj vērī similis
reality n rēs f, rēs ipsa f, vērum nt; **in ~** rēvērā
realize vt intellegere, animadvertere; (aim) efficere, peragere; (money) redigere
really adv vērē, rēvērā, profectō; **really?** itane vērō?
realm n rēgnum nt
reap vt metere; **~ the reward of** fructum percipere ex
reaper n messor m
reappear vi revenīre
rear vt alere, ēducāre; (structure) exstruere ▶ vi sē ērigere ▶ n tergum nt; (MIL) novissima aciēs f, novissimum agmen nt; **in the ~** ā tergō; **bring up the ~** agmen claudere, agmen cōgere ▶ adj postrēmus, novissimus
rearguard n novissimum agmen nt, novissimī mpl
rearrange vt ōrdinem mūtāre (gen)
reason n (faculty) mēns f, animus m, ratiō f; (sanity) sānitās f; (argument) ratiō f; (cause) causa f; (moderation) modus m; **by ~ of** propter (acc); **for this ~** idcircō, ideō, proptereā; **in ~** aequus, modicus; **with good ~** iūre; **without ~** temerē, sine causā; **without good ~** frūstrā, iniūriā; **give a ~ for** ratiōnem adferre (gen); **I know the ~ for** sciō cūr, quamobrem (subj); **there is no ~ for** nōn est cūr, nihil est quod (subj); **lose one's ~** īnsānīre ▶ vi ratiōcinārī, disserere
reasonable adj aequus, iūstus; (person) modestus; (amount) modicus
reasonably adv ratiōne, iūstē; modicē
reasoning n ratiō f, ratiōcinātiō f
reassemble vt colligere, cōgere
reassert vt iterāre
reassume vt recipere
reassure vt firmāre, cōnfirmāre
rebate vt dēdūcere
rebel n rebellis m ▶ adj sēditiōsus ▶ vi rebelliōnem facere, rebellāre, dēscīscere
rebellion n sēditiō f, mōtus m
rebellious adj sēditiōsus
rebound vi resilīre
rebuff n repulsa f ▶ vt repellere, āversārī
rebuild vt renovāre, restaurāre
rebuke n reprehēnsiō f, obiūrgātiō f ▶ vt reprehendere, obiūrgāre, increpāre
rebut vt refūtāre, redarguere
recalcitrant adj invītus
recall n revocātiō f, reditus m ▶ vt revocāre; (from exile) redūcere; (to mind) reminīscī (gen), recordārī (gen)
recant vt retractāre
recantation n receptus m

recapitulate vt repetere, summātim dīcere
recapitulation n ēnumerātiō f
recapture vt recipere
recast vt reficere, retractāre
recede vi recēdere
receipt n (act) acceptiō f; (money) acceptum nt; (written) apocha f
receive vt accipere, capere; (in turn) excipere
receiver n receptor m
recent adj recēns
recently adv nūper, recēns
receptacle n receptāculum nt
reception n aditus m, hospitium nt
receptive adj docilis
recess n recessus m, angulus m; (holiday) fēriae fpl
recharge vt replēre
recipe n compositiō f
recipient n quī accipit
reciprocal adj mūtuus
reciprocally adv mūtuō, inter sē
reciprocate vt referre, reddere
reciprocity n mūtuum nt
recital n nārrātiō f, ēnumerātiō f; (LIT) recitātiō f
recitation n recitātiō f
recite vt recitāre; (details) ēnumerāre
reciter n recitātor m
reck vt ratiōnem habēre (gen)
reckless adj temerārius, incautus, praeceps
recklessly adv incautē, temerē
recklessness n temeritās f, neglegentia f
reckon vt (count) computāre, numerāre; (think) cēnsēre, dūcere; (estimate) aestimāre; ~ on cōnfīdere (dat); ~ up dīnumerāre; (cost) aestimāre; ~ with contendere cum
reckoning n ratiō f
reclaim vt repetere; (from error) revocāre
recline vi recumbere; (at table) accumbere; (pl) discumbere
recluse n homō sōlitārius m
recognition n cognitiō f
recognizance n vadimōnium nt
recognize vt agnōscere; (approve) accipere; (admit) fatērī
recoil vi resilīre; ~ from refugere; ~ upon recidere in (acc)
recollect vt reminīscī (gen)
recollection n memoria f, recordātiō f
recommence vt renovāre, redintegrāre
recommend vt commendāre; (advise) suādēre (dat)
recommendation n commendātiō f; (advice) cōnsilium nt; **letter of ~** litterae commendātīciae
recompense vt remūnerārī, grātiam referre (dat) ▶ n praemium nt, remūnerātiō f
reconcile vt compōnere, reconciliāre; **be reconciled** in grātiam redīre
reconciliation n reconciliātiō f, grātia f
recondite adj reconditus, abstrūsus
recondition vt reficere
reconnaissance n explōrātiō f

reconnoitre vt, vi explōrāre; **without reconnoitring** inexplōrātō
reconquer vt recipere
reconsider vt reputāre, retractāre
reconstruct vt restituere, renovāre
reconstruction n renovātiō f
record n monumentum nt; (LIT) commentārius m; **records** pl tabulae fpl, fāstī mpl, ācta ntpl; **break the ~** priōrēs omnēs superāre ▶ vt in commentārium referre; (history) perscrībere, nārrāre
recount vt nārrāre, commemorāre
recourse n: **have ~ to** (for safety) cōnfugere ad; (as expedient) dēcurrere ad
recover vt recipere, recuperāre; (loss) reparāre; ~ **oneself** sē colligere; ~ **one's senses** ad sānitātem revertī ▶ vi convalēscere
recovery n recuperātiō f; (from illness) salūs f
recreate vt recreāre
recreation n requiēs f, remissiō f, lūdus m
recriminate vi in vicem accūsāre
recrimination n mūtua accūsātiō f
recruit n tīrō m ▶ vt (MIL) cōnscrībere; (strength) reficere
recruiting officer n conquīsītor m
rectify vt corrigere, ēmendāre
rectitude n probitās f
recumbent adj supīnus
recuperate vi convalēscere
recur vi recurrere, redīre
recurrence n reditus m, reversiō f
recurrent adj assiduus
red adj ruber
redden vi ērubēscere ▶ vt rutilāre
reddish adj subrūfus
redeem vt redimere, līberāre
redeemer n līberātor m
redemption n redemptiō f
red-haired adj rūfus
red-handed adj: **catch ~** in manifestō scelere dēprehendere
red-hot adj fervēns
red lead n minium nt
redness n rubor m
redolent adj: **be ~ of** redolēre
redouble vt ingemināre
redoubt n prōpugnāculum nt
redoubtable adj īnfestus, formīdolōsus
redound vi redundāre; **it redounds to my credit** mihī honōrī est
redress n remedium nt; **demand ~** rēs repetere ▶ vt restituere
reduce vt minuere, attenuāre; (to a condition) redigere, dēdūcere; (MIL) expugnāre; ~ **to the ranks** in ōrdinem cōgere
reduction n imminūtiō f; (MIL) expugnātiō f
redundancy n redundantia f
redundant adj redundāns; **be ~** redundāre
reduplication n gemīnātiō f
re-echo vt reddere, referre ▶ vi resonāre
reed n harundō f
reedy adj harundineus

reef n saxa ntpl ▶ vt (sail) subnectere
reek n fūmus m ▶ vi fūmāre
reel vi vacillāre, titubāre
re-enlist vt rescrībere
re-establish vt restituere
refashion vt reficere
refer vt (person) dēlēgāre; (matter) rēicere,
  remittere ▶ vi: **~ to** spectāre ad; (in speech)
  attingere, perstringere
referee n arbiter m
reference n ratiō f; (in book) locus m
refine vt excolere, expolīre; (metal) excoquere
refined adj hūmānus, urbānus, polītus
refinement n hūmānitās f, cultus m,
  ēlegantia f
refit vt reficere
reflect vt reddere, repercutere ▶ vi meditārī;
  ~ upon cōnsīderāre, sēcum reputāre; (blame)
  reprehendere
reflection n (of light) repercussus m; (image)
  imāgō f; (thought) meditātiō f, cōgitātiō f;
  (blame) reprehēnsiō f; **cast reflections on**
  maculīs aspergere, vitiō vertere; **with due ~**
  cōnsīderātē; **without ~** incōnsultē
reflux n recessus m
reform n ēmendātiō f ▶ vt (lines) restituere;
  (error) corrigere, ēmendāre, meliōrem facere
  ▶ vi sē corrigere
reformation n corrēctiō f
reformer n corrēctor m, ēmendātor m
refract vt īnfringere
refractory adj contumāx
refrain vi pūrgāre, abstinēre (dat),
  supersedēre (infin)
refresh vt recreāre, renovāre, reficere; (mind)
  integrāre
refreshed adj requiētus
refreshing adj dulcis, iūcundus
refreshment n cibus m
refuge n perfugium nt; (secret) latebra f;
  take ~ with perfugere ad (acc); **take ~ in**
  confugere
refugee n profugus m
refulgence n splendor m
refulgent adj splendidus
refund vt reddere
refusal n recūsātiō f, dētrectātiō f
refuse n pūrgāmenta ntpl; (fig) faex f ▶ vt
  (request) dēnegāre; (offer) dētrectāre, recūsāre;
  (with verb) nōlle
refutation n refūtātiō f, reprehēnsiō f
refute vt refellere, redarguere, revincere
regain vt recipere
regal adj rēgius, rēgālis
regale vt excipere, dēlectāre; **~ oneself** epulārī
regalia n īnsignia ntpl
regally adv rēgāliter
regard n respectus m, ratiō f; (esteem) grātia f;
  with ~ to ad (acc), quod attinet ad ▶ vt (look)
  intuērī, spectāre; (deem) habēre, dūcere; **send
  regards to** salūtem dīcere (dat)
regarding prep dē (abl)

regardless adj neglegēns, immemor
regency n interrēgnum nt
regent n interrēx m
regicide n (person) rēgis interfector m; (act)
  rēgis caedēs f
regime n administrātiō f
regimen n vīctus m
regiment n legiō f
region n regiō f, tractus m
register n tabulae fpl, album nt ▶ vt in tabulās
  referre, perscrībere; (emotion) ostendere,
  sūmere
registrar n tabulārius m
registry n tabulārium nt
regret n dolor m; (for past) dēsīderium nt; (for
  fault) paenitentia f ▶ vt dolēre; **I ~ mē paenitet,
  mē piget** (gen)
regretful adj maestus
regretfully adv dolenter
regrettable adj īnfēlīx, īnfortūnātus
regular adj (consistent) cōnstāns; (orderly)
  ōrdinātus; (habitual) solitus, adsiduus; (proper)
  iūstus, rēctus
regularity n moderātiō f, ōrdō m; (consistency)
  cōnstantia f
regularly adv ōrdine, cōnstanter, iūstē, rēctē
regulate vt ōrdināre, dīrigere; (control)
  moderārī
regulation n lēx f, dēcrētum nt
rehabilitate vt restituere
rehearsal n meditātiō f
rehearse vt meditārī
reign n rēgnum nt; (emperor's) prīncipātus m;
  in the ~ of Numa rēgnante Numā ▶ vi rēgnāre;
  (fig) dominārī
reimburse vt rependere
rein n habēna f; **give full ~ to** habēnās immittere
  ▶ vt īnfrēnāre
reindeer n rēnō m
reinforce vt firmāre, cōnfirmāre
reinforcement n subsidium nt;
  reinforcements pl novae cōpiae fpl
reinstate vt restituere, redūcere
reinstatement n restitūtiō f, reductiō f; (to
  legal privileges) postlīminium nt
reinvigorate vt recreāre
reiterate vt dictitāre, iterāre
reiteration n iterātiō f
reject vt rēicere; (with scorn) respuere,
  aspernārī, repudiāre
rejection n rēiectiō f, repulsa f
rejoice vi gaudēre, laetārī ▶ vt dēlectāre
rejoicing n gaudium nt
rejoin vt redīre ad ▶ vi respondēre
rejoinder n respōnsum nt
rejuvenate vt: **be rejuvenated** repuērāscere
rekindle vt suscitāre
relapse vi recidere
relate vt (tell) nārrāre, commemorāre,
  expōnere; (compare) cōnferre ▶ vi pertinēre
related adj propinquus; (by birth) cognātus;
  (by marriage) adfīnis; (fig) fīnitimus

relation n (tale) nārrātiō f; (connection) ratiō f; (kin) necessārius m, cognātus m, adfinis m
relationship n necessitūdō f; (by birth) cognātiō f; (by marriage) adfīnitās f; (connection) vīcīnitās f
relative adj cum cēterīs comparātus ▶ n propinquus m, cognātus m, adfinis m, necessārius m
relatively adv ex comparātiōne
relax vt laxāre, remittere ▶ vi languēscere
relaxation n remissiō f, requiēs f, lūdus m
relay n: relays of horses dispositī equī mpl
release vt solvere, exsolvere, līberāre, expedīre; (LAW) absolvere ▶ n missiō f, līberātiō f
relegate vt relēgāre
relent vi concēdere, plācārī, flectī
relentless adj immisericors, inexōrābilis; (things) improbus
relevant adj ad rem
reliability n fīdūcia f
reliable adj fīdus
reliance n fīdūcia f, fidēs f
reliant adj frētus
relic n rēliquiae fpl
relief n levātiō f, levāmen nt, adlevāmentum nt; (aid) subsidium nt; (turn of duty) vicēs fpl; (art) ēminentia f; (sculpture) toreuma nt; bas ~ anaglypta ntpl; in ~ ēminēns, expressus; throw into ~ exprimere, distinguere
relieve vt levāre, sublevāre; (aid) subvenīre (dat); (duty) succēdere (dat), excipere; (art) distinguere
religion n religiō f, deōrum cultus m
religious adj religiōsus, pius; ~ feeling religiō f
religiously adv religiōsē
relinquish vt relinquere; (office) sē abdicāre (abl)
relish n sapor m; (sauce) condīmentum nt; (zest) studium nt ▶ vt dēlectārī (abl)
reluctance n: with ~ invītus
reluctant adj invītus
reluctantly adv invītus, gravātē
rely vi fīdere (dat), cōnfīdere (dat)
relying adj frētus (abl)
remain vi manēre, morārī; (left over) restāre, superesse
remainder n reliquum nt
remaining adj reliquus; the ~ cēterī pl
remains n rēliquiae fpl
remand vt (LAW) ampliāre
remark n dictum nt ▶ vt dīcere; (note) observāre
remarkable adj īnsignis, ēgregius, memorābilis
remarkably adv īnsignītē, ēgregiē
remediable adj sānābilis
remedy n remedium nt ▶ vt medērī (dat), sānāre
remember vt meminisse (gen); (recall) recordārī (gen), reminīscī (gen)
remembrance n memoria f, recordātiō f
remind vt admonēre, commonefacere
reminder n admonitiō f, admonitum nt
reminiscence n recordātiō f
remiss adj dissolūtus, neglegēns

remission n venia f
remissness n neglegentia f
remit vt remittere; (fault) ignōscere (dat); (debt) dōnāre; (punishment) condōnāre; (question) referre
remittance n pecūnia f
remnant n fragmentum nt; remnants pl rēliquiae fpl
remonstrance n obtestātiō f, obiūrgātiō f
remonstrate vi reclāmāre; ~ with obiūrgāre; ~ about expostulāre
remorse n paenitentia f, cōnscientia f
remorseless adj immisericors
remote adj remōtus, reconditus
remotely adv procul
remoteness n longinquitās f
removal n āmōtiō f; (going) migrātiō f
remove vt āmovēre, dēmovēre, eximere, removēre; (out of the way) dēmovēre ▶ vi migrāre, dēmigrāre
remunerate vt remūnerārī
remuneration n mercēs f, praemium nt
rend vt scindere, dīvellere
render vt reddere; (music) interpretārī; (translation) vertere; (thanks) referre
rendering n interpretātiō f
rendez-vous n cōnstitūtum nt
renegade n dēsertor m
renew vt renovāre, integrāre, īnstaurāre, redintegrāre
renewal n renovātiō f; (ceremony) īnstaurātiō f
renounce vt renūntiāre, mittere, repudiāre
renovate vt renovāre, reficere
renown n fāma f, glōria f
renowned adj praeclārus, īnsignis, nōtus
rent n (tear) fissum nt; (pay) mercēs f ▶ vt (hire) condūcere; (lease) locāre
renunciation n cessiō f, repudiātiō f
repair vt reficere, sarcīre ▶ vi sē recipere ▶ n: keep in good ~ tuērī; in bad ~ ruīnōsus
reparable adj ēmendābilis
reparation n satisfactiō f
repartee n facētiae fpl, salēs mpl
repast n cēna f, cibus m
repay vt remūnerārī, grātiam referre (dat); (money) repōnere
repayment n solūtiō f
repeal vt abrogāre ▶ n abrogātiō f
repeat vt iterāre; (lesson) reddere; (ceremony) īnstaurāre; (performance) referre
repeatedly adv identidem, etiam atque etiam
repel vt repellere, dēfendere
repellent adj iniūcundus
repent vi: I ~ mē paenitet (+ gen of thing)
repentance n paenitentia f
repentant adj paenitēns
repercussion n ēventus m
repertory n thēsaurus m
repetition n iterātiō f
repine vi conquerī
replace vt repōnere, restituere; ~ by substituere

replacement n supplēmentum nt
replenish vt replēre, supplēre
replete adj plēnus
repletion n satietās f
replica n apographon nt
reply vi respondēre ▶ n respōnsum nt
report n (talk) fāma f, rūmor m; (repute) opīniō f; (account) renūntiātiō f, litterae fpl; (noise) fragor m; **make a ~** renūntiāre ▶ vt referre, dēferre, renūntiāre
repose n quiēs f, requiēs f ▶ vt repōnere, pōnere ▶ vi quiēscere
repository n horreum nt
reprehend vt reprehendere, culpāre
reprehensible adj accūsābilis, improbus
reprehension n reprehēnsiō f, culpa f
represent vt dēscrībere, effingere, exprimere, imitārī; (character) partēs agere (gen), persōnam gerere (gen); (case) prōpōnere; (substitute for) vicārium esse (gen)
representation n imāgō f, imitātiō f; **make representations to** admonēre
representative n lēgātus m
repress vt reprimere, cohibēre
repression n coercitiō f
reprieve n mora f, venia f ▶ vt veniam dare (dat)
reprimand vt reprehendere, increpāre ▶ n reprehēnsiō f
reprisals npl ultiō f
reproach vt exprobrāre, obicere (dat) ▶ n exprobrātiō f, probrum nt; (cause) opprobrium nt
reproachful adj contumēliōsus
reprobate adj perditus
reproduce vt propāgāre; (likeness) referre
reproduction n prōcreātiō f; (likeness) imāgō f
reproductive adj genitālis
reproof n reprehēnsiō f, obiūrgātiō f
reprove vt reprehendere, increpāre, obiūrgāre
reptile n serpēns f
republic n lībera rēspūblica f, cīvitās populāris f
republican adj populāris
repudiate vt repudiāre
repudiation n repudiātiō f
repugnance n fastīdium nt, odium nt
repugnant adj invīsus, adversus
repulse n dēpulsiō f; (at election) repulsa f ▶ vt repellere, āversārī, prōpulsāre
repulsion n repugnantia f
repulsive adj odiōsus, foedus
reputable adj honestus
reputation n fāma f, existimātiō f; (for something) opīniō f (gen); **have a ~** nōmen habēre
repute n fāma f, existimātiō f; **bad ~** īnfāmia f
reputed adj: **I am ~ to be** dīcor esse
request n rogātiō f, postulātum nt; **obtain a ~** impetrāre ▶ vt rogāre, petere; (urgently) dēposcere
require vt (demand) imperāre, postulāre; (need) egēre (abl); (call for) requīrere
requirement n postulātum nt, necessārium nt

requisite adj necessārius
requisition n postulātiō f ▶ vt imperāre
requital n grātia f, vicēs fpl
requite vt grātiam referre (dat), remūnerārī
rescind vt rescindere, abrogāre
rescript n rescrīptum nt
rescue vt ēripere, expedīre, servāre ▶ n salūs f; **come to the ~ of** subvenīre (dat)
research n investigātiō f
resemblance n similitūdō f, imāgō f, īnstar nt
resemble vt similem esse (dat), referre
resent vt aegrē ferre, indignārī
resentful adj īrācundus
resentment n dolor m, indignātiō f
reservation n (proviso) exceptiō f
reserve vt servāre, (store) recondere; (in a deal) excipere ▶ n (MIL) subsidium nt; (disposition) pudor m, reticentia f; (caution) cautiō f; **in ~** in succenturiātus; **without ~** palam
reserved adj (place) adsignātus; (disposition) taciturnus, tēctus
reservedly adv circumspectē
reserves npl subsidia ntpl
reservoir n lacus m
reside vi habitāre; **~ in** incolere
residence n domicilium nt, domus f
resident n incola m/f
residual adj reliquus
residue, residuum n reliqua pars f
resign vt cēdere; (office) abdicāre mē, tē etc dē (abl); **~ oneself** acquiēscere ▶ vi sē abdicāre
resignation n abdicātiō f; (state of mind) patientia f, aequus animus m
resigned adj patiēns; **be ~ to** aequō animō ferre
resilience n mollitia f
resilient adj mollis
resist vt resistere (dat), adversārī (dat), repugnāre (dat)
resistance n repugnantia f; **offer ~** obsistere (dat)
resistless adj invictus
resolute adj fortis, cōnstāns
resolutely adv fortiter, cōnstanter
resolution n (conduct) fortitūdō f, cōnstantia f; (decision) dēcrētum nt, sententia f; (into parts) sēcrētiō f
resolve n fortitūdō f, cōnstantia f ▶ vt dēcernere, cōnstituere; (into parts) dissolvere; **the senate resolves** placet senātuī
resonance n sonus m
resonant adj canōrus
resort n locus celeber m; **last ~** ultimum auxilium nt ▶ vi frequentāre, ventitāre; (have recourse) dēcurrere, dēscendere, cōnfugere
resound vi resonāre, personāre
resource n subsidium nt; (means) modus m; **resources** pl opēs fpl, cōpiae fpl
resourceful adj versūtus, callidus
resourcefulness n calliditās f, versūtus animus m
respect n (esteem) honōs m, observantia f; (reference) ratiō f; **out of ~** honōris causā; **pay**

one's respects to salūtāre; **show ~ for**
observāre; **in every ~** ex omnī parte, in omnī
genere; **in ~ of** ad (acc), ab (abl) ▶ vt honōrāre,
observāre, verērī
respectability n honestās f
respectable adj honestus, līberālis, frūgī
respectably adv honēstē
respectful adj observāns
respectfully adv reverenter
respectfulness n observantia f
respective adj suus (with quisque)
respectively adv alius ... alius
respiration n respīrātiō f, spīritus m
respire vi respīrāre
respite n requiēs f, intercapēdō f, intermissiō f
resplendence n splendor m
resplendent adj splendidus, illūstris
resplendently adv splendidē
respond vi respondēre
response n respōnsum nt
responsibility n auctōritās f, cūra f
responsible adj reus; (witness) locuplēs;
be ~ for praestāre
responsive adj (pupil) docilis; (character) facilis
rest n quiēs f, ōtium nt; (after toil) requiēs f;
(remainder) reliqua pars f; **be at ~** requiēscere;
set at ~ tranquillāre; **the ~** (others) cēterī mpl;
the ~ of reliquī ▶ vi requiēscere, acquiēscere;
~ on nītī (abl), innītī in (abl) ▶ vt (hope) pōnere
in (abl)
resting place n cubīle nt, sēdēs f
restitution n satisfactiō f; **make ~** restituere;
demand ~ rēs repetere
restive adj contumāx
restless adj inquiētus, sollicitus; **be ~** fluctuārī
restlessness n sollicitūdō f
restoration n renovātiō f; (of king) reductiō f
restore vt reddere, restituere; (to health)
recreāre; (to power) redūcere; (damage) reficere,
redintegrāre
restorer n restitūtor m
restrain vt coercēre, comprimere, cohibēre
restraint n moderātiō f, temperantia f, frēnī
mpl; **with ~** abstinenter
restrict vt continēre, circumscrībere
restricted adj artus; **~ to** proprius (gen)
restriction n modus m, fīnis m; (limitation)
exceptiō f
result n ēventus m, ēventum nt, exitus m;
the ~ is that quō fit ut ▶ vi ēvenīre, ēvādere
resultant adj cōnsequēns
resume vt repetere
resuscitate vt excitāre, suscitāre
retail vt dīvēndere, vēndere
retailer n caupō m
retain vt retinēre, tenēre, cōnservāre
retainer n satelles m
retake vt recipere
retaliate vi ulcīscī
retaliation n ultiō f
retard vt retardāre, remorārī
retention n cōnservātiō f

retentive adj tenāx
reticence n taciturnitās f
reticent adj taciturnus
reticulated adj rēticulātus
retinue n satellitēs mpl, comitātus m
retire vi recēdere, abscēdere; (from office) abīre;
(from province) dēcēdere; (MIL) pedem referre, sē
recipere
retired adj ēmeritus; (place) remōtus
retirement n (act) recessus m, dēcessus m;
(state) sōlitūdō f, ōtium nt; **life of ~** vīta prīvāta
retiring adj modestus, verēcundus
retort vt respondēre, referre ▶ n respōnsum nt
retouch vt retractāre
retrace vt repetere, iterāre
retract vt revocāre, renūntiāre
retreat n (MIL) receptus m; (place) recessus m,
sēcessus m; **sound the ~** receptuī canere ▶ vi
sē recipere, pedem referre; regredī
retrench vt minuere, recīdere
retrenchment n parsimōnia f
retribution n poena f
retributive adj ultor, ultrīx
retrieve vt reparāre, recipere
retrograde adj (fig) dēterior
retrogression n regressus m
retrospect n: **in ~** respicientī
retrospective adj: **be ~** retrōrsum sē referre
retrospectively adv retrō
return n reditus m; (pay) remūnerātiō f; (profit)
fructus m, pretium nt; (statement) professiō f;
make a ~ of profitērī; **in ~ for** prō (abl); **in ~** in
vicem, vicissim ▶ vt reddere, restituere, referre
▶ vi redīre, revenīre, revertī; (from province)
dēcēdere
reunion n convīvium nt
reunite vt reconciliāre
reveal vt aperīre, patefacere
revel n cōmissātiō f, bacchātiō f; **revels** pl orgia
ntpl ▶ vi cōmissārī, bacchārī; **~ in** luxuriārī
revelation n patefactiō f
reveller n cōmissātor m
revelry n cōmissātiō f
revenge n ultiō f; **take ~ on** vindicāre in (acc)
▶ vt ulcīscī
revengeful adj ulcīscendī cupidus
revenue n fructus m, reditus m, vectīgālia ntpl
reverberate vi resonāre
reverberation n repercussus m
revere vt venerārī, colere
reverence n venerātiō f; (feeling) religiō f;
reverentia f
reverent adj religiōsus, pius
reverently adv religiōsē
reverie n meditātiō f, somnium nt
reversal n abrogātiō f
reverse adj contrārius ▶ n contrārium nt; (MIL)
clādēs f ▶ vt invertere; (decision) rescindere
reversion n reditus m
revert vi redīre, revertī
review n recognitiō f, recēnsiō f ▶ vt (MIL)
recēnsēre

revile vt maledīcere (dat)
revise vt recognōscere, corrigere; (LIT) līmāre
revision n ēmendātiō f; (LIT) līma f
revisit vt revīsere
revival n renovātiō f
revive vt recreāre, excitāre ▶ vi revīvīscere, renāscī
revocation n revocātiō f
revoke vt renūntiāre, īnfectum reddere
revolt n sēditiō f, dēfectiō f ▶ vi dēficere, rebellāre
revolting adj taeter, obscēnus
revolution n (movement) conversiō f; (change) rēs novae fpl; (revolt) mōtus m; **effect a ~** rēs novāre
revolutionary adj sēditiōsus, novārum rērum cupidus
revolve vi volvī, versārī, convertī ▶ vt (in mind) volūtāre
revulsion n mūtātiō f
reward n praemium nt, mercēs f ▶ vt remūnerārī, compēnsāre
rhapsody n carmen nt; (epic) rhapsōdia f
rhetoric n rhētorica f; **of ~** rhētoricus; **exercise in ~** dēclāmātiō f; **practise ~** dēclāmāre; **teacher of ~** rhētōr m
rhetorical adj rhētoricus, dēclāmātōrius
rhetorically adv rhētoricē
rhetorician n rhētōr m, dēclāmātor m
rhinoceros n rhīnocerōs m
rhyme n homoeoteleuton nt; **without ~ or reason** temerē
rhythm n numerus m, modus m
rhythmical adj numerōsus
rib n costa f
ribald adj obscēnus
ribaldry n obscēnitās f
ribbon n īnfula f
rice n oryza f
rich adj dīves, locuplēs; opulentus; (fertile) ūber, opīmus; (food) pinguis
riches npl dīvitiae fpl, opēs fpl
richly adv opulentē, largē, lautē
richness n ūbertās f, cōpia f
rid vt līberāre; **get rid of** dēpōnere, dēmovēre, exuere
riddle n aenigma nt; (sieve) cribrum nt ▶ vt (with wounds) cōnfodere
ride vi equitāre, vehī; **~ a horse** in equō vehī; **~ at anchor** stāre; **~ away** abequitāre, āvehī; **~ back** revehī; **~ between** interequitāre; **~ down** dēvehī; **~ into** invehī; **~ off** āvehī; **~ out** ēvehī; **~ past** praetervehī; **~ round** circumvehī (dat), circumequitāre; **~ up and down** perequitāre; **~ up to** adequitāre ad, advehī ad
rider n eques m
ridge n iugum nt
ridicule n lūdibrium nt, irrīsus m ▶ vt irrīdēre, illūdere, lūdibriō habēre
ridiculous adj rīdiculus, dērīdiculus
ridiculously adv rīdiculē
riding n equitātiō f

rife adj frequēns
riff-raff n faex populī f
rifle vt expīlāre, spoliāre
rift n rīma f
rig vt (ship) armāre, ōrnāre ▶ n habitus m
rigging n rudentēs mpl
right adj rēctus; (just) aequus, iūstus; (true) rēctus, vērus; (proper) lēgitimus, fās; (hand) dexter; **it is ~** decet (+acc and infin); **it is not ~** dēdecet (+acc and infin); **you are ~** vēra dīcis; **if I am ~** nisi fallor; **in the ~ place** in locō; **at the ~ time** ad tempus; **at ~ angles** ad parēs angulōs; **on the ~** ā dextrā ▶ adv rēctē, bene, probē; (justifiably) iūre; **~ up to** usque ad (acc); **~ on** rēctā ▶ n (legal) iūs nt; (moral) fās nt ▶ vt (replace) restituere; (correct) corrigere; (avenge) ulcīscī
righteous adj iūstus, sanctus, pius
righteously adv iūstē, sanctē, piē
righteousness n sanctitās f, pietās f
rightful adj iūstus, lēgitimus
rightfully adv iūstē, lēgitimē
right hand n dextra f
right-hand adj dexter; **~ man** comes m
rightly adv rēctē, bene; iūre
right-minded adj sānus
rigid adj rigidus
rigidity n rigor m; (strictness) sevēritās f
rigidly adv rigidē, sevērē
rigmarole n ambāgēs fpl
rigorous adj dūrus; (strict) sevērus
rigorously adv dūriter, sevērē
rigour n dūritia f; sevēritās f
rile vt irrītāre, stomachum movēre (dat)
rill n rīvulus m
rim n labrum nt
rime n pruīna f
rind n cortex m
ring n ānulus m; (circle) orbis m; (of people) corōna f; (motion) gȳrus m ▶ vt circumdare; (bell) movēre ▶ vi tinnīre, sonāre
ringing n tinnītus m ▶ adj canōrus
ringleader n caput nt, dux m
ringlet n cincinnus m
rinse vt colluere
riot n tumultus m, rixa f; **run ~** exsultāre, luxuriārī, tumultuārī, turbās efficere; (revel) bacchārī
rioter n cōmissātor m
riotous adj tumultuōsus, sēditiōsus; (debauched) dissolūtus; **~ living** cōmissātiō f, luxuria f
riotously adv tumultuōsē; luxuriōsē
rip vt scindere
ripe adj mātūrus; **of ~ judgment** animī mātūrus
ripen vt mātūrāre ▶ vi mātūrēscere
ripeness n mātūritās f
ripple n unda f ▶ vi trepidāre
rise vi orīrī, surgere; (hill) ascendere; (wind) cōnsurgere; (passion) tumēscere; (voice) tollī; (in size) crēscere; (in rank) ascendere; (in revolt) coorīrī, arma capere; **~ and fall** (tide)

reciprocāre; **~ above** superāre; **~ again**
resurgere; **~ in** (river) orīrī ex (abl); **~ out**
ēmergere; **~ up** exsurgere ▸ n ascēnsus m; (slope)
clīvus m; (increase) incrēmentum nt; (start) ortus
m; **give ~ to** parere
rising n (sun) ortus m; (revolt) mōtus m ▸ adj
(ground) ēditus
risk n perīculum nt; **run a ~** perīculum subīre,
ingredī ▸ vt perīclitārī, in āleam dare
risky adj perīculōsus
rite n rītus m
ritual n caerimōnia f
rival adj aemulus ▸ n aemulus m, rīvālis m ▸ vt
aemulārī
rivalry n aemulātiō f
river n flūmen nt, fluvius m ▸ adj fluviātilis
riverbed n alveus m
riverside n rīpa f
rivet n clāvus m ▸ vt (attention) dēfīgere
rivulet n rīvulus m, rīvus m
road n via f, iter nt; **on the ~** in itinere, ex itinere;
off the ~ dēvius; **make a ~** viam mūnīre
roadstead n statiō f
roam vi errāre, vagārī; **~ at large** ēvagārī
roar n fremitus m ▸ vi fremere
roast vt torrēre ▸ adj āssus ▸ n āssum nt
rob vt spoliāre, exspoliāre, expīlāre; (of hope)
dēicere dē
robber n latrō m, fūr m; (highway) grassātor m
robbery n latrōcinium nt
robe n vestis f; (woman's) stola f; (of state) trabea
f ▸ vt vestīre
robust adj rōbustus, fortis
robustness n rōbur nt, firmitās f
rock n saxum nt; (steep) rūpēs f, scopulus m ▸ vt
agitāre ▸ vi agitārī, vacillāre
rocky adj saxōsus, scopulōsus
rod n virga f; (fishing) harundō f
roe n (deer) capreolus m, caprea f; (fish) ōva ntpl
rogue n veterātor m
roguery n nēquitia f, scelus nt
roguish adj improbus, malus
role n partēs fpl
roll n (book) volūmen nt; (movement) gȳrus m;
(register) album nt; **call the ~ of** legere; **answer
the ~ call** ad nōmen respondēre ▸ vt volvere ▸ vi
volvī, volūtārī; **~ down** vt dēvolvere ▸ vi dēfluere;
~ over vi prōvolvere ▸ vi prōlābī; **~ up** vt
convolvere
roller n (AGR) cylindrus m; (for moving) phalangae
fpl; (in book) umbilīcus m
rollicking adj hilaris
rolling adj volūbilis
Roman adj Rōmānus ▸ n: **the Romans** Rōmānī
mpl
romance n fābula f; amor m
romantic adj fābulōsus; amātōrius
Rome n Rōma f; **at ~** Rōmae; **from ~** Rōmā; **to ~**
Rōmam
romp vi lūdere
roof n tēctum nt; (of mouth) palātum nt ▸ vt
tegere, integere

rook n corvus m
room n conclāve nt, camera f; (small) cella f;
(bed) cubiculum nt; (dining) cēnāculum nt;
(dressing) apodytērium nt; (space) locus m;
make ~ for locum dare (dat), cēdere (dat)
roominess n laxitās f
roomy adj capāx
roost vi stabulārī
rooster n gallus gallīnāceus m
root n rādīx f; **take ~** coalēscere ▸ vt: **~ out**
ērādīcāre
rooted adj (fig) dēfīxus; **deeply ~** (custom)
inveterātus; **be ~ in** īnsidēre (dat); **become
deeply ~** inveterāscere
rope n fūnis m; (thin) restis f; (ship's) rudēns m;
know the ropes perītum esse
rose n rosa f
rosemary n rōs marīnus m
rostrum n rōstra ntpl, suggestus m
rosy adj roseus, purpureus
rot n tābēs f ▸ vi putrēscere, pūtēscere ▸ vt
putrefacere
rotate vi volvī, sē convertere
rotation n conversiō f; (succession) ōrdō m,
vicissitūdō f; **in ~** ōrdine; **move in ~** in orbem īre
rote n: **by ~** memoriter
rotten adj putridus
rotund adj rotundus
rotundity n rotunditās f
rouge n fūcus m ▸ vt fūcāre
rough adj asper; (art) incultus, rudis; (manners)
agrestis, inurbānus; (stone) impolītus;
(treatment) dūrus, sevērus; (weather) atrōx,
procellōsus ▸ vi: **~ it** dūram vītam vīvere
rough-and-ready adj fortuītus
rough draft n (LIT) silva f
roughen vt asperāre, exasperāre
rough-hew vt dolāre
roughly adv asperē, dūriter; (with numbers)
circiter
roughness n asperitās f
round adj rotundus; (spherical) globōsus;
(cylindrical) teres ▸ n (circle) orbis m; (motion)
gȳrus m; (series) ambitus m; **go the rounds** (MIL)
vigiliās circumīre ▸ vt (cape) superāre; **~ off**
rotundāre; (sentence) concludere; **~ up**
compellere ▸ adv circum, circā; **go ~** ambīre
▸ prep circum (acc), circā (acc)
roundabout adj: **~ story** ambāgēs fpl; **~ route**
circuitus m, ānfrāctus m
roundly adv (speak) apertē, līberē
rouse vt excīre, excitāre; (courage) adrigere
rousing adj vehemēns
rout n fuga f; (crowd) turba f ▸ vt fugāre, fundere;
in fugam conicere, prōflīgāre
route n cursus m, iter nt
routine n ūsus m, ōrdō m
rove vi errāre, vagārī
rover n vagus m; (sea) pīrāta m
row n (line) ōrdō m; (noise) turba f, rixa f ▸ vi (boat)
rēmigāre ▸ vt rēmīs incitāre
rowdy adj turbulentus

rower n rēmex m
rowing n rēmigium nt
royal adj rēgius, rēgālis
royally adv rēgiē, rēgāliter
royalty n (power) rēgnum nt; (persons) rēgēs mpl, domus rēgia f
rub vt fricāre, terere; **rub away** conterere; **rub hard** dēfricāre; **rub off** dētergēre; **rub out** dēlēre; **rub up** expolīre
rubbing n trītus m
rubbish n quisquiliae fpl; (talk) nūgae fpl
rubble n rūdus nt
rubicund adj rubicundus
rudder n gubernāculum nt, clāvus m
ruddy adj rubicundus, rutilus
rude adj (uncivilized) barbarus, dūrus, inurbānus; (insolent) asper, importūnus
rudely adv horridē, rusticē; petulanter
rudeness n barbariēs f; petulantia f, importūnitās f
rudiment n elementum nt, initium nt
rudimentary adj prīmus, incohātus
rue n (herb) rūta f ▶ vt: **I rue** mē paenitet (gen)
rueful adj maestus
ruffian n grassātor m
ruffle vt agitāre; (temper) sollicitāre, commovēre
rug n strāgulum nt
rugged adj horridus, asper
ruggedness n asperitās f
ruin n ruīna f; (fig) exitium nt, perniciēs f; **go to ~** pessum īre, dīlābī ▶ vt perdere, dēperdere, pessum dare; (moral) corrumpere, dēprāvāre; **be ruined** perīre
ruined adj ruīnōsus
ruinous adj exitiōsus, damnōsus
rule n (instrument) rēgula f, amussis f; (principle) nōrma f, lēx f, praeceptum nt; (government) dominātiō f, imperium nt; **ten-foot ~** decempeda f; **as a ~** ferē; **lay down rules** praecipere; **make it a ~ to** īnstituere (infin); **~ of thumb** ūsus m ▶ vt regere, moderārī ▶ vi rēgnāre, dominārī; (judge) ēdīcere; (custom) obtinēre; **~ over** imperāre (dat)
ruler n (instrument) rēgula f; (person) dominus m, rēctor m
ruling n ēdictum nt
rumble vi mūgīre
rumbling n mūgītus m
ruminate vi rūminārī
rummage vi: **~ through** rīmārī
rumour n fāma f, rūmor m
rump n clūnis f
run vi currere; (fluid) fluere, mānāre; (road) ferre; (time) lābī ▶ n cursus m; **run about** discurrere, cursāre; **run across** incidere in (acc); **run after** sectārī; **run aground** offendere; **run away** aufugere, terga vertere; (from) fugere, dēfugere; **run down** dēcurrere, dēfluere ▶ vt (in words) obtrectāre; **run high** (fig) glīscere; **run into** incurrere in (acc), īnfluere in (acc); **run off with** abripere, abdūcere; **run on** pergere; **run out**

(land) excurrere; (time) exīre; (supplies) dēficere; **run over** vt (with car) obterere; (details) percurrere; **run riot** luxuriārī; **run through** (course) dēcurrere; (money) disperdere; **run short** dēficere; **run up to** adcurrere ad; **run up against** incurrere in (acc); **run wild** lascīvīre ▶ vt gerere, administrāre
runaway adj fugitīvus
rung n gradus m
runner n cursor m
running n cursus m ▶ adj (water) vīvus
rupture n (fig) dissidium nt ▶ vt dīrumpere
rural adj rūsticus, agrestis
ruse n fraus f, dolus m
rush n (plant) cārex f, iuncus m; (movement) impetus m ▶ vi currere, sē incitāre, ruere; **~ forward** sē prōripere; prōruere; **~ in** inruere, incurrere; **~ out** ēvolāre, sē effundere ▶ adj iunceus
russet adj flāvus
rust n (iron) ferrūgō f; (copper) aerūgō f ▶ vi rōbīginem trahere
rustic adj rūsticus, agrestis
rusticate vi rūsticārī ▶ vt relēgāre
rusticity n mōrēs rūsticī mpl
rustle vi increpāre, crepitāre ▶ n crepitus m
rusty adj rōbīginōsus
rut n orbita f
ruthless adj inexōrābilis, crūdēlis
ruthlessly adv crūdēliter
rye n secāle nt

S

sabbath n sabbata ntpl
sable adj āter, niger
sabre n acīnacēs m
sacerdotal adj sacerdōtālis
sack n saccus m; (MIL) dīreptiō f ▶ vt dīripere, expīlāre; spoliāre
sackcloth n cilicium nt
sacred adj sacer, sanctus
sacredly adv sānctē
sacredness n sanctitās f
sacrifice n sacrificium nt, sacrum nt; (act) immolātiō f; (victim) hostia f; (fig) iactūra f ▶ vt immolāre, sacrificāre, mactāre; (fig) dēvovēre, addīcere ▶ vi sacra facere; (give up) prōicere
sacrificer n immolātor m
sacrilege n sacrilegium nt
sacrilegious adj sacrilegus
sacristan n aedituus m
sacrosanct adj sacrōsanctus
sad adj maestus, tristis; (thing) tristis
sadden vt dolōre adficere
saddle n strātum nt ▶ vt sternere; (fig) impōnere
saddlebags n clītellae fpl
sadly adv maestē
sadness n tristitia f, maestitia f
safe adj tūtus; (out of danger) incolumis, salvus; (to trust) fīdus; ~ and sound salvus ▶ n armārium nt
safe-conduct n fidēs pūblica f
safeguard n cautiō f, prōpugnāculum nt ▶ vt dēfendere
safely adv tūtō, impūne
safety n salūs f, incolumitās f; seek ~ in flight salutem fugā petere
saffron n crocus m ▶ adj croceus
sag vi dēmittī
sagacious adj prūdēns, sagāx, acūtus
sagaciously adv prūdenter, sagāciter
sagacity n prūdentia f, sagācitās f
sage n sapiēns m; (herb) salvia f ▶ adj sapiēns
sagely adv sapienter
sail n vēlum nt; set ~ vēla dare, nāvem solvere; shorten ~ vēla contrahere ▶ vi nāvigāre; ~ past legere, praetervehī

sailing n nāvigātiō f
sailor n nauta m
sail yard n antenna f
saint n vir sanctus m
sainted adj beātus
saintly adj sanctus
sake n: for the ~ of grātiā (gen), causā (gen), propter (acc); (behalf) prō (abl)
salacious adj salāx
salad n morētum nt
salamander n salamandra f
salary n mercēs f
sale n vēnditiō f; (formal) mancipium nt; (auction) hasta f; for ~ vēnālis; be for ~ prōstāre; offer for ~ vēnum dare
saleable adj vēndibilis
salient adj ēminēns; ~ points capita ntpl
saline adj salsus
saliva n salīva f
sallow adj pallidus
sally n ēruptiō f; (wit) facētiae fpl ▶ vi ērumpere, excurrere
salmon n salmō m
salon n ātrium nt
salt n sal m ▶ adj salsus
saltcellar n salīnum nt
saltpetre n nitrum nt
salt-pits n salīnae fpl
salty adj salsus
salubrious adj salūbris
salubriously adv salūbriter
salubriousness n salūbritās f
salutary adj salūtāris, ūtilis
salutation n salūs f
salute vt salūtāre
salvage vt servāre, ēripere
salvation n salūs f
salve n unguentum nt
salver n scutella f
same adj īdem; ~ as īdem ac; all the ~ nihilōminus; one and the ~ ūnus et īdem; from the ~ place indidem; in the ~ place ibīdem; to the ~ place eōdem; at the ~ time simul, eōdem tempore; (adversative) tamen; it is all the ~ to me meā nōn interest
Samnites n Samnītēs, Samnītium mpl
sample n exemplum nt, specimen nt ▶ vt gustāre
sanctify vt cōnsecrāre
sanctimony n falsa rēligiō f
sanction n comprobātiō f, auctōritās f ▶ vt ratum facere
sanctity n sanctitās f
sanctuary n fānum nt, dēlubrum nt; (for men) asỹlum nt
sand n harēna f
sandal n (outdoors) crepida f; (indoors) solea f
sandalled adj crepidātus, soleātus
sandpit n harēnāria f
sandstone n tōfus m
sandy adj harēnōsus; (colour) flāvus
sane adj sānus

sangfroid n aequus animus m
sanguinary adj cruentus
sanguine adj laetus
sanitary adj salūbris
sanity n mēns sāna f
sap n sūcus m ▶ vt subruere
sapience n sapientia f
sapient adj sapiēns
sapling n surculus m
sapper n cunīculārius m
sapphire n sapphīrus f
sarcasm n aculeī mpl, dicācitās f
sarcastic adj dicāx, acūleātus
sardonic adj amārus
sash n cingulum nt
satchel n loculus m
sate vt explēre, satiāre
satellite n satelles m
satiate vt explēre, satiāre, saturāre
satiety n satietās f
satire n satura f; (pl, of Horace) sermōnēs mpl
satirical adj acerbus
satirist n saturārum scrīptor m
satirize vt perstringere, notāre
satisfaction n (act) explētiō f; (feeling) voluptas f; (penalty) poena f; **demand ~** rēs repetere
satisfactorily adv ex sententiā
satisfactory adj idōneus, grātus
satisfied adj: **be ~** satis habēre, contentum esse
satisfy vt satisfacere (dat); (desire) explēre
satrap n satrapēs m
saturate vt imbuere
satyr n satyrus m
sauce n condīmentum nt; (fish) garum nt
saucer n patella f
saucily adv petulanter
saucy adj petulāns
saunter vi ambulāre
sausage n tomāculum nt, hīllae fpl
savage adj ferus, efferātus; (cruel) atrōx, inhūmānus; saevus
savagely adv ferōciter, inhūmānē
savagery n ferōcitās f, inhūmānitās f
savant n vir doctus m
save vt servāre; **~ up** reservāre ▶ prep praeter (acc)
saving adj parcus; **~ clause** exceptiō f ▶ n compendium nt; **savings** pl peculium nt
saviour n līberātor m
savory n thymbra f
savour n sapor m; (of cooking) nīdor m ▶ vi sapere; **~ of** olēre, redolēre
savoury adj condītus
saw n (tool) serra f; (saying) prōverbium nt ▶ vt serrā secāre
sawdust n scobis f
say vt dīcere; **say that … not** negāre; **say no** negāre; **he says** (quoting) inquit; **he says yes** āit; **they say** ferunt (+ acc and infin)
saying n dictum nt
scab n (disease) scabiēs f; (over wound) crusta f

scabbard n vāgīna f
scabby adj scaber
scaffold, scaffolding n fala f
scald vt ūrere
scale n (balance) lanx f; (fish, etc) squāma f; (gradation) gradūs mpl; (music) diagramma nt ▶ vt scālīs ascendere
scallop n pecten m
scalp n capitis cutis f
scalpel n scalpellum nt
scamp n verberō m
scamper vi currere
scan vt contemplārī; (verse) mētīrī
scandal n īnfāmia f, opprobrium nt; (talk) calumnia f
scandalize vt offendere
scandalous adj flāgitiōsus, turpis
scansion n syllabārum ēnārrātiō f
scant adj exiguus, parvus
scantily adv exiguē, tenuiter
scantiness n exiguitās f
scanty adj exiguus, tenuis, exīlis; (number) paucus
scapegoat n piāculum nt
scar n cicātrīx f
scarce adj rārus; **make oneself ~** sē āmovēre, dē mediō recēdere ▶ adv vix, aegrē
scarcely adv vix, aegrē; **~ anyone** nēmō ferē
scarcity n inopia f, angustiae fpl
scare n formīdō f ▶ vt terrēre; **~ away** absterrēre
scarecrow n formīdō f
scarf n focāle nt
scarlet n coccum nt ▶ adj coccinus
scarp n rūpēs f
scathe n damnum nt
scatter vt spargere; dispergere, dissipāre; (violently) disicere ▶ vi diffugere
scatterbrained adj dēsipiēns
scattered adj rārus
scene n spectāculum nt; (place) theātrum nt
scenery n locī faciēs f, speciēs f; (beautiful) amoenitās f
scent n odor m; (sense) odōrātus m; **keen ~** sagācitās f ▶ vt odōrārī; (perfume) odōribus perfundere
scented adj odōrātus
sceptic n Pyrrhōnēus m
sceptical adj incrēdulus
sceptre n scēptrum nt
schedule n tabulae fpl, ratiō f
scheme n cōnsilium nt, ratiō f ▶ vt māchinārī, mōlīrī
schemer n māchinātor m
schism n discidium nt, sēcessiō f
scholar n vir doctus m, litterātus m; (pupil) discipulus m
scholarly adj doctus, litterātus
scholarship n litterae fpl, doctrīna f
scholastic adj umbrātilis
school n (elementary) lūdus m; (advanced) schola f; (high) gymnasium nt; (sect) secta f, domus f ▶ vt īnstituere

schoolboy n discipulus m
schoolmaster n magister m
schoolmistress n magistra f
science n doctrīna f, disciplīna f, ars f
scimitar n acīnacēs m
scintillate vi scintillāre
scion n prōgeniēs f
Scipio n Scīpiō, Scipiōnis m
scissors n forfex f
scoff vi irrīdēre; ~ **at** dērīdēre
scoffer n irrīsor m
scold vt increpāre, obiūrgāre
scolding n obiūrgātiō f
scoop n trulla f ▶ vt: ~ **out** excavāre
scope n (aim) fīnis m; (room) locus m, campus m;
  ample ~ laxus locus
scorch vt exūrere, torrēre
scorched adj torridus
score n (mark) nota f; (total) summa f; (reckoning)
  ratiō f; (number) vīgintī ▶ vt notāre ▶ vi vincere
scorn n contemptiō f ▶ vt contemnere, spernere
scorner n contemptor m
scornful adj fastīdiōsus
scornfully adv contemptim
scorpion n scorpiō m, nepa f
scot-free adj immūnis, impūnītus
scoundrel n furcifer m
scour vt (clean) tergēre; (range) percurrere
scourge n flagellum nt; (fig) pestis f ▶ vt
  verberāre, virgīs caedere
scout n explōrātor m, speculātor m ▶ vi
  explōrāre, speculārī ▶ vt spernere, repudiāre
scowl n frontis contractiō f ▶ vi frontem
  contrahere
scraggy adj strigōsus
scramble vi: ~ **for** certātim captāre; ~ **up**
  scandere
scrap n frūstum nt
scrape vt rādere, scabere; ~ **off** abrādere
scraper n strigilis f
scratch vt rādere; (head) perfricāre; ~ **out**
  exsculpere, ērādere
scream n clāmor m, ululātus m ▶ vi clāmāre,
  ululāre
screech n ululātus m ▶ vi ululāre
screen n obex m/f; (from sun) umbra f; (fig)
  vēlāmentum nt ▶ vt tegere
screw n clāvus m; (of winepress) cochlea f
scribble vt properē scrībere
scribe n scrība m
script n scrīptum nt; (handwriting) manus f
scroll n volūmen nt
scrub vt dētergēre, dēfricāre
scruple n religiō f, scrūpulus m
scrupulous adj religiōsus; (careful) dīligēns
scrupulously adv religiōsē, dīligenter
scrupulousness n religiō f; dīligentia f
scrutinize vt scrūtārī, intrōspicere in (acc),
  excutere
scrutiny n scrūtātiō f
scud vi volāre
scuffle n rixa f

scull n calvāria f; (oar) rēmus m
scullery n culīna f
sculptor n fictor m, sculptor m
sculpture n ars fingendī f; (product) statuae fpl
  ▶ vt sculpere
scum n spūma f
scurf n porrīgō f
scurrility n maledicta ntpl
scurrilous adj maledicus
scurvy adj (fig) turpis, improbus
scythe n falx f
sea n mare nt; aequor nt; **open sea** altum nt; **put
  to sea** solvere; **be at sea** nāvigāre; (fig) in errōre
  versārī ▶ adj marīnus; (coast) maritimus
seaboard n lītus nt
seafaring adj maritimus, nauticus
seafight n nāvāle proelium nt
seagull n larus m
seal n (animal) phōca f; (stamp) signum nt ▶ vt
  signāre; ~ **up** obsignāre
seam n sūtūra f
seaman n nauta m
seamanship n scientia et ūsus nauticārum
  rērum
seaport n portus m
sear vt adūrere, torrēre
search n investīgātiō f ▶ vi investīgāre,
  explōrāre ▶ vt excutere, scrūtārī; **in ~ of** causa
  (gen); ~ **for** quaerere, exquīrere, investīgāre;
  ~ **into** inquīrere, anquīrere; ~ **out** explōrāre,
  indāgāre
searcher n inquīsītor m
searching adj acūtus, dīligēns
seashore n lītus nt
seasick adj: **be** ~ nauseāre
seasickness n nausea f
seaside n mare nt
season n annī tempus nt, tempestās f; (right
  time) tempus nt, opportūnitās f; **in** ~ tempestīvē
  ▶ vt condīre
seasonable adj tempestīvus
seasonably adv tempestīvē
seasoned adj (food) condītus; (wood) dūrātus
seasoning n condīmentum nt
seat n sēdēs f; (chair) sedīle nt; (home) domus f,
  domicilium nt; **keep one's** ~ (riding) in equō
  haerēre ▶ vt collocāre; ~ **oneself** īnsidēre
seated adj: **be** ~ sedēre
seaweed n alga f
seaworthy adj ad nāvigandum ūtilis
secede vi sēcēdere
secession n sēcessiō f
seclude vt sēclūdere, abstrūdere
secluded adj sēcrētus, remōtus
seclusion n sōlitūdō f, sēcrētum nt
second adj secundus, alter; **a** ~ **time** iterum ▶ n
  temporis pūnctum nt; (person) fautor m; ~ **sight**
  hariolātiō f ▶ vt favēre (dat), adesse (dat)
secondary adj īnferior, dēterior
seconder n fautor m
second-hand adj aliēnus, trītus
secondly adv deinde

secrecy n sēcrētum nt, silentium nt
secret adj secretus; occultus, arcānus; (stealth)
fūrtīvus ▶ n arcānum nt; **keep ~** dissimulāre,
cēlāre; **in ~** clam; **be ~** latēre
secretary n scrība m, ab epistolīs, ā manū
secrete vt cēlāre, abdere
secretive adj tēctus
secretly adv clam, occultē, sēcrētō
sect n secta f, schola f, domus f
section n pars f
sector n regiō f
secular adj profānus
secure adj tūtus ▶ vt (MIL) firmāre, ēmūnīre;
(fasten) religāre; (obtain) parāre, nancīscī
securely adv tūtō
security n salūs f, impūnitās f; (money) cautiō f,
pignus nt, spōnsiō f; **sense of ~** sēcūritās f; **give**
good ~ satis dare; **on good ~** (loan) nōminibus
rēctis cautus; **stand ~ for** praedem esse prō (abl)
sedan n lectīca f
sedate adj placidus, temperātus, gravis
sedately adv placidē
sedateness n gravitās f
sedge n ulva f
sediment n faex f
sedition n sēditiō f, mōtus m
seditious adj sēditiōsus
seditiously adv sēditiōsē
seduce vt illicere, pellicere
seducer n corruptor m
seduction n corruptēla f
seductive adj blandus
seductively adv blandē
sedulity n dīligentia f
sedulous adj dīligēns, sēdulus
sedulously adv dīligenter, sēdulō
see vt vidēre, cernere; (suddenly) cōnspicārī;
(performance) spectāre; (with mind) intelligere;
go and see vīsere, invīsere; **see to** vidēre,
cōnsulere (dat); curare (+acc and gerundive); **see**
through dīspicere; **see that you are** vidē ut sīs,
fac sīs; **see that you are not** vidē nē sīs, cavē sīs
seed n sēmen nt; (in a plant) grānum nt; (in fruit)
acinum nt; (fig) stirps f, prōgeniēs f
seedling n surculus m
seed-time n sēmentis f
seeing that conj quōniam, siquidem
seek vt petere, quaerere
seeker n indāgātor m
seem vi vidērī
seeming adj speciōsus ▶ n speciēs f
seemingly adv ut vidētur
seemly adj decēns, decōrus; **it is ~** decet
seep vi mānāre, percōlārī
seer n vātēs m/f
seethe vi fervēre
segregate vt sēcernere, sēgregāre
segregation n sēparātiō f
seize vt rapere, corripere, adripere, prehendere;
(MIL) occupāre; (illness) adficere; (emotion)
invādere, occupāre
seizure n ēreptiō f, occupātiō f

seldom adv rārō
select vt ēligere, excerpere, dēligere ▶ adj lēctus,
ēlēctus
selection n ēlēctiō f, dēlēctus m; (lit) ecloga f
self n ipse; (reflexive) sē; **a second ~** alter īdem
self-centred adj glōriōsus
self-confidence n cōnfidentia f, fidūcia f
self-confident adj cōnfīdēns
self-conscious adj pudibundus
self-control n temperantia f
self-denial n abstinentia f
self-evident adj manifestus; **it is ~** ante pedēs
positum est
self-governing adj līber
self-government n lībertās f
self-important adj adrogāns
self-interest n ambitiō f
selfish adj inhūmānus, avārus; **be ~** suā causā
facere
selfishly adv inhūmānē, avārē
selfishness n inhūmānitās f, incontinentia f,
avāritia f
self-made adj (man) novus
self-possessed adj aequō animō
self-possession n aequus animus m
self-reliant adj cōnfīdēns
self-respect n pudor m
self-restraint n modestia f
self-sacrifice n dēvōtiō f
selfsame adj ūnus et īdem
sell vt vēndere; (in lots) dīvēndere; **be sold** vēnīre
seller n vēnditor m
selvage n limbus m
semblance n speciēs f, imāgō f
semicircle n hēmicyclium nt
senate n senātus m; **hold a meeting of the ~**
senātum habēre; **decree of the ~** senātus
cōnsultum nt
senate house n cūria f
senator n senātor m; (provincial) decuriō m;
senators pl patrēs mpl
senatorial adj senātōrius
send vt mittere; **~ across** trānsmittere; **~ ahead**
praemittere; **~ away** dīmittere; **~ back**
remittere; **~ for** arcessere; (doctor) adhibēre;
~ forth ēmittere; **~ forward** praemittere; **~ in**
immittere, intrōmittere; **~ out** ēmittere; (in
different directions) dīmittere; **~ out of the way**
ablēgāre; **~ up** submittere
senile adj senīlis
senility n senium nt
senior adj nātū māior; (thing) prior
sensation n sēnsus m; (event) rēs nova f; **lose ~**
obtorpēscere; **create a ~** hominēs
obstupefacere
sensational adj novus, prōdigiōsus
sense n (faculty) sēnsus m; (wisdom) prūdentia f;
(meaning) vis f, sententia f; **common ~**
prūdentia f; **be in one's senses** apud sē esse,
mentis suae esse; **out of one's senses** dēmēns;
recover one's senses resipīscere; **what is**
the ~ of quid sibī vult? ▶ vt sentīre

senseless adj absurdus, ineptus, īnsipiēns
senselessly adv īnsipienter
senselessness n īnsipientia f
sensibility n sēnsus m
sensible adj prūdēns, sapiēns
sensibly adv prūdenter, sapienter
sensitive adj mollis, inrītābilis, patibilis
sensitiveness n mollitia f
sensual adj libīdinōsus
sensuality n libīdō f, voluptās f
sensually adv libīdinōsē
sentence n (judge) iūdicium nt, sententia f;
  (GRAM) sententia f; **pass ~** iūdicāre; **execute ~**
  lēge agere ▸ vt damnāre; **~ to death** capitis
  damnāre
sententious adj sententiōsus
sententiously adv sententiōsē
sentient adj patibilis
sentiment n (feeling) sēnsus m; (opinion)
  sententia f; (emotion) mollitia f
sentimental adj mollis, flēbilis
sentimentality n mollitia f
sentimentally adv molliter
sentries npl statiōnēs fpl, excubiae fpl
sentry n custōs m, vigil m; **be on ~ duty** in
  statiōne esse
separable adj dīviduus, sēparābilis
separate vt sēparāre, dīvidere, disiungere;
  (forcibly) dīrimere, dīvellere ▸ vi dīgredī ▸ adj
  sēparātus, sēcrētus
separately adv sēparātim, seōrsum
separation n sēparātiō f; (violent) discidium nt
September n mēnsis September m; **of ~**
  September
sepulchral adj fūnebris
sepulchre n sepulcrum nt
sepulture n sepultūra f
sequel n exitus m, quae sequuntur
sequence n seriēs f, ōrdō m
sequestered adj sēcrētus
serenade vt occentāre
serene adj tranquillus, sēcūrus
serenely adv tranquillē
serenity n sēcūritās f
serf n servus m
serfdom n servitūs f
sergeant n signifer m
series n seriēs f, ōrdō m
serious adj gravis, sērius, sevērus
seriously adv graviter, sēriō, sevērē
seriousness n gravitās f
sermon n ōrātiō f
serpent n serpēns f
serpentine adj tortuōsus
serrated adj serrātus
serried adj cōnfertus
servant n (domestic) famulus m, famula f;
  (public) minister m, ministra f; **family servants**
  familia f
servant maid n ancilla f
serve vt servīre (dat); (food) ministrāre,
  adpōnere; (interest) condūcere (dat) ▸ vi (MIL)

stīpendia merēre, mīlitāre; (suffice) sufficere;
  ~ as esse prō (abl); **~ in the cavalry** equō
  merēre; **~ in the infantry** pedibus merēre;
  having served one's time ēmeritus; **~ a**
  sentence poenam subīre; **~ well** bene merērī
  dē (abl)
service n (status) servitium nt, famulātus m;
  (work) ministerium nt; (help) opera f; (by an
  equal) meritum nt, beneficium nt; (MIL) mīlitia f,
  stīpendia ntpl; **be of ~ to** prōdesse (dat), bene
  merērī dē; **I am at your ~** adsum tibī; **complete**
  one's ~ stīpendia ēmerērī
serviceable adj ūtilis
servile adj servīlis; (fig) abiectus, humilis
servility n adūlātiō f
servitude n servitūs f
session n conventus m; **be in ~** sedēre
sesterce n sēstertius m, **10 sesterces** decem
  sēstertiī; **10,000 sesterces** dēna sēstertia ntpl;
  1,000,000 sesterces deciēs sēstertium
set vt pōnere, locāre, statuere, sistere; (bone)
  condere; (course) dīrigere; (example) dare; (limit)
  impōnere; (mind) intendere; (music) modulārī;
  (sail) dare; (sentries) dispōnere; (table) īnstruere;
  (trap) parāre ▸ vi (ASTR) occidere; **set about**
  incipere; **set against** oppōnere; **set apart**
  sēpōnere; **set aside** sēpōnere; **set down**
  (writing) perscrībere; **set eyes on** cōnspicere;
  set foot on ingredī; **set forth** expōnere, ēdere;
  set free līberāre; **set in motion** movēre; **set in**
  order compōnere, dispōnere; **set off**
  (decoration) distinguere; (art) illūmināre; **set on**
  (to attack) immittere; **set on foot** īnstituere; **set**
  on fire incendere; **set one's heart on** exoptāre;
  set out vi proficīscī; **set over** praeficere,
  impōnere; **set up** statuere; (fig) cōnstituere
  ▸ adj (arrangement) status; (purpose) certus;
  (rule) praescrīptus; (speech) compositus; **of set**
  purpose cōnsultō ▸ n (persons) numerus m;
  (things) congeriēs f; (current) cursus m
setback n repulsa f
settee n lectulus m
setting n (ASTR) occāsus m; (event) locus m
settle n sella f ▸ vt statuere; (annuity) praestāre;
  (business) trānsigere; (colony) dēdūcere; (debt)
  exsolvere; (decision) cōnstituere; (dispute)
  dēcīdere, compōnere ▸ vi (abode) cōnsīdere;
  (agreement) cōnstituere, convenīre; (sediment)
  dēsīdere; **~ in** īnsidēre (dat)
settled adj certus, explōrātus
settlement n (of a colony) dēductiō f; (colony)
  colōnia f; (of dispute) dēcīsiō f, compositiō f;
  (to wife) dōs f
settler n colōnus m
set to n pugna f
seven num septem; **~ each** septēnī; **~ times**
  septiēns
seven hundred num septingentī
seven hundredth adj septingentēsimus
seventeen num septendecim
seventeenth adj septimus decimus
seventh adj septimus; **for the ~ time** septimum

seventieth adj septuāgēsimus

seventy num septuāgintā; **~ each** septuāgēnī; **~ times** septuāgiēns

sever vt incīdere, sēparāre, dīvidere

several adj complūrēs, aliquot

severally adv singulī

severe adj gravis, sevērus, dūrus; (style) austērus; (weather) asper; (pain) ācer, gravis

severely adv graviter, sevērē

severity n gravitās f; asperitās f; sevēritās f

sew vt suere; **sew up** cōnsuere; **sew up in** īnsuere in (acc)

sewer n cloāca f

sex n sexus m

shabbily adv sordidē

shabbiness n sordēs fpl

shabby adj sordidus

shackle n compēs f, vinculum nt ▸ vt impedīre, vincīre

shade n umbra f; (colour) color m; **shades** pl mānēs mpl; **put in the ~** officere (dat) ▸ vt opācāre, umbram adferre (dat)

shadow n umbra f

shadowy adj obscūrus; (fig) inānis

shady adj umbrōsus, opācus

shaft n (missile) tēlum nt, sagitta f; (of spear) hastīle nt; (of cart) tēmō m; (of light) radius m; (excavation) puteus m

shaggy adj hirsūtus

shake vt quatere, agitāre; (structure) labefacere, labefactāre; (belief) īnfīrmāre; (resolution) labefactāre, commovēre; **~ hands with** dextram dare (dat) ▸ vi quatī, agitārī, tremere, horrēscere; **~ off** dēcutere, excutere; **~ out** excutere

shaking n tremor m

shaky adj īnstābilis, tremebundus

shall aux vb use fut indic

shallot n caepa Ascalōnia f

shallow adj brevis, vadōsus; (fig) levis

shallowness n vada ntpl; (fig) levitās f

shallows n brevia ntpl, vada ntpl

sham adj fictus, falsus, fūcōsus ▸ n simulātiō f, speciēs f ▸ vt simulāre

shambles n laniēna f

shame n (feeling) pudor m; (cause) dēdecus nt, ignōminia f; **it shames** pudet (+ acc of person, gen of thing); **it is a ~** flāgitium est ▸ vt rubōrem incutere (dat) ▸ interj prō pudor!

shamefaced adj verēcundus

shameful adj ignōminiōsus, turpis

shamefully adv turpiter

shameless adj impudēns

shamelessly adv impudenter

shamelessness n impudentia f

shank n crūs nt

shape n fōrma f, figūra f ▸ vt fōrmāre, fingere; (fig) īnfōrmāre ▸ vi: **~ well** prōficere

shapeless adj īnfōrmis, dēfōrmis

shapelessness n dēfōrmitās f

shapeliness n fōrma f

shapely adj fōrmōsus

shard n testa f

share n pars f; (plough) vōmer m; **go shares with** inter sē partīrī ▸ vt (give) partīrī, impertīre; (have) commūnicāre, participem esse (gen)

sharer n particeps m/f, socius m

shark n volpēs marīna f

sharp adj acūtus; (fig) ācer, acūtus; (bitter) amārus

sharpen vt acuere; (fig) exacuere

sharply adv ācriter, acūtē

sharpness n aciēs f; (mind) acūmen nt, argūtiae fpl; (temper) acerbitās f

shatter vt quassāre, perfringere, adflīgere; (fig) frangere

shave vt rādere; **~ off** abrādere

shavings n rāmenta ntpl

she pron haec, ea, illa

sheaf n manipulus m

shear vt tondēre, dētondēre

shears n forficēs fpl

sheath n vāgīna f

sheathe vt recondere

shed vt fundere; (blood) effundere; (one's own) profundere; (tears) effundere; (covering) exuere; **~ light on** (fig) lūmen adhibēre (dat)

sheen n nitor m

sheep n ovis f; (flock) pecus m

sheepfold n ovīle nt

sheepish adj pudibundus

sheepishly adv pudenter

sheer adj (absolute) merus; (steep) praeruptus

sheet n (cloth) linteum nt; (metal) lāmina f; (paper) carta f, scheda f; (sail) pēs m; (water) aequor nt

shelf n pluteus m, pēgma nt

shell n concha f; (egg) putāmen nt; (tortoise) testa f

shellfish n conchȳlium f

shelter n suffugium nt, tegmen nt; (refuge) perfugium nt, asȳlum nt; (lodging) hospitium nt; (fig) umbra f ▸ vt tegere, dēfendere; (refugee) excipere ▸ vi latēre; **~ behind** (fig) dēlitēscere in (abl)

sheltered adj (life) umbrātilis

shelve vt differre ▸ vi sē dēmittere

shelving adj dēclīvis

shepherd n pastor m

shield n scūtum nt; clipeus m; (small) parma f; (fig) praesidium nt ▸ vt prōtegere, dēfendere

shift n (change) mūtātiō f; (expedient) ars f, dolus m; **make ~ to** efficere ut; **in shifts** per vicēs ▸ vt mūtāre; (move) movēre ▸ vi mūtārī; discēdere

shiftless adj iners, inops

shifty adj vafer, versūtus

shilling n solidus m

shimmer vi micāre ▸ n tremulum lūmen nt

shin n tībia f

shine vi lūcēre, fulgēre; (reflecting) nitēre; (fig) ēminēre; **~ forth** ēlūcēre, ēnitēre, effulgēre; **~ upon** adfulgēre (dat) ▸ n nitor m

shingle n lapillī mpl, glārea f

shining adj lūcidus, splendidus; (fig) illūstris

shiny adj nitidus
ship n nāvis f; **admiral's ~** nāvis praetōria;
  decked ~ nāvis tēcta, nāvis cōnstrāta ▶ vt
  (cargo) impōnere; (to a place) nāvī invehere
shipowner n nāviculārius m
shipping n nāvēs fpl
shipwreck n naufragium nt; **suffer ~**
  naufragium facere
shipwrecked adj naufragus
shirk vt dēfugere, dētrectāre
shirt n subūcula f
shiver n horror m ▶ vi horrēre, tremere ▶ vt
  perfringere, comminuere
shivering n horror m
shoal n (fish) exāmen nt; (water) vadum nt;
  shoals pl brevia ntpl
shock n impulsus m; (battle) concursus m,
  cōnflictus m; (hair) caesariēs f; (mind) offēnsiō f
  ▶ vt percutere, offendere
shocking adj atrōx, dētestābilis, flāgitiōsus
shoddy adj vīlis
shoe n calceus m
shoemaker n sūtor m
shoot n surculus m; (vine) pampinus m ▶ vi
  frondēscere; (movement) volāre; **~ up** ēmicāre
  ▶ vt (missile) conicere, iaculārī; (person) iaculārī,
  trānsfīgere
shop n taberna f
shore n lītus nt, ōra f ▶ vt fulcīre
short adj brevis; (broken) curtus; (amount)
  exiguus; **for a ~ time** parumper, paulisper; **~ of**
  (number) intrā (acc); **be ~ of** indigēre (abl); **cut ~**
  interpellāre; **in ~** ad summam, dēnique; **very ~**
  perbrevis; **fall ~ of** nōn pervenīre ad, abesse ab;
  run ~ dēficere; **to cut a long story ~** nē multīs
  morer, nē multa
shortage n inopia f
shortcoming n dēlictum nt, culpa f
short cut n via compendiāria f
shorten vt curtāre, imminuere, contrahere;
  (sail) legere
shorthand n notae fpl
shorthand writer n āctuārius m
short-lived adj brevis
shortly adv (time) brevī; (speak) breviter; **~ after**
  paulō post, nec multō post
shortness n brevitās f, exiguitās f; (difficulty)
  angustiae fpl
short-sighted adj (fig) imprōvidus, imprūdēns
short-sightedness n imprūdentia f
short-tempered adj īrācundus
shot n ictus m; (range) iactus m
should vi (duty) dēbēre
shoulder n umerus m; (animal) armus m ▶ vt
  (burden) suscipere
shout n clāmor m, adclāmātiō f ▶ vt, vi clāmāre,
  vōciferārī; **~ down** obstrepere (dat); **~ out**
  exclāmāre
shove vt trūdere, impellere
shovel n rutrum nt
show n speciēs f; (entertainment) lūdī mpl,
  spectāculum nt; (stage) lūdicrum nt; **for ~** in

speciem; **put on a ~** spectācula dare ▶ vt
  mōnstrāre, indicāre, ostendere, ostentāre;
  (point out) dēmōnstrāre; (qualities) praestāre;
  ~ off vi sē iactāre ▶ vt ostentāre
shower n imber m ▶ vt fundere, conicere
showery adj pluvius
showiness n ostentātiō f
showing off n iactātiō f
showy adj speciōsus
shred n fragmentum nt, minūtātim;
  tear to shreds dīlaniāre ▶ vt concīdere
shrew n virāgō f
shrewd adj acūtus, ācer, sagāx
shrewdly adv acūtē, sagāciter
shrewdness n acūmen nt, sagācitās f
shriek n ululātus m ▶ vi ululāre
shrill adj acūtus, argūtus
shrine n fānum nt, dēlubrum nt
shrink vt contrahere ▶ vi contrahī; **~ from**
  abhorrēre ab, refugere ab, dētrectāre
shrivel vt corrūgāre ▶ vi exārēscere
shroud n integumentum nt; **shrouds** pl
  rudentēs mpl ▶ vt involvere
shrub n frutex m
shrubbery n fruticētum nt
shudder n horror m ▶ vi exhorrēscere; **~ at**
  horrēre
shuffle vt miscēre ▶ vi claudicāre; (fig)
  tergiversārī
shun vt vītāre, ēvītāre, dēfugere
shut vt claudere; (with cover) operīre; (hand)
  comprimere; **~ in** inclūdere; **~ off** interclūdere;
  ~ out exclūdere; **~ up** inclūdere
shutter n foricula f, lūmināre nt
shuttle n radius m
shy adj timidus, pudibundus, verēcundus
shyly adv timidē, verēcundē
shyness n verēcundia f
sibyl n sibylla f
sick adj aeger, aegrōtus; **be ~** aegrōtāre; **feel ~**
  nauseāre; **I am ~ of** mē taedet (gen)
sicken vt fastīdium movēre (dat) ▶ vi nauseāre,
  aegrōtāre
sickle n falx f
sickly adj invalidus
sickness n nausea f; (illness) morbus m,
  aegritūdō f
side n latus nt; (direction) pars f; (faction) partēs
  fpl; (kin) genus nt; **on all sides** undique; **on both
  sides** utrimque; **on one ~** ūnā ex parte; **on our ~**
  ā nōbīs; **be on the ~ of** stāre ab, sentīre cum; **on
  the far ~ of** ultrā (acc); **on this ~** hīnc; **on
  this ~ of** cis (acc), citrā (acc) ▶ vi: **~ with** stāre ab,
  facere cum
sideboard n abacus m
sidelong adj oblīquus
sideways adv oblīquē, in oblīquum
sidle vi oblīquō corpore incēdere
siege n obsidiō f, oppugnātiō f; **lay ~ to** obsidēre
siege works npl opera ntpl
siesta n merīdiātiō f; **take a ~** merīdiāre
sieve n crībrum nt

sigh n suspīrium nt; (loud) gemitus m ▶ vi suspīrāre, gemere

sight n (sense) vīsus m; (process) aspectus m; (range) cōnspectus m; (thing seen) spectāculum nt, speciēs f; **at** ~ ex tempore; **at first** ~ prīmō aspectū; **in** ~ in cōnspectū; **come into** ~ in cōnspectum sē dare; **in the** ~ **of** in oculīs (gen); **catch** ~ **of** cōnspicere; **lose** ~ **of** ē cōnspectū āmittere; (fig) oblīvīscī (gen) ▶ vt cōnspicārī

sightless adj caecus

sightly adj decōrus

sign n signum nt, indicium nt; (distinction) īnsigne nt; (mark) nota f; (trace) vestīgium nt; (proof) documentum nt; (portent) ōmen nt; (Zodiac) signum nt; **give a** ~ innuere ▶ vi signum dare, innuere ▶ vt subscrībere (dat); (as witness) obsignāre

signal n signum nt; **give the** ~ **for retreat** receptuī canere ▶ vi signum dare ▶ adj īnsignis, ēgregius

signalize vt nōbilitāre

signally adv ēgregiē

signature n nōmen nt, manus f, chīrographum nt

signet n signum nt

signet ring n anulus m

significance n interpretātiō f, significātiō f, vīs f; (importance) pondus nt

significant adj gravis, clārus

signification n significātiō f

signify vt significāre, velle; (omen) portendere; **it does not** ~ nōn interest

silence n silentium nt; **in** ~ per silentium ▶ vt comprimere; (argument) refūtāre

silent adj tacitus; (habit) taciturnus; **be** ~ silēre, tacēre; **be** ~ **about** silēre, tacēre; **become** ~ conticēscere

silently adv tacitē

silhouette n adumbrātiō f

silk n bombȳx m; (clothes) sērica ntpl ▶ adj bombȳcinus, sēricus

silken adj bombȳcinus

sill n līmen nt

silliness n stultitia f, ineptiae fpl

silly adj fatuus, ineptus; stultus; **be** ~ dēsipere

silt n līmus m

silver n argentum nt ▶ adj argenteus

silver mine n argentāria f

silver plate n argentum nt

silver-plated adj argentātus

silvery adj argenteus

similar adj similis

similarity n similitūdō f

similarly adv similiter

simile n similitūdō f

simmer vi lēniter fervēre

simper vi molliter subrīdēre

simple adj simplex; (mind) fatuus; (task) facilis

simpleton n homō ineptus m

simplicity n simplicitās f; (mind) stultitia f

simplify vt faciliōrem reddere

simply adv simpliciter; (merely) sōlum, tantum

simulate vt simulāre

simulation n simulātiō f

simultaneously adv simul, ūnā, eōdem tempore

sin n peccātum nt, nefās nt, dēlictum nt ▶ vi peccāre

since adv abhinc; **long** ~ iamdūdum ▶ conj (time) ex quō tempore, postquam; (reason) cum (subj), quōniam; ~ **he** quippe quī ▶ prep ab (abl), ex (abl), post (acc); **ever** ~ usque ab

sincere adj sincērus, simplex, apertus

sincerely adv sincērē, ex animō

sincerity n fidēs f, simplicitās f

sinew n nervus m

sinewy adj nervōsus

sinful adj improbus, impius, incestus

sinfully adv improbē, impiē

sing vt canere, cantāre; ~ **of** canere

singe vt adūrere

singer n cantor m

singing n cantus m ▶ adj canōrus

single adj ūnus, sōlus, ūnicus; (unmarried) caelebs ▶ vt: ~ **out** ēligere, excerpere

single-handed adj ūnus

singly adv singillātim, singulī

singular adj singulāris; (strange) novus

singularly adv singulāriter, praecipuē

sinister adj īnfaustus, malevolus

sink vi dēsīdere; (in water) dēmergī; ~ **in** inlābī, īnsīdere ▶ vt dēprimere, mergere; (well) fodere; (fig) dēmergere

sinless adj integer, innocēns, castus

sinner n peccātor m

sinuous adj sinuōsus

sip vt gustāre, lībāre

siphon n siphō m

sir n (to master) ere; (to equal) vir optime; (title) eques m

sire n pater m

siren n sīrēn f

sirocco n Auster m

sister n soror f; **sister's** sorōrius

sisterhood n germānitās f; (society) sorōrum societās f

sister-in-law n glōs f

sisterly adj sorōrius

sit vi sedēre; **sit beside** adsidēre (dat); **sit down** cōnsīdere; **sit on** īnsidēre (dat); (eggs) incubāre; **sit at table** accumbere; **sit up** (at night) vigilāre

site n situs m, locus m; (for building) ārea f

sitting n sessiō f

situated adj situs

situation n situs m; (circumstances) status m, condiciō f

six num sex; **six each** sēnī; **six or seven** sex septem; **six times** sexiēns

six hundred num sēscentī; **six hundred each** sēscēnī; **six hundred times** sēscentiēns

six hundredth adj sēscentēsimus

sixteen num sēdecim; ~ **each** sēnī dēnī; ~ **times** sēdeciēns

sixteenth adj sextus decimus

sixth adj sextus; **for the ~ time** sextum
sixtieth adj sexāgēsimus
sixty num sexāgintā; **~ each** sexāgēnī; **~ times** sexāgiēns
size n māgnitūdō f, amplitūdō f; (*measure*) mēnsūra f, fōrma f
skate vi per glaciem lābī; **~ on thin ice** (*fig*) incēdere per ignēs suppositōs cinerī dolōsō
skein n glomus nt
skeleton n ossa ntpl
sketch n adumbrātiō f, dēscrīptiō f ▶ vt adumbrāre, īnfōrmāre
skewer n verū nt
skiff n scapha f, lēnunculus m
skilful adj perītus, doctus, scītus; (*with hands*) habilis
skilfully adv perītē, doctē; habiliter
skill n ars f, perītia f, sollertia f
skilled adj perītus, doctus; **~ in** perītus (*gen*)
skim vt dēspūmāre; **~ over** (*fig*) legere, perstringere
skin n cutis f; (*animal*) pellis f ▶ vt pellem dētrahere (*dat*)
skinflint n avārus m
skinny adj macer
skip vi exsultāre ▶ vt praeterīre
skipper n magister m
skirmish n leve proelium nt ▶ vi vēlitārī
skirmisher n vēles m, excursor m
skirt n īnstita f; (*border*) limbus m ▶ vt contingere (*dat*); (*motion*) legere
skittish adj lascīvus
skulk vi latēre, dēlitēscere
skull n caput nt
sky n caelum nt; **of the sky** caelestis
skylark n alauda f
slab n tabula f
slack adj remissus, laxus; (*work*) piger, neglegēns
slacken vt remittere, dētendere ▶ vi laxārī
slackness n remissiō f; pigritia f
slag n scōria f
slake vt restinguere, sēdāre
slam vt adflīgere
slander n maledicta ntpl, obtrectātiō f; (*LAW*) calumnia f ▶ vt maledīcere (*dat*), īnfāmāre, obtrectāre (*dat*)
slanderer n obtrectātor m
slanderous adj maledicus
slang n vulgāria verba ntpl
slant vi in trānsversum īre
slanting adj oblīquus, trānsversus
slantingly adv oblīquē, ex trānsversō
slap n alapa f ▶ vt palmā ferīre
slapdash adj praeceps, temerārius
slash vt caedere ▶ n ictus m
slate n (*roof*) tēgula f; (*writing*) tabula f ▶ vt increpāre
slatternly adj sordidus, incōmptus
slaughter n caedēs f, strāgēs f ▶ vt trucīdāre
slaughterhouse n laniēna f

slave n servus m; (*domestic*) famulus m; (*home-born*) verna m; **be a ~ to** īnservīre (*dat*); **household slaves** familia f
slave girl n ancilla f
slavery n servitūs f
slavish adj servīlis
slavishly adv servīliter
slay vt interficere, occīdere
slayer n interfector m
sleek adj nitidus, pinguis
sleep n somnus m; **go to ~** obdormīscere ▶ vi dormīre; **~ off** vt ēdormīre
sleeper n dormītor m
sleepiness n sopor m
sleepless adj īnsomnis, vigil
sleeplessness n īnsomnia f
sleepy adj somniculōsus; **be ~** dormītāre
sleeve n manica f
sleight of hand n praestīgiae fpl
slender adj gracilis, exīlis
slenderness n gracilitās f
slice n frūstum nt ▶ vt secāre
slide n lāpsus m ▶ vi lābī
slight adj levis, exiguus, parvus ▶ n neglegentia f ▶ vt neglegere, offendere
slightingly adv contemptim
slightly adv leviter, paululum
slightness n levitās f
slim adj gracilis
slime n līmus m
slimness n gracilitās f
slimy adj līmōsus, mūcōsus
sling n funda f ▶ vt mittere, iaculārī
slinger n funditor m
slink vi sē subdūcere
slip n lāpsus m; (*mistake*) offēnsiuncula f; (*plant*) surculus m ▶ vi lābī; **~ away** ēlābī, dīlābī; **~ out** ēlābī; (*word*) excidere; **give the ~ to** ēlūdere; **let ~** āmittere, ēmittere; (*opportunity*) ōmittere; **there's many a ~ twixt the cup and the lip** inter ōs et offam multa interveniunt
slipper n solea f
slippery adj lūbricus
slipshod adj neglegēns
slit n rīma f ▶ vt findere, incīdere
sloe n spīnus m
slope n dēclīve nt, clīvus m; (*steep*) dēiectus m ▶ vi sē dēmittere, vergere
sloping adj dēclīvis, dēvexus; (*up*) adclīvis
slot n rīma f
sloth n inertia f, segnitia f, dēsidia f, ignāvia f
slothful adj ignāvus, iners, segnis
slothfully adv ignāvē, segniter
slouch vi languidē incēdere
slough n (*skin*) exuviae fpl; (*bog*) palūs f
slovenliness n ignāvia f, sordēs fpl
slovenly adj ignāvus, sordidus
slow adj tardus, lentus; (*mind*) hebes
slowly adv tardē, lentē
slowness n tarditās f
sludge n līmus m
slug n līmāx f

sluggard n homō ignāvus m
sluggish adj piger, segnis; (mind) hebes
sluggishly adv pigrē, segniter
sluggishness n pigritia f, inertia f
sluice n cataracta f
slumber n somnus m, sopor m ▶ vi dormīre
slump n vīlis annōna f
slur n nota f; **cast ~ on** dētrectāre ▶ vt: **~ words** balbūtīre
sly adj astūtus, vafer, callidus; **on the sly** ex opīnātō
slyly adv astūtē, callidē
slyness n astūtia f
smack n (blow) ictus m; (with hand) alapa f; (boat) lēnunculus m; (taste) sapor m ▶ vt ferīre ▶ vi: **~ of** olēre, redolēre
small adj parvus, exiguus; (gathering) īnfrequēns; **how ~** quantulus, quantillus; **so ~** tantulus; **very ~** perexiguus, minimus
smaller adj minor
smallest adj minimus
smallness n exiguitās f, brevitās f
small talk n sermunculus m
smart adj (action) ācer, alacer; (dress) concinnus, nitidus; (pace) vēlōx; (wit) facētus, salsus ▶ n dolor m ▶ vi dolēre; (fig) ūrī, mordērī
smartly adv ācriter; nitidē; vēlōciter; facētē
smartness n alacritās f; (dress) nitor m; (wit) facētiae fpl, sollertia f
smash n ruīna f ▶ vt frangere, comminuere
smattering n: **get a ~ of** odōrārī, prīmīs labrīs attingere; **with a ~ of** imbūtus (abl)
smear vt oblinere, ungere
smell n (sense) odōrātus m; (odour) odor m; (of cooking) nīdor m ▶ vt olfacere, odōrārī ▶ vi olēre
smelly adj olidus
smelt vt fundere
smile n rīsus m ▶ vi subrīdēre; **~ at** adrīdēre (dat); **~ upon** rīdēre ad; (fig) secundum esse (dat)
smiling adj laetus
smirk vi subrīdēre
smith n faber m
smithy n fabrica f
smock n tunica f
smoke n fūmus m ▶ vi fūmāre
smoky adj fūmōsus
smooth adj lēvis; (skin) glaber; (talk) blandus; (sea) placidus; (temper) aequus; (voice) lēvis, teres ▶ vt sternere, līmāre
smoothly adv lēviter, lēnīter
smoothness n lēvitās f, lēnitās f
smother vt opprimere, suffocāre
smoulder vi fūmāre
smudge n macula f
smug adj suī contentus
smuggle vt fūrtim importāre
smugness n amor suī m
smut n fūlīgō f
snack n cēnula f; **take a ~** gustāre
snag n impedīmentum nt, scrūpulus m
snail n cochlea f
snake n anguis m, serpēns f

snaky adj vīpereus
snap vt rumpere, praerumpere; **~ the fingers** digitīs concrepāre ▶ vi rumpī, dissilīre; **~ at** mordēre; **~ up** corripere
snare n laqueus m, plaga f, pedica f ▶ vt inrētīre
snarl n gannītus m ▶ vi gannīre
snatch vt rapere, ēripere, adripere, corripere; **~ at** captāre
sneak n perfidus m ▶ vi conrēpere; **~ in sē** īnsinuāre; **~ out** ēlābī
sneaking adj humilis, fūrtīvus
sneer n irrīsiō f ▶ vi irrīdēre, dērīdēre
sneeze n sternūtāmentum nt ▶ vi sternuere
sniff vt odōrārī
snip vt praecīdere, secāre
snob n homō ambitiōsus m
snood n mitra f
snooze vi dormītāre
snore vi stertere
snoring n rhoncus m
snort n fremitus m ▶ vi fremere
snout n rōstrum nt
snow n nix f ▶ vi ningere; **snowed under** nive obrutus; **it is snowing** ningit
snowy adj nivālis; (colour) niveus
snub vt neglegere, praeterīre
snub-nosed adj sīmus
snuff n (candle) fungus m
snug adj commodus
snugly adv commodē
so adv (referring back) sīc; (referring forward) ita; (with adj and adv) tam; (with verb) adeō; (consequence) ergō, itaque, igitur; **and so** itaque; **so great** tantus; **so-so** sīc; **so as to ut; so be it** estō; **so big** tantus; **so far** usque adeō, adhūc; **so far as** quod; **so far from** adeō nōn; **so little** tantillus; **so long as** dum; **so many** tot; **so much** adj tantus ▶ adv tantum; (with compar) tantō; **so often** totiēns; **so that** ut (subj); **so that ... not** (purpose) nē; (result) ut nōn; **and so on** deinceps; **not so very** haud ita; **say so** id dīcere
soak vt imbuere, madefacere
soaking adj madidus
soap n sāpō m
soar vi in sublīme ferrī, subvolāre; **~ above** superāre
sob n singultus m ▶ vi singultāre
sober adj sobrius; (conduct) modestus; (mind) sānus
soberly adv sobriē, modestē
sobriety n modestia f, continentia f
so-called adj quī dīcitur
sociability n facilitās f
sociable adj facilis, cōmis
sociably adv faciliter, cōmiter
social adj sociālis, commūnis
socialism n populāris ratiō f
socialist n homō populāris m/f
society n societās f; (class) optimātēs mpl; (being with) convīctus m; **cultivate the ~ of** adsectārī; **secret ~** sodālitās f

sod n caespes m, glaeba f
soda n nitrum nt
sodden adj madidus
soever adv -cumque
sofa n lectus m
soft adj mollis; (fruit) mītis; (voice) submissus; (character) dēlicātus; (words) blandus
soften vt mollīre; (body) ēnervāre; (emotion) lēnīre, mītigāre ▸ vi mollēscere, mītēscere
soft-hearted adj misericors
softly adv molliter, lēniter; blandē
softness n mollitia f, mollitiēs f
soil n solum nt, humus f ▸ vt inquināre, foedāre
sojourn n commorātiō f, mānsiō f ▸ vi commorārī
sojourner n hospes m, hospita f
solace n sōlātium nt, levātiō f ▸ vt sōlārī, cōnsōlārī
solar adj sōlis
solder n ferrūmen nt ▸ vt ferrūmināre
soldier n mīles m; **be a ~** mīlitāre; **common ~** manipulāris mīles m; **gregārius mīles** m; **fellow ~** commīlitō m; **foot ~** pedes m; **old ~** veterānus m ▸ vi mīlitāre
soldierly adj mīlitāris
soldiery n mīles m
sole adj sōlus, ūnus, ūnicus ▸ n (foot) planta f; (fish) solea f
solecism n soloecismus m
solely adv sōlum, tantum, modō
solemn adj gravis; (religion) sanctus
solemnity n gravitās f; sanctitās f
solemnize vt agere
solemnly adv graviter; rītē
solicit vt flāgitāre, obsecrāre
solicitation n flāgitātiō f
solicitor n advocātus m
solicitous adj anxius, trepidus
solicitously adv anxiē, trepidē
solicitude n cūra f, anxietās f
solid adj solidus; (metal) pūrus; (food) firmus; (argument) firmus; (character) cōnstāns, spectātus; **become ~** concrēscere; **make ~** cōgere
solidarity n societās f
solidify vt cōgere ▸ vi concrēscere
solidity n soliditās f
solidly adv firmē, cōnstanter
soliloquize vi sēcum loquī
soliloquy n ūnīus ōrātiō f
solitary adj sōlus, sōlitārius; (instance) ūnicus; (place) dēsertus
solitude n sōlitūdō f
solo n canticum nt
solstice n (summer) sōlstitium nt; (winter) brūma f
solstitial adj sōlstitiālis, brūmālis
soluble adj dissolūbilis
solution n (of puzzle) ēnōdātiō f
solve vt ēnōdāre, explicāre
solvency n solvendī facultās f
solvent adj: **be ~** solvendō esse

sombre adj obscūrus; (fig) tristis
some adj aliquī; (pl) nonnūllī, aliquot; **~ people** sunt quī (subj); **~ ... other** alius ... alius; **for ~ time** aliquamdiū; **with ~ reason** nōn sine causā ▸ pron aliquis; (pl) nonnūllī, sunt quī (subj), erant quī (subj)
somebody pron aliquis; **~ or other** nescioquis
somehow adv quōdammodō, nescio quōmodō
someone pron aliquis; (negative) quisquam; **~ or other** nescioquis; **~ else** alius
something pron aliquid; **~ or other** nescioquid; **~ else** aliud
sometime adv aliquandō; (past) quondam
sometimes adv interdum, nonnumquam; **~ ... ~** modo ... modo
somewhat adv aliquantum, nōnnihil, paulum; (with compar) paulō, aliquantō
somewhere adv alicubi; (to) aliquō; **~ else** alibī; (to) aliō; **from ~** alicunde; **from ~ else** aliunde
somnolence n somnus m
somnolent adj sēmisomnus
son n fīlius m; **small son** fīliolus m
song n carmen nt, cantus m
son-in-law n gener m
sonorous adj sonōrus, canōrus
soon adv mox, brevi, citō; **as ~ as** ut prīmum, cum prīmum (+ fut perf), simul āc/atque (+ perf indic); **as possible** quam prīmum; **too ~** praemātūrē, ante tempus
sooner adv prius, mātūrius; (preference) libentius, potius; **~ or later** sērius ōcius; **no ~ said than done** dictum factum
soonest adv mātūrissimē
soot n fūlīgō f
soothe vt dēlēnīre, permulcēre
soothing adj lēnis, blandus
soothingly adv blandē
soothsayer n hariolus m, vātēs m/f, haruspex m
sooty adj fūmōsus
sop n offa f; (fig) dēlēnīmentum m
sophism n captiō f
sophist n sophistēs m
sophistical adj acūleātus, captiōsus
sophisticated adj lepidus, urbānus
sophistry n captiō f
soporific adj sopōrifer, somnifer
soprano adj acūtus
sorcerer n veneficus m
sorceress n venefica f, saga f
sorcery n venēficium nt; (means) venēna ntpl, carmina ntpl
sordid adj sordidus; (conduct) illīberālis
sordidly adv sordidē
sordidness n sordēs fpl; illīberālitās f
sore adj molestus, gravis, acerbus; **feel ~** dolēre ▸ n ulcus nt
sorely adv graviter, vehementer
sorrel n lapathus f, lapathum nt
sorrow n dolor m, aegritūdō f; (outward) maeror m; (for death) lūctus m ▸ vi dolēre, maerere, lūgēre

sorrowful adj maestus, tristis
sorrowfully adv maestē
sorry adj paenitēns; (poor) miser; **I am ~ for** (remorse) mē paenitet, mē piget (gen); (pity) mē miseret (gen)
sort n genus nt; **a ~ of** quīdam; **all sorts of** omnēs; **the ~ of** tālis; **this ~ of** huiusmodī; **the common ~** plēbs f; **I am not the ~ of man to** nōn is sum quī (subj); **I am out of sorts** mihī displiceō ▶ vt dīgerere, compōnere; (votes) diribēre
sortie n excursiō f, excursus m, ēruptiō f; **make a ~** ērumpere, excurrere
sot n ēbriōsus m
sottish adj ēbriōsus, tēmulentus
sottishness n vīnolentia f
soul n anima f, animus m; (essence) vīs f; (person) caput nt; **not a ~** nēmō ūnus; **the ~ of** (fig) medulla f
soulless adj caecus, dūrus
sound n sonitus m, sonus m; (articulate) vōx f; (confused) strepitus m; (loud) fragor m; (strait) fretum nt ▶ vt (signal) canere; (instrument) īnflāre; (depth) scrūtārī, temptāre; (person) animum temptāre (gen) ▶ vi canere, sonāre; (seem) vidērī; **~ a retreat** receptuī canere ▶ adj sānus, salūbris; (health) firmus; (sleep) artus; (judgment) exquīsītus; (argument) vērus; **safe and ~** salvus, incolumis
soundly adv (beat) vehementer; (sleep) artē; (study) penitus, dīligenter
soundness n sānitās f, integritās f
soup n iūs nt
sour adj acerbus, amārus, acidus; **turn ~** acēscere; (fig) coacēscere ▶ vt (fig) exacerbāre
source n fōns m; (river) caput nt; (fig) fōns m, orīgō f; **have its ~ in** orīrī ex; (fig) proficīscī ex
sourness n acerbitās f; (temper) mōrōsitās f
souse vt immergere
south n merīdiēs f ▶ adj austrālis ▶ adv ad merīdiem
south-east adv inter sōlis ortum et merīdiem
southerly adj ad merīdiem versus
southern adj austrālis
south-west adv inter occāsum sōlis et merīdiem
south wind n auster m
souvenir n monumentum nt
sovereign n rēx m, rēgīna f ▶ adj prīnceps, summus
sovereignty n rēgnum nt, imperium nt, prīncipātus m; (of the people) māiestās f
sow¹ n scrōfa f, sūs f
sow² vt serere; (field) cōnserere ▶ vi sementem facere
sower n sator m
sowing n sēmentis f
spa n aquae fpl
space n (extension) spatium nt; (not matter) ināne nt; (room) locus m; (distance) intervallum nt; (time) spatium nt; **open ~** ārea f; **leave a ~ of** intermittere ▶ vt: **~ out** dispōnere

spacious adj amplus, capāx
spaciousness n amplitūdō f
spade n pāla f, rūtrum nt
span n (measure) palmus m; (extent) spatium nt ▶ vt iungere
spangle n bractea f
spangled adj distinctus
spar n tignum nt
spare vt parcere (dat); (to give) suppeditāre; **~ time for** vacāre (dat) ▶ adj exīlis; (extra) subsecīvus
sparing adj parcus
sparingly adv parcē
spark n scintilla f; (fig) igniculus m
sparkle vi scintillāre, nitēre, micāre
sparrow n passer m
sparse adj rārus
spasm n convulsiō f
spasmodically adv interdum
spatter vt aspergere
spawn n ōva ntpl
speak vt, vi loquī; (make speech) dīcere, contiōnārī, ōrātiōnem habēre; **~ out** ēloquī; **~ to** adloquī; (converse) colloquī cum; **~ well of** bene dīcere (dat); **it speaks for itself** rēs ipsa loquitur
speaker n ōrātor m
speaking n: **art of ~** dīcendī ars f; **practise public ~** dēclāmāre ▶ adj: **likeness ~** vīvida imāgō
spear n hasta f
spearman n hastātus m
special adj praecipuus, proprius
speciality n proprium nt
specially adv praecipuē, praesertim
species n genus nt
specific adj certus
specification n dēsignātiō f
specify vt dēnotāre, dēsignāre
specimen n exemplar nt, exemplum nt
specious adj speciōsus
speciously adv speciōsē
speciousness n speciēs f
speck n macula f
speckled adj maculīs distinctus
spectacle n spectāculum nt
spectacular adj spectābilis
spectator n spectātor m
spectral adj larvālis
spectre n larva f
speculate vi cōgitāre, coniectūrās facere; (COMM) forō ūtī
speculation n cōgitātiō f, coniectūra f; (COMM) ālea f
speculator n contemplātor m; (COMM) āleātor m
speech n ōrātiō f; (language) sermō m, lingua f; (to people or troops) cōntiō f; **make a ~** ōrātiōnem/cōntiōnem habēre
speechless adj ēlinguis, mūtus
speed n celeritās f, cursus m, vēlōcitās f; **with all ~** summā celeritāte; **at full ~** māgnō cursū,

speedily *adv* celeriter, citō
speedy *adj* celer, vēlōx, citus
spell *n* carmen *nt*
spellbound *adj*: be ~ obstipēscere
spelt *n* far *nt*
spend *vt* impendere, īnsūmere; (*public money*) ērogāre; (*time*) agere, cōnsūmere, terere; (*strength*) effundere; ~ **itself** (*storm*) dēsaevīre; ~ **on** īnsūmere (*acc and dat*)
spendthrift *n* nepōs *m*, prōdigus *m*
sphere *n* globus *m*; (*of action*) prōvincia *f*
spherical *adj* globōsus
sphinx *n* sphinx *f*
spice *n* condīmentum *nt*; **spices** *pl* odōrēs *mpl* ▶ *vt* condīre
spicy *adj* odōrātus; (*wit*) salsus
spider *n* arānea *f*; **spider's web** arāneum *nt*
spike *n* dēns *m*, clāvus *m*
spikenard *n* nardus *m*
spill *vt* fundere, profundere ▶ *vi* redundāre
spin *vt* (*thread*) nēre, dēdūcere; (*top*) versāre; ~ **out** (*story*) prōdūcere ▶ *vi* circumagī, versārī
spindle *n* fūsus *m*
spine *n* spīna *f*
spineless *adj* ēnervātus
spinster *n* virgō *f*
spiral *adj* intortus ▶ *n* spīra *f*
spire *n* cōnus *m*
spirit *n* (*life*) anima *f*; (*intelligence*) mēns *f*; (*soul*) animus *m*; (*vivacity*) spīritus *m*, vigor *m*, vīs *f*; (*character*) ingenium *nt*; (*intention*) voluntās *f*; (*of an age*) mōrēs *mpl*; (*ghost*) anima *f*; **spirits** *pl* mānēs *mpl*; **full of** ~ alacer, animōsus
spirited *adj* animōsus, ācer
spiritless *adj* iners, frāctus, timidus
spiritual *adj* animī
spit *n* verū *nt* ▶ *vi* spuere, spūtāre; ~ **on** cōnspūtāre; ~ **out** exspuere
spite *n* invidia *f*, malevolentia *f*, līvor *m*; **in** ~ **of me** mē invītō; **in** ~ **of the difficulties** in his angustiīs ▶ *vt* incommodāre, offendere
spiteful *adj* malevolus, malignus, invidus
spitefully *adv* malevolē, malignē
spitefulness *n* malevolentia *f*
spittle *n* spūtum *nt*
splash *n* fragor *m* ▶ *vt* aspergere
spleen *n* splēn *m*; (*fig*) stomachus *m*
splendid *adj* splendidus, lūculentus; īnsignis; (*person*) amplus
splendidly *adv* splendidē, optimē
splendour *n* splendor *m*, fulgor *m*; (*fig*) lautitia *f*, adparātus *m*
splenetic *adj* stomachōsus
splice *vt* iungere
splint *n* ferula *f*
splinter *n* fragmentum *nt*, assula *f* ▶ *vt* findere
split *vt* findere ▶ *vi* dissilīre ▶ *adj* fissus ▶ *n* fissum *nt*; (*fig*) dissidium *nt*
splutter *vi* balbūtīre

spoil *n* praeda *f* ▶ *vt* (*rob*) spoliāre; (*mar*) corrumpere ▶ *vi* corrumpī
spoiler *n* spoliātor *m*; corruptor *m*
spoils *npl* spolia *ntpl*, exuviae *fpl*
spoke *n* radius *m*; **put a ~ in someone's wheel** inicere scrūpulum (*dat*)
spokesman *n* interpres *m*, ōrātor *m*
spoliation *n* spoliātiō *f*, dīreptiō *f*
spondee *n* spondēus *m*
sponge *n* spongia *f*
sponsor *n* spōnsor *m*; (*fig*) auctor *m*
spontaneity *n* impulsus *m*, voluntās *f*
spontaneous *adj* voluntārius
spontaneously *adv* suā sponte, ultrō
spoon *n* cochlear *nt*
sporadic *adj* rārus
sporadically *adv* passim
sport *n* lūdus *m*; (*in Rome*) campus *m*; (*fun*) iocus *m*; (*ridicule*) lūdibrium *nt*; **make ~ of** illūdere (*dat*) ▶ *vi* lūdere
sportive *adj* lascīvus
sportiveness *n* lascīvia *f*
sportsman *n* vēnātor *m*
sportsmanlike *adj* honestus, generōsus
spot *n* macula *f*; (*place*) locus *m*; (*dice*) pūnctum *nt*; **on the ~** īlicō ▶ *vt* maculāre; (*see*) animadvertere
spotless *adj* integer, pūrus; (*character*) castus
spotted *adj* maculōsus
spouse *n* coniunx *m/f*
spout *n* (*of jug*) ōs *nt*; (*pipe*) canālis *m* ▶ *vi* ēmicāre
sprain *vt* intorquēre
sprawl *vi* sē fundere
sprawling *adj* fūsus
spray *n* aspergō *f* ▶ *vt* aspergere
spread *vt* pandere, extendere; (*news*) dīvulgāre; (*infection*) vulgāre ▶ *vi* patēre; (*rumour*) mānāre, incrēbrēscere; (*feeling*) glīscere
spreadeagle *vt* dispandere
spreading *adj* (*tree*) patulus
spree *n* cōmissātiō *f*
sprig *n* virga *f*
sprightliness *n* alacritās *f*
sprightly *adj* alacer, hilaris
spring *n* (*season*) vēr *nt*; (*water*) fōns *m*; (*leap*) saltus *m* ▶ *vi* (*grow*) crēscere, ēnāscī; (*leap*) salīre; ~ **from** orīrī ex, proficīscī ex; ~ **on to** īnsilīre in (*acc*); ~ **up** exorīrī, exsilīre ▶ *vt*: ~ **a leak** rīmās agere; ~ **a surprise on** admīrātiōnem movēre (*dat*) ▶ *adj* vērnus
springe *n* laqueus *m*
sprinkle *vt* aspergere; ~ **on** īnspergere (*dat*)
sprint *vi* currere
sprout *n* surculus *m* ▶ *vi* fruticārī
spruce *adj* nitidus, concinnus
sprung *adj* ortus, oriundus
spume *n* spūma *f*
spur *n* calcar *nt*; ~ **of a hill** prōminēns collis; **on the** ~ **of the moment** ex tempore ▶ *vt* incitāre; ~ **the willing horse** currentem incitāre; ~ **on** concitāre
spurious *adj* falsus, fūcōsus, fictus

spurn vt spernere, aspernārī, respuere

spurt vi ēmicāre; (run) sē incitāre ▶ n impetus m

spy n speculātor m, explōrātor m ▶ vi speculārī ▶ vt cōnspicere; **spy out** explōrāre

squabble n iūrgium nt ▶ vi rixārī

squad n (MIL) decuria f

squadron n (cavalry) āla f, turma f; (ships) classis f

squalid adj sordidus, dēfōrmis

squall n procella f

squally adj procellōsus

squalor n sordēs fpl, squālor m

squander vt dissipāre, disperdere, effundere

squanderer n prōdigus m

square n quadrātum nt; (town) ārea f ▶ vt quadrāre; (account) subdūcere ▶ vi cōnstāre, congruere ▶ adj quadrātus

squash vt conterere, contundere

squat vi subsīdere ▶ adj brevis atque obēsus

squatter n (on land) agripeta m

squawk vi crōcīre

squeak n strīdor m ▶ vi strīdēre

squeal n vāgītus m ▶ vi vāgīre

squeamish adj fastīdiōsus; **feel ~** nauseāre, fastīdīre

squeamishness n fastīdium nt, nausea f

squeeze vt premere, comprimere; **~ out** exprimere

squint adj perversus ▶ n: **person with a ~** strabō m ▶ vi strabō esse

squinter n strabō m

squinting adj paetus

squire n armiger m; (landed) dominus m

squirm vi volūtārī

squirrel n sciūrus m

squirt vt ēicere, effundere ▶ vi ēmicāre

stab n ictus m, vulnus nt ▶ vt fodere, ferīre, percutere

stability n stabilitās f, firmitās f, cōnstantia f

stabilize vt stabilīre, firmāre

stable adj firmus, stabilis ▶ n stabulum nt, equīle nt; **shut the ~ door after the horse has bolted** clipeum post vulnera sūmere

stack n acervus m ▶ vt congerere, cumulāre

stadium n spatium nt

staff n scīpiō m, virga f; (augur's) lituus m; (officers) contubernālēs mpl

stag n cervus m

stage n pulpitum nt, proscēnium nt; (theatre) scēna f, theātrum nt; (scene of action) campus m; (of journey) iter nt; (of progress) gradus m ▶ adj scēnicus ▶ vt (play) dare, docēre

stage fright n horror m

stagger vi titubāre ▶ vt obstupefacere

stagnant adj iners

stagnate vi (fig) cessāre, refrīgēscere

stagnation n cessātiō f, torpor m

stagy adj scēnicus

staid adj sevērus, gravis

stain n macula f, lābēs f; (fig) dēdecus nt, ignōminia f ▶ vt maculāre, foedāre, contāmināre; **~ with** īnficere (abl)

stainless adj pūrus, integer

stair n scālae fpl, gradus mpl

staircase n scālae fpl

stake n pālus m, stīpes m; (pledge) pignus nt; **be at ~** agī, in discrīmine esse ▶ vt (wager) dēpōnere

stale adj obsolētus, effētus; (wine) vapidus

stalemate n: **reach a ~** ad incitās redigī

stalk n (corn) calamus m; (plant) stīpes m ▶ vi incēdere ▶ vt vēnārī, īnsidiārī (dat)

stall n (animal) stabulum nt; (seat) subsellium nt; (shop) taberna f ▶ vt stabulāre

stallion n equus m

stalwart adj ingēns, rōbustus, fortis

stamina n patientia f

stammer n haesitātiō f ▶ vi balbūtīre

stammering adj balbus

stamp n fōrma f; (mark) nota f, signum nt; (of feet) supplōsiō f ▶ vt imprimere; (coin) ferīre, signāre; (fig) inūrere; **~ one's feet** pedem supplōdere; **~ out** exstinguere

stampede n discursus m; (fig) pavor m ▶ vi discurrere; (fig) expavēscere

stance n status m

stanchion n columna f

stand n (position) statiō f; (platform) suggestus m; **make a ~** resistere, restāre ▶ vi stāre; (remain) manēre; (matters) sē habēre ▶ vt statuere; (tolerate) ferre, tolerāre; **~ against** resistere (dat); **~ aloof** abstāre; **~ by** adsistere (dat); (friend) adesse (dat); (promise) praestāre; **~ convicted** manifestum tenērī; **~ down** concēdere; **~ fast** cōnsistere; **~ one's ground** in locō perstāre; **~ for** (office) petere; (meaning) significāre; (policy) postulāre; **~ in awe of** in metū habēre; **~ in need of** indigēre (abl); **~ on** īnsistere in (abl); **~ on end** horrēre; **~ on one's dignity** gravitātem suam tuērī; **~ out** ēminēre, exstāre; (against) resistere (dat); (to sea) in altum prōvehī; **~ out of the way of** dēcēdere (dat); **~ over** (case) ampliāre; **~ still** cōnsistere, īnsistere; **~ to reason** sequī; **~ trial** reum fierī; **~ up** surgere, cōnsurgere; **~ up for** dēfendere, adesse (dat); **~ up to** respōnsāre (dat)

standard n (MIL) signum nt; (measure) nōrma f; **~ author** scrīptor classicus m; **up to ~** iūstus; **judge by the ~ of** referre ad

standard-bearer n signifer m

standing adj perpetuus ▶ n status m; (social) locus m, ōrdō m; **of long ~** inveterātus; **be of long ~** inveterāscere

stand-offish adj tēctus

standstill n: **be at a ~** haerēre, frīgēre; **bring to a ~** ad incitās redigere; **come to a ~** īnsistere

stanza n tetrastichon nt

staple n uncus m ▶ adj praecipuus

star n stēlla f, astrum nt; sīdus nt; **shooting stars** acontiae fpl

starboard adj dexter

starch n amylum nt

stare n obtūtus m ▶ vi intentīs oculīs intuērī, stupēre; **~ at** contemplārī

stark adj rigidus; simplex ▶ adv plānē, omnīnō

starling n sturnus m
starry adj stēllātus
start n initium nt; (movement) saltus m; (journey) profectiō f; ~ **a day's** ~ **on** diē antecēdere ▶ vt incipere, īnstituere; (game) excitāre; (process) movēre ▶ vi (with fright) resilīre; (journey) proficīscī; ~ **up** exsilīre
starting place n carcerēs mpl
startle vt excitāre, terrēre
starvation n famēs f
starve vi fame cōnficī; (cold) frīgēre ▶ vt fame ēnecāre
starveling n famēlicus m
state n (condition) status m, condiciō f; (pomp) adparātus m; (POL) cīvitās f, rēs pública f; **the ~ of affairs is** ita sē rēs habet; **I know the ~ of affairs** quō in locō rēs sit sciō; **of the ~** pública ▶ adj pública ▶ vt adfirmāre, expōnere, profitērī; ~ **one's case** causam dīcere
stateliness n māiestās f, gravitās f
stately adj gravis, grandis, nōbilis
statement n adfirmātiō f, dictum nt; (witness) testimōnium nt
state of health n valētūdō f
state of mind n adfectiō f
statesman n vir reī pública gerendae perītus m, cōnsilī pública auctor m
statesmanlike adj prūdēns
statesmanship n cīvīlis prūdentia f
static adj stabilis
station n locus m; (MIL) statiō f; (social) locus m, ōrdō m ▶ vt collocāre, pōnere; (in different places) dispōnere
stationary adj immōtus, statārius, stabilis
statistics n cēnsus m
statuary n fictor m
statue n statua f, signum nt, imāgō f
statuette n sigillum nt
stature n fōrma f, statūra f
status n locus m
status quo n: **restore the** ~ ad integrum restituere
statutable adj lēgitimus
statute n lēx f
staunch vt (blood) sistere ▶ adj fīdus, cōnstāns
stave vt perrumpere, perfringere; ~ **off** arcēre
stay n firmāmentum nt; (fig) columen nt; (sojourn) mānsiō f, commorātiō f ▶ vt (prop) fulcīre; (stop) dētinēre, dēmorārī ▶ vi manēre, commorārī
stead n locus m; **stand someone in good** ~ prōdesse (dat)
steadfast adj firmus, stabilis, cōnstāns; ~ **at home** tenēre sē domī
steadfastly adv cōnstanter
steadfastness n firmitās f, cōnstantia f
steadily adv firmē, cōnstanter
steadiness n stabilitās f; (fig) cōnstantia f
steady adj stabilis, firmus; (fig) gravis, cōnstāns
steak n offa f

steal vt surripere, fūrārī ▶ vi: ~ **away** sē subdūcere; ~ **over** subrēpere (dat); ~ **into** sē īnsinuāre in (acc); ~ **a march on** occupāre
stealing n fūrtum nt
stealth n fūrtum nt; **by** ~ fūrtim, clam
stealthily adv fūrtim, clam
stealthy adj fūrtīvus, clandestīnus
steam n aquae vapor m, fūmus m ▶ vi fūmāre
steed n equus m
steel n ferrum nt, chalybs m ▶ adj ferreus ▶ vt dūrāre; ~ **oneself** obdūrēscere
steely adj ferreus
steelyard n statēra f
steep adj arduus, praeceps, praeruptus; (slope) dēclīvis ▶ vt imbuere
steeple n turris f
steepness n arduum nt
steer vi, vt gubernāre, regere, dīrigere ▶ n iuvencus m
steering n gubernātiō f
steersman n gubernātor m; rector m
stellar adj stēllārum
stem n stīpes m, truncus m; (ship) prōra f ▶ vt adversārī (dat); ~ **the tide of** (fig) obsistere (dat)
stench n foetor m
stenographer n exceptor m, āctuārius m
stenography n notae fpl
stentorian adj (voice) ingēns
step n gradus m; (track) vestīgium nt; (of stair) gradus m; ~ **by** ~ gradātim; **flight of steps** gradus mpl; **take a** ~ gradum facere; **take steps to** ratiōnem inīre ut, vidēre ut; **march in** ~ in numerum īre; **out of** ~ extrā numerum ▶ vi gradī, incēdere; ~ **aside** dēcēdere; ~ **back** regredī; ~ **forward** prōdīre; ~ **on** insistere (dat)
stepdaughter n prīvīgna f
stepfather n vītricus m
stepmother n noverca f
stepson n prīvīgnus m
stereotyped adj trītus
sterile adj sterilis
sterility n sterilitās f
sterling adj integer, probus, gravis
stern adj dūrus, sevērus; (look) torvus ▶ n puppis f
sternly adv sevērē, dūriter
sternness n sevēritās f
stew vt coquere
steward n prōcūrātor m; (of estate) vīlicus m
stewardship n prōcūrātiō f
stick n (for beating) fūstis m; (for walking) baculum nt ▶ vi haerēre; ~ **at nothing** ad omnia dēscendere; ~ **fast in** inhaerēre (dat), inhaerēscere in (abl); ~ **out** ēminēre; ~ **to** adhaerēre (dat); ~ **up for** dēfendere ▶ vt (with glue) conglūtināre; (with point) fīgere; ~ **into** īnfīgere; ~ **top on** praefīgere
stickler n dīligēns (gen)
sticky adj lentus, tenāx
stiff adj rigidus; (difficult) difficilis; **be** ~ rigēre
stiffen vt rigidum facere ▶ vi rigēre
stiffly adv rigidē

stiff-necked adj obstinātus
stiffness n rigor m
stifle vt suffocāre; (fig) opprimere, restinguere
stigma n nota f
stigmatize vt notāre
stile n saepēs f
still adj immōtus, tranquillus, quiētus; tacitus
▶ vt lēnīre, sēdāre ▶ adv etiam, adhūc,
etiamnum; (past) etiam tum; (with compar)
etiam; (adversative) tamen, nihilōminus
stillness n quiēs f; silentium nt
stilly adv tacitus
stilted adj (language) īnflātus
stilts n grallae fpl
stimulant n stimulus m
stimulate vt stimulāre, acuere, exacuere,
excitāre
stimulus n stimulus m
sting n aculeus m; (wound) ictus m; (fig) aculeus
m, morsus m ▶ vt pungere, mordēre
stingily adv sordidē
stinginess n avāritia f, sordēs fpl, tenācitās f
stinging adj (words) aculeātus, mordāx
stingy adj sordidus, tenāx
stink n foetor m ▶ vi foetēre; ~ **of** olēre
stinking adj foetidus
stint n modus m; **without** ~ abundē ▶ vt
circumscrībere
stipend n mercēs f
stipulate vt pacīscī, stipulārī
stipulation n condiciō f, pactum nt
stir n tumultus m ▶ vt movēre, agitāre; (fig)
commovēre; ~ **up** excitāre, incitāre ▶ vi movērī
stirring adj impiger, tumultuōsus; (speech)
ārdēns
stitch vt suere ▶ n sūtūra f; (in side) dolor m
stock n stirps f, genus nt, gēns f; (equipment)
īnstrūmenta ntpl; (supply) cōpia f; (investment)
pecūniae fpl; **livestock** rēs pecuāria f ▶ vt
īnstruere ▶ adj commūnis, trītus
stockade n vallum nt
stock dove n palumbēs m/f
stock in trade n īnstrūmenta ntpl
stocks n (ship) nāvālia ntpl; (torture)
compedēs fpl
stock-still adj plānē immōtus
stocky adj brevis atque obēsus
stodgy adj crūdus, īnsulsus
stoic n Stōicus m ▶ adj Stōicus
stoical adj dūrus, patiēns
stoically adv patienter
stoicism n Stōicōrum ratiō f, Stōicōrum
disciplīna f
stoke vt agitāre
stole n stola f
stolid adj stolidus
stolidity n īnsulsitās f
stolidly adv stolidē
stomach n stomachus m; venter m ▶ vt patī,
tolerāre
stone n lapis m, saxum nt; (precious) gemma f,
lapillus m; (of fruit) acinum nt; **leave**

no ~ **unturned** omnia experīrī; **kill two birds
with one** ~ ūnō saltū duōs aprōs capere;
hewn ~ saxum quadrātum; **unhewn** ~
caementum nt ▶ vt lapidibus percutere
▶ adj lapideus; ~ **blind** plānē caecus; ~ **deaf**
plānē surdus
stonecutter n lapicīda m
stony adj (soil) lapidōsus; (path) scrūpōsus;
(feeling) dūrus, ferreus
stool n sēdēcula f
stoop vi sē dēmittere; ~ **to** dēscendere in (acc)
stop n mora f; (punctuation) pūnctum nt; **come
to a** ~ īnsistere; **put a** ~ **to** comprimere, dirimere
▶ vt sistere, inhibēre, fīnīre; (restrain) cohibēre;
(hole) obtūrāre; ~ **up** occlūdere, interclūdere
▶ vi dēsinere, dēsistere; (motion) īnsistere
stopgap n tībīcen m
stoppage n interclūsiō f, impedīmentum nt
stopper n obtūrāmentum nt
store n cōpia f; (place) horreum nt; (for wine)
apothēca f; **be in** ~ **for** manēre; **set great** ~ **by**
magnī aestimāre ▶ vt condere, repōnere;
~ **away** recondere; ~ **up** repōnere, congerere
storehouse n (fig) thēsaurus m
storekeeper n cellārius m
storeship n nāvis frūmentāria f
storey n tabulātum nt
stork n cicōnia f
storm n tempestās f, procella f; **take by** ~
expugnāre ▶ vt (MIL) expugnāre ▶ vi saevīre; ~ **at**
īnsectārī, invehī in (acc)
stormbound adj tempestāte dētentus
stormer n expugnātor m
storming n expugnātiō f
stormy adj turbidus, procellōsus; (fig)
turbulentus
story n fābula f, nārrātiō f; (short) fābella f;
(untrue) mendācium nt
storyteller n nārrātor m; (liar) mendāx m
stout adj pinguis; (brave) fortis; (strong) validus,
rōbustus; (material) firmus
stouthearted adj māgnanimus
stoutly adv fortiter
stove n camīnus m, fornāx f
stow vt repōnere, condere; ~ **away** vi in nāvī
dēlitēscere
straddle vi vāricāre
straggle vi deerrāre, pālārī
straggler n pālāns m
straggling adj dispersus, rārus
straight adj rēctus, dīrēctus; (fig) apertus,
vērāx; **in a** ~ **line** rēctā, ē regiōne; **set** ~ dīrigere
▶ adv dīrēctō, rēctā
straighten vt corrigere, extendere
straightforward adj simplex, dīrēctus; (easy)
facilis
straightforwardness n simplicitās f
straightness n (fig) integritās f
straightway adv statim, extemplō
strain n contentiō f; (effort) labor m; (music)
modī mpl; (breed) genus nt ▶ vt intendere,
contendere; (injure) nimiā contentiōne

dēbilitāre; (*liquid*) dēliquāre, percōlāre ▸ *vi* ēnītī, vīrēs contendere

strained *adj* (*language*) accessītus

strainer *n* cōlum *nt*

strait *adj* angustus ▸ *n* fretum *nt*; **straits** *pl* angustiae *fpl*

straiten *vt* coartāre, contrahere; **straitened circumstances** angustiae *fpl*

strait-laced *adj* tristis, sevērus

strand *n* lītus *nt*; (*of rope*) fīlum *nt* ▸ *vt* (*ship*) ēicere

strange *adj* novus, īnsolitus; (*foreign*) peregrīnus; (*another's*) aliēnus; (*ignorant*) rudis, expers

strangely *adv* mīrē, mīrum in modum

strangeness *n* novitās *f*, īnsolentia *f*

stranger *n* (*from abroad*) advena *f*; peregrīnus *m*; (*visiting*) hospes *m*, hospita *f*; (*not of the family*) externus *m*; (*unknown*) ignōtus *m*

strangle *vt* strangulāre, laqueō gulam frangere

strap *n* lōrum *nt*, habēna *f*

strapping *adj* grandis

stratagem *n* cōnsilium *nt*, fallācia *f*

strategic *adj* (*action*) prūdēns; (*position*) idōneus

strategist *n* artis bellicae perītus *m*

strategy *n* ars imperātōria *f*; cōnsilia *ntpl*

straw *n* (*stalk*) culmus *m*; (*collective*) strāmentum *nt*; **not care a ~ for** floccī nōn facere ▸ *adj* strāmenticius

strawberry *n* frāgum *nt*

strawberry tree *n* arbutus *m*

stray *vt* aberrāre, deerrāre; vagārī ▸ *adj* errābundus

streak *n* līnea *f*, macula *f*; (*light*) radius *m*; (*character*) vēna *f* ▸ *vt* maculāre

stream *n* flūmen *nt*, fluvius *m*; **down ~** secundō flūmine; **up ~** adversō flūmine ▸ *vi* fluere, sē effundere; **~ into** īnfluere in (*acc*)

streamlet *n* rīvus *m*, rīvulus *m*

street *n* via *f*, platea *f*

strength *n* vīrēs *fpl*; (*of material*) firmitās *f*; (*fig*) rōbur *nt*, nervī *mpl*; numerus *m*; **know the enemy's ~** quot sint hostēs scīre; **on the ~ of** frētus (*abl*)

strengthen *vt* firmāre, corrōborāre; (*position*) mūnīre

strenuous *adj* impiger, strēnuus, sēdulus

strenuously *adv* impigrē, strēnuē

strenuousness *n* industria *f*

stress *n* (*words*) ictus *m*; (*meaning*) vīs *f*; (*importance*) mōmentum *nt*; (*difficulty*) labor *m*; **lay great ~ on** in māgnō discrīmine pōnere ▸ *vt* exprimere

stretch *n* spatium *nt*, tractus *m*; **at a ~** sine ūllā intermissiōne ▸ *vt* tendere, intendere; (*length*) prōdūcere, extendere; (*facts*) in māius crēdere; **~ a point** indulgēre; **~ before** obtendere; **~ forth** porrigere; **~ oneself** (*on ground*) sternī; **~ out** porrigere, extendere ▸ *vi* extendī, patēscere

strew *vt* (*things*) sternere; (*place*) cōnsternere

stricken *adj* saucius

strict *adj* (*defined*) ipse, certus; (*severe*) sevērus, rigidus; (*accurate*) dīligēns

strictly *adv* sevērē; dīligenter; **~ speaking** scīlicet, immo

strictness *n* sevēritās *f*; dīligentia *f*

stricture *n* vituperātiō *f*

stride *n* passus *m*; **make great strides** (*fig*) multum prōficere ▸ *vi* incēdere, ingentēs gradūs ferre

strident *adj* asper

strife *n* discordia *f*, pugna *f*

strike *vt* ferīre, percutere; (*instrument*) pellere, pulsāre; (*sail*) subdūcere; (*tent*) dētendere; (*mind*) venīre in (*acc*); (*camp*) movēre; (*fear into*) incutere in (*acc*); **~ against** offendere; **~ out** dēlēre; **~ up** (*music*) incipere; **~ a bargain** pacīscī; **be struck** vāpulāre ▸ *vi* (*work*) cessāre

striking *adj* īnsignis, īnsīgnītus, ēgregius

strikingly *adv* īnsīgnītē

string *n* (*cord*) restícula *f*; (*succession*) seriēs *f*; (*instrument*) nervus *m*; (*bow*) nervus *m*; **have two strings to one's bow** duplicī spē ūtī ▸ *vt* (*bow*) intendere; (*together*) coniungere

stringency *n* sevēritās *f*

stringent *adj* sevērus

strip *vt* nūdāre, spoliāre, dēnūdāre; **~ off** exuere; (*leaves*) stringere, dēstringere ▸ *n* lacinia *f*

stripe *n* virga *f*; (*on tunic*) clāvus *m*; **stripes** *pl* verbera *ntpl*

striped *adj* virgātus

stripling *n* adulescentulus *m*

strive *vi* nītī, ēnītī, contendere; (*contend*) certāre

stroke *n* ictus *m*; (*lightning*) fulmen *nt*; (*oar*) pulsus *m*; (*pen*) līnea *f*; **~ of luck** fortūna secunda *f* ▸ *vt* mulcēre, dēmulcēre

stroll *vi* deambulāre, spatiārī

strong *adj* fortis, validus; (*health*) rōbustus, firmus; (*material*) firmus; (*smell*) gravis; (*resources*) pollēns, potēns; (*feeling*) ācer, māgnus; (*language*) vehemēns, probrōsus; **be ~** valēre; **be twenty ~** vīgintī esse numerō

strongbox *n* arca *f*

stronghold *n* arx *f*

strongly *adv* validē, vehementer, fortiter, ācriter, graviter

strong-minded *adj* pertināx, cōnstāns

strophe *n* stropha *f*

structure *n* aedificium *nt*; (*form*) strūctūra *f*; (*arrangement*) compositiō *f*

struggle *n* (*effort*) cōnātus *m*; (*fight*) pugna *f*, certāmen *nt* ▸ *vi* nītī; certāre, contendere; (*fight*) luctārī; **~ upwards** ēnītī

strut *vi* māgnificē incēdere

stubble *n* stipula *f*

stubborn *adj* pertināx, pervicāx

stubbornly *adv* pertināciter, pervicāciter

stubbornness *n* pertinācia *f*, pervicācia *f*

stucco *n* gypsum *nt*

stud *n* clāvus *m*; (*horses*) equī *mpl*

studded *adj* distinctus

student *n* discipulus *m*; **be a ~ of** studēre (*dat*)

studied *adj* meditātus, accūrātus; (*language*) exquīsītus
studio *n* officīna *f*
studious *adj* litterīs dēditus, litterārum studiōsus; (*careful*) attentus
studiously *adv* dē industriā
study *vt* studēre (*dat*); (*prepare*) meditārī; ~ **under** audīre ▶ *n* studium *nt*; (*room*) bibliothēca *f*
stuff *n* māteria *f*; (*cloth*) textile *nt* ▶ *vt* farcīre, refercīre; (*with food*) sagīnāre
stuffing *n* sagīna *f*; (*of cushion*) tōmentum *nt*
stultify *vt* ad inritum redigere
stumble *vi* offendere; ~ **upon** incidere in (*acc*), offendere
stumbling block *n* offēnsiō *f*
stump *n* stīpes *m*
stun *vt* stupefacere; (*fig*) obstupefacere, cōnfundere
stunned *adj* attonitus
stunt *vt* corporis auctum inhibēre
stunted *adj* curtus
stupefaction *n* stupor *m*
stupefied *adj*: **be ~** stupēre, obstupefierī
stupefy *vt* obstupefacere
stupendous *adj* mīrus, mīrificus
stupid *adj* stultus, hebes, ineptus
stupidity *n* stultitia *f*
stupidly *adv* stultē, ineptē
stupor *n* stupor *m*
sturdily *adv* fortiter
sturdiness *n* rōbur *nt*, firmitās *f*
sturdy *adj* fortis, rōbustus
sturgeon *n* acipēnser *m*
stutter *vi* balbūtīre
stuttering *adj* balbus
sty *n* hara *f*
style *n* (*kind*) genus *nt*, ratiō *f*; (*of dress*) habitus *m*; (*of prose*) ēlocūtiō *f*, ōrātiō *f*; (*pen*) stilus *m* ▶ *vt* appellāre
stylish *adj* ēlegāns, lautus, expolītus
stylishly *adv* ēleganter
suasion *n* suāsiō *f*
suave *adj* blandus, urbānus
suavity *n* urbānitās *f*
subaltern *n* succenturiō *m*
subdivide *vt* dīvidere
subdivision *n* pars *f*, mōmentum *nt*
subdue *vt* subigere, dēvincere, redigere, domāre; (*fig*) cohibēre
subdued *adj* dēmissus, summissus
subject *n* (*person*) cīvis *m/f*; (*matter*) rēs *f*; (*theme*) locus *m*, argūmentum *nt* ▶ *adj* subiectus; ~ **to** obnoxius (*dat*) ▶ *vt* subicere; obnoxium reddere
subjection *n* servitūs *f*
subjective *adj* proprius
subject matter *n* māteria *f*
subjoin *vt* subicere, subiungere
subjugate *vt* subigere, dēbellāre, domāre
sublime *adj* sublīmis, ēlātus, excelsus
sublimely *adv* excelsē
sublimity *n* altitūdō *f*, ēlātiō *f*

submarine *adj* submersus
submerge *vt* dēmergere; (*flood*) inundāre ▶ *vi* sē dēmergere
submersed *adj* submersus
submission *n* obsequium *nt*, servitium *nt*; (*fig*) patientia *f*
submissive *adj* submissus, docilis, obtemperāns
submissively *adv* submissē, oboedienter, patienter
submit *vi* sē dēdere; ~ **to** pārēre (*dat*), obtemperāre (*dat*), patī, subīre ▶ *vt* (*proposal*) referre
subordinate *adj* subiectus, secundus ▶ *vt* subiungere, subicere
suborn *vt* subicere, subōrnāre
subpoena *vt* testimōnium dēnūntiāre (*dat*)
subscribe *vt* (*name*) subscrībere; (*money*) cōnferre
subscription *n* collātiō *f*
subsequent *adj* sequēns, posterior
subsequently *adv* posteā, mox
subserve *vt* subvenīre (*dat*), commodāre
subservience *n* obsequium *nt*
subservient *adj* obsequēns; (*thing*) ūtilis, commodus
subside *vi* dēsīdere, resīdere; (*fever*) dēcēdere; (*wind*) cadere; (*passion*) dēfervēscere
subsidence *n* lābēs *f*
subsidiary *adj* subiectus, secundus
subsidize *vt* pecūniās suppeditāre (*dat*)
subsidy *n* pecūniae *fpl*, vectīgal *nt*
subsist *vi* cōnstāre, sustentārī
subsistence *n* vīctus *m*
substance *n* (*matter*) rēs *f*, corpus *nt*; (*essence*) nātūra *f*; (*gist*) summa *f*; (*reality*) rēs *f*; (*wealth*) opēs *fpl*
substantial *adj* solidus; (*real*) vērus; (*important*) gravis; (*rich*) opulentus, dīves
substantially *adv* rē; māgnā ex parte
substantiate *vt* cōnfirmāre
substitute *vt* subicere, repōnere, substituere ▶ *n* vicārius *m*
substratum *n* fundāmentum *nt*
subterfuge *n* latebra *f*, perfugium *nt*
subterranean *adj* subterrāneus
subtle *adj* (*fine*) subtīlis; (*shrewd*) acūtus, astūtus
subtlety *n* subtīlitās *f*; acūmen *nt*, astūtia *f*
subtly *adv* subtīliter; acūtē, astūtē
subtract *vt* dētrahere, dēmere; (*money*) dēdūcere
subtraction *n* dētractiō *f*, dēductiō *f*
suburb *n* suburbium *nt*
suburban *adj* suburbānus
subvention *n* pecūniae *fpl*
subversion *n* ēversiō *f*, ruīna *f*
subversive *adj* sēditiōsus
subvert *vt* ēvertere, subruere
subverter *n* ēversor *m*
succeed *vi* (*person*) rem bene gerere; (*activity*) prosperē ēvenīre; ~ **in obtaining** impetrāre ▶ *vt* īnsequī, excipere, succēdere (*dat*)

success n bonus ēventus m, rēs bene gesta f
successful adj fēlīx; (thing) secundus; **be ~** rem bene gerere; (play) stāre
successfully adv fēlīciter, prosperē, bene
succession n (coming next) successiō f; (line) seriēs f, ōrdō m; **alternate ~** vicissitūdō f; **in ~** deinceps, ex ōrdine
successive adj continuus, perpetuus
successively adv deinceps, ex ōrdine; (alternately) vicissim
successor n successor m
succinct adj brevis, pressus
succinctly adv breviter, pressē
succour n auxilium nt, subsidium nt ▶ vt subvenīre (dat), succurrere (dat), opem ferre (dat)
succulence n sūcus m
succulent adj sūcidus
succumb vi succumbere, dēficere
such adj tālis, eiusmodī, hūiusmodī; (size) tantus; **at ~ a time** id temporis; **~ great** tantus
suchlike adj hūiusmodī, ēiusdem generis
suck vt sūgere; **~ in** sorbēre; **~ up** exsorbēre, ēbibere
sucker n surculus m
sucking adj (child) lactēns
suckle vt nūtrīcārī, mammam dare (dat)
suckling n lactēns m/f
sudden adj subitus, repentīnus
suddenly adv subitō, repente
sue vt in iūs vocāre, lītem intendere (dat); **sue for** rogāre, petere, ōrāre
suffer vt patī, ferre, tolerāre; (injury) accipere; (loss) facere; (permit) patī, sinere ▶ vi dolōre adficī; **~ defeat** clādem accipere; **~ from** labōrāre ex, adficī (abl) **~ for** poenās dare (gen)
sufferable adj tolerābilis
sufferance n patientia f, tolerantia f
suffering n dolor m
suffice vi sufficere, suppetere
sufficiency n satis
sufficient adj idōneus, satis (gen)
sufficiently adv satis
suffocate vt suffocāre
suffrage n suffrāgium nt
suffuse vt suffundere
sugar n saccharon nt
suggest vt admonēre, inicere, subicere; **~ itself** occurrere
suggestion n admonitiō f; **at the ~ of** admonitū (gen); **at my ~** mē auctōre
suicidal adj fūnestus
suicide n mors voluntāria f; **commit ~** mortem sibī cōnscīscere
suit n (LAW) līs f, āctiō f; (clothes) vestītus m ▶ vt convenīre (dat), congruere (dat); (dress) sedēre (dat), decēre; **it suits** decet; **to ~ me** dē meā sententiā
suitability n convenientia f
suitable adj aptus (+ dat or 'ad' + acc), idōneus (+ dat or'ad'+ acc)
suitably adv aptē, decenter

suite n comitēs mpl, comitātus m
suitor n procus m, amāns m
sulk vi aegrē ferre, mōrōsum esse
sulky adj mōrōsus, tristis
sullen adj tristis, mōrōsus
sullenness n mōrōsitās f
sully vt īnfuscāre, contāmināre
sulphur n sulfur nt
sultriness n aestus m
sultry adj aestuōsus
sum n summa f; **sum of money** pecūnia f ▶ vt subdūcere, computāre; **sum up** summātim dēscrībere; **to sum up** ūnō verbō, quid plūra?
summarily adv strictim, summātim; sine morā
summarize vt summātim dēscrībere
summary n summārium nt, epitomē f ▶ adj subitus, praesēns
summer n aestās f ▶ adj aestīvus; **of ~** aestīvus
summit n vertex m, culmen nt; (fig) fastīgium nt; **the ~ of** summus
summon vt arcessere; (meeting) convocāre; (witness) citāre; **~ up courage** animum sūmere
summons n (LAW) vocātiō f ▶ vt in iūs vocāre, diem dīcere (dat)
sumptuary adj sūmptuārius
sumptuous adj sūmptuōsus, adparātus, māgnificus, lautus
sumptuously adv sūmptuōsē, māgnificē
sun n sōl m ▶ vt: **sun oneself** aprīcārī
sunbeam n radius m
sunburnt adj adūstus
sunder vt sēparāre, dīvidere
sundial n sōlārium nt
sundry adj dīversī, complūrēs
sunlight n sōl m
sunlit adj aprīcus
sunny adj aprīcus, serēnus
sunrise n sōlis ortus m
sunset n sōlis occāsus m
sunshade n umbella f
sunshine n sōl m
sup vi cēnāre
superabundance n abundantia f
superabundant adj nimius
superabundantly adv satis superque
superannuated adj ēmeritus
superb adj māgnificus
superbly adv māgnificē
supercilious adj adrogāns, superbus
superciliously adv adroganter, superbē
superciliousness n adrogantia f, fastus m
supererogation n: **of ~** ultrō factus
superficial adj levis; **acquire a ~ knowledge of** prīmīs labrīs gustāre
superficiality n levitās f
superficially adv leviter, strictim
superfluity n abundantia f
superfluous adj supervacāneus, nimius; **be ~** redundāre
superhuman adj dīvīnus, hūmānō māior
superimpose vt superimpōnere
superintend vt prōcūrāre, praeesse (dat)

superintendence n cūra f

superintendent n cūrātor m, praefectus m

superior adj melior, amplior; **be ~** praestāre, superāre ▸ n prīnceps m, praefectus m

superiority n praestantia f; **have the ~** superāre; (in numbers) plūrēs esse

superlative adj ēgregius, optimus

supernatural adj dīvīnus

supernaturally adv dīvīnitus

supernumerary adj adscrīptīcius; **~ soldiers** accēnsī mpl

superscription n titulus m

supersede vt succēdere (dat), in locum succēdere (gen); **~ gold with silver** prō aurō argentum suppōnere

superstition n rēligiō f, superstitiō f

superstitious adj rēligiōsus, superstitiōsus

supervene vi īnsequī, succēdere

supervise vt prōcūrāre

supervision n cūra f

supervisor n cūrātor m

supine adj supīnus; (fig) neglegēns, segnis

supinely adv segniter

supper n cēna f; **after ~** cēnātus

supperless adj iēiūnus

supplant vt praevertere

supple adj flexibilis, mollis

supplement n appendix f ▸ vt amplificāre

supplementary adj additus

suppleness n mollitia f

suppliant n supplex m/f

supplicate vt supplicāre, obsecrāre

supplication n precēs fpl

supplies npl commeātus m

supply n cōpia f ▸ vt suppeditāre, praebēre; (loss) supplēre

support n firmāmentum nt; (help) subsidium nt, adiūmentum nt; (food) alimenta ntpl; (of party) favor m; (of needy) patrōcinium nt; **I ~** subsidiō sum (dat); **lend ~ to rumours** alimenta rūmōribus addere ▸ vt fulcīre; (living) sustinēre, sustentāre; (with help) adiuvāre, opem ferre (dat); (at law) adesse (dat)

supportable adj tolerābilis

supporter n fautor m; (at trial) advocātus m; (of proposal) auctor m

supporting cast n adiūtōrēs mpl

suppose vi (assume) pōnere; (think) existimāre, opīnārī, crēdere; **~ it is true** fac vērum esse

supposedly adv ut fāma est

supposing conj sī; (for the sake of argument) sī iam

supposition n opīniō f; **on this ~** hōc positō

supposititious adj subditus, subditīvus

suppress vt opprimere, comprimere; (knowledge) cēlāre, reticēre; (feelings) coercēre, reprimere

suppression n (of fact) reticentia f

supremacy n imperium nt, dominātus m, prīncipātus m

supreme adj summus; **be ~** dominārī; **~ command** imperium nt

supremely adv ūnicē, plānē

sure adj certus; (fact) explōrātus; (friend) fīdus; **be ~ of** compertō habēre; **feel ~** persuāsum habēre, haud scīre an; prō certō habēre; **make ~ of** (fact) comperīre; (action) efficere ut; **to be ~** quidem; **~ enough** rē vērā

surely adv certō, certē, nonne; (tentative) scīlicet, sānē; **~ you do not think?** num putās?; **~ not** num

surety n (person) vās m, praes m, spōnsor m; (deposit) fīdūcia f; **be ~ for** spondēre prō

surf n fluctus m

surface n superficiēs f; **~ of the water** summa aqua

surfeit n satietās f ▸ vt satiāre, explēre

surge n aestus m, fluctus m ▸ vi tumēscere

surgeon n chīrūrgus m

surgery n chīrūrgia f

surlily adv mōrōsē

surliness n mōrōsitās f

surly adj mōrōsus, difficilis

surmise n coniectūra f ▸ vi suspicārī, conicere, augurārī

surmount vt superāre

surmountable adj superābilis

surname n cognōmen nt

surpass vt excellere, exsuperāre, antecēdere

surpassing adj excellēns

surplus n reliquum nt; (money) pecūniae residuae fpl

surprise n admīrātiō f; (cause) rēs inopīnāta f; **take by ~** dēprehendere ▸ adj subitus ▸ vt dēprehendere; (MIL) opprimere; **be surprised** dēmīrārī; **be surprised at** admīrārī

surprising adj mīrus, mīrābilis

surprisingly adv mīrē, mīrābiliter

surrender vt dēdere, trādere, concēdere ▸ vi sē dēdere; **~ unconditionally to** sē suaque omnia potestātī permittere (gen) ▸ n dēditiō f; (legal) cessiō f; **unconditional ~** permissiō f

surreptitious adj fūrtīvus

surreptitiously adv fūrtim, clam; **get in ~** inrēpere in (acc)

surround vt circumdare, cingere, circumvenīre, circumfundere

surrounding adj circumiectus; **surroundings** npl vīcīnia f

survey vt contemplārī, cōnsīderāre; (land) mētārī ▸ n contemplātiō f; (land) mēnsūra f

surveyor n fīnītor m, agrimēnsor m, mētātor m

survival n salūs f

survive vt superāre; superesse (dat)

survivor n superstes m/f

susceptibility n mollitia f

susceptible adj mollis

suspect vt suspicārī; **be suspected** in suspīciōnem venīre

suspend vt suspendere; (activity) differre; (person) locō movēre; **be suspended** pendēre

suspense n dubitātiō f; **be in ~** animī pendēre, haerēre

suspicion n suspiciō f; **direct ~ to** suspiciōnem adiungere ad
suspicious adj (suspecting) suspiciōsus; (suspected) dubius, anceps
sustain vt (weight) sustinēre; (life) alere, sustentāre; (hardship) ferre, sustinēre; (the part of) agere
sustenance n alimentum nt, vīctus m
sutler n lixa m
suzerain n dominus m
swaddling clothes n incūnābula ntpl
swagger vi sē iactāre
swaggerer n homō glōriōsus m
swallow n hirundō f ▸ vt dēvorāre; **~ up** absorbēre
swamp n palūs f ▸ vt opprimere
swampy adj ūlīginōsus
swan n cycnus m; **swan's** cycnēus
swank vi sē iactāre
sward n caespes m
swarm n exāmen nt; (fig) nūbēs f ▸ vi: **~ round** circumfundī
swarthy adj fuscus, aquilus
swathe vt conligāre
sway n diciō f, imperium nt; **bring under one's ~** suae diciōnis facere ▸ vt regere ▸ vi vacillāre
swear vi iūrāre; **~ allegiance to** iūrāre in verba (gen)
sweat n sūdor m ▸ vi sūdāre
sweep vt verrere; **~ away** rapere; **~ out** ēverrere
sweet adj dulcis, suāvis
sweeten vt dulcem reddere
sweetheart n dēliciae fpl
sweetly adv dulciter, suāviter
sweetness n dulcitūdō f, suāvitās f
sweet-tempered adj suāvis, cōmis
swell n tumor m ▸ vi tumēre, tumēscere; (fig) glīscere ▸ vt inflāre
swelling adj tumidus ▸ n tumor m
swelter vi aestū labōrāre
swerve vi dēclīnāre, dēvertere ▸ n dēclīnātiō f
swift adj celer, vēlōx, incitātus
swiftly adv celeriter, vēlōciter
swiftness n celeritās f, vēlōcitās f
swill vt (rinse) colluere; (drink) ēpōtāre
swim vi nāre, innāre; (place) natāre; **~ across** trānāre; **~ ashore** ēnāre; **~ to** adnāre
swimming n natātiō f
swindle vt circumvenīre, verba dare (dat) ▸ n fraus f
swine n sūs m/f
swineherd n subulcus m
swing n (motion) oscillātiō f ▸ vi oscillāre ▸ vt lībrāre
swinish adj obscēnus
swirl n vertex m ▸ vi volūtārī
switch n virga f ▸ vt flectere, torquēre
swivel n cardō f
swollen adj tumidus, turgidus, īnflātus
swoon n dēfectiō f ▸ vi intermorī
swoop n impetus m ▸ vi lābī; **~ down on** involāre in (acc)

sword n gladius m; **put to the ~** occīdere; **with fire and ~** ferrō ignīque
swordsman n gladiātor m
sworn adj iūrātus
sybarite n dēlicātus m
sycophancy n adsentātiō f, adūlātiō f
sycophant n adsentātor m, adūlātor m
syllable n syllaba f
syllogism n ratiōcinātiō f
sylvan adj silvestris
symbol n signum nt, īnsigne nt
symmetrical adj concinnus, aequus
symmetry n concinnitās f, aequitās f
sympathetic adj concors, misericors
sympathetically adv misericorditer
sympathize vi cōnsentīre; **~ with** miserērī (gen)
sympathy n concordia f, cōnsēnsus m; misericordia f
symphony n concentus m
symptom n signum nt, indicium nt
syndicate n societās f
synonym n verbum idem dēclārāns nt
synonymous adj idem dēclārāns
synopsis n summārium nt
syringe n clystēr m
system n ratiō f, fōrmula f; (PHILOS) disciplīna f
systematic adj ōrdinātus, cōnstāns
systematically adv ratiōne, ōrdine
systematize vt in ōrdinem redigere

t

tabernacle n tabernāculum nt

table n mēnsa f; (inscribed) tabula f; (list) index m; **at ~** inter cēnam; **turn the tables on** pār parī referre

tablet n tabula f, tabella f

taboo n rēligiō f

tabulate vt in ōrdinem redigere

tacit adj tacitus

tacitly adv tacitē

taciturn adj taciturnus

taciturnity n taciturnitās f

tack n clāvulus m; (of sail) pēs m ▶ vt: **~ on** adsuere ▶ vi (ship) reciprocārī, nāvem flectere

tackle n armāmenta ntpl ▶ vt adgredī

tact n iūdicium nt, commūnis sēnsus m, hūmānitās f

tactful adj prūdēns, hūmānus

tactfully adv prūdenter, hūmāniter

tactician n reī mīlitāris perītus m

tactics n rēs mīlitāris f, bellī ratiō f

tactless adj ineptus

tactlessly adv ineptē

tadpole n rānunculus m

tag n appendicula f

tail n cauda f; **turn ~** terga vertere

tailor n vestītor m

taint n lābēs f, vitium nt ▶ vt inquināre, contāmināre, īnficere

take vt capere, sūmere; (auspices) habēre; (disease) contrahere; (experience) ferre; (fire) concipere; (meaning) accipere, interpretārī; (in the act) dēprehendere; (person) dūcere; **~ after** similem esse (dat, gen); **~ across** trānsportāre; **~ arms** arma sūmere; **~ away** dēmere, auferre, adimere, abdūcere; **~ back** recipere; **~ by storm** expugnāre; **~ care that** cūrāre ut/nē (subj); **~ down** dētrahere; (in writing) exscrībere; **~ for** habēre prō; **~ hold of** prehendere; **~ in** (as guest) recipere; (information) percipere, comprehendere; (with deceit) dēcipere; **~ in hand** incipere, suscipere; **~ off** dēmere; (clothes) exuere; **~ on** suscipere; **~ out** eximere, extrahere; (from store) prōmere; **~ over** excipere; **~ place** fierī, accidere; **~ prisoner** capere;

~ refuge in cōnfugere ad (acc); **~ the field** in aciem dēscendere; **~ to** sē dēdere (dat), amāre; **~ to oneself** suscipere; **~ up** sūmere, tollere; (task) incipere, adgredī ad; (in turn) excipere; (room) occupāre; **~ upon oneself** recipere, sibī sūmere

taking adj grātus ▶ n (MIL) expugnātiō f

tale n fābula f, fābella f

talent n (money) talentum nt; (ability) ingenium nt, indolēs f

talented adj ingeniōsus

talk n sermō m; (with another) colloquium nt; **common ~** fāma f; **be the ~ of the town** in ōre omnium esse ▶ vi loquī; (to someone) colloquī cum; **~ down to** ad intellectum audientis dēscendere; **~ over** cōnferre, disserere dē

talkative adj loquāx

talkativeness n loquācitās f

tall adj prōcērus, grandis

tallness n prōcēritās f

tallow n sēbum nt

tally n tessera f ▶ vi congruere

talon n unguis m

tamarisk n myrīca f

tambourine n tympanum nt

tame vt domāre, mānsuēfacere ▶ adj mānsuētus; (character) ignāvus; (language) īnsulsus, frīgidus

tamely adv ignāvē, lentē

tameness n mānsuētūdō f; (fig) lentitūdō f

tamer n domitor m

tamper vi: **~ with** (person) sollicitāre; (writing) interpolāre

tan vt imbuere

tang n sapor m

tangible adj tāctilis

tangle n nōdus m ▶ vt implicāre

tank n lacus m

tanned adj (by sun) adūstus

tanner n coriārius m

tantalize vt lūdere

tantamount adj pār, īdem

tantrum n īra f

tap n epitonium nt; (touch) plāga f ▶ vt (cask) relinere; (hit) ferīre

tape n taenia f

taper n cēreus m ▶ vi fastīgārī

tapestry n aulaea ntpl

tar n pix f

tardily adv tardē, lentē

tardiness n tarditās f, segnitia f

tardy adj tardus, lentus

tare n lolium nt

targe n parma f

target n scopus m

tariff n portōrium nt

tarn n lacus m

tarnish vt īnfuscāre, inquināre ▶ vi īnfuscārī

tarry vi morārī, commorārī, cunctārī

tart adj acidus, asper ▶ n scrīblīta f

tartly adv acerbē

tartness n asperitās f

task n pēnsum nt, opus nt, negōtium nt; **take to ~** obiūrgāre
taskmaster n dominus m
tassel n fimbriae fpl
taste n (sense) gustātus m; (flavour) sapor m; (artistic) iūdicium nt, ēlegantia f; (for rhetoric) aurēs fpl; **in good ~** ēlegāns ▶ vt gustāre, dēgustāre ▶ vi sapere; **~ of** resipere
tasteful adj ēlegāns
tastefully adv ēleganter
tastefulness n ēlegantia f
tasteless adj īnsulsus, inēlegāns
tastelessly adv īnsulsē, inēleganter
tastelessness n īnsulsitās f
taster n praegustātor m
tasty adj dulcis
tattered adj pannōsus
tatters n pannī mpl
tattoo vt compungere
taunt n convīcium nt, probrum nt ▶ vt exprobrāre, obicere (dat of pers, acc of charge)
taunting adj contumēliōsus
tauntingly adv contumēliōsē
taut adj intentus; **draw ~** addūcere
tavern n taberna f, hospitium nt
tawdry adj vīlis
tawny adj fulvus
tax n vectīgal nt, tribūtum nt; **a 5 per cent tax** vīcēsima f; **free from tax** immūnis ▶ vt vectīgal impōnere (dat); (strength) contendere; **tax with** (charge) obicere (acc and dat), īnsimulāre
taxable adj vectīgālis
taxation n vectīgālia ntpl
tax collector n exāctor m
tax farmer n pūblicānus m
taxpayer n assiduus m
teach vt docēre, ērudīre, īnstituere; (thoroughly) ēdocēre; (passive) discere; **~ your grandmother** sūs Minervam
teachable adj docilis
teacher n magister m, magistra f, doctor m; (PHILOS) praeceptor m; (of literature) grammaticus m; (of rhetoric) rhētor m
teaching n doctrīna f, disciplīna f
team n (animals) iugum nt
tear n lacrima f; **shed tears** lacrimās effundere ▶ vt scindere; **~ down** revellere; **~ in pieces** dīlaniāre, discerpere, lacerāre; **~ off** abscindere, dēripere; **~ open** rescindere; **~ out** ēvellere; **~ up** convellere
tearful adj flēbilis
tease vt lūdere, inrītāre
teat n mamma f
technical adj (term) proprius
technique n ars f
tedious adj longus, lentus, odiōsus
tediously adv molestē
tedium n taedium nt, molestia f
teem vi abundāre
teeming adj fēcundus, refertus
teens n: **in one's ~** adulescentulus
teethe vi dentīre

tell vt (story) nārrāre; (person) dīcere (dat); (number) ēnumerāre; (inform) certiōrem facere; (difference) intellegere; (order) iubēre (+ acc and infin), imperāre (+ 'ut' +subj or + 'ne' +subj); **~ the truth** vēra dīcere; **~ lies** mentīrī ▶ vi valēre; **~ the difference between** discernere; **I cannot ~** nesciō
telling adj validus
temerity n temeritās f
temper n animus m, ingenium nt; (bad) īra f, īrācundia f; (of metal) temperātiō f ▶ vt temperāre; (fig) moderārī (dat)
temperament n animī habitus m, animus m
temperamental adj incōnstāns
temperance n temperantia f, continentia f
temperate adj temperātus, moderātus, sobrius
temperately adv moderātē
temperature n calor m, frīgus nt; **mild ~** temperiēs f
tempest n tempestās f, procella f
tempestuous adj procellōsus
temple n templum nt, aedēs f; (head) tempus nt
temporal adj hūmānus, profānus
temporarily adv ad tempus
temporary adj brevis
temporize vi temporis causā facere, tergiversārī
tempt vt sollicitāre, pellicere, invītāre
temptation n illecebra f
tempter n impulsor m
ten num decem; **ten each** dēnī; **ten times** deciēns
tenable adj inexpugnābilis, stabilis, certus
tenacious adj tenāx, firmus
tenaciously adv tenāciter
tenacity n tenācitās f
tenant n inquilīnus m, habitātor m; (on land) colōnus m
tenantry n colōnī mpl
tend vi spectāre, pertinēre ▶ vt cūrāre, colere
tendency n inclīnātiō f, voluntās f
tender adj tener, mollis ▶ vt dēferre, offerre
tenderhearted adj misericors
tenderly adv indulgenter
tenderness n indulgentia f, mollitia f
tendon n nervus m
tendril n clāviculus m
tenement n habitātiō f; **block of tenements** īnsula f
tenet n dogma nt, dēcrētum nt
tennis court n sphaeristērium nt
tenor n (course) tenor m; (purport) sententia f
tense adj intentus ▶ n tempus nt
tension n intentiō f
tent n tabernāculum nt; (general's) praetōrium nt
tentacle n bracchium nt
tentatively adv experiendō
tenterhooks n: **on ~** animī suspēnsus
tenth adj decimus; **for the ~ time** decimum; **men of the ~ legion** decumānī mpl

tenuous *adj* rārus
tenure *n* possessiō *f*
tepid *adj* tepidus; **be ~** tepēre
tergiversation *n* tergiversātiō *f*
term *n* (*limit*) terminus *m*; (*period*) spatium *nt*; (*word*) verbum *nt* ▶ *vt* appellāre, nuncupāre
terminate *vt* termināre, fīnīre ▶ *vi* dēsinere; (*words*) cadere
termination *n* fīnis *m*, terminus *m*
terminology *n* vocābula *ntpl*
terms *npl* condiciō *f*, lēx *f*; **propose ~** condiciōnem ferre; **be on good ~** in grātiā esse; **we come to ~** inter nōs convenit
terrain *n* ager *m*
terrestrial *adj* terrestris
terrible *adj* terribilis, horribilis, horrendus
terribly *adv* horrendum in modum
terrific *adj* formīdolōsus; vehemēns
terrify *vt* terrēre, perterrēre, exterrēre
terrifying *adj* formīdolōsus
territory *n* ager *m*, fīnēs *mpl*
terror *n* terror *m*, formīdō *f*, pavor *m*; **object of ~** terror *m*; **be a ~ to** terrōrī esse (*dat*)
terrorize *vt* metum inicere (*dat*)
terse *adj* pressus, brevis
tersely *adv* pressē
terseness *n* brevitās *f*
tessellated *adj* tessellātus
test *n* experīmentum *nt*, probātiō *f*; (*standard*) obrussa *f*; **put to the ~** experīrī, perīclitārī; **stand the ~** spectārī ▶ *vt* experīrī, probāre, spectāre
testament *n* testāmentum *nt*
testamentary *adj* testāmentārius
testator *n* testātor *m*
testify *vt* testificārī
testifying *n* testificātiō *f*
testily *adv* stomachōsē
testimonial *n* laudātiō *f*
testimony *n* testimōnium *nt*
testy *adj* difficilis, stomachōsus
tether *n* retināculum *nt*, vinculum *nt* ▶ *vt* religāre
tetrarch *n* tetrarchēs *m*
tetrarchy *n* tetrarchia *f*
text *n* verba *ntpl*
textbook *n* ars *f*
textile *adj* textilis
textual *adj* verbōrum
texture *n* textus *m*
than *conj* quam (*abl*); **other ~** alius ac
thank *vt* grātiās agere (*dat*); **~ you** bene facis; **no, ~ you** benīgnē
thankful *adj* grātus
thankfully *adv* grātē
thankfulness *n* grātia *f*
thankless *adj* ingrātus
thanklessly *adv* ingrātē
thanks *n* grātiae *fpl*, grātēs *fpl*; **return ~** grātiās agere, grātēs persolvere; **~ to you** operā tuā, beneficiō tuō; **it is ~ to somebody that ... not** per aliquem stat quominus (*subj*)

thanksgiving *n* grātulātiō *f*; (*public*) supplicātiō *f*
that *pron* (*demonstrative*) ille; (*rel*) quī ▶ *conj* (*statement*) acc and infin; (*command, purpose, result*) ut; (*fearing*) nē; (*emotion*) quod; **oh ~** utinam
thatch *n* culmus *m*, strāmenta *ntpl* ▶ *vt* tegere, integere
thaw *vt* dissolvere ▶ *vi* liquēscere, tābēscere
the *art not expressed*; (*emphatic*) ille; (*with compar*) quō ... eō
theatre *n* theātrum *nt*
theatrical *adj* scēnicus
theft *n* fūrtum *nt*
their *adj* eōrum; (*ref to subject*) suus
theme *n* māteria *f*, argūmentum *nt*
themselves *pron* ipsī; (*reflexive*) sē
then *adv* (*time*) tum, tunc; (*succession*) deinde, tum, posteā; (*consequence*) igitur, ergō; **now and ~** interdum; **only ~** tum dēmum
thence *adv* inde
thenceforth *adv* inde, posteā, ex eō tempore
theologian *n* theologus *m*
theology *n* theologia *f*
theorem *n* prōpositum *nt*
theoretical *adj* contemplātīvus
theory *n* ratiō *f*; **~ and practice** ratiō atque ūsus
there *adv* ibī, illīc; (*thither*) eō, illūc; **from ~** inde, illinc; **here and ~** passim; **~ is** est; (*interj*) ecce
thereabout, thereabouts *adv* circā, circiter, prope
thereafter *adv* deinde, posteā
thereby *adv* eā rē, hōc factō
therefore *adv* itaque, igitur, ergō, idcircō
therein *adv* inibī, in eō
thereof *adv* ēius, ēius reī
thereon *adv* īnsuper, in eō
thereupon *adv* deinde, statim, inde, quo factō
therewith *adv* cum eō
thesis *n* prōpositum *nt*
thews *n* nervī *mpl*
they *pron* iī, hī, illī
thick *adj* dēnsus; (*air*) crassus
thicken *vt* dēnsāre ▶ *vi* concrēscere
thickening *n* concrētiō *f*
thicket *n* dūmētum *nt*
thickheaded *adj* stupidus, hebes
thickly *adv* dēnsē; **~ populated** frequēns
thickness *n* crassitūdō *f*
thickset *adj* brevis atque obēsus
thick-skinned *adj*: **be ~** callēre; **become ~** occallēscere
thief *n* fūr *m*
thieve *vt* fūrārī, surripere
thievery *n* fūrtum *nt*
thievish *adj* fūrāx
thigh *n* femur *nt*
thin *adj* exīlis, gracilis, tenuis; (*attendance*) īnfrequēns ▶ *vt* attenuāre, extenuāre; **~ out** rārefacere; **~ down** dīluere
thine *adj* tuus
thing *n* rēs *f*; **as things are** nunc, cum haec ita sint

think vi cōgitāre; (*opinion*) putāre, existimāre, arbitrārī, rērī, crēdere; **as I ~** meā sententiā; **~ about** cōgitāre dē; **~ highly of** māgnī aestimāre; **~ nothing of** nihilī facere; **~ out** excōgitāre; **~ over** reputāre, in mente agitāre

thinker n philosophus m

thinking adj sapiēns ▶ n cōgitātiō f; **~ that** ratus, arbitratus

thinly adv exīliter, tenuiter; rārē

thinness n exīlitās f, gracilitās f; (*person*) maciēs f; (*number*) exiguitās f, īnfrequentia f; (*air*) tenuitās f

thin-skinned adj inrītābilis

third adj tertius; **for the ~ time** tertium ▶ n tertia pars f, triēns m; **two thirds** duae partēs, bēs m

thirdly adv tertiō

thirst n sitis f ▶ vi sitīre; **~ for** sitīre

thirstily adv sitienter

thirsty adj sitiēns

thirteen num tredecim; **~ each** ternī dēnī; **~ times** terdeciēns

thirteenth adj tertius decimus

thirtieth adj trīcēsimus

thirty num trīgintā; **~ each** trīcēnī; **~ times** trīciēns

this pron hīc

thistle n carduus m

thither adv eō, illūc

thole n scalmus m

thong n lōrum nt, habēna f

thorn n spīna f, sentis m

thorny adj spīnōsus

thorough adj absolūtus, germānus; (*work*) accūrātus

thoroughbred adj generōsus

thoroughfare n via f

thoroughly adv penitus, omnīnō, funditus

thoroughness n cūra f, dīligentia f

thou pron tū

though conj etsī, etiamsī, quamvīs (*subj*), quamquam (+ *indic*)

thought n (*faculty*) cōgitātiō f, mēns f, animus m; (*an idea*) cōgitātum nt, nōtiō f; (*design*) cōnsilium nt, prōpositum nt; (*expressed*) sententia f; (*heed*) cautiō f, prōvidentia f; (*RHET*) inventiō f; **second thoughts** posteriōrēs cōgitātiōnēs

thoughtful adj cōgitābundus; prōvidus

thoughtfully adv prōvidē

thoughtless adj incōnsīderātus, incōnsultus, imprōvidus, immemor

thoughtlessly adv temerē, incōnsultē

thoughtlessness n incōnsīderantia f, imprūdentia f

thousand num mīlle; **thousands** (*pl*) mīlia (*ntpl* + *gen*); **~ each** mīllēnī; **~ times** mīlliēns; **three ~** tria mīlia

thousandth adj mīllēsimus

thraldom n servitūs f

thrall n servus m

thrash vt verberāre

thrashing n verbera ntpl

thread n fīlum nt; **hang by a ~** (*fig*) fīlō pendēre ▶ vt: **~ one's way** sē īnsinuāre

threadbare adj trītus, obsolētus

threat n minae fpl, minātiō f

threaten vt minārī (*dat of pers*), dēnūntiāre ▶ vi imminēre, impendēre

threatening adj mināx, imminēns

threateningly adv mināciter

three num trēs; **~ each** ternī; **~ times** ter; **~ days** trīduum nt; **~ years** triennium nt; **~ quarters** trēs partēs fpl, dōdrāns m

three-cornered adj triangulus, triquetrus

threefold adj triplex

three hundred num trecentī; **three hundred each** trecēnī; **three hundred times** trecentiēns

three hundredth adj trecentēsimus

three-legged adj tripēs

three-quarters n dōdrāns m, trēs partēs fpl

thresh vt terere

threshing floor n ārea f

threshold n līmen nt

thrice adv ter

thrift n frūgālitās f, parsimōnia f

thriftily adv frūgāliter

thrifty adj parcus, frūgī

thrill n horror m ▶ vt percellere, percutere ▶ vi trepidāre

thrilling adj mīrābilis

thrive vi vigēre, valēre, crēscere

thriving adj valēns, vegetus; (*crops*) laetus

throat n faucēs fpl, guttur nt; **cut the ~ of** iugulāre

throaty adj gravis, raucus

throb vi palpitāre, micāre ▶ n pulsus m

throe n dolor m; **be in the throes of** labōrāre ex

throne n solium nt; (*power*) rēgnum nt

throng n multitūdō f, frequentia f ▶ vt celebrāre; **~ round** stīpāre, circumfundī (*dat*)

throttle vt strangulāre

through prep per (*acc*); (*cause*) propter (*acc*), abl ▶ adv: **~ and ~** penitus; **carry ~** exsequī, peragere; **go ~** trānsīre; **run ~** percurrere; **be ~ with** perfūnctum esse (*abl*)

throughout adv penitus, omnīnō ▶ prep per (*acc*)

throw n iactus m, coniectus m ▶ vt iacere, conicere; **~ about** iactāre; **~ across** trāicere; **~ away** abicere; (*something precious*) prōicere; **~ back** rēicere; **~ down** dēturbāre, dēicere; **~ into** inicere; **~ into confusion** perturbāre; **~ off** excutere, exsolvere; **~ open** patefacere; **~ out** ēicere, prōicere; **~ over** (*fig*) dēstituere; **~ overboard** iactūram facere (*gen*); **~ to** (*danger*) obicere; **~ up** ēicere; (*building*) exstruere; **~ a bridge over** pontem inicere (*dat*), pontem faciendum cūrāre in (*abl*); **~ light on** (*fig*) lūmen adhibēre (*dat*); **~ a rider** equitem excutere

throwing n coniectiō f, iactus m

thrum n līcium nt

thrush n turdus m

thrust vt trūdere, pellere, impingere; **~ at** petere; **~ away** dētrūdere; **~ forward** prōtrūdere; **~ home** dēfīgere; **~ into** īnfīgere, impingere; **~ out** extrūdere

thud n gravis sonitus m

thug n percussor m, sīcārius m

thumb n pollex m; **have under one's ~** in potestāte suā habēre

thump n plāga f ▸ vt tundere, pulsāre

thunder n tonitrus m ▸ vi tonāre, intonāre; **it thunders** tonāt

thunderbolt n fulmen nt

thunderer n tonāns m

thunderstruck adj attonitus

thus adv (referring back) sīc; (referring forward) ita; **~ far** hāctenus

thwack vt verberāre

thwart vt obstāre (dat), officere (dat), remorārī, frustrārī ▸ n (boat's) trānstrum nt

thy adj tuus

thyme n thymum nt; (wild) serpyllum nt

tiara n diadēma nt

ticket n tessera f

tickle vt titillāre

tickling n titillātiō f

ticklish adj lūbricus

tidal adj: **~ waters** aestuārium nt

tide n aestus m; (time) tempus nt; **ebb ~** aestūs recessus m; **flood ~** aestūs accessus m; **turn of the ~** commūtātiō aestūs; **the ~ will turn** (fig) circumagētur hīc orbis

tidily adv concinnē, mundē

tidiness n concinnitās f, munditia f

tidings n nūntius m

tidy adj concinnus, mundus

tie n (bond) vinculum nt, cōpula f; (kin) necessitūdō f ▸ vt ligāre; (knot) nectere; **tie fast** dēvincīre, cōnstringere; **tie on** illigāre; **tie to** adligāre; **tie together** colligāre; **tie up** adligāre; (wound) obligāre

tier n ōrdō m

tiff n dissēnsiō f

tiger n tigris usu f

tight adj strictus, astrictus, intentus; (close) artus; **draw ~** intendere, addūcere

tighten vt adstringere, contendere

tightly adv artē, angustē

tightrope n extentus fūnis; **~ walker** n fūnambulus m

tigress n tigris f

tile n tegula f, imbrex f, later nt

till conj dum, dōnec ▸ prep usque ad (acc), in (acc); **not ~** dēmum ▸ n arca f ▸ vt colere

tillage n cultus m

tiller n (AGR) cultor m; (ship) clāvus m, gubernāculum nt

tilt vt inclīnāre

tilth n cultus m, arvum nt

timber n (for building) māteria f; (firewood) lignum nt

timbrel n tympanum nt

time n tempus nt; (lifetime) aetās f; (interval) intervallum nt, spatium nt; (of day) hōra f; (leisure) ōtium nt; (rhythm) numerus m; **another ~** aliās; **at times** aliquandō, interdum; **at all times** semper; **at any ~** umquam; **at one ~ ... at another** aliās ... aliās; **at that ~** tunc, id temporis; **at the right ~** ad tempus, mātūrē, tempestīvē; **at the same ~** simul; tamen; **at the wrong ~** intempestīvē; **beating ~** percussiō f; **convenient ~** opportūnitās f; **for a ~** aliquantisper, parumper; **for a long ~** diū; **for some ~** aliquamdiū; **for the ~ being** ad tempus; **from ~ to ~** interdum, identidem; **have a good ~** geniō indulgēre; **have ~ for** vacāre (dat); **in ~** ad tempus, tempore; **in a short ~** brevī; **in good ~** tempestīvus; **in the ~ of** apud (acc); **keep ~** (marching) gradum cōnferre; (music) modulārī; **many times** saepe, saepenumerō; **pass ~, spend ~** tempus sūmere, dēgere; **several times** aliquotiēns; **some ~** aliquandō; **waste ~** tempus terere; **what is the time?** quota hōra est?; **~ expired** ēmeritus

time-honoured adj antīquus

timeliness n opportūnitās f

timely adj opportūnus, tempestīvus, mātūrus

timid adj timidus

timidity n timiditās f

timidly adv timidē

timorous adj timidus

timorously adv timidē

tin n stannum nt, plumbum album nt ▸ adj stanneus

tincture n color m, sapor m ▸ vt īnficere

tinder n fōmes m

tinge vt imbuere, īnficere, tingere

tingle vi horrēre

tingling n horror m

tinkle vi tinnīre ▸ n tinnītus m

tinsel n bractea f; (fig) speciēs f, fūcus m

tint n color m ▸ vt colōrāre

tiny adj minūtus, pusillus, perexiguus

tip n apex m, cacūmen nt, extrēmum nt; **the tip of** prīmus, extrēmus ▸ vt praefīgere; **tip over** invertere

tipple vi pōtāre

tippler n pōtor m, ēbrius m

tipsy adj tēmulentus

tiptoes n: **on ~** suspēnsō gradū

tirade n obiūrgātiō f, dēclāmātiō f

tire vt fatīgāre; **~ out** dēfatīgāre ▸ vi dēfetīscī, fatīgārī; **I ~ of** mē taedet (gen); **it tires** taedet (+ acc of person, gen of thing)

tired adj (dē)fessus, lassus; **~ out** dēfessus; **I am ~ of** mē taedet

tiresome adj molestus, difficilis

tiring adj labōriōsus, operōsus

tiro n tīrō m, rudis m

tissue n textus m

tit n: **give tit for tat** pār parī respondēre

Titan n Tītān m

titanic adj immānis

titbit n cuppēdium nt

tithe n decuma f

tithe gatherer n decumānus m
titillate vt titillāre
titillation n titillātiō f
title n (book) īnscrīptiō f, index m; (inscription) titulus m; (person) nōmen nt, appellātiō f; (claim) iūs nt, vindiciae fpl; **assert one's ~ to** vindicāre; **give a ~ to** īnscrībere
titled adj nōbilis
title deed n auctōritās f
titter n rīsus m ▶ vi rīdēre
tittle-tattle n sermunculus m
titular adj nōmine
to prep ad (acc), in (acc); (attitude) ergā (acc); (giving) dat; (towns, small islands, domus, rūs) acc ▶ conj (purpose) ut ▶ adv: **come to** animum recipere; **to and fro** hūc illūc
toad n būfō m
toady n adsentātor m, parasītus m ▶ vt adsentārī (dat)
toadyism n adsentātiō f
toast n: **drink a ~** prōpīnāre ▶ vt torrēre; (drink) prōpīnāre (dat)
today adv hodiē; **today's** hodiernus
toe n digitus m; **big toe** pollex m
toga n toga f
together adv ūnā, simul; **bring ~** cōgere, congerere; **come ~** convenīre, congregārī; **put ~** cōnferre, compōnere
toil n labor m; (snare) rēte nt ▶ vi labōrāre; **~ at** ēlabōrāre in (abl)
toilet n (lady's) cultus m
toilsome adj labōriōsus, operōsus
toil-worn adj labōre cōnfectus
token n īnsigne nt, signum nt, indicium nt
tolerable adj tolerābilis, patibilis; (quality) mediocris; (size) modicus
tolerably adv satis, mediocriter
tolerance n patientia f, tolerantia f
tolerant adj indulgēns, tolerāns
tolerantly adv indulgenter
tolerate vt tolerāre, ferre, indulgēre (dat)
toleration n patientia f; (freedom) lībertās f
toll n vectīgal nt; (harbour) portōrium nt
toll collector n exāctor m; portitor m
tomb n sepulcrum nt
tombstone n lapis m
tome n liber m
tomorrow adv crās; **tomorrow's** crāstinus; **the day after ~** perendiē; **put off till ~** in crāstinum differre
tone n sonus m, vōx f; (painting) color m
tongs n forceps m/f
tongue n lingua f; (shoe) ligula f; **on the tip of one's ~** in prīmōribus labrīs
tongue-tied adj ēlinguis, īnfāns
tonnage n amphorae fpl
tonsils n tōnsillae fpl
tonsure n rāsūra f
too adv (also) etiam, īnsuper, quoque; (excess) nimis ▶ compar adj: **too far** extrā modum; **too much** nimium; **too long** nimium diū; **too great to** māior quam quī (subj);

too late sērius; **too little** parum (gen)
tool n īnstrūmentum nt; (AGR) ferrāmentum nt; (person) minister m
tooth n dēns m; **~ and nail** tōtō corpore atque omnibus ungulīs; **cast in someone's teeth** exprobrāre, obicere; **cut teeth** dentīre; **in the teeth of** obviam (dat), adversus (acc); **with the teeth** mordicus
toothache n dentium dolor m
toothed adj dentātus
toothless adj ēdentulus
toothpick n dentiscalpium nt
toothsome adj suāvis, dulcis
top n vertex m, fastīgium nt; (tree) cacūmen nt; (toy) turbō m; **from top to toe** ab īmīs unguibus usque ad verticem summum; **the top of** summus ▶ vt exsuperāre; **top up** supplēre ▶ adj superior, summus
tope vi pōtāre
toper n pōtor m
topiary adj topiārius ▶ n topiārium opus nt
topic n rēs f; (RHET) locus m; **~ of conversation** sermō m
topical adj hodiernus
topmost adj summus
topography n dēscrīptiō f
topple vi titubāre; **~ over** prōlābī
topsail n dolō m
topsyturvy adv praeposterē; **turn ~** sūrsum deōrsum versāre, permiscēre
tor n mōns m
torch n fax f, lampas f
torment n cruciātus m; (mind) angor m ▶ vt cruciāre; (mind) discruciāre, excruciāre, angere
tormentor n tortor m
tornado n turbō m
torpid adj torpēns; **be ~** torpēre; **grow ~** obtorpēscere
torpor n torpor m, inertia f
torrent n torrēns m
torrid adj torridus
torsion n tortus m
torso n truncus m
tortoise n testūdō f
tortoiseshell n testūdō f
tortuous adj flexuōsus
torture n cruciātus m, supplicium nt; **instrument of ~** tormentum nt ▶ vt torquēre, cruciāre, excruciāre
torturer n tortor m, carnifex m
toss n iactus m ▶ vt iactāre, excutere; **~ about** agitāre; **be tossed** (at sea) fluitāre
total adj tōtus, ūniversus ▶ n summa f
totality n ūniversitās f
totally adv omnīnō, plānē
totter vi lābāre, titubāre; **make ~** labefactāre
tottering n titubātiō f
touch n tāctus m; **a ~ of** aliquantulum (gen); **finishing ~** manus extrēma f ▶ vt tangere, attingere; (feelings) movēre, tangere ▶ vi inter sē contingere; **~ at** nāvem appellere ad; **~ on** (topic) attingere, perstringere; **~ up** expolīre

touch-and-go adj anceps ▶ n discrīmen nt
touching adj (place) contiguus; (emotion)
flexanimus ▶ prep quod attinet ad (acc)
touchstone n (fig) obrussa f
touchy adj irrītābilis; stomachōsus
tough adj dūrus
toughen vt dūrāre
toughness n dūritia f
tour n iter nt; (abroad) peregrīnātiō f
tourist n viātor m, peregrīnātor m
tournament n certāmen nt
tow n stuppa f; **of tow** stuppeus ▶ vt adnexum
trahere, remulcō trahere
toward, towards prep ad (acc), versus (after
noun, acc); (feelings) in (acc), ergā (acc); (time)
sub (acc)
towel n mantēle nt
tower n turris f ▶ vi ēminēre
towered adj turrītus
town n urbs f, oppidum nt; **country ~**
mūnicipium nt ▶ adj urbānus
town councillor n decuriō m
townsman n oppidānus m
townspeople npl oppidānī mpl
towrope n remulcum nt
toy n crepundia ntpl ▶ vi lūdere
trace n vestīgium nt, indicium nt ▶ vt
investīgāre; (draw) dēscrībere; **~ out** dēsignāre
track n (mark) vestīgium nt; (path) callis m,
sēmita f; (of wheel) orbita f; (of ship) cursus m
▶ vt investīgāre, indāgāre
trackless adj invius
tract n (country) tractus m, regiō f; (book) libellus
m
tractable adj tractābilis, facilis, docilis
trade n mercātūra f, mercātus m; (a business)
ars f, quaestus m; **freedom of ~** commercium nt
▶ vi mercātūrās facere, negōtiārī; **~ in** vēndere,
vēnditāre
trader n mercātor m, negōtiātor m
tradesman n opifex m
tradition n fāma f, mōs māiōrum m, memoria f
traditional adj ā māiōribus trāditus, patrius
traditionally adv mōre māiōrum
traduce vt calumniārī, obtrectāre (dat)
traducer n calumniātor m, obtrectātor m
traffic n commercium nt; (on road) vehicula ntpl
▶ vi mercātūrās facere; **~ in** vēndere, vēnditāre
tragedian n (author) tragoedus m; (actor) āctor
tragicus m
tragedy n tragoedia f; (fig) calamitās f,
malum nt
tragic adj tragicus; (fig) tristis
tragically adv tragicē; male
tragicomedy n tragicōcōmoedia f
trail n vestīgia ntpl ▶ vt trahere ▶ vi trahī
train n (line) agmen nt, ōrdō m; (of dress) īnstita f;
(army) impedīmenta ntpl; (followers) comitēs
mpl, satellitēs mpl, cohors f ▶ vt īnstituere,
īnstruere, docēre, adsuēfacere; exercēre;
(weapon) dīrigere
trainer n (sport) lanista m, aliptēs m

training n disciplīna f, īnstitūtiō f; (practice)
exercitātiō f
trait n līneāmentum nt
traitor n prōditor m
traitorous adj perfidus, perfidiōsus
traitorously adv perfidiōsē
trammel vt impedīre
tramp n (man) planus m; (of feet) pulsus m ▶ vi
gradī
trample vi: **~ on** obterere, prōterere, prōculcāre
trance n stupor m; (prophetic) furor m
tranquil adj tranquillus, placidus, quiētus,
sēdātus
tranquility n tranquillitās f, quiēs f, pāx f
tranquillize vt pācāre, sēdāre
tranquilly adv tranquillē, placidē, tranquillō
animō
transact vt agere, gerere, trānsigere
transaction n rēs f, negōtium nt
transactor n āctor m
transalpine adj trānsalpīnus
transcend vt superāre, excēdere
transcendence n praestantia f
transcendent adj eximius, ēgregius, excellēns
transcendental adj dīvīnus
transcendentally adv eximiē, ēgregiē, ūnicē
transcribe vt dēscrībere, trānscrībere
transcriber n librārius m
transcript n exemplar nt, exemplum nt
transfer n trānslātiō f; (of property) aliēnātiō f
▶ vt trānsferre; (troops) trādūcere; (property)
abaliēnāre; (duty) dēlēgāre
transference n trānslātiō f
transfigure vt trānsfōrmāre
transfix vt trānsfīgere, trāicere, trānsfodere;
(mind) obstupefacere; **be transfixed** stupēre,
stupēscere
transform vt commūtāre, vertere
transformation n commūtātiō f
transgress vt violāre, perfringere ▶ vi
dēlinquere
transgression n dēlictum nt
transgressor n violātor m
transience n brevitās f
transient adj fluxus, cadūcus, brevis
transit n trānsitus m
transition n mūtātiō f; (speech) trānsitus m
transitory adj brevis, fluxus
translate vt vertere, reddere; **~ into Latin**
Latīnē reddere
translation n: **a Latin ~ of Homer** Latīnē
redditus Homērus
translator n interpres m
translucent adj perlūcidus
transmarine adj trānsmarīnus
transmission n missiō f
transmit vt mittere; (legacy) trādere, prōdere
transmutable adj mūtābilis
transmutation n mūtātiō f
transmute vt mūtāre, commūtāre
transom n trabs f
transparency n perlūcida nātūra f

transparent adj perlūcidus; (fig) perspicuus
transparently adv perspicuē
transpire vi (get known) ēmānāre, dīvulgārī; (happen) ēvenīre
transplant vt trānsferre
transport n vectūra f; (ship) nāvis onerāria f; (emotion) ēlātiō f, summa laetitia f ▶ vt trānsportāre, trānsvehere, trānsmittere; **be transported** (fig) efferrī, gestīre
transportation n vectūra f
transpose vt invertere; (words) trāicere
transposition n (words) trāiectiō f
transverse adj trānsversus, oblīquus
transversely adv in trānsversum, oblīquē
trap n laqueus m; (fig) īnsidiae fpl ▶ vt dēcipere, excipere; (fig) inlaqueāre
trappings npl ōrnāmenta ntpl, īnsignia ntpl; (horse's) phalerae fpl
trash n nūgae fpl
trashy adj vīlis
Trasimene n Trasimēnus m
travail n labor m, sūdor m; (woman's) puerperium nt ▶ vi labōrāre, sūdāre; parturīre
travel n itinera ntpl; (foreign) peregrīnātiō f ▶ vi iter facere; (abroad) peregrīnārī; **~ through** peragrāre; **~ to** contendere ad, in (acc), proficīscī in (acc)
traveller n viātor m; (abroad) peregrīnātor m
traverse vt peragrāre, lūstrāre; **~ a great distance** multa mīlia passuum iter facere
travesty n perversa imitātiō f ▶ vt perversē imitārī
tray n ferculum nt
treacherous adj perfidus, perfidiōsus; (ground) lūbricus
treacherously adv perfidiōsē
treachery n perfidia f
tread vi incēdere, ingredī; **~ on** īnsistere (dat) ▶ n gradus m, incessus m
treadle n (loom) īnsilia ntpl
treadmill n pistrīnum nt
treason n māiestās f, perduelliō f; **be charged with ~** māiestātis accūsārī; **be guilty of high ~ against** māiestātem minuere, laedere (gen)
treasonable adj perfidus, perfidiōsus
treasure n gāza f, thēsaurus m; (person) dēliciae fpl ▶ vt māximī aestimāre, dīligere, fovēre; **~ up** condere, congerere
treasure house n thēsaurus m
treasurer n aerāriī praefectus m; (royal) dioecētēs m
treasury n aerārium nt; (emperor's) fiscus m
treat n convīvium nt; dēlectātiō f ▶ vt (in any way) ūtī (abl), habēre, tractāre, accipere; (patient) cūrāre; (topic) tractāre; (with hospitality) invītāre; **~ with** agere cum; **~ as a friend** amīcī locō habēre
treatise n liber m
treatment n tractātiō f; (MED) cūrātiō f
treaty n foedus nt; **make a ~** foedus ferīre
treble adj triplus; (voice) acūtus ▶ n acūtus sonus m ▶ vt triplicāre

tree n arbor f
trek vi migrāre ▶ n migrātiō f
trellis n cancellī mpl
tremble vi tremere, horrēre
trembling n tremor m, horror m ▶ adj tremulus
tremendous adj immānis, ingēns, vastus
tremendously adv immāne quantum
tremor n tremor m
tremulous adj tremulus
trench n fossa f
trenchant adj ācer
trenchantly adv ācriter
trend n inclīnātiō f ▶ vi vergere
trepidation n trepidātiō f
trespass n dēlictum nt ▶ vi dēlinquere; **~ on** (property) invādere in (acc); (patience, time, etc) abūtī (abl)
trespasser n quī iniussū dominī ingreditur
tress n crīnis m
trial n (essay) experientia f; (test) probātiō f; (LAW) iūdicium nt, quaestiō f; (trouble) labor m, aerumna f; **make a ~** experīrī, perīculum facere (gen); **be brought to ~** in iūdicium venīre; **put on ~** in iūdicium vocāre; **hold a ~ on** quaestiōnem habēre dē (abl)
triangle n triangulum nt
triangular adj triangulus, triquetrus
tribe n tribus m; gēns f; (barbarian) nātiō f
tribulation n aerumna f
tribunal n iūdicium nt
tribune n tribūnus m; (platform) rōstra ntpl
tribuneship, tribunate n tribūnātus m
tribunician adj tribūnicius
tributary adj vectīgālis ▶ n: **be a ~ of** (river) īnfluere in (acc)
tribute n tribūtum nt, vectīgal nt; (verbal) laudātiō f; **pay a ~ to** laudāre
trice n: **in a ~** mōmentō temporis
trick n dolus m, fallācia f, fraus f, īnsidiae fpl, ars f; (conjurer's) praestīgiae fpl; (habit) mōs m ▶ vt fallere, dēcipere, ēlūdere; (with words) verba dare (dat); **~ out** ōrnāre, distinguere
trickery n dolus m, fraus f, fallāciae fpl
trickle n guttae fpl ▶ vi mānāre, dēstillāre
trickster n fraudātor m, veterātor m
tricky adj lūbricus, difficilis
trident n tridēns m, fuscina f
tried adj probātus, spectātus
triennial adj trietēricus
triennially adv quartō quōque annō
trifle n nūgae fpl, paululum nt ▶ vi lūdere, nūgārī; **~ with** lūdere
trifling adj levis, exiguus
triflingly adv leviter
trig adj lepidus, concinnus
trigger n manulea f
trim adj nitidus, concinnus ▶ vt putāre, tondēre; (lamp) oleum īnstillāre (dat) ▶ vi temporibus servīre
trimly adv concinnē
trimness n nitor m, munditia f
trinket n crepundia ntpl

trip n iter nt ▶ vt supplantāre ▶ vi lābī, titubāre;
~ along currere; **~ over** incurrere in (acc)
tripartite adj tripartītus
tripe n omāsum nt
triple adj triplex, triplus ▶ vt triplicāre
triply adv trifāriam
tripod n tripus m
trireme n trirēmis f
trite adj trītus
triumph n triumphus m; (victory) victōria f
▶ vi triumphāre; vincere; **~ over** dēvincere
triumphal adj triumphālis
triumphant adj victor; laetus
triumvir n triumvir m
triumvirate n triumvirātus m
trivial adj levis, tenuis
triviality n nūgae fpl
trochaic adj trochaicus
trochee n trochaeus m
Trojan n Trōiānus m
troop n grex f, caterva f; (cavalry) turma f
▶ vi cōnfluere, congregārī
trooper n eques m
troops npl cōpiae fpl
trope n figūra f, trānslātiō f
trophy n tropaeum nt; **set up a ~** tropaeum
pōnere
tropic n sōlstitiālis orbis m; **tropics** pl loca
fervida ntpl
tropical adj tropicus
trot vi tolūtim īre
troth n fidēs f
trouble n incommodum nt, malum nt, molestia
f, labor m; (effort) opera f, negōtium nt;
(disturbance) turba f, tumultus m; **take the ~ to**
operam dare ut; **be worth the ~** operae pretium
esse ▶ vt (disturb) turbāre; (make uneasy)
sollicitāre, exagitāre; (annoy) incommodāre,
molestiam exhibēre (dat); **~ oneself about**
cūrāre, respicere; **be troubled with** labōrāre ex
troubler n turbātor m
troublesome adj molestus, incommodus,
difficilis
troublesomeness n molestia f
troublous adj turbidus, turbulentus
trough n alveus m
trounce vt castīgāre
troupe n grex f, caterva f
trousered adj brācātus
trousers n brācae fpl
trow vi opīnārī
truant adj tardus ▶ n cessātor m; **play ~** cessāre,
nōn compārēre
truce n indutiae fpl
truck n carrus m; **have no ~ with** nihil commerciī
habēre cum
truckle vi adsentārī
truculence n ferōcia f, asperitās f
truculent adj truculentus, ferōx
truculently adv ferōciter
trudge vi rēpere, pedibus incēdere
true adj vērus; (genuine) germānus, vērus;

(loyal) fīdus, fidēlis; (exact) rēctus, iūstus
truism n verbum trītum nt
truly adv rēvērā, profectō, vērē
trumpery n nūgae fpl ▶ adj vīlis
trumpet n tuba f, būcina f
trumpeter n būcinātor m, tubicen m
trump up vt ēmentīrī, cōnfingere
truncate vt praecīdere
truncheon n fustis m, scīpiō m
trundle vt volvere
trunk n truncus m; (elephant's) manus f; (box)
cista f
truss n fascia f ▶ vt colligāre
trust n fidēs f, fīdūcia f; **breach of ~** mala fidēs;
held in ~ fīdūciārius; **put ~ in** fidem habēre (dat)
▶ vt confīdere (dat), crēdere (dat); (entrust)
committere, concrēdere
trustee n tūtor m
trusteeship n tūtēla f
trustful adj crēdulus, fīdēns
trustfully adv fīdenter
trustily adv fidēliter
trustiness n fidēs f, fidēlitās f
trusting adj fīdēns
trustingly adv fīdenter
trustworthily adv fidēliter
trustworthiness n fidēs f, integritās f
trustworthy adj fīdus, certus; (witness)
locuplēs; (authority) certus, bonus
trusty adj fīdus, fidēlis
truth n vēritās f, vērum nt; **in ~** rē vērā
truthful adj vērāx
truthfully adv vērē
truthfulness n fidēs f
try vt (attempt) cōnārī; (test) experīrī, temptāre;
(harass) exercēre; (judge) iūdicāre, cognōscere;
try for petere, quaerere
trying adj molestus
tub n alveus m, cūpa f
tubby adj obēsus
tube n fistula f
tufa n tōfus m
tuft n crista f
tug vt trahere, tractāre
tuition n īnstitūtiō f
tumble vi concidere, corruere, prōlābī
▶ n cāsus m
tumbledown adj ruīnōsus
tumbler n pōculum nt
tumid adj tumidus, īnflātus
tumour n tūber nt
tumult n tumultus m, turba f; (fig) perturbātiō f
tumultuous adj tumultuōsus, turbidus
tumultuously adv tumultuōsē
tumulus n tumulus m
tun n dōlium nt
tuna n thunnus m
tune n modī mpl, carmen nt; **keep in ~**
concentum servāre; **out of ~** absonus, dissonus;
(strings) incontentus ▶ vt (strings) intendere
tuneful adj canōrus
tunefully adv numerōsē

tunic n tunica f; **wearing a ~** tunicātus
tunnel n cunīculus m
turban n mitra f, mitella f
turbid adj turbidus
turbot n rhombus m
turbulence n tumultus m
turbulent adj turbulentus, turbidus
turbulently adv turbulentē, turbidē
turf n caespes m
turgid adj turgidus, īnflātus
turgidity n (RHET) ampullae fpl
turgidly adv īnflātē
turmoil n turba f, tumultus m; (mind)
  perturbātiō f
turn n (motion) conversiō f; (bend) flexus m,
  ānfrāctus m; (change) commūtātiō f, vicissitūdō
  f; (walk) spatium nt; (of mind) adfectus m; (of
  language) sententia f, cōnfōrmātiō f; **~ of events**
  mutātiō rērum f; **bad ~** iniūria f; **good ~**
  beneficium nt; **~ of the scale** mōmentum nt;
  take a ~ for the worse in pēiōrem partem vertī;
  in turns invicem, vicissim, alternī; **in one's ~**
  locō ōrdine ▶ vt vertere, convertere, flectere;
  (change) vertere, mūtāre; (direct) intendere,
  dīrigere; (translate) vertere, reddere; (on a lathe)
  tornāre; **~ the edge of** retundere; **~ the head**
  mentem exturbāre; **~ the laugh against** rīsum
  convertere in (acc); **~ the scale** (fig) mōmentum
  habēre; **~ the stomach** nauseam facere; **~ to**
  account ūtī (abl), in rem suam convertere ▶ vi
  versārī, circumagī; (change) vertere, mūtārī;
  (crisis) pendēre; (direction) convertī; (scale)
  prōpendēre; **~ against** vt aliēnāre ab; **~ king's/**
  queen's evidence indicium prōfitērī ▶ vi
  dēscīscere ab; **~ around** (se) circumvertere;
  ~ aside vt dēflectere, dēclīnāre ▶ vi dēvertere,
  sē dēclīnāre; **~ away** vt āvertere, dēpellere ▶ vi
  āversārī, discēdere; **~ back** vi revertī; **~ down** vt
  invertere; (proposal) rēicere; **~ into** vi vertere in
  (acc), mūtārī in (acc); **~ out** vt ēicere, expellere
  ▶ vi cadere, ēvenīre, ēvādere; **~ outside in**
  excutere; **~ over** vt ēvertere; (book) ēvolvere; (in
  mind) volūtāre, agitāre; **~ round** vt circumagere
  ▶ vi convertī; **~ up** vt retorquēre; (earth) versāre;
  (nose) corrūgāre ▶ vi adesse, intervenīre;
  ~ upside down invertere
turncoat n trānsfuga m
turning n flexus m, ānfrāctus m
turning point n discrīmen nt, mēta f
turnip n rāpum nt
turpitude n turpitūdō f
turquoise n callais f ▶ adj callainus
turret n turris f
turreted adj turrītus
turtle n testūdō f; **turn ~** invertī
turtle dove n turtur m
tusk n dēns m
tussle n luctātiō f ▶ vi luctārī
tutelage n tūtēla f
tutelary adj praeses
tutor n praeceptor m, magister m ▶ vt docēre,
  praecipere (dat)

tutorship n tūtēla f
twaddle n nūgae fpl
twang n sonus m ▶ vi increpāre
tweak vi vellicāre
tweezers n forceps m/f, volsella f
twelfth adj duodecimus ▶ n duodecima pars f,
  ūncia f; **eleven twelfths** deūnx m; **five twelfths**
  quīncūnx m; **seven twelfths** septūnx m
twelve num duodecim; **~ each** duodēnī; **~ times**
  duodeciēns
twelvemonth n annus m
twentieth adj vīcēsimus ▶ n vīcēsima pars f;
  (tax) vīcēsima f
twenty num vīgintī; **~ each** vīcēnī; **~ times**
  vīciēns
twice adv bis; **~ as much** duplus, bis tantō;
  ~ a day bis diē, bis in diē
twig n virga f, rāmulus m
twilight n (morning) dīlūculum nt; (evening)
  crepusculum nt
twin adj geminus ▶ n geminus m, gemina f
twine n resticula f ▶ vt nectere, implicāre,
  contexere ▶ vi sē implicāre; **~ round** complectī
twinge n dolor m
twinkle vi micāre
twirl vt intorquēre, contorquēre ▶ vi circumagī
twist vt torquēre, intorquēre ▶ vi torquērī
twit vt obicere (dat)
twitch vt vellicāre ▶ vi micāre
twitter vi pīpilāre
two num duo; **two each** bīnī; **two days** biduum
  nt; **two years** biennium nt; **two years old**
  bīmus; **two by two** bīnī; **two feet long**
  bipedālis; **in two parts** bifāriam, bipartītō
two-coloured adj bicolor
two-edged adj anceps
twofold adj duplex, anceps
two-footed adj bipēs
two-headed adj biceps
two-horned adj bicornis
two hundred num ducentī; **two hundred**
  each ducēnī; **two hundred times** ducentiēns
two hundredth adj ducentēsimus
two-oared adj birēmis
two-pronged adj bidēns, bifurcus
two-way adj bivius
type n (pattern) exemplar nt; (kind) genus nt
typhoon n turbō m
typical adj proprius, solitus
typically adv dē mōre, ut mōs est
typify vt exprimere
tyrannical adj superbus, crūdēlis
tyrannically adv superbē, crūdēliter
tyrannize vi dominārī, rēgnāre
tyrannous adj see **tyrannical**
tyrannously adv see **tyrannically**
tyranny n dominātiō f, rēgnum nt
tyrant n rēx m, crūdēlis dominus m; (Greek)
  tyrannus m
tyro n tīrō m, rudis m

u

ubiquitous *adj* omnibus locīs praesēns
ubiquity *n* ūniversa praesentia *f*
udder *n* über *nt*
ugliness *n* foeditās *f*, dēfōrmitās *f*, turpitūdō *f*
ugly *adj* foedus, dēfōrmis, turpis
ulcer *n* ulcus *nt*, vomica *f*
ulcerate *vi* ulcerārī
ulcerous *adj* ulcerōsus
ulterior *adj* ulterior
ultimate *adj* ultimus, extrēmus
ultimately *adv* tandem, ad ultimum
umbrage *n* offēnsiō *f*; **take ~ at** indignē ferre,
patī
umbrageous *adj* umbrōsus
umbrella *n* umbella *f*
umpire *n* arbiter *m*, disceptātor *m*
unabashed *adj* intrepidus, impudēns
unabated *adj* integer
unable *adj* impotēns; **be ~** nōn posse, nequīre
unacceptable *adj* ingrātus
unaccompanied *adj* sōlus
unaccomplished *adj* īnfectus, imperfectus;
(*person*) indoctus
unaccountable *adj* inexplicābilis
unaccountably *adv* sine causā, repentē
unaccustomed *adj* īnsuētus, īnsolitus
unacquainted *adj* ignārus (*gen*), imperītus
(*gen*)
unadorned *adj* inōrnātus, incōmptus; (*speech*)
nūdus, ēnucleātus
unadulterated *adj* sincērus, integer
unadvisedly *adv* imprūdenter, incōnsultē
unaffected *adj* simplex, candidus
unaffectedly *adv* simpliciter
unaided *adj* sine auxiliō, nūdus
unalienable *adj* proprius
unalloyed *adj* pūrus
unalterable *adj* immūtābilis
unaltered *adj* immūtātus
unambiguous *adj* apertus, certus
unambitious *adj* humilis, modestus
unanimity *n* cōnsēnsiō *f*, ūnanimitās *f*
unanimous *adj* concors, ūnanimus; **be ~** idem
omnēs sentīre

unanimously *adv* ūnā vōce, omnium
cōnsēnsū
unanswerable *adj* necessārius
unanswerably *adv* sine contrōversiā
unappreciative *adj* ingrātus
unapproachable *adj* inaccessus; (*person*)
difficilis
unarmed *adj* inermis
unasked *adj* ultrō, suā sponte
unassailable *adj* inexpugnābilis
unassailed *adj* intāctus, incolumis
unassuming *adj* modestus, dēmissus;
~ manners modestia *f*
unassumingly *adv* modestē
unattached *adj* līber
unattempted *adj* intentātus; **leave ~**
praetermittere
unattended *adj* sōlus, sine comitibus
unattractive *adj* invenustus
unauthentic *adj* incertō auctōre
unavailing *adj* inūtilis, inānis
unavenged *adj* inultus
unavoidable *adj* necessārius
unavoidably *adv* necessāriō
unaware *adj* īnscius, ignārus
unawares *adv* inopīnātō, dē imprōvīsō;
incautus
unbalanced *adj* turbātus
unbar *vt* reserāre
unbearable *adj* intolerābilis, intolerandus
unbearably *adv* intoleranter
unbeaten *adj* invictus
unbecoming *adj* indecōrus, inhonestus; **it is ~**
dēdecet
unbeknown *adj* ignōtus
unbelief *n* diffīdentia *f*
unbelievable *adj* incrēdibilis
unbelievably *adv* incrēdibiliter
unbelieving *adj* incrēdulus
unbend *vt* remittere, laxāre ▶ *vi* animum
remittere, aliquid dē sevēritāte remittere
unbending *adj* inexōrābilis, sevērus
unbiassed *adj* integer, incorruptus, aequus
unbidden *adj* ultrō, sponte
unbind *vt* solvere, resolvere
unblemished *adj* pūrus, integer
unblushing *adj* impudēns
unblushingly *adv* impudenter
unbolt *vt* reserāre
unborn *adj* nōndum nātus
unbosom *vt* patefacere, effundere
unbound *adj* solūtus
unbounded *adj* īnfīnītus, immēnsus
unbridled *adj* īnfrēnātus; (*fig*) effrēnātus,
indomitus, impotēns
unbroken *adj* integer; (*animal*) intractātus;
(*friendship*) inviolātus; (*series*) perpetuus,
continuus
unburden *vt* exonerāre; **~ oneself of** aperīre,
patefacere
unburied *adj* inhumātus, īnsepultus
unbusinesslike *adj* iners

uncalled-for adj supervacāneus
uncanny adj mīrus, mōnstruōsus
uncared-for adj neglectus
unceasing adj perpetuus, adsiduus
unceasingly adv perpetuō, adsiduē
unceremonious adj agrestis, inurbānus
unceremoniously adv inurbānē
uncertain adj incertus, dubius, anceps; **be ~** dubitāre, pendēre
uncertainly adv incertē, dubitanter
uncertainty n incertum nt; (state) dubitātiō f
unchangeable adj immūtābilis; (person) cōnstāns
unchanged adj immūtātus, īdem; **remain ~** permanēre
uncharitable adj inhūmānus, malignus
uncharitableness n inhūmānitās f
uncharitably adv inhūmānē, malignē
unchaste adj impudīcus, libīdinōsus
unchastely adv impudīcē
unchastity n incestus m, libīdō f
unchecked adj līber, indomitus
uncivil adj inurbānus, importūnus, inhūmānus
uncivilized adj barbarus, incultus, ferus
uncivilly adv inurbānē
uncle n (paternal) patruus m; (maternal) avunculus m
unclean adj immundus; (fig) impūrus, obscēnus
uncleanly adv impūrē
uncleanness n sordēs fpl; (fig) impūritās f, obscēnitās f
unclose vt aperīre
unclothe vt nūdāre, vestem dētrahere (dat)
unclothed adj nūdus
unclouded adj serēnus
uncoil vt explicāre, ēvolvere
uncomely adj dēfōrmis, turpis
uncomfortable adj incommodus, molestus
uncomfortably adv incommodē
uncommitted adj vacuus
uncommon adj rārus, īnsolitus, inūsitātus; (eminent) ēgregius, singulāris, eximius
uncommonly adv rārō; ēgregiē, ūnicē
uncommonness n īnsolentia f
uncommunicative adj tēctus, taciturnus
uncomplaining adj patiēns
uncompleted adj imperfectus
uncompromising adj dūrus, rigidus
unconcern n sēcūritās f
unconcerned adj sēcūrus, ōtiōsus
unconcernedly adv lentē
uncondemned adj indemnātus
unconditional adj absolūtus
unconditionally adv nūllā condiciōne
uncongenial adj ingrātus
unconnected adj sēparātus, disiūnctus; (style) dissolūtus
unconquerable adj invictus
unconquered adj invictus
unconscionable adj improbus
unconscionably adv improbē

unconscious adj: **~ of** īnscius (gen), ignārus (gen); **become ~** sōpīrī, animō linquī
unconsciousness n sopor m
unconsecrated adj profānus
unconsidered adj neglectus
unconstitutional adj illicitus
unconstitutionally adv contrā lēgēs, contrā rem pūblicam
uncontaminated adj pūrus, incorruptus, integer
uncontrollable adj impotēns, effrēnātus
uncontrollably adv effrēnātē
uncontrolled adj līber, solūtus
unconventional adj īnsolitus, solūtus
unconvicted adj indemnātus
unconvincing adj incrēdibilis, nōn vērī similis
uncooked adj crūdus
uncorrupted adj incorruptus, integer
uncouple vt disiungere
uncouth adj horridus, agrestis, inurbānus
uncouthly adv inurbānē
uncouthness n inhūmānitās f, rūsticitās f
uncover vt dētegere, aperīre, nūdāre
uncritical adj indoctus, crēdulus
uncultivated adj incultus; (fig) agrestis, rūsticus, impolītus
uncultured adj agrestis, rudis
uncut adj intōnsus
undamaged adj integer, inviolātus
undaunted adj intrepidus, fortis
undecayed adj incorruptus
undeceive vt errōrem tollere (dat), errōrem ēripere (dat)
undecided adj dubius, anceps; (case) integer
undecked adj (ship) apertus
undefended adj indēfēnsus, nūdus
undefiled adj integer, incontāminātus
undemonstrative adj taciturnus
undeniable adj certus
undeniably adv sine dubiō
undependable adj inconstāns, mōbilis
under adv īnfrā, subter ▶ prep sub (abl), īnfrā (acc); (number) intrā (acc); (motion) sub (acc); **~ arms** in armīs; **~ colour** (pretext of) speciē (gen), per speciem (gen); **~ my leadership** mē duce; **~ the circumstances** cum haec ita sint; **labour ~** labōrāre ex; **~ the eyes of** in cōnspectū (gen); **~ the leadership of** abl + duce
underage adj impūbēs
undercurrent n: **an ~ of** lātēns
underestimate vt minōris aestimāre
undergarment n subūcula f
undergo vt subīre, patī, ferre
underground adj subterrāneus ▶ adv sub terrā
undergrowth n virgulta ntpl
underhand adj clandestīnus, fūrtīvus ▶ adv clam, fūrtim
underline vt subscrībere
underling n minister m, satelles m/f
undermine vt subruere; (fig) labefacere, labefactāre
undermost adj īnfimus

underneath adv īnfrā ▶ prep sub (abl), īnfrā (acc); (motion) sub (acc)
underprop vt fulcīre
underrate vt obtrectāre, extenuāre, minōris aestimāre
understand vt intellegere, comprehendere; (be told) accipere, comperīre; (in a sense) interpretārī; ~ **Latin** Latīnē scīre
understandable adj crēdibilis
understanding adj sapiēns, perītus ▶ n intellegentia f; (faculty) mēns f, intellectus m; (agreement) cōnsēnsus m; (condition) condiciō f
undertake vt suscipere, sūmere, adīre ad; (business) condūcere; (case) agere, dēfendere; (promise) recipere, spondēre
undertaker n dissignātor m
undertaking n inceptum nt, inceptiō f
undervalue vt minōris aestimāre
underwood n virgulta ntpl
underworld n īnferī mpl
undeserved adj immeritus, iniūstus
undeservedly adv immeritō, indignē
undeserving adj indignus
undesigned adj fortuītus
undesignedly adv fortuītō, temerē
undesirable adj odiōsus, ingrātus
undeterred adj immōtus
undeveloped adj immātūrus
undeviating adj dīrēctus
undigested adj crūdus
undignified adj levis, inhonestus
undiminished adj integer
undiscernible adj invīsus, obscūrus
undisciplined adj lascīvus, immoderātus; (MIL) inexercitātus
undiscovered adj ignōtus
undisguised adj apertus
undisguisedly adv palam, apertē
undismayed adj impavidus, intrepidus
undisputed adj certus
undistinguished adj ignōbilis, inglōrius
undisturbed adj tranquillus, placidus
undo vt (knot) expedīre, resolvere; (sewing) dissuere; (fig) īnfectum reddere
undoing n ruīna f
undone adj infectus; (ruined) perditus; **be ~** perīre, disperīre; **hopelessly ~** dēperditus
undoubted adj certus
undoubtedly adv sine dubiō, plānē
undress vt exuere, vestem dētrahere (dat)
undressed adj nūdus
undue adj nimius, immoderātus, inīquus
undulate vi fluctuāre
undulation n spīra f
unduly adv nimis, plūs aequō
undutiful adj impius
undutifully adv impiē
undutifulness n impietās f
undying adj immortālis, aeternus
unearth vt ēruere, dētegere
unearthly adj mōnstruōsus, dīvīnus, hūmānō māior

uneasily adv aegrē
uneasiness n sollicitūdō f, perturbātiō f
uneasy adj sollicitus, anxius, inquiētus
uneducated adj illitterātus, indoctus, rudis; **be ~** litterās nescīre
unemployed adj ōtiōsus
unemployment n cessātiō f
unencumbered adj expedītus, līber
unending adj perpetuus, sempiternus
unendowed adj indōtātus
unendurable adj intolerandus, intolerābilis
unenjoyable adj iniūcundus, molestus
unenlightened adj rudis, inērudītus
unenterprising adj iners
unenviable adj nōn invidendus
unequal adj impār, dispār
unequalled adj ūnicus, singulāris
unequally adv inaequāliter, inīquē
unequivocal adj apertus, plānus
unerring adj certus
unerringly adv certē
unessential adj adventīcius, supervacāneus
uneven adj impār; (surface) asper, inīquus, inaequābilis
unevenly adv inīquē, inaequāliter
unevenness n inīquitās f, asperitās f
unexamined adj (case) incognitus
unexampled adj inaudītus, ūnicus, singulāris
unexceptionable adj ēmendātus; (authority) certissimus
unexpected adj imprōvīsus, inopīnātus, īnspērātus
unexpectedly adv dē imprōvīsō, ex īnspērātō, inopīnātō, necopīnātō
unexplored adj inexplōrātus
unfading adj perennis, vīvus
unfailing adj perennis, certus, perpetuus
unfailingly adv semper
unfair adj inīquus, iniūstus
unfairly adv inīquē, iniūstē
unfairness n inīquitās f, iniūstitia f
unfaithful adj īnfidēlis, īnfīdus, perfidus
unfaithfully adv īnfidēliter
unfaithfulness n īnfidēlitās f
unfamiliar adj novus, ignōtus, īnsolēns; (sight) invīsitātus
unfamiliarity n īnsolentia f
unfashionable adj obsolētus
unfasten vt solvere, refīgere
unfathomable adj īnfīnītus, profundus
unfavourable adj inīquus, adversus, importūnus
unfavourably adv inīquē, male; **be ~ disposed** āversō animō esse
unfed adj iēiūnus
unfeeling adj dūrus, crūdēlis, ferreus
unfeelingly adv crūdēliter
unfeigned adj sincērus, vērus, simplex
unfeignedly adv sincērē, vērē
unfilial adj impius
unfinished adj īnfectus, imperfectus
unfit adj inūtilis, incommodus, aliēnus

unfix vt refigere
unflinching adj impavidus, firmus
unfold vt explicāre, ēvolvere; (story) expōnere, ēnārrāre
unfolding n explicātiō f
unforeseen adj imprōvīsus
unforgettable adj memorābilis
unforgiving adj implācābilis
unformed adj īnfōrmis
unfortified adj immūnītus, nūdus
unfortunate adj īnfēlīx, īnfortūnātus
unfortunately adv īnfēlīciter, male; **~ you did not come** male accidit quod nōn vēnistī
unfounded adj inānis, vānus
unfrequented adj dēsertus
unfriendliness n inimīcitia f
unfriendly adj inimīcus, malevolus; **in an ~ manner** inimīcē
unfruitful adj sterilis; (fig) inānis, vānus
unfruitfulness n sterilitās f
unfulfilled adj īnfectus, inritus
unfurl vt explicāre, pandere
unfurnished adj nūdus
ungainly adj agrestis, rūsticus
ungallant adj inurbānus, parum cōmis
ungenerous adj illīberālis; **~ conduct** illīberālitās f
ungentlemanly adj illīberālis
ungirt adj discinctus
ungodliness n impietās f
ungodly adj impius
ungovernable adj impotēns, indomitus
ungovernableness n impotentia f
ungraceful adj inconcinnus, inēlegāns
ungracefully adv inēleganter
ungracious adj inhūmānus, petulāns, importūnus
ungraciously adv acerbē
ungrammatical adj barbarus; **be ~** soloecismum facere
ungrateful adj ingrātus
ungrudging adj largus, nōn invītus
ungrudgingly adv sine invidiā
unguarded adj intūtus; (word) incautus, incōnsultus
unguardedly adv temerē, incōnsultē
unguent n unguentum nt
unhallowed adj profānus, impius
unhand vt mittere
unhandy adj inhabilis
unhappily adv īnfēlīciter, miserē
unhappiness n miseria f, tristitia f, maestitia f
unhappy adj īnfēlīx, miser, tristis
unharmed adj incolumis, integer, salvus
unharness vt disiungere
unhealthiness n valētūdō f; (climate) gravitās f
unhealthy adj invalidus, aeger; (climate) gravis, pestilens
unheard adj inaudītus; (LAW) indictā causā
unheard-of adj inaudītus
unheeded adj neglectus
unheeding adj immemor, sēcūrus

unhelpful adj difficilis, invītus
unhesitating adj audāx, prōmptus
unhesitatingly adv sine dubitātiōne
unhewn adj rudis
unhindered adj expedītus
unhinged adj mente captus
unhistorical adj fictus, commentīcius
unholiness n impietās f
unholy adj impius
unhonoured adj inhonōrātus
unhoped-for adj īnspērātus
unhorse vt excutere, equō dēicere
unhurt adj integer, incolumis
unicorn n monocerōs m
uniform adj aequābilis, aequālis ▸ n īnsignia ntpl; (MIL) sagum nt; **in ~** sagātus; **put on ~** saga sūmere
uniformity n aequābilitās f, cōnstantia f
uniformly adv aequābiliter, ūnō tenōre
unify vt coniungere
unimaginative adj hebes, stolidus
unimpaired adj integer, incolumis, illībātus
unimpeachable adj (character) integer; (style) ēmendātus
unimportant adj levis, nullīus mōmentī
uninformed adj indoctus, ignārus
uninhabitable adj inhabitābilis
uninhabited adj dēsertus
uninitiated adj profānus; (fig) rudis
uninjured adj integer, incolumis
unintelligent adj īnsipiēns, tardus, excors
unintelligible adj obscūrus
unintelligibly adv obscūrē
unintentionally adv imprūdēns, temerē
uninteresting adj frīgidus, āridus
uninterrupted adj continuus, perpetuus
uninterruptedly adv continenter, sine ullā intermissiōne
uninvited adj invocātus; **~ guest** umbra f
uninviting adj iniūcundus, invenustus
union n coniūnctiō f; (social) cōnsociātiō f, societās f; (POL) foederātae cīvitātēs fpl; (agreement) concordia f, cōnsēnsus m; (marriage) coniugium nt
unique adj ūnicus, ēgregius, singulāris
unison n concentus m; (fig) concordia f, cōnsēnsus m
unit n ūniō f
unite vt coniungere, cōnsociāre, cōpulāre ▸ vi coīre; cōnsentīre, cōnspīrāre; (rivers) cōnfluere
unity n (concord) concordia f, cōnsēnsus m
universal adj ūniversus, commūnis
universally adv ūniversus, omnis; (place) ubīque
universe n mundus m, rērum nātūra f
university n acadēmia f
unjust adj iniūstus, inīquus
unjustifiable adj indignus, inexcūsābilis
unjustly adv iniūstē, iniūriā
unkempt adj horridus
unkind adj inhūmānus, inīquus
unkindly adv inhūmānē, asperē

unkindness n inhūmānitās f
unknowingly adv imprūdēns, īnscius
unknown adj ignōtus, incognitus; (fame) obscūrus
unlawful adj vetitus, iniūriōsus
unlawfully adv iniūriōsē, iniūriā
unlearn vt dēdiscere
unlearned adj indoctus, inēruditus
unless conj nisī
unlettered adj illitterātus
unlike adj dissimilis (+ gen or dat), dispār
unlikely adj nōn vērīsimilis
unlimited adj īnfīnītus, immēnsus
unload vt exonerāre, deonerāre; (from ship) expōnere
unlock vt reserāre, reclūdere
unlooked-for adj īnspērātus, inexpectātus
unloose vt solvere, exsolvere
unlovely adj invenustus
unluckily adv īnfēlīciter
unlucky adj īnfēlīx, īnfortūnātus; (day) āter
unmake vt īnfectum reddere
unman vt mollīre, frangere, dēbilitāre
unmanageable adj inhabilis
unmanly adj mollis, ēnervātus, muliebris
unmanneriness n importūnitās f, inhūmānitās f
unmannerly adj importūnus, inhūmānus
unmarried adj (man) caelebs; (woman) vidua
unmask vt nūdāre, dētegere
unmatched adj ūnicus, singulāris
unmeaning adj inānis
unmeasured adj īnfīnītus, immoderātus
unmeet adj parum idōneus
unmelodious adj absonus, absurdus
unmentionable adj īnfandus
unmentioned adj indictus; **leave** ~ ōmittere
unmerciful adj immisericors, inclēmēns
unmercifully adv inclēmenter
unmerited adj immeritus, indignus
unmindful adj immemor
unmistakable adj certus, manifestus
unmistakably adv sine dubiō, certē
unmitigated adj merus
unmixed adj pūrus
unmolested adj intāctus
unmoor vt solvere
unmoved adj immōtus
unmusical adj absonus, absurdus
unmutilated adj integer
unnatural adj (event) mōnstruōsus; (feelings) impius, inhūmānus; (style) accersītus, pūtidus
unnaturally adv contrā nātūram; impiē, inhūmānē; pūtidē
unnavigable adj innāvigābilis
unnecessarily adv nimis
unnecessary adj inūtilis, supervacāneus
unnerve vt dēbilitāre, frangere
unnoticed adj: **be** ~ latēre, fallere
unnumbered adj innumerus
unobjectionable adj honestus, culpae expers
unobservant adj tardus

unobserved adj: **be** ~ latēre, fallere
unobstructed adj apertus, pūrus
unobtrusive adj verēcundus; **be** ~ fallere
unobtrusiveness n verēcundia f
unoccupied adj vacuus, ōtiōsus
unoffending adj innocēns
unofficial adj prīvātus
unorthodox adj abnōrmis
unostentatious adj modestus, verēcundus
unostentatiously adv nullā iactātiōne
unpaid adj (services) grātuītus; (money) dēbitus
unpalatable adj amārus; (fig) iniūcundus, īnsuāvis
unparalleled adj ūnicus, inaudītus
unpardonable adj inexcūsābilis
unpatriotic adj impius
unpitying adj immisericors, ferreus
unpleasant adj iniūcundus, ingrātus, īnsuāvis, gravis, molestus
unpleasantly adv iniūcundē, ingrātē, graviter
unpleasantness n iniūcunditās f, molestia f
unpleasing adj ingrātus, invenustus
unploughed adj inarātus
unpoetical adj pedester
unpolished adj impolītus; (person) incultus, agrestis, inurbānus; (style) incondītus, rudis
unpopular adj invidiōsus, invīsus
unpopularity n invidia f, odium nt
unpractised adj inexercitātus, imperītus
unprecedented adj īnsolēns, novus, inaudītus
unprejudiced adj integer, aequus
unpremeditated adj repentīnus, subitus
unprepared adj imparātus
unprepossessing adj invenustus, illepidus
unpretentious adj modestus, verēcundus
unprincipled adj improbus, levis, prāvus
unproductive adj īnfēcundus, sterilis
unprofitable adj inūtilis, vānus
unprofitably adv frustrā, ab rē
unpropitious adj īnfēlīx, adversus
unpropitiously adv malīs ōminibus
unprotected adj indēfēnsus, intūtus, nūdus
unprovoked adj ultrō (adv)
unpunished adj impūnītus ▸ adv impūne
unqualified adj nōn idōneus; (unrestricted) absolūtus
unquestionable adj certus
unquestionably adv facile, certē
unquestioning adj crēdulus
unravel vt retexere; (fig) ēnōdāre, explicāre
unready adj imparātus
unreal adj falsus, vānus
unreality n vānitās f
unreasonable adj inīquus, importūnus
unreasonableness n inīquitās f
unreasonably adv inīquē
unreasoning adj stolidus, temerārius
unreclaimed adj (land) incultus
unrefined adj impolītus, inurbānus, rudis
unregistered adj incēnsus
unrelated adj aliēnus
unrelenting adj implācābilis, inexōrābilis

unreliable *adj* incertus, levis
unreliably *adv* leviter
unrelieved *adj* perpetuus, adsiduus
unremitting *adj* adsiduus
unrequited *adj* inultus, inānis
unreservedly *adv* apertē, sine ullā exceptiōne
unresponsive *adj* hebes
unrest *n* inquiēs f, sollicitūdō f
unrestrained *adj* līber, impotēns, effrēnātus, immoderātus
unrestricted *adj* līber, absolūtus
unrevenged *adj* inultus
unrewarded *adj* inhonōrātus
unrewarding *adj* ingrātus, vānus
unrighteous *adj* iniūstus, impius
unrighteously *adv* iniūstē, impiē
unrighteousness *n* impietās f
unripe *adj* immātūrus, crūdus
unrivalled *adj* ēgregius, singulāris, ūnicus
unroll *vt* ēvolvere, explicāre
unromantic *adj* pedester
unruffled *adj* immōtus, tranquillus
unruliness *n* licentia f, impotentia f
unruly *adj* effrēnātus, impotēns, immoderātus
unsafe *adj* perīculōsus, dubius; (*structure*) īnstābilis
unsaid *adj* indictus
unsatisfactorily *adv* nōn ex sententiā, male
unsatisfactory *adj* parum idōneus, malus
unsatisfied *adj* parum contentus
unsavoury *adj* īnsuāvis, taeter
unscathed *adj* incolumis, integer
unschooled *adj* indoctus, inērudītus
unscrupulous *adj* improbus, impudēns
unscrupulously *adv* improbē, impudenter
unscrupulousness *n* improbitās f, impudentia f
unseal *vt* resignāre, solvere
unseasonable *adj* intempestīvus, importūnus
unseasonableness *n* incommodītās f
unseasonably *adv* intempestīvē, importūnē
unseasoned *adj* (*food*) nōn condītus; (*wood*) viridis
unseat *vt* (*rider*) excutere
unseaworthy *adj* īnfirmus
unseeing *adj* caecus
unseemly *adj* indecōrus
unseen *adj* invīsus; (*ever before*) invīsitātus
unselfish *adj* innocēns, probus, līberālis
unselfishly *adv* līberāliter
unselfishness *n* innocentia f, līberālitās f
unserviceable *adj* inūtilis
unsettle *vt* ad incertum revocāre, turbāre, sollicitāre
unsettled *adj* incertus, dubius; (*mind*) sollicitus, suspēnsus; (*times*) turbidus
unsew *vt* dissuere
unshackle *vt* expedīre, solvere
unshaken *adj* immōtus, firmus, stabilis
unshapely *adj* dēfōrmis
unshaven *adj* intōnsus
unsheathe *vt* dēstringere, stringere

unshod *adj* nūdis pedibus
unshorn *adj* intōnsus
unsightliness *n* dēfōrmitās f, turpitūdō f
unsightly *adj* foedus, dēfōrmis
unskilful *adj* indoctus, īnscītus, incallidus
unskilfully *adv* indoctē, īnscītē, incallidē
unskilfulness *n* īnscītia f, imperītia f
unskilled *adj* imperītus, indoctus; ~ **in** imperitus (*gen*)
unslaked *adj* (*lime*) vīvus; (*thirst*) inexplētus
unsociable *adj* īnsociābilis, difficilis
unsoiled *adj* integer, pūrus
unsolicited *adj* voluntārius ▸ *adv* ultrō
unsophisticated *adj* simplex, ingenuus
unsound *adj* īnfirmus; (*mind*) īnsānus; (*opinion*) falsus, perversus
unsoundness *n* īnfirmitās f; īnsānitās f; prāvitās f
unsparing *adj* inclēmēns, immisericors; (*lavish*) prōdigus
unsparingly *adv* inclēmenter; prōdigē
unspeakable *adj* īnfandus, incrēdibilis
unspeakably *adv* incrēdibiliter
unspoilt *adj* integer
unspoken *adj* indictus, tacitus
unspotted *adj* integer, pūrus
unstable *adj* īnstābilis; (*fig*) incōnstāns, levis
unstained *adj* pūrus, incorruptus, integer
unstatesmanlike *adj* illīberālis
unsteadily *adv* incōnstanter; **walk ~** titubāre
unsteadiness *n* (*fig*) incōnstantia f
unsteady *adj* īnstābilis; (*fig*) incōnstāns
unstitch *vt* dissuere
unstring *vt* retendere
unstudied *adj* simplex
unsubdued *adj* invictus
unsubstantial *adj* levis, inānis
unsuccessful *adj* īnfēlīx; (*effort*) inritus; **be ~** offendere; **I am ~** mihi nōn succēdit
unsuccessfully *adv* īnfēlīciter, rē īnfectā
unsuitable *adj* incommodus, aliēnus, importūnus; **it is ~** dēdecet
unsuitableness *n* incommodītās f
unsuitably *adv* incommodē, ineptē
unsuited *adj* parum idōneus
unsullied *adj* pūrus, incorruptus
unsure *adj* incertus, dubius
unsurpassable *adj* inexsuperābilis
unsurpassed *adj* ūnicus, singulāris
unsuspected *adj* latēns, nōn suspectus; **be ~** latēre, in suspīciōnem nōn venīre
unsuspecting *adj* imprōvidus, imprūdēns
unsuspicious *adj* nōn suspīcāx, crēdulus
unswerving *adj* cōnstāns
unsworn *adj* iniūrātus
unsymmetrical *adj* inaequālis
untainted *adj* incorruptus, integer
untamable *adj* indomitus
untamed *adj* indomitus, ferus
untaught *adj* indoctus, rudis
unteach *vt* dēdocēre
unteachable *adj* indocilis

untenable *adj* inānis, īnfirmus
unthankful *adj* ingrātus
unthankfully *adv* ingrātē
unthankfulness *n* ingrātus animus *m*
unthinkable *adj* incrēdibilis
unthinking *adj* incōnsīderātus, imprōvidus
unthriftily *adv* prōdigē
unthrifty *adj* prōdigus, profūsus
untidily *adv* neglegenter
untidiness *n* neglegentia *f*
untidy *adj* neglegēns, inconcinnus, squālidus
untie *vt* solvere
until *conj* dum, dōnec ▸ *prep* usque ad (acc), in (acc); **~ now** adhūc
untilled *adj* incultus
untimely *adj* intempestīvus, immātūrus, importūnus
untiring *adj* impiger; (effort) adsiduus
unto *prep* ad (acc), in (acc)
untold *adj* innumerus
untouched *adj* intāctus, integer
untoward *adj* adversus, malus
untrained *adj* inexercitātus, imperītus, rudis
untried *adj* intemptātus, inexpertus; (trial) incognitus
untrodden *adj* āvius
untroubled *adj* tranquillus, placidus, quiētus; (mind) sēcūrus
untrue *adj* falsus, fictus; (disloyal) īnfīdus, īnfidēlis
untrustworthy *adj* infīdus, mōbilis
untruth *n* mendācium *nt*, falsum *nt*
untruthful *adj* mendāx, falsus
untruthfully *adv* falsō, falsē
untuneful *adj* absonus
unturned *adj*: **leave no stone ~** nihil intemptātum relinquere, omnia experīrī
untutored *adj* indoctus, incultus
unused *adj* (person) īnsuētus, īnsolitus; (thing) integer
unusual *adj* īnsolitus, inūsitātus, īnsolēns, novus
unusually *adv* īnsolenter, praeter cōnsuētūdinem
unusualness *n* īnsolentia *f*, novitās *f*
unutterable *adj* īnfandus, inēnārrābilis
unvarnished *adj* (fig) simplex, nūdus
unveil *vt* (fig) aperīre, patefacere
unversed *adj* ignārus (gen), imperītus (gen)
unwanted *adj* supervacāneus
unwarily *adv* imprudenter, incautē, incōnsultē
unwariness *n* imprūdentia *f*
unwarlike *adj* imbellis
unwarrantable *adj* inīquus, iniūstus
unwarrantably *adv* iniūriā
unwary *adj* imprūdēns, incautus, incōnsultus
unwavering *adj* stabilis, immōtus
unwearied, unwearying *adj* indēfessus, adsiduus
unweave *vt* retexere
unwedded *adj* (man) caelebs; (woman) vidua
unwelcome *adj* ingrātus

unwell *adj* aeger, aegrōtus
unwept *adj* indēflētus
unwholesome *adj* pestilēns, gravis
unwieldy *adj* inhabilis
unwilling *adj* invītus; **be ~** nolle
unwillingly *adv* invītus
unwind *vt* ēvolvere, retexere
unwise *adj* stultus, īnsipiēns, imprūdēns
unwisely *adv* īnsipienter, imprūdenter
unwittingly *adv* imprūdēns, īnsciēns
unwonted *adj* īnsolitus, inūsitātus
unworthily *adv* indignē
unworthiness *n* indignitās *f*
unworthy *adj* indignus (abl)
unwounded *adj* intāctus, integer
unwrap *vt* ēvolvere, explicāre
unwritten *adj* nōn scrīptus; **~ law** mōs *m*
unwrought *adj* īnfectus, rudis
unyielding *adj* dūrus, firmus, inexōrābilis
unyoke *vt* disiungere
up *adv* sūrsum; **up and down** sūrsum deōrsum; **up to** usque ad (acc), tenus (abl, after noun); **bring up** subvehere; (child) ēducāre; **climb up** ēscendere; **come up to** aequāre; **lift up** ērigere, sublevāre; **from childhood up** ā puerō; **it is all up with** āctum est dē; **well up in** gnārus (gen), perītus (gen); **what is he up to?** quid struit? ▸ *prep* (motion) in (acc) ▸ *n*: **ups and downs** (fig) vicissitūdinēs *fpl*
upbraid *vt* exprobrāre (dat of pers, acc of charge); obicere (dat and acc), increpāre, castīgāre
upbringing *n* ēducātiō *f*
upheaval *n* ēversiō *f*
upheave *vt* ēvertere
uphill *adj* acclīvis ▸ *adv* adversō colle, in adversum collem
uphold *vt* sustinēre, tuērī, servāre
upholstery *n* supellex *f*
upkeep *n* impēnsa *f*
upland *adj* montānus
uplift *vt* extollere, sublevāre
upon *prep* in (abl), super (abl); (motion) in (acc), super (acc); (dependence) ex (abl); **~ this** quō factō
upper *adj* superior; **gain the ~ hand** superāre, vincere
uppermost *adj* suprēmus, summus
uppish *adj* superbus
upright *adj* rēctus, ērēctus; (character) integer, probus, honestus
uprightly *adv* rēctē; integrē
uprightness *n* integritās *f*
upriver *adj*, *adv* adversō flūmine
uproar *n* tumultus *m*; clāmor *m*
uproarious *adj* tumultuōsus
uproariously *adv* tumultuōsē
uproot *vt* ērādīcāre, exstirpāre, ēruere
upset *vt* ēvertere, invertere, subvertere; **~ the apple cart** plaustrum percellere ▸ *adj* (fig) perturbātus
upshot *n* ēventus *m*
upside-down *adv*: **turn ~** ēvertere, invertere; (fig) miscēre

upstart n novus homō m ▶ adj repentīnus

upstream adj, adv adversō flūmine

upward, upwards adv sūrsum; **upward(s) of** (number) amplius

urban adj urbānus, oppidānus

urbane adj urbānus, cōmis

urbanely adv urbānē, cōmiter

urbanity n urbānitās f

urchin n (boy) puerulus m; (animal) echīnus m

urge vt urgēre, impellere; (speech) hortārī, incitāre; (advice) suādēre; (request) sollicitāre; **~ on** incitāre ▶ n impulsus m; dēsīderium nt

urgency n necessitās f

urgent adj praesēns, gravis; **be ~** instāre

urgently adv graviter

urn n urna f

usage n mōs m, īnstitūtum nt, ūsus m

use n ūsus m; (custom) mōs m, cōnsuētūdō f; **be of use** ūsuī esse, prōdesse, condūcere; **out of use** dēsuētus; **go out of use** exolēscere; **in common use** ūsitātus; **it's no use** nīl agis, nīl agimus ▶ vt ūtī (abl); (improperly) abūtī; (for a purpose) adhibēre; (word) ūsurpāre; **use up** cōnsūmere, exhaurīre; **used to** adsuētus (dat); solēre (infin); **I used to do** faciēbam

useful adj ūtilis; **be ~** ūsuī esse

usefully adv ūtiliter

usefulness n ūtilitās f

useless adj inūtilis; (thing) inānis, inritus; **be ~** nihil valēre

uselessly adv inūtiliter, frustrā

uselessness n inānitās f

usher n (court) appāritor m; (theatre) dēsignātor m ▶ vt: **~ in** indūcere, intrōdūcere

usual adj ūsitātus, solitus; **as ~** ut adsolet, ut fert cōnsuētūdō, ex cōnsuētūdine; **out of the ~** īnsolitus, extrā ōrdinem

usually adv ferē, plērumque; **he ~ comes** venīre solet

usufruct n ūsus et frūctus m

usurer n faenerātor m

usurp vt occupāre, invādere in (acc), ūsurpāre

usurpation n occupātiō f

usury n faenerātiō f, ūsūra f; **practise ~** faenerārī

utensil n īnstrūmentum nt, vās nt

utility n ūtilitās f, commodum nt

utilize vt ūtī (abl); (for a purpose) adhibēre

utmost adj extrēmus, summus; **at the ~** summum; **do one's ~** omnibus vīribus contendere

utter adj tōtus, extrēmus, summus ▶ vt ēmittere, ēdere, ēloquī, prōnūntiāre

utterance n dictum nt; (process) prōnūntiātiō f

utterly adv funditus, omnīnō, penitus

uttermost adj extrēmus, ultimus

V

vacancy n inānitās f; (office) vacuitās f; **there is a ~** locus vacat; **elect to fill a ~** sufficere

vacant adj inānis, vacuus; **be ~** vacāre

vacate vt vacuum facere

vacation n fēriae fpl

vacillate vi vacillāre, dubitāre

vacillation n dubitātiō f

vacuity n inānitās f

vacuous adj vacuus

vacuum n ināne nt

vagabond n grassātor m ▶ adj vagus

vagary n libīdō f

vagrancy n errātiō f

vagrant n grassātor m, vagus m

vague adj incertus, dubius

vaguely adv incertē

vain n vānus, inānis, inritus; (person) glōriōsus; **in ~** frustrā

vainglorious adj glōriōsus

vainglory n glōria f, iactantia f

vainly adv frustrā, nēquīquam

vale n vallis f

valet n cubiculārius m

valiant adj fortis, ācer

valiantly adv fortiter, ācriter

valid adj ratus; (argument) gravis, firmus

validity n vīs f, auctōritās f

valley n vallis f

valorous adj fortis

valour n virtūs f

valuable adj pretiōsus

valuation n aestimātiō f

value n pretium nt; (fig) vīs f, honor m ▶ vt aestimāre; (esteem) dīligere; **~ highly** māgnī aestimāre; **~ little** parvī aestimāre, parvī facere

valueless adj vīlis, minimī pretī

valuer n aestimātor m

van n (in battle) prīma aciēs f; (on march) prīmum agmen nt

vanguard n prīmum agmen nt

vanish vi diffugere, ēvānēscere, dīlābī

vanity n (unreality) vānitās f; (conceit) glōria f

vanquish vt vincere, superāre, dēvincere

vanquisher n victor m

vantage n (*ground*) locus superior m
vapid adj vapidus, īnsulsus
vapidly adv īnsulsē
vaporous adj nebulōsus
vapour n vapor m, nebula f; (*from earth*) exhālātiō f
variable adj varius, mūtābilis
variableness n mūtābilitās f, incōnstantia f
variance n discordia f, dissēnsiō f, discrepantia f; **at ~** discors; **be at ~** dissidēre, inter sē discrepāre; **set at ~** aliēnāre
variant adj varius
variation n varietās f, vicissitūdō f
variegate vt variāre
variegated adj varius
variety n varietās f; (*number*) multitūdō f; (*kind*) genus nt; **a ~ of** dīversī
various adj varius, dīversus
variously adv variē
varlet n verberō m
varnish n pigmentum nt; (*fig*) fūcus m
varnished adj (*fig*) fūcātus
vary vt variāre, mūtāre; (*decorate*) distinguere ▶ vi mūtārī
vase n vās nt
vassal n ambāctus m; (*fig*) cliēns m
vast adj vastus, immānis, ingēns, immēnsus
vastly adv valdē
vastness n māgnitūdō f, immēnsitās f
vat n cūpa f
vault n (ARCH) fornix f; (*jump*) saltus m ▶ vi salīre
vaulted adj fornicātus
vaunt vt iactāre, ostentāre ▶ vi sē iactāre, glōriārī
vaunting n ostentātiō f, glōria f ▶ adj glōriōsus
veal n vitulīna f
vedette n excursor m
veer vi sē vertere, flectī
vegetable n holus nt
vehemence n vīs f, violentia f; (*passion*) ārdor m, impetus m
vehement adj vehemēns, violentus, ācer
vehemently adv vehementer, ācriter
vehicle n vehiculum nt
Veii n Vēiī, Vēiorum mpl
veil n rīca f; (*bridal*) flammeum nt; (*fig*) integumentum nt ▶ vt vēlāre, tegere
vein n vēna f
vellum n membrāna f
velocity n celeritās f, vēlōcitās f
venal adj vēnālis
vend vt vēndere
vendetta n simultās f
vendor n caupō m
veneer n (*fig*) speciēs f, fūcus m
venerable adj gravis, augustus
venerate vt colere, venerārī
veneration n venerātiō f, cultus m
venerator n cultor m
vengeance n ultiō f, poena f; **take ~ on** ulcīscī, vindicāre in (*acc*); **take ~ for** ulcīscī, vindicāre
vengeful adj ultor

venial adj ignōscendus
venison n dāma f, ferīna f
venom n venēnum nt; (*fig*) vīrus nt
venomous adj venēnātus
vent n spīrāculum nt; (*outlet*) exitus m; **give ~ to** profundere, ēmittere ▶ vt ēmittere; (*feelings on*) profundere in (*acc*), ērumpere in (*acc*)
ventilate vt perflāre; (*opinion*) in medium prōferre, vulgāre
ventilation n perflāre
venture n perīculum nt; (*gamble*) ālea f; **at a ~** temerē ▶ vi audēre ▶ vt perīclitārī, in āleam dare
venturesome adj audāx, temerārius
venturesomeness n audācia f, temeritās f
veracious adj vērāx, vēridicus
veracity n vēritās f, fidēs f
verb n verbum nt
verbally adv per colloquia; (*translate*) ad verbum, verbum prō verbō
verbatim adv ad verbum, totidem verbīs
verbiage n verba ntpl
verbose adj verbōsus
verbosity n loquendī prōfluentia f
verdant adj viridis
verdict n sententia f, iūdicium nt; **deliver a ~** sententiam prōnūntiāre; **give a ~ in favour of** causam adiūdicāre (*dat*)
verdigris n aerūgō f
verdure n viriditās f
verge n ōra f; **the ~ of** extrēmus, on **the ~ of** (*fig*) prope (*acc*) ▶ vi vergere
verification n cōnfirmātiō f
verify vt cōnfirmāre, comprobāre
verily adv profectō, certē
verisimilitude n vērī similitūdō f
veritable adj vērus
veritably adv vērē
verity n vēritās f
vermilion n sandīx f
vermin n bestiolae fpl
vernacular adj patrius ▶ n patrius sermō m
vernal adj vērnus
versatile adj versūtus, varius
versatility n versātile ingenium nt
verse n (*line*) versus m; (*poetry*) versus mpl, carmina ntpl
versed adj īnstructus, perītus, exercitātus
versification n ars versūs faciendī
versify vt versū inclūdere ▶ vi versūs facere
version n (*of story*) fōrma f; **give a Latin ~ of** Latīnē reddere
vertex n vertex m, fastīgium nt
vertical adj rēctus, dīrēctus
vertically adv ad līneam, rēctā līneā, ad perpendiculum
vertigo n vertīgō f
vervain n verbēna f
verve n ācrimōnia f
very adj ipse ▶ adv admodum, valdē, vehementer ▶ superl: **at that ~ moment** tum māximē; **not ~** nōn ita
vessel n (*receptacle*) vās nt; (*ship*) nāvigium nt

vest n subúcula f ▶ vt: ~ **power in** imperium
  déferre (dat); **vested interests** nummī
  locātī mpl
vestal adj vestālis ▶ n virgō vestālis f
vestibule n vestibulum nt
vestige n vestīgium nt, indicium nt
vestment n vestīmentum nt
vesture n vestis f
vetch n vicia f
veteran adj veterānus ▶ n (MIL) veterānus m;
  (fig) veterātor m
veto n interdictum nt; (tribune's) intercessiō f
  ▶ vt interdīcere (dat); (tribune's) intercēdere (dat)
vex vt vexāre, sollicitāre, stomachum movēre
  (dat); **be vexed** aegrē ferre, stomachārī
vexation n (caused) molestia f; (felt) dolor m,
  stomachus m
vexatious adj odiōsus, molestus
vexatiously adv molestē
vexed adj īrātus; (question) anceps
via prep per (acc)
viaduct n pōns m
viands n cibus m
vibrate vi vībrāre, tremere
vibration n tremor m
vicarious adj vicārius
vice n (general) prāvitās f, perditī mōrēs mpl;
  (particular) vitium nt, flāgitium nt; (clamp)
  fībula f
viceroy n prōcūrātor m
vicinity n vīcīnia f, vīcīnitās f
vicious adj prāvus, vitiōsus, flāgitiōsus; (temper)
  contumāx
viciously adv flāgitiōsē; contumāciter
vicissitude n vicissitūdō f; **vicissitudes** pl
  vicēs fpl
victim n victima f, hostia f; (fig) piāculum nt;
  (exploited) praeda f; **be the ~ of** labōrāre ex; **fall
  a ~ to** morī (abl); (trickery) circumvenīrī (abl)
victimize vt nocēre (dat), circumvenīre
victor n victor m
victorious adj victor m, victrīx f; **be ~** vincere
victory n victōria f; **win a ~** victōriam reportāre;
  win a ~ over vincere, superāre
victory message n laureātae litterae fpl
victory parade n triumphus m
victual vt rem frūmentāriam suppeditāre (dat)
victualler n caupō m; (MIL) frūmentārius m
victuals n cibus m; (MIL) frūmentum nt,
  commeātus m
vie vi certāre, contendere; **vie with** aemulārī
view n cōnspectus m; (from far) prōspectus m;
  (from high) dēspectus m; (opinion) sententia f;
  exposed to ~ in mediō; **entertain a ~** sentīre;
  in ~ of propter (acc); **in my ~** meā sententiā,
  meō iūdiciō; **end in ~** prōpositum nt; **have in ~**
  spectāre; **point of ~** iūdicium nt; **with a ~ to** eō
  cōnsiliō ut ▶ vt īnspicere, spectāre, intuērī
vigil n pervigilium nt; **keep a ~** vigilāre
vigilance n vigilantia f, dīligentia f
vigilant adj vigilāns, dīligēns
vigilantly adv vigilanter, dīligenter

vigorous adj ācer, vegetus, integer; (style)
  nervōsus
vigorously adv ācriter, strēnuē
vigour n vīs f, nervī mpl, integritās f
vile adj turpis, impūrus, abiectus
vilely adv turpiter, impūrē
vileness n turpitūdō f, impūritās f
vilification n obtrectātiō f, calumnia f
vilify vt obtrectāre, calumniārī, maledīcere (dat)
villa n vīlla f
village n pāgus m, vīcus m; **in every ~** pāgātim
villager n pāgānus m, vīcānus m
villain n furcifer m, scelerātus m
villainous adj scelestus, scelerātus, nēquam
villainously adv scelestē
villainy n scelus nt, nēquitia f
vindicate vt (right) vindicāre; (action) pūrgāre;
  (belief) arguere; (person) dēfendere, prōpugnāre
  prō (abl)
vindication n dēfēnsiō f, pūrgātiō f
vindicator n dēfēnsor m, prōpugnātor m
vindictive adj ultor, ulcīscendī cupidus
vine n vītis f; **wild ~** labrusca f
vinedresser n vīnitor m
vinegar n acētum nt
vineyard n vīnea f, vīnētum nt
vintage n vindēmia f
vintner n vīnārius m
violate vt violāre
violation n violātiō f
violator n violātor m
violence n violentia f, vīs f, iniūria f; **do ~ to**
  violāre; **offer ~ to** vim īnferre (dat)
violent adj violentus, vehemēns; (passion) ācer,
  impotēns; **~ death** nex f
violently adv vehementer, per vim
violet n viola f
viper n vīpera f
viperous adj (fig) malignus
virgin n virgō f ▶ adj virginālis
virginity n virginitās f
virile adj virīlis
virility n virtūs f
virtually adv rē vērā, ferē
virtue n virtūs f, honestum nt; (woman's)
  pudīcitia f; (power) vīs f, potestās f; **by ~ of**
  ex (abl)
virtuous adj honestus, probus, integer
virtuously adv honestē
virulence n vīs f, vīrus nt
virulent adj acerbus
virus n vīrus nt
visage n ōs nt, faciēs f
vis-à-vis prep exadversus (acc)
viscosity n lentor m
viscous adj lentus, tenāx
visible adj ēvidēns, cōnspicuus, manifestus;
  be ~ appārēre
visibly adv manifestō
vision n (sense) vīsus m; (power) aspectus m;
  (apparition) vīsum nt, vīsiō f; (whim) somnium nt
visionary adj vānus ▶ n somniāns m

visit n adventus m; (formal) salūtātiō f; (long) commorātiō f; **pay a ~ to** invīsere ▸ vt vīsere; **~ occasionally** intervīsere; **go to ~** invīsere

visitation n (to inspect) recēnsiō f; (to punish) animadversiō f

visitor n hospes m, hospita f; (formal) salūtātor m

visor n buccula f

vista n prōspectus m

visual adj oculōrum

visualize vt animō cernere, ante oculōs pōnere

visually adv oculīs

vital adj (of life) vītālis; (essential) necessārius, māximī mōmentī

vitality n vīs f; (style) sanguis m

vitally adv praecipuē, imprīmīs

vitals n viscera ntpl

vitiate vt corrumpere, vitiāre

vitreous adj vitreus

vitrify vt in vitrum excoquere

vituperate vt vituperāre, obiūrgāre

vituperation n vituperātiō f, maledicta ntpl

vituperative adj maledicus

vivacious adj alacer, vegetus, hilaris

vivaciously adv hilare

vivacity n alacritās f, hilaritās f

vivid adj vīvidus, ācer

vividly adv ācriter

vivify vt animāre

vixen n vulpēs f

vocabulary n verbōrum cōpia f

vocal adj: **~ music** vōcis cantus m

vocation n officium nt, mūnus nt

vociferate vt, vi vōciferārī, clāmāre

vociferation n vōciferātiō f, clāmor m

vociferous adj vōciferāns

vociferously adv māgnīs clāmōribus

vogue n mōs m; **be in ~** flōrēre, in honōre esse

voice n vōx f ▸ vt exprimere, ēloquī

void adj inānis, vacuus; **~ of** expers (gen); **null and ~** inritus ▸ n ināne nt ▸ vt ēvomere, ēmittere

volatile adj levis, mōbilis

volatility n levitās f

volition n voluntās f

volley n imber m

volubility n volūbilitās f

voluble adj volūbilis

volume n (book) liber m; (mass) mōlēs f; (of sound) māgnitūdō f

voluminous adj cōpiōsus

voluntarily adv ultrō, suā sponte

voluntary adj voluntārius; (unpaid) grātuītus

volunteer n (MIL) ēvocātus m ▸ vt ultrō offerre ▸ vi (MIL) nōmen dare

voluptuary n dēlicātus m, homō voluptārius m

voluptuous adj voluptārius, mollis, dēlicātus, luxuriōsus

voluptuously adv molliter, dēlicātē, luxuriōsē

voluptuousness n luxuria f, libīdō f

vomit vt vomere, ēvomere; **~ up** ēvomere

voracious adj vorāx, edāx

voraciously adv avidē

voracity n edācitās f, gula f

vortex n vertex m, turbō m

votary n cultor m

vote n suffrāgium nt; (opinion) sententia f; **take a ~** (senate) discessiōnem facere ▸ vi (election) suffrāgium ferre; (judge) sententiam ferre; (senator) cēnsēre; **~ against** (bill) antīquāre; **~ for** (candidate) suffrāgārī (dat); (senator's motion) discēdere in sententiam (gen) ▸ vt (senate) dēcernere

voter n suffrāgātor m

votive adj vōtīvus

vouch vi spondēre; **~ for** praestāre, testificārī

voucher n (person) auctor m; (document) auctōritās f

vouchsafe vt concēdere

vow n vōtum nt; (promise) fidēs f ▸ vt vovēre; (promise) spondēre

vowel n vōcālis f

voyage n nāvigātiō f, cursus m ▸ vi nāvigāre

vulgar adj (common) vulgāris; (low) plēbēius, sordidus, īnsulsus

vulgarity n sordēs fpl, īnsulsitās f

vulgarly adv vulgō; īnsulsē

vulnerable adj nūdus; (fig) obnoxius; **be ~** vulnerārī posse

vulture n vultur m; (fig) vulturius m

W

wad n massa f
wade vi per vada īre; **~ across** vadō trānsīre
waft vt ferre, vehere
wag n facētus homō m, ioculātor m ▶ vt movēre, mōtāre, agitāre ▶ vi movērī, agitārī
wage n mercēs f; (pl) mercēs f, manupretium nt; (fig) pretium nt, praemium nt ▶ vt gerere; **~ war on** bellum īnferre (dat)/gerere
wager n spōnsiō f ▶ vi spōnsiōnem facere ▶ vt dēpōnere, oppōnere
waggery n facētiae fpl
waggish adj facētus, rīdiculus
waggle vt agitāre, mōtāre
wagon n plaustrum nt, carrus m
waif n inops m/f
wail n ēiulātus m ▶ vi ēiulāre, dēplōrāre, lāmentārī
wailing n plōrātus m, lāmentātiō f
waist n medium corpus nt; **hold by the ~** medium tenēre
wait n: **have a long ~** diū exspectāre; **lie in ~** īnsidiārī ▶ vi manēre, opperīrī, exspectāre; **~ for** exspectāre; **~ upon** (accompany) adsectārī, dēdūcere; (serve) famulārī (dat); (visit) salūtāre
waiter n famulus m, minister m
waive vt dēpōnere, remittere
wake vt excitāre, suscitāre ▶ vi expergīscī ▶ n vestīgia ntpl; **in the ~** pōne, ā tergō; **follow in the ~ of** vestīgiīs īnstāre (gen)
wakeful adj vigil
wakefulness n vigilantia f
waken vt excitāre ▶ vi expergīscī
walk n (act) ambulātiō f, deambulātiō f; (gait) incessus m; (place) ambulātiō f, xystus m; **~ of life** status m; **go for a ~** spatiārī, deambulāre ▶ vi ambulāre, īre, gradī; (with dignity) incēdere; **~ about** obambulāre; **~ out** ēgredī
wall n mūrus m; (indoors) pariēs m; (afield) māceria f; **walls** pl (of town) moenia ntpl ▶ vt mūnīre, saepīre; **~ up** inaedificāre
wallet n pēra f
wallow vi volūtārī
walnut n iūglāns f

wan adj pallidus
wand n virga f
wander vi errāre, vagārī; (in mind) ālūcinārī; **~ over** pervagārī
wanderer n errō m, vagus m
wandering adj errābundus, vagus ▶ n errātiō f, error m
wane vi dēcrēscere, senēscere
want n inopia f, indigentia f, egestās f, pēnūria f; (craving) dēsīderium nt; **in ~** inops; **be in ~** egēre ▶ vt (lack) carēre (abl), egēre (abl), indigēre (abl); (miss) dēsīderāre; (wish) velle
wanting adj (missing) absēns; (defective) vitiōsus, parum idōneus; **be ~** deesse, dēficere ▶ prep sine (abl)
wanton adj lascīvus, libīdinōsus ▶ vi lascīvīre
wantonly adv lascīvē, libīdinōsē
war n bellum nt; **regular war** iūstum bellum; **fortunes of war** fortūna bellī; **outbreak of war** exortum bellum; **be at war with** bellum gerere cum; **declare war** bellum indīcere; **discontinue war** bellum dēpōnere; **end war** (by agreement) compōnere; (by victory) cōnficere; **enter war** bellum suscipere; **give the command of a war** bellum mandāre; **make war** bellum īnferre; **prolong a war** bellum trahere; **provoke war** bellum movēre; **wage war** bellum gerere; **wage war on** bellum īnferre (dat) ▶ vi bellāre
warble vi canere, cantāre
warbling adj garrulus, canōrus ▶ n cantus m
war cry n clāmor m
ward n custōdia f; (person) pupillus m, pupilla f; (of town) regiō f ▶ vt: **~ off** arcēre, dēfendere, prōpulsāre
warden n praefectus m
warder n custōs m
wardrobe n vestiārium nt
wardship n tūtēla f
warehouse n apothēca f
wares n merx f, mercēs fpl
warfare n bellum nt
warily adv prōvidenter, cautē
wariness n circumspectiō f, cautiō f
warlike adj ferōx, bellicōsus
warm adj calidus; (fig) ācer, studiōsus; **be ~** calēre; **become ~** calefierī, incalēscere; **keep ~** fovēre; **~ baths** thermae fpl ▶ vt calefacere, tepefacere, fovēre ▶ vi calefierī
warmly adv (fig) ferventer, studiōsē
warmth n calor m
warn vt monēre, admonēre
warning n (act) monitiō f; (particular) monitum nt; (lesson) documentum nt, exemplum nt
warp n stāmina ntpl ▶ vt dēprāvāre, īnflectere
warped adj (fig) prāvus
warrant n auctōritās f ▶ vt praestāre
warranty n cautiō f
warrior n bellātor m, bellātrīx f, mīles m
warship n nāvis longa f
wart n verrūca f
wary adj prōvidus, cautus, prūdēns
wash vt lavāre; (of rivers, sea) adluere; **~ away**

dīluere; **~ clean** abluere; **~ out** (*fig*) ēluere ▶ *vi* lavārī

washbasin *n* aquālis *m*

washing *n* lavātiō *f*

wasp *n* vespa *f*

waspish *adj* acerbus, stomachōsus

waste *n* dētrīmentum *nt*, intertrīmentum *nt*; (*extravagance*) effūsiō *f*; (*of time*) iactūra *f*; (*land*) sōlitūdō *f*, vastitās *f* ▶ *adj* dēsertus, vastus; **lay ~** vastāre, populārī ▶ *vt* cōnsūmere, perdere, dissipāre; (*time*) terere, absūmere; (*with disease*) absūmere ▶ *vi*: **~ away** tābēscere, intābēscere

wasteful *adj* prōdigus, profūsus; (*destructive*) damnōsus, perniciōsus

wastefully *adv* prōdigē

wasting *n* tābēs *f*

wastrel *n* nebulō *m*

watch *n* (*being awake*) vigilia *f*; (*sentry*) statiō *f*, excubiae *fpl*; **keep ~** excubāre; **keep ~ on, keep ~ over** custōdīre, invigilāre (*dat*); **set ~** vigiliās dispōnere; **at the third ~** ad tertiam būcinam ▶ *vt* (*guard*) custōdīre; (*observe*) intuērī, observāre, spectāre ad (*acc*); **~ for** observāre, exspectāre; (*enemy*) īnsidiārī (*dat*); **~ closely** adservāre

watcher *n* custōs *m*

watchful *adj* vigilāns

watchfully *adv* vigilanter

watchfulness *n* vigilantia *f*

watchman *n* custōs *m*, vigil *m*

watchtower *n* specula *f*

watchword *n* tessera *f*, signum *nt*

water *n* aqua *f*; **deep ~** gurges *m*; **fresh ~** aqua dulcis; **high ~** māximus aestus; **running ~** aqua prōfluēns; **still ~** stagnum *nt*; **fetch ~** aquārī; **fetching ~** aquātiō *f*; **cold ~** frīgida *f*; **hot ~** calida *f*; **troubled waters** (*fig*) turbidae rēs ▶ *vt* (*land*) inrigāre; (*animal*) adaquāre

water carrier *n* aquātor *m*; (*Zodiac*) Aquārius *m*

water clock *n* clepsydra *f*

waterfall *n* cataracta *f*

watering *n* aquātiō *f*; **~ place** *n* (*spa*) aquae *fpl*

water pipe *n* fistula *f*

watershed *n* aquārum dīvortium *nt*

water snake *n* hydrus *m*

water spout *n* prēstēr *m*

watery *adj* aquōsus, ūmidus

wattle *n* crātēs *f*

wave *n* unda *f*, fluctus *m* ▶ *vt* agitāre, iactāre ▶ *vi* fluctuāre

waver *vi* dubitāre, fluctuārī, nūtāre, vacillāre, labāre, inclīnāre

wavering *adj* dubius, incōnstāns ▶ *n* dubitātiō *f*, fluctuātiō *f*

wavy *adj* undātus; (*hair*) crispus

wax *n* cēra *f* ▶ *vt* cērāre ▶ *vi* crēscere

waxen *adj* cēreus

waxy *adj* cērōsus

way *n* via *f*; (*route*) iter *nt*; (*method*) modus *m*, ratiō *f*; (*habit*) mōs *m*; (*ship's*) impetus *m*; **all the way to, all the way from** usque ad, ab; **by the way** (*parenthesis*) etenim; **get in the way of**

intervenīre (*dat*), impedīre; **get under way** nāvem solvere; **give way** (*structure*) labāre; (*MIL*) cēdere; **give way to** indulgēre (*dat*); **go out of one's way to do** ultrō facere; **have one's way** imperāre; **in a way** quōdam modō; **in this way** ad hunc modum; **it is not my way to** nōn meum est (*infin*); **lose one's way** deerrāre; **make way** dē viā dēcēdere; **make way for** cēdere (*dat*); **make one's way into** sē īnsinuāre in (*acc*); **on the way** inter viam, in itinere; **out of the way** āvius, dēvius; (*fig*) reconditus; **pave the way for** praeparāre; **put out of the way** tollere; **right of way** iter; **stand in the way of** obstāre (*dat*); **that way** illāc; **this way** hāc; **ways and means** opēs *fpl*, reditūs *mpl*

wayfarer *n* viātor *m*

waylay *vt* īnsidiārī (*dat*)

wayward *adj* protervus, incōnstāns, levis

waywardness *n* libīdō *f*, levitās *f*

we *pron* nōs

weak *adj* dēbilis, īnfirmus, imbēcillus; (*health*) invalidus; (*argument*) levis, tenuis; (*senses*) hebes

weaken *vt* dēbilitāre, īnfirmāre; (*resistance*) frangere, labefactāre ▶ *vi* minuī, labāre

weakling *n* imbēcillus *m*

weakly *adj* invalidus, aeger ▶ *adv* īnfirmē

weak-minded *adj* mollis

weakness *n* dēbilitās *f*, īnfirmitās *f*; (*of argument*) levitās *f*; (*of mind*) mollitia *f*, imbēcillitās *f*; (*flaw*) vitium *nt*; **have a ~ for** dēlectārī (*abl*)

weal *n* salūs *f*, rēs *f*; (*mark of blow*) vībex *f*; **the common ~** rēs pūblica *f*

wealth *n* dīvitiae *fpl*, opēs *fpl*; **a ~ of** cōpia *f*, abundantia *f*

wealthy *adj* dīves, opulentus, locuplēs, beātus; **make ~** locuplētāre, dītāre; **very ~** praedīves

wean *vt* lacte dēpellere; (*fig*) dēdocēre

weapon *n* tēlum *nt*

wear *n* (*dress*) habitus *m*; **~ and tear** intertrīmentum *nt* ▶ *vt* gerere, gestāre; (*rub*) terere, conterere; **~ out** cōnficere ▶ *vi* dūrāre; **~ off** minuī

wearily *adv* cum lassitūdine, languidē

weariness *n* fatīgātiō *f*, lassitūdō *f*; (*of*) taedium *nt*

wearisome *adj* molestus, operōsus, labōriōsus

weary *adj* lassus, fessus, dēfessus, fatīgātus ▶ *vt* fatīgāre; **I am ~ of** me taedet (*gen*)

weasel *n* mustēla *f*

weather *n* tempestās *f*, caelum *nt*; **fine ~** serēnitās *f* ▶ *vt* superāre

weather-beaten *adj* tempestāte dūrātus

weave *vt* texere

weaver *n* textor *m*, textrix *f*

web *n* (*on loom*) tēla *f*; (*spider's*) arāneum *nt*

wed *vt* (*a wife*) dūcere; (*a husband*) nūbere (*dat*)

wedding *n* nūptiae *fpl*

wedge *n* cuneus *m* ▶ *vt* cuneāre

wedlock *n* mātrimōnium *nt*

weed *n* inūtilis herba *f* ▶ *vt* runcāre

weedy *adj* exīlis

week n hebdomas f
ween vt arbitrārī, putāre
weep vi flēre, lacrimārī; ~ **for** dēflēre, dēplōrāre
weeping n flētus m, lacrimae fpl
weevil n curculiō m
weft n subtēmen nt; (web) tēla f
weigh vt pendere, exāmināre; (anchor) tollere; (thought) ponderāre; ~ **down** dēgravāre, opprimere; ~ **out** expendere ▶ vi pendere
weight n pondus nt; (influence) auctōritās f, mōmentum nt; (burden) onus nt; **have great** ~ (fig) multum valēre; **he is worth his ~ in gold** aurō contrā cōnstat
weightily adv graviter
weightiness n gravitās f
weighty adj gravis
weir n mōlēs f
weird adj mōnstruōsus ▶ n fātum nt
welcome vt grātus, exspectātus, acceptus ▶ n salūtātiō f ▶ vt excipere, salvēre iubēre ▶ interj salvē, salvēte
welfare n salūs f
well n puteus m; (spring) fōns m ▶ vi scatēre ▶ adj salvus, sānus, valēns; **be** ~ valēre ▶ adv bene, probē; (transition) age ▶ interj (concession) estō; (surprise) heia; ~ **and good** estō; ~ **begun is half done** dīmidium factī quī coepit habet; ~ **done!** probē!; ~ **met** opportūnē venis; ~ **on in years** aetāte prōvectus; **all is** ~ bene habet; **as** ~ etiam; **as** ~ **as** cum … tum, et … et; **let** ~ **alone** quiēta nōn movēre; **take** ~ in bonam partem accipere; **wish** ~ favēre (dat); **you may** ~ **say** iūre dīcis; **you might as** ~ **say** illud potius dīcās
well-advised adj prūdēns
well-behaved adj modestus
wellbeing n salūs f
well-bred adj generōsus, līberālis
well-disposed adj benevolus, amīcus
well-informed adj ērudītus
well-judged adj ēlegāns
well-knit adj dēnsus
well-known adj nōtus, nōbilis; (saying) trītus
well-nigh adv paene
well-off adj beātus, fortūnātus; **you are** ~ bene est tibī
well-read adj litterātus
well-timed adj opportūnus
well-to-do adj beātus, dīves
well-tried adj probātus
well-turned adj rotundus
well-versed adj perītus, expertus
well-wisher n amīcus m, benevolēns m
well-worn adj trītus
welter n turba f ▶ vi miscērī, turbārī; (wallow) volūtārī
wench n muliercula f
wend vt: ~ **one's way** īre, sē ferre
west n occidēns m, sōlis occāsus m ▶ adj occidentālis
westerly, western adj occidentālis
westwards adv ad occidentem
west wind n Favōnius m

wet adj ūmidus, madidus; **be wet** madēre; **wet weather** pluvia f ▶ vt madefacere
wether n vervēx m
wet nurse n nūtrīx f
whack n ictus m, plāga f ▶ vt pulsāre, verberāre
whale n bālaena f
wharf n crepīdō f
what pron (interrog) quid; (adj) quī; (rel) id quod, ea quae; ~ **kind of?** quālis
whatever, whatsoever pron quidquid, quodcumque; (adj) quīcumque
wheat n trīticum nt
wheaten adj trīticeus
wheedle vt blandīrī, pellicere
wheedling adj blandus ▶ n blanditiae fpl
wheel n rota f ▶ vt flectere, circumagere ▶ vi sē flectere, circumagī
wheelbarrow n pabō m
wheeze vi anhēlāre
whelm vt obruere
whelp n catulus m
when adv (interrog) quandō, quō tempore ▶ conj (time) cum (subj), ubī (+ indic)
whence adv unde
whenever conj quotiēns, utcumque, quandocumque, cum (+ perf indic/pluperf indic); (as soon as) simul āc
where adv ubī; (to) quō; ~ … **from** unde; ~ **to** quō (interrog and rel)
whereabouts n locus m; **your** ~ quō in locō sīs
whereas conj quoniam; (contrast) not expressed
whereby adv quō pāctō, quō
wherefore adv (interrog) quārē, cūr; (rel) quamobrem, quāpropter
wherein adv in quō, in quā
whereof adv cūius, cūius reī
whereon adv in quō, in quā
whereupon adv quō factō
wherever conj ubiubī, quācumque
wherewith adv quī, cum quō
wherry n linter f
whet vt acuere; (fig) exacuere
whether conj (interrog) utrum; (single question) num; (condition) sīve, seu; ~ … **or** utrum … an (in indirect question); (in conditional clauses) seu (sive) … seu (sive); ~ … **not** utrum … necne (in indirect question)
whetstone n cōs f
whey n serum nt
which pron (interrog) quis; (of two) uter; (rel) quī ▶ adj quī; (of two) uter
whichever pron quisquis, quīcumque; (of two) utercumque
whiff n odor m
while n spatium nt, tempus nt; **for a** ~ parumper; **a little** ~ paulisper; **a long** ~ diū; **it is worth** ~ expedit, operae pretium est; **once in a** ~ interdum ▶ conj (during the time that) dum (+ pres indic); (all the time that) dum (+ imperf indic) ▶ vt: ~ **away** dēgere, fallere
whilst conj dum
whim n libīdō f, arbitrium nt

whimper n vāgītus m ▸ vi vāgīre
whimsical adj facētus, īnsolēns
whimsically adv facētē
whimsy n dēliciae fpl, facētiae fpl
whine n quirītātiō f ▸ vi quirītāre
whinny n hinnītus m ▸ vi hinnīre
whip n flagellum nt, flagrum nt ▸ vt flagellāre, verberare
whirl n turbō m ▸ vt intorquēre, contorquēre ▸ vi contorquērī
whirlpool n vertex m, vōragō f
whirlwind n turbō m
whisper n susurrus m ▸ vt, vi susurrāre, īnsusurrāre; **~ to** ad aurem admonēre, in aurem dīcere
whistle n (instrument) fistula f; (sound) sībilus m ▸ vi sībilāre
white adj albus; (shining) candidus; (complexion) pallidus; (hair) cānus; **turn ~** exalbēscere ▸ n album nt; (egg) albūmen nt
white-hot adj: **to be ~** excandēscere
whiten vt dealbāre ▸ vi albēscere
whiteness n candor m
whitewash n albārium nt ▸ vt dealbāre
whither adv quō; **whithersoever** quōcumque
whitish adj albulus
whizz n strīdor m ▸ vi strīdere, increpāre
who pron quis; (rel) quī
whoever pron quisquis, quīcumque
whole adj tōtus, cūnctus; (unhurt) integer, incolumis; (healthy) sānus ▸ n tōtum nt, summa f, ūniversitās f; **on the ~** plērumque
wholehearted adj studiōsissimus
wholeheartedly adv ex animō
wholesale adj māgnus, cōpiōsus; **~ business** negōtiātiō f; **~ dealer** mercātor m, negōtiātor m
wholesome adj salūtāris, salūbris
wholesomeness n salūbritās f
wholly adv omnīnō, tōtus
whoop n ululātus m ▸ vi ululāre
whose pron cūius
why adv cūr, quāre, quamobrem, qua dē causa
wick n mergulus m
wicked adj improbus, scelestus; (to gods, kin, country) impius
wickedly adv improbē, scelestē, impiē
wickedness n improbitās f, scelus nt, impietās f
wicker adj vīmineus ▸ n vīmen nt
wide adj lātus, amplus; **be ~ of** aberrāre ab ▸ adv lātē; **far and ~** longē lātēque
widely adv lātē; (among people) vulgō
widen vt laxāre, dīlātāre
widespread adj effūsus, vulgātus
widow n vidua f
widowed adj viduus, orbus
widower n viduus m
widowhood n viduitās f
width n lātitūdō f, amplitūdō f
wield vt tractāre, gestāre, ūtī (abl)
wife n uxor f
wifely adj uxōrius

wig n capillāmentum nt
wild adj ferus, indomitus, saevus; (plant) agrestis; (land) incultus; (temper) furibundus, impotens, āmēns; (shot) temerārius; **~ state** feritās f
wild beast n fera f
wilderness n sōlitūdō f, loca dēserta ntpl
wildly adv saevē
wildness n feritās f
wile n dolus m, ars f, fraus f
wilful adj pervicāx, contumāx; (action) cōnsultus
wilfully adv contumāciter, cōnsultō
wilfulness n pervicācia f, libīdō f
wilily adv astūtē, vafrē
wiliness n astūtia f
will n (faculty) voluntās f, animus m; (intent) cōnsilium nt; (decision) arbitrium nt; (of gods) nūtus m; (document) testāmentum nt; **~ and pleasure** libīdō f; **against one's ~** invītus; **at ~** ad libīdinem suam; **good ~** studium nt; **ill ~** invidia f; **with a ~** summō studiō; **without making a ~** intestātus, intestātō ▸ vt (future) velle; (legacy) lēgāre; **as you ~** ut libet
willing adj libēns, parātus; **be ~** velle; **not be ~** nōlle
willingly adv libenter
willingness n voluntās f
willow n salix f ▸ adj salignus
willowy adj gracilis
wilt vi flaccēscere
wily adj astūtus, vafer, callidus
wimple n mitra f
win vt ferre, obtinēre, adipisci; (after effort) auferre; (victory) reportāre; (fame) cōnsequī, adsequī; (friends) sibī conciliāre; **win the day** vincere; **win over** dēlēnīre, conciliāre ▸ vi vincere
wince vi resilīre
winch n māchina f, sucula f
wind¹ n ventus m; (north) aquilō m; (south) auster m; (east) eurus m; (west) favōnius m; **I get ~ of** subolet mihī; **run before the ~** ventō sē dare; **take the ~ out of (someone's) sails** ad inritum redigere; **there is something in the ~** nesciouid olet; **which way the ~ blows** quōmodo sē rēs habeat
wind² vt torquēre; **~ round** intorquēre ▸ vi flectī, sinuāre; **~ up** (speech) perōrāre
windbag n verbōsus m
winded adj anhēlāns
windfall n repentīnum bonum nt
winding adj flexuōsus, tortuōsus ▸ n flexiō f, flexus m; **windings** pl (speech) ambāgēs fpl
windlass n māchina f, sucula f
window n fenestra f
windpipe n aspera artēria f
windward adj ad ventum conversus ▸ adv: **to ~** ventum versus
windy adj ventōsus
wine n vīnum nt; (new) mustum nt; (undiluted) merum nt

winebibber n vīnōsus m
wine cellar n apothēca f
wine merchant n vīnārius m
wine press n prēlum nt
wing n āla f; (MIL) cornū nt, āla f; (of bird) penna f;
take ~ ēvolāre; **take under one's ~** patrōnus
fierī (gen), clientem habēre, in custōdiam
recipere
winged adj ālātus, pennātus, volucer
wink n nictus m ▶ vi nictāre; **~ at** cōnīvēre (dat)
winner n victor m
winning adj blandus, iūcundus
winningly adv blandē, iūcundē
winning post n mēta f
winnings n lucra ntpl
winnow vt ventilāre; (fig) excutere
winnowing-fan n vannus f
winsome adj blandus, suāvis
winter n hiems f; (mid) brūma f ▶ adj hiemālis,
hībernus ▶ vi hībernāre
winter quarters n hīberna ntpl
wintry adj hiemālis, hībernus
wipe vt dētergēre; **~ away** abstergēre; **~ dry**
siccāre; **~ off** dētergēre; **~ out** dēlēre; **~ the nose**
ēmungere
wire n fīlum aēneum nt
wiry adj nervōsus
wisdom n sapientia f; (in action) prūdentia f;
(in judgment) cōnsilium nt
wise adj sapiēns, prūdēns
wisely adv sapienter, prūdenter
wish n optātum nt, vōtum nt; (for something
missing) dēsīderium nt; **wishes** pl (greeting)
salūs f ▶ vt optāre, cupere, velle; **~ for** exoptāre,
expetere, dēsīderāre; **~ good-day** salvēre
iubēre; **as you ~** ut libet; **I ~ I could** utinam
possim
wishful adj cupidus
wishing n optātiō f
wisp n manipulus m
wistful adj dēsīderī plenus
wistfully adv cum dēsīderiō
wistfulness n dēsīderium nt
wit n (humour) facētiae fpl, salēs mpl; (intellect)
argūtiae fpl, ingenium nt; **caustic wit** dicācitās
f; **be at one's wits' end** valdē haerēre; **be out of
one's wits** dēlīrāre; **have one's wits about one**
prūdens esse; **to wit** nempe, dīcō
witch n sāga f, strīga f
witchcraft n veneficium nt, magicae
artēs fpl
with prep (person) cum (abl); (thing) abl; (in
company) apud (acc); (fight) cum (abl), contrā
(acc); **be angry ~** īrāscī (dat); **begin ~** incipere ab;
rest ~ esse penes (acc); **end ~** dēsinere in (acc);
what do you want ~ me? quid mē vīs?
withdraw vt dēdūcere, dētrahere; (fig)
āvocāre; (words) retractāre ▶ vi discēdere,
abscēdere, sē recipere, sē subdūcere
withdrawal n (MIL) receptus m
wither vt torrēre ▶ vi dēflōrēscere
withered adj marcidus

withhold vt abstinēre, retinēre, supprimere
within adv intus, intrā; (motion) intrō ▶ prep
intrā (acc), in (abl)
without adv extrā, forīs; **from ~** extrīnsecus;
be ~ vacāre (abl), carēre (abl) ▶ prep sine (abl),
expers (gen); **I admire ~ fearing** ita laudō ut nōn
timeam; **~ breaking the law** salvīs lēgibus; **you
cannot see ~ admiring** vidēre nōn potes quīn
laudēs; **you cannot appreciate ~ seeing for
yourself** aestimāre nōn potes nisī ipse vīderis;
~ doubt sine dubiō; **~ the order of** iniussū (gen);
~ striking a blow rē integrā
withstand vt resistere (dat), obsistere (dat);
(attack) ferre, sustinēre
withy n vīmen nt
witless adj excors, ineptus, stultus
witness n (person) testis m/f; (to a document)
obsignātor m; (spectator) arbiter m; (evidence)
testimōnium nt; **call as ~** testificārī; **bear ~**
testificārī; **call to ~** testārī ▶ vt testificārī; (see)
vidēre, intuērī
witnessing n testificātiō f
witticism n dictum nt; **witticisms** pl
facētiae fpl
wittily adv facētē, salsē
wittingly adv sciēns
witty adj facētus, argūtus, salsus; (caustic) dicāx
wizard n magus m, veneficus m
wizardry n magicae artēs fpl
wizened adj marcidus
woad n vitrum nt
wobble vi titubāre; (structure) labāre
woe n luctus m, dolor m, aerumna f; **woes** pl
mala ntpl, calamitātēs fpl; **woe to** vae (dat)
woeful adj tristis, maestus, aerumnōsus
woefully adv triste, miserē
wolf n lupus m, lupa f; **wolf's** lupīnus
woman n fēmina f, mulier f; **old ~** anus f;
married ~ mātrōna f; **woman's** muliebris
womanish adj muliebris, effēminātus
womanly adj muliebris
womb n uterus m
wonder n admīrātiō f; (of a thing) admīrābilitās
f; (thing) mīrāculum nt, mīrum nt, portentum nt
▶ vi mīrārī; **~ at** admīrārī, dēmīrārī
wonderful adj mīrus, mīrābilis, admīrābilis;
~ to relate mīrābile dictū
wonderfully adv mīrē, mīrābiliter, mīrum
quantum
wonderfulness n admīrābilitās f
wondering adj mīrābundus
wonderment n admīrātiō f
wondrous adj mīrus, mīrābilis
wont n mōs m, cōnsuētūdō f
wonted adj solitus
woo vt petere
wood n silva f, nemus nt; (material) lignum nt;
gather ~ lignārī; **touch wood!** absit verbō
invidia ▶ adj ligneus
woodcutter n lignātor m
wooded adj silvestris, saltuōsus
wooden adj ligneus

woodland n silvae fpl ▸ adj silvestris
woodman n lignātor m
wood nymph n dryas f
woodpecker n pīcus m
wood pigeon n palumbēs m/f
woodwork n tigna ntpl
woodworker n faber tignārius m
woody adj silvestris, silvōsus
wooer n procus m
woof n subtēmen nt
wool n lāna f
woollen adj lāneus
woolly adj lānātus
word n verbum nt; (spoken) vōx f; (message)
nūntius m; (promise) fidēs f; (term) vocābulum nt;
~ **for** ~ ad verbum, verbō; **a** ~ **with**
you! paucīs tē volō!; **break one's** ~ fidem fallere;
bring back ~ renūntiāre; **by** ~ **of mouth** ōre; **fair**
words blanditiae fpl; **give one's** ~ fidem dare;
have a ~ **with** colloquī cum; **have words with**
iūrgāre cum; **have a good** ~ **for** laudāre; **in a** ~
ūnō verbō, dēnique; **keep one's** ~ fidem
praestāre; **of few words** taciturnus; **take at**
someone's ~ crēdere (dat)
wording n verba ntpl
wordy adj verbōsus
work n (energy) labor m, opera f; (task) opus nt;
(thing done) opus nt; (book) liber m; (trouble)
negōtium nt; **works** (MIL) opera ntpl;
(mechanism) māchinātiō f; (place) officīna f ▸ vi
labōrāre ▸ vt (men) exercēre; (metal) fabricārī;
(soil) subigere; (results) efficere; ~ **at** ēlabōrāre;
~ **in** admiscēre; ~ **off** exhaurīre; ~ **out** ēlabōrāre;
~ **up** (emotion) efferre; ~ **one's way up** prōficere
▸ vi gerī
workaday adj cottīdiānus
workhouse n ergastulum nt
working n (mechanism) māchinātiō f; (soil)
cultus m
workman n (unskilled) operārius m; (skilled)
opifex m, faber m; **workmen** operae fpl
workmanship n ars f, artificium nt
workshop n fabrica f, officīna f
world n (universe) mundus m; (earth) orbis
terrārum m; (nature) rērum nātūra f; (mankind)
hominēs mpl; (masses) vulgus nt; **of the** ~
mundānus; **man of the** ~ homō urbānus m;
best in the ~ rērum optimus, omnium optimus;
where in the ~ ubī gentium
worldliness n quaestūs studium nt
worldly adj quaestuī dēditus
worm n vermis m ▸ vi: ~ **one's way** sē īnsinuāre
worm-eaten adj vermiculōsus
wormwood n absinthium nt
worn adj trītus
worried adj sollicitus, anxius
worry n cūra f, sollicitūdō f ▸ vi sollicitārī ▸ vt
vexāre, sollicitāre; (of dogs) lacerāre
worse adj pēior, dēterior; **grow** ~ ingravēscere;
make matters ~ rem exasperāre ▸ adv pēius,
dēterius
worsen vi ingravēscere, dēterior fierī

worship n venerātiō f, deōrum cultus m; (rite)
sacra ntpl, rēs dīvīnae fpl ▸ vt adōrāre, venerārī,
colere
worst adj pessimus, dēterrimus; ~ **enemy**
inimīcissimus m; **endure the** ~ ultima patī ▸ vt
vincere
worsted n lāna f
worth n (value) pretium nt; (moral) dignitās f,
frūgālitās f, virtūs f; (prestige) auctōritās f ▸ adj
dignus; **for all one's** ~ prō virīlī parte; **how**
much is it worth? quantī vēnit?; **it is** ~ **a lot**
multum valet; **it is** ~ **doing** operae pretium est
worthily adv dignē, meritō
worthiness n dignitās f
worthless adj (person) nēquam; (thing) vīlis,
inānis
worthlessness n levitās f, nēquitia f; vīlitās f
worthy adj dignus; (person) frūgī, honestus; ~ **of**
dignus (abl)
wound n vulnus nt ▸ vt vulnerāre; (feelings)
offendere
wounded adj saucius
wrangle n iūrgium nt, rixa f ▸ vi iūrgāre, rixārī,
altercārī
wrap vt involvere, obvolvere; ~ **round**
intorquēre; ~ **up** involvere
wrapper n involucrum nt
wrapping n integumentum nt
wrath n īra f, īrācundia f
wrathful adj īrātus
wrathfully adv īrācundē
wreak vt: ~ **vengeance on** saevīre in (acc), ulcīscī
wreath n corōna f, sertum nt
wreathe vt (garland) torquēre; (object) corōnāre
wreck n naufragium nt ▸ vt frangere; (fig)
perdere; **be wrecked** naufragium facere
wreckage n fragmenta ntpl
wrecked adj (person) naufragus; (ship) frāctus
wrecker n perditor m
wren n rēgulus m
wrench vt intorquēre, extorquēre; ~ **away**
ēripere; ~ **open** effringere
wrest vt extorquēre
wrestle vi luctārī
wrestler n luctātor m, athlēta m
wrestling n luctātiō f
wretch n scelerātus m, nēquam homō m;
poor ~ miser homō m
wretched adj īnfēlīx, miser; (pitiful) flēbilis
wretchedly adv miserē
wretchedness n miseria f; maestitia f
wriggle vi sē torquēre
wriggling adj sinuōsus
wright n faber m
wring vt torquēre; ~ **from** extorquēre
wrinkle n rūga f ▸ vt corrūgāre
wrinkled adj rūgōsus
wrist n prīma palmae pars f
writ n (legal) auctōritās f
write vt scrībere; (book) cōnscrībere; ~ **off**
indūcere; ~ **on** īnscrībere (dat); ~ **out** exscrībere,
dēscrībere; ~ **out in full** perscrībere

writer n (lit) scrīptor m, auctor m; (clerk) scrība m
writhe vi torquērī
writing n (act) scrīptiō f; (result) scrīptum nt
wrong adj falsus, perversus, prāvus; (unjust)
iniūstus, inīquus; **be ~, go ~** errāre ▶ n iniūria f,
culpa f, noxa f, malum nt; **do ~** peccāre,
dēlinquere; **right and ~** (moral) honesta ac
turpia ntpl ▶ vt laedere, nocēre (dat); (by deceit)
fraudāre
wrongdoer maleficus m, scelerātus m
wrongdoing n scelus nt
wrongful adj iniūstus, iniūriosus, inīquus
wrongfully adv iniūriā, iniūstē, inīquē
wrong-headed adj perversus
wrong-headedness n perversitās f
wrongly adv falsō, dēprāvātē, male, perperam
wroth adj īrātus
wrought adj factus
wry adj dētortus; **make a wry face** ōs dūcere
wryness n prāvitās f

yacht n phasēlus m
yard n (court) ārea f; (measure) trēs pedēs
yardarm n antenna f
yarn n fīlum nt; (story) fābula f
yawn n hiātus m ▶ vi hiāre, ōscitāre; (chasm)
dehiscere
ye pron vōs
yean vt parere
year n annus m; **every ~** quotannīs; **for a ~** in
annum; **half ~** sēmēstre spatium nt; **this year's**
hōrnus; **twice a ~** bis annō; **two years**
biennium nt; **three years** triennium nt; **four
years** quadriennium nt; **five years**
quinquennium nt
yearly adj annuus, anniversārius ▶ adv
quotannīs
yearn vi: **~ for** dēsīderāre, exoptāre
yearning n dēsīderium nt
yeast n fermentum nt
yell n clāmor m; (of pain) ēiulātiō f ▶ vi clāmāre,
eiulāre
yellow adj flāvus; (pale) gilvus; (deep) fulvus;
(gold) luteus; (saffron) croceus
yelp n gannītus m ▶ vi gannīre
yeoman n colōnus m
yes adv ita vērō (est), māximē; (correcting) immo
yesterday adv herī ▶ n hesternus diēs m;
yesterday's hesternus; **the day before ~** nudius
tertius
yet adv (contrast) tamen, nihilōminus, attamen;
(time) adhūc, etiam; (with compar) etiam; **and
yet** atquī, quamquam; **as yet** adhūc; **not yet**
nōndum
yew n taxus f
yield n frūctus m ▶ vt (crops) ferre, efferre;
(pleasure) adferre; (concession) dare, concēdere;
(surrender) dēdere ▶ vi cēdere; (surrender) sē
dēdere, sē trādere; **~ to the wishes of** mōrem
gerere (dat), obsequī (dat)
yielding adj (person) facilis, obsequēns; (thing)
mollis ▶ n cessiō f; dēditiō f
yoke n iugum nt ▶ vt iungere, coniungere
yokel n agrestis m
yolk n vitellus m

yonder *adv* illīc ▸ *adj* ille, iste
yore *n*: **of ~** quondam, ōlim
you *pron* tū, vōs
young *adj* iuvenis, adulēscēns; (*child*) parvus;
  younger iūnior, nātū minor; **youngest** nātū
  minimus ▸ *n* fētus *m*, pullus *m*, catulus *m*
young man *n* iuvenis *m*; adulēscēns *m*
youngster *n* puer *m*
your *adj* tuus, vester
yourself *pron* ipse
youth *n* (*age*) iuventūs *f*, adulescentia *f*; (*person*)
  iuvenis *m*, adulēscēns *m*; (*collective*) iuventūs *f*
youthful *adj* iuvenīlis, puerīlis
youthfully *adv* iuvenīliter

Z

zeal *n* studium *nt*, ārdor *m*
zealot *n* studiōsus *m*, fautor *m*
zealous *adj* studiōsus, ārdēns
zealously *adv* studiōsē, ārdenter
zenith *n* vertex *m*
zephyr *n* Favōnius *m*
zero *n* nihil *nt*
zest *n* (*taste*) sapor *m*; (*fig*) gustātus *m*,
  impetus *m*
zigzag *n* ānfrāctus *m* ▸ *adj* tortuōsus
zither *n* cithara *f*
zodiac *n* signifer orbis *m*
zone *n* cingulus *m*